Why You Need This New Edition

If you're wondering why you should buy this new edition of *Writing Today*, here are a few great reasons!

Two new chapters on Research Papers. A new Part 2 chapter offers you guidance on inventing, organizing, drafting, designing, and revising one of the most commonly assigned genres in college: the research paper (Ch. 13). The companion Part 7 chapter provides many contextualized examples of summary, paraphrase, quotation, citation, and documentation of sources in MLA and APA styles (Ch. 42).

More attention to thesis statements. Effective thesis statements for each genre in Chapters 4–13 are explored in the sections on Drafting and include examples of strong and weak theses, reinforced with reminders in the Quick Start Guides. Additional coverage is provided in chapters on Topic, Angle, and Purpose as well as on Drafting Introductions and Conclusions (Chs. 2, 19).

Expanded treatment of Profiles. New instruction and examples in Chapters 5 and 34 help you profile organizations, places, and events—as well as people. New readings profile the Grand Canyon and Griffith Park, among others.

Additional microgenres. Three new full microgenre assignments include the annotated bibliography, the bio, and the explainer. Fifty new microgenres at the end of chapters in Part 2 suggest activities for in-class or out-of-class work (Chs. 4–13).

Strengthened connection between At-A-Glances and One Student's Works. Expanded instruction in the At-A-Glance diagrams in Part 2 aligns more closely with the sample readings in One Student's Work, helping you better see the elements of genres fleshed out in real student writing (Chs. 4–13).

New engaging, effective readings. Over 20 new readings profile the Foo Fighters, review Hawaii 5-0, research serial killers, propose eradicating athletic scholarships, analyze how Homer Simpson speaks, and more to keep class discussion lively and suggest a range of topics you might consider for you own writing.

Revised treatment of Arguments. The newly revised chapter on arguments explains why rich arguable issues have more than two sides and helps you address a range of perspectives strategically as you argue your own position (Ch. 10).

More coverage of rhetorical patterns. New coverage of using "cause and effect" as a strategy and new examples of other writing strategies help you build effective paragraphs or sections within your papers (Ch. 20).

New Media enhancements available in the Pearson eText. The dynamic, online version of *Writing Today* links you to videos, animations, interactive documents, and more in MyCompLab to create a rich, interactive learning experience. Resources that support and extend *Writing Today's* instructional content let you access additional help as needed.

PEARSON

Writing
Today

SECOND EDITION

RICHARD JOHNSON-SHEEHAN
Purdue University

CHARLES PAINE
University of New Mexico

PEARSON

Boston Columbus Indianapolis New York San Francisco Upper Saddle River
Amsterdam Cape Town Dubai London Madrid Milan Munich Paris Montreal Toronto
Delhi Mexico City São Paulo Sydney Hong Kong Seoul Singapore Taipei Tokyo

Senior Acquisitions Editor: Lauren A. Finn
Director of Development: Mary Ellen Curley
Senior Development Editor: David B. Kear
Senior Marketing Manager: Sandra McGuire
Senior Supplements Editor: Donna Campion
Executive Digital Producer: Stefanie Snajder
Digitial Project Manager: Janell Lantana
Digital Editor: Sara Gordus
Production Manager: Eric Jorgensen
Project Coordination, Text Design, and Electronic Page Makeup: Cenveo Publisher Services/Nesbitt Graphics, Inc.
Cover Designer/Manager: Wendy Ann Fredericks
Cover Art: iStockphoto and Shutterstock images
Senior Manufacturing Buyer: Roy L. Pickering Jr.
Printer/Binder: R. R. Donnelley Crawfordsville
Cover Printer: Lehigh-Phoenix/Hagerstown

This title is restricted to domestic sales and distribution only.

Credits and acknowledgments borrowed from other sources and reproduced, with permission, in this textbook appear on the appropriate page within text [or on page 842].

Library of Congress Cataloging-in-Publication Data

Johnson-Sheehan, Richard.
  Writing today / Richard Johnson-Sheehan, Charles Paine.—2nd ed.
     p. cm.
  ISBN-13: 978-0-205-21008-4
  ISBN-10: 0-205-21008-2
  1. English language—Rhetoric. 2. Report writing. 3. Study skills. I.
Paine, Charles. II. Title.
  PE1408.J7533 2012
  808'.042—dc23   2011045702

10—DOC—14

Student copy
ISBN 10: 0-205-21008-2
ISBN 13: 978-0-205-21008-4

A-la Carte copy
ISBN 10: 0-205-22945-X
ISBN 13: 978-0-205-22945-1

www.pearsonhighered.com

Detailed Contents

PART 3
Developing a Writing Process   342

PART 4

Strategies for Shaping Ideas 404

PART 5
Doing Research   464

PART 6
Getting Your Ideas Out There   552

PART 7

Anthology of Readings 598

PART 8
Handbook   790

Preface

Writing Today began with a few basic assumptions. First, we believe students want to learn writing skills that will help them succeed in college and in their careers. Second, students need a writing guide that presents information clearly, simply, and in a way that is easy to reference. Third, writing instructors prefer a teaching tool that is both practical and flexible, allowing them to adapt its content to their own pedagogical approaches and teaching styles.

To help students with the kinds of writing they do in college courses and in their lives outside of the classroom, *Writing Today* provides tools they can use to respond effectively to many different writing situations. This book teaches *genres* of writing (memoirs, analyses, reports, proposals, etc.) and *strategies* for writing (narration, comparison, argumentation, etc.) as well as *processes* for writing (planning, drafting, revising, etc.).

Writing Today is an easy-to-use book that fits the way today's students read and learn. We believe they respond best to an interactive writing style, so our instruction is brief and to the point; key concepts are immediately defined and reinforced; sections and paragraphs are short; and important points are clearly labeled and supported by instructional visuals. This straightforward presentation of complex information creates a reading experience in which students access information *when they are ready for it*.

Our own experiences as teachers and writing program administrators tell us that pedagogical approaches and teaching styles vary—and that the best writing guides support a range of instructors. The variety of writing purposes (expressive, informative, persuasive, argumentative, etc.) and writing projects in *Writing Today* support a broad range of curricular goals. Writing instructors can choose the order in which they teach these chapters and combine them into units that fit their course designs.

Genres are not rigid templates but are rather a set of versatile tools that guide every aspect of the writing process. We want students to develop *genre awareness* and *genre know-how*, and we emphasize paying attention to how communities get things done with words and images. We also believe that people learn best by doing, so we emphasize inquiry, practice, production, and active research. Students need to become versatile writers who can respond effectively to a changing world.

Our approach is informed by personal observations and by much of the research done in the field of writing studies over the last twenty years. The approach is also supported by findings emerging from our research with the Consortium for the Study of Writing in College (a collaboration between the National Survey of Student Engagement and the Council of Writing Program Administrators). Surveys conducted since 2008 by the CSWC of more than 200,000 students at over 200 different schools found that when faculty assigned challenging and diverse writing assignments, students reported deeper learning, increased practical competence, and greater personal and social gains.

New to This Edition

Two New Chapters on Research Papers.
A new Part 2 chapter offers guidance on inventing, organizing, drafting, designing, and revising one of the most commonly assigned genres in college: the research paper (Chapter 13). The companion Part 7 chapter provides many contextualized examples of summary, paraphrase, quotation, citation, and documentation of sources in MLA and APA styles (Chapter 42).

More Attention to Thesis Statements.
Effective thesis statements for each genre in Chapters 4–13 are explored in the sections on drafting and include examples of strong and weak theses, reinforced with reminders in the Quick Start Guides. Additional coverage is provided in chapters on topic, angle, and purpose as well as on drafting introductions and conclusions (Chapters 2, 19).

Expanded Treatment of Profiles and Revised Treatment of Arguments.
New instruction and examples in Chapter 5 help students profile organizations, places, and events (as well as people), and new end-of-chapter activities provide practice opportunities. New readings profile the Foo Fighters and Griffith Park. The revised chapter on arguments helps students recognize that rich arguable issues have more than two sides and encourages them to address the range of perspectives as they argue for their position (Chapter 10).

Additional Microgenres.
Three new full microgenres include the annotated bibliography (in Research Papers), the bio (in Profiles), and the explainer (in Reports). Fifty new microgenres are suggested at the ends of chapters in Part 2 so that students can explore families of related genres (Chapters 4–13).

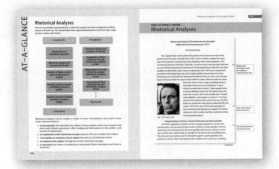

Strengthened Connection between At-A-Glances and One Student's Works Sections.

Expanded instruction in the At-A-Glance diagrams in Part 2 aligns more closely with the sample readings in One Student's Work, helping students better see the elements of genres fleshed out in real student writing (Chapters 4–13).

New Engaging, Effective Readings.

Over 20 new readings profile the Grand Canyon, review *Hawaii 5-0*, research serial killers, propose eradicating athletic scholarships, analyze how Homer Simpson speaks, and more to keep class discussion lively and suggest a range of topics students might consider for their own writing, including five new MLA and five new APA readings to model student papers.

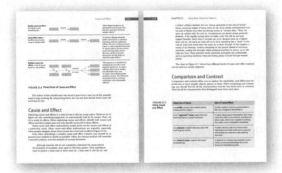

More Coverage of Rhetorical Patterns.

New coverage of using "cause and effect" as a rhetorical strategy and new examples of other rhetorical patterns help students build effective paragraphs or sections in their papers (Chapter 21).

Watch the Animation presents abstract concepts or processes using animated text with audio narrative to extend discussions in the book.

Watch the Video shows conferences or peer collaboration to illustrate writing processes.

Analyze the Interactive Document provides additional sample texts with annotations or commentary to help students think critically about decisions writers make.

Apply the Concept suggests additional activities and opportunities to practice new concepts.

New Media Enhancements Available in the Pearson eText.

The dynamic, online version of *Writing Today* links students to videos, animations, interactive documents, and more in MyCompLab to create a rich, interactive learning experience. Resources that support and extend *Writing Today's* instructional content let students access additional help as needed and help students with different learning styles understand key concepts. The icons link the Pearson eText directly to this content.

Features of This Book

Interactive Writing Style. Instruction is brief and to the point. Key concepts are immediately defined and reinforced. Paragraphs are short and introduced by heads that preview content. This interactive style helps students skim, ask questions, and access information when they are ready for it—putting them in control of their learning.

At-A-Glance. Each Part 2 chapter opens with a diagram that shows one or two common ways to organize a genre's key elements, giving an immediate and visual orientation to the genre. Students learn to adapt this organization to suit their rhetorical situation as they read the chapter.

End-of-Chapter Activities. Exercises conclude every chapter in the book to help students understand and practice concepts and strategies.

- **Talk About This** questions prompt classroom discussion.
- **Try This Out** exercises suggest informal writing activities students can complete in class or as homework.
- **Explore This** suggests other related microgenres for students to examine.
- **Write This** prompts facilitate longer, formal writing assignments.

One Student's Work. A student-written example in each writing project chapter shows the kinds of issues students might explore in a specific genre of writing as well as the angles they might take. Annotations highlight the writer's key rhetorical decisions so the reading can be used either for discussion or as a model.

Quick Start Guide.
This practical review includes action steps and appears in each chapter to get students writing quickly. Students spend less time reading about writing and more time working on their own compositions. They can also use the Quick Start Guide as a quick way to gain familiarity with a genre before reading the chapter.

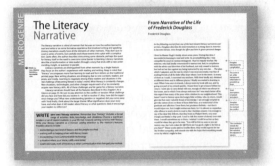

Microgenre.
A microgenre applies features of major genres to narrow rhetorical situations. For example, in Chapter 11, students apply features of a proposal to a pitch; in Chapter 5, those of a memoir to a literacy narrative. Each microgenre in Part 2 includes a description, an example, and a writing activity, encouraging students to experiment and play by stretching genre conventions.

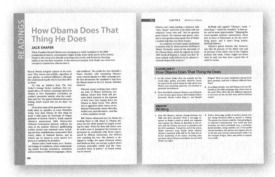

Readings and Prompts.
Six readings—two in each project chapter and four in the anthology—offer models of each genre. Question sets after each reading encourage critical engagement.

- **A Closer Look** questions facilitate analytical reading.
- **Ideas for Writing** questions prompt responses, analyses, and different genres of writing.
- **A Few Ideas for Composing** activities (in the anthology) encourage writing that further explores each genre's possibilities.

A Multimodal Approach.
Today's writers compose electronic texts, work with visual and audio tools, insert graphics, and collaborate with others online. Each chapter includes strategies for working in a multimodal environment. Multimodal assignments appear in "Write This" and in "A Few Ideas for Composing." Chapters in Part 6 offer guidance on creating and posting compositions in online environments.

How This Book Is Organized

Writing Today features brief chapters and plainly labeled sections, creating obvious access points that help students find what they need when they need it.

PART 1

Getting Started

Purposefully brief, the first three chapters are designed to get students up and running right away. They introduce the five elements of rhetorical situations (topic, angle, purpose, readers, and context) and explain why and how using genres will help students to write successfully.

PART 2

Using Genres to Express Ideas

These chapters help students master ten commonly assigned kinds of writing that form the foundation of an adaptable portfolio of skills. Students explore expressive, informative, analytical, persuasive, and argumentative genres that help them respond effectively to a majority of academic and workplace writing situations.

PART 3

Developing a Writing Process

Stand-alone chapters on planning, organization, style, design, and revision offer strategies students can apply to any writing situation. Instructors can assign them alongside the genre chapters.

PART 4

Strategies for Shaping Ideas

Straightforward chapters on drafting introductions and conclusions, developing paragraphs and sections, and incorporating rhetorical strategies (such as narration, classification, and comparison and contrast) provide resources for writing those sections of papers where students often find themselves stuck. A chapter on argument explores appeals and fallacies, and a chapter on collaboration helps students work effectively in groups.

PART 5

Doing Research

The ability to research effectively is critical to students' success in college and in their careers. Students learn to engage in inquiry-driven research, evaluate sources, and work with sources by paraphrasing, quoting, and synthesizing. Up-to-date coverage of MLA and APA styles includes citation examples and model papers.

PART 6

Getting Your Ideas Out There

Today's students have more opportunities to present their work publicly than ever before. Students learn how to use social networking and other Web applications for rhetorical purposes. Students learn best practices for creating a professional portfolio of their work. Basics such as succeeding on essay exams and giving presentations are covered in depth as well.

PART 7

Anthology of Readings

The anthology showcases the ten genres of writing explored in Part 2. These additional readings serve as models, suggest situations in which specific genres are particularly effective, offer material for response, and help students discover their own research topics.

PART 8

Handbook

Designed to be as accessible and usable as possible, the handbook gives students a quick resource for issues of grammar, usage, and punctuation.

Ways to Fit This Book to Your Teaching Approach

Flexibility is a chief strength of *Writing Today*. The first three chapters form a foundation, but remaining chapters can be taught in any order or combination to suit individual teaching approaches and objectives.

A Process Approach. Students want to learn a writing process that suits their own working habits and writing styles. The chapters in Part 2 tailor the writing process with strategies specific to different genres. Part 3, "Developing a Writing Process," provides additional chapters on prewriting, drafting, designing, revising, and editing that can be assigned with any project.

A Genre-Based Approach. Genres aren't templates into which writers pour words: they are tools writers can use to help them invent ideas and plan, research and draft, and design and edit. *Writing Today* covers real-world writing—such as analyses, reviews, reports, and proposals—that help students solve real problems and achieve specific goals.

A Purposes or Aims-Based Approach. Instructors who teach an aims approach to writing encourage students to be aware of their audience and purpose as they write to express, inform, analyze, or persuade. This approach works hand-in-hand with a genre-based approach: knowing the genre helps writers better understand a text's purpose, readers, and context.

A Strategies or Patterns-Based Approach. Instructors who teach rhetorical patterns (narrative, description, comparison and contrast, cause and effect, etc.), will find them embedded in this book. Part 4, "Strategies for Shaping Ideas," shows how strategies work with and within genres to help students organize and shape their ideas. *Writing Today* applies the strengths of a patterns-based approach to more complex kinds of documents.

An Academic Approach. Students learn the kinds of writing common in the General Education curriculum, such as narratives, rhetorical analyses, literary analyses, reviews, and argument essays. They also learn the foundations of the kinds of writing common in advanced academic classes, such as profiles, commentaries, reports, and proposals. Strategies for writing from sources—including paraphrasing, quoting, citing, and documenting sources—are covered in Part 5.

An Argument-Based Approach. *Writing Today* presents a rhetorical approach to writing. Several genres in Part 2, such as rhetorical analyses, commentaries, arguments, and proposals, are purposefully designed to be argument-based; this content is labeled with ARGUMENT in the table of contents. Chapter 22 helps students determine what is arguable and anticipate opposing points of view while also explaining the four stases, the classical appeals, and logical fallacies.

An Integrated, Multimodal Approach. Instructors teaching multimodal composition courses know there are few writing guides that teach critical twenty-first-century composing skills and even fewer that offer multimodal assignments. *Writing Today* assumes that students compose electronically and research online, and it offers strategies for writers to plan and collaborate online, include visuals in print texts, create visual texts, create media projects, and post compositions to the Web.

Distance Learning and Online Teaching. *Writing Today* was designed to be easily adaptable to online and hybrid learning environments. The book's comprehensiveness and flexibility provide strong scaffolding on which distance learning, online, and hybrid courses can be developed. Its highly accessible design allows students to quickly find the information they need while learning on their own and composing at their computers. The Pearson eText can be used alone or embedded in a suite of online writing, research, and grammar resources delivered in MyCompLab.

Correlation to the WPA Outcomes Statement

Writing Today helps teachers and students address learning outcomes for first-year composition courses identified by the Council of Writing Program Administrators: rhetorical knowledge; critical thinking, reading, and writing; processes; knowledge of conventions; and composing in electronic environments. Both of us have been leaders in this organization, and we believe strongly that these outcomes reflect the kinds of abilities that students should master in these courses. Specific connections between chapters and the WPA Outcomes appear in the Instructor's Manual.

Supplements

The Instructor's Manual. The Instructor's Manual opens discussing how genre theory can be applied to the first-year writing curriculum. Subsequent chapters discuss classroom management, syllabus building, and teacher-student communication in traditional, hybrid, or online learning spaces. The second section is a collection of syllabi that facilitates rhetorical strategies/patterns approaches or purposes/aims-based approaches. The third section offers teaching strategies and support for *every* chapter in the book, as well as discussion of how each chapter aligns with WPA Outcomes. The last section provides additional support for teaching the readings and using the activities and prompts in the Anthology.

PEARSON **mycomplab** **Interactive Pearson eText in MyCompLab.** A dynamic, online version of *Writing Today* is available in MyCompLab. This eText brings together the many resources of MyCompLab with the instruction and content of this successful writing guide to create an enriched, interactive learning experience for students. MyCompLab, an eminently flexible application, empowers student writers and teachers by integrating a composing space and assessment tools with multimedia tutorials, including online tutoring and exercises for writing, grammar, and research. Visit www.mycomplab.com to learn more.

CourseSmart. Students can subscribe to *Writing Today* at CourseSmart.com. Ebook functionality includes the ability to search the text, bookmark passages, save students' own notes, and print reading assignments that incorporate lecture notes.

Acknowledgments

We would like to thank our editors, Lauren Finn, David Kear, and Joe Opiela for their great ideas and persistence. We would also like to thank our colleagues, Scott Sanders, Susan Romano, Wanda Martin, Michelle Kells, Karen Olson, David Blakesley, Irwin Weiser, and Shirley Rose, for their feedback on our ideas. We also want to thank our students, especially our graduate students, for trying out some of these materials in their classes and helping us refine the ideas and approaches in this book. We would like to thank Christine Tulley, The University of Findlay, for her additional editorial guidance. We are appreciative of our thoughtful reviewers, whose feedback helped us improve the effectiveness of *Writing Today*.

Shawn Adamson, *Genesee Community College*; Ryan Allen, *University of Louisville*; Jennifer Aly, *University of Hawai'i Maui College*; Ellen Arnold, *Coastal Carolina University*; Katherine Baker, *College of Southern Nevada*; John Barrett, *Richland College*; Lisa Bickmore, *Salt Lake Community College*; Jacqueline A. Blackwell, *Thomas Nelson Community College*; Patricia Webb Boyd, *Arizona State University*; Jo Ann Buck, *Guilford Technical Community College*; Genesea M. Carter, *The University of New Mexico*; Marlys Cervantes, *Cowley College*; Ron Christiansen, *Salt Lake Community College*; Gail S. Corso, *Neumann University*; T. Allen Culpepper, *Tulsa Community College, Southeast Campus*; Tamera Davis, *Northern Oklahoma College*; Dominic Delli Carpini, *York College of Pennsylvania*; Jason DePolo, *North Carolina A&T State University*; Paul Dombrowski, *University of Central Florida*; Carlton Downey, *Houston Community College*; Chitralekha Duttagupta, *Utah Valley University*; Jeremiah Dyehouse, *The University of Rhode Island*; William FitzGerald, *Rutgers University–Camden*; Mary Sue Fox, *Central New Mexico Community College*; MacGregor Frank, *Guilford Technical Community*

College; Dayna V. Goldstein, *Georgia Southern University*; Susanmarie Harrington, *The University of Vermont*; Matthew Hartman, *Ball State University*; Dave Higginbotham, *University of Nevada, Reno*; Krista Jackman, *The University of New Hampshire*; Jay Jordan, *The University of Utah*; Chad Jorgensen, *Metropolitan Community College*; Margaret Konkol, *University at Buffalo, The State University of New York*; Andrew J. Kunka, *University of South Carolina Sumter*; Betty LaFace, *Bainbridge College*; Karen Laing, *College of Southern Nevada*; William B. Lalicker, *West Chester University of Pennsylvania*; Steve Lazenby, *University of North Carolina at Charlotte*; Robert Lively, *Truckee Meadows Community College*; Joleen Malcolm, *University of West Florida*; Terri Mann, *El Paso Community College*; Rachel Maverick, *Richland College*; Miles McCrimmon, *J. Sargeant Reynolds Community College*; James McWard, *Johnson County Community College*; Eileen Medeiros, *Johnson & Wales University*; Shellie Michael, *Volunteer State Community College*; Susan Miller, *The University of Utah*; Rhonda Morris, *Santa Fe College*; Mary Ellen Muesing, *University of North Carolina at Charlotte*; Lori Mumpower, *University of Alaska Anchorage*; Margie Nelson, *El Paso Community College*; Annie Nguyen, *Community College of Baltimore County*; Matthew Oliver, *Old Dominion University*; Michael Pennell, *The University of Rhode Island*; Jason Pickavance, *Salt Lake Community College*; Jennifer Pooler-Courtney, *The University of Texas at Tyler*; Sarah A. Quirk, *Waubonsee Community College*; Timothy D. Ray, *West Chester University of Pennsylvania*; Peggy L. Richards, *The University of Akron*; Shewanda Riley, *Tarrant County College–Northeast Campus*; Christy Rishoi, *Mott College*; Mauricio Rodriguez, *El Paso Community College*; Jane Rosecrans, *J. Sargeant Reynolds Community College*; Dan Royer, *Grand Valley State University*; Stephen Ruffus, *Salt Lake Community College*; Andrew Scott, *Ball State University*; Brittany Stephenson, *Salt Lake Community College*; Stacey Tartar-Esch, *West Chester University of Pennsylvania*; Bradley A. Waltman, *College of Southern Nevada*; Elizabeth Wardle, *University of Central Florida*; Louise Dekreon Watsjold, *University of Alaska Chugia—Eagle River Campus*; Leah Williams, *The University of New Hampshire*; Margaret Wintersole, *Laredo Community College*; Kristy Wooten, *Catawba Valley Community College*; and John Ziebell, *College of Southern Nevada*.

About the Authors

Richard Johnson-Sheehan is a Professor of Rhetoric and Composition at Purdue University. At Purdue, he has directed the Introductory Composition program, and he has mentored new teachers of composition for many years. He teaches a variety of courses in composition, professional writing, and writing program administration, as well as classical rhetoric and the rhetoric of science. He has published widely in these areas. His prior books on writing include *Technical Communication Today,* now in its fourth edition, and *Writing Proposals,* now in its second edition. Professor Johnson-Sheehan was awarded 2008 Fellow of the Association of Teachers of Technical Writing and has been an officer in the Council for Writing Program Administrators.

Charles Paine is a Professor of English at the University of New Mexico, where he teaches undergraduate courses in first-year, intermediate, and professional writing as well as graduate courses in writing pedagogy, the history of rhetoric and composition, and other areas. At UNM, he directed the Rhetoric and Writing Program and the First-Year Writing Program. He is an active member of the Council of Writing Program Administrators and currently serves on its Executive Board. He cofounded and coordinates the Consortium for the Study of Writing in College, a joint effort of the National Survey of Student Engagement and the Council of Writing Program Administrators. The Consortium conducts general research into the ways that undergraduate writing can lead to enhanced learning, engagement, and other gains related to student success.

PART 1

Getting Started

PART OUTLINE

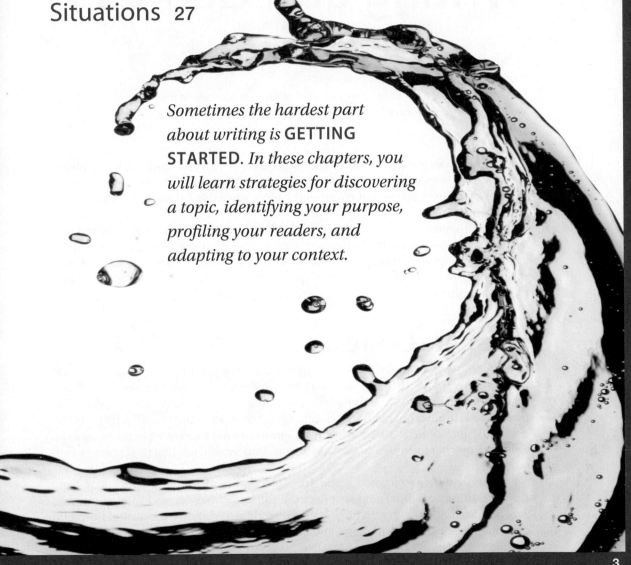

Sometimes the hardest part about writing is **GETTING STARTED**. *In these chapters, you will learn strategies for discovering a topic, identifying your purpose, profiling your readers, and adapting to your context.*

1

Writing and Genres

In this chapter, you will learn how to—

- use genres to communicate with readers.
- use "genre know-how" to become a versatile writer in college and in the workplace.
- develop a writing process that will help you write efficiently and effectively.

Writing gives you the power to get things done with words and images. It allows you to respond successfully to the events and people around you, whether you are trying to improve your community, pitch a new idea at work, or just text with your friends.

The emergence of new writing situations—new places for writing, new readers, and new media—means writing today involves more than just getting words and images onto a page or screen. Writers need to handle a wide variety of situations with diverse groups of people and technologies. Learning to navigate among these complex situations is the real challenge of writing in today's world.

What Are Genres?

In this book, you will learn how to use writing *genres* to interpret these complex situations and respond to them successfully. Defining the word *genre* is difficult. Mistakenly, genres are sometimes defined by their structure alone (e.g., "A report has five parts: introduction, methods, results, discussion, and conclusion"). But this understanding of genre is a bit misleading. Genres are not fixed or rigid patterns to be followed mechanically. They are not forms into which we insert sentences and paragraphs.

Genres are ways of writing and speaking that help people interact and work together. In other words, genres reflect the things people do, and they are always evolving because human activities change over time to suit new social situations and new challenges. Genres *do* offer somewhat stable patterns for responding to typical situations. More importantly, though, they reflect how people act, react, and interact in these situations. Genres are meeting places—and *meaning* places.

Up until now, your writing courses have probably taught you how to master one genre—the academic essay—and write for one kind of reader—your teachers. In college, you will need to master and write in a variety of genres that help you to achieve different kinds of goals. This book will help you develop this "genre know-how," which you can use to strengthen your writing in college courses and in your career. You will also master a useful "genre set" that will allow you to respond successfully to a variety of important situations.

With this book, you will learn how to recognize and adapt genres for your own needs. You will become a more agile writer with a greater awareness of the differences among readers and contexts. You will become more proficient at analyzing specific writing situations and at adapting your writing to them.

Using Genres to Write Successfully

For writers, genres offer flexible approaches to writing that reflect how people in communities interact with each other. They provide strategies for analyzing and interpreting what is happening around you. Once you understand your current situation, you can then use genres to focus your creativity, generate new ideas, and present those ideas to others. You can use words and images to mold reality to your advantage.

Readers use genres, too. They use genres as guideposts to orient themselves to a text, helping them to anticipate what they are likely to find in the document and how they can use the information in it. Readers are never passive spectators. They bring specific expectations with them and they respond to your writing, in part, according to those expectations. As a writer, when you understand what your readers expect to find, you can make strategic choices about what information you will include and how you will present your ideas (Figure 1.1). Knowing what your readers expect of a particular genre gives you insight about how to compose your text. It gives you power.

FIGURE 1.1 College Writing Requires Genre Know-How

Writing matters because it is one way people get things done. College writing will teach you "genre know-how," the ability to size up writing situations and respond to them appropriately.

Writing with Genres

As a writer, you can use a genre to help you make sense of a complex situation, invent your ideas, and write a text that achieves your purpose and meets the expectations of your readers. Here are the most important things to remember about genres:

Genres Are Flexible. Genres are as flexible and changeable as the human activities they represent. It is important to know the common features of each genre, so you can use them to help you interpret and write, but keep in mind that genres reflect human activities. As a result, you should look at genres as flexible and adaptable to the evolving reality around you.

Genres Are Adaptable to Various Situations. When the audience or context changes, a genre needs to be adjusted to suit the new situation. An argument that worked previously with some readers or in a particular context might not work with different readers or in another context.

Genres Evolve to Suit Various Fields. Each discipline adapts common genres to its own needs and purposes. A report written by a biologist, for example, will share many characteristics with a report written by a manager at a corporation, but there will also be notable differences in the content, organization, style, and design of the text.

Genres Shape Situations and Readers. When you choose a particular genre, you are deciding what kinds of issues will be highlighted and what role your readers will play. For instance, readers know that when they encounter a memoir (a type of literary genre), they should read thoroughly and follow the story line. Quite differently, when readers encounter a report (a workplace genre), they assume that they can "raid" the text for the specific information they need—that is, they can skip and skim.

Genres Can Be Played With. You can be creative and play with the conventions of genres. You can combine, blend, or even "mash up" genres into new ones. Can you use a memoir to review a book? Can you use a rhetorical analysis to study a painting? Sure you can. Genres are stretchy. But if you are going to go against your readers' expectations of the genre, you need to do so consciously and for a specific purpose.

Genres in Movies

You are already familiar with the concept of genres in media and entertainment. To illustrate how genres work, let's take a look at how they function in the movie industry. Movies can be sorted by the genres that were used to make them (Figure 1.2). Movie genres include romantic comedies, action flicks, documentaries, murder mysteries, musicals, science fiction and fantasy, horror, thrillers, and others. These genres aren't formulas that the writers and directors must follow. Instead, they are familiar patterns that audiences will recognize and understand.

Once the audience recognizes the genre of the movie, they form specific expectations about what kinds of things they will—and will not—experience. For example, a romantic comedy usually explores the amusing awkwardness and pratfalls of a new relationship. Two people meet and feel an attraction to each other. But then, events beyond their control keep them apart and cause humorous misunderstandings. Eventually, the two star-crossed lovers realize they truly do love each other and find a way at the end of the movie to be together.

Directors of successful romantic comedies use the boundaries and conventions of this genre to help them work creatively and produce something that is both

FIGURE 1.2 Movie Genres

Usually, moviegoers recognize the genre of a movie even before they step into the theatre. Movie studios use posters and previews to help audiences know what to expect and how to interpret the movie.

recognizable and new. Genres aid the director's creativity by providing guidelines about how the movie should be structured, scripted, visually designed, musically scored, and even edited. Genres also constrain movies by helping directors determine what is "in bounds" and what is "out of bounds." Good directors work creatively within a genre to produce something original.

Movies that flop often fail to follow a recognizable genre or—even worse—they follow a common genre in a trite way. A movie that strictly uses a genre formulaically feels painfully predictable and shallow. The people in the audience get bored and tune out when they realize that the movie is mechanically following a genre in a predictable way.

Like successful movie directors, effective writers need to fully understand the genres they are using. Genres help writers figure out where to start and how to proceed. They allow writers to create something fresh and new, while also helping them to organize and control their message in a way that readers will recognize and comprehend. In this sense, good writers (like good movie directors) are always balancing the old, familiar, and stable with the new, creative, and dynamic.

Genre and the Writing Process

So, how can genres help you write better? Think of something you already do well. Perhaps you are a good swimmer or a solid basketball player. Maybe you are a great video game player. Do you play the guitar, or do you like to make pottery? Have you learned a martial art? Do you practice yoga?

To do something well, you first needed to learn the *process* for doing it. Someone else, perhaps a teacher, coach, parent, or friend, showed you the process and helped you get better at it (Figure 1.3). Then, once you knew that process, you worked on

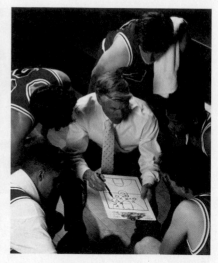

FIGURE 1.3 Learning to Do Something Involves Learning a Process

In order to do something you enjoy, you first had to learn a step-by-step process for doing it. Once you mastered the process and it became second nature, you could make it yours by refining and adapting it.

improving and refining your skills. You gained confidence. Before long, you developed the "know-how" for that activity—not just the skill to do it, but also an ability to be innovative and original. When you reached this point, you could then start being creative and trying out new ideas.

Writing is similar to the other things you enjoy doing. To write well, you first need to develop your own writing process. Strong writers aren't born with a special gift, and they aren't necessarily smarter than anyone else. Strong writers have simply learned and mastered a reliable writing process that allows them to generate new ideas and shape those ideas into something readers will find interesting and useful.

Using a Writing Process

A writing process is a series of steps that leads you from your basic idea to a finished document. Over time, you will develop your own unique writing process, but the following six steps work well as a starting place:

Analyze the rhetorical situation. Identify the genre you are being asked to use or the genre that best fits the needs of your project. Then define your topic, state your purpose, and analyze your readers and the contexts in which your text will be read or used.

Invent your ideas. Use inquiry and research to generate your own ideas and discover what others already know about your topic.

Organize and draft your paper. Arrange and compose your ideas into familiar patterns that your readers will recognize and find useful.

Choose an appropriate style. Use techniques of plain and persuasive style to clarify your writing and make it more compelling.

Design your document. Develop an appropriate page layout and use visual or audio features to make your ideas more accessible and attractive to readers.

Revise and edit your work. Improve your writing by rewriting, reorganizing, editing, and proofreading your work.

Experienced writers tend to handle each of these steps separately, but a writing process shouldn't be followed mechanically from one step to the next. Instead, experienced writers tend to move around among these steps as needed (Figure 1.4). For instance, while drafting your paper, you may find you need to invent more content. Or, while revising, you may decide that you need to rethink the style of the text.

Why bother with a writing process at all? Can't you just write the paper? Truth is, as projects grow more complex and important, you need to give yourself time to generate and refine your ideas. A reliable writing process helps you do things one step at

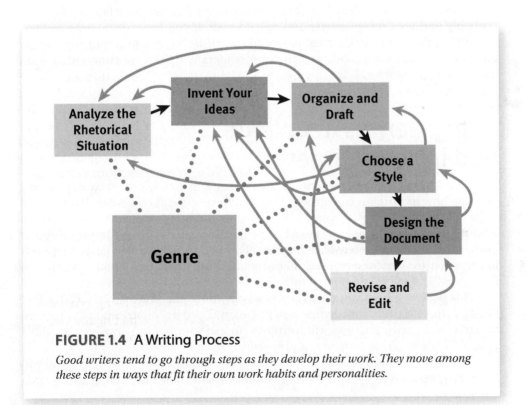

FIGURE 1.4 A Writing Process

Good writers tend to go through steps as they develop their work. They move among these steps in ways that fit their own work habits and personalities.

a time. In the long run, following a writing process will save you time and will help you to write something that is more creative and interesting to your readers.

Using Genre as a Guiding Concept

Watch the Animation on **Genres** at **mycomplab.com**

The genre you are using should influence each stage of your writing process, as shown in Figure 1.4. The genre will help you make decisions about the content of your paper, how your paper should be organized, what style would be appropriate, and what kind of design would work best. Then, as you revise and edit, you can use the genre to guide your decisions. So as you write, keep the genre you are following in mind. Use the genre as a source for guidance and creativity.

For example, if you are writing a movie review, the "review genre" (discussed in Chapter 6, "Reviews") will help you make decisions about what kinds of information your readers will expect. Should you tell them the plot of the movie? Should you describe the characters? Should you give away the ending? The genre will provide you with a model organization, so you can arrange your ideas in a pattern that your readers will expect. The genre also helps you to make informed decisions about what kind of style and design would work.

The purpose of a genre is to help you figure out how people tend to act, react, and interact in the situation in which you are writing. So if you tell your readers you are giving them a "movie review," they will have some expectations about the content, organization, style, and design of your text. If you meet those expectations, they will probably find your review useful and easy to read. If you bend those expectations, they might find your review creative or unique. However, if you completely violate their expectations for a movie review, your readers will likely be confused or frustrated with your work.

Using Genres in College and in Your Career

This genre-based approach to writing might be new to you. It's the next step toward learning how to write for college and in your future career. You already have a good sense about how the "essay genre" is used, and you know what your professors, as readers, expect from academic essays. Now that you are in college, you will need to master and write in a variety of genres that allow you to achieve new goals. You need to learn how to write for advanced college courses and workplace situations in which the academic essay would not be suitable.

This book will help you develop genre know-how, the practical knowledge and skill to write effectively with genres. You will learn how to recognize and adapt genres for your own needs, and you will learn how to use your genre know-how to adjust your writing for unique situations and specific readers.

This book will help you to become a versatile, flexible, and agile writer. You will learn how to analyze specific writing situations and then take action with words and images.

At the end of each chapter in this book, you will find something called the "Quick Start Guide." The purpose of the Quick Start Guides is to help you get up and running as soon as possible. You can use these guides for review or to preview the essential information in the chapter. Here is the essential information in this chapter.

KNOW What a Genre Is

Genres are ways of writing and speaking that help people communicate and work together in specific situations. Genres offer relatively stable patterns for writing, but more importantly they reflect how humans act, react, and interact in everyday situations. Genres are meeting places—and *meaning* places.

GET Some "Genre Know-How"

Genre know-how is the ability to use genres to analyze and interpret what is happening around you. When you have genre know-how, you can use genres to focus your creativity, generate new ideas, and present those ideas to others.

KEEP in Mind That Genres Are Flexible

Genres are as flexible and changeable as the human activities they represent. They need to be adjusted to suit evolving situations. They can be stretched, blended, and messed around with to fit unique situations.

DEVELOP Your Writing Process

A writing process leads you from your basic idea to a finished document, from inventing ideas to final editing. Developing and refining your writing process will save you time and effort in the long run.

USE Genres in College and in Your Career

A genre-based approach to writing helps you master a "genre set" that you can use in advanced college courses and in the workplace. The genre set taught in this book will cover most of the texts you will write in college and in your career.

1. In a group, first ask each person to talk briefly about his or her favorite movie genre; then, as a group, choose one of those genres to discuss. Describe the genre and its characteristics: What do all or most movies in this genre include? What kinds of characters do they have? What happens in them? Then talk about some of the best and worst movies that fit the genre. What do the best movies do well? Why do the worst movies fail?

2. In your group, brainstorm and list all the television shows you can think of. Then divide these shows into genres. What characteristics did you use to sort these shows into categories? What elements made you choose to put a show in one genre instead of another? Are there any shows that seem to stretch or bend genres, or that straddle more than one genre? If so, how do the producers of these shows bend the genres to come up with something new?

3. With your group, brainstorm and list all the restaurant genres you can think of. Then choose one restaurant genre to explore further. (For instance, one restaurant genre might be the coffee shop, which might include Starbucks, Caribou Coffee, and a variety of local coffee shops.) Describe the characteristics that all or most of the restaurants in the genre share. What guideposts signal to customers what kind of restaurant they are in? How are restaurant customers expected to behave, and how do the restaurants' characteristics encourage or require such behaviors?

1. On the Internet, find a Web page or Web site that conforms to a familiar Web site genre. For your professor (who may not know about this genre), write a one-page document that describes the Web site and explains the genre and how it works (how people use Web sites like this one, the genre's general features, how and why writers create texts in that genre, how and why readers come to such texts). You should also explain whether you think the Web site uses the genre properly and highlight any places where you think it could be improved by using the genre better.

2. When a movie uses the well-known features of a genre to make fun of that genre, it's called a parody. For instance, the *Scary Movie* movies are parodies of horror flicks. *Get Smart* is a parody of spy movies. Think of other parodies that use a genre in order to poke fun at it. For your professor or your group, write a one-page description of a movie that parodies a particular genre, the genre it makes fun of, and the features of the genre that are specifically targeted by the parody.

3. For five minutes, freewrite about your favorite movie or television show. Freewriting means just putting your pen on the paper (or your fingers on the keyboard) and writing anything that comes to mind. Don't stop until the five minutes are up. Don't correct any errors or change anything. After five minutes of writing, read through your freewrite and underline any of your comments that relate to the genre of the movie. Then, in your group, discuss the parts you underlined.

4. Consider a kind of writing activity that you are good at. It might be texting your friends, e-mailing people, updating on a social networking profile, or writing college application essays or the five-paragraph essay. Describe this kind of writing and discuss how people use it (both writers and readers). Describe the setting of such writing (where it occurs and in what medium). Finally, describe the writing itself: What kind of content is typical; how is that content organized; what kind of language is used? In what ways does the genre determine who the participants can and cannot be?

5. Imagine that you have been asked to direct a movie that crosses two very different genres. For example, you might be asked to tell a horror story as a romantic comedy, or you might be asked to convert a historical documentary into an action flick. In a one-page paper written for your professor, explain how this merging of genres might offer some creative opportunities. What kinds of problems would it cause? Do you know any movies that do this kind of genre bending or genre merging? Are these movies successful, and do you find them entertaining?

1. **Analyze a genre.** Find a longer nonfiction document that seems to be using a specific genre. Write a three-page analysis in which you describe the document's content, organization, style, and design. Then explain how its genre highlights certain kinds of information and ignores other kinds of information. Show how the style and design of the document is well suited (or ill suited) for the intended readers.

2. **Review a movie for a Web site or blog.** Write a three-page review of a movie you saw recently for a blog or movie review Web site. In your review, identify the genre of the movie and the common characteristics of that genre. Then show your readers how the movie exhibited those characteristics. Toward the end of your review, tell your readers whether you thought the movie was good or not by discussing how well it worked within its genre. Compare it to other successful movies in that genre.

PEARSON
mycomplab

For support in meeting this chapter's objectives, follow this path in MyCompLab: Resources ⟹ Writing ⟹ More Writing Resources. Review the Instruction and Multimedia resources about writing successfully, then complete the Exercises and click on Gradebook to measure your progress.

2

Topic, Angle,
Purpose

In this chapter, you will learn how to—

- develop and narrow your topic to respond to any writing situation.
- develop your angle, the unique perspective you'll bring to the topic.
- identify your purpose, or what you want to accomplish.
- use your identified purpose to develop a thesis sentence (or main point).

Imagine that one of your professors has given you a new writing assignment. What should you do first? Of course, you should read the assignment closely. Take a deep breath. Then ask yourself a few specific questions about what you are being asked to do:

> *What am I being asked to write about?* (Topic)
>
> *What is new or has changed recently about this topic?* (Angle)
>
> *What exactly is the assignment asking me to do or accomplish?* (Purpose)
>
> *Who will read this document and what do they expect?* (Readers)
>
> *Where and when will they be reading this document?* (Context)

These kinds of questions are also helpful in the workplace. When you are writing something for a client or your supervisor, you can use these five questions to help you figure out what you need to accomplish.

These questions are the basic elements of what we will be calling the "rhetorical situation" throughout this book (Figure 2.1). Before you start writing any text, you should first gain an understanding of your rhetorical situation: topic, angle, purpose, readers, and context. In this chapter, we will discuss the first three of these elements. Then, in Chapter 3, "Readers, Contexts, and Rhetorical Situations," we will discuss

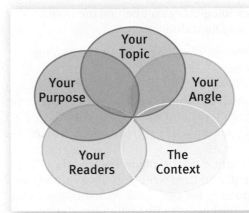

FIGURE 2.1 Five Elements of the Rhetorical Situation

Before you start writing, consider these five elements of the rhetorical situation, which will help you get started on your work.

techniques and strategies for profiling your readers and anticipating the contexts in which they will experience your document.

Gaining a clear understanding of your topic, angle, and purpose will help you decide which genre is most appropriate for your writing project.

Topic: What Am I Writing About?

In college, your professors will either provide the topics for your papers or ask you to come up with your own. When your professor supplies the topic, he or she might define the topic broadly, saying something like this:

> For this paper, I want you to write about the Civil Rights movement in the 1960s.

> Shakespeare's *King Lear* is often held up as a masterpiece of Renaissance tragedy. We will explore why this play is still popular today.

> Our next subject will be "mating and dating" in college, and we will be using our own campus for field research.

If your professor does not supply a topic, you will need to decide for yourself what you are writing about. In these cases, you should pick a topic that intrigues you and one about which you have something interesting to say.

In the workplace, you will write about different topics than the issues you handled in college, but you should still begin by identifying clearly what you are writing about. A client or your supervisor may request a written document from you in the following way:

> Our organization is interested in receiving a proposal that shows how we can lower our energy costs with sustainable energy sources, especially wind and solar.

Please write a report that explains the sociological causes behind the sudden rise in violence in our city's south side neighborhoods.

Evaluate these three road surfaces to determine which one would be best for repaving 2nd Street in the downtown area.

Once you have clearly identified your topic, you should explore its boundaries or scope, trying to figure out what is "inside" your topic and what is "outside" the topic. A good way to determine the boundaries of your topic is to create a concept map like the one shown in Figure 2.2.

To make a concept map, start out by writing your topic in the middle of your computer screen or a sheet of paper. Circle it, and then write down everything connected with it that comes to mind. For example, let's say your sociology professor wants you to write about the romantic relationships of college students. Put "dating and mating in college" in the middle of a sheet of paper and circle it. Then start mapping around that topic, as shown in Figure 2.2.

FIGURE 2.2 Creating a Concept Map About Your Topic

A concept map is a helpful way to get your ideas onto the screen or a piece of paper.

Write down all the things you already know about your topic. Then, as you begin to run out of ideas, go online and enter some of the words from your map into a search engine like *Google*, *Yahoo!*, or *Bing*. The search engine will bring up links to numerous other ideas and sources of information about your topic. Read through these sources and add more ideas to your concept map.

As your map fills out, you might ask yourself whether the topic is too large for the amount of time you have available. If so, pick the most interesting ideas from your map and create a second concept map around them alone. This second map will often help you narrow your topic to something you can handle.

Angle: What Is New About the Topic?

Completely new topics are rare. On just about every issue, someone has already said something. That's fine. You don't need to discover a completely new topic for your writing project. Instead, you need to come up with a new *angle* on a topic. Your angle is your unique perspective or view on the issue.

One way to come up with your angle is to ask yourself, "What has changed recently about this topic that makes it especially interesting right now?" For example, let's say you are searching the Internet for articles about college dating trends. You find a 2001 report from the Institute for American Values called "Hooking Up, Hanging Out, and Hoping for Mr. Right: College Women on Dating and Mating Today" (Figure 2.3). The report is a little out of date, but you mostly agree with the sociologists who wrote it, especially the part about college students wanting marriage but shying away from commitment.

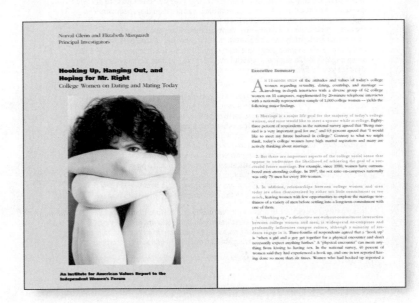

FIGURE 2.3
A Report on Your Topic

This report, published in 2001, looks like a great source for information on your topic, but it's a little dated. Your own experiences as a college student today may give you some new ways to see the topic.

Another way to come up with your angle is to ask yourself, "What unique experiences, expertise, or knowledge do I possess that I can bring to the topic?" For example, your experiences as a college student give you some additional insights or "angles" into college dating. Plus, times have changed a little since the report came out. Your own experiences tell you that the hooking-up culture has been replaced by a culture of "serial monogamy" in which many college students now go through a series of short-term emotional and physical relationships while they are in college. These so-called monogamous relationships may last a few months or perhaps a year, but most people don't expect them to lead to marriage. That's your angle.

You decide to do a little freewriting to see if your angle works. Freewriting involves opening a new page in your word processor and writing anything that comes to mind for about five minutes (Figure 2.4). When freewriting, don't stop to correct or revise. Just keep writing anything that comes into your head.

Dating and mating in college is a very large topic—too large for a five- to ten-page paper. But if you decide to write a paper that explores a specific angle (e.g., the shift from a hooking-up culture to a culture of serial monogamous relationships)

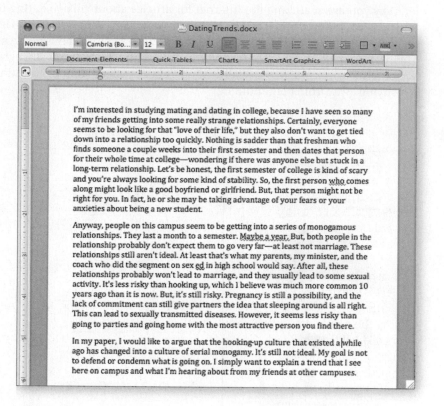

Watch the Video on **Narrowing a Topic** at **mycomplab.com**

FIGURE 2.4
Freewriting to Find Your Angle

Freewriting about your topic helps you test your new angle. Just write freely for five to ten minutes without making revisions or corrections.

you can say something new and interesting about how people date and mate in college.

Purpose: What Should I Accomplish?

Your purpose is what you want to accomplish. Figuring out your topic and angle has helped you determine *what* you are writing about. Now, you need to clearly state your purpose—*why* you are writing. Everything you write has a purpose, even informal texts. Whenever you speak or write, you are trying to inform, ask a question, flirt, impress, or just have fun. When writing for college or the workplace, however, you should clearly identify the purpose of every document you create.

Your professor may have already identified a purpose for your paper in the assignment, so check there first. Assignments based on the topics given on page 15 might look like this:

> Your objective in this paper is to show how Martin Luther King's use of nonviolence changed the dynamics of racial conflict in the 1960s, undermining the presumption of white dominance among blacks and whites.

> In your paper, show how Shakespeare's *King Lear* is similar to and different from his other tragedies. Then discuss why the themes in *Lear* still resonate with today's audiences.

> Use close observation of students on our campus to support or debunk some of the common assumptions about dating and mating in college.

If you need to come up with your own purpose for the paper, ask yourself what you believe and what you would like to prove about your topic. For example, at the end of the freewrite in Figure 2.4, a purpose statement is starting to form:

> In my paper, I would like to argue that the hooking-up culture that existed a decade ago has changed into a culture of serial monogamy. It's still not ideal. My goal is not to defend or condemn what is going on. I simply want to explain a trend that I see here on campus and what I'm hearing about from my friends at other campuses.

This statement is still a bit rough and it lacks a clear focus, but the purpose of the project is starting to take shape.

Your purpose statement also defines what genre you are likely to follow. For example, the word "argue" in the rough purpose statement above signals that the author will likely be writing an argument, a commentary, or a research report. It helps to remember that documents in college and in the workplace tend to be written for two primary reasons: to *inform* and to *persuade*. So your purpose statement will usually be built around some of the verbs shown in Figure 2.5 on the next page.

FIGURE 2.5
Common Verbs
Used in Purpose
Statements

Informative Papers	Persuasive Papers
to inform	to persuade
to describe	to convince
to define	to influence
to review	to argue
to notify	to recommend
to instruct	to change
to advise	to advocate
to announce	to urge
to explain	to defend
to demonstrate	to justify
to illustrate	to support

You can consult this list of verbs if you are having trouble coming up with your purpose statement. Start by determining whether you are trying to *inform* your readers or trying to *persuade* them. Then pick the key word that best describes what you want to accomplish.

Thesis Statement (Main Claim)

 Watch the Animation on **Writing a Thesis Statement** at mycomplab.com

Closely related to your purpose statement is your *thesis statement* (also known as your "main point" or "main claim"). A purpose statement guides you, as the *writer*, helping you develop your ideas and draft your paper. Your thesis statement guides your *readers* by announcing the main point or claim of the paper.

The thesis statement in your paper will usually first appear in your introduction (Figure 2.6 on the next page). Then, it reappears, usually with more emphasis, in the conclusion.

In special cases, you may choose to use a "question thesis" or "implied thesis" in which a question or open-ended comment in the introduction sets up a thesis statement that appears only in the conclusion of the document.

There are four major types of thesis statements:

Informative Thesis. As its name implies, an informative thesis is appropriate when your purpose is to inform readers, not to persuade them:

Natural threats to Florida's cities include hurricanes, floods, and even tsunamis.

Irish and Chinese immigrants were the bulk of the labor force that built the First Transcontinental Railroad.

Turnbow 1

Katelyn Turnbow

Professor Thompson

English 102

6 May 2009

Lives Not Worth the Money?

The idea of a forgotten disease is almost absurd, a disease for which a cure is

available but not given, effective, but never given a chance to work. We are often of the

belief that human life is invaluable that it cannot be bought with money and that a sick

person should be treated whether he is an enemy or a friend, poor or rich. In reality,

however, the cures that do not make money for the manufacturer are simply not made at

all. One need only look at African Sleeping Sickness (WHO). There is a cure, but the

victims who would benefit from the drug are poor and considered "unprofitable" by the

pharmaceutical industry. It remains, however, a drug company's ethical responsibility to

care for the people that its drugs can save, even when helping others is not profitable.

West African Sleeping Sickness, also known as African Trypanosomiasis or

HAT, was discovered in 1902 and it kills over 50,000 people a year. These victims,

FIGURE 2.6
A Prominent Thesis Statement Orients Readers

Your thesis statement should help readers understand your main point or claim quickly and clearly.

Argumentative Thesis. An argumentative thesis is a claim that your readers can choose to agree or disagree with. This kind of thesis usually has two features, an *assertion* and *backing*:

The Federal Communications Commission (FCC) should re-exert its authority over violence on television, because American children who watch violent shows are becoming desensitized to the consequences of cruel behavior.

← Assertion

← Backing

Engineering students should not be required to take liberal arts courses since these courses do not prepare them for their career.

← Assertion

← Backing

Both of these thesis statements are "arguable," meaning someone could agree or disagree with them.

Question or Open-Ended Thesis. Occasionally you may want to hold off stating your main point, saving it for the end of the paper. In these situations, a question or open-ended thesis may be your best choice, especially if you are arguing about something controversial or making a controversial point:

> What is the best way to ensure that guns are not used to commit crimes while also protecting the constitutional rights of gun owners?

> The question explored in this research paper is whether teachers' unions are beneficial or harmful to the American educational system.

The conclusion of your paper needs to clearly express your thesis statement. That way, the question or open-ended sentence you posed in your introduction is answered at the end of your paper.

Implied Thesis. In some situations, you might choose not to state your thesis explicitly. For genres that use the narrative pattern, such as memoirs, some profiles, and narrative argument papers, readers may not expect or need a thesis statement. In these situations, the author's purpose is to move readers toward thoughtful reflection rather than to inform or persuade them about a single specific point. Other times, the author might feel the overall message will be more powerful if readers figure out the main point for themselves. If you choose not to include a thesis statement, you need to make sure the message of your text comes through for the readers, even though you aren't stating it explicitly.

Choosing the Appropriate Genre

Once you have sketched out your topic, angle, and purpose, you can choose which genre would be appropriate for your project. The appropriate genre depends on what you are trying to do and who you are writing for. Perhaps your professor has already identified the genre by asking you to write a "review," a "literary analysis," a "proposal," or a "research paper." If so, you can turn to that chapter in this book to learn about the expectations for that genre (Chapters 4–13).

If you are allowed to choose your own genre, or if you are writing something on your own, the best way to figure out which genre would work best is to look closely at your purpose statement. Keep in mind, though, that genres are not formulas or recipes to be followed mechanically. Instead, each one reflects how people in various communities and cultures do things with words and images. They are places where people make meaning together. Figure 2.7 shows how your purpose statement can help you figure out which genre is most appropriate for your writing situation.

My Purpose	The Appropriate Genre
"I want to write about the meaning of something I experienced in my life."	Memoirs (Chapter 4)
"I want to describe someone else."	Profiles (Chapter 5)
"I need to critique something I saw, experienced, or read."	Reviews (Chapter 6)
"I need to explain and interpret a work of literature or art."	Literary Analyses (Chapter 7)
"I need to explain why a text or speech was effective or persuasive, or not."	Rhetorical Analyses (Chapter 8)
"I want to express my opinion about the people and events around me."	Commentaries (Chapter 9)
"I want to argue for my beliefs or opinions."	Arguments (Chapter 10)
"I want to propose a solution to a problem."	Proposals (Chapter 11)
"I need to explain an issue by doing research about it."	Reports (Chapter 12)
"I want to use research to explain an issue or argue a point."	Research Papers (Chapter 13)

FIGURE 2.7
Identifying the Appropriate Genre

The genre that fits your purpose statement will help you make strategic decisions about how you are going to invent the content of your document, organize it, develop an appropriate style, and design it for your readers.

Ready to start right now? Here are some techniques and strategies for identifying your topic, angle, and purpose.

IDENTIFY Your Topic

Your topic will be assigned by your professor or you will need to come up with it yourself. Either way, figure out what interests you about the topic. Then use a concept map to determine what issues are related to your topic.

NARROW Your Topic

Ask yourself whether the topic is too large for the amount of time you have available. If it seems too large, pick the most interesting ideas from your concept map and create a second map around them. This second map should help you narrow your topic to something you can handle.

DEVELOP Your Angle

Your angle is your unique perspective on the topic. A good way to develop an angle is to ask yourself, "What has changed recently about this topic that makes it especially interesting right now?" You might also ask what unique perspective you could offer on this issue.

WRITE Down Your Purpose

Your purpose is what you want to accomplish—that is, what you want to explain or prove to your readers. Decide whether you are *informing* or *persuading* your readers, or doing something else. Then write a thesis statement that says exactly what you are going to do. The verbs shown in Figure 2.5 can help. Keep in mind that your thesis will probably change as you develop your drafts.

CHOOSE the Appropriate Genre

The best way to figure out which genre would work best for your project is to look closely at your purpose statement. The chart in Figure 2.7 will help you decide which genre would work for the document you want to write. In some cases, your professor will tell you which genre to use.

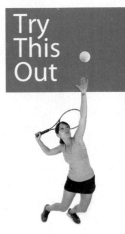

1. With a small group, list some topics that people often discuss and argue about. For example, what do people talk about on television or the radio? What do they argue about at local gathering places like cafés, restaurants, or bars? What are some things people discuss with their friends or families? With your group, come up with ten things that you yourselves have discussed or argued about over the last few days.

2. Take a look at today's news on Web sites like *CNN.com, FoxNews.com,* or *MSNBC .com.* What are some of the topics in the news today? You will notice that totally new topics aren't all that common. However, there are new angles developing all the time. With your group, discuss the new angles you notice on these topics. How do reporters come up with these new angles? What has changed recently to create some of these new angles?

3. Find an opinion piece in your local or campus newspaper or on the Internet. Examine the thesis. Does the author accurately and clearly announce the main point in a thesis statement? If the thesis is not stated, is it clear to you what point the author wanted to make? What kind of thesis is used—informational, argumentative, question, or implied? Do you think the author chose the best kind of thesis for this piece, or would a different kind of thesis statement have worked better?

1. List five topics that you might be interested in writing about this semester. They can include anything that captures your imagination. Then, for each of these topics, ask yourself, "What is new or has changed recently about this topic?" Using your answers to this question, write down two possible angles for each topic.

2. Think of a topic that catches your interest. For five minutes, create a concept map that includes everything you can think of about this topic. Now, look at your concept map and find a part of this topic that you would like to explore further. Then freewrite on that part for five more minutes and see what kinds of ideas begin to emerge. Would this "narrower" topic be easier to write about than the topic you started with?

3. Pick a topic that interests you and develop a purpose statement for a paper about that topic. Your purpose statement doesn't need to be perfect right now, but try to describe what you want to achieve in your paper. Do you want to inform your readers about your topic or do you want to persuade them? Now, build your purpose statement around one of the words shown in the chart in Figure 2.5.

4. Using the topic and purpose statement from the exercise above, identify which genre would be most appropriate for writing about this topic. Figure 2.7 provides a chart that shows how to use your purpose statement to figure out which genre you should use. Once you've determined which genre to use, flip to that chapter in Part 2, "Using Genres to Express Ideas," to see what that genre usually involves.

5. Using the topic and purpose statement from Exercise 3, first decide what kind of thesis statement you think would work best (informative, argumentative, question, or implied). Now, write down your thesis statement. Try to come up with a thesis statement that captures your main point clearly and completely.

1. **Identify the topic, angle, and purpose of an assignment.** Choose a writing assignment from one of your professors. Using the steps and concepts discussed in this chapter, determine the topic you are being asked to write about and come up with a unique angle on it. Then draft a purpose statement for your assignment. Write an e-mail to your professor in which you identify the topic, angle, and purpose of the paper you will be writing. Then discuss which genre would be appropriate for this assignment and why.

2. **E-mail your professor about a new angle on a topic.** Pick any topic that interests you and find a new angle on that topic. Use concept mapping to explore and narrow your topic. Then write a rough purpose statement that shows what you want to achieve in your paper.

   Using the chart in Figure 2.7, choose a genre that would help you to say something meaningful and interesting about this issue. Turn to the chapter in Part 2 that discusses the genre you chose. Using the At-a-Glance diagram that appears early in the chapter, sketch a brief outline on this topic.

   Finally, write an e-mail to your professor in which you explain how you would go about writing an argument on this topic. Explain your topic, angle, purpose, readers, and the genre you would use. Tell your professor why you think your approach to the topic would be effective for your readers.

Readers, Contexts, and Rhetorical Situations

In this chapter, you will learn how to—

- profile your readers to understand their expectations, values, and attitudes.
- figure out how context—the place readers read and the medium you use—shapes your readers' experience.
- use the rhetorical situation (topic, angle, purpose, readers, and context) to help you respond to any writing situation.

In your college courses and in your career, you will need to write to people who will read and use your documents in specific times and places. Your writing needs to inform them, persuade them, achieve your purpose, and get something done.

In the previous chapter, you learned how to identify your topic, angle, and purpose. In this chapter, you will learn how to achieve your purpose by developing *reader profiles* and sizing up the *contexts* in which people will read your work. Together, this information makes up the *rhetorical situation*—that is, the topic, angle, purpose, readers, and context. Each rhetorical situation is unique, because every new situation puts into play a specific writer with a purpose, writing for specific readers who are encountering the work at a unique time and place.

When you have sized up the rhetorical situation, you can use genres more successfully to accomplish what you want to achieve. Identifying your topic, angle, and purpose allows you to figure out which genre would work best. Understanding your readers and the contexts in which they will experience your text will help you adjust the genre to fit their expectations and communicate most effectively.

Watch the Animation about **Knowing Your Audience** at **mycomplab.com**

Profiling Readers

In college and in the workplace, you will usually be writing for other people, not yourself. So before writing, you need to develop a reader profile that helps you adapt your ideas to their expectations and the situations in which they will use your document.

A profile is an overview of your readers' traits and characteristics. At a minimum, you should develop a *brief reader profile* that gives you a working understanding of the people who will be reading your text. If time allows, you should create an *extended reader profile* that will give you a more in-depth view of their expectations, values, and attitudes.

A Brief Reader Profile

To create a brief reader profile, you can use the Five-W and How questions to help you describe the kinds of people who will be reading your text (Figure 3.1).

Who Are My Readers? What are their personal characteristics? How old are they? What cultures do they come from? Do they have much in common with you? Are they familiar with your topic already or are they completely new to it?

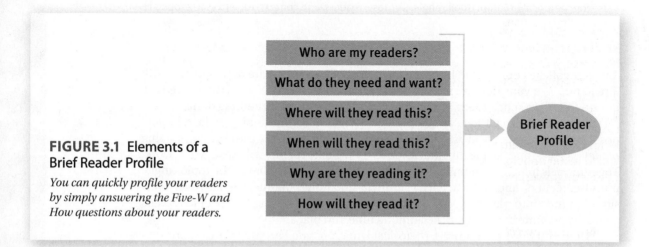

FIGURE 3.1 Elements of a Brief Reader Profile

You can quickly profile your readers by simply answering the Five-W and How questions about your readers.

What Are Their Expectations? What do they need from you and your document? What do they want, exactly? What ideas excite them, and what bores them? What information do they need to help them accomplish their personal and professional goals?

Where Will They Be Reading? In what locations might they read your document? Will your readers be sitting at their desks, in a meeting, or on an airplane? Will they be reading from a printed page, a computer screen, a tablet computer, or a small-screen reading device like a smartphone?

When Will They Be Reading? Does the time of day affect how they will read your document? Will they be reading it when the issues are hot and under discussion? Will they be reading it at a time when they can think about your ideas slowly and carefully?

Why Will They Be Reading? Why will they pick up your document? Do their reasons for reading the document match your purpose in writing it? Do they want to be informed, or do they need to be persuaded?

How Will They Be Reading? Will they read slowly and carefully? Will they skip and skim? Will they read some parts carefully and some parts quickly or not at all?

Your answers to the Five-W and How questions will give you a brief reader profile to help you start writing. For simple documents, a brief profile like this one might be enough. For larger, more complex documents, you will need to dig a little deeper to develop a more thorough understanding of your readers.

An Extended Reader Profile

Keep in mind that your readers probably understand issues differently than you do. Their expectations, values, and attitudes will be unique, and sometimes even contradictory to yours. Meanwhile, complex genres, like the genres discussed in this book, usually require a more thorough understanding of the people who will be reading the text.

To write successfully in these complex rhetorical situations, you might find it helpful to create an *extended reader profile* that goes beyond answering the Who, What, Where, When, Why, and How questions. An extended reader profile will help you to better anticipate what your readers expect, what they value, and what their attitudes are toward you and your topic.

 **Analyze** the Interactive Document for **Audience** at **mycomplab.com**

What Are Their Expectations? Your readers probably picked up your document because they *expect* or *need* something. Do they need to know something specific? What do they need in order to do something or achieve a goal? Make a list of the two to five items that your readers expect you to address in your document for it to be useful to them.

The genre you've chosen will shape your readers' expectations in powerful but predictable ways. Every genre has a certain look and feel. Readers get a sense of which genre they're in by noticing cues in the title, contents, organization, writing style, design, and other features. So developing genre know-how is important because it helps you anticipate your readers' expectations.

- For a memoir or profile, your readers will expect you to use descriptive detail and capture their interest with an engaging narrative.

- For an evaluation or a review, your readers may expect you to define and explain the evaluation criteria you are using and the reasons you have chosen that criteria.

- For a literary analysis or rhetorical analysis, you may need to summarize the text you are analyzing and use examples to illustrate its style.

- For an argument or commentary, they will expect you to back up your claims with facts, examples, and solid reasoning.

- For a report or a proposal, your readers will expect you to provide background information to allow them to understand the current situation. They will also be looking for specific plans and recommendations to help them solve problems.

If you can figure out and then shape your readers' expectations, you are well on your way to knowing what to include in your document and how to present it.

What Are Their Values? *Values* involve personal beliefs, social conventions, and cultural expectations. Your readers' values have been formed through their personal experiences, family or religious upbringing, and social/cultural influences.

Personal values. Your readers' personal beliefs can be hard to predict, but you can take a few educated guesses. Think about your readers' upbringings and experiences. What are their core beliefs? What makes your readers different or unique? How are your readers similar to you and what personal values do you and your readers likely hold in common?

Customs of their society. How do people do things in their social circles? What expectations does their society place on them? What traditions or codes govern their behavior?

Cultural values. Your readers' culture may influence their behavior in ways even they don't fully understand. What do people in your readers' culture value? How are these cultural values similar to or different from your cultural values?

Mistakenly, writers sometimes assume that their readers hold the same values they do. Even people very similar to you in background and upbringing may hold values that are different from yours. Meanwhile, people whose cultures and up-bringings are different from yours may have distinctly different ways of seeing the world.

What Is Their Attitude Toward You and the Issue? Your readers will also have a particular *attitude* about your topic and, perhaps, about you. Are they excited, or are they bored? Are they concerned or apathetic, happy or upset about your topic? Do they already accept your ideas, or are they deeply skeptical? Are they feeling positive toward you or negative? Will they welcome your views or be hostile toward them? Are they joyful or angry, optimistic or pessimistic?

If your readers are positive and welcoming toward your views, you will want to take advantage of their goodwill by giving them persuasive reasons to agree with you. If they are negative or resistant, you will want to use solid reasoning, sufficient examples, and good style to counter their resistance and win them over.

Anticipating all of your readers' expectations, values, and attitudes can be especially difficult if you try to do it all in your head. That's why professional writers often like to use a Reader Analysis Worksheet like the one shown in Figure 3.2 to help them create an extended profile of their readers.

Types of Readers	Expectations	Values	Attitudes
Most Important Readers:			
Second Most Important Readers:			
Third Most Important Readers:			

FIGURE 3.2 A Reader Analysis Worksheet

A Reader Analysis Worksheet is a helpful tool for understanding your readers and making good decisions about the content, organization, style, and design of your document.

Using the Reader Analysis Worksheet is easy. On the left, list the types of readers who are likely to read your document, ranking them by importance. Then fill in what you know about their expectations, values, and attitudes. If you don't know enough to fill in a few of the squares on the worksheet, just put question marks (?) there. Question marks signal places where you may need to do some additional research on your readers.

An extended reader profile blends your answers to the Five-W and How questions with the information you added to the Reader Analysis Worksheet. These two reader analysis tools should give you a strong understanding of your readers and how they will interpret your document.

Analyzing the Context

The *context* of your document involves the external influences that will shape how your readers interpret and react to your writing. It is important to remember that readers react to a text moment by moment. So the happenings around them can influence their understanding of your document.

Your readers will be influenced by three kinds of contexts: place, medium, and social and political issues.

Place

Earlier, when you developed a brief profile of your readers, you answered the Where and When questions to figure out the locations and times in which your readers would use your document. Now go a little deeper to put yourself in your readers' place.

What are the physical features of this place?

What is visible around the readers, and what can they hear?

What is moving or changing in this place?

Who else is in this place, and what do they want from my readers?

What is the history and culture of this place, and how does it shape how people view things?

FIGURE 3.3 The Influence of Place

The place where your readers encounter your writing will strongly influence their interpretation of your ideas.

A place is never static. Places are always changing. So figure out how this changing, evolving place influences your readers and their interpretation of your text (Figure 3.3).

The genre of your document may help you to imagine the places where people are likely to read it. Proposals and reports tend to be read in office settings, and they are often discussed in meetings. Memoirs, profiles, reviews, and commentaries tend to be read in less formal settings—at home, on the bus, or in a café. Once you know the genre of your document, you can make decisions about how it should be designed and what would make it more readable in a specific place.

Medium

The medium is the technology that your readers will use to experience your document. Each medium (e.g., paper, Web site, public presentation, video, podcast) will shape how they interpret your words and react to your ideas:

Paper documents. Paper documents are often read more closely than on-screen documents. With paper, your readers may be more patient with longer documents and longer paragraphs. Document design, which is discussed in Chapter 17, "Designing," makes the text more attractive and helps your readers read more efficiently. People appreciate graphics and photographs that enhance and reinforce the words on the page, but visuals aren't mandatory. Paper documents, however, are often less accessible than on-screen documents, because they are harder to store and keep track of.

Electronic documents. When people read text on a screen, like a Web site or a blog, they usually scan it, reading selectively for the information they need. In other words, your on-screen readers will be "raiding" the text to locate specific facts and information. They are not going to be patient with a long document, and they will tend to avoid reading large paragraphs. They will appreciate any visuals, like graphs, charts, and photographs, that you can add to enhance their understanding. You can turn to Chapter 29, "Using the Internet," for more ideas about how to write for the screen.

Public presentations. Presentations tend to be much more visual than on-screen and print documents. A presentation made with *PowerPoint* or *Keynote* usually boils an original text down to bullet points that highlight major issues and important facts. Your readers will focus on the items you choose to highlight, and they will rely on you to connect these items and expand on them. Turn to Chapter 32, "Presenting Your Work," for more ideas about how to make great presentations.

Podcasts or videos. A podcast or video needs to be concise and focused. Hearing or seeing a text can be very powerful in this multimedia age; however, amateurs are easy to spot. So your readers will expect a polished, tight presentation that is carefully produced. Your work should get to the point and not waste their time, or they will turn to something else. You can turn to Chapter 29, "Using the Internet," to learn how to make podcasts and videos and upload them to the Internet.

Paper is no longer the only medium for writing. So you should always keep in mind that your texts will likely appear in electronic media. These various media shape how readers will experience your text and interpret your ideas.

Social and Political Influences

Now, think about how current trends and events will influence how your readers interpret what you are telling them. Always keep in mind that your readers will encounter your writing in specific and real contexts that are always changing. The change can be quick and dramatic, or it can be slow and almost imperceptible.

Social trends. Pay attention to the social trends that are influencing you, your topic, and your readers. You originally decided to write about this topic because you believe it is important right now. What are the larger social trends that will influence how people in the near and distant future understand this topic? What is changing in your society that makes this issue so important? Most importantly, how do these trends directly or indirectly affect your readers?

Economic trends. For many issues, it all comes down to money. What economic factors will influence your readers? How does their economic status shape how they will interpret your arguments? What larger economic trends are influencing you and your readers?

Political trends. Also, keep any political trends in mind as you analyze the context for your document. On a micropolitical level, how will your ideas affect your readers' relationships with you, their families, their colleagues, or their supervisors? On a macropolitical level, how will political trends at the local, state, federal, and international levels shape how your readers interpret your ideas?

Readers, naturally, respond to the immediate context in which they live (Figure 3.4 on page 35). If you understand how place, medium, and social and political trends influence your readers, you can better adapt your work to their specific expectations, values, and attitudes.

◉ Watch the Animation
on **Genres and the
Rhetorical Situation**
at **mycomplab.com**

Genres and the Rhetorical Situation

We threw quite a bit of material at you in this chapter and in the previous one. Here's the point and a brief overview. Genres are used to respond to specific types of rhetorical situations. So when choosing the appropriate genre, you first need to completely understand the situation to which you are responding:

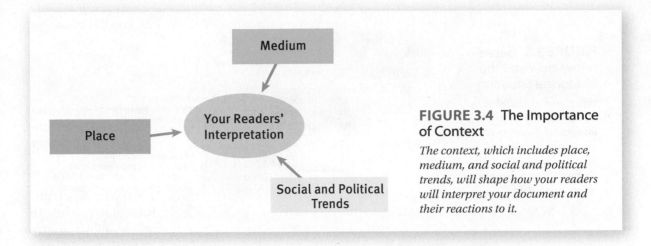

FIGURE 3.4 The Importance of Context

The context, which includes place, medium, and social and political trends, will shape how your readers will interpret your document and their reactions to it.

Topic. What is the exact topic your document is going to discuss? What information is "inside" the topic's boundaries and what is "outside" those boundaries? Have you sharpened your topic enough to allow you to handle it in the time and space you have available?

Angle. What is new or different about your approach to this topic? What has happened recently that makes your topic especially interesting to you and your readers right now? What makes your ideas about this topic different than the ideas of others?

Purpose. What exactly do you want to achieve in this document? What do you want your readers to believe or do after they are finished reading it? What are your goals in writing this text?

Readers. What are your readers' expectations, values, and attitudes? How do these characteristics shape the content, organization, style, and design of your document?

Contexts. In what places do you expect your readers to encounter your document? How does the medium of your text shape how they will read it? What economic and social-political trends will influence how they react to what you are saying?

Figure 3.5 shows how these elements work together. It might seem like a lot of work to figure all these things out, especially when the deadline is not that far away.

FIGURE 3.5 Genre Know-How and the Rhetorical Situation

When you've analyzed the rhetorical situation and understand how genres work, you can more efficiently create documents that will have an impact on your readers.

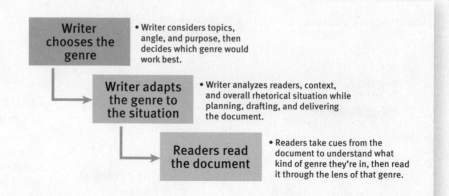

Writer chooses the genre
• Writer considers topics, angle, and purpose, then decides which genre would work best.

Writer adapts the genre to the situation
• Writer analyzes readers, context, and overall rhetorical situation while planning, drafting, and delivering the document.

Readers read the document
• Readers take cues from the document to understand what kind of genre they're in, then read it through the lens of that genre.

In reality, though, analyzing the rhetorical situation only takes a few minutes for most documents. Once you have developed a full understanding of the rhetorical situation, you will find that writing the document is faster and more efficient. In other words, you will save time, because you won't hit dead ends or spend time collecting information you don't need. A few minutes invested at the beginning will pay off with better writing that takes less time and effort.

Need to quickly analyze your readers and the context for your document? Here are some steps to help you get started.

CREATE a Brief Profile of Your Readers

Using the Five-W and How questions, figure out *who* your readers are, *what* they need, *where* and *when* they will be reading the document, *why* they are reading it, and *how* they will be reading it. A sentence or two for each question should be enough to develop a brief profile.

KNOW Your Readers' Expectations

On a basic level, what are the two to five pieces of information your readers *expect* or *need* you to tell them for your document to be useful?

FIGURE OUT Your Readers' Values

Write down your readers' personal, social, and cultural values, and try to anticipate how these values will shape your document.

ANTICIPATE Your Readers' Attitudes About You and Your Topic

Try to figure out what your readers' mind-set will be. Will they be excited or bored, concerned or apathetic, happy or upset? Are they already convinced or deeply skeptical? Are they feeling positive toward you or negative? Will they welcome your views or be hostile toward them? Are they glad or angry, optimistic or pessimistic?

THINK About How Place and Medium Affect Your Readers

The physical place where they are reading may affect how closely they are reading and dictate what they need you to highlight for them. The medium of your document (e.g., paper, screen, presentation, podcast) will also shape how readers interpret your ideas.

CONSIDER Social and Political Trends

Identify any current trends or events that might color your readers' understanding of your writing. What social trends affect your topic? How does money influence the situation? How does your project touch on micropolitical and macropolitical trends?

QUICK START GUIDE

1. Choose an advertisement from a magazine or a newspaper. In a group, figure out the advertisement's purpose, target readers, and the contexts in which it was used. Be as specific and thorough as you can as you define the following:

   • *Purpose:* What is the advertisement trying to do? Use key words like *persuade, inform, entertain,* and others to describe its objectives.

   • *Readers:* What are the expectations, values, and attitudes of the target readers? How does the advertisement try to use those expectations, values, and attitudes to its advantage?

   • *Context:* Describe the place and medium of the advertisement as well as the social, economic, and political trends that might influence how it is interpreted. How do these contextual factors influence how readers respond to this ad?

   Finally, do you think the ad is effective in persuading or influencing its intended readers? For which readers would it be most effective, and for which ones would it be least effective?

2. Think of a time when you did not communicate effectively. With your group, discuss why the communication failed. What happened? Describe how you misread the situation, and why the audience or readers reacted as they did. How could you have handled the situation better if you had known the expectations, values, and attitudes of the audience or readers? If you had better understood the social and political issues, how might you have been more successful?

3. With your group, make a list of ten things that motivate people to agree with others or to take action. Discuss how these motives influence the ways people make decisions in real life. What are some ways you could use these motivations in your written work to persuade or influence people?

1. Imagine that you are an advertising specialist who has been asked to develop an advertising campaign to sell digital audio players (MP3, iPod, or other audio device) to people over 60 years old. Figure out these customers' expectations, values, and attitudes toward the product. Then figure out how place and social and political factors shape their decisions about buying this kind of product. In a one-page memo to your professor, explain how you might use this knowledge to create an advertising campaign for this new market.

2. You have probably seen those electronic billboards that use light-emitting diodes (LEDs) to display content. These billboards offer more flexibility than traditional billboard media, because different advertisements can be displayed at different times of the day.

   Imagine that you are creating ads for these kinds of billboards. First, choose a product you want to advertise. Now create two thumbnail sketches (with images and words) for the billboard for two different contexts:

   • *Context A:* rush hour, when drivers are stopped at traffic lights in front of the billboard for as long as 90 seconds.

   • *Context B:* normal drive time, when drivers may not stop at all, but drive by and have as little as two seconds to glance at the billboard.

Write a one-page memo explaining how the two versions differ in response to the differing contexts. Explain why each version's design and content is right for the context.

3. For your next project in this class, do a brief reader analysis in which you answer the Five-W and How questions about your readers. Then do an expanded reader analysis in which you explore their expectations, values, and attitudes. In a one-page memo to your professor, explain the differences between your brief analysis and the extended analysis. What does the extended analysis reveal that the brief analysis didn't reveal? Would the brief analysis be enough for this project? Why? Or do you think the extended analysis would help you write a more effective document?

Write This

1. **Evaluate an argument.** Find an opinion article about an issue that interests you and write a two-page evaluation in which you discuss how well the writer has adapted his or her article for its context. You can find a variety of opinion articles in your local or school newspapers (in the "opinion" section) or on the Internet (blogs, personal pages, online newspaper opinion sections and the responses to them). Mark up the text, paying attention to how the writer addresses the following contextual issues:

   • *Place:* First, note how the place in which the article was published and where it will likely be read influence the way readers interact with it.

   • *Medium:* How does the medium shape the way people read the text and what they will focus on?

   • *Social and Political Trends:* What have people been saying about the issue? If it's a hot topic, what makes it hot? What larger trends have motivated the writer to write this argument?

   In your evaluation, explain how the author of this opinion article adjusted his or her argument to the context in which it appears. Discuss whether you felt the opinion article succeeded. How might it be improved?

2. **Rewrite an online text for a different reader.** Find a brief document on the Internet that is aimed toward a specific kind of reader. Then rewrite the document for a completely different type of reader. For example, if it was originally aimed at a young reader, rewrite it for an older reader.

   To complete this assignment, you will need to do a brief and extended reader analysis of your new readers.

   When you are finished rewriting the document, write a brief e-mail to your professor in which you explain how the change in readers changed the content, organization, style, and design of your rewrite. Attach your new version of the text to your e-mail.

PEARSON
mycomplab

For support in meeting this chapter's objectives, follow this path in MyCompLab: Resources ⟹ Writing ⟹ Writing Process ⟹ Revising. Review the Instruction and Multimedia resources about speaking to your audience, then complete the Exercises and click on Gradebook to measure your progress.

Using Genres to Express Ideas

PART OUTLINE

Writing well means responding effectively to diverse situations. In these chapters, you will learn how to use ten GENRES and ten "MICROGENRES" that will help you write about yourself, be critical, take a stand, pitch your ideas, and argue with others.

4

Memoirs

In this chapter, you will learn how to—
- generate content for your memoir.
- use the memoir genre to organize a story.
- develop an engaging voice to tell your story.

The words *memoir* and *memory* come from the same root word, but memoirs involve more than an author sharing his or her memories. While telling an autobiographical story, good memoirs explore and reflect on a central theme or question. They rarely provide explicit answers to those questions. Instead, they invite readers to explore and reflect with the narrator to try to unravel the deeper significance of the recounted events.

Writers create memoirs when they have true personal stories that they hope will inspire others to reflect on or understand interesting questions or social issues. Readers come to memoirs expecting to engage with authors and their stories. They expect to encounter new perspectives and insights that are fresh and meaningful.

Today, memoirs are more popular than ever. They are common on best-seller lists of books. Some recent memoirs, such as Jeanette Walls' *The Glass Castle* about growing up in a dysfunctional family and Frank McCourt's *Angela's Ashes* about his childhood in Ireland, sold millions of copies. Meanwhile, blogs and social networking sites give ordinary people opportunities to post their reflections on their lives.

In college, professors will sometimes ask you to write about your life to explore where you came from and how you came to hold certain beliefs. In these assignments, the goal is not just to recount events but to unravel their significance and arrive at insights that help you explore and engage more deeply with the issues discussed in the class.

Memoirs

This diagram shows a basic organization for a memoir, but other arrangements of these sections will work, too. You should alter this organization to fit the features of your topic, angle, purpose, readers, and context.

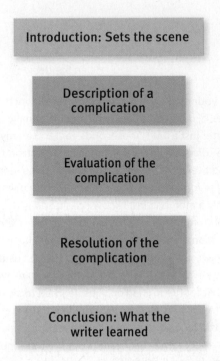

Using rich detail, memoirs tell a personal story in which an event or series of events leads the writer to new insights about life. They tend to have these main features:

- **An engaging title** that hints at the memoir's overall meaning or "theme."
- **An introduction with a "lead"** that captures the reader's interest or sets a scene.
- **A complication** that must be resolved in some way—a tension or conflict between people's values and beliefs, or a personal inner conflict the author faces.
- **A plot** that draws the reader forward as the memoir moves through a series of scenes or stages.
- **Intimacy between the narrator and the reader,** allowing the writer to speak with readers in a personal one-on-one way.
- **Rich and vivid details** that give the story greater imagery, texture, and impact.
- **A central theme or question** that is rarely announced or answered explicitly, but that the narrator explores and reflects on with the reader.
- **A new understanding or revelation** that presents a moment of growth, transformation, or clarity in the writer.

ONE STUDENT'S WORK
Memoirs

Engaging title that forecasts the subject of swimming and also hints at the memoir's theme.

Introduction starts fast with a lead that sets the scene, and it ends in a surprising way.

The complication is introduced, an inner struggle the narrator faces.

Background moves the plot forward.

Diving In

Helen Sanderson

Take your mark. Anticipation builds as I crouch and grip the edge of the rough plastic, ready to strike at any second. I finally hear the sound of the electronic starter just a few nanoseconds earlier than my competition. I hit a block of ice before I dive just below the surface. A few strong kicks and I'm taking my first stroke, and then another as fast as I can. Breathe as little as possible. By the time I'm on the second lap, I'm going nowhere. I am dying to take in gulps of air and rest for only a moment, but I know I can't. Surely this is almost over. My lungs and muscles burn for oxygen as I dig in for the final stretch; the end of the pool could not come soon enough. I look up to find that I have shaved a second off of my time and have achieved last place in my heat, as usual.

I have never been an athlete. My motions are awkward, uncoordinated, and uncertain. At fourteen, I had only just learned to swim the butterfly with a dozen eight year olds as my classmates. Deciding to try out for my high school swim team was the biggest challenge I had ever undertaken. I will never forget the day of my first tryouts. The coach had posted tryout times that were way beyond my reach: thirty-five seconds for fifty yards. I had never even come within twenty seconds of that time. All that time I had spent the summer before my freshman year swimming lap after lap, practicing for this day, seemed like wasted effort. I knew I could swim those fifty yards ahead of me, but only if I was given a full minute, not just thirty-five seconds. Holding back tears, I watched my classmates, fearless, dive into the water. Should I dive in behind them knowing I will fail?

It's not as though I've never failed before: a Latin test, a piano audition, or even as a friend. But I had personal experience behind me to reassure myself that I would get better. I started swimming with a stone cold slate and only a few months of summer training with a private instructor. No summer leagues or competitive teams. I just swam back and forth. Up to this point, I had never physically pushed myself so hard. All I wanted was to make the team.

Practices were much worse. Though no one was cut, I knew I was the slowest. My teammates passed me, and I always finished each set last. I can hear the

coach yelling out the next set of drills: "Ten 100's! Ready . . . go!" Meanwhile I am still struggling to get to the end of the previous set, deprived of energy, oxygen, and morale. I cried countless times out of frustration and self-pity, wanting to quit. I had made the team, but I was failing my teammates. I cramped my team's efforts and embarrassed myself, but I swam every lap. I may have been the slowest, but I was going to work the hardest.

> Rich and vivid details give the story texture and intensify the complication.

I improved tremendously after just a few weeks of rigorous practice. Although I was still the slowest, I was slower by a smaller margin. Fifty yards in thirty-nine seconds. No one else could say they had improved by seventeen seconds, a tremendous accomplishment. I persevered through every meet, practice, lap, and stroke. I had attained my goal: I was a swimmer.

> Narrator's personal tone is maintained throughout.

Swimming is the hardest challenge I have ever undertaken. I have always been very driven academically and socially, but I was very afraid to push myself to be an athlete because balance, endurance, and coordination were so unfamiliar to me. However, I did not allow myself to accept failure. Just dive in and keep swimming. There is only me and the pool, a full immersion of body and mind.

Take your mark. My muscles and mind lock into place, attentive and poised. I hear the starter sound and take a leap, already stretching toward the end of the pool. My strokes are fluid, deliberate, and quick. Breathe as little as possible. I do a flip turn, tight and well executed, as I push myself harder and faster. I don't think about the air I need to fill my lungs or the other girls in my race; I only concentrate on what I feel. This time as I reach the end of the pool, I look up to find that I have reached a new personal record of thirty-six seconds and have achieved next-to-last place in my heat. I have won.

> Conclusion resolves the conflict as narrator describes a newly gained clarity.

Inventing Your Memoir's Content

Your goal in a memoir is to uncover the meaning of your past for your readers *and* for yourself. When starting out, you shouldn't be too concerned about what your point will be. Instead, begin with an interesting event or series of events from your life that you want to explore.

Inquiring: Finding an Interesting Topic

With your whole life as potential subject matter, deciding what to write about and narrowing your topic can be a challenge. Think about the times in your life when you did something challenging, scary, or fun. Think about the times when you felt pain or great happiness. Think about the times when something important happened to you, helping you make a discovery about yourself or someone else.

Now, on your screen or a piece of paper, make a brainstorming list of as many of these events as you can remember (Figure 4.1). Don't think too much about what you are writing down. These events don't need to be earth-shattering. Just list the stories you like to tell others about yourself.

Inquiring: Finding Out What You Already Know

Memoirs are about memories—of course—but they are also about your reflections on those memories. You need to do some personal inquiry to pull up those memories and then reflect on them to figure out what they meant at the time and what they mean to you now. Pick an event from your brainstorming list and use some of the following techniques to reflect on it.

Make a Map of the Scene. In your mind's eye, imagine the place where the event happened. Then draw a map of that place (Figure 4.2). Add as many details as you can remember—names, buildings, people, events, landmarks. You can use this map to help you tell your story.

Record Your Story as a Podcast or Video. Tell your story into your computer's audio recorder or into a camcorder. Afterwards, you may want to transcribe it to the written page. Sometimes it's easier to tell the story orally and then turn it into written text.

Storyboard the Event. In comic strip form, draw out the major scenes in the event. It's fine to use stick figures, because these drawings are only for you. They will help you remember and sort out the story you are trying to tell.

Do Some Role Playing. Use your imagination to put yourself into the life of a family member or someone close to you. Try to work through events as that person might have experienced them, even events that you were part of. Then compare and contrast that person's experiences with your own, paying special attention to any tensions or conflicts.

> **Possible Topics for a Memoir**
> Breaking my leg skiing
> Winning the clothing design competition
> Failing that geometry class
> The trip to Mexico
> Death of Fred Sanders
> Leaving home to go to college
> Meeting Senator Wilkins
> Discovering Uncle Jim is gay
> When Bridgeport's downtown flooded
> When the car broke down in Oklahoma
> Going to the state volleyball finals
> Not making the cheerleading team

FIGURE 4.1 Brainstorming to Find Topics

Brainstorming is a good way to list possible topics for your memoir. Try to think of moments when something important happened that changed your life or led to a new insight.

Researching: Finding Out What Others Know

Research can help you better understand the event or times you are writing about. For instance, a writer describing her father's return from the Persian Gulf War (1990–1991) might want to find out more about the history of this war. She could

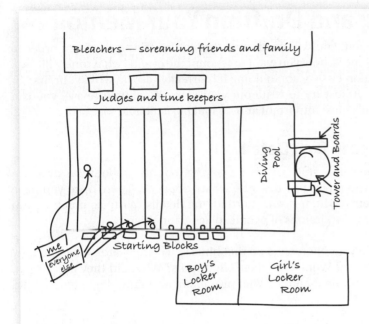

FIGURE 4.2 Making a Map of the Scene

Sometimes drawing a map of the scene where an event happened can help you reconstruct it and remember important details. Here is a map of the pool described in Helen Sanderson's memoir.

find out about soldiers' experiences by reading personal stories about the Gulf War (and other recent wars) at *The Memory Archive* (memoryarchive.org). When researching your topic, you should try to find information from the following three types of sources:

Online Sources. Use Internet search engines to find information that might help you understand the people or situations in your memoir. This information can be especially helpful if you are recounting an experience from a time when you were very young and had little or no awareness of what was happening in the world. Understanding the historical context better might help you to frame your memoir. Or maybe you could find information on psychology Web sites that could help explain your behavior or the behavior you witnessed.

Print Sources. At your campus or public library, look for newspapers or magazines that might have reported something about the event you are describing. Or find historical information in magazines from the period or a history textbook. These resources can help you explain the conditions that shaped how people behaved.

Empirical Sources. Research doesn't only happen on the Internet and in the library. Interview people who were involved with the events you are describing in your memoir. If possible, revisit the place you are writing about. Write down any observations, describe things as they are now, and look for details that you might have forgotten or missed.

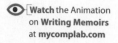 Watch the Animation on **Writing Memoirs** at **mycomplab.com**

Organizing and Drafting Your Memoir

To create a good memoir, you will need to go through a series of drafts in order to discover what your theme is, how you want to recount the events, what tone will work best, and so forth. So don't worry about doing it "correctly" as you write your first, or even your second, draft. Just try to write out your story. When you revise, you can work on deciding what's most important and on making it all hold together.

Setting the Scene in Rich Detail

Start out by telling the whole story without worrying too much about the structure you will use. At first, you might just describe what happened. Then, once you have the basic series of events written down, start adding details. Write as much as you can. Be sure to give rich descriptions of people, places, and things.

The People. What did your characters do that hints at who they are? What did they say? How did they behave? What were their blind spots? What did they care about, and what were they ambivalent about? What prominent or quirky characteristics did they have?

The Scenes. What did each scene look like? How did it feel or smell? What did you taste or hear? What is the history of this place—both its public history and your personal history?

Dialogue. What was said before and after the event? Who said what to whom? How did they say it? Were they angry? excited? thrilled? scared?

These kinds of details are some of the most important features of your memoir. Your memoir will be more realistic if you give the readers enough detail to reconstruct the scene, people, and events for themselves.

Main Point or Thesis

Memoirs explore and reflect on a central theme or question, but they rarely provide explicit answers or explicit thesis statements early in the text. When writing a memoir, put your point in the conclusion, using an implied thesis. In other words, don't state your main point or thesis in your introduction unless you have a good reason for doing so.

Describing the Complication

The *complication* in your memoir is the problem or challenge that you or others needed to resolve. So pay special attention to how this complication came about and why people reacted to it in a particular way.

The Event. What exactly happened? Who did it and what did they do? Was the event sudden or did it take a long time to develop?

The Complication. What was really at stake here? What was the essential conflict or complication that caused this story to be something more than an everyday event? How did you or the other people in the story feel about that tension?

The Immediate Reaction. How did people react to the event? What were their emotions? What did their reactions look like? Did they do anything that they later regretted?

Evaluating and Resolving the Complication

After the initial reaction, you should show how you and others evaluated and resolved the complication. The complication isn't necessarily a problem that needs to be fixed. Instead, you should show how the people involved tried to make sense of the complication, reacted to the change, and moved forward.

The Evaluation. What did you and other people think was happening? Were there any misunderstandings? Did you talk about the appropriate ways to respond? Did you or others come up with a plan?

The Resolution. What did you decide to do? Were you successful in resolving the complication, or partially successful? If so, how did you handle it? If you weren't successful, how did you make changes to adjust to the new situation? How did other people make adjustments?

Concluding with a Point—an Implied Thesis

Your conclusion describes, directly or indirectly, not only what you learned but also what your reader should have learned from your experiences. Memoirs usually have an "implied thesis." You should avoid writing a "and the moral of the story is . . ." or a "they lived happily ever after" ending. Instead, you should strive for something that feels like the events or people reached some kind of closure.

Your conclusion is where you are going to make your point. For example, you might state it directly, as in Wang Ping's "Book War" at the end of this chapter:

> When I saw stars rising from their eyes, I knew I hadn't lost the battle. The books had been burnt, but the story went on.

If, however, you think your point is obvious to readers, or if you want to have your readers reflect on the overall meaning, you can leave it unstated. In these situations, you can give readers a glimpse into the future. Or you can provide a final sentence or passage that hints at your memoir's meaning. For instance, Joe Mackall's "Words of My Youth," which appears at the end of this chapter, does not end with a tidy message but with an evocative set of images that foster reflection:

> An excellent question. I honestly do not know. I have no idea. The slur just seems to have been out there, there and somehow not there, like incense, like the way a Wiffle ball whips and dips, the way adults laugh at things kids don't

Mackall's final paragraph provides a sense of closure but asks readers to reflect on the central theme for themselves.

understand, the way background noise from a baseball game leaks out of transistor radios, the way bits of gravel bounce out of pickup truck beds, the way factory fires flirt with the night sky, the way sonic booms burst the lie of silence.

Whether you choose to state your main point directly or not, your readers should come away from your memoir with a clear sense of closure.

Choosing an Appropriate Style

Your memoir's style and tone depend on how you want to portray yourself as the narrator of the story. Choose a style that works for you, your story, and your readers. If you want your narrator (you) to have a casual attitude, that's the style and tone you want to strive for. If the narrator's relationship to the story is more formal, then the style will be more formal.

Evoking an Appropriate Tone

Tone refers to the attitude, or stance, that is taken toward the subject matter and the reader. That is, a certain "tone of voice" arises from the words on a page. For instance, in the story about joining her high-school swim team, Helen Sanderson combines past tense with present tense, evoking a vivid and tell-it-straight tone, to paint a frank picture of what was happening around her and inside her head. Wang Ping's tone in the memoir at the end of this chapter is serious and sincerely reverent, which mirrors the author's attitude about books, stories, and their power.

At times, whether you're writing the first draft or polishing your final draft, you may want to strategically establish a certain tone. Here's how to do it with concept mapping. First think of a key word that describes the tone you want to set. Then put that word in the middle of your screen or a piece of paper and circle it (Figure 4.3). Now create a concept map around that key word. Write down any words that you tend to associate with this tone. Then, as you put words on the screen or paper, try to come up with more words that are associated with these new words. Eventually, you will fill the screen or sheet.

In the draft of your memoir, look for places where you can use these words. If you use them strategically throughout the memoir, your readers will sense the tone, or attitude you are trying to convey. This will help you develop your central "theme," the idea or question that the entire memoir explores. You only need to use a few of these words to achieve the effect you want. If you use too many of them, your readers will feel that you are overdoing it.

Using Dialogue

Allow the characters in your memoir to reveal key details about themselves through dialogue rather than your narration. Use dialogue occasionally to reveal themes and ideas that are *key* to understanding your memoir. Here are some guidelines for using dialogue effectively:

Use Dialogue to Move the Story Forward. Anytime you use dialogue, the story should move forward. Dialogues between characters are key moments that should change the flow of the story in an important way.

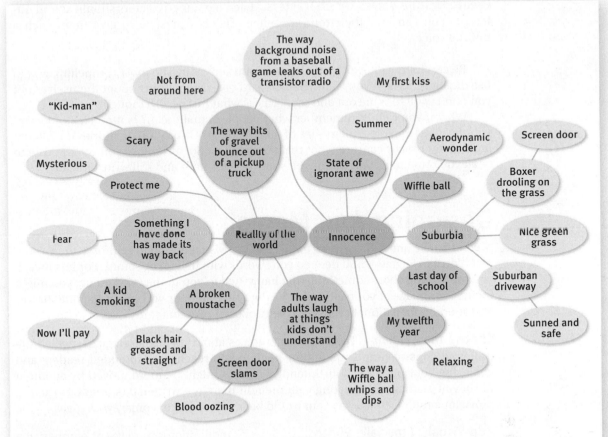

FIGURE 4.3 Creating a Tone with a Concept Map

A concept map is a good tool for helping you set a tone in your memoir. Simply choose the words or phrases that best describe the tone you are looking for and create a concept map around them. Here, a concept map has the ideas of "innocence" and "reality of the world" in the center, with other word and phrase clusters surrounding them.

Write the Way Your Characters Speak. People often don't speak in proper English, grammatical sentences, or full thoughts. When using dialogue, take advantage of opportunities to show how people really talk.

Trim the Extra Words. In real dialogue, people often say more than they need to say. You can trim out the unnecessary details, most of the "ums" and "ahs," and the repetitions. Your dialogue should be as crisp and tight as possible.

Identify Who Is Talking. The readers should know who is talking, so make sure you use dialogue tags (e.g., *he said, she said, he growled, she yelled*). Not every statement needs a dialogue tag; however, if you leave off the tag, make sure it's obvious who said the line.

Create Unique Voices for Characters. Each of your characters should sound different. You can vary their tone, cadence, dialects, or style to give them each a unique voice.

Be careful not to overuse dialogue in your memoir. The most compelling way to use dialogue is when you want characters to reveal something about themselves but you don't want to come out and say, "This is what this person thought."

What if you cannot remember what people actually said? Is it ethical to present your best but imperfect memories of that dialogue? Clearly, all memories are filtered and do not exactly capture what really happened. So, as long as you remain true to what you remember, you can invent some of the details and still write ethically.

Designing Your Memoir

Memoirs, like almost all genres today, can use visual design to reinforce the written text. You can augment and deepen your words with images or sound. For instance, if you are writing about something that happened to you in the third grade, you might include an image of yourself and a third-grade friend, or you might include images and sound from national events that were occurring at that time.

Choose the Medium. To guide your choices about media, strategically weigh the pros and cons of various media for helping you reach your intended readers and achieving your purpose. Your intended readers might be more moved by an audio file of you reading and enacting your memoir than by a written document. Perhaps a movie or a multimedia document would better allow you to convey your ideas.

Add Visuals, Especially Photos. Use one or more photos to make or emphasize a key point, set a tone, or add a new dimension. For instance, on her Web page for "Book War" (end of this chapter), Wang Ping (wangping.com) includes pictures of herself as a young girl and as a grown woman. These photos, like the words the author strategically employs, highlight the human being, with a human face, who is living through a massive revolution involving millions of people.

Find a Place to Publish. You might want to go a step further to get your story out there. Web sites, like the *Memory Archive,* offer places where you can share your memories (Figure 4.4). Otherwise, you might consider putting your memoirs on a blog or on your *Facebook* page. Remember, though, not to reveal private information that might embarrass you or put you at any kind of risk. Save your most personal information and photographs for yourself.

Revising and Editing Your Memoir

A good memoir is lean, with little or no fat. After drafting and gathering feedback from your classmates, professor, and/or friends and family, work toward a final draft that is as polished as possible. Cut out anything that does not advance the story or help you develop your characters or message.

FIGURE 4.4 The *Memory Archive*

The Memory Archive *is a great place to publish your memoir or read others' memoirs. Go to www.memoryarchive.org.*

Make Your Title Enticing. Keep trying out new titles. Work toward a title that sounds interesting to a reader who knows nothing about your memoir and captures something essential about your story. Try reading through your memoir to find an arresting image or statement that you can turn into a title.

Craft the Perfect Lead. Look at your lead, the beginning sentence or short paragraph that is supposed to capture the readers' interest. A compelling lead casts your readers into the drama of your memoir and makes them lean forward with questions they hope your memoir will answer. Does your lead introduce some idea or question that is important to the memoir's point? Does your lead focus down to an important image, idea, or point? Does it set the right tone for the rest of the memoir? You can turn to Chapter 19, "Drafting Introductions and Conclusions," for more ideas about crafting your lead.

Reevaluate the Details and Cut the Fat. Look at every aspect of the memoir—the narrative, the dialogue, the setting—and take out what is not absolutely necessary. Long stories are simply boring. When it comes to storytelling, less is often more. Provide your readers with just enough detail and character development to make them want to keep reading.

The revision and editing phase is where you are going to take your story from interesting to compelling. So leave plenty of time to rework your ideas and words. In some cases, you might need to "re-vision" your whole memoir because you figure out something important as you are writing. If so, have the courage and take the time to make those changes. The effort will be worth it.

The Literacy Narrative

The literacy narrative is a kind of memoir that focuses on how the author learned to read and write or on some formative experience that involved writing and speaking. Literacy narratives usually have all the elements of other memoirs. They don't just re-count a series of events, but carefully work those events into a plot with a complication. Quite often, the author describes overcoming some obstacle, perhaps the quest for literacy itself or the need to overcome some barrier to learning. Literacy narratives describe a transformation or take readers through a story that ends with a new under-standing, insight, or question to ponder.

Watch the Video **Literacy Narrative** at **mycomplab** .com

Literacy narratives are distinguished from other memoirs by a single feature: they focus on the author's experiences with reading and writing. Keep in mind that "literacy" encompasses more than learning to read and form letters on the traditional printed page. New writing situations are emerging due to new contexts, readers, pur-poses, and media. Learning to negotiate among these readers and situations is the real challenge of becoming literate in today's world. What literacy *is* constantly changes. New situations, technologies, and other changes require each of us to constantly acquire new literacy skills. All of these challenges are fair game for a literacy narrative.

Literacy narratives should have all the features described in this chapter's At-a-Glance on page 43. Be sure to pay attention to the conflict or tension: What challenge did you face and how did you resolve it—or fail to resolve it? Also, how did the experi-ence change you? What new understanding (positive or negative) did you come away with? And finally, think about the larger theme: What significance does your story have, and what does it tell readers about literacy or what questions does it encourage your readers to reflect on?

WRITE **your own literacy narrative.** Remember that "literacy" includes a broad range of activities, skills, knowledge, and situations. Choose a significant incident or set of related incidents in your life that involved coming to terms with literacy. Write your literacy narrative as a memoir, paying attention to the memoir's features. Possible subjects include:

- encountering a new kind of literacy, and the people involved
- working with or helping others with literacy issues
- encountering a new communication technology
- a situation where your literacy skills were tested
- a particular book, work of literature, or other communication that changed your outlook

From *Narrative of the Life of Frederick Douglass*

Frederick Douglass

In the following excerpt from one of the best-known literacy narratives ever written, Douglass describes his determination as a young slave in America to become literate, even though the effort put him in grave personal danger.

I lived in Master Hugh's family about seven years. During this time, I succeeded in learning to read and write. In accomplishing this, I was compelled to resort to various stratagems. I had no regular teacher. My mistress, who had kindly commenced to instruct me, had, in compliance with the advice and direction of her husband, not only ceased to instruct, but had set her face against my being instructed by any one else.... The plan which I adopted, and the one by which I was most successful, was that of making friends of all the little white boys whom I met in the street. As many of these as I could, I converted into teachers. With their kindly aid, obtained at different times and in different places, I finally succeeded in learning to read. When I was sent of errands, I always took my book with me, and by going one part of my errand quickly, I found time to get a lesson before my return. I used also to carry bread with me, enough of which was always in the house, and to which I was always welcome; for I was much better off in this regard than many of the poor white children in our neighborhood. This bread I used to bestow upon the hungry little urchins, who, in return, would give me that more valuable bread of knowledge. I am strongly tempted to give the names of two or three of those little boys, as a testimonial of the gratitude and affection I bear them; but prudence forbids;—not that it would injure me, but it might embarrass them; for it is almost an unpardonable offence to teach slaves to read in this Christian country. It is enough to say of the dear little fellows, that they lived on Philpot Street, very near Durgin and Bailey's ship-yard. I used to talk this matter of slavery over with them. I would sometimes say to them, I wished I could be as free as they would be when they got to be men. "You will be free as soon as you are twenty-one, *but I am a slave for life!* Have not I as good a right to be free as you have?" These words used to trouble them; they would express for me the liveliest sympathy, and console me with the hope that something would occur by which I might be free.

Douglass introduces the complication.

The scene is set, while background information is provided up front.

Vivid descriptions of people and places.

Douglass shows how he resolved the conflict.

The conclusion reveals the larger point of the narrative: the injustice of slavery.

Here's one basic approach for creating an engaging memoir that makes a point.

CHOOSE the Event or Series of Events You Want to Write About

Use the brainstorming exercises to come up with a list of events and choose the one that could become an effective memoir.

QUESTION Your Memory About the Event(s)

Figure out what you know and what you can imagine about the event. What can you find out about the place, the objects in that place, and the people and what they did?

DO Some Research

If you want to find out more about the time, the place, or a person in your memoir, do some background research to find out what things were really like.

DRAFT the Story

Write the story, including all the events that relate to it. Describe people, their actions, and places with rich and vivid detail.

FIND the Theme

Reflect on what you've written and decide what "theme" you want this story to evoke for your readers. "Pets and people" is a topic not a theme; "To what degree can pets replace people in our lives?" is a theme.

STATE the Message Directly or Indirectly

Whether you choose to make the main point directly or indirectly, your final paragraphs should provide a sense of closure that points readers to your overall message.

DEVELOP an Appropriate Tone or Voice

Develop your narrator's voice and use dialogue to add different voices to your story.

EDIT the Story to Its Essentials

When you ask yourself, *What is essential to the theme of my memoir?* you'll probably end up cutting a lot out of your original draft. Good memoirs are to the point; they should include only what is essential.

Book War

WANG PING

In this memoir, author Wang Ping writes about learning to read and growing up during the Cultural Revolution, a tumultuous time in Chinese history. As you read, pay attention to how she uses even simple events to draw out meaning and relevance.

I discovered "The Little Mermaid" in 1968. That morning, when I opened the door to light the stove to make breakfast, I found my neighbor reading under a streetlight. The red plastic wrap indicated it was Mao's collected work. She must have been there all night long, for her hair and shoulders were covered with frost, and her body shivered from cold. She was sobbing quietly. I got curious. What kind of person would weep from reading Mao's words? I walked over and peeked over her shoulders. What I saw made me shiver. The book in her hands had nothing to do with Mao; it was Hans Christian Andersen's fairy tales, and she was reading "The Little Mermaid," the story that had lit my passion for books since my kindergarten. I had started school a year earlier so that I could learn how to read the fairy tales by myself. By the end of my first grade, however, the Cultural Revolution began. Schools were closed, libraries sealed. Books, condemned as "poisonous weeds," were burnt on streets. And I had never been able to get hold of "The Little Mermaid."

My clever neighbor had disguised Andersen's "poisonous weed" with the scarlet cover of Mao's work. Engrossed in the story, she didn't realize my presence behind her until I started weeping. She jumped up, fairy tales clutched to her budding chest. Her panic-stricken face said she was ready to fight me to death if I dared to report her. We stared at each other for an eternity. Suddenly she started laughing, pointing at my tear-stained face. She knew then that her secret was safe with me.

She gave me 24 hours to read the fairy tales, and I loaned her *The Arabian Nights*, which was missing the first fifteen pages and the last story. But the girl squealed and started dancing in the twilight. When we finished each other's books, we started an underground book group with strict rules for safety, and we had books to read almost every day, all "poisonous" classics.

Soon I excavated a box of books my mother had buried beneath the chicken coop. I pried it open with a screwdriver, and pulled out one treasure after another: *The Dream of the Red Chamber, The Book of Songs, Grimm's Fairy Tales, The Tempest, The Hunchback of Notre Dame, Huckleberry Finn, American Dream,* each wrapped with waxed paper to keep out moisture.

I devoured them all, in rice paddies and 5 wheat fields, on my way home from school and errands. I tried to be careful. If I got caught, the consequence would be catastrophic, not only for myself, but also for my entire family. But my mother finally discovered I had unearthed her treasure box, and set out to destroy these "time bombs"—if I was caught reading these books, the whole family would be destroyed. She combed every possible place in the house: in the deep of drawers, under the mattress and floor boards. It was a hopeless battle: my mother knew every little trick of mine. Whenever she found a book, she'd order me to tear the pages and place them in the stove, and she'd sit nearby watching, tears in her eyes. And my heart, our hearts, turned into cinder.

When the last book went, I sat with my chickens. Hens and roosters surrounded me, pecking at my closed fists for food. As tears flowed, the Little Mermaid became alive from inside. She stepped onto the sand, her feet bled terribly, and she could not speak, yet how her eyes sang with triumph. Burning with a fever similar to the Little Mermaid's, I started telling stories to my siblings, friends, and neighbors—stories I'd read from those forbidden treasures, stories I made up for myself and my audience. We gathered on summer nights, during winter darkness. When I saw stars rising from their eyes, I knew I hadn't lost the battle.

The books had been burnt, but the story went on.

A CLOSER LOOK AT
Book War

1. What happens to the reader in the first paragraph? Pretend you are reading in slow motion and pinpoint the moment at which some detail draws you in to surprise you. Is it effective?

2. Make a list of the events that occur. What happens in each scene? What changes in each scene? How do these events work together to form a plot?

3. What is the complication in "Book War"? What is at stake in this memoir, and whose values does the narrator struggle with? In the resolution of the story, whose values win out in the end, and how clear is that resolution?

IDEAS FOR
Writing

1. Which of your family's stories do you remember most? Freewrite for five minutes, telling this story. Be sure to note details about the setting and characters. What happened? What did it mean to you then, and what does it mean to you now?

2. Memoirs like "Book War" are sometimes called "literacy narratives." They tell the story of learning to read or write, or they tell the story of coming to grips with some new aspect of literacy—for example, the power of stories to make change, the promise of literacy and education for achieving one's dreams, and so on. What is your literacy narrative? Write a brief memoir in which you tell a story about how you learned to read and/or write.

Words of My Youth

JOE MACKALL

Joe Mackall is an author of books about culture and his own life. In this memoir, he talks about growing up in the suburbs. Notice how his voice seems to emerge from the text as he tells his story.

I stand at the edge of my suburban driveway on Fairlawn Drive, sunned and safe. My friend Mick and I play Wiffle ball. Each swing of the bat sends the ball flying into the mystery grip of physics and aerodynamic wonder. The ball appears headed straight up before some hidden hand of wind and speed and serrated plastic jerks it over to the lawn of the widow next door. Mrs. Worth's boxer drools the day away, watching from the backyard in its own state of ignorant awe.

We take turns "smacking the shit" out of the plastic ball. I don't notice, not right away, an older kid—a man really—walking down the other side of the street, his eyes straight ahead. Not from around here. As the kid-man gets closer, I focus more intently on the game, as if this focus will protect me from what's about to happen. I chase the ball as if catching it matters more than anything, more than my first kiss or my last day of school. I make careful throws, keeping my eye on the ball, trying to anticipate the direction of its flight and fall.

I fear—as I so often fear—that something I have done has found its way back to me. And now I'll pay. Five or six houses away now, the kid-man crosses the street. He's not from around here, but I recognize him from somewhere. There's something in the way the kid-man never looks around, as if his entire world centers on a horizon only he can see. He's smoking. Not a good sign. I pick the ball up off the boxer's drool-wet lawn, wipe the drool on my jeans, and toss it a few feet in the air. When I look up I see the kid-man— black hair greased and straight, a broken mustache, patches of dirt and beard—punch Mick in the nose. Mick bends over and covers his nose with cupped hands in one motion. Blood oozes through his summer-stained fingers and drips onto the hot cement. Although the kid-man—eighteen, nineteen, probably—has just punched Mick in the face, I'm stunned stupid when the kid-man walks over to me and slams me in the nose. We run to the porch.

"My girlfriend's not a dyke," the kid-man says, as he lights a new cigarette from the old and walks off.

It's true. We have called the man's girl-friend a dyke. Often and repeatedly. But still, standing behind the harsh-sounding, cool-sounding word with blood dripping from my nose, I who only a minute ago was playing Wiffle ball on a summer afternoon, realize I cannot define nor do I understand the word we all so love to use. 5

II

Again on the Wiffle ball driveway, also summer, also my twelfth year, I call one of my Gentile friends a dumb Jew. Soon all of us revel in the discovery of this new slur. This new way of degrading each other catches on quickly. Not one of the Catholic boys schooled in the Judeo-Christian tradition is sure why calling somebody a dumb Jew is derogatory.

But we celebrate this new slur anyway. But wait. Wasn't Jesus a Jew? Isn't Bill Rosenberg a Jew? We all love Bill. This must be something else. It sounds different. It sounds like it shouldn't be said. So we say it and love saying it, we boys without weapons.

The screen door slams. My mother has caught the sound of the slur. She motions for me to come inside. "Tell your friends to go home," she says. I do not have to. They're gone. This is 1971, and the suburbs. Somebody's parent is everybody's parent. Parents stick together. They know who the real enemy is.

She grabs my hair and pulls me into the house. Inside my head I'm screaming.

I do not say a word.

"What did you say out there? What were 10 you saying?"

I understand that my mother knows the answer to her questions. I realize I had better not repeat what I said outside, not even in answer to her questions. I know she never wants to hear that again. Not ever. Not from me. Not from anybody.

"Where did you ever hear a thing like that? That kind of talk?" she asks.

An excellent question. I honestly do not know. I have no idea. The slur just seems to have been out there, there and somehow not there, like incense, like the way a Wiffle ball whips and dips, the way adults laugh at things kids don't understand, the way background noise from a baseball game leaks out of transistor radios, the way bits of gravel bounce out of pickup truck beds, the way factory fires flirt with the night sky, the way sonic booms burst the lie of silence.

A CLOSER LOOK AT
Words of My Youth

1. A memoir doesn't just recount events but selects and arranges those events into a "plot" that helps the reader infer causation, or a sense of what causes what. There seem to be two stories here, but is there a single plot? What single question or theme is evoked from this plot? Outline the two stories and show how they follow a single plot.

2. In this memoir, the Wiffle ball is more than an object that the narrator and his friends throw and smack.

The Wiffle ball itself—the actual object and the way it behaves when it is thrown—serves as a symbol of some other idea or problem. How is the Wiffle ball used to illustrate other concepts in this memoir? Examine the memoir's final sentence closely.

3. Compare the ending of "Words of My Youth" with the ending of "Book War" or the ending of "Diving In." How do the endings differ and how do they help the memoirs achieve their purposes?

IDEAS FOR
Writing

1. Explain the purpose of "Words of My Youth." What theme or question is Mackall encouraging readers to explore with him? Try to articulate that question or theme in a single sentence. Write a one-page response in which you identify that question and explain what Mackall wants readers to take away from his memoir.

2. Mackall chooses to use strong and perhaps offensive language, and to describe violent events and offensive behavior. In a one-page response to this memoir, discuss whether you feel the language and events were warranted, considering what you believe is the central theme/question of the story.

1. Ask each member of your group to tell a funny story about himself or herself (something PG-13, please). After each person tells his or her story, compare the organization of the story to the typical organization of a memoir. What are some of the similarities and differences between these funny stories and memoirs?

2. With a group of people in your class, talk about the physical space where you did a lot of your learning in elementary school. Is there a classroom or other space prominent in your memories? Describe sensory details: how the furniture was arranged, who sat or stood where, the background noises, perhaps even the smells of that place.

3. Do some people who don't really know you have a false idea about who you are? Perhaps it's an impression or image that you yourself have adopted, encouraged, or just never bothered to correct. Describe this mistaken or alternative impression of yourself that some people hold to your group. Tell a story that illustrates the "you" others see, and how that image or impression just doesn't capture the real you.

Talk About This

1. All families have stories that have been told so often they have become "famous." Choose a story about you that stands out as especially celebrated in your family.

   a. Briefly relate that story. If you're writing the story, make it less than 300 words; if you're telling it in a small group, make it less than three minutes.

   b. Now explain (in writing or orally) *why* that story is a favorite. What does it *mean* to those who tell it? Does it mean the same thing for everyone involved? *When* is it told? What purpose does it serve? What *point* does it make about your family—what is its significance? Do different people draw different meanings from the story? What general *theme* does it evoke, and why is that theme important for your family?

2. Find a memoir in a book or magazine, or on the Internet. Think about how changing the intended audience and/or the medium might help the memoir reach a different set of readers. What other medium would you choose, and how would you alter the original memoir to adapt it to this medium?

3. Authors write memoirs because they have a point they want to get across to their readers. If you wanted to "repurpose" your memoir to, say, a profile, a proposal, or a research report, how might you do it? How would its angle and purpose change? When you change genres, the nature of the text changes. The readers themselves may change and their expectations change significantly; tone needs to change, as does style and many other factors. List specifically what would change if you used a different genre to handle the subject of your memoir.

Try This Out

Ready to search for your own microgenres? Here are some microgenres that are related to memoirs. Choose a microgenre from the list below and find three examples in print or on the Internet. Compare and contrast their content, organization, style, and design.

Manifesto—a statement of your personal beliefs based on your experiences

Confessional—a story about something you did wrong

"This I Believe"—a story that illustrates a belief or value you hold as true

Graphic-Novel Memoir—an illustrated memoir, designed like a comic or storyboard

Digital Literacy Narrative—a story about how you learned to use technology (e.g., texting, e-mail, mobile phone) to communicate with others

Write
This

1. **Write a memoir.** Write a five-page memoir in which you explore your relationship with another member of your family. Choose an event or series of events that could illustrate that relationship and explore its tensions. Identify a complication or a struggle of values. Then show how you and this other family member evaluated the complication and resolved it. End your memoir by telling your readers what you learned from this experience.

2. **Create a map or a storyboard.** Create a map or a storyboard and write a three-page memoir about a specific event in your life. Develop your memoir by paying special attention to the scene, the people, and the events (actions, dialogue, thoughts) that make up the plot. Be sure that your memoir evokes some significant message or theme that you want your reader to understand.

3. **Write a "six-word memoir."** A six-word memoir tries to tell a story in just six words. For instance, when the famous writer Ernest Hemingway was challenged to tell a story in just six words, he responded: "For sale: baby shoes, never worn." *Smith Magazine* challenged famous and unknown writers to contribute and received over 11,000 responses, some of which were collected in *Not Quite What I Was Planning: Six-Word Memoirs by Writers Famous and Obscure*. Here are a few of them:

   • I'm ten, and have an attitude.
   • Anything's possible with an extension cord.
   • Revenge is living well, without you.
   • My reach always exceeds my grasp.
   • Never should have bought that ring.
   • Found true love after nine months.

For support in meeting this chapter's objectives, follow this path in MyCompLab: Resources ⟹ Writing ⟹ Writing Purposes ⟹ Writing to Reflect. Review the Instruction and Multimedia resources about writing to reflect, then complete the Exercises and click on Gradebook to measure your progress.

Profiles

In this chapter, you will learn how to—

- observe people closely as subjects.
- describe a person, place, or event in detail.
- tell an interesting story about someone or something.

P rofiles are used to describe interesting people, their significance, and their contributions. They are not full-blown life stories. Instead, profiles try to create a snapshot of a person by taking a specific angle that allows the writer to capture something
essential—an insight, idea, theme, or social cause. Some of the best profiles focus on
people who seem ordinary but are representative of a larger issue.

You can also use a profile to describe groups of people, places, and events. For
example, you could write a profile of a campus organization or club, giving it a unique
personality. You could profile a town or building, describing it as a living being. Or,
you might write a profile of an event (e.g., a basketball game, a historical battle, an
earthquake) that describes the subject as alive in some way.

When writing a profile, you should strive to reveal a fundamental quality of your
subject. Keep this question in mind: "What larger idea about this subject do I want to
emerge from the profile?" For instance, if you are writing a profile of someone from
your hometown (e.g., the mayor, a coach, or a family member), you would want to
show what makes this person unique or special in some way. You want to make him
or her representative of something greater.

Profiles appear in a variety of print and online publications. They are common in
magazines like *People, Rolling Stone*, and *Time*. Web sites like *Slate.com, National
Review Online,* and *Politico* regularly feature profiles. Profiles are also mainstays on
cable channels like ESPN, the History Channel, and the Biography Channel.

In college and in your career, you will likely need to write profiles about others
and yourself for Web sites, brochures, reports, and proposals. Profiles are sometimes
called backgrounders, biographies, or bios, and they appear under titles like "About
Us" or "Our Team." You might also want to write your own profile for social networking sites like *Facebook, Bebo,* or *LinkedIn.*

Profiles

Here are two possible organizational patterns for writing a profile. The pattern on the left is good for describing your subject. The pattern on the right is best for telling a story about your subject. Other arrangements of these sections will work, too. You should organize your profile to fit your topic, angle, purpose, readers, and context.

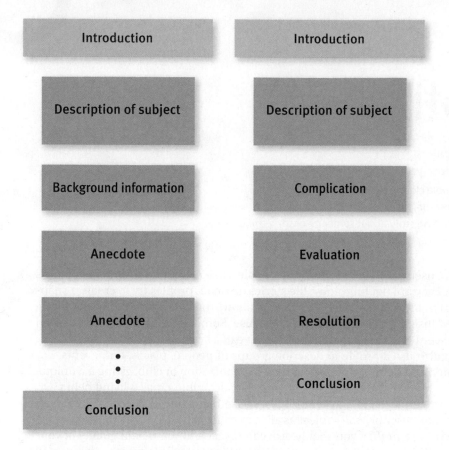

A profile can stick to the basic facts (as in a biographical sketch) or provide an intimate depiction of the subject. Profiles have some or all of these features:

- **A person, organization, place, or event** that allows you to explore a topic, issue, idea, or theme that is interesting to you and your readers.
- **An interesting angle** that captures a single dominant impression about the subject.
- **A description of the subject** that allows readers to visualize and imagine it.
- **Background information** that describes the setting or social context of the subject.
- **Anecdotes** that reveal the character of the subject through actions and dialogue.
- **A theme,** or central issue about the subject that goes beyond the surface and factual details to address larger questions.

Profiles

Brother, Life Coach, Friend

Katie Koch

On a spring morning at a Boston high school, Wyatt Posig, a caseworker in the Massachusetts Department of Youth Services, has some good news for Chris, an affable seventeen-year-old with a sleepy smile and an armed robbery conviction. Posig thinks he may have found Chris an office job for the summer.

> The profile starts fast, setting a scene that shows the subject at work, what he *does*.

There's only one problem—the internship calls for business attire. Posig has been trying to get clothing vouchers for Chris, whose wardrobe runs to the type of oversized checked shirts and baggy pants he's wearing today. "I might have some ties for you," Posig says. Chris shrugs indifferently at the dilemma. (Some names and details have been changed.)

Photo by Kathleen Dooher.

It wasn't too long ago that Posig was an intern himself. Now, just a year out of college, he is one of a handful of caseworkers assigned to a pilot program designed to give Boston's juvenile offenders some much-needed support as they leave detention centers and reenter their communities. In search of a better way to cut recidivism, the state introduced the program last year, tweaking a model developed by the National Center on Addiction and Substance Abuse at Columbia University. Each of Boston's neighborhood community centers now has a dedicated caseworker to act as a consistent presence in these troubled kids' lives: an amalgam of older brother, life coach, negotiator, and friend. For Dorchester's teens, that person is Posig.

> Background information: where the subject came from, the context of his work.

He started prepping for the role years ago, studying sociology at BU and coordinating the Big Siblings program. He worked summer internships at the Department for Children and Families in his hometown of Burlington, Vermont. "I've always known I wanted to work with young people in this situation," Posig says. "I really thrive on being able to help them out. And for whatever reason, I've been able to connect with kids really easily my entire life."

continued

It helps that he could almost pass for a teenager. Tall and lanky, with a smattering of freckles and a dark red beard, he sticks to a uniform of loose shirts and jeans. He spends most of his day checking up on his clients, taking them to dental appointments, or letting the kids vent to him in his office. For the ten boys in his caseload, none of whom have fathers living at home, Posig is a role model, but not in the traditional sense.

"The other caseworkers are the parent figures," he says. "I'm more of a brother. The difficult part is that you want to be the kids' friend, but you also want to get that respect"—a hard thing to earn as the youngest guy in the office. But Posig brings a youthful energy to the Dorchester Community Reentry Center: he leads the daily staff meeting, chats up his coworkers, and—perhaps a first for world-weary social workers—does it all without caffeine. (He's never had a cup of coffee, he says.)

"I turned twenty-three yesterday," Posig says. "But none of the kids knows that."

Curtis, one of the center's charges, just celebrated a birthday as well. There were no parties, as Posig and coworker Sheila Cooper learn when they visit him that afternoon at Casa Isla, a lockup in Quincy for twenty boys ages eleven to seventeen. Curtis arrives in the visitors' room, and Cooper and Posig quickly assume their roles: Cooper, the tough-love veteran caseworker, and Posig, the tentative, encouraging upstart. "It's good to see you," Posig says. "It's not good to see you locked up, but it's good to see you."

Cooper starts to grill him: why did he call them down for a meeting? "I miss y'all," Curtis finally confesses. Just seven days away from his release, the fifteen-year-old is tense. "Don't tell the other kids you're waiting to get out," Posig advises, "or they'll test you." He later explains that it's not uncommon for an offender to slip up near the end of a sentence, back for a new crime just weeks after being let out. When Curtis is released, Posig's task will be to help him navigate the everyday challenges of school, family, and work that can make life on the inside seem relatively easy—even desirable.

Still, Posig is optimistic about Curtis's chances, perhaps more so than Curtis himself. In the year he's been on the job, he's witnessed success stories: one of his kids has never missed a day of work, and another recently made the honor roll. His attitude, he hopes, is contagious.

> Physical description allows readers to visualize the subject.

> Quotes and dialogue are used to bring the subject to life and develop the overall theme.

> Anecdotes show readers who Posig is and the role he plays for the young men he works with.

> Profile ends with a feeling of closure, *implying* rather than stating the main point (or thesis).

Inventing Your Profile's Content

Begin by choosing a subject that is fascinating to you and that would be interesting to your readers. Although it's tempting to choose a celebrity, it is hard to get beyond the hype to the reality of his or her life. Instead, look for someone or some place that is unique but not famous. Here are some possible places where you can find your subject:

- People who have influenced you
- Historical figures
- People you have met at work or while volunteering
- A place of special importance to you (a building, an indoor or outdoor space)
- People you know through social and cultural groups
- People or groups of people whose lifestyles are different or unusual
- A club, organization, or social group that you belong to or that has helped you
- People who are doing things that you would like to be doing one day
- People who have done something wrong

It is usually best to pick a subject you can easily access or about which much information is already available. If your subject is a person, choose someone you can shadow, interview, or research. If your subject is a group, place, or event that has had a significant impact on you or others, then describe your subject as a living being that moves, has emotions, and changes. The key is finding a subject that is interesting to *you*, because if you are not interested, it will be very difficult to spark an interest in your readers.

Inquiring: Finding Out What You Already Know

Once you find your subject, take some time to think about what makes this subject unique or interesting. Your aim is to find an angle that will depict your subject in a way that makes your profile interesting and meaningful. Use one or more of the following methods to generate ideas for your profile.

Answer the Five-W and How Questions. Journalists often use the Five-W and How questions (who, what, where, when, why, how) to start generating ideas for a profile. Who or what is your subject? Who has been influenced by your subject? Who is involved with your subject regularly? What has your subject done that is especially interesting to you and your readers? Where did your subject come from? When and where did your subject do the things that interest you and your readers? What is unique about your subject? How does your subject react to people and events? What does your subject look like? How did this person's origins shape his or her outlook on life?

Freewrite. Darken your computer screen or take out a blank sheet of paper. Then, for about five minutes, write down everything you know about your subject without stopping. Write about what makes this person, group, place, or event interesting. Just write.

Use Cubing. Cubing involves using writing to explore your subject from six different viewpoints or perspectives (Figure 5.1). *Describe* your subject by paying attention to

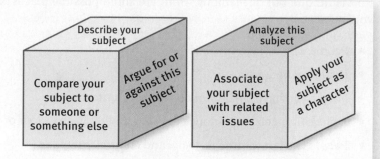

FIGURE 5.1 Using Cubing to Inquire About Your Subject

Cubing is a good way to study your subject from different viewpoints or perspectives. Each side of the cube urges you to see the subject you are profiling somewhat differently, generating new ideas and insights.

your senses. *Compare* your subject to someone or something else. *Associate* this subject with related issues or things you already know about. *Analyze* this subject, looking for any patterns, hidden questions, or unique characteristics. *Apply* your subject as a character by describing it in action. *Argue* for or against this subject: Is this person or group of people right or wrong, a saint or a scoundrel, or has this place helped bring about good or bad results?

Try a few different prewriting and invention methods to draw out what you already know about your subject. Chapter 14, "Inventing Ideas and Prewriting," describes some other methods you might try.

Researching: Finding Out What Others Know

Good research is essential to writing an interesting profile. When you start researching your subject, you should begin by identifying a variety of online, print, and empirical sources.

Online Sources. Use an Internet search engine to gather biographical or historical information on this person, group, place, or event. Then gather background information on the time period you are writing about.

Print Sources. Consult newspapers, magazines, and books to find out about your subject. These print sources are probably available at your campus library or a local public library.

Empirical Sources. Interview your subject and/or talk to people who know or knew this person. You might also ask whether you can observe or even shadow your subject or someone in the group. For a profile about a place or an event, you can interview people who live in the place you are profiling or who experienced the event you are writing about.

Interviewing. An interview is often the best way to gather information for a profile. If you want to do an interview, keep in mind that phone calls or e-mails are often good ways to ask people questions about themselves or others.

Remember to script your questions before your interview. Then, while conducting the interview, be sure to *listen and respond*—asking follow-up questions that engage with what the interviewee has told you. Some open-ended questions you might ask include:

- "What do you think is most interesting/important about what you do?"

- "In all, what did this experience mean for you, and what do you think it should mean for others?"

- "What's the most important idea you want people to understand about your story/work?"

Shadowing. If your subject is a person, you could "shadow" him or her (with the person's permission, of course), learning more about your subject's world, the people in it, and how your subject interacts with them. For a place or event profile, spend some time exploring and observing, either by visiting the physical location or examining pictures and firsthand accounts. Keep your notebook, a camera, and perhaps a digital recorder handy to capture anything that might translate into an interesting angle or a revealing quotation.

In Chapter 25, "Finding Sources and Collecting Information," you can learn more about interviewing and other empirical forms of research.

As you collect information, make sure you are using reliable sources. There is a great amount of gossip and misinformation out there, especially on the Internet. So anything you find should be confirmed by at least a few different sources. If something sounds too good (or too far-fetched) to be true, it probably is.

Organizing and Drafting Your Profile

Watch the Animation on **Writing Profiles** at **mycomplab.com**

The organization of a profile should help you draw readers in and keep their attention. As you organize your ideas and write your first draft, you should keep a couple of key questions in mind:

What do you find most interesting, surprising, or important? As you researched your subject, what did you discover that you weren't expecting? How can you make this discovery interesting for your readers?

What important conflicts does your subject face? People are most interesting when they face important challenges. Groups, like individuals, also face challenges. Places and events are scenes of conflict and change. What is the principal conflict for your subject?

Keep in mind that the profile is one of the most flexible genres. Don't feel as though the information needs to appear in any specific order. You can arrange the information you collected in a variety of ways to suit your topic, purpose, and readers and the contexts in which they will read the profile.

The Introduction

Get a quick, strong start with a lead that hints at or captures the theme of the profile. For instance, in her profile of Jay McCarroll at the end of this chapter, Jennifer Senior begins with a rich description of McCarroll and his workspace. Then she ends that first paragraph with a brisk description of the drama and the conflict: "Though he's the first-season winner of *Project Runway*, Jay, 32, is still homeless in New York."

Identify Your Subject and Purpose. Your introduction should identify your subject, directly or indirectly reveal your purpose, and stress the importance of the subject.

State Your Main Point or Thesis. In some types of profiles, you might want to state a main point, or thesis, in the introduction. Most profiles "show" rather than "tell"; so they use unstated or implied theses. In these kinds of profiles, you should not state the main points (or thesis) directly, but you should leave your readers with a strong impression about what your subject stands for or typifies. Usually, the strongest overall impression comes at or near the end of the profile.

Description of the Subject

Your readers should be able to visualize the person or place you are describing and perhaps describe your subject in other ways. Use plenty of details to describe how this subject looks, moves, and sounds. In some situations, you might describe how he, she, or it smells or would feel if touched.

Background on the Subject

As you describe your subject, you might also place him, her, or it in a setting or tell your readers something about the time periods and places in which your subject lives or lived.

Anecdotes

Tell one or more stories that reveal your subject's character and beliefs. Your stories should also illustrate the theme or point of your profile.

Dialogue or Quotes

Keep your ears open for dialogue and quotable statements from your subject and from others, especially quotes that capture important ideas. Try to find dialogue or quotes that reflect your overall theme or your dominant impression of this person. However, don't overdo the use of dialogue or quotes. Because quotes receive special attention from readers, reserve them for ideas that are especially important.

The Conclusion

Profiles shouldn't just end; they should leave an impression. Because endings, like beginnings, get special notice from readers, your conclusion should include information, ideas, or images that leave readers with a sense of the point (or thesis) you want to make about your subject. Conclude with a strong impression that will stay with your readers.

For example, in "Brother, Life Coach, Friend" (earlier in this chapter), the author concludes with two final paragraphs that avoid a simple "happily ever after" ending. Instead, she carefully chooses her words, leaving readers with a final impression that is both optimistic and anxious about the continuing challenges her subject faces:

> **Good (Tells Rather Than Shows).** In conclusion, through his tireless efforts, Posig has done a great service to the families and children of the Boston area. He doesn't always succeed, but his optimism inspires the young men he works with. His work is far more than just a job; he is like a brother, friend, and life coach.

> **Better (Leaves a Strong Impression).** Still, Posig is optimistic about Curtis's chances, perhaps more so than Curtis himself. In the year he's been on the job, he's witnessed success stories: one of his kids has never missed a day of work, and another recently made the honor roll. His attitude, he hopes, is contagious.

Choosing an Appropriate Style

If possible, the style of your profile should reflect your subject's essence—an individual's personality and voice, or the unique character of a group, place, or event. For instance, if you are profiling a person who is energetic and restless, you should use words that express that energy (e.g., dynamic, on the go, lively, brisk, vibrant), while using abruptly short sentences and phrases to quicken the readers' pace. But if you want your readers to perceive this person's calm thoughtfulness, you might choose words that imply calm, while using longer sentences to slow down the pace.

For instance, in the student example above, Katie Koch's word choices and sentences echo her subject's "youthful energy."

> But Posig brings a youthful energy to the Dorchester Community Reentry Center: he leads the daily staff meeting, chats up his coworkers, and—perhaps a first for world-weary social workers—does it all without caffeine. (He's never had a cup of coffee, he says.)

Similarly, in the profile of the Grand Canyon at the end of this chapter, Walter Kirn describes the middle of his journey with words and sentence structures that connote the mixture of awe and disorientation he feels upon arriving at the bottom of the "Abyss." To punctuate these emotions, Kirn combines direct statements with questions and long sentences with short ones, showing his readers the connections between the Grand Canyon's changes across millions of years and the parallel changes he recognizes in himself across his much shorter lifetime. And he ends the paragraph with an impression that could be about the Grand Canyon, himself, or both.

> My real reaction, it turned out, was almost impossible to characterize, as was the new world around me and beneath me. The canyon seemed to make human emotion irrelevant. Where should I focus my vision? No idea. What direction should I face? No clue. I was standing before an inverted mountain range, a fantastically detailed, colossal absence. It confounded my senses and rendered them nearly useless. The moment (which lasted 20 minutes,

in fact) reminded me of scary tales I'd heard about skiers who'd been buried in avalanches and lost track of up and down, of left and right. What I was buried in wasn't snow, however, but a far more abstract substance. Time. Or what preceded time.

Quite differently, when he describes the ending of the journey and his new understanding about the Grand Canyon and himself, Kirn's sentences are measured and calm.

> Going up, we went by faded geometric murals by Hopi artist Fred Kabotie, and when we reached the topmost floor, the canyon was not the same one I'd first encountered at the conclusion of the mule ride. It no longer disoriented and terrified but, in accordance with Colter's ideals, it elevated the mind, enlarged the heart. And that was what I craved just then, I realized, after so many, so many decades of traveling toward a place that felt suddenly, uncannily like home.

This calmer style mirrors the author's own meditative state. It also mirrors what for Kirn is the essence of the Grand Canyon—a place that can be frightening and disorienting but in the end gives visitors an opportunity to arrive at a deeper understanding of themselves.

You might find that the best way to develop a voice or tone in your profile is to imagine your subject's personality and feelings. Then put yourself into that character (develop a persona) and write from that perspective. Chapter 16, "Choosing a Style," offers some other strategies for developing a specific tone or voice in your writing.

Designing Your Profile

Profiles usually take on the design of the medium (e.g., magazine, newspaper, Web site, television documentary) in which they will appear. A profile written for a magazine or newspaper will look different than a profile written for a report or proposal. So as you think about the appropriate design for your profile, think about what would work with the kind of medium in which it will appear.

Using Photography. When writing for any medium, consider using photographs of your subject, especially ones that reflect the theme of your profile. For example, the photograph of Wyatt Posig in Katie Koch's profile of him effectively portrays his personality and the place where he works. Posig looks serious but confident. He is pictured with the young men he works with, one of whom is diligently working on a math problem, while the others stare out the window.

Captions are helpful for explaining the picture and reinforcing the profile's theme. Captions can simply state the subject's name, describe a detail, or summarize. Captions might also include a direct quotation from your subject, taken from an interview or from material you have collected. Captions should provide important details that you want your readers to notice.

Adding Pull Quotes or Breakouts. Readers often skim profiles to see if the subject interests them. You want to stop them from skimming by giving them an access point into the text. One way to catch their attention is to use a pull quote or breakout that quotes something from the text. Pull quotes appear in a large font and are usually placed in the margins or a gap in the text. These kinds of quotes will grab the readers' attention and encourage them to start reading. You can turn to Chapter 17, "Designing," to learn more about using pull quotes and other page design features.

Revising and Editing Your Profile

Since your profile describes someone or something you care about, you want it to be as polished as possible. More than likely, your first draft will be a bit plain and static. Usually, it takes two or three drafts to bring forward the theme you want and to find the appropriate style.

Trim the Details That Do Not Advance Your Theme. Remember that this is a profile, not a life story or complete history. While details are important, make sure that you carefully choose only those details that advance the theme you want your readers to carry away. Unnecessary details will only distract your readers and blur your meaning.

Rethink the Organization. If your first drafts follow a strictly chronological sequence (e.g., "Babe Ruth was born on February 6, 1895, in . . ."), you might look for another organization that allows you to better highlight important facts about your subject. For instance, you might begin by building a setting before you introduce the person you are profiling. Maybe you want to tell an anecdote that grabs the readers.

Refine Your Voice. Your voice and tone are not going to emerge fully in your first draft. Professional writers know that, so they wait until the revision phase to sharpen these elements of their text. Try reading your profile out loud to yourself, or have someone read it to you. Mark places where your style seems flat. Then use better word choices to enhance the voice and tone you are seeking.

Enhance and Amplify the Theme. Ultimately, the theme is what your readers will take away from your profile. So trace the theme through your profile to make sure it plays a role in each part of your profile. In most cases, the theme will be most apparent in the conclusion, so make sure it is properly amplified at this point. You can use quotes to bring out this theme in the conclusion, or perhaps you might just come out and tell the readers what this person, place, or event means to you.

Proofread. Don't weaken the impression you want to make with a bunch of typos, spelling errors, and grammatical mistakes. Proofread your profile at least a few times to find those flaws that undermine the quality of your work.

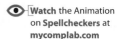
Watch the Animation on **Spellcheckers** at **mycomplab.com**

The Bio

Bios are used to describe a person's life and accomplishments. When you are applying for internships, scholarships, awards, and jobs, you will likely need to write a bio about yourself. A bio usually runs about 100–300 words, and it describes a person's major accomplishments.

In your college classes, you may be asked to write bios of prominent people and fictional characters, such as famous scientists, presidents, social activists, protagonists, and villains. You may enjoy writing bios of musicians, sports figures, actors, and fictional characters for popular Web sites. A bio is a good way to explore a person's personality, characteristics, and motives.

When writing a bio about yourself or someone else, you should concentrate on your subject's personality, upbringing, education, career, relationships, memberships in organizations, awards, interests, and hobbies. You might also spend some time figuring out what makes you or the person you are describing unique and interesting. Here's how to write a bio:

Provide the basic biographical facts.   Identify full name, date of birth, place of birth, date of marriage, and names of parents, spouse, and siblings. These personal facts would usually not be included in a professional bio.

Describe major life events.   Locate information about the places where the person lived, schools and colleges attended, awards received, disappointments, and special moments that have happened.

Describe major interests and activities.   Look for information on this person's career, hobbies, religion, clubs, sports teams, volunteer work, pets, pleasures, and frustrations.

Tell one or two stories.   Use anecdotes to reveal this person's personality or something interesting that this person has accomplished.

Organize these materials in a way that fits the bio's purpose.   If the bio is for a career-related purpose, such as a job, scholarship, corporate Web site, or internship, you should put career-related information early in the bio and any personal information that you feel is pertinent later. If you are writing a description of a person's life, including your own, then order the information chronologically.

WRITE your retirement bio. Imagine you are in your late 60s and getting ready to retire after a successful career and an enriched personal life. Write a 300-word bio in which you describe what you want said about you when you are reflecting on your career and life.

About John Charles Cook

John Charles Cook

A distinguished gentleman with a distinct style, John Charles Cook plays a superb eclectic guitar with an extensive repertoire, which includes classical, jazz standards, and popular music. Some of his favorite artists and composers include Johann Sebastian Bach, George Gershwin, and Stevie Wonder.

Starts with an overall description of the bio's subject.

John Charles is a rare performer who embodies professionalism, class, grace, and elegance in each performance. He attributes his success to his supportive audiences throughout his musical career. During each of his appearances, he attempts to share with his audience the beauty, joy, and versatility of the guitar. To him, music is not just an art; it is life.

Uses details to distinguish the subject from similar artists.

John Charles Cook has been performing for over thirty years in the private sector as well as for major corporate businesses, non-profit agencies, universities, colleges, TV, radio, concert halls, and country clubs. He brings a warm and classy style to each and every performance, whether he is playing background music or commanding center stage.

Uses specific words to set a theme for the bio.

He studied with John Knowles while attending Fisk University and took Master Classes with David Tanenbaum at Hart School of Music. He currently teaches guitar at Carondelet Music in Latham, New York, and conducts private lessons as well. John Charles facilitates guitar workshops at various area schools where he provides an overview of his music and performances. John Charles is in the development stages of starting his own music school. This school will focus on learning instruments, composing, arranging, and performance. John Charles enjoys his music and loves to share his gift with all who are willing to listen.

Offers specific details about his career.

Concludes with an overall point about the subject.

Need to get going with your profile? Here are some ideas to help you start.

CHOOSE an Interesting Subject

Find a person, group, place, or event that is fascinating to you and would be interesting to your readers. The best subjects are unique or symbolic.

FIGURE OUT What You Already Know About Your Subject

Use invention tools like the Five-W and How questions, freewriting, and cubing to study your subject from a variety of perspectives.

RESEARCH Your Subject

Find information on the Internet or in print sources. Also, if possible, interview your subject or visit the place. Talk to people who know your subject well.

DRAFT Your Profile

Start out strong by grabbing the readers in your introduction. Then, in the body, use detail to paint a portrait of your subject. Avoid writing a complete history. Instead, pick an event or series of anecdotes that capture your subject.

DEVELOP an Appropriate Style

The appropriate style for your profile usually reflects the personality of your subject. You can use word choice and sentence length to portray a specific voice or tone.

LOCATE Some Photographs, If Available

Look for photographs that illustrate your subject and the theme of your profile.

STRESS the Theme

You want your profile to do more than simply describe your subject. Use your subject's history and actions as a symbol of something larger or more significant. That's your theme.

REVISE and Edit

Always remember that your profile needs to capture your subject's essence. So clarify the content, straighten out the organization, and refine your writing style.

The Near-Fame Experience

JENNIFER SENIOR

Project Runway is one of the many reality shows that came out in the last decade. These shows often take otherwise ordinary people and give them the opportunity to pursue their dreams. In this profile, which appeared in New York Magazine *in August 2007, Jennifer Senior follows up with one of the winners. Pay attention to the contrast between what people think happens to these celebrities and what sometimes really happens.*

McCarroll, baby-faced and hoodie-clad, works in the sort of space you'd expect from a fellow who dreams in fabric. It's outfitted with four sewing machines and oceans of material arranged in brilliant spectral sequence; his spring 2007 collection hangs on a rack in the corner, anchored by a quilt skirt so audaciously outsized it could easily double as a bedspread. But bedding itself is missing from this studio, as is a kitchen and a shower, which matters more in this case than it ordinarily would: Though he's the first-season winner of *Project Runway*, Jay, 32, is still homeless in New York.

"I haven't been living anywhere for two years," he says. "I sleep at other people's houses. I sleep here if I'm drunk."

Jay was one of the Bravo network's first guinea pigs in the competition reality genre, a brightly imaginative new form that mixes the more mundane conceits of *The Real World* and *Survivor* with contests involving genuine skill. In exchange for a few weeks of reality-style exploitation, contestants have a chance to show the world what they can do—with a sewing machine, with a pair of scissors, in a kitchen, in an undecorated room—and in the aftermath find their careers in full bloom. But the shows, it turns out, are the easy part.

"I have a fucking gazillion e-mails from all over the world from people asking, *Why isn't your stuff out there?*" says Jay. "Yet financially, I have no way to get them a product because I got pushed out of a boat and into the ocean, as if, *Oh, you can survive now.*"

This isn't what one would assume, of course. One would assume he'd be a money magnet after his star turn. Certainly Jay assumed as much. "You don't think I took the fucking bus to New York the day after I won the show, thinking someone was going to come up to me on the street and say, *You're awesome, here's money?*" he asks. "I thought that for two years. But I've given up on that."

Had Bravo not invented *Project Runway*, Jay would probably still be back in Lehman, Pennsylvania, where he ran a vintage-clothing store (before that, he was producing online porn). But because of the show, Bravo and Bravo watchers expected quite a bit more from him. *Project Runway* wasn't some competition gimmick like *Fear Factor* or *The Amazing Race*, where the contestants' skills only served the needs of the show. Jay's talents were practical and real, and Bravo gave him a platform to showcase them. If he couldn't succeed in the aftermath, why were we watching? Of what use was the show?

That's pretty much how Jay saw it, too. He'd worked for five straight months, with zero pay and little sleep, to appear on *Project Runway* and create a collection for Bryant Park. Audiences adored him. The show owed much of its success, let's face it, to him. So what did Jay get out of it?

The trouble is, celebrity came easily to Jay. Business did not. On the show, Jay was wicked and entertaining and cheerfully provocative, but he hardly had the means, savvy, or professional temperament to navigate the New York fashion world. (His first voice-mail message to me, ever: *Hey Jen, this is Jay McCarroll . . . Um, I am free tonight and all day tomorrow to do this bullshit. Fucking call me, would you?*) "A week after I won the show, I met with two ladies from Banana Republic at the top of the Soho House, which is like, big time," he says. "And they were like, 'Oh, we can give you numbers for factories to get your clothes produced.' But that was totally not anything like what I needed. What I needed was someone to sit down with me and say, *Here's how you start a fashion label.*"

Before long, the blogs started to howl that Jay's work was nowhere to be seen, and Tim Gunn, the kindly host and soul of *Project Runway*, was wondering aloud to the press why Jay hadn't gained more momentum; he also castigated him for being a diva.

"My hands have been creatively crippled for two years—all those fucking eyes on me, reading that I'm a waste on blogs," he says. He looks genuinely unhappy now, and younger than his 32 years—a reminder that there's an *enfant* in *enfant terrible*, a person one feels just as apt to protect as to throttle. "I was just an artist before this happened," he adds. "Now I'm an artist with a fucking clock ticking."

A CLOSER LOOK AT
The Near-Fame Experience

1. One of the themes in this profile is that Jay is sometimes his own worst enemy. How does the writer of the profile convey that characteristic without coming out and directly saying it?

2. This profile uses a narrative structure to tell its story. Find the typical elements of a narrative (i.e., setting, complication, evaluation, resolution, conclusion). How is this profile similar to a typical narrative, and how is it different?

3. How does the writer use dialogue to give insight into Jay's thoughts and character? Why do you think dialogue rather than description is sometimes the best way to give insight into who a person really is? What advantages does dialogue have over description? What are some potential disadvantages to using dialogue?

IDEAS FOR
Writing

1. Freewrite for five minutes about how you feel about Jay after reading this profile. Do you feel sympathetic? Do you think he has wasted his time and talents? If you were in Jay's place, how might you have handled things differently?

2. Play the *believing/doubting game* with this profile. Write a brief response in which you believe Jay and understand his troubles. What is the root of his problems? Why has he struggled to get a start, despite his talent and his success on *Project Runway*? Then write a response in which you doubt Jay's sincerity and abilities. Why do you think he has caused some of his own struggles? What is it about creative people (or perhaps humans in general) that causes them to self-destruct in this way?

The Grand Canyon: A Whole New World

WALTER KIRN

One of the best-known and most-visited places on earth is the Grand Canyon. Why would anyone write—or want to read—a profile on something everyone knows about? What more could possibly be said about the place? Novelist and memoirist Walter Kirn takes up those questions in this brief place profile. As you read, pay attention to the way that the narration starts fast with a "grabber" and ends with energy. Notice how the place brings the narrator to a new understanding about himself, a "whole new world."

It's never too late, my traveler friends kept telling me, to visit the Grand Canyon for the first time—but, for me, it was definitely getting there. I was 47 years old. I'd lived in the West (Montana) for 20 years and was growing immune, I thought, to natural wonders.

Plus, life was getting busier by the month. My editor was clamoring to see a sample chapter of my next novel, and Twitter was catching on among my colleagues. And something about the canyon's iconic rep, its very grandeur, seemed off-putting. I wondered if one reason I'd avoided it was a vague lifelong fear of being dwarfed by something much larger than my own ego.

After a night spent driving across northern Arizona in an unseasonable blizzard, my girlfriend, Amanda, and I were tired and cranky as we headed toward the South Rim. Because we were late for a mule ride that we'd signed up for, neither of us was in Great Expectations mode. We parked our rental car in a crowded lot next to the stately old El Tovar Hotel at the center of Grand Canyon Village, then raced into the lobby to check in, skipping the overlook 20 yards away. What shameful, hectic, narrow lives we led.

By the time we found the mule corral that has served for almost a century as the jumping-off point for the rides, the startlingly colorful crew of wranglers who run the operation were already settling tourists' posteriors into rigid, scuffed-up leather saddles.

Still not knowing what lay before us or whether we'd feel let down by perhaps the most postcarded vista on planet Earth, we bounced along on our sturdy but naughty animals (my mule required constant reining in, so determined was he to chew branches near the trail) through a shadowy forest of piñon pines. The animals' hooves raised fine, dry puffs of dust that blew back into my face and tickled my nostrils. Whenever my mule, the tallest of the bunch, chose to pick up his pace, the mule in front of me decided to slow down or stop entirely, leading to several near-collisions and one ornery kick in my mule's chest that his muscular body serenely absorbed but whose shuddering impact shook my saddle and ran straight up through my spine.

The mule train stopped at a spot called the Abyss, where we dismounted and trudged toward the railed lookout. Suddenly, I wasn't hurrying anymore. I'd glimpsed, for less than a second and not clearly, an orange corner of the primeval chasm that I'd come all-too-close to never seeing. Now I was afraid that when I did, I'd either be overtaken by regret or crushed by disappointment.

My real reaction, it turned out, was almost impossible to characterize, as was the new world around me and beneath me. The canyon seemed to make human emotion irrelevant. Where should I focus my vision? No idea. What direction should I face? No clue. I was standing before an inverted mountain range, a fantastically detailed, colossal absence. It confounded my senses and rendered them nearly useless. The moment (which lasted 20 minutes, in fact) reminded me of scary tales I'd heard about skiers who'd been buried in avalanches and lost track of up and down, of left and right. What I was buried in wasn't snow, however, but a far more abstract substance. Time. Or what preceded time.

A Temple of the Gods

At supper in El Tovar's dining room, surrounded by mid-20th-century murals depicting a simplistic yet evocative version of Native American customs, I gradually regained my bearings. The thick-cut lamb chops helped, as did the meticulous, formal wait staff who kept refilling my glass of ice water with hushed efficiency. By dessert I felt like a human being again, capable of performing our species's great trick: using thought to make the incomprehensible intelligible.

The Grand Canyon is not just a geological spectacle. It's also a cultural artifact, a myth, imbued with a conscious, manmade aura of romance. Or a woman-made aura of romance, one should say. The Santa Fe Railroad, which opened El Tovar in 1905 as a sanctuary in the wilderness for well-heeled visitors from more civilized parts, assigned the job of defining the canyon's meaning to an architect named Mary Colter. She designed El Tovar's interior, which blends European and Southwestern motifs. And she designed a series of structures (including Hopi House, a simulated pueblo where tribal crafts are sold, and the Lookout Studio gift shop) whose inspiration was Native American. The result is a distinctive monumental vision. The Grand Canyon: a temple of the Gods. A spot where ancient human spirituality meets eternal natural artistry.

On our second day, we lit out for the Watchtower, which, for me, is Colter's masterpiece: a turret constructed of thousands of small stacked rocks, at the South Rim's far eastern end. The vista there is particularly expansive. It allows a vivid prospect of the winding Colorado River as well as the plateaus and ridgelines of the nearby Navajo Nation. Amanda climbed the twisting stone staircase ahead of me, passing notchlike windows that framed the huge view in little portrait-size fragments.

Going up, we went by faded geometric murals by Hopi artist Fred Kabotie, and when we reached the topmost floor, the canyon was not the same one I'd first encountered at the conclusion of the mule ride. It no longer disoriented and terrified but, in accordance with Colter's ideals, it elevated the mind, enlarged the heart. And that was what I craved just then, I realized, after so many, so many decades of traveling toward a place that felt suddenly, uncannily like home.

A CLOSER LOOK AT
The Grand Canyon: A Whole New World

1. This place profile tells a complete story in a short space. Like all stories, it introduces a complication (a tension or conflict within or between people) and a resolution (a moment of transformation or clarity).

   a. Look at the beginning and ending. Is Kirn's opening "lead" effective? Does it grab you? Does he end on an up note or with a surprising revelation?

   b. Describe the tension the narrator feels within himself. What is he afraid of? And how is the conflict resolved?

   c. Ultimately, what insight does the narrator come to?

   d. Find the places where the narrator sets the scene with rich detail about his physical surroundings. Which of those details seem to reflect his inner state? How do the details help readers understand how he arrives at his insights?

2. Whether its subject is a person, place, organization, or event, a profile should bring that subject to life by capturing something essential about it. What larger idea about the Grand Canyon does Kirn evoke? Point to specific places in the profile that make the Grand Canyon seem "alive," with an identity, personality, and purpose.

3. Like most profiles, this one provides some background for its subject. Here, Kirn provides a slice of history (in paragraph 10). Why does he choose *this* slice? How does this bit of history help readers understand the essence of the Grand Canyon and the narrator's revelation?

4. Is this really a profile, or is it a memoir about the author? Or is it both? Does the author's story about himself provide energy and substance, or is it just self-centered?

IDEAS FOR
Writing

1. Recall a place that you have traveled to and write a profile that, like Kirn's, describes how you made a startling discovery about yourself and the place. Describe your expectations and what happened. Bring the place to life with rich details.

2. Write a "place obituary," a profile of place that has meaning for you and others (either positive or negative) but that has disappeared or is no longer accessible. Obituaries, of course, are written for deceased persons. Gain some insight into the obituary genre by finding some on the Web and use the conventions of the genre to help you make your point about this special place.

Talk About This

1. Pair off with a partner. Interview your partner about his or her life at college. Ask about his or her daily routine. Ask about what this person does that's unique or different from a typical college student. Ask about what this person believes about life and the college experience.

2. With your group, discuss the portrait below, taken by Charles C. Ebbets (1905–1978) of workmen perched on a steel beam on the 69th floor of the Rockefeller Center in 1932. How are these workers portrayed? What word or phrase captures their attitude? Considering the historical context of this picture—the Great Depression—what message is conveyed about America at the time?

© Charles C. Ebbets/Ebbets Photo Graphics.

3. With your group, come up with five national issues that you all seem to care about. They don't have to be enormous issues. For each of these issues, pick a specific person, group, place, or event that is symbolic of that problem or its solution. Then talk about how a profile of these subjects could be used to help readers understand the issue you linked with them.

Try This Out

1. Choose one of the profiles included in this chapter and analyze it using the features listed in the At-a-Glance on page 64. Does the profile adhere exactly to these features? List three ways the profile matches this description of the genre. Then list three ways the profile does not match the description.

2. On the Internet, find a profile of someone who interests you. Present this profile to your writing group, identifying its strengths and weaknesses. Then identify the theme of the profile and show your group how the author uses the profile to make a larger point.

3. With your group, list five places or buildings on campus that seem to come alive when people are in them. Pick one of these places and describe it as though it is a person or a living being of some kind. How can a place be similar to a person? How can personifying a place make it more interesting for readers?

Go find your own examples of microgenres! Here are a few microgenres that are related to profiles. Choose a microgenre from the list below and find three examples in print or on the Internet. What are some common features of this microgenre?

Explore This

Portrait—a short sketch that describes how another person looks and behaves

Snapshot—a description of a place or event as though everything has stopped

Social Networking Profile—a brief profile for a social networking site

Obituary—an end-of-life profile for a celebrity or someone you know

Personal Ad—a description of yourself for a dating Web site

Write This

1. **Profile someone you know.** Write a profile of someone you know well and like. Think about why you find this person interesting: they're quirky, hardworking, funny, unusual, and so on. Talk to others about this person to collect a variety of viewpoints and possibly gain new insights. Paint a verbal portrait of this person that views him or her from a specific angle and that captures something essential about him or her—an idea, social cause, insight, or theme.

2. **Create a profile with graphics or audio/video elements.** Write a profile about a historical figure or place from your state or country. Using the Internet and print sources, find out as much as you can. Then interview an expert who has studied this person or place in depth. Paint a verbal portrait, viewing your subject from a specific angle and capturing something essential—an idea, social cause, insight, or theme. Add pictures taken from the Internet or elsewhere.

3. **Write a profile of a person or group of people that is supposed to represent your generation.** Choose a subject that is used as a cultural icon to explain young people in general and your generation in particular. What common experiences do you and your friends share with this person or group? What is it about the subject's unique experiences or persona that has made your subject an icon (for better or worse) for your generation?

For support in meeting this chapter's objectives, follow this path in MyCompLab: Resources ⟹ Writing ⟹ Writing Purposes ⟹ Writing to Describe. Review the Instruction and Multimedia resources about writing a description, then complete the Exercises and click on Gradebook to measure your progress.

6

Reviews

In this chapter you will learn how to—

- invent and organize a review.
- determine common expectations with readers.
- improve your writing style for a popular readership.

While in college and during your career, you will be asked to write reviews in which you discuss whether something was or was not successful. Reviews offer critical discussions of movies, books, software, music, products, services, performances, and many other items, helping readers to understand the subject's strengths and limitations.

In essence, a review expresses the reviewer's informed opinion about the subject and explains why the reviewer came to that opinion. Reviewers need to do more than simply state whether they did or didn't like something. Instead, they need to base their opinions on some *common expectations* that they share with their readers. When writing a review, your opinion is important, but it needs to be based on your shared assumptions with readers about what makes something successful or unsuccessful.

Reviews tend to be found in magazines and newspapers and on the Internet. You probably check out the reviews before deciding to see a movie, buy a book, go to a performance, or download some music. Reviews can help you determine whether you would enjoy something before you buy it. Sometimes people like to read reviews after they experience something to see if others agree with their opinion about it.

In college courses, professors will assign reviews to give you a chance to express your opinion about the arts, architecture, books, politics, education, fashion, and other issues. When assigning a review, professors are typically looking for your ability to support your opinions and to demonstrate your understanding of a subject, while also allowing you to express your opinion in an informed way.

Reviews

These diagrams show two possible organizations for a review, but other arrangements of these sections will work, too. You should alter these organizations to fit your topic, angle, purpose, readers, and context.

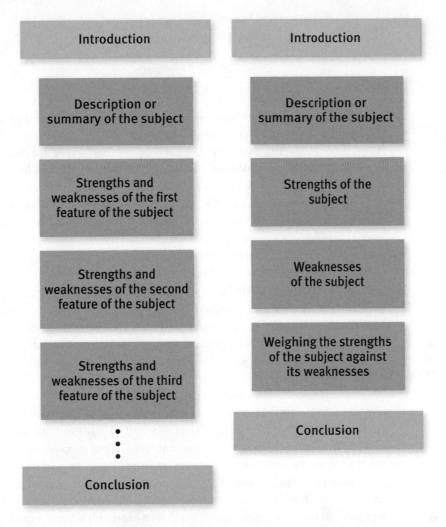

A review typically has the following features:

- **An introduction** that identifies the subject being reviewed or evaluated.
- **A description** or summary of the subject.
- **A discussion** of the subject that determines whether it meets, exceeds, or falls short of common expectations.
- **A conclusion** that offers an overall judgment of the subject.

ONE STUDENT'S WORK
Reviews

Toy Story 3 Is an Adult's Film for Children

Yair Rosenberg

Immediately identifies the subject of the review

Sets the tone through an engaging and entertaining style with plays on words.

As the intrepid plastic heroes of Pixar's *Toy Story 3* approach their new home—a much dreaded day care center to which they are being donated, as their owner Andy departs for college—one of them cries out in surprised delight, "Look, it's nice! See, the door has a rainbow on it!" Of course, only in a children's film would colorful decorations on a door act as a plausible predictor for what lies behind it. Disney movies always make sure to helpfully dress up characters and locales in accordance with their essential nature. When the toys are welcomed with open arms by the local population and meet strawberry-scented leader Lotso (short for "Lots-o-Huggin' Bear," voiced brilliantly by Ned Beatty), the initial perception of the cheerfully named Sunnyside Day Care Center seems to be confirmed. But the genius of *Toy Story 3* is that it straddles the line between childlike simplicity and mature reality such that audiences—like the toys—are constantly being misled by its jovial, happy veneer. As the day care center is unmasked as a fascist police state ruled by the ostensibly wholesome Lotso, *Toy Story 3* is unmasked as a film that uses the conventions of children's cinema to ponder adult questions, where the answers and characters do not fall into easily distinguishable boxes.

States the main point (thesis) of the review at the end of the introduction.

The toys find themselves at the day care center because their owner has outgrown them. The fiercely loyal Woody (Tom Hanks) argues that the toys ought to stick by 17-year-old Andy and go into storage until he might have need of them. The rest of the toys are less than enthused by this proposition, and, feeling abandoned by Andy, pack themselves into a box that is being donated to day care, hoping to be played with once more. Beneath the cartoon exterior of this debate is a profound question: What is the nature of a committed relationship, and just how far do its obligations extend? At its heart, this is the question that the movie sets out to answer.

Discusses strengths.

Along the way, *Toy Story 3* offers witty dialogue, creative plotting, an evocative score, and the sparkling animation viewers have come to expect from Pixar, and especially from writers John Lasseter, Andrew Stanton, and Lee Unkrich (the team behind the prior *Toy Story* films, as well as *Finding Nemo* and *Monsters Inc.*). There are deft nods to pop culture and, less congruously, to John Locke (whose mantra, "Authority should derive from the consent of the governed, not from the threat of force," is channeled by none other than Barbie, voiced by Jodi Benson). Beyond the specifics, *Toy Story 3* also showcases all the cinematic qualities that have made Pixar such a successful critical and commercial juggernaut for over a decade.

Most notably, though, it boasts an all-star vocal cast: leads Woody and Buzz Lightyear are voiced by Tom Hanks and Tim Allen, supported by Joan Cusack, Wallace Shawn, and Michael Keaton, among others. Yet not a single billboard or trailer for *Toy Story 3* mentioned even one celebrity vocal actor. Animated features allow filmmakers to escape their actors' previous work and avoid the persona and viewer expectations that a known actor normally brings to the table. Here, Tim Allen can play a hero, rather than a slapstick comedian, and Wallace M. Shawn can play a bashful dinosaur without anyone thinking about Vizzini and land wars in Asia. But overemphasize the actors—splashing their names on billboards or making their CGI counterparts match their facial expressions, as was done with Will Smith and Angelina Jolie in the Dreamworks misfire *Shark Tale*—and one risks bringing all that baggage back into play and hampering the freedom of the film to present truly original characters. Dispensing with physical presence—from star power to sex appeal—allows *Toy Story 3* to focus more on themes, and less on theatrics.

In this way, *Toy Story 3* is a grown-up's film for kids. It doesn't resort to winking at adults with double entendres or on-the-nose pop culture references like so many animated flicks, but instead engages them deeply in the subtext of the film, which, at its core, is about the bittersweet truth of growing up. Though kids will walk out of the theater excitedly repeating the movie's jokes and plot points, their parents will have appreciated its deeper resonance.

> Writes critically throughout the review, stating his reactions and explaining why he reacted as he did.

> A strong conclusion repeats the overall judgment from the first paragraph but also adds emphasis or a special twist.

Inventing Your Review's Content

Of course, in order to write a review of something, you need to spend some time experiencing it. If you're reviewing a movie, you need to go see it. If you're reviewing a book, you need to read it. If you're reviewing a product or service, you need to use it. That's the fun part.

But wait. Before you see the movie, read the book, or use the product, you should do some inquiry and background research to help you view your subject from a critical perspective. Inquiry will help you determine what you and your readers expect of your subject. Background research will help you develop a fuller understanding of your subject's history and context.

Inquiring: Finding Common Expectations

The foundation of a good review is the set of common expectations that you and your readers share about what makes something successful or unsuccessful. Those expectations are not usually stated directly in the review itself. Instead, the reviewer takes

FIGURE 6.1
Using Brainstorming to List Common Expectations

Brainstorming is a good way to come up with a list of elements that you and your readers would expect the subject of your review to have.

Features of a Good Action Movie

*Great hero
Memorable lines
*Love interest that doesn't sidetrack movie
Real or potential victims of villain
Character evolution, especially hero
Suspense
Interesting setting
Something unexpected
Chase scenes
Use of weapons
*Complex and sinister villain
*Fast-paced plot
Fighting scenes
Some irony, but not too much
Hero needs to be flawed in some way
Mystery to be solved
*Amazing stunts

Cool special effects
Unexpected humor
Intense music soundtrack
Strong set of values
Villain is brilliant
*Music that sets the moods for scenes
Hero's desire for revenge
Opening scene that grabs audience
Social pressures on hero to give up
Good friends for hero
Low expectations for hero
Recognizable actors
Dark lighting
Somewhat realistic, even if fantasy
Characters worth caring about
Rivalry between hero and villain
Violence that has purpose and meaning

for granted that his or her readers share some assumptions about the thing being reviewed.

For example, let's say you want to write a review of an action movie that just arrived in theaters. Your first challenge is to decide what features make an action movie successful. In other words, you need to figure out what moviegoers, namely you and your readers, expect from a movie like the one you are going to review.

So use an invention strategy like brainstorming to help you list all the things most people would expect from the kind of movie you are reviewing. As fast as you can, make a list like the one shown in Figure 6.1. Then put a star or asterisk next to the three to six items that are most important to you.

More than likely, if you asked a group of people to make their own lists of expectations for an action movie, they would produce lists similar to yours. They might use different words and they might put stars next to a few other items, but most people would agree on what makes a good action film. That's what we mean by "common expectations." They are expectations that you and your readers already share.

Once you have identified the features you believe are most important, group the unstarred items on your list under the starred ones. For example, the list shown in Figure 6.1 could be sorted into six major categories:

- Noble But Flawed Hero

- Complex and Sinister Villain

- A Romantic Relationship

- Fast-Paced Plot
- Stunts and Chase Scenes
- Music That Enhances Scenes

Having created your list of common expectations, you will have a better idea about what you and your readers will be looking for in this kind of movie.

Researching: Gathering Background Information

The best reviewers do some background research before they experience their subject. Background research will help you to better understand what is going on as you experience your subject.

Answer the Five-W and How Questions. Using the Internet or print sources like magazines and newspapers, find out as much about your subject as possible. When collecting information to write a review, you might start out with an Internet search, typing your subject's name or title into the search line. Look for answers to the Five-W and How questions:

- Who were its creators or original developers?
- What exactly are you reviewing?
- When and where was it created?
- Why was it created—for what purpose?
- How was it made?

Then follow up with print sources, which are available at your campus library. In magazines, newspapers, and academic journals, look for more background information on your subject and the people who created or participated in it.

Locate Other Reviews of Your Subject. You might also use an Internet search engine or your library's indexes and databases to help you find other reviews on your subject. What have others said about the movie, album, performance, restaurant, or product that you are reviewing? Other reviewers might bring up issues that you hadn't thought about.

While taking notes, be very careful not to use the words or ideas of another reviewer without citing your source. In academic settings, borrowing ideas without citation is plagiarism. In professional settings, such borrowing could violate copyright laws. Of course, it is not uncommon for reviews to arrive at similar conclusions and even to refer to each other, but your review needs to be original in wording and presentation.

Interview or Survey Others. Depending on your subject, you might find an expert you could interview. On almost any college campus, someone is an expert about your subject. This person might help you understand what to look for when you experience your subject. You could also survey others who have already seen the movie, eaten at the restaurant, listened to the music, and so on. What did they think of your subject? How did they react to it? What did they like and dislike about it?

Watch the Animation on **Writing Surveys** at **mycomplab.com**

Prepare to Do Field Observations. Grab your laptop or notebook and get ready to do some field observations of your subject. In a field observation, you would watch your subject closely *and* pay attention to how others react to it. For example, while watching an action movie, take notes about how the audience reacted to particular scenes. Did they laugh? Did they groan? Did they seem to enjoy themselves, or were they dismissive of the film?

Researching: Go Experience It

This might sound obvious, but part of your research involves experiencing your subject. Go see the movie. Go eat at the restaurant. Read the book. Your inquiry and background research should help you experience your subject from an informed and critical perspective.

Being critical means being aware of your own reactions to your subject. For example, when you are reviewing a movie, allow yourself to experience the movie as a regular moviegoer. But also step back and experience the movie critically as a reviewer. If something in the movie is funny, go ahead and laugh, but then ask yourself *why* you laughed. If you thought the food at a restaurant was bland, ask yourself *why* you had that reaction.

It helps if you can take down some notes as you are experiencing your subject. Your inquiry and research should have given you some things to keep in mind as you experience your subject. During the experience, keep notes about whether your subject measures up to common expectations. Also keep notes about why you came to these conclusions.

After you experience your subject, you might also spend some time playing the Believing and Doubting Game to draw out some ideas for your review.

Believing. First, imagine that you are going to write an overly positive review. What did you like? What were your subject's strengths? What stood out as superior? How did your subject exceed your expectations?

Doubting. Now imagine that you are going to write a very negative review. What didn't you like? What didn't work? What were the weakest aspects of your subject? What annoyed or irritated you? What didn't fit your expectations or the genre?

Synthesizing to Find Common Ground. Now examine the two sides of the game to consider which features are most important to you and your readers. Where do they agree, and where do they strongly disagree? Which side do you think is right?

While synthesizing, try to figure out how you really feel about your subject. Where do you stand among the people who would totally dislike your subject or would totally love it?

Organizing and Drafting Your Review

The organization of a review tends to be rather straightforward, so drafting these kinds of documents is often easier than drafting other documents.

Watch the Animation on **Writing Reviews** at **mycomplab.com**

The Introduction

Your introduction is the basis for the rest of the review. It will typically make some or all of these moves:

Identify Your Topic and Offer Background Information. Tell your readers your topic (the subject of your review) and offer enough background information to familiarize your readers with it.

State Your Purpose. You should also identify your purpose directly or indirectly. You don't need to say something like "My purpose is to review . . ." but it should be clear to your readers that you are writing a review.

> Reviewing a classic action movie like *The Bourne Identity* is always challenging, because these kinds of movies develop a cult following of fans who are no longer able to watch from a critical perspective.

> When I decided to dine at Bistro 312, I was determined to begin with an open mind and leave behind my usual biases against French food.

State Your Main Point or Thesis. Later in the introduction, you may want to tell your readers your overall assessment of your subject (your main point or thesis). Your main point or thesis statement should do more than say whether you liked or didn't like the subject of your review. You should be specific about what you liked or didn't like.

> **Weak:** *Halo: Reach* is a very good video game.

> **Stronger:** The narrative and characters in *Halo: Reach* tend to be superficial, but the combat sequences are realistic, the soundtrack is engaging, and the multiplayer features add exciting dimensions to the game.

Often, your main point or thesis statement will state your expectations or the criteria on which you based your review.

Your main point or thesis statement, however, doesn't need to be stated in the introduction. In some reviews, you may not want to tell your readers your verdict up front. Reviewers of movies, music, and performances, for instance, will often wait until the conclusion before they finally give their overall judgment.

Description or Summary of the Subject

Now you need to familiarize your readers with the subject of your review. Begin by assuming that your readers have not seen the movie, read the book, eaten at the restaurant, or gone to the performance. You will need to give them a brief description or summary of your subject. You have a couple of options:

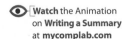
Watch the Animation on **Writing a Summary** at **mycomplab.com**

Chronological Description or Summary. Describe or summarize your subject by leading your readers through the major scenes of the movie, book, or performance. At this point in your review, you should offer an objective description without making any evaluative comments. Your goal is to describe or summarize your subject well enough that your readers do not need to actually see your subject or read it to understand your review.

Feature-by-Feature Description. If you are reviewing something that is stationary, like a meal, a building, or a piece of artwork, your best approach would be to describe your subject feature by feature. Divide your subject into two to five major parts and then describe each part separately. Make sure you use your senses to include plenty of detail. What does it look like? How does it sound, taste, smell, and feel?

In most reviews, this description or summary tends to be one or two substantial paragraphs. This part of the review rarely goes over three paragraphs unless the review or evaluation is particularly long.

Discussion of Strengths and Shortcomings

Earlier, you generated a list of three to six common expectations that you and your readers have about your subject. Point out the strengths of your subject for your readers—how the subject met these expectations. Then discuss any shortcomings—how the subject failed to meet these expectations—and explore why your subject came up short.

> The primary strength of the *The Bourne Identity* is the characters of Jason Bourne and his reluctant partner, Marie. Both Jason and Marie have typical desires and fears that make them very human. Jason seems like a regular guy, even though he discovers that he has unexplainable fighting abilities and expertise with weaponry. The audience wants Jason and Marie to survive and escape. . . .
>
> On the downside, the absence of a great villain means *The Bourne Identity* lacks some of the intensity of a typical action movie. The forces of evil in this movie are mostly faceless bureaucrats who send one-dimensional assassins to kill Jason Bourne. The audience has trouble focusing its anger on one person or a few people, because there is no single evil-doer in the movie. Instead. . . .

Early in each paragraph, make a direct claim about a strength or shortcoming of your subject. Then, in the rest of the paragraph, support that claim with reasoning, examples, quotes, facts, and any other evidence you need to prove your point.

In this part of the review, go ahead and express your opinion. That's what readers expect from you. They want you to tell them exactly how you felt about the movie, the book, the restaurant, or the performance.

Conclusion

The conclusion of your review will usually be brief, perhaps a few sentences. In your conclusion, you should state or restate your overall assessment of the subject. Then you might offer a look to the future.

> Overall, I found *The Bourne Identity* to be a thoroughly entertaining film, despite its few weaknesses. Matt Damon carries the film with one of his best performances. The film also leaves plenty of loose ends to be explored in its two equally entertaining sequels, *The Bourne Supremacy* and *The Bourne Ultimatum*. This movie certainly deserves to be listed among the classics of action movies.

Avoid introducing any new information in the conclusion. Your conclusion should bring readers around to your main point.

Choosing an Appropriate Style

The style of your review depends on your readers and the places where they will encounter your review. Most readers will expect your review to be entertaining as well as factually correct. A review written for a mainstream newspaper, magazine, or Web site should use a lively style that matches your reaction to the movie, book, or performance.

Use Plenty of Detail

Reviews need detail. Whether you are reviewing a movie or a restaurant, you need to provide lots of descriptive detail to help your readers envision what you are discussing. For example, when you are summarizing a movie, you want to describe the characters and the action in vivid detail. You want the readers to be able to imagine what the movie actually looked like and sounded like. Similarly, if you are reviewing a new restaurant, you want your readers to imagine the taste of the food, while hearing the same sounds you heard and smelling the same smells.

One way to add detail to your review or evaluation is to concentrate on your senses:

Sight: What colors did you see? How were people dressed and how did they behave? What objects did you notice as you were observing? What were the reactions of other people around you?

Hearing: What sounds did you hear? How did people talk? What sounds did you enjoy and which noises irritated you? Were people laughing? If you closed your eyes, what did you hear?

Taste: If you had a chance to sample some food or drink, what did it taste like? Did you enjoy the taste? If so, what made it pleasurable? Did something taste awful? Use specific details to tell your readers why you felt that way.

Touch: How did things feel? Did you brush your hands over any surfaces? What did that feel like? Were surfaces rough or smooth, cold or hot, hard or soft?

Smell: What scents did your nose pick up? Did you enjoy the smells, or did they turn you off? What smells came through the strongest and which ones were not immediately obvious?

Of course, you don't need to use something from all five senses in your review. Movie reviews are about what you saw and heard, not what you smelled or touched. Restaurant reviews are mostly about what you saw, tasted, and smelled. Keep all your senses open and take notes on what you detected. You never know what kinds of details might be useful as you draft and revise your review.

Set the Appropriate Tone

The tone of your review should reflect your reaction to the subject, and your voice should be entertaining to your readers. If you were really excited by the movie you saw, the tone of your review should reflect your excitement. If you thought a particular restaurant was disgusting, your readers should sense that disgust in the tone of your writing. A concept map can help you set a specific tone in your writing.

If you occasionally use words from your concept map in your writing, your readers will sense the tone you are trying to set. So if you thought a movie like *The Bourne Identity* was intense, using words associated with "intense" will give your readers that feeling, too. If you thought the restaurant was disgusting, using words from a cluster around the word "disgusting" will signal that tone to your readers.

Changing the Pace

You might also pay added attention to pace in your review. Typically, shorter sentences will make the pace of your writing feel faster, because they increase the heartbeat of the text. So if you are describing action scenes in a movie, you might try using shorter sentences to increase the intensity of your writing. If you want to describe a hectic day at a restaurant, shorter sentences can help to create a feeling of frantic chaos. Longer sentences slow the pace down. So if you are describing a calm, peaceful restaurant or a slow scene in a movie, use longer sentences to slow down the pace of your writing.

Designing Your Review

Typically, the format and design of reviews depend on where they will appear or be used. A review written to appear in a newspaper, magazine, or blog should be designed to fit that setting.

Choose the Appropriate Medium. Paper is fine, but you should consider other media, like a Web site, a blog, or even a podcast, for making your review available to the public. Today, the vast majority of movie, book, and product reviews appear on the Internet.

Add Photographs, Audio, or Video Clips. Depending on what you are reviewing, you might consider adding a photograph of the item, such as a book cover, a still from the movie, or a picture of the product (Figure 6.2). For some reviews, such as a movie review, you might be able to add in a link to a trailer or a clip from a scene. If you plan to publish your review or post it on a Web site, though, make sure you ask permission to use any photos or screenshots.

Revising and Editing Your Review

When you are finished drafting and designing your review, leave yourself an hour or more to revise and edit your work. Revising and editing will help you sharpen your claims and develop better support for your opinions.

Determine Whether Your Opinion Has Evolved. Sometimes while you are reviewing something, your opinion will evolve or change. Watching a movie closely or reading a book carefully, for example, might cause you to gain more respect for it, or you might see some flaws that you did not notice before. If your opinion has evolved, you will need to rewrite and revise the review to fit your new opinion.

Review Your Expectations. Now that you are finished reviewing your subject, look at your list of common expectations again. Did you cover all these expectations in your review? Did any new expectations creep into your draft?

Improve Your Tone. The tone of a review is important, because readers expect to be entertained while reading. Look for places where your voice seems a little flat and revise those parts of the review to add interest for readers.

Edit and Proofread. As always, carefully check your work for grammar mistakes, typos, and misspellings. Your credibility with readers will be harmed if they notice mistakes in your writing. Errors make you look careless at best, and uninformed and unintelligent at worst.

FIGURE 6.2 Adding a Still or Clip from a Movie

In your review, you might add a still from a movie or even a link to the trailer.

While you are finishing up your review or evaluation, put yourself in your readers' place. What kinds of information and details would help you make a decision about whether to see a movie, eat at a restaurant, or read a book? Keep in mind that your readers have not seen or experienced your subject. Your job is to let them experience it through you, so they can make a decision about whether they want to see it, read it, or buy it.

The Rave

Did you ever really like something? Did you really, really, really like it? Have you ever been completely blown away by a movie, song, play, novel, meal, or concert?

You should write a rave about it. A rave is an over-the-top review that is more about feelings and reactions than reason. In a rave, the reviewer suspends his or her ability to think rationally about the subject of the review. Instead, he or she shares that out-of-control feeling with the readers.

But how do you write a rave review without looking like you've lost it, gone off the deep end, drank the Kool-Aid? Here are some strategies:

Figure out what you liked best about it.   There were probably one or two qualities that made this one "the best ever." What were those qualities and why did they make the experience so incredible?

Summarize it briefly.   Summarize or describe your subject briefly, but use only positive terms and graphic details to illustrate your points.

Compare it favorably to the classics.   Tell readers that your subject belongs with the classics and name those classics. Don't say it's better than the classics, because your readers will be skeptical. Instead, tell the readers it's just as good.

Use metaphors and similes to describe your experience.   Metaphors and similes that use food and fighting work well: "It left us hungry for more." "The crowd was drooling with anticipation." "It was delicious." "We were stunned." "It knocked me for a loop." "I felt like I had been elbowed in the head."

Tell the readers they *must* experience it.   You're not just recommending they experience it; you're telling them they *must* do it.

Amplify and exaggerate.   Liberally use words like "awesome," "incredible," "unbelievable," "fantastic," "amazing," and "astounding." Use the word "very" a little too often. Tell the readers it's one of the most important things ever written, filmed, created, cooked, played. Call it an instant classic.

Don't let up.   In a rave review, there is no going halfway. This was the best thing that has happened to you in your life, this year, this month, this week, or at least today (pick one).

Have fun.   Raves are about expressing your raw emotions about the things you love. You want readers to feel what you felt. They know you're being irrational. That's the best part about a rave.

WRITE **your own rave.** Think of a movie, television show, book, restaurant, or place that you really, really enjoyed. Then write a three-page rave review in which you share your enthusiasm with your readers. Let yourself go a little.

Review: The Black Keys Shake Up the Orpheum in Vancouver

Francois Marchand

The Black Keys—guitarist Dan Auerbach and drummer Pat Carney—brought their brotherly brand of garage blues-rock to the Orpheum in Vancouver Sunday night, performing in front of a sold-out crowd that couldn't have asked for more.

For 90 minutes, the dynamic combo from Akron, Ohio, blasted a crunchy barrage of drums/guitars-driven, blues and soul-laden tunes, including a fair number from their latest album, *Brothers*, which, Auerbach announced with a grin between songs, has gone "gold" in Canada—a first for the band, in any country.

The Keys were unrelenting, sweaty and wild right from the very beginning with old-school numbers like "Thickfreakness" (from the album of the same name, released in 2003), "Girl Is On My Mind," and "10 A.M. Automatic" (both from 2004's *Rubber Factory*), shaking the foundations of the theatre.

It would only get crazier from then on: A display of raw and pure R 'n' R energy from start to finish, the duo knocking back a few other hidden gems from their back catalogue, including "The Breaks" (from their 2002 debut *The Big Come Up*), "Stack Shot Billy," and "Busted."

Within a few songs, both Carney and Auerbach were soaked, barreling as they did through their material without too much pause for respite, the crowd constantly pushing and clamoring for more. The duo then brought on a few backup guys, Nick Movshon on bass and Leon Michels on keys (both have been seen playing in the Dap-Kings in the past), to assist them on the more intricate songs from their latest album.

For some, it may have been an odd sight: the Keys are a duo to the core, even when it comes to playing songs from the multi-layered, Danger Mouse-produced *Attack & Release* ("Strange Times," for example, turns into an almost atonal, swampy guitar mess in concert, a far cry from its loopy studio version), but the songs from *Brothers*, more moody and less buzz-driven, truly require the extra textures to really hit the mark (on record, if anything, the songs have less of an edge than they do in concert, which is a bit of a shame).

With Movshon and Michels in the background, the spotlights still firmly focused on Auerbach and Carney, the Keys delivered nuggets like

The author uses words that amplify and even exaggerate.

Show is summarized briefly.

continued

"Everlasting Light" (with its gigantic mirror ball coming up from behind the stage and casting a swirling, speckled glow throughout the theatre), before pushing the groove even deeper with "Howlin' For You" and the whistle-laden "Tighten Up," which got a massive response from the audience.

The Keys have come a long way from their early garage days and have mutated into a fully realized band that deserves no comparison. Their modern tales of love and betrayal, deeply rooted in the spirit of the Delta, have come to maturity over the last few years, best exemplified by a song like "Ten Cent Pistol," which truly blends the soul, blues and country roots of the Keys both lyrically and musically.

Still, when the Keys get back to two-piece mode and deliver the devastating attack of "I Got Mine" or encore closer "Your Touch" (easily two of their best songs), that's when the sparks truly come flying out, the crowd simply erupting, bodies flailing, mouths screaming in unison. Mind-blowing stuff.

The Black Keys

Add to the Keys Brooklynite Nicole Atkins and her band, the Black Sea, in the opening slot, and you had quite an evening of live music on your hands. Atkins' voice is something to behold, mashing the bombast of Etta James with the rawness of Janis Joplin, and her band can sure kick out some jams. However, it's easy to wonder what a different, less classic bar rock style would do for Atkins. There really is a lot of soul that needs to be dug up in there.

Metaphors are used to amplify and explain.

The reviewer doesn't let up with her positive review.

Need to write a review? Here's what you need to get going.

FIND Something You Want to Review

Your professor may tell you what you should review. If not, choose something that you can analyze critically, not something you absolutely adore or detest. You want to pick something you can assess fairly.

FIGURE OUT Your and Your Readers' Common Expectations

List two to seven qualities that you and your readers would expect something like your subject to have.

GATHER Background Information on Your Subject

Using online and print sources, collect background information on your subject and read other reviews. You might also interview an expert.

GO Experience It

As you are experiencing your subject, pay attention to your own reactions as a regular participant and as a critical observer.

DRAFT Your Review

Introduce your subject and describe it. Figure out your main point or thesis statement. Then describe your subject's strengths and weaknesses. Finish with a conclusion that offers your overall judgment.

DEVELOP an Appropriate Writing Style

The style of your review depends on where it will appear and who will read it. Most reviews use a lively tone that is entertaining to readers.

ADD Graphics to Support Your Written Text

A few graphics, like photographs and movie stills, will help you to visually illustrate what you are talking about.

REVISE and Edit

Keep in mind that your opinion of the subject may have changed while you were reviewing it. If so, you may need to revise the whole argument to fit your current opinion.

Long Overdue: A Review of the Movie *Juno*

CARINA CHOCANO

The movie Juno *went on to be one of the big hits of 2008. But when it first came out, reviewers weren't quite sure what to make of it.* Juno *was quirky, even for an independent film, and it played on the boundaries between conservative and liberal values. In this review, which was one of the first reviews of* Juno, *Carina Chocano, writing for the* Los Angeles Times, *explores the quirks and playfulness of this unique movie.*

In *Juno*, a spunky teenage girl (Ellen Page) named after the Roman goddess of women and childbirth gets herself accidentally knocked-up and decides to carry the pregnancy to term and then give "the thing" (as she fondly refers to her unborn progeny) up for adoption to a picture-perfect couple she finds advertised in the local *PennySaver*.

If the premise sounds like just the thing to raise a few eyebrows at some conservative media watchdog groups, wait until they see how it turns out. Of course, any forthcoming blasts of righteous condemnation will probably only add to the overall experience of the movie, which is already about as entertaining as it gets. Directed by Jason Reitman (*Thank You for Smoking*) from a screenplay by hot newcomer and media darling Diablo Cody, whose memoir *Candy Girl* recounted her year as an "unlikely stripper" in Minnesota, *Juno* is hilarious and sweet-tempered, perceptive and surprisingly grounded. It's also a gust of fresh air, perspective-wise, in that it follows the gestational misadventures of a girl, whose hotness is not actually her most salient characteristic, from the girl's point of view.

At first, it seems as if the script is going to stay glib and superficial and that Juno will communicate via rimshot zingers exclusively, even in moments of crisis. Page first appears on-screen walking to the drugstore, chugging Sunny Delight from a gallon jug on her way to buy yet another home pregnancy test. Pint-sized and intense, Juno has a sardonic nonchalance that masks whatever emotional turmoil she's going through. But her deadpan stance occasionally falls away to reveal what she is—a young kid in a tough spot, which only makes her earlier bravado feel all the more authentic. Although some of her one-liners feel forced, others capture the sardonic lack of affect that cool adolescent girls—and we haven't seen them on-screen, it seems, since *Ghost World* came out in 2001—find so comforting. "I'm going to call Women Now," she tells her best friend, Leah (Olivia Thirlby), after breaking the news of her pregnancy, "because they help women now."

It also helps that the sublime Michael Cera has been cast as Bleeker, Juno's buddy and secret admirer and the unlikely father of her baby. A track geek whose milky, short-clad thighs, intense (possibly myopic) gaze and terry cloth headbands make him more intriguing than he knows, Bleeker belongs to the same genus as the characters Cera played in *Superbad* and *Arrested Development*—smart, awkward, sincere, serious, weirdly irresistible. A gruff-but-lovable J.K. Simmons and a saucy Allison Janney are equally adorable as Juno's dad and stepmom, Mac and Brenda MacGuff, whom Cody and Reitman treat with a degree of affection and respect rarely afforded to parents in teen comedies. ("You're not going to be a Pop-Pop," Brenda tells Mac at one point. "Someone else is going to find a blessing from Jesus in this garbage dump of a situation.")

But the movie doesn't truly blossom until Juno meets and starts to get to know Mark and Vanessa Loring (Jennifer Garner and Jason Bateman), a beautiful couple in their mid-30s who live in a lovingly sterilized McMansion in a gated community. A serious, soft-spoken executive who is desperate for a baby but has been unable to conceive, Vanessa comes across at first like a type-A control freak. Juno identifies more easily with Mark, a former musician who writes commercial jingles and yearns for his lost youth. 5

Despite having opted for a "closed" adoption, which means she'll have no involvement in the baby's life as it grows up, Juno finds herself nonetheless drawn to the Lorings' house as she feels the need to share the experience with someone who cares and feels more and more alienated from her classmates.

Mark, who works from home alone, is always glad to see her, though for him, Juno's visits are a chance to regress, haul out the comic books and swap music mixes. As much as Juno enjoys their camaraderie, it's tinged with a sense that they're communicating from parallel dimensions—she's hanging out with his inner high-schooler while her grown-up self finds his immaturity appalling.

Meanwhile, the more she gets to know Vanessa, the more she understands what her choice means. In one of the movie's most beautiful scenes—Garner is touchingly awkward in it—Juno encourages Vanessa to talk to the baby in her belly, and Vanessa delivers what is perhaps the movie's least clever, most heartbreaking line, a shy "I can't wait to meet you" so intimate you forget she's talking to the baby through another person, at a mall. Funny as *Juno* is, it's scenes like these that ultimately make it so satisfying. Deceptively superficial at the outset, the movie deepens into something poignant and unexpected.

A CLOSER LOOK AT
Long Overdue: A Review of the Movie *Juno*

1. The writer of the review, Chocano, summarizes the plot of the movie early in the article. What features of the movie does she decide to share with the readers? How much does she reveal, and what did she decide to leave out of the summary? If you haven't seen the movie, *Juno*, did she offer you enough information to give you an overall sense of it?

2. What are some common expectations the reviewer assumes that her readers share with her about a movie like *Juno*? List three to five of these common expectations. How does this particular movie bend or play with those common expectations to come up with something original or new?

3. Does the review give away the ending of the movie? Where would the ending of the movie appear if the reviewer decided to "spoil" it for the readers? How close does the reviewer get to giving it away, and how much did she reveal about the ending?

1. *Juno* received mostly positive but mixed reviews. In 2008, there were few major movies, so critics had reservations about putting this movie on their nomination lists for awards. Find three other reviews on the Internet that show a mixture of responses to this movie. Then write a brief position paper in which you show both sides of the argument and express your opinion about whether the movie was award-winning caliber or not. You will need to see the movie to answer this question.

2. One of the interesting aspects of the movie *Juno* was the inability of critics to pin down its politics, especially regarding the abortion issue. On one hand, the character Juno is doing exactly what conservatives would recommend for a teenager who cannot raise the child herself—that is, putting her baby up for adoption. But Juno's and others' cavalier attitudes about sex and relationships took away some of the idealism of the adoption process. On the other hand, for progressives, Juno seems to be an odd messenger for pro-choice positions or a liberal understanding of sexuality. Write a three-page commentary in which you discuss the political complexities of this film. Discuss whether you feel these complexities were helpful or harmful toward understanding the political issues around teen pregnancy and adoption.

Violent Media Is Good for Kids

GERARD JONES

In this article from Mother Jones *magazine, Gerard Jones, a well-known comic book author, uses the review genre to make a broader argument: that children should be exposed to violence through the media.*

At 13 I was alone and afraid. Taught by my well-meaning, progressive, English-teacher parents that violence was wrong, that rage was something to be overcome and cooperation was always better than conflict, I suffocated my deepest fears and desires under a nice-boy persona. Placed in a small, experimental school that was wrong for me, afraid to join my peers in their bumptious rush into adolescent boyhood, I withdrew into passivity and loneliness. My parents, not trusting the violent world of the late 1960s, built a wall between me and the crudest elements of American pop culture.

Then the Incredible Hulk smashed through it.

One of my mother's students convinced her that Marvel Comics, despite their apparent juvenility and violence, were in fact devoted to lofty messages of pacifism and tolerance. My mother borrowed some, thinking they'd be good for me. And so they were. But not because they preached lofty messages of benevolence. They were good for me because they were juvenile. And violent.

The character who caught me, and freed me, was the Hulk: overgendered and undersocialized, half-naked and half-witted, raging against a frightened world that misunderstood and persecuted him. Suddenly I had a fantasy self to carry my stifled rage and buried desire for power. I had a fantasy self who was a self: unafraid of his desires and the world's disapproval, unhesitating and effective in action. "Puny boy follow Hulk!" roared my fantasy self, and I followed.

I followed him to new friends—other 5 sensitive geeks chasing their own inner brutes—and I followed him to the arrogant, self-exposing, self-assertive, superheroic decision to become a writer. Eventually, I left him behind, followed more sophisticated heroes, and finally my own lead along a twisting path to a career and an identity. In my 30s, I found myself writing action movies and comic books. I wrote some Hulk stories, and met the geek-geniuses who created him. I saw my own creations turned into action figures, cartoons, and computer games. I talked to the kids who read my stories. Across generations, genders, and ethnicities I kept seeing the same story: people pulling themselves out of emotional traps by immersing themselves in violent stories. People integrating the scariest, most fervently denied fragments of their psyches into fuller senses of selfhood through fantasies of superhuman combat and destruction.

I have watched my son living the same story—transforming himself into a bloodthirsty dinosaur to embolden himself for the plunge into preschool, a Power Ranger to muscle through a social competition in kindergarten. In the first grade, his friends started climbing a tree at school. But he was afraid: of falling, of the centipedes crawling on the trunk, of sharp branches, of his friends' derision. I took my cue from his own fantasies and read him old Tarzan comics, rich in combat and bright with flashing knives. For two weeks he lived in them. Then he put them aside. And he climbed the tree.

But all the while, especially in the wake of the recent burst of school shootings, I heard pop psychologists insisting that violent stories are harmful to kids, heard teachers begging parents to keep their kids away from "junk culture," heard a guilt-stricken friend with a son who loved Pokémon lament, "I've turned into the bad mom who lets her kid eat sugary cereal and watch cartoons!"

That's when I started the research.

"Fear, greed, power-hunger, rage: these are aspects of our selves that we try not to experience in our lives but often want, even need, to experience vicariously through stories of others," writes Melanie Moore, Ph.D., a psychologist who works with urban teens. "Children need violent entertainment in order to explore the inescapable feelings that they've been taught to deny, and to reintegrate those feelings into a more whole, more complex, more resilient selfhood."

Moore consults to public schools and lo- 10 cal governments, and is also raising a daughter. For the past three years she and I have been studying the ways in which children use violent stories to meet their emotional and developmental needs—and the ways in which adults can help them use those stories healthily. With her help I developed Power Play, a program for helping young people improve their self-knowledge and sense of potency through heroic, combative storytelling.

We've found that every aspect of even the trashiest pop-culture story can have its own developmental function. Pretending to have superhuman powers helps children conquer the feelings of powerlessness that inevitably come with being so young and small. The dual-identity concept at the heart of many superhero stories helps kids negotiate the conflicts between the inner self and the public self as they work through the early stages of socialization. Identification with a rebellious, even destructive, hero helps children learn to push back against a modern culture that cultivates fear and teaches dependency.

At its most fundamental level, what we call "creative violence"—head-bonking cartoons, bloody videogames, playground karate, toy guns—gives children a tool to master their rage. Children will feel rage. Even the sweetest and most civilized of them, even those whose parents read the better class of literary magazines, will feel rage. The world is uncontrollable and incomprehensible; mastering it is a terrifying, enraging task. Rage can be an energizing emotion, a shot of courage to push us to resist greater threats, take more control than we ever thought we could. But rage is also the emotion our culture distrusts the most. Most of us are taught early on to fear our own. Through immersion in imaginary combat and identification with a violent protagonist, children engage the rage they've stifled, come to fear it less, and become more capable of utilizing it against life's challenges.

I knew one little girl who went around exploding with fantasies so violent that other moms would draw her mother aside to whisper, "I think you should know something about Emily. . . ." Her parents were separating, and she was small, an only child, a tomboy at an age when her classmates were dividing sharply along gender lines. On the playground she acted out "Sailor Moon" fights, and in the classroom she wrote stories about people being stabbed with knives. The more adults tried to control her stories, the more she acted out the roles of her angry heroes: breaking rules, testing limits, roaring threats.

Then her mother and I started helping her tell her stories. She wrote them, performed them, drew them like comics: sometimes bloody, sometimes tender, always blending the images of pop culture with her own most private fantasies. She came out of it just as fiery and strong, but more self-controlled and socially competent: a leader among her peers, the one student in her class who could truly pull boys and girls together.

I worked with an older girl, a middle-class "nice girl," who held herself together through a chaotic family situation and a tumultuous adolescence with gangsta rap. In the mythologized street violence of Ice T, the rage and strutting of his music and lyrics, she found a theater of the mind in which she could be powerful, ruthless, invulnerable. She avoided the heavy drug use that sank many of her peers, and flowered in college as a writer and political activist.

I'm not going to argue that violent entertainment is harmless. I think it has helped inspire some people to real-life violence. I am going to argue that it's helped hundreds of people for every one it's hurt, and that it can help far more if we learn to use it well. I am going to argue that our fear of "youth violence" isn't well-founded on reality, and that the fear can do more harm than the reality. We act as though our highest priority is to prevent our children from growing up into murderous thugs—but modern kids are far more likely to grow up too passive, too distrustful of themselves, too easily manipulated.

We send the message to our children in a hundred ways that their craving for imaginary gun battles and symbolic killings is wrong, or at least dangerous. Even when we don't call for censorship or forbid "Mortal Kombat," we moan to other parents within our kids' earshot about the "awful violence" in the entertainment they love. We tell our kids that it isn't nice to play-fight, or we steer them from some monstrous action figure to a pro-social doll. Even in the most progressive households, where we make such a point of letting children feel what they feel, we rush to substitute an enlightened discussion for the raw material of rageful fantasy. In the process, we risk confusing them about their natural aggression in the same way the Victorians confused their children about their sexuality. When we try to protect our children from their own feelings and fantasies, we shelter them not against violence but against power and selfhood.

15

A CLOSER LOOK AT
Violent Media Is Good for Kids

1. In this review, Gerard Jones argues that violent media prepares kids for a violent world while letting them work out their aggression in a constructive way. His review mostly talks about how comic books can do this. Should parents use violent media to help children conquer their fears and channel their aggressive feelings? If you agree with Jones, are there limits to the amount of violent media that children can consume? If you disagree with him, do you think it is best to shield children from all forms of violence?

2. Jones uses a clear voice, or tone, in this review. How would you describe his voice or tone? What words in the review signal that tone for you? How does the length of his sentences speed up or slow down the pace of the reading? How does his use of emotion draw readers in, so they can empathize with his position?

3. This review is not typical, because it reviews several forms of violent media. What is Jones using as his common expectations for deciding whether a form of violent media is good or bad for a child? Locate the places in his review where he directly or indirectly identifies these common expectations.

IDEAS FOR
Writing

1. Write a rebuttal of Jones's argument in this review (see Chapter 10, "Arguments," to learn about rebuttal). Evidence shows that children are negatively affected by violent media and that it might cause them to be more aggressive. How can you use this evidence to argue against Jones's persuasive argument? Where are the weaknesses in his argument? Is he relying on faulty assumptions or drawing unsound conclusions? Do you think he is altogether wrong, or is he generally correct? How might you modify his argument to make it more in line with your own experiences?

2. Television seems to be increasingly violent, especially as networks compete with cable channels for viewers. Pick a show that you have never seen before that includes some violence. Write a review of the television show, paying special attention to whether the violence is being used to propel the story or just to keep the attention of the audience. What are your common expectations for acceptable violence in a television show? Does the episode you watched meet or exceed your expectations? Do you think more violence would have made the show better? Could the show still be good without the violence?

1. With a group in your class, discuss a movie that you all have seen. What did you like about the movie, and what were some of its limitations? As you discuss the movie, take note of the issues that seem to be part of the discussion. What are some expectations that your group members seem to have in common? Are there any issues that some members seem to care about but others don't? When people disagree, what do they disagree about?

2. In class, talk about what you want a reviewer to discuss in a typical music or movie review. How much do you want the reviewer to reveal about the movie? What kinds of reviews do you find most helpful when you are considering whether to buy music? Do you like reviewers whose work reveals their personalities or do you prefer objective reviewers who seem to stick to the facts? Are there any movie, music, or book reviewers that you seem to trust more than others? Why?

3. Examine and critique the following passage, which is taken from a review of a Greek restaurant. Describe which aspects of the review work well. Explain how it could be improved so that it meets the expectations readers have for reviews.

Among the appetizers, everybody in the group agreed that the spanakopita was by far the best but that the hummus was not up to par. There was some disagreement about the entrees. Personally, I liked the chicken souvlaki and dolmades plate, but two members of the group preferred the "Greek Combo," which includes dolman, spanakopita, souvlaki, broiled scampi, and mousaka.

1. On the Internet, find a video advertisement that you can review. Most companies put their most recent advertisements on their Web sites, or you can find them on video sharing Web sites like *YouTube* or *Hulu*. Write a review of the advertisement in which you critique its effectiveness. Tell your readers why you thought it worked, failed, or just irritated you. Your review should run about two pages.

2. Choose a movie and write two one-page reviews for it. Your first review should be positive. Focus on your and your readers' common expectations and say mostly positive things about the movie. The second review should be negative. Focus on elements that would cast the movie in a negative light. Then, in a memo to your professor, explore how your decisions about what to consider changed your review and what you had to say about the movie. Could you reconcile these two reviews into one that is balanced?

3. Find a review on the Internet. The review can be about music, movies, television, or just about anything. In a one-page response to your professor, explain how the review works. Discuss its content, organization, style, and design. Did you find the review effective? What were its strengths and how could it be improved?

Now it's your turn to find some microgenres. There are several microgenres that are similar to reviews. Choose a microgenre from the list below and find three examples in print or on the Internet. How is the microgenre you studied similar to and different from a regular review?

Slam—a review of something you really disliked

Customer Review—a brief statement about a product you purchased

Complaint—a complaint to a company about a product or service

Synthesis—a review that summarizes what other reviewers have said

Star Rating—a rating for something (e.g., five stars, 1–10, thumbs up/thumbs down, rotten tomatoes) with a brief explanation of the rating

Explore This

1. **Write a review for your campus newspaper.** Imagine that you are a reviewer for your campus newspaper or another local newspaper. You can review music, books, poetry, movies, video games, television, sports teams, or just about anything that you enjoy doing. Write a three- to four-page review of a subject you choose. Be sure to summarize your subject for your readers, who may not have seen, heard, or experienced it. Then discuss your subject based on expectations that you and your readers share. Explain to your readers why you are giving your subject a positive or negative review.

Write This

2. **Write an opposing review.** Find a review on the Internet that you disagree with. Then, in a brief response to the Web site, write an opposing review. Your review should be written as a response to the original review, showing why you felt differently about the subject. Next, write a one-page cover memo to your professor in which you explain your strategy for rebutting the original review. Also, discuss why you believe someone might find your review of the subject stronger than the original review.

3. **Write a rave about something you *despise*.** Here's an opportunity to really challenge yourself. Think of something you have experienced recently that you absolutely loathed. You should choose something that other people would be able to experience for themselves—a book, a class, a sport, a restaurant, a vacation spot. First, as a brainstorming exercise, write down exactly what you hated about the experience, just to get it out of your system. Then put yourself in the position of someone who would have actually enjoyed the same thing. Write your rave from that imagined point of view, using as many details from your original brainstorming as possible. (However tempted you may be, don't get carried away by sarcasm or irony.)

PEARSON
mycomplab

For support in meeting this chapter's objectives, follow this path in MyCompLab: Resources ⟹ Writing ⟹ Writing Purposes ⟹ Writing to Evaluate. Review the Instruction and Multimedia resources about writing to evaluate, then complete the Exercises and click on Gradebook to measure your progress.

Literary Analyses

In this chapter, you will learn how to—

- analyze literary texts by exploring genre, plot, characters, setting, language, and tone.
- organize your literary analysis to highlight your interpretations of the text.
- use an appropriate voice and quotations to add authority to your analysis.

A literary analysis poses an *interpretive question* about a literary text and then uses that question to explain the text, its author, or the historical context in which it was written. Your purpose is to provide your readers with new and interesting insights into the work.

Literary analyses explain the meaning of a text, analyze its structure and features, and examine it through the lenses of historical, cultural, social, biographical, and other contexts. An effective literary analysis helps readers understand what makes a literary work thought provoking, revealing, or enjoyable. Literary analyses also contribute to the larger scholarly conversation about the meaning and purpose of literature.

When writing a literary analysis, you shouldn't feel like you need to prove that you have the "correct" or "right" interpretation. Instead, your literary analysis should invite your readers to consider the work from new and interesting angles, while showing them how a particular angle can lead to fresh insights.

The literary analysis genre overlaps in many ways with the rhetorical analysis genre, which is discussed in Chapter 8. Both genres study texts closely to understand why they have particular effects on readers. Rhetorical analyses, however, tend to study all forms of texts, while literary analyses usually examine fictional or poetic texts, often using them as ways to understand humanity and culture.

Literary analyses are used in a variety of courses, not just English courses. For example, a history class studying the Progressive Era in America might read Upton Sinclair's novel *The Jungle.* A class examining the sociology of poverty might read a short story by Edwidge Danticat (one of which is included in this chapter). Professors across the disciplines assign literary works that provide insights into the subjects they want to explore with their students.

Literary Analyses

These diagrams show two possible basic organizations for a literary analysis, but other arrangements will work, too. You should adjust these organizational patterns to fit your topic, angle, purpose, readers, and context.

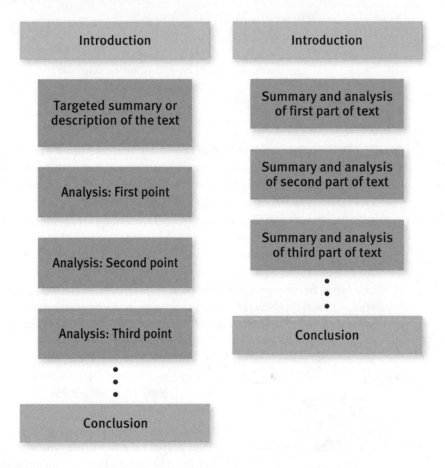

Literary analyses have these features:

- **An introduction** that identifies the literary work you are analyzing and its background. It should also state your interpretive question about the text and a main point (thesis statement) that answers that question.

- **Targeted summaries or descriptions of the text** that focus *only* on the events or features that play a key role in your interpretation.

- **Quoted material** taken directly from the text that helps to move your interpretation forward and illustrate your points.

- **Support for your interpretation** that shows how your interpretation makes sense and offers insights into the interpretive question.

- **A conclusion** that discusses the significance of the interpretation.

ONE STUDENT'S WORK
Literary Analyses

(Turn to page 126 to read "A Wall of Fire Rising.")

Doing the Right Thing in Edwidge Danticat's
"A Wall of Fire Rising"

Nick Baca

The writer begins with a single-sentence statement that introduces the literary work under consideration.	Edwidge Danticat's "A Wall of Fire Rising" is on the surface a fairly simple story, but it concludes mysteriously as a powerful and disturbing meditation about love, memory, and doing what's right. The story includes just three main characters. Guy and Lili are the dreadfully poor but happy, loving, and responsible parents of Little Guy. The parents' greatest hope is to protect Little Guy from the meanness of their world and to provide him with the possibility of a bright future. The action is also quite simple, most of it occurring among just the three of them. However, in the final climactic scene, both the characters and action become complex, strange, and disturbing. In fact, Guy's actions— stealing the factory owner's balloon and jumping to his death as his family looks on—seem completely out of character. He is clearly a loving and responsible father and husband, but his final deed seems perverse, selfish, and horribly irresponsible.

A targeted summary/description focuses only on aspects that are crucial to understanding the interpretive question.

Prominently states the interpretive question.

This analysis will explore why Guy does this crazy, horrible final deed, depriving his family of a father and husband, just for a few self-indulgent moments on a joy ride. Strangely enough, seen from the perspective of Haitian poverty and Guy's desire to leave something important for his son, Guy's final deed, perhaps, makes terribly perfect sense. It could be that Little Guy's memorized speeches bring Guy to a new understanding about his desires for the "true freedom" of Boukman's speeches. Guy wants more for his son than food and shelter; he wants Little Guy to have a lasting memory of his father that gives him the courage to pursue true freedom. Guy also wants to pursue true freedom for the sake of his own father's memory, breaking the intergenerational chain of oppression and poverty. Guy's final deed is described best, perhaps, by one of the market women's shouts—"Beautiful."

The thesis statement answers the interpretive question.

Guy's final deed could be interpreted as merely a cowardly escape from a hopeless life of crushing poverty and meanness, but that interpretation does

An alternative interpretation is described in this paragraph and argued against in the next.

not match up with what we learn about Guy and about his relationship to Lili and Little Guy. It's true that hunger and despair are always close at hand. For instance, the narrator spends several paragraphs describing Lili's methods for "kill[ing] the vermin in the stomach that made poor children hungry" (58). We learn also that Lili spends much of her effort each day trying "to scrape together that night's meal" (70). Their home is small and dark; Guy has never even seen his wife unclothed "in broad daylight" (69). The outside world is described always as menacing. For instance, the sounds outside their shack are described this way: "Lilly could hear the whispers of the market women, their hisses and swearing as their sandals dug into the sharp-edged rocks on the road" (69). It's true, such a world might drive a person to despair and suicide.

However, while Guy's life is certainly full of despair, it is also full of love and hope. That hope is energized powerfully by his son's memorized speeches from the Haitian revolutionary, Boukman. The Boukman of Little Guy's speeches, like Guy, looks forward to creating a better world, and not for himself but for those living now and those from the past: "*Not only those people whose dark hollow faces I see daily in the fields, but all those souls who have gone ahead to haunt my dreams.*" Boukman, like Guy, struggles not just for himself but also for the memories of "*a loving father, a valiant love, a beloved friend*" (79). Similarly, Guy is no self-centered father, as all his actions show. For instance, his son "never goes to bed hungry" (74), and Guy does "not want to set a bad example for his son by indulging in very small pleasures" (70). Furthermore, Guy has a soul mate in Lili. Although they have their disagreements, Lili understands Guy's deepest longings, and Guy knows that very well, as he explains the night before he steals the balloon:

> "Sometimes I know you want to believe in me," he said. "I know you're wishing things for me. You want me to work at the mill. You want me to get a pretty house for us. I know you want these things too, but mostly you want me to feel like a man. That's why you're not one to worry about, Lili. I know you can take things as they come." (73)

Although Guy's life is difficult, he is neither selfish nor irresponsible. On the contrary, the meaning of his life seems to come from his hopes for his Lili and especially for Little Guy.

The final scene of this short story is horrible and sad, but it could also be seen, strangely, as beautiful and even uplifting. Actually, both sets of emotions are present, and the tension between them is what gives the conclusion so

Interpretation is supported with quotations from story (some quotations are complete sentences, others are phrases).

Long quotations (more than three lines) are in block quotes.

Interpretation goes beyond the surface by showing how a deeper and more careful reading leads to interesting insights.

continued

much power. It seems pretty clear that Guy waits until Lili and Little Guy have arrived at the market before "climbing over the side of the basket" and then, apparently, letting go, "hurtling down towards the crowd" so that he "crash[es] not far from where Lili and the boy were standing, his blood immediately soaking the landing spot" (77). How strange and awful. What kind of person commits suicide in front of his loved ones? Isn't that the deed of the "disgruntled" family member who wants to take the ultimate revenge on his family? But that is not the case here, and both Little Guy and Lili seem to understand that immediately. Lili claims him, proudly it seems: "'He is mine,' she said to young Assad. 'He is my family. He belongs to me'" (78). Over his corpse, Little Guy once again recites his lines from Boukman, this time not in the character of Boukman but perhaps in the character of his own father, this time not as a boy in a play but with "his voice rising to a man's grieving roar" (79). Lili too seems to understand perfectly. When the foreman asks her "Do you want to close the eyes?" she responds with a knowing "No, leave them open. . . . My husband, he likes to look at the sky" (80).

Danticat's story is so disturbing because it just doesn't make sense that Guy's suicide could result merely from despair and self-indulgence, as both Lili and Little Guy seem to understand immediately. And yet Guy's horrible final deed, his horrible suicide carried out in the sight of his family, actually makes a kind of perfect sense in the context of Guy's world. It is still hard to accept that suicide is ever "doing the right thing," but there is much more to Guy's action, at least in his mind and perhaps in actuality. Stealing the balloon is a symbolic gesture *toward* freedom, not an actual attempt to *gain* freedom. (If Guy had wanted to actually pursue freedom, he would have remained in the balloon to try and land in a place where freedom is possible.) Little Guy's Boukman says, "*I call on everyone and anyone so that we shall all let out one piercing cry that we may either live freely or we should die*" (71). Perhaps Guy has answered Boukman's call with his own "piercing cry" to "live freely or die." His cry looks both to the future, to inspire his own son, and to the past, as a son in memory of his "loving father." In this way, this horrible, mysterious, and tragic tale is actually uplifting and beautiful.

Works Cited

Danticat, Edwidge. "A Wall of Fire Rising." *Krik? Krak?* New York: Random House, 1996. 51–80. Print.

Quotation omits some words from the original text, indicated with an ellipsis.

The conclusion does not merely summarize or repeat the analysis but addresses new and larger questions.

Inventing Your Literary Analysis's Content

The first challenge in writing a literary analysis is finding an interesting *interpretive question* about the work you are studying. As you read and research the text, look for signs and evidence that might offer insights that go beyond the obvious.

Read, Reread, Explore

If the literary work is a short story or novel, read it at least twice. If it is a poem, read it again and again, silently and aloud, to get a feel for how the language works and how the poem makes you feel. As you read the text, mark or underline anything that intrigues or puzzles you. Write observations and questions in the margins.

Inquiring: What's Interesting Here?

As you are reading and exploring the text, try to come up with an interesting question that focuses on the work's genre, plot, characters, or use of language. The goal here is to find your interpretive question, which will serve as your angle into the text.

Explore the Genre. In your literature classes, your professors will use the term *genre* somewhat differently than it is used in this book. Literary works fall into four major genres: fiction, poetry, drama, and literary nonfiction.

Literary Genre	Subgenres
Fiction	short stories, novellas, novels, detective novels, science fiction, romance, mysteries, horror, fantasy, historical fiction
Poetry	limericks, sonnets, ballads, epic poems, haikus, ballads, villanelle, odes, sestinas, open verse
Drama	plays, closet dramas, comedies, tragedies, romances, musicals, operas
Literary nonfiction (or nonfiction prose)	memoirs, profiles (of people, places, events), biographies, histories, essays, nature writing, religion, politics

While examining the text, ask yourself why the author chose this genre or subgenre of literature and not another one. Why a poem rather than a story? Why a short story rather than a novel?

Also, look for places where the author follows the genre or strays from it. How does the genre constrain what the author can do? How does the author bend the genre to fit the story that he or she wants to tell? How does the author use this genre in a unique or interesting way?

Explore the Plot.

Plot refers not just to the sequence of events but also to how the events arise from the main conflict in the story. How do the events in the story unfold? Which events are surprising or puzzling? What is the complication or conflict on which the narrative is based? How do the characters react to it? And how is this conflict resolved?

Keep in mind that conflict often arises from characters' values and beliefs and from the setting in which the characters reside. What conflicts do you sense in the story as you read? Are there conflicts between characters, between characters and their surroundings, between characters' aspirations, or between competing values and beliefs?

Finally, pay special attention to the critical moment in the story, called the *climax*. What happens and why is this moment so crucial? How is the conflict resolved, for better or worse?

Explore the Characters.

The characters are the people who inhabit the story or poem. Who are they? What kinds of people are they? Why do they act as they do? What are their values, beliefs, and desires? How do they interact with each other, or with their environment and setting? You might explore the psychology or motives of the characters, trying to figure out the meaning behind their decisions and actions.

Explore the Setting.

What is the time and place of the story? What is the broader setting—culture, social sphere, historic period? What is the narrow setting—the details about the particular time and place? How does the setting constrain the characters by establishing their beliefs, values, and actions? How does the setting become a symbol that colors the way readers interpret the work? Is the setting realistic, fantastical, ironic, or magical?

Analyze the Interactive Poem for Tone at mycomplab.com

Explore the Language and Tone.

How does the author's tone or choices of words color your attitude toward the characters, setting, or theme? What feeling or mood does the work's tone evoke, and how does that tone evolve as the story or poem moves forward?

Also, pay attention to the author's use of metaphors, similes, and analogies. How does the author use these devices to deepen the meaning of the text or bring new ideas to light? What images are used to describe the characters, events, objects, or setting? Do those images become metaphors or symbols that color the way readers understand the work, or the way the characters see their world?

Literary works usually cannot be broken down into simple tidy messages or lessons, but authors want their work to affect readers in some way. They want their words to influence the way readers view the world and what they believe. So as you are exploring the text from different angles, try to figure out what message or theme the author is trying to convey.

Researching: What Background Do You Need?

While most literary analyses focus primarily on the literary text itself, you should also research the historical background of a work or author. Depending on the assignment and where you want to take it, you can use Internet or print sources that provide insights into the work, its impact, and the author's intentions.

Research the Author. Learning about the author can often lead to interpretive insights. The author's life experiences may help you understand his or her intentions. You might study the events that were happening in the author's time, because the work itself might directly or indirectly respond to them.

Research the Historical Setting. You could also do research about the text's historical setting. If the story takes place in a real setting, you can read about the historical, cultural, social, and political forces that were in play at that time and in that place.

Research the Science. Human and physical sciences can often give insights into human behavior, social interactions, or natural phenomena. Sometimes additional research into psychology, sociology, biology, and other sciences can give you interesting insights into characters and events.

Organizing and Drafting Your Literary Analysis

So far, you have read the literary work carefully, taken notes, done some research, and perhaps written some informal responses. Now, how should you dive in and begin drafting? Here are some ideas for getting your ideas down on the page.

The Introduction

Introductions in literary analyses usually include a few common features:

Include Background Information That Leads to Your Interpretive Question.
Draw your reader into your analysis by starting with a question or information that
your reader is already familiar with, and then move steadily toward your interpretive
question and your thesis. Show your reader why this is an interesting question that
will lead to new insights about the work or other broader concerns.

Watch the Animation
on **Introductions**
at **mycomplab.com**

State Your Interpretive Question Prominently and Clearly. Make sure your
reader understands the question that your analysis will investigate. If necessary,
make it obvious by saying something like, "This analysis will explore why. . . ." That
way, your readers will clearly understand your purpose.

Place Your Thesis Statement at or Near the End of the Introduction. Provide a
clear thesis that answers your interpretive question (Figure 7.1). Since a literary analysis is academic in nature, your readers will expect you to state your main point or
thesis statement somewhere in the introduction. Here are examples of a weak thesis
statement and a stronger one:

> **Weak:** Jane Austen's *Emma* is a classic early nineteenth-century novel that
> has stood the test of time.

> **Stronger:** Jane Austen's *Emma* is especially meaningful now, because Emma
> herself is a complex female character whose passion for matchmaking
> resonates with today's socially networked women.

The Body of Your Analysis

In the body paragraphs, you should take your reader through your analysis point by
point, showing them that your interpretation makes sense and leads to interesting
new insights.

Summarize and Describe Key Aspects of the Work. You can assume that your
readers will be familiar with the literary work, so you don't need to provide a complete summary or fully explain who the characters are. But there may be aspects of
the work that are crucial to your analysis and that need to be brought to your readers'
attention. You may wish to focus on a particular scene, or on certain features, such as
a character, interactions between characters, language, symbols, plot features, and
so forth. Discuss *only* those aspects of the work that are crucial to understanding
your analysis.

Build Your Case, Step by Step. Keep in mind that the goal of a literary analysis is
not to prove that your interpretation is correct but to show that it is plausible and
leads to interesting insights into the text and related matters. Take your readers
through your analysis point by point. Back up each key point with reasoning and evidence, and make connections to your interpretive question and thesis statement.

Interpretive Questions	Interpretive Claims
Why does Guy (who seems to be a loving and responsible parent and husband) steal the balloon and jump to his death?	Guy has been deeply affected by Boukman's words, believing that the ultimate gift he can give to his family is to follow Boukman's rallying words that "we shall all let out one piercing cry that we may either live freely or we should die." Stealing the balloon is such a "piercing cry."
	Little Guy's recitation of Boukman's great speeches about living freely inspires Guy to break the cycle of despair that has devastated his father's life and his own life, and that will likely devastate Little Guy's life. It is the ultimate gift both for his father (justifying his struggles) and for his son (inspiring him to live freely).
	The damage to the psyche caused by pervasive poverty is so strong that even a loving and responsible father and husband like Guy can be driven to horrible deeds.
What does the balloon represent for Guy?	Representing the possibility of escape and freedom, the balloon provides Guy with the opportunity to prove himself as a capable man (not just a man whose only worth is as a latrine cleaner), one who deserves to pursue his freedom.
How and why does the narrator contrast the home setting with the public settings of the Haitian shantytown?	By moving back and forth between Guy and Lili's loving shanty and the inhospitable shantytown, the story paints a stark contrast between the two worlds and shows how love and responsibility are perhaps impossible in a world of such dreadful poverty.
How does the setting drive the character and plot?	The environment in which Guy lives is all-important, as it drives his character toward feeling deep sadness about the past and keen anxiety about the future. Hence, the setting drives the characters, and the characters drive the plot. By showing the reader how powerful such an environment can be, Danticat creates a story that makes an emotional and very effective argument against poverty.

FIGURE 7.1
Interpretive Questions and Possible Thesis Statements

Cite and Quote the Text to Back Up and Illustrate Your Points. The evidence for your interpretation should come mostly from the text itself. Show your readers what the text says by quoting and citing it, or by describing and citing key scenes and events.

Include Outside Support, Where Appropriate. Although you can bring in concepts and ideas from outside the text, make sure your ideas are anchored by

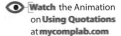
Watch the Animation on **Using Quotations** at **mycomplab.com**

what is actually written in the text you are studying. Don't just use the text as a springboard to dive off into some other topic. Stay focused on what happens in the literary work.

The Conclusion

Your conclusion should bring your readers around to the thesis that you expressed in the introduction. Your conclusion should also point the reader in new directions. Up to this point in the literary analysis, your readers will expect you to closely follow the text. In the conclusion, though, they will allow more leeway. In a sense, you've earned the right to speculate and consider other ideas.

So, if you want, take on the larger issues that were dealt with in this literary work. What conclusions or questions does your analysis suggest? What challenges does the author believe we face? What is the author really trying to say about people, events, and the world we live in?

Choosing an Appropriate Style

Literary analyses invite readers into a conversation about a literary work. Therefore, the style should be straightforward but also inviting and encouraging.

Use the "Literary Present" Tense

The literary present tense involves talking about the work and the characters as though they live in the present day. For example, you might say,

> Little Guy is excited about his role in the play, and while his mother is happy for Little Guy, his father's reactions suggest he is troubled by the speech.

> Many of Langston Hughes's poems recount the struggles of African Americans but are often tinged with definite optimism and hope.

When discussing the author historically, however, use the past tense.

> Langston Hughes was well-known in his time as a Harlem Renaissance poet. He often touched on themes of equality and expressed a guarded optimism about equality of treatment for all races.

Integrate Quoted Text

Weave words and ideas from the literary text into your words and ideas, and avoid quotations that are detached from your ideas. For example, you can include a quotation at the end of your own sentence:

The outside world is described always as menacing. For instance, the sounds outside their shack are described this way: "Lilly could hear the whispers of the market women, their hisses and swearing as their sandals dug into the sharp-edged rocks on the road" (69).

You could also take the same sentence from the story and weave a "tissue" of quotations into your words:

> The world outside their home is described as menacing. Even "the whispers of the market women" are just "hisses and swearing," and even the road's "sharp-edged rocks" seem hostile (69).

Make sure any sentences that include quotations remain grammatically correct. When you omit words from your quotation, use ellipses.

When You Quote, Tell Readers What You Want Them to Notice. Whenever you take a quote from the text, explain how the quotation supports the point you are trying to make. Don't leave your readers hanging with a quotation and no commentary. Tell them what the quote means.

Move Beyond Personal Response

Literary analyses are always partly personal, but they are not merely personal. While your professor may encourage you to delve into your personal reactions in your response papers, in your literary analysis you will need to move beyond that personal response to a discussion of the literary work itself. In other words, describe what the text does, not just what it does to you.

Cast Interpretations as Speculative. Literary analyses are interpretive, not absolute and final. When you want your readers to understand that you are interpreting, use words and phrases such as "seems," "perhaps," "it could be," "may," "it seems clear that," and "probably."

> Little Guy and Lili seem to immediately understand that Guy has been motivated by something more noble than just a joy ride in a balloon. For instance, Lili expresses no sense of shame about her husband's actions, as she claims his body proudly: "'He is mine,' she said to young Assad. 'He is my family. He belongs to me'" (78).

Designing Your Literary Analysis

Typically, literary analyses use a simple and traditional design, following the MLA format for manuscripts: double-spaced, easy-to-read font, one-inch margins, MLA documentation style (see Chapter 27). Always consult with your professor about which format to use.

Headings and graphics are becoming more common in literary analyses. If you want to use headings or graphics, ask your professor if they are allowed. Headings will help you organize your analysis and make transitions between larger sections. In some cases, you may want to add graphics, especially if the literary work you are analyzing uses illustrations or if you have a graphic that would illustrate or help explain a key element in your analysis.

Design features like headers and page numbers are usually welcome, because they help professors and your classmates keep the pages in order. Also, if you discuss your work in class, page numbers help your readers easily find what is being discussed.

Revising and Editing Your Literary Analysis

Once you have drafted your literary analysis, take the time to make sure that you have created a piece that will engage readers and lead them to new and interesting insights about the literary work you are analyzing. Here are some issues to consider as you revise and edit your draft:

Make Sure the Interpretive Question and Its Importance Are Clearly Stated. If your readers are to engage with you in a conversation about the literary work, they first need to understand your interpretive question and the angle you are exploring. They also need to understand why your interpretive question is important or interesting and how it will lead to insights about the work that go beyond a surface reading.

Check Your Main Claim, or What Your Interpretation Reveals About the Work. Your readers will also want to completely understand what your interpretation reveals about the work. State your main point or thesis clearly, prominently, and completely near the end of your introduction. You may have already written a working thesis early in the drafting process, but as you fill out your analysis, you will get a better and better sense of exactly what your interpretation is about and why it is interesting and important. Return to your thesis statement again and again to adjust and refine it.

Check Whether Your Analysis Remains Focused on Your Interpretive Question and Main Claim. Every paragraph should further develop your interpretation. Examine your topic sentences and make sure each paragraph moves your interpretation further along. If you find yourself going off on a tangent, revise or eliminate that part of the analysis.

Make Sure You Cite, Quote, and Explain Specific Parts of the Literary Text.
Use the text as evidence to support your major claims. Although you may wish to bring in ideas and sources from outside the text, make sure your readers understand exactly how the material in the literary text itself leads you to your interpretation.

Verify That You Have Cited the Text Appropriately. When you quote the text or describe a specific part of it, your readers will want to know exactly where in the text they can find that material. So use MLA documentation style to cite any quotes or sources. Also, include a "Works Cited" page that identifies the edition of your literary text and any other sources you consulted.

Make sure you spend ample time revising and editing your work. The real reader of your literary analysis is probably a professor, perhaps an English professor. That kind of reader is more sensitive than most to good (and bad) organization and style. So the extra time spent revising and editing will greatly improve his or her impression of your work.

The Reading Response

Here's something that happens more and more in courses in every college discipline. Your professor assigns a reading response as "informal writing." A literature professor might ask you to write about your first reaction to a poem to help you explore its meaning. An anthropology professor might ask you to describe your reactions to the rituals of a different culture. In the workplace, trainers and consultants often use informal writing exercises to help teams of employees explore ideas together—a kind of brainstorming.

Your professors may assign a wide variety of reading response assignments, but no matter what the specific assignment, make sure you do the following:

Read the prompt carefully.   Make sure you understand exactly what your professor wants you to do. Pay attention to the verbs. Are you supposed to summarize, explore, speculate, analyze, identify, explain, define, evaluate, apply, or something else?

Try out new ideas and approaches.   Informal writing can be your chance to speculate, explore, and be creative. Be sure you understand what your professor expects, but reading responses can allow you to stretch your thinking into new areas.

Show that you have read, understand, and can work with the material.
Ground your response in the material you are being asked about. When writing about a story or poem, come back to the text with quotes, summaries, and descriptions. If the reading involves a concept, make sure your response shows that you understand or can use the concept to address the prompt.

Branch out and make connections (if appropriate).   Look for the broader implications and for connections with other issues from the course. With informal writing like reading responses, you're usually allowed to or even encouraged to take risks and speculate. If you're not sure whether your professor wants you to do this, ask.

WRITE your own reading response. Ground your response in the text itself by describing or summarizing aspects of the text or by quoting it. Then move to generating new ideas and insights, making connections between the text and something else (something you know about from personal experience). Because this is an informal response, speculate and take risks. Have fun exploring the text while you write your response.

Reading response assignment

Here is an example of the kind of response prompt you might be assigned in a literature class. This prompt is about a poem written in 1896 by the African American writer Paul Laurence Dunbar (1872–1906). The professor's prompt follows the poem; the student's response is on the next page.

Paul Laurence Dunbar

We Wear the Mask (1896)

We wear the mask that grins and lies,
It hides our cheeks and shades our eyes,—
This debt we pay to human guile;
With torn and bleeding hearts we smile,   5
And mouth with myriad subtleties.

Why should the world be over-wise,
In counting all our tears and sighs?
Nay, let them only see us, while
    We wear the mask.   10

We smile, but, O great Christ, our cries
To thee from tortured souls arise.
We sing, but oh the clay is vile
Beneath our feet, and long the mile;
But let the world dream otherwise,   15
    We wear the mask!

Reading response prompt for "We Wear the Mask"

Write a response paper that is at least 400 words long and that incorporates at least two quotations from the poem. Paul Laurence Dunbar's poem renders a general social issue concrete and tangible with his central metaphor of "the mask." Examine this metaphor closely. Explain how it works in the poem and how it adds to the impact or meaning of the poem in terms of tone, theme, or overall message. Finally, speculate about whether you believe the metaphor is still appropriate in today's world, even though the poem was written over one hundred years ago.

Specifies use of at least two quotes

Be sure to discuss concept of "mask" metaphor.

The three key verbs are *examine*, *explain*, and *speculate*.

continued

A Student's Reading Response

Informal reading response uses personal pronouns *I* and *me*.

Satisfies the prompt by quoting the poem, and discussing the metaphor.

Connects poem and its context.

Directly addresses the prompt (why Dunbar "chose *this* metaphor").

Satisfies prompt by speculating about appropriateness of metaphor for the present day.

When I first read this, it *sounded* kind of happy, almost like a nursery rhyme. So at first I thought the mask metaphor was kind of happy, because when you hear "mask," you think fun, childhood, and parties. And also there's the movie *The Mask* with Jim Carrey, which is pretty funny. But reading it a few more times, I noticed all those words that are the opposite of happy: "grins and lies," "human guile," "bleeding hearts," "tears and sighs," "tortured souls," and many others. So, this is not a happy mask at all. I also wondered about who is the "We" in "We wear the mask." Then I noticed the picture of Dunbar and his life span. That made me think about my history class, where we're learning about the Jim Crow laws in America, from around 1875 to the 1960s, when whites passed laws that put blacks into incredibly brutal segregation. Bringing all these things together, the "We" and "the mask" started to make sense. The "We" is "We black Americans" around 1896, when the poem was written. "The mask" is not a physical thing. It's a façade that blacks wear that makes whites *think* they're happy but really *hides* total despair: "But let the world dream otherwise, / We wear the mask." In 1896, blacks could not show even a hint of disobedience. So the black person, who has to *act* ignorant and happy, actually knows *more* than the white person who "dream[s] otherwise."

But why not just come out and say that racism and Jim Crow laws are hurting black Americans? With this metaphor, the poem is much more emotional and has more impact than just a straight argument. The message is more *memorable* because it gives us a human face. It's almost like a story inside the metaphor. The mask metaphor gives the poem more impact because it makes us see and feel something we might not have. It makes the message much more powerful.

But is the metaphor still appropriate today? You might say it's not appropriate because the Jim Crow laws aren't around anymore. Besides, everyone wears a mask sometimes because everyone faces situations where they can't show their real selves. But on the other hand, even today, certain groups have to pretend they're not angry about inequality and injustice because it makes some people say "Quit your complaining!" I know that this is true for Hispanics, and it's also true for other groups, like Muslims. People in power don't like to hear it. Sometimes it's still just the smart thing to do to wear "the mask," because most people just don't understand what it's like to walk in shoes of someone else. Maybe they should read this poem. Maybe they're the ones Dunbar is talking to.

Here are some quick steps to get you going on your literary analysis.

READ the Literary Work at Least Twice and Narrow Your Topic

Make sure you're very familiar with the work you'll be analyzing so you can examine the text closely. If you have response papers or other notes, look at them closely, too.

STATE Your Interpretive Question

In one sentence, try to write down the question that you want to answer in your analysis. This will probably change as you draft your analysis and continue delving deeply into the text, so don't worry about making it perfect. This is just to get you started; you'll refine this later.

DO Some Inquiry and Research

Using your reading notes, decide what intrigues you most about the work. Then do some outside research on the text, its author, and the historical period in which it was written.

STATE Your Main Point or Thesis

Come up with a main point or thesis that answers your interpretive question. Your thesis will probably change and evolve, so just write down your best guess at this point.

DRAFT Your Analysis

Take your reader through the analysis step by step. Use targeted summaries and quotes to direct readers' attention to specific aspects of the text (not the whole text).

REVISIT Your Introduction and Conclusion

After drafting, go back to your introduction and refine your interpretive question and thesis. After reading through your analysis once more, go to your conclusion and make sure that it brings readers back to your thesis and then branches out in new directions.

DESIGN, Revise, and Edit

The design of a literary analysis is typically simple and straightforward. However, make sure you format the document the way your professor requests. Then revise by sharpening your topic sentences and making sure each paragraph stays focused on answering your interpretive question. Make sure you use the literary present tense and cite the text properly.

A Wall of Fire Rising

EDWIDGE DANTICAT

Edwidge Danticat was born in the city of Port-au-Prince, Haiti, in 1969 and immigrated to the United States with her parents (a cab driver and textile worker) at the age of twelve. She is the author of three plays and seven novels. She has edited books and published a memoir, Brother, I'm Dying, *in 2007. In 1995, she published* Krik? Krak!, *her only collection of short stories, which includes "A Wall of Fire Rising" and was a finalist for the National Book Award. More information about Danticat's personal background can be found in* Edwidge Danticat: Return to Haiti *on page 136.*

"Listen to what happened today," Guy said as he barged through the rattling door of his tiny shack.

His wife, Lili, was squatting in the middle of their one-room home, spreading cornmeal mush on banana leaves for their supper.

"Listen to what happened *to me* today!" Guy's seven-year-old son—Little Guy—dashed from a corner and grabbed his father's hand. The boy dropped his composition notebook as he leaped to his father, nearly stepping into the corn mush and herring that his mother had set out in a trio of half gourds on the clay floor.

"Our boy is in a play." Lili quickly robbed Little Guy of the honor of telling his father the news.

"A play?" Guy affectionately stroked the 5 boy's hair.

The boy had such tiny corkscrew curls that no amount of brushing could ever make them all look like a single entity. The other boys at the Lycée Jean-Jacques called him "pepper head" because each separate kinky strand was coiled into a tight tiny ball that looked like small peppercorns.

"When is this play?" Guy asked both the boy and his wife. "Are we going to have to buy new clothes for this?"

Lili got up from the floor and inclined her face towards her husband's in order to receive her nightly peck on the cheek.

"What role do you have in the play?" Guy asked, slowly rubbing the tip of his nails across the boy's scalp. His fingers made a soft grating noise with each invisible circle drawn around the perimeters of the boy's head. Guy's fingers finally landed inside the boy's ears, forcing the boy to giggle until he almost gave himself the hiccups.

"Tell me, what is your part in the play?" 10 Guy asked again, pulling his fingers away from his son's ear.

"I am Boukman," the boy huffed out, as though there was some laughter caught in his throat.

"Show Papy your lines," Lili told the boy as she arranged the three open gourds on a piece of plywood raised like a table on two bricks, in the middle of the room. "My love, Boukman is the hero of the play."

The boy went back to the corner where he had been studying and pulled out a thick book carefully covered in brown paper.

"You're going to spend a lifetime learning those." Guy took the book from the boy's hand and flipped through the pages quickly. He had to strain his eyes to see the words by the light of an old kerosene lamp, which that night—like all others—flickered as though it was burning its very last wick.

"All these words seem so long and heavy," Guy said. "You think you can do this, son?"

"He has one very good speech," Lili said. "Page forty, remember, son?"

The boy took back the book from his father. His face was crimped in an of-course-I-remember look as he searched for page forty.

"Bouk-man," Guy struggled with the letters of the slave revolutionary's name as he looked over his son's shoulders. "I see some very hard words here, son."

"He already knows his speech," Lili told her husband.

"Does he now?" asked Guy.

"We've been at it all afternoon," Lili said. "Why don't you go on and recite that speech for your father?"

The boy tipped his head towards the rusting tin on the roof as he prepared to recite his lines.

Lili wiped her hands on an old apron tied around her waist and stopped to listen.

"Remember what you are," Lili said, "a great rebel leader. Remember, it is the revolution."

"Do we want him to be all of that?" Guy asked.

"He is Boukman," Lili said. "What is the only thing on your mind now, Boukman?"

"Supper," Guy whispered, enviously eyeing the food cooling off in the middle of the room. He and the boy looked at each other and began to snicker.

"Tell us the other thing that is on your mind," Lili said, joining in their laughter.

"Freedom!" shouted the boy, as he quickly slipped into his role.

"Louder!" urged Lili.

"Freedom is on my mind!" yelled the boy.

"Why don't you start, son?" said Guy. "If you don't, we'll never get to that other thing that we have on our minds."

The boy closed his eyes and took a deep breath. At first, his lips parted but nothing came out. Lili pushed her head forward as though she were holding her breath. Then like the last burst of lightning out of clearing sky, the boy began.

"A wall of fire is rising and in the ashes, I see the bones of my people. Not only those people whose dark hollow faces I see daily in the fields, but all those souls who have gone ahead to haunt my dreams. At night I relive once more the last caresses from the hand of a loving father, a valiant love, a beloved friend."

It was obvious that this was a speech written by a European man, who gave to the slave revolutionary Boukman the kind of European phrasing that might have sent the real Boukman turning in his grave. However, the speech made Lili and Guy stand on the tips of their toes from great pride. As their applause thundered in the small space of their shack that night, they felt as though for a moment they had been given the rare pleasure of hearing the voice of one of the forefathers of Haitian independence in the forced baritone of their only child. The experience left them both with a strange feeling that they could not explain. It left the hair on the back of their necks standing on end. It left them feeling much more love than they ever knew that they could add to their feeling for their son.

"Bravo," Lili cheered, pressing her son into the folds of her apron. "Long live Boukman and long live my boy."

"Long live our supper," Guy said, quickly batting his eyelashes to keep tears from rolling down his face.

• • •

The boy kept his eyes on his book as they ate their supper that night. Usually Guy and Lili would not have allowed that, but this was a special occasion. They watched proudly as the boy muttered his lines between swallows of cornmeal.

The boy was still mumbling the same words as the three of them used the last of the rainwater trapped in old gasoline containers and sugarcane pulp from the nearby sugarcane mill to scrub the gourds that they had eaten from.

When things were really bad for the fam- 40 ily, they boiled clean sugarcane pulp to make what Lili called her special sweet water tea. It was supposed to suppress gas and kill the vermin in the stomach that made poor children hungry. That and a pinch of salt under the tongue could usually quench hunger until Guy found a day's work or Lili could manage to buy spices on credit and then peddle them for a profit at the marketplace.

That night, anyway, things were good. Everyone had eaten enough to put all their hunger vermin to sleep.

The boy was sitting in front of the shack on an old plastic bucket turned upside down, straining his eyes to find the words on the page. Sometimes when there was no kerosene for the lamp, the boy would have to go sit by the side of the road and study under the street lamps with the rest of the neighborhood children. Tonight, at least, they had a bit of their own light.

Guy bent down by a small clump of old mushrooms near the boy's feet, trying to get a better look at the plant. He emptied the last drops of rainwater from a gasoline container on the mushroom, wetting the bulging toes sticking out of his sons' sandals, which were already coming apart around his endlessly growing feet.

Guy tried to pluck some of the mushrooms, which were being pushed into the dust as though they wanted to grow beneath the ground as roots. He took one of the mushrooms in his hand, running his smallest finger over the round bulb. He clipped the stem and buried the top in a thick strand of his wife's hair.

The mushroom looked like a dried insect 45 in Lili's hair.

"It sure makes you look special," Guy said, teasing her.

"Thank you so much," Lili said, tapping her husband's arm. "It's nice to know that I deserve these much more than roses."

Taking his wife's hand, Guy said, "Let's go to the sugar mill."

"Can I study my lines there?" the boy asked.

"You know them well enough already," 50 Guy said.

"I need many repetitions," the boy said.

• • •

Their feet sounded as though they were playing a wet wind instrument as they slipped in and out of the puddles between the shacks in the shantytown. Near the sugar mill was a large television screen in a iron grill cage that the government had installed so that the shantytown dwellers could watch the state-sponsored news at eight o'clock every night. After the news, a gendarme would come and turn off the television set, taking home the key. On most nights, the people stayed at the site long after this gendarme had gone and told stories to one another beneath the big blank screen. They made bonfires with dried sticks, corn husks, and paper, cursing the authorities under their breath.

There was a crowd already gathering for the nightly news event. The sugar mill workers sat in the front row in chairs or on old buckets.

Lili and Guy passed the group, clinging to their son so that in his childhood naïveté he wouldn't accidentally glance at the wrong person and be called an insolent child. They didn't like the ambiance of the nightly news watch. They spared themselves trouble by going instead to the sugar mill, where in the past year they had discovered their own wonder.

Everyone knew that the family who 55 owned the sugar mill were eccentric "Arabs," Haitians of Lebanese or Palestinian descent whose family had been in the country for generations. The Assad family had a son who, it seems, was into all manner of odd things, the most recent of which was a hot-air balloon, which he had brought to Haiti from America and occasionally flew over the shantytown skies.

As they approached the fence surrounding the field where the large wicker basket and deflated balloon rested on the ground, Guy let go of the hands of both his wife and the boy.

Lili walked on slowly with her son. For the last few weeks, she had been feeling as though Guy was lost to her each time he reached this point, twelve feet away from the balloon. As Guy pushed his hand through the barbed wire, she could tell from the look on his face that he was thinking of sitting inside the square basket while the smooth rainbow surface of the balloon itself floated above his head. During the day, when the field was open, Guy would walk up to the basket, staring at it with the same kind of longing that most men display when they admire very pretty girls.

Lili and the boy stood watching from a distance as Guy tried to push his hand deeper, beyond the chain link fence that separated him from the balloon. He reached into his pants pocket and pulled out a small pocketknife, sharpening the edges on the metal surface of the fence. When his wife and child moved closer, he put the knife back in his pocket, letting his fingers slide across his son's tightly coiled curls.

"I wager you I can make this thing fly," Guy said.

"Why do you think you can do that?" Lili 60 asked.

"I know it," Guy replied.

He followed her as she circled the sugar mill, leading to their favorite spot under a watch light. Little Guy lagged faithfully behind them. From this distance, the hot-air balloon looked like an odd spaceship.

Lili stretched her body out in the knee-high grass in the field. Guy reached over and tried to touch her between her legs.

"You're not one to worry, Lili," he said. "You're not afraid of the frogs, lizards, or snakes that could be hiding in this grass?"

"I am here with my husband," she said. 65 "You are here to protect me if anything happens."

Guy reached into his shirt pocket and pulled out a lighter and a crumpled piece of paper. He lit the paper until it burned to an ashy film. The burning paper floated in the night breeze for a while, landing in fragments on the grass.

"Did you see that, Lili?" Guy asked with a flame in his eyes brighter than the lighter's. "Did you see how the paper floated when it was burned? This is how that balloon flies."

"What did you mean by saying that you could make it fly?" Lili asked.

"You already know all my secrets," Guy said as the boy came charging towards them.

"Papa, could you play *Lago* with me?" 70 the boy asked.

Lili lay peacefully on the grass as her son and husband played hide-and-seek. Guy kept hiding and his son kept finding him as each time Guy made it easier for the boy.

"We rest now." Guy was becoming breathless.

The stars were circling the peaks of the mountains, dipping into the cane fields belonging to the sugar mill. As Guy caught his breath, the boy raced around the fence, running as fast as he could to purposely make himself dizzy.

"Listen to what happened today," Guy whispered softly in Lili's ear.

"I heard you say that when you walked in 75 the house tonight," Lili said. "With the boy's play, I forgot to ask you."

The boy sneaked up behind them, his face lit up, though his brain was spinning. He wrapped his arms around both their necks.

"We will go back home soon," Lili said.

"Can I recite my lines?" asked the boy.

"We have heard them," Guy said. "Don't tire your lips."

The boy mumbled something under his [80] breath. Guy grabbed his ear and twirled it until it was a tiny ball in his hand. The boy's face contorted with agony as Guy made him kneel in the deep grass in punishment.

Lili looked tortured as she watched the boy squirming in the grass, obviously terrified of the crickets, lizards, and small snakes that might be there.

"Perhaps we should take him home to bed," she said.

"He will never learn," Guy said, "if I say one thing and you say another."

Guy got up and angrily started walking home. Lili walked over, took her son's hand, and raised him from his knees.

"You know you must not mumble," she [85] said.

"I was saying my lines," the boy said.

"Next time say them loud," Lili said, "so he knows what is coming out of your mouth."

That night Lili could hear her son muttering his lines as he tucked himself in his corner of the room and drifted off to sleep. The boy still had the book with his monologue in it clasped under his arm as he slept.

• • •

Guy stayed outside in front of the shack as Lili undressed for bed. She loosened the ribbon that held the old light blue cotton skirt around her waist and let it drop past her knees. She grabbed half a lemon that she kept in the corner by the folded mat that she and Guy unrolled to sleep on every night. Lili let her blouse drop to the floor as she smoothed the lemon over her ashen legs.

Guy came in just at that moment and [90] saw her bare chest by the light of the smaller castor oil lamp that they used for the later hours of the night. Her skin had coarsened a bit over the years, he thought. Her breasts now drooped from having nursed their son

for two years after he was born. It was now easier for him to imagine their son's lips around those breasts than to imagine his anywhere near them.

He turned his face away as she fumbled for her nightgown. He helped her open the mat, tucking the blanket edges underneath.

Fully clothed, Guy dropped onto the mat next to her. He laid his head on her chest, rubbing the spiky edges of his hair against her nipples.

"What was it that happened today?" Lili asked, running her fingers along Guy's hairline, an angular hairline, almost like a triangle, in the middle of his forehead. She nearly didn't marry him because it was said that people with angular hairlines often have very troubled lives.

"I got a few hours' work for tomorrow at the sugar mill," Guy said. "That's what happened today."

"It was such a long time coming," Lili [95] said.

It was almost six months since the last time Guy had gotten work there. The jobs at the sugar mill were few and far between. The people who had them never left, or when they did they would pass the job on to another family member who was already waiting on line.

Guy did not seem overjoyed about the one day's work.

"I wish I had paid more attention when you came in with the news," Lili said. "I was just so happy about the boy."

"I was born in the shadow of that sugar mill," Guy said. "Probably the first thing my mother gave me to drink as a baby was some sweet water tea from the pulp of the sugarcane. If anyone deserves to work there, I should."

"What will you be doing for your day's [100] work?"

"Would you really like to know?"

"There is never any shame in honest work," she said.

"They want me to scrub the latrines."

"It's honest work," Lili said, trying to console him.

"I am still number seventy-eight on the permanent hire list," he said. "I was thinking of putting the boy on the list now, so maybe by the time he becomes a man he can be up for a job."

Lili's body jerked forward, rising straight up in the air. Guy's head dropped with a loud thump onto the mat.

"I don't want him on that list," she said. "For a young boy to be on any list like that might influence his destiny. I don't want him on the list."

"Look at me," Guy said. "If my father had worked there, if he had me on the list, don't you think I would be working?"

"If you have any regard for me," she said, "you will not put him on the list."

She groped for her husband's chest in the dark and laid her head on it. She could hear his heart beating loudly as though it were pumping double, triple its normal rate.

"You won't put the boy on any lists, will you?" she implored.

"Please, Lili, no more about the boy. He will not go on the list."

"Thank you."

"Tonight I was looking at that balloon in the yard behind the sugar mill," he said. "I have been watching it real close."

"I know."

"I have seen the man who owns it," he said. "I've seen him get in it and put it in the sky and go up there like it was some kind of kite and he was the kite master. I see the men who run after it trying to figure out where it will land. Once I was there and I was one of those men who were running and I actually guessed correctly. I picked a spot in the sugarcane fields. I picked the spot from a distance and it actually landed there."

"Let me say something to you, Guy—"

"Pretend that this is the time of miracles and we believed in them. I watched the owner for a long time, and I think I can fly that balloon. The first time I saw him do it, it looked like a miracle, but the more and more I saw it, the more ordinary it became."

"You're probably intelligent enough to do it," she said.

"I am intelligent enough to do it. You're right to say that I can."

"Don't you think about hurting yourself?"

"Think like this. Can't you see yourself up there? Up in the clouds somewhere like some kind of bird?"

"If God wanted people to fly, he would have given us wings on our backs."

"You're right, Lili, you're right. But look what he gave us instead. He gave us reasons to want to fly. He gave us the air, the birds, our son."

"I don't understand you," she said.

"Our son, your son, you do not want him cleaning latrines."

"He can do other things."

"Me too. I can do other things too."

A loud scream came from the corner where the boy was sleeping. Lili and Guy rushed to him and tried to wake him. The boy was trembling when he opened his eyes.

"What is the matter?" Guy asked.

"I cannot remember my lines," the boy said.

Lili tried to string together what she could remember of her son's lines. The words slowly came back to the boy. By the time he fell back to sleep, it was almost dawn.

• • •

The light was slowly coming up behind the trees. Lili could hear the whispers of the market women, their hisses and swearing as their sandals dug into the sharp-edged rocks on the road.

She turned her back to her husband as she slipped out of her nightgown, quickly putting on her day clothes.

"Imagine this," Guy said from the mat on the floor. "I have never really seen your entire body in broad daylight." [135]

Lili shut the door behind her, making her way out to the yard. The empty gasoline containers rested easily on her head as she walked a few miles to the public water fountains. It was harder to keep them steady when the containers were full. The water splashed all over her blouse and rippled down her back.

The sky was blue as it was most mornings, a dark indigo-shaded turquoise that would get lighter when the sun was fully risen.

Guy and the boy were standing in the yard waiting for her when she got back.

"You did not get much sleep, my handsome boy," she said, running her wet fingers over the boy's face.

"He'll be late for school if we do not go right now," Guy said. "I want to drop him off before I start work." [140]

"Do we remember our lines this morning?" Lili asked, tucking the boy's shirt down deep into his short pants.

"We just recited them," Guy said. "Even I know them now."

Lili watched them walk down the footpath, her eyes following them until they disappeared.

As soon as they were out of sight, she poured the water she had fetched into a large calabash, letting it stand beside the house.

She went back into the room and slipped into a dry blouse. It was never too early to start looking around, to scrape together that night's meal. [145]

• • •

"Listen to what happened again today," Lili said when Guy walked through the door that afternoon.

Guy blotted his face with a dust rag as he prepared to hear the news. After the day he'd had at the factory, he wanted to sit under a tree and have a leisurely smoke, but he did not want to set a bad example for his son by indulging his very small pleasures.

"You tell him, son," Lili urged the boy, who was quietly sitting in a corner, reading.

"I've got more lines," the boy announced, springing up to his feet. "Papy, do you want to hear them?"

"They are giving him more things to say in the play," Lili explained, "because he did such a good job memorizing so fast." [150]

"My compliments, son. Do you have your new lines memorized too?" Guy asked.

"Why don't you recite your new lines for your father?" Lili said.

The boy walked to the middle of the room and prepared to recite. He cleared his throat, raising his eyes towards the ceiling.

"There is so much sadness in the faces of my people. I have called on their gods, now I call on our gods. I call on our young. I call on our old. I call on our mighty and the weak. I call on everyone and anyone so that we shall all let out one piercing cry that we may either live freely or we should die."

"I see your new lines have as much drama as the old ones," Guy said. He wiped a tear away, walked over to the chair, and took the boy in his arms. He pressed the boy's body against his chest before lowering him to the ground. [155]

"Your new lines are wonderful, son. They're every bit as affecting as the old." He tapped the boy's shoulder and walked out of the house.

"What's the matter with Papy?" the boy asked as the door slammed shut behind Guy.

"His heart hurts," Lili said.

• • •

After supper, Lili took her son to the field where she knew her husband would be. While the boy ran around, she found her husband sitting in his favorite spot behind the sugar mill.

"Nothing, Lili," he said. "Ask me nothing 160 about this day that I have had."

She sat down on the grass next to him, for once feeling the sharp edges of the grass blades against her ankles.

"You're really good with that boy," he said, drawing circles with his smallest finger on her elbow. "You will make a performer of him. I know you will. You can see the best in that whole situation. It's because you have those stars in your eyes. That's the first thing I noticed about you when I met you. It was your eyes, Lili, so dark and deep. They drew me like danger draws a fool."

He turned over on the grass so that he was staring directly at the moon up in the sky. She could tell that he was also watching the hot-air balloon behind the sugar mill fence out of the corner of his eye.

"Sometimes I know you want to believe in me," he said. "I know you're wishing things for me. You want me to work at the mill. You want me to get a pretty house for us. I know you want these things too, but mostly you want me to feel like a man. That's why you're not one to worry about, Lili. I know you can take things as they come."

"I don't like it when you talk this way," 165 she said.

"Listen to this, Lili. I want to tell you a secret. Sometimes, I just want to take that big balloon and ride it up in the air. I'd like to sail off somewhere and keep floating until I got to a really nice place with a nice plot of land where I could be something new. I'd build my own house, keep my own garden. Just *be* something new."

"I want you to stay away from there."

"I know you don't think I should take it. That can't keep me from wanting."

"You could be injured. Do you ever think about that?"

"Don't you ever want to be something 170 new?"

"I don't like it," she said.

"Please don't get angry with me," he said, his voice straining almost like the boy's.

"If you were to take that balloon and fly away, would you take me and the boy?"

"First you don't want me to take it and now you want to go?"

"I just want to know that when you 175 dream, me and the boy, we're always in your dreams."

He leaned his head on her shoulders and drifted off to sleep. Her back ached as she sat there with his face pressed against her collar bone. He drooled and the saliva dripped down to her breasts, soaking her frayed polyester bra. She listened to the crickets while watching her son play, muttering his lines to himself as he went in a circle around the field. The moon was glowing above their heads. Winking at them, as Guy liked to say, on its way to brighter shores.

Opening his eyes, Guy asked her, "How do you think a man is judged after he's gone?"

How did he expect her to answer something like that?

"People don't eat riches," she said. "They eat what it can buy."

"What does that mean, Lili? Don't talk to 180 me in parables. Talk to me honestly."

"A man is judged by his deeds," she said. "The boy never goes to bed hungry. For as long as he's been with us, he's always been fed."

Just as if he had heard himself mentioned, the boy came dashing from the other side of the field, crashing in a heap on top of his parents.

"My new lines," he said. "I have forgotten my new lines."

"Is this how you will be the day of this play, son?" Guy asked. "When people give you big responsibilities, you have to try to live up to them."

The boy had relearned his new lines by 185 the time they went to bed.

That night, Guy watched his wife very closely as she undressed for bed.

"I would like to be the one to rub that piece of lemon on your knees tonight," he said.

She handed him the half lemon, then raised her skirt above her knees.

Her body began to tremble as he rubbed his fingers over her skin.

"You know that question I asked you be- 190 fore," he said, "how a man is remembered after he's gone? I know the answer now. I know because I remember my father, who was a very poor struggling man all his life. I remember him as a man that I would never want to be."

• • •

Lili got up with the break of dawn the next day. The light came up quickly above the trees. Lili greeted some of the market women as they walked together to the public water fountain.

On her way back, the sun had already melted a few gray clouds. She found the boy standing alone in the yard with a terrified expression on his face, the old withered mushrooms uprooted at his feet. He ran up to meet her, nearly knocking her off balance.

"What happened?" she asked. "Have you forgotten your lines?"

The boy was breathing so heavily that his lips could not form a single word.

"What is it?" Lili asked, almost shaking 195 him with anxiety.

"It's Papa," he said finally, raising a stiff finger in the air.

The boy covered his face as his mother looked up at the sky. A rainbow-colored balloon was floating aimlessly above their heads.

"It's Papa," the boy said. "He is in it."

She wanted to look down at her son and tell him that it wasn't his father, but she immediately recognized the spindly arms, in a bright flowered shirt that she had made, gripping the cables.

• • •

From the field behind the sugar mill a group 200 of workers were watching the balloon floating in the air. Many were clapping and cheering, calling out Guy's name. A few of the women were waving their head rags at the sky, shouting, "Go! Beautiful, go!"

Lili edged her way to the front of the crowd. Everyone was waiting, watching the balloon drift higher up into the clouds.

"He seems to be right over our heads," said the factory foreman, a short slender mulatto with large buckteeth.

Just then, Lili noticed young Assad, his thick black hair sticking to the beads of sweat on his forehead. His face had the crumpled expression of disrupted sleep.

"He's further away than he seems," said young Assad. "I still don't understand. How did he get up there? You need a whole crew to fly these things."

"I don't know," the foreman said. "One 205 of my workers just came in saying there was a man flying above the factory."

"But how the hell did he start it?" Young Assad was perplexed.

"He just did it," the foreman said.

"Look, he's trying to get out!" someone hollered.

A chorus of screams broke out among the workers.

The boy was looking up, trying to see if his 210 father was really trying to jump out of the balloon. Guy was climbing over the side of the basket. Lili pressed her son's face into her skirt.

Within seconds, Guy was in the air hurtling down towards the crowd. Lili held her breath as she watched him fall. He crashed not far from where Lili and the boy were standing, his blood immediately soaking the landing spot.

The balloon kept floating free, drifting on its way to brighter shores. Young Assad rushed towards the body. He dropped to his knees and checked the wrist for a pulse, then dropped the arm back to the ground.

"It's over!" The foreman ordered the workers back to work.

Lili tried to keep her son's head pressed against her skirt as she moved closer to the body. The boy yanked himself away and raced to the edge of the field where his father's body was lying on the grass. He reached the body as young Assad still knelt examining the corpse. Lili rushed after him.

"He is mine," she said to young Assad. 215 "He is my family. He belongs to me."

Young Assad got up and raised his head to search the sky for his aimless balloon, trying to guess where it would land. He took one last glance at Guy's bloody corpse, then raced to his car and sped away.

The foreman and another worker carried a cot and blanket from the factory.

Little Guy was breathing quickly as he looked at his father's body on the ground. While the foreman draped a sheet over Guy's corpse, his son began to recite the lines from his play.

"A wall of fire is rising and in the ashes, I see the bones of my people. Not only those people whose dark hollow faces I see daily in the fields, but all those souls who have gone ahead to haunt my dreams. At night I relive once more the last caresses from the hand of a loving father, a valiant love, a beloved friend."

"Let me look at him one last time," Lili 220 said, pulling back the sheet.

She leaned in very close to get a better look at Guy's face. There was little left of that countenance that she had loved so much. Those lips that curled when he was teasing her. That large flat nose that felt like a feather when rubbed against hers. And those eyes, those night-colored eyes. Though clouded with blood, Guy's eyes were still bulging open. Lili was searching for some kind of sign—a blink, a smile, a wink—something that would remind her of the man that she had married.

"His eyes aren't closed," the foreman said to Lili. "Do you want to close them, or should I?"

The boy continued reciting his lines, his voice rising to a man's grieving roar. He kept his eyes closed, his fists balled at his side as he continued with his newest lines.

"There is so much sadness in the faces of my people. I have called on their gods, now I call on our gods. I call on our young. I call on our old. I call on our mighty and the weak. I call on everyone and anyone so that we shall all let out one piercing cry that we may either live freely or we should die."

"Do you want to close the eyes?" the 225 foreman repeated impatiently.

"No, leave them open," Lili said. "My husband, he likes to look at the sky."

A CLOSER LOOK AT
A Wall of Fire Rising

1. Make a list of specific words and phrases that characterize or describe the story's settings, characters, and interpersonal relationships: the family's home; the shantytown and other areas outside the home; Guy's personality and character; Lili's personality and character; the relationships among family members; the relationship between Guy and Lili. (If you form groups, each group can take one or two of these topics and present their lists to the class.) Now, write a paragraph that describes

that setting, character, or relationship. It should have a strong topic sentence and should include quoted words, phrases, sentences, and possibly passages. Use the strategies in "Choosing an Appropriate Style" to help you integrate the story's words with your own (and be sure to use the literary present tense when appropriate).

2. The setting for this story is a Haitian shantytown. Do some research on Haitian shantytowns to find

out what they're like and what it's like to live in one. Try to find pictures depicting them and life there. What role does the setting itself play in the story? Our environment affects us in ways that are both profound and subtle. How does this setting affect the reader's view of the story and its characters, and how does the setting affect the characters' views of themselves?

3. If you were going to produce a movie based on this short story, how would you do it? Which actors would you choose to play the roles of each character? How would you try to capture the mood of the story with visual effects: lighting, camera angles, and so on? If you wanted to be as true to the story as possible (not just the events, but its mood and tone), what would this movie look like? Write a one-minute "pitch" for your movie and present it to the class. (The pitch is a microgenre similar to proposals; see Chapter 11.)

IDEAS FOR
Writing

1. After reading Corine Milano's "Edwidge Danticat: Return to Haiti," write a reading response that addresses how learning about the author has colored or even changed your interpretation of "A Wall of Fire Rising." What is it about Danticat's background, values, beliefs, or motivations that made you see things differently? What do you understand about the story that you didn't understand before? What do you see in the story that you didn't see before? In general, does knowing an author's background help you to understand and appreciate a literary work?

2. Develop your own interpretive question about "A Wall of Fire Rising" and write a literary analysis about the short story. Use the strategies described in "Inventing Your Literary Analysis's Content" to help you develop your question. Focus your analysis on the text.

Edwidge Danticat: Return to Haiti

CORINE MILANO

On January 12, 2010, a catastrophic earthquake devastated Haiti. The number of deaths has been estimated to be an incredible 316,000, with as many injuries and one million made homeless. In this interview, conducted and written up by Corine Milano, Edwidge Danticat discusses Haiti before and after the earthquake. Although this is not an example of a literary analysis, Danticat's words provide insights into what she is trying to accomplish in her literary work.

You lived in Port-au-Prince until you were 12. Can you describe the Haiti of your childhood?

Everyone, including my parents, idealizes the Haiti of their childhood; and lately, we've all been idealizing the Haiti of before January's earthquake.

I'll try not to do that here. I grew up in a very poor hillside neighborhood called Bel Air in Port-au-Prince. We woke up to the sounds of street peddlers singing about their wares and to the radio blasting the news from the neighbor's house. School was strict, and we were made to speak French there even though we spoke Creole at home.

I saw my aunts and grandmothers as goddesses. One of my aunts sold notebooks, pencils, and books in downtown Port-au-Prince. She managed to put five kids through school and buy a house all on her own. My Aunt Denise helped raise me. If someone gave her $100, she would increase it five fold in a week, in a way that still seems magical to me.

I'm realizing now that I haven't given 5 due credit to their stories—the stories these women lived; their ingenuity; their entrepreneurial skills; their intelligence despite a lack of book learning.

How has your image of Haiti shifted over the years, especially in the aftermath of the earthquake?

There is a Haiti that lives in my imagination, the Haiti I write about. I think all writers, all artists have that. But Haiti is very complex. You can say that my image of Haiti is ever-changing, just as Haiti is ever-changing.

Since the earthquake, there is a constant ache in my heart. When I visit family members and they're in tents in front of their houses, in the countryside, or when you get dozens of calls a week from people saying they are hungry, or they fear rape, or need to go to school, it's not about image or nostalgia anymore. I ask myself every day when things will change, and what I can do about it.

What was it like to watch the earthquake unfold from the US?

The evening of the earthquake itself, when 10 there was so little information, I had a sense that the whole country had been flattened, that everyone was lost. The weight of that possibility was overwhelming. My cousin and his 10-year-old son died that day. Many friends died.

I have two small children, and I was offered opportunities to go back right away, but I couldn't get there. My youngest was not eating, so I had to stay with her. I've never had such a pressing question of loyalty in my life. It's the eternal female dilemma, I think. But then there was also this feeling of helplessness. Like what could I do? I'm not a doctor. I'm not a rescue worker. People were saying that going back meant eating food that survivors could otherwise eat.

When I did go back 23 days later, you had the feeling that you just wanted to hug the ground, wrap your arms around everyone, every broken place. But in a situation like this, there is very little room for sentimentality. Everyone does what little he or she can. And looking at wounded people or the dead bodies that were still all coiled up and dried on the side of the road, you felt really helpless and guilty that you could leave.

Soon after the quake, I went to church in Miami, and there was a man there who survived. He was talking about what he saw and how he survived. There was a woman who was inconsolable listening to him. She had lost 25 family members, and she could not go back to find and bury her parents.

There are degrees of trauma, and sometimes, if people can hear you, or read you, your trauma seems more pressing. But there are people who suffered so much more; I render this space to them. . . .

In terms of earthquake recovery efforts, what 15 *has been disappointing to you and what has given you hope?*

I've been encouraged by the smaller efforts that I see everywhere: People who have decided that they are not going to wait for the billions of dollars the international community has promised in aid.

I have been very proud of the Haitian-American community: the doctors, nurses, teachers, young men, and young women who have returned to do what they can. Churches, hometown associations are working harder than ever. That's the part we don't hear a lot about.

The saddest part is that even in the middle of hurricane season there seems to be no more urgency to it. The tent cities are looking more and more permanent. There is a new wave of trauma as Haitians begin to realize that nothing is going to change anytime soon.

A lot has been said about Haitian resilience, but sometimes I think that is being used to let people continue to live in these deplorable conditions. So much rubble is still in the streets; so many people are still homeless. You see so many hungry people; so many hungry children; people with no job prospects. People feel abandoned. Those in power tell them to be patient, elections first. But will the elections change anything? Will they change the lives of the poorest?

We've hit bottom, so we have to hope 20 that it will get better. We have to make sure that Haitians are empowered to rebuild their country. They ultimately must be unified in building a more egalitarian Haiti with more opportunities for the poor, for women, for the disadvantaged, which now includes thousands and thousands of disabled people as well.

What is the situation for women like now?

The last time I was in Haiti, I saw all these little girls with big bellies. I had never seen that before: little girls walking in the neighborhoods with big bellies. I was in Jalousie, one of those precarious neighborhoods perched on the hills, and I saw all these little girls in corridors and alleys with those bellies. I asked someone what was going on and she said, "phenomene de tente"—the tent phenomenon. Young girls have been raped and are now pregnant. A health worker I talked to said she had treated a pregnant 10-year-old. And there is gang rape, what people call "beton."

But we have some extraordinary women leaders rising out of these same camps. There are some you will never hear about. I know a woman who had 100 people in her yard after the earthquake, and she fed them and gave them water. She would have never considered herself a leader before but she organized everyone.

Women want to take charge, but they need our support.

What is your vision for the future of Haiti?   25

Ultimately, we should be asking the people in Haiti what they would like to see, what their vision is. But if I'm being Utopian, I'd like to see a society emerge out of this rubble where every child can go to school, where every person can eat every day, and have a roof over his head that won't blow away or crumble at the slightest wind.

What many don't know is that the women of Haiti have been trying to build this for years; they try to work miracles. The people who are in charge of this "rebuilding" should study these efforts very well. I believe recovery efforts can learn a lot from the way women have been recovering for years—from droughts, from floods, from hurricanes.

Let's not leave those folks out of the conversation.

As a mother, what do you tell your children about your country?

My children—they are 5 and 1-year-old—have been to Haiti many times, and will always know the good and the bad because that is the way we have experienced it.

I will continue to tell my daughters the stories of the great historical and everyday women (and men) of Haiti. I will probably ₃₀ drive them crazy, but they'll know all about them.

People often pity or idealize Haitians: They are seen as either "poor Haitians" or "super-resilient Haitians." Somewhere in the middle lies the truth.

It's worth remembering that Haitians have a lot to teach the world. I will continue to teach my children that we are often in positions where we need a lot from others, but as Haitians, we also have a lot to give to each other and a lot to contribute to the world.

A CLOSER LOOK AT
Edwidge Danticat: Return to Haiti

1. What do you remember about the Haitian earthquake? You may remember many news reports and other coverage. How does this interview change your understanding of that devastating event?

2. In this interview, Danticat provides rich portraits of the Haitian people, especially Haitian women. She says, "Women want to take charge, but they need our support" and "the women of Haiti have been trying to build this [a vision for a better Haiti] for years; they try to work miracles." Does this match the portrait of Lili in "A Wall of Fire Rising"? In what ways does it match or not?

3. At the end of the interview, Danticat makes a very clear and direct statement about the Haitian people and their experience: "Haitians have a lot to teach the world. I will continue to teach my children that we are often in positions where we need a lot from others, but as Haitians, we also have a lot to give to each other and a lot to contribute to the world." Was Danticat striving to provide a similar message in "A Wall of Fire Rising"? If so, why didn't she just come out and say that in her story, as she does in this interview? What can literature do that other writing (like an interview or essay) cannot?

IDEAS FOR
Writing

1. Practice summarizing and quoting. Choose one of the extended passages in this interview that most interested you. Write a brief summary of that passage in which you use your own words to capture the message. If you quote, do not quote entire sentences, but limit yourself to quotes that are one to six words long and incorporate them into your own sentences. (For help with summarizing and quoting, consult "Choosing an Appropriate Style" from this chapter and "Quoting, Paraphrasing, and Citing Sources" from Chapter 26.

2. Near the end of the interview, Danticat makes this statement about the usual perceptions of Haitians: "People often pity or idealize Haitians: They are seen as either 'poor Haitians' or 'super-resilient Haitians.' Somewhere in the middle lies the truth." Write a five-page literary analysis that examines

"A Wall of Fire Rising" in light of this statement. Incorporate the words written by Milano, spoken by Danticat, or both. Be sure to provide context for your quotations or summaries, so that your readers understand where the quoted words come from.

3. Conduct an interview with someone about their work (whatever that is) and create a three-page interview written in a style and structure that is inspired by or is similar to Milano's. Like Milano, you should try to capture something essential and interesting about your interviewee. You can interview a friend, classmate, family member, acquaintance, or stranger. It doesn't have to be someone famous, or someone whose work is fascinating, but try to get at some feature of the work that is remarkable.

1. In a group, consider how you could analyze a movie in the same way that you analyze a literary work. Start out by selecting a movie that most of you have seen or are familiar with. Then generate an "interpretive question" about the movie. Ask yourself, "What do I/we want to understand by going beneath the surface of the movie?" In a single sentence, write down your interpretive question, and in another single sentence, write down your thesis.

2. Ask each member of your group to bring in a short poem. Discuss the poem as a literary work by paying attention to its genre, plot, characters, setting, and use of language and tone. What intrigues you about each poem?

3. Find a literary analysis on the Internet. Point to specific places in the analysis where the author makes the following moves:

   a. Identifies an interpretive question

   b. States a thesis that addresses that question

   c. Examines the text itself to support the interpretation

   d. Goes outside the text (with information about the author, the social or historical setting, etc.) to develop the interpretation

   e. Provides insights that go beyond the obvious

Talk About This

1. Read Paul Laurence Dunbar's "We Wear the Mask" (page 123). Generate an "interprctive question" about the poem. Ask yourself, "What do I want to understand by going beneath the surface of the poem?" Focus on just one question.

   a. Address your interpretive question by discussing the specifics of the poem. Focus at first on the poem itself rather than what you might know about the author or the time it was written. Finally, come up with one aspect of the poem that makes a plausible case about its message, what makes it effective, thought provoking, revealing, or enjoyable.

   b. In a single sentence, write down your interpretive question. In another single sentence, write down your thesis.

2. Practice summarizing, describing, and quoting by choosing a scene or feature (character, plot, setting, etc.) from "A Wall of Fire Rising" that you find interesting. First, summarize that scene or feature as clearly and efficiently as possible in two or three sentences. Second, rework what you've written to weave in quoted words and phrases that are particularly important to the summary. Be sure to use quotation marks and parenthetical citations to show which words are quoted.

3. Search the Internet to find literary definitions of the word "genre." Cut and paste those definitions into a single file. Now, look back at the definition of genre in Chapter 1, "Writing and Genres." How are the literary definitions of genre different than the one used in this book? Are there any similarities? In a response to your professor, try to reconcile these two definitions of genre in a way that makes both useful.

Try This Out

There are many microgenres that are similar to literary analyses. Choose a microgenre from the list below and find three examples in print or on the Internet. Using these examples, try to figure out the common features common to this microgenre.

Book Cover Blurb—a brief description of the book that can run anywhere from one to five lines on the back of the book. A blurb tries to capture the spirit of the book, enticing potential readers to buy it

Movie or TV Episode Analysis—analysis of a movie or TV episode that uses the strategies and features of a literary analysis

Literary Review—a review that discusses the strengths and weaknesses of a literary work (novel, short story, or poem)

Imitation Piece—imitation of a literary work that uses the style, tone, themes, and structures of the original work (can be serious or humorous)

Literary Analysis Parody—a literary analysis of a literary work (or movie or TV show) that you really think is shallow and terrible but written as if you think it's great art (using the conventions of the literary analysis)

1. **Analyze a short story or poem.** Write a four- to five-page literary analysis of a short story or poem that poses an interesting interpretive question and offers an interpretive thesis that explains the work's message or significance or that analyzes its structure and features (character, symbol, setting, etc.). Be sure that you focus on the text itself for your interpretation.

2. **Create a multimedia literary analysis of a song or poem.** Drawing on a variety of media (images, sound, or text), create an electronic multimedia presentation of a song or poem. Choose whatever medium you are comfortable with (or that you want to learn), such as a podcast, Web page, or *PowerPoint* slide presentation. Combine these media to provide your audience with an experience that goes beyond the text and presents them with something new—a new insight, analysis, or interesting juxtaposition.

3. **Turn a review into a literary analysis.** Write an informal two-page review of a movie, a TV show, or a work in some other medium. Then transform the review into a more formal three- to four-page literary analysis using the strategies described in this chapter. Pose an interpretive question and state a thesis that answers the question. Quote and describe the text. Then explain the message or significance of the work you are analyzing.

PEARSON
mycomplab

For support in meeting this chapter's objectives, follow this path in MyCompLab: Resources ⟹ Writing ⟹ Writing Purposes ⟹ Writing to Analyze. Review the Instruction and Multimedia resources about writing to analyze, then complete the Exercises and click on Gradebook to measure your progress.

Rhetorical Analyses

In this chapter, you will learn how to—

- analyze rhetorical elements of a text.
- use *logos*, *ethos*, and *pathos* as means of persuasion.
- write in an academic style for academic readers.

The purpose of a rhetorical analysis is to determine how and why texts are or are not influential. Advertisers, marketing analysts, and public relations agents use rhetorical analyses to understand how well their messages are influencing target audiences and the general public. Political scientists and consultants use rhetorical analyses to determine which ideas and strategies will be most persuasive to voters and consumers. Meanwhile, historians and rhetoricians use rhetorical analyses to study historic speeches and documents to understand how and why they were influential in their day and perhaps are still influential today.

Ultimately, the objective of a rhetorical analysis is to show why a text was *effective* or *persuasive*. By studying texts closely, you can learn how writers and speakers sway others and how you can be more persuasive yourself.

In your college courses, you may be asked to write rhetorical analyses that explore historical and present-day documents, advertisements, and speeches. These assignments are not always called "rhetorical analyses," but anytime you are being asked to analyze a nonfiction text, you are probably being asked to write a rhetorical analysis. Also, depending on your career after college, your supervisors may ask you to closely analyze your organization's marketing materials and messages to determine their effectiveness. These critiques are rhetorical analyses, too.

Rhetorical Analyses

Here are two possible organizations for a rhetorical analysis, but other arrangements of these sections will work, too. You should adjust these organizational patterns to fit your topic, angle, purpose, readers, and context.

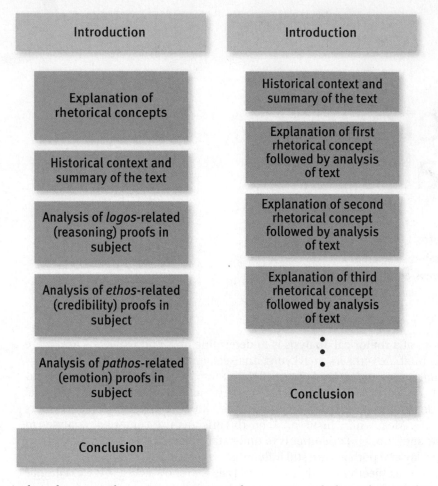

Rhetorical analyses can be written a variety of ways. Nevertheless, they tend to have some common features:

- **An introduction** that identifies the subject of your analysis, states your purpose and main point (thesis statement), offers background information on the subject, and stresses its importance.

- **An explanation of the rhetorical concepts** that you will use to analyze the subject.

- **A description or summary of your subject** that sets it in a historical context.

- **An analysis of the subject** through the chosen rhetorical concepts.

- **A conclusion** that states or restates your main point (thesis statement) and looks to the future.

ONE STUDENT'S WORK
Rhetorical Analyses

**Rhetorical Analysis of the *Keep America Beautiful*
Public Service Announcement (1971)**

Wes Rodenburg

The original *Keep America Beautiful* public service announcement (PSA) aired for the first time on Earth Day in 1971, and it is widely credited for inspiring environmental consciousness and changing minds about pollution. The commercial features Iron Eyes Cody (fig. 1), a movie actor who has since become an icon of the environmental movement. At the beginning of the PSA, Iron Eyes paddles his birch bark canoe down an American river. The river is natural and beautiful at the beginning, but as Iron Eyes paddles downstream it is transformed into an industrial and mechanical world of black oil, soot, coal, and garbage. Iron Eyes makes his way to shore with his canoe. After he pulls his canoe from the water, he has a bag of garbage thrown at his feet from a car on an interstate. A stern-voiced narrator then intones, "Some people have a natural abiding respect for the beauty that was once this country, and some people don't. People start pollution, and people can stop it." Iron Eyes turns to the camera with a tear in his eye. The PSA ends as a symbol for *Keep America Beautiful* fills the screen. This PSA is one of the best examples of how environmental groups can appeal to broader audiences with emotion (*pathos*), authority (*ethos*), and reasoning (*logos*).

Fig. 1. Iron Eyes Cody.

> Background information helps the readers to understand the text.

> Here is the author's thesis statement.

Using Emotions to Draw a Contrast between the Ideal and Real

This PSA's appeals to emotion are its strongest arguments. As the commercial starts, we can see Iron Eyes Cody in what we could consider to be his native land. He sits proud and tall as he paddles downstream. We can see his eyes and his face, and he looks as though he has heard some troubling news. The shot pans out and we see his silhouette against a gold-splashed river, pristine as can be. Then, the beauty of this natural scene comes to a crashing

> The advertisement is summarized here.

continued

halt as a crumpled newspaper page floats by the canoe. The music shifts from a native-sounding melody to a mechanical booming sound. The silhouette of Iron Eyes and his canoe—the only reminder we have of what nature is intended to look like—is then shadowed as we reach an apex of filth: garbage-ridden water, smoggy air, oil, and a massive steel barge. This scene dwarfs his canoe, and the music begins to sound desperate as it reaches its peak. Iron Eyes is turned transparent, a ghost of what respect humankind had for the earth, and he is juxtaposed against what is now: smoke stacks and pollution. Quietly overwhelmed, Iron Eyes pulls his canoe ashore where still more waste permeates the surroundings. The trash thrown at Iron Eyes' feet feels like a final insult that punctuates the scene.

The use of *pathos* is discussed.

We now know who is responsible for this tragedy: it is us. Our sense of emotional shame is triggered by the contrasts we have just seen. The floating newspaper, the smog, sludge, smoke, muck, oil, grease, fumes, and garbage. Pollution is everywhere, and we now know that we are the cause. It is our fault—humanity's fault. The appeal to *pathos* then reaches its pinnacle as Iron Eyes sheds a tear for what we have done to this land. We see a great contrast between the environment as he knew it and the way it is now.

Using a Symbolic Figure to Create a Sense of Authority

Credibility proofs (*ethos*) are discussed here.

Dressed in classic Native American clothing, Iron Eyes Cody is a symbol of our fading past that appeals to our sense of *ethos*. When most people think of Native Americans, they think of how they taught the original settlers to live off of the land. They think about the respect that American natives had for the land and nature. When the narrator says, "Some people have a natural abiding respect for the beauty that was once this country, and some people don't," the contrast between Iron Eyes Cody and his polluted surroundings feels sharp. In this way, the symbolic *ethos* of Iron Eyes demonstrates that the ruination around him is our doing, not his. He takes us on a journey that slowly opens our eyes to what we are responsible for—ruining nature. One might even suggest that Iron Eyes may be analogous to the earth itself. As the pollution thickens, the image of the Iron Eyes fades from a vibrantly dressed Native American to a silhouette until he becomes a ghost of the past. Iron Eyes does nothing to change the pollution, nor does he attempt to change it. Instead he observes it and feels it with pain, remorse, and despair. That's the only thing that he and the earth can do.

Analysis explains the meaning of the advertisement.

Using Reasoning to Drive Home the Point

The PSA's use of an appeal to reason is analyzed here.

Finally, the PSA uses *logos* to drive home its point: "Some people have a deep and abiding respect for the natural beauty that was once this country.

And some people don't. People start pollution. People can stop it." After this logical statement, we are given a five-second display of the *Keep America Beautiful* symbol, suggesting an answer. In the Web version, a Web site address is given where people can access information on how they can do something about pollution. The logic is inescapable: If you really care about the environment, stop doing more damage and start getting active in cleaning up the mess. The viewer's next logical question is almost inescapably, "How can I do something?"

> The conclusion returns to the main point of the rhetorical analysis.

The *Keep America Beautiful* PSA has been a model for reaching out to the public about environmental issues. Its use of emotion, authority, and reasoning brings us face to face with our transgressions against nature. This PSA woke many people up and urged them to change their ways. Of course, the pollution problem has not been solved, but we seem to have turned the corner. Iron Eyes Cody is watching to see if we succeed.

> Ends by stressing the importance of the subject and looks to the future.

Inventing Your Rhetorical Analysis's Content

When preparing to write a rhetorical analysis, the first thing you need to do is closely read the text you are analyzing. Read through it at least a couple of times, taking special note of any places where the author seems to make important points or perhaps misses an opportunity to do so.

Inquiring: Highlight Uses of Proofs

Now, do some analysis. When looking closely at the text, you will notice that authors tend to use three kinds of *proofs* to persuade you:

Watch the Animation on **Appeals** at **mycomplab.com**

Reasoning (*logos*): appealing to readers' common sense, beliefs, or values

Credibility (*ethos*): using the reputation, experience, and values of the author or an expert to support claims

Emotion (*pathos*): using feelings, desires, or fears to influence readers

Rhetoricians often use the ancient Greek terms, *logos, ethos,* and *pathos,* to discuss these three kinds of proofs, so we have used them here. Let's look at these concepts more closely.

Highlighting Uses of Reasoning (*Logos*). The word *logos* in ancient Greek means "reasoning" in English. This word is the basis for the English word, "logic," but *logos*

involves more than using logic to prove a point. *Logos* also involves appealing to someone else's common sense and using examples to demonstrate a point. Here are some common ways people use reasoning to influence the beliefs and opinions of others:

If . . . then: "If you believe X, then you should believe Y also."

Either . . . or: "Either you believe X, or you believe Y."

Cause and effect: "X is the reason Y happens."

Costs and benefits: "The benefits of doing X are worth/not worth the cost of Y."

Better and worse: "X is better/worse than Y because . . ."

Examples: "For example, X and Y demonstrate that Z happens."

Facts and data: "These facts/data support my argument that X is true or Y is false."

Anecdotes: "X happened to these people, thus demonstrating Y."

As you analyze the text, highlight these uses of reasoning so you can figure out how the writer uses *logos* to influence people.

Highlighting Uses of Credibility (*Ethos*). The Greek word *ethos* means "credibility," "authority," or "character" in English. It's also the basis for the English word, "ethics." *Ethos* could mean the author's credibility or the use of someone else's credibility to support an argument.

Highlight places in the text where the author is using his or her authority or credibility to prove a point:

Personal experience: "I have experienced X, so I know it's true and Y is not."

Personal credentials: "I have a degree in Z" or "I am the director of Y, so I know about the subject of X."

Good moral character: "I have always done the right thing for the right reasons, so you should believe me when I say that X is the best path to follow."

Appeal to experts: "According to Z, who is an expert on this topic, X is true and Y is not true."

Identification with the readers: "You and I come from similar backgrounds and we have similar values; therefore, you would likely agree with me that X is true and Y is not."

Admission of limitations: "I may not know much about Z, but I do know that X is true and Y is not."

Expression of good will: "I want what is best for you, so I am recommending X as the best path to follow."

Use of "insider" language: Using special terminology or referring to information that only insiders would understand.

When you are searching for *ethos*-related proofs, look carefully for places where the author is trying to use his or her character or experience to sway readers' opinions.

Highlighting Uses of Emotion (*Pathos*). Finally, look for places where the author is trying to use *pathos,* or emotions, to influence readers. The psychologist Robert Plutchik suggests there are eight basic emotions: joy, acceptance, fear, surprise, sadness, disgust, anger, and anticipation. As you analyze the text, highlight places where the author is using these basic emotions to persuade readers.

Promise of gain: "By agreeing with us, you will gain trust, time, money, love, advancement, reputation, comfort, popularity, health, beauty, or convenience."

Promise of enjoyment: "If you do things our way, you will experience joy, anticipation, fun, surprises, enjoyment, pleasure, leisure, or freedom."

Fear of loss: "If you don't do things this way, you risk losing time, money, love, security, freedom, reputation, popularity, health, or beauty."

Fear of pain: "If you don't do things this way, you may feel pain, sadness, grief, frustration, humiliation, embarrassment, loneliness, regret, shame, vulnerability, or worry."

Expressions of anger or disgust: "You should be angry or disgusted because X is unfair to you, me, or someone else."

Some other common emotions that you might find are annoyance, awe, calmness, confidence, courage, disappointment, delight, embarrassment, envy, frustration, gladness, grief, hate, happiness, hope, horror, humility, impatience, inspiration, joy, jealousy, loneliness, love, lust, nervousness, nostalgia, paranoia, peace, pity, pride, rage, regret, resentment, shame, sorrow, shock, suffering, thrill, vulnerability, worry, and yearning.

Frequently, writers will not state emotions directly. Instead, they will inject feelings by using emotional stories about others or by incorporating images that illustrate the feelings they are trying to invoke. Advertisements, for example, rely heavily on using emotions to sell products (Figure 8.1).

Researching: Finding Background Information

Once you have highlighted the proofs (i.e., *logos, ethos, pathos*) in the text, it's time to do some background research on the author, the text, and the context in which the work was written and used.

FIGURE 8.1 Advertising and Emotions

Advertising relies heavily on pathos *arguments, because there isn't much time available to persuade a customer to buy something.*

Online Sources. Using Internet search engines and electronic databases, find out as much as you can about the person or company who wrote the text and any issues that he, she, or they were responding to. What historical events led up to the writing of the text? What happened after the text was released to the public? What have other people said about it?

Print Sources. Using your library's catalog and article databases, dig deeper to understand the historical context of the text you are studying. How did historical events or pressures influence the author and the text? Did the author need to adjust the text in a special way to fit the audience? Was the author or organization that published the text trying to achieve particular goals or make a statement of some kind?

Empirical Sources. In person or through e-mail, you might interview an expert who knows something about this text, its author, or the context of the text you are analyzing. An expert can help you gain a deeper understanding of the issues and people involved in the text. You might also show the text to others and note their reactions to it. You can use surveys or informal focus groups to see how people respond to the text.

As always, keep track of your sources. You will need to cite them in your text and list them in the works cited list at the end of your rhetorical analysis.

Organizing and Drafting Your Rhetorical Analysis

Watch the Animation on **Writing Rhetorical Analyses** at **mycomplab.com**

At this point, you should be ready to start drafting your rhetorical analysis. As mentioned earlier, rhetorical analyses can follow a variety of organizational patterns, but those shown on page 144 are good models to follow. You can modify these where necessary as you draft your ideas.

Keep in mind that you don't actually need to use rhetorical terms, such as *logos, ethos,* and *pathos,* in your rhetorical analysis, especially if your readers don't know what these terms mean. Instead, you can use words like "reasoning," "credibility," and "emotion," which will be more familiar to your readers.

The Introduction

Usually, the introduction to a rhetorical analysis is somewhat brief. In this part of your analysis, you want to make some or all of these moves:

Identify the Subject of Your Analysis and Offer Background Information. Clearly state what you are analyzing and provide some historical or other background information that will familiarize your readers with it.

State the Purpose of Your Analysis. Explain that the purpose of your analysis is to determine whether or not your subject was effective or persuasive.

State Your Main Point or Thesis Statement. Rhetorical analyses are usually used in academic settings, so they often include a clear main point or thesis statement in the introduction. Here are examples of a weak thesis statement and a stronger one:

> **Weak:** The *Messin' with Sasquatch* commercials for Jack's Links Beef Jerky are effective because they are funny.

> **Stronger:** The *Messin' with Sasquatch* commercials for Jack's Links Beef Jerky are effective because they humorously show their target consumers (i.e., males in their twenties) playing pranks in nature and then paying for those pranks in degrading but funny ways.

Stress the Importance of the Text. Tell readers why your subject's rhetorical strategies are interesting or worth paying attention to.

These introductory moves can be arranged in just about any order, so write them down and then figure out what order best suits your rhetorical analysis and your readers.

Explanation of Rhetorical Concepts

After the introduction, you should define and explain the rhetorical concepts you are using to analyze the text. So if you are using *logos*, *ethos*, and *pathos*, you need to explain how these concepts are defined. For example, here is how a student defined *pathos* in her rhetorical analysis:

> *Pathos,* which involves using emotion to influence someone else, is a commonly used rhetorical tactic in advertisements aimed at teenage girls. Emotional scenes and images are used to grab the teen's attention and often make her feel something negative, like less confident, insecure, undesirable, unattractive, anxious, or dependent (Holt et al. 84).
>
> Of course, the product being pushed by the advertiser is then put forward as a solution to that supposed inadequacy in the teen's life. For example, as psychologist Tina Hanson points out, teenage girls don't really need a cabinet full of haircare products (73). The typical teenage girl's hair is already healthy, shiny, full, and rich in color. Yet, television and magazine advertisements from haircare companies, which make shampoo, conditioner, and dye, routinely show frustrated teens unsatisfied with their hair. Usually the message being sent to a teen is "You don't even know you need this product, but everyone else knows you do, especially guys." The images show a discouraged girl who risks losing friends or being embarrassed because her hair isn't perfect.

In your rhetorical analysis, you don't need to cover all three of the rhetorical proofs mentioned in this chapter. Instead, you might decide to concentrate on just one of them, like *pathos*, so you can develop a fuller definition of that concept for your readers.

Also as mentioned earlier, keep in mind that other rhetorical concepts besides *logos, ethos,* and *pathos* are available. For instance, you could choose to study the metaphors used in a text, or perhaps its genre, style, or use of narrative. If you choose one of these other rhetorical concepts, you will need to define and explain that concept to your readers.

Provide Historical Context and Summary

To give your readers an overall understanding of the text you are analyzing, give them some historical background on it. Then summarize the text for them.

Historical Context. Tell your readers the history of the text. Who wrote it or presented it? Who was the target reader or audience? Where and when did the text appear? Why was the text produced or written?

Summary. Spend anywhere from one to five paragraphs summarizing the content of the text. Most summaries follow the organization of the text itself, highlighting the main points and stressing the most important features. Your summary of the text should be completely in your own words, with select quotes taken from the text. When summarizing, do not express your own opinions about the text or its message. Instead, just give readers an objective overview of the content of the text.

The aim of this historical context section is to give your readers enough background to understand the text you are analyzing. For example, here is the historical context and a summary of an advertisement for Red Bull:

Fig. 1. "Red Bull Gives You Wings."

Advertisements for energy drinks rely heavily on emotion to make sales to college students. These unique soft drinks, which usually contain high amounts of caffeine and calories, began to grow in popularity in the late 1990s.

Red Bull, one of the most popular brands, actually was invented in the 1970s in Thailand, and it was first exported to the United States in 1997 (FundingUniverse). From the beginning, Red Bull's advertising has been squarely aimed at college students, telling them that they need to have extra energy to get through their hectic days. One of its recent advertising campaigns, which is called "Red Bull Gives You Wings," began in 2005 with simple hand-drawn movies like the one shown in fig. 1.

In this advertisement, a bird relieves himself on a man who looks a lot like a professor. The man then drinks a can of Red Bull and sprouts wings. He flies above the bird, pulls down his pants, and proceeds to return the favor (offscreen, thankfully). The viewer hears the bird screech in horror as an image of a can of Red Bull fills the screen, but we can all imagine what happened.

During the span of the 30-second advertisement, the man transforms from being a seemingly helpless victim to a superheroic figure who can take vengeance on the bird. Drinking Red Bull is shown to be the way he gains this new power.

The length of your summary depends on your readers. If they are already familiar with the text you are analyzing, your summary should be brief. You don't want to bore your readers by telling them something they already know. If, however, they are not familiar with the text, your summary should be longer and more detailed.

Analysis of the Text

Watch the Animation on **Analyzing Texts** at **mycomplab.com**

Now it is time to analyze the text for your readers. Essentially, you are going to interpret the text for them, using the rhetorical concepts you defined earlier in the rhetorical analysis.

There are two main ways to organize this section:

- You can follow the organization of the text you are analyzing, starting from the beginning and working to the end of the text. Apply the rhetorical concepts to each major section of the text you are analyzing.

- You can discuss the text through each rhetorical concept separately. For instance, if you are analyzing the uses of *logos*, *ethos*, and *pathos* in a text, you would separately discuss the text's use of each kind of proof.

For example, here is a discussion of *pathos* in the Red Bull advertisement:

Using Emotion to Sell Red Bull

Like much advertising aimed at young people, the Red Bull advertisement uses emotions to bring home its argument. In this advertisement, the use of humor is what gives the message its emotional punch.

Many young people feel like the professor in this advertisement, because they perceive that they are ultimately powerless in society. So when someone else treats them badly, young people usually assume they need to just take it. In this case, the Red Bull advertisement shows the bird relieving itself on the professor-like character. In most situations, the man would simply need to suffer that humiliation. But, he has a secret weapon, Red Bull. He drinks a can, sprouts wings, and humorously takes revenge on the bird.

The story itself is an emotional parable that reflects the life of most young people. The bird represents all the things in young peoples' lives that humiliate and embarrass them but that they cannot fix. The professor-like man, though not young, is a figure that students can relate to, because he is still in the educational system and seems powerless in his own way. So when he is able to actually use a product like Red Bull to take revenge, young people not only laugh but also feel an emotional release of their own frustration. The emotional message to young people is, "Drink Red Bull, and you can get back at all those people who crap on you."

The humor, coupled with the revenge theme, makes the advertisement's use of emotion very effective. According to Mark Jefferson, a professor at Penn State who studies advertisements, the use of revenge is very effective for reaching college students. "Students often feel powerless in a world that tells them they are adults but refuses to give them power. Advertisements that tap into that frustration in a humorous way are very powerful" (23).

In this discussion of emotion, the writer is applying her definition of *pathos* to the advertisement. This allows her to explain the use of emotion to sell Red Bull. She can now go on to discuss the use of *logos* and *ethos* in the ad. Or, if she has more to say about *pathos*, she might make her rhetorical analysis about the use of *pathos* alone.

The Conclusion

When you have finished your analysis, it's time to wrap up your argument. Keep this part of your rhetorical analysis brief. A paragraph or two should be enough. You should answer one or more of the following questions:

- Ultimately, what does your rhetorical analysis reveal about the text you studied?

- What does your analysis tell your readers about the rhetorical concept(s) you used to analyze the text?

- Why is your explanation of the text or the rhetorical concept(s) important to your readers?

- What should your readers look for in the future with this kind of text or this persuasion strategy?

Minimally, the key to a good conclusion is to restate your main point (thesis statement) about the text you analyzed.

Choosing an Appropriate Style

The style of a rhetorical analysis depends on your readers and where your analysis might appear. If you are writing your analysis for an online magazine like *Slate* or *Salon*, readers would expect you to write something colorful and witty. If you are writing the argument for an academic journal, your tone would need to be more formal. Here are some ideas for using an appropriate style in your rhetorical analysis:

Use Lots of Detail to Describe the Text. In as much detail as possible, tell readers the *who, what, where, when, why,* and *how* of the text you are analyzing. Also, use details to describe what the text looks like, sounds like, and feels like. Above all, you want readers to experience the text, even if they haven't seen or read it themselves.

Minimize the Jargon and Difficult Words. When analyzing something, you might be tempted to puff up your language with lots of specialized terminology and complex words. These kinds of complex words will unnecessarily make your text harder to read.

Improve the Flow of Your Sentences. Rhetorical analyses are designed to explain a text as clearly as possible, so you want your writing to flow easily from one sentence to the next. The best way to create this kind of flow is to use the "given-new" strategies that are discussed in Chapter 20, "Developing Paragraphs and Sections." Given-new involves making sure each new sentence takes something like a word, phrase, or idea from the previous sentence.

Pay Attention to Sentence Length. If you are writing a lively or witty analysis, you will want to use shorter sentences to make your argument feel more active and fast-paced. If you are writing for an academic audience, longer sentences will make your analysis sound more formal and proper. Keep in mind that your sentences should be "breathing length."

As mentioned earlier in this chapter, rhetorical terms like *logos, ethos,* and *pathos* do not need to appear in your rhetorical analysis. If you are writing for readers who probably don't know what these terms mean, you are better off using words like "reasoning," "credibility," or "emotion." If you want to use the actual rhetorical terms, make sure you define them for readers.

Designing Your Rhetorical Analysis

Computers make it possible to use visuals in a rhetorical analysis. You can download pictures from the Internet, use a scanner to insert an image of the text, or take a picture with a digital camera. You could even include a video or audio podcast, so your readers can experience the text you are analyzing. Here are some things you might try out:

Download Images from the Internet. If you are reviewing a book or a historical document, you can download an image of its cover and include that image in your rhetorical analysis. This way, readers can actually see what you are talking about.

"Red Bull Gives You Wings"

Energy drinks are a product that relies heavily on emotion for sales to high school and college students. These soft drinks, which usually contain high amounts of caffeine and calories, began to grow in popularity in the late 1990s. Red Bull, one of the most popular brands, actually was invented in the 1970s in Thailand, and it was first exposed to the United States in 1997 (FundingUniverse). From the beginning, Red Bull's advertising has been squarely aimed at college students, telling them that they need to have extra energy to get through their hectic days. It's current version of the "Red Bull Gives You Wings" slogan began in 2005 with simple hand-drawn movies like the one shown in Fig. 1.

Fig. 1. "Red Bull Gives You Wings."

In this advertisement, a bird relieves himself on a man who looks a lot like a professor. The man then drinks a can of Red Bull and sprouts wings. He flies above the bird, pulls down his pants, and proceeds to return the favor (offscreen, thankfully). The viewer hears the bird screech in horror as an image of a can of Red Bull fills the screen, but we can all imagine what happened.

During the span of 30-second advertisement, the man transforms from being a seemingly weak victim to a *superheroic* figure who can take vengeance on the bird. Drinking Red Bull is shown to be the way he gains this new power.

FIGURE 8.2 Adding a Screen Shot to Your Analysis

A screen shot is an easy way to put an image into your rhetorical analysis.

Add a Screen Shot. If you are writing about an advertisement from the Internet, you can take a picture of your screen (i.e., a screen shot). Then you can include that screen shot in your analysis (Figure 8.2). On a PC, you can push the Print Screen button to capture a screen shot. Then you can use the cropping tool to remove the parts of the image you don't want. On a Mac, just type Command-Shift-3 for a shot of the whole screen or Command-Shift-4 for a cursor that allows you to take a picture of part of the screen.

Include a Link to a Podcast. If you are analyzing a video or audio text (perhaps something you found on *YouTube*), you can put a link to that text in your analysis. Or you can include the Web address so readers can find the text themselves. If your analysis will appear online, you can use a link to insert the podcast right into your document.

Make a Web Site. Your rhetorical analysis can be made into a Web site. The home page can be the introduction, and you can provide links to the rest of your analysis. You can add images and links to other sites, which will allow readers to better experience the text you are analyzing.

Why not be creative? Look for ways to use technology to let your readers access the text you are analyzing.

Revising and Editing Your Rhetorical Analysis

Rhetorical analyses tend to be medium-sized documents, so they are easy to revise and edit. One of the challenges of editing a rhetorical analysis is keeping your definitions of key terms consistent throughout the argument. If you aren't careful, your definitions of rhetorical concepts will evolve as you analyze a text. So you want to make sure you are using your terms consistently.

Recheck Definitions of the Rhetorical Concepts. Early in the analysis, you defined one or more rhetorical concepts you used to analyze the text. Now that you have finished drafting your analysis, make sure you actually used those definitions in the same way that you described them. You might find that you need to revise or refine your definitions, or you might need to rewrite parts of your analysis to fit those original definitions.

Expand Your Analysis. Did you cover all the angles? Could you say more? Look for gaps in your analysis of the text. For example, if you were talking about the use of emotion in a Red Bull ad, are there some additional emotional elements you didn't talk about or could expand on?

Copyedit for Clarity. Take a closer look at your paragraphs and sentences. Can you make them plainer? Can you put better claims at the beginnings of paragraphs? Can you work on improving the flow of the sentences?

Read Your Work Out Loud. Your ears are more sensitive to phrasing problems than your eyes. So read your rhetorical analysis out loud to yourself, or have someone read it to you. Mark any places where something sounds odd or makes you stumble. Then edit those marked places.

As always, a solid effort at proofreading will only improve your work (and your professor's response to it). Some people find it helpful to print out the document, so they can proofread on paper. Errors are often easier to find on paper than they are on the screen.

The Ad Critique

An ad critique evaluates an advertisement to show why it was or was not effective. If the ad is persuasive, show the readers why it works. An ad critique can also help you explain why you like or dislike a particular type of advertisement. You should aim your critique at people like you who are consumers of mass media and products.

Today, ad critiques are becoming common on the Internet, especially on blogs. They give people a way to express their reactions to the kinds of advertisements being thrown at them. Here are some strategies for writing an ad critique:

Summarize the ad.   If the ad appeared on television or the Internet, describe it objectively in one paragraph. Tell your readers the *Who, What, Where,* and *When* of the ad. If the ad appeared in a magazine or other print medium, you can scan it or download the image from the sponsor's Web site and insert the image into your document.

Highlight the unique quality that makes the advertisement stand out. There must be something remarkable about the ad that caught your attention. What is it? What made it stand out from all the other ads that are similar to it?

Describe the typical features of ads like this one.   Identify the three to five common features that are usually found in this type of advertisement. You can use examples of other ads to explain how a typical ad would look or sound.

Show how this ad is different from the others.   Compare the features of the ad to those of similar advertisements. Demonstrate why this ad is better or worse than its competitors.

Include many details.   Throughout your critique, use plenty of detail to help your readers visualize or hear the ad. You want to replicate the experience of seeing or hearing it.

WRITE **your own ad critique.**   While watching television or reading a magazine, find an ad that seems different. Then write a two-page critique in which you explain why it was or was not effective. Don't forget to scan, download, or take a picture of the ad so you can include it in your critique.

Chrysler's Super Bowl Ad Sells Detroit

Theo Keith

As mid-Missouri's apparent expert on Detroit, I've received texts, phone calls and had conversations with people who want to tell me they loved Chrysler's Super Bowl ad.

It was pretty neat.

The ad, which promoted the Chrysler 200 mid-size sedan, ran 2 minutes and cost "less than $9 million," CEO Sergio Marchionne told the *Detroit Free Press*. It looked like a short documentary, starting with images of a tough, gritty, industrial Detroit. The voiceover asks, "What does a town that's been to hell and back know about the finer things in life?" Then, the answer: "More than most."

The commercial turns to shots of the Joe Louis fist in Hart Plaza, scenes from the ice skating rink at Campus Martius, the Spirit of Detroit statue, and Diego Rivera's "Detroit Industry" frescos at the Detroit Institute of Arts. Here, the voiceover says, "It's the hottest fires that make the hardest steel. Add hard work and conviction, and the know-how that runs generations deep in every last one of us. That's who we are. That's our story."

Then, a swing at journalists who parachute in for a quick story about Detroit's ruins with photos of the crumbling Packard plant and Michigan Central Station. "Now, it's probably not the one you've been reading in papers. The one being written by folks who've never even been here and don't know what we're capable of."

Detroit has always been about hard work and making things. Chrysler, one of two U.S. automakers who went bankrupt in 2009 and relied on a U.S. government bailout to survive, used that theme on Super Bowl Sunday. The rapper Eminem made an appearance, capping the commercial with his only line: "This is the Motor City, and this is what we do."

It's not the first time Chrysler has used Detroit's glory days of inventions and building great things. The automaker debuted its redesigned Jeep Grand Cherokee last year with the slogan, "The things we make, make us." When I last drove by, those words were plastered on the exterior of Chrysler headquarters in Auburn Hills, Mich.

> The ad is summarized.

> The ad is summarized.

> The who, what, where, and when are described.

> Lots of detail helps readers visualize the ad.

continued

Chrysler's Super Bowl Ad Sells Detroit (continued)

As a Michigander, I've seen firsthand Detroit's downfall. I certainly hope the Motor City can live up to its other nickname — the Renaissance City.

Did the ad do enough to sell the car? The 200 is an important vehicle to Chrysler. It replaces the struggling Sebring, which other automakers' mid-sized sedans were hammering in sales. Does the commercial make anyone want to buy a 200? Probably not, a few who watched it on TV told me. The car isn't the star of the show.

Detroit is.

Chrysler's marketing strategy, which one of my friends studying public relations at MU called "great," might not sell more 200s. But by using Detroit and the American ideal that hard work pays off, it may help sell the company. For an automaker that analysts openly questioned could survive just one year ago, that's a victory.

Speaking of unlikely winners, this phrase was lighting up Twitter after the game:

"In a stunning turn of events, Detroit wins the Super Bowl."

Here are the unique qualities that make the ad stand out.

The reviewer shows how this ad is different from the others.

Need to write a rhetorical analysis? Here are some steps to get you going.

FIND a Text You Want to Analyze

Pick something you find intriguing. The best texts are ones that seem curiously persuasive to you (or not persuasive at all). You might also look for texts that are historically important.

HIGHLIGHT the Uses of *Logos, Ethos,* and *Pathos*

Read through the text, marking places in the text where the author uses reasoning (*logos*), credibility (*ethos*), or emotion (*pathos*).

RESEARCH the Context

Use a variety of sources to do background research on the text you are analyzing. Find out as much as you can about the author and the historical context in which he or she created the text. Use interviews or surveys to measure how others react to the text you are studying. Interview experts who know about this kind of text.

DRAFT Your Rhetorical Analysis

A rhetorical analysis typically has the following sections: Introduction (with a solid thesis statement), Definitions of Rhetorical Concepts, Historical Context and Summary, Analysis, and Conclusion. Draft each section separately.

CHOOSE an Appropriate Style

Your style depends on your readers, the place where your analysis will appear, and the text you are analyzing. Use ample details and good pacing to match your analysis's style to the place where it could be published.

DESIGN Your Rhetorical Analysis

Some graphics, especially screen shots, would make the text you are analyzing easier for readers to understand. If you want to do something more advanced, you might try creating a Web site or an audio or video podcast to an on-screen text.

REVISE and Edit

You have gone this far. Now finish the job. Do some revising and editing to make your rhetorical analysis shine. Look for any inconsistencies. Fill out places where more information might be helpful.

How Obama Does That Thing He Does

JACK SHAFER

When President Barack Obama was emerging as a viable candidate in the 2008 presidential primaries, commentators began to take notice of the power of his oratory. People in the crowd were literally swooning at his words, and he had an amazing ability to tap into their emotions. In this rhetorical analysis, Jack Shafer uses rhetorical concepts to explain how Obama does it.

Barack Obama bringeth rapture to his audience. They swoon and wobble, regardless of race, gender, or political affiliation, although few understand exactly why he has this effect on them.

No less an intellect than *The New Yorker*'s George Packer confesses that moments after a 25-minute campaign speech by Obama in New Hampshire concluded, he couldn't remember exactly what the candidate said. Yet "the speech dissolved into pure feeling, which stayed with me for days," he writes.

Given that many of his speeches are criminally short on specifics, as Leon Wieseltier writes, how does Obama do that thing he does? A 2005 paper by University of Oregon professor of rhetoric David A. Frank unpeels Obama's momentous 2004 Democratic National Convention keynote address for clues to his method. Obama's spellbinding oration earned near-universal raves, including one from establishment conservative Rich Lowry, editor of *National Review*, and its echoes can be heard in every speech he's given as a candidate for president.

Obama relies, Frank writes, on a "rhetorical strategy of consilience, where understanding results through translation, mediation, and an embrace of different languages, values, and traditions." He credits the *New Republic*'s Noam Scheiber with translating Obama's cross-cultural signals in a 2004 campaign profile that documents the candidate's leap from the Illinois senate to the U.S. Senate. Scheiber observes:

> Whereas many working-class voters are wary of African American candidates, whom they think will promote black interests at the expense of their own, they simply don't see Obama in these terms. This allows him to appeal to white voters on traditional Democratic issues like jobs, health care, and education—just like a white candidate would.

Bill Clinton disarmed race for blacks by 5 inviting them to talk about it. Obama disarms race for white people by largely avoiding the topic. When he does talk about race, he makes sure to juxtapose the traumas experienced by nonblacks with those experienced by African Americans, but without ever equating the two. His rhetoric is designed to bridge the space between whites and blacks so they can occupy a place where common principles reside and the "transcendent value of justice," as Frank writes, can be shared.

For instance, in a 2005 speech honoring civil rights hero John Lewis, Obama talks about campaigning for the Senate in Cairo, Ill., a town synonymous with overt racism. Obama is accompanied by Sen. Dick Durbin, to whom he directly compares himself. Obama calls himself "a black guy born in Hawaii with a father from Kenya and a mother from Kansas" and Durbin "the son of Lithuania immigrants born into very modest means in east St. Louis." They're both improbable success stories, and had the pair visited Cairo together 30 years previous, who knows what would have happened?

Obama's worries about what sort of reception he and Durbin will receive turn out to be baseless: It's an enthusiastic, mixed crowd, a living demonstration of the racial progress we've made, thanks to the courage of John Lewis and people like him.

In his 2004 convention speech, Obama concedes that we Americans have our differences. While race, geography, politics, and sexual orientation may separate individuals, he insists "there is not a liberal America and a conservative America—there is the United States of America. There is not a black America and a White America and Latino America and Asian America—there's the United States of America." The same words issued by George W. Bush's mouth would move nobody, but a boundary walker like Obama has a way of making them sound genuine. The bonus point for Obama is that by calling for unity, he can also subtly reject the identity politics that have crippled the Democratic Party.

As the candidate who prides himself on disagreeing without being disagreeable, Obama takes on a Christlike quality for lots of people, especially white people. If a white American doesn't feel guilty about race, you can be almost certain that he feels anxious about it. Believe me, if these people had a street address where they could go and get absolution, they'd take the next taxi. Obama has a talent for extending forgiveness to the guilty and the anxious without requiring an apology from them first. Go forth and sin no more, he almost says, and never mind the reparations. No wonder they call him the brother from another planet.

He also knows how to comfort voters with a national narrative of his own invention. As Frank writes, the Song of Obama usually begins with references to Thomas Jefferson, a self-contradicting political thinker whose stock—for good reason—has not always been high in African American circles. Next, he ropes in Abraham Lincoln, whom he describes as less than a perfect emancipator in a 2005 speech. And yet Obama, a tall, gangly lawyer whose political career was made in Springfield, Ill., slyly compared himself to Lincoln when he declared for the presidency. Lincoln, Obama said, was "a tall, gangly, self-made Springfield lawyer" who "tells us that there is power in words" and "tells us there is power in conviction."

Obama's national narrative notes both Roosevelts before calling on Martin Luther King Jr. and, as everybody knows, Ronald Reagan. The implication, of course, is that the Obama candidacy stands as the fulfillment of the American ideal, and by casting their ballot for him, voters can participate in that transcendent moment. It's a dizzying notion. No wonder George Packer's mind went vacant after he heard Obama speak.

In his speeches, Obama pretends to be a hero out of Joseph Campbell. He talks about being on a journey that is about more than just *hope* and *change*. If you want to walk together down his American road, he wants you to be prepared for hard work. It's never going to be easy. He warns his listeners to beware of the cynics and the they-say and they-said naysayers who believe the quest is hopeless.

Obama speeches aren't all nonstop inspiration, mind you. Just as John McCain is stuck on addressing "my friends" in his speeches,

Obama can't resist starting a sentence with "now, I know" and loves to do battle with the nefarious "some who will." But his genuine good humor, his bassoon-and-gravel voice, and a trust quotient that equals that of Walter Cronkite help him over those humps.

In a response to Frank's paper (published in tandem with it), Mark Lawrence McPhail of Miami University warns of the downside of the Obama vision, which he regards as, in the 1994 words of Stephen L. Carter, one that "almost nobody really believes in but almost everybody desperately wants to."

McPhail rails against "Obama's 'audacious hope,'" which he considers "at best naïve, and at worst opportunistic." Skipping the much-needed national conversation about race in favor of Obamaism in the sky won't bring peace, and it won't bring justice, McPhail believes. 15

Obama's grand rhetoric did, however, win him 90 percent of the black vote and 52 percent of the white vote in the Virginia primary this week. Voters might not know what he said, but they have a good idea of what he means.

A CLOSER LOOK AT
How Obama Does That Thing He Does

1. In this review, Shafer does not actually use the words *logos, pathos,* and *ethos.* However, locate the places in the article where he talks about how Obama uses reasoning, authority, and emotion to persuade his audiences.

2. How does Shafer compare Obama's use of rhetoric to that of other great orators, like Franklin Delano Roosevelt, Martin Luther King Jr., and Ronald Reagan? What are some similarities among these great speakers, and how is Obama different from them?

3. According to Shafer, how did Obama treat race differently in the 2008 campaign than others have in the past? What effect did this different approach to race have on his own life story and his political career?

IDEAS FOR
Writing

1. How did Obama's rhetoric change between the 2008 and 2012 elections? Write a two-page response to Shafer's article in which you compare and contrast the Obama he describes in this article with the Obama you know as president and the 2012 candidate. Toward the end of the article, Shafer expresses some doubts about whether Obama's oratorical skills will be the basis for effective leadership of the nation. Knowing what you know about Obama as president, do you think Shafer was right?

2. Write a three-page profile of another person who has strong rhetorical skills in speech or writing. The person you choose could be a historical figure or someone contemporary. You could also pick someone you know personally (e.g., a professor, family member, clergy member, etc.). Your profile should introduce this person and explain why he or she has such strong communication skills. Use the concepts of *logos, ethos,* and *pathos* to support your profile.

What's a Girl to Read?

LIZA FEATHERSTONE

In this article, Liza Featherstone discusses magazines that are aimed toward teenage girls. Traditionally, these kinds of magazines have been about image, fashion, and relationships. Featherstone detects a shift, with some magazines changing for the better and others repackaging the same old themes. In this rhetorical analysis, pay attention to how she criticizes and applauds the ways some magazines use emotion and credibility to attract young women.

Trying to seduce as many underage girls as possible, corporate publishing has adopted the buzzword "real" as its come-on of the moment. Rightly sensing that there is a vacuum in the teen magazine market—the fastest-growing segment of the population has, like, nothing to read—publishers have dreamed up *Jump, Teen People, Twist* and *Glossy. Teen People*, which hit the newsstands this month, promises "real teens, real style." *Jump*'s slogan is "For girls who dare to be real." It makes sense that realness should become a market niche—existing teen magazines like *Seventeen* and *YM* being so decidedly unreal.

But how much realer is this new crop? "Reality" is a place where bodies come in all shapes and sizes, and girls have a political, intellectual and creative life of their own. Despite their pretenses, commercial teen magazines' reality bureaus are still pretty short-staffed.

Time Inc.'s Joe Camel, *Teen People*, deserves some credit for putting out a model-free magazine. Only a third of *Teen People* is devoted to fashion and beauty, and it has refreshingly little advice about how to find a boyfriend. *Teen People* also nods to the not-so-girly girls with profiles of girl sportclimbers and in-line streetskaters. But it's a sad commentary on the state of the glossies that these achievements are even worth mentioning, since *Teen People* is clearly nothing more than a way to hook future *People* readers on celebrity worship—and on a made-in-Hollywood world view (movies are praised for making you "believe in love"). Worse, *Teen People* trivializes girls' achievements; a profile of *Party of Five*'s Jennifer Love Hewitt is almost entirely dedicated to her clothes and her love life. But *Teen People*'s most heinous crime is unskeptically quoting—just five pages away from a full-page *Dawson's Creek* ad, but who's noting such minutia—one of the cast members of *Dawson's Creek* as claiming, "We're a mouthpiece for real teens." Did *Teen People* even "watch" that show? Talk to the hand.

Jump, just a few issues old, from the fitness-oriented Weider Publishing, is a refreshing paean to the active girl—"stylin' snowboarders" and girl hockey players fill its pages; nail polishes recommended are quick-drying (which assumes you have something better to do than sit around and fan your nails). *Jump* clearly has feminist intentions; a first-person story by a girl who suffered from chronic acne offers a powerful indictment of how girls are made to suffer over any physical flaw. But at points *Jump* reads like a 90s *Cosmo*: Pressure to be skinny is replaced by pressure to be "buff," and a plea to girls not to worry about being model-perfect is written by a boy. The message is clear: It's OK that boys and magazines still have the last word on what makes you sexy.

Twist, a bimonthly launched this month 5 by Bauer Publishing, fails at realness even more dismally. It does try to boost girls' body images; "Do our bellies really need busting?" is an eloquent plea for self-acceptance, and the magazine commendably names "Anti-Waifs" as a "Trend We Love . . . Finally! Hollywood is recognizing that you don't have to be scary skinny to shine." But check out their wussy examples—Jewel, Jennifer Aniston, Neve Campbell—no Janeane Garofalo or, hello, Kate Winslet, who was the romantic lead in the blockbuster of the year? Is it too utopian to hope that actresses with real meat on their bones could be presented as sexy icons in a commercial teen magazine? *Twist* shows some models of color, and recently ran a short item on how Janet Jackson gets her "rad red highlights," but these half-hearted hi-fives to multiculturalism are dwarfed by a full-page feature on "How can I get smooth silky hair"—in which the strived-after tresses shown are, you guessed it, blonde.

Aggravating as these body problems are, *Twist*'s assault on girls' minds is even worse. We know only one thing for certain about a girl who picks up a magazine: She doesn't spend every single minute of her life watching TV. So what else does *Twist* recommend she read? Books that might as well be TV shows because they are: the *Party of Five, Buffy the Vampire Slayer, Moesha* and *X-Files* book series. *Twist* also plugs supermodel autobiography *Veronica Webb Sight.* Whatever. *Twist* manages to have even less respect for readers' intelligence than its older sister glossies; while *Seventeen*, to its credit, has always featured fiction-writing contests, *Twist*'s idea of reader participation is—no joke—a "love quiz" contest.

Then there's *Glossy*, a Web magazine newly launched in print, which doesn't remotely aspire to realness. It makes *YM* look like the Seneca Falls Declaration.

OK, OK. My catty sniping is all very well, but ultimately, what's a girl to read? Luckily there are a number of alternatives to these mind-numbing infomercials: independently published magazines written by and for teenage girls. These magazines are not only more feminist than their glossy counterparts, they're far smarter, more racially diverse, and yes, more real.

Rochester, N.Y.-based *Blue Jean*, an ad-free bimonthly, offers, to use its own words, an "alternative to the fashion and beauty magazines targetting young women." Ani "I-refuse-to-sell-out-to-the-McMusic-industry" diFranco graces the cover of the January/February "Women We Love" issue with gritty style—not your father's *Esquire*'s "Women We Love": in addition to Ani, *Blue Jean* loves Third Wave activist Rebecca Walker, soccer star Mia Hamm, tennis pro Venus Williams (and "the sassy swing of her beaded hair"), author Veronica Chambers, teen novelist Jean Crowell and Hard Candy nail polish entrepreneur Dineh Mohajer, and features interviews with both Missy "Misdemeanor" Elliott and Rosa Parks.

Teen Voices, a national quarterly run out 10 of Boston that roughly estimates its readership at 45,000, focuses on urban girls—taking on issues from teen pregnancy and body mutilation to "Snowboarding on the Cheap!" Articles ask: Was the court decision in the Boston Latin affirmative action case fair? Are cartoons sexist? Do animals have rights? How do you get over shyness? Should you get a tattoo? *Teen Voices* has a fine mix of politics, personal stuff, book and record reviews, fiction and poetry.

Hues, a feisty, multi-cultural quarterly, has a high-quality, attractive, innovative layout—on shiny paper (none of this hard-to-read, self-marginalizing newsprint). Its current issue features "Get On the Bus!" an account of Philadelphia's little-covered Million Woman March; "Making It Big," a profile of a successful and gorgeous 190-pound model who's outspoken in her criticism of the fashion industry; advice on looking for a good job "before you give up and accept a lifetime position at Minimum-Wages-R-Us"; an undercover look at phone sex; and a cultural dialogue between two young Indian women about arranged marriage. They've also run pieces on "Ghetto Feminism" and a "Swimsuit Issue" featuring women of all colors, shapes and sizes. *Hues* was recently acquired by New Moon publishing, the creator of the younger girls' magazine *New Moon*; it will go bimonthly next year.

Reluctant Hero is a Canadian quarterly with some serious feminist analysis—"Birds do it, Bees do it, Boys sure do. Why is it so taboo for girls to have a libido?"—asking why boys on TV shows don't listen to girls' desires (they pursue girls who aren't interested, harass them endlessly, and end up winning them over in the end). *Reluctant Hero* also explores cliques, sexual harassment and peer

mediation, and asks that timeless question that you will probably never see in a commercial teen magazine—"Why Are Girls So Mean?" Other features cheer girls' creativity and ambitions: "Be a Mega Zine Queen," "Does Science Have a Gender?" and "Getting a Record Deal."

These magazines are so good that rereading them actually made me dislike *Jump, Teen People* and *Twist* even more. Though these commercial ventures are, considering the territory, a step in the right direction, girls themselves can do so much better. It's too soon to say for sure how many readers the mainstream newcomers have attracted, but *Teen People* is reportedly selling like the Titanic. The independents don't attract Gap ads, and, at least in *Blue Jean*'s case, wouldn't even if they could; they need support. Subscribe, request them at your bookstore or library, make a contribution, show them to your favorite teenager—or millionaire investor. Let's hope the talent behind this girls' alternative press gets the encouragement it deserves to keep on keeping it real.

A CLOSER LOOK AT
What's a Girl to Read?

1. In her article, Featherstone says this about these new magazines: "The message is clear: It's OK that boys and magazines still have the last word on what makes you sexy." What does Featherstone believe is the alternative to this common theme in magazines aimed at teenage girls? How do the magazines she supports change this dynamic?

2. How do images, especially images of the body, become an issue of credibility (*ethos*) in teen magazines? How do these magazines use or

misuse images of celebrities and models to promote a specific ideal of what teenage girls should aspire to?

3. According to Featherstone, how do these kinds of magazines play on the emotions of teenage girls? Does she suggest that there are good ways to use emotional arguments aimed at girls? What are some of the inappropriate ways that emotions are used in these magazines and their advertisements?

IDEAS FOR
Writing

1. At your campus library or local library, find a magazine that is aimed toward women. Write a two-page review in which you use the concepts of *logos, ethos,* and *pathos* to discuss how this magazine and its advertisers try to persuade its readers. Your review should be aimed at the target audience for the magazine. Tell them whether the magazine is effective or not.

2. Write a proposal in which you pitch an idea for a new kind of magazine aimed at college-age women or men. Pick a specific angle or niche that sets your magazine apart from the magazines that are already aimed at these markets. Your proposal should first discuss the absence of magazines like yours. Then describe the magazine and its market.

1. With a group in your class, discuss the ways people try to persuade you. How do family members try to persuade you? How do your friends try to persuade you? In what ways do their persuasive strategies differ from the ways advertisers try to persuade people?

2. List some ways people try to use their credibility (*ethos*) or emotion (*pathos*) to persuade others. Supposedly, using reason (*logos*) is the most reliable way to persuade someone, and yet we use credibility and emotion all the time to get our points across. Why? When are arguments from credibility and emotion even more persuasive than arguments that rely on reason?

3. With a group, make a list of your favorite five commercials on television and a list of five commercials you cannot stand. Why do people in your group find some of these commercials interesting and worth watching? Why are some commercials so irritating that you want to turn the television off? As a group, create a list of ten do's and don'ts of advertising to college students.

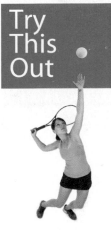

1. Find an advertisement in a magazine that you think is persuasive (or not). Then write a one-page analysis of the advertisement in which you discuss why you think it is effective (or not). Look closely at its uses of reasoning, credibility, and emotion. What kinds of support does the advertiser rely on most? What do these rhetorical strategies say about the people the advertiser is targeting?

2. Imagine that a political candidate has hired you to explain how to persuade college students to vote for him or her. The candidate sees college students as very important, but is frustrated by some students' ability to see through the political spin. In a one- to two-page brief, explain what college students find persuasive these days and what kinds of message would get them to go to the polls.

3. Find a rhetorical analysis on the Internet that you can study. These documents are rarely called "rhetorical analyses." Instead, they tend to be critiques of advertisements, speeches, or documents. You can find good examples on Web sites like Slate.com or the *New York Times* Web site (nytimes.com). Write a one-page discussion in which you study the organization, style, and design of the rhetorical analysis. How does it work? What kinds of rhetorical elements does the reviewer pay attention to? Do you agree with the reviewer's analysis?

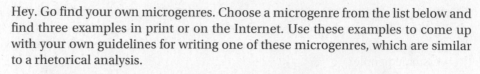

Hey. Go find your own microgenres. Choose a microgenre from the list below and find three examples in print or on the Internet. Use these examples to come up with your own guidelines for writing one of these microgenres, which are similar to a rhetorical analysis.

Ad Buster—demonstrates whether an ad's claims are true or false

Critique—brief discussion of a recent speech by a public figure

Song Analysis—exploration of the rhetorical meaning of a song

Ad Report Card—grading of advertisements with brief explanation of grade

Pundit's Response—partisan review of a speech by a candidate

Write
This

1. **Analyze a text.** Choose a historical, nonfiction text you find interesting and write a five-page rhetorical analysis of it. Your analysis should define the rhetorical concepts you will use to study the document. It should summarize the text and offer some historical background on it. Then offer a close analysis of the text, explaining why it is or is not effective.

2. **Analyze something else as a rhetorical text.** Find something other than a written text for your rhetorical analysis. You could study the architecture of a building, the design of a sculpture, the way someone dresses, or perhaps how someone acts. Using the rhetorical concepts of *logos*, *ethos*, and *pathos*, discuss how designs or people can be persuasive in nonverbal ways. Write a five-page paper or create a Web site in which you explain the ways in which reason, credibility, and emotion can be conveyed without using words.

3. **Critique an advertisement or advertising campaign.** Choose an advertisement or a series of advertisements that you enjoy or detest. Then write a five-page rhetorical analysis in which you explain why the ad or series is effective or ineffective. You should embed a visual, like a screen shot, scan, or video, somewhere in your analysis so your readers can see what you are analyzing.

For support in meeting this chapter's objectives, follow this path in MyCompLab: Resources ⟹ Writing ⟹ Writing Purposes ⟹ Writing to Analyze. Review the Instruction and Multimedia resources about writing to analyze, then complete the Exercises and click on Gradebook to measure your progress.

Commentaries

In this chapter, you will learn how to—
- respond to the arguments of others.
- do research about a current event or debate.
- use emotion and character to add life and energy to an argument.

Do you like to express your opinions about what's happening around you? Writing commentaries will give you a chance to get your ideas out there. Commentaries are used to express opinions on current issues and events, offering new and interesting perspectives that help readers understand the world in which they live.

When writing a commentary, you are contributing something new to an ongoing public conversation. Your goal is to convince readers to agree with you and, perhaps, to change their minds. Meanwhile, readers of commentaries want to grasp the issue under discussion and understand the author's angle quickly and easily. They want to learn something new and figure out how someone else views an important issue. To catch their attention, a commentary needs to snap, making its point quickly and memorably.

Many college writing assignments are forms of commentary. Your professors will ask you to write your opinions about current events or describe your reactions to a reading. They will ask you to take a stand on an issue or consider opposing sides of a controversy. In upper-level courses, professors often ask students to write opinion pieces to demonstrate that they have a firm grasp on a subject and to express what they believe.

You will likely find plenty of opportunities to write commentaries in your career. In this age of around-the-clock news coverage, the Internet and television are overflowing with commentaries. Editorials, op-ed essays, and letters to the editor are regular features of news Web sites, newspapers, and magazines. Meanwhile, blogs and social networking sites, like *Facebook* and *MySpace*, allow people to write commentaries on current events and the world around them.

Commentaries

This diagram shows a basic organization for a commentary. When writing a commentary, you should explain the current event or issue. Then offer support for your opinion. Other arrangements of these sections can be used, so you should alter this organization to fit your topic, angle, purpose, readers, and context.

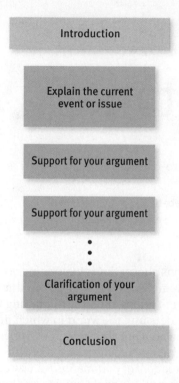

Commentaries take a new angle on a timely topic and back up their claims with good reasoning and solid evidence. They include some or all of these features:

- **A topic** based on current events or current issues.

- **An introduction** that immediately engages the reader by clearly announcing the *issue* under examination, the writer's thesis, and the angle he or she will take on this topic.

- **An explanation of the current event or issue** that reviews what happened and the ongoing conversation about it.

- **An argument for a specific position** that includes reasoning, evidence, examples, and observations.

- **A clarification** that qualifies the argument, avoiding the tendency to overgeneralize or oversimplify the topic.

- **A conclusion** that offers an overall assessment of the issue, highlights its importance to readers, and looks to the future.

ONE STUDENT'S WORK
Commentaries

Why My Generation Doesn't Care About Performance Enhancement

David Meany

Steroids in sports might come as a big shock to most of America, but not to my generation. Here's why. When it comes to sports stars, Hollywood celebrities, and political leaders, my generation (I'm 18 years old) has very low expectations. It's not that we're cynical or completely jaded; it's just that we don't hold these people up as role models. We don't really care if their morals are pure. We would say that we're simply realistic, that we see the world as it is. These celebrities—politicians, movie and TV stars, and, yes, sports figures—do whatever it takes to get ahead. The rest of us are different.

> Identifies the topic, purpose, angle, and thesis.

Let me back up just a little. I'm a huge baseball fan and always have been. I love baseball's history, in fact, all of sports history. Way back in grade school, when it was time to do a book report, I'd find a sports biography: Babe Ruth, Cal Ripkin, Babe Didrikson, Roy Campanella, Joe Namath, Julius "Dr. J" Erving. Even nonhuman sports stars, like Sea Biscuit and Dan Patch, made great reads and reports. I grew up obsessed with Cal Ripken and his quest to break Lou Gehrig's record for consecutive games played. When I was younger and had more time, I could tell you the starting lineup and batting order for every Major League baseball team. So, yes, I was a total baseball nerd.

So now Barry Bonds and Roger Clemens have been caught shooting up, or creaming up, or doing whatever athletes do nowadays to get those steroids into their systems and build muscle, giving them strength and stamina that no steroid-free human could ever hope for. Talking heads on ESPN express outrage (Bryant and Quinn). Sports radio personalities howl in disgust. Even eggheads like commentator George Will moan about a "stain on baseball" (A31). Meanwhile, the Mitchell Report, a tell-all treatise written for the Commissioner of Baseball, says that investigations are "critical to effectively identifying and disciplining players who continue to violate Major League Baseball's rules and policies" (286).

> Explains the current issue and reviews the ongoing conversation.

And you know what, I don't care, and most of my generation doesn't care because we're more realistic than older generations. Some might say we're

continued

more cynical, but it's a question of expectations. We expect our celebrities and leaders to have low ethical standards.

Uses reasoning and examples to support his argument.

Having low ethical standards, doing whatever it takes, that's how people get to be prominent figures in the first place. A person still has to work hard, but a person has to be willing to succeed "at any cost" if they want to really make it big. Look at our recent presidents and members of Congress. You can't stay out of the gutter and make it through an election successfully. Barack Obama and John McCain tried, but they ended up slinging the mud. Look at our Hollywood celebrities, like Paris Hilton, Justin Timberlake, and Lindsay Lohan. Sure, they have talent, but lots of people have talent, maybe even more talent than the stars who "make it." But not everyone has the will to succeed at any cost. That's how people get to be really successful. They're not normal people. Look what happens to celebrities between films or concerts: they're exposed as drug-using, law-breaking creeps. A little sunshine reveals some very dark corners.

I don't know if it's always been that way, or if scandals are just more out in the open these days. The Internet and other never-ending news shows have made it easier to uncover celebrity secrets, and harder to maintain the myth that those who have made it got there fair and square. We know better. I think we're just a little more realistic than people were a generation back.

Americans of my generation just don't expect their sports figures, Hollywood celebrities, and political leaders to be pure and free from the taint of scandal and unfair play. We know that these people probably abide by the credo that "If you're not cheatin', you're not trying." These people are not our heroes and don't deserve to be. They know it, and we know it.

Clarifies and qualifies his position.

I'm not saying we are a cynical generation, just that we are cynical about one thing in particular: celebrities of all kinds. When it comes to how we expect ourselves to behave, our standards are as high as any generation's. We expect ourselves, for the most part, to abide by common decency and commonsense values. My friends and I (and most of my generation) believe in fair play and honesty, and we expect the same from the people we have to deal with. For example, we play by the rules (most of us) when it comes to academics, too. Most of us don't cheat; most of us look down on people who do.

Concludes by restating the main point.

I'm talking about the people who really make it big. I don't trust them. I don't look up to them to help me figure out how to live my life. They're not my heroes, and that's just fine with me. It's just the way America works right now. We look elsewhere to find out how to live. We're pretty smart that way. I think we're a little more savvy about these things than previous celebrity-worshipping generations of Americans.

Works Cited

Bryant, Howard, and T.J. Quinn. "Has MLB Changed since the Mitchell Report?" *ESPN.com*. ESPN, 12 Dec. 2008. Web. 4 Mar. 2009.

Mitchell, George. *Report to the Commissioner of Baseball of an Independent Investigation into the Illegal Use of Steroids and Other Performance Enhancing Substances by Players in Major League Baseball*. New York: Office of the Commissioner of Baseball, 2007. Print.

Will, George. "A Stain on Baseball." *Washington Post* 8 Dec. 2004: A31. Print.

Inventing Your Commentary's Content

When writing a commentary about a current event or issue, you should begin by listening. After all, if you want to join a conversation, you first need to understand it. Nobody wants to hear from someone who dives right into a debate but hasn't taken the time to figure out what people have said so far. Also, listen carefully for the important things people are *not* saying, for the insightful angle they are *not* pursuing. In other words, attend to the gaps in the conversation that you can fill in.

To start, you need a good topic. Commentaries are usually written in response to events that are happening right now. So watch the news, read news Web sites, or search newspapers and magazines to find an event or issue that people are talking about. Your topic should be something you personally care about and something about which you could say something interesting.

Inquiring: Finding Out What You Already Know

Once you have a topic, find out what you already know about it. A great way to get your ideas out there is to play the Believing and Doubting Game. Playing this game with your topic can help you see different sides of an issue while coming up with an angle that is uniquely your own. There are three steps in the game—believing, doubting, and synthesizing:

Believing. Begin by studying one side of your topic from the perspective of a true believer. Assume that this side is completely correct and that all assertions—even if they are contradictory—are valid. Then freewrite or brainstorm for five minutes to figure out the arguments a true believer might come up with. What evidence might support this side of the argument? From what vantage point would the believer's side make the most sense? Even if you initially disagree with this side of the argument, try to imagine yourself in agreement and come up with reasons that support the position or idea.

Doubting. Now, imagine that you are a staunch critic, a complete skeptic. Do another five-minute freewrite or brainstorm in which you look for errors in the believer's side of the argument. What logical weaknesses can you find in the believer's argument? How could you undermine that argument and get others to doubt it too? If you take everything the believer says literally, what problems will arise? What are your greatest fears about the consequences of the believer's argument? How would you show others that the believer's side of the argument cannot be true?

Synthesizing. Finally, put the true believer and the true doubter at the two ends of a spectrum and figure out where you personally would stand on this issue. If you did a good job of playing the Believing and Doubting Game, you should better understand both sides of the issue. You should also be able to figure out your angle on this topic—that is, your personal point of view. What are the major issues that separate the two sides? What are some of the assumptions and key terms that each side uses and how do they use them differently? Where might the two sides actually find common ground?

Figure 9.1 shows a worksheet that you might find helpful when playing the Believing and Doubting Game. In the two top columns, list everything you can think of to support these opposing positions. Then, in the "Synthesis" area, write down the issues that the two sides hold in common and find out where you fit between the two positions. Concisely state your position in the section "Where I Stand on This Issue."

Researching: Finding Out What Others Know

A successful commentary needs to be built on a foundation of solid research. However, commentaries are different from other texts because they usually respond to issues that are in the news right now. As a writer, you are commenting about events that are still unfolding and about which all the facts are not known. So your goal is to figure out what others are saying and where their support comes from. That way, you can find information that will let you add something meaningful to the conversation.

Online Sources. Because you are commenting on events that are happening right now, online sources may be your most useful resources for information. Using Internet search engines, start out by collecting other commentaries on your topic. Then try to sort these commentaries into two or more sides, and figure out where the

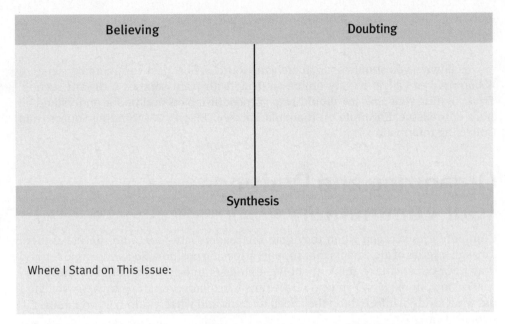

FIGURE 9.1 A Worksheet for Playing the Believing and Doubting Game

Try using this worksheet when playing the Believing and Doubting Game. On the left, list everything a true believer might say. On the right, list everything a true skeptic might say. Then try to find common ground in the "Synthesis" area between the two positions. Also, identify where you stand on this issue.

sides disagree. Also, pay close attention to where these commentators found their support, so you can track down those sources yourself. Make sure you assess the bias and reliability of each source. They will all be biased to some extent, but some will be better grounded in factual information than others.

Print Sources. Print sources are useful for doing background research on your topic. Articles in newspapers and magazines can give you a sense of the debate and who is involved. Books, meanwhile, may help you explore the history of the topic and develop a better understanding of the sides of the issue. Keep in mind that commentaries are usually about issues that are happening in real time, so the information in some print sources will be outdated. Look for the most recent print sources on your subject.

Empirical Sources. Chances are good that someone on your campus is an expert on your topic. So find the faculty member or local expert on your campus who knows about this issue. Then set up an interview or correspond through e-mail. Other empirical methods you could use might include surveys or field observations, depending on your topic.

As always, you should triangulate your sources. For most commentary topics, it is common to collect mostly online sources, with print sources a distant second. Triangulating your sources should help you confirm facts and better understand all sides of the issue. For more on triangulation, see Chapter 25, "Finding Sources and Collecting Information."

Organizing and Drafting Your Commentary

Watch the Animation on **Writing Commentaries** at mycomplab.com

Commentaries succeed when they grab the readers' attention and then lead them through a series of arguments that support a specific position. So as you organize and draft your commentary, think about what kinds of information would be most persuasive to your readers. You won't have time to explain everything to them, so figure out what kinds of information they need to know and what would help you make the strongest case.

The Introduction

While drafting your introduction, always remember that your readers will be interested in what you have to say only if you offer them something new and interesting that they had not considered before.

State Your Purpose. Readers want to know—quickly—what topic you are addressing, what your purpose is, and what new angle you are bringing to the conversation. For example:

> In her recent commentary in the *Indiana Daily Student*, Sarah Hann describes her classmates' use of laptops during class lectures and complains, quite reasonably, "You're a distraction for the rest of us." Hann proposes that the problem could be addressed by turning off the Internet in classrooms. But would that remedy actually solve the problem? More important, would it be fair to responsible Internet users?

In this introduction, the author identifies his topic and reveals his angle on the issue.

State Your Main Point or Thesis Statement. Your introduction should also be clear about what you want to prove (your main point or thesis statement). Sometimes it is helpful to just come right out and tell your readers your position:

Weak: People worry too much about crime around here.

Stronger: The local media's tendency to sensationalize the rare violent crimes in this town has changed people's perception of their safety, especially at night.

Weak: The Great Recession, which hit full stride in 2008, had a big impact on young people's lives.

Stronger: The Great Recession, which hit full stride in 2008, significantly changed how young people thought about their futures, and it shaped how they made decisions about which colleges to attend and what majors to pursue.

A solid thesis statement gives your readers a good sense of where you are going with your commentary.

Watch the Animation on **Thesis Statements** at **mycomplab.com**

Explain the Current Event or Issue

Depending on your readers' familiarity with the topic, you should explain what has happened already and summarize the ongoing conversation about that event. If your readers are already familiar with the topic, you can keep this section of the commentary brief. Just give them enough background to remember the event or the origins of the debate.

If the topic is not familiar to your readers, you should provide enough background information to help them understand the event or issue. Start out by explaining what happened, who was involved, where and when it happened, how it happened, and why. As much as possible, you should show them both sides (or all sides) of the issue. Summarize what others have said about this topic.

The objective of this section is to show your readers that you understand the conversation and that you are able to see more than one side. You will have more credibility if people believe you are considering all sides seriously and giving everyone a fair hearing.

Support Your Position

After explaining the current event or issue, it is time to present support for your side of the argument. Look at your notes and identify the strongest two to five major reasons why you believe you are right about this issue. You don't need to include every bit of evidence you've collected—your readers would find it tiresome and tedious. Instead, pick your best reasons and devote your time to explaining them.

In a brief commentary, each of these major reasons will likely receive a paragraph or two of coverage. State a claim (topic sentence) early in the paragraph and then use examples, details, reasoning, facts, data, quotations, anecdotes, and anything else you can think of to support that claim:

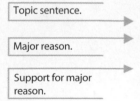

Topic sentence.

Major reason.

Support for major reason.

> Furthermore, shutting off the Internet would actually make some excellent learning activities impossible. Specifically, many professors use the Internet to engage students and motivate them to use all the features in our textbooks. For instance, my astronomy professor, an exciting and demanding teacher, had us pull up our e-books and click on a link to an animation showing two galaxies colliding. Then we answered her multiple-choice questions in groups, and reported back using our clickers. This five-minute exercise had us working together and *using* the knowledge she just gave us. None of us will forget that lesson. Also, it made us understand how helpful the textbook actually could be, motivating us to prepare for class by reading it and using its electronic features.

Each major reason for your argument should support the main point, or thesis, you stated in the introduction. Your support needs to steadily build up your argument for your side of the issue.

Clarification of Your Position

Before concluding your commentary, you might want to show readers that you are aware of the complexities of the issue. So you should clarify your argument by pointing out that new information or events might alter your ideas and approaches to the topic. Also, you can qualify your argument by conceding that the issue is not simple and the problem is not easy to solve. Writers often signal such clarifications with phrases like these:

> I'm not arguing here for a complete . . . , but only . . .
>
> I understand, of course, that . . .
>
> I'm only suggesting that . . .
>
> I recognize that the people on the other side want to do the right thing, too.

Typically a clarification will only need a paragraph, depending on the length of your commentary.

Without this clarification, your readers might accuse you of "painting with too broad a brush"—that is, generalizing too far or failing to consider the fine but important points of an issue. Your clarification will help deflect or prevent those kinds of criticisms.

The Conclusion

Your final words should leave readers with a clear statement of your position and a sense of your commitment to it. Restate your main point or thesis, preferably in stronger terms than you used in the introduction. You might also reemphasize the importance of the topic and offer a look to the future. Then finish the conclusion with a memorable anecdote, figure of speech, turn of phrase, or arresting image that will give readers something to think about. For example:

> However distracting the Internet abusers may be, we should remember the Internet's value for teaching and learning. One student's diversion is another's road to learning and exploration. Hann's remedy doesn't solve the problem. It simply erects a roadblock for everyone.

In this brief two-sentence conclusion, the writer states the main point, stresses the importance of the topic, looks to the future, and provides a clever turn of phrase that gives the readers something to think about.

Watch the Animation on **Closing Paragraphs** at **mycomplab.com**

Choosing an Appropriate Style

The commentary genre tends to use a spirited style, which often sets it apart from other argumentative genres, such as position papers or proposals. To catch your readers' attention, you need to develop a strong sense of your persona with your commentary's style. Start out by thinking about how you want to sound to your readers. How do you want them to imagine you? How do you want them to react to your voice? What tone should they hear as they read? Here are a few ways to develop your style.

Get into Character

As you draft and revise your commentary, try to imagine yourself playing a role like an actor. If you want to sound angry, imagine being angry as you write. If you want to sound upbeat, imagine being in an upbeat mood. You need to get into character before you start drafting or revising.

Getting into character works because it allows you to write with less inhibition. You're playing a role, so you can freely let those emotions and that tone spill onto the screen or page. As you draft, use your writing to explore the specific emotion or tone you are trying to project to your readers.

Imitate a Well-Known Writer

Try imitating the style of a well-known critic or commentator whose work you like to read. Then find a few articles written by this person that use a style similar to the one you want to use in your commentary. Look closely at how this person achieves that particular style or tone. Does he or she use details or words in a particular way? Are the sentences long or short? Does he or she use analogies, metaphors, or similes to express complex thoughts? How does this writer convey excitement, anger, or other emotions you are seeking to express?

It's best if you *avoid* imitating the style of an article on the topic you are writing about. That way, while imitating the style of an article, you won't mistakenly plagiarize the writer's ideas or words.

Match Your Tone to Your Readers' Expectations

It's important to know the context for your document—that is, *where* your commentary will appear and *who* your potential readers are. If your potential readers expect an informal, colloquial commentary, then you should adopt that informal style. For instance, if you're writing for an online discussion and the writers all speak in casual terms, you should probably do the same. On the other hand, if you're writing to a local newspaper or magazine with a more formal tone, then you should match that level of formality.

Use Analogies, Similes, and Metaphors

Since commentaries typically handle complex topics that can be difficult to understand, writers often turn to analogies, similes, and metaphors to make the unfamiliar seem more familiar. For example, note how this commentator uses an analogy to explain that banning the Internet in classrooms is wrongheaded:

Metaphor suggesting the Internet is a tool.

The analogy draws a parallel to more familiar classroom learning tools.

We should remember that the Internet is a tool, which like any tool can be used for good or bad. Certainly, it's extremely annoying and distracting to see fellow students misusing the Internet to surf vacation spots or post to Facebook. However, you could make an argument like that against any learning tool. For instance, in my economics recitation just last week, the instructor had to ask the immature lovebirds in front of me to stop passing notes, but I doubt anyone was thinking that we should ban pens and paper from the classroom. The point is, banning these learning tools may lessen some irresponsible and annoying behavior, but it also prevents responsible students from taking full advantage of the education they're trying to attain.

Essentially, the writer draws an analogy between laptops and other tools used to communicate (pens, paper) and explains why shutting down classroom Internet access would be foolish.

Analogies, similes, and metaphors also have the benefit of adding a visual element to an argument. In the paragraph above, for example, it is easy to visualize the

Internet as a "tool" for the classroom rather than a distraction. Tools can be used for good or bad, as the author argues, so automatically banning them from the class-room might be an overreaction.

Designing Your Commentary

As you design your document, pay attention to its medium and what's possible in that medium. For example, if your commentary will appear on a Web site or blog, adding design features like photos and other graphics is much easier than it would be in an opinion article written for a newspaper or magazine.

Commentaries rarely appear in a stand-alone format. Instead, they appear within larger documents, like Web sites, newsletters, newspapers, and magazines. So as you are thinking about what design would be appropriate, pay attention to the place where your commentary is likely to appear.

Include Photography. Because commentaries address current events and issues, you may want to snap a few pictures or download photographs from the Internet to show what you are talking about. If you are taking your own photographs with a digital camera or a mobile phone, you can download them to your computer and then insert them into your document. Most word processors have an Insert function in their top menu that will put the picture wherever you set your cursor on the page.

You can also insert pictures that you have downloaded from the Internet. When using a PC, you can use the right button on your mouse to download a picture you want. Click on the picture. A menu will appear that allows you to download the image to your hard drive. Then use the Insert function to put the photograph into your document.

If you are using the picture for a strictly academic purpose (e.g., a paper for class), you don't need to ask permission to use it. However, if you are using the pic-ture in a public way (e.g., on a Web site or blog, in a publication, on a poster, etc.) you will need to ask permission from the person who owns it. An e-mail to the owner of the Web site where you found the photo is usually the best way to ask permission. If you don't get permission to use it, you will be in violation of copyright law. Don't do that.

Add Pull Quotes to Emphasize Important Points. You have probably seen pull quotes in print and online magazines. Pull quotes draw attention to a key sen-tence or short passage from the text that captures some essential point, question, or idea (Figure 9.2). Sometimes the pull quote functions as a subtitle, or an alter-native title.

When readers are deciding whether they want to read a particular commentary, they usually skim the page or screen for the following elements: the title, a pull quote, and the first and maybe the second paragraph. A pull quote that grabs their attention

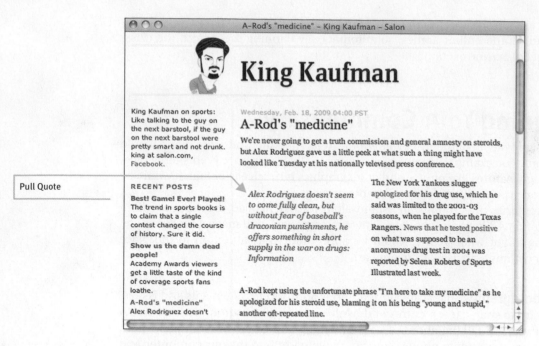

Pull Quote

FIGURE 9.2 A Pull Quote

A pull quote captures an essential point, question, or idea from the text. They are helpful for drawing the readers' attention to the text.

and tells them the angle and tone of your commentary will help readers decide whether they should read your commentary. But don't overdo it. Reserve pull quotes for the really big, attention-grabbing ideas. As a rule of thumb, use only one or two pull quotes per written page, and no more than one per screen.

Revising and Editing Your Commentary

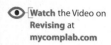

Watch the Video on **Revising** at mycomplab.com

As you revise, keep in mind that you want your commentary to be noticed, to stand out among all the other commentaries your readers have available. But you also want to seem reasonable so that readers will listen, take your ideas seriously, and consider your ideas as they think about the issue and carry the conversation forward.

Strengthen the Sense That You're Listening to All Sides. Refer to what others have said and done. Incorporate the ideas of others with brief summaries, paraphrases, and quotations. When appropriate, recognize the value of others' viewpoints and the importance of listening to all sides. Make sure that you come across not as a naysayer or cynic, but as someone who listens carefully and considers all reasonable sides of an issue.

Set Your Ideas Apart from Those of Others. Make sure your readers understand how and why your views are different from those of others. Tell the readers what sets your views apart, but be careful not to sound condescending or dismissive about people who disagree with you.

Refine Your Persona. As you finish your final draft, look back at what you have written and make sure that you are projecting the intended persona. Do you want to be seen as a reasonable peacemaker who strives to bring people together and manage conflict so that the conversation is productive? Or do you want to be viewed as someone who is raising tough issues and telling uncomfortable truths?

Proofread (and Proofread Again). Fair or not, if there are grammatical errors, misspellings, and typos littering your argument, the ideas in your commentary will be judged negatively. So spend plenty of time going through your commentary to fix these kinds of errors. Your readers are more likely to trust your reasoning if your text is error-free.

Watch the Animation on **Proofreading** at **mycomplab.com**

Before you hand in your commentary, let it sit for at least a few hours. Then read it through one last time, looking for problems in content, organization, style, and design. A little distance will help you polish it.

Letter to the Editor

A letter to the editor is a brief commentary that is written for the opinions section of a newspaper, magazine, or news Web site. Though addressed "to the editor," they are written for the larger readership. Letters to the editor usually respond directly to a specific news item or an opinion piece in the publication.

Letters to the editor often force you to distill your argument to 250 words or less. Here's how to write a great one:

Address and summarize a specific issue, story, or opinion piece. Editors tend to publish only letters that respond directly to an issue or current event that was written about or reported in their publication.

State your purpose precisely. If you are challenging what was said previously, express concisely what you believe was inaccurate, misstated, or misunderstood. If you are agreeing with the original text, explain why you agree with it.

Support your argument with personal experiences. Letters to the editor often use personal experiences to challenge or validate a story or opinion piece.

Support your argument with factual evidence. Back up your argument or challenge the text to which you are responding with carefully researched data, historical facts, quotations, and other details.

Recognize logical fallacies. Target logical fallacies in the text to which you are responding, and be careful not to use them yourself. See Chapter 22, "Using Argumentative Strategies."

Avoid condescension. When you disagree with a news story or opinion piece, it's tempting to be sarcastic or insulting. But if you keep your tone professional, readers will be more receptive to your views and your letter will have a better chance at publication.

Keep revising until you have expressed your views as concisely as possible.

WRITE **your own letter to the editor.** Find an article on a news Web site, in a magazine, or from a newspaper that is no more than a week old. Then write a letter to the editor that reacts in a positive or critical way. Give your professor contact information (address, e-mail address) for the editors to whom you could send your letter.

Why I'm Against the Statewide Smoking Ban

Michael Spatz

It could be easily argued that when it comes to statewide smoking bans, typical 18- to 22-year-old college students are the ones most affected. Smoking is a habit often picked up during a person's college years. And while Lawrence's smoking ban has already been law for half a decade, I do not think a statewide smoking ban is what the state of Kansas needs right now.

> Identifies specific issue being addressed.

> Main point (or thesis).

The economic effects of a statewide smoking ban are obvious. Bars and taverns lose the business of smokers, which, in some cases, is enough to close down the establishment. According to the Department of Labor, the unemployment rate in Kansas for March 2009 was 6.5 percent, the highest in 26 years. A statewide smoking ban would only further handcuff bars and taverns across the state in their fight to stay above water during this recession.

> Supports argument with factual evidence.

More important than the economic effects are the health effects. The effects that smoking has on a smoker are proven. The effects of second-hand smoke, however, are extremely debatable. According to the *Health News Digest*, "The results do not support a causal relation between environmental tobacco smoke and tobacco-related mortality, although they do not rule out a small effect."

> Factual evidence.

One last defense against a smoking ban deals with a core American value: freedom. If a bar owner wants to cater to smokers in his or her privately owned establishment, what gives a state government the right to deny that bar owner? Smoking is legal.

On a personal note, I am a social smoker. On average, I smoke probably twice a month. I won't ever be picking up the habit of being a regular smoker. My solution is simple. If a bar owner chooses to accommodate smokers, that's his or her right. If a bar owner chooses to keep his establishment a nonsmoking place, that is equally his or her right.

> Supports his argument with personal experiences.

A few months ago, I saw an anti-smoking poster on campus. One of the ways it stated to avoid picking up the habit was to not associate with smokers. This disgusted me. It gave the impression that smokers are less than human and need to be completely isolated from non-smokers. Smoking bans have already hit my home state and my college town. I can only hope for significant resistance in the 29 states, Kansas included for now, that they haven't reached.

> Restates his main point/thesis in a memorable way.

Are you ready to start writing your commentary? Here are some ideas to help you do it.

FIND a Current Event or Current Issue That Interests You

Pay attention to the news or the events happening around you. Commentaries are typically written about things that are currently happening.

FIND OUT What You Already Know and Believe About Your Topic

Use invention techniques like freewriting, brainstorming, or the Believing and Doubting Game to find out what you already know or believe about your topic.

DO Research on the Event or Issue

Online sources are especially helpful when writing about current events or issues. Print and empirical sources are helpful for collecting background information on the topic.

DRAFT Your Commentary

Your introduction needs to grab the readers' attention. Then, in the body of your commentary, explain the current event or issue. Support your side of the argument and clarify your position. Use a brief conclusion to restate your main point (thesis statement), and try to end with a clever turn of phrase that gives the readers something to think about.

LIVEN UP Your Style

Commentaries are known for their lively and engaging style. People enjoy reading them for the content and the colorful way the ideas are expressed. So get into character and let your emotions show on the page.

CONSIDER the Design

Because they often appear in larger documents, commentaries tend to follow the design of the Web site, newspaper, or magazine in which they appear. Nevertheless, you should look for photography that will support or illustrate your argument. Pull quotes will allow you to highlight important ideas and quotes.

REVISE and Edit

Spend some time working and reworking your ideas. While revising and editing, pay special attention to your voice and tone. You want to polish your writing so that it stands out from the other commentaries available on the topic.

Are Jobs Obsolete?

DOUGLAS RUSHKOFF

In this commentary, Douglas Rushkoff, a media theorist and commentator, speculates about the nature of jobs in the United States' future. Pay attention to how he raises questions about what is needed for a functioning society.

The U.S. Postal Service appears to be the latest casualty in digital technology's slow but steady replacement of working humans. Unless an external source of funding comes in, the post office will have to scale back its operations drastically, or simply shut down altogether. That's 600,000 people who would be out of work, and another 480,000 pensioners facing an adjustment in terms.

We can blame a right wing attempting to undermine labor, or a left wing trying to preserve unions in the face of government and corporate cutbacks. But the real culprit—at least in this case—is e-mail. People are sending 22% fewer pieces of mail than they did four years ago, opting for electronic bill payment and other net-enabled means of communication over envelopes and stamps.

New technologies are wreaking havoc on employment figures—from EZpasses ousting toll collectors to Google-controlled self-driving automobiles rendering taxicab drivers obsolete. Every new computer program is basically doing some task that a person used to do. But the computer usually does it faster, more accurately, for less money, and without any health insurance costs.

We like to believe that the appropriate response is to train humans for higher level work. Instead of collecting tolls, the trained worker will fix and program toll-collecting robots. But it never really works out that way, since not as many people are needed to make the robots as the robots replace.

And so the president goes on television 5 telling us that the big issue of our time is jobs, jobs, jobs—as if the reason to build high-speed rails and fix bridges is to put people back to work. But it seems to me there's something backwards in that logic. I find myself wondering if we may be accepting a premise that deserves to be questioned.

I am afraid to even ask this, but since when is unemployment really a problem? I understand we all want paychecks—or at least money. We want food, shelter, clothing, and all the things that money buys us. But do we all really want jobs?

We're living in an economy where productivity is no longer the goal, employment is. That's because, on a very fundamental level, we have pretty much everything we need. America is productive enough that it could probably shelter, feed, educate, and even provide health care for its entire population with just a fraction of us actually working.

According to the U.N. Food and Agriculture Organization, there is enough food produced to provide everyone in the world with 2,720 kilocalories per person per day. And that's even after America disposes of thousands of tons of crop and dairy just to keep market prices high. Meanwhile, American banks overloaded with foreclosed properties are demolishing vacant dwellings to get the empty houses off their books.

Our problem is not that we don't have enough stuff—it's that we don't have enough ways for people to work and prove that they deserve this stuff.

Jobs, as such, are a relatively new concept. People may have always worked, but until the advent of the corporation in the early Renaissance, most people just worked for themselves. They made shoes, plucked chickens, or created value in some way for other people, who then traded or paid for those goods and services. By the late Middle Ages, most of Europe was thriving under this arrangement.

The only ones losing wealth were the aristocracy, who depended on their titles to extract money from those who worked. And so they invented the chartered monopoly. By law, small businesses in most major industries were shut down and people had to work for officially sanctioned corporations instead. From then on, for most of us, working came to mean getting a "job."

The Industrial Age was largely about making those jobs as menial and unskilled as possible. Technologies such as the assembly line were less important for making production faster than for making it cheaper, and laborers more replaceable. Now that we're in the digital age, we're using technology the same way: to increase efficiency, lay off more people, and increase corporate profits.

While this is certainly bad for workers and unions, I have to wonder just how truly bad is it for people. Isn't this what all this technology was for in the first place? The question we have to begin to ask ourselves is not how do we employ all the people who are rendered obsolete by technology, but how can we organize a society around something other than employment? Might the spirit of enterprise we currently associate with "career" be shifted to something entirely more collaborative, purposeful, and even meaningful?

Instead, we are attempting to use the logic of a scarce marketplace to negotiate things that are actually in abundance. What we lack is not employment, but a way of fairly distributing the bounty we have generated through our technologies, and a way of creating meaning in a world that has already produced far too much stuff.

The communist answer to this question 15 was just to distribute everything evenly. But that sapped motivation and never quite worked as advertised. The opposite, libertarian answer (and the way we seem to be going right now) would be to let those who can't capitalize on the bounty simply suffer. Cut social services along with their jobs, and hope they fade into the distance.

But there might still be another possibility— something we couldn't really imagine for ourselves until the digital era. As a pioneer of virtual reality, Jaron Lanier, recently pointed out, we no longer need to make stuff in order to make money. We can instead exchange information-based products.

We start by accepting that food and shelter are basic human rights. The work we do— the value we create—is for the rest of what we want: the stuff that makes life fun, meaningful, and purposeful.

This sort of work isn't so much employment as it is creative activity. Unlike Industrial Age employment, digital production can be done from the home, independently, and even in a peer-to-peer fashion without going through big corporations. We can make games for each other, write books, solve problems, educate and inspire one another—all through bits instead of stuff. And we can pay one another using the same money we use to buy real stuff.

For the time being, as we contend with what appears to be a global economic slowdown by destroying food and demolishing homes, we might want to stop thinking about jobs as the main aspect of our lives that we want to save. They may be a means, but they are not the ends.

A CLOSER LOOK AT
Are Jobs Obsolete?

1. What are the major technology-related *causes* of America's economic downturn, according to Rushkoff? How do these technological shifts change the nature of employment and work in the United States?

2. Early in the commentary, Rushkoff states, "We're living in an economy where productivity is no longer the goal, employment is." What do you think he means by this statement? Why does he think American's obsession with employment, rather than productivity, is a problem in the long-run?

3. Later in the article, Rushkoff describes the kinds of work that Americans might do instead of "make stuff." What are some of the kinds of careers he describes? Why does he think they are more advantageous to people than traditional manufacturing jobs?

IDEAS FOR
Writing

1. This commentary sounds reasonable on the surface, but there are still some underlying problems. For example, Rushkoff says "food and shelter are basic human rights." If so, who would create that food and shelter in this post jobs world? Write a rebuttal in which you highlight some of the holes in his argument.

2. Write a proposal in which you try to describe the kind of job-free world that Rushkoff imagines. His commentary is rather abstract. Use more concrete details to propose a society in which people treated employment as a "creative activity." What would that world look like? How would people still meet their basic needs in this job-free society?

Faith in a Globalized Age

TONY BLAIR

Tony Blair was the Prime Minister of the United Kingdom from 1997 to 2007. As leader of the British Labour Party, he steered his party toward a centrist position and away from traditional left-wing views. He converted to Roman Catholicism in 2007 and began the Tony Blair Faith Foundation in 2008. In this commentary, pay attention to how he anticipates and responds to the arguments of potential critics of his views.

For years, it was assumed, certainly in the West, that, as society developed, religion would wither away. But it hasn't, and, at the start of a new decade, it is time for policymakers to take religion seriously.

The number of people proclaiming their faith worldwide is growing. This is clearly so in the Islamic world. Whereas Europe's birthrate is stagnant, the Arab population is set to double in the coming decades, and the population will rise in many Asian Muslim-majority countries. Christianity is also growing–in odd ways and in surprising places.

Religion's largest growth is in China. Indeed, the religiosity of China is worth reflecting on. There are more Muslims in China than in Europe, more practicing Protestants than in England, and more practicing Catholics than in Italy. In addition, according to the latest surveys, around 100 million Chinese identify themselves as Buddhist. And, of course, Confucianism—a philosophy rather than a religion—is deeply revered.

There is a huge Evangelical movement in Brazil and Mexico. Faith remains for many in the United States a vital part of their lives. Even in Europe, the numbers confessing to a belief in God remain high. And, of course there are hundreds of millions of Hindus and still solid numbers of Sikhs and Jews.

Those of faith do great work because of it. Around 40% of health care in Africa is delivered by faith-based organizations. Muslim, Hindu, and Jewish relief groups are active the world over in combating poverty and disease. In any developed nation, you will find selfless care being provided to the disabled, the dying, the destitute, and the disadvantaged, by people acting under the impulse of their faith. Common to all great religions is love of neighbors and human equality before God.

Unfortunately, compassion is not the only context in which religion motivates people. It can also promote extremism, even terrorism. This is where faith becomes a badge of identity in opposition to those who do not share it, a kind of spiritual nationalism that regards those who do not agree—even those within a faith who live a different view of it—as unbelievers, infidels, and thus enemies.

To a degree, this has always been so. What has changed is the pressure of globalization, which is pushing the world's peoples ever closer together as technology advances and shrinks the world. Growing up 50 years ago, children might rarely meet someone of a different cultural or faith background. Today, when I stand in my ten-year-old son's playground or look at his friends at his birthday party, I find myriad different languages, faiths, and colors.

Personally, I rejoice in this. But such a world requires that mutual respect replace mutual suspicion. Such a world upends traditions and challenges old thinking, forcing us to choose consciously to embrace it. Or not. And there is the rub: for some, this force is a threat. It menaces deeply conservative societies. And, for those for whom religion matters, globalization can sometimes be accompanied by an aggressive secularism or hedonism that makes many uneasy.

So we must make sense of how the world of faith interacts with the compulsive process of globalization. Yet it is extraordinary how little political time or energy we devote to doing so. Most of the conflicts in today's world have a religious dimension. Extremism based on a perversion of Islam shows no sign of abating; indeed, it will not abate until it is taken on religiously, as well as by security measures.

This extremism is, slowly but surely, pro- 10 ducing its own reaction, as we see from Islamaphobic parties' electoral gains in Europe, and statements by European leaders that multiculturalism has failed.

Of course, throughout time, religion has often been part of a political conflict. But that doesn't mean that religion should be discounted. On the contrary, it requires a special focus. I see this very plainly spending so much time in Jerusalem, where—East and West—there is an emphatic increase in religiosity.

I started my Faith Foundation precisely to create greater understanding between the faiths. My reasoning is simple. Those advocating extremism in the name of religion are active, well resourced, and—whatever the reactionary nature of their thinking—brilliant

at using modern communication and technology. We estimate that literally billions of dollars every year are devoted to promoting this view of religion.

So my Foundation has a university program—now underway in nine countries—that is designed to take religion out of the sole preserve of divinity schools and start analyzing its role in the world today. We have another program—in 15 countries, with others set to join—that links high school students across the world through interactive technology to discuss their faith and what it means to them. And we have an action program through which young people work with those of another faith to raise awareness of the Millennium Development Goals, the United Nations-led program to combat world poverty.

We are just one organization. There are others starting. But governments should start to take this far more seriously. The Alliance of Civilizations, begun by Spain and Turkey, is one example. The King of Saudi Arabia has also shown great leadership in this sphere. Yet this is not just about bringing high-level people together. It has to be taken down into the grassroots of nations, especially into the media of their young people.

Finally, religious leaders must accept a 15 new responsibility: to stand up firmly and resolutely for respecting those of faiths different from their own. Aggressive secularists and extremists feed off each other. Together, they do constitute a real challenge to people of faith. We must demonstrate the loving nature of true faith; otherwise, religion will be defined by a battle in which extremists seize control of faith communities and secularists claim that such attitudes are intrinsic to religion.

This would be a tragedy. For, above all, it is in this era of globalization that faith can represent reason and progress. Religion isn't dying; nor should it. The world needs faith.

A CLOSER LOOK AT
Faith in a Globalized Age

1. Blair claims that "Christianity is also growing—in odd ways and surprising places. What are three examples he uses to back up this claim? Why are these changes odd or surprising?

2. According to Blair, why is globalization often viewed as threatening to people who hold conservative religious beliefs?

3. Blair is promoting faith as a solution to the world's problems in this commentary. How does he defend faith in a time when extremists sometimes exploit religion for their own purposes?

4. Blair argues that religious leaders must accept a new responsibility in an age of globalization. What is that new responsibility?

IDEAS FOR
Writing

1. Imagine you want to create a foundation that supports a cause you feel strongly about. Write a proposal in which you explain the problem your foundation would try to solve and its methods for solving that problem. As you describe the problem, identify what is causing it and discuss some of its effects. How would your foundation use its resources (research and money) to address some of those causes and effects?

2. Write a memoir in which you explore how you came to your religious beliefs (or agnosticism or atheism). A faith narrative is similar to a literacy narrative. Tell a story in which you reconstruct a key moment or series of events that helped you develop your views on religion.

1. Ask each member of your group to describe a conversation he or she had with friends or family about a controversial current event or issue. What was the content and style of that discussion? How did you try to get your ideas across to the others? Did any participant in the discussion become upset or stop listening? If so, what went wrong? Why couldn't your friends or family get along well enough to discuss ideas in depth?

2. With your group, list seven issues or events being covered in the news right now. Pick two of these issues and discuss the different sides of the debate. Then go around the group and talk about how each member would approach writing a commentary about these two topics. What would your angle be? What could you add to the conversation about each topic?

3. Do you know someone whose participation in a discussion almost always results in discomfort, negative feelings, or anger? Do you enjoy conversing with this person, or do you avoid it? What does this person do that prompts such negative consequences? With your group, list five things that some people do to undermine discussions of important issues.

Talk About This

1. Listen to at least two news and opinion shows from different television or radio networks. Be attentive to how the pundits represent and exchange their differing viewpoints and (supposedly) try to influence each other as they influence the audience. What do you notice about the "conversation" and its characteristics? Is there a reasonable exchange of ideas? Do the people in the discussion seem to want to persuade the other participants to adopt their viewpoints, or simply to dominate the others? Do they ever seem to really listen to each other?

2. Find an interesting opinion piece from a print or online magazine and bring it to class. With your group, talk about the written and visual features that make this piece effective. Then discuss the features that were not used that *could have* made it more effective. For instance, what is the writer's angle? What is he or she trying to achieve (purpose)? What is his or her main point? What does the commentary do to grab readers' attention and help them decide quickly whether it's worth reading?

3. Find a commentary in a newspaper or magazine, or on a news Web site. In a one-page analysis written to your professor, describe the commentary's content, organization, style, and design. What kinds of information does the writer use to support his or her points? Does the organization reflect the commentary organization described in this chapter? How would you describe the style, and how does the writer achieve this style? Finally, what design features are used to support the written text and make it more visually attractive?

Try This Out

These five microgenres are in many ways similar to commentary but are different in important ways. Try your hand at one or two of these and notice how you need to reconsider features such as the writer-author relationship, angle, purpose, tone, and style.

Rant—anger-fueled response about a current event

Believing/Doubting Game—discussion of both sides of an issue

Arguing the Opposite—brief argument for the side you disagree with

Call to Action—a rallying cry for your readers to take action on an issue

Mock Commentary—argue passionately but reasonably about a silly issue (e.g., "the best flavor of gum," "which is better: pie or cake?")

Write
This

1. **Express your opinion.** Imagine that you've been invited to begin writing a weekly opinion piece (editorial) for your local community newspaper, campus newspaper, or some other regularly published venue that regularly carries commentaries. Pick an issue or current event that is in the news right now. Write a four-page commentary in which you express your own view on this issue. While inventing your argument, first figure out what you already know by using invention techniques, such as the Believing and Doubting Game. Then draft your argument, paying special attention to how you organize and support your ideas.

2. **Post your views on a Web site.** Most news Web sites allow readers to comment on the articles. Find one of these commentary areas and read the twenty most recent comments posted. What are some of the points of contention? Can you detect two or more sides to the debate? Write a two-page contribution to the discussion. Be sure to respond to the original article as well as to what others have written. Hand in your commentary to your professor along with a one-page reflection in which you discuss the original article, the comments others had written, and the approach you took with your commentary.

3. **Start your own blog.** Blogs are popular places for writers to publish their commentaries on current events. Imagine that you would like to start your own blog. What topics would you write about? What angles would you take on them? Write a half-page description of your blog for your professor. Then write three 250-word entries, which you would publish on your blog. If you want, you could use this assignment to start your own blog on a free blogging service like *Blogger*, *Blogspot*, or *WordPress*.

PEARSON
mycomplab

For support in meeting this chapter's objectives, follow this path in MyCompLab: Resources ⟹ Writing ⟹ Writing Purposes ⟹ Writing to Discuss. Review the Instruction and Multimedia resources about writing to discuss, then complete the Exercises and click on Gradebook to measure your progress.

10

Arguments

In this chapter, you will learn how to—

- develop an argumentative thesis about a controversial issue.
- describe the strengths and limitations of opposing viewpoints.
- use evidence and reasoning to back up your thesis.

If you like to argue and engage with other people about important issues, you will enjoy writing arguments. The purpose of an argument is to explore two or more sides of a controversial topic and then to argue fairly and reasonably for one side over the others. When you consider all sides of a controversial issue and explain them fairly, you will deepen your own understanding and you might even alter your position, either slightly or radically. By fairly presenting all viewpoints, you will also strengthen your argument because readers will see you as fair-minded and knowledgeable.

This balanced approach is what makes arguments different from commentaries, which usually express only the author's opinion. An argument describes other positions and discusses why one is stronger or better than the others.

In college, your professors will ask you to write arguments that analyze and evaluate both (or all) sides of an issue and then argue for one side or another. In the workplace, documents called "position papers" are used to argue for or against business strategies or policies. The ability to argue effectively is an essential skill that will help you throughout your life.

Arguments

This diagram shows two basic organizations for an argument, but other arrangements of these sections will work, too. In the pattern on the left, opposing positions are described up front; then your own position is explained. In the pattern on the right, you make a point-by-point comparison, explaining why your position is better than others. You should alter this organization to fit your topic, angle, purpose, readers, and context.

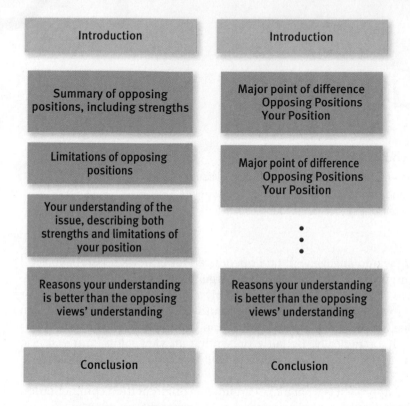

Arguing can be fun, but you need to argue fairly and reasonably if you want to win over your readers. The strongest arguments address differing viewpoints as objectively and fairly as possible and then persuade readers that one side is superior to the others. They tend to have the following features:

- **An introduction** that states the issue being debated, identifies the issue's two or more sides, and usually offers an explicit thesis that the argument will support.
- **An objective summary** of opposing views, including their strengths.
- **A point-by-point discussion** of the limitations of opposing views.
- **A summary** of your viewpoint and your understanding of the issue.
- **A point-by-point discussion** of both strengths and limitations of your position, arguing overall that yours is superior.
- **A conclusion** that drives home your thesis and looks to the future.

ONE STUDENT'S WORK
Arguments

Allowing Guns on Campus Will Prevent Shootings, Rape

Tyler Ohmann

A graduate student leaving an evening class walks along the poorly lit sidewalk to the parking lot—it is a long, cold walk in the pitch-black night, and the student grows wary as shadows begin lurking in the distance. Suddenly, someone jumps out in front of the student, immediately threatening her with force. Before the student can react, she is raped and robbed. This is a very scary scenario, and one that happens on the SCSU campus every year. It seems like every week we get an e-mail citing another attack on students somewhere on or near campus. However, all of these attacks could be prevented if we allowed students to carry guns as a means of self-defense.

Although safety is my biggest concern, there are other arguments that point to this solution as well. First, it is our Second Amendment right to bear arms. Although debates have gone on about how it should be interpreted, I believe it means that if law-abiding, trained, and eligible citizens would like to carry a gun with them in self-defense, they should be able to. Right now, that does not include campus. "The law, as it stands now, does not prohibit carry on campus," said Terence McCloskey, SCSU campus leader for Students for Concealed Carry on Campus (SCCC). "It allows universities to establish rules restricting carry on campus by students and staff." According to the March 2007 Safety and Security bulletin in section 2.1, "Alcoholic beverages, non-regulated drugs, explosives, guns and ammunition are not permitted on SCSU property." This rule, I believe, is a violation of my Second Amendment rights.

The second reason guns should be allowed is because it will give students, such as the one in the scenario, a sense of security and comfort when they are in a normally uncomfortable situation or area. The opposition would say that although the person with the gun is comfortable, it makes others around that person uncomfortable or afraid to speak up in class. Well, let me ask you this: How often do you feel uncomfortable or scared about someone near you having a gun when you go to a movie theater? Probably not too often. However, McCloskey said that 1 percent of Minnesotans have a permit to carry guns. "That means that every time they go to a movie theater with around 200 people

The writer sets the scene to grab readers.

Here is his explicitly stated thesis.

Point-by-point comparison of two positions.

Opposing views are presented.

continued

inside, they are sitting with two people that are carrying a gun," McCloskey said. There are people all around us that have guns, and it seems to be handled just fine.

After all, the 1 percent that do carry guns have to meet certain requirements—guns are not handed out to just anyone. Minnesota law requires everyone to have a permit in order to own a handgun, and to obtain one you must be 21 years of age, be a U.S. citizen, have training in the safe use of a pistol, not be a felon, not have a domestic violence offense in the last 10 years, not be a person convicted of stalking, as well as many other restrictions. You can find these laws on the State of Minnesota Web site.

The final reason that guns should be allowed to be carried by students who obtain a permit is that it could prevent a tragic shooting like the one at Virginia Tech a couple of years ago. "Our best and our brightest are in an unprotected environment and are essentially being led to the slaughter," said Keith Moum in an article in the *Missourian*. "It's not as graphic as that, but it clearly shows that there is an element out there that has targeted college students, and campus policy has left them with no way to defend themselves." If guns had been allowed on that campus, that tragedy may have been either averted or at least minimized.

So in order to make the SCSU campus and other campuses nationwide a safe, comfortable environment for everyone, we need to allow the ability to carry a gun on campus. Not only will it make a student carrying a gun feel safe, it can prevent a tragic shooting, a robbery, or a rape. It is our right. Let us exercise it.

The thesis is driven home.

Inventing Your Argument's Content

Watch the Video on **Finding an Argument Topic** at **mycomplab.com**

When writing an argument, you will need to summarize the issue as thoroughly as possible. Here is the hard part: you need to present the various sides of the controversy fairly. In other words, when reading your argument, a person with an opposing viewpoint would say, "Yes, that's a fair presentation of my view." If readers sense that you are distorting opposing positions, they will question whether you are presenting the argument fairly. So let your facts and reasoning do the talking for you. If your position is truly stronger, you should be able to explain all sides fairly and then demonstrate to readers why your side is better.

Inquiring: Identifying Your Topic

When writing an argument, you should choose a topic (or question) that is narrow enough for you to manage, while allowing you to offer new insights. If you choose a very broad and well-worn topic, such as gun control or abortion, you will find it difficult to say anything new or interesting. But you can take even a broad topic and narrow it by asking what is new or what has changed about the topic recently.

Too Broad: Should we allow people to carry concealed handguns?

Better: Should students, faculty, and staff be allowed to carry concealed handguns on college campuses?

Even Better: Considering recent violence on and near our campus, should we allow students, faculty, and staff to carry concealed handguns on our college campus?

New topics for arguments are rare; however, new angles on topics are readily available. Pay attention to what has changed about your topic or how recent events have made your topic important today.

Inquiring: Identifying Points of Contention

To begin generating content for your argument, first identify the major points on which your viewpoint and opposing viewpoints differ. A brainstorming list like the one shown in Figure 10.1 is often the best way to identify these major points.

When brainstorming, use two columns. In the left column, write "My position" and list all the arguments you can think of to support your case. In the right column, write "Opposing positions" and list the best arguments for the other sides of the controversy. When listing the ideas of people who disagree with you, try to see things from their perspective. What are their strongest arguments? Why do they hold these views or values? What goals are they trying to achieve that are different from yours?

When you have filled out your brainstorming lists, put checkmarks next to the two to five most important issues on which you disagree with the other sides. These are your controversy's "points of contention."

Researching: Finding Out What Others Believe and Why

Now it is time to do some research. At this point, you should have identified the two to five major points of contention on which people disagree about this topic. You can use them as a starting place for your research.

Begin by researching the opposing viewpoints first. By finding out what people who disagree with you believe, you can identify the strengths and weaknesses of your own position. And, if necessary, you can shift your position as you become more informed about the issue.

As you research positions that differ from yours, imagine that you are arguing for these opposing positions. How would you build your argument? What would be your strongest points? What weaknesses would you point out in the other sides' positions? What kinds of sources would you use to support these sides? Your goal is to figure out why people hold viewpoints different than yours.

Then find sources that support your position. Your research on other viewpoints should help you pinpoint the kinds of sources that will support your side of the

My position: Concealed weapons on campus are a greater risk than no handguns on campus.

Students, faculty, and staff will feel less safe on campus if guns are allowed.

✓ Alcohol could cause a lapse in judgment.

✓ Campus police don't want guns on campus.

Universities may be liable if an accident happens.

✓ In a shooting incident, police cannot tell the criminals from the people defending themselves with guns.

Bullets from a defender's gun may strike innocent people in a classroom.

Students are less mature and may use their guns to threaten others or play games.

Some students will carry guns without a concealed-carry permit.

Guns on campus will cause parents to fear sending their students to our university.

✓ Guns locked in cars won't be any use in a shooting.

Less stable students are the ones most interested in carrying guns.

We can strengthen security if campus is thought to be unsafe.

Accidents do happen, and the university will be liable.

Opposing positions: Students, faculty, and staff should be able to carry concealed handguns on campus.

More shootings on college campuses have happened recently.

Gun-free campuses disarm citizens who could end campus shootings.

Violent people would think twice about shooting at a campus.

More mentally ill students are going to college these days.

Universities would not be such easy targets for shooters.

A shooting could be ended quickly.

It may take minutes for security to arrive at the scene of a shooting.

Gun accidents are very rare.

Gun ownership is a constitutional right.

People with guns would need to be licensed and weapons concealed.

People will carry guns anyway, so it's best to have it regulated.

Only way to stop someone with a gun is to use a gun.

Guns on campus could be left in car.

People will feel more confident and less scared on campus.

People will be able to be on campus at night.

FIGURE 10.1 Brainstorming to Identify Major Points of Contention

When brainstorming about your topic, just write down anything about your topic that comes to mind.

argument. You should look for credible sources that both support your position and answer the criticisms that opposing positions might use against you.

Keep in mind that using a variety of sources will make your argument stronger. So you should look for a mix of online, print, and empirical sources that support all sides of the issue.

Online Sources. The Internet can be helpful for generating content, but you need to be especially careful about your sources when you are preparing to write an argument. Countless people will offer their opinions on blogs and Web sites, but these sources are often heavily biased and may provide little support to back up their opinions. When researching, you should look for factual sources on the Internet and avoid sources that are too biased. Also, keep an eye out for credible television documentaries and radio broadcasts on your subject, because they will often address both sides of the issue in a journalistic way.

Print Sources. Print documents will likely be your most reliable sources of factual information. Look for magazines, academic journals, books, and other documents, because these sources tend to be more careful about their facts than online sources and they usually have less bias. Through your library's Web site, try using the *Readers' Guide* to find magazine articles. Use periodical indexes to find academic articles. Your library's online catalog is a good place to search for books.

Empirical Sources. Facts you investigate or gather yourself will be very useful for backing up your claims about your topic. Set up an interview with an expert on your topic. You might find it especially helpful to interview an expert who holds an opposing view. This kind of interview will help you understand both sides of the issue much better. You might also create a survey that will generate some data or do some field observations.

Remember, you are looking for information that is credible and not too biased. It is fine to use sources that make a strong argument for one side or the other, but you need to make sure these sources are backed up with facts, data, and solid sources.

Organizing and Drafting Your Argument

The key to organizing an argument is to remember that you need to treat all sides of the issue fairly and thoroughly. As you are drafting your argument, it might help to imagine yourself in a debate with another person or a group of people (Figure 10.2). If you were in a public debate, how would you express your best points and persuade the audience that yours is the most reasonable position? How would you counter criticisms of your position? Meanwhile, try to really understand and explain the opposing perspectives while countering their best arguments.

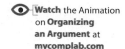
Watch the Animation on **Organizing an Argument** at **mycomplab.com**

The Introduction

Your introduction should prepare readers for your argument. It will usually include some or all of these moves:

> **Start with a Grabber or Lead.** Look for a good grabber or lead to catch readers' attention at the beginning of your introduction.

> **Identify Your Topic.** State the controversial issue your argument will explore. You might state it as a question.

FIGURE 10.2 Imagining a Debate with the Opposing Side

When drafting an argument, imagine yourself debating people who hold positions that oppose yours. How would you win them over? Would they say you understand their perspective, even though you disagree with it?

Offer Background. Briefly provide an overview of the various positions on the issue.

State Your Purpose. State your purpose clearly by telling readers that you will explain all sides of the issue and demonstrate why yours is stronger.

State Your Main Point or Thesis. You should state your main point or thesis clearly and completely. In most arguments, the main point or thesis statement often appears in the first or last sentences of your introduction. In some situations, you might save your main point or thesis statement for the conclusion, especially if you think readers might resist your argument. Your main point or thesis statement should be as specific as possible.

Weak: Only qualified police officers should be allowed to carry weapons on campus.

Stronger: Only qualified police officers should be allowed to carry weapons on campus, because the dangers of allowing students and faculty to carry weapons clearly outweigh the slight chance that a concealed weapon would be used in self-defense.

Summary and Limitations of Opposing Positions

Here is the tough part. Try to explain the opposing position's argument in a way that your readers would consider fair, reasonable, and complete. Acknowledge its strong points. Where possible, use quotes from opposing arguments to explain those perspectives. Paraphrasing or summarizing their argument is fine too, as long as you do it fairly.

As straightforwardly as possible, explain the limitations of opposing positions. What exactly are they missing? What have they neglected to consider? What are they ignoring in their argument? Again, you want to highlight these limitations as objectively as possible. This is not the place to be sarcastic or dismissive. You want to fairly point out the weaknesses in your opponents' argument.

Your Understanding of the Issue

Then it's your turn. Explain your side of the argument by taking your readers through the two to five points of contention, showing them why your side of the argument is stronger. Here is where you need to use your sources to back up your argument. You need to use good reasoning, examples, facts, and data to show readers why your opinion is more credible.

Reasons Why Your Understanding Is Stronger

Before moving to your conclusion, you might spend a little time comparing and contrasting the opposing views with your own. Briefly, compare the two sides head to head, showing readers why your view is stronger. At this point, it is all right to concede some points to your opponents. Your goal is to show readers that your view is stronger *on balance.* In other words, both sides probably have their strengths and weaknesses. You want to show that your side has more strengths and fewer weaknesses than your opponents' side.

Conclusion

Bring your argument to a close by stating or restating your thesis and looking to the future. Here is where you want to drive your main point or thesis home by telling your readers exactly what you believe. Then show how your position leads to a better future than opposing positions. Overall, your conclusion should be brief (a paragraph in most arguments).

Watch the Animation on **Conclusions** at **mycomplab.com**

Choosing an Appropriate Style

The style of your argument will help you distinguish your side from opposing sides. Even though your goal is to be *factually* fair to all sides, there is nothing wrong with using style to make your side sound more appealing and exciting.

Use Plain Style to Describe the Opposing Positions

When dealing with opposing perspectives, you should not be sarcastic or dismissive. Instead, describe opposing arguments as plainly as possible. In Chapter 16, "Choosing a Style," you will find helpful strategies for writing plainly, like putting the subjects of your sentences up front and using active verbs. You will also find techniques for writing better paragraphs that use clear topic sentences. By using these plain-style techniques to describe opposing perspectives, you will convey fairness and objectivity.

Use Similes, Metaphors, and Analogies When Describing Your Position

When you are describing your side of the argument, you want to present your case as visually as possible. Similes, metaphors, and analogies are a great way to help your readers visualize your argument and remember its key points.

A simile compares something unfamiliar to something familiar:

Simile (X Is Like Y)

A college campus in which students carry guns would be like a tense Old West frontier town.

Sharing music is like lending a good book to a friend, not pirating a ship on the high seas.

Metaphor (X Is Y)

If a shooting incident did occur, the classroom would turn into a deadly crossfire zone, with armed students and police firing away at anyone with a gun in his or her hand. No one would be able to tell the difference between the original shooter and students with their weapons drawn.

The purpose of the music industry's lawsuits is to throw a few unfortunate college students to the lions. That way, they can hold up a few bloody carcasses to scare the rest of us.

Analogy (X Is to Y Like A Is to B)

For some people, a gun has the same comforting effect as a safety blanket to a baby. Neither a gun nor a blanket will protect you from those imaginary monsters, but both can give you a make-believe feeling of security.

The music industry's lawsuits are like your old Aunt Martha defending her tin of chocolate chip cookies at the church potluck. The industry offers a plate of delicious songs, but only the "right people" are allowed to enjoy them. College students aren't the right people because we don't have enough money.

Try some of these "persuasive style" techniques to enhance the power of your argument. Similes, metaphors, and analogies will make your writing more visual and colorful, and they will also help you come up with new ways to think and talk about your topic. You can learn more about persuasive style in Chapter 16, "Choosing a Style."

Use Top-Down Paragraphs

Your argument needs to sound confident, and your readers should be able to find your major points easily. So, in your paragraphs, put each major point in the first or second sentence. Don't put your major points in the middle of your paragraphs or at the end because your readers won't find them easily. A top-down style will make you sound more confident, because you are stating your major claims and then proving them.

Define Unfamiliar Terms

Your readers may or may not be familiar with the topic of your argument. So if you use any specialized or technical terms, you should provide quick parenthetical or sentence definitions to explain them.

Sentence Definition

A conceal-carry permit is the legal authorization that allows private citizens to carry a handgun or other weapon on their person or in a secure place nearby.

Peer-to-peer file sharing involves using a network of computers to store and share files without charge.

Parenthetical Definitions

Colleges have traditionally invoked an "opt-out" statute, a law that allows the ban of weapons where posted, to keep concealed handguns off their campuses.

Music sharing should become illegal when a person *burns* the songs (i.e., puts them on a CD) and sells them to someone else.

Designing Your Argument

More and more, you will find that your professors appreciate the addition of helpful visuals and the use of good page design. If your work looks professional, they will likely have a more favorable impression of it.

Use Descriptive Headings. Each of the major sections in your argument should start with a clear heading that identifies what the section is about. For example, you could use headings like these:

The Case for Allowing Concealed Guns on Campus

The Limitations of Allowing Guns on Campus

Why Concealed Guns on Campus Are Dangerous

Conclusion: Why the Risks of Concealed Weapons Aren't Worth It

You might use bold type to help your headings stand out, and you might use a larger font size where appropriate. Make sure your headings are formatted consistently.

Add Photographs and Illustrations. If you are writing about a local issue or an issue with a local angle, you might grab a digital camera and take a few pictures to use in your paper. The Internet might also be a good place to find a few pictures and illustrations you can download to add a visual element to your text.

In your document, make sure you label your visuals with a number and title, and include a caption to explain them. If you download a photograph or other illustration from the Internet, you will need to cite your source in the caption and in your bibliography. If you want to put your argument on the Internet, you will need to ask permission from the owners of the photograph to use it on your Web site.

Include Helpful Graphs, Diagrams, and Charts. Arguments often discuss trends in society, so you might look for ways to use graphs that illustrate those trends. If you collected data or found data on the Internet, you might create a graph or chart to present that data visually. Or, if you found a helpful graph on the Internet, you could use it in your own document, as long as you cite it properly. Graphs and charts should have a title, and you should use figure numbers in your written text to refer readers to the visual (e.g., "In Figure 2, the graph shows . . .").

Design the Page to Make It More Readable and Attractive. Let's be honest. A double-spaced paper with 1-inch margins just looks boring. Your professors might appreciate your efforts to design a document that is more readable and more attractive (Figure 10.3). A header or footer would be nice. Maybe you could use two columns instead of one. Your headings could be bolder and more colorful. Of course, if your professor asks for something specific, like "Your essay must use 12-point Times, be double-spaced, and use 1-inch margins," then you will need to format it that way. But if there are no guidelines, you might ask whether designing the document is acceptable.

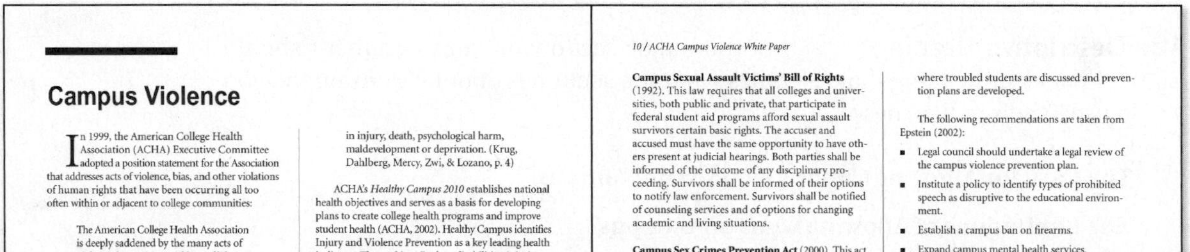

Campus Violence

In 1999, the American College Health Association (ACHA) Executive Committee adopted a position statement for the Association that addresses acts of violence, bias, and other violations of human rights that have been occurring all too often within or adjacent to college communities:

> The American College Health Association is deeply saddened by the many acts of violence, hate crimes and loss of life over this past year. We, the members of the Association, believe that for a campus community to be truly healthy, it must be guided by the values of multicultural inclusion, respect, and equality. Intolerance has no place at an institution of higher learning. The Association supports all individuals regardless of sexual orientation, race, national origin, age, religion, or disability. We encourage all campus health professionals to be actively engaged in the struggle to end oppression, to prevent bias-related violence in our campus communities, and to take action to eradicate injustice. (ACHA, 1999)

Since this timely position statement was developed, acts of violence have continued to force U.S. colleges and universities to address the dangerous and alarming violent events that send shockwaves throughout many campuses and compromise students' and employees' health and safety. Campus shootings, murder-suicides, homicides, hate crimes based on gender, race, ethnicity, or sexual orientation, suicides, assaults, hazing, and arson require us to conduct fresh analyses and create new paradigms for preventing and decreasing all campus violence.

This paper will adopt the World Health Organization definition of violence as:

> The intentional use of physical force or power, threatened or actual, against oneself, another person, or against a group or community, that either results in or has a high likelihood of resulting in injury, death, psychological harm, maldevelopment or deprivation. (Krug, Dahlberg, Mercy, Zwi, & Lozano, p. 4)

ACHA's *Healthy Campus 2010* establishes national health objectives and serves as a basis for developing plans to create college health programs and improve student health (ACHA, 2002). Healthy Campus identifies Injury and Violence Prevention as a key leading health indicator. The goal is to "reduce disabilities, injuries and deaths due to injury and violence" (p. 51). Specifically, ACHA seeks to reduce homicides, physical assaults, intimate partner violence, emotional abuse, sexual abuse, rape and attempted rape, physical fighting, and weapon carrying. In addition, a goal is to increase the annual rate of reporting of rape and attempted rape to the police *and* via surveys.

The purpose of this ACHA White Paper is to confront this serious college health issue through analyzing campus violence patterns, types of violence, methodological problems with collecting campus crime data, underlying issues related to campus violence, and promising practices to prevent and address campus violence.

Scope of the Problem

There are approximately 16 million students enrolled in 4,200 colleges and universities (U.S. Department of Education, 2002). The Violence Against Women Act (1994) mandated the study of campus victimization. The National Crime Victimization Survey (NCVS) gathers data on crimes reported and not reported to the police from a nationally representative sample of U.S. households. Beginning in 1995, the Bureau of Justice Statistics added new items to the survey regarding student victims of crime.

According to the Violent Victimization of College Students report (Baum & Klaus, 2005), between 1995 and 2002, college students ages 18-24 were victims of approximately 479,000 crimes of violence annually: rape/sexual assault, robbery, aggravated assault, and simple assault. Overall, the violent crime rate declined 54%. These data include both part-time and full-time students attending private or public

10 / ACHA Campus Violence White Paper

Campus Sexual Assault Victims' Bill of Rights (1992). This law requires that all colleges and universities, both public and private, that participate in federal student aid programs afford sexual assault survivors certain basic rights. The accuser and accused must have the same opportunity to have others present at judicial hearings. Both parties shall be informed of the outcome of any disciplinary proceeding. Survivors shall be informed of their options to notify law enforcement. Survivors shall be notified of counseling services and of options for changing academic and living situations.

Campus Sex Crimes Prevention Act (2000). This act provides for the collection and disclosure of information about convicted, registered sex offenders either enrolled in or employed at institutions of higher education.

University duty to warn

Courts have held that policy and federal law permit notification of family or others (usually by the dean of students) but do not create a duty to notify (Jain v. State of Iowa, 2000). The Family Educational Rights and Privacy Act (FERPA) permits notification as a health or safety issue. Psychologists and psychiatrists have a duty to warn if specific threats are made against specific people by their clients. Privacy obligations of administrators may provide greater flexibility than confidentiality obligations of professional counseling or medical staff. Courts have ruled that colleges have a duty to provide "reasonable supervision of students" and "take reasonable steps to protect students" (Jain v. State of Iowa).

Recommendations

These recommendations are based on the ACHA 2003 Annual Meeting Legal Symposium on High-Risk Students, an invited address by Nancy Tribbensee (2003) (see also Lake & Tribbensee, 2002).

- Make necessary a consultative approach across departments and administrative lines to manage high-risk student behavior.
- Educate faculty and graduate assistants, staff, and other students about the importance of early referral for distressed students.
- Address environmental issues such as drugs and alcohol.
- Develop an early warning system, such as a Student Assistance Coordinating Committee, where troubled students are discussed and prevention plans are developed.

The following recommendations are taken from Epstein (2002):

- Legal council should undertake a legal review of the campus violence prevention plan.
- Institute a policy to identify types of prohibited speech as disruptive to the educational environment.
- Establish a campus ban on firearms.
- Expand campus mental health services.
- Encourage students/staff to report verbal and written threats, weapons, and bizarre behaviors.
- Have protocols in place for conveying information regarding dangerous situations and threats.

Epstein (2002) recommends development of a protocol that addresses bystander reports for each college or university campus. While recognizing conflicting issues of unjust accusations vs. not reporting potential risks that become actual hazards, the policy should ensure due process, confidentiality of the bystander whenever possible, rights of the suspected student, and constitutional validity of the policy itself. College administration must be aware of the risks associated with bystander disclosure and protect that person's rights and safety.

It is extremely important to have protocols in place for conveying information regarding dangerous situations and threats and search and seizure, as well as checking the reliability of third-party tips. A strong emphasis must be placed on increasing staff and student awareness of policies and procedures so that untrained personnel minimize risk. With regard to concerns for violation of privacy issues, Epstein (2002) suggested that one way to involve students is to ask incoming students to sign a release that will allow administrators to take action if their behavior warrants concern and becomes erratic.

Resources: Innovative Programs and Suggested Readings

Promising and innovative sexual violence prevention programs have been developed that are intended for college males only, females only, mixed-gendered audiences, athletes, fraternity members, and

FIGURE 10.3 Designing an Argument

Your argument doesn't need to look boring or hard to read. The designers of this paper on campus violence use headings, bullets, indentation, and columns to make the text more accessible.

Number the Pages. Page numbers might seem like a simple thing, but they are helpful when discussing your argument with other students or with your professor. Your word processor can add them automatically to the top or bottom of each page.

Revising and Editing Your Argument

As you draft your argument, your ideas will evolve. Some shift in your opinion is natural because writing about something gives you the opportunity to think about it in greater depth and consider other viewpoints. Drafting your argument will also force you to back up your claims. This may cause you to rethink your position a little or to reconsider it completely.

Now that you are finished drafting, you need to spend time revising and "re-visioning" your argument to make sure it holds together. In other words, you don't want to argue one thing at the beginning of the paper and then argue something a little different at the end. The whole argument needs to work together to prove your main point or thesis.

Remove Any Digressions. When arguing, you might find yourself temporarily drifting off topic. These moments are called *digressions*, and you should remove them from the final version of your paper. Check each paragraph to make sure you are discussing your topic and not going off in a direction that expands or sidetracks your argument.

Back-Check the Evidence for Your Claims. Make sure your claims are backed up with solid support. If you make a claim about your position or opposing positions, that statement should be followed up with facts, data, examples, reasoning, or quotations. Short paragraphs are usually a signal that you are not backing up your claims, because such paragraphs typically include only a claim with minimal support.

Improve the Flow of Your Sentences. Try reading your draft out loud to yourself or someone else. Mark any places where you stumble or hear something that doesn't sound right. Then use the "plain style" methods discussed in Chapter 16, "Choosing a Style," to make your sentences flow better.

Make Your Writing More Visual. Look for places where you can use more detail and color to bring your writing to life. Describe things and people. Look for places where you can use similes and metaphors to add a visual component to your writing.

Ask a friend or roommate to read through your argument and highlight places where you could revise. Also, your university may have a Writing Lab where you can get help with locating places in your argument that need revision.

Revising and editing are critical to developing a solid argument because your readers (i.e., your professors) place a high value on clear, thoughtful writing. If they sense that you did not revise and edit your work, they will rate your work lower.

Watch the Animation on **Revising from Peer Review** at **mycomplab.com**

The Rebuttal

A rebuttal counters or refutes a specific argument. Rebuttals often appear as letters to the editor. They are also used in the workplace to argue against potentially damaging reviews, evaluations, position papers, and reports. Knowing how to write a rebuttal is an important part of defending your beliefs, projects, and research.

The main difference between a rebuttal and an argument is that a rebuttal responds directly to the points made in the original argument. After responding to that argument point by point, you then offer a better counterargument. Here are some strategies for writing a successful rebuttal:

Review the original argument briefly.   Objectively summarize the original argument's thesis and its main points.

Challenge any hidden assumptions behind the author's claims.   Look for unstated assumptions in each major claim of the original argument. These are weak points that you can challenge.

Watch the Animation on **Investigating Assumptions** at **mycomplab** **.com**

Challenge the evidence.   If the author leaves out important facts and other evidence or uses evidence that is not accurate or typical, point that out. Locate the original source to see if any data or details are outdated, inaccurate, exaggerated, or taken out of context.

Challenge the authority of the sources.   If possible, question whether the author's sources are truly authoritative on the issue. Unless a source is rock solid, you can question the reliability of the information taken from it.

Examine whether emotion is overcoming reason or evidence.   If the author is allowing his or her feelings to fuel the argument, you can suggest that these emotions are clouding his or her judgment on the issue.

Look for logical fallacies.   Logical fallacies are forms of weak reasoning that you can use to challenge your opponents' ideas. You can learn more about logical fallacies in Chapter 22, "Using Argumentative Strategies."

Offer a solid counterargument.   Offer a different understanding of the issue supported by authoritative research.

WRITE your own rebuttal. Find an argument or similar document in a newspaper or on a Web site that you disagree with. Write a two-page rebuttal in which you refute the original argument and offer a counterargument. Your goal is to win readers over to your side.

Letter to the Editor on Climate Story

Russ Walker and David Roberts

Politico did a disservice to its readers in publishing the Nov. 25 story, "Scientists urge caution on global warming." It reports that "climate change skeptics"—the too-charitable name given those who deny the existence of climate change in the face of overwhelming evidence and the testimony of every reputable scientific organization—are watching "a growing accumulation of global cooling science and other findings that could signal that the science behind global warming may still be too shaky to warrant cap-and-trade legislation."

Opposing position is reviewed.

While reasonable people may debate the value of cap-and-trade legislation, and it is certainly worth reporting on how its congressional opponents are strategizing to block it, it is simply false to point to a "growing accumulation" of evidence rendering basic climate science "shaky." There is no such accumulation; there is no such science. If there were, perhaps the author would have cited some of it—it is telling that she did not.

Instead, she relies on the work of Joseph D'Aleo, a meteorologist (meteorology is the study of weather, not climate). D'Aleo's lack of qualifications in climate science would be less relevant if he had published his work on "global cooling" in peer-reviewed scientific journals. Instead, it appears in the *Farmers' Almanac.*

Challenges authority of sources.

Incidentally, D'Aleo's professional association, the American Meteorological Association, is one of dozens of leading national and international scientific groups to endorse the broad consensus on anthropogenic climate change. For some reason, the author did not reference or quote a single one of the hundreds if not thousands of scientists who might have vouchsafed that consensus (inexplicably, the one countervailing quote is given to Al Gore's spokeswoman). If she had spoken with mainstream climate scientists, she would have discovered that they are not "urging caution" on global warming—they are running around, to paraphrase ex-CIA chief George Tenet, with their hair on fire, increasingly radicalized by the ignorance and delay of the world's governments in the face of the crisis.

Points out that the original article left out key sources of information.

Also glossed over is the fact that the organizations backing D'Aleo's work—National Consumer Coalition, Americans for Tax Reform, the

continued

National Center for Policy Analysis and Citizens for a Sound Economy—are (for better or worse) conservative interest groups, not science organizations. Similarly, the "Global Warming Petition Project" the author cites is one of the oldest, most discredited hoaxes in the "skeptic" handbook. It first emerged in 1998, when it was promptly disavowed and disowned by the Academy of Sciences. The petition is deceptive: Only a handful of signatories come from relevant scientific disciplines, it is open to signature by anyone willing to fill out an online form and there is no clear way to document the scientific credentials of those who have signed. (One clever blogger signed up his dog.) The petition is rereleased every few years and debunked all over again, inevitably after snookering a few journalists.

Offers a counterargument.

Meanwhile, respected and nonpolitical scientific bodies are firmly united when it comes to climate change—humanity's reliance on carbon-based fuels is pumping dangerous amounts of CO_2 into the atmosphere, leading to a steady rise in average global temperature and attendant ill effects including droughts, the spread of infectious diseases, and sea level rise. This basic consensus is as well-established in mainstream science as any finding in biology or chemistry, endorsed with a greater than 90 percent degree of confidence by the reports of the Intergovernmental Panel on Climate Change.

Journalists working on climate issues will recognize the bogus evidence and outlier scientists featured in *Politico*'s piece; they are regularly highlighted by the office of Sen. James Inhofe. Though Inhofe's long campaign of disinformation on climate science is eagerly consumed and propagated by political allies dead set on opposing any government action on global warming, mainstream science and climate journalists have long since learned to disregard it. There's a reason Inhofe's campaign is waged via press conferences and online petitions rather than peer-reviewed science.

Here is the thesis with an ending that snaps.

Climate change is an incredibly complex topic; the policy prescriptions for addressing it are wide open for debate; the maneuverings of various industries and interest groups are well worth documenting. But the basic science is quite clear, and *Politico* should take the subject seriously enough not to equate the views of a small group of ideological deniers with a consensus reached over decades of intense data collection, study, and peer review.

IDENTIFY an Arguable Topic

An arguable topic has at least two sides. Choose the side that you agree with. Then narrow your topic to something suitable for an argument.

IDENTIFY the Points Separating Your Views from Opposing Views

Using brainstorming or another prewriting tool, put down everything you know about your topic. Then write down everything someone who holds the opposing view believes.

RESEARCH Both Sides of the Topic

Collect materials that support both (or all) sides of the issue, because you want to discover the best reasons for supporting opposing positions. You can then authoritatively counter these positions as you support your own.

DEVELOP Your Main Point or Thesis Statement

State the main point or thesis that you will be supporting in your argument. This main point or thesis statement will help you draft and revise your argument.

ORGANIZE Your Materials and Draft Your Argument

Arguments are organized to explain competing sides of an issue. Describe the strengths of the opposing positions fully and fairly before you challenge them.

CHOOSE Your Style

When explaining opposing positions, use a "plain style" with simple, clear sentences and paragraphs. When you explain your own position, add energy to your argument by using similes, metaphors, and analogies.

DESIGN the Document

Arguments tend to be rather plain in design. However, you might look for opportunities to add visuals to support your argument.

REVISE and Edit

As you draft your argument, your position may evolve. Give yourself time to modify your argument and refine your points. Proofreading is critical because readers will see errors as evidence that your argument has not been fully thought through.

In Defense of Torture

SAM HARRIS

This argument, written by Sam Harris, who is best known for his book The End of Faith, *makes an argument that "torture may be an ethical necessity." Harris uses a combination of emotional and logical appeals to persuade his readers. Notice how he concedes points to the opposing side in strategic ways, which allows him to bring forward his own arguments for torture.*

Imagine that a known terrorist has planted a bomb in the heart of a nearby city. He now sits in your custody. Rather than conceal his guilt, he gloats about the forthcoming explosion and the magnitude of human suffering it will cause. Given this state of affairs—in particular, given that there is still time to prevent an imminent atrocity—it seems that subjecting this unpleasant fellow to torture may be justifiable. For those who make it their business to debate the ethics of torture this is known as the "ticking-bomb" case.

While the most realistic version of the ticking bomb case may not persuade everyone that torture is ethically acceptable, adding further embellishments seems to awaken the Grand Inquisitor in most of us. If a conventional explosion doesn't move you, consider a nuclear bomb hidden in midtown Manhattan. If bombs seem too impersonal an evil, picture your seven-year-old daughter being slowly asphyxiated in a warehouse just five minutes away, while the man in your custody holds the keys to her release. If your daughter won't tip the scales, then add the daughters of every couple for a thousand miles—millions of little girls have, by some perverse negligence on the part of our government, come under the control of an evil genius who now sits before you in shackles. Clearly, the consequences of one person's uncooperativeness can be made so grave,

and his malevolence and culpability so transparent, as to stir even a self-hating moral relativist from his dogmatic slumbers.

I am one of the few people I know of who has argued in print that torture may be an ethical necessity in our war on terror. In the aftermath of Abu Ghraib, this is not a comfortable position to have publicly adopted. There is no question that Abu Ghraib was a travesty, and there is no question that it has done our country lasting harm. Indeed, the Abu Ghraib scandal may be one of the costliest foreign policy blunders to occur in the last century, given the degree to which it simultaneously inflamed the Muslim world and eroded the sympathies of our democratic allies. While we hold the moral high ground in our war on terror, we appear to hold it less and less. Our casual abuse of ordinary prisoners is largely responsible for this. Documented abuses at Abu Ghraib, Guantanamo Bay, and elsewhere have now inspired legislation prohibiting "cruel, inhuman or degrading" treatment of military prisoners. And yet, these developments do not shed much light on the ethics of torturing people like Osama bin Laden when we get them in custody.

I will now present an argument for the use of torture in rare circumstances. While many people have objected, on emotional grounds, to my defense of torture, no one has pointed out a flaw in my argument. I hope my case for torture is wrong, as I would be much happier standing side by side with all the good people who oppose torture categorically. I invite any reader who discovers a problem with my argument to point it out to me in the comment section of this blog. I would be sincerely grateful to have my mind changed on this subject.

Most readers will undoubtedly feel at 5 this point that torture is evil and that we are wise not to practice it. Even if we can't quite muster a retort to the ticking bomb case, most of us take refuge in the fact that the paradigmatic case will almost never arise. It seems, however, that this position is impossible to square with our willingness to wage modern war in the first place.

In modern warfare, "collateral damage"—the maiming and killing of innocent noncombatants—is unavoidable. And it will remain unavoidable for the foreseeable future. Collateral damage would be a problem even if our bombs were far "smarter" than they are now. It would also be a problem even if we resolved to fight only defensive wars. There is no escaping the fact that whenever we drop bombs, we drop them with the knowledge that some number of children will be blinded, disemboweled, paralyzed, orphaned, and killed by them.

The only way to rule out collateral damage would be to refuse to fight wars under any circumstances. As a foreign policy, this would leave us with something like the absolute pacifism of Gandhi. While pacifism in this form can constitute a direct confrontation with injustice (and requires considerable bravery), it is only applicable to a limited range of human conflicts. Where it is not applicable, it seems flagrantly immoral. We would do well to reflect on Gandhi's remedy for the Holocaust: he believed that the Jews should have committed mass suicide, because this "would have aroused the world

and the people of Germany to Hitler's violence." We might wonder what a world full of pacifists would have done once it had grown "aroused"—commit suicide as well? There seems no question that if all the good people in the world adopted Gandhi's ethics, the thugs would inherit the earth.

So we can now ask, if we are willing to act in a way that guarantees the misery and death of some considerable number of innocent children, why spare the rod with known terrorists? I find it genuinely bizarre that while the torture of Osama bin Laden himself could be expected to provoke convulsions of conscience among our leaders, the perfectly foreseeable (and therefore accepted) slaughter of children does not. What is the difference between pursuing a course of action where we run the risk of inadvertently subjecting some innocent men to torture, and pursuing one in which we will inadvertently kill far greater numbers of innocent men, women, and children? Rather, it seems obvious that the misapplication of torture should be far *less* troubling to us than collateral damage: there are, after all, no *infants* interned at Guantanamo Bay. Torture need not even impose a significant risk of death or permanent injury on its victims; while the collaterally damaged are, almost by definition, crippled or killed. The ethical divide that seems to be opening up here suggests that those who are willing to drop bombs might want to abduct the nearest and dearest of suspected terrorists—their wives, mothers, and daughters—and torture *them* as well, assuming anything profitable to our side might come of it. Admittedly, this would be a ghastly result to have reached by logical argument, and we will want to find some way of escaping it. But there seems no question that accidentally torturing an innocent man is better than accidentally blowing him and his children to bits.

In this context, we should note that many variables influence our feelings about an act of physical violence. The philosopher Jonathan Glover points out that "in modern war, what is most shocking is a poor guide to what is most harmful." To learn that one's grandfather flew a bombing mission over Dresden in the Second World War is one thing; to hear that he killed five little girls and their mother with a shovel is another. We can be sure that he would have killed many more women and girls by dropping bombs from pristine heights, and they are likely to have died equally horrible deaths, but his culpability would not appear the same. There is much to be said about the disparity here, but the relevance to the ethics of torture should be obvious. If you think that the equivalence between torture and collateral damage does not hold, because torture is up close and personal while stray bombs aren't, you stand convicted of a failure of imagination on at least two counts: first, a moment's reflection on the horrors that must have been visited upon innocent Afghanis and Iraqis by our bombs will reveal that they are on par with those of any dungeon. If our intuition about the wrongness of torture is born of an aversion to how people generally behave while being tortured, we should note that this particular infelicity could be circumvented pharmacologically, because paralytic drugs make it unnecessary for screaming ever to be heard or writhing seen. We could easily devise methods of torture that would render a torturer as blind to the plight of his victims as a bomber pilot is at thirty thousand feet. Consequently, our natural aversion to the sights and sounds of the dungeon provide no foothold for those who would argue against the use of torture.

To demonstrate just how abstract the torments of the tortured can be made to seem, we need only imagine an ideal "torture pill"—a drug that would deliver both the instruments of torture and the instrument of their concealment. The action of the pill would be to produce transitory paralysis and transitory misery of a kind that no human being would willingly submit to a second time. Imagine how we torturers would feel if, after giving this pill to captive terrorists, each lay down for what appeared to be an hour's nap only to arise and immediately confess everything he knows about the workings of his organization. Might we not be tempted to call it a "truth pill" in the end? No, there is no ethical difference to be found in how the suffering of the tortured or the collaterally damaged appears.

Opponents of torture will be quick to argue that confessions elicited by torture are notoriously unreliable. Given the foregoing, however, this objection seems to lack its usual force. Make these confessions as unreliable as you like—the chance that our interests will be advanced in any instance of torture need only equal the chance of such occasioned by the dropping of a single bomb. What was the chance that the dropping of bomb number 117 on Kandahar would effect the demise of Al Qaeda? It had to be pretty slim. Enter Khalid Sheikh Mohammed: our most valuable capture in our war on terror. Here is a character who actually seems to have stepped out of a philosopher's thought experiment. U.S. officials now believe that his was the hand that decapitated the *Wall Street Journal* reporter Daniel Pearl. Whether or not this is true, his membership in Al Qaeda more or less rules out his "innocence" in any important sense, and his rank in the organization suggests that his knowledge of planned atrocities must be extensive. The bomb has been ticking ever since September 11th, 2001. Given the damage we were willing to cause to the bodies and minds of innocent children in Afghanistan and Iraq, our disavowal of torture in the case of Khalid Sheikh

10

Mohammed seems perverse. If there is even one chance in a million that he will tell us something under torture that will lead to the further dismantling of Al Qaeda, it seems that we should use every means at our disposal to get him talking. (In fact, the *New York Times* has reported that Khalid Sheikh Mohammed was tortured in a procedure known as "waterboarding," despite our official disavowal of this practice.)

Which way should the balance swing? Assuming that we want to maintain a coherent ethical position on these matters, this appears to be a circumstance of forced choice: if we are willing to drop bombs, or even risk that rifle rounds might go astray, we should be willing to torture a certain class of criminal suspects and military prisoners; if we are unwilling to torture, we should be unwilling to wage modern war.

A CLOSER LOOK AT
In Defense of Torture

1. Harris uses several hypothetical situations to argue that torture may be needed in some special cases. What are these hypothetical situations, and do you find them persuasive in convincing you to accept torture as an option?

2. Find two places where Harris concedes a point to his opponents about torture. How does he make a concession without undermining his own argument? Do these concessions make his argument stronger or weaker?

3. Harris's final sentence says, "if we are unwilling to torture, we should be unwilling to wage modern war." He comes to this conclusion by comparing the deaths of innocent people (i.e., collateral damage) with the treatment of terrorists. Do you find his comparison between innocent people and terrorists effective or not?

IDEAS FOR
Writing

1. This argument was published in 2005. Now we know much more about the Bush administration's use of torture before and during the Iraq war. Write a brief report in which you objectively describe how torture was used during the Iraq war.

2. Write a rebuttal to Harris's argument. Where are the weak points in his argument? Can you see any ways to use his own arguments against him? What does he seem to be missing and what kinds of questionable claims does he make?

Friends with Benefits: Do *Facebook* Friends Provide the Same Support as Those in Real Life?

KATE DAILEY

Social networking sites like Facebook *and* MySpace *have challenged our ideas about what it means to be a "friend." Today, people can keep in touch with others who might otherwise have faded into the past. Also, we can be "friends" with people we barely know who share common interests or backgrounds. In this argument, pay attention to how Dailey builds her case and notice where she summarizes the other side of the debate.*

I have a friend named Sue. Actually, "Sue" isn't her real name, and she isn't really a friend: she's something akin to a lost sorority sister—we went to the same college, participated in the same activities and had a lot of mutual respect and admiration for one another. But since graduation, we've fallen out of touch, and the only way I know about Sue, her life and her family is through her *Facebook* updates. That's why I felt almost like a voyeur when Sue announced, via *Facebook*, the death of her young son. I was surprised she had chosen to share something so personal online—and then ashamed, because since when did I become the arbiter of what's appropriate for that kind of grief?

The more I thought about it, the more I realized *Facebook* might be the perfect venue for tragic news: it's the fastest way to disseminate important information to the group without having to deal with painful phone calls; it allowed well-meaning friends and acquaintances to instantly pass on condolences, which the family could read at their leisure, and it eliminated the possibility that were I to run into Sue in the supermarket, I'd ask unknowingly about her son and force her to replay the story over again.

Numerous studies have shown that a strong network of friends can be crucial to getting through a crisis, and can help you be healthier in general. But could virtual friends, like the group of online buddies that reached out to Sue, be just as helpful as the flesh-and-blood versions? In other words, do *Facebook* friends—and the support we get from them—count? These questions are all the more intriguing as the number of online social-network users increases. *Facebook* attracted 67.5 million visitors in the U.S. in

April (according to ComScore Inc.), and the fastest-growing demographic is people over 35. It's clear that connecting to friends, both close and distant, via the computer will become more the norm than novelty.

Researchers have yet to significantly study the social implications of *Facebook*, so what we do know is gleaned from general studies about friendship, and some of the emerging studies about online networking. First, a definition of "friend": In research circles, experts define a friend as a close, equal, voluntary partnership—though Rebecca G. Adams, a professor of sociology at the University of North Carolina, Greensboro, says that in reality, "friendships don't have to be equal or close, and we know from research that friendships aren't as voluntary as they seem," because they're often constricted by education, age and background. Friends on *Facebook* seem to mimic, if not replicate, this trend—there are people online that you are more likely to chat with every day, while others only make an appearance once or twice a year, content to spend the rest of the time residing silently in your friend queue. (Though the *Facebook* friends with whom you have frequent social interaction might not be people you interact with often in "real life.")

In life, having 700 people in your circle of 5 friends could get overwhelming, but that's less of an issue online. "Research suggests that people are only intermittently in touch with many of their online 'friends' but correspond regularly with only a few good friends," says Shelley E. Taylor, professor of psychology at The University of California, Los Angeles. "That said, creating networks to ease the transition to new places can be hugely helpful to people, offsetting loneliness until new friends are made."

In other words, *Facebook* may not replace the full benefits of real friendship, but it definitely beats the alternative. I conducted a very informal poll via my *Facebook* status update, asking if *Facebook* makes us better friends. A

high-school pal, with whom I haven't spoken in about 10 years, confessed that since she had her baby, corresponding via *Facebook* has been a lifeline—and even if she wasn't actively commenting, it was nice to know what people were up to. "Any electronic communication where you don't have to be in the same physical space is going to decrease feelings of isolation," says Dr. Adams.

Several people in my online network admit that *Facebook* doesn't make them a better friend, but a better acquaintance, more likely to dash off a quick happy birthday e-mail, or to comment on the photo of a new puppy. But that's not a bad thing. Having a large group of "friends" eager to comment on your daily life could be good for your self-esteem. When you get a new job, a celebratory lunch with your best friends will make you feel good and make for a fantastic memory. But the boost you get from the 15 *Facebook* friends who left encouraging comments can also make you happy.

"The way to think of this is before the Internet, we wouldn't see our acquaintances very often: every once in a while, we might show up at a wedding and suddenly have 100 of our closest friends around," says James Fowler, associate professor of political science at the University of California, San Diego. "With *Facebook*, it's like every day is a wedding." And just like leaving a wedding may leave you feeling energized and inspired by reconnecting to old pals, so can spending time on *Facebook*, says Fowler.

While Fowler's research also shows that bad habits like smoking and weight gain can be contagious among close friends, emotions like happiness and sadness are easily transferable through acquaintances. The good news? "Because happiness spreads more easily then unhappiness, getting positive comments from your *Facebook* friends is more likely to make you happy than sad," he says.

Shy people who may not always be able 10 to engage friends in the real world are finding solace in the structure of *Facebook*. Though people who identify as shy have a smaller circle of *Facebook* friends than those who don't, they are better able to engage with the online friends they do have. "Because people don't have to interact face-to-face, that's why we're seeing them having relationships: they can think more about what they have to say and how they want to say it," says Craig Ross, a graduate student in psychology at the University of Windsor who studies online social networks.

And what of my "friend" "Sue"? Can the support she received from *Facebook* friends upon learning about the death of her son replicate the support that would come from friends stopping by the house? It's impossible to replace the warm feelings—or brain-boosting endorphins—that come from human-on-human contact, and you can't send someone a casserole through *Facebook*. But grieving online can have powerful and productive benefits. Diana Nash, professor of psychology at Marymount Manhattan College, who has studied how college students use *MySpace* to deal with grief, notes that, "One of the primary desires that we all have is for someone to really listen to us in a deep kind of way. They want to be listened to," she says. Her research shows that by sharing their grief on *MySpace*, her subjects felt more listened to and more visible, and doing so helped them heal.

Posting personal experiences, no matter how painful, also allows acquaintances who have lived through similar experiences to reach out, either with information about support groups or just an empathetic ear. "The idea of sharing a commonality helps make it a little more bearable. You're not alone, and there are others going through what you went through," says Nash. "It doesn't take away the pain, but it can lessen the pain and make you feel not so alone."

The majority of times we reach out on *Facebook*, however, it's not about a tragedy, but a smaller problem for which we need advice: good movers in the San Francisco area, a copy of yesterday's newspaper, answers to a question about taxes. This is another place where the large *Facebook* networks come in handy. In real life, people tend to befriend people who think thoughts and live very similar lives to their own, but because on *Facebook* people often "friend" classmates, people met at parties, and friends-of-friends, the networks include individuals who wouldn't make the "real friend" cut. Having that diversity of opinion and experience available online increases the diversity of responses received when posting a question, which allows you to make a better-informed decision.

Still, there are experts who worry that too much time online keeps us from living satisfying lives in the real world. "It's great to have a lot of *Facebook* friends, but how many of those will friends will show when you're really in trouble?" asks Michael J. Bugeja, a professor of communications at Iowa State University of Science and Technology and author of *Interpersonal Divide: The Search for Community in a Technological Age*. He notes the world of difference between someone typing a frowny emoticon upon hearing that you've been in a car crash and showing up to help you get home. He also says that *Facebook*, with its focus on existing relationships—and its ability to codify and categorize those relationships—in some ways belies the promise of the Internet. "Rather than opening us up to a global community, it is putting us into groups," he says.

That's why *Facebook* works best as an amplification of a "real life" social life, not a replacement—even as time and technology progress and the lines between online interactions and real-world experiences continue to blur. [15]

A CLOSER LOOK AT
Friends with Benefits

1. In this argument, the definition of the word "friend" seems open for debate. Dailey offers a couple of different definitions of a friend, a traditional definition and a social-networking site definition. How are these two types of friends similar, and how are they different?

2. This argument talks about how habits can be contagious among friends, like smoking and weight gain. Bailey, however, sees this kind of contagiousness as a good thing because of *Facebook*. Why?

3. A good argument fairly describes the other side of the debate, usually early in the argument. However, in this one, Dailey waits until the end to clearly state the opposing argument. What do these people find wrong with calling people on *Facebook* "friends"?

IDEAS FOR
Writing

1. Write a three-page commentary in which you discuss the future of friendships in an electronically networked world. Do you think people will lose touch with each other, because they are mostly interacting through texting, social networking sites, or e-mail? Or do you think electronic networking is actually making relationships stronger? What are some of the benefits of friendships through electronic networking? What are some of the downsides?

2. Find one of your childhood friends on *Facebook, MySpace*, or another social networking site. Write a two-page profile of your friend using only evidence drawn from his or her page. On his or her page, your friend has tried to project a particular image. What is that image? How is that image similar to or different from the person you know or knew personally?

1. With a small group, make a list of some challenging issues facing our society to-day. Pick an issue and explore both sides. What are the two to five major points of contention between the two sides of the issue? What are the strengths of each side? What are the limitations of each side?

2. With your class, list ten effective and ineffective ways to argue. What is the best way to get your point across to someone else? What are your most effective strategies? Then list some of the worst ways to argue. What are some of the annoying ways in which other people have tried to persuade you? How did you react to some of these less effective methods?

3. Think about arguments you have had with friends, family members, and other people you care about. With a small group, discuss why these arguments are sometimes more difficult than arguments with people who are not so close to you. Do you have any strategies for arguing effectively with people you care strongly about? Do you avoid these kinds of arguments? If so, why?

1. Look at the opinions section of your local newspaper. Pick an issue that is being discussed in the editorials, commentaries, or letters to the editor. On your screen or a piece of paper, list the positions and the kinds of support offered by one of the writers. Then list the points opponents might make to counter these positions and support their own opinions. In a memo to your professor, explain both sides of the argument as fairly as possible. Then show why you think one side or the other has the stronger argument.

2. Find an argument or similar document on the Internet. You might look for these arguments in the online versions of newspapers or magazines. In a two-page memo to your professor, analyze the argument and explain whether you think the author is arguing effectively or not. Did the author fairly represent both sides of the issue? Is the author too biased, or does he or she neglect any strengths of the opponents' position or limitations of his or her own position?

3. Pick a topic that you feel strongly about. Create a two-column brainstorming list that explores the issues involved with this topic. Then identify the two to five main points of contention that separate you from someone who disagrees with you about this topic. In a one-page memo to your professor, discuss the strengths and limitations of your side of the issue and your opponents'. Explain what kinds of information you would need to collect to support your best arguments and highlight the limitations of your opponents' views.

Working with one or two of the microgenres listed below can be fun and instructive about arguments generally. If you are working in a group, write just the introduction and conclusion and report back to the class. If you are doing an informal writing assignment, include a memo to your professor that describes how the microgenre differs from the basic argument.

Mock Argument—a parody that pretends to argue seriously about a silly (or nonarguable) issue

Argumentum Ad Absurdum—an argument taken to ridiculous extremes

Devil's Advocate—argument for the side you disagree with

Debate Dialogue—imagined dialogue between two people on opposite sides of an issue

Letter of Recommendation—argument about the qualifications of someone for a certain position

1. **Write an argument about a local issue.** Write a five-page argument in which you explore both sides of a contentious local issue. Pick an issue that affects you directly and try to fairly represent both sides of the issue. Explain opposing sides of the issue as clearly and fairly as possible. Then point out their limitations. Explain your side of the issue and concede any limitations of your side. Then persuade your readers that your understanding of the issue is stronger and more reasonable than your opponents' understanding.

2. **Create a multimedia presentation.** Illegal downloading of music has been an important issue on college campuses recently. Some students are being sued by the music industry, and they are being forced to pay thousands of dollars in damages and fines. Create a ten-slide presentation in which you state your opinion about downloading music "illegally" off the Internet. Explain how people with opposing perspectives understand the issue. Then explain your side and show why you think your understanding is stronger. Your presentation could be made with *PowerPoint*, *Keynote*, or any other presentation software. Try adding photographs, charts, video, and audio, where appropriate.

3. **Argue that something bad for people is really good for them.** In a five-page argument, make and support the claim that something people traditionally assume is "bad" (e.g., playing video games, being overweight, seeing violence in movies, watching television, cramming for an exam) is actually good. Summarize the conventional assumptions about why something is bad. Then use research to show that it is actually good for people.

For support in meeting this chapter's objectives, follow this path in MyCompLab: Resources ⟹ Writing ⟹ Writing Purposes ⟹ Writing to Argue or Persuade. Review the Instruction and Multimedia resources about writing to argue or persuade, then complete the Exercises and click on Gradebook to measure your progress.

11

Proposals

In this chapter, you will learn how to—

- use proposals to invent your ideas and explain them clearly and persuasively to your readers.
- analyze problems in terms of their causes and effects.
- synthesize your ideas into well-defined and workable plans.

People write proposals to explore problems and offer plans for solving those problems. In your advanced college courses, your professors will ask you to write proposals that explain how to improve your community or that describe research projects you want to do. In the workplace, proposals are used to develop new strategies, take advantage of new opportunities, and pitch new projects and products.

The aim of a proposal is to help readers understand the *causes* and *effects* of a problem and to persuade them that your step-by-step plan offers the best solution for that problem. Your readers will expect your proposal to be clearly written and persuasive. They expect you to try to win them over with strong reasoning, good examples, and appropriate appeals to authority and emotion.

In college, proposals are growing more popular, because advanced courses are becoming more team-oriented and project-centered. Your professors may put you into teams and ask you to write proposals that describe the projects you want to pursue.

In today's workplace, the proposal is one of the most common genres. Anytime someone wants to solve a problem or present new ideas, he or she will be asked to "write the proposal." *Internal proposals* are written for people inside a company or organization to pitch new ideas, with *external proposals* written for clients to sell a company's services. *Solicited proposals* respond to "Requests for Proposals" (RFPs). *Grant proposals* are used by researchers and not-for-profit groups to obtain funding for their projects.

Proposals

This diagram shows a basic organization for a proposal, but other arrangements of these sections will work, too. You should alter this organization to fit your topic, angle, purpose, readers, and context.

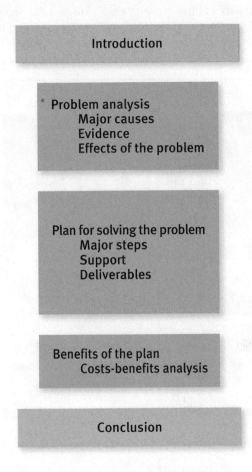

A proposal is one of the more complicated genres you will be asked to write. Here are a proposal's typical features:

- **An introduction** that defines a problem, stresses its importance, and offers a brief description of the proposed solution (the thesis).
- **An analysis** of the problem, discussing its causes, and its effects.
- **A detailed plan** that shows step by step how to solve the problem.
- **A costs-benefits analysis** that measures the benefits of the plan against its costs.
- **A conclusion** that looks to the future and stresses the importance of taking action.

ONE STUDENT GROUP'S WORK
Proposals

This proposal was written by Matthew Steele and the Associated Students of the University of Washington (Seattle Campus). Responding to a request for proposals (RFP) soliciting proposals for replacing an underused café space, they propose a new food-services facility that offers healthy and local alternatives.

Descriptive title tells readers what the proposal is about.

Descriptive headers and table of contents help readers see the big picture.

Color and images attract readers' attention.

The purpose of the proposal is stated here.

Introduction defines the topic and links it to larger campus issues.

SCC Café Proposal

Spring 2010

Proposed by the ASUW Food Cooperative Task-Force

Contents

Appendices

Executive Summary

The UW Student Food Cooperative proposes operating a food Café offering a local, healthy, and affordable menu in the former SCC café space. The need for food service was identified as a significant concern of students in a 2006 report created by a taskforce of health sciences administrators and students. The low traffic that the building currently receives makes a food enterprise difficult to financially sustain. However, the co-op caters to a niche market and thus has magnet market qualities that will be able to pull traffic to the site.

We believe this niche market makes the co-op uniquely able to sustain itself in that space. Furthermore, the food co-op has similar goals as those stated by the School of Public Health and its department of Nutritional Sciences. The co-op will support the SCC as a hub for health and food interests, both for its students and staff and the campus at large. The enterprise will provide healthy, sustainable, and affordable eating options while utilizing student participation and creating opportunities for collaboration, education, and leadership.

1

SCC Café Proposal   Spring 2010

Background

The South Campus Center (SCC) was originally built by funds from UW students in the 1970s. Generally its use has waned in recent years and since 2004 both the Café space and the industrial kitchen have not been operating. Traffic for food service was absorbed by the creation of the Rotunda in the main Health Sciences building. Due to its under-use by the student body at large, daily operational responsibilities will appropriately transfer to Health Sciences Administration on July 1st, 2010.

The idea of the food co-op has developed out of the growing excitement and interest in food issues on campus evidenced by the proliferation of food-related curriculum and public events on campus, the influx of applications for the graduate department of Nutritional Sciences, and the envisioning of an interdisciplinary program collaborating across the fields of Anthropology, Public Health, Biology, Geography, the Program on the Environment, Urban Horticulture and Urban Planning. Campus activities around food have also expanded, for example, the UW Farm has grown substantially over the last few years to a community of over 400 students with various projects constantly underway. Due to the student interest in urban agriculture, the UW Farm is poised to expand to a full acre plot on campus.

The food co-op will be supported by students and their concern for issues of health, environmental degradation, loss of biodiversity, and exploitation of workers' rights implicated by large-scale industrial farming practices, the corporate dominance of food choices, and the far-flung transportation of food. As a solution to these issues, the café will source organic food exclusively from local farmers and producers, including the UW farm. The café 's commitment to sustainability, which will be extended to include waste recycling practices, will create awareness of issues surrounding the food system at every level. Student demand for healthy and sustainable options is overwhelming. Recently, café s with comprehensive approaches to healthy food and sustainability have opened and enjoyed overwhelming success like the vegetarian café Chaco Canyon on 50th and 12th and Thrive raw food café in Ravenna. UW students, especially those in residence halls who are required to purchase HFS meal plans, suffer from the lack of organic, vegetarian, and vegan food options. Currently, healthy on-campus venues that accept husky cards are limited.

In January 2010, the Associated Students of the University of Washington (ASUW) formed a taskforce to research the formation of a food co-op, similar to the entities that exist at University of British Columbia, University of California Berkeley, Evergreen State College, Puget Sound University, and many other universities around the United States. The ASUW Food Co-op Taskforce's conclusion is that the former SCC café space would meet the need for food service by students, draw more foot traffic to the area, and provide local, healthy, affordable food.

Problem Statement

In 2006 a taskforce of university administrators and students produced a report for Provost Phyllis Wyse on the current and potential Health Sciences uses of the South Campus Center (SCC). The specific conclusions of 2006 SCC Taskforce Report were that "food service, at least on a small scale, was a major priority and would be needed in order to revitalize the usage of the SCC." Specifically, they recommended a "small specialty food service that would offer something different such as an emphasis on a healthy menu." In addition, they wanted to fully utilize the beautiful views of Portage Bay. Based on a student survey the taskforce sent, 70.7% of the comments were related to the availability of food service in the building. In particular, specific comments from the students expressed their desire for food options that were healthy, local, affordable, and provided an alternative to what is currently offered at the Rotunda. The closure of the newspaper and candy stand on June 18, 2010 will further limit the food options in the SCC and make the concern of providing healthy, affordable food in SCC more pressing. Though the transfer of the building to Health Sciences Administration will more fully utilize the space, the lack of food traffic and food service will persist until another food provider is identified.

The background explains the current situation.

The benefits of implementing the plan are described up front.

The problem and its causes are described.

Proposed Solution

Opening for plan section.

Based on findings of the 2006 SCC taskforce, the reopening of the SCC Café space would help to address the lack of alternative and affordable food choices. A food cooperative would provide excellent food service to the SCC, while catering to a growing niche market of those concerned with nutrition, sustainability, affordability, and democratic business structures. The opening of a Café focused on these priorities and values will attract a community of conscientious eaters and will bring additional foot traffic to the SCC as well as spread awareness of food-related topics.

The benefits are discussed at the end of the plan.

Spring 2010 Food Survey - Conducted by ASUW Food Cooperative Task-Force

(1250 total students surveyed)

20% of students responded: *"I can't get food on campus that meets my dietary preferences – I eat off campus or pack food"*

35% of students responded: *"I'd like to eat more local and organic produce, but am limited by budget"*

18% of students *identified as vegetarian (almost 100% of diet), 13% identified vegan food as at least a large portion of their diet*

53% of students *expressed interest in participating in working for the Co-op, in exchange for meal credits.*

Intro on the Food Co-op

UW students are following the models of prominent universities across the nation in creating a student food cooperative whose purpose is to achieve food sovereignty on campus and address food justice issues through the affordable provision of healthy and organic high-quality prepared foods that are locally sourced and sustainably grown and produced, possibly right on the UW campus. The UW Farm is currently undergoing major visioning and administrative partnering as it embarks on an expansion to an acre of land on the campus. If their current production capabilities are any indicator of what they will be able to do with that acre, they will be a major producer of food for students in years to come. Working directly with the UW Farm, the idea is to create a localized food system where students can gain an understanding of not only what real food is, but also where it comes from. In addition to sourcing locally and establishing partnerships with the UW Farm, the student-run food co-op will further create a localized and contextualized food system on campus through projects such as a bulk-buying club, a CSA program, and the operation of the cooperative for food credit.

We are seeking a collaborative partnership with the department of Nutritional Sciences. The Nutritional Sciences wants to expand their undergraduate program and the number of classes offered and students served. A Student Food Co-op will aid in these efforts. Specifically, the department of Nutritional Sciences will repurpose the SCC commercial kitchen into a gastronomy teaching laboratory.

The cooperative could prove instrumental to engage students in the cooking classes that the department hopes to conduct and be involved in the activities occurring there. The food co-op will link Nutritional Sciences and all the Health Sciences Schools with the sustainability movement at this university.

How a Student-Run Food Cooperative Addresses These Problems

The 2006 SCC taskforce specifically identified "the need to provide a magnet use in the SCC that will bring students to the facility." As previously mentioned, interest in food issues as it relates to urban agriculture, social and food justice, environmentalism, and alternative agrifood movements are quickly building momentum on campus. Thus, by addressing popular food-related issues on campus, the cooperative can be a magnet for student activity and presence along with the repurposing the building to teaching spaces and student lounge/study areas. This emphasis, in addition to providing students with healthy and affordable food and an extraordinary, waterfront study and meeting space, will meet the goal from the 2006 Task Force report that a unique Café will be able to pull traffic past the Rotunda and E Court Café. Our plans will revitalize the SCC space, while functioning largely with the existing plans for the building.

3

SCC Café Proposal   Spring 2010

Vision for Café Space

We envision a hub for community building and a place to engender a culture of sustainability. Our objective is to establish a food node in the South Campus region where the UW Farm is poised to expand their operations. The Café could also serve as a gallery space to showcase the work of local artists from the UW community and beyond. We can work in collaboration with Parnassus Café and Gallery in the UW School of Art to identify artists. Community bulletin boards in the Café will serve as a central information resource for housing notices, skill-sharing opportunities, and promotional material for student and community events.

We propose to offer local, sustainable, organic food sourced from the UW Farm and local producers at affordable prices for the entire UW community.

See Appendix A for the design of the Café space.

Students expressed the most interest in *Healthy Snack Food Alternatives*: homemade energy bars, fresh produce, dips, nuts, natural juices, etc.

> Authors look ahead to the next phase of the project.

> The use of color draws readers' attention to these graphics.

Sample Menu

Sandwich Options:
Curry tofu salad (vegan)
Egg, green onion, avocado & greens
Roasted vegetables & cheese
Artichoke Melts

Soups (all vegan):
Bean, pea, or lentil Stews
Pureed roasted vegetables
Raw vegetable purees & avocado

Salads:
Seasonal greens with lemon-tahini, balsamic, or apple vinaigrette
Wheatberry salad with dried fruit, toasted nuts & roasted squash
Farro salad with roasted vegetables & lemon dressing

Fresh Juices Made From:
Kale, spinach, beets, carrots, celery, garlic, cucumber, ginger, apples, pears, berries, seasonal fruit

Snacks:
Homemade energy bars
Crackers, flat breads, spreads & cheeses
Fresh produce
Roasted nuts & dried fruit

Stumptown Coffee
Direct-exchange, organic drip coffee
Assorted Teas

all ingredients will be organic and locally sourced whenever possible!

Recommendation

- To operate a student run food cooperative within the former SCC café space.

4

SCC Café Proposal · Spring 2010

Appendix A: Floor Plan for SCC Café Space

UW Student Food Cooperative Cafe Floor Plan

prep. counter · sink · freezer

espresso stand · smothie tray blender · register · front counter · deli/ veggies/ fruit display · kitchen · freezer · freezer

produce stand/ bulk bins · community pantry

SCC Café Proposal · Spring 2010

Appendix D: Health Sciences Student Petition

To All UW Students and Faculty,

Do you want to have more control in what food choices are available to you on the UW campus or in the University District? Do you care about having an idea of where and how your food was grown or raised? Do you want to see alternative yet affordable food options that align with your values, be they environmental sustainability, farm worker and animal rights, or community development UW students are following prominent universities (like Berkeley, Evergreen, and UBC) in creating a student food cooperative whose purpose is to address food justice issues and achieve a level of sovereignty over their food system.

The idea of the Food Co-op is to not just create another café, but to build a community space where people can prepare foods together, learn about canning and preserving foods, purchase bulk goods, and pick up affordable, healthy snacks and meals on the go!

If you are hungry for change, please sign our petition!

Statement of Support for the UW Student Food Cooperative:

I support the University of Washington students organizing for a campus food cooperative and find their presence on campus to be in alignment with my own personal values. The co-op will introduce students to the importance of sustainable food production and provide alternative food options to students who care about environmental sustainability, strengthening our local food economy, and supporting social justice. Further, the Co-op has the potential to create greater self-sufficiency and sustainability within our local food system.

This project will run through the ASUW as a student enterprise. I give the UW Student Food Coop my full support for building a campus cafe and food cart to provide students with alternative yet affordable food options and for building a greater sense of community on campus through food.

*131 Student Signatures collected, listed bellow

Inventing Your Proposal's Content

When writing a proposal, your first challenge is to fully understand the problem you are trying to solve. Then you can come up with a plan for solving it.

Inquiring: Defining the Problem

You should start out by figuring out the boundaries of your topic and what you want to achieve with your proposal.

State Your Proposal's Purpose. A good first step is to state the purpose of your proposal in one sentence. A clear statement of your purpose will help you focus your research and save you time.

> The purpose of this proposal is to show how college students can help fight global climate change.

Narrow Your Topic and Purpose. Make sure you aren't trying to solve a problem that is too big. Look at your purpose statement again. Can you narrow the topic to something more manageable? Specifically, can you take a local approach to your subject by discussing how the problem affects people where you live or in your state? Can you talk about your topic in terms of recent events?

> The purpose of this proposal is to show how our campus can significantly reduce its greenhouse gas emissions, which are partly responsible for global climate change.

Find Your Angle. Figure out what might be unique or different about how you would approach the problem. What is your new angle?

> We believe attempts to conserve energy offer a good start toward cutting greenhouse emissions, but these effects will only take us part of the way. The only way to fully eliminate greenhouse gas emissions here on campus is to develop new sources of clean, renewable energy.

Inquiring: Analyzing the Problem

Now you need to identify and analyze the major causes of the problem, so you can explain them to your readers.

Identify the Major and Minor Causes of the Problem. A good way to analyze a problem is to use a concept map to determine what you already know about the causes of the problem. To create a concept map, put the problem you are analyzing in the middle of your screen or a sheet of paper. Then write the two to five major causes of that problem around it (Figure 11.1, page 232).

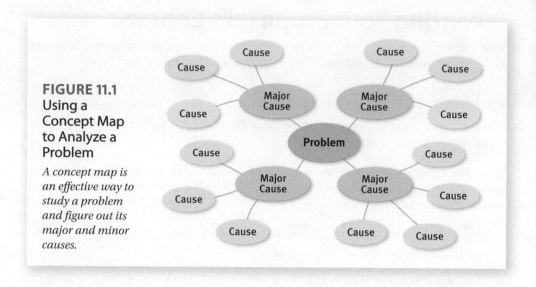

FIGURE 11.1 Using a Concept Map to Analyze a Problem

A concept map is an effective way to study a problem and figure out its major and minor causes.

Keep Asking "What Changed?"   As you explore the problem's major causes, keep asking yourself, "What has changed to create this problem?" If you pay attention to the things that are changing about your topic, you will find it easier to identify what is causing the problem itself.

Analyze the Major and Minor Causes.   Once you have identified two to five major causes, find the minor causes that are causing them. Ask yourself, "What are the two to five minor causes of each major cause? What has changed recently that created each of the major causes or made them worse?" Figure 11.1 shows how a concept map can illustrate both major and minor causes, allowing you to develop a comprehensive analysis of the problem.

Researching: Gathering Information and Sources

Your concept map will give you a good start, but you are going to need to do some solid research on your topic. When doing research, you need to collect information from a variety of sources. You should "triangulate" your research by drawing material from online, print, and empirical sources.

Online Sources.   Choose some keywords from your concept map, and use Internet search engines to gather background information on your topic. Pay special attention to Web sites that identify the causes of the problem you are exploring. Also, look for documentaries, podcasts, or broadcasts on your subject. You might find some good sources on *YouTube, Hulu,* or the Web sites of television networks.

Print Sources.   Your best print sources will usually be newspapers and magazine articles, because most proposals are written about current or local problems. You can run keyword searches in newspaper and magazine archives on the Internet, or you can use the *Readers' Guide* at your library to locate magazine sources. On your library's Web site, you might also use research indexes to find articles in academic journals. These articles tend to offer more empirically grounded discussions of issues.

Empirical Sources. Set up interviews, do field observations, or survey people to gather empirical evidence that supports or challenges your online and print sources. Someone on your campus, perhaps a professor or a staff member, probably knows a great amount about the topic you have chosen to study. So send that person an e-mail to set up an interview. If you aren't sure who might know something about your topic, call over to the department that seems closest to your topic.

As always, you should use a combination of online, print, and empirical sources to gather information. Solid research is the backbone of any proposal. If you don't fully research and understand the problem, you will not be able to come up with a good solution. So give yourself plenty of time to gather and triangulate your sources.

Inquiring: Planning to Solve the Problem

With your preliminary research finished, you are now ready to start developing a plan to solve the problem. A plan is a step-by-step strategy for getting something done. Essentially, when writing a plan, you are telling your readers, "If we take these steps, we will solve the problem I just described to you."

Map Out Your Plan. Again, a concept map is a useful tool for figuring out your plan. Start out by putting your best solution in the middle of your screen or a piece of paper. Then ask yourself, "What are the two to five major steps we need to take to achieve this goal?" Write those major steps around your solution and connect them to it with lines (Figure 11.2, page 234).

Explore Each Major Step. Now, consider each of the major steps one at a time. Ask yourself, "What are the two to five steps we need to take to achieve each of these major steps?" For example, if one of your major steps is "develop alternative sources of energy," what steps would your university need to take to do that?

1. The university might look for grants or donations to help it do research on converting its campus to renewable energy sources like wind power or solar energy.

2. The university might explore ways to replace the inefficient heating systems in campus buildings with geothermal heating and cooling systems.

3. The university might convert its current fleet of buses and service vehicles to biodiesel or plug-in hybrids.

Each major step can be broken down further into minor steps that offer more detail.

Figure Out the Costs and Benefits of Your Plan. With your plan mapped out, you should now identify its costs and benefits. Essentially, your goal is to determine

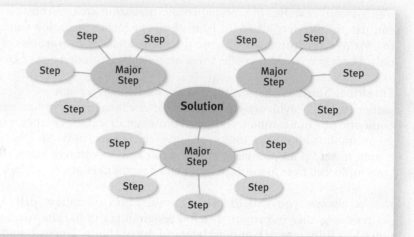

FIGURE 11.2 Using a Concept Map to Develop a Plan

A concept map is one of the most useful tools available for planning. It will help you figure out the steps needed to solve the problem.

whether the benefits of your plan outweigh the costs. After all, nothing is free. So someone, probably your readers, will need to give up something (like money) to put your plan into action. You want to prove to your readers that the benefits are worth the costs. When figuring out the costs and benefits, brainstorming is an especially helpful tool. You can use it to list all the costs of your plan and then use it to list all the benefits (Figure 11.3).

Researching: Find Similar Projects

Now that you have developed your plan, do some more research. Again, you should gather information from online, print, and empirical sources. This time, though, look for projects similar to the one you are proposing.

Of course, you don't want to copy their solution—their plan probably won't work for your situation anyway—but you might learn what others have tried before, what has worked, and what hasn't worked.

As you do your research, also try to find sources that will help you fill out and support your plan. More than likely, your research is going to uncover new strategies and complications that you would not have thought of yourself. Incorporate those strategies into your own plan, and try to come up with ways to work around the complications. Always make sure you keep track of your sources, so you can cite them in your proposal.

Organizing and Drafting Your Proposal

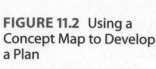

Watch the Animation on **Organizing Proposals** at **mycomplab.com**

Organizing and drafting a large document like a proposal can be challenging, but here is where your hard work doing inquiry and research will finally pay off. The best way to draft a proposal is to write each of its major sections separately. Draft each major section as though it is a small argument on its own.

Benefits of My Plan to Make Our Campus
Carbon Neutral

Help save humanity from apocalyptic end (!)

Reduce this university's dependence on foreign oil

Help clean up local air, water, and soil

Widely distributed power sources, which will make us less
vulnerable to energy system failures

Not contribute to ecological destruction involved with mining
coal and drilling for oil

Help create more local jobs for a "green economy"

Millions of dollars in energy savings, starting in 10 years

Be ahead of energy policy changes that are coming anyway

Make our campus modern and forward thinking, which is
attractive to top students

Costs of My Plan

Transformation costs will be high, perhaps
even $100 million

University will need to invest in energy
research and training

Need to retrain current power plant
employees

University will need to stress energy
conservation as system evolves

FIGURE 11.3 Costs and Benefits of Your Plan

Brainstorming can help you list the costs and benefits of your plan. Your goal is to show your readers that the benefits of your plan outweigh the costs.

The Introduction

An introduction to a proposal will typically make up to five moves, which can be made in just about any order:

State the topic. Tell your readers what the proposal is about.

State the purpose. State the purpose of your proposal in one or two sentences.

Provide background information. Give readers just enough historical information to understand your topic.

Stress the importance of the topic to the readers. Tell readers why they should care about this topic.

State your main point (thesis). Offer a straightforward statement that summarizes your plan and explains why your plan will succeed.

Weak: We think Hanson Gym should be open for longer hours.

Stronger: We propose keeping Hanson Gym open 24 hours a day, so students can work off stress, stay fit, and have a safe, beneficial place to socialize at night.

Heading

Section opening that states and defines the problem

Discussion of major cause 1

Discussion of major cause 2

•
•
•

Discussion of the effects of the problem

Heading

Section opening that states and defines the problem

Discussion of major cause 1 and its effects

Discussion of major cause 2 and its effects

•
•
•

Closing that stresses the importance of solving the problem

FIGURE 11.4 Drafting the Problem Section

An effective analysis of the problem will discuss its causes and effects. Make sure you offer good support for your statements. Here are two possible ways to organize this section of the proposal.

In the introduction to a proposal, you should almost always state your topic, purpose, and main point (thesis). The other two moves are optional, but they become more important and necessary in larger proposals.

Description of the Problem, Its Causes, and Its Effects

You should now describe and analyze the problem for your readers, showing them its causes and effects. Look at your concept map and your research notes to identify the two to five major causes of the problem. Then draft this section of the proposal around those causes (Figure 11.4).

Opening Paragraph. Use the opening paragraph to clearly describe the problem and perhaps stress its importance.

> The problem we face is that our campus is overly dependent on energy from the Anderson Power Facility, a 20-megawatt coal-fired plant on the east side of campus that belches out many tons of carbon dioxide each year. At this point, we have no alternative energy source, and our backup source of energy is the Bentonville Power Plant, another coal-fired plant 50 miles away. This dependence on the Anderson Plant causes our campus's carbon footprint to be large, and it leaves us vulnerable to power shortages and rising energy costs.

Body Paragraphs. Explain the causes of the problem, providing plenty of support for your claims. Here is an example discussion of one cause among a few others that the writers want to include.

The primary reason the campus is so reliant on coal-fired energy is the era when the campus was built. Our campus is like many others in the United States. The basic infrastructure and many of the buildings were built in the early twentieth century when coal was cheap and no one could have anticipated problems like global warming. A coal-fired plant, like the one on the east side of campus, seemed like the logical choice. As our campus has grown, our energy needs have increased exponentially. Now, on any given day, the campus needs anywhere from 12 to 22 megawatts to keep running (Campus Energy Report, 22).

Closing Paragraph. You might consider closing this section with a discussion or summary of the effects of the problem if no action is taken. In most cases, problems grow worse over time, so you want to show readers what will happen if they choose not to do anything.

Our dependence on fossil fuels for energy on this campus will begin to cost us more and more as the United States and the global community are forced to address global climate change. More than likely, coal-fired plants like ours will need to be completely replaced or refitted with expensive carbon capture equipment (Gathers, 12). Also, federal and state governments will likely begin putting a "carbon tax" on emitters of carbon dioxide to encourage conservation and conversion to alternative energy. These costs could run our university many millions of dollars. Moreover, the costs to our health cannot be overlooked. Coal-fired plants, like ours, put particulates, mercury, and sulfur dioxide into the air that we breathe (Vonn, 65). The costs of our current coal-fired plant may seem hidden now, but they will eventually bleed our campus of funds and continue to harm our health.

Figure 11.4 shows two of the more common patterns for the Problem section, but other patterns will work, too. You can use whichever pattern helps you best explain the causes and effects of the problem to your readers.

Description of Your Plan

Draft the Plan section next. In this section, you want to describe step by step how the problem can be solved (Figure 11.5, page 238). The key to success in this section is to tell your readers *how* you would solve the problem and *why* you would do it this way.

Opening Paragraph. The opening paragraph of this section should be brief. Tell the readers your solution and give them a good reason why it is the best approach to the problem. Give your plan a name that is memorable and meaningful. For example:

The best way to make meaningful cuts in greenhouse gas emissions on our campus would be to replace our current coal-fired power plant with a 12-turbine wind farm and install solar panels on all campus buildings. The "Cool Campus Project" would cut greenhouse gas emissions by half within ten years, and we could eliminate all greenhouse emissions within twenty years.

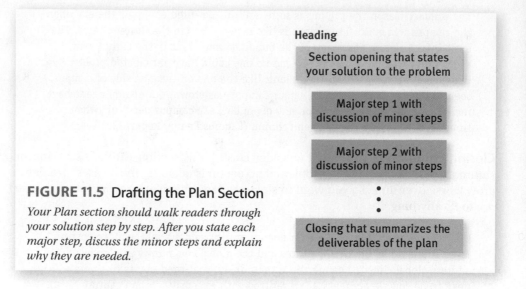

FIGURE 11.5 Drafting the Plan Section

Your Plan section should walk readers through your solution step by step. After you state each major step, discuss the minor steps and explain why they are needed.

Body Paragraphs. The body paragraphs for this section should then tell the readers step by step how you would carry out your plan. Usually, each paragraph will start out by stating a major step.

Step Three: Install a 12-Turbine Wind Farm at the Experimental Farm

The majority of the university's electricity needs would be met by installing a 12-turbine wind farm that would generate 18 megawatts of energy per day. The best place for this wind farm would be at the university's Experimental Farm, which is two miles west of campus. The university already owns this property, and the area is known for its constant wind. An added advantage to placing a wind farm at this location is that the Agriculture Department could continue to use the land as an experimental farm. The turbines would be operating above the farm, and the land would still be available for planting crops.

Closing Paragraph. In the closing paragraph of this section, you should summarize the *deliverables* of the plan. Deliverables are the things you will deliver to the readers when the project is completed:

When the Cool Campus Project is completed, the university will be powered by a 12-turbine wind farm and an array of solar panels mounted on campus buildings. This combination of wind and solar energy will generate the 20 megawatts needed by campus on regular days, and it should be able to satisfy the 25 megawatts needed on peak usage days.

Don't get locked into the pattern shown in Figure 11.5. You might find other, more effective patterns for describing your plan, depending on the solution you are proposing.

Discussing the Costs and Benefits of Your Plan

A good way to round out your argument is to discuss the costs and benefits of your plan. You want to show readers the two to five major benefits of your plan and then argue that these benefits outweigh the costs.

> In the long run, the benefits of the Cool Campus Project will greatly outweigh the costs. The major benefits of converting to wind and solar energy include—
>
> - A savings of $1.2 million in energy costs each year once the investment is paid off.
> - The avoidance of millions of dollars in refitting costs and carbon tax costs associated with our current coal-fired plant.
> - The improvement of our health due to the reduction of particulates, mercury, and sulfur dioxide in our local environment.
> - A great way to show that this university is environmentally progressive, thus attracting students and faculty who care about the environment.
>
> We estimate the costs of the Cool Campus Project will be approximately $20 million, much of which can be offset with government grants. Keep in mind, though, that our coal-fired plant will need to be refitted or replaced soon anyway, which would cost millions. So the costs of the Cool Campus Project would likely be recouped within a decade.

Costs do not always involve money, or money alone. Sometimes, the costs of the plan will be measured in effort or time.

The Conclusion

Your proposal's conclusion should be brief and to the point. By now, you have told the readers everything they need to know, so you just need to wrap up and leave your readers in a position to say yes to your plan. Here are a few moves you might consider making in your conclusion:

Restate your main point (thesis). Again, tell the readers what you wanted to prove in your proposal. Your main point (thesis) first appeared in the introduction. Now bring the readers back around to it, showing that you proved your argument.

Restress the importance of the topic. Briefly, tell the readers why this topic is important. You want to leave them with the sense that this issue needs to be addressed as soon as possible.

Look to the future. Proposal writers often like to leave readers with a description of a better future. A "look to the future" should only run a few sentences or a brief paragraph.

Offer contact information. Tell readers who to contact and how to contact that person if they have questions, want more information, or are interested in discussing the proposal.

Your conclusion should not be more than a couple brief paragraphs, even in a large proposal. The goal of your conclusion is to wrap up quickly.

Choosing an Appropriate Style

Proposals are persuasive documents by nature, so your style should be convincing to match your proposal's content. In Chapter 16, "Choosing a Style," you can learn about how to use persuasive style techniques. For now, here are some easy strategies that will make your proposal sound more convincing:

Create an Authoritative Tone. Pick a tone that expresses a sense of authority. Then create a concept map around it (Figure 11.6). You should weave these terms from your concept map into your proposal, creating a theme that sets the desired tone.

Use Metaphors and Similes. Metaphors and similes allow you to compare new ideas to things that are familiar to your readers. For example, calling a coal-fired plant a "smoke-belching tailpipe" will make it sound especially unattractive to your readers, making them more inclined to agree with you. Or, you might use a metaphor

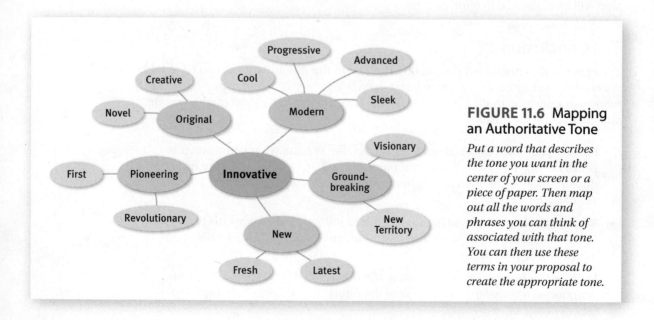

FIGURE 11.6 Mapping an Authoritative Tone

Put a word that describes the tone you want in the center of your screen or a piece of paper. Then map out all the words and phrases you can think of associated with that tone. You can then use these terms in your proposal to create the appropriate tone.

to discuss your wind turbines in terms of "farming" (e.g., harvesting the wind, planting wind turbines in a field, reaping the savings) because that will sound good to most people.

Pay Attention to Sentence Length. Proposals should generate excitement, especially at the moments when you are describing your plan and its benefits. To raise the heartbeat of your writing, shorten the sentences at these key places in your proposal. Elsewhere in the proposal, keep the sentences regular length (breathing length). See Chapter 16, "Choosing a Style," for more on sentence length and style.

Minimize the Jargon. Proposals can get somewhat technical, depending on the topic. So look for any jargon words that could be replaced with simpler words or phrases. If a jargon word is needed, make sure you define it for readers.

Designing Your Proposal

Your proposal needs to be attractive and easy to use, so leave yourself some time to design the document and include graphics. Good design will help your proposal stand out, while making it easy to read. Your readers will also appreciate graphics that enhance and support your message.

Create a Look. Figure out what image your proposal should project to the readers. Do you want your proposal to appear progressive or conservative? Do you want it to look exciting or traditional? Then make choices about fonts, columns, and photographs that reflect that design (Figure 11.7, page 242).

Use Meaningful Headings. When they first pick up your proposal, your readers will likely scan it before reading. So your headings need to be meaningful and action-oriented. Don't just use headings like "Problem" or "Plan." Instead, use headings like "Our Campus's Global Warming Problem" or "Introducing the Cool Campus Initiative."

Include Relevant, Accurate Graphics. Proposals often talk about trends, so you should look for places where you can use charts or graphs to illustrate those trends. Where possible, put data into tables. Use photographs to help you explain the problem or show examples of your solution.

Use Lists to Highlight Important Points. Look for places in your proposal where you list key ideas or other items. Then, where appropriate, put those ideas into bulleted lists that are more scannable for readers.

Create White Space. You might want to expand your margins to add some white space. Readers often like to take notes in the margins of proposals, so a little extra white space is useful. Also, extra white space makes the proposal seem more welcoming and easier to understand.

FIGURE 11.7
Setting a Proposal's Tone with Design

Your proposal shouldn't look boring. Instead, use design to create a tone for your proposal and make it easier to read. The photographs, bulleted lists, graphic icons, and color used in this proposal set a professional tone that gives the authors credibility and engages the readers.

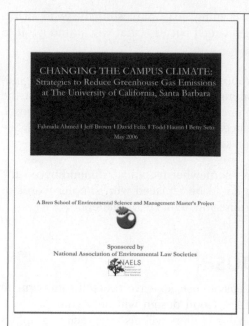
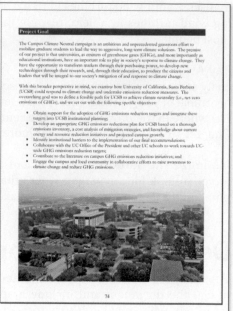

Revising and Editing Your Proposal

Proposals are often large, complex documents, so make sure you save time for revising and editing. Solid revision and careful editing will help you raise the quality of your document to a higher level.

Look for Inconsistencies in Content. As you drafted your proposal, your ideas about the topic probably evolved and changed as you learned more about it. So make sure your analysis of the problem matches up with your plan for solving it. In your Costs and Benefits section, make sure you have summarized the most important benefits mentioned in your plan and listed out the costs. Finally, your introduction and conclusion should be consistent with each other in both content and style.

Get Rid of the Extra Stuff. Look for places where you have included material that goes beyond the readers' need to know. It is always tempting to tell the readers everything you know about your topic, but they only need information that will help them make a decision. So cut out any extra information they probably don't need or want.

Tweak the Design. When the whole proposal is put together, look for places where the design is inconsistent or looks odd. Then make adjustments to get rid of those problems. Check the headings to make sure they are consistent. Look over the graphics to ensure that they are properly placed and easy to read.

Don't Forget to Proofread! Proofreading is always important, but it is essential for proposals. If your readers see misspellings and grammatical errors, they are going to doubt the soundness of your ideas. Even small problems like typos will sabotage your entire proposal. So read it through carefully, and have others look it over as well.

As you are editing your proposal, keep in mind that you are trying to persuade readers to trust you and your ideas. A professional, polished proposal will build their confidence in you and your ideas. Inconsistencies and small errors will undermine your whole argument.

The Pitch

Pitches are brief proposals made to people who can offer their support (usually money) for your ideas. Pitches tend to be about one minute long, which means you need to be focused, concise, and confident. You're promoting yourself as much as you are selling your idea.

Here are some good strategies for making a persuasive one-minute pitch:

Introduce yourself and establish your credibility.   Remember that people invest in other *people,* not in projects. So tell them *who* you are and *what* you do.

Grab them with a good story.   You need to capture your listeners' attention right away, so ask them, "What if _____?" or explain, "Recently, _____ happened and we knew there must be a better way."

Present your big idea in one sentence.   Don't make them wait. Hit them with your best idea up front in one sentence.

Give them your best two or three reasons for doing it.   The secret is to sell your idea, not explain it. List your best two or three reasons with minimal explanation.

Mention something that distinguishes you and your idea from the others.   What is unique about your idea? How does your idea uniquely fit your listeners' prior investments?

Offer a brief cost-benefits analysis.   Show them very briefly that your idea is worth their investment of time, energy, or money. If relevant, tell them what you need to make this project a reality

Make sure they remember you.   End your pitch by telling them something memorable about you or your organization. Make sure you put your contact information in their hand (e.g., a business card or résumé). If they allow it, leave them a written version of your pitch.

The pitch shown here was written by two Syracuse University students to promote their online game, graFighters.

WRITE your own pitch. Think of an original product, company, service, or idea that you can offer (please keep it PG-13). Then write a one-minute pitch that sells your idea to someone who can say yes and give you the resources to make it a reality.

Elevator Pitch: graFighters

Dave Chenell and Eric Cleckner

The first online fighting game for your hand-drawn characters is graFighters. Upload your drawings to the site, challenge your friends, and watch as they battle it out from any computer or mobile device.

The introduction identifies the product and states the big idea in a sentence

The idea for the game was spawned by the countless number of hours we spent drawing characters in our notebooks during class. At one point, we were sitting next to each other arguing about whose drawing would win in a fight. After wasting a healthy amount of class time on the discussion, we decided that it would be awesome if there were a way to let the characters decide for themselves. That moment is what inspired us to develop the game.

Here is a good story that readers can identify with.

What makes graFighters really different than any other fighting game is that you don't control your character during the fight. When you upload your drawing, the computer analyzes how that character has been drawn and then determines its strengths, weaknesses, and fighting style. The algorithm that makes all of these decisions is something we've code named "Cornelius."

These qualities distinguish the ideas from similar ideas.

So what we're trying to get across is that the most important part of the game happens with your pencil and paper. That's where your fights are really won or lost. Once you have uploaded your character to the site, your drawing has essentially become a living, breathing, fighting machine. At this point, the player's role has changed from creator to coach, setting up matches and determining what changes he or she could make to the fighter to develop it into a better warrior. In essence, we're letting players "Lose Control" (graFighters tag-line) in exchange for a more creative type of gameplay.

We are excited about creating a game with art and design right at the core of it. For us, it's all about the creativity. The game is played with your pencil and paper—the rest, everything that happens on the site, is the aftermath of your creation.

To date, with the help of our awesome team of programmers, we have been able to develop the game engine, which is the part that actually animates the characters and allows them to fight. We are also in the midst of refining the character uploading process. But the reason that we've reached out to the kickstarter community is because we need money to build "Cornelius," which truly is the most important part of the game.

continued

Elevator Pitch: graFighters (continued)

This website is a key part of the pitch for this new product.

Identifies what they need to make the project a reality.

We are asking for $20,000, all of which will go toward the development of "Cornelius." This algorithm is truly the most important part of graFighters. With it in place, we will be able to accurately portray your drawings in the game just as you have imagined them. This means that if your characters have the ability to fly and breathe fire, they will actually do that in-game. Or if you gave your character a double-barrelled shotgun, you can expect to see paper bullets wreaking havoc on your opponent.

The pitch ends with a request and a clever closing.

Please help us raise the money to build this algorithm. Drawings all over the world will be eternally grateful for your donation.

Here are some quick steps to get you working on your proposal.

IDENTIFY the Problem You Want to Solve

In one sentence, write down the topic and purpose of your proposal. Then narrow the topic to something you can manage.

ANALYZE the Problem's Causes and Effects

Use a concept map to analyze the problem's two to five major causes. Then use another concept map to explore the effects of the problem if nothing is done about it.

DO Your Research

Search the Internet and your library to collect sources. Then use empirical methods like interviews or surveys to help you support or challenge the facts you find.

DEVELOP Your Plan for Solving the Problem

Using a concept map, figure out the two to five major steps needed to solve the problem. Then figure out what minor steps will be needed to achieve each of these major steps.

FIGURE OUT the Costs and Benefits of Your Plan

Look at your Plan section closely. Identify any costs of your plan. Then list all the benefits of solving the problem your way. You want to make sure the benefits of your solution outweigh the costs.

DRAFT the Proposal

Try drafting each major section separately, treating each one like a small document on its own. Your introduction should include a main point or thesis statement that expresses your solution to the problem in a straightforward way.

DESIGN Your Proposal

Your proposal needs to look professional and easy to read. Make choices about fonts, graphics, and document design that best suit the materials you are presenting to your readers.

REVISE and Edit

Proposals are complicated documents, so you should leave plenty of time to revise and edit your work.

For True Reform, Athletics Scholarships Must Go

JOHN R. GERDY

In this proposal, Professor Gerdy argues that college athletics would be improved if athletic scholarships were based on need rather than athletic ability. This proposal does not exactly follow the organizational pattern described in this chapter; however, it is a good example of the proposal genre. Pay attention to the ways Gerdy adjusts the genre to fit the needs of his argument.

The president of the National Collegiate Athletics Association, Myles Brand, created a stir recently when he forcefully defended the NCAA's commercial efforts to raise revenues for its member institutions. "Commercialism per se" is not incompatible with the values of higher education, he contended in his 2006 "State of the Association" address. "It depends entirely on how the commercial activity is conducted."

Despite the outcry his comments generated among critics of college athletics, Brand is absolutely correct. If only he had stopped there.

Responding to those who think that "working too hard to generate revenue somehow taints the purity of college sports," Brand cried, "Nonsense! This type of thinking is both a misinterpretation and a misapplication of amateurism. 'Amateur' defines the participants, not the enterprise."

Talk about nonsense!

Division I scholarship athletes are pro- 5 fessionals — and to claim otherwise is to ignore reality.

Consider the essence of professional athletics: pay for play. Despite Brand's idealistic rhetoric, the contract between the college athlete and the institution no longer represents the "amateur" ideal of "pay (scholarship) for education" when it is plain to everyone — coaches, fans, faculty members, media, and especially the athletes — that they are on the campus, first and foremost, to play ball. That, by any definition, is "pay for play."

The professional model is also about paying whatever you must for coaches, staff members, facilities, scouting, travel, and anything else that coaches believe might make the difference between winning and losing, regardless of how outrageous or remote the actual impact. Professional sports is also about playing anywhere at anytime to reap television revenues. And professional athletics is about the expectation that athletes train year-round and sacrifice their bodies for "the program." In short, Division I athletics, as currently structured and conducted, operates on the same basic principles as professional sports teams.

Yet educational institutions have no business being in the business of professional sports. It is time to dismantle the professional model of college athletics and rebuild it in the image of an educational institution.

Specifically, the athletics scholarship must be eliminated in favor of institutional need-based aid. The athletics scholarship at its foundation is the biggest barrier to athletes' getting a genuine educational opportunity. When you are paid to play, regardless of the form of "payment," everything takes a back seat to athletic performance.

Calls to eliminate the athletics scholarship in favor of need-based aid are not new. In 1952 the Special Committee on Athletic Reform of the American Council on Education recommended that scholarships be awarded based solely on academic need rather than athletic ability. In 1989 the NCAA President's Commission proposed establishing a need-based system for all sports — with the exceptions of football and men's basketball and two women's sports selected by the institution. More recently, the faculty-led Drake Group suggested changing to a need-based aid system as part of its reform agenda. While some may interpret those failed attempts to adopt a need-based aid model as evidence that it will never pass, an alternative view would be that it is an idea whose time has simply yet to come. [10]

At first glance, it would appear that eliminating athletics scholarships in favor of a need-based formula would not be in the best interest of athletes. However, if judged on what is in their best interest for the next 50 years of their lives, rather than the four or five years they are on a campus, it becomes clear that eliminating the athletics grant will contribute significantly to athletes' chances of obtaining a well-balanced college experience.

An athletics scholarship represents a contractual agreement between the athlete and the coach. That contract allows coaches to view athletes as employees, bought and paid for by the athletics department, and has little to do with education and everything to do with athletic performance and control. If the athlete does not do what the coach wants, or fails to meet expectations on the field or court, he or she can be "fired."

A need-based financial aid agreement, however, is a contractual agreement between the student and the institution. Under such a contract, the student would continue to receive his or her financial aid regardless of what transpires on the athletics field. As a result, the student would be less beholden to the athletics department's competitive and business motives and freer to explore the wide diversity of experiences college offers. There is no more effective way to "empower" the athlete because it would fundamentally change the relationships among the athlete, the coach, and the institution.

Some argue that eliminating athletics scholarships would deny opportunity and limit access for many students, most notably black athletes. The question is, access to what? The fields of competition or an opportunity to earn a meaningful degree? With the six-year graduation rates of black basketball players hovering in the high 30-percent range, and black football players in the high 40-percent range, despite years of "academic reform," earning an athletics scholarship under the current system is little more than a chance to play sports.

A more likely result of the change would be that the black athletes would simply be replaced by other black athletes. While they might be a bit less talented and obsessed with athletics, they would probably be better students — or at least somewhat interested in academic achievement rather than simply using college as a springboard to the pros. What's the better lifelong deal: receiving need-based aid that leads to a meaningful degree, or receiving an athletics scholarship that provides an educational experience that is a sham? [15]

Another potential benefit of this change relates to the athletics culture on campus.

How much of an impact does receiving a scholarship, and all the benefits and special treatment that accompany it, have on an athlete's sense of entitlement? How much does it contribute not only to the isolation of the athlete and the team from the general student body, but also to the creation of a team culture that is often at odds with broader academic mores and behavioral expectations? Could it be that much of the deviant athlete behavior that has been revealed in recent scandals at the University of Colorado at Boulder in football and now, apparently, Duke University in lacrosse is in part the result of athletes' believing their status exempts them from the behavioral standards applied to other students? Dropping the athletics scholarship would help to recast the image of the athlete from the current hired mercenary of the gladiator class to simply a student who happens to be a good athlete.

Finally, the elimination of athletics scholarships would have a tremendous impact beyond the walls of academe. As a society, we have lost perspective regarding the role that sports should play in our schools, communities, and lives. For proof, one has only to read the daily newspaper to see how high-school and youth programs have become increasingly competitive: coaches scream at 7-year-olds for committing errors; parents and coaches push children to specialize in a sport at earlier and earlier ages; parents sue a coach because their child doesn't get enough playing time; parents attack Little League umpires or even fatally beat each other at a youth-hockey game. Far too many parents and youngsters believe sports, rather than education, is the ticket to future success. While moving to a need-based aid system may not completely change that myth, our educational institutions should have absolutely no part in perpetuating it.

Other aspects of the professional model must also be changed. College freshmen should not be eligible for varsity competition. Spring football and out-of-season practices should be eliminated, as should off-campus recruiting. Basketball and football coaching staffs should be cut in half. Seasons should be shortened, schedules reduced, and travel more restricted.

Such changes would significantly shrink the sizes, budgets, and campus influence of athletics departments. Yet if you operate a business where expenses outpace revenue and where revenue streams are almost tapped out, as is the case with athletics at most colleges and universities—how many more stadium boxes can you build, and how much more stadium signage can you sell? — there is only one way to become solvent: Cut expenses and overhead. Shrink the operation. Many college programs and departments have been downsized or shut down when it has become apparent that they fail to meet their purposes or are drains on institutional resources.

Although college presidents have worked [20] diligently to reform athletics, their efforts have failed to change the fundamental culture and operating principles surrounding Division I programs. Raising academic standards may result in a few more athletes' graduating, but history tells us that, more often, it simply heightens the bar for academic fraud, fosters a greater dependence on athletics-department tutoring services, creates pseudomajors to keep athletes eligible, and incites an arms race in the area of academic-support programs and facilities. Change that is more fundamental must occur.

That is not to say that intercollegiate athletics should be eliminated from higher education. To the contrary, the benefits and positive influence of university-sponsored athletics programs that are operated in a fiscally sound and academically responsible manner can be enormous. Even programs with commercial ties can advance an academic agenda and contribute to the institutional mission in meaningful ways.

Indeed, we must accept the notion that as long as we have athletics, commercialism will be a part of it. We must also recognize that the financing of American higher education is radically different from 20 years ago. Corporate-sponsored research, naming rights, and the commercialization of myriad other aspects of colleges' operations are increasingly common. And given a future economic outlook of increasing costs and declining revenues and state support, the pressure on institutions to set up partnerships with commercial entities to maintain academic excellence will only increase. Against that backdrop, the commercialism of athletics will look increasingly less radical and out of line with the financing of higher education in general.

In such an environment, athletics' potential to generate resources becomes more important. Thus, what's at issue is not whether athletics can or should be used as a commercial entity to advance institutional mission, but rather how to construct and operate the enterprise to maximize both its commercial and its educational values. The fundamental question regarding that challenge is whether the professional model, with its runaway costs, undermining of academic integrity, and win-at-all-cost culture, is the most effective way to achieve those ends.

Despite the growing evidence that the professional model is not, we continue to buy into the notion advanced by the athletics community that what makes college athletics commercially viable is the "level of play." That has led to a drive to mirror professional sports in training and playing, as well as in behavioral and management styles. It has been the athletics establishment's unyielding adherence to that notion of the "quality of the game," coupled with higher-education leaders' lack of courage to confront such claims, that is most responsible for the misguided professionalization and fiscal excesses of college athletics.

Little evidence, however, suggests that [25] changes such as those that I've recommended would have enough impact on the "quality of the game" to adversely affect the long-term entertainment value of the University of Florida, Pennsylvania State University, or the University of California at Los Angeles in the marketplace. The appeal of college athletics rests not only in how high the players jump, how fast they run, whether they participated in spring practice, or whether they are on an athletics scholarship. Rather, a big part of the commercial draw is that the activity is steeped in university tradition and linked to the higher purpose of education. Alabama-Auburn, Harvard-Yale, Michigan-Ohio State, and Oklahoma-Texas will always draw crowds, be covered by the media, and captivate the public's imagination, regardless of the level of play.

The key to a successful athletic-entertainment business is maintaining public confidence and interest. Public perception of your "brand," or what your business stands for, is critical. Like it or not, the current NCAA brand does not stand for students who are pursuing an education, but rather for pampered, mercenary athletes who have little interest in attending class and are using college as a vehicle to play in the pros. A poll released by the Knight Commission on Intercollegiate Athletics in January found that by a 2-to-1 margin, Americans believe that college sports are more like professional sports than amateur sports.

Most people want college athletics to stand for something other than turning a buck, preparing the next generation of professional stars, and winning at any cost. Deprofessionalizing the operation would actually increase college athletics' public and commercial appeal. Not only would its fan base hold steady and probably even expand, but corporate interest would also increase, as companies prefer to associate their products with positive and wholesome institutions.

The public would be more likely to continue to support college sports, or, for those who have become disengaged, to reconnect with them.

Realizing change of this magnitude, however, will be neither quick nor easy. It will require the courage and will of college and university leaders to make athletics look like and represent what they want.

Higher education has been at the reform game, with limited success, for decades. That does not mean that there has not been significant progress in building the foundation and critical mass that can serve as backdrop for significant change. Despite a rash of recent scandals that has led many to suggest that reform is a lost cause, upon closer examination, there are many signs that suggest, for the first time, that the table of reform may finally be set. The writer Malcolm Gladwell describes the one dramatic moment or event in a social movement when everything can change at once as the "tipping point," in his book of that title (Little, Brown, 2000). We may finally be approaching the tipping point for revolutionary change in college sports.

Over the past few years, we have been 30 treated to out-of-control coaches, several cases of academic fraud, and even a murder of a basketball player at Baylor University. Despite such discouraging examples, the third incarnation of the Knight Commission in 2003 represented the continuation of what has been a 24-year process of envisioning, articulating, building, and institutionalizing the structure necessary to support meaningful reform. This movement began in earnest in 1983 when the NCAA adopted a set of academic standards that significantly raised the bar for freshman eligibility.

The significance of the type and duration of the reform effort cannot be overemphasized. Reform of college athletics requires the building and coalescing of a critical mass of people, institutions, and organizations over an extended period of time to drive change. Besides the Knight Commission, other "outside" groups such as the Drake Group, the Coalition on Intercollegiate Athletics, and the Association of Governing Boards of Universities and Colleges have been pressing for it.

Further, the context in which college athletics operates has changed — and, in some ways, rather significantly. For example, not only has public pressure for reform increased, but Congress is beginning to look more critically at the business of college athletics. Title IX continues to exert pressure on athletics departments regarding how best to appropriate resources. Increasingly, research is beginning to paint a more critical picture of athletics' impact on institutional values and outcomes. And where 20 years ago, talk of institutional control and compliance was unheard of, a firmly entrenched and growing compliance community now works to instill a culture of accountability and integrity in intercollegiate athletics.

The situation is far different from the athletics cultures that existed during previous reform efforts. The seeds of reform that were advanced in the 1929 report on athletics of the Carnegie Foundation for the Advancement of Teaching, the "Sanity Code" (or "Principles for the Conduct of Intercollegiate Athletics") of 1946, and the ACE proposals of 1952 were strewn on a barren cultural landscape. Today that landscape is much more fertile for seeds of reform to take root. We may finally be on the verge of the intersection of people, institutions, and ideas, coupled with a series of changing contextual factors, needed to transform the role of sports in our educational institutions. As those forces coalesce, the time for systemic change has never been better. All that is needed is the initiative that begins the avalanche of change.

That initiative is the elimination of the athletics scholarship, which would provide American higher education the much-needed opportunity to recalibrate every aspect of its relationship with athletics. We must get beyond the fear that eliminating the athletics scholarship and the department of professional athletics will cause the entire enterprise to collapse. To the contrary, it will make it more educationally sound, more commercially viable, and thus more effective in contributing to larger university purposes.

A CLOSER LOOK AT
For True Reform, Athletics Scholarships Must Go

1. In this proposal, John Gerdy mentions several problems with today's athletic programs at Division I schools. List five of the major problems that he identifies. Why does he believe athletic scholarships are partly to blame for these problems?

2. Gerdy's main solution is to eliminate athletic scholarships and replace them with need-based scholarships. What are some of the benefits, according to him, of changing from scholarships based on athletic ability to scholarships based on need alone?

3. Based on what you have heard in the news and at your own campus, do you think the problems mentioned by Gerdy are widespread? Or, is he picking out a few cases that support his point, while most college athletic programs are credible?

IDEAS FOR
Writing

1. Write a two-page rebuttal to Gerdy's proposal in which you point out potential flaws in his argument. Do you think he is being too idealistic? Do you have a different way to solve the problem?

2. Choose a stand-out athlete who played for your university or another university. Write a two-page profile of that athlete that discusses his or her preparation for college competition, his or her athletic and academic career while at the university, and his or her career after leaving college. You may find that the most interesting subjects for your profile are athletes that did not go on to play professional sports.

3. Write a ten-page research report in which you explore the athletics program at your university or another university. Find out how athletes are recruited and what standards they need to meet to gain admission to the university. What kinds of athletic scholarships are available, and how many students receive scholarships? If possible, interview athletes, coaches, and others at the athletics department to find out what they think.

From Degrading to De-Grading

ALFIE KOHN

In this proposal, which was published in High School *magazine, Alfie Kohn first explains the problems with using grades to motivate students in high school. Then he describes how high schools could evaluate students in other ways. Kohn, an education reformer, has published numerous books, has been featured in a variety of magazines and newspapers, and has appeared on the* Oprah Winfrey Show.

You can tell a lot about a teacher's values and personality just by asking how he or she feels about giving grades. Some defend the practice, claiming that grades are necessary to "motivate" students. Many of these teachers actually seem to enjoy keeping intricate records of students' marks. Such teachers periodically warn students that they're "going to have to know this for the test" as a way of compelling them to pay attention or do the assigned readings—and they may even use surprise quizzes for that purpose, keeping their grade books at the ready.

Frankly, we ought to be worried for these teachers' students. In my experience, the most impressive teachers are those who despise the whole process of giving grades. Their aversion, as it turns out, is supported by solid evidence that raises questions about the very idea of traditional grading.

Three main effects of grading

Researchers have found three consistent effects of using—and especially, emphasizing the importance of—letter or number grades:

1. *Grades tend to reduce students' interest in the learning itself.* One of the most well-researched findings in the field of motivational psychology is that the more people are rewarded for doing something, the more they tend to lose interest in whatever they had to do to get the reward (Kohn, 1993). Thus, it shouldn't be surprising that when students are told they'll need to know something for a test—or, more generally, that something they're about to do will count for a grade—they are likely to come to view that task (or book or idea) as a chore.

While it's not impossible for a student to 5 be concerned about getting high marks and also to like what he or she is doing, the practical reality is that these two ways of thinking generally pull in opposite directions. Some research has explicitly demonstrated that a "grade orientation" and a "learning orientation" are inversely related (Beck et al., 1991; Milton et al., 1986). More strikingly, study after study has found that students—from elementary school to graduate school, and across cultures—demonstrate less interest in learning as a result of being graded (Benware and Deci, 1984; Butler, 1987; Butler and Nisan, 1986; Grolnick and Ryan, 1987; Harter and Guzman, 1986; Hughes et al., 1985; Kage, 1991; Salili et al., 1976). Thus, anyone who wants to see students get hooked on words and numbers and ideas already has reason to look for other ways of assessing and describing their achievement.

2. *Grades tend to reduce students' preference for challenging tasks.* Students of all ages who have been led to concentrate on getting a good grade are likely to pick the easiest possible assignment if given a choice (Harter, 1978; Harter and Guzman, 1986; Kage, 1991; Milton et al., 1986). The more pressure to get an A, the less inclination to truly challenge oneself. Thus, students who cut corners may not be lazy so much as rational; they are adapting to an environment where good grades, not intellectual exploration, are what count. They might well say to us, "Hey, you told me the point here is to bring up my GPA, to get on the honor roll. Well, I'm not stupid: the easier the assignment, the more likely that I can give you what you want. So don't blame me when I try to find the easiest thing to do and end up not learning anything."

3. *Grades tend to reduce the quality of students' thinking.* Given that students may lose interest in what they're learning as a result of grades, it makes sense that they're also apt to think less deeply. One series of studies, for example, found that students given numerical grades were significantly less creative than those who received qualitative feedback but no grades. The more the task required creative thinking, in fact, the worse the performance of students who knew they were going to be graded. Providing students with comments in addition to a grade didn't help: the highest achievement occurred only when comments were given instead of numerical scores (Butler, 1987; Butler, 1988; Butler and Nisan, 1986).

In another experiment, students told they would be graded on how well they learned a social studies lesson had more trouble understanding the main point of the text than did students who were told that no grades would be involved. Even on a measure of rote recall, the graded group remembered fewer facts a week later (Grolnick and Ryan, 1987). A brand-new study discovered that students who tended to think about current events in terms of what they'd need to know for a grade were less knowledgeable than their peers, even after taking other variables into account (Anderman and Johnston, 1998).

More Reasons to Just Say No to Grades

The preceding three results should be enough to cause any conscientious educator to rethink the practice of giving students grades. But as they say on late-night TV commercials, Wait—there's more.

4. *Grades aren't valid, reliable, or objective.* [10] A "B" in English says nothing about what a student can do, what she understands, where she needs help. Moreover, the basis for that grade is as subjective as the result is uninformative. A teacher can meticulously record scores for one test or assignment after another, eventually calculating averages down to a hundredth of a percentage point, but that doesn't change the arbitrariness of each of these individual marks. Even the score on a math test is largely a reflection of how the test was written: what skills the teacher decided to assess, what kinds of questions happened to be left out, and how many points each section was "worth."

Moreover, research has long been available to confirm what all of us know: any given assignment may well be given two different grades by two equally qualified teachers. It may even be given two different grades by a single teacher who reads it at two different times (for example, see some of the early research reviewed in Kirschenbaum et al., 1971). In short, what grades offer is spurious precision—a subjective rating masquerading as an objective evaluation.

5. *Grades distort the curriculum.* A school's use of letter or number grades may encourage what I like to call a "bunch o' facts" approach to instruction because that sort of learning is easier to score. The tail of assessment thus comes to wag the educational dog.

6. *Grades waste a lot of time that could be spent on learning.* Add up all the hours that teachers spend fussing with their grade books. Then factor in all the (mostly unpleasant) conversations they have with students and their parents about grades. It's tempting to just roll our eyes when confronted with whining or wheedling, but the real problem rests with the practice of grading itself.

7. *Grades encourage cheating.* Again, we can continue to blame and punish all the students who cheat—or we can look for the structural reasons this keeps happening. Researchers have found that the more students are led to focus on getting good grades, the more likely they are to cheat, even if they themselves regard cheating as wrong (Anderman et al., 1998; Milton et al., 1986; also see "Who's Cheating Whom?").

8. *Grades spoil teachers' relationships with students.* Consider this lament, which could have been offered by a teacher in your district:

> I'm getting tired of running a classroom in which everything we do revolves around grades. I'm tired of being suspicious when students give me compliments, wondering whether or not they are just trying to raise their grade. I'm tired of spending so much time and energy grading your papers, when there are probably a dozen more productive and enjoyable ways for all of us to handle the evaluation of papers. I'm tired of hearing you ask me 'Does

this count?' And, heaven knows, I'm certainly tired of all those little arguments and disagreements we get into concerning marks which take so much fun out of the teaching and the learning . . . (Kirschenbaum et al., 1971, p. 115).

9. *Grades spoil students' relationships with each other.* The quality of students' thinking has been shown to depend partly on the extent to which they are permitted to learn cooperatively (Johnson and Johnson, 1989; Kohn, 1992). Thus, the ill feelings, suspicion, and resentment generated by grades aren't just disagreeable in their own right; they interfere with learning.

The most destructive form of grading by far is that which is done "on a curve," such that the number of top grades is artificially limited: no matter how well all the students do, not all of them can get an A. Apart from the intrinsic unfairness of this arrangement, its practical effect is to teach students that others are potential obstacles to their own success. The kind of collaboration that can help all students to learn more effectively doesn't stand a chance in such an environment.

Sadly, even teachers who don't explicitly grade on a curve may assume, perhaps unconsciously, that the final grades "ought to" come out looking more or less this way: a few very good grades, a few very bad grades, and the majority somewhere in the middle. But as one group of researchers pointed out, "It is not a symbol of rigor to have grades fall into a 'normal' distribution; rather, it is a symbol of failure—failure to teach well, failure to test well, and failure to have any influence at all on the intellectual lives of students" (Milton et al., 1986, p. 225).

The competition that turns schooling into a quest for triumph and ruptures relationships among students doesn't just happen within classrooms, of course. The same effect is witnessed at a schoolwide level when kids are not just rated but ranked, sending the message that the point isn't to learn, or even to perform well, but to defeat others. Some students might be motivated to improve their class rank, but that is completely different from being motivated to understand ideas. (Wise educators realize that it doesn't matter how motivated students are; what matters is how students are motivated. It is the type of motivation that counts, not the amount.)

Grade Inflation . . . and Other Distractions

Most of us are directly acquainted with at [20] least some of these disturbing consequences of grades, yet we continue to reduce students to letters or numbers on a regular basis. Perhaps we've become inured to these effects and take them for granted. This is the way it's always been, we assume, and the way it has to be. It's rather like people who have spent all their lives in a terribly polluted city and have come to assume that this is just the way air looks—and that it's natural to be coughing all the time.

Oddly, when educators are shown that it doesn't have to be this way, some react with suspicion instead of relief. They want to know why you're making trouble, or they assert that you're exaggerating the negative effects of grades (it's really not so bad—cough, cough), or they dismiss proven alternatives to grading on the grounds that our school could never do what others schools have done.

The practical difficulties of abolishing letter grades are real. But the key question is whether those difficulties are seen as problems to be solved or as excuses for perpetuating the status quo. The logical response to the arguments and data summarized here is to say: "Good Heavens! If even half of this is true, then it's imperative we do whatever we can, as soon as we can, to phase out

traditional grading." Yet many people begin and end with the problems of implementation, responding to all this evidence by saying, in effect, "Yeah, yeah, yeah, but we'll never get rid of grades because . . ."

It is also striking how many educators never get beyond relatively insignificant questions, such as how many tests to give, or how often to send home grade reports, or what grade should be given for a specified level of achievement (e.g., what constitutes "B" work), or what number corresponds to what letter. Some even reserve their outrage for the possibility that too many students are ending up with good grades, a reaction that suggests stinginess with A's is being confused with intellectual rigor. The evidence indicates that the real problem isn't grade inflation; it's grades. The proper occasion for outrage is not that too many students are getting A's, but that too many students have accepted that getting A's is the point of going to school.

Common objections

Let's consider the most frequently heard responses to the above arguments—which is to say, the most common objections to getting rid of grades.

First, it is said that students expect to re- [25] ceive grades and even seem addicted to them. This is often true; personally, I've taught high school students who reacted to the absence of grades with what I can only describe as existential vertigo. (Who am I, if not a B+?) But as more elementary and even some middle schools move to replace grades with more informative (and less destructive) systems of assessment, the damage doesn't begin until students get to high school. Moreover, elementary and middle schools that haven't changed their practices often cite the local high school as the reason they must get students used to getting grades regardless of their damaging effects—just as high schools point the finger at colleges.

Even when students arrive in high school already accustomed to grades, already primed to ask teachers, "Do we have to know this?" or "What do I have to do to get an A?", this is a sign that something is very wrong. It's more an indictment of what has happened to them in the past than an argument to keep doing it in the future.

Perhaps because of this training, grades can succeed in getting students to show up on time, hand in their work, and otherwise do what they're told. Many teachers are loath to give up what is essentially an instrument of control. But even to the extent this instrument works (which is not always), we are obliged to reflect on whether mindless compliance is really our goal. The teacher who exclaims, "These kids would blow off my course in a minute if they weren't getting a grade for it!" may be issuing a powerful indictment of his or her course. Who would be more reluctant to give up grades than a teacher who spends the period slapping transparencies on the overhead projector and lecturing endlessly at students about Romantic poets or genetic codes? Without bribes (A's) and threats (F's), students would have no reason to do such assignments. To maintain that this proves something is wrong with the kids—or that grades are simply "necessary"—suggests a willful refusal to examine one's classroom practices and assumptions about teaching and learning.

"If I can't give a child a better reason for studying than a grade on a report card, I ought to lock my desk and go home and stay there." So wrote Dorothy De Zouche, a Missouri teacher, in an article published in February . . . of 1945. But teachers who can give a child a better reason for studying don't need grades. Research substantiates this: when the curriculum is engaging—for example, when it involves hands-on, interactive learning activities—students who aren't graded

at all perform just as well as those who are graded (Moeller and Reschke, 1993).

Another objection: it is sometimes argued that students must be given grades because colleges demand them. One might reply that "high schools have no responsibility to serve colleges by performing the sorting function for them"—particularly if that process undermines learning (Krumboltz and Yeh, 1996, p. 325). But in any case the premise of this argument is erroneous: traditional grades are not mandatory for admission to colleges and universities.

Making change

A friend of mine likes to say that people don't resist change—they resist being changed. Even terrific ideas (like moving a school from a grade orientation to a learning orientation) are guaranteed to self-destruct if they are simply forced down people's throats. The first step for an administrator, therefore, is to open up a conversation—to spend perhaps a full year just encouraging people to think and talk about the effects of (and alternatives to) traditional grades. This can happen in individual classes, as teachers facilitate discussions about how students regard grades, as well as in evening meetings with parents, or on a website—all with the help of relevant books, articles, speakers, videos, and visits to neighboring schools that are farther along in this journey.

The actual process of "de-grading" can be done in stages. For example, a high school might start by freeing ninth-grade classes from grades before doing the same for upperclassmen. (Even a school that never gets beyond the first stage will have done a considerable service, giving students one full year where they can think about what they're learning instead of their GPAs.)

Another route to gradual change is to begin by eliminating only the most pernicious practices, such as grading on a curve or ranking students. Although grades, per se, may continue for a while, at least the message will be sent from the beginning that all students can do well, and that the point is to succeed rather than to beat others.

Anyone who has heard the term "authentic assessment" knows that abolishing grades doesn't mean eliminating the process of gathering information about student performance—and communicating that information to students and parents. Rather, abolishing grades opens up possibilities that are far more meaningful and constructive. These include narratives (written comments), portfolios (carefully chosen collections of students' writings and projects that demonstrate their interests, achievement, and improvement over time), student-led parent-teacher conferences, exhibitions and other opportunities for students to show what they can do.

Of course, it's harder for a teacher to do these kinds of assessments if he or she has 150 or more students and sees each of them for 45–55 minutes a day. But that's not an argument for continuing to use traditional grades; it's an argument for challenging these archaic remnants of a factory-oriented approach to instruction, structural aspects of high schools that are bad news for reasons that go well beyond the issue of assessment. It's an argument for looking into block scheduling, team teaching, interdisciplinary courses—and learning more about schools that have arranged things so each teacher can spend more time with fewer students (e.g., Meier, 1995).

Administrators should be prepared to respond to parental concerns, some of them completely reasonable, about the prospect of edging away from grades. "Don't you value excellence?" You bet—and here's the evidence that traditional grading undermines excellence. "Are you just trying to spare the self-esteem of students who do poorly?" We are concerned that grades may be making things worse for such students, yes, but the problem isn't just that some kids won't get A's and will have their feelings hurt. The real problem is that almost all kids (including yours) will come to focus on grades and, as a result, their learning will be hurt.

If parents worry that grades are the only window they have into the school, we need to assure them that alternative assessments provide a far better view. But if parents don't seem to care about getting the most useful information or helping their children become more excited learners—if they demand grades for the purpose of documenting how much better their kids are than everyone else's, then we need to engage them in a discussion about whether this is a legitimate goal, and whether schools exist for the purpose of competitive credentialing or for the purpose of helping everyone to learn (Kohn, 1998; Labaree, 1997).

Above all, we need to make sure that objections and concerns about the details don't obscure the main message, which is the demonstrated harm of traditional grading on the quality of students' learning and their interest in exploring ideas.

High school administrators can do a world of good in their districts by actively supporting efforts to eliminate conventional grading in elementary and middle schools. Working with their colleagues in these schools can help pave the way for making such changes at the secondary school level.

In the meantime

Finally, there is the question of what classroom teachers can do while grades continue to be required. The short answer is that they should do everything within their power to make grades as invisible as possible for as long as possible. Helping students forget about grades is the single best piece of advice for creating a learning-oriented classroom.

When I was teaching high school, I did a
lot of things I now regret. But one policy that
still seems sensible to me was saying to students on the first day of class that, while I was
compelled to give them a grade at the end of
the term, I could not in good conscience ever
put a letter or number on anything they did
during the term—and I would not do so. I
would, however, write a comment—or, better, sit down and talk with them—as often as
possible to give them feedback.

At this particular school I frequently
faced students who had been prepared for
admission to Harvard since their early childhood—a process I have come to call
"Preparation H." I knew that my refusal to
rate their learning might only cause some
students to worry about their marks all the
more, or to create suspense about what
would appear on their final grade reports,
which of course would defeat the whole purpose. So I said that anyone who absolutely
had to know what grade a given paper would
get could come see me and we would figure it
out together. An amazing thing happened: as
the days went by, fewer and fewer students
felt the need to ask me about grades. They
began to be more involved with what we were
learning because I had taken responsibility
as a teacher to stop pushing grades into their
faces, so to speak, whenever they completed
an assignment.

What I didn't do very well, however, was
to get students involved in devising the criteria for excellence (what makes a math solution elegant, an experiment well-designed,
an essay persuasive, a story compelling) as
well as deciding how well their projects met
those criteria. I'm afraid I unilaterally set the
criteria and evaluated the students' efforts.
But I have seen teachers who were more willing to give up control, more committed to
helping students participate in assessment
and turn that into part of the learning.
Teachers who work with their students to

design powerful alternatives to letter grades
have a replacement ready to go when the
school finally abandons traditional grading—
and are able to minimize the harm of such
grading in the meantime.

References

Anderman, E. M., and J. Johnston. "Television News in the Classroom: What Are Adolescents Learning?" *Journal of Adolescent
Research* 13 (1998): 73–100.

Beck, H. P., S. Rorrer-Woody, and L. G. Pierce.
"The Relations of Learning and Grade
Orientations to Academic Performance."
Teaching of Psychology 18 (1991): 35–37.

Benware, C. A., and E. L. Deci. "Quality of
Learning With an Active Versus Passive
Motivational Set." *American Educational
Research Journal* 21 (1984): 755–65.

Butler, R. "Task-Involving and Ego-Involving
Properties of Evaluation: Effects of Differ-
ent Feedback Conditions on Motivational
Perceptions, Interest, and Performance."
Journal of Educational Psychology 79
(1987): 474–82.

Butler, R. "Enhancing and Undermining Intrinsic Motivation: The Effects of Task-
Involving and Ego-Involving Evaluation on
Interest and Performance." *British Journal
of Educational Psychology* 58 (1988): 1–14.

Butler, R., and M. Nisan. "Effects of No
Feedback, Task-Related Comments, and
Grades on Intrinsic Motivation and Performance." *Journal of Educational Psychology* 78 (1986): 210–16.

De Zouche, D. "'The Wound Is Mortal':
Marks, Honors, Unsound Activities." *The
Clearing House* 19 (1945): 339–44.

Grolnick, W. S., and R. M. Ryan. "Autonomy
in Children's Learning: An Experimental
and Individual Difference Investigation."
*Journal of Personality and Social Psychol-
ogy* 52 (1987): 890–98.

Harter, S. "Pleasure Derived from Challenge
and the Effects of Receiving Grades on

Children's Difficulty Level Choices." *Child Development* 49 (1978): 788–99.

Harter, S. and Guzman, M. E. "The Effect of Perceived Cognitive Competence and Anxiety on Children's Problem-Solving Performance, Difficulty Level Choices, and Preference for Challenge." Unpublished manuscript, University of Denver. 1986.

Hughes, B., H. J. Sullivan, and M. L. Mosley. "External Evaluation, Task Difficulty, and Continuing Motivation." *Journal of Educational Research* 78 (1985): 210–15.

Kage, M. "The Effects of Evaluation on Intrinsic Motivation." Paper presented at the meeting of the Japan Association of Educational Psychology, Joetsu, Japan, 1991.

Kohn, A. *Punished by Rewards: The Trouble with Gold Stars, Incentive Plans, A's, Praise, and Other Bribes.* Boston: Houghton Mifflin, 1993.

Kohn, A. "Only for My Kid: How Privileged Parents Undermine School Reform." *Phi Delta Kappan,* April 1998: 569–77.

Krumboltz, J. D., and C. J. Yeh. "Competitive Grading Sabotages Good Teaching." *Phi Delta Kappan,* December 1996: 324–26.

Labaree, D. F. *How to Succeed in School Without Really Learning: The Credentials Race in American Education.* New Haven, Conn.: Yale University Press, 1997.

Meier, D. *The Power of Their Ideas: Lessons for America from a Small School in Harlem.* Boston: Beacon, 1995.

Milton, O., H. R. Pollio, and J. A. Eison. *Making Sense of College Grades.* San Francisco: Jossey-Bass, 1986.

Moeller, A. J., and C. Reschke. "A Second Look at Grading and Classroom Performance: Report of a Research Study." *Modern Language Journal* 77 (1993): 163–69.

Salili, F., M. L. Maehr, R. L. Sorensen, and L. J. Fyans, Jr. "A Further Consideration of the Effects of Evaluation on Motivation." *American Educational Research Journal* 13 (1976): 85–102.

A CLOSER LOOK AT
From Degrading to De-Grading

1. This article follows the organization of a traditional proposal. Look through the article and identify the places where Kohn describes (a) the problem, its causes, and its effects; (b) a solution to the problem, including any major and minor steps; and (c) the benefits of accepting his plan.

2. Some of Kohn's major points are supported with empirical evidence and some aren't. Do you think the use of empirical evidence in this proposal makes parts of his argument more credible? Why or why not? In places where he has not backed up his argument with empirical sources, do you find his arguments reasonable and solid? Why or why not?

3. In your opinion, what are Kohn's three strongest arguments against grading and what are his two weakest arguments? What are his three best ideas for alternative ways to evaluate and motivate students? What are the two ideas in his plan that you are most skeptical about?

IDEAS FOR
Writing

1. Write a letter to the editor or rebuttal for *High School* magazine in which you agree or disagree with Kohn's argument. If you agree with his argument, how do your experiences as someone who graduated from (survived) high school match up with Kohn's descriptions? What parts of his plan do you think would work? If you are writing a rebuttal, where do his criticisms and ideas for reform fall short? Do you think he is wrong, or do you have a better way to reform the system of grades that is used in high school (and college)?

2. Write an argument essay in which you argue for or against the use of grading in college. Many of Kohn's criticisms against grading might be applicable to college, too. But what are some important differences between grading in college and high school? If you are arguing for keeping grades, can you think of a way to improve the system? If you are against grades in college, can you offer a solution that would still keep students motivated and allow professors to gauge whether students had learned the materials?

1. What are some of the problems on your college's campus? With a group in your class, list them and pick one that seems especially troublesome. What do you think are the causes of this problem? What has changed recently to bring this problem about or make it worse? Discuss this problem with a group of other people in your class.

2. Now try to figure out a way to solve this campus problem. What would be a good solution to this problem? Can you think of a few other solutions? With a small group, discuss the costs and benefits of solving the problem in different ways.

3. With a group in class, find a proposal on the Internet that you can discuss. Look closely at the proposal's content, organization, style, and design. Do you think the proposal is effective? What are its strengths? What are its weaknesses? If you were going to revise this proposal, what are some of the things you would change?

1. Find a proposal on the Internet by entering keywords like "proposal" and your topic into a search engine. Write a one-page analysis of the proposal, describing how it explains the problem and offers a plan for solving it. In your analysis, tell your readers whether you think the proposal is or is not effective. Explain why you think so, and offer suggestions about how the proposal could be improved.

2. List five problems that are facing our society right now. Pick one that interests you and then try to narrow the topic down to something you can manage in a small proposal. Use a concept map to explore what you already know about the problem, its causes, and its effects. Then do research on the subject by collecting online and print sources on it. Draft a one- or two-page analysis of the problem that explores its causes and effects.

3. Find a proposal on the Internet that is badly designed. Do a makeover of the design to improve the look and usability of the proposal. What would make it more appealing to readers? How could design techniques be used to make it easier to scan or easier to understand? You should create two sample pages that illustrate your design.

Here are some other microgenres that are similar to proposals. Choose a microgenre from the list below and find three examples in print or on the Internet. Create your own set of guidelines for writing one of these microgenres.

Ridiculous-invention proposal—a "mock proposal" for an outrageous invention (perhaps a overly complex solution to a simple problem)

Marriage (or date) proposal—a proposal of marriage (or a romantic date) with someone using all the features of a formal proposal

Assignment prospectus—description of your proposed approach to a particular writing or other assignment, addressed to a professor

Job application letter—a letter that describes how you can help a business or organization solve its problems

Letter to politician or campus leader—a proposed solution to a pressing national, local, or campus problem

1. **Propose your own solution.** Write a proposal that solves a problem in our society or in your life. Explore the causes of the problem and then come up with a plan that solves it. Then identify all the benefits that would come about if the problem were solved according to your plan. The best topics for proposals are ones that affect your life in some way. Pick a problem that you feel strongly about or something that affects your everyday life. Your proposal should run about seven to ten pages. Include graphics and make sure the document is well designed.

2. **Remake a proposal into a multimedia presentation.** Using a search engine, find a proposal available on the Internet. Transform the proposal into a presentation that incorporates multimedia features. You can use presentation software, overhead projector slides, flipcharts, or posters. Then write a one-page rhetorical analysis for your professor that introduces the proposal and describes how you altered the original proposal's content, organization, style, and design to make it work as a multimedia presentation.

3. **Propose something absurd.** One of the most famous "proposals" is Jonathan Swift's "A Modest Proposal" in which he suggests consuming Irish children as a way to solve a famine. Swift's intent was to draw attention to the desperation of the Irish, while shaming absent English landlords. Write an ironic five-page proposal like Swift's that proposes an absurd solution for an important problem. Remember that the key to irony is to bring about a positive change by shaming the people who are at fault.

PEARSON
mycomplab

For support in meeting this chapter's objectives, follow this path in MyCompLab: Resources ⟹ Writing ⟹ Writing Samples ⟹ Writing Samples: Proposals. Review the Instruction and Multimedia resources about writing proposals, then complete the Exercises and click on Gradebook to measure your progress.

Reports

In this chapter, you will learn how to—

- use the report genre to describe your research, findings, and recommendations.
- develop a narrow research question.
- turn your research question into a working hypothesis that you can test and refine through your research.

Reports are used to describe research findings, analyze those findings, and make recommendations. When writing a report, you need to do more than present the facts. You also need to interpret your results and help your readers understand the information you've collected.

In college, your professors will ask you to write reports about important issues and projects. As you take more advanced courses, your projects will grow more complex, creative, and collaborative. Professors in your advanced courses will ask you to use reports to analyze specific issues and present your findings.

In the workplace, the report genre has many versions, including *research reports, recommendation reports, completion reports, feasibility reports,* and *scientific reports.* No matter what career you choose, from business to engineering to fashion design to science, writing reports will be an important part of your professional life. You will need to write reports regularly to explain issues and offer recommendations to supervisors, clients, and customers.

Learning to write reports is an important skill that you should master right now. Reports tend to be complex documents, but once you know how they work, you can write these kinds of documents more effectively and efficiently.

Reports

To help you remember this structure, you might memorize the acronym IMRaD, which is widely used by professional researchers. IMRaD stands for Introduction, Methods, Results, and Discussion.

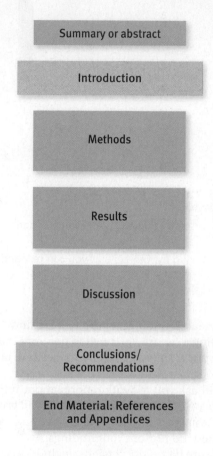

A typical report tends to have the following features:

- **Executive summary or abstract** that summarizes the major sections of the report.
- **Introduction** that defines a research question or problem and explains why it is important to the reader. The introduction clearly states the purpose and main point of the report, while offering background information on the topic.
- **Methods section** that describes how the research was carried out.
- **Results or Findings section** that presents the results of the research objectively.
- **Discussion section** that analyzes the results and explains what they mean.
- **Conclusion/Recommendations** that restates the main point of the report and offers specific recommendations.
- **End Material: References** that provides a list of references or works cited. **Appendices** that offer additional sources and other materials.

ONE STUDENT'S WORK
Reports

This report was written for a class that assigned research reports on "gender identity," our sense of self in terms of being male or female, and how this identity is shaped by both cultural and biological factors.

Gender Stereotypes and Toys: Is It Nature or Nurture?

Scott Walker, University of New Mexico

Abstract

In order to better understand the roles that nature vs. nurture play in the formation of gender identity, I performed a field research study at a large-chain toy store. There I recorded information about how toys were marketed to young children in terms of images, gender stereotypes, and other factors. I found that almost all toys were marked by gender, with the exception of learning materials and some products associated with movies, music, or television. Older children's toys were only slightly more gender distinctive than infants' toys. Finally, I speculate about the repercussions of such marketing on gender identity and how parents might help children resist such stereotyping.

A brief abstract summarizes the entire report, section by section.

Introduction

Scientists and cultural theorists have long argued about whether nature or nurture (biology or culture) is responsible for gender differences between men and women. Both sides, however, agree that gender differences can be seen even in very young children. Researchers who argue that gender differences are due to "nature" usually emphasize the role played by evolution (Lippa, 2002). They suggest that the differences in behavior between boys and girls exist because human evolution has manipulated genes and hormones over time to increase behavioral differences (Choi, 2001). They even argue that girls and boys respond differently to specific colors, especially pink, for biological reasons (Alexander, 2003).

Those who argue that gender differences are due to "nurture" usually focus on the differences between boys' and girls' socialization in their culture. They maintain that children are taught by their culture, through rewards and modeling, to engage in certain gender behaviors and hold specific attitudes

Report follows the IMRaD organization, with each section marked by headings.

Introduction begins by establishing the question that the field research will address.

continued

(Lippa, 2002; Paige, 2008). The nurture side of the debate says that as an individual grows up, he or she begins to become aware of how males and females
are expected to behave (Ball, 2006). These gender roles, they argue, are taught
almost from the moment we are born: boys are expected to be strong, tough, independent, and unemotional, while girls are expected to be nurturing, sensitive,
dependent, and expressive. According to the nurture side of the debate, these
behaviors are drilled so deeply into our heads from the moment we are born that
they seem natural and inborn.

The toys that boys and girls play with offer a good way to study gender differences, because toys are some of the earliest and strongest shapers of gender
identity (Blakemore, LaRue, & Olejnik, 1979). Through reinforcement and modeling, boys and girls are taught to play with toys that are considered appropriate
for their gender. Infant boys get fire trucks and infant girls get baby dolls. Then
the adults around them continue to reinforce gender stereotypes consciously
and unconsciously by buying specific kinds of toys for their children and others'
children (Pollitt, 1995; Clark, 2000). The stereotyping is less for infants, according
to Campenni (1999), and it grows greater for older children.

In this research study, my aim was to explore how toys affect gender socialization. My research will not, of course, settle the nature vs. nurture debate once
and for all. However, by conducting field research at a large toy store, my goal
was to gain some insights into how toys shape boys' and girls' sense of gender.
My hypothesis is that gender differences in toys help establish gender identity
from the beginning of life and that these differences become more apparent as
children grow older. As I will show, I discovered definite differences between toys
marketed to girls and boys, and these gender differences are more marked for
older children than for very young children. But, I also learned that these differences are established earlier than I originally expected.

Methodology: Visiting a Toy Store

To test my hypothesis, my methodology included collecting sources at the
university library and running searches for sources on the Internet. My Internet
and library sources helped me prepare for the empirical part of my study, which
was a visit to a well-known chain toy store, where I observed the marketing of
toys and how children interacted with them. Chain toy stores are arranged by
children's ages because people shop with a particular child of a particular age in
mind. So I began my observations in the infant and toddlers' (ages 0–3) section.
Then I moved to the young children's (ages 4–6) section and finished in the
preteens' (ages 7–12) section.

In each section, I spent a half hour taking careful field notes about the characteristics of toys and how they were marketed, noting (a) the name of the toy,

(b) its stated or unstated purpose, and (c) any visual features such as choice of colors, decals, images of boys or girls, and other visual cues that signaled gender. In the left column of a two-column notebook, I described the features of the toys, their packaging, and the ways in which they were displayed.

Then I returned to each section of the store for an hour each to observe how children in the store interacted with the toys. In the right column of my two-column notebook, I recorded how they reacted similarly or differently to various types of toys.

When possible, I also described situations in which adults, usually parents, seemed to be encouraging or discouraging children from playing with specific kinds of toys. I listened carefully for clues from parents directing children in gendered terms (e.g., "Caleb, those ponies are for girls" or "Brittany, did you see the dolls over there?").

Admittedly, my methods are influenced by my own cultural biases. I, too, have been raised by my culture to view some toys, colors, and images as associated with one gender or the other. For example, while observing, I assumed that the pink toys are aimed at girls, and the camouflage toys are aimed at boys. As I wrote my field notes, though, I tried to set those cultural biases aside and pay attention to children's voluntary reactions to specific toys and their displays.

> Author concedes his own potential biases, which may affect his research.

Results: Three Types of Areas in Each Section

As I entered each area of the store, it was immediately obvious which toys were directed at boys and which were directed at girls. Even from a distance, the toys were made distinct by color: the pink and purple areas were the girls' sections, while the red, black, and blue areas were the boys' sections.

> Results describe his most important findings.

Infant and Toddler (0 to 3 Years Old) Area

In the Infant and Toddler area, the boys' and girls' areas were clearly marked with signs that said "Boys" and "Girls."

In the boys' area, there were toys like construction trucks and equipment, fire engines, trains, and racecars. They were usually painted with bold and bright colors (red, blue, yellow, and orange). Human figures in this area were always male (construction workers, repairmen, firemen, police officers, etc.). Sports were a common theme, with lots of toddler-sized equipment for baseball, golf, soccer, and basketball.

In the girls' area, the products were surprisingly "mommy" or "princess" oriented—more than I expected. There were rolling "activity walkers," which

> Details in this section are used to describe what was observed.

continued

looked suspiciously like baby strollers. Dolls, especially babies, were common. Animals seemed to be a common theme, especially puppies and kittens. The colors in this section were pink, purple, light blue, and yellow. These colors were generally much softer than the ones in the boys' section. All the characters were female, and most of them were wearing makeup. Pictures of princesses were common, and there was a wide assortment of cuddly, soft, and polka-dot patterned toys. There was no sports equipment in this area.

Young Children (4 to 6 Years) Area

In the Young Children area, there were clear differences between the male and female parts of the aisle, although the learning materials were, once again, directed at both genders.

The boys' area consisted of a wide assortment of male action figures, as well as toy lions, gorillas, sharks, tigers, and aliens. I noted a wide variety of construction and sports toys, including toolboxes and balls. There were huge, intricate play sets with cars, soldiers, pirates, and male workers (they often had tool belts or fire hats). Nearly everything was colored blue, black, orange, and other dark and bold colors. Flames were a common design on the toys for this age.

Then, as I entered the female section, I had to stop to let my eyes adjust to the change in color. Almost every toy was pink with white or purple accents. The dolls were all female and nearly always had makeup on (even the baby dolls). One toy set typified the girls' toys in this area: the "Little Mommy" toy set that comes with dolls (wearing lipstick and blush), strollers, and cribs.

Preteen (7 to 12 Years) Area

The Preteen area continued many of the patterns I noticed in the earlier areas.

The boys' area was, again, dominated by reds, blues, and blacks. Nearly everything had a "cool" or aggressive design on it, like flames or fangs. The boys' bikes had names like "Hummer," "Rhino," and "Corruption." There was a lot of sports equipment here.

The girls' area, on the other hand, consisted almost entirely of pink and purple toys covered in flowers and bubbles. The most common sight in this area was a variety of Hannah Montana toys. There were many Barbie-doll sets, one with "Up to 2000 combinations!" of clothes and shoes. There were at least 25 different cooking sets. There were bikes here as well, but they were clearly painted pink or purple for girls with flower decals, and they had names like "Belly," "Twirl," "Malibu," and "Hannah Montana." Any sports equipment in this area had pink or purple splashed on it.

Author maintains an objective tone in the Results section.

Adult Redirection

I only observed a few instances in which adults seemed to be redirecting their children toward toys designed for their gender. In the Infant and Toddler area, a boy was attracted to some stuffed animals that were in the girls' section. His father asked him if he wanted to "check out" the sports equipment. In a few cases, parents entered the aisle and pointed out where their girl or boy could find the toys for them. A mother directed her young boy to a display with pirates. For the most part, though, even the youngest children seemed to go immediately to the toys that were marked for their gender. In a couple situations, young boys seemed especially eager to get out of the girls section to go over to the boys part of the aisle. I didn't notice girls feeling equally uncomfortable in the boys part of the aisle.

Discussion: Divided from the Start

Overall, I found that the differences between toys marketed to boys and girls were very distinct with few exceptions. These gender distinctions were clear even in the Infant and Toddler toys area, which I did not expect. My findings show that gender stereotypes are reinforced early and consistently in the marketing of toys.

The discussion analyzes the findings and explains what they mean.

As might have been predicted, the dolls and action figures for boys and girls were very different and clearly reinforced gender stereotypes. Baby dolls and supplies were aimed at girls, even in the toddler years. The Barbie-doll sets for preteen girls seemed to suggest that shopping and spending money on clothing, makeup, and accessories is a good thing. The dolls themselves reinforced the "skinny, blonde, big-breasted, and most often white" stereotype. Almost always, the preteen dolls and even the dolls for young children were outfitted with revealing clothes. The female characters for young children and preteens were mostly princesses and fashion dolls. The dolls (excuse me, "action figures") that represented males were all construction workers, soldiers, policemen, superheroes, firefighters, and so forth. There were no chefs, fathers, or fashion models in the boys' toys sections.

Interestingly, color seemed to be an important way to distinguish one gender's toys from the other. Pinks and purples, as expected, were used to mark products for girls. The packaging for girls' toys usually had muted, soft colors, like pastels and other homey tones. But there wasn't an equivalent exclusive color scheme for boys, except perhaps black. Red, blue, and green tended to be in the boys' area, but most girls would not have a problem with using with a blue soccer ball or wearing a red bike helmet. Black was a color that seemed exclusive

continued

to boys, but not in the same way pink marked a product for girls. This seems in line with Campenni's conclusion that feminine toys are "stereotyped more than masculine toys" (121).

Author discusses his main conclusions about what he observed.

Originally, when I started my research, I assumed that toys would start out mostly gender neutral and differ as children grew older. That's actually not true. Even toddler toys were clearly marked as appropriate for boys and girls. I cannot imagine that it matters to an infant boy if he plays with a pink kitten or to a toddler girl if she plays with a flame-streaked fire truck. In the marketing world of toys, however, these kinds of gendered distinctions are obviously important and parents go along with it.

I also expected to see more parental prompting about which toys were appropriate for their boys and girls. In the end, I didn't see much of that kind of behavior. The girls, even toddlers, seemed to know immediately which toys were designed for them. The boys didn't hesitate to run over to their toys either. As I mentioned before, I did notice that the boys were more distressed when they were being held up in the girls' area. It seems like they were aware that the toys in the girls' area were not for them.

Conclusions: Nurture Is Important

So, what insights can we gain into the how the differences in toys affect children's sense of gender? I don't think I resolved the nature vs. nurture debate, but I am convinced that nurture is a powerful force in determining how children figure out what a culture expects for their gender.

The main point of the report is expressed clearly.

All in all, toys reinforce gender expectations for children, probably more than most people realize. They tell little boys that they should grow up to be tough workers or sports stars, that they should love cars, trucks, sports, and anything ferocious, and that they should be aggressive and adventurous. Little girls should grow up to be clean, neat mothers, shoppers, performers, and fashion models.

However, gender is not destiny. There is somehow still room for individuality that breaks free of the stereotypes. As long as parents participate actively in the raising of their children, they can overcome the gender expectations and stereotypes of today's world.

References

List of references gives bibliographic information for everything cited in the text.

Alexander, G. M. (2003). An evolutionary perspective on sex-typed toy preferences: Pink, blue, and the brain. *Archives of Sexual Behavior, 32,* 7–14.

Ball, R. (2006). Dreaming of a pink Christmas. *The F Word: Contemporary UK Feminism.* Retrieved from http://www.thefword.org.uk/features/2006/12/pink_christmas.

Blakemore, J. E., LaRue, A. A., & Olejnik, A. B. (1979). Sex-appropriate toy preference and the ability to conceptualize toys as sex-role related. *Developmental Psychology, 15,* 339–340.

Campenni, C. E. (1999). Gender stereotyping of children's toys: A comparison of parents and non-parents. *Sex Roles, 40,* 121–138.

Choi, P. (2001). Genes and gender roles: Why is the nature argument so appealing? *Sexualities, Evolution, and Gender, 3,* 279–285.

Clark, B. (2000). *Girls, boys, books, toys: Gender in children's literature and culture.* Baltimore, MD: Johns Hopkins University Press.

Lippa, R. A. (2002). *Gender, nature, and nurture.* Mahwah, NJ: Lawrence Erlbaum Associates, Inc.

Paige, J. (2008). Why action figures and dolls are bad gifts for gender stereotyping. Retrieved from http://www.helium.com/items/700248-reflections-why -action-figures-and-dolls-are-bad-gifts-for-gender-stereotyping

Pollitt, K. (1995, October 8). HERS: Why boys don't play with dolls. *The New York Times.* Retrieved from http://www.nytimes.com

Inventing Your Report's Content

When starting a research project, you first need to figure out your topic, your research question, and your hypothesis. Your hypothesis will serve as your thesis statement while you are drafting your report. Then you need to discover what you already know about your topic and come up with a systematic way to find out what others know. And finally, you need to use your research skills to generate findings, analyze those findings, and develop your conclusions or recommendations. In other words, much needs to happen before you sit down to draft your report.

Inquiring: Developing Your Research Question and Hypothesis

Start out by identifying your topic, angle, research question, and hypothesis.

Topic. Define your topic and then narrow it down to something you can handle in the time you have available. Reports tend to be large compared to other documents, so you may be tempted to pick a topic that is very large (e.g., violence, eating disorders, alternative energy), but these topics are way too broad. Instead, you need to choose a much narrower topic within a larger topic (e.g., recent incidents of violence on campus, how first-year college students with eating disorders adapt to dorm food, using wind energy to power your dormitory). A narrower topic will allow you to focus your research and come up with more useful results and recommendations.

Angle. The best way to narrow down your topic is to find the *angle* you want to pursue. Completely new topics are rare, but there are always new angles you can explore on existing topics. To help you find your angle, ask yourself: What has changed about this topic recently? How does this topic affect us locally?

Research Question. Now, it's time to develop your *research question*. Your research question should state your topic and identify an issue that your research will address. As discussed in Chapter 24, "Starting Research," your research question also needs to be as focused as possible.

> **Too Broad:** Why do people eat so much fast food?
>
> **Focused Research Question:** Why do college students turn to fast food as a way to help them handle stressful situations?
>
> **Too Broad:** Why do crows behave the way they do?
>
> **Focused Research Question:** Why do crows tend to live here on campus in the winter and how can we encourage them to go somewhere else?
>
> **Too Broad:** Are children becoming more violent?
>
> **Focused Research Question:** Do violent video games cause children to act out more violently in their everyday lives?

Hypothesis. Once you have figured out your research question, you should turn it into a *hypothesis* that will guide your research. Your hypothesis is your best guess—for the moment—about how your research question will be answered.

> My hypothesis is that fast food contains ingredients like salt, protein, carbohydrates, and fat that give our bodies short-term fuel for overcoming threatening moments. This craving is due to evolution. Our minds, when anxious or stressed, start thinking about the needs of short-term survival, not long-term health.

> My hunch is that crows congregate on our campus in the winter because there is ample food available and sources of warmth. Also, they are intelligent birds and have strong social bonds, so campus provides a consistent safe place for them to live together through the winter.

> My hypothesis is that today's children fantasize more about violence due to video games, but these games actually make children less violent because they can work through their aggression in a virtual environment.

Your hypothesis serves as your report's "working thesis." It is your best guess for now, and it will probably change as you move forward with your research. You're not committed to proving it. Instead, you are proposing this hypothesis with an open mind, gathering evidence that confirms or contradicts it. Then you will need to revise your hypothesis to fit your findings. You can turn to Chapter 24, "Starting Research," for help with creating a good hypothesis.

Inquiring: Finding Out What You Already Know

There is a good chance you already know quite a bit about your topic. That's why you or your professor chose it in the first place. So first discover what is already stored away in your gray matter about your topic.

Begin by brainstorming about your topic (Figure 12.1). Put your topic at the top of a piece of paper. Then list everything you know about that topic. Do this for five minutes or more. When you are finished brainstorming, identify two to five major

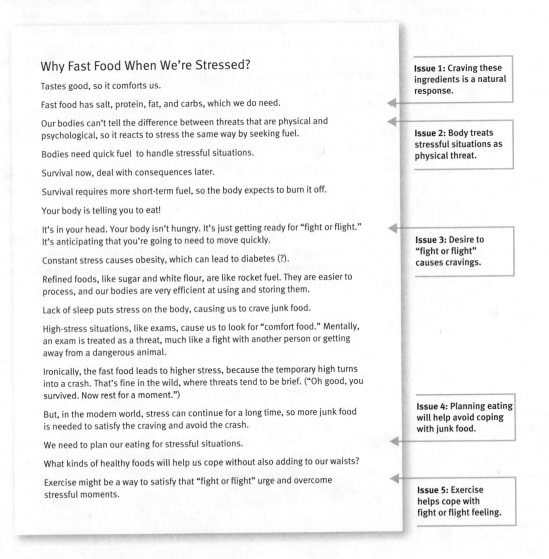

Why Fast Food When We're Stressed?

Tastes good, so it comforts us.

Fast food has salt, protein, fat, and carbs, which we do need.

Our bodies can't tell the difference between threats that are physical and psychological, so it reacts to stress the same way by seeking fuel.

Bodies need quick fuel to handle stressful situations.

Survival now, deal with consequences later.

Survival requires more short-term fuel, so the body expects to burn it off.

Your body is telling you to eat!

It's in your head. Your body isn't hungry. It's just getting ready for "fight or flight." It's anticipating that you're going to need to move quickly.

Constant stress causes obesity, which can lead to diabetes (?).

Refined foods, like sugar and white flour, are like rocket fuel. They are easier to process, and our bodies are very efficient at using and storing them.

Lack of sleep puts stress on the body, causing us to crave junk food.

High-stress situations, like exams, cause us to look for "comfort food." Mentally, an exam is treated as a threat, much like a fight with another person or getting away from a dangerous animal.

Ironically, the fast food leads to higher stress, because the temporary high turns into a crash. That's fine in the wild, where threats tend to be brief. ("Oh good, you survived. Now rest for a moment.")

But, in the modern world, stress can continue for a long time, so more junk food is needed to satisfy the craving and avoid the crash.

We need to plan our eating for stressful situations.

What kinds of healthy foods will help us cope without also adding to our waists?

Exercise might be a way to satisfy that "fight or flight" urge and overcome stressful moments.

Issue 1: Craving these ingredients is a natural response.

Issue 2: Body treats stressful situations as physical threat.

Issue 3: Desire to "fight or flight" causes cravings.

Issue 4: Planning eating will help avoid coping with junk food.

Issue 5: Exercise helps cope with fight or flight feeling.

FIGURE 12.1 Brainstorming on Your Topic

A brainstorming list is a great way to put your ideas on the screen or a piece of paper. It will also help you identify the two to five major issues you will probably explore as you do research for your report.

issues on your list that you could explore further in your research. Circle these issues or make a special mark next to them. At this point, you could do some freewriting or Internet research to see which issue might make a good topic for your report.

Researching: Creating a Research Plan

When you are finished writing down what you already know, you should have a good idea about where your research project is going. Now it's time to figure out how you are going to do your research (i.e., your research methods) to test your hypothesis.

You will need to develop a step-by-step plan for finding information. A concept map is an especially helpful tool for developing your research methods. It will help you figure out the steps you need to take when you are doing your research (Figure 12.2). You can map out your research methods like this:

1. In the middle of the screen or page, write down your research question.

2. Write down the two to five *major steps* you will need to take to answer that research question. Circle them.

3. For each major step, write down two to five *minor steps* that you would need to take to achieve that major step. Circle them and draw lines to connect them to the major steps.

The key question you should keep asking yourself is, "How?" "*How* am I going to answer that question? *How* am I going to find that information? *How* am I going to generate that data?" To help you answer these questions, you might turn to Chapter 24, "Starting Research," for ideas about doing your research.

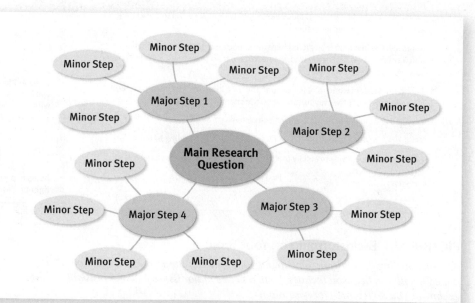

FIGURE 12.2
Inventing Your Methods with a Concept Map

Even the most experienced researchers find it difficult to develop their research methods. Making a concept map allows you to get your thoughts down in front of you and to organize them spatially.

FIGURE 12.3
Outlining a
Methodology

Research Question: Why Do Stressed Out People Eat So Much Fast Food?

Major Step 1: Search for Online Sources

- Review hospital Web sites for information about fast food
- Look on *WebMD* and other medical Web sites
- Find documentaries about fast food at library or through Netflix
- Search fast food companies' Web sites for nutrition information

Major Step 2: Find Print Sources

- Visit the Student Health Center to collect pamphlets on stress and diet
- Use *Readers' Guide* to find articles in health magazines
- Find articles in medical journals at library
- Check out nutrition and health textbooks in library
- Go to bookstore to browse books that discuss stress and food

Major Step 3: Do Empirical Research

- Interview nutritionist here on campus or in the community
- Create survey for college students
- Observe stressed people at the Student Union
- Interview spokesperson for McDonalds, Taco Bell, or Arby's

A concept map can easily be turned into an outline like the one shown here. List your major steps and then arrange the minor steps beneath them.

You can then turn your concept map into an outline, as shown in Figure 12.3. Your methodology should include all three kinds of sources (i.e., online, print, and empirical) so you can "triangulate" the facts you discover while doing your research. Triangulation, as discussed in Chapter 25, "Finding Sources and Collecting Information." This allows you to cross-reference your sources to determine the strength and the usefulness of the information they offer.

Researching: Gathering Sources and Revisiting Your Hypothesis

Your research will inevitably turn up new ideas and concepts that you didn't know about when you started the project. That's good. When doing research for a report, your objective is *not* to simply find sources that prove your working thesis. Instead, your objective is to do open-ended inquiry into your topic, letting the facts *lead* you to answers.

As you do research for your report, you will probably find information and facts that challenge your hypothesis. That's not a bad thing. Your original hypothesis was only your best guess when you began your research. Now that you know more about your topic, you should be willing to modify or even completely change your hypothesis to fit the information you've collected.

Good research is a cyclical process (Figure 12.4). You should keep returning to your hypothesis to see if you have changed your mind about how you will answer your research question. Your ideas will evolve as you figure things out. Eventually, as you

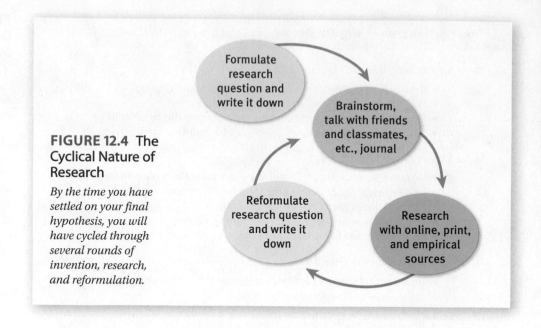

FIGURE 12.4 The Cyclical Nature of Research

By the time you have settled on your final hypothesis, you will have cycled through several rounds of invention, research, and reformulation.

finish doing your research, your hypothesis will solidify and become the main point (or thesis) of your report. At that point, you can start drafting your report with confidence.

Organizing and Drafting Your Report

The best way to draft a report is to write each major section separately. If you draft each section one at a time, you will avoid feeling overwhelmed by the size of the document.

Executive Summary or Abstract

Executive summaries usually devote a small paragraph to each major section of the report. Abstracts tend to be only one paragraph, devoting a sentence or two to each section of the report. The executive summary or abstract should be written after you have finished drafting the rest of the report.

Analyze the Interactive Abstract at mycomplab.com

Introduction

An introduction in a report will typically make up to five moves.

State the topic. Tell your readers what the report is about.

State the purpose. In one or two sentences, explain what the report is going to do or achieve.

State the main point or thesis of the report. State the overall conclusion of your report (i.e., what you discovered in your research).

Weak: Our research has turned up some interesting things about the food served in campus dining halls.

Stronger: Based on our research, we have found that the unhealthy food served at campus food courts is in part responsible for the "freshman fifteen" weight gain of new students.

Provide background information. Briefly, give readers enough historical information about your topic to help them understand it.

Explain why the topic is important to readers. Tell readers why they should care about this topic.

These moves can be made in just about any order, and they are not all necessary. Minimally, your introduction should tell your readers the report's topic, purpose, and main point.

Methods Section

Explain your research methods step by step in a way that would allow your readers to replicate your research. Each major step will usually receive at least one paragraph of coverage (Figure 12.5). Explain *how* you did each step and *why* you did it that way.

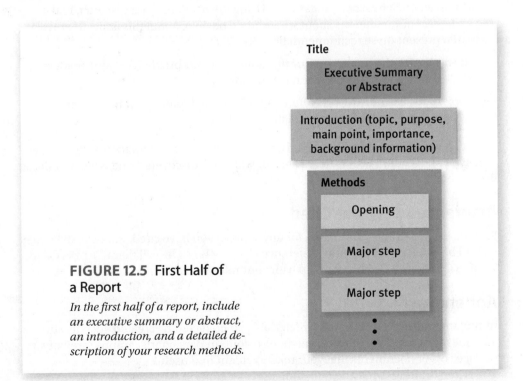

FIGURE 12.5 First Half of a Report

In the first half of a report, include an executive summary or abstract, an introduction, and a detailed description of your research methods.

Findings or Results Section

Choose the two to five most important findings or results from your research. In larger reports, each major finding should at least receive its own paragraph. Your job in this section is to describe what you found. Where possible, use graphics, such as charts, graphs, and tables, to present the data you've collected.

Discussion Section

Discuss your results and what they mean. Show how your results answer your research question. Researchers often boil their results down to two to five "conclusions." In most reports, each conclusion will need a paragraph to discuss how it supports the hypothesis and its implications. As shown in Figure 12.6, the Discussion section can be merged with the Findings/Results section if the findings and discussion of those findings can be handled together.

Conclusion/Recommendations

The conclusion of your report should be brief. A report's conclusion typically makes all or some of the following moves.

Restate your main point. One more time, state the report's overall main point or finding.

Make two to five recommendations. Using the results of your research, make some recommendations about what should be done about this issue. Reports often present these recommendations in a list.

Reemphasize the importance of the topic. Explain briefly why your readers should care about this topic and take action.

Look to the future. Reports often end with a small paragraph that describes what will happen in the near and distant future.

Your conclusion should be brief, perhaps only two or three paragraphs. Your goal is to leave your readers with a clear sense of what you discovered and what should be done about it.

References or Works Cited

Provide bibliographic information for any sources you have cited. For APA style, they should be listed under the title "References." For MLA style, call them "Works Cited." Turn to Chapters 27 and 28 for help with your references.

Appendices

In the appendices, put any other materials you collected or created such as surveys and questionnaires. Appendices might also contain data charts, graphs, previous reports, or other documents that your readers might find useful.

When drafting, it may help to draft larger sections in the report as separate documents, each with its own opening paragraph and a few body paragraphs. Figure 12.6

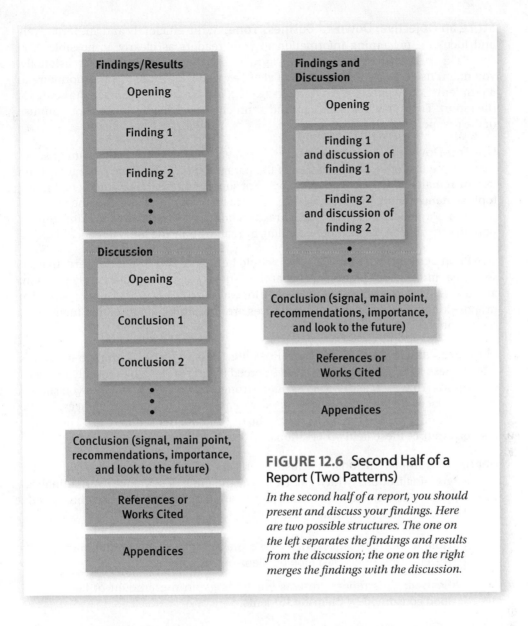

FIGURE 12.6 Second Half of a Report (Two Patterns)

In the second half of a report, you should present and discuss your findings. Here are two possible structures. The one on the left separates the findings and results from the discussion; the one on the right merges the findings with the discussion.

shows several different patterns that will help you organize the more complicated sections of your report.

Choosing an Appropriate Style

Reports usually sound neutral and objective. Your readers expect you to give them information in a straightforward way. As a result, reports are usually written in a plain style. Here are some plain style techniques that work particularly well with the report genre.

Strike an Objective, Down-to-Business Tone. Write efficiently and authoritatively and focus on presenting information to your readers as clearly as possible. You should let the information be the main attraction of the report, not you. Occasionally, you might use the first person point of view (e.g., "I distributed the questionnaire to 35 students" or "We ran the experiment again"), but don't make yourself the center of the report. Try to stay in the background as much as possible by minimizing your use of the first person point of view.

Use Top-Down Paragraphs. Consistently put each paragraph's main claim or statement in the first or second sentence of the paragraph (i.e., the topic sentence). Then use the remainder of the paragraph to prove or support that claim or statement. Putting topic sentences at the top of each paragraph will help your readers locate the most important information. Moreover, if your readers only have limited time to skim your report, they can get an overall understanding by reading only the topic sentences.

Use Plain Sentences. Your sentences should be simple and straightforward. In each sentence, move your subject (i.e., what the sentence is about) to an early position, and use active verbs where possible. Look for ways to minimize your use of excessive prepositional phrases. Make sure sentences are "breathing length"—not too long to be said out loud in one breath.

Minimize Passive Voice as Much as Possible. Passive voice is common in reports (e.g., "These field observations were reinforced by our survey."), especially in scientific reports. However, active voice is often stronger and easier to read, so you should look for places where you can turn passive sentences into active sentences. Active voice will help your readers understand who or what did the action (e.g., "The survey results reinforce these field observations.").

Get Rid of Nominalizations. Because reports are usually technical, they sometimes overuse nominalizations, which can cloud the meaning of sentences. A nominalization happens when the action in the sentence appears as a noun rather than a verb. *Hint:* Look for words that end in "-tion."

> **Nominalization:** This report offers a presentation of our findings on the consumption of fast food by Clemson students.
>
> **Revised:** This report presents our findings on the amount of fast food consumed by Clemson students.

> **Nominalization:** We make a recommendation that stressed-out students get exercise instead of turning to junk foods that harm their health.
>
> **Revised:** We recommend that stressed-out students get exercise instead of turning to junk foods that harm their health.

Nominalizations make your writing less clear because they hide the action in a sentence. If you move the action into the sentence's verb, your meaning will be much clearer to your readers.

Define Jargon and Other Technical Terms. In research reports, jargon words and technical terms are common and often unavoidable. When you use a jargon word or a technical term for the first time, give your readers a sentence definition or parenthetical definition to clarify its meaning.

> **Sentence Definition:** Low-density lipoprotein cholesterol (LDL) is a waxy substance that causes fat to build up in the walls of larger arteries.

> **Parenthetical Definition:** The extreme amount of salt in most fast food can cause hypertension, a condition in which a person's blood pressure rises to an abnormally high level and potentially does damage to the heart.

In moderation, jargon and technical terms are fine. Just define these words so your readers understand what you are talking about.

In Chapter 16, "Choosing a Style," you can find additional helpful advice about how to write clearly and plainly. Plain style will make your report sound authoritative and objective.

Designing Your Report

Reports usually aren't flashy documents, but that doesn't mean they should look unattractive and difficult to read. Your report's page design and graphics will often determine whether your readers actually read your report and whether they can quickly find the information they are looking for.

Design a "Raidable" Page Layout. People rarely read reports from front to back. Instead, they "raid" reports for the information they need. So use clear headings to highlight key sections and important information. Put critical pieces of information in lists, tables, or graphics to make them easy to find. Figure 12.7 shows a report that uses an attractive, raidable page layout. The headings are easy to locate, and the graphics support the written text. The use of color attracts the reader to the text. In other words, there are plenty of *access points* to begin reading this document.

Use Meaningful Headings. Your report's headings should give readers a clear idea about what is in each section of the report. You don't need to use *Methods, Results, Discussion,* and *Conclusion* as headings. Instead, you can give readers a sense of what they will find in each section with descriptive and interesting headings:

Our Research Methods: Going Undercover in the World of Fast Food

Our Findings: Stress Drives People to Fast Food

Our Recommendations: Battling the Expanding Waistline with Good Information

FIGURE 12.7
A Raidable Page Layout

The design of a report needs to be attractive and accessible to readers. In this report, the authors use headings, graphics, color, and boxes to highlight important information.

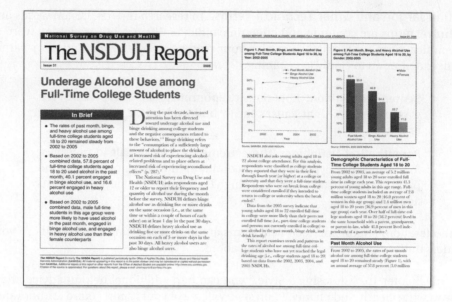

Use Tables, Graphs, and Charts to Reinforce Written Text. Where possible, find ways to put your data and other facts into tables, graphs, and charts. Your graphics should reinforce the written text, not replace it.

Use Photographs to Illustrate or Emphasize Key Points. With the availability of digital cameras, photographs are now common in research reports. If you find something difficult to describe, perhaps you can take a picture of it and add it to your report.

Insert a Table of Contents. If your report is over six pages long, insert a table of contents to help readers see the big picture and locate specific information easily. Most word-processing programs can generate a table of contents for you.

Designing a report does not take long, and your readers will appreciate a document that is attractive and easy to use.

Revising and Editing Your Report

Because research reports tend to be large documents, the revising and editing phase is critical to improving your report's quality. Here are some guidelines that will help you revise and edit your document:

Clarify the Purpose of the Report. In your introduction, make sure your purpose is stated clearly and prominently. Does this statement clearly tell your readers what the report will do? Now that you are finished drafting, would it be possible to state your purpose in an even clearer, more direct way? Did your purpose evolve while you were drafting your report?

Look for Gaps in Content. Search out places where you are making any unsupported statements or claims. Each major point needs to be backed up with some evidence that you have drawn from online, print, or empirical sources. If you find a gap in your support, look in your notes for evidence to fill that gap.

Find Nonessential Information That Can Be Cut. Include only need-to-know information and locate any places where your report goes off topic. Keep in mind that you probably found more information than you need. So slash any information that does not help you support or prove your major points in the report.

Pay Special Attention to Your Report's Paragraphs. Strong paragraphs are essential in a report because they help people scan and read quickly (reports are rarely read for enjoyment). Spend some extra time making sure you use good topic sentences early in your paragraphs.

Review Your Recommendations. Your recommendations are key to the success of your report. So make sure your recommendations follow logically from your findings and discussion.

Proofread Carefully. Reports are typically large, complex documents, so there are plenty of opportunities for typos, garbled sentences, spelling mistakes, and grammatical errors. Proofread carefully. Read your report out loud to help you find errors and weak sentences. Ask your friends to read your report carefully. Proofreading is especially important because errors in your report will signal shoddy research to your readers. If they find errors, they will be less likely to trust your findings.

Yes, time is short when you reach the revision and editing phase. The deadline is here. But don't skimp on revising and editing your report. Your hard work doing research, drafting, and designing will be undermined if your report isn't thoroughly revised.

The Explainer

An "explainer" is very brief report that addresses a specific question that your readers want to understand. The question might be one that people are curious about—"Does truth serum really work?" "Why do school grades go from *A* to *F* with no *E*?" Or it could be used to inform people about a local issue—"How do you apply for student financial aid on our campus?" Or it could be used to inform an organization's management or other group about an important issue—"How are businesses using social networking to increase sales?" "How does a student apply for financial aid on our campus?" The ability to write explainers is a valuable skill in the workplace, and it's becoming increasingly important in college as well.

Assignments similar to the explainer are becoming more popular in advanced college courses and on the Internet. Your professors may ask you to examine a very specific question that leads into a larger project. News Web sites publish briefs that offer factual information on important stories. For example, *Slate.com* publishes "The Explainer" to address questions that are in the news. Think tanks, like the Pew Foundation and the Brookings Institution, publish in a related genre called "The Brief" on their Web sites to influence public policy. Briefs are miniature reports that include most of a regular report's features.

Here is how to write an explainer:

Offer a title that asks your question.   Introduce your topic and purpose in the title itself.

Explain why the topic is interesting, important, or timely.   Relate your question to current events or to issues that your readers are interested in.

Provide context for your topic.   If readers don't know about your topic, define it, explain its function, or briefly review the history of your topic's origins and how it changed over the years.

Do your research and state the facts.   As objectively as possible, state the facts that you have collected. You should cite any sources you have collected, but you don't need to explain fully how you collected the facts you are providing.

Add a graphic.   If possible, put your data into a graph, chart, or table. Add a photograph if it would help illustrate your point or draw your readers in.

WRITE **your own explainer.** Choose a question related to an issue on your campus that interests you. Write a two-page explainer in which you objectively answer that question. Keep your opinions to a minimum.

Planking: What is it and Why it is Popular

IBTimes: San Francisco

Planking is a game that is gaining a lot of popularity where people (known as "plankers") lie down on the ground—usually in an unusual location—and post the picture of planking on online community such as Facebook.

The rules of planking are simple, as a planking page on Facebook page posts, "You got a body, you got a Plank." The planker must lie face down, on the ground or aerial, body straight like a wooden board, and palms attached to the side. The more innovative is the situation, the more popular it gets. Sounds random and silly, but people are posting hundreds of pictures on Facebook of their planking activities, and the numbers are increasing.

The planking game has developed gradually in the past decade. According to Tom Meltzer of *Guardian*, the game traces back 14 years by two English boys Gary Clarkson and Langbon who called it "the lying down game".

While Clarkson and Langbon do not remember what inspired their beginning, some believe the video for Radiohead song "Just" from 1995 to be the beginning where a man lies down on a road, ignoring the surrounded crowd—and by the end, everyone lie down together. The *Washington Post* suspects a 1993 film The Program might have had influence where a scene featured the quarterback lying down on the yellow line in the middle of the road as cars passed by. The scene was later deleted because some people were reported to have been killed or injured by trying to imitate the "brave" quarterback.

Clarkson and Langbon's game continued to grow, little-by-little, until they began a Facebook group in 2007, gaining thousands of followers. Plankers take pictures of their activities, usually in an unusual—and sometimes dangerous—situation, and post them on the social network site.

One person put her picture on the stairs of a subway station, while another person put his picture of planking on a railroad. Sometimes it is a group effort—seniors of Treasure Coast High School in Port St. Lucie, Florida decided to hold a senior plank rather than a prank. If this does not amuse the viewer, there was a man who planked across two opened overhead bins on the opposite end of an airplane—his neck on one and his ankle on the other.

continued

Planking: What is it and Why it is Popular? (continued)

The game may sound like a simple and harmless way of having fun for some. However, there is a growing number of voices that oppose such activity for having caused problems. In 2009, a group of doctors and nurses in Swindon, England were suspended for planking on duty. On May 13, 2011, a 20-year-old Nate Shaw in Australia was charged for planking on a police vehicle. Two days later, there was a first reported death while planking—Acton Beale of Australia fell from a seventh floor while planking on a balcony.

Despite the risk of danger, and ironically because of the media attention they were getting, planking is gaining more popularity. As of May 27, Facebook has over 700 groups related to planking, and several planking pages have drawn over 100,000 "likes."

Works Cited

Flock, Elizabeth. "Planking: Why Do People Do It?" *Washington Post Blog*. The Washington Post, 25 May 2011. Web. 26 May 2011.

Meltzer, Tom. "Planking: A Brief History." *Guardian.co.uk*. The Guardian, 16 May 2011. Web. 26 May 2011.

Here are some quick strategies to get you going on that report.

DEVELOP Your Research Question and Hypothesis

Write down an interesting research question about your topic—a question you would like to answer with some research. Then turn that question into a hypothesis (your best guess about how that research question will be answered).

FIND Out What You Already Know

Use prewriting tools to get your ideas out on the screen or a piece of paper. Star or highlight your best ideas. Then share your ideas with your friends and classmates.

FIND Out What Others Know

Develop a research plan that uses a combination of online, print, and empirical sources to find information. Interview experts on campus to find out more.

REVISIT Your Hypothesis

After you have done a good amount of research, look at your hypothesis again. Does it need to be modified or refined?

ORGANIZE and Draft Your Report

Organize your draft into sections and write one section at a time. The most common organization for a report is this: Executive Summary/Abstract, Introduction, Methods, Findings/Results, Discussion, Conclusion/Recommendations, References, and Appendices.

CHOOSE an Appropriate Style

Reports are almost always written in plain style, because this style sounds objective and authoritative. Use plain sentences and top-down paragraphs with solid topic sentences. The best style is one that sounds neutral and objective.

DESIGN the Document

Create an attractive and accessible page layout. Use active headings to help readers locate important information. Put your data and facts into tables, graphs, and charts, so your readers can see how they support the written text.

REVISE and Edit

Revise headings so they clearly state the points you want to make. Edit your paragraphs to make them easy to scan.

"How Many Zombies Do You Know?" Using Indirect Survey Methods to Measure Alien Attacks and Outbreaks of the Undead

ANDREW GELMAN AND GEORGE A. ROMEROY

Andrew Gelman, a respected and award-winning professor of statistics and political science at Columbia University, wrote on his blog that he created this unpublished paper to do some "humorous fun-poking" but also to illustrate how a very real cutting-edge survey method could be used for solving difficult research problems. As you read and enjoy this, notice he uses the conventions of the scientific-article genre.

1 Introduction

Zombification is a serious public-health and public-safety concern (Romero, 1968, 1978) but is difficult to study using traditional survey methods. Zombies are believed to have very low rates of telephone usage and in any case may be reluctant to identify themselves as such to a researcher. Face-to-face surveying involves too much risk to the interviewers, and internet surveys, although they originally were believed to have much promise, have recently had to be abandoned in this area because of the potential for zombie infection via computer virus.

In the absence of hard data, zombie researchers[1] have studied outbreaks and their dynamics using differential equation models (Munz, Hudea, Imad, & Smith, 2009, Lakeland, 2010) and, more recently, agent-based models (Messer, 2010). Figure 1 shows an example of such work.

But mathematical models are not enough. We need data.

2 Measuring zombification using network survey data

Zheng, Salganik, and Gelman (2006) discuss how to learn about groups that are not directly sampled in a survey. The basic idea is to ask respondents questions such as, "How many people do you know named Stephen/Margaret/etc." to learn the sizes of their social networks, questions such as "How many

---

[1] By "zombie researchers," we are talking about people who research zombies. We are not for a moment suggesting that these researchers are themselves zombies. Just to be on the safe side, however, we have conducted all our interactions with these scientists via mail.

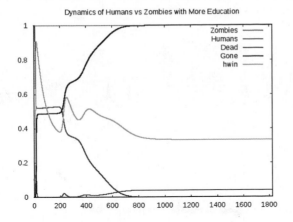

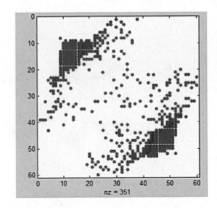

Figure 1: From Lakeland (2010) and Messer (2010). There were other zombie graphs at these sites, but these were the coolest.

lawyers/teachers/police officers/etc. do you know," to learn about the properties of these networks, and questions such as "How many prisoners do you know" to learn about groups that are hard to reach in a sample survey. Zheng et al. report that, on average, each respondent knows 750 people; thus, a survey of 1500 Americans can give us indirect information on about a million people.

This methodology should be directly applicable to zombies or, for that matter, ghosts, aliens, angels, and other hard-to-reach entities. In addition to giving us estimates of the populations of these groups, we can also learn, through national surveys, where they are more prevalent (as measured by the residences of the people who know them), and who is more likely to know them.

A natural concern in this research is potential underreporting; for example, what if your wife[2] is actually a zombie or an alien and you are not aware of the fact. This bias can be corrected via extrapolation using the estimates of different populations with varying levels of reporting error; Zheng et al.

(2006) discuss in the context of questions ranging from names (essentially no reporting error) to medical conditions such as diabetes and HIV that are often hidden.

3 Discussion

As Lakeland (2010) puts it, "Clearly, Hollywood plays a vital role in educating the public about the proper response to zombie infestation." In this article we have discussed how modern survey methods based on social networks can help us estimate the size of the problem.

Other, related, approaches are worth studying too. Social researchers have recently used Google Trends to study hard-to-measure trends using search volume (Askitas & Zimmerman, 2009, Goel, Hofman, Lahaie, Pennock, & Watts, 2010); Figure 2 illustrates how this might be done in the zombie context. It would also make sense to take advantage of social networking tools such as Facebook (Goel, Mason, & Watts, 2010) and more zombie-specific sites such as ZDate. We envision vast unfolding vistas of funding in this area.

4 Technical note

We originally wrote this article in Word, but then we converted it to Latex to make it look more like science.

---

[2] Here we are choosing a completely arbitrary example with absolutely no implications about our marriages or those of anyone we know.

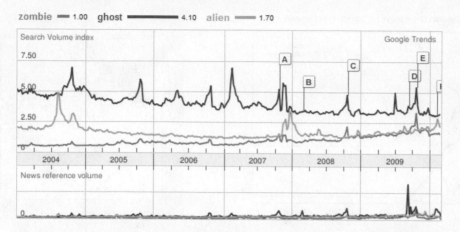

zombie ▬ 1.00   ghost ▬▬▬ 4.10   alien ▬▬ 1.70

Figure 2: Google Trends report on "zombie," "ghost," and "alien." The patterns show fascinating trends from which, we feel, much could be learned if resources were made available to us in the form of a sizable research grant from the Department of Defense, Department of Homeland Security, or a major film studio. Please make out any checks to the first author or deposit directly to his PayPal account.

5 References

Askitas, N., and Zimmermann, K. F. (2009). Google econometrics and unemployment forecasting. *Applied Economics Quarterly*, 55, 107-120.

Goel, S., Hofman, J. M., Lahaie, S., Pennock, D. M., & Watts, D. J. (2010). What can search predict? Technical report, Yahoo Research.

Goel, S., Mason, W., & Watts, D. J. (2010). Real and perceived attitude homophily in social networks. Technical report, Yahoo Research.

Lakeland, D. (2010). Improved zombie dynamics. Models of Reality blog, 1 March. http://models.street-artists.org/?p=554

Messer, B. (2010). Agent-based computational model of humanity's prospects for post zombie outbreak survival. The Tortise's Lens blog, 10 March. http://thetortoiseslens.blogspot.com/2010/03/agent-based-computational-model-of.html

Munz, P., Hudea, I., Imad, J., & Smith, R. J. (2009). When zombies attack!: Mathematical modelling of an outbreak of zombie infection. In *Infectious Disease Modelling Research Progress*, ed. J. M. Tchuenche and C. Chiyaka, 133-150. Hauppage, New York: Nova Science Publishers.

Romero, G. A. (1968). *Night of the Living Dead*. Image Ten.

Romero, G. A. (1978). *Dawn of the Dead*. Laurel Group.

Zheng, T., Slaganik, M., & Gelman, A. (2006). "How many people do you know in prison?": Using overdispersion in count data to estimate social structure in networks. *Journal of the American Statistical Association*, 101, 409-423.

A CLOSER LOOK AT

How Many Zombies Do You Know?

1. How well does this mock scientific-research report use the features (organization, feature, style, etc.) of the report genre? Where does it differ from the typical report genre?

2. All of the books and articles cited are real. Some are serious articles written by scientists and some are added for humorous effect. Run through the References section and try to predict which are

serious and which are silly. Use Google or another search engine to actually find these articles and test the accuracy of your predictions.

3. The introduction of a report should define a research question and explain why it is important to the reader. What is the question defined here? Does the author explain its importance?

IDEAS FOR
Writing

1. Write a mock research report in the style Gelman's article. (In fact, this zombies article is a parody of the last item in the Research section, which Gelman coauthored.) Choose a silly topic and write a report similar to Gelman's. Be sure to follow the report-genre. Try to make the moves he makes, and try to come up with a few of your own moves.

2. Write a bio of Andrew Gelman. Using Google or another search engine, find Andrew Gelman's professional page at Columbia University and take a look at his papers and some of his blog entries. Do Internet research into his areas of specialization. Try to capture what distinguishes the work that he does and how he approaches his work. We usually think of the scientist as a very, very serious, almost non-human figure who is devoted to seeking the scientific truth. How is Gelman different?

Report of the APA Task Force on the Sexualization of Girls: Executive Summary

EILEEN L. ZUBRIGGEN, REBECCA L. COLLINS, SHARON LAMB, TONI-ANN ROBERTS, DEBORAH L. TOLMAN, L. MONIQUE WARD, AND JEANNE BLAKE

This report was published by the American Psychological Association (APA). It offers a broad review of research done on portrayals of girls in the media. The report's methodology describes how the researchers analyzed a variety of articles on this important and complex topic. We have included only the executive summary here. Pay attention to how it follows the report genre pattern and uses an objective style.

Report of the Task Force on the Sexualization of Girls

Executive Summary

Journalists, child advocacy organizations, parents, and psychologists have argued that the sexualization of girls is a broad and increasing problem and is harmful to girls. The APA Task Force on the Sexualization of Girls was formed in response to these expressions of public concern.

APA has long been involved in issues related to the impact of media content on children. In 1994, APA adopted a policy resolution on Violence in Mass Media, which updated and expanded an earlier resolution on televised violence. In 2004, the APA Task Force on Advertising and Children produced a report examining broad issues related to advertising to children. That report provided recommendations to restrict advertising that is primarily directed at young children and to include developmentally appropriate disclaimers in advertising, as well as recommendations regarding research, applied psychology, industry practices, media literacy, advertising, and schools. In 2005, APA adopted the policy resolution on Violence in Video Games and Interactive Media, which documented the negative impact of exposure to violent interactive media on children and youth and called for the reduction of violence in these media. These resolutions and reports addressed how violent media and advertising affect children and youth, but they did not address sexualization.

The APA Task Force on the Sexualization of Girls was tasked with examining the psychological theory, research, and clinical experience addressing the sexualization of girls via media and other cultural messages, including the prevalence of these messages and their impact on girls and the role and impact of race/ethnicity and socioeconomic status. The task force was charged with producing a report, including recommendations for research, practice, education and training, policy, and public awareness.

This report examines and summarizes psychological theory, research, and clinical experience addressing the sexualization of girls. The report (a) defines sexualization; (b)

examines the prevalence and provides examples of sexualization in society and in cultural institutions, as well as interpersonally and intrapsychically; (c) evaluates the evidence suggesting that sexualization has negative consequences for girls and for the rest of society; and (d) describes positive alternatives that may help counteract the influence of sexualization.

There are several components to sexualization, and these set it apart from healthy sexuality. Sexualization occurs when

- a person's value comes only from his or her sexual appeal or behavior, to the exclusion of other characteristics;
- a person is held to a standard that equates physical attractiveness (narrowly defined) with being sexy;
- a person is sexually objectified—that is, made into a thing for others' sexual use, rather than seen as a person with the capacity for independent action and decision making; and/or
- sexuality is inappropriately imposed upon a person.

All four conditions need not be present; any one is an indication of sexualization. The fourth condition (the inappropriate imposition of sexuality) is especially relevant to children. Anyone (girls, boys, men, women) can be sexualized. But when children are imbued with adult sexuality, it is often imposed upon them rather than chosen by them. Self-motivated sexual exploration, on the other hand, is not sexualization by our definition, nor is age-appropriate exposure to information about sexuality.

Evidence for the Sexualization of Girls

Virtually every media form studied provides ample evidence of the sexualization of women, including television, music videos, music lyrics, movies, magazines, sports media, video games, the Internet, and advertising (e.g., Gow, 1996; Grauerholz & King, 1997; Krassas, Blauwkamp, & Wesselink, 2001, 2003; Lin, 1997; Plous & Neptune, 1997; Vincent, 1989; Ward, 1995). Some studies have examined forms of media that are especially popular with children and adolescents, such as video games and teen-focused magazines.

In study after study, findings have indicated that women more often than men are portrayed in a sexual manner (e.g., dressed in revealing clothing, with bodily postures or facial expressions that imply sexual readiness) and are objectified (e.g., used as a decorative object, or as body parts rather than a whole person). In addition, a narrow (and unrealistic) standard of physical beauty is heavily emphasized. These are the models of femininity presented for young girls to study and emulate.

In some studies, the focus was on the sexualization of female characters across all ages, but most focused specifically on young adult women. Although few studies examined the prevalence of sexualized portrayals of girls in particular, those that have been conducted found that such sexualization does occur and may be increasingly common. For example, O'Donohue, Gold, and McKay (1997) coded advertisements over a 40-year period in five magazines targeted to men, women, or a general adult readership. Although relatively few (1.5%) of the ads portrayed children in a sexualized manner, of those that did, 85% sexualized girls rather than boys. Furthermore, the percentage of sexualizing ads increased over time.

Although extensive analyses documenting the sexualization of girls, in particular, have yet to be conducted, individual examples can easily be found. These include advertisements (e.g., the Skechers "naughty and nice" ad that featured Christina Aguilera dressed as a schoolgirl in pigtails, with her shirt unbuttoned, licking a lollipop), dolls (e.g., Bratz dolls dressed in sexualized clothing such as miniskirts, fishnet stockings, and feather boas), clothing (thongs sized for 7– to 10-year-olds, some printed with slogans such as "wink wink"), and television programs (e.g., a televised fashion show in which adult models in lingerie were presented as young girls). Research documenting the pervasiveness and influence of such products and portrayals is sorely needed.

Societal messages that contribute to the sexualization of girls come not only from media and merchandise but also through girls' interpersonal relationships (e.g., with parents, teachers, and peers; Brown & Gilligan, 1992). Parents may contribute to sexualization in a number of ways. For example, parents may convey the message that maintaining an attractive physical appearance is the most important goal for girls. Some may allow or encourage plastic surgery to help girls meet that goal. Research shows that teachers sometimes encourage girls to play at being sexualized adult women (Martin, 1988) or hold beliefs that girls of color are "hypersexual" and thus unlikely to achieve academic success (Rolón-Dow, 2004). Both male and female peers have been found to contribute to the sexualization of girls—girls by policing each other to ensure conformance with standards of thinness and sexiness (Eder, 1995; Nichter, 2000) and boys by sexually objectifying and harassing girls. Finally, at the extreme end, parents, teachers, and peers, as well as others (e.g., other family members, coaches, or strangers) sometimes sexually abuse, assault, prostitute, or traffic girls, a most destructive form of sexualization.

If girls purchase (or ask their parents to purchase) products and clothes designed to make them look physically appealing and sexy, and if they style their identities after the sexy celebrities who populate their cultural landscape, they are, in effect, sexualizing themselves. Girls also sexualize themselves when they think of themselves in objectified terms. Psychological researchers have identified *self-objectification* as a key process whereby girls learn to think of and treat their own bodies as objects of others' desires (Frederickson & Roberts, 1997; McKinley & Hyde, 1996). In self-objectification, girls internalize an observer's perspective on their physical selves and learn to treat themselves as objects to be looked at and evaluated for their appearance. Numerous studies have documented the presence of self-objectification in women more than in men. Several studies have also documented this phenomenon in adolescent and preadolescent girls (McConnell, 2001; Slater & Tiggemann, 2002).

Consequences of the Sexualization of Girls

Psychology offers several theories to explain how the sexualization of girls and women could influence girls' well-being. Ample evidence testing these theories indicates that sexualization has negative effects in a variety of domains, including cognitive functioning, physical and mental health, sexuality, and attitudes and beliefs.

Although most of these studies have been conducted on women in late adolescence (i.e., college age), findings are likely to generalize to younger adolescents and to girls, who may be even more strongly affected because their sense of self is still being formed.

Cognitive and Emotional Consequences

Cognitively, self-objectification has been repeatedly shown to detract from the ability to concentrate and focus one's attention, thus leading to impaired performance on mental activities such as mathematical computations or logical reasoning (Frederickson, Roberts, Noll, Quinn, & Twenge, 1998; Gapinski, Brownell, & LaFrance, 2003; Hebl, King, & Lin, 2004). One study demonstrated this fragmenting quite vividly (Fredrickson et al., 1998). While alone in a dressing room, college students were asked to try on and evaluate either a swimsuit or a sweater. While they waited for 10 minutes wearing the garment, they completed a math test. The results revealed that young women in swimsuits performed significantly worse on the math problems than did those wearing sweaters. No differences were found for young men. In other words, thinking about the body and comparing it to sexualized cultural ideals disrupted mental capacity. In the emotional domain, sexualization and objectification undermine confidence in and comfort with one's own body, leading to a host of negative emotional consequences, such as shame, anxiety, and even self-disgust. The association between self-objectification and anxiety about appearance and feelings of shame has been found in adolescent girls (12–13-year-olds) (Slater & Tiggemann, 2002) as well as in adult women.

Mental and Physical Health

Research links sexualization with three of the most common mental health problems of girls and women: eating disorders, low self-esteem, and depression or depressed mood (Abramson & Valene, 1991; Durkin & Paxton, 2002; Harrison, 2000; Hofschire & Greenberg, 2001; Mills, Polivy, Herman, & Tiggemann, 2002; Stice, Schupak-Neuberg, Shaw, & Stein, 1994; Thomsen, Weber, & Brown, 2002; Ward, 2004). Several studies (on both teenage and adult women) have found associations between exposure to nar-row representations of female beauty (e.g., the "thin ideal") and disordered eating attitudes and symptoms. Research also links exposure to sexualized female ideals with lower self-esteem, negative mood, and depressive symptoms among adolescent girls and women. In addition to mental health consequences of sexualization, research suggests that girls' and women's physical health may also be negatively affected, albeit indirectly.

Sexuality

Sexual well-being is an important part of healthy development and overall well-being, yet evidence suggests that the sexualization of girls has negative consequences in terms of girls' ability to develop healthy sexuality. Self-objectification has been linked directly with diminished sexual health among adolescent girls (e.g., as measured by decreased condom use and diminished sexual assertiveness; Impett, Schooler, & Tolman, 2006). Frequent exposure to narrow ideals of attractiveness is associated with unrealistic and/or negative expectations concerning sexuality. Negative effects (e.g., shame) that emerge during adolescence may lead to sexual problems in adulthood (Brotto, Heiman, & Tolman, in press).

Attitudes and Beliefs

Frequent exposure to media images that sexualize girls and women affects how girls conceptualize femininity and sexuality. Girls and young women who more frequently consume or engage with mainstream media content offer stronger endorsement of sexual stereotypes that depict women as sexual objects (Ward, 2002; Ward & Rivadeneyra, 1999; Zurbriggen & Morgan, 2006). They also place appearance and physical attractiveness at the center of women's value.

Impact on Others and on Society

The sexualization of girls can also have a negative impact on other groups (i.e., boys, men, and adult women) and on society more broadly. Exposure to narrow ideals of female sexual attractiveness may make it difficult for some men to find an "acceptable" partner or to fully enjoy intimacy with a female partner (e.g., Schooler & Ward, 2006).

3

Adult women may suffer by trying to conform to a younger and younger standard of ideal female beauty. More general societal effects may include an increase in sexism; fewer girls pursuing careers in science, technology, engineering, and mathematics (STEM); increased rates of sexual harassment and sexual violence; and an increased demand for child pornography.

Positive Alternatives to the Sexualization of Girls

Some girls and their supporters, now and in the past, have resisted mainstream characterizations of girls as sexual objects. A variety of promising approaches exist to reduce the amount of sexualization that occurs and to ameliorate its effects.

Because the media are important sources of sexualizing images, the development and implementation of school-based media literacy training programs could be key in combating the influence of sexualization. There is an urgent need to teach critical skills in viewing and consuming media, focusing specifically on the sexualization of women and girls. Other school-based approaches include increased access to athletic and other extracurricular programs for girls and the development and presentation of comprehensive sexuality education programs.

Strategies for parents and other caregivers include learning about the impact of sexualization on girls and co-viewing media with their children in order to influence the way in which media messages are interpreted. Action by parents and families has been effective in confronting sources of sexualized images of girls. Organized religious and other ethical instruction can offer girls important practical and psychological alternatives to the values conveyed by popular culture.

Girls and girls' groups can also work toward change. Alternative media such as "zines" (Web-based magazines), "blogs" (Web logs), and feminist magazines, books, and Web sites encourage girls to become activists who speak out and develop their own alternatives. Girl empowerment groups also support girls in a variety of ways and provide important counterexamples to sexualization.

Recommendations

I. Research

A solid research base has explored the effects of having an objectified body image or viewing objectified body images in the media. Much previous work, however, has focused on women. Future studies focusing on girls are needed. In addition, more culturally competent, focused work is required to document the phenomenon of the sexualization of girls; to explore the short- and long-term harm of viewing, listening to, and buying into a sexualized pathway to power; and to test alternative presentations of girlhood, sexuality, and power. We recommend that psychologists conduct research to:

1. Document the frequency of sexualization, specifically of girls, and examine whether sexualization is increasing.

2. Examine and inform our understanding of the circumstances under which the sexualization of girls occurs and identify factors involving the media and products that either contribute to or buffer against the sexualization of girls.

3. Examine the presence or absence of the sexualization of girls and women in all media but especially in movies, music videos, music lyrics, video games, books, blogs, and Internet sites. In particular, research is needed to examine the extent to which girls are portrayed in sexualized and objectified ways and whether this has increased over time. In addition, it is important that these studies focus specifically on sexualization rather than on sexuality more broadly or on other constructs such as gender-role stereotyping.

4. Describe the influence and/or impact of sexualization on girls. This includes both short- and long-term effects of viewing or buying into a sexualizing objectifying image, how these effects influence girls' development, self-esteem, friendships, and intimate relationships, ideas about femininity, body image, physical, mental, and sexual health, sexual satisfaction, desire for plastic surgery, risk factors for early pregnancy, abortion, and sexually transmitted infections, attitudes toward women, other girls, boys, and men, as well as educational aspirations and future career success.

5. Explore issues of age compression ("adultification" of young girls and "youthification" of adult women), including prevalence, impact on the emotional well-being of girls and women, and influences on behavior.

6. Explore differences in presentation of sexualized images and effects of these images on girls of color; lesbian, bisexual, questioning, and transgendered girls; girls of different cultures and ethnicities; girls of different religions; girls with disabilities; and girls from all socioeconomic groups.

7. Identify media (including advertising) and marketing alternatives to sexualized images of girls, such as positive depictions of sexuality.

8. Identify effective, culturally competent protective factors (e.g., helping adolescent girls develop a nonobjectified model of normal, healthy sexual development and expression through school or other programs).

9. Evaluate the effectiveness of programs and interventions that promote positive alternatives and approaches to the sexualization of girls. Particular attention should be given to programs and interventions at the individual, family, school, and/or community level.

10. Explore the relationship between the sexualization of girls and societal issues such as sexual abuse, child pornography, child prostitution, and the trafficking of girls. Research on the potential associations between the sexualization of girls and the sexual exploitation of girls is virtually nonexistent, and the need for this line of inquiry is pressing.

11. Investigate the relationships between international issues such as immigration and globalization and the sexualization of girls worldwide. Document the global prevalence of the sexualization of girls and the types of sexualization that occur in different countries or regions and any regional differences in the effects of sexualization. Assess the effects of sexualization on immigrant girls and determine whether these effects are moderated by country of origin, age at immigration, and level of acculturation.

12. Conduct controlled studies on the efficacy of working directly with girls and girls' groups that address these issues, as well as other prevention/intervention programs.

13. Researchers who are conducting studies on related topics (e.g., physical attractiveness, body awareness, or acceptance of the thin ideal) should consider the impact of sexualization as they develop their findings.

II. Practice

As practitioners, psychologists can perform a valuable service by raising awareness of the negative impact of the sexualization of girls—on girls, as well as on boys, women, and men. As individuals and in collaboration with others, practitioners are encouraged to address the sexualization of girls. We recommend:

1. That APA make the Report of the Task Force on the Sexualization of Girls available to practitioners working with children and adolescents in order to familiarize them with information and resources relevant to the sexualization of girls and objectifying behavior on the part of girls.

2. That APA make the Report of the Task Force on the Sexualization of Girls available to practitioners as a source of information on assisting girls in developing the skills necessary to advocate for themselves and counter these adverse messages, taking into account the impact and influence of family and other relationships.

III. Education and Training

Education and training focusing on the prevalence and impact of the sexualization of girls are needed at all levels of psychology to raise awareness within the discipline of psychology and among psychologists about these important issues. We recommend:

1. That APA disseminate information about the Report of the Task Force on the Sexualization of Girls to instructors at the middle-school, high-school, and undergraduate levels and to chairs of graduate departments of psychology.

2. That information from the Report of the Task Force on the Sexualization of Girls be considered for inclusion in future revisions of the *National Standards for High School Psychology Curricula* and *Guidelines on the Undergraduate Psychology Major* by the groups charged with revising these documents.

5

3. That chairs of graduate departments of psychology and of graduate departments in other areas in which psychologists work be encouraged to consider information from the Report of the Task Force on the Sexualization of Girls as curricula are developed within their programs and to aid in the dissemination of the report.

4. That information from the Report of the Task Force on the Sexualization of Girls be considered for development as continuing education and online academy programming, in partnership with APA's Continuing Education in Psychology Office.

5. That the Ethics Committee and APA Ethics Office consider and use this report in developing ethics educational and training materials for psychologists and make this report available to the group responsible for the next revision of the APA "Ethical Principles of Psychologists and Code of Conduct."

IV. Public Policy

APA, in collaboration with other organizations and through its advocacy efforts, is encouraged to advocate for and better support understanding of the nature and impact of the sexualization of girls, as well as identification and broad implementation of strategies to combat this serious societal problem. We recommend:

1. That APA advocate for funding to support needed research in the areas outlined above.

2. That APA advocate for funding to support the development and implementation by public agencies and private organizations of media literacy programs, including interactive media, in schools that combat sexualization and objectification.

3. That APA advocate for the inclusion of information about sexualization and objectification in health and other related programs, including comprehensive sex education and other sexuality education programs.

4. That APA encourage federal agencies to support the development of programming that may counteract damaging images of girlhood and test the effects of such pro-

grams, for example, Web "zines" (i.e., Web magazines), extracurricular activities (such as athletics), and programs that help girls feel powerful in ways other than through a sexy appearance.

5. That APA work with Congress and relevant federal agencies and industry to reduce the use of sexualized images of girls in all forms of media and products.

V. Public Awareness

The task force offers the following recommendations with the goal of raising public awareness about this important issue. Achieving this goal will require a comprehensive, grassroots, communitywide effort. Participants and stakeholders will include parents and other caregivers, educators, young people, community-based organizations, religious communities, the media, advertisers, marketing professionals, and manufacturers. Overarching strategies will be needed to build linkages and partnerships among the community members. If the goal of raising public awareness is left unmet, the mission of this work will be significantly curtailed. We recommend:

1. That APA seek outside funding to support the development and implementation of an initiative to address the issues raised in this report and identify outside partners to collaborate on these goals. The long-term goals of this initiative, to be pursued in collaboration with these outside partners, should include the following:

- Develop age-appropriate multimedia education resources representing ethnically and culturally diverse young people (boys and girls) for parents, educators, health care providers, and community-based organizations, available in English and other languages, to help facilitate effective conversations about the sexualization of girls and its impact on girls, as well as on boys, women, and men.

- Convene forums that will bring together members of the media and a panel of leading experts in the field to examine and discuss (a) the sexualization of girls in the United States, (b) the findings of this task force report, and (c) strategies to increase awareness about this issue and reduce negative images of girls in the media.

- Develop media awards for positive portrayals of girls as strong, competent, and nonsexualized (e.g., the best television portrayal of girls or the best toy).
- Convene forums with industry partners, including the media, advertisers, marketing professionals, and manufacturers, to discuss the presentation of sexualized images and the potential negative impact on girls and to develop relationships with the goal of providing guidance on appropriate material for varying developmental ages and on storylines and programming that reflect the positive portrayals of girls.

2. That school personnel, parents and other caregivers, community-based youth and parenting organizations, and local business and service organizations encourage positive extracurricular activities that help youth build nurturing connections with peers and enhance self-esteem based on young people's abilities and character rather than on their appearance.

References

Abramson, E., & Valene, P. (1991). Media use, dietary restraint, bulimia, and attitudes toward obesity: A preliminary study. *British Review of Bulimia and Anorexia Nervosa, 5,* 73-76.

Brotto, L., Heiman, J., & Tolman, D. (in press). Towards conceptualizing women's desires: A mixed methods study. *Journal of Sex Research.*

Brown, L. M., & Gilligan, C. (1992). *Meeting at the crossroads: Women's psychology and girls' development.* Cambridge, MA: Harvard University Press.

Durkin, S. J., & Paxton, S. J. (2002). Predictors of vulnerability to reduced body image satisfaction and psychological well-being in response to exposure to idealized female media images in adolescent girls. *Journal of Psychosomatic Research, 53,* 995-1005.

Eder, D. (with Evans, C. C., & Parker, S). (1995). *School talk: Gender and adolescent culture.* New Brunswick, NJ: Rutgers University Press.

Fredrickson, B. L., & Roberts, T-A. (1997). Objectification theory: Toward understanding women's lived experience and mental health risks. *Psychology of Women Quarterly, 21,* 173-206.

Fredrickson, B. L., Roberts, T., Noll, S. M., Quinn, D. M., & Twenge, J. M. (1998). That swimsuit becomes you: Sex differences in self-objectification, restrained eating, and math performance. *Journal of Personality and Social Psychology, 75,* 269-284.

Gapinski, K. D., Brownell, K. D., & LaFrance, M. (2003). Body objectification and "fat talk": Effects on emotion, motivation, and cognitive performance. *Sex Roles, 48,* 377-388.

Gow, J. (1996). Reconsidering gender roles on MTV: Depictions in the most popular music videos of the early 1990s. *Communication Reports, 9,* 151-161.

Grauerholz, E., & King, A. (1997). Primetime sexual harassment. *Violence Against Women, 3,* 129-148.

7

Harrison, K. (2000). The body electric: Thin-ideal media and eating disorders in adolescents. *Journal of Communication, 50,* 119-143.

Hebl, M. R., King, E. G., & Lin, J. (2004). The swimsuit becomes us all: Ethnicity, gender, and vulnerability to self-objectification. *Personality and Social Psychology Bulletin, 30,* 1322-1331.

Hofschire, L. J., & Greenberg, B. S. (2001). Media's impact on adolescents' body dissatisfaction. In J. D. Brown & J. R. Steele (Eds.), *Sexual teens, sexual media* (pp. 125-149). Mahwah, NJ: Erlbaum.

Impett, E. A., Schooler, D., & Tolman, D. L. (2006). To be seen and not heard: Femininity ideology and adolescent girls' sexual health. *Archives of Sexual Behavior, 21,* 628-646.

Krassas, N., Blauwkamp, J. M., & Wesselink, P. (2001). Boxing Helena and corseting Eunice: Sexual rhetoric in *Cosmopolitan* and *Playboy* magazines. *Sex Roles, 44,* 751-771.

Krassas, N. R., Blauwkamp, J. M., & Wesselink, P. (2003). "Master your Johnson": Sexual rhetoric in *Maxim* and *Stuff* magazines. *Sexuality & Culture, 7,* 98-119.

Lin, C. (1997). Beefcake versus cheesecake in the 1990s: Sexist portrayals of both genders in television commercials. *Howard Journal of Communications, 8,* 237-249.

Martin, K. A. (1998). Becoming a gendered body: Practices in preschools. *American Sociological Review, 63,* 494-511.

McConnell, C. (2001). An object to herself: The relationship between girls and their bodies. *Dissertation Abstracts International, 61*(8B), p. 4416.

McKinley, N. M., & Hyde, J. S. (1996). The Objectified Body Consciousness Scale. *Psychology of Women Quarterly, 20,* 181-215.

Mills, J., Polivy, J., Herman, C. P., & Tiggemann, M. (2002). Effects of exposure to thin media images: Evidence of self-enhancement among restrained eaters. *Personality and Social Psychology Bulletin, 28,* 1687-1699.

Nichter, M. (2000). *Fat talk: What girls and their parents say about dieting.* Cambridge, MA: Harvard University Press.

O'Donohue, W., Gold, S. R., & McKay, J. S. (1997). Children as sexual objects: Historical and gender trends in magazines. *Sexual Abuse: Journal of Research & Treatment, 9,* 291-301.

Plous, S., & Neptune, D. (1997). Racial and gender biases in magazine advertising: A content analytic study. *Psychology of Women Quarterly, 21,* 627-644.

Rolón-Dow, R. (2004). Seduced by images: Identity and schooling in the lives of Puerto Rican girls. *Anthropology and Education Quarterly, 35,* 8-29.

Schooler, D., & Ward, L. M. (2006). Average joes: Men's relationships with media, real bodies, and sexuality. *Psychology of Men and Masculinity, 7,* 27-41.

Slater, A., & Tiggemann, M. (2002). A test of objectification theory in adolescent girls. *Sex Roles, 46,* 343-349.

Stice, E., Schupak-Neuberg, E., Shaw, H., & Stein, R. (1994). Relation of media exposure to eating disorder symptomatology: An examination of mediating mechanisms. *Journal of Abnormal Psychology, 103,* 836-840.

Thomsen, S. R., Weber, M. M., & Brown, L. B. (2002). The relationship between reading beauty and fashion magazines and the use of pathogenic dieting methods among adolescent females. *Adolescence, 37,* 1-18.

Vincent, R. C. (1989). Clio's consciousness raised? Portrayal of women in rock videos, re-examined. *Journalism Quarterly, 66,* 155-160.

Ward, L. M. (1995). Talking about sex: Common themes about sexuality in the prime-time television programs children and adolescents view most. *Journal of Youth & Adolescence, 24,* 595-615.

Ward, L. M. (2002). Does television exposure affect emerging adults' attitudes and assumptions about sexual relationships? Correlational and experimental confirmation. *Journal of Youth and Adolescence, 31,* 1-15.

Ward, L. M. (2004). Wading through the stereotypes: Positive and negative associations between media use and Black adolescents' conceptions of self. *Developmental Psychology, 40,* 284-294.

Ward, L. M., & Rivadeneyra, R. (1999). Contributions of entertainment television to adolescents' sexual attitudes and expectations: The role of viewing amount versus viewer involvement. *Journal of Sex Research, 36,* 237–249.

Zurbriggen, E. L., & Morgan, E. M. (2006). Who wants to marry a millionaire? Reality dating television programs, attitudes toward sex, and sexual behaviors. *Sex Roles, 54,* 1-17.

9

Report of the APA Task Force on the Sexualization of Girls: Executive Summary

A CLOSER LOOK AT
Report of the APA Task Force on the Sexualization of Girls

1. The report concludes that girls are victimized by oversexualization in American culture. Look closely at this report, and identify three to five *causes* of the sexualization of girls. Then identify three to five *effects* of this sexualization on girls, women, and American culture.

2. Where and how does the report define "sexualization"? Based on your own experiences, do you agree with these definitions? Have you experienced these kinds of conditions in your own life?

3. Look over the recommendations of the report. Which of these recommendations would make the most significant changes in American culture? Which of these recommendations could actually change how girls and women perceive themselves and how they are portrayed in the American media?

IDEAS FOR
Writing

1. Write a three-page memoir describing an event in which you, or someone else, were sexualized as described in this report. First, set the scene and describe the event as a complication that disrupts that scene. Then describe how the event was evaluated and resolved. End your memoir by discussing what was learned. Keep in mind that sexualization is not the same as sexual assault.

2. Write a two-page response to this report in which you react to its findings and recommendations. What parts of the report do you agree with? What parts do you disagree with? Would you expand or narrow the report's definitions of sexualization? How might you expand or alter the study?

1. With your group, brainstorm all of the different "reports" that you can think of—lab reports, research reports, recommendation reports, police reports, credit reports, and other report types that you might have come across. Come up with five characteristics that all these reports have in common. Then list one thing about each report that makes it unique.

2. Find and download a report from the Internet. To find a report, put "Report" and a topic that interests you into an Internet search engine like *Google, Yahoo!,* or *Ask.* (You might include ".pdf" or ".doc" in the search line to narrow the search.) A list of reports should pop up. With your group, discuss whether the report's topic, purpose, and main point are clearly stated in the introduction.

3. After reading the student example in this chapter, discuss with your group how well this report follows the genre of the research report. Separately, consider its content, organization, style, and design. What could be improved?

1. Make a list of five topics on which you might want to do research. Then pick three of these topics, choose an angle, and narrow them down to something that you could handle in a report. When choosing an angle, try to figure out why this issue is interesting right now. Share your topic ideas with your group.

2. Devise a research question that interests you. Then turn it into a hypothesis. Using a prewriting tool, such as brainstorming or a concept map, sketch out a research methodology that would allow you to answer this question and prove or disprove your hypothesis. Turn your methodology into an outline. Then write a one-page memo to your professor that reviews your outline and discusses why you would pursue this research question this way.

3. Use an Internet search engine to find a report on the issue you are or will be investigating. Write a one-page analysis of the report. Does the report have all the elements described in this chapter? Were there gaps in the report? Was the report organized well? Is the style and design appropriate for the topic?

There are many, many microgenres related to the report. Choose a microgenre from the list below and find three examples in print or on the Internet. Then, come up with your own guidelines that explain how to write one of these microgenres.

Explainer for an outsider—explainer about a well-understood question but addressed to an outsider (e.g., older person, foreigner, extraterrestrial being) unfamiliar with your world

Incident report—description of an event (an accident or unusual occurrence) that you witnessed or experienced

Consumer report—a report describing head-to-head testing of two or more products

Letter of complaint—description of a negative experience with a product or service, addressed to a decision maker and requesting specific actions from that person

Research-activity report—a report describing how you conducted your print, online, and empirical research (listing search engines, search terms, etc.) and how you assessed the reliability of those sources (consult Chapters 24 and 25)

Write This

1. **Turn a print report into a multimedia presentation.** On the Internet, find a report and transform it into a multimedia presentation that has ten to fifteen slides. Use presentation software like *PowerPoint* or *Keynote* to help you organize the information and make it attractive to an audience. Where possible, add graphs, charts, photographs, and other visuals that will help explain the topic.

2. **Write a field research report.** A field research report gives you a chance to collect data about local issues in your community or on campus. To write one, you need to pose a research question, devise a method for answering it, do the research, and interpret your findings. With a small group, do these activities:

   a. Make a list of interesting or urgent issues or questions that your community or campus faces. What are some of the more annoying problems on your college's campus that you know about or that are in the news?

   b. Choose one that seems especially annoying. What has changed recently to bring this problem to a head?

   c. Discuss this problem with a group of other people in your class.

   d. Choose one angle of that issue and turn it into a research question that could be answered by doing field research (interviews, surveys, observations). State that research question briefly but clearly and thoroughly.

   e. Turn your research question into a hypothesis.

   Show your research question and hypothesis to your professor. If he or she approves it, begin your research. Write an eight-page report on your topic.

3. **Answer an eccentric question in an experimental report.** Pose an odd question that you would like to answer (e.g., "How big are the splatters from eggs dropped from different heights?" "How do people react when they see a strangely worded sign?"). Then devise a research methodology and come up with some results. Write a report that presents your findings. Include pictures or other graphics.

13

Research Papers

In this chapter, you will learn how to—

- figure out what kind of research paper your professor is asking for.
- develop a topic and angle for an effective research paper.
- properly cite sources and format your research paper.

The research paper is one of the most common large assignments you will write in college, but it is also one of the most misunderstood. Research papers, which are also called "term papers," are typically assigned in the last month of a college course. They involve doing substantial research at the library and on the Internet. They are used to explain a historical period or event, study a social trend or natural phenomenon, or argue for a position about culture, art, science, technology, or religion.

When a professor assigns a research paper, he or she is most likely asking you to do a substantial amount of research on a subject, synthesize the results of your research, and explain your subject in a clear and engaging way. Research papers tend to be about ten double-spaced pages with a list of "Works Cited" or "References" at the end. However, your professors may ask for research papers that are longer or shorter, depending on the course and the subject matter.

Research paper assignments can be misunderstood because each of your professors may have a different idea about the content, organization, style, and format. For example, some professors have an "expository" research paper in mind. They want you to explain an issue without making an overt argument for one side or the other. Other professors will want an "argumentative" research paper in which you take a side on an issue and use your research to support your position. When you are assigned a research paper, one of your first tasks is to find out what kind of research paper—expository or argumentative—your professor expects.

Outside of college, you probably won't be asked to write something called a "research paper." In the workplace, *white papers* and *analytical reports* are similar to research papers because they rely on sources to explain an issue or support an argument.

Research Papers

Research papers can be organized a variety of ways. These models show two basic patterns that you can adjust to fit your topic, angle, purpose, readers, and context.

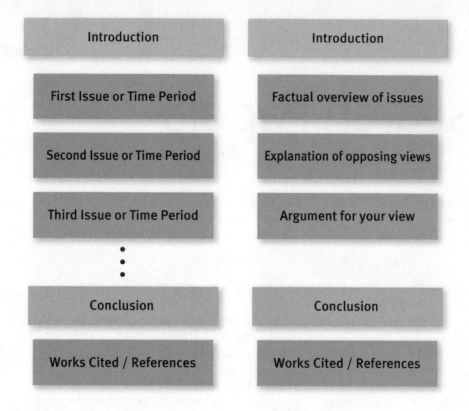

An effective research paper uses sources to explain an issue or argue for a position. They tend to have the following major features:

- **An introduction** that identifies the research paper's topic and purpose, while clearly stating a thesis or main point that you will support or prove; the introduction should offer background information and explain why the topic is important.

- **Body paragraphs** that use an issue-by-issue or chronological pattern to present the results of your research; the body is divided into sections with headings.

- **A Conclusion** that restates the thesis or main point of the research paper and summarizes your major points.

- **A References or Works Cited** that includes a list of references or works cited in a standardized citation style (usually MLA or APA style).

Turnbow 1

Katelyn Turnbow
Professor Thompson
English 102
6 May 2009

Lives Not Worth the Money?

The idea of a forgotten disease is almost absurd—a disease for which a cure is available and effective but never given a chance to work. We are often of the belief that human life is invaluable, that it cannot be bought with money and that a sick person should be treated whether he is an enemy or a friend, poor or rich. In reality, however, the cures that do not make money for some manufacturer are simply not made at all. According to the World Health Organization (WHO), one need only look at African sleeping sickness (WHO). There is a cure, but the victims who would benefit from the drug are poor and considered "unprofitable" by the pharmaceutical industry. It remains, however, a drug company's ethical responsibility to care for people its drugs can save, even when helping them is not profitable.

African sleeping sickness, also known as Human African Trypanosomiasis or HAT, was discovered in 1902 and kills more than 50,000 people a year. These victims, however, are often forgotten because they are poor and live in sub-Saharan Africa, not a prosperous Western nation (see Fig. 1). The disease is caused by a parasite and transmitted to humans by the Tsetse fly. Some villages in the region report that sleeping sickness is the "first or second cause of mortality," and that it is "even ahead of HIV/AIDS" (WHO). WHO estimates that on top of the 17,616 cases reported in 2005, about 50,000-70,000 cases were never diagnosed.

Sleeping sickness manifests in two distinct stages. The haemolymphatic stage (blood-lymph node) occurs shortly after exposure to the parasite and causes headache, fever, joint pain, and itching (WHO). The neurological stage follows, occurring months or even years after initial infection (see Fig. 2). This phase begins when the deadly parasite invades its host's central nervous system (CNS) and is accompanied by a large array of neurological symptoms including confusion, loss or disturbance of the senses, personality changes, and decreased coordination as well as the "disturbance of the sleep cycle which gives the disease its

Specific statistics from credible sources provide credibility for the paper's arguments.

continued

Turnbow 2

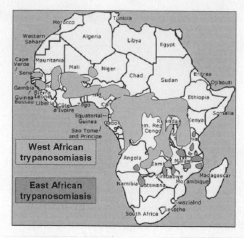

Maps, illustrations, and photographs should be placed in the paper where they provide the most support for in-text arguments.

Fig. 1. Distribution of West African or Gambian Sleeping Sickness and East African or Rhodesian Sleeping Sickness.
University of South Carolina, School of Medicine; *Parasitology*; *Microbiology and Immunology Online*; 1 Jan. 2009; Web; 1 May 2009; Fig. 4.

name" (WHO). Sleeping sickness is always fatal if not treated, and by the time the disease reaches its neurological stage, it is usually too late (WHO).

Effective treatments for sleeping sickness have been available since 1921, but they are dangerous and extremely painful. If diagnosed and treated in the early stages, sleeping sickness responds well to Pentamidine or, in extreme cases, Suramin. Both drugs, while sometimes accompanied by serious side effects such as heart and kidney failure, are fairly safe and inexpensive (WHO). Victims in the CNS stage of HAT, however, have for a long time been treated with a drug called Melarsoprol. Melarsoprol is widely available and cheap, but is derived from arsenic, and, acting as the potent poison that it is, can kill 5-20 percent of patients. The drug is also excruciatingly painful, described by many victims as "fire in the veins" ("Sleeping Sickness"). Although Melarsoprol "wouldn't pass a single ethical or drug-safety test" in the developed world, it is still used in Africa because it is the only treatment readily available to victims of this fatal but neglected disease (Gombe).

When there is no author, use an abbreviated title of the article.

It is surprising, then, to learn that a new and highly effective treatment was developed almost 40 years ago. The chemotherapy drug, defluoro-methyl-ornithine (DFMO), was developed in the 1970s but failed as a cancer treatment, causing only hair loss in patients (Wickware 908-09). It would have been the end of the pharmaceutical, but in 1983, New York parasite biologist Cyrus Bacchi dis-covered DFMO's effectiveness on the later stage of sleeping sickness (Shah 22).

Turnbow 3

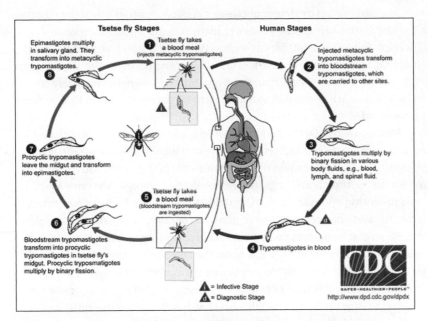

Fig. 2. Life Cycle of *T.b. gamienese* and *T.b. rhodesiense*.
Alexander J. da Silva and Melanie Moser; Centers for Disease Control Public Health Image
Library; n.d.; Web; 27 Apr. 2009.

Shortly after this discovery, Belgian doctor Henri Taelman used DFMO to treat
an infected woman who had already fallen into a coma, and, almost miraculously, DFMO brought the woman out of her coma within 24 hours. Dr. Taelman
renamed the drug eflornithine, but it quickly became known as the "resurrection
drug" because it was "so effective at reviving even comatose patients" (Wickware
909; McNeil A1). Other than the highly toxic Melarsoprol, eflornithine is the only
drug effective against late-stage Trypanosomiasis (McNeil A1). In addition to a
much lower drug-induced mortality rate, eflornithine has fewer and milder side
effects than Melarsoprol, and patients who receive eflornithine are more than
twice as likely to survive the year following treatment as those treated with the
older drug (Chappuis et al. 748-50).

    It is clear that the drug is sorely needed by those who suffer the formidable
symptoms of sleeping sickness. Despite this, eflornithine was very short-lived.
The pharmaceutical company, Sanofi-Aventis, halted production of the resurrection drug in 1995 along with two other antitrypanosome drugs (Wickware 909).

When quoting more than one author, separate the information with a semicolon.

When a work has more than three authors, use the name of the first author listed followed by "et al." meaning "and others."

continued

A drug aimed toward treatment of diseases in poor countries was simply "not considered to be a profitable venture to many pharmaceutical companies" (Thomas). This attitude left groups such as WHO and Doctors without Borders struggling to control the disease and save their dying patients without the drugs they needed to do so. Once again these organizations were forced to rely on Melarsoprol, which seemed almost as likely to kill patients as it was to save them (Jackson and Healy 6).

> The topic sentence at the beginning of each paragraph should state your point.

Although WHO, Doctors without Borders, and similar groups petitioned Aventis to continue production of the drug that would save thousands, it was not until 2001 that production of eflornithine resumed. Aventis had found a new use for the "resurrection drug"—hair removal. The company was once again

> Illustrations that support your point (topic sentence) can include quotations, statistics, figures, and other evidence.

mass producing eflornithine as an ingredient in a $54-a-tube facial hair removal cream for women. Aventis was even generous enough to donate 60,000 doses to WHO so that its doctors could treat HAT in sub-Saharan Africa (Jackson and Healy 6). Although this in itself was good, the company's reasons for doing so are less admirable. It placed "money before all" in all of its decisions, showing the "crass commodification of health" by an industry that was once "driven by a motive to improve human health" (Gombe). It is clear from the initial decision to halt production and Aventis's willingness to donate the drug only after a more cost-efficient use for it was found, that the company only helps others when it can make money by being kind. WHO's agreement with Aventis is only guaranteed for five years and the contract will expire soon (Chappuis et al. 751). The drug is already in short supply, and WHO can only afford to give it to those victims who survive their dose of arsenic and still need to be treated with the safer and more effective alternative (Gastellu-Etchegorry et al. 958). Aventis claims that the drug is "corrosive and destroys the equipment used to make it," suggesting that the pharmaceutical giant will once again refuse help to those in need and charge WHO and Doctors without Borders $70.00 a dose (McNeil A1).

> The end of the paragraph should explain the significance of the point and illustrations for the reader, and support the paper's thesis.

This is a price that neither organization can afford and that is far out of reach for the thousands of indigent victims who suffer from trypanosomiasis every year (McNeil A1).

Lifestyle drugs currently account for over "eighty percent of the world's pharmaceutical market," while companies are "ignoring diseases, like sleeping sickness and malaria, that affect only the poor" (McNeil A1). While I understand that pharmaceutical companies are big businesses committed to raising profits, it is unfortunate that the "$406 billion dollar global industry" feels it cannot spare its extra doses of eflornithine, a gesture that would save so many human lives (Shah 20).

Turnbow 5

A pharmaceutical company, which specializes in manufacturing medical products, should have at least some commitment to treating those who suffer from strategically forgotten diseases. Because it manufactures treatments for diseases and makes billions of dollars off of health care, Aventis has an unspoken responsibility for the people it can afford to save and must continue to provide the drug to the organizations that devote all of their time and money to fighting diseases in developing countries. Unlike a vial of chemicals, no price tag can be placed on a human life. Our responsibility is the same, even if those we help cannot give us anything in return. Here, there are truly no excuses.

> The beginning of the conclusion is a summary of the key arguments, which also reflects the thesis claim.

Turnbow 6

Works Cited

Chappuis, Francois, Nitya Udayraj, Kai Stietenroth, Ann Meussen, and Patrick A. Bovier. "Eflornithine Is Safer Than Melarsoprol for the Treatment of Second-Stage Trypanosoma Brucei Gambiense Human African Trypanosomiasis." *Clinical Infectious Diseases* 41.5 (2005): 748-51. Print.

Gastellu-Etchegorry, M. J. P. Helenport, B. Pecoul, J. Jannin, and D. Legros. "Availability and Affordability of Treatment for Human African Trypanosomiasis." *Tropical Medicine and International Health* 6.11 (2001): 957-59. Print.

Gombe, Spring. "Epidemic, What Epidemic: Treating Sleeping Sickness." *Bulletin of Medicus Mundi Switzerland*. Medicus Mundi Switzerland, Apr. 2004. Web. 12 Apr. 2009.

Jackson, Nicolette, and Sean Healy. "Facial Hair Cream to the Rescue." *New Internationalist* (2002): 6. Print.

McNeil, Donald G., Jr. "Cosmetic Saves a Cure for Sleeping Sickness." *New York Times* (2001): A1. *EBSCOhost*. Web. 28 Apr. 2009.

Shah, Sonia. "An Unprofitable Disease." *The Progressive* Sept. 2002: 20-23. Print.

"Sleeping Sickness." Doctors without Borders. 2009. Web. 12 Apr. 2009.

Thomas, Susan L. "African Sleeping Sickness." *Insect Science at Boston College*. 1 Mar. 2002. Web. 12 Apr. 2009.

Wickware, Potter. "Resurrecting the Resurrection Drug." *Nature Medicine* 8.9 (2002): 908-09. *EBSCOhost*. Web. 28 Apr. 2009.

World Health Organization. "African Trypanosomiasis." WHO, Aug. 2006. Web. 27 April 2009.

Inventing Your Research Paper's Content

The content of your research paper will be primarily based on your research at your campus library and on the Internet. For some kinds of research papers, you might also want to use empirical tools for gathering information, such as surveys, interviews, or observations.

It's no secret that your professor wants you to use sources that back up your claims and statements. Your professor does *not* want to you to simply write your opinion and then sprinkle in a few citations to make it look like you did research. Professors will know the difference between a research paper that is grounded in solid research and one that merely mentions a few sources.

Inquiring: Defining Your Topic, Angle, Purpose

Your first task is to figure out what kind of research paper you are being asked to write. There are two major types of research papers:

Expository Research Paper—expository means to "exhibit" or "explain" what you have discovered about your topic. Expository research papers explain an issue, event, or trend, without making an overt argument for one side.

Argumentative Research Paper—argumentation involves choosing one side of the issue and using your research to support your side while disputing opposing views.

If it's not clear whether you are *explaining* something (exposition) or *arguing* a point (argumentation), you should ask your professor to clarify the assignment.

Then, define your topic and figure out your angle. Your professor probably assigned you a specific topic or a range of topics on which to do research. For example, let's say you are studying the causes of the American Revolutionary War in a sophomore-level history course. Let's imagine your professor has asked you to write a ten-page expository research paper in which you explain how and why the war began.

Topic: The Main Causes of the American Revolutionary War

Possible Angles: Financial pressures on British colonies; overtaxation or perceived overtaxation; governance without representation; political miscalculations by King George III; French interference in British colonies; British military abuses of colonists

Obviously, a topic like the American Revolutionary War is too large to be handled in a ten-page paper. So, you need to choose an angle that will help you narrow the topic. Choosing an angle will also help you write your purpose statement. For example, here is a possible purpose statement for an *expository* research paper:

My purpose is to demonstrate that the American Revolutionary War was the result of several key political miscalculations by King George III and the British government.

For an argumentative research paper, developing a topic, angle, and purpose is similar. Let's say your psychology professor wants you to write a research paper in which you argue for or against the use of brain-enhancing drugs to help college students perform better on exams.

Topic: Use of brain-enhancing drugs to help college students perform better on exams

Possible Angles: Using technology to increase student learning; bringing brain-enhancing drugs out of the shadows; leveling the playing field for all students; potential negative health implications of drug use; ethical problems with turning to drugs to enhance our abilities

Your "argumentative" purpose statement for this kind of research paper might be something like the following:

In my research paper, I will argue that students should have access to drugs that help them study better and perform better on exams, because the purpose of education is to help them learn as much as possible and succeed.

Figure 13.1 shows some verbs that could be used as the basis of your research paper's purpose statement and thesis statement.

Expository Research Papers	Argumentative Research Papers
to describe	to persuade
to explain	to convince
to review	to influence
to instruct	to argue
to demonstrate	to recommend
to illustrate	to change
to inform	to advocate
to appraise	to urge
to educate	to defend
to show	to justify
to display	to support
to exhibit	to propose
to present	to encourage
	to promote

FIGURE 13.1
Common Verbs Used in Purpose Statements

Researching: Finding Out What Others Know

Chapter 24 of *Writing Today* goes over the research process in depth, so here is a brief review here that is targeted toward the needs of research papers.

Watch the Animation on **Evaluating Sources** at **mycomplab.com**

Library Research. Your university's library has a variety of books, magazines, and academic journals that you can use to collect information about your topic. Use your library's electronic catalog, usually available through its Web site, to search for books on your topic. Then, when you track down a useful book on the library shelves, look at the books around it to determine if there are others that you might use. Similarly, if you find an academic journal article about your topic through a journal database, look at its Works Cited or References list to see if there are other articles and books that might be useful to you.

Internet Research. The Internet can be useful, but you need to be careful about the sources you collect, especially for research papers. For example, Wikipedia and similar Web sites can be helpful for gaining an overall understanding of your topic, but Wikipedia is not an authoritative and citable source. After all, just about anyone can write or alter an entry on Wikipedia. So, when collecting sources from the Internet, you should thoroughly check the background of the organization that offers the information.

Empirical Research. On campus and in your community, you can find experts on your topic. For example, most professors would be willing to meet with you during office hours even if you aren't in one of the classes they are teaching. You should set up interviews with these experts or send them questions via e-mail. Depending on your topic, you might also want to do some field observations that will help you confirm or challenge some of things you found in print sources and electronic sources.

Turn to Chapter 25 on Finding Sources and Collecting Information for more help on doing research. Collecting reliable sources is the key to writing a solid research paper. Plus, if you collect good sources, drafting the research paper will be much easier because you will have most of the content you need.

Organizing and Drafting Your Research Paper

Watch the Animation on **Drafting a Research Paper** at **mycomplab.com**

After collecting your sources, you might feel a little overwhelmed by the amount of information available on your topic. How will you fit all this stuff into your paper and still write something worth reading? Don't panic. It's not that difficult.

When you begin the drafting phase, your first task is to figure out which issues you want to cover and how you want to organize your research paper. The models in the At-A-Glance at the beginning of this chapter should give you a few ideas about how you might organize your paper.

The Introduction

Your research paper needs an engaging introduction that will clearly identify your topic, purpose, and main point (thesis). You should also offer some background information on your topic, stress its importance to the readers, and perhaps forecast how the body of the research paper is organized.

In your introduction, you're basically saying, "Here is my topic, and here is what I am going to explain/prove in this paper." A solid introduction will typically make most or all of the following five opening moves.

Identify Your Topic. Your readers should be able to clearly figure out what your research paper is about (and perhaps what it is not about).

State Your Purpose. In one sentence, tell your readers what you are trying to demonstrate or prove. You can be straightforward with this statement.

> In this research paper, I will argue that King George III was not the inept monarch described in many history books, but his economic miscalculations and his strict code of values added fuel to a growing independence movement in the American colonies.

> My objective is to prove that the mental health services on our campus are not adequate.

State Your Main Point or Thesis Statement. In a research paper, your main point or thesis should be clearly stated somewhere in the introduction.

> **Weak:** King George III's mistakes were partially responsible for the American Revolutionary War.

> **Stronger:** The United States would have eventually gained its independence through peaceful means, but King George III's heavy-handed tactics sparked a violent revolt among the American colonists, igniting an expensive and humiliating war for the British Empire.

> **Weak:** We need better mental health services on our campus.

> **Stronger:** Our university needs better mental health services because untreated psychological problems can lead to greater substance abuse, increased stress, underachievement, and even violence.

Offer Background Information on the Topic. Give the readers just enough historical information or factual evidence to familiarize themselves with the topic.

Watch the Animation on **Introductions** at **mycomplab.com**

Stress the Importance of the Topic to the Readers. Briefly mention why this topic is significant, especially to the readers. You might also consider using a grabber or a lead to catch the readers' attention at the beginning of your research paper. In Chapter 19, you can learn more about using grabbers or leads to spark the readers' interest in your topic.

These five introductory moves can be made in almost any order. Many research papers, for example, start out with a little background information to catch the readers' attention. Others begin by identifying the topic and stressing its importance. If you make these five moves, you will probably have a good start to your research paper.

The Body

The body of your research paper can be organized in a variety of ways. Here are a few common ways to organize your draft:

Issues Divide your information into two to five major issues that you want to discuss in your research paper. Specifically, pay attention to issues on which people tend to disagree or major points that people tend to discuss when they consider this topic.

Chronological Divide your information into two to five historical time periods (e.g., 1980s, 1990s, 2000s; or before the event, start of the event, during the event, end of the event, aftermath of the event). Then, arrange your information by sorting out what happened in each of those time periods.

Argumentation Divide your information into three categories: Review of the facts; discussion of how others, especially people with opposing views, interpret the facts; discussion of how you and people who agree with you interpret the facts.

Carving the Body into Sections. The body of your research paper will probably have two to five major sections (Figure 13.2). These major sections will then have two to five paragraphs apiece.

Each section in your research paper can follow a variety of patterns. The following organizational strategies can be helpful for organizing the material in each section:

Narrative—Use true stories and anecdotes to illustrate your points in a chronological way.

Description—Divide something into its major parts and describe them separately.

Cause and Effect—Explain the causes of a problem and the effects.

Classification—Divide something into major and minor categories.

Comparison and Contrast—Identify similarities and differences between two things.

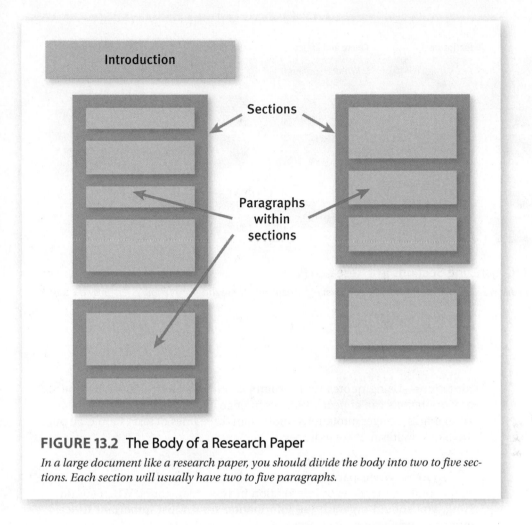

FIGURE 13.2 The Body of a Research Paper

In a large document like a research paper, you should divide the body into two to five sections. Each section will usually have two to five paragraphs.

Figure 13.3 on page 318 shows some models for how sections might be organized. You might also turn to Chapter 20, "Developing Paragraphs and Sections," for some other ideas about how to organize information in sections.

Using and Citing Your Sources. While drafting the body of your research paper, you need to carefully quote and thoroughly cite your sources. Chapter 26, "Quoting, Paraphrasing, and Citing Sources," will help you use your sources properly. Here is a quick review:

Watch the Animation on **Avoiding Plagiarism** at **mycomplab.com**

> **In-Text Parenthetical Citations**—Each time you take an idea or quote from a text, you need to use an in-text citation to signal where it came from. In-text MLA citations will usually include the author's last name and the page number, e.g., (Author 34). In-text APA citations will usually include the author's last name, the year published, and a page number, e.g., (Author, 20XX, p. 43).

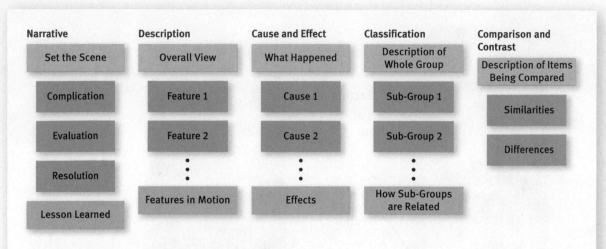

FIGURE 13.3 Organizing Sections in a Research Paper

Each section in your research paper should have its own organization. These diagrams show a few possibilities.

Watch the Animation
on **Quotations** at
mycomplab.com

Quotations—Using quotes from experts is encouraged in research papers. Brief quotations can appear within a sentence and are highlighted with quotation marks. Longer quotations (more than three lines of text) should be put into block quotes that are indented.

Paraphrasing and Summarizing—You can also paraphrase or summarize your sources. When paraphrasing, you should follow the structure of the source, putting the ideas or information in your own words. When summarizing, you should organize the information from most important to least important, using your own words.

Turn to Chapter 26 for more help with using your sources. In a research paper, it's critical that you properly quote, paraphrase, and cite your sources.

The Conclusion

The conclusion of your research paper should be similar in many ways to your introduction. It should restate your main point (thesis) and stress the importance of your subject one final time. You should also briefly discuss the future of your topic.

Your research paper's conclusion should make up to five moves:

- Make an obvious transition from the body to the conclusion.

- State your main point, or thesis statement.

- Stress again the importance of the topic to the readers.

- Call your readers to action (in argumentative research paper).

- Briefly discuss the future of this topic.

The transition to your conclusion should be obvious to the readers. A heading like "Conclusion: Brain-Enhancing Drugs Need to Be Banned" will signal that you are concluding. Otherwise, you can start your conclusion with a phrase like "In conclusion," "In summary," or "In closing" to signal that you are making your final points.

Your main point or thesis statement should be similar to the sentence you used in your introduction but not exactly the same. State your main point in different words, perhaps with a little more emphasis.

Finally, you should end your research paper by discussing the future of the topic. If you're arguing a point, call the readers to action (e.g., "Now is the time to do something about this problem"). If you're writing an expository research paper, you can briefly discuss what happened next with this topic (e.g., "The American Revolution sparked other colonial revolts in other parts of the Americas"). You can also discuss what you think will happen next.

Your conclusion should be brief, perhaps one or two paragraphs. Once you signal that you are concluding, your readers will expect you to wrap up in a short amount of time. The conclusion is not the place to add in any new information. Sometimes, it's tempting to throw in all the stuff you didn't have a chance to talk about. Don't do it. If that information is important, you should put it in the body of your research paper. New information in your conclusion will only cloud your message and make it difficult for your readers to find your main point.

Works Cited or References

The final page(s) of your research paper will be your list of Works Cited (MLA) or References (APA). You should turn to Chapter 27, "Using MLA Style," or Chapter 28, "Using APA Style," to determine how to format your list of sources.

You should pay special attention to accurately listing out your Works Cited or References. Your readers, especially your professors, will want to check the sources that you used while you did your research. If your sources are formatted accurately, they will easily find the information you used to develop your ideas and reach your conclusions. If you are sloppy with your sources, your readers may be skeptical about the credibility of your research.

Choosing an Appropriate Style

Expository research papers tend to be written in the plain style, while argumentative research papers use both plain and persuasive styles. The plain style is especially helpful for explaining the facts about your topic and discussing what happened. The persuasive style should be used when you are trying to influence the readers to accept your point of view.

Use Doers as the Subjects of Your Sentences. When drafting a research paper, writers tend to use passive voice (e.g., "In a 2011 study, brain-enhancing drugs were given by scientists to 200 college students"). When revising, change this kind of sentences into active voice by moving the doers into the subject of your sentences (e.g., "In a 2011 study, scientists gave brain-enhancing drugs to 200 college students"). Active voice will make your research paper sound more authoritative.

Avoid Weak Sentence Constructions. When drafting, writers also tend to rely too heavily on weak sentence constructions, such as "It is . . .," "There are . . .," and "This is. . . ." These sentences considerably weaken your style and make your ideas harder to understand. You can strengthen these sentences by using real subjects and active verbs, such as "Students know . . .," "Researchers discovered . . .," and "This experiment demonstrated. . . ."

Keep Sentences Breathing Length. Research papers are often plagued with long, overly complex sentences that are difficult to read. As you revise, look for sentences that are longer than breathing length. Then, cut them down or divide them into two sentences.

Use Similes and Analogies to Explain Difficult Concepts. If you are trying to explain something complicated to your readers, try using a simile or analogy. For example, you might use a simile like "After the skirmish at Concord, the American Revolution spread like a wave throughout the colonies." You could also use analogies, such as "Using brain-enhancing drugs to study for an exam is like putting rocket fuel in your car. The benefits are noticeable but also short-lived and dangerous." Similes and analogies will help you explain difficult concepts by making comparisons to things that are familiar to your readers.

Organize Sections and Paragraphs in a Top-Down Structure. Each paragraph should have a clear topic sentence (a statement or claim) preferably early in the paragraph. Then, support that topic sentence with examples, details, reasoning, facts, data, quotations, definitions, or descriptions. Similarly, the opening paragraph of each section should include a statement or claim that the paragraphs in the section will support or prove.

Designing Your Research Paper

More than likely, your professor will have some specific guidelines about how the research paper should be formatted. He or she might ask you to double-space the text and use one-inch margins (Figure 13.4). You might also be asked to use a specific typeface (e.g., Times or Arial) and a specific type size (e.g., 12-point).

In some cases, your professor may ask you to follow MLA format or APA format, which might mean the format spelled out in the *MLA Handbook for Writers of Research Papers* or the *Publication Manual of the American Psychological Association*.

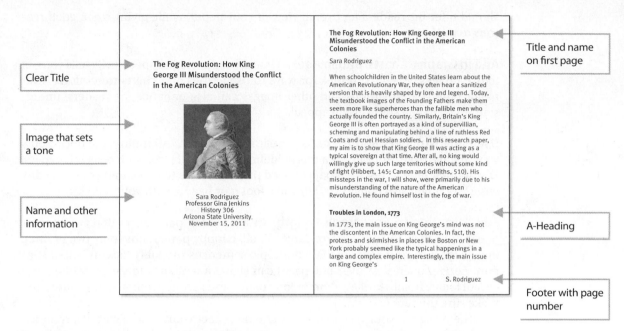

FIGURE 13.4 Designing a Research Paper

Even a traditional design for a research paper, like the one shown here, can be attractive.

These handbooks, which should be available at your library or on the Internet, offer clear guidelines about how to format research papers.

You should look carefully at the assignment sheet to determine exactly what kind of design or format your professor is requiring. Part of your grade, after all, may be based on whether you followed the assignment's formatting directions. If your professor does not spell out a specific format or design, you should ask for some guidance.

If you are given flexibility to choose your own design, here are some design features you might consider:

Include a Cover Page. A cover page, like the one shown in Figure 13.4, can add a professional touch to your research paper. Your cover page should include the title of your paper, your name, your professor's name, and the date the research paper was submitted. An appropriate image on the cover can also set a specific tone for the research paper.

Use Meaningful Headings. The headings in your research paper should be descriptive and accurate but not boring. For example, instead of "Start of Revolutionary War," you might use "The Shot Heard Around the World." Your headings together should offer the readers an overall view of your paper, while giving them good reasons to read each section.

Add in Graphs, Charts, and Images. Unless your professor specifically tells you not to use images, you should look for ways to use graphs and charts to reinforce your major points. Photographs and other images can also enhance the readers' understanding and add some visual appeal.

Use Page Numbers and Perhaps a Header or Footer. All multi-page documents should have page numbers, but this guideline is especially true with research papers. Due to their length, research papers need page numbers to make them easier to discuss. You might also consider adding in a footer or header with your name.

Pay Attention to Paragraph Length. In a research paper, you don't want your paragraphs to be too small or too large. Small, choppy paragraphs (only two or three lines) signal to your readers that your topic sentences probably lack sufficient support. Long paragraphs (over one page) can signal a tendency toward rambling or a lack of focus. In some cases, short or long paragraphs are appropriate, but you should make sure they are needed.

The design of your research paper should reflect your topic. Typically, research papers are more formal, so their designs tend to be traditional and not too splashy.

Revising and Editing Your Research Paper

Leave yourself a few days to revise the text. Since a research paper is often the final project in a course, your professor will view it as your best work. If it is well written and thoroughly researched, chances are good that your professor will consider your whole semester successful. So, additional time spent on revising and rewriting will be worth the effort.

Watch the Video on
Giving a Peer Review
at **mycomplab.com**

Ask Someone Else to Read It Out Loud. Ask your roommate or a friend to read your research paper out loud to you. When she or he stumbles or seems confused, mark those places so you can revise them later.

Revising Is Re-Visioning and Rewriting. Your first draft is just a starter draft. When you are finished with the first draft, remind yourself that you will need to rethink and rewrite much of the text. In many cases, your ideas and opinions will have evolved as you did your research and drafted the paper. Make sure you revise and rewrite the sections that aren't in line with your current understanding of your topic.

Challenge Each Paragraph. Research papers are long, so it's easy to lose track of your overall argument. So, check or "challenge" each paragraph to make sure it belongs in the paper. If a paragraph is not supporting your overall point, then you should consider removing it or revising it.

Look for Gaps in the Content. Underline your main point (thesis statement). Then, go through the research paper section by section and paragraph by paragraph to check whether you have actually supported or proven this point. Specifically, look for gaps where need-to-know information is missing.

Revise Paragraphs to Improve Flow. Look closely at each paragraph to determine whether it has a clear topic sentence, usually early in the paragraph. Then, work sentence by sentence to improve the flow of each paragraph by aligning the subjects of the sentences or using given/new strategies to weave the sentences together. Turn to Chapter 20, "Developing Paragraphs and Sections," for some extra help.

Proofread, Darn It! Even a well-written research paper will be graded lower if your professor stumbles across typos, grammar errors, and spelling errors. Some professors are highly concerned about correctness, meaning they will grade harshly if they find errors. Your research paper needs to be flawless, so your message will come through clearly.

Here's a tip. If your research paper is thoroughly revised and edited, your professor will have more trust in your work. He or she will often overlook one or two weak aspects of your research paper's content if the rest of the paper flows well and doesn't have mistakes. Solid revision builds confidence in your work (and a better grade).

The Annotated Bibliography

Your professor may ask you to prepare an *annotated bibliography* that summarizes and evaluates the sources you collected for your research paper. An annotated bibliography is an alphabetical list of your sources that briefly summarizes and sometimes assesses how each will be useful in your research paper.

An annotated bibliography is a great way to collect and better understand the print and electronic sources on your topic. It is a good way to sort out the facts of a topic and figure out the larger arguments and trends that influence your topic.

Here are some strategies for creating a useful annotated bibliography:

Locate a variety of sources on your topic.   Find a variety of print and electronic sources on your topic. Determine what each source contains and how this information relates to your project. Don't collect only Web-based sources. You need to go over to the library, too.

Don't include sites like Wikipedia as sources.   Wikipedia and similar Web sites can give you an overview of your topic and help you locate sources. However, since the entries on these Web sites are written anonymously and can be altered by the public, you should not consider them authoritative.

Format your sources accurately.   List out your sources and format them in MLA or APA style. If you format them properly as you are creating your annotated bibliography, they will be easier to include at the end of your research paper.

Offer a brief summary or commentary on each source.   Your summary should run the length of a typical paragraph. The first line should state the main point of the text. The remaining sentences should each express the major points of the source.

Consider each source in depth and figure out how it fits into your research project.   Your professors will also use your annotated bibliography to review the kinds of sources you have collected and make suggestions about other possible sources. At the end of each source in your list, write a couple sentences about how it might be used in your research paper.

Be careful not to plagiarize your sources.   If you take a quote or ideas from a source, carefully label these items with page numbers and the necessary quotation marks. This labeling is especially important while writing a research paper, because as you draft your text, you may forget which words and ideas originally came from your sources.

WRITE your own annotated bibliography. Create an annotated bibliography for the research paper you have been assigned to write. Your annotated bibliography should include at least ten sources from a variety of print and electronic texts.

Annotated Bibliography: The Fog of Revolution

Sara Rodriguez Professor Gina Jenkins History 306

Allen, Thomas. "One Revolution, Two Wars." *Military History* 27 (2011): 58-63. Print.

This article points out that the American Revolution was in many ways a civil war between Patriots, who wanted revolution, and Loyalists who supported King George III. As Allen points out, "the signers [of the Declaration of Independence] knew they did not speak for 'one people' but for a people including Americans who opposed the Revolution" (58). Many members of established families acted as informants for the British. Many Loyalists would join the British forces in battles against the Patriots. These divisions led to much distrust among the Patriots, because they weren't certain who was on their side and who was against them (61).

My assessment: This article can be helpful for my argument. Part of my argument is that we are given a rather cleaned-up version of the American Revolution in our classes and textbooks. This article demonstrates that the war was not one that pitted American patriots against British oppressors. Instead, there were many factions in the colonies who had reasons to support or fight against independence.

Black, Jeremy. *George III: America's Last King*. New Haven, CT: Yale UP, 2006. Print.

The author points out that King George III has become a caricature in American history. In some accounts, he is portrayed as a cruel dictator. In other accounts, he is a bumbling monarch, unable to hold together the vast empire he inherited from greater monarchs. Black looks at the historical context in which King George III found himself. He points out that many pressures were being placed on the British Empire at that time. So, it's not surprising that the uprising of some colonists was not handled with full concern. Discussing the king's values, Black writes, "George's conception of his task was always led by a commitment to restore and maintain the moral order of society, a position that greatly influenced his attitude towards dissatisfaction in the American colonies" (1). Also, he was distracted by numerous upheavals among his ministers in London, so George may not have given the rebellion in the American colonies much thought until it was too late (107).

continued

My assessment: This book is critical toward my argument about the state of mind of King George III. The author includes several chapters that delve into the king's family, values, religion, and his psychological state. These chapters will be especially helpful toward showing that George was handling a great number of other matters that may have distracted him from the problems in the American colonies. The book also shows how George's strict adherence to values may have kept him from compromising with the colonists at key points in the conflict.

Bonwick, Colin. *The American Revolution.* **Charlottesville, VA: U of Virginia P, 1991. Print.**

This book suggests that the American Revolution is generally misunderstood by the general public. Typically, Bonwick argues, the American Revolution is portrayed as an uprising among colonists who were seeking their freedom from Britain. This revolutionary narrative glosses over the many "internal debates and processes which gave birth to the United States from 1776 onwards" implying they "were little more than necessary consequences of independence" (1). The book steps back and shows that each colony had its own reasons for seeking independence. Overall, though, much of the tension between the colonies and Britain were due to economic rather than ideological reasons (56). The final move toward Revolution was more about preserving economic strength rather than freeing people from any kind of bondage.

My assessment: This book makes a similar argument to the one I am making. I'm arguing that King George III's actions, especially increased taxation, made the economic situation in the colonies more difficult, which made it easier for arguments for independence to take hold.

Here are some quick strategies to get you going on your research paper.

DEFINE Your Research Topic and Find a New Angle

Your professor may have given you a topic or asked you to find one of your own. You should first narrow your topic to something specific that you can handle in about a ten-page paper. Then, look for an angle on that topic that is new or different.

STATE Your Purpose

In one sentence, state exactly what you want to achieve in your research paper. Your purpose statement will evolve as you do research and draft.

STATE Your Main Point or Thesis Statement

In one sentence, state exactly what your research paper will demonstrate or prove. An expository research paper will offer a thesis that guides the discussion. An argumentative research paper will state a thesis that you intend to prove.

RESEARCH Your Topic

Research papers rely heavily on print and electronic sources. Use your computer to access databases at your campus library. If you use sources from the Internet, make sure they are reliable. Go to the library!

ORGANIZE Your Research Paper

A variety of organizations are available for your research paper. They almost always include an introduction and conclusion. The body should be organized in a way that allows you to present your research in a logical way.

CHOOSE an Appropriate Style

The style of a research paper tends to be straightforward and formal. You can use stylistic devices like similes, metaphors, and analogies. For the most part, though, a plain style is best.

DESIGN and Format the Document

Your professor will likely have some specific guidelines for how to format your paper (e.g., double-spaced, one-inch margins, 12-point font). You should ask if you can include images and if there is any flexibility in designing the document.

REVISE and Edit Your Writing

Pay special attention to your paragraphs, especially the topic sentences. Also, your research paper needs to be error-free if you want your readers to take your work seriously.

Nervous Nellies

TAYLOR CLARK

People usually assume, in general, that women are naturally more nervous or anxious than men. In this research paper, which is based on the book Nerve: Poise Under Pressure, Serenity Under Stress, and the Brave New Science of Fear and Cool, *Taylor Clark argues that scientists have demonstrated that women are not biologically inclined to be more anxious. Instead, they are socialized to be this way. While reading this argument, look at the ways Clark uses sources to back up his arguments.*

In the jittery world of anxiety research, one of the field's most consistent findings is also perhaps its biggest source of controversy: Women, according to countless studies, are twice as prone to anxiety as men (Kendler & Prescott, 1999; Todero, Biing-Jiun, Raffa, Tilkemeier & Niaura, 2007). When pollsters call women up, they always confess to far higher levels of worry than men about everything from crime to the economy. Psychologists diagnose women with anxiety disorders two times as often as men, and research confirms—perhaps unsurprisingly—that women are significantly more inclined toward negative emotion, self-criticism, and endless rumination about problems. From statistics like these, some have even leapt to the Larry Summers-esque claim that women are simply built to be much more nervous than men—an idea that has outraged many women inside (and outside) the psychology community (Summers, 2005).

According to new evidence, however, the outraged are right: When it comes to our preconceived notions about women and anxiety, women are unfairly being dragged through the mud. While women are indeed more fretful than men on average right now, this difference is mostly the result of a cultural setup—one in which major social and parenting biases lead to girls becoming needlessly nervous adults. In reality, the idea that women are "naturally" twice as anxious as men is nothing more than a pernicious illusion.

Before we can unleash the vengeance of the furies on this falsehood, though, there's some bad news we need to get out of the way first: a few recent studies have indicated that the hormonal differences between the sexes really do make women a touch more biologically inclined toward anxiety than men. One noteworthy experiment from last year, for example, found that female brains—well, female rat brains—get more rattled by small levels of a major stress hormone called corticotrophin-releasing factor than male brains (Valentino, 2010). Another 2010 study, at Florida State University, likewise revealed that male rats' higher testosterone levels seem to give them a larger buffer against anxiety than female rats have (Hartung, 2010). (Don't get hung up on the fact that these studies were on rodents; most of what we know about the neuroscience of fear actually comes from tormenting lab rats.) Just how big a role these biological factors play in human women's anxiety isn't yet clear.

But one thing we do know for certain is that the way we raise children plays a huge role in determining how disposed toward anxiety they are later in life, and thus the difference in the way we treat boys and girls explains a lot about the heightened nerves we see in many adult women. To show just how important this is, let's start at the very beginning. If women really were fated to be significantly more anxious than men, we would expect them to start showing this nervousness at a very young age, right? Yet precisely the opposite is true: According to the UCLA anxiety expert Michelle Craske, in the first few months of infants' lives, it's boys who show greater emotional neediness. While girls become slightly more prone to negative feelings than boys at two years (which, coincidentally, is the age at which kids begin learning gender roles), research has shown that up until age 11, girls and boys are equally likely to develop an anxiety disorder. By age 15, however, girls are six times more likely to have one than boys are (McGee, Feehan, Williams & Anderson, 1992).

Why the sudden gap in diagnosed anxiety? Well, one answer is that as a flood of adolescent hormones sends these boys' and girls' emotions into overdrive, the difference in their upbringings finally catches up with them. After all, whether parents intend to or not, they usually treat the emotional outbursts of girls far differently than those of boys. "From a socialization angle, there's quite a lot of evidence that little girls who exhibit shyness or anxiety are reinforced for it, whereas little boys who exhibit that behavior might even be punished for it," Craske told me.

In my book *Nerve*, I call this the "skinned knee effect": Parents coddle girls who cry after a painful scrape but tell boys to suck it up, and this formative link between emotional outbursts and kisses from mom predisposes girls to react to unpleasant situations with "negative" feelings like anxiety later in life. On top of this, cultural biases about boys being more capable than girls also lead parents to push sons to show courage and confront their fears, while daughters are far more likely to be sheltered from life's challenges. If little Olivia shows fear, she gets a hug; if little Oliver shows fear, he gets urged to overcome it.

The result of these parenting disparities is that by the time girls grow into young women, they've learned fewer effective coping strategies than their male counterparts, which translates to higher anxiety. The sexes learn to deal with fear in two very different ways: men have been conditioned to tackle problems head-on, while women have been taught to worry, ruminate, and complain to each other (hey, I'm just reporting the research) rather than actively confront challenges. These are generalizations, of course; the fact that I have always been an Olympic-caliber worrier offers us just one example of how men can fret with the best of them, and everyone knows at least one woman who appears not even to know what fear is. Still, these differences in upbringing clarify quite a bit about the gender gap in anxiety.

Yet parenting doesn't tell the full story of feminine nerves, because even if a young woman emerges from childhood as a relatively cool and resilient adult, she still has to do battle with social forces that seem bent on making her anxious. You may expect me to dwell here on the viselike pressure that contemporary culture exerts on women to look beautiful and young forever (one highly questionable survey found that women worry about their bodies an average of 252 times a week), but while this is a significant issue, the cultural biases about women and anxiety run deeper still (Alexander, 2009).

We have an odd tendency to label women as anxious even when they aren't. A recent, highly revealing study showed that even in situations in which male and female subjects experience the same level of an emotion, women are consistently seen—and even see themselves—as being "more emotional" than men. It shouldn't be too surprising, then, that this bias holds for anxiety as well; we buy into the fretful-women stereotypes far too often. Another report, for

5

example, found significant differences in the way doctors respond to patients who report common stress symptoms like chest pain: Whereas men get full cardiac workups, women are more often told that they're just stressed or anxious, and that their symptoms are in their heads.

It should be pretty clear by now that the claims about women being far more innately anxious than men are suspect, but before I depart in a blaze of justice, one final point is in order: Men are getting off much too easily in the anxiety discussion. Probably the most significant reason why women get diagnosed with anxiety disorders twice as often as men isn't that they're doubly fearful. It's because anxious men are much less likely to seek psychological help.

The flip side of being raised to always show strength is that men come to feel that going to a therapist is a sign of weakness or failure (think of Tony Soprano's mopey resistance to the benefits of psychiatry), which is why men constitute just 37 percent of therapy patients, by some estimates. If nearly twice as many women seek help from a psychologist, then they'll obviously be diagnosed more often with anxiety disorders. Troublingly enough, the evidence shows that while women deal with anxiety and stress by worrying, men are more likely to try to bury these feelings with alcohol or drugs—which offers one rationale for why men are at higher risk for "antisocial" disorders like alcoholism.

So take heart, women of the world: You're not necessarily bioengineered to be worry machines. The deeper truth behind the great anxiety divide is this: We all get stressed-out and nervous sometimes. Women are simply more honest about their anxiety, because they've been taught to deal with it through unencumbered fretting. Of course, I'm not about to declare that if we raised boys and girls exactly the same, eradicated the cultural

anxiety bias against women, and frog-marched more men into therapy, the gender nervousness gap would magically disappear. We would almost certainly see, though, that this gap is far smaller than we think.

References

Alexander, H. (2009, November 23). Women worry about their bodies 252 times a week. *Telegraph.co.uk. The Telegraph.* Retrieved from http://www.telegraph.co.uk/news/uknews/6634686/Women-worry-about-their-bodies-252-times-a-week.html

Clark, T. (2011). *Nerve: Poise under pressure, serenity under stress, and the brave new science of fear and cool.* Little, Brown and Company.

Harting, R. (2010, September 1). Why does anxiety target women more? *Florida State University.* Retrieved April 27, 2011, from http://www.fsu.com/News-Archive/2010/September/Why-does-anxiety-target-women-more-FSU-researcher-awarded-1.8M-grant-to-find-out

Kendler, K., & Prescott, C. (1999). A population-based twin study of lifetime major depression in men and women. *Archives of General Psychology, 56,* 39-44.

McGee, R., Feehan, M., Williams, S., & Anderson, J. (1992). DSM-III disorders from age 11 to age 15 years. *Journal of American Academy of Child Adolescent Psychology, 31*(1), 50-59.

Summers, L. (2005, January 14). Remarks at NBER Conference on diversifying the science & engineering workforce. *Office of the President, Harvard University.* Retrieved April 27, 2011, from http://classic-web.archive.org/web/20080130023006/http://www.president.harvard.edu/speeches/2005/nber.html

Todaro, J., Biing-Jiun, S., Raffa, S., Tilke-meier, P., & Niaura, R. (2007). Prevalence of anxiety disorders in men and women with established coronary heart disease.

Journal of Cardiopulmonary Rehabilitation & Prevention, 27(2), 86-91. doi:10.1097/01. HCR.0000265036.24157.e7

Valentino, R. (2010, August 20). Stress hormone receptors less adaptive in female brain. *National Institute of Mental Health.* Retrieved April 27, 2011, from http://www.nimh.nih.gov/media/audio/stress-hormone-receptors-less-adaptive-in-female-brain.shtml

A CLOSER LOOK AT
Nervous Nellies

1. In this research paper, Clark argues against the assumption that women are *naturally* more nervous or anxious than men. Instead, he is arguing that women are socialized to be this way. Where in the article does he use evidence from sources to prove his point?

2. This essay can be considered an "argumentative" research paper. Where in the text does the author signal that he is arguing, not only explaining? Where does he reveal the main point (thesis) of his argument? What are three or four major arguments in support of his main point? What strategies does he use to argue for his position?

3. Clark agrees that women are in general more nervous and anxious than men. Where and how does he agree to this assumption? What are the reasons he gives for these differences between women and men? What suggestions does he offer to lessen women's tendencies to be more nervous or anxious than men?

IDEAS FOR
Writing

1. Write a two-page rhetorical analysis in which you explain why you find Clark's argument effective or ineffective. Look closely at his use of reasoning (*logos*), authority (*ethos*), and emotions (*pathos*) to support his arguments. Your rhetorical analysis should not argue for or against Clark's main point. Instead, explain why you find his argument strategies effective or not.

2. Write a rebuttal in which you argue against Clark's main point or one of his major arguments. You can argue from your own experience, but you should also back up your arguments with your own sources. Also, you can agree with Clark's overall argument, but you could disagree with his reasoning or his suggestions for dealing with anxiousness in women.

Serial Murder: A Forensic Psychiatric Perspective

JAMES KNOLL, MD

TV shows and magazine articles about serial killers are common in today's media, but what do we really know about serial murder? To answer that question, forensic psychiatrist James Knoll reports on the scientific and medical research and reveals what we know and what we need to find out through further research. As you read, pay attention to the way that Knoll takes on myths and misconceptions about serial murder and the kind of research he uses to reach his conclusions.

'You feel the last bit of breath leaving their body. You're looking into their eyes. A person in that situation is God!'

—Ted Bundy

Ressler: "Do you have any idea at all, of what would start bringing this type of fantasy to mind . . .?"

Dahmer: "It all revolved around having complete control. Why or where it came from, I don't know."

—How to Interview a Cannibal
Robert K. Ressler

When law enforcement apprehends a serial murderer, the event is consistently the focus of unswerving media coverage. For local communities, the ordeal can be particularly shocking and upsetting. Residents living in a community that is exposed to serial murder may even experience posttraumatic stress disorder symptoms for varying periods of time (Herkov and Beirnat, 1997).

Over the past three decades, our society has become fascinated by the phenomenon of serial murder as evidenced by the numerous books, movies and television shows on the subject. Yet, despite the high level of interest, there is no current theory that adequately explains the etiology of serial murder (Holmes et al., 2002). This is primarily due to the fact that serial murder is an event with an extremely low base rate and therefore is difficult to study via rigorous scientific methods (Dietz, 1986).

While serial murder is a universally terrifying concept, it is an extraordinarily rare event. In a study of the frequency of serial sexual homicide, McNamara and Morton (2004) found that it accounted for only 0.5% of all homicides over a 10-year period in Virginia. In contrast to the sensationalized perception that serial murder is a growing epidemic, there is no solid evidence that this is the case. An analysis of homicide victims from 1960 to 1998 indicated that the percentages of female homicide victims have actually decreased (Schlesinger, 2001a). Because the victims of serial murderers are overwhelmingly female, these data fail to support the notion that serial murder is increasing in frequency.

Historically, the term serial murder may be relatively new, but its occurrence is not. In the United States alone there have been documented cases as far back as the 1800s. In 16th-century France, it is likely that myths such as "werewolves" were used to explain the deeds of serial murderers that were too horrifying to attribute to human beings (Everitt, 1993). In all likelihood, serial murderers have always been among us.

In 1886, psychiatry professor Richard [5] von Krafft-Ebing wrote the classic *Psychopathia Sexualis,* in which he described the characteristics of individuals who appeared to obtain sexual gratification from acts of sadistic domination. The next major psychiatric contribution to our understanding of serial murderers was in 1970 when forensic psychiatrist Robert Brittain produced detailed descriptions of sadistic murderers he had encountered over his career. Beginning in the early '70s, media coverage of notorious cases such as Ted Bundy and the Hillside Strangler produced a sense of urgency to study and explain the phenomenon.

Thus far, the study of serial murder has been somewhat hampered by lack of a unanimously agreed upon definition. However, most experts agree on the criteria that the offender must have murdered at least two victims in temporally unrelated incidents. This phenomenon usually involves a cooling off or refractory period between killings that varies in duration for each individual offender. To date, our greatest source of knowledge and data on serial murder has come from experts working in the Federal Bureau of Investigation's Behavioral Science Unit, now called the Behavioral Analysis Unit. To emphasize the sexual nature of the crimes, and to distinguish these offenders from others who murder serially for other reasons (e.g., contract killers), Douglas et al. (1997) have used the term sexual homicide. For each individual serial sexual homicide offender, the performance and meaning of the sexual element may vary.

Researchers at the FBI gathered data from detailed interviews of 36 convicted serial murderers and were able to extract and analyze important personality and behavioral characteristics that helped distinguish different types of serial murderers. For ease of communication and conceptualization, the offenders were categorized into either "organized" or "disorganized" types (Table 1). These terms were initially meant to help law enforcement interpret crime scenes and can be understood as generally applicable concepts. They may also have appeal to forensic mental health professionals in that they

TABLE 1 Offender Traits

Organized	Disorganized
Good verbal skills, socially adept	Poor verbal and social skills
May live with spouse	Loner or lives with parents
Reasonably intelligent	Low intelligence
Usually employed	Under- or unemployed
Planning of crime	Little to no planning of crime
Ruse or con to gain control of victim	Blitz or surprise attack of victim
Targeted victim	Victim of opportunity
Crime scene: suggests control, order	Crime scene: disarray
Crime scene and death scene not the same	Crime scene and death scene often the same
Movement of body	Body left at death scene
Attempts to conceal evidence	Little to no attempts to conceal evidence

Source: Knoll J (2006)

provide illustrative descriptors of personality and behavior. The term mixed sexual homicide is used to describe the offender whose crime scene reflected aspects of both the organized and disorganized types. Finally, the term sadistic murderer describes the offender who is primarily a sexual sadist and derives the greatest satisfaction from the victim's response to torture.

Meloy (2002) has advanced a similar typology, but with a clinical emphasis. Sexual homicide perpetrators may be described as either "compulsive" or "catathymic." The compulsive perpetrators are similar to the FBI's organized killers. They leave organized crime scenes and can be diagnosed with sexual sadism and antisocial/narcissistic personality disorders. The catathymic perpetrators leave disorganized crime scenes and may be diagnosed with a mood disorder and varying personality traits. While the compulsive type display emotional detachment and autonomic hyporeactivity, the catathymic type are less psychopathic. In contrast, the catathymic type are autonomically hyperreactive and may have histories of abuse. Again, these types were intended to be generalities, and any individual case is likely to fall on a continuum between the two.

Psychiatric Findings

In terms of formal psychiatric diagnoses, most data come from individual case studies and retrospective analyses. When these studies are reviewed, they do suggest a common collection of diagnoses: psychopathy, antisocial personality, sexual sadism and other paraphilias (voyeurism, fetishism and sometimes necrophilia). The sexual sadism seen in serial murderers must be distinguished from sexual sadism between consenting adults that would not be considered criminal. The variant of sexual sadism seen in serial murderers is at the extreme end of the spectrum. Dietz et al. (1990) have provided an analysis of individuals who engaged in torturing victims to the

point of death to obtain the "pleasure in complete domination" over them.

Paraphilias, particularly voyeurism and [10] fetishism, have been described in many serial murderers. In fact, over 70% of sexual murderers had these paraphilias in Ressler et al.'s 1988 study. Schlesinger and Revitch (1999) have suggested that some individuals with voyeurism and fetishism may engage in burglaries that actually serve the purpose of gratifying these two paraphilias.

Focusing on the compulsive nature of the offenses, researchers have speculated on the significance of the seemingly obsessive qualities of the serial murderer, particularly the organized type. These individuals demonstrate a tendency toward orderliness, obsessive fantasy and ritualistic behavior (e.g. posing the body, biting, inserting objects and so forth) during their murders that suggest compulsive qualities. Experts believe that these obsessive and compulsive traits, combined with higher than average intelligence, permit organized offenders to improve their predatory skills and ability to avoid apprehension over time.

There is a notable absence of psychosis among serial murderers, and approximately half of perpetrators report substance use prior to their offenses (Ressler et al., 1988). At the present time, there is no conclusive evidence that specific organic factors play a causal role in the creation of a serial murderer. However, studies have found right temporal lobe abnormalities (Hucker et al., 1988) and other neurological abnormalities (Gratzer and Bradford, 1995) in sexual sadists.

Silva and colleagues (2004, 2002) have used neuropsychiatric concepts to approach the study of serial murderers, most notably Jeffrey Dahmer. They describe an association between autism spectrum disorders and a subgroup of serial murders, and propose that Dahmer may have suffered from Asperger's syndrome. Along these lines, it is interesting to note that after exhaustive interviews with

Dahmer, legendary FBI profiler Robert Ressler was impressed by the peculiar nature of Dahmer's presentation. In fact, Ressler held the opinion that Dahmer should have been sent to a psychiatric hospital instead of prison (Ressler, 2004a).

One of the most reliable psychological findings in the mental lives of serial murderers is the presence of violent fantasy. Convicted serial murderers have consistently described a high frequency of violent fantasies that are both persistent and arousing (Brittain, 1970; Johnson and Becker, 1997; Warren et al., 1996). Behavioral theorists have speculated that an early developmental pairing of sexual arousal with aggression is responsible for the deviant fantasy life seen in serial murderers.

Developmental Theories

Over the past several decades, there have been a number of different psychosocial theories put forth on the etiology of serial murder. Investigators with significant experience interviewing serial murderers have speculated that the behavior may result from a deadly convergence of: 1) early childhood attachment disruptions; 2) psychopathy; and 3) early traumatogenic abuse (Myers et al., 2005).

However, there is conflicting evidence on the presence of child abuse in the development of serial murderers. When the FBI studied 36 serial murderers, many of them had a history of either abuse or neglect: 43% reported a history of childhood sexual abuse, and 74% reported a history of psychological abuse that typically involved humiliation (Ressler et al., 1988). In contrast, other studies have found that the majority of sexually sadistic murderers had no evidence of childhood abuse (Dietz et al., 1990; Gratzer and Bradford, 1995). One possibility accounting for these differences may be due to heterogeneity in the populations studied.

When sexual murderers with a history of sexual abuse were compared to murderers without such a history, Ressler et al. (2004) found significant differences. Sexual murderers with a history of early sexual abuse were significantly more likely to begin fantasizing about rape earlier, in addition to developing more severe sexual deviancy. In addition to abuse, the family histories of many sexual murderers reveal unstable environments that may predispose them to disordered early life attachments. In one study, 70% of the sexual murderers' families had histories of alcohol abuse, and about 50% had family members with criminal histories (Ressler, 2004b). It is hypothesized that parental neglect from either absence or preoccupation with their own problems might have further exacerbated these men's ability to form healthy attachments.

Animal cruelty appears to be a common finding in the childhood and adolescent developmental stages of many serial murderers. The link between animal cruelty during childhood and subsequent physical violence during adulthood has been demonstrated in a number of studies (Kellert and Felthouse, 1985; Tingle et al., 1986), leading animal cruelty to be added to the DSM III-TR as a symptom under the diagnosis of conduct disorder in 1987. In keeping with the developmental theme of conduct disorder symptoms, researchers have also commented on a possible link between childhood fire setting and adult serial murder (Singer and Hensley, 2004).

Obviously, children who are diagnosed with conduct disorder or engage in animal cruelty do not all go on to become serial murderers. Nevertheless, it is thought that in the cases of those who do, an early "practicing" of violent and/or sadistic behavior on a living creature plays a role in desensitizing the individual to violence against humans. This notion has been termed "the graduation hypothesis" (Wright and Hensley, 2003). Indeed, some individuals progress past mere desensitization and actually derive pleasure and satisfaction from acts of animal cruelty.

Psychodynamically oriented investigators [20] have theorized that a sexually provocative mother may contribute to the formation of a serial murderer (Fox and Levin, 1994; Meloy, 2002). It is important to note that this premise is far from another "blaming of the mother" theory. Rather, investigators point to documented instances of strikingly inappropriate sexual behavior on the part of the mother that in some cases would easily qualify as sexual abuse. Evaluations of some convicted serial murderers suggest that a displacement of aggression from their mothers onto to their female victims was present during their offenses.

In summarizing both developmental theories and individual case studies of serial murderers, some relatively consistent traits are observed: a strong need for control/domination, an active deviant fantasy life, deviant sexual interests and psychopathic traits. Upon synthesizing these traits into a gestalt, the following picture emerges: an individual who spends excessive time in a reverie of deviant fantasy and has a tendency toward isolation, a need for totally submissive partners and a preference for autoerotic pleasure (Grubin, 1994). As can be imagined, such an individual will have a lack of healthy relationships and subsequently must depend on fantasy for gratification.

At some point, mere fantasy becomes an insufficient source of pleasure for the potential offender. It is theorized that a gradually progressive series of "tryouts" occur where he attempts to turn his fantasies into reality. For example, an offender may begin by simply following a potential victim. This may next progress to voyeurism or breaking into victims' homes as suggested by Schlesinger and Revitch (1999).

During a burglary, the offender may steal fetishistic items for sexual pleasure, such as undergarments. When this fails to provide sufficient satisfaction, the offender may progress to rape and ultimately murder. Such behavior is positively reinforced over time through paired association with masturbation, making the deviant fantasies extremely refractory to extinction (Prentky et al., 1989). Each time the serial murderer takes a victim, there is further stimulation of fantasy and an overall reinforcement of the cycle.

Assessment and Prevention

Forensic assessments of suspected serial murderers are best done by those with experience evaluating psychopathic and serial sexual offenders. Dishonesty and underreporting of deviant fantasies and offenses are commonplace, and a meticulous review of collateral data prior to the evaluation is necessary. Individuals who have already confessed to murders may nevertheless be unwilling to discuss the sexual nature of their offenses for a variety of reasons, the most common being the fact that sex offenders are severely harassed by other inmates in prison.

In an effort to help guide forensic risk assessments, Schlesinger (2001b) has put forth a list of 10 ominous signs (Table 2). The list consists of traits, characteristics and behaviors that were frequently found in the backgrounds [25]

TABLE 2 Ominous Signs (When Seen in Combination) Indicate Risk for a Potential Sex Murderer

1. Childhood abuse
2. Inappropriate maternal (sexual) conduct
3. Pathological lying and manipulation
4. Sadistic fantasy with a compulsion to act
5. Animal cruelty, particularly against cats
6. Need to control and dominate others
7. Repetitive firesetting
8. Voyeurism, fetishism, and (sexual) burglary
9. Unprovoked attacks on females, associated with generalized misogynous emotions
10. Evidence of ritualistic (signature) behavior

Source: Schlesinger LB (2001), The potential sex murderer: ominous signs, risk assessment. Journal of Threat Assessment 1(1):47-62. Reprinted with permission from The Haworth Press, Inc.

of perpetrators of sexual homicides. It is suggested that when these signs are seen in combination, the individual may be predisposed to committing sexual homicides.

Most experts believe that the prognosis for individuals who have committed serial murder is extremely poor (Douglas and Olshaker, 1995; Revitch and Schlesinger, 1989). At the present time, a preventive approach is most widely endorsed. Children and adolescents who demonstrate sexually sadistic fantasies or other ominous signs should be followed closely by mental health professionals who can direct efforts toward extinguishing the reinforcing cycle and conducting periodic risk assessments (Johnson and Becker, 1997).

Conclusions

Regarding the origins of serial murder, Park Dietz, MD (1986), arguably forensic psychiatry's leading expert on the subject, cautioned us:

The tendency of the press, public and public officials to regard such individuals as mad solely on the basis of their crimes reflects the widespread needs to attribute such behavior to alien forces.

As difficult as it is to fathom, serial murder may "simply be part of the spectrum of human possibility, a brutal dark side of man, not representing demons or disease" (Drukteinis, 1992).

It is important to recognize how limited our present understanding is in terms of the etiology and development of serial murder, so that erroneous conclusions are not drawn. While researchers have identified traits and abnormalities common to serial murderers, there are many who possess these traits and do not go on to become serial murderers. What is it then that leads some to act on their deviant fantasies while others do not? Until future research can help further clarify this question, Dietz suggested that, in his experience, "the leap from fantasy to action has much to do with character and the vicissitudes of life" (Simon, 1996).

References

Brittain RP (1970), The sadistic murderer. Med Sci Law 10(4):198-207.

Dietz PE (1986), Mass, serial and sensational homicides. Bull NY Acad Med 62(5): 477-491.

Dietz PE, Hazelwood RR, Warren J (1990), The sexually sadistic criminal and his offenses. Bull Am Acad Psychiatry Law 18(2):163-178.

Douglas JE, Burgess AW, Burgess AG, Ressler R, eds. (1997), Crime Classification Manual: A Standard System for Investigating and Classifying Violent Crimes. San Francisco: Jossey Bass Publishers.

Douglas JE, Olshaker M (1995), Mind Hunter: Inside the FBI's Elite Serial Crime Unit. New York: Scribner.

Drukteinis AM (1992), Serial murder—the heart of darkness. Psychiatr Ann 22(10):532-538.

Everitt D (1993), Human Monsters: An Illustrated Encyclopedia of the World's Most Vicious Murderers. Chicago: Contemporary Books.

Fox JA, Levin J (1994), Overkill: Mass Murder and Serial Killing Exposed. New York: Plenum Press.

Gratzer T, Bradford JM (1995), Offender and offense characteristics of sexual sadists: a comparative study. J Forensic Sci 40(3):450-455.

Grubin D (1994), Sexual sadism. Criminal Behavior and Mental Health 4:3-9 [editorial].

Herkov MJ, Biernat M (1997), Assessment of PTSD symptoms in a community exposed to serial murder. J Clin Psychol 53(8):809-815.

Holmes ST, Tewksbury R, Holmes RM (2002), Fractured identity syndrome: a new theory of serial murder. In: Current Perspectives on Sex Crimes, Holmes RM, Holmes ST, eds. Thousand Oaks, Calif.: Sage Publications.

Hucker SJ, Langevin R, Wortzman G et al. (1988), Cerebral damage and dysfunction in sexually aggressive men. Annals of Sex Research 1:33-47.

Johnson BR, Becker JV (1997), Natural born killers?: the development of the sexually sadistic serial killer. J Am Acad Psychiatry Law 25(3):335-348.

Kellert SR, Felthouse AR (1985), Childhood cruelty toward animals among criminals and noncriminals. Human Relations 38(12):1113-1129.

McNamara JJ, Morton RJ (2004), Frequency of serial sexual homicide victimization in Virginia for a ten-year period. [Published erratum J Forensic Sci 49(5):1148.] J Forensic Sci 49(3):529-533.

Meloy JR (2002), The nature and dynamics of sexual homicide: an integrative review. Aggression and Violent Behavior 5(1):1-22.

Myers WC, Gooch E, Meloy JR (2005), The role of psychopathy and sexuality in a female serial killer. J Forensic Sci 50(3):652-657.

Prentky RA, Burgess AW, Rokous F et al. (1989), The presumptive role of fantasy in serial sexual homicide. Am J Psychiatry 146(7):887-891.

Ressler RK (2004a), How to interview a cannibal. In: Profilers: Leading Investigators Take You Inside the Criminal Mind, Campbell JH, DeNevi D, eds. Amherst, N.Y.: Prometheus Books.

Ressler RK (2004b), The men who murdered. In: Profilers: Leading Investigators Take You Inside the Criminal Mind, Campbell JH, DeNevi D, eds. Amherst, N.Y.: Prometheus Books.

Ressler RK, Burgess AW, Douglas JE (1988), Sexual Homicide: Patterns and Motives. Lexington, Mass.: Lexington Books.

Ressler RK, Burgess AW, Hartman CR et al. (2004), Murderers who rape and mutilate. In: Profilers: Leading Investigators Take You Inside the Criminal Mind, Campbell JH, DeNevi D, eds. Amherst, N.Y.: Prometheus Books.

Revitch E, Schlesinger LB (1989), Sex Murder and Sex Aggression: Phenomenology, Psychopathology, Psychodynamics and Prognosis. Springfield, Ill.: Charles C. Thomas.

Schlesinger LB (2001a), Is serial homicide really increasing? J Am Acad Psychiatry Law 29(3):294-297.

Schlesigner LB (2001b), The potential sex murderer: ominous signs, risk assessment. Journal of Threat Assessment 1(1):47-62.

Schlesinger LB, Revitch E (1999), Sexual burglaries and sexual homicide: clinical, forensic, and investigative considerations. J Am Acad Psychiatry Law 27(2):227-238.

Silva JA, Ferrari MM, Leong GB (2002), The case of Jeffrey Dahmer: sexual serial homicide from a neuropsychiatric developmental perspective. J Forensic Sci 47(6):1347-1359.

Silva JA, Leong GB, Ferrari MM (2004), A neuropsychiatric developmental model of serial homicidal behavior. Behav Sci Law 22(6):787-799.

Simon RI (1996), Bad Men Do What Good Men Dream: A Forensic Psychiatrist Illuminates the Darker Side of Human Behavior. Washington, D.C.: American Psychiatric Press, Inc., p312.

Singer SD, Hensley C (2004), Applying social learning theory to childhood and adolescent firesetting: can it lead to serial murder? Int J Offender Ther Comp Criminol 48(4):461-476.

Tingle D, Barnard GW, Robbins L et al. (1986), Childhood and adolescent characteristics of pedophiles and rapists. Int J Law Psychiatry 9(1):103-116.

Warren JI, Hazelwood RR, Dietz PE (1996), The sexually sadistic serial killer. J Forensic Sci 41(6):970-974.

Wright J, Hensley C (2003), From animal cruelty to serial murder: applying the graduation hypothesis. Int J Offender Ther Comp Criminol 47(1):71-88.

A CLOSER LOOK AT
Serial Murder: A Forensic Psychiatric Perspective

1. According to Knoll's findings in the medical research, why do psychiatrists and other forensic experts still know so little about serial murder?

2. Do a brief rhetorical analysis of "Serial Murder."

   a. What are Knoll's purpose and main point/thesis? In other words, what is he trying to provide for his readers, and what single idea does he want them to understand? Go through the text and mark the sentence or sentences that best express the main point. What are some other major points that Knoll makes?

   b. Who are the readers Knoll is writing for? This report appeared in *Psychiatric Times.* Go to the magazine's Web site and find out who they are and what they would need and want in an article like this.

   c. In what ways is this report written for these readers? Overall, how well would it achieve its purpose for these readers?

3. Highlight or make a list of the myths and misconceptions about serial murder that Knoll addresses. Now write a single sentence that sums up how those misconceptions compare to the reality. Write a sentence that follows a pattern like this: "Most people believe that _____, but actually _____."

4. After reading Knoll's report on the scientific research about serial murder, in what ways have your views on the topic changed?

IDEAS FOR
Writing

1. Write a 200-word abstract for this research report. Be sure to explain what topic and question is addressed, the main findings, and implications.

2. Search the Internet for a report or article about serial killers that takes a more "sensational" angle. That is, find an article that is written in a way that is intended merely to excite and shock readers rather than informing them seriously and accurately. Using what you know from Knoll's article, write a rhetorical analysis of that sensational article. How does it seek to excite and shock its readers? Does it succeed in informing them as well as exciting them?

1. Using an Internet search engine, find a research paper written by a college student. With your group, discuss the strengths and weaknesses of this research paper. Determine whether this research paper is an expository research paper or an argumentative one. Can you find a clear purpose statement or thesis? Do you think the writer covered the topic in enough depth, or can you find gaps in his or her research?

2. The research paper is often criticized as a genre that is mostly used in school. With your group, come up with five ways in which a research paper could be used outside of college. What kinds of readers would find a research paper interesting and worth reading?

3. With your group, discuss the student example of a research paper included at the beginning of this chapter. How well does the student follow the research paper genre, as described in this chapter? Where does she deviate from the genre? How is she creative with the content, organization, style, and design of the document?

1. More than likely, your professor has asked you to write a research paper. With your group, read through the assignment sheet carefully. List ten topics that would be appropriate for this assignment. Then, identify a new angle for each of these topics. A good way to find a new angle is to ask, "What is new or has changed recently about this topic?"

2. Find an annotated bibliography on the Internet. What kinds of sources did the author include in the bibliography? Do you find the summaries of the sources helpful, or could the writer have described the sources in more depth? Using your library's Web site, find five additional sources that could have been included in this bibliography. Put them in APA or MLA style and send them to your professor.

3. Even a brief search on the Internet will turn up many of those "Buy a Research Paper" Web sites. Looking at these Web sites, write down ten ways that would help you detect whether a research paper was bought or plagiarized. Do these Web sites promise results that they cannot possibly deliver?

Here's your chance to play around with some other microgenres. Choose a microgenre from the list below and find three examples in print or on the Internet. Use these examples to come up with your own guidelines for writing one of these microgenres, which are similar to a research paper.

Brief—answers a simple scientific or historical question with a factual response

Abstract—a one-paragraph summary of a book or article, using the original wording from the source

White Paper—a brief report that explains an important concept or event with factual research

340

Overview—a concise explanation of an event or phenomenon that gives readers some helpful background on that subject

Q&A—In a question and answer format, addresses potential questions that might be asked by readers or an audience about a specific topic

1. **Collect sources and create an annotated bibliography.** For a research paper you are writing, collect ten documents from a variety of print and electronic sources. Read these sources and create an annotated bibliography. Each source should be put into MLA or APA bibliographic format. Then, each should include a three-sentence or more summary.

2. **Write a research paper.** Research papers can be written on a variety of topics. More than likely, your professor has asked you to write one for the course you are taking. Working on your own or in a small group, do these activities:

   a. Identify a topic that you would be interested in writing about and come up with a new angle.

   b. In one sentence write down a statement of purpose that describes what you want the research paper to demonstrate or prove.

   c. Write down two possible thesis statements that could be used to guide this research paper. Which one is stronger? Why?

   d. Create an outline of your research paper. Start out with the diagrams shown in the At-A-Glance at the beginning of this chapter. Which of these patterns will be most useful for your project? How can this pattern be modified to fit your topic's needs?

   e. Find at least ten items from print and electronic sources. Create a Works Cited or References list from these sources. Then, use them as support in your research paper.

3. **Invent an electronic research paper.** Research papers have traditionally been handed in on paper. If you were to completely rethink the research paper as an electronic document, what would it look like and how would it work? Write a two-page proposal for a new kind of research paper that is multimedia-based. Your proposal should describe how written text, images, audio, and video could be used make a more dynamic document for the readers.

PEARSON
mycomplab

For support in meeting this chapter's objectives, follow this path in MyCompLab: Resources ⟹ Research ⟹ The Research Assignment ⟹ Writing the Research Paper. Review the Instruction and Multimedia resources about drafting and revising a research paper, then complete the Exercises and click on Gradebook to measure your progress.

Developing a Writing Process

PART OUTLINE

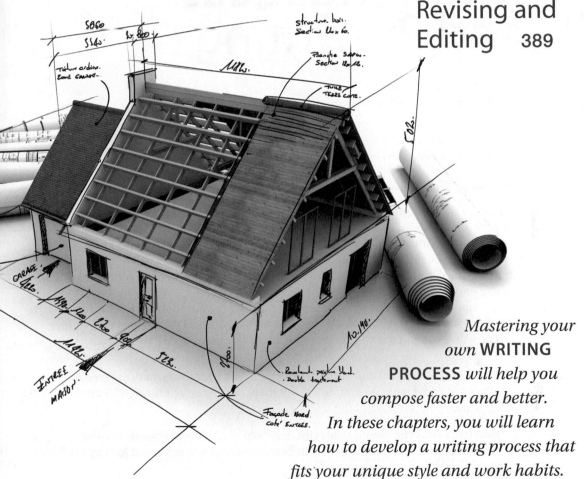

Mastering your own **WRITING PROCESS** *will help you compose faster and better. In these chapters, you will learn how to develop a writing process that fits your unique style and work habits.*

14

Inventing Ideas
and Prewriting

In this chapter, you will learn how to—

- use prewriting techniques to get your ideas flowing.
- develop your ideas with heuristics.
- reflect on your ideas with exploratory writing and extend them in new directions.

Invention involves generating new ideas and inquiring into topics that you find interesting. Invention also helps you discover and create the content of your document. In this chapter, you will learn some simple but powerful invention strategies that will help you tap into your natural creativity. These strategies will help you figure out what you already know about your topic and get those ideas onto your screen or a piece of paper.

Writers use a variety of techniques to help them invent their ideas and see their topic from new perspectives. In this chapter, we will discuss three types of invention strategies that you can use to generate new ideas and inquire into your topic:

Prewriting uses visual and verbal strategies to put your ideas on the screen or a piece of paper, so you can think about them and figure out how you want to approach your topic.

Heuristics use time-tested strategies that help you ask good questions about your topic and figure out what kinds of information you will need to support your claims and statements.

Exploratory writing uses reflective writing to help you better understand how you feel about your topic and turn those thoughts into sentences, paragraphs, and outlines.

Some of these invention strategies will work better for you than others. So try them all to see which ones help you best tap into your creativity.

Prewriting

Prewriting helps you put your ideas on the screen or a piece of paper, though usually not in an organized way. Your goal while prewriting is to figure out what you already know about your topic and to start coming up with new ideas that go beyond what you already know.

Concept Mapping

One of the most common prewriting tools is *concept mapping*. To create a concept map, write your topic in the middle of your screen or a piece of paper (Figure 14.1). Put a circle around it. Then write down as many other ideas as you can about your topic. Circle those ideas and draw lines that connect them with your original topic and with each other.

Watch the Video on **Concept Maps** at mycomplab.com

The magic of concept mapping is that it allows you to start throwing your ideas onto the screen or a blank page without worrying about whether they make sense at the moment. Each new idea in your map will help you come up with other new ideas. Just keep going. Then, when you run out of new ideas, you can work on connecting ideas together into larger clusters.

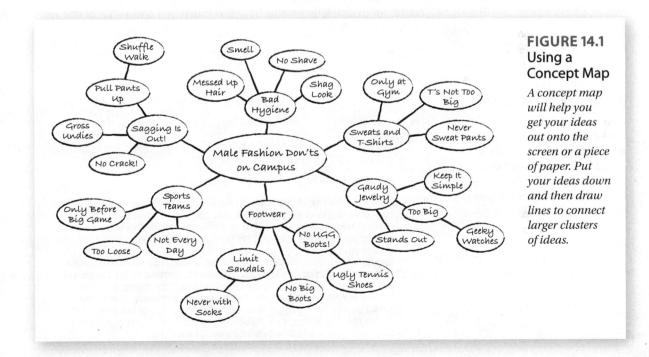

**FIGURE 14.1
Using a
Concept Map**

A concept map will help you get your ideas out onto the screen or a piece of paper. Put your ideas down and then draw lines to connect larger clusters of ideas.

For example, Figure 14.1 shows a concept map about the pitfalls of male fashion on a college campus. A student made this concept map for an argument paper. She started out by writing "Male Fashion Don'ts on Campus" in the middle of a sheet of paper. Then she began jotting down anything that came to mind. Eventually, the whole sheet was filled out. She then linked ideas together into larger clusters.

With her ideas in front of her, she can now figure out what she wants to write about. The larger clusters might become major topics in her argument (e.g., sweats and T-shirts, jewelry, footwear, hygiene, saggy pants, and sports uniforms). Or she could pick one of those clusters (e.g., footwear) and structure her argument around that narrower topic.

If you like concept mapping, you might try one of the free mapping software packages available online, including *Compendium, Free Mind, Connected Mind, MindMeister,* and *VUE,* among others.

Freewriting

When *freewriting*, all you need to do is open a page on your computer or pull out a piece of notebook paper. Then write as much as you can for five to ten minutes, putting down anything that comes into your mind. Don't worry about making real sentences or paragraphs. If you find yourself running out of words, try finishing phrases like "What I mean is . . ." or "Here's my point. . . ."

When using a computer, try turning off the monitor or closing your eyes as you freewrite. That way, the words you have already written won't distract you from writing down new ideas. Plus, a dark screen will help you avoid the temptation to go back and fix those typos and garbled sentences.

Figure 14.2 shows an example freewrite. The text has typos and some of the sentences make no sense. That's fine.

FIGURE 14.2 Freewriting

When you are freewriting, just let the ideas flow and see where they lead you. In this sample, the writer didn't stop to correct typos. She just moved from one topic to the next. The result is a little chaotic, but now she has several new ideas to work with.

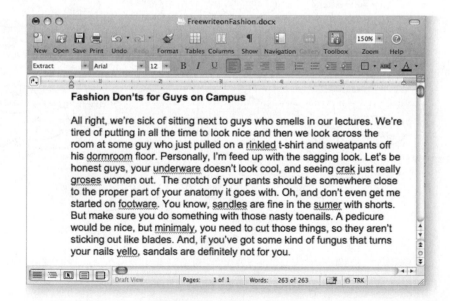

Fashion Don'ts for Guys on Campus

All right, we're sick of sitting next to guys who smells in our lectures. We're tired of putting in all the time to look nice and then we look across the room at some guy who just pulled on a rinkled t-shirt and sweatpants off his dormroom floor. Personally, I'm feed up with the sagging look. Let's be honest guys, your underware doesn't look cool, and seeing crak just really groses women out. The crotch of your pants should be somewhere close to the proper part of your anatomy it goes with. Oh, and don't even get me started on footware. You know, sandles are fine in the sumer with shorts. But make sure you do something with those nasty toenails. A pedicure would be nice, but minimaly, you need to cut those things, so they aren't sticking out like blades. And, if you've got some kind of fungus that turns your nails yello, sandals are definitely not for you.

When you are finished freewriting, go through your text, highlighting or under-lining your best ideas. Some people find it helpful to do a second, follow-up freewrite that focuses just on the best ideas.

Brainstorming or Listing

Another kind of prewriting is *brainstorming*, which is also called *listing*. To brain-storm about your topic, open a new page on your screen or pull out a piece of paper. Then list everything that comes to mind about your topic. As in freewriting, you should just keep listing ideas for about five to ten minutes without stopping.

Next, pick your best idea and create a second brainstorming list in a second col-umn. Again, list everything that comes to mind about this best idea. Making two lists will help you narrow your topic and deepen your thoughts about it.

Storyboarding

Movie scriptwriters and advertising designers use a technique called storyboarding to help them sketch out their ideas. *Storyboarding* involves drawing a set of pictures that show the progression of your ideas. Storyboards are especially useful when you are working with genres like memoirs, reports, or proposals, because they help you visualize the "story."

The easiest way to storyboard about your topic is to fold a regular piece of paper into four or eight panels (Figure 14.3, page 348). Then, in each of the panels, draw a scene or a major idea involving your topic. Stick figures are fine. Don't worry about making your drawings look good. We can't all be artists.

Storyboarding is similar to turning your ideas into a comic strip. You add panels to your storyboards and cross them out as your ideas evolve. You can also add dia-logue into the scenes and put captions underneath each panel to show what is hap-pening. Storyboarding often works best for people who like to think in drawings or pictures rather than in words and sentences.

Using Heuristics

You already use heuristics, but the term is probably not familiar to you. A *heuristic* is a discovery tool that helps you ask insightful questions or follow a specific pattern of thinking. Writers often memorize the heuristics that they find especially useful. Here, we will review some of the most popular heuristics, but many others are available.

Asking the Journalist's Questions

The most common heuristic is a tool called the *journalist's questions*, which we like to call the "Five-W and How questions." Writers for newspapers, magazines, and televi-sion use these questions to help them sort out the details of a story.

Who was involved?   **When** did it happen?

What happened?   **Why** did it happen?

Where did the event happen?   **How** did it happen?

**FIGURE 14.3
A Storyboard
That Illustrates
the Major
Parts of a Text**

*Some writers find
it helpful to draw
out their ideas
as a storyboard.
Each scene in
the storyboard
becomes a major
part of the text.*

Write each of these questions separately on your screen or a piece of paper. Then answer each question in as much detail as you can. Make sure your facts are accurate, so you can reconstruct the story from your notes. If you don't know the answer to one of these questions, put down a question mark. A question mark signals a place where you might need to do some more research.

When using the Five-W and How questions, you might also find it helpful to ask, "What has changed recently about my topic?" Paying attention to change will also help you determine your "angle" on the topic (i.e., your unique perspective or view).

Using the Five Senses

Writers also like to use their five senses as a heuristic to explore a topic and invent their ideas. When trying to describe something to your readers, concentrate on each of your senses one by one:

Sight What can you see? What does it look like? What colors or shapes do you see?

Hearing What sounds can you hear? What do people or objects sound like?

Smell What can you smell? Does anything have a distinctive scent?

Touch What do things feel like? Are they rough or smooth? Are they cold or hot?

Taste Are there any tastes? If so, are they sweet, salty, sour, delicious?

Using all five senses will help you experience your topic from various stand-points. These vivid descriptions will give your readers a richer understanding of your subject.

Investigating *Logos, Ethos, Pathos*

Aristotle, a philosopher and rhetorician, realized that arguments tend to draw on three kinds of proof: reasoning (*logos*), authority (*ethos*), and emotion (*pathos*). Today, writers still use these Greek terms to remind themselves to gather evidence from all three kinds of proof. This heuristic works especially well for persuasive texts, such as commentaries, position papers, and proposals.

Logos. *Logos* includes any reasoning and examples that will support your claims. You can use logical statements to prove your points, or you can use real or realistic examples to back up your claims. Here are some basic strategies that you can use to support your ideas with *logos:*

> *If . . . then:* "If you believe X, then you should believe Y also."
>
> *Either . . . or:* "Either you believe X, or you believe Y."
>
> *Cause and effect:* "X is the reason Y happens."
>
> *Costs and benefits:* "The benefits of doing X are worth/not worth the cost Y."
>
> *Better and worse:* "X is better/worse than Y because . . ."
>
> *Examples:* "For example, X and Y demonstrate that Z happens."
>
> *Facts and data:* "These facts/data support my argument that X is true (or Y is false)."
>
> *Anecdotes:* "X happened to these people, thus demonstrating Y."

Ethos. *Ethos* involves information that will help you build your authority and reputation with readers. If you are an expert on a particular topic, you can use your own experiences to support your argument. For example, on the topic of clothing, someone majoring in fashion design would have more *ethos*. If you are not an expert on your topic, then you can draw from sources written by experts to add *ethos* to your writing. Here are a few ways to use *ethos* in your writing:

> *Personal experience:* "I have experienced X, so I know it's true and Y is not."
>
> *Personal credentials:* "I have a degree in Z" or "I am the director of Y." "So I know a lot about the subject of X."
>
> *Good moral character:* "I have always done the right thing for the right reasons, so you should believe me when I say that X is the best path to follow."
>
> *Appeal to experts:* "According to Z, who is an expert on this topic, X is true and Y is not true."

Identification with the readers: "You and I come from similar backgrounds and we have similar values; therefore, you would likely agree with me that X is true and Y is not."

Admission of limitations: "I may not know much about Z, but I do know that X is true and Y is not."

Expression of goodwill: "I want what is best for you, so I am recommending X as the best path to follow."

Use of "insider" language: Using jargon or referring to information that only insiders would understand.

Pathos.   *Pathos* relates to emotional support for your argument. Think about the aspects of your topic that make people happy, mad, sad, anxious, concerned, surprised, disgusted, joyful, or fearful. You can appeal to these emotions to persuade people to see things your way. Here are some strategies for using emotion:

Promise of gain: "By agreeing with us, you will gain trust, time, money, love, advancement, reputation, comfort, popularity, health, beauty, or convenience."

Promise of enjoyment: "If you do things our way, you will experience joy, anticipation, fun, surprises, enjoyment, pleasure, leisure, or freedom."

Fear of loss: "If you don't do things this way, you risk losing time, money, love, security, freedom, reputation, popularity, health, or beauty."

Fear of pain: "If you don't do things this way, you may feel pain, sadness, grief, frustration, humiliation, embarrassment, loneliness, regret, shame, vulnerability, or worry."

Expressions of anger or disgust: "You should be angry or disgusted because X is unfair to you, me, or others."

Emotion alone usually won't create the strongest arguments. Instead, you should use emotion to support your *logos*-based or *ethos*-based arguments. Emotion will add power and feeling to your argument, while heightening the intensity for your readers. Figure 14.4 on page 351 shows the introduction to a first draft in which the author uses emotion to support her *logos* and *ethos* arguments.

Cubing

A cube has six sides, and cubing asks you to explore your topic through six "sides" or angles.

1. **Describe it.** What does your topic look like? What are its color and shape? How big or small is it? What is it made of?

2. **Compare it.** What is it like? What is it *not* like? In what ways is it similar to or different from things that are more familiar to your readers?

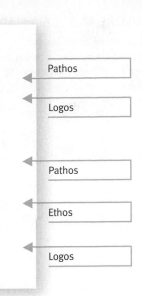

As a fashion design major (and a woman), let me offer you guys a little helpful advice about attracting women on campus. College women view campus differently than most men. Guys see campus as a place to go to class and study, perhaps throw a frisbee. So, showing up in a faded t-shirt, sweatpants, and flipflops might seem all right. Quite differently, women see campus as a place to socialize and meet friends, in addition to doing class-related stuff. For women, campus is a place to see people and be seen. Consequently, women don't like to be seen with guys who look like they were just shot out of a wrinkle gun. But, if you guys make a few simple wardrobe changes, women are going to notice you.

Pathos
Logos
Pathos
Ethos
Logos

FIGURE 14.4   A First Draft That Uses *Logos, Pathos,* **and** *Ethos* **for Support**

In this first draft of an essay's introduction, the author uses a combination of reasoning, authority, and emotional appeals to persuade her readers.

3. **Associate it.** What does it remind you of? What other topics is it related to that you know something about?

4. **Analyze it.** What patterns run through your topic? What are its hidden questions or meanings? Who created it? What has changed that makes it important?

5. **Apply it.** How could you or someone else use it? Who would use it? What good would it do them? What harm might it do?

6. **Argue for or against it.** What arguments could you or someone else make for or against your topic?

Exploratory Writing

Exploratory writing helps you reflect on your ideas and get your thoughts down for further consideration. Essentially, exploratory writing is "writing about writing" that allows you to examine your writing projects from a little more distance.

Journaling, Blogging, or Microblogging

Some writers find it helpful to keep a regular journal or blog to reflect on their experiences and generate new ideas. In these forums, you can write down your thoughts and think about your life without the pressure of drafting the full argument.

FIGURE 14.5 A Blog

Journals or blogs can be helpful for coming up with new ideas and reflections. This blog was found on Blogger.com, *a free blogging Web site.*

Journaling. This kind of exploratory writing can be done in a notebook or on your computer. The key to successful journaling is to add something new every day. You can talk about the things that happen to you and what is going on in your world.

Blogging. Blogging is very similar to journaling, but blogs are public texts (Figure 14.5). You can sign up for a blog at several blogging Web sites, usually for free. You may not want everyone to read your innermost ideas—but then, of course, you might! Some personal blogs develop their own cult followings. For more on blogging, see Chapter 29, "Using the Internet."

Microblogging. You can use a microblog like *Twitter, Tumblr, Plurk, Jaiku, identi.ca,* and others to describe what is happening to you. Besides keeping your friends informed about where you are and what you are doing, your microblog can track your thoughts and experiences.

Before writing a new entry into your journal or blog, go back and read what you wrote previously. That way, you can build from your previous thoughts or use them as a springboard for coming up with new ideas.

Writing an Exploratory Draft

Sometimes it is helpful to write an "exploratory draft" before you begin trying to write a rough draft. In an exploratory draft, write about how you feel about the topic and what you already know about it. Write down some of the main points you want to make in your paper and what kinds of information or examples you will need to support your points. Your exploratory draft is also a good place to express your concerns about the project and come up with some strategies for handling them.

> In this paper, I want to argue that guys should dress nicer on campus. But I don't want to come off as some kind of fashion snob or diva. I also don't want to give the impression that I think everyone has enough money to buy designer clothes. I strongly believe that looking good is not a matter of money or being physically attractive. It's about making good choices and taking a few minutes to think about what looks good to others. I guess my main goal in this paper is to give guys good reasons to dress nicer on campus. Yeah, I'll need to tweak them a little to get their attention. My writing style will probably need to be funny or even teasing. If they get a little angry, maybe they'll think a little more about how they look. It would be nice if I could find some pictures that demonstrate good fashion choices. Nothing GQ. Just normal guys on campus making good choices about clothing. That would help me show my readers what I mean.

The purpose of an exploratory draft is not to write the paper itself but to use writing to help you explore your topic and sort out your ideas.

Exploring with Presentation Software

Presentation software can be a powerful tool for doing exploratory writing about your subject. There are many software packages, such as Microsoft's *PowerPoint*, Apple's *KeyNote*, and free programs like *Prezi, SlideRocket, 280 Slides,* and OpenOffice's *Impress.* The software can help you create slides, making a bulleted list of your major subjects and key points. Then you can fill out the slides with details, pictures, and graphs. Try this:

1. Create a new page in your favorite presentation software.

2. On the title slide, type a title for your paper that identifies your topic. In the subtitle area, type in your angle on that topic.

3. Think of two to five major topics that will be discussed in your argument. Create separate slides for each of those major topics.

4. On the slide for each major topic, list two to five issues that you might need to talk about in your paper.

5. As you fill in each slide, look for opportunities to add visuals, such as photographs, charts, and graphs.

If you don't know something about one of your major topics, just leave that slide blank for now. These gaps in slides signal places where you need to do more exploration or research.

When you are finished filling in the slides as best you can, you might find it helpful to change your screen to Slide Sorting View, so you can see an overview of your

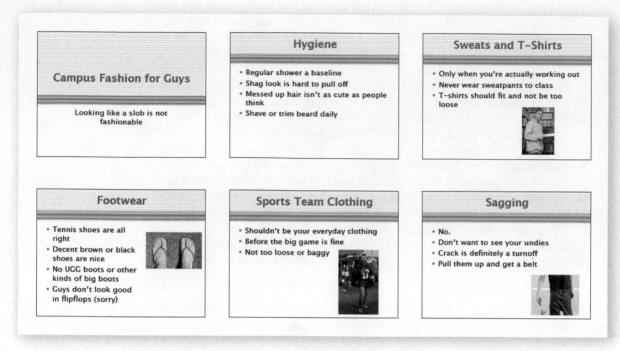

FIGURE 14.6 Outlining with Presentation Software

Presentation software can help you make a quick outline of your argument and insert graphics.

whole text (Figure 14.6). This view will allow you to move slides around to figure out how to best organize your ideas.

When you are finished exploring your topic with the presentation software, you will have a good outline for writing your paper. Plus, you will have collected the photographs, charts, and other visuals you need to design the document.

Taking Time to Invent and Prewrite

When writing a paper, it is tempting to jump straight to the drafting stage of the writing process. After all, time spent prewriting, using heuristics, and doing exploratory writing might seem like time away from your real task—getting that assignment finished. In the end, the secret to invention is to give yourself the time and space to explore your ideas.

Above all, think of "invention" as a separate stage in your writing process. Set aside some time to discover and form your ideas before you start trying to draft your paper. You will be more productive and more creative. Plus, you will actually save time, because you won't just sit at your computer staring into the screen.

Start developing the content of your document. Here are some techniques for prewriting, using heuristics, and doing some exploratory writing.

DO Some Prewriting to Get the Ideas Flowing

Prewriting uses visual and verbal strategies to help you figure out what you already know about your topic and how you want to approach it. Try making a concept map, freewriting, doing some brainstorming, or making a storyboard on your topic.

USE Heuristics to Draw Out Your Ideas

A heuristic is a discovery tool that helps you ask insightful questions or follow a specific pattern of thinking. Some of the common heuristics are the Five-W and How questions, the five human senses, *logos/ethos/pathos*, and cubing.

REFLECT on Your Topic with Exploratory Writing

Exploratory writing is "writing about writing" that allows you to think about your writing projects from a little more distance. You can do some journaling or blogging. Or you can write an exploratory draft that lets you talk through what you want to write about. Presentation software can be a useful tool for putting your ideas on the screen in an organized way.

GIVE Yourself Time to Invent Your Ideas

It's tempting to jump right to the drafting stage. That deadline is looming. But you will find that you write more efficiently and better if you give yourself time to sort through your ideas first.

1. List three times in your life when you have been especially inventive or innovative. Why did you decide to take the more creative path rather than the ordinary path? Tell your group about these creative moments and how they came about.

2. With your group, list five celebrities who you think are especially original and innovative. What unique characteristics make each of them creative? Can you find any common characteristics that they all share?

3. What kinds of invention strategies have you learned previously, and what has worked for you in the past? With your group, talk about methods you have used in the past to come up with new ideas for projects.

Try This Out

1. Create a concept map about a topic that interests you. What are the one or two most interesting issues in your concept map? Put one of those issues in the middle of your screen or a piece of paper and create a second concept map on this narrower version of the topic. Ask yourself, "What has changed to make this topic interesting right now?" Doing so will help you find a new angle on your topic.

2. For about five minutes, freewrite about a topic for your next paper in this class. When you are finished, pick your best idea and freewrite for another five minutes. This second freewrite will help you develop a solid understanding of the topic, purpose, and angle for your paper.

3. Check into some of the free blogging services available online. What are some of the pros and cons of each blogging site? If you don't have a blog of your own, what kind of blog might you enjoy keeping?

Write This

1. **Invent with presentation software.** For your next project in this class, start out by creating a version of your document with presentation software. Begin with a title slide that includes your title and main point. Then create slides for the major points in your paper. Add a slide for the conclusion. Then go back and fill in the bullet points for each of your major points. Find any graphics you can and add them to the slides. When you have finished creating your "presentation," use the slide sorter feature to move slides around. When you are finished, talk through your presentation with your group.

2. **Start keeping a journal or blog.** For the next two weeks, keep a journal or a blog. Spend a little time each day writing something about the topic of your next paper. Then, as you draft, design, and edit your paper, write about your successes and challenges while developing the document. Hand in your journal or your blog's URL with the final draft of your paper.

PEARSON
mycomplab

For support in meeting this chapter's objectives, follow this path in MyCompLab: Resources ⟹ Writing ⟹ The Writing Process ⟹ Planning. Review the Instruction and Multimedia resources about freewriting and prewriting, then complete the Exercises and click on Gradebook to measure your progress.

Organizing and Drafting

In this chapter, you will learn how to—

- use genres to organize your ideas.
- sketch out your ideas with an outline.
- overcome writer's block with solid writing habits.

In the previous chapter, you learned how to "invent" the content of your paper by using prewriting, heuristics, and exploratory writing to be creative and gather information. In this chapter, you will learn about the second stage in the writing process: how to use genres to organize your ideas and write a draft of your paper.

The genre you choose will help you determine where your ideas and the information you gathered should appear in the text. The genre helps you organize your ideas into a shape that is familiar to you and your readers. Remember, genres are not formulas to be followed mechanically. Instead, genres follow flexible patterns that reflect how people act, react, and interact in the real world. The organization of a genre, in other words, reflects how people get things done.

Using Genres to Organize Your Ideas

As your documents grow longer and more complex, genres will help you dramatically improve your writing. Genres follow organizational patterns that reflect the activities you will do in your college classes and in the workplace. For example, the report genre, (discussed in Chapter 12) reflects the steps that you should follow when doing research on a topic:

1. Define a research question and hypothesis

2. Develop a method for answering that research question

3. Gather results

4. Discuss those results

5. Draw conclusions and/or recommendations

It's no coincidence, then, that the report genre calls for five sections that reflect this research process: *introduction, methods, results, discussion*, and *recommendations*. Once you know that a report tends to be organized into these five sections, you can arrange the information you have gathered to fit what your readers expect.

Should you mechanically follow a genre as a fixed pattern? Absolutely not. A genre's organization can be adjusted to suit your purpose and the unique characteristics of the rhetorical situation. Genres are flexible and "stretchy," allowing you to move, combine, and divide sections according to your specific writing situation.

Drafting Introductions, Bodies, and Conclusions

Genres commonly used in college and in the workplace have some organizational features that you can commit to memory. Specifically, genres used in college and the workplace almost always include an introduction, body, and conclusion:

Introduction. The purpose of the introduction is to set a "context" for the body of the document. The introduction usually tells readers your topic, purpose, and thesis statement. It might also offer background information on your topic and stress its importance to readers. Introductions can range in size from one small paragraph to several paragraphs.

Body. The body presents the "content" of the document. Essentially, the body provides the facts, reasoning, examples, quotations, data, and anything else needed to support or prove your document's thesis statement and achieve its purpose.

Conclusion. At the end of the document, the conclusion reestablishes the context for the document by restating your main point or thesis (usually with more emphasis), restating why your topic is important to your readers, and offering a look to the future. Your conclusion should be as brief as possible, from one small paragraph to a few paragraphs at most.

To help you remember this three-part pattern, sometimes it helps to keep the time-tested speechwriter's pattern in mind: "Tell them what you're going to tell them. Tell them. Then tell them what you told them."

In Chapter 19, "Drafting Introductions and Conclusions," you will learn more about how to write strong beginnings and endings. You can turn there now if you are looking for immediate advice on writing introductions and conclusions.

Sketching an Outline

An outline can be an important tool for organizing your ideas, especially as the documents you write grow larger and more complex. In the workplace, most people sketch out a rough outline to help them sort out their ideas or to get input from others. Your outline doesn't need to be formal, but it should list the major parts of your document. Your outline is a map that guides you as you draft your document.

Creating a Basic Outline

When creating a basic outline, you first need to decide which genre you are using and turn to that chapter in Part 2 of this book. At the beginning of each genre chapter, you will see an "At a Glance" diagram illustrating one or two organizational patterns that the genre tends to follow. These patterns should give you an overall idea about which sections should appear in your outline.

Here's the easy part. Type or write "I. Introduction" on your screen or a piece of paper. Then type or write "X. Conclusion" at the bottom. After all, you already know your document will need an introduction and a conclusion. For now, use an "X" with the conclusion, because you aren't sure how many sections will be needed for the body of your text.

*Watch the Video on **Creating a Basic Outline** at **mycomplab.com***

Filling Out Your Outline

Here's the hard part. Start listing the major sections that will appear in your document. Give each one an uppercase roman numeral (e.g., II, III, IV, V, VI, VII, etc.). The genre you are following should give you a good idea about how many sections you will need (Figure 15.1, page 360). *Hint:* If your roman numerals are nearing X (that's ten sections), you probably have too many sections. If that's the case, some of your sections should be combined or removed.

When you have finished listing the major sections, list the issues or subsections that will appear in each of these major sections. Each major section should include about two to five issues or subsections.

How will you know what to include in each section? That's where the invention strategies you learned about in the previous chapter will help you. Look at the ideas and keywords you came up with during the invention phase, and put them into your outline.

*Watch the Animation on **Outlining with a Computer** at **mycomplab.com***

Drafting Through Writer's Block

Writer's block happens to everyone, even the most experienced writers. Here are some strategies for keeping the words flowing, and for working through those moments of writer's block.

Drafting (Almost) Every Day

The worst thing you can do is start drafting the night before your paper is due. You will often hear people say things like, "I write best under pressure" or "I need to figure

**FIGURE 15.1
A Starter
Outline**

*An outline of your
paper does not
need to be formal
or complex. Use
the genre to help
you identify the
major sections.
Then list the
likely issues
or subsections
beneath each
major section.*

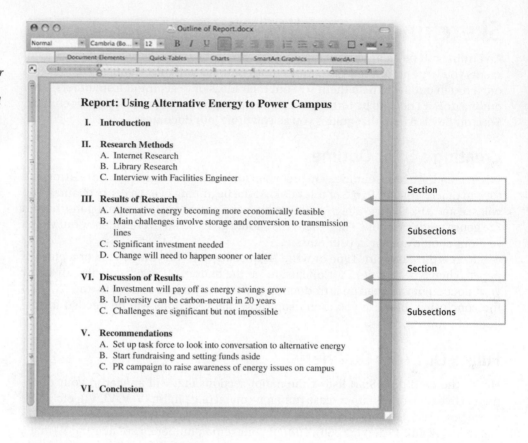

Report: Using Alternative Energy to Power Campus

I. **Introduction**

II. **Research Methods**
   A. Internet Research
   B. Library Research
   C. Interview with Facilities Engineer

III. **Results of Research**
   A. Alternative energy becoming more economically feasible
   B. Main challenges involve storage and conversion to transmission lines
   C. Significant investment needed
   D. Change will need to happen sooner or later

VI. **Discussion of Results**
   A. Investment will pay off as energy savings grow
   B. University can be carbon-neutral in 20 years
   C. Challenges are significant but not impossible

V. **Recommendations**
   A. Set up task force to look into conversation to alternative energy
   B. Start fundraising and setting funds aside
   C. PR campaign to raise awareness of energy issues on campus

VI. **Conclusion**

Section

Subsections

Section

Subsections

out what I'm going to say before I start writing." These kinds of statements are warning signals that a writer is procrastinating. After all, people don't really write well under pressure, and the best way to figure out what you have to say is to *get started and write something down.*

Our best advice is to do half an hour of drafting every day. Each day, set aside a regular time in the morning or evening to work on your writing assignments. Writing is like exercising at the gym. If you exercise for half an hour every day, you will improve steadily—much more than if you exercised for four hours on one day. In the same way, if you say, "I'm setting aside Sunday afternoon to write that paper," you are not going to do your best work. But if you write for half an hour every day, you will write better and faster. Try it, and you'll see that it makes a big difference.

Overcoming Writer's Block

Almost all writers find themselves blocked at some point. Here are some of the most popular techniques for overcoming writer's block:

Watch the Video
on **Overcoming
Writer's Block** at
mycomplab.com

"What I Really Mean Is. . . ."   Whenever you are blocked, finish the sentence "What I really mean is. . . ." You will discover that simply finishing this sentence will help you get past the temporary block.

Lower Your Standards While Drafting.   Stop trying to get it right on the first try. Instead, put your ideas on the screen without worrying about whether they are intelligent or grammatically correct. Then spend extra time during the revision phase turning those ideas into a document that has the high quality you expect.

Talk It Out.   Professional writers can often be found talking to friends about their work or even talking to themselves. Sometimes it helps to just say out loud what you want to write—to yourself or someone else who is willing to listen. Then, after you have rehearsed the text a few times, you should find it easier to write your ideas down.

Change How and Where You Write.   If you normally draft on a computer, try switching over to pen and paper for a little while. If you normally write in your dorm room, try a change of scenery by going over to the library or out on central campus. Sometimes the change in medium or location will help you loosen up.

Use Both Sides of Your Brain.   The right side of your brain is more visual than the left. So use invention techniques like concept mapping, freewriting, and cubing to tap into that visual creativity. These techniques will help you put your ideas on the screen. Then the left side of your brain can organize them into sentences and paragraphs.

Write an E-mail.   Start writing your document as an e-mail to a friend. E-mail is often a more familiar writing environment, allowing you to relax as you write.

Talk to Your Professors.   Your professors probably have some helpful ideas about how to draft your papers. Visit your professors during office hours. They are there to help you.

Go to the Writing Center.   If your campus has a writing center, you should drop by for some help. You can talk your ideas over with an experienced writer who can offer you some advice and strategies.

Stop Procrastinating.   Procrastination is the usual culprit behind writer's block. The pressure of a deadline can cause your brain to freeze. So start each project early, and write a little every day. Your writer's block will evaporate.

Your first year of college is the best time to develop good writing habits. Don't wait until your advanced courses or your first job to form these habits, because it will be too late.

Organization is the key to presenting your ideas in a meaningful, orderly way. It also allows you to highlight the important information that your readers need.

USE Genres to Organize Your Ideas

Genres are not formulas, but they do offer helpful patterns for organizing the content of your document. Chapters 4–13 will give you a good idea of how each genre is typically organized.

DIVIDE Your Document into an Introduction, Body, and Conclusion

Almost all nonfiction genres include an introduction, body, and conclusion. The introduction "tells them what you're going to tell them." The body "tells them." And the conclusion "tells them what you told them."

SKETCH an Outline

Outlines may seem a bit old-fashioned, but an informal outline is often a good way to sort your ideas into sections of a document. Don't worry about all those roman numerals. Just list the subjects you want to cover in your document.

DRAFT Your Document

Drafting is about putting your rear end in the seat and keeping your hands on the keyboard. Try drafting for half an hour almost every day.

OVERCOME Writer's Block

It happens to everyone. The techniques discussed in this chapter should help you get through those moments.

1. With a group, discuss how you were taught to outline papers in high school. Do you think outlining works well for you? In which situations do outlines seem to work best?

2. Have you ever waited until the last moment to write a paper for one of your classes? If you got a good grade, why do you think you did well despite procrastinating? If you didn't do well, what do you think you should have done differently to avoid waiting until the last moment?

3. When does writer's block happen most frequently to you? Can you think of ways to avoid writer's block in the first place? When writer's block happens, which strategies have you used to get writing again?

Talk About This

1. As you draft your next paper, keep a log of how much time you spend drafting. When you hand your paper in, look at your log. Where have you devoted more or less time to the project? How can you spread your time out better on the next project to strengthen your writing?

2. Do some research on the writing habits of one of your favorite contemporary authors. How often do they write, and how much time do they devote to it each day? Do they offer any wisdom about how to overcome writer's block? Write an e-mail to your professor about this author's writing habits.

Try This Out

1. **Analyze your writing process.** In a brief report, describe how you currently draft your documents. How much time do you usually devote to drafting? Which strategies or routines help you draft a paper? Next, offer some ideas for improving how you draft documents. Which techniques for overcoming writer's block in this chapter would be most helpful for you?

2. **Interview a professional via e-mail.** Set up an e-mail interview with a professional in your desired career or a professor in your major. Ask that person about his or her writing process and pay special attention to what he or she says about organizing ideas and drafting documents. Ask how documents are organized in his or her field. Ask how he or she learned how to write those kinds of documents. In a brief profile, describe how your subject uses writing in his or her personal life.

Write This

PEARSON mycomplab

For support in meeting this chapter's objectives, follow this path in MyCompLab: Resources ⟹ Writing ⟹ The Writing Process ⟹ Planning. Review the Instruction and Multimedia resources about organizing and outlining, then complete the Exercises and click on Gradebook to measure your progress.

16

Choosing a Style

In this chapter, you will learn how to—

- use plain style to write clearly and confidently.
- establish a voice or tone in your papers.
- use persuasive style to add energy and impact to your writing.

Style is not something you have or you don't have. Instead, style is a way of expressing your attitude and feelings about a topic. It is a way of establishing your character and a sense of authority with your readers. In a word, style is about the quality of your writing.

Style is *not* flowery language or fancy words. It's *not* about sprinkling in a few adjectives to make dull sentences more interesting or colorful. Sometimes inexperienced writers will talk about "my style," as though each writer possesses one unique voice or way of writing. In reality, the best style for your document depends on your topic, the rhetorical situation, and the genre that you are using.

There is no correct style for a particular genre; however, some genres are associated with specific styles. Scientific reports tend to be written in a plain, objective style. Movie reviews are often colorful and upbeat. In some circumstances, though, a scientific report could use an upbeat style and a movie review could be serious. Ultimately, the style you choose depends on the rhetorical situation for your document.

Writing in Plain Style

Plain style is the foundation for all other writing styles. The usual advice to writers is to "write clearly" or "write in concrete language," as though making up your mind to do so is all it takes. Actually, using plain style is a skill that requires some practice. Once you learn a few basic guidelines, writing plainly will become a natural strength.

Guideline 1: Clarify What or Who the Sentence Is About

Often, difficult sentences simply lack a clear subject. For example, consider the following sentence:

Original:

Seven months after our Spring Break trip to Vail in which a bunch of us travelled around the front range of the Rockies, my roommates' fond memories of the trip were enough to ignore the nagging reality that the trip itself had yet to be fully paid for.

What is this sentence about? The word "memories" is currently in the subject position, but the sentence might also be about "months," "vacation," "bunch of us," "my roommates," or "trip." A sentence like this one is hard to understand because readers cannot easily locate the subject of the sentence.

You first need to decide what the sentence is about. Then you can move that subject into the subject position of the sentence. For example, when this sentence is reconstructed around "my roommates and I" it is much easier to understand.

Revised:

Seven months after our Spring Break trip to Vail, my roommates and I still have fond memories of travelling around the front range of the Rockies, which helps us ignore the nagging reality that we haven't paid for the trip yet.

This sentence is still difficult to read, but it is clearer now because the noun in the subject position (i.e., "my roommates and I") is what the sentence is about.

Guideline 2: Make the "Doer" the Subject of the Sentence

Readers tend to focus on who or what is doing something in a sentence, so whenever possible, try to move the "doer" into the subject position. For example, which of the following sentences is clearer?

On Monday morning, the report was completed just in time by Sheila.

On Monday morning, Sheila completed the report just in time.

Most readers would point to the second sentence, because Sheila, who is the subject of this sentence, is doing something. Meanwhile, the subject of the first sentence, the report, is just sitting still, not doing anything.

Guideline 3: Put the Subject Early in the Sentence

Subconsciously, your readers start every sentence looking for the subject. The subject is the anchor of the sentence, so the longer you make them wait for it, the harder the sentence will be to read.

Original:

If the Sandia Mountains ecosystem experiences another drought like the one observed from 2000–2009, black bears will suffer severely from a lack of available food and water.

Revised:

Black bears will suffer severely from lack of available food and water if the Sandia Mountains ecosystem experiences another drought like the one from 2000–2009.

The second sentence is easier to read, because the subject appears early in the sentence. When readers find that anchor, they know how to read the sentence.

Guideline 4: State the Action in the Verb

In each sentence, ask yourself what the doer is doing. Then move that action into the verb position and put the verb as close to the subject as possible.

Original:

The detective is the person who conducted an investigation into the homicide that happened last night on 4th Avenue.

Revised:

The detective investigated last night's homicide on 4th Avenue.

The original sentence is harder to understand because the action (investigation) is not a verb, and it's buried later in the sentence. The revised sentence is easier to understand because the action (investigate) is a verb, and it's close to the subject.

Guideline 5: Eliminate Nominalizations

Nominalizations are perfectly good verbs and adjectives that have been turned into awkward nouns.

Original:

Students have an expectation that all professors will be rigorous and fair in the assignment of grades.

Revised:

Students expect all professors to be rigorous and fair when assigning grades.

Original:

Our discussion about the matter allowed us to make a decision to go to Florida for spring break this year.

Revised:

We discussed our spring break options and decided to go to Florida this year.

By turning nominalizations into verbs, you can simplify and shorten a sentence. You also make the sentence more active because the action is being expressed in the verb.

Guideline 6: Boil Down the Prepositional Phrases

Prepositional phrases follow prepositions, like *in, of, by, about, over,* and *under.* These phrases are necessary in writing, but they can be overused.

Original:

This year's increase *in* the success *of* the basketball team *called* the Hokies *of* Virginia Tech offered a demonstration *of* the importance *of* a coach *with* a national reputation *for* the purposes *of* recruiting.

Revised:

This year's successful Virginia Tech Hokies basketball team demonstrated the importance *of* a nationally known coach *for* recruiting.

In the examples above, the prepositions have been italicized and the prepositional phrases are blue. Notice how prepositional phrases can create "chains" of phrases that make the sentence harder to read.

Try turning some of them into adjectives. For example, "in the success of the basketball team called the Hokies of Virginia Tech" was boiled down to "successful Virginia Tech basketball team." You don't need to eliminate all prepositional phrases, but you can simplify a sentence by eliminating some of them.

Guideline 7: Eliminate Redundancies

To stress an important idea, some writers mistakenly turn to redundant phrasing. For example, they might say "unruly mob" as though some mobs are controlled and orderly. Or, they might talk about "active participants" as though people can participate without doing anything. In some cases, they use two or more synonyms with the same meaning to modify a noun.

Watch the Animation on **Achieving Variety** at **mycomplab.com**

Original:

We are demanding important, significant changes to university policies.

Revised:

We are demanding significant changes to university policies.

Original:

The London plague of 1665 was especially deadly and lethal for the poor, who could not escape to the countryside.

Revised:

The London plague of 1665 was especially deadly for the poor, who could not escape to the countryside.

Redundancies should be eliminated because they use two or more words to do the work of one.

Guideline 8: Use Sentences That Are Breathing Length

You should be able to read a sentence out loud in one comfortable breath. If one of your sentences runs on and on—even if it is grammatically correct—your readers will feel like they are mentally holding their breath. Your readers will be more concerned about when the sentence will end than what it means.

On the other hand, if you only use short sentences, your readers will feel like they are breathing too quickly. Each period signals, "Take a breath." Many short sentences together will make readers feel like they are hurrying.

Here are two ways to make your sentences breathing length:

- Sentences that cannot be said out loud comfortably in one breath should be shortened or cut into two sentences. (Don't asphyxiate your readers with overly long sentences!)

- Sentences that are too short should be combined with other short sentences around them. (Don't make your readers hyperventilate, either!)

Plain style takes some practice, but writing clearly is not that hard to master. These eight guidelines will help you transform your writing into something that is easy to read. This is the essence of plain style.

Establishing Your Voice

When reading, all of us, including your readers, hear a voice that sounds out the words. The best way to create a specific voice in a text is to decide what *tone* you want your readers to hear as they read your writing.

In other words, think about how you want your voice to sound: excited, angry, joyful, sad, professional, disgusted, objective, happy, compassionate, surprised, optimistic, aggressive, regretful, anxious, tense, affectionate, or sympathetic.

After you choose a specific tone, you can create your voice by getting into character or imitating other writers.

Get into Character

While drafting, one easy way to establish your voice is to imagine yourself playing a role, as in a movie or a play. You need to get into character before you start drafting.

For instance, you may need to write about a topic that is serious or tragic, but you happen to be in a good mood that day. Or perhaps you are writing about something that should be exciting, but you just aren't feeling thrilled.

The best way to handle these situations is to pretend that you are feeling "serious" or "excited" while you are working on the first draft of your document. You might even imagine that you are someone else who is serious or excited about your topic. Get into character, and then let that character compose from his or her point of view.

Imitate Other Writers

Imitation was once a common way for people to learn how to improve their voice and tone. Teachers of speech and writing would regularly ask their students to imitate the style of well-known speakers and writers to practice new stylistic techniques.

Imitation is not widely used to teach writing today, but you can still use it to improve your own style. Choose an author whose work you enjoy. Pay close attention to his or her style. How does the choice of words shape what the writer says? How do the writer's sentences convey his or her meaning? As you are drafting or revising your next paper, use some of those word choices and sentence strategies to convey your own ideas. When imitating someone else, you will usually end up blending elements of his or her writing style with elements of yours.

Be careful not to use the exact words or ideas of the writer or text you are imitating. That's plagiarism. To avoid any chance of plagiarism, try imitating the style of a text that was written on a different topic than the one you are writing about.

Writing Descriptively with Tropes

Tropes, which are usually referred to as "figurative language," are good devices for helping you write visually. They include analogies, similes, metaphors, and onomatopoeia, which use language in ways that invite readers to see an issue from new and different perspectives. Trope, in the ancient Greek, means "turn." Tropes bend or turn words and phrases, so people can view familiar things from new angles.

Use Similes and Analogies

A *simile* is a figure of speech in which one thing is compared to something that has similar features but is also very different.

> My car is like an old boyfriend. I still love it and we've had some great times together, but it's becoming unreliable and a little clunky. For now, I'm hanging on to it until something sleeker and sportier comes along.

> Up ahead, two dozen white pelicans were creating a spiral staircase as they flew. It looked like a feathered DNA molecule. Their wings reflected the sun. The light shifted, and they disappeared. (Terry Tempest Williams, *Refuge*)

A simile makes a comparison, "X is like Y," or "X is as Y," asking the readers to make visual connections between two different things. Comparing a car to an old boyfriend, for instance, calls up all kinds of interesting visual relationships.

Analogies are similes that work at two levels. When using an analogy, you are saying, "X is like Y, as A is like B."

> Like police keeping order in a city, white blood cells patrol your body's bloodstream controlling viruses and bacteria that want to do you harm.

> In the 17th century, England's reliance on imported salt was similar to the United States' dependence on foreign oil today. England's Queen Elizabeth I was especially anxious about her nation's reliance on salt from France, her nation's old enemy (Kurlansky, *Salt*, 195). So, she pushed hard for increased domestic production and sought to open other, more dependable sources of salt. England's navy was built in part to protect its salt supply, much as the United States' navy is responsible for ensuring the flow of oil.

Analogies are used to highlight and explain complex relationships. A good analogy allows readers to visualize similar features between two things.

Use Metaphors

Metaphors are much more powerful than similes and analogies, and they tend to work at a deeper level. There are two types of metaphors that you can use to add power and depth to your writing: simple metaphors and cultural metaphors.

A *simple metaphor* states that one thing is something else, "X is Y."

> Mr. Lewis's face is an aged parchment, creased and wrinkled from his years of sailing.

> Vince, our boss, threw one grenade after another in our meeting.

> This year, my bike is my car—because I can't afford gas anymore!

On the surface, these metaphors say something obviously false (i.e., a face is a parchment, the boss threw grenades in the meeting, a bike is a car). Their falseness on the surface urges readers to figure out an alternative meaning.

A simple metaphor can be extended:

> Mr. Lewis's face is an aged parchment, creased and wrinkled from his years of sailing. In his bronze skin, you can see months spent sailing in the Caribbean. The wrinkles around his eyes reveal many years of squinting into the wind. His bent nose and a scar on his chin bear witness to the storms that have thrown him to the deck. His bright eyes peer out from beneath his white brow, hinting at memories that nonsailors like me will never have.

In this example, you can see the power of a fertile metaphor. A good metaphor can be used to create a perspective or a unique way of "seeing" something.

There are also larger *cultural* metaphors that shape the way people think about issues. For example, here are some common metaphors that we almost take for granted:

Time is money (e.g., spend time, waste time, saved time, lost time)

Thought is light (e.g., he is bright, she was in the dark, they enlightened me)

Argument is war (e.g., she defended her argument, she attacked my claims)

Cultural metaphors like the "war on cancer" or the "war on drugs" have become so ingrained in our culture that we rarely challenge them. And yet, the "war on X" metaphor urges us to think of a subject in a certain way that may not be beneficial. It suggests, for example, that we need to respond to illegal drug use or cancer with weapons and surveillance rather than managing them as diseases.

Use Onomatopoeia

Onomatopoeia is a big word that stands for a rather simple idea. It means using words that sound like the things you are describing.

The fire *crackled* in the fireplace.   She *screeched*, "I hate this class!"

He *shuffled* down the hallway.   The trees *fluttered* in the wind.

Using onomatopoeia isn't difficult. Think about the sounds that are associated with your subject. Then look for words that capture those sounds.

Improving Your Writing Style

With a little practice, you can dramatically improve the power and intensity of your writing by simply paying attention to its style. You can help your readers "see" and "hear" what you are writing about.

If you practice these techniques, they will become a natural part of your writing skills. Then you will be able to use them without even trying.

Remember that style is a choice that you can and should make. Style is a way to express your attitude and feelings about a topic, while establishing your character and a sense of authority.

USE Plain Style

Plain style is the basis of all other writing styles. By choosing an appropriate subject for each sentence and moving it to an early place, you can clarify your writing for readers. Put the action of the sentence in the verb. Then eliminate nominalizations, boil down prepositional phrases, and eliminate redundancies.

ESTABLISH Your Voice

Think of a voice or tone that would be appropriate for your text. Then put that voice into your writing by getting into character or imitating other writers. Practice using other writers' styles and adapt their strategies to your own context and purpose.

USE Similes, Analogies, and Metaphors

Similes, analogies, and metaphors highlight relationships among different things and ideas. They allow readers to see your topic in new and interesting ways.

EXPLORE and Challenge Cultural Metaphors

Pay attention to the cultural metaphors that shape how we think. You can use those cultural metaphors or challenge them.

EVOKE Atmosphere with Sound

You can also describe something by using sound. An onomatopoeia is a word that sounds like the thing it is describing (e.g., crackling fire, shuffling walk, screeching voice). You can also use shorter and longer sentences to speed up or slow down the pace of the text.

1. With a group of people from your class, make a list of ten people who you consider stylish. What about them signals that they have good style?

2. With your group, talk about the ways people adopt a particular style or voice. Are there situations in your life when you need to adopt a different style or voice than you normally would?

3. Find three texts on the Internet that demonstrate three different styles. Have each member of your group explain why he or she likes or dislikes the style of each document. How does the style of each document fit or not fit the needs of its readers and contexts?

Try This Out

1. Find a text or author that you would like to imitate. Then, with that text on your desk or screen, try to write about a different topic but use the style of that text. Try to match its use of tone, metaphors, similes, detail, and sentence length.

2. Searching the Internet, explore the different uses of a common cultural metaphor. What does this cultural metaphor say about how we think about these subjects in our culture?

3. Come up with your own simile or metaphor—perhaps something absurd. Pick any metaphor that comes to mind. Try freewriting for three minutes with your simile or metaphor in front of you. Does the simile or metaphor give you any new insights? At what point does the simile or metaphor become far-fetched or absurd?

Write This

1. **Analyze a cultural metaphor.** Find a common cultural metaphor and write an analysis in which you discuss its strengths and weaknesses. Where does the metaphor fail to capture the full meaning of its subject?

2. **Review the style of an online document.** Choose a document on the Internet that exhibits good style and write a review of the document's use of any figurative language, rich descriptions, or other stylistic strategies.

For support in meeting this chapter's objectives, follow this path in MyCompLab: Resources ⟹ Writing ⟹ The Writing Process ⟹ Finishing and Editing. Review the Instruction and Multimedia resources about checking your voice, then complete the Exercises and click on Gradebook to measure your progress.

17

Designing

In this chapter, you will learn how to—

- design documents that suit your paper's purpose, readers, context, and genre.
- use principles of design to lay out a document.
- enhance and reinforce written text with graphs and charts.

Imagine your own reaction to a large document with no pictures, no headings, no graphics, and no lists. Every page looks like a brick wall of words, throwing big blocks of paragraphs at you, page after page. If you're like most people, you wouldn't even want to start reading.

Good design makes the information in a document more accessible, and it makes reading that document more pleasurable. A well-designed text helps readers quickly locate the information they need. If your document looks accessible and attractive, readers are going to want to spend more time reading it. If it looks difficult and unattractive, they might not read it at all.

In this chapter, you will learn some basic strategies for designing your documents and creating graphics. These strategies work with any genre, depending on the kinds of information you want to share with your readers.

Before You Begin Designing

After drafting, spend some time thinking about what kind of design features would work best in this kind of text.

Genre. What design features and graphics are typical for the genre of this document? You might search for examples of the genre on the Internet to gain a sense of how they tend to look.

Purpose. How can you use design and graphics to achieve your purpose? Think about how your document's page layout (e.g., headings, columns, margin notes, color, tables, graphs, photographs) could be used to highlight important information and make it more accessible to readers.

Readers. What kinds of design features and graphics will your readers expect or prefer? For some genres, like reports, readers are "raiders," so they expect the design to help them locate the information they need. Other genres, like memoirs, are designed to be read in a more leisurely way.

Context. In what places will readers use the document, and how do these places shape how it should look?

Now you're ready to design your text. To get you started, we will begin by describing a few basic principles of design.

Five Basic Principles of Design

Good design creates a sense of order and gives your readers *access points* to help them locate the information they need. Here are five basic principles of design that will help you make your documents accessible and attractive:

1. **Balance.** Your text should look balanced from left to right and top to bottom.

2. **Alignment.** Related words and images should be aligned vertically on the page to reveal the text's structure and its hierarchy of information.

3. **Grouping.** Related images and ideas should be put near each other on the page, so readers see them as groups.

4. **Consistency.** Design features should be used consistently and predictably, helping readers quickly interpret the layout of each page and locate the information they need.

5. **Contrast.** Items on the page that are different should *look* different, creating a feeling of boldness and confidence.

These five principles are based on the Gestalt theory of design, which is used by many graphic designers, clothing designers, architects, and artists. Once you learn these principles, you should find it easy—and perhaps even fun—to design your texts.

Design Principle 1: Balance

To balance a text, imagine that a page from your document has been placed on a point, like a pencil point. Everything you add to the left side of the page needs to be balanced with something on the right. For example, if you add a picture to the left side, you will need to add text or perhaps another picture on the right.

To illustrate, look at the page from a report shown in Figure 17.1 on page 376. On this page, the drawing of an owl on the left has what graphic designers call "weight."

FIGURE 17.1
A Balanced Design

Balance creates a sense of order in documents. This page is balanced both left to right and top to bottom.

The drawing of the owl is balanced with the written text on the right.

The header and footer balance the page on the top and bottom.

This drawing strongly attracts the readers' eyes to it. So to offset this drawing, the designers decided to put a large block of two-column text on the right. Meanwhile, the heavy green borders at the top and bottom of the sheet balance with each other, making the page feel stable and steady from top to bottom.

Balance is not a matter of making the page look symmetric (the same on the left and right). The items should balance, but they don't need to mirror each other.

Balancing a Page

Watch the Animation on **Working with Illustrations** at mycomplab.com

When graphic designers talk about how much the items on the page "weigh," they are talking about how strongly these elements will attract the readers' eyes to them. For example, on a Web page, animated images weigh more than images that don't move. (That's why advertisers often use dancing people in their Internet ads.)

Here are some guidelines for balancing the features on a page:

- Pictures weigh more than written text.
- Color items weigh more than black and white items.
- Big items weigh more than small ones.
- Strange shapes weigh more than standard shapes.
- Things on the right side of the page weigh more than things on the left.
- Things on the top of the page weigh more than things on the bottom.
- Moving features, like Web page animations, weigh more than static ones.

You can use these guidelines to help you balance just about any page. Don't be afraid to move items around on the page to see how they look.

Design Principle 2: Alignment

Your readers will subconsciously search for visual relationships among items on the page. If two items line up on the page, they will assume that those two items are related in some way. If a picture, for example, is vertically aligned with a caption, list, or block of text on a page, readers will naturally assume that they go together.

For example, in Figure 17.2, the absence of alignment means the page on the left gives no hint about the levels of information, making it difficult for readers to find what they are looking for in the text. The page on the right, on the other hand, uses vertical alignment to highlight the levels in the text. Most readers would find the text on the right easier to read, because they immediately understand how the information is structured.

To create vertical alignment in your page design:

- Use margins and indentation consistently to highlight the hierarchy of the information.

- Use bulleted lists or numbered lists whenever possible to set off related information from the main text.

- Adjust the placement of any photographs or graphics to align vertically with the text around them, so readers see them as belonging together.

Design Principle 3: Grouping

The design principle "grouping" takes advantage of your readers' tendency to see any items on a page that are close together as belonging to a group. If a photograph appears near a block of text, your readers will naturally assume that the image and text

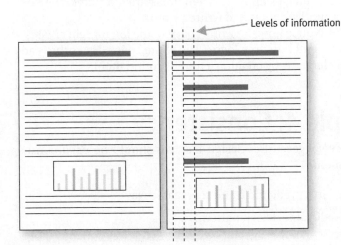

FIGURE 17.2 Using Vertical Alignment

Aligning text vertically allows you to show different levels of information in the text, making the document easier to read and scan. The page on the left is harder to read because it has minimal alignment. The page on the right uses alignment to signal the levels of information in the text.

FIGURE 17.3
Using Grouping

Grouping is a good way to help readers put items together on the page. In this page, for example, you can see four distinct blocks of information that are grouped together, making the text easier to read.

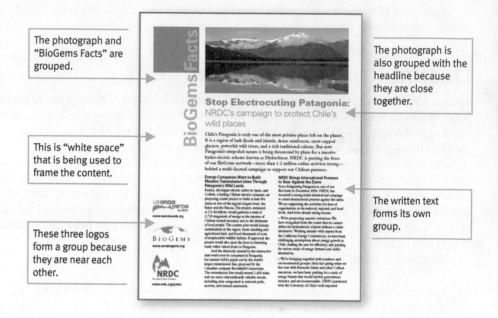

The photograph and "BioGems Facts" are grouped.

The photograph is also grouped with the headline because they are close together.

This is "white space" that is being used to frame the content.

The written text forms its own group.

These three logos form a group because they are near each other.

are related. Similarly, if a heading appears near a block of written text, the readers will see the heading as belonging with the written text.

Figure 17.3 shows a page design that uses grouping well. The "BioGems Facts" on the top left of the page is put close to the picture of mountains on the top right, creating a group. The three logos in the bottom left are grouped together, forming a unit. Also, the picture and the green headline, "Stop Electrocuting Patagonia," can be seen as one group because they appear close together. Finally, the columns of text are naturally seen as a group, too, because they are so close together on the page.

One key to using grouping well is to be aware of the white spaces in your document's design where no text or images appear. When areas are left blank, they become eye-catching frames around graphics and written words.

Look again at Figure 17.3. Notice how the white space in the left margin creates a frame for the "BioGems Facts" and the three logos. The white space draws the readers' attention to these visual elements by creating a frame around them.

Design Principle 4: Consistency

The principle of consistency suggests that design features should be used consistently throughout the document:

• Headings should be used in a predictable and repeatable way.

• Pages should follow a predictable design pattern.

- Lists should use consistent bullets or numbering schemes.

- Headers, footers, and page numbers should be used to help make each page look similar to the others.

Consistency creates a sense of order, so your readers know what to expect. If the page design or features like headings or images are used consistently, your readers will find it easier to understand how your document is structured.

Choosing Typefaces

A good first step toward consistency is to choose appropriate typefaces. A typeface is the design of the letters in your written text (e.g., Times Roman, Arial, Bookman, Helvetica). As a basic guideline, you should only choose one or two typefaces for your document. Many graphic designers like to choose one typeface for the headings and a different typeface for the main text.

There are two basic types of typeface: serif and sans serif. A serif typeface, like Times Roman, New York, or Bookman, has small tips (serifs) at the ends of the main strokes in each letter (Figure 17.4). Sans serif typefaces like Arial and Helvetica do not have these small tips. ("Sans serif" means "without serifs" in French.)

Serif fonts are considered more formal and traditional. They are useful for the main text and parts of a document where readability is important. Most people think sans serif fonts, like Helvetica and Arial, look more modern. They are especially useful for titles, headings, footers, captions, and parts of a document where you want to catch readers' eyes.

Using Headings Consistently

Headings are very useful visual elements in any kind of document, but you need to use them consistently (Figure 17.5, page 380). Make some choices up front about the levels of headings you will use.

Watch the Animation on **Using Headings** at **mycomplab.com**

Title. The title of the document should be sized significantly larger than other headings. You might consider using color to set off the title, or you could center it.

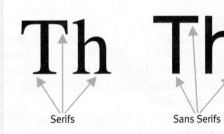

FIGURE 17.4 Serif vs. Sans Serif Typefaces

Serif fonts, like Times Roman on the left, have serifs, while sans serif fonts, like Arial on the right, do not have them.

FIGURE 17.5 Levels of Headings

The headings you choose for your document should be clearly distinguishable from the body text and from each other. That way, your readers can clearly see the hierarchy of your text.

> ## Document Title:
> ## The Best College Paper
> ## Ever Written
>
> ### First-Level Headings
> These "A heads" divide a document into its major sections. They are usually significantly larger and bolder and use a different font than the body text.
>
> *Second-Level Headings*
> These "B heads" divide sections into smaller subsections. While these use the same font as the first-level headings, they should differ significantly in size or style (such as italics).
>
> **Third-Level Headings.** These "C heads" might be the same font and size as the body text (and appear on the same line), but use bold or italics to distinguish them.

First-Level Headings ("A Heads"). These are the most common headings. They divide your text into its major sections. First-level headings are often bold and slightly larger than the text used in the body of the document.

Second-Level Headings ("B Heads"). These are used when you need to divide a large section in your document into even smaller parts. These headings tend to use italics and can be the same size as the body text.

Third-Level Headings ("C Heads"). These are usually the smallest level of headings. They are often italicized or boldfaced and placed on the same line as the body text.

Headings help readers in a few important ways. First, they offer access points into the text, giving readers obvious places to locate the information they need. Second, they highlight the structure of the text, breaking the larger document down into smaller blocks of information. Third, they give readers places to take breaks from reading sentence after sentence, paragraph after paragraph.

Headings are also beneficial to you as the writer, because they help you make transitions between large sections of the document. Instead of a clumsy, "And now, let me move on to the next issue" kind of statement, you can use a heading to quickly and cleanly signal the transition to a new subject.

Design Principle 5: Contrast

The fifth and final design principle is *contrast*. Using contrast means making different items on the page look significantly different. Your headings, for example, should look significantly different than the main text.

There are a variety of ways to create contrast in your document's design. You can change the size of the font, add color, use shading, and use highlighting features like boldface, italics, or underlining. The sample report shown in Figure 17.6 uses contrast in several important ways:

- The blue banner across the top, "Geothermal Technologies Program, Colorado," clearly contrasts with the rest of the items on the page because it uses big lettering and a bold color.

- Below the banner, the italicized text contrasts sharply with the body text, helping it stand out on the page.

- The blue heading "Current Development" is clearly distinguishable from the body text because it is larger and uses color.

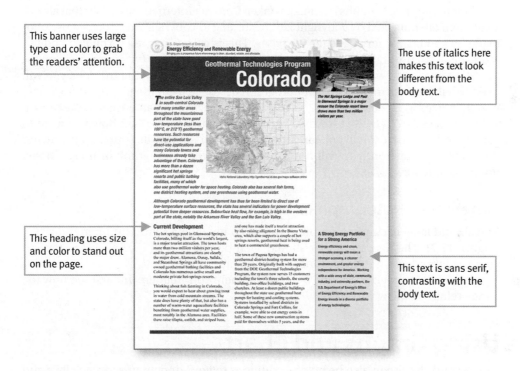

This banner uses large type and color to grab the readers' attention.

The use of italics here makes this text look different from the body text.

This heading uses size and color to stand out on the page.

This text is sans serif, contrasting with the body text.

FIGURE 17.6 Using Contrast

Contrast makes a page look more readable and attractive. This page uses several kinds of contrast to capture the readers' attention.

- In the blue screened box on the right of the page, the use of a sans serif font helps to distinguish this text from the body text just to its left.

The secret to using contrast is experimenting with the page design to see how things look. So be daring and explore how items on the page look when you add contrast. Try making visual features larger, bolder, more colorful, or different.

Using Photography and Images

With the capabilities of today's computers, you should always look for ways to add photography to your document. To add a picture, you can use a digital camera or a mobile phone to snap the picture, or you can download a picture from the Internet.

Downloading Photographs and Images from the Internet

If you find a photograph or image on the Internet that you want to use, save the image to your hard drive, and insert it into your document.

Some popular sources for photographs include *Flickr.com, Photobucket.com, Google Images,* and *Zooomr.com.* The Library of Congress (http://www.loc.gov) offers many historical pictures that you can use for free.

When using photographs and images taken from the Internet, remember that almost all of them are protected by copyright law. According to copyright law, you can use photographs and images for academic purposes. This is called "fair use." You can find out more about fair use and copyright law at the U.S. Copyright Office (www.copyright.gov).

However, if you want to publish your document or put it on the Internet, you will need to ask permission to use the photograph or image from the person or organization that owns it. The easiest way to ask permission is to send an e-mail to the person who manages the Web site on which you found the image. Explain how you want to use the image, where it will appear, and how you will identify its source. If the owner denies you permission, you will not be able to use the photograph or image in any nonacademic way.

Watch the Animation on **Using Visuals** at **mycomplab.com**

Labeling a Photograph or Image

You should label each photograph or image by giving it a figure number and a title (Figure 17.7). The figure number should then be mentioned in the written text, so your readers know when to look for the photograph.

Captions are not mandatory, but they can help your readers understand how the image relates to the written text.

Using Graphs and Charts

Graphs and charts can also be helpful additions to your documents, especially if you are presenting data to your readers. Genres like reports and proposals routinely use graphs and charts to illustrate data. These graphics can also be useful in evaluations and position papers to provide support for claims in the written text.

FIGURE 17.7 Labeling a Photograph

Proper labeling will help readers understand how the graphic supports the written text.

Fig. 1: A Tiktaalik

The Tiktaalik was a prehistoric fish that had four legs. Paleontologists think this creature fills the fossil gap between fish and early limbed animals.

Source: Natl. Sci. Found., Oct. 2008; Web; 19 Mar. 2009.

Figure number and title.

Caption and source information.

Creating a Graph or Chart

Your best option for making a visual might be to use the spreadsheet program, such as *Excel* or *Quattro Pro,* that came with your word-processing software (Figure 17.8). Simpler graphs can be made in presentation software, like *PowerPoint* or *Keynote.*

These spreadsheet and presentation software packages can help you create quick graphs and charts from a data set. Then you can insert the graphic right into your document. (Your word processor will probably have a Chart feature that will take you to the spreadsheet program.) Once you have created the graph, you should add a title and label the horizontal x-axis and vertical y-axis (Figure 17.8, page 384).

After you have inserted your graph into your document, make sure you have labeled it properly and provided a citation for the source of the data. To label the graph, give it a number or letter and a title. For example, the graph in Figure 17.8 is called "Figure A: Obesity Rates (Percentage) By County." After you have labeled the graph, include your source below the graph using a common citation style (e.g., MLA, APA).

In the written part of your document, refer to the graphic by its number, so readers know when to refer to it. When you want the readers to consider the graph, write something like, "As shown in Figure A, the local obesity rate. . . ." Or, you can simply put "(Figure A)" at the end of the sentence where you refer to the graph.

Choosing the Appropriate Graph or Chart

You can use various kinds of graphs and charts to display your data. Each graph or chart allows you to tell a different story to your readers.

 Analyze the Interactive Document for **Using Graphs and Charts** at mycomplab.com

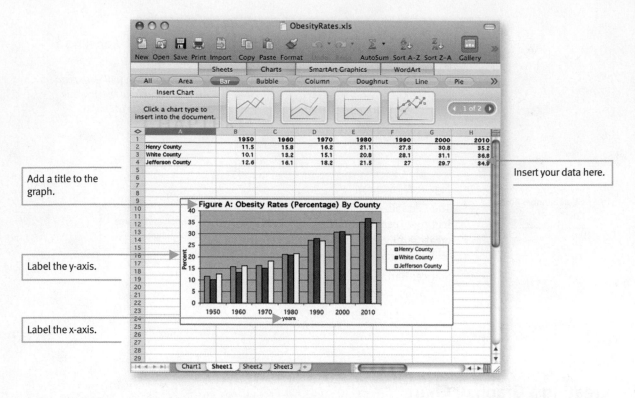

FIGURE 17.8 Using Spreadsheet Software to Make a Graph

A spreadsheet is a helpful tool for creating a graph. Enter your data and then click the graphing button to create a graph. Then you can insert the graph into your document.

Line Graph. A line graph is a good way to show measurements or trends over time. In a line graph, the vertical axis (y-axis) displays a measured quantity, such as temperature, sales, growth, and so on. The horizontal axis (x-axis) is usually divided into time increments such as years, months, days, or hours. See Figure 17.9.

Bar Chart. Bar charts are used to show quantities, allowing readers to make visual comparisons among different amounts. Like line graphs, bar charts can be used to show fluctuations in quantities over time. See Figure 17.10.

Pie Charts. Pie charts are useful for showing how a whole quantity is divided into parts. These charts are a quick way to add a visual element into your document, but you should use them sparingly. They take up a lot of space in a document while usually presenting only a small amount of data. See Figure 17.11.

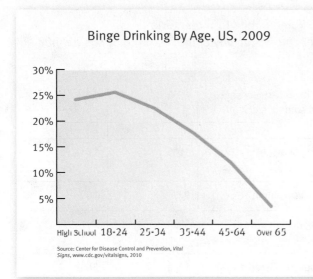

Binge Drinking By Age, US, 2009

Source: Center for Disease Control and Prevention, *Vital Signs*, www.cdc.gov/vitalsigns, 2010

FIGURE 17.9 Line Graph

A line graph is a good way to show a trend over time. In this graph, the line reveals a trend that would not be apparent from the data alone.

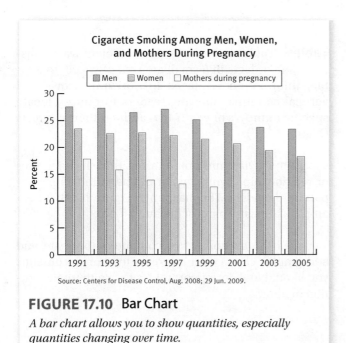

Cigarette Smoking Among Men, Women, and Mothers During Pregnancy

Source: Centers for Disease Control, Aug. 2008; 29 Jun. 2009.

FIGURE 17.10 Bar Chart

A bar chart allows you to show quantities, especially quantities changing over time.

Many Firearms Remain Accessible to Children

Source: Schuster et al., 2000.

FIGURE 17.11 Pie Chart

A pie chart is a good way to show how a whole is divided into parts. When using a pie chart, you should label the slices of the pie and add the numerical information that was used to create the chart.

FIGURE 17.12
Table

A table offers a great way to show data efficiently. This table combines words and data to illustrate differences between boys' and girls' malicious uses of the Internet.

Online Rumors Tend to Target Girls *Have you, personally, ever experienced any of the following things online?*		
	Boys	*Girls*
Someone taking a private e-mail, IM, or text message you sent them and forwarding it to someone else or posting it where others could see it	13%	17%
Someone sending you a threatening or aggressive e-mail, IM, or text message	10%	15%
Someone spreading a rumor about you online	9%	16%
Someone posting an embarrassing picture of you online without your permission	5%	7%
At least one of the forms of cyberbullying listed above	23%	36%

Source: *Pew Internet and American Life Project Parents and Teens Survey,* 2006.

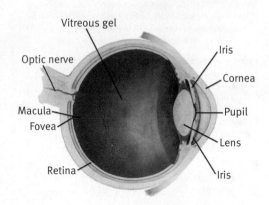

FIGURE 17.13 A Diagram

A diagram is only partially realistic. It shows only the most important features and concentrates on relationships instead of showing exactly what the subject looks like.

Tables. Tables provide the most efficient way to display data or facts in a small amount of space. In a table, information is placed in horizontal rows and vertical columns, allowing readers to quickly locate specific numbers or words that address their interests (Figure 17.12).

Diagrams. Diagrams are drawings that show features or relationships, which might not be immediately apparent to readers. The diagram in Figure 17.13, for example, shows the parts of the human eye.

With the capabilities of computers to create and add graphs, charts, and diagrams to your documents, you should look for opportunities to use these illustration methods.

Now it's time to make your document look better. Here are some basic strategies for designing your document.

REVIEW Your Genre, Purpose, Readers, and Context

Your document's design should reflect and reinforce the genre and the overall purpose of your text. Design features should also be appropriate for your readers and the contexts in which your document will be used.

BALANCE the Text

Use design features to balance elements on the left and right as well as on the top and bottom of the page.

ALIGN Items Vertically on the Page

Look for opportunities to vertically align items on the page. Indenting text and aligning graphics with text will help create a sense of hierarchy and structure in your document.

GROUP Related Items Together

Put items together that are meant to be seen together. Photos should be near any text they reinforce. Headings should be close to the paragraphs they lead off. Use white space to frame items you want to be seen as a group.

CHECK the Document for Consistency

Your headings and other design features should be used consistently throughout the document. Make sure you use lists consistently.

ADD Some Contrast

Items on the page that are different should look significantly different. Use color and font size to make written text stand out.

INCLUDE Photographs, Graphs, and Charts

Add your own photographs or images downloaded from the Internet to your document. Create graphs or charts to illustrate data and complex ideas. Number, title, and caption these visuals so readers understand how the images connect to your text.

Talk About This

1. Ask each member in your group to bring a favorite magazine. Discuss the magazine's full-page advertisements and their use of design features. Pay special attention to the use of balance, alignment, grouping, consistency, and contrast.

2. Discuss the design of your favorite Web sites. What kinds of design features make it a favorite? What design features help you access information more easily?

3. On campus or in the community, find a flyer or brochure that you think is a failure in design. With your group, discuss how the document could be redesigned to make it more accessible and attractive.

Try This Out

1. Find a document on the Internet, on campus, or at your workplace that shows minimal attention to design. Then do a "design makeover" to make the document more accessible and attractive to readers.

2. Write a brief critique of the visual elements of a document you found on campus or at your workplace. Show how each of the five design principles makes its design effective or ineffective.

3. Practice downloading photographs and images and inserting them into a document. Add figure numbers and titles to the images. Include captions that explain the images and their relevance to your document.

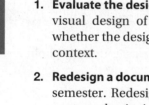

Write This

1. **Evaluate the design of a document.** Write an evaluation in which you discuss the visual design of a document of your choice. Your analysis should consider whether the design is appropriate for the document's topic, purpose, readers, and context.

2. **Redesign a document on a computer.** Choose a document you wrote earlier in the semester. Redesign the document with your computer, using some of the concepts and principles discussed in this chapter. Then write a brief evaluation in which you discuss your design decisions.

PEARSON
myccomplab

For support in meeting this chapter's objectives, follow this path in MyCompLab: Resources ⟹ Writing ⟹ The Writing Process ⟹ Finishing and Editing. Review the Instruction and Multimedia resources about designing your document, then complete the Exercises and click on Gradebook to measure your progress.

Revising
and
Editing

In this chapter, you will learn how to—

- edit the content, organization, and design of your paper.
- copyedit paragraphs and sentences to make them clearer.
- proofread your work carefully and quickly.

N ow it's time to take your text from "good" to "excellent" by revising and editing it. This chapter shows you how to revise and edit your work at four different levels. Each level asks you to concentrate on different aspects of your text, moving from global issues to small details.

> **Level 1: Global Revision** reexamines and adjusts the document's overall approach, using genre to sharpen its topic, angle, purpose, thesis, and appropriateness for the readers and context.

> **Level 2: Substantive Editing** pays attention to the document's content, organization, and design.

> **Level 3: Copyediting** focuses on revising the style for clarity, persuasion, and consistency, paying close attention to paragraphs and sentences.

> **Level 4: Proofreading** examines and revises surface features, such as grammatical correctness, spelling, and usage.

As shown in Figure 18.1, on page 390, you should work from the "global level" (global editing) to the "local level" (proofreading). That way, you can start out making

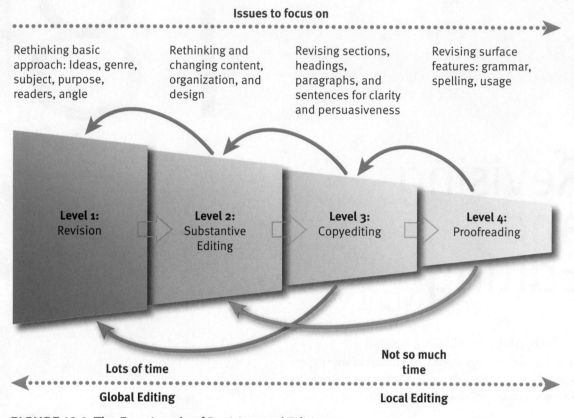

FIGURE 18.1 The Four Levels of Revising and Editing

Whether you are revising and editing your own work or helping someone else revise and edit their work, the process can be broken down into four levels. The idea is to progress toward a final, polished draft efficiently, taking care of the big issues first (purpose, audience) and then moving toward final editing and polishing.

large-scale changes to your document. Then, as the paper gets closer to finished, you can focus exclusively on style and correctness.

Level 1: Global Revision

All right. You finished your first draft. Now it's time to reexamine and reconsider your project's topic, angle, and purpose, and your understanding of the readers and the context.

Figure 18.2 shows an excerpt of a student's proposal when it was a first draft. Figure 18.3 (on page 393) shows how Brad's original notes helped him challenge his ideas and rethink how he could persuade his readers to agree with him.

Watch the Animation on **Global Peer Review Responses** at **mycomplab.com**

**FIGURE 18.2
Rough Draft**
With global revision, you need to look at the big picture and rethink your basic approach. Here is an excerpt from student writer Brad's rough draft of a proposal. Figure 18.3 shows part of his global revision.

America Is Addicted to Oil

When I hear all the whining about gas prices, it makes me really mad. After all, it's not like we haven't been warned. Economists and environmentalists have been telling the American people for years that this day of reckoning would come. Now it's here, and everyone is acting like they have been completely caught off guard. They don't have solutions. They just want another hit of their drug.

This crisis reminds me of people trying to quit smoking. I started smoking when I was 16 and I smoked for three years until I started college. Why did I stop? Well, I knew it was bad for me, but mostly I couldn't afford it anymore. That's kind of where America is right now. We know our addiction to oil is bad for us, but as long as it doesn't cost too much, we keep using. We'll deal with the effects later. So, why can't we break our addiction to oil like a smoker breaks the nicotine addiction?

How do we stop being addicted to oil? One of my friends gave me a book that helped me stop smoking. It is called *Seven Tools to Beat Addiction*, and it's by a social/clinical psychologist who has helped many people beat their addictions to smoking, sex, pornography, drugs, gambling, etc. The seven tools he describes would work well to help American get off its oil habit, like when I stopped smoking:

1. *Values:* Build a foundation of values—We need to rethink what it means to be a nation again. Americans need to stop being so greedy and selfish.

2. *Motivation:* Activate our desire to quit—It's not going to happen until we admit we have a problem and want to break our addiction.

3. *Reward:* Weigh the costs and benefits of addiction—Imagine all the money we'll save if it's not all going over to Saudi Arabia and Russia! Plus, pollution will go down and we'll be more healthy.

4. *Resources:* Identify strengths and weaknesses—We have lots of possible sources of alternative energy. Plus, we already have lots of highly educated people who can figure this stuff out.

Brad notices that his topic is mostly about gasoline prices, not about other oil-related issues (see his notes in Figure 18.3).

Brad figures out that his best angle is "Our addiction to oil is like an addiction to nicotine." He decides to stress that angle in the next draft.

Brad realizes that this list is messy and long. So he decides to trim it down, while expanding on some of the more important concepts.

continued

FIGURE 18.2
Rough Draft
(continued)

5. *Support:* Get help from those nearest to us—Right now, other nations are a little upset with us. But, if they see us on the right track, they will probably start working with us, not against us.

6. *A Mature Identity:* Grow into self-respect and responsibility—For the last decade, our nation has been acting like an immature brat on the world stage. It's time to start acting like a mature country again.

7. *Higher Goals:* Pursue and accomplish things of value—Maybe we can strive for a better, cleaner world instead of just trying figure out how we can keep the cheap gas flowing.

He sees that he needs to expand on the argument in this paragraph. Right now it's mostly broad statements with minimal concrete support.

Getting over an addiction is tough. I still feel those cravings for nicotine. Getting ourselves off oil is going to be hard and even a little painful. We are going to be tested, and our pushers will be waiting for us to fail. But the benefits of ending our oil addiction has so many benefits. We will save money, our health, and improve our national security. We've taken the first step. We admitted we have a problem. Now, let's get to work.

Here are Brad's notes to help him with the global revision process.

Brad realizes that he needs to narrow his topic.

Notes on First Draft (Global Revision)

I'm writing a proposal to fix our dependence on oil as an energy source.

Topic: My topic is how to solve the oil crisis that we are facing right now. I need to concentrate mostly on consumer's need for gasoline to drive. Also, I want to bring in some of the environmental benefits of transitioning to alternative fuels. I want to show how seeing oil as an addiction can be a path to solving the problem.

Angle: My angle is the metaphor "America is addicted to oil." What happens if we take that metaphor seriously and treated oil as a drug that America is addicted to? As someone who was addicted to nicotine, I think I have some insight into how it feels to fight an addiction and what it takes to win.

FIGURE 18.3 Global Revision
Brad's professor asked him to reflect on his first draft. In these notes, Brad is examining what he hopes to accomplish with a global revision of his proposal draft.

Purpose: I don't think my purpose is clearly stated in this draft. So, here it is in one sentence: The purpose of my paper is to argue that America needs to treat oil as a drug and we need to recognize that we are addicted to that drug; so, we need to use drug rehab steps to end our addiction. (That's messy.)

Thesis statement: I also don't really state my thesis the way I probably should. I'm arguing, so I need an argumentative thesis statement. I've done this pretty well in the third paragraph, but I think I could sharpen it a little.

Readers: Mostly, I thought I was writing to everyone, but now I realize that I am writing mostly to younger people who can't afford these gas prices and really want to do something to change the world.

Expectations—First my readers need to understand the real problem. Then they need a clear strategy for solving that problem. The media keeps acting as though this problem is really about gas prices. That's just a symptom of the deeper problem underneath. My readers need to see that the prices are not the real problem.

Values—My values are similar to my readers' values. They care about the environment, but they also like the freedom of driving and traveling. They're also realistic about this problem. They want to do the right thing, but they know an easy solution isn't out there.

Attitudes—They are probably frustrated with the gas prices like most people. I would like to tap into their frustration, turn it into anger, and then get my readers to consider my solution. Get angry at that drug! It's the best way to fight it!

> Remember, we say in Chapter 2 that "the purpose statement guides you, as the writer.... Your thesis statement guides your readers."

> Brad analyzes his readers to figure out how he can use their expectations, values, and attitudes to persuade them.

FIGURE 18.3 Global Revision *(continued)*

Challenge Your Draft's Topic, Angle, and Purpose

You need to challenge your first draft to make sure it's doing what you intended. Reread your draft, paying special attention to the following global issues:

Topic. How has your topic evolved since you started? Do you now have a better understanding of the boundaries of your topic? Can you sharpen the topic, or does it need to be broadened a little? Can you find any places where your paper strays from the topic? Can you find any gaps in coverage where you don't address a key issue about your topic?

Angle. Have you shown what is new about your topic or what has changed recently? Have you connected your paper to any recent events or changes in our culture? Have you uncovered any unexpected issues that complicate or challenge your own views?

Purpose. Is your purpose clear in the introduction of your paper, and have you achieved that purpose by the conclusion? Does your purpose need to be more focused?

Thesis Statement. If you are writing in a genre that calls for an explicit thesis statement, have you announced your thesis clearly, completely, and prominently? Have you considered carefully what kind of thesis statement to use: informative, argumentative, question/open-ended, or implied?

Think About Your Readers (Again) and the Context

As you drafted your paper, chances are good that you gained a better understanding of your readers' expectations, values, and attitudes. Now try to put yourself in your readers' place to imagine how they will react to your ideas and the way you have expressed them.

Expectations. Have you considered how the genre leads readers to have certain expectations? Have you given readers all the information they need to make a decision? What additional information do they need if they are going to agree with you? Are they expecting an explicit thesis statement?

Values. Are your readers' values different from yours? If so, have you anticipated their values and how their values might cause them to react differently to your ideas than you would? Can you add anything that would help build trust between you and them?

Attitudes. Have you adjusted the text to fit your primary readers' attitude about your topic? If they have a positive attitude about your topic, have you reinforced that attitude? If they have a negative attitude, have you given them good reasons to think differently about your topic?

Now look at the context for your document to check whether you have addressed issues of place, medium, and social and political influences.

Place. How will the physical place in which readers experience your document shape how they read it? What will they see, hear, and feel? How will the history and culture of this place shape how readers will interpret what you are saying?

Medium. How will your paper's medium (e.g., paper, podcast, presentation) influence how people react to your message or interpret what you have to say?

Social and Political Influences. How will current social, economic, and political trends influence how your readers feel about what your paper has to say?

If you need more help profiling your readers turn to Chapter 3, "Readers, Contexts, and Rhetorical Situations."

Watch the Animation on **Peer Review, Editing, and Proofreading** at **mycomplab.com**

Level 2: Substantive Editing

When doing "substantive editing," you should look closely at the content, organization, and design of your document.

Determine Whether You Have Enough Information (or Too Much)

Your paper needs to have enough information to support your claims and explain your ideas to readers, but you don't want to include more content than you need.

- ❒ Does your thesis statement and main claim (usually in the introduction and/or the conclusion) describe what you're achieving in this paper?

- ❒ Are your claims in the body of the paper expressed completely and accurately? Could you express them in a more prominent, precise, or compelling way?

- ❒ Can you find any places where your ideas need more support or where your thesis and claims need more evidence drawn from sources?

- ❒ Are there any digressions? Can you trim the text down?

If you need more information or sources to back up your ideas, turn to Chapter 25, "Finding Sources and Collecting Information."

Reorganize Your Work to Better Use the Genre

Your readers will expect your document to conform to the genre's typical organizational pattern. This does not mean mechanically following a formula, but it does mean that your document should reflect the features your readers will expect in this genre.

- ❒ Does your paper have each of the sections included in this genre? If not, are you making a conscious choice to leave out a section or merge it with something else?

- ❒ Does your introduction do its job according to the conventions of the genre? Does it draw your readers in, introduce them to the topic, state the thesis and main claim, and stress the importance of the subject?

- ❒ Are your main ideas prominent enough? If not, can you move these main ideas to places where your readers are more likely to see them?

- ❒ Does the conclusion do its job according to the conventions of the genre? Does it restate the thesis or main point of the whole paper, reemphasize the importance of the topic, and offer a look to the future?

- ❒ Do the introduction and conclusion echo each other? If not, can you adjust your introduction and conclusion so they are clearly talking about the same topic, angle, purpose, and thesis?

Chapter 19 discusses introductions and conclusions, and Chapter 20 discusses paragraphing and sections.

Look for Ways to Improve the Design

Review how your document looks, focusing on whether the design is a good fit for your readers. The design should make your text easier to read and more attractive.

❐ Does the design of the document match your readers' expectations for the genre? Is the visual "tone" of the design appropriate for this genre?

❐ From a distance, does the text look inviting, interesting, and easy to read? Can you use page design, images, or color to make it more attractive and inviting to your readers?

❐ Have you used the design principles of balance, alignment, grouping, consistency, and contrast to organize and structure the page layout?

❐ Have you used graphics and charts to reinforce and clarify the written text while making your text more visually interesting?

Chapter 17, "Designing," offers some helpful strategies for improving the design of your document.

Watch the Animation on **Benefitting from Peer Review** at **mycomplab.com**

Ask Someone Else to Read Your Work

Substantive editing is a good time to ask others to review your work. Ask a friend or someone from your class to read through your text. Tell him or her to concentrate on content, organization, and design. Your editor can ignore any typos or grammatical errors, because right now you need feedback on higher-level features and problems.

For example, Figure 18.4 shows some helpful substantive editing comments from Rachel, a person in Brad's class, on his second draft. Brad has made significant improvements to his first draft. Rachel's thorough comments will help him improve it even more, because they highlight the proposal's weaknesses in content, organization, and design.

Level 3: Copyediting

Copyediting involves improving the "flow" of your text by making it *clear, concise, consistent*, and *correct* (sometimes called the "Four Cs" by professional copyeditors). When you are copyediting, focus exclusively on your document's title and headings, paragraphs, and sentences. Your ideas need to be as clear as possible and stated as concisely as possible. Also, make sure your ideas are consistent and that your facts are accurate.

Review Your Title and Headings

Your title should grab the readers' attention, and the headings in your document should help them quickly grasp your ideas and understand how the document is structured.

❐ Is the title unique, and does it grab the readers' attention? If your readers saw the title alone, would they be interested in reading your paper?

❐ Do the headings accurately reflect the information that follows them?

❐ Do the headings grab the readers' attention and draw them into the text?

❐ Are the headings consistent in grammar and parallel to each other in structure?

America Is Addicted to Oil

When gasoline prices rose dramatically in the summer of 2008, American citizens whined and complained. They called for more oil to be pumped from the arctic, from the shores of California and Florida, from shale oil deposits in Colorado. They yelled at gas station attendants and wrote angry letters to newspapers and members of Congress.

But it's not as though we didn't see this coming. For years, economists, conservationists, and political leaders have been telling the American public that the cheap ride on foreign oil would be coming to an end. The demand for oil was continually going up, especially with emerging economies like those in China, India, and Brazil demanding more oil. Yet, people kept buying big cars and commuting longer and longer distances. It's not as though we weren't warned.

> **Rachel**
> Back up these claims with cites from sources.

America is a junkie, and oil is our heroin. In this proposal, I would like to show how treating oil as an addiction can help us get out of this terrible situation and perhaps even save the planet.

> **Rachel**
> Your thesis statement is clear, but you might want to state it more plainly.

How do we stop being addicted to oil? As someone who stopped smoking, I know just how difficult it can be to break an addiction. After smoking for almost three years, I decided that I wanted to quit. One of my friends gave me a book written by psychologist Stanton Peele called *Seven Tools to Beat Addiction,* which I will discuss below.

> **Rachel**
> I noticed that you don't really have a section that discusses the problem. Instead, you just go straight to the solution. Maybe you should spend a little more time talking about the causes and effects of the problem. Also, I noticed you don't really discuss what someone with the opposing viewpoint would say about the problem and your solution.

Values: Build a foundation of values—We need to have a national conversation about what we value as Americans. Right now, our society is running on consumerism, greed, and selfishness. We need to build or rebuild a sense of common values in which the community's needs balance with the desires of the individual.

Motivation: Activate our desire to quit—Both major political parties need to reach consensus on this issue and then work together to solve it. We cannot kick the habit if one party or the other is telling us we don't really have a problem.

> **Rachel**
> This is cool, but some outside support would make it stronger.

continued

FIGURE 18.4 Substantive Editing

Brad revised his first draft for a peer review session the next day. Here is the second draft and substantive editing comments from Rachel, a classmate in his writing group.

Reward: Weigh the costs and benefits of addiction—Our government needs to commission scientific studies that show Americans the real costs of oil, such as the costs to our health, our environment, and the military we need to protect our flow of the drug. Only then will be able to truly measure the benefits of getting off the junk.

> **Rachel**
> A picture, chart, or graph would support what you are saying here.

Resources: Identify strengths and weaknesses—Our nation needs to recognize that our scientific, technological, and manufacturing capabilities would allow us to make a relatively quick conversion to other forms of energy, like solar, wind, and nuclear. Our weaknesses, however, include short-sighted thinking and selfishness, which is a downside of American individualism.

> **Rachel**
> This list could be designed better to make it more readable.

Support: Get help from those nearest to us—Like any addict, the United States is going to need support. Certainly, our Allies in Europe and Asia would be willing to help. They're recovering addicts too. But, we also have good neighbors in Canada and Mexico, who we could work with to bring about this change. Each of our neighbors has alternative energy strengths that we could tap into.

> **Rachel**
> Some quotes from sources would make this much stronger.

A Mature Identity: Grow into self-respect and responsibility—The United States has been behaving like a young addict, who lacks care for himself and lacks responsibility for his actions. This nation needs to mature and start taking on the priorities of an adult, such as caring for others, making tough decisions, and protecting those who are weaker than us.

Higher Goals: Pursue and accomplish things of value—Our addiction has caused us to give up on many of those "American ideals" that made us strong in the first place. We're cutting exploration, innovation, diplomacy, and creativity, so we can continue our flow of the drug. It's time to get back to what America once was—a beacon of freedom and hope. A place

FIGURE 18.4 Substantive Editing *(continued)*

where people could dream big and fill those dreams. Once the drug is out of our system, we can start to think about the future again, rather than just our next fix. Let's be honest. Getting ourselves off oil is going to be hard and a little painful. It's a life change, and we are going to be tested. But the benefits of ending our oil addiction are enormous. We will save money, our health, and improve our national security. We've taken the first step. We admitted we have a problem. Now, let's do something about it.

> **Rachel**
> Perhaps you can expand on the benefits of doing this. More discussion of the benefit might help win over your readers.

> Overall, Brad, I really like your paper. Comparing America's need for oil to a drug addiction really helped me see the problem we have. Your purpose seems clear enough, and I think I understand your thesis. One big problem is that you make some pretty big claims that aren't really supported with evidence in your paper. The design is pretty boring (sorry). Can't you find some images or graphs that would strengthen your argument and make the text more attractive?

FIGURE 18.4 Substantive Editing *(continued)*

You can learn more about using effective titles and headings in Chapter 15, "Organizing and Drafting," and Chapter 17, "Designing."

Edit Paragraphs to Make Them Concise and Consistent

Work through your document paragraph by paragraph, paying attention to how each one is structured and how it works with the paragraphs around it.

As you read through each paragraph, ask yourself these questions:

❏ Would a transition sentence at the beginning of the paragraph help make a bridge from the prior paragraph?

❏ Would transitions help bridge any gaps between sentences in the paragraph?

❏ Is each paragraph unified? Does each sentence in the paragraph stick to a consistent topic? Do any sentences seem to stray from the paragraph's claim or statement?

❏ Does each paragraph logically follow from the paragraph that preceded it and does it prepare readers for the paragraph that follows?

❏ If the paragraph is long or complex, would it benefit from a "point sentence" at its end that states or restates the paragraph's overall point?

Revise Sentences to Make Them Clearer

After you reshape and refine each paragraph, focus your attention on the clarity and style of individual sentences.

- ❏ Are the subjects of your sentences easy to locate? Do they tend to be placed early in the sentence where your readers can easily find them?

- ❏ Do the verbs express the action of the sentence? Can you remove any passive verbs (e.g., *is, was, be, has been*) by replacing them with active verbs?

- ❏ Can you eliminate any unnecessary prepositional phrases?

- ❏ Are your sentences breathing length? Are any sentences too long (i.e., do they take longer than one breath to say out loud)?

In Chapter 16, "Choosing a Style," you can find some "plain style" techniques for improving the clarity of your sentences while making them more concise.

Revise Sentences to Make Them More Descriptive

Now, work on giving your sentences more impact and power.

- ❏ Do your sentences use vivid detail to help readers see, hear, touch, taste, and smell what you are writing about?

- ❏ Would any similes, metaphors, or analogies help your readers to understand or visualize what you are talking about?

- ❏ Do your sentences generally use a consistent tone and voice? Can you describe in one word the tone you are trying to set in your paper?

Level 4: Proofreading

Proofreading is the final step in editing your document, during which you should search for any typos, grammatical errors, spelling mistakes, and word usage problems. Proofreading takes patience and practice, but it is critical to successful writing.

Read Your Writing Out Loud

Your ear will often detect problems that slip past your eyes. Errors that slip by when you are reading your work silently will stick out when you read aloud.

Read Your Draft Backwards

By reading your draft backwards, sentence by sentence, you can concentrate on the words rather than their meaning. You will find yourself noticing any odd sentence constructions and misspelled words.

Read a Hard Copy of Your Work

If you have been drafting and editing onscreen, reading a print copy will help you to see your writing from a fresh perspective. You might even try changing the font or line spacing to give the text a different look.

Know Your Grammatical Weaknesses

If you know you tend to make certain grammatical mistakes, devote one proofreading pass to those problems. For instance, if you tend to use run-on sentences, devote one entire proofreading session to that kind of mistake, looking only for it.

Use Your Spellchecker

Spellcheck has become a reliable tool over the years. A spellchecker can flag most of those annoying typos and spelling errors. (Look for the squiggly red lines that highlight potential problems.) You should not, however, rely exclusively on your spellchecker for proofreading. Instead, read through your document looking for possible spelling problems. If you aren't sure whether a word is being spelled or used correctly, then use your word processor's dictionary to look it up.

Peer Review: Asking for Advice

The keys to productive peer review are focus and honesty. As the writer, you need to tell your reviewers specifically what kind of help you need. For example, you might say:

- This is an early draft, so don't pay any attention to the grammar and wording. Look at my ideas and my thesis. Could they be stronger or sharper?

- My readers are high school students who are considering skipping college. Do you think this draft addresses their needs and answers the questions they would have?

- My thesis is X. What can I do to make sure that it comes through clearly and persuasively?

- Please look at the introduction closely. Do I introduce the topic clearly and grab the readers' attention?

Encourage your reviewers to be honest about your draft. You need them to do more than say "I like it," "It looks good," or "I would give it an A." Ask them to be as tough as possible, so you can find places to improve your writing.

When you are editing someone else's paper, write your comments and suggestions for improvements on a sheet of paper or in an e-mail, so the author has something concrete to work with when revising the draft. Also, make sure you tell the author what you liked about his or her paper, not just the negative stuff. Authors need to know what they are doing well.

Ready to finish your document? Follow the "Four Levels of Editing" to revise and edit your text like a professional.

REVISE Globally (Level 1)

Revision means "re-visioning" the text. Challenge your draft's topic, angle, purpose, and thesis. Then think further about your readers and the contexts in which they will read or use your document.

EDIT the Content, Organization, and Design (Level 2)

Substantive editing involves looking closely at the content, organization, and design of your document. Determine whether you have enough (or too much) content. Then make sure the organization of your document highlights your major ideas. Also, look for ways you can improve the design.

COPYEDIT Paragraphs and Sentences (Level 3)

Copyediting involves improving the "flow" of your text by making it *clear, concise, consistent*, and *correct*. Review your title and headings to make sure they are meaningful and consistent. Work paragraph by paragraph to make the text concise and consistent. Then revise the style of your sentences to make them clear and descriptive.

PROOFREAD Your Work (Level 4)

As a last step, proofreading is your final opportunity to catch any errors, like typos, grammatical errors, spelling mistakes, and word usage problems. To help you proofread, try reading your writing out loud, reading the draft backwards, and reading a hard copy of your work. Be aware of your grammatical weaknesses and look for those specific errors. Meanwhile, use your computer's spellchecker to catch any smaller errors.

ASK Someone Else to Review Your Work

By now, you are probably unable to see your document objectively. So have someone else look over your work and give you an honest assessment. Your professor may even give you and the members of your group time to "peer review" each other's writing.

1. On the Internet, find a document that seems to be poorly edited. With your group, discuss the impact that the lack of editing has on you and other readers. What do the errors say about the author and perhaps the company or organization he or she works for?

2. Choose a grammar rule with which you have problems. Explain in your own words what the rule is (use the "Handbook" section of this book for help). Then explain why you have trouble with it. Why do you have trouble remembering to follow it during composing?

3. Find a text on the Internet that you think is pretty strong but that lacks a clearly stated thesis statement. As a group, write a few thesis statements that could help guide readers about the main claim. Try the different kinds of thesis statements described in Chapter 2: an informative, argumentative, or question/open-ended thesis. Discuss which would work best for this text and explain your reasons.

Talk About This

1. On your own or with a colleague, choose a draft of your writing and decide which level of revising and editing it needs. Then, using the appropriate section in this chapter, walk through the steps for editing the document at that level.

2. Write a brief e-mail explaining the main differences between the levels of revising and editing to someone unfamiliar with the concept.

3. Find a text on the Internet that you think is poorly written. Using the four levels of editing, read through the text four separate times. Each time, explain what you would need to do to the text to make it stronger.

Try This Out

1. **Edit a text from someone in your class.** Exchange drafts with another person or within a small group during peer review. In addition to the draft itself, write a memo to your reviewers telling them exactly what you'd like them to focus on. Use the language from this chapter (level 1, level 2, global, local, etc.) and define as precisely as you can what you think might be an issue.

2. **Copyedit a text onscreen with Track Changes.** Find a rough draft (one of your own, a colleague's, or something from the Internet) and use Track Changes to do a level 3 edit (copyediting) on it. When you have finished, write an e-mail to your professor explaining your edits.

Write This

 **mycomplab**

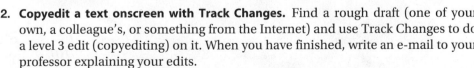

For support in meeting this chapter's objectives, follow this path in MyCompLab: Resources ⟹ Writing ⟹ The Writing Process ⟹ Revising. Review the Instruction and Multimedia resources about revising and editing, then complete the Exercises and click on Gradebook to measure your progress.

PART 4

Strategies for Shaping Ideas

PART OUTLINE

These chapters go way beyond just tips and tricks. Instead, you will learn time-tested STRATEGIES *for arranging your ideas and writing with strength and authority.*

19

Drafting Introductions and Conclusions

In this chapter, you will learn how to—

- start your papers with clear, engaging introductions.
- catch your readers' attention with a grabber or lead.
- finish your papers with strong conclusions.

Introductions and conclusions are important because they are the places where the readers are paying the most attention. If readers don't like your introduction, chances are good that they won't like the rest of your text either. And if they don't like how your paper ends, they will be left with doubts about what you had to say.

In this chapter, you are going to learn some easy-to-use strategies for writing great introductions and conclusions. By mastering some basic "moves" that are commonly made in introductions and conclusions, you can learn how to write powerful, engaging openings and closings for your texts.

Drafting Introductions

Put yourself in your readers' place. Before you start reading any text, you have some questions you want answered: "What is this? Why was this sent to me? What is this writer trying to get me to believe or do? Is this important? Do I care about this?" Your readers will be asking the same kinds of questions when they begin reading your text.

Five Introductory Moves

Watch the Animation on **Introductions** at **mycomplab.com**

Your introduction should answer your readers' questions up front by making some or all of the following five introductory moves:

Move 1: Identify your topic.

Move 2: State your purpose.

Move 3: State your main point, thesis statement, or a question you will answer.

Move 4: Offer background information on your topic.

Move 5: Stress the importance of the topic to your readers.

These opening moves can be made in just about any order. The first three are the most important, because these moves tell readers (a) what you are writing about, (b) why you are writing, and (c) what you want to explain or prove. The other two moves will help your readers familiarize themselves with your topic. Here is a sample introduction that uses all five moves:

> **Streets of Death: The Perils of Street Racing**
>
> That night, Davey Yeoman hadn't planned on almost killing himself. He was out cruising with a couple of friends in his blue turbo-charged Honda Accord. The other guy was in a yellow Pontiac GTO with katana rims. The driver of the GTO asked if Davey wanted to race. He said yeah. So they agreed to meet at 11:00 p.m. on a two-laner outside town. It was a popular place for street racing.
>
> When the stoplight changed, Davey hit 120 mph almost right away. The GTO was running beside him, a little off his right quarter panel. His Accord was shaking, and its engine was screaming. Suddenly, ahead, Davey saw the headlights of a semitrailer turning into his lane from a side road. The last thing Davey remembered thinking was, "Not me, God, not me." He knew he was dead.
>
> Street racing is a craze that has grown steadily in the last decade. Last year, over two hundred young people were killed in street racing incidents (FARS). Some of the dead and maimed were the drivers or their passengers, and some were people who just got in the way. Street racing has turned some of our roads into deadly places. These street racers need to understand the deadly dangers of turning our roads into racetracks.

Topic identified.

Background information.

Importance of the topic stressed.

Main point (thesis) stated.

Purpose identified in thesis statement.

In this introduction, the author *identifies the topic* (street racing) up front and then offers some *background information*. In the next paragraph, he *stresses the importance of the topic* with some data. Then he finishes the introduction by stating his *purpose* and *main point*.

Generally, your paper's main point, or thesis statement, should arrive somewhere near the end of the introduction, but you don't need to put it there. In the sample introduction above, for example, the writer could easily move the sentences and paragraphs around to put the main point earlier if that seemed to work better.

Using a Grabber to Start Your Introduction

To catch readers' attention, some writers like to use a *grabber* or *hook* at the beginning of their introduction. A grabber can gently spark your readers' curiosity, or it can shout, "Listen to me!" Here are some good grabbers you can use:

Ask an Interesting Question.   A question draws readers into the text by prompting them for an answer.

> Have you ever thought about becoming a professional chef? The training is
> rigorous and the work can be difficult, but the rewards are worth it.

State a Startling Statistic.   An interesting statistic can immediately highlight the importance of the topic.

> A shocking survey recently showed that 73 percent of teens in Bloomington
> have smoked marijuana, and 23 percent report using it at least once a week
> ("Weed" A3).

Make a Compelling Statement.   Make a statement that challenges readers at the beginning of the text.

> Unless we take action now on global warming, we are likely to see massive
> storms and rising ocean levels that will drown coastal cities.

Begin with a Quotation.   A quote is a good way to pique your readers' curiosity.

> That great American, Ben Franklin, once said, "They who would give up an
> essential liberty for temporary security deserve neither liberty nor security."
> Today, it seems like our fellow citizens are more willing than ever to make
> this trade.

Use Dialogue.   Dialogue offers a quick way to bring your readers into the story you are telling.

> One morning at breakfast, I heard a couple of other students from my dorm
> talking about the terrorist attacks on September 11th. One of them said,
> "September 11th was just like when the Germans bombed Pearl Harbor."
> The other gave a confused look and asked, "You mean the Chinese, right?
> The Chinese bombed Pearl Harbor." That's when I came to the troubling
> conclusion that many people my age have a dangerously flawed understanding
> of American history.

Address Readers as "You." Addressing the readers directly with "you" is a good way to get their attention.

> Has this ever happened to you? You finally have a chance to take your significant other out for a night out on the town. You're dressed up, and you're dining at one of the finest restaurants in the city. But then, the maître d' escorts you to the worst table in the place, right next to the swinging doors to the kitchen or the station where they fill the water glasses. Right away, you realize that you're being discriminated against because you're young.

The best grabber is one that (1) identifies your topic, (2) says something that intrigues your readers, and (3) makes the point of your paper in a concise way.

Using a Lead to Draw in the Readers

You can also use a lead (sometimes spelled "lede") to introduce your text. A lead is the first one or two paragraphs of a news story in a magazine, newspaper, or Web site. Like a grabber, the aim of a lead is to capture the readers' attention while giving them good reasons to continue reading. Here are some commonly used types of leads:

Scene Setter. A scene setter describes the place in which something important or interesting happened.

> The young men wade through thigh-high grass beneath the firs and ponderosa pines, calmly setting the forest on fire. With flicks of the wrist, they paint the landscape in flame. The newborn fires slither through the grass and chew into the sagging branches. Every few minutes a fire ignites, flames devouring it in a rush of light, the roar of rockets. It is over in seconds. Only a smoking skeleton remains. (Neil Shea, "Under Fire")

Anecdote. An anecdote starts out the introduction with an interesting true story that happened to the author or someone else.

> My parents didn't know, once again, that I was wide awake at 4:00 in the morning on a school night, inside an enormous and beautiful world, chatting and playing with twenty of my closest friends. Sometimes, I'd stay there for two or three days without a break. Yes, *World of Warcraft* is addictive, and you could say I was one of its countless victims.

Case Histories. A case history tells two to three very short true stories about different people who have had similar problems or experiences.

> Fred Jenkins never thought he was the kind of person to declare bankruptcy. He was a successful businessman with money in the bank. When his wife discovered she had ovarian cancer, though, his bank accounts were soon emptied by the costs of treatment. Mira Johanson took a different path to bankruptcy. She racked up $24,000 in credit card debt, because she bought a

house she couldn't afford. When she was laid off at Gerson Financial, she could no longer make the minimum payments on her credit cards. Then, with her credit in ruins, she could not refinance her mortgage. Her personal finances collapsed, causing her to lose everything.

Personal Sketch. Articles that are about a person often begin with a description of the person and a small biography.

> In mid-January 1959, Fidel Castro and his comrades in revolution had been in power less than a month. Criticized in the international press for threatening summary justices and execution for many members of the government of ousted dictator Fulgencio Batista, Castro called on the Cuban people to show their support at a rally in front of Havana's presidential palace.
>
> Castro, 32, wore a starched fatigue cap as he faced the crowd. With him were two of his most trusted lieutenants, Camilo Cienfuegos, unmistakable in a cowboy hat, and Ernesto (Che) Guevara in his trademark black beret. (Guy Gugliotta, "Comrades in Arms")

The lead comes before your main point (i.e., your thesis) in the introduction. Its job is to draw your readers into your paper and encourage them to keep reading.

Drafting Conclusions

● Watch the Animation on **Conclusions** at **mycomplab.com**

What happens when one of your professors says, "In conclusion . . . ," or "Finally," or "Here is what I really want you to take away from today's lecture"? Everyone in the class wakes up and starts paying close attention. Why? Because everyone knows the professor is going to state his or her main points.

The same is true of the conclusion at the end of your document. When your readers realize they have arrived at the conclusion, they will start paying closer attention because they know you are going to state your main points.

Here are five moves that you could make in your conclusion.

Move 1: Signal clearly that you are concluding.

Move 2: Restate your main point or thesis statement with added emphasis.

Move 3: Stress the importance of your topic again.

Move 4: Call your readers to action (if needed).

Move 5: Look to the future.

Your conclusion should be as short as possible, and it should be similar to your introduction in content and tone. In your conclusion, you need to bring readers back around to the beginning of your argument, showing them that you have achieved your purpose. For example, consider the following conclusion:

Street Racing Must Stop

Signal conclusion. →

In the end, street racing just isn't worth it. A few seconds of thrill can cause a lifetime of suffering or even get someone killed—maybe you. Davey Yeoman found that out the hard way, and he wants his wrecked life to be an example to others. He's paralyzed and eats through a straw. The Accord he once loved is a mangled heap that is towed around to local high schools as a warning to others. Davey hopes he can use his destroyed life to save the lives of others.

← Importance of topic.

Call to action. →

Look to the future. →

The laws against street racing are already on the books. We don't need more laws. What we need is more education and tougher enforcement to stop street racing. Only then will we be able to end this dangerous craze that leaves so many lives destroyed. Only then will our streets be safe again.

← Main point.

This conclusion makes all five concluding moves in two brief paragraphs. First, the author *signals that he is concluding* in the first sentence with the phrase "In the end."

Phrases that signal a conclusion include the following:

In conclusion,	Put briefly,	Ultimately,
To sum up,	In brief,	Overall,
In summary,	Finally,	As a whole,
In closing,	To finish up,	On the whole,

Then the author stresses the *importance of the topic* by returning to the story of Davey Yeoman, who crashed while street racing. By returning to this story, which started in the introduction, the author also brings the reader around to the beginning of the argument, making it feel whole.

A *call to action* and the *main point* appear in the paragraph that follows. Pairing the main point (thesis statement) with a call to action gives it more power because the author is stating it directly and telling readers what should be done.

Finally, the conclusion ends with a *look to the future* in which the author looks beyond the boundaries of the argument to talk about what should happen or will happen in the future.

You don't need to include all five of these concluding moves in your paper, and they don't need to appear in any specific order. If you find yourself writing a conclusion that goes longer than one or two paragraphs, you might move some of the information into the body of the paper.

Here are some basic strategies for writing an introduction and conclusion for your paper.

DIVIDE Your Argument into a Beginning, Middle, and End

Nonfiction documents should have an introduction (tell them what you are going to tell them), a body (tell them), and a conclusion (tell them what you told them).

DRAFT Your Introduction

A typical introduction includes up to five moves: (1) identify your topic, (2) state your purpose, (3) state your main point or thesis, (4) stress the importance of the topic, and (5) provide background information on the topic.

DEVELOP a Good Grabber or Lead for Your Introduction

Your introduction needs to capture the readers' interest right away. So use a question, intriguing statistic, compelling statement, interesting story, or quotation to hook them.

DRAFT Your Conclusion

A conclusion should make up to five moves: (1) signal that you are concluding, (2) restate the main point or thesis with more emphasis, (3) reemphasize the importance of the topic, (4) call for action, and (5) look to the future.

VERIFY That Your Introduction and Conclusion Work Together

The introduction and conclusion should work together, containing similar information, restating your main point, and using a similar tone. Often, the conclusion will complete a story that was started in the introduction. Here is also where the main point of the paper should be repeated once again.

1. Find a document on the Internet and identify its introduction and conclusion. With a group of people in your class, talk about whether you think the introduction and conclusion are effective in this text.

2. With your group, find an example of each kind of grabber and lead listed in this chapter. Print out or copy your examples and label which kind of grabber or lead they use.

3. Look closely at four conclusions from four different sample texts. With your group, rank the conclusions from best to worst. What aspects of some of the conclusions made them superior to the others?

1. Find an argument or other text that you have enjoyed reading this semester. Then write a one-page rhetorical analysis in which you discuss the structure of the text. Explain how the text's introduction, body, and conclusion work.

2. Find a text that you think has a weak introduction and/or conclusion. Write a one-page rhetorical analysis in which you diagnose the structural problems with the text's introduction and conclusion. What could the author have done better to build a stronger introduction and/or conclusion?

3. From the Internet, cut and paste an argument into your word processor. Then, with one or two people from your class, start experimenting with the introduction and conclusion. In an e-mail to your professor, explain how changing the arrangement of the introduction and conclusion has different effects on readers.

1. **Evaluate the organization of a reading.** Choose a reading from this book and write a two-page structural analysis of it. Using the criteria described in this chapter, analyze its introduction, body, and conclusion to determine whether they are well organized and whether they are the appropriate length.

2. **Describe the qualities of a good Internet article lead.** Internet readers are notoriously impatient, and they make quick decisions about whether to click to something else. Find three different kinds of leads used in articles on the Internet. Write a brief evaluation in which you discuss how the electronic medium changes the way readers enter the text.

For support in meeting this chapter's objectives, follow this path in MyCompLab: Resources ⟹ Writing ⟹ The Writing Process ⟹ Drafting. Review the Instruction and Multimedia resources about introductions and conclusions, then complete the Exercises and click on Gradebook to measure your progress.

20

Developing Paragraphs and Sections

In this chapter, you will learn how to—

- write a paragraph with an effective topic sentence and support.
- get paragraphs to flow from one sentence to the next.
- make sections out of related groups of paragraphs.

Paragraphs and sections help your readers understand at a glance how you have structured your ideas. Good paragraphs and sections help your readers figure out your main points and how you are supporting them.

A paragraph's job is actually rather straightforward: a paragraph presents a claim or statement, and then it supports or proves that claim or statement with facts, reasoning, examples, data, anecdotes, quotations, or descriptions. A paragraph isn't just a bunch of sentences that seem to fit together. Instead, a solid paragraph is a unit that is built around a central topic, idea, issue, or question. There are no hard-and-fast rules for writing paragraphs in terms of length or structure. A paragraph's length and structure need to fit its purpose and the genre you are using.

A section is a group of paragraphs that supports a common idea or claim. A section offers a broad claim and then uses a series of paragraphs to support or prove that claim. Longer college-length papers and most workplace documents are usually carved up into a few or several sections so they are easier to read.

In this chapter, you will learn how to develop great paragraphs and sections that will make your writing stronger and better organized.

Creating a Basic Paragraph

Paragraphs tend to include up to four elements: a *transition,* a *topic sentence, support sentences,* and a *point sentence.* The diagram in Figure 20.1 shows where these kinds of sentences usually appear in any given paragraph. Here is a typical paragraph with these four elements highlighted.

Watch the Animation on **Creating a Basic Paragraph** at **mycomplab.com**

> Of course, none of this happened overnight (transition). In fact, more important than the commercialization of rap was the less visible cultural movement on the ground in anyhood USA (topic sentence). In rap's early days, before it became a thriving commercial entity, dj party culture provided the backdrop for this off-the-radar cultural movement (support). What in New York City metropolitan area took the form of dj battles and the MC chants emerged in Chicago as the house party scene, and in D.C. it was go-go (support). In other regions of the country, the local movement owed its genesis to rap acts like Run DMC, who broke through to a national audience in the early 1980s (support). In any case, by the mid-1980s, this local or underground movement began to emerge in the form of cliques, crews, collectives, or simply kids getting together primarily to party, but in the process of rhyming, dj-ing, dancing, and tagging (support). Some, by the early 1990s, even moved into activism (support). In large cities like Chicago, San Francisco, Houston, Memphis, New Orleans, Indianapolis, and Cleveland and even in smaller cities and suburban areas like Battle Creek, Michigan, and Champaign, Illinois, as the '80s turned to the '90s, more and more young Blacks were coming together in the name of hip-hop (point sentence). (Bakari Kitwana, *Hip Hop Generation*)

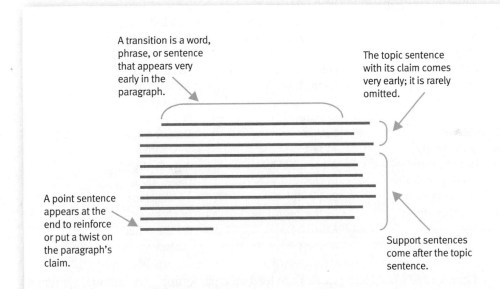

A transition is a word, phrase, or sentence that appears very early in the paragraph.

The topic sentence with its claim comes very early; it is rarely omitted.

A point sentence appears at the end to reinforce or put a twist on the paragraph's claim.

Support sentences come after the topic sentence.

FIGURE 20.1 The Shape of a Paragraph

Although paragraphs vary in terms of function and structure, the core of a paragraph includes the topic sentence with a claim followed by support sentences. Transition and point sentences can, in many cases, improve the flow of the paragraph.

Transition or Transitional Sentence (Optional)

The purpose of a transition or transitional sentence is to make a smooth bridge from the prior paragraph to the current paragraph. These kinds of transitions are especially useful when you want to shift or change the direction of the discussion.

A transition, if needed, should appear at the beginning of the paragraph. It might be as brief as a single word or phrase (e.g., *finally, in the past*) or as long as a complete sentence. A transitional sentence might ask a question or make an obvious turn in the discussion:

> If fast food is causing America's expanding waistlines, what are our options for counteracting the power of fast food over young people?

A question like this one sets up the topic sentence, which usually follows immediately. Here is a transitional sentence that makes an obvious turn in the discussion:

> Before moving ahead, though, we first need to back up and discuss some of the root causes of poverty in the United States.

A transitional sentence often redirects the readers' attention to a new issue while setting up the paragraph's claim (topic sentence).

A transitional word or phrase can also make an effective bridge between two paragraphs. Here are some transitional words and phrases that you can try out:

Watch the Animation on **Transitional Words** at **mycomplab.com**

For example	Nevertheless	Even though
To illustrate	At the same time	While it may be
For this reason	To summarize	true that
As an illustration	While this may or	Above all
Besides	may not be true	In addition
Of course	Equally important	With this in mind
In the past	As a result	For this purpose
In the future	Consequently	To this end
The next step	Meanwhile	At this point
In any event	In contrast	Subsequently
On the whole	Despite	Whenever
Likewise	Rather	Occasionally
Accordingly	At last	Inevitably
In conclusion	All of a sudden	Admittedly
More specifically	In the future	Under these
In the same way	Suddenly	conditions
In other words	In the meantime	In this way
Specifically	At any rate	On the other
On the contrary	At least	hand

Transitional words and phrases can lead off a paragraph's transitional sentence, or they can be used to start out a paragraph's topic sentence.

Topic Sentence (Needed)

A topic sentence announces the paragraph's subject and makes a statement or claim that the rest of the paragraph will support or prove.

> At the beginning of his presidency, Barack Obama was confronted with a number of pressing economic issues.

> A good first step would be to remove fast food options from junior high and high school lunch programs.

> Debt on credit cards is the greatest threat to the American family's financial security.

In most paragraphs, the topic sentence will be the first or second sentence. You may have been told in the past that a topic sentence can be put anywhere in a paragraph. That's true. But if you want your reader to understand the paragraph's subject and identify its key statement or claim quickly, put that topic sentence up front.

Of course, any guideline will have exceptions. For example, if you are telling your readers a story or leading them toward a controversial or surprising point, your topic sentence might arrive at the end of the paragraph. In the following paragraph, the topic sentence appears at the end, because the author is showing how something changed over time:

> My second grade homeroom teacher was a young graduate from a missionary school. When she found out I spoke English, she began to practice her English on me. One day she used English when asking me to run an errand for her. As I turned to close the door behind me, I noticed the puzzled faces of my classmates. I had the same sensation I had often experienced when some stranger in a crowd would turn on hearing me speak English. I was more intensely pleased on this occasion, however, because I suddenly felt that my family language had been singled out from the family languages of my classmates. Since we were not allowed to speak any dialect other than Standard Chinese in the classroom, having my teacher speak English to me in class made English an official language of the classroom. I began to take pride in my ability to speak it (topic sentence). (Min Zhan Lu, "From Silence to Struggle")

In some paragraphs, like this narrative paragraph, the topic sentence can appear at the end.

Support Sentences (Needed)

Support sentences make up the body of most paragraphs. These sentences provide examples, details, reasoning, facts, data, quotations, anecdotes, definitions, descriptions, and anything else needed to back up the paragraph's topic sentence. Support sentences usually appear after the topic sentence.

> With over 4,210 acres of both natural chapparal-covered terrain and landscaped parkland and picnic areas, Griffith Park is the largest municipal park with urban wilderness area in the United States (topic sentence).

Situated in the eastern Santa Monica Mountain range, the Park's elevations range from 384 to 1,625 feet above see level (support). With an arid climate, the Park's plant communities vary from coastal sage scrub, oak and walnut woodlands to riparian vegetation with trees in the Park's deep canyons (support). The California native plants represented in Griffith Park include the California species of oak, walnut, lilac, mountain mahogany, sages, toyon, and sumac (support). Present, in small quantities, are the threatened species of manzanita and berberis (support). ("Griffith Park," par.3)

Point Sentence (Optional)

Point sentences state, restate, or amplify the paragraph's main point at the end of the paragraph. A point sentence is especially useful in longer paragraphs when you want to reinforce or restate the topic sentence of the paragraph in different words.

That early anti-commercial intent symbolised the ethos of the alternative music scene (topic sentence). In 1990, Grohl became the drummer for Seattle-based band Nirvana, which had been formed by singer Kurt Cobain and bass player Krist Novoselic in 1987. Nirvana had already released a debut album, *Bleach* (1989), and the three-piece—Cobain, Novoselic and Grohl—toured small venues in a tiny van. It was a love of music that fuelled them, not the desire to become rich, famous rock stars (point sentence). (Wilkinson, "David Grohl")

As shown in the paragraph above, a point sentence is a good way to stress the point of a complex paragraph. The topic sentence at the beginning of the paragraph states a claim and the point sentence drives it home.

Getting Paragraphs to Flow (Cohesion)

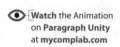

Watch the Animation on **Paragraph Unity** at **mycomplab.com**

Getting your paragraphs to flow is not difficult, but it takes a little practice. Flow, or *cohesion*, is best achieved by paying attention to how each paragraph's sentences are woven together. You can use two techniques, *subject alignment* and *given-new chaining*, to achieve this feeling of flow.

Subject Alignment in Paragraphs

A well-written paragraph keeps the readers' focus on a central subject, idea, issue, or question. For example, the following paragraph does not flow well because the subjects of the sentences are inconsistent:

Watching people at the park on a Saturday afternoon is a true pleasure. Frisbee golf is played by a group of college students near the trees. Visiting with each other are dog owners with their pets running around in playful packs.

Picnic blankets have been spread out, and parents are chatting and enjoying their lunch. The playground is full of children sliding down slides and playing in the sand.

One way to get a paragraph to flow is to align the paragraph's sentences around a common set of subjects.

> Watching people at the park on a Saturday afternoon is a true pleasure. Near the trees, a group of college students play frisbee golf. Off to the side, dog owners visit with each other as their pets run around in playful packs. Parents chat and enjoy their lunch on spread-out picnic blankets. On the playground, children slide down slides and play in the sand.

This paragraph flows better (it is coherent) because the subjects of the sentences are all people. In other words, the paragraph is about the people at the park, so making people the subjects creates the feeling that the paragraph is flowing.

First decide what the paragraph is about. Then revise its sentences so they use a consistent set of subjects. Subject alignment means keeping a consistent set of subjects, not necessarily the same subject, through most or all of the paragraph.

Given-New in Paragraphs

Another good way to create flow is to use something called "given-new chaining" to weave the sentences in a paragraph together. Here's how it works.

Each sentence should start out with something that appeared in the prior sentence (called the "given"). Then the remainder of the sentence offers something that the readers didn't see in the prior sentence (called the "new"). That way, each sentence takes something given from the prior sentence and adds something new.

> Recently, an art gallery exhibited the mysterious paintings of Irwin Fleminger, a modernist artist whose vast Mars-like landscapes contain cryptic human artifacts. One of Fleminger's paintings attracted the attention of some young schoolchildren who happened to be walking by. At first, the children laughed, pointing out some of the strange artifacts in the painting. Soon, though, the strange artifacts in the painting drew the students into a critical awareness of the painting, and they began to ask their bewildered teacher what the artifacts meant. Mysterious and beautiful, Fleminger's paintings have this effect on many people, not just schoolchildren.

In this paragraph, the beginning of each sentence takes something from the previous sentence or an earlier sentence. This creates a given-new chain, causing the text to feel coherent and flowing.

A combination of subject alignment and given-new chaining will allow you to create good flow in your paragraphs.

Organizing a Section

A section is a group of paragraphs that supports a major point in your text. When used properly, sections break a larger document into manageable portions. They also provide readers with a bird's-eye view of the document, allowing them to take in the gist of a longer document at a glance.

Opening, Body, Closing

Like a paragraph, a section usually supports or proves a major statement or claim. This statement or claim tends to be placed at the beginning of the section, often in a brief *opening paragraph*. Then the *body paragraphs* in the section each contribute something to support that statement or claim. Finally, an optional *closing paragraph*, which tends to be only a couple of sentences, can be used to restate the major statement or claim that the section was supporting or trying to prove.

Organizational Patterns for Sections

When organizing a section, begin by asking yourself what you want to achieve. Then identify a pattern that will help you structure and fill out that space. Figure 20.2 on page 422 shows a variety of patterns that you might consider when organizing sections in your text. These are some of the most common patterns, but others, including variations of the ones shown here, are possible.

Using Headings in Sections

Headings are especially helpful for marking where sections begin and end. They can help you and your readers make transitions between larger ideas. Also, they give readers an overview of the structure of the document.

All headings within a certain level should follow consistent phrasing patterns. A consistent pattern might use gerunds (-*ing* words), questions, or statements.

Inconsistent Headings	Performance Enhancement
	Is Performance Enhancement Unethical?
	Kinds of Performance Enhancement
Consistent Headings Using Gerunds	Defining Performance Enhancement
	Understanding the Ethics of Performance Enhancement
	Determining the Downside
Consistent Headings Using Questions	What Is Performance Enhancement?
	What Are the Risks?
	What's Really the Issue Here?

Consistent Headings	Cognitive Performance Enhancement Is Possible
Using Claims	Enhancement Will Improve Student Performance
	A Better National Conversation Is Needed

Headings should also be specific, clearly signaling the content of the sections that follow them.

Unspecific Headings	Fast Food
	The High School Scene
	Solutions
Specific Headings	Fast Food and High School Students: A Bad Mix
	The Effects of Fast Food on Health and Performance
	Alternatives to Fast Food

Using Sections and Paragraphs Together

A well-organized document is a structure that contains structures (sections) that contain structures (paragraphs) that contain structures (sentences). The purpose of a paragraph is to support or prove a statement or claim. The purpose of a section is to support a larger claim. The sections, altogether, support the thesis or main point of the document.

If you learn how to write solid paragraphs and sections, you will find that the structures of paragraphs and sections will help you figure out what you need to include in each part of your document. That will save you time, while improving your writing dramatically.

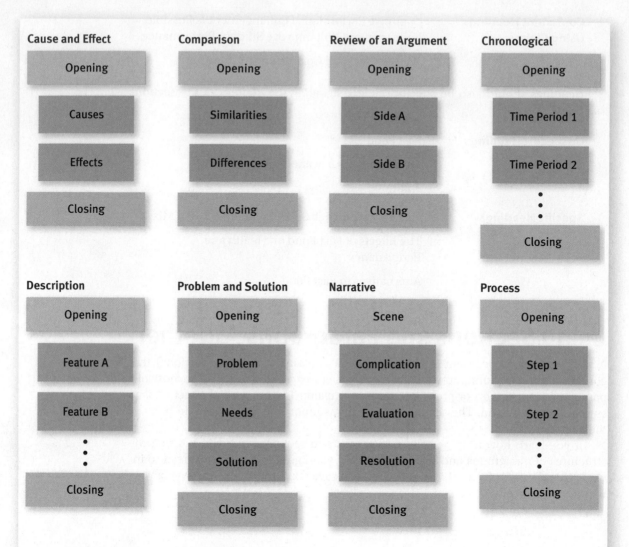

FIGURE 20.2 Organizational Patterns for Sections

Simple patterns like these can help you organize sections in your document. These patterns should not be followed mechanically, though. You should adapt them to suit your purpose.

Here are some basic strategies for creating clear, logical paragraphs and sections in your documents.

IDENTIFY the Four Kinds of Sentences in a Paragraph

A typical paragraph has a *topic sentence* and *support sentences.* As needed, a paragraph can also include a *transition sentence,* word, or phrases and a *point sentence.*

STATE Each Paragraph's Topic Sentence Clearly

A topic sentence announces the paragraph's subject—the central idea or issue covered in the paragraph. Your topic sentences should make a statement or claim that the rest of the paragraph will support or prove.

DEVELOP Support Sentences for Each Paragraph

Support sentences make up the body of most paragraphs. These sentences provide examples, details, reasoning, facts, data, anecdotes, definitions, descriptions, and anything else that backs up the paragraph's topic sentence.

DECIDE If a Transition Sentence or Transition Is Needed

If the prior paragraph is talking about something significantly different from the current paragraph, you might consider using a transition sentence or transitional word or phrase to bridge the gap.

DECIDE If a Point Sentence Would Be Helpful

In a longer paragraph, you might decide to use a point sentence to state or restate the paragraph's main point. Usually, the point sentence makes a claim that is similar to the topic sentence at the beginning of the paragraph.

COMBINE Paragraphs into Sections

Larger documents should be carved into sections. A typical section has an opening paragraph and body paragraphs. A closing paragraph is optional.

1. In studies of high school students' writing, researchers have found that inexperienced writers tend to place topic sentences at the end of their paragraphs, not the beginning. Why do you think inexperienced writers compose this way?

2. In this chapter, you learned that topic sentences should usually appear at the beginning of a paragraph and occasionally at the end. Can you think of any situations in which burying the topic sentence in the middle of the paragraph would be a good idea?

3. With your group, choose a reading in Part 2 of this book and pull its paragraphs apart, identifying their topic sentences, support sentences, transition sentences, and point sentences.

1. Go to the Internet and collect some interesting paragraphs. Identify the topic sentence and support sentences in each paragraph. If transition sentences and point sentences are used, highlight them, too. In a presentation to your class, choose one of your paragraphs and show how it works.

2. Find a badly written paragraph in a printed or online text. First, improve the flow of the paragraph by aligning the subjects of the sentences. Second, use given-new strategies to revise the paragraph's sentences. Finally, use a combination of subject alignment and given-new strategies to improve its flow. Which of these methods (subject alignment, given-new, or a combination) worked best?

3. On the Internet or on campus, find a document that is divided into sections. Look at each section carefully to determine what patterns are used. Which patterns for sections described in this chapter are most common? Are the sections following any patterns that aren't shown in this chapter?

1. **Diagnose and solve a paragraph's organizational problems.** Find a paragraph that has a confusing organization (one of your own, a colleague's, or something from the Internet). Diagnose the problems with this paragraph using the guidelines in this chapter. Then write a one-page analysis of the paragraph in which you explain its problems and offer two to five suggestions for improving it.

2. **Use a computer to revise the structure of a section.** Find a poorly organized multiple-page document on the Internet that is divided into sections. Revise the organization of one section so that it includes a clear opening paragraph and body paragraphs. Write an e-mail to the document's author (you don't have to actually send it) in which you discuss the problems with the original section and describe your strategy for improving it.

PEARSON
mycomplab

For support in meeting this chapter's objectives, follow this path in MyCompLab: Resources ⟹ Writing ⟹ The Writing Process ⟹ Drafting. Review the Instruction and Multimedia resources about writing body paragraphs, then complete the Exercises and click on Gradebook to measure your progress.

21

Using Basic
Rhetorical
Patterns

In this chapter you will learn how to—

- use rhetorical patterns to organize your ideas.
- organize paragraphs and sections into familiar patterns.
- combine rhetorical patterns to make sophisticated arguments.

When drafting, writers will often use *rhetorical patterns* to arrange their ideas into sections and paragraphs. Rhetorical patterns are familiar forms and strategies that help you to organize information in ways your readers will easily comprehend. Teachers of rhetoric, like Aristotle, called these patterns *topoi,* or commonplaces. *Topoi* (from the Greek word "place") are familiar patterns or strategies that you can use in a variety of situations.

Rhetorical patterns are not formulas to be followed mechanically. You can alter, bend, and combine these patterns to fit your purpose and the genre of your text.

Narrative

A narrative describes a sequence of events or tells a story in a way that illustrates a specific point.

Narratives can be woven into just about any genre. In reviews, literary analyses, and rhetorical analyses, narrative can be used to summarize or describe what you are analyzing. In proposals and reports, narratives can be used to recreate events and give historical background on a topic. Other genres, such as memoirs and profiles, often rely on narrative to organize the entire text.

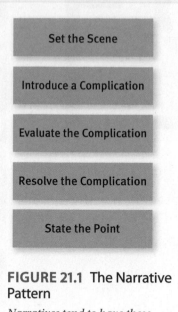

FIGURE 21.1 The Narrative Pattern

Narratives tend to have these five parts. Parts can be moved or removed to fit the rhetorical situation.

The diagram in Figure 21.1 shows the typical pattern for a narrative. When telling a story, writers will usually start out by *setting the scene* and *introducing a complication* of some kind. Then the characters in the story *evaluate the complication* to figure out how they are going to respond. They then *resolve the complication*. At the end of the narrative, the writer *states the point* of the story, if needed.

Consider, for example, the following paragraph, which follows the narrative pattern:

> Yesterday, I was eating at Gimpy's Pizza on Wabash Street (scene). Suddenly, some guy started yelling for everyone to get on the floor, because he was robbing the restaurant (complication). At first, I thought it was a joke (evaluation). But then everyone else got on the floor. I saw the guy waving a gun around, and I realized he was serious. I crawled under the table. Fortunately, the guy just took the money and ran (resolution). That evening, on the news, I heard the guy was arrested a couple of hours later. This brush with crime opened my eyes about the importance of personal safety (point). We all need to be prepared for the unexpected.

The narrative pattern is probably already familiar to you, even if you didn't know it before. This is the same pattern used in television sitcoms, novels, story jokes, and just about any story. In nonfiction writing, though, narratives are not "just stories." They help writers make specific points for their readers. The chart in Figure 21.2 shows how narratives can be used in a few different genres.

Description

Watch the Animation on **Description** at mycomplab.com

Descriptions often rely on details drawn from the five senses—seeing, hearing, touching, smelling, and tasting. In situations where the senses don't offer a full description, writers can turn to other rhetorical devices, like metaphor, simile, and onomatopoeia, to deepen the readers' experience and understanding.

Describing with the Senses

Like you, your readers primarily experience the world through their senses. So when you need to describe someone or something, start out by considering your subject from each of the five senses:

What Does It Look Like? List its colors, shapes, and sizes. What is your eye drawn toward? What makes your subject visually distinctive?

Objective of Genre	Use of Narrative
In a **proposal,** use a story to explain a problem in rich detail, including its causes and effects.	In a proposal about food safety, a writer motivates the reader to care about the issue by telling the story of a girl who died from food poisoning.
In a **commentary,** tell a story that demonstrates your expertise.	In a commentary that criticizes the inadequate training of soldiers, an army veteran uses a story from his deployment to illustrate his combat know-how.
In a **review,** summarize a movie's plot for readers.	In a movie review of a new romantic comedy, the writer gives an overview of the movie's main events, without giving away how the conflict in the movie was resolved.
In a **literary analysis,** use a historical narrative to offer background information on the text.	In a literary analysis, the writer tells an interesting story about the poet whose poem is being analyzed. This story offers insight into the meaning of the poem.
In a **report,** make an abstract concept easier to understand by narrating a series of events.	In explaining the concept of metamorphosis in a research report, the writer describes the luna moth's life cycle as a fight for survival from egg, to caterpillar, to chrysalis, to adult moth.

FIGURE 21.2 Using Narratives

What Sounds Does It Make? Are the sounds sharp, soothing, irritating, pleasing, metallic, harmonious, or erratic? What effect do these sounds have on you and others?

What Does It Feel Like? Is it rough or smooth, hot or cold, dull or sharp, slimy or firm, wet or dry?

How Does It Smell? Does your subject smell fragrant or pungent? Does it have a particular aroma or stench? Does it smell fresh or stale?

How Does It Taste? Is your subject spicy, sweet, salty, or sour? Does it taste burnt or spoiled? What foods taste similar to the thing you are describing?

Describing with Similes, Metaphors, and Onomatopoeia

Some people, places, and objects cannot be fully described using the senses. Here is where similes, metaphors, and onomatopoeia can be especially helpful. These stylistic devices are discussed in depth in Chapter 16, "Choosing a Style," so we will only discuss them briefly here.

Simile. A simile ("X is like Y"; "X is as Y") helps you describe your subject by making a simple comparison with something else:

> Directing the flow of traffic, the police officer moved as mechanically and purposefully as a robot on an assembly line.

Objective of Genre	Use of Description
In a **memoir,** describe characters and their setting.	In a memoir about a writer's Brazilian hometown, she uses sights, sounds, and textures to describe how her neighbors enjoyed playing and watching soccer in the streets.
In a **review,** describe the product being reviewed.	In a review of a new snowboard, the writer describes the visual features of the board, stressing what makes it different from others.
In a **commentary,** describe people or places of interest.	A writer uses description to show the hard life of people who are living without health care in southern Iowa.
In a **proposal,** describe a plan or a product.	A team of writers uses description to show how a new playground would look in a local park.
In a **report,** describe the laboratory setup for an experiment.	The methodology section describes how a laboratory experiment was put together, allowing the readers to verify and replicate it.

FIGURE 21.3 Using Descriptions

Metaphor. A metaphor ("X is Y") lets you describes your subject in more depth than a simile by directly comparing it to something else.

> When the fall semester starts, a college campus becomes a chaotic bazaar, with colorful people, cars, and buses moving frantically from here to there.

Onomatopoeia. Onomatopoeia uses words that sound like the thing being described.

> The flames crackled and hissed as the old farmhouse teetered on its charred frame.

Description is commonly used in all genres. The chart in Figure 21.3 shows how descriptions could be used in several kinds of writing situations.

Describing with a Mixture of the Senses and Tropes

A full, vivid description will usually include a combination of sensory details and tropes. In this description of an earthquake, the author uses both the senses and tropes to create a vivid picture of a graphic scene.

> When an earthquake happens, the waves sent through the earth are like waves made by a tree falling into a still lake. The fault snaps, sending ripples through the earth. The first waves, called primary waves (P-waves) move away from the

fault the quickest. P-waves push and pull, causing the earth to compress and expand like a spring ("Earthquakes"). For this reason, P-waves are also called "compression waves." Many people say that P-waves feel like a truck is pushing back and forth on their building. The secondary waves (S-waves), which are also called "shear waves," shake the earth sideways and up and down. People feel like they are being shaken or bounced, and they can hear rumbling. These vibrations can cause much more damage to buildings and bridges because S-waves move the earth more violently and last longer than P-waves ("Earthquakes"). Just like waves on a lake, the S-waves only stop when the earth settles down again.

The combination of sensory details and tropes makes this scene particularly visual and disturbing.

Definition

A definition states the exact meaning of a word or phrase. Definitions explain how a particular term is being used and why it is being used that way.

Sentence definitions, like the ones in a dictionary, typically have three parts: the term being defined, the category in which the term belongs, and the distinguishing characteristics that set it apart from other things in its category.

Category

Term

Cholera is a potentially lethal illness that is caused by the

Distinguishing characteristics

bacterium, *Vibrio cholerae*, with symptoms of vomiting and watery diarrhea.

An *extended definition* is longer than a sentence definition. An extended definition usually starts with a sentence definition and then continues to define the term further. You can extend a definition with one or more of the following techniques:

Word Origin (Etymology). Exploring the historical origin of a word can provide some interesting insights into its meaning.

According to the *Online Etymology Dictionary*, the word *escape* comes from the Old French word "eschaper," which literally meant "to get out of one's cape, leave a pursuer with just one's cape."

Examples. Giving examples can put a word's meaning into context.

For example, when someone says she "drank the Kool-Aid" for Barack Obama, it means she became a mindless follower of him and his ideas.

Negation. When using negation, you explain something by telling what it is not.

> St. John's wort is not a stimulant, and it won't cure all kinds of depression. Instead, it is a mild sedative.

Division. You can divide the subject into parts, which are then defined separately.

> There are two kinds of fraternities. The first kind, a "social fraternity," typically offers a dormitory-like place to live near a campus, as well as a social community. The second kind, an "honorary fraternity," allows members who share common backgrounds to network and support fellow members.

Similarities and Differences. When using similarities and differences, you compare and contrast the thing being defined to other similar things.

> African wild dogs are from the same biological family, *Canidae,* as domestic dogs, and they are similar in size to a labrador. Their coats, however, tend to have random patterns of yellow, black, and white. Their bodies look like those of domestic dogs, but their heads look like those of hyenas.

Analogy. An analogy compares something unfamiliar to something that readers would find familiar.

> Your body's circulatory system is similar to a modern American city. Your arteries and veins are like roads for blood cells to travel on. These roadways contain white blood cells, which act like state troopers patrolling for viruses and bacteria.

The chart in Figure 21.4 shows how definitions can be used in a variety of genres.

Objective of Genre	Use of Definition
In a **literary analysis,** explain a literary concept.	The writer defines words like "irony" or an important concept in the novel or poem.
In a **rhetorical analysis,** define a rhetorical term that helps explain why something is persuasive.	A person critiquing an advertisement defines the word *"pathos"* to help her explain how emotion is used to sway an audience.
In a **commentary,** define an important but unfamiliar term.	A commentator uses a specific term, like "Taliban," that calls for a definition to explain what it means.
In a **report,** clarify an important technical term.	In a research report about the great apes, a writer defines what a bonobo is and how it is different from other apes.

FIGURE 21.4 Using Definitions

Objective of Genre	Use of Classification
In a **review,** identify common subgenres.	A reviewer uses classification to identify where a new vampire movie fits in the horror movie genre.
In a **profile,** sort people into types.	A writer explains her best friend by categorizing college students into common groups.
In a **commentary,** explain a culture by describing its demographic groups.	A commentator tries to explain why different Islamic sects in the Middle East are sometimes mistrustful of each other.
In a **report,** divide a number of species into smaller subspecies.	A researcher uses classification to describe a family of insects.

FIGURE 21.5 Using Classifications

Classification

Classification allows you to divide objects and people into groups, so they can be discussed in greater depth. A classification can take up a single paragraph, or it might be used to organize an entire section (Figure 21.5). There are three basic steps to using classification to organize a paragraph or section.

Step One: List Everything That Fits into the Whole Class

List all the items that can be included in a specific class. Brainstorming is a good tool for coming up with this kind of list.

If you discuss all of these items individually, you will bore your readers to tears. So you need to find a way to break this long list down into smaller classifications.

Step Two: Decide on a Principle of Classification

The key to classifying something is to come up with a *principle of classification* that helps you do the sorting.

For example, let's imagine you are classifying all the ways to stop smoking. You would list all the methods you can find. Then you would try to sort them into categories:

Lifestyle changes—exercise daily, eat healthy snacks, break routines, distract yourself, set up rewards, keep busy.

Smoking-like activities—chew gum, drink hot tea, breathe deeply, eat vegetables, eat nuts that need to be shelled.

Nicotine replacement—nicotine patch, nicotine gum, sprays, inhalers, lozenges, nicotine fading.

Medical help—acupuncture, hypnosis, antidepressants, support group.

Step Three: Sort into Major and Minor Groups

If you choose an effective principle of classification, you should be able to sort all the items from your brainstorming list cleanly into the major and minor categories you came up with. In other words, an item that appears in one category should not appear in another. Also, no items on your list should be left over.

Here is a classification that was written by someone trying to stop smoking:

I really want to quit smoking because it wastes my money and I'm tired of feeling like a social outcast. Plus, someday, smoking is going to kill me if I don't stop. I have tried to go cold turkey, but that hasn't worked. The cravings for nicotine are just too strong, and I miss doing something with my hands. So, I began searching for other ways to stop. While doing my research, I found that there are four basic paths:

Lifestyle Changes. The first and perhaps easiest path is to make some changes in your life. Break any routines that involve smoking, like smoking after meals or going outside for a smoke break. Start exercising daily and set personal rewards for reaching milestones (e.g., dinner out, treat, movie). Mostly, it's important to distract yourself by keeping busy. And, if needed, keep pictures of charcoal lungs around to remind yourself what happens if you don't give up smoking.

Smoking-Like Activities. For many of us, the physical aspects of smoking are important, especially doing something with the hands and mouth. Some people keep a bowl of peanuts around in the shells, so they have something to do with their hands. Drinking hot tea or breathing deeply can replicate the warmth and sensation of smoking on the throat and lungs. Healthy snacks, like carrots, pretzels, or chewing gum, offer ways to keep the mouth busy.

Nicotine Replacement. Let's be honest—smokers want the nicotine. A variety of products, like nicotine gum, patches, sprays, and lozenges can hold down those cravings. Also, nicotine fading is a good way to use weaker and weaker cigarettes to step down the desire for nicotine.

Medical Help. Medical help is also available. Here on campus, the Student Health Center offers counseling and support groups to help people stop. Meanwhile some people have had success with hypnosis and acupuncture.

My guess is that a combination of these methods will help me quit this habit. This time I'm going to succeed.

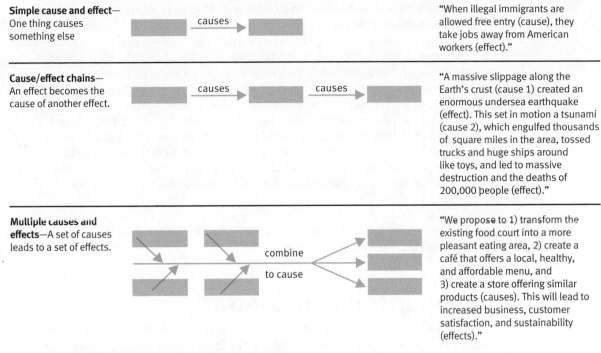

FIGURE 21.6 Three Kinds of Cause and Effect

The author of this classification has found a good way to sort out all the possible ways to stop smoking. By categorizing them, she can now best decide which ones will work best for her.

Cause and Effect

Exploring causes and effects is a natural way to discuss many topics. When we try to figure out why something happened, we automatically look for its causes. Then, we try to study its effects. When explaining causes and effects, identify both causes and effects and then explain *how* and *why* specific causes led to those effects.

Some cause-and-effect explanations simply point out the causes and effects of a particular event. Other cause-and-effect explanations are *arguable,* especially when people disagree about what causes the event and its effects (Figure 21.6).

Even when describing a complex cause-and-effect scenario, you should try to present your analysis as clearly as possible. Often, the clearest analysis will resemble a narrative pattern, as in this analysis of tornado formation:

Although scientists still do not completely understand the causes behind the formation of tornadoes, most agree on this basic pattern. Three ingredients must be present: a large mass of warm moist air, a large mass of cold dry air, and a violent collision between the two. During springtime in the central United States, enormous masses of warm moist air can move rapidly northeastward from the Gulf of Mexico into what has become known as "tornado alley." When the warm air collides with the cold air, thunderstorms are almost always produced. However, if the rapidly moving warm air slides *under* the cold air and gets trapped beneath, that's when a tornado can occur. Because warm air is lighter than cold air, the warm-air mass will try to form something like a "drain" in the cold-air mass that would allow the warm air to shoot through. If this happens, a vortex of air develops, sucking everything on the ground upward at enormous velocities, causing the strongest winds produced anywhere in nature, up to 300 miles per hour. These powerful winds sometimes accomplish the unbelievable, such as uprooting enormous trees and driving pieces of straw through wooden planks.

The chart in Figure 21.7 shows how different kinds of cause-and-effect analyses can be used in a variety of genres.

Comparison and Contrast

Comparison and contrast allow you to explore the similarities and differences between two or more people, objects, places, or ideas. When comparing and contrasting, you should first list all the characteristics that the two items have in common. Then list all the characteristics that distinguish them from each other.

FIGURE 21.7 Using Cause and Effect

Objective of Genre	Use of Cause/Effect
In a **profile,** explain how certain events influenced the subject.	A writer explains how her grandmother's life was changed by World War II.
In an **"argument" essay,** argue that one event has led to a certain outcome.	A writer argues open immigration laws have made the nation more diverse and lowered labor costs, which has resulted in making the nation more competitive worldwide.
In a **proposal,** explain how your plan will lead to good results.	A writer pitches a plan to increase bus ridership and shows it will save money by eliminating the need for a new parking structure.
In a **research paper,** explain the cause of something.	A student in a history class explains how a series of misunderstandings led to the American Revolutionary War.

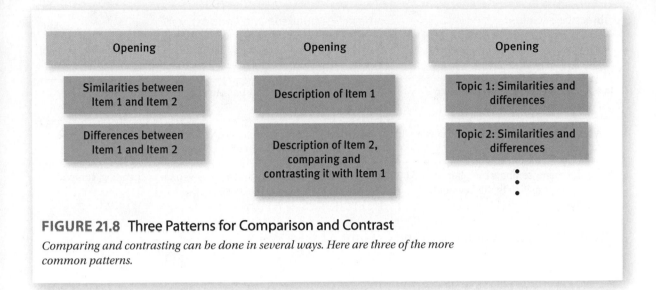

FIGURE 21.8 Three Patterns for Comparison and Contrast
Comparing and contrasting can be done in several ways. Here are three of the more common patterns.

You can then show how these two things are similar to and different from each other. Figure 21.8 shows three patterns that could be used to organize the information in your list. As an example of comparison and contrast, see the paragraph that follows:

> The differences between first-degree and second-degree murder can seem subtle. Both are forms of homicide, which is "the act of taking someone's life through murder" ("Homicide"). Also, in both types of murder, the perpetrator intentionally killed the victim. First-degree murder happens when the perpetrator planned in advance to kill someone. He or she wanted to murder someone else, made a plan, and carried out the act. Usually, he or she then tried to cover up the murder. Second-degree murder happens when the alleged killer was in the act of committing another crime, but he or she did not plan in advance to murder the victim. For example, a burglar commits second-degree murder if he intentionally kills a security guard who discovers him committing the crime. In this case, the burglar did not set out to kill the security guard, but he did it on purpose when he was discovered. Second-degree murder might occur as a result of arson, rape, robbery, or kidnapping.

Comparison and contrast is a useful way to describe something by comparing it to something else. Or you can use it to show how two or more things measure up against each other. Figure 21.9 on page 436 describes how comparison and contrast can be used in a variety of genres.

Objective of Genre	Use of Comparison and Contrast
In a **memoir,** compare a new experience to something familiar.	A writer compares her first day of college to her first day of high school to help new students understand how challenging college is.
In a **profile,** compare a new person to someone readers know.	A writer compares his new boss to cartoon character Homer J. Simpson.
In a **proposal,** compare the plan to successful plans used in the past.	While pitching a plan for a new dog park, a writer shows that similar plans have worked in other cities.
In an **argument,** compare the plan offered by the opposing position to the one being supported.	An economist argues against more government spending, comparing growth in the 1960s to the 1980s.

FIGURE 21.9 Using Comparison and Contrast

Combining Rhetorical Patterns

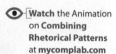
Watch the Animation on **Combining Rhetorical Patterns** at **mycomplab.com**

Rhetorical patterns can be combined to meet a variety of purposes. For example, you can embed a comparison and contrast within a narrative. Or you can use a classification within a description. In other words, you shouldn't get hung up on a particular pattern as *the* way to make your point. You can mix and match these rhetorical patterns to fit your needs. All of the readings in *Writing Today* use combinations of rhetorical patterns, so you should turn to them for examples.

Here are some easy ways to start using and combining basic rhetorical patterns in your writing.

NARRATE a Story

Look for places in your writing where you can tell a story. Set the scene and then introduce a complication. Discuss how you or others evaluated and resolved the complication. Then tell readers the main point of the story.

DESCRIBE People, Places, or Objects

Consider your subject from your five senses: sight, sound, touch, smell, and taste. Pay attention to movement and features that make your subject unique or interesting.

DEFINE Your Words or Concepts

Look for important words or concepts that need to be defined. A sentence definition should have three parts: the term, the category, and distinguishing characteristics. To extend the definition, describe the word's history, offer examples of its usage, use negation to show what it isn't, divide the subject into two or more parts, or discuss its similarities and differences with other things.

CLASSIFY Items by Dividing Them into Groups

If you are discussing something large or complex, list all its parts. Then use a principle of classification to sort that list into two to five major groups. Each group can be divided further into minor groups.

USE CAUSE AND EFFECT To Explain What Causes What

Examine your subject in terms of causes and effects. When analyzing a problem, explain what has changed to cause it. When pitching a solution, describe how your plan will lead to good results.

COMPARE AND CONTRAST Things

Find something that is similar to your subject. List all the similarities between the two items. Then list all the differences. Describe their similarities and differences.

MIX It Up!

Rhetorical patterns are not recipes or formulas to be mechanically followed. You should combine these patterns in ways that enhance their strengths.

1. Have each member of your group find two print examples of one of the basic rhetorical patterns discussed in this chapter and give a brief presentation in which he or she shows how the examples illustrate the pattern.

2. Make a list of ten slang words or phrases. With your group, come up with definitions for each of these words in which you identify the term, the category, and the distinguishing characteristics.

3. Basic rhetorical patterns are sometimes used as structures for essays. With your group, discuss and list the advantages and disadvantages of using these patterns to learn how to write whole documents.

1. Pick a place where you can sit undisturbed for half an hour. Write down everything you hear, feel, smell, and taste. Do *not* write down what you see. Then try to write a one-page description of the place where you were sitting. Try not to include any visual elements. Instead, use only your other senses to describe the place.

2. Pick two things that are similar in most ways but different in some important ways. Write three one-paragraph comparison and contrasts of these two things using each of the patterns shown in Figure 21.8. Which pattern worked best for your comparison and contrast, and why?

3. With your group, create a concept map that classifies the men and women at your university. When you are finished, discuss whether it is possible to appropriately sort people into groups without resorting to stereotypes.

4. In a group or on your own, think of a major problem that your school, community, or nation faces. What are the two to five major causes of this problem? What are the two to five major effects of this problem? Would everyone agree completely with your cause-effect analysis? If not, how would others analyze the issues?

1. **Examine something using six basic rhetorical patterns.** Think of something you know a lot about but with which others are unfamiliar. Using the six basic rhetorical patterns (narrative, description, definition, classification, cause and effect, comparison and contrast), help someone who knows little about your topic to understand it.

2. **Find rhetorical patterns on the Internet.** Write a two-page rhetorical analysis of a Web site in which you identify these basic rhetorical patterns and discuss how they are used on the site.

PEARSON
mycomplab

For support in meeting this chapter's objectives, follow this path in MyCompLab: Resources ⟹ Writing ⟹ Writing Purposes. Review the Instruction and Multimedia resources about the basic rhetorical patterns, then complete the Exercises and click on Gradebook to measure your progress.

Using Argumentative Strategies

In this chapter, you will learn how to—

- determine the source and nature of an arguable claim.
- use reasoning, authority, and emotion to support your argument.
- identify and avoid logical fallacies.

For some people, the word *argument* brings up images of fingerpointing, glares, outbursts, or quiet resentment. Actually, these aren't arguments at all. They are quarrels. When people quarrel, they no longer listen to each other or consider each other's ideas.

An argument is something quite different. An argument involves making reasonable claims and then backing up those claims with evidence and support. The objective of an argument is not to "win" and prove you have the truth. Instead, your primary goal is to persuade others that you are *probably* right. Arguments rarely end with one side proving the other side wrong. Instead, both sides strive to persuade others that their position is stronger or more beneficial, perhaps reaching agreement in the middle.

In college and in the professional world, arguments are used to think through ideas and debate uncertainties. Arguments are about getting things done by gaining the cooperation of others. In most situations, an argument is about agreeing as much as disagreeing, about cooperating with others as much as competing with them. The ability to argue effectively will be an important part of your success in college courses and in your career.

Argument can be used in any genre, but it is more prominent in some than in others. Memoirs and profiles, for example, do not typically make straightforward arguments with explicit claims, because they are primarily based on personal experience or historical facts. Other genres, such as reviews, evaluations, literary analyses, rhetorical analyses, proposals, and reports, are more obviously argumentative because their authors are deliberately trying to persuade readers to accept a particular view or idea.

In this chapter, you will learn some helpful strategies for persuading people to accept your ideas. You can use these strategies to argue effectively with your friends and family. They are also useful for arguing about important issues in college and in the workplace.

What Is Arguable?

Watch the Animation on **What is Arguable** at **mycomplab.com**

Let's begin by first discussing what is "arguable." Some people will say that you can argue about anything. And in a sense, they are right. We *can* argue about anything, no matter how trivial or pointless.

"I don't like chocolate."	"Yes, you do."
"The American Civil War began in 1861."	"No, it didn't."
"It really bugs me when I see a pregnant woman smoking."	"No way. You think that's cool."

These kinds of arguments are rarely worth the time and effort. Of course, we can argue that our friend is lying when she tells us she doesn't like chocolate, and we can challenge the historical fact that the Civil War really started in 1861. (Ultimately, anything is arguable.) However, debates over *personal judgments,* such as liking or not liking chocolate, quickly devolve into "Yes, I do. No, you don't!" kinds of quarrels. Meanwhile, debates about *proven facts,* like the year the American Civil War started, can be resolved by consulting a trusted source. To be truly arguable, a claim should exist somewhere between personal judgments and proven facts (Figure 22.1).

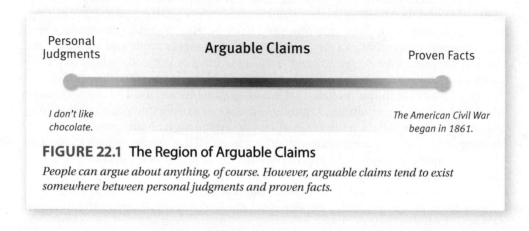

FIGURE 22.1 The Region of Arguable Claims

People can argue about anything, of course. However, arguable claims tend to exist somewhere between personal judgments and proven facts.

Arguable Claims

When laying the groundwork for an argument, you need to first define an arguable claim that you will try to persuade your readers to accept as probably true. For example, here are two arguable claims on two sides of the same topic:

Arguable Claim: The United States made a mistake when it invaded Iraq in 2003 because the invasion was based on faulty intelligence that suggested Iraq possessed weapons of mass destruction.

Arguable Claim: Despite faulty intelligence, the United States was justified in invading Iraq because Saddam Hussein was a dangerous dictator who was threatening Iraq's neighboring countries, supporting worldwide terrorism, and lying in wait for an opportunity to purchase or build weapons of mass destruction that could be used against the United States and its allies.

These claims are "arguable" because neither side can prove that it is factually right or that the other side is factually wrong. Meanwhile, neither side is based exclusively on personal judgments. Instead, both sides want to persuade you, the reader, that they are *probably* right.

When you invent and draft your argument, your goal is to support your position to the best of your ability, but you should also imagine your readers' views and viewpoints that might disagree with yours. Keeping opposing views in mind will help you to clarify your ideas, generate support, and identify any weaknesses in your argument. Then, when you draft your argument, you will be able to show readers that you have considered both sides fairly.

On the other hand, if you realize that opposing views are really not credible or that they are extremely weak, then you may not have an arguable claim in the first place.

Four Sources of Arguable Claims

Once you have a rough idea of your arguable claim, you should refine and clarify it. Toward this end, it is helpful to figure out what kind of arguable claim you are trying to support. Arguable claims generally arise from four different sources: issues of definition, causation, evaluation, and recommendation (Figure 22.2, page 442).

Watch the Animation on **Types of Claims** at **mycomplab.com**

Issues of Definition. Some arguments hinge on how to define an object, event, or person. For example, here are a few arguable claims that debate how to define something:

Animals, like humans, are sentient beings who have inalienable rights; therefore, killing and eating animals is an unethical act.

The terrorist acts of September 11, 2001, were an unprovoked act of war, not just a criminal act. Consequently, the United States was justified in declaring war on Al-Qaeda and its ally, the Taliban government of Afghanistan.

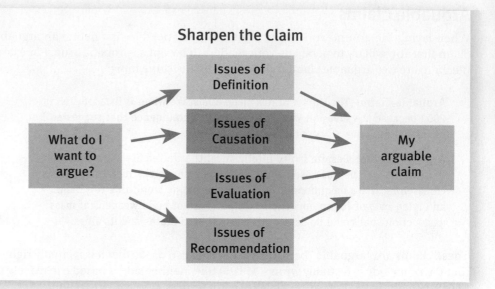

FIGURE 22.2 Developing and Sharpening an Arguable Claim

First, figure out what you want to argue. Then sharpen your claim by figuring out which type of argument you are making. The result will be a much clearer arguable claim.

A pregnant woman who smokes is a child abuser who needs to be stopped before she further harms her unborn child.

Issues of Causation. Humans tend to see events in terms of cause and effect. Consequently, we often argue about whether one thing caused another.

The main cause of boredom is a lack of variety. People become bored when nothing changes in their lives, causing them to lose their curiosity about the people, places, and events around them.

Advocates of gun control blame the guns when a school shooting happens. Instead, we need to look at the sociological and psychological causes of school violence, such as mental illness, bullying, gang violence, and the shooters' histories of aggression.

Pregnant mothers who choose to smoke are responsible for an unacceptable number of birth defects in children.

Issues of Evaluation. We also argue about whether something is *good* or *bad, right* or *wrong,* or *better* or *worse.*

Usually, the Part 3 sequel of a movie series is awful, but *Toy Story 3* is arguably the best animated film of all time with its thrills, heartbreaks, and moments of redemption.

The current U.S. taxation system is unfair, because the majority of taxes fall most heavily on people who work hard and corporations who are bringing innovative products to the marketplace.

Although both are dangerous, drinking alcohol in moderation while pregnant is less damaging to an unborn child than smoking in moderation.

Issues of Recommendation. We also use arguments to make recommendations about the best course of action to follow. These kinds of claims are signaled by words like "should," "must," "ought to," and so forth.

Tompson Industries should convert its Nebraska factory to renewable energy sources, like wind, solar, and geothermal, using the standard electric grid only as a backup supply for electricity.

The meat industry is heavily subsidized by the American taxpayer; therefore, we recommend removing all subsidies, making vegetarianism a financially viable choice.

We must help pregnant women to stop smoking by developing smoking-cessation programs that are specifically targeted toward this population.

To refine and sharpen your arguable claim, you should figure out which of these four types of arguable claims you are making, as shown in Figure 22.2. Then revise your claim to fit neatly into one of the four categories.

Using Reason, Authority, and Emotion

Once you have developed an arguable claim, you can start figuring out how you are going to support it with evidence and reasoning. There are three ways to support your position: reason, authority, and emotion (Figure 22.3). A solid argument will usually employ all three; however, one type will usually be the dominant mode of argument.

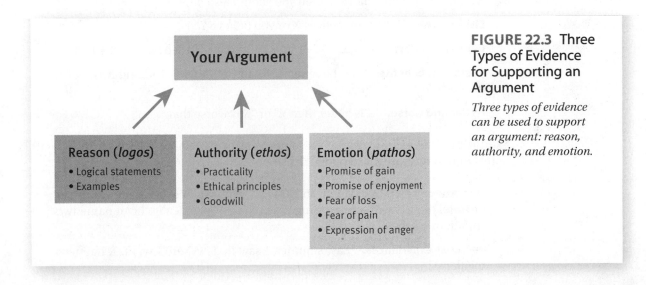

FIGURE 22.3 Three Types of Evidence for Supporting an Argument

Three types of evidence can be used to support an argument: reason, authority, and emotion.

FIGURE 22.4 A Cause and Effect Argument

In this advertisement from Health Canada, the primary argument strategy is cause and effect (i.e., smoking hurts unborn babies, or "X causes Y"). The argument also uses emotion (pathos).

Greek rhetoricians like Aristotle originally used the words *logos* (reason), *ethos* (authority), and *pathos* (emotion) to discuss these three kinds of evidence.

Reason (*Logos*)

Reasoning involves appealing to your readers' common sense or beliefs.

⊙ Watch the Animation
on **Reason (*Logos*)** at
mycomplab.com

Logical Statements. The first type of reasoning, logical statements, allows you to use your readers' existing beliefs to prove they should agree with a further claim. Here are some common patterns for logical statements:

> **If . . . then.** "If you believe X, then you should also believe Y."
>
> **Either . . . or.** "Either you believe X or you believe Y."
>
> **Cause and effect.** "X causes Y." or "Y is caused by X." (See Figure 22.4.)
>
> **Costs and benefits.** "The benefits A, B, and C show that doing X is worth the costs."
>
> **Better and worse.** "X is better than Y." or "X is worse than Y."

Examples. The second type of reasoning, examples, allows you to illustrate your points or demonstrate that a pattern exists.

> **"For example."** "For example, in 1994 . . ." "For instance, last week . . ." "To illustrate, there was the interesting case of . . ." "Specifically, I can name two situations when . . ."
>
> **Personal experiences.** "Last summer, I saw . . ." "Where I work, X happens regularly."

Facts and data. "According to our experiment, . . ." "Recently published data show that . . ."

Patterns of experiences. "X happened in 2000, 2004, and 2008. Therefore, we expect it to happen again in 2012." "In the past, each time X happened, Y has happened also."

Quotes from experts. "Dr. Jennifer Xu, a scientist at Los Alamos National Laboratory, recently stated . . ." "In his 2009 article, historian George Brenden claimed . . ." "My position is backed up by prominent leaders in the field, such as animal-rights advocate Jane Goodall, who shows that . . ."

Authority (*Ethos*)

Authority involves using your own experience or the reputations of others to support your arguments. Another way to strengthen your authority is to demonstrate your practicality, ethical principles, and goodwill (Figure 22.5). These three types of authority were first mentioned by Aristotle as a way to show your readers that you are fair and therefore credible, and these strategies still work well today.

Watch the Animation on **Authority (*Ethos*)** at **mycomplab.com**

Practicality. Show your readers that you are primarily concerned about solving problems and getting things done, not lecturing, theorizing, or simply winning.

FIGURE 22.5

Celebrities are often used to promote causes, such as the It Gets Better Project, because they have credibility with the public.

Where appropriate, admit that the issue is complicated and cannot be fixed easily. You can also point out that reasonable people can disagree about the issue. Being "practical" involves being realistic about what is possible, not idealistic about what would happen in a perfect world.

Ethical Principles. Demonstrate that you are arguing for an outcome that meets a specific set of ethical principles. An ethical argument can be based on any of three types of ethics:

- *Rights:* Using human rights or constitutional rights to back up your claims.
- *Laws:* Showing that your argument is in line with civic laws.
- *Utilitarianism:* Arguing that your position is more beneficial for the majority.

In some situations, you can demonstrate that your position is in line with your own and your readers' religious beliefs or other deeply held values.

Goodwill. Demonstrate that you have your readers' interests in mind, not just your own. Of course, you may be arguing for something that benefits you. So show your readers that you care about their needs and interests, too. Show them that you understand their concerns and that your position is fair or a "win-win" for you and them.

Emotion (*Pathos*)

Watch the Animation on **Emotion (***Pathos***)** at **mycomplab.com**

Using emotional appeals to persuade your readers is appropriate if the feelings you draw on are suitable for your topic and readers. As you develop your argument, think about how your and your readers' emotions might influence how their decisions will be made.

Begin by listing the positive and negative emotions that are associated with your topic or with your side of the argument.

Promise of Gain. Demonstrate to your readers that agreeing with your position will help them gain things they need or want, like trust, time, money, love, advancement, reputation, comfort, popularity, health, beauty, or convenience.

Promise of Enjoyment. Show that accepting your position will lead to more satisfaction, including joy, anticipation, surprise, pleasure, leisure, or freedom.

Fear of Loss. Suggest that not agreeing with your opinion might cause the loss of things readers value, like time, money, love, security, freedom, reputation, popularity, health, or beauty.

Fear of Pain. Imply that not agreeing with your position will cause feelings of pain, sadness, frustration, humiliation, embarrassment, loneliness, regret, shame, vulnerability, or worry.

Expressions of Anger or Disgust. Show that you share feelings of anger or disgust with your readers about a particular event or situation.

FIGURE 22.6
Using Emotions in an Argument
This advertisement uses emotional appeals to influence readers.

Use positive emotions as much as you can, because they will build a sense of happiness and goodwill in your readers. Generally, people like to feel good. Show readers that your position will bring them gain, enjoyment, and happiness.

Negative emotions should be used sparingly. Negative emotions can energize your readers and spur them to action (Figure 22.6). However, you need to be careful not to threaten or frighten your readers, because people tend to reject bullying or scare tactics. Any feelings of anger or disgust you express in your argument must be shared by your readers, or they will reject your argument as unfair, harsh, or reactionary.

Avoiding Logical Fallacies

A logical fallacy is an error in reasoning. Try to avoid logical fallacies because they can undermine your argument. Plus, they can keep you from gaining a full understanding of the issue because fallacies usually lead to inaccurate or ambiguous conclusions.

Figure 22.7 on page 448 defines and gives examples of common logical fallacies. Watch out for them in your own arguments. When an opposing viewpoint depends on a logical fallacy, you can point to it as a weakness.

Fallacies tend to occur for three primary reasons:

False or weak premises. In these situations, the author is overreaching to make a point. The argument uses false or weak premises (bandwagon, *post hoc* reasoning, slippery slope, or hasty generalization), or it relies on comparisons or authorities that are inappropriate (weak analogy, false authority).

Irrelevance. The author is trying to distract readers by using name calling (*ad hominem*) or bringing up issues that are beside the point (red herring, *tu quoque, non sequitur*).

Watch the Animation on **Logical Fallacies** at **mycomplab.com**

Logical Fallacy	Definition	Example
Ad Hominem	Attacking the character of the arguer rather than the argument.	"Mary has no credibility on the smoking ban issue, because she was once a smoker herself."
Bandwagon (*Ad Populum*)	Suggesting that a person should agree to something because it is popular.	"Over one thousand people have decided to sign up, so you should too."
Begging the Question	Using circular reasoning to prove a conclusion.	"Conservatives believe in hard work and strong values. That's why most Americans are conservative."
Either/Or	Presenting someone with a limited choice, when other choices are possible.	"We either buy this car now, or we spend the rest of the year walking to school."
Straw Man	Arguing against a position that no one is defending.	"Letting children play soccer on a busy highway is wrong, and I won't stand for it."
Weak Analogy	Making an improper comparison between two things that share a common feature.	"Paying taxes to the government is the same as handing your wallet over to a mugger in the park."
Post Hoc Reasoning	Arguing that one event caused another when they are unrelated.	"Each time my roommate is out of town, it causes my car to break down and I can't get to work."
Hasty Generalization	Using a part to make an inaccurate claim about a whole.	"The snowboarder who cut me off proved that all snowboarders are rude."
Slippery Slope	Suggesting that one event will automatically lead to a chain of other events.	"If we allow them to ban assault weapons, soon handguns, rifles, and all other guns will be banned, too."
Red Herring	Saying something that distracts from the issue being argued about.	"So, because books can now be found on the Internet, you're suggesting we burn our libraries?"
False Authority	Defending a claim with a biased or untrustworthy source.	"My mother read my paper, and she thinks it deserves an A."
Non Sequitur	Stating a conclusion that does not follow from the premises.	"Watching *30 Rock* each week will make you smarter and more popular."
Tu Quoque	Improperly turning an accusation back on the accuser.	"If you cared about global warming, as you claim, you wouldn't have driven a car to this meeting."

FIGURE 22.7 Common Logical Fallacies

Ambiguity. The author is clouding the issue by using circular reasoning (begging the question), arguing against a position that no one is defending (straw man), or presenting the reader with an unreasonable choice of options (either/or).

Logical fallacies do not prove that someone is wrong about a topic. They simply mean that the person is using weak or improper reasoning to reach his or her conclusions. In some cases, especially in advertising, logical fallacies are used deliberately. The advertiser wants to slip a sales pitch past the audience. Savvy arguers can also use logical fallacies to trip up their opponents. When you learn to recognize these fallacies, you can counter them when necessary.

Rebuttals and Refutations

Because we argue *with* others in an effort to gain their understanding and cooperation, you need to understand opposing viewpoints fully. You also need to anticipate how your readers will feel about your claims and your support. You need to imagine their possible objections or misunderstandings. After all, something that sounds like a good reason to you may not seem as convincing to your reader.

Summarize Your Opponents' Position Objectively

If you're discussing something "arguable," then there must be at least one other side to the issue. Show your readers that you understand those other sides before you offer a rebuttal or counter it. If you ignore the opposing viewpoints, your readers will think you are either unfairly overlooking potential objections or you just don't understand the other side of the argument. You can show readers that you understand other viewpoints by summarizing them objectively early in your argument. Try to frame their argument in a way that makes your readers say, "Yes, that's a fair and complete description of the opposing position."

Summarizing opposing viewpoints does three things for your argument. First, it lays out the specific points that you can refute or concede when you explain your own position. Second, it takes away some of your opponents' momentum, because your readers will slow down and consider both sides of the issue carefully. Third, it will make you look more reasonable and well-informed about the issue.

Recognize When the Opposing Position May Be Valid

The opposing viewpoint probably isn't completely wrong. There are likely to be situations, both real and hypothetical, where the other views may be valid. For example, let's say you are arguing that the U.S. automobile industry needs to convert completely to manufacturing electric cars within twenty years. Your opponents might argue that this kind of dramatic conversion is not technically or economically feasible.

To show that you are well informed and reasonable, you could name a few situations in which they are correct.

Converting fully to electric vehicles within twenty years may not be possible in some circumstances. For example, it is unlikely that large trucks, like semitrailers, will be able to run on electricity two decades from now because batteries will not be strong enough to provide the amount of energy required to move their weight for long distances. Furthermore, even if we stopped manufacturing gasoline-powered vehicles immediately, they would still be on the road for decades, requiring gas stations and mechanical repair. We cannot, after all, ask all drivers to immediately switch over to electric vehicles, especially if they cannot afford it.

By identifying situations in which the opposing position may be valid, you give some ground to the opposing side while limiting the effectiveness of their major points.

Concede Some of the Opposing Points

When you concede a point, you are acknowledging that some aspects of the opposing viewpoints or objections are valid in a limited way. It's true that you will be highlighting potential weaknesses in your own position but you will strengthen your argument by candidly acknowledging these limitations and addressing them fairly.

For instance, if you were arguing that the federal government should use taxpayer money to help the auto industry develop electric cars, you could anticipate two objections to your argument:

- As X points out, production of electric cars cannot be ramped up quickly because appropriate batteries are not being manufactured in sufficient numbers.

- It is of course true that the United States' electric grid could not handle millions of new electric cars being charged every day.

These objections are important, but they do not undermine your whole argument. Simply concede that they are problems while demonstrating that they are problems that can be fixed or that do not matter in the long run.

It is true that the availability of car batteries and the inadequacy of the United States' electricity grid are concerns. As Stephen Becker, a well-respected consultant to the auto industry, points out, "car manufacturers are already experiencing a shortage of batteries," and there are no plans to build more battery factories in the future (109). Meanwhile, as Lauren King argues, the United States' electric grid "is already fragile, as the blackouts a few years ago showed. And there has been very little done to upgrade our electric-delivery infrastructure." King states that the extra power "required to charge 20 million cars would bring the grid to a grinding halt" (213).

However, there are good reasons to believe that these problems, too, can be dealt with if the right measures are put in place. First, if investors had more confidence that there would be a steady demand for electric cars, and if the government guaranteed loans for new factories, the growing demand for batteries would encourage manufacturers to bring them to market (Vantz, 12). Second, experts have been arguing for years that the United States needs to invest in a *nationalized* electricity grid that will meet our increasing needs for electricity. King's argument that the grid is "too fragile" misses the point. We already need to build a better grid, because the current grid *is* too fragile, even for today's needs. Moreover, it will take years to build a fleet of 20 million cars. During those years, the electric grid can be rebuilt.

By conceding some points, you weaken their effectiveness. By anticipating your readers' doubts or the other side's arguments, you can minimize the damage to your own argument.

Refute or Absorb Your Opponents' Major Points

In some situations, your opponents will have one or two major points that cannot be conceded without completely undermining your argument. In these situations, you should study each major point to understand why it challenges your own argument. Is there a chance your opponents have a good point? Could your argument be flawed in some fundamental way? Do you need to rethink or modify your claims?

If you still believe your side of the argument is stronger, you have a couple of choices at this point. First, you can refute your opponents' major point by challenging its factual correctness. It helps to look for a "smoking gun" moment in which the opposing side makes a mistake or overstates a claim.

> Critics of electric cars argue that the free market should determine whether electric cars and the infrastructure to support them should be built. They argue that the government should not determine which automotive technologies survive and thrive. However, this kind of argument goes against the historical record. The US government has always been involved in building roads, railways, and airports. For decades, it has given tax breaks to support the manufacturing of gasoline vehicles. We are simply asking for these supports to be shifted in ways that will meet future needs, not the needs of the past.

In other situations, you can absorb your opponents' arguments by suggesting that your position is necessary or is better for the majority.

> The skeptics are correct that the conversion from gasoline cars to electric cars will not be easy and may even be economically painful. At this point, though, we have little choice. Our dependence on foreign oil, which is something we all agree is a problem, is a threat to our economic and political freedom. Moreover, our planet is already experiencing the negative effects of global climate change, which could severely damage the fragile ecosystems on which we depend for food, air, and water. We aren't talking about lifestyle choices at this point. We are talking about survival.

When absorbing your opposing points, you should show that you are aware that they are correct but that the benefits of your position outweigh the costs.

Qualify Your Claims

You might be tempted to state your claims in the strongest language possible, perhaps even overstating them.

> **Overstatement.** The government must use its full power to force the auto industry to develop and build affordable electric cars for the American consumer. The payoff in monetary and environmental benefits will more than pay for the investment.

> **Qualified Statement.** Although many significant challenges must be dealt with, the government should begin taking steps to encourage the auto industry to develop and build affordable electric cars for the American consumer. The payoff in monetary and environmental impact could very well pay for the effort and might even pay dividends.

When qualifying your claims and other points, you are softening your position a little. This softening gives readers the sense that they are being asked to make up their own minds. Few people want to be told that they "must" do something or "cannot" do something else. If possible, you want to avoid pushing your readers into making an either/or, yes/no kind of decision, because they may reject your position altogether.

Instead, remember that all arguments have gray areas. No one side is absolutely right or wrong. Qualifying your claims allows you to show your readers that your position has some flexibility. You can use the following words and phrases to qualify your claims:

unless	would	in all probability
except	perhaps	usually
if	maybe	frequently
even though	reasonably	probably
not including	plausibly	possibly
aside from	in most circumstances	conceivably
in some cases	almost certainly	often
although	most likely	may
could	if possible	might
should		

You can also soften your claims by acknowledging that you are aware of the difficulties and limitations of your position. Your goal is to argue reasonably while strongly advocating for your side of the argument.

Here are some strategies for becoming more effective at argument.

DEVELOP an "Arguable Claim"

An arguable claim is a statement that exists between personal judgments and proven facts. It should also be a claim that others would be willing to dispute.

IDENTIFY the Source of Your Arguable Claim

Arguable claims tend to emerge from four types of issues: issues of definition, causation, evaluation, and recommendation. You can sharpen your claim by figuring out what kind of issue you are arguing about.

FIND Reason-Based Evidence to Back Up Your Claims

Reasoning (*logos*) consists of using logical statements and examples to support your arguments.

LOCATE Authoritative Evidence to Back Up Your Claims

You can use your own experience if you are an expert, or you can draw quotes from other experts who agree with you. You should also build up your authority (*ethos*) by demonstrating your practicality, ethical principles, and goodwill toward readers.

USE Emotional Evidence to Back Up Your Claims

Identify any emotions (*pathos*) that shape how your readers will be influenced by your argument. You can use promise of gain, promise of enjoyment, fear of loss, fear of pain, and expressions of anger and disgust to influence them.

COUNTER the Claims of the Opposing View

There are a variety of ways to counter or weaken the opposing argument through rebuttal and refutation including (a) summarizing the position objectively, (b) identifying limited situations in which the opposing position may be valid, (c) conceding your opponents' minor points, (d) refuting or absorbing your opponents' major points, and (e) qualifying your claims.

AVOID Logical Fallacies

Look for logical fallacies in your argument and locate them in the opposing position's arguments. A logical fallacy is a weak spot that should be addressed in your own work and can be exploited as you counter the opposing sides' arguments.

1. With a group of people from your class, talk about how you usually argue with your friends and family. When are arguments productive? At what point do they become quarrels?

2. Discuss whether each of the following claims is "arguable." Explain why each is or is not arguable. For each that is not arguable, alter it enough to make it arguable.

   a. I always like to bring a water bottle with me when I work out at the gym.

   b. The Dallas Cowboys were America's favorite team during the 1970s.

   c. The major message behind the television show *Modern Family* is that all families are really messed up.

3. With your group, identify five reasons why arguing can be useful, productive, or even entertaining.

1. On the Internet, find a fairly short opinion article about an issue that interests you. Identify its main claim and determine which kind of evidence (*logos, ethos,* or *pathos*) is most dominant.

2. Find three different Web sites that persuade people to stop smoking. Compare and contrast their argument strategies. In a presentation, show why you think one Web site is more persuasive than the others.

3. With a group of three or four people from your class, divide up the list of fallacies in Figure 22.7 (on page 453). Then find or create examples of these fallacies. Share your examples with other groups in your class.

1. **Generate four claims and four counterclaims.** Choose an issue that you care about and develop an "arguable claim" from each of the sources of arguable claims discussed in this chapter (i.e., definition, causation, evaluation, recommendation). Then, for each of these arguable claims, develop a counterclaim that an opposing arguer might use against your positions.

2. **Find the fallacies in an advertisement.** Find an advertisement on television that uses one or more logical fallacies to support its points. In a two-page ad critique (see page 158), draw attention to the logical fallacies and use them as weak spots to undermine the advertisement.

PEARSON
mycomplab

For support in meeting this chapter's objectives, follow this path in MyCompLab: Resources ⟹ Writing ⟹ Writing Purposes ⟹ Writing to Argue or Persuade. Review the Instruction and Multimedia resources about writing arguments, then complete the Exercises and click on Gradebook to measure your progress.

Working Collaboratively with Other Writers

In this chapter, you will learn how to—

- work productively in groups and teams.
- assign specific roles to team members.
- understand and overcome conflicts that can arise in collaborative work.

In college and throughout your career, you will be asked to collaborate with other people on a variety of projects. Working in teams allows people to concentrate their personal strengths and take advantage of each other's abilities. Working with others also helps you to be more creative and take on larger and more complex projects.

Computers and the Internet have significantly increased our ability to collaborate with others (Figure 23.1, page 456). You probably already use e-mail, texting, mobile phones, blogs, microblogs, social networking sites, chat, and virtual worlds to keep in touch with your friends and family. In your career, you will use these same kinds of communication tools to interact with people at your office, across the country, and throughout the world.

In your college classes and in the workplace, collaboration will tend to take on two forms:

Working in Groups. Groups involve people who are working on separate but related assignments. Each member of the group shares his or her ideas and research, and everyone helps review and edit each other's work. Each person completes and hands in his or her own assignment.

Working in Teams. Teams involve people who are working on the same project. Each member of the team is responsible for completing one or more parts of the project, and the team hands in one common assignment or set of assignments.

Working with a Group of Other Writers

In your college classes, professors will regularly ask you to work in groups. Often, these groups are informal, made up of the people who happen to be sitting near you in class that day. Your professor may also put you into a group with people who are working on a similar topic or who have a major similar to yours.

Watch the Video on **Group Dynamics** at mycomplab.com

Choosing Group Roles

When you are put into a group, each person should choose a role:

FIGURE 23.1 Working Collaboratively in Your Career

The ability to work with others in groups and teams is essential in today's networked workplace.

Facilitator. The facilitator is responsible for keeping the group moving forward toward completing the task. His or her responsibility is to make sure the group stays on task, always keeping an eye on the clock. When the group goes off on a tangent or becomes distracted, the facilitator should remind the group members what they are trying to achieve and how much time is left to complete the task.

Scribe. The scribe takes notes on what the group says or decides. These notes can be shared with the group, helping everyone remember what was decided. If the group runs out of issues to talk about, the scribe should look back through the notes to pick topics that could benefit from more discussion.

Innovator. The innovator should feel free to come up with new and unique ideas that help the group see the issue from other perspectives. The innovator should look for ways to be creative and different, even though he or she might come up with something that the rest of the group will probably not agree with.

Designated Skeptic. The designated skeptic's job is to keep the group from reaching easy consensus on issues. He or she should bring up concerns that someone else might use to raise doubts about what the members of the group have decided.

These roles should be rotated among the group members. Give everyone a chance to be a facilitator, scribe, innovator, and skeptic.

Figuring Out What the Group Needs to Do

Soon after your professor puts you into groups, you can warm up by answering the following questions:

What Is Our Primary Goal? Figure out what your group is being asked to accomplish. The facilitator can state what he or she thinks the task is. Other group members can elaborate on that statement until everyone settles on a common goal.

What Else Should We Achieve? Your professor may ask your group to achieve secondary goals, too. Figure out what they are and have the scribe write them down.

How Much Time Do We Have? With your goals listed, figure out how much time you can devote to each one. Accomplishing the primary goal will usually take up the most time, but save some time for those secondary goals.

What Are We Expected to Deliver? When time is up, what is the group supposed to have finished? Does the professor expect someone to summarize the group's ideas for the class? Does the group need to produce something on paper to be handed in?

Who Will Speak for Our Group? Pick someone who can speak for the group when the activity is over. This choice should be made early, so the designated speaker can think about what he or she is going to say. This responsibility should rotate among group members, so the same person doesn't end up always speaking for the group.

These questions are designed to get everyone on the same page, so you are all sure about what you are doing and what you are supposed to deliver.

Getting the Work Done

Now it's time to get to work. Here are some ways your group can work together to help each other succeed:

Generate Ideas. Your group can brainstorm ideas and help each other see different perspectives on issues. Your group can use any prewriting technique, such as concept mapping, listing, or brainstorming, to generate ideas. The scribe should write down the ideas while the other group members talk.

Serve as a Sounding Board. The people in your group can serve as a forum for talking out your ideas for an assignment and figuring out your angle on the project. The group's facilitator should ask each person in the group to take turns sharing his or her ideas. Then, after each person speaks, every group member should say something positive about the speaker's project and offer at least one suggestion for improving it.

Discuss Readings. Your group will be asked to discuss the course readings to figure out the meaning of the text and its implications. Each person should be asked to contribute. Meanwhile, the designated skeptic should keep the group from reaching quick consensus about what a reading means. Your professor will likely ask each group to offer a brief report to the class about your discussion.

Review Works-in-Progress. Members of your group can read and comment on your writing, helping you strengthen and clarify your ideas. You can rotate papers among members of the group. If time allows, each member of the group might take a turn reading someone else's paper out loud. While listening, other members of the group should take notes about the paper's strengths and what could be improved.

Working with a Team

Throughout your college career, especially in advanced courses for your major, you will be asked to work on team projects. Working in teams usually involves developing one project (i.e., a document, presentation, product, experiment) that your team will hand in together. You and your team members will need to set goals and deadlines, negotiate with each other, divide up the work, and overcome disagreements.

One helpful way to successfully work as a team is to use the "Four Stages of Teaming" developed by management guru Bruce Tuckman (Figure 23.2). Tuckman noticed that teams tend to go through four stages when working on a project:

Forming. Getting to know each other, defining goals, describing outcomes, setting deadlines, dividing up the work.

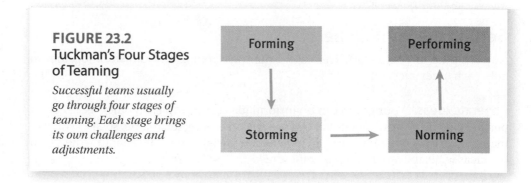

**FIGURE 23.2
Tuckman's Four Stages of Teaming**

Successful teams usually go through four stages of teaming. Each stage brings its own challenges and adjustments.

Storming. Experiencing disagreements, sensing tension and anxiety, doubting the leadership, experiencing conflict, feeling uncertain and frustrated.

Norming. Forming consensus, revising the project's goals, refining expectations of outcomes, solidifying team roles.

Performing. Sharing a common vision, delegating tasks, feeling autonomous, resolving conflicts and differences in constructive ways.

The secret to working in teams is recognizing that these stages are normal—including storming—and knowing what to do at each stage.

Forming: Planning a Project

When your team is first formed, you should give team members an opportunity to get to know each other and figure out the expectations of the project.

Watch the Video on **Planning a Project** at mycomplab.com

Hold a Planning Meeting. Your first task should be to plan the project and set some deadlines. To help you get started, do some or all of the following:

❐ Ask all team members to introduce themselves.

❐ Define the purpose of the project and its goals.

❐ Describe the expected outcomes of the project.

❐ Identify the strengths and interests of each team member.

❐ Divide up the work.

❐ Create a project calendar and set deadlines.

❐ Agree on how conflicts will be solved when they arise (because they will).

Choose Team Responsibilities. Each member of the team should be given a specific role on the project. When writing a collaborative document, here are four roles that your team might consider assigning:

Coordinator. This person is responsible for maintaining the project schedule and running the meetings. The coordinator is not the "boss." Rather, he or she is responsible for keeping people in touch and keeping the project on schedule.

Researchers. One or two group members should be assigned to collect information. They are responsible for digging up material at the library, running searches on the Internet, and coordinating any empirical research.

Editor. The editor is responsible for the organization and style of the final document. He or she identifies missing content and places where the document needs to be reorganized.

Designer. This person designs the document, gathers images from the Internet, creates graphs and charts, and takes photographs.

Notice that there is no "writer" in this list. Everyone on your team should be responsible for writing part of the document. Everyone should be responsible for reading and responding to all the parts, even those originally written by another person.

Storming: Overcoming Differences

Conflict is a normal part of any team project, so you need to learn how to manage the conflicts that come up. In fact, one of the reasons your professors put you into work teams is so you can learn how to manage conflict in constructive ways. Conflict may seem uncomfortable at the time, but it can lead to new ideas and more creativity.

Here are some strategies and tips for managing conflict:

Run Efficient Meetings. Choose a facilitator for the meeting and decide up front what will happen, what will be achieved, and when it will end. At the end of each meeting, each team member should state what he or she will do on the project before the next meeting.

Encourage Participation from Everyone. Each team member should have an opportunity to contribute ideas and opinions. No one should be allowed to sit back and let the others make decisions. Also, no one should dominate the meeting.

Allow Dissent (Even Encourage It). Everyone should feel welcome to disagree or offer alternative ideas for consideration. In fact, dissent should be encouraged, because it often leads to new and better ways of completing the project.

Mediate Conflicts. Conflicts will come up, and people will become irritated and even angry with each other. When conflicts happen, give each side time to consider and state their position. Then identify the two to five issues that the two sides disagree about. Rank these issues from most important to least. Address each of these issues separately, and try to negotiate a solution to the conflict.

Motivate Any Slackers. Slackers can kill the momentum of a team and undermine its ability to finish the project. If someone is slacking, your team should make your expectations clear to that person as soon as possible. Often, slackers simply need a straightforward list of responsibilities.

Conflict is normal and inevitable. When you see conflict developing in your team, remind yourself that the team is just going through the storming stage of the teaming process. You are going to experience plenty of conflict in advanced classes and in your career, so here is a good place to practice managing it.

Norming: Getting Down to Work

The storming stage can be frustrating, but soon afterward your team will usually enter the norming stage. Norming gives your group an opportunity to refine the goals of the project and finish the majority of the work.

Revise Project Goals and Expected Outcomes. At a meeting or through e-mail or Web conferencing, your team should look back at the original goals and outcomes you identified during the planning stage. Sharpen your goals and clarify what your team will accomplish by the end of the project.

Adjust Team Responsibilities. Your team should redistribute the work so the burden is shared fairly among team members. Doing so will raise the morale of the group and allow more work to be done in the time allowed.

Revise the Project Calendar. More than likely, unexpected challenges and events have put your team a little behind schedule. So spend some time with your team working out some new deadlines. These deadlines will need to be firmer than the ones you set in the forming stage.

Hold Regular Meetings. Your team should meet once or twice a week. Each person in the team should bring something new to each meeting.

Use Online Collaborative Tools. You can't always meet face to face, but you can still collaborate. Online collaborative software such as *Google Docs* allows team members to view the document's editing history, revert to previous versions of a document, and even work on the same document simultaneously. When you do work together online, it's best to also have a voice connection.

Keep in Touch with Each Other. Depending on the project deadline, your group should be in touch with each other every day or every other day. Texting or e-mailing works well. If you aren't hearing regularly from someone, give that person a call. Regular contact will help keep the project moving forward.

Performing: Working as a Team

When performing, each team member needs to recognize and understand the others' talents, needs, and capabilities. Your team is doing more than just trying to finish the project. Now, everyone on the team is looking for ways to improve the project, leading to higher-quality results (and more satisfaction among team members).

This is as much as we are going to say about performing in this book. Teams usually need to be together for several months before they reach this stage. If your team in a college class reaches the performing stage, that's fantastic. If not, that's fine too. The performing stage is a goal you should work toward in your advanced classes and in your career, but it's not typical in a college writing course.

Here are some useful strategies and tips that will help you get going on a group or team project.

CHOOSE Group Member Roles

A group works best when each person chooses a specific role. Some popular roles include facilitator, scribe, innovator, and designated skeptic.

DETERMINE What the Group Is Being Asked to Do

Talk with your group about its main goal and other objectives, while determining how much time is available, what is expected of the group, and who will speak for the group.

PURSUE Goals by Doing a Variety of Activities

Your group can be used to generate new ideas, serve as a sounding board, discuss readings, and review and edit each other's work.

REMEMBER That Teams Go Through Stages

When working on a team project, keep in mind that teams go through four stages: forming, storming, norming, and performing.

PLAN the Team Project

While forming, hold a planning meeting and have each team member choose his or her responsibilities on the project.

WORK Through Any Conflicts

When the team reaches the storming phase, work on running good meetings, encouraging participation from everyone, allowing dissent, mediating conflict, and motivating any slackers.

RETHINK the Team's Goals and Roles

After storming, teams usually enter a norming phase in which project goals are modified and team roles are adjusted.

IMPROVE Your Team's Quality

Teams that are together for a long time reach the performing stage, allowing them to concentrate on improving quality and satisfaction.

1. With a group in class, discuss the positive and negative experiences you have had while working in groups or teams. Describe two or three specific things group members can do to get a struggling group back on track.

2. In your group, discuss situations in which slackers have hurt a project you were working on. What are some ways to remove slackers from a project if they won't get to work?

3. What are some of the qualities of a successful sports team? How do the leaders of the team behave? How do the others on the team contribute?

Talk About This

1. Using the Internet to do research, list five ways in which you will need to use collaborative skills to be successful in your chosen career path. Write a brief report in which you discuss the kinds of collaborative work that happens in your field.

2. With a team of people in your class, pick a topic that you are all interested in. Then, in less than an hour, put together a visual report on that topic. While your team is working, pay attention to how each person contributes to the project. Before your next class, each person in the group should write two to three paragraphs describing (a) what happened, (b) what went well, and (c) what could have gone better. Compare experiences with your team members.

3. Research the future of virtual offices, telecommuting, and teleworking. In a brief report, explain how new media and technology will change how people work and how people will communicate with each other.

Try This Out

1. **Imagine that your classroom is a workplace.** With a group in your class, evaluate your writing class as a workplace. Write a proposal for restructuring the classroom as an effective and collaborative workplace. In your report, explain whether or not you think this kind of change would be a good idea.

2. **Use an online collaborative tool.** Write a pitch to your professor in which you advocate for the use of online collaborative tools in your writing class.

Write This

PEARSON
mycomplab

For additional help with writing, reading, and research, go to www.mycomplab.com.

PART OUTLINE

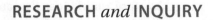

RESEARCH *and* **INQUIRY**

are the keys to discovery. In these

chapters, you will learn how to

do thoughtful and thorough research,

discovering answers to the questions

that intrigue you.

24

Starting
Research

In this chapter, you will learn how to—

- develop your own dependable "research process" that will help you inquire into topics that interest you.
- devise a "research plan" for your projects that allows you to stay on schedule and keep track of sources and information.
- assess whether sources are reliable and trustworthy.

Research systematically explores topics, using hands-on experience, factual evidence, and secondary sources. Research is used to do three important things:

- **Inquire:** A researcher gathers information in order to investigate an issue and explain it to other people.

- **Advance knowledge:** Researchers, especially scientists, collect and analyze facts to increase or strengthen our knowledge about a subject.

- **Support an argument:** In some situations, research can be used to persuade others and support a particular side of an argument while gaining a full understanding of the opposing view.

Research requires more than simply finding books or articles that agree with your preexisting opinion or using the first page of hits from an Internet search engine like *Google*. Instead, research is about pursuing truth and developing knowledge.

A dependable research process allows you to write and speak with authority, because you will be more confident about the reliability of your sources. Following a research process will actually save you time in the long run while helping you find more useful and trustworthy sources of information.

Starting Your Research Process

A reliable research process, as shown in Figure 24.1, is "recursive," which means the researcher collects sources and modifies the working thesis in a cyclical way. The process ends when the working thesis fits the facts available.

When starting your research, you should do three things:

1. Define a *research question* and sharpen it.

2. Develop a *working thesis* or *hypothesis* that offers your best guess about how you will answer the research question.

3. Devise a *research plan* to systematically collect the information needed to answer your research question and determine whether your working thesis is verifiable.

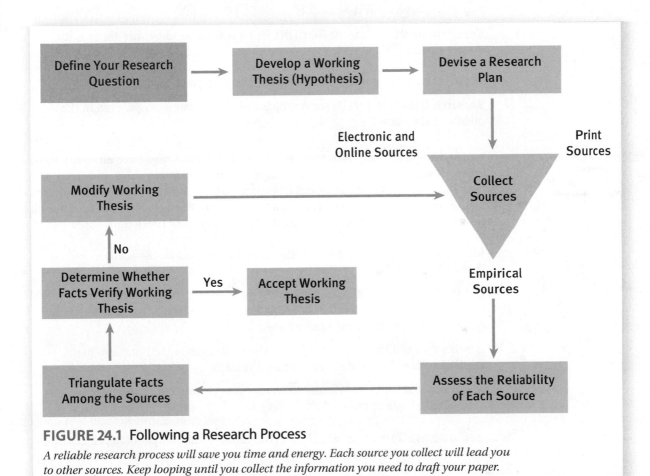

FIGURE 24.1 Following a Research Process

A reliable research process will save you time and energy. Each source you collect will lead you to other sources. Keep looping until you collect the information you need to draft your paper.

Step One: Define Your Research Question

Your research question names the topic you are studying and states specifically what you want to find out about that topic. Write down the exact question your research will try to answer:

Topic: Illegal immigrants and the economy.

Research Question: Is the flow of illegal immigrants into the United States helping or harming our economy?

Topic: The reasons Confederate states seceded before the Civil War.

Research Question: Why did the Confederate states decide to secede from the United States, thus sparking the US Civil War?

Topic: The severity of the threat of swine flu (H1N1 Flu).

Research Question: Is swine flu (H1N1 Flu) a real threat to our health, or is it mostly media hype?

Topic: The oddity of wearing shorts and flipflops in wintertime.

Research Question: Why do some people wear shorts and flipflops, even in the middle of the winter?

Watch the Animation on **Narrowing a Research Topic** at **mycomplab.com**

Notice that in moving from topic to research question, you have already begun to narrow down your research. The best research questions are short and simple.

Once you have drafted a research question, you should spend some time sharpening it. The research questions mentioned above, for example, are too broad for a typical college research paper. Here are sharper versions of these questions:

Are illegal immigrants having a positive or negative affect on the economy of Tucson, Arizona?

Was the constitutional disagreement over "states' rights" the real reason the Confederate states decided to secede from the United States, or did they secede to protect slavery as a cheap labor source?

Is swine flu a real threat to people in northern Michigan, or is it just another media-generated frenzy about an obscure disease?

Why do some students at Syracuse University always wear shorts and flipflops, even in the middle of the winter?

Sharper research questions will help you narrow the scope of your research, saving you time and effort by allowing you to target the best of sources and information.

Step Two: Develop a Working Thesis

After defining your research question, you should then develop a *working thesis*, which is also called a "hypothesis" in some fields. Your working thesis is your best guess about how you will answer your research question.

In one sentence, try to write down your overall claim about your topic. For example, here are some working theses based on the research questions above:

> I believe illegal immigration helps the Tucson economy by attracting low-wage labor, thus keeping costs down; but illegal immigrants also use up valuable public resources and take jobs away from legal citizens who already live here.

> Slavery was one of the key reasons the Confederate states decided to secede; however, other issues also sparked secession, such as Constitutional disagreements about states' rights, the economic disparities between North and South, and the formation of new non-slave states in the West that threatened to weaken the South politically.

> In northern Michigan, we need to be on guard against H1N1 Flu because we spend much of the winter confined indoors, increasing the chances that the flu will spread from person to person.

> Some Syracuse students wear shorts and flipflops in the winter because they prefer light, comfortable clothing, and they can keep warm by staying inside and walking from building to building across campus.

As you do your research, it is likely your working thesis will change, eventually becoming the main claim for your project. If possible, boil your working thesis down into one sentence. If you require two or three sentences to state your working thesis, your topic may be too complex or broad.

Step Three: Devise a Research Plan

Before you begin collecting sources, take some time to sketch out your *research plan*. Your plan should describe the kinds of sources you will need to collect to answer your research question. It should also describe how you are going to collect these sources and your deadlines for finding them. A typical research plan has these elements:

- Research question
- Working thesis
- Results of start-up research
- Description of electronic, online, print, and empirical sources available
- Schedule for conducting and completing the research
- Bibliography

Even if your professor does not ask for a research plan, you should spend some time considering these items to better target sources and streamline your research.

Doing Start-Up Research

Watch the Animation on **Start-up Research** at mycomplab.com

Now that you have created a research question, working thesis, and research plan, you're ready to start tracking down sources and collecting information. Some researchers find it helpful to begin by doing an hour of "start-up" research. This kind of research will help you to gain an overall view of the topic, figure out the various sides of the issue, and identify the kinds of sources available.

In Chapter 25, "Finding Sources and Collecting Information," we will talk about doing formal research, which is much more targeted and structured. For now, though, let's look at some good ways to do start-up research:

Surf the Internet. Put your research question or its keywords into *Google, Yahoo!, Bing,* or *Ask.com.* See what pops up. Jot down notes about the kinds of information you find. Identify some of the major issues and people involved with your topic and take note of any key sources of information that you might want to look up later. Bookmark Web sites that seem especially useful.

Look Through Online Encyclopedias. Major online encyclopedias include *Wikipedia, MSN Encarta,* and *Encyclopaedia Britannica Online.* Again, note the major issues and people involved with your topic. Identify key terms and any controversies about your topic.

One note: Professors probably won't let you cite online encyclopedias like *Wikipedia* or *Encyclopaedia Britannica* as authoritative sources, because the entries are often written by nonexperts. Nevertheless, online encyclopedias are useful for gaining a quick overview of your topic and finding sources that are authoritative. That's why they can be especially helpful when doing start-up research.

Browse Your Library's Catalog. Log on to your school's online library catalog and type in keywords to see what kinds of materials are available on your topic. Write down the names of any authors and titles that look like they might be helpful. In some cases, your library's catalog can e-mail your selections to you.

Start-up research should take you an hour or less. Your goal is to gain an overall sense of your topic, not to make up your mind or form your final opinion. Keep your options open and don't become too occupied by one source or perspective.

Assessing a Source's Reliability

Watch the Animation on **Evaluating Online Sources** at mycomplab.com

All information is not created equal. Some people who claim to be "authorities" are downright wrong or even dishonest. Even more problematic are people who have agendas or biases and whose print and online writings aren't always honest or truthful about the facts. To assess the reliability of your sources, consider these questions:

Is the Source Credible?

To determine whether a source's author and publisher are trustworthy, you should use an Internet search engine to check out their backgrounds and expertise. If you cannot find information about the author or publisher—or if you find questionable credentials or reputations—you should look for something more reliable.

How Biased Are the Author and the Publisher?

All sources have some bias because authors and publishers have their own ideas and opinions. When you are assessing the reliability of a source, consider how much the author or publisher *wants* the information to be true. If it seems like the author or publisher would only accept one kind of answer from the outset (e.g., "smoking does not cause cancer"), the information should be considered too biased to be a reliable source. On the other hand, if the author and publisher were open to a range of possible conclusions, you can feel more confident about using the source.

How Biased Are You?

As a researcher, you need to keep your own biases in mind as you assess your sources. Try viewing your sources from alternative perspectives, even (or especially) perspectives you disagree with. Knowing your own biases and seeing the issue from other perspectives will help you gain a richer understanding of your topic.

Is the Source Up to Date?

Depending on your topic, information can quickly become obsolete. In some fields, like cancer research, information that is only a few years old might already be out of date. In other fields, like geology, information that is decades old might still be usable today. So pay attention to how rapidly the field is changing. Consult your professor or a research librarian about whether a source can be considered up to date.

Can You Verify the Information in the Source?

You should be able to confirm your source's information by consulting other, independent sources. If a source is the only one that offers information that you want to use, you should treat it as unverified and use it only cautiously, if at all. If multiple sources offer the same or similar kinds of information, then you can use each source with much more confidence.

Evaluating Your Sources: A Checklist

❏ Is the source reliable?

❏ How biased are the author and the publisher?

❏ How biased are you?

❏ Is the source up to date?

❏ Can you independently verify the information in the source?

Managing Your Research Process

When you finish your start-up research, you should have enough information to create a schedule for completing your research. At this point, you should also start a bibliographic file to help you keep track of your sources.

Creating a Research Schedule

You might find "backward planning" helpful when creating your research schedule. Backward planning means working backward from the deadline to today, filling in all the tasks that need to be accomplished. Here's how to do it:

1. On your screen or a piece of paper, list all the tasks you need to complete.

2. On your calendar, set a deadline for finishing your research. You should also fill in your deadlines for drafting, designing, and revising your project.

3. Work backwards from your research deadline, filling in the tasks you need to accomplish and the days on which each task needs to be completed.

Online calendars like those from *Scrybe, Google,* or *Yahoo!* or calendars on your mobile phone or computer are great tools for making research schedules. A low-tech paper calendar still works well, too.

Starting Your Bibliography File

One of the first tasks on your research schedule should be to set up a file on your computer that holds a working bibliography of the sources you find. Each time you find a useful source, add it to your bibliography file.

As you find sources, record all the information for a full bibliographic citation (you will learn how to cite sources in Chapters 27, "Using MLA Style," and 28, "Using APA Style"). When you are ready to create your works cited page at the end of your paper, you will have a list of your sources ready to go.

Following and Modifying Your Research Plan

You should expect to modify your research plan as you move forward with the project. In some cases, you will find yourself being pulled away from your research plan by interesting facts, ideas, and events that you didn't know about when you started. Let your research take you wherever the facts lead you.

While researching, check in regularly with your research question and working thesis to make sure you are not drifting too far away from your original idea for the project. Or, you might need to adjust your research question and working thesis to fit some of the sources or new issues you have discovered.

When Things Don't Go as Expected

Research is a process of inquiry—of exploring, testing, and discovering. You are going to encounter ideas and issues that will require you to modify your approach, research question, or working thesis. Expect the unexpected and move forward.

Roadblocks to Research. You may not be able to get access to all the sources you had planned on using. For example, you might find that the expert you wanted to interview is unavailable, or that the book you needed is checked out or missing from the library, or that you simply cannot find certain data or information. Don't give up. Instead, modify your approach and move around the roadblock.

Information and Ideas That Change Your Research Question or Working Thesis. You might find something unexpected that changes how you see your topic. For instance, sources might not support your working thesis after all. Or, you might find that a different, more focused research question is more interesting to you. Rather than getting distracted or disappointed, look at this as an opportunity to discover something new. Modify your research question or working thesis and move forward.

These temporary roadblocks can be frustrating, but these inevitable surprises can also make research fun. If research were just mechanical plugging and chugging, then we wouldn't need to do it in the first place.

⊙ Watch the Animation on **Using Evidence** at **mycomplab.com**

Uses these guidelines to begin your research process.

UNDERSTAND Why Writers Do Research

Keep in mind that the purpose of research is to inform and support your ideas. Research is not just a regurgitation of others' ideas.

DEFINE Your Research Question

Name your topic and state your research question as specifically as possible. This is the question that your research will help you answer. Improve the efficiency of your research by sharpening that research question as much as possible.

DEVELOP a Working Thesis

In a single sentence, write down your working thesis. This is your best guess, or "hypothesis," for what you think will be your main claim.

DO Some "Start-Up" Research

Take half an hour to an hour to scan the kinds of sources available and get an overall sense of the various views on your research question. This informal start-up should include the Internet, online encyclopedias, and your library's online catalog.

DEVISE Your Research Plan

Avoid the temptation to just dive in. Take a little time to make a written plan that describes your research question, working thesis, start-up research results, schedule, and an early bibliography.

CREATE a Schedule

Use "backward planning" to break your research into manageable chunks. After listing all the tasks you will need to complete, work backward from your deadline, filling in the tasks and the days they need to be completed.

KEEP a Bibliography File

Keep a computer file of your working bibliography and maintain it. Your readers will need this bibliographic information to see where your sources can be found.

EXPECT the Unexpected

As you find new information, you will want to modify your research approach, research question, and working thesis. This is all part of the research process.

1. List five possible research questions that you find personally interesting. Then turn each of your research questions into a working thesis. With a small group, talk about these research questions and your working theses. Do group members have any ideas about how you could narrow your research?

2. With a small group, develop a research question on a topic that is interesting to all of you. Go online and use a variety of keywords to explore that topic. What are some possible answers to the research question?

3. In class, discuss what kinds of sources you think are most reliable. Do you believe online sources can be as reliable as print sources? When are hands-on empirical sources, like interviews or surveys, better than online and print sources?

Talk About This

1. Do about 30 minutes of start-up research on something that interests you. In an e-mail, describe to your professor what kinds of issues you will face if you want to do some formal research on this topic.

2. In a brief memo to your professor, describe your research plan for your next project. Explain why you think specific types of sources will be most helpful and why other kinds of sources probably will not be helpful.

3. On the Internet, find three sources of information that you would consider "heavily biased." Write an evaluation of these sources, explaining why you consider them biased and perhaps unreliable as sources.

Try This Out

1. **Create a research plan.** Write a full research plan. Identify your research question and your working thesis, show the results of your start-up research, and identify the kinds of sources you plan to target.

2. **Start a research journal.** Keep a journal while you do research for your next assignment. Keep track of the kinds of research you did and the amount of time you devoted to those activities. Determine what kinds of research yielded the most useful information and what kinds of research cost you too much time.

Write This

25

Finding Sources and Collecting Information

In this chapter, you will learn how to—

- triangulate your research by collecting information from electronic, print, and empirical resources.
- use reliable strategies to find and evaluate sources.
- do your own empirical research with interviews, surveys, and field observations.

N ow that you have figured out your working thesis and research plan, you are ready to start collecting sources. In this chapter, you will learn how to collect a variety of *primary* and *secondary* sources that will help you inquire into your topic and find useful information. The ability to collect reliable sources will be critical to doing useful, dependable research in college and in the workplace.

Evaluating Sources with Triangulation

When doing any kind of research, you should try to draw information from a variety of perspectives. If you rely on just one type of source, especially the Internet, you risk developing a limited or inaccurate understanding of your topic. To avoid this problem, *triangulate* your research by looking for information from three different types of sources:

Electronic and online sources: Web sites, CD-ROMs, listservs, television, radio, podcasts, videos, and blogs.

Print sources: Books, journals, magazines, newspapers, government publications, reference materials, and microform/microfiche.

Empirical sources: Personal experiences, field observations, interviews, surveys, case studies, and experiments.

Together, these three types of sources are called the *research triangle* (Figure 25.1). Here's how the research triangle works. If you collect similar facts from all three kinds of sources, the information you found is probably reliable. If you gather comparable facts from only two points of the triangle, your findings are probably still reliable but open to some doubt. However, if you can only find facts from one point on the triangle, then you probably need to do more research to back up your findings.

Of course, finding similar information in all three types of sources doesn't make something true. It just means the information is probably trustworthy. Triangulation is a good way to evaluate your sources and corroborate the facts you uncover about your topic. Keep in mind that "facts" and the "truth" are more slippery than we like to admit.

Also, remember that there are always at least two sides to any issue. So don't just look for sources that support your working thesis. Instead, use triangulation to find sources that also challenge what you believe. Even if you completely disagree with one of your sources, the argument it makes might give you a stronger understanding of your own position.

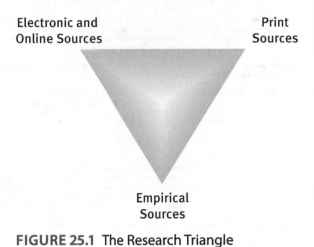

FIGURE 25.1 The Research Triangle

Triangulating your sources is a good way to ensure that you are drawing information from a variety of places. If you find similar information from all three corners of the triangle, it is probably reliable.

Using Primary and Secondary Sources

Researchers tend to distinguish between two types of sources: *primary sources* and *secondary sources*. Both kinds are important to doing reliable research.

Primary Sources. These are the actual records or artifacts, such as letters, photographs, videos, memoirs, books, or personal papers, that were created by the people involved in the issues and events you are researching (Figure 25.2, page 478). Primary sources can also include any data or observations collected from empirical research.

Secondary Sources. These are the writings of scholars, experts, and other knowledgeable people who have studied your topic. For example, scholarly books by

KENEDY COUNTY SHERIFF'S DEPARTMENT
TX 1310000
INCIDENT REPORT
02/11/2006
NUMBER: 06020136   REPORT DATE: 02/15/2006   ORI: TX1310000
LOCATION: ARMSTRONG RANCH   ZONE: ARMSTRONG

At approximately 1830 hrs on Saturday February 11, 2006, Kenedy County Sheriff Ramon Salinas contacted me, Chief Deputy Gilberto San Miguel Jr. The phone call was in reference to a hunting accident that occurred on the Armstrong Ranch. I was told by Sheriff Salinas to report to the main house on the Armstrong Ranch on Sunday February 12, at 0800 hrs and I would receive more information when I got there.

On Sunday, February 12, 2006, at approximately 0805 hrs, I Chief Deputy Gilberto San Miguel Jr., arrived at the bump gate to the Armstrong Ranch. This ranch is located approximately twenty-one miles south of Sarita, Texas in Kenedy County. There at the bump gate, Secret Service, and Border Patrol personnel met me. I identified myself and told everyone I was to report to the main house. I was instructed to park my vehicle so it could be inspected before I could proceed to the main house. While my vehicle was getting inspected, a Secret Service agent approached me and he advised me he would be riding with me to the main house. As I was approaching the main house, I was instructed to park my vehicle by the cattle guard. There I walked across the cattle guard and was turned over to another agent who identified himself to me as Michael A. Lee, Special Agent in charge with the Secret Service.

As we entered the main house, Mr. Lee introduced me to Vice President Cheney. Mr. Cheney shook my hand and told me he was there to cooperate in any way with the interview. As I got comfortable at a table inside the main house, I asked Mr. Cheney if he could explain to me what had happened the day of the incident.

Mr. Cheney told me that on Saturday, February 11, 2006 at approximately 5:30 pm on the Armstrong Ranch there was a three vehicle hunting party that consisted of himself, Bo Hubert, Pam Willeford, Jerry Medellin, Katharine Armstrong, Sarita Armstrong Hixon, Harry Whittington, and Oscar Medellin. Mr. Cheney told me the sun was setting to the west when the dogs had located a covey. Around the same time, Oscar Medellin notified the hunters he had also located a covey. After the group shot at the first covey he and Pam Willeford proceeded to the second covey because Harry Whittington was looking for his downed birds. Mr. Cheney told me he and Pam Willeford had walked approximately 100 yards from the first location and met up with Oscar Medellin and the hunting guide Bo Hubert. There was a single bird that flew behind him and he followed the bird by line of sight in a counter clockwise direction not realizing Harry Whittington had walked up from behind and had positioned himself approximately 30 yards to the west of him. Mr. Cheney told me the reason Harry Whittington sustained the injuries to his face and upper body was that Mr. Whittington was standing on ground that was lower than the one he was standing on. Mr. Cheney told me if Mr. Whittington was on the same ground level the injuries might have been lower on Mr. Whittington's body.

STATUS: CLOSED   STATUS DATE: 02/15/2006
OFFICER: SAN MIGUEL, GILBERTO JR.   502

02/15/2006 16:00 P.M.   1   *Gilberto San Miguel Jr*

FIGURE 25.2 Primary Sources of Information

Primary sources were created by the people involved in the events you are studying or through empirical research.

historians are secondary sources because their authors analyze and reflect on events from the past. Secondary sources can include books, academic journals, magazines, newspapers, and blogs.

For most research projects in college, you will usually rely on secondary sources. However, you should always look for opportunities to collect information from primary sources because they allow you to get closer to your topic than secondary sources.

Finding Electronic and Online Sources

The Internet is a good place to start doing research on your topic. Keep in mind, though, that the Internet is only a starting place for your research. You will need to triangulate, using print and empirical sources to support anything you find on the Internet.

Using Internet Search Engines

Search engines let you use keywords to locate information about your topic. If you type your topic into *Google, Bing,* or *Ask,* the search engine will return dozens or even millions of links. A handful of these links will be useful, and the vast majority of them will not.

With a few easy tricks, though, you can target your search with some common symbols and strategies. For example, let's say you are researching how sleep deprivation affects college students. You might start by entering the phrase:

sleep and college students

With this generic subject, a search engine will pull up millions of Web pages that might refer to this topic. Of course, there is no way you are going to have time to look through all those pages to find what you need, even if the search engine ranks them for you.

So you need to target your search to pull up only the kinds of materials you want. Here are some tips for pulling up better results:

Use Exact Words. Choose words that exactly target your topic, and use as many as you need to sharpen your results. For example,

sleep deprivation effects on students test taking

Use Quotation (" ") Marks. If you want to find a *specific phrase*, use quotation marks to target those phrases.

"sleep deprivation" +effects on students and "test taking" –insomnia –apnea

Use the Plus (+) Sign. If you put a plus (+) sign in front of a word or phrase, that tells the search engine to only find pages that have that exact word or phrase in them.

sleep +deprivation effects on +students +test +taking

Use the Minus (–) Sign. If you want to eliminate any pages that refer to words or phrases you don't want to see, you can use the minus sign to eliminate pages that refer to them.

sleep deprivation +effects on students +test +taking –insomnia –apnea

Watch the Animation on **Internet Search Engines** at **mycomplab.com**

Use Wildcard Symbols. Some search engines have symbols for "wildcards," such as ?, *, or %. These symbols are helpful when you know most of a phrase, but not all of it.

"sleep deprivation" +effects on students and "test taking" neural* behavioral* –insomnia –apnea

These search engine tips will help you pull up the pages you need. Figure 25.3 shows the results of an *Ask.com* search using the phrase

"sleep deprivation" effects on students "test taking" –insomnia –apnea.

Something to remember is that the first items pulled up by search engines are usually *sponsored links*. In other words, these companies paid to have their links show up at the top of your list. Most search engines highlight these links in a special way. You might find these links useful, but you should keep in mind that the sponsors are biased because they want to sell you something.

Using the Internet Cautiously

You already know that information from the Internet can be unreliable. Many of the so-called "facts" on the Internet are really just opinions and hearsay with little basis

◉ **Watch** the Animation on **Evaluating Online Sources** at **mycomplab.com**

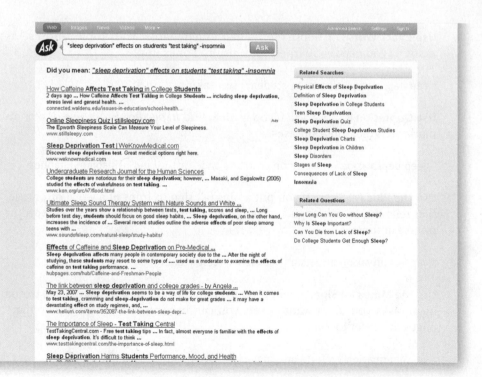

FIGURE 25.3 Targeting Your Search

In this search, the use of symbols has helped narrow the search to useful pages.

in reality. Also, many quotes that appear on the Internet have been taken out of context or corrupted in some way. So you need to use information from the Internet critically and even skeptically. Don't get fooled by a professional-looking Web site, because a good Web designer can make just about anything look professional.

Chapter 24, "Starting Research," offers some questions for checking the reliability of any source. Here are some additional questions you should use to challenge Internet sources:

- Can you identify and trust the author(s) of the source?

- What organization is this source associated with and why is it publishing this information?

- What does the source's author or organization have to gain from publishing this information?

- Does the source clearly distinguish between opinions and independent facts?

- Does the source fairly discuss two or more sides of the issue?

- Does the source use other independent sources to back up claims and can you access those sources?

- Does the information seem too incredible, too terrible, or too good to be true?

- Has the Web site been updated recently?

The Internet has plenty of useful, reliable information, but there is also a great amount of junk. It's your responsibility as a researcher to critically decide what is reliable and what isn't.

Using Documentaries and Television/Radio Broadcasts

Multimedia resources such as television and radio broadcasts are available online through network Web sites as well as sites like *YouTube* and *Hulu*. Depending on who made them, documentaries and broadcasts can be reliable sources. If the material is from a trustworthy source, you can take quotes and cite these kinds of electronic sources in your own work.

Documentaries. A documentary is a nonfiction movie or program that relies on interviews and factual evidence about an event or issue. A documentary can be biased, though, so check into the background of the person or organization that made it.

Television Broadcasts. Cable channels and news networks like HBO, the History Channel, the National Geographic Channel, and the Biography Channel are producing excellent broadcasts that are reliable and can be cited as support for your argument. Programs on news channels that feature just one or two highly opinionated commentators are less reliable because they tend to be sensationalistic and are often biased.

Radio Broadcasts. Radio broadcasts, too, can be informative and authoritative. Public radio broadcasts, such as National Public Radio and American RadioWorks, offer well-researched stories on the air and at their Web sites. On the other hand, political broadcasts like *The Sean Hannity Show, The Rush Limbaugh Show, The Rachel Maddow Show,* and *Doing Time with Ron Kuby,* are notorious for slanting the news and playing loose with the facts. You cannot rely on these broadcasts as factual sources in your argument.

Using Wikis, Blogs, and Podcasts

As a general rule, you should not use wikis, blogs, or podcasts as your main sources for academic research projects, because they are too opinion-based and their "facts" are often unreliable. Nevertheless, they are helpful for defining issues and pointing you toward more established sources.

Wikis. You probably already know about *Wikipedia,* the most popular wiki, but a variety of other wikis are available, like *WikiHow, Wikibooks,* and *Wikitravel.* Wikis allow their users to add and revise content, and they rely on other users to back-check facts. On some topics, such as popular culture (e.g., television programs, music, celebrities), a wiki might be the best or only source of up-to-date information. On more established topics, however, you should always be skeptical about the reliability of their information. Your best approach is to use these sites primarily for start-up research on your topic and to help you find other, more reliable sources.

⊙ Watch the Animation
on **Evaluating Blogs**
at **mycomplab.com**

Blogs. Blogs can be helpful for exploring a range of opinions on a particular topic. However, even some of the most established and respected blogs like *Daily Kos, Power Line*, and *Wonkette* are little more than opinionated commentaries on the day's events. Like wikis, blogs can help you identify the issues involved with your topic and locate more reliable sources, but most of them are not reliable sources themselves.

Podcasts. Most news Web sites offer podcasts, but the reliability of these sources depends on who made the audio or video file. Today, anyone with a video camera or digital tape recorder can make a podcast, even a professional-looking podcast, so you need to carefully assess the credibility and experience of the person who made it.

On just about every topic, you will find plenty of people on the Internet who have opinions. The problem with online sources is that just about anyone can create or edit them. That's why the Internet is a good place to start collecting sources, but you need to also collect print and empirical sources to back up what you find.

Finding Print Sources

With such easy access to electronic and online sources, people sometimes forget to look for print sources on their topic. That's a big mistake. Print sources are typically the most reliable forms of information on a topic.

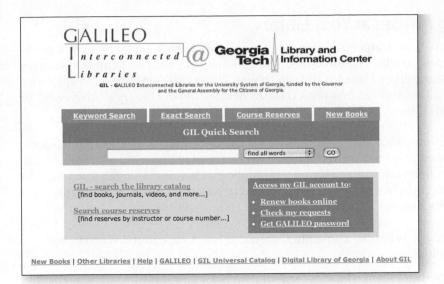

FIGURE 25.4
Searching Your Library's Catalog

Your library's catalog is easy to search online. Here is the Georgia Tech library's Web page for searching its catalog. Finding books is almost as easy as using a search engine to find information on the Internet.

Locating Books at Your Library

Finding useful books on your topic at your campus or local public library is actually rather easy. More than likely, your library's Web site has an online search engine that you can access from any networked computer (Figure 25.4). This search engine will allow you to locate books in the library's catalog. Meanwhile, your campus library will usually have research librarians on staff who can help you find useful print sources. Ask for them at the Information Desk.

Books. The most reliable information on your topic can usually be found in books. Authors and editors of books work closely together to check their facts and gather the best information available. So books tend to be more reliable than Web sites. The downside of books is that they tend to become outdated in fast-changing fields.

Government Publications. The U.S. government produces an amazing amount of printed material on almost any topic you could imagine. Government Web sites, like *The Catalog of U.S. Government Publications,* are a good place to find these sources. Your library probably collects many of these materials because they are usually free or inexpensive.

Reference Materials. The reference section of your library collects helpful reference tools, such as almanacs, directories, encyclopedias, handbooks, and guides. These reference materials can help you find facts, data, and information about people, places, and events.

Right now, entire libraries of books are beings scanned and put online. Out-of-copyright books are appearing in full-text versions as they become available. Meanwhile, online versions of copyrighted books are searchable, allowing you to see excerpts and identify pages on which you can locate the specific information you need.

Finding Articles at Your Library

◉ Watch the Animation on **Researching Periodicals** at **mycomplab.com**

At your library, you can also find articles in academic journals, magazines, and newspapers. These articles can be located using online databases or periodical indexes available through your library's Web site. If your library does not have these databases available online, you can find print versions of them in your library's "Reference" or "Periodicals" areas.

Academic Journals.   Articles in journals are usually written by scientists, professors, consultants, and subject matter experts (SMEs). These journals will offer some of the most exact information available on your topic. To find journal articles, you should start by searching in a *periodical index* related to your topic. Some of the more popular periodical indexes include:

> *ArticleFirst.* Business, humanities, medicine, popular culture, science, and technology
>
> *EBSCOhost.* Academic, business, science, psychology, education, and liberal arts
>
> *ERIC.* Education research and practice
>
> *Humanities Index.* Literature, history, philosophy, languages, and communication
>
> *LexisNexis.* News, business, medical, and legal issues
>
> *OmniFile.* Education, science, humanities, social science, art, biology, and agriculture
>
> *PsycINFO.* Psychology and related fields
>
> *Web of Science.* Physics, chemistry, biology, and life sciences
>
> *IEEE Xplore.* Engineering and science

Magazines.   You can find magazine articles about your topic with the *Readers' Guide to Periodical Literature*, which is likely available through your campus library's Web site. Print versions of the *Readers' Guide* should be available in your library's periodical or reference rooms. Other useful online databases for finding magazine articles include *Find Articles, MagPortal,* and *InfoTrac.*

Newspapers.   For research on current issues or local topics, newspapers often provide the most recent information. At your library or through its Web site, you can use newspaper indexes to search for information. Past editions of newspapers are often stored on microform or microfiche, which can be read on projectors at your campus library. Some of the more popular newspaper indexes include *ProQuest Newspapers, Chronicling America, LexisNexis, New York Times Index,* and *EBSCOhost.*

Doing research at your campus or local public library is almost as easy as doing research on Internet search engines. You will find that the librarians working there can help you locate the materials you need. While at the library, you will likely stumble across useful materials you didn't expect, and the librarians might be able to help you find materials you would never have found on your own.

Using Empirical Sources

Empirical sources include observations, experiments, surveys, and interviews. They are especially helpful for confirming or challenging the claims made in your electronic, online, and print sources. For example, if one of your electronic or online sources claims that "each day, college students watch an average of five hours of television but spend less than one hour on their coursework," you could use observations, interviews, or surveys to confirm or debunk that statement.

Interviewing People

Interviews are a great way to go behind the facts to explore the experiences of experts and regular people. Plus, interviewing others is a good way to collect quotes that you can add to your text. Here are some strategies for interviewing people:

Prepare for the Interview

1. **Do your research.** You need to know as much as possible about your topic before you interview someone about it. If you do not understand the topic before going into the interview, you will waste your own and your interviewee's time by asking simplistic or flawed questions.

2. **Create a list of three to five factual questions.** Your research will probably turn up some facts that you want your interviewee to confirm or challenge.

3. **Create a list of five to ten open-ended questions.** Write down five to ten questions that cannot be answered with a simple "yes" or "no." Your questions should urge the interviewee to offer a detailed explanation or opinion.

4. **Decide how you will record the interview.** Do you want to record the interview as a video or make an audio recording? Or do you want to take written notes? Each of these methods has its pros and cons. For example, audio recording captures the whole conversation, but interviewees are often more guarded about their answers when they are being recorded.

5. **Set up the interview.** The best place to do an interview is at a neutral site, like a classroom, a room in the library, or perhaps a café. The second best place is at the interviewee's office. If necessary, you can do interviews over the phone.

Conduct the Interview

1. **Explain the purpose of your project and how long the interview will take.** Start out by explaining to the interviewee the purpose of your project and how the information from the interview will be used. Also, tell the interviewee how long you expect the interview will take.

2. **Ask permission to record.** If you are recording the interview in any way, ask permission to make the recording. First, ask if recording is all right before you turn on your recorder. Then, once the recorder is on, ask again so you record the interviewee's permission.

3. **Ask your factual questions first.** Warm up the interviewee by asking questions that allow him or her to confirm or deny the facts you have already collected.

4. **Ask your open-ended questions next.** Ask the interviewee about his or her opinions, feelings, experiences, and views about the topic.

5. **Ask if he or she would like to provide any other information.** Often people want to tell you things you did not expect or know about. You can wrap up the interview by asking, "Is there anything else you would like to add about this topic?"

6. **Thank the interviewee.** Don't forget to thank the interviewee for his or her time and information.

Interview Follow-Up

1. **Write down everything you remember.** As soon as possible after the interview, describe the interviewee in your notes and fill out any details you couldn't write down during the interview. Do this even if you recorded the interview.

2. **Get your quotes right.** Clarify any direct quotations you collected from your interviewee. If necessary, you might e-mail your quotes to the interviewee for confirmation.

3. **Back-check the facts.** If the interviewee said something that was new to you or that conflicted with your prior research, use electronic, online, or print sources to back-check the facts. If there is a conflict, you can send an e-mail to the interviewee asking for clarification.

4. **Send a thank-you note.** Usually an e-mail that thanks your interviewee is sufficient, but some people prefer to send a card or brief letter of thanks.

Using an Informal Survey

Informal surveys are especially useful for generating data and gathering the views of many different people on the same questions. Many free online services, such as *SurveyMonkey* and *Zoomerang,* allow you to create and distribute your own surveys. They will also collect and tabulate the results for you. Here is how to create a useful, though not a scientific, survey:

1. **Identify the population you want to survey.** Some surveys target specific kinds of people (e.g., college students, women from ages 18–22, medical doctors). Others are designed to be filled out by anyone.

2. **Develop your questions.** Create a list of five to ten questions that can be answered quickly. Surveys typically use four basic types of questions: rating scales,

multiple choice, numeric open-ended, and text open-ended. Figure 25.5 shows examples of all four types.

3. **Check your questions for neutrality.** Make sure your questions are as neutral as possible. Don't lead the people you are surveying with biased or slanted questions that fit your own beliefs.

4. **Distribute the survey.** Ask a number of people to complete your survey, and note the kinds of people who agree to do it. Not everyone will be interested in completing your survey, so remember that your results might reflect the views of specific kinds of people.

5. **Tabulate your results.** When your surveys are returned, convert any quantitative responses into data. In written answers, pull out phrases and quotes that seem to reflect how the people you surveyed felt about your topic.

Rating Scales

Going skiing is a good Spring Break activity.

Strongly Agree	Agree	Disagree	Strongly Disagree	No Opinion
☐	☐	☐	☐	☐

Multiple Choice

In what region did you spend most of your childhood?

☐ Northeast States   ☐ Mountain Western States
☐ Midwest States   ☐ West Coast States
☐ Southern States   ☐ Other

Numeric Open-Ended

How many times have you gone downhill skiing in your life? _____

Text Open-Ended

What do you enjoy most about skiing in Minnesota?

_____
_____
_____
_____

FIGURE 25.5
Types of Survey Questions

Make sure your questions are easy to understand to help your survey takers provide answers quickly and accurately.

Professional surveyors will point out that your informal survey is not objective and that your results are not statistically valid. That's fine, as long as you are not using your survey to make important decisions or support claims about how people really feel. Your informal survey will still give you some helpful information about the opinions of others.

Doing Field Observations

Conducting a field observation can help you generate ideas and confirm facts. Field observations involve watching something closely and taking detailed notes.

1. **Choose an appropriate location (field site).** You want to choose a field site that allows you to see as much as possible, while not making it obvious that you are watching and taking notes. People will typically change their behavior if they think someone is watching them.

2. **Take notes in a two-column format.** A good field note technique is to use two columns to record what you see. On the left side, list the people, things, and events you observed. On the right side, write down how you interpret what you observed.

3. **Use the Five-W and How questions.** Keep notes about the *who, what, where, when, why,* and *how* elements that you observe. Try to include as much detail as possible.

4. **Use your senses.** Take notes about the things you see, hear, smell, touch, and taste while you are observing.

5. **Pay attention to things that are moving or changing.** Take special note of the things that moved or changed while you were observing, and what caused them to do so.

When you are finished taking notes, spend some time interpreting what you observed. Look for patterns in your observations to help you make sense of your field site.

Reliable research involves collecting sources from a variety of electronic, online, print, and empirical sources.

TRIANGULATE Your Sources

Make sure your research plan will allow you to triangulate your sources. Collect electronic, print, and empirical sources that will allow you to confirm or challenge any facts or information you find.

SEARCH Online Sources

Use Internet search engines, listservs, podcasts, and other online sources to collect information on your subject. As you are searching, consider the reliability of each source. A professional-looking Web site does not mean the source is reliable.

FIND Documentaries or Broadcasts about Your Topic

You can download documentaries and broadcasts online. Your library may have documentaries you can borrow as well.

READ Books on Your Topic

You can access many books through your library's online catalog. Books are often the most reliable sources of information.

USE Indexes and Databases to Find Articles

Access indexes and databases through your library's Web site to find articles in academic journals, magazines, and newspapers.

TRY Empirical Methods to Gather Information

You can interview experts, conduct surveys, or do field observations to confirm or challenge the online and print sources you have gathered about your topic.

LOOK for Gaps in Your Information

Each source you find will raise more questions. When you notice gaps, do some more research to fill them.

Talk About This

1. With your group, discuss your plans for triangulating two or three sources for your research project.

2. In a small group, talk about which kinds of sources you believe will be most helpful for your research. Depending on your topic, you will find different kinds of information helpful.

3. How reliable is the Internet as a source of information for your research? With a group in your class, come up with a list of ten ways you could back-check an Internet source.

Try This Out

1. Using your library's Web site, locate at least five books and five articles for your next assignment. Create an annotated bibliography using either MLA or APA citation style. You can learn about how to create an annotated bibliography in Chapter 13 on page 324.

2. Using an Internet search engine, locate ten sources of information on your topic. Try using symbols in the search engine (+, –, "", *) to target your searches and find the most useful information available. Now try the same search with at least one other search engine and compare the results. Write an evaluation in which you discuss the ten best sources you found and how the search engines differed.

3. Choose one of the empirical tools discussed in this chapter (i.e., interview, survey, or field observation). Create the materials you would need to use this tool for your own research. Write a brief memo explaining this empirical tool to your professor and discuss the kinds of results you hope it will yield.

Write This

1. **Learn how professionals do research.** Using the Internet, research how people in your field of study do their own research. In a report or profile, discuss your field's research practices.

2. **Find some suspicious sources.** Locate three to five online sources on your topic that you consider suspicious or misleading. Write a brief report that explains why you consider these electronic sources to be suspicious and how people can determine whether a source on this topic is reliable.

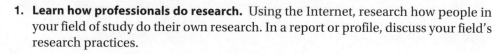

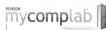

PEARSON
mycomplab

For support in meeting this chapter's objectives, follow this path in MyCompLab: Resources ⟹ Research ⟹ The Research Assignment. Review the Instruction and Multimedia resources about finding sources, then complete the Exercises and click on Gradebook to measure your progress.

26

Quoting, Paraphrasing, and Citing Sources

In this chapter you will learn how to—

- quote, paraphrase, and summarize your sources.
- frame quotes, paraphrases, and summaries in your texts.
- avoid plagiarizing the works and ideas of others.

In college and in the workplace, you need to do more than simply collect sources when you're doing research. You also need to take the next step and engage with your sources, using them to develop your ideas and support your claims. As Chapter 24, "Starting Research," explained, research allows you to extend the work of others and advance your ideas with greater efficiency, clarity, authority, and persuasiveness. This chapter explains how to incorporate that research into your own writing.

When you use sources to inform and support your ideas, your writing has more authority. Also, by engaging with the ideas of others, you enter a larger conversation about those ideas within a particular discipline or profession.

When using a quotation, you are taking a key word, phrase, or passage directly from a source. A direct quote conveys the original text's immediacy and authority while capturing its tone and style.

When paraphrasing, you are explaining a specific idea or describing a specific portion of the source using your own words and your own sentence structures. Typically, your paraphrase will be about the same length as the material you are using from the source. Unlike a direct quotation, paraphrase allows you to clarify or draw attention to a particular issue or point in the original. That way, you can show readers how the author's ideas fit in with your overall work.

When summarizing, you are describing the major ideas of a source in your own words. Often you will summarize not only *what* authors say but *how* they say it. For instance, you might describe their underlying values, their reasoning process, or their evidence. A summary should be much shorter than the original, and it should be structured so that the major points you want to make stand out.

This chapter will show you how to incorporate the ideas and words of others into your work while giving appropriate credit. Chapters 27 and 28 will show you how to cite your sources properly using MLA and APA documentation styles.

Whether something is common knowledge, you should go ahead and cite it.

Quoting

◉ Watch the Animation on **Quoting** at **mycomplab.com**

When quoting an author or speaker, you are importing their exact words into your document and placing quotation marks around those words. It sounds pretty easy, but you can confuse your readers or even get yourself in trouble if you don't properly incorporate and cite the words of others. In some cases, you could be accused of plagiarism. Here are some ways to quote properly.

Brief Quotations

A brief quotation takes a word, phrase, or sentence directly from an original source. Always introduce and give some background on quotations: Do not expect a quotation to make your point by itself.

Words. If an author uses a word in a unique way, you can put quotes around it in your own text. After you tell your reader where the word comes from, you don't need to continue putting it inside quotation marks.

> **Acceptable quotation:** Using Gladwell's terms, some important differences exist between "explicit" learning and "collateral" learning (36).

> **Unacceptable quotation:** Using Gladwell's terms, some important differences exist between explicit learning and collateral learning (36).

Phrases. If you want to use a whole phrase from a source, you need to put quotation marks around it. Then weave the quote into a sentence, making sure it flows with the rest of your writing.

> **Acceptable quotation:** Tomorrow's educators need to understand the distinction between, as Gladwell puts it, "two very different kinds of learning" (36).

> **Unacceptable quotation:** Tomorrow's educators need to understand the distinction between, as Gladwell puts it, two very different kinds of learning (36).

Sentences. You can also bring entire sentences from another source into your document. Use a *signal phrase* (e.g., "As Gladwell argues,") or a colon to indicate that you are quoting a whole sentence.

Acceptable quotation: As Gladwell argues, "Meta-analysis of hundreds of studies done on the effects of homework shows that the evidence supporting the practice is, at best, modest" (36).

Unacceptable quotation: Meta-analysis of hundreds of studies done on the effects of homework shows that the evidence supporting the practice is, at best, modest, according to Gladwell.

Acceptable quotation using a colon: Gladwell summarizes the research simply: "Meta-analysis of hundreds of studies done on the effects of homework shows that the evidence supporting the practice is, at best, modest" (36).

Unacceptable quotation using a colon: Gladwell summarizes the research simply: Meta-analysis of hundreds of studies done on the effects of homework shows that the evidence supporting the practice is, at best, modest.

Long Quotations

Occasionally, you may need to quote a source at length. A quote longer than four lines should be formatted as a *block quote*. A block quote indents the entire quotation to separate it from your normal text. No quotation marks are used, and the citation appears at the end of the quote, outside the final punctuation.

A child is unlikely to acquire collateral learning through books or studying for the SAT exams, Gladwell explains. They do acquire it through play:

> The point is that books and video games represent two very different kinds of learning. When you read a biology textbook, the content of what you read is what matters. Reading is a form of explicit learning. When you play a video game, the value is in how it makes you think. Video games are an example of collateral learning, which is no less important. ("Brain" 2)

Block quote.

In asserting that collateral learning "is no less important" than explicit learning, Gladwell implies that American education may be producing students who are imbalanced—with too much content knowledge and too little facility in dealing with unstructured situations, the kinds of situations that a person is likely to face every day of his or her working life.

Author explains what the quote means.

Use block quotes only when the original quotation cannot be paraphrased and must be preserved in its full length. Don't expect a long quotation to make your point for you. Instead, use the quote to support the point you are making.

Paraphrasing and Summarizing

When paraphrasing or summarizing, you are putting someone else's ideas into your own words. In some situations, using a paraphrase or summary is preferable to using a quote. Using too many quotations can make a text look choppy and might lead the reader to think that you are just stitching together other people's words. Paraphrasing allows you to maintain the tone and flow of your writing.

There are three main differences between a summary and a paraphrase:

- A summary often covers the entire content of the source, while a paraphrase handles only a portion of it.

- A summary organizes the source's main ideas in a way that may differ from the source's organization. A paraphrase usually follows the organization of the original.

- A summary is shorter than the original, while a paraphrase is sometimes about the same length or a little shorter.

Figure 26.1 includes a source text that we will be using to discuss paraphrasing and summarizing in the remainder of this chapter.

Paraphrasing

👁 Watch the Animation on **Paraphrasing** at **mycomplab.com**

The goal of paraphrasing is to explain and describe a portion of the source's text in your own words. A paraphrase is usually about the same length or a little shorter than the material being paraphrased. For example, the following acceptable and unacceptable paraphrases explain Gladwell's distinction between "explicit" and "collateral" learning.

Acceptable Paraphrase

Gladwell explains that we can think of intelligence (or "smart," as he calls it) as having two related but distinct dimensions (36). On the one hand, there is the intelligence dimension we associate with storing, accessing, and reproducing information and with the ability to solve certain kinds of problems. This is the kind of intelligence a person gets from reading books and, generally, from school—what Gladwell calls "explicit" learning. Then there's another kind of intelligence that we get through "collateral" learning. When people develop this kind of intelligence, they have the practical know-how needed to enter a confusing, complex, chaotic situation and quickly and perhaps intuitively develop a hierarchy of what needs to be done, how it should be done, and when it should be done. Both kinds of intelligence are important, Gladwell assures us, but we probably need to think long and hard about the "right balance" between them.

In this acceptable paraphrase, the writer used primarily her own words. When she used exact words from Gladwell's article, she placed them inside quotations. Now let's look at a paraphrase that is too close to the original source:

Unacceptable Paraphrase

Gladwell explains that being smart requires two kinds of thinking. When a person reads a textbook, he or she is engaging in explicit learning. Here the crystallized knowledge that comes from the content of what you read is what

FIGURE 26.1
Source Text

This excerpt from Malcolm Gladwell's Outliers *will be used in this chapter to demonstrate paraphrasing and summarizing.*

The point is that books and video games represent two very different kinds of learning. When you read a biology textbook, the content of what you read is what matters. Reading is a form of explicit learning. When you play a video game, the value is in how it makes you think. Video games are an example of collateral learning, which is no less important.

Being "smart" involves facility in both kinds of thinking—the kind of fluid problem solving that matters in things like video games and I.Q. tests, but also the kind of crystallized knowledge that comes from explicit learning. If Johnson's book has a flaw, it is that he sometimes speaks of our culture being "smarter" when he's really referring just to that fluid problem-solving facility. When it comes to the other kind of intelligence, it is not clear at all what kind of progress we are making, as anyone who has read, say, the Gettysburg Address alongside any Presidential speech from the past twenty years can attest. The real question is what the right balance of these two forms of intelligence might look like. *Everything Bad Is Good for You* doesn't answer that question. But Johnson does something nearly as important, which is to remind us that we shouldn't fall into the trap of thinking that explicit learning is the only kind of learning that matters.

One of the ongoing debates in the educational community, similarly, is over the value of homework. Meta-analysis of hundreds of studies done on the effects of homework shows that the evidence supporting the practice is, at best, modest. Homework seems to be most useful in high school and for subjects like math. At the elementary-school level, homework seems to be of marginal or no academic value. Its effect on discipline and personal responsibility is unproved. And the causal relation between high-school homework and achievement is unclear: it hasn't been firmly established whether spending more time on homework in high school makes you a better student or whether better students, finding homework more pleasurable, spend more time doing it. So why, as a society, are we so enamored of homework? Perhaps because we have so little faith in the value of the things that children would otherwise be doing with their time. They could go out for a walk, and get some exercise; they could spend time with their peers, and reap the rewards of friendship. Or, Johnson suggests, they could be playing a video game, and giving their minds a rigorous workout.

matters. Playing video games is an example of collateral learning. Here the value lies in how the game makes you think and results in adaptable problem-solving skills. Although many people think that explicit learning is the only kind that matters, both kinds are important (36).

The highlighted words and phrases are taken directly from Gladwell's article. Even though the writer cites the source many words are lifted directly without quotation or attribution. If the writer felt it was important to use these exact words and phrases, she should have placed them inside quotation marks.

When paraphrasing, don't allow your own voice to be overwhelmed by your source's tone or voice. Notice how the unacceptable paraphrase has almost the same voice as the original source. In the acceptable paraphrase, the writer's voice comes through clearly. Her paraphrase is accurate even as she uses her own words.

Summarizing

Watch the Animation on **Summarizing** at mycomplab.com

When you summarize a source, you are capturing its principal idea or ideas. A summary often explains the source's structure; its tone, angle, or thesis; its style; its underlying values; or the persuasive strategies it uses to drive home its points. In the following summaries, the writers address the main idea in Gladwell's review: the right balance between "explicit" and "collateral" learning.

Acceptable Paragraph-Length Summary

In the final portion of "Brain Candy," Gladwell accepts Johnson's argument that video games can help develop valuable capacities and extends it further, suggesting that we overvalue "explicit" learning and undervalue "collateral" learning. But the real issue, Gladwell tells us, is not whether Americans are getting better at collateral learning or whether collateral learning is important. "The real question," asserts Gladwell, "is what the right balance of these two forms of intelligence might look like" (36). We need to discuss this question, Gladwell suggests, as a nation because many of the decision makers in education seem to think that explicit learning is all that matters without a healthy debate. We have failed to acknowledge, Gladwell reminds us, that play also results in an important kind of intelligence.

Notice how this summary focuses on an explicit point and makes it prominent.

An unacceptable summary usually relies too much on the wording of the original text, and it often does not prioritize the most important points in the source text.

Unacceptable Summary

In the final portion of "Brain Candy," Gladwell accepts Johnson's argument that playing video games is valuable because of how it makes you think and extends it further, asking what the right balance between these two forms of intelligence would look like. Gladwell explains that books and video games deliver two very different kinds of learning (36). When you read, it's the content that matters. Reading is a form of explicit learning. Playing a video game is valuable because of the way it makes you think. Collateral learning is no less important than explicit learning. But the real question, Gladwell tells us, is figuring out the right balance of these two forms of intelligence. We need to discuss this question, Gladwell suggests, as a nation because many of the decision makers in education seem to be proceeding as if explicit learning is all that matters without a healthy debate. For example, a number of elementary schools have eliminated recess and replaced it with math or English (36). They have also increased the amount of homework, even though nobody knows whether spending more time on homework in high school makes you a better student or whether better students spend more time on their homework. Gladwell concludes that as a society, we are so enamored of homework because we do not understand the value of the things that children would otherwise be doing with their time. This is the triumph of the explicit over the collateral.

The highlighted phrases in the unacceptable summary show where the writer uses almost the same wording as the original text. This is called "patchwriting," which writing scholar Rebecca Moore Howard defines as "copying from a source text and then deleting some words, altering grammatical structures, or plugging in one synonym for another" (xvii). Patchwriting is a form of plagiarism and is discussed later in this chapter.

Framing Quotes, Paraphrases, and Summaries

Your readers need to easily see the boundaries between your work and the material you are taking from your sources. To help them identify these boundaries, you should properly frame your quotations, paraphrases, and summaries by using signal phrases, and citations, and by making connections to your own ideas (Figure 26.2).

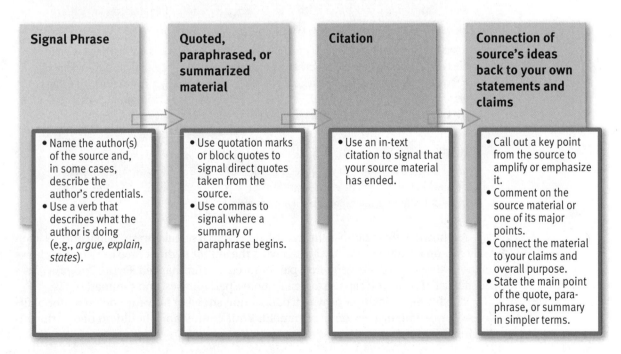

Signal Phrase
- Name the author(s) of the source and, in some cases, describe the author's credentials.
- Use a verb that describes what the author is doing (e.g., *argue*, *explain*, *states*).

Quoted, paraphrased, or summarized material
- Use quotation marks or block quotes to signal direct quotes taken from the source.
- Use commas to signal where a summary or paraphrase begins.

Citation
- Use an in-text citation to signal that your source material has ended.

Connection of source's ideas back to your own statements and claims
- Call out a key point from the source to amplify or emphasize it.
- Comment on the source material or one of its major points.
- Connect the material to your claims and overall purpose.
- State the main point of the quote, paraphrase, or summary in simpler terms.

FIGURE 26.2 Framing Material from a Source

Material taken from a source should be clearly framed with a signal phrase, a citation, and a connection to your own statements and claims.

Signal Phrase. A signal phrase indicates where the source material came from. The words "as" and "in" are often at the heart of a signal phrase (e.g., "As Gladwell argues," "In his article, 'Brain Candy,' Gladwell states").

Direct Quotation. Material quoted directly from your source should be separated from your own words with commas, quotation marks, and other punctuation to indicate which words came directly from the source and which are your own.

Citation. A citation allows readers to find the exact page or Web site of the source. In MLA or APA documentation style, an in-text citation is used to cite the source. In other documentation styles, you might use a footnote or endnote.

Connection. When you connect the source's ideas to your ideas, you will make it clear how the source material fits in with your own statements and claims.

Figure 26.2 color codes these features. The following examples use these colors to highlight signal phrases, source material, citations, and connections.

> As Malcolm Gladwell reminds us, many American schools have eliminated recess in favor of more math and language studies, favoring "explicit" learning over "collateral" learning ("Brain" 36). This approach is problematic, because it takes away children's opportunities to interact socially and problem-solve, which are critical skills in today's world. [MLA]

> Speculating about why we so firmly believe that homework is critical to academic success, Gladwell suggests, "Perhaps because we have so little faith in the value of the things that children would otherwise be doing with their time" (36). In other words, Gladwell is arguing that we are so fearful of letting children play that we fill up their time with activities like homework that show little benefit. [MLA]

> Studies show that the careers of the future will rely heavily on creativity and spatial recognition, which means people who can think with the right side of their brain will have the advantage (Pink, 2006, p. 65). If so, we need to change our educational system so that we can strengthen our abilities to think with both sides of the brain, not just the left side. [APA]

As shown in this example, the frame begins with a signal phrase. Signal phrases typically rely on an action verb that signals what the author of the source is trying to achieve in the material that is being quoted, paraphrased, or summarized. Figure 26.3 provides a helpful list of verbs you can use to signal quotes, paraphrases, and summaries.

The frame typically ends with a connection showing how the source material fits into your overall discussion or argument. Your connection should do one of the following things for your readers:

- Call out a key point from the source to amplify or emphasize it.

- Expand on the source material or one of its major points.

accepts	accuses	acknowledges
adds	admits	advises
agrees	alleges	allows
analyzes	announces	answers
argues	asks	asserts
believes	charges	claims
comments	compares	complains
concedes	concludes	confirms
considers	contends	countercharges
criticizes	declares	demonstrates
denies	describes	disagrees
discusses	disputes	emphasizes
explains	expresses	finds
grants	holds	illustrates
implies	insists	interprets
maintains	notes	objects
observes	offers	point outs
proclaims	proposes	provides
quarrels	reacts	reasons
refutes	rejects	remarks
replies	reports	responds
reveals	shows	states
suggests	supports	thinks
urges	writes	

FIGURE 26.3
Verbs for Signal Phrases

Use verbs like these to introduce quotations, paraphrases, and summaries. You can also use them in signal phrases.

- Connect the source material to your claims and overall purpose.

- Rephrase the main point of the source material in simpler terms.

When handled properly, framing allows you to clearly signal the boundaries between your source's ideas and your ideas.

Avoiding Plagiarism

The Council of Writing Program Administrators defines plagiarism this way:

> **In an instructional setting, plagiarism occurs when a writer deliberately uses someone else's language, ideas, or other original (not common-knowledge) material without acknowledging its source.**

In college, plagiarism is a form of academic dishonesty, and it can lead to a failing grade on an assignment or even for the class. In the workplace, plagiarism is a form of copyright infringement in which one person illegally takes the ideas or words of someone else without that person's permission. Copyright infringement can lead to costly lawsuits and the firing of any employee who commits it.

Watch the Animation on **Avoiding Plagiarism** at mycomplab.com

Plagiarism is not always intentional. Sometimes writers forget to copy down their sources in their notes. Even accidental plagiarism may result in serious trouble with your professors, your university, or your employer. So it is crucial that you understand the kinds of plagiarism and learn to avoid them.

Academic Dishonesty

The most obvious form of plagiarism occurs when someone hands in work that is not his or her own. Everyone, including your professors, knows about "cheater Web sites" that sell or give away college papers. Everyone also knows about "borrowing" someone else's paper. And everyone knows it's easy to cut and paste a sample paper from the Internet. (If you found it, chances are good your professor will find it, too.)

And yet, some students foolishly try to get away with these kinds of plagiarism. Your professors aren't naive. If you hand in a paper that's not your own, you're being dishonest. When students get caught, they often fail the class, which looks bad on their transcripts and is difficult to explain to future employers or graduate school admissions committees. They might even be expelled. This kind of plagiarism is clearly intentional, and few people have sympathy for someone who is so obviously cheating.

Ironically, people who buy, download, or copy papers often spend more time and energy finding the paper and worrying about the consequences of getting caught than they would if they just wrote the paper in the first place.

Patchwriting

Patchwriting was mentioned earlier in this chapter. Usually, patchwriting happens when someone cuts and pastes one or more paragraphs from a Web page or other source and then alters words and sentences to make them look like his or her own.

When done intentionally, patchwriting is clearly a form of academic dishonesty, because the writer is presenting someone else's ideas as his or her own without attribution. Some students have even tried to patchwrite an entire paper. They cut and paste several paragraphs from one source or a variety of sources. Then they add some transitions and a few of their own sentences, while altering the words and sentences from the original. As a result, little of the paper is based on their own ideas. This kind of dishonesty usually leads to a failing grade on the paper and for the class.

Patchwriting can happen unintentionally, especially when a writer copies sentences or paragraphs from a source and then forgets the material was taken from somewhere else. The writer might even cite the source, not realizing that the text they included is too close to the original. Unfortunately, your professor cannot tell whether you were intentionally being dishonest or just made an honest mistake.

To avoid patchwriting, carefully identify your sources in your notes. Clearly mark any quotes taken from your sources with quotation marks, brackets, or some other kind of distinguishing mark. Then, when you use these materials in your document, make sure you quote, paraphrase, summarize, and cite them properly.

Ideas and Words Taken without Attribution

In college and in the workplace, you will often need to use the exact ideas, words, phrases, or sentences from a source. When you do this, *you must correctly quote and cite that source.* That is, you must place those words inside quotation marks (or block quote them) and provide a citation that tells your reader precisely where you got those words. If you use ideas, words, phrases, or sentences without attribution, you could be charged with academic dishonesty or copyright infringement.

Sometimes it is difficult to determine whether someone else owns the ideas that you are using. If you aren't sure, cite the source. Citing a source will only add support to your work, and it will help you avoid being accused of plagiarism.

The Real Problem with Plagiarism

No doubt, plagiarism is easier than ever with the Internet. It's also easier than ever to catch someone who is plagiarizing. Your professors can use *Google* too, and they have access to plagiarism-checking Web sites like *Turnitin*. They often have access to collections of prior papers that were handed in before.

If you plagiarize, there is a good chance you will get caught. But the real problem with plagiarism is that you are cheating yourself. You're probably paying thousands of dollars for your education. Cheating robs you of the chance to strengthen your communication skills and prepare for advanced courses and your career.

Of course, there is pressure to do well in your classes, and you don't always have enough time to do everything you want. In the end, though, doing your own work will help you improve and strengthen your mind and abilities. Don't miss that opportunity.

Here are some helpful guidelines for quoting, paraphrasing, and summarizing sources and avoiding plagiarism.

DECIDE What to Quote, Paraphrase, or Summarize

Ask yourself what kinds of materials should be quoted, summarized, or paraphrased in your document. To guide your decision, keep your readers' needs and the genre in mind.

INCLUDE Short Quotations and Cite Them Properly

Any words, phrases, or sentences should be placed in quotation marks and cited with MLA or APA documentation style.

USE Block Quotes for Longer Quotations

If a quote is longer than three lines or contains more than one sentence, set it off in a block quote. A block quote indents the quotation to separate it from the normal text.

PARAPHRASE Important Sources and Cite Them

A paraphrase puts someone else's ideas into your own words. Paraphrases are usually about the same length or a little shorter than the original. Make sure you do not use words from the original text unless you quote them. Paraphrases need to be cited.

SUMMARIZE Sources with Important Ideas and Cite Them

A summary captures the principal ideas of a source by summarizing the entire work or a major portion of it. Summaries are shorter than paraphrases, and they usually present the source's main ideas from most important to least important.

USE Signal Phrases and Verbs to Mark Quotes, Paraphrases, and Summaries

A *signal phrase* uses words like "as" or "in" to highlight for the readers where a source is being referenced. A variety of *signal verbs* can also highlight the beginning of a quote, paraphrase, or summary.

DON'T Plagiarize Intentionally or Unintentionally

Plagiarism, whether intentional or unintentional, is a form of academic dishonesty. It involves using someone else's words or ideas without giving that person proper credit. Intentional plagiarism usually leads to a failing grade for the paper and the course. Don't do it.

1. What kinds of research have you done in the past, and how did you incorporate sources into your work? How do you think research in college will be handled differently?

2. Look at the example of "patchwriting" on page 496. Discuss how you can avoid patchwriting in your own work.

3. With your group, discuss how professors should keep students from plagiarizing, and what should be done when someone does plagiarize.

Talk
About
This

1. Choose a television commercial and try to paraphrase it and summarize it. How challenging is it to do this accurately?

2. Choose three quotations from a source and practice incorporating them into something you are writing for this class. Be sure to use a signal phrase or signal verb.

3. Choose three paragraphs from a source and purposely create an inappropriate "patchwritten" text. Then transform your patchwritten text into an appropriate paraphrase. As you rewrite the text, pay attention to the kinds of alterations you need to make.

Try
This
Out

1. **Summarize a source.** Choose a source text and write down a single sentence that summarizes the source's main point in your own words. Now write a one-paragraph summary of the source, highlighting its major ideas. Finally, turn your one-paragraph summary into a multiple-paragraph summary that includes quotes and citations.

2. **Explain how to handle plagiarism.** Write a brief position paper in which you discuss how universities should handle plagiarism in the age of the Internet. Offer some ideas about how professors can steer students away from the temptation to plagiarize.

Write
This

mycomplab

For support in meeting this chapter's objectives, follow this path in MyCompLab: Resources ⟹ Research ⟹ The Research Assignment. Review the Instruction and Multimedia resources about integrating sources, then complete the Exercises and click on Gradebook to measure your progress.

27

Using MLA Style

In this chapter you will learn how to—

- use MLA parenthetical citations in your texts.
- create bibliographic entries for a Works Cited list.
- prepare a Works Cited list in MLA style.

odern Language Association (MLA) documentation style helps you to keep track of your sources, while showing your readers where you found the supporting information in your document. MLA style is most commonly used in the humanities (i.e., English, history, philosophy, languages, art history). This style is also used in other scholarly fields because of its flexibility and familiarity.

In the previous chapter, you learned how to quote, paraphrase, and cite your sources. In this chapter, you will learn how to use MLA style to reference your sources and create a list of "Works Cited" at the end of your document. The models of MLA citations shown here are the ones most commonly used in college and in the workplace. If you cannot find a model that fits the source you are trying to cite, you should turn to the *MLA Handbook for Writers of Research Papers*, 7th ed. (2009).

On the Internet, an increasing number of online citation generators are available, or your word-processing software may include one. We recommend using these online tools because they can help you quickly generate MLA-style documentation. However, you should always make sure the generator is following the most up-to-date MLA documentation style. Also, double-check all citations to make sure they were created correctly.

Parenthetical Citations

When citing a source with MLA style, you first need to include a *parenthetical reference*. A parenthetical reference appears in the text of your document, usually at the end of the sentence where the information that you used from another source appears. For example:

Watch the Video on **Parenthetical Citations** at **mycomplab.com**

> Archeologists have shown that wild dogs diverged from wolves about ten thousand years ago (Jones 27).

> For example, in *The Robber Bride*, Atwood depicts the response of second wave feminism to postfeminism (Tolan 46), through the complex interactions of three friends with an aggressive vampire, Zenia, who has recently returned from the dead.

Note: For a key to the color highlighting used here and throughout this chapter, see the bottom of this page.

As shown here, a parenthetical reference includes two important pieces of information: the source's name (usually an author's name), a single space with no comma, and the page number from the source where the information appeared. The first parenthetical reference above signals that the information was taken from page 27 in a work from someone named "Jones." The second parenthetical reference signals that its information can be found on page 46 in a source written by someone named "Tolan."

If readers want to, they can then turn to the "Works Cited" at the end of the document to see the full citation, which will look like this:

> Jones, Steve. *Darwin's Ghost*. New York: Ballantine, 2000. Print.

> Tolan, Fiona. "Sucking the Blood Out of Second Wave Feminism: Postfeminist Vampirism in Margaret Atwood's *The Robber Bride*." *Gothic Studies* 9.2 (2007): 45-57. Print.

The parenthetical reference and the full citation work together. The reference points to the work-cited list, which provides the information needed for locating the source.

When the Author's Name Appears in the Sentence

You don't always need to include the author's name in the parenthetical reference. If you name the author in the sentence, you only need to provide the page number in parentheses. For example:

According to Steve Jones, a genetic scientist, archeologists have shown that wild dogs diverged from wolves about ten thousand years ago (27).

In her recent article, Tolan (46) argues that Atwood's *The Robber Bride* is really an allegory of postfeminism, in which three second-wave feminists are confronted with the anxieties brought about by the postfeminist backlash.

Typically, a parenthetical reference appears at the end of the sentence, but as shown above, it can also appear immediately after the name of the source.

If the first part of your sentence draws information from a source but the remainder of the sentence represents your own thoughts, you should put the reference immediately after the source's material is used. For example:

Glassner argues that naive Americans are victimized by a news media that is engaged in "fear-mongering" and other scare tactics (205), but I believe the American people are able to distinguish between real news and sensationalism.

Citing More Than One Source in the Same Sentence

If you want to cite multiple sources that are basically saying the same thing, you can use one parenthetical reference, separating the sources with semicolons:

George Washington was the only logical choice for President of the United States, because he had the respect of the competing political factions that emerged after the signing of the Treaty of Paris in 1783 (Irving 649; Ellis 375).

If you are citing more than one source in the same sentence but they are making different points, you should put the parenthetical reference as close as possible to the information taken from each source. For example:

Some historians view Cicero as a principled defender of the dying Roman Republic (Grant 29), while others see him as an idealistic statesman who stood helplessly aside as the Republic crumbled (Everett 321).

Citing a Source Multiple Times

In some situations, you will need to cite a source multiple times. If your document continues using a single source, you only need to include the page number in following references as long as no other source comes between them.

New owners often misread the natural signals from their puppy (Monks 139). One common problem is submissive urination in which a puppy shows submission by peeing. Owners often believe the puppy is acting defiantly, but it is really trying to signal submission. So punishing the dog is exactly the wrong thing to do, because it only encourages the puppy to be even more submissive, resulting in even more puddles on the floor (140).

In the example above, the full parenthetical reference is included early in the paragraph. The second reference, which is only a page number, is clearly referring back to the source in the first reference.

However, if another source is cited between two parenthetical references to the same source, the author's name from the first source would need to be repeated in a subsequent reference. For example:

New owners often misread the natural signals from their puppy (Monks 139). One common problem is submissive urination in which a puppy shows submission by peeing. Owners often believe the puppy is acting defiantly, but it is really trying to signal submission (Kerns 12). So punishing the dog is exactly the wrong thing to do, because it only encourages the puppy to be even more submissive, resulting in even more puddles on the floor (Monks 140).

In the example above, the author includes "Monks" in the last sentence's reference because the reference "(Kerns 12)" appears between the two references to the source written by Monks.

Other Parenthetical References

A wide variety of parenthetical references are possible. Figure 27.1 shows models of some common parenthetical references. Choose the one that best fits your source. If none of these models fits the source you are trying to cite, you can use combinations of these models. If you still cannot figure it out, turn to the *MLA Handbook* for help.

Preparing the List of Works Cited

Your list of Works Cited appears at the end of your document. In this list, you should include full citations for all the sources you cite. A typical entry includes features like the name of the author, the name of the text, the place where it was published, the medium in which it was published, and the date it was published. Here are three entries from three types of sources:

Chew, Robin. "Charles Darwin, Naturalist, 1809-1882." *Lucidcafe* 1 Feb. 2008. Web. 8 Feb. 2009.

Author Title Publication Online Source

FIGURE 27.1
Types of MLA
Parenthetical
References

Type of Source	Example Parenthetical Reference
Single author	(Gerns 12)
Single author, multiple pages	(Barnes 5-9) or (Barnes 34, 121) *The hyphen signals a range of pages. The comma suggests similar information can be found on two different pages.*
Two authors	(Hammonds and Gupta 203)
Three authors	(Gym, Hanson, and Williams 845)
More than three authors	*First reference:* (Wu, Gyno, Young, and Reims 924) *Subsequent references:* (Wu et al. 924)
Multiple sources in same reference	(Yu 34; Thames and Cain 98; Young, Morales, and Cato 23) *The semicolon divides the sources.*
Two or more works by the same author	(Tufte, *Visual* 25) and (Tufte, "Powerpoint" 9) *The first prominent word in the source's title is used. Italics signals a book, while quotation marks signal an article.*
Different authors with the same last name	(M. Smith 54) and (A. Smith 34) *The first letter abbreviates each author's first name.*
Corporate author	(NASA 12) or (Amer. Beef Assn. 232) *Abbreviate as much of the corporate name as possible. Periods are needed with abbreviations that are not known acronyms.*
No author for book	(*Handling* 45) *Use the first prominent word in the title and put it in italics.*
No author for journal article or newspaper article	("Genomics" 23) *Use the first prominent word in the title and put it in quotation marks.*
No author for newspaper article	("Recession" A4) *The letter "A" is the section of the newspaper and the number is the page.*
Quoted in another source	(qtd. in Franks 94) *"qtd." stands for "quoted."*

continued

Type of Source	Example Parenthetical Reference
Web page or other document with no pagination	(Reynolds, par. 3) *"par." stands for paragraph, as counted down from the top of the page. The comma separates the name from the paragraph number.*
Web page or other document with no author and no pagination	("Friendly," par. 7) *Put the first prominent word in the title in quotes, with "par." standing for the paragraph, as counted down from the top of the page. The comma separates the title from the paragraph number.*

FIGURE 27.1
Types of MLA Parenthetical References
(continued)

Not all possible parenthetical references are shown here. If you have a unique source that doesn't fit these examples, you can usually figure out how to cite it by combining the above reference models. If you still cannot figure out how to cite your source, turn to the *MLA Handbook* for help.

Poresky, Louise. "Cather and Woolf in Dialogue: The Professor's House to the Light House." *Papers on Language and Literature* 44.1 (2008): 67-86. Print.

Shreve, Porter. *When the White House Was Ours*. Boston: Houghton Mifflin, 2008. Print.

Only sources you reference in your document should appear in your Works Cited. The works-cited list is not a bibliography of all the sources you found.

List the entries in alphabetical order by the authors' last names. When the author's name is not known, alphabetize by the first prominent word in its title. Ignore words like *The, A,* or *An* if they are the first word in the title.

Including More Than One Source from an Author

If your works-cited list includes two or more sources from the same author, only the first entry should include the author's name. Afterward, entries should use three hyphens instead of the name. Multiple entries from one author should be alphabetized by the first prominent words in the titles.

Murphy, James. *Rhetoric in the Middle Ages: A History of Rhetorical Theory from Saint Augustine to the Renaissance*. Berkeley, CA: U of California P, 1974. Print.

---. *A Short History of Writing Instruction: From Ancient Greece to Modern America*. 2nd ed. Mahwah, NJ: Erlbaum, 2001. Print.

--- ed. *Three Medieval Rhetorical Arts*. Berkeley, CA: U of California P, 1971. Print.

Author Title Publication Online Source

Torres 12

Works Cited

Barber, Paul. *Vampires, Burial, and Death*. New Haven, NJ: Yale UP, 1989.
Print.

Bluestein, Gene. *Poplore: Folk and Pop in American Culture*. Amherst:
U of Massachusetts P, 1994. Print.

Keyworth, Donald. "Was the Vampire of the Eighteenth Century a
Unique Type of Undead Corpse?" *Folklore* 117.3 (2006): 1-16. Print.

Todorova, Maria. *Imagining the Balkans*. Oxford: Oxford UP, 1996. Print.

FIGURE 27.2 Formatting a List of Works Cited
MLA style requires that the heading "Works Cited" be centered on the page. The margins should be one inch on all sides. The entries should be double-spaced.

Murphy, James, Richard Katula, Forbes Hill, and Donovan Ochs. *A Synoptic History of Classical Rhetoric*. 3rd ed. Mahwah, NJ: Erlbaum, 2003. Print.

As shown above, if a single author is also listed as a coauthor for another entry, you should include the full name again without the three hyphens.

Formatting a List of Works Cited

Start the works-cited list on a new page with the centered heading "Works Cited" at the top (Figure 27.2). Entries are double-spaced, in hanging indent format, which means the first line of each entry is not indented, but the rest are indented a half inch.

In professional texts, however, your works-cited list should match the design of your document. The "Works Cited" heading should be consistent with other headings. If you are single-spacing the rest of your document, the works-cited list should be single-spaced, too, perhaps with spaces between entries.

Citing Sources in the List of Works Cited

Watch the Animation on **Citing Sources using MLA** at mycomplab.com

The following examples of MLA citations are based on the guidelines in the *MLA Handbook for Writers of Research Papers* (7th ed., 2009). This list is not comprehensive. However, we have included models of the most common kinds of entries in a works-cited list. You can use these examples as models for your own citations. If you do not find a model for a source, you should turn to the *MLA Handbook*.

MLA List of Works Cited

Books and Other Nonperiodical Publications

1. Book, One Author
2. Book, Two Authors
3. Book, Three Authors
4. Book, Four or More Authors
5. Book, Corporate or Organization Author
6. Book, Edited Collection
7. Book, Translated
8. Book, Author Unknown
9. Book, Second Edition or Beyond
10. Book, in Electronic Form
11. Document, Government Publication
12. Document, Pamphlet
13. Foreword, Introduction, Preface, or Afterword
14. Sacred Text
15. Dissertation, Unpublished

Journals, Magazines, and Other Periodical Publications

16. Article, Journal with Volume and Issue Numbers
17. Article, Journal with Issue Number Only
18. Article, Edited Book
19. Article, Magazine
20. Article, Newspaper
21. Article, Author Unknown

22. Article, CD-ROM
23. Editorial
24. Letter to the Editor
25. Review

Web Publications

26. Web Site, Author Known
27. Web Site, Corporate Author
28. Web Site, Author Unknown
29. Article from an Online Periodical
30. Article from an Online Scholarly Journal
31. Periodical Article Accessed through a Database (Web)
32. Blog Posting
33. Wiki Entry
34. Podcast

Other Kinds of Sources

35. Film or Video Recording
36. Television or Radio Program
37. Song or Audio Recording
38. CD-ROM
39. Personal Correspondence, E-Mail, or Interview
40. Work of Art
41. Print Advertisement
42. Commercial
43. Speech, Lecture, or Reading
44. Map
45. Cartoon

Citing Books and Other Nonperiodical Publications

Books and other nonperiodical publications are perhaps the easiest to list in the works-cited list. A book citation will have some of the following features:

1. Name of the author, corporation, or editor with last name first (add "ed." or "eds." if the work is listed by the name of the editor)

2. Title of the work

3. City where the work was published

4. Publisher

5. Year of publication

6. Medium of publication

①   ②   ③   ④   ⑤   ⑥

Author. *Title.* City of publication: Publisher, year of publication. Medium of publication.

1. Book, One Author

Ambrose, Stephen. *Band of Brothers.* 3rd ed. New York: Simon, 2001. Print.

2. Book, Two Authors

Brett, Michael, and Elizabeth Fentress. *The Berbers: The Peoples of Africa.* Malden: Wiley-Blackwell, 1996. Print.

3. Book, Three Authors

Fellman, Michael, Daniel E. Sutherland, and Lesley J. Gordon. *This Terrible War: The Civil War and Its Aftermath.* New York: Longman, 2007. Print.

4. Book, Four or More Authors

Huss, Bernard, et al. *The Unknown Socrates.* New York: Bolchazy-Carducci, 2002. Print.

5. Book, Corporate or Organization Author

American Psychiatric Association. *Diagnostic and Statistical Manual of Mental Disorders.* 4th ed. Washington: APA, 1994. Print.

6. Book, Edited Collection

Mueller-Vollmer, Kurt, ed. *The Hermeneutics Reader.* New York: Continuum, 1990. Print.

7. Book, Translated

Dostoevsky, Fyodor. *Notes from Underground.* 2nd ed. Trans. Michael Katz. New York: Norton, 2001. Print.

8. Book, Author Unknown

Physical Science. New York: McGraw, 1998. Print.

9. Book, Second Edition or Beyond

Kottak, Conrad. *Anthropology: The Exploration of Human Diversity*. 12th ed. New York: McGraw, 2008. Print.

10. Book, in Electronic Form

Darwin, Charles. *On the Various Contrivances by Which British and Foreign Orchids Are Fertilised by Insects*. London: Murray, 1862. Web. 1 Jan. 2008.

11. Document, Government Publication

Arguin, Paul M., Phyllis E. Kozarsky, and Ava W. Navin, eds. *Health Information for International Travel 2007-2008: The Yellow Book*. St. Louis: Centers for Disease Control, 2007. Print.

12. Document, Pamphlet

Historians Against the War. *Torture, American Style*. Somerville: Historians Against the War, 2006. Print.

13. Foreword, Introduction, Preface, or Afterword

Parker, Hershel. Foreword. *Moby Dick*. By Herman Melville. Evanston: Northwestern UP, 2001. xiii-xvi. Print.

14. Sacred Text

The New Oxford Annotated Bible. 3rd ed. New York: Oxford UP, 2001. Print.

15. Dissertation, Unpublished

Charlap, Marie-Helene. "Once with Women, Now with Women: A Qualitative Study of Identity." Diss. New York U, 2008. Print.

Citing Journals, Magazines, and Other Periodicals

Citations for periodicals, such as journals, magazines, and other regularly published documents, need to include additional information. The title of the article should appear in quotation marks. The volume number and issue number appear after the title of the periodical. The page numbers follow the year the work was published.

A citation for a journal, magazine, or other periodical publication includes the following features:

1. Name of the author, corporation, or editor with last name first

2. Title of the work in quotation marks

3. Name of the periodical in italics

4. Volume number and issue number

5. Date of publication (year for scholarly journal; day, month, year for other periodicals)

6. Range of page numbers for whole article

7. The medium in which the work was published ("Print" for a journal, periodical, or newspaper)

①　　　　②　　　　③　　　　　④　　　　⑤　　　　⑥
Author. "Article Title." *Journal Title* Date or Volume.Issue (Year): page numbers.

⑦
Medium of publication.

16. Article, Journal with Volume and Issue Numbers

Jovanovic, Franck. "The Construction of the Canonical History of Financial Economics." *History of Political Economy* 40.2 (2008): 213-42. Print.

17. Article, Journal with Issue Number Only

Lee, Christopher, "Enacting the Asian Canadian." *Canadian Literature* 199 (2008): 28-44. Print.

18. Article, Edited Book

Goodheart, George. "Innate Intelligence Is the Healer." *Healers on Healing*. Ed. Richard Carlson and Benjamin Shield. New York: Putnam, 1989. 53-57. Print.

19. Article, Magazine

Zakaria, Fareed. "Obama's Vietnam: How to Salvage Afghanistan." *Newsweek* 9 Feb. 2009: 36-37. Print.

20. Article, Newspaper

Herszenhorn, David. "Bipartisan Push to Trim Size of Stimulus Plan." *New York Times* 5 Feb. 2009, New York ed.: A1. Print.

21. Article, Author Unknown

"The Big Chill Leaves Bruises." *Albuquerque Tribune* 17 Jan. 2004: A4. Print.

22. Article, CD-ROM

Hanford, Peter. "Locating the Right Job for You." *The Electronic Job Finder*. San
Francisco: Career Masters, 2001. CD.

23. Editorial

"A Vital Boost for Education." Editorial. *New York Times* 4 Feb. 2009, New York ed.:
A30. Print.

24. Letter to the Editor

Bertin, Joan. Letter. *New York Times* 6 Feb. 2009, New York ed.: A22. Print.

25. Review

Leonhardt, David. "Chance and Circumstance." Rev. of *Outliers,* by Malcolm Gladwell.
New York Times 30 Nov. 2008, New York ed.: BR9. Print.

Citing Web Publications

In the most recent update of the *MLA Handbook* (2009), Web addresses (URLs) have
been removed. When possible, you should include two dates: the date the material
appeared on the Internet, and the date you accessed the material. If you cannot find
the first date, then put *n.d.* for "no date." If you cannot find the publisher of the information, put *n.p.* for "no publisher."

Watch the Animation
on **Citing Websites**
at **mycomplab.com**

26. Web Site, Author Known

Nagel, Michael. "Biography." *The Official Mark Twain Website*. CMG Solutions, n.d.
Web. 2 Feb. 2009.

27. Web Site, Corporate Author

United States Fish and Wildlife Service. *Arctic National Wildlife Refuge*. Dept. of the
Interior, 12 Sept. 2008. Web. 12 Mar. 2009.

28. Web Site, Author Unknown

"Pentagon Sets Sights on Public Opinion." *MSNBC.com*. Microsoft, 5 Feb. 2009. Web. 6
Feb. 2009.

29. Article from an Online Periodical

Leier, Andrew. "How Martian Winds Make Rocks Walk." *ScienceDaily*. ScienceDaily, 12
Jan. 2009. Web. 4 Feb. 2009.

FIGURE 27.3 CITATION MAP: Citing All or Part of a Web Site

A citation for a Web publication will have some or all of the following features:

① Name of the author, corporation, editor, webmaster with last name first

② Title of the work (in quotation marks if an article; italicized if a stand-alone work)

③ Name of the Web site in italics if different than the title of the Web site

④ Publisher of the Web site. (If not available, use *N.p.* for "no publisher.")

⑤ Date of publication, including day, month, year. (If not available, use *n.d.* for "no date.")

⑥ The medium in which the work was published ("Web" for Web sites)

⑦ Date on which you accessed the Web site

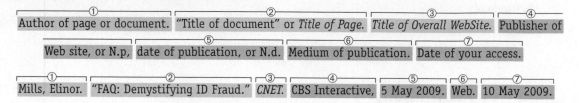

Author of page or document. "Title of document" or *Title of Page*. *Title of Overall WebSite*. Publisher of Web site, or N.p, date of publication, or N.d. Medium of publication. Date of your access.

Mills, Elinor. "FAQ: Demystifying ID Fraud." *CNET*. CBS Interactive, 5 May 2009. Web. 10 May 2009.

③ Name of Web site

② Title of work

① Author

⑤ Date of publication

⑥ Medium of publication

⑦ Date of access

④ Publisher of Web site

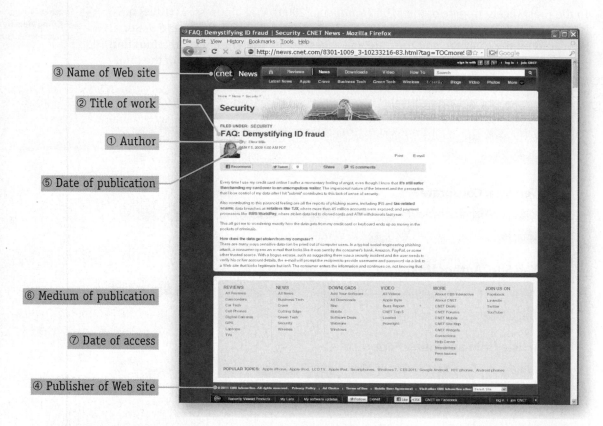

FIGURE 27.4 CITATION MAP: Citing a Scholarly Journal on the Web

A citation for an article from a scholarly journal on the Web includes the following features:

① Name of the author, last name first

② Title of the work in quotation marks

③ Name of the journal in italics

④ Volume number and issue number

⑤ Date of publication (year for scholarly journal)

⑥ Range of page numbers for whole article

⑦ The medium in which the work was published

⑧ Your date of access

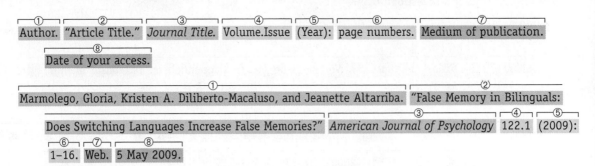

Author. "Article Title." *Journal Title.* Volume.Issue (Year): page numbers. Medium of publication.
Date of your access.

Marmolego, Gloria, Kristen A. Diliberto-Macaluso, and Jeanette Altarriba. "False Memory in Bilinguals: Does Switching Languages Increase False Memories?" *American Journal of Psychology* 122.1 (2009): 1–16. Web. 5 May 2009.

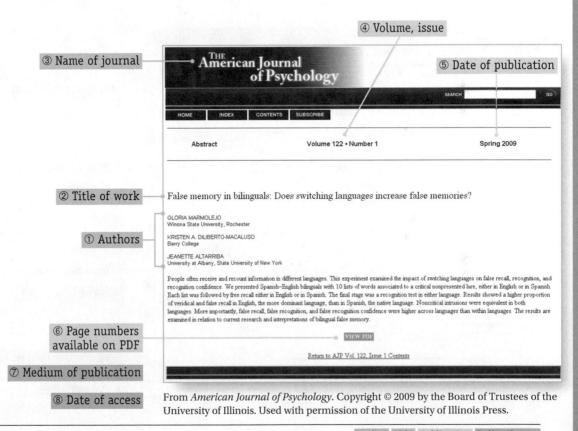

④ Volume, issue

③ Name of journal

⑤ Date of publication

② Title of work

① Authors

⑥ Page numbers available on PDF

⑦ Medium of publication

⑧ Date of access

FIGURE 27.5 CITATION MAP: Citing a Scholarly Journal from a Database

A citation for an article from a scholarly journal accessed through a database includes the following features:

① Name of the author, last name first

② Title of the work in quotation marks

③ Name of the journal in italics

④ Volume number and issue number

⑤ Date of publication (year for scholarly journal)

⑥ Range of page numbers for whole article

⑦ Name of database

⑧ Medium of publication

⑨ Your date of access

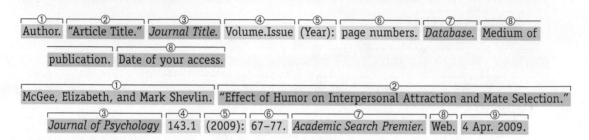

Author. "Article Title." *Journal Title*. Volume.Issue (Year): page numbers. *Database*. Medium of publication. Date of your access.

McGee, Elizabeth, and Mark Shevlin. "Effect of Humor on Interpersonal Attraction and Mate Selection." *Journal of Psychology* 143.1 (2009): 67–77. *Academic Search Premier*. Web. 4 Apr. 2009.

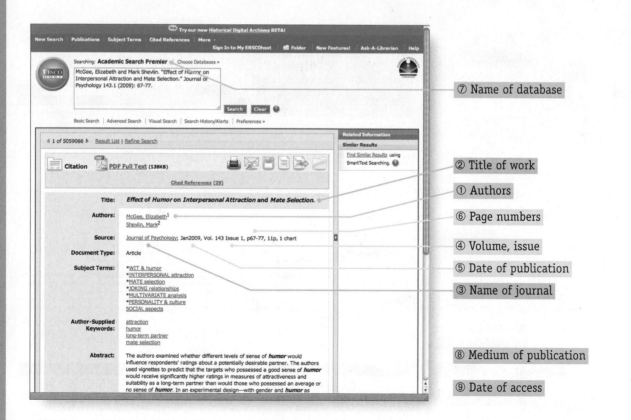

30. Article from an Online Scholarly Journal

Ochiagha, Terri. "The Literary Fantastic in African and English Literature." *CLCWeb*:
   10.4 (2008): n. pag. Web. 5 Feb. 2009.

31. Periodical Article Accessed through a Database (Web)

Sklansky, David. "Police and Democracy." *Michigan Law Review* 103.7 (2005):
   1699-1830. *JSTOR*. Web. 5 Feb. 2009.

32. Blog Posting

Isaacson, Walter. "A Bold Idea for Saving Journalism." *The Huffington Post*.
   HuffingtonPost.com, 5 Feb. 2009. Web. 5 Feb. 2009.

33. Wiki Entry

"Galileo Galilei." *Wikipedia*. Wikimedia, n.d. Web. 5 Feb. 2009.

34. Podcast

"Interview with Neil Gaiman." *Just One More Book*. N.p., 27 Jan. 2009. Web. 3 Feb. 2009.

Citing Other Kinds of Sources

There are many other kinds of sources. Especially for performances, you may choose
to begin a citation with either an artist's name, a director or producer's name, or the
title of the work. Consult the *MLA Handbook* for specific examples.

1. Title of the work (italics for a complete work; quotation marks for a work that is a
   segment, episode, or part of a whole) OR name of a specific performer, director,
   writer, etc. (last name, first name)

2. Title of the program, in italics, if applicable

3. Name of the network that aired or produced the work

4. Call letters and city of the station that aired the work, if available

5. Date of broadcast (day, month, year)

6. The medium of the work (e.g., television, radio, DVD, CD, film)

35. Film or Video Recording

Fiddler on the Roof. Dir. Norman Jewison. Prod. Norman Jewison. The Mirisch
   Production Company, 1971. Film.

Harris, Rosalind, perf. *Fiddler on the Roof*. Dir. Norman Jewison. The Mirisch
   Production Company, 1971. Film.

36. Television or Radio Program

"Destination: The South Pole." Narr. Richard Harris. *All Things Considered.* Natl.
Public Radio. 6 Jan. 2003. Web. 4 Feb. 2004.

37. Song or Audio Recording

Myer, Larry. "Sometimes Alone." *Flatlands.* People's Productions, 1993. CD.

38. CD-ROM

Lilley, Linda, Scott Harrington, and Julie Snyder. *Pharmacology and the Nursing
Process Companion CD.* 5th ed. St. Louis: Mosby, 2007. CD-ROM.

39. Personal Correspondence, E-Mail, or Interview

Schimel, Eric. Personal interview. 12 Dec. 2008.

40. Work of Art

Vermeer, Johannes. *Girl with a Pearl Earring.* N.d. Oil on canvas. Mauritshuis, The
Hague.

41. Print Advertisement

Sprint. Advertisement. *Newsweek.* 9 Feb. 2009. Print.

42. Commercial

Toyota. Advertisement. MSNBC. 5 Feb. 2009. Television.

43. Speech, Lecture, or Reading

Obama, Barack. "Inauguration Address." Capital Building, Washington DC. 21 Jan.
2009. Address.

44. Map

"Japan." Map. *Rand McNally World Atlas.* New York: Rand, 2004. 31. Print.

45. Cartoon

Adams, Scott. "Dilbert." Comic strip. *Journal and Courier* 8 Apr. 2009: C8. Print.

A Student's MLA-Style Research Paper

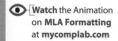
Watch the Animation
on **MLA Formatting**
at **mycomplab.com**

The document shown here uses MLA citation style. You can use this document to
observe how an author uses MLA citation style under real conditions, including parenthetical references and a list of works cited.

Naidus 1

Brian Naidus

Dr. Will Crampton

PCD 3442

6 May 2011

A Whole New World: A Background on the

Life of the Freshwater Shark

The shark has easily become one of the most popular and
recognizable marine species in our culture today. This animal is a
cartilaginous fish of the subclass Selachimorpha, which belongs to the
more notorious class, Chondrichthyes ("Chondrichtyes"). This diverse
group has a plethora of variation and diversity; over 2,000 recorded,
fossilized species. The first sharks were thought to be introduced
between 450 and 420 million years ago, with the earliest known fossil
to be a 400 million year old shark known as Leonodus (Martin,
"Earliest" par. 3). Although the shark had evolved to inhabit almost
strictly marine environments, this species had specialized teeth,
indicating that it may have lived in freshwater habitats. This ancient
species belonged to a family, known as xenacanths, a group of early
freshwater sharks that existed at this time.

Currently, there are a few freshwater species of shark, which
remain mostly under the radar, due to their more popular oceanic
family members (Compagno, Dando, and Folwer 54). The bull shark,
Carcharhinus leucas, is a species that is not only common in warm,
coastal waters, but is also able to tolerate freshwater (Curtis, par. 2).
It is often showcased for its extremely aggressive behavior, and is
undoubtedly the most recognized of the 43 members of the
Selachimorpha that are said to have been reported in freshwater
habitats. Among these are the six members of the "River Sharks,"
which reside in the East-Indian and West-Central Pacific Oceans.
There is very little known of these rare and possibly endangered

> Dates and figures
> from credible
> sources strengthen
> the report.

Fig. 1: Shark Teeth. Ancient multi-cusped teeth for grasping and swallowing prey whole.

species, although they resemble, cohabit and are sometimes mistaken for bull sharks themselves. Some sharks may tolerate brackish water; however some have seemed to prefer water with low or no salinity. All these species share an interesting evolutionary past and their behavior and biology continues to mystify and question those who study them.

The history of sharks is far-branching and can lead to heavy debate. Some species may grow and shed tens of thousands of teeth within a matter of years. It is this reason that their species remains a personal favorite with paleontologists and have been extensively identified. The first fossilized sharks were recognized by their double-cusped teeth, which heavily favors the possibility that these individuals were a freshwater species (Martin, "Origin," par. 3). The teeth of these ancient fish were different than those of modern sharks (Fig. 1).

Naidus 3

Multi-cusped teeth primarily serve the shark to grasp its prey and swallow it whole, while modern teeth have evolved as serrated, single-cusped teeth, which allow the shark to tear and gouge its prey and to refrain from swallowing its food whole.

Freshwater sharks can be found in two separate habitats. First they will arrive in coastal rivers via the sea. Secondly, sharks can be found in lakes, which have little or no direct contact with the sea (Budker 137). In the first scenario, freshwater sharks can choose in which habitat to live; temporal or seasonal factors allow the shark to either remain in the freshwater or return to brackish or marine coastal waters. However, if rivers dry up or change course, sharks may be quarantined in lakes, where they are subject to allopatric speciation. If they happen to survive, they will eventually give rise to the formation of new specialized species.

One of these sharks is the bull shark, or *Carcharhinus leucas*, the most infamous of all sharks to have freshwater ties. It could be the fish's broad habitat or resounding aggressiveness which has labeled it as the world's most dangerous shark. Not only can attacks occur in warm coastal waters, but bull shark incidents have been reported hundreds of miles up inland river systems! This species, which can get up to 500 pounds and 11 feet in length, can be known as other names such as the Zambezi Shark in Africa, or the Lake Nicaragua shark in Central America (Curtis). Their habitat stretches the globe; however these sharks prefer to stay in warm, shallow, murky waters either on the coast or in inland brackish or freshwaters.

Bull sharks presently have a vast habitat in the lakes of Central America. Sharks and sawfish can be seen in Lake Izabel, the largest lake in Guatemala; however they are most known to reside in the waters of Lake Nicaragua. These sharks were first believed to be Brown Sharks, and it wasn't until the 1960's however, that scientists determined that

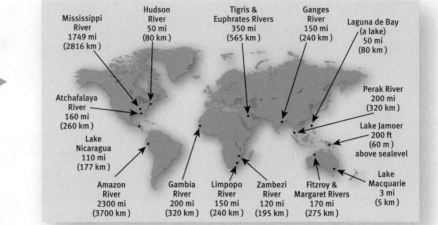

Fig. 2: Sightings of Bull Sharks in Fresh Water. Aiden Martin, Martin, R. Aidan; "Freshwater Sharks and Rays"; ReefQuest Centre for Shark Research; n.d.; Web; 20 Mar 2008.

> Maps and other graphics should be placed where they can support specific points.

the sharks in Lake Nicaragua were in fact species of *Carcharhinus Leucas*. Much of what we know about these animals is because of the research put together by "The Status of the Freshwater Shark in Lake Nicaragua" assembled by Thomas Thorson, Donald Watson, and Michael Cowan in 1966.

Lake Nicaragua is connected to the sea by the San Juan River which distributes sharks from lake to sea. These 1966 studies reported that sharks use this path, and during times where the river level was low, they discovered that the sharks actually navigate upriver through rapids from the Caribbean, much like spawning salmon do (McCollam, par. 5).

As shown in Figure 2, the Bull Shark can be found in the Mississippi River in the United States and has been recorded in the Amazon River as far as 4000 km from sea! *Leucas* is also extremely prevalent in the Ganges River in India. These sharks have an indiscriminate palate; they will eat almost everything. In the Ganges, they often feed on deceased bodies fed to the river during funerals, a tradition practiced by many locals. Many shark attacks will appear in this area and this species is often confused with the Ganges Shark, *Glyphis gangeticus*. (Martin, "Bull Shark, par. 8")

Sharks, which are primarily marine organisms, are only able to withstand and tolerate fresh water, depending on the animal's capability to change. History shows that the first recorded shark was thought to be a freshwater species. Many marine biologists and psychologists believe that all of the earliest marine specimens actually inhabited freshwater or slightly brackish water. Elasmobranches were thought to transition from freshwater into the sea in the mid-Devonian Period, and ultimately, be able to transfer back and forth between habitats (Gilbert, Mathewson, and Hall 265).

This point of view would be a definite milestone; if sharks evolved from their freshwater ancestors, then the ability for Elasmobranches to survive in saline water would likely be viewed as an impressive applied adaptation. The argument that freshwater precedents saltwater species is based on the fact that an organism's kidneys are more developed in freshwater fish species. This subject is extremely controversial, yet there is not enough evidence to deduce where the first sharks lived.

Most organisms would more than likely have trouble adjusting their eyesight from the different densities of water salinity. However, sharks as a whole rarely rely on their eyes; their other senses are much more important to them. River sharks inhabit murky waters with little or no visibility so it can be suggested that their small beady eyes are not much of a factor for deciding whether or not to venture into new salinities.

On the other hand, osmoregulation in sharks seems to ask the main question; how can shark's circulatory and urinary systems deal with the change in the salinities? As we know, teleost fishes constantly drink sea water to keep a higher concentration of salt in their bodies. Unlike these fish, a shark's salt concentrations are hypertonic to the surrounding water, meaning they must keep a constant supply of water running through their gills. A few experiments have been done comparing the freshwater Bull Shark to its marine counter part.

Looking at the Lake Nicaragua species, Thorson and his co-workers concluded that when juxtaposed with its marine equivalent, the freshwater species showcased a loss of osmotic pressure; it measured about two-thirds of that of the marine species. They concluded that the loss of pressure was due to a 20 percent reduction in bodily sodium and chloride (excreted by the rectal gland) and a reduction of half of the animal's urea production. These freshwater animals adapt by critically diluting their urine and increasing their urine rate to around 20 times of those in the ocean. In sum, the internal salt concentration of freshwater Elasmobranches is lower than their marine counterparts, but it is still extremely higher than the internal concentrations of saltwater game fishes (Martin, "Freshwater," par. 3).

Freshwater sharks have lived a life in the shadows, while the abundant groups of marine sharks have shined in the spotlight. Nonetheless, many species do spend plenty of time in waters with lower salinities, and history reveals that our first sharks may have been freshwater-dwelling. Bull Sharks continue to have the most freshwater influence, and their broad habitat sometimes allows people to mistake them for other species, such as the river sharks of the Ganges River. These sharks have adapted to new waters mostly through techniques of osmoregulation and reduced osmotic pressure. Freshwater sharks can tell us a lot about the past, present, and future of any shark species, and they truly invoke a feeling of appreciation for one of the oldest and magnificent animals on the planet.

Works Cited

Budker, Paul. *The Life of Sharks*. New York: Columbia UP, 1971. Print.

"Chondrichthyes." Bowdoin College, n.d. Web. 27 Mar. 2008.

Compagno, Leonard, Marc Dando, and Sarah Folwer. *Sharks of the World*. Princeton: Princeton UP, 2005. Print.

Curtis, Tobey. "Bull Shark." *Ichthyology*. Florida Museum of Natural History, n.d. Web. 18 Mar. 2008.

Gilbert, Perry, Robert Mathewson, and David Rall. *Sharks, Skates, and Rays*. Baltimore: Johns Hopkins P, 1967. Print.

Martin, R. Aidan. "Bull Shark." *Biology of Sharks and Rays*. ReefQuest Centre for Shark Research., n.d. Web. 20 Mar 2008.

Martin, R. Aidan. "Earliest Sharks." *Biology of Sharks and Rays*. ReefQuest Centre for Shark Research., n.d. Web. 20 Mar 2008.

Martin, R. Aidan. "Freshwater Sharks and Rays." *Biology of Sharks and Rays*. ReefQuest Centre for Shark Research, n.d. Web. 20 Mar. 2008.

Martin, R. Aidan. "Origin of Modern Sharks." *Biology of Sharks and Rays*. ReefQuest Centre for Shark Research, n.d. Web. 20 Mar. 2008.

McCollam, Douglass. "The Bull Shark." *Slate*. The Slate Group, 18 July 2001. Web. 21 Mar. 2008.

Skelton, Jamie. "The Evolution of Sharks." *Helium*. Helium, n.d. Web. 30 Mar. 2008.

Thorson, Thomas, Donald Watson, and Michael Cowan. "The Status of the Freshwater Shark of Lake Nicaragua." *American Society of Ichthyologists and Herpetologists* 3 (1966): 386. Print.

28

Using APA Style

In this chapter you will learn how to—

- use APA parenthetical citations in your texts.
- create bibliographic entries for a References list.
- prepare a References list in APA style.

A merican Psychological Association (APA) documentation style, like MLA style (Chapter 27), is a method for keeping track of your sources, while letting readers know where you found the support for your claims. APA style is commonly used in the social sciences, physical sciences, and technical fields.

In this chapter, you will learn how to use APA style to reference your sources and create a list of "References" at the end of your document. The models of APA citations shown here are the ones most commonly used in college and in the workplace. For more information on APA style, consult the *Publication Manual of the American Psychological Association,* 6th ed. (2010).

Parenthetical Citations

When citing a source with APA style, you first need to include a parenthetical citation, which appears in the text of your document, usually at the end of the sentence where the information that you used from another source appears. For example:

Children and adults see the world differently, which can make their parents'
divorce especially unsettling (Neuman, 1998, p. 43).

Among Africa's other problems, the one that is most significant may be its lack
of reliable electrical energy (Friedman, 2008, p. 155).

As shown here, a full parenthetical citation includes three important pieces of information: the source's name (usually an author's name), the year the source was published, and the page number from the source where the information appeared.

If readers want to, they can then turn to the list of "References" at the end of the
document to see the full citation, which will look like this:

Neuman, G. (1998). *Helping your kids cope with divorce the sandcastles way.*
New York, NY: Random House.

In other words, the parenthetical citation and the full reference work together. The
parenthetical citation points readers to the reference list, where they can find the information needed to locate the source.

Note: For a key to the color highlighting used here and throughout this chapter,
see the bottom of this page.

APA style also allows you to refer to a whole work by simply putting the author's
name and the year of the source. For example:

Genetics are a new frontier for understanding schizophrenia (Swaminathan, 2008).

Autism and psychosis have been shown to be diametrical disorders of the brain
(Crespi & Badcock, 2008).

These parenthetical references without page numbers are common in APA style, but
not in MLA style.

In situations where you are specifically highlighting a study or author, you should
move the full parenthetical reference up in the sentence:

According to one study (Adreason & Pierson, 2008), the cerebellum plays a key
role in the onset of schizophrenia.

Three books (Abraham & Llewellyn-Jones, 1992; Boskind-White & White, 2000;
Burby, 1998) have tried to explain bulimia to nonscientists.

When the Author's Name Appears in the Sentence

If you name the author in the sentence, you only need to provide the year of the source
and the page number in parentheses. The year should follow the name of the source
and the page number is usually placed at the end of the sentence. For example:

Author Title Publication Online Source

Neuman (1998) points out that children and adults see the world differently, which can make their parents' divorce especially unsettling (p. 43).

Friedman (2008) argues that Africa's most significant problem may be its lack of electrical energy (p. 155).

If one part of your sentence draws information from a source but the remainder of the sentence states your own thoughts, you should put the reference immediately after the source's material is used. For example:

As Dennet (1995) points out, scientists are uncomfortable with the idea that nature uses a form of reason (p. 213), but I think we must see nature as a life form that is looking out for its best interests.

Citing More Than One Source in the Same Sentence

In APA style, it is common to cite multiple sources making the same point, separated with semicolons:

Several researchers (Crespi & Badcock, 2008; Shaner, Miller, & Mintz, 2004, p. 102; Swaminatha, 2008) have shown the toll that schizophrenia takes on a family.

In the sentence above, the writer is referring to the whole work by Crespi and Badcock and Swaminatha, but she is only referring to page 102 in the article by Shaner, Miller, and Mintz.

If you are citing more than one source in the same sentence but they are making different points, you should put the parenthetical reference as close as possible to the information taken from each source. For example:

Depression is perhaps one of the most common effects of bulimia (McCabe, McFarlane, & Olmstead, 2004, p. 19), and this depression "almost always impairs concentration" (Sherman & Thompson, 1996, p. 57).

Citing a Source Multiple Times

In some situations, you will need to cite a source multiple times. If your document continues using a single source, you only need to include the page number in subsequent references as long as no other source comes between them.

> The side effects of brain tumor treatment can include fatigue, brain swelling, hair loss, and depression (Black, 2006, p. 170). Hair loss and other outward signs of treatment can be the most disturbing. Depression, however, perhaps needs more attention because it often requires patients to take antidepressants and stimulants (p. 249).

In the example above, the full parenthetical citation is included early in the paragraph. The second reference, which is only a page number, is clearly referring back to the source in the first reference.

However, if another source is cited between two parenthetical citations to the same source, the author's name from the first source would need to be repeated in a subsequent reference. For example:

> The side effects of brain tumor treatment can include fatigue, brain swelling, hair loss, and depression (Black, 2006, p. 170). Hair loss and other outward signs of treatment can be the most disturbing. For instance, Becker (2003) discusses her obsession with hiding the incision where the tumor was removed (p. 231). Depression, however, perhaps needs more attention because it often requires patients to take antidepressants and stimulants (Black, 2006, p. 249).

In the example above, the author includes a full parenthetical reference to Black in the final sentence of the paragraph, because the reference to Becker (2003) appears between the first and second references to Black.

Other Parenthetical References

Figure 28.1 on page 532 shows models of some common parenthetical citations. Choose the one that best fits your source. If none of these models fits the source you are trying to cite, you can use combinations of these models. If you still cannot figure it out, turn to the APA's *Publication Manual*.

Preparing the List of References

Your list of references appears at the end of your document. In this list, you should include full citations for all the sources you cite. A typical entry includes features like the name of the author, the date of publication, the title of the text, and the place of publication. Here are three different entries from three different types of sources.

FIGURE 28.1
Types of APA
Parenthetical
References

Type of Source	Example Parenthetical Reference
Single author	(Gerns, 2009, p. 12)
Single author, multiple pages	(Barnes, 2007, pp. 5–9) or (Barnes, 2007, pp. 34, 121) *The dash signals a range of pages. The comma suggests similar information can be found on two different pages. The "pp." signals multiple pages.*
Two authors	(Hammonds & Gupta, 2004, p. 203) *The ampersand (&) is used instead of "and."*
Three authors	(Gym, Hanson, & Williams, 2005, p. 845) *The ampersand (&) is used instead of "and."*
More than three authors	First reference: (Wu, Gyno, Young, & Reims, 2003, p. 924) Subsequent references: (Wu et al., 2003, p. 924)
Six or more authors	First and subsequent references: (Williamson et al., 2004, p. 23)
Multiple sources in same reference	(Thames & Cain, 2008; Young, Morales, & Cato, 2009; Yu, 2004) *The semicolon divides the sources.*
Two or more works by the same author	(Tufte, 2001, p. 23) and (Tufte, 2003) *The author's name is used with the date.*
Two or more works by the same author in the same year	(Tufte, 2001a, p. 23) and (Tufte, 2001b, p. 11) *The "a" and "b" signal two different works and will appear in the list of references also.*
Different authors with the same last name	(M. Smith, 2005, p. 54) and (A. Smith, 2007, p. 34) *The first letters abbreviate each author's first name.*
Corporate author	(National Aeronautics and Space Administration [NASA], 2009, p. 12) or (American Beef Association, 2006, p. 232 *Well-known acronyms, such as NASA, can be put in brackets the first time and then used in any following parenthetical references.* (NASA, 2009, p. 14)

continued

FIGURE 28.1
Types of APA
Parenthetical
References
(continued)

Type of Source	Example Parenthetical Reference
No author for book	(*Handling Bulimia,* 2004, p. 45) *Use the full title of the source in italics.*
No author for journal article or newspaper article	("Genomics as the New Frontier," 2008, p. 23) *Put the full title in quotation marks.*
No author for newspaper article	("Recession," 2009, p. A4) *The letter "A" is the section of the newspaper and the number is the page.*
Cited in another source	(as cited in Franks, 2007, p. 94)
Web page or other document with no pagination	(Reynolds, 2006, para. 3) *"para." stands for "paragraph," as counted down from the top of the page.*
Web page or other document with no author and no pagination	("Friendly," 2008, para. 7) *Put the first prominent word in the title in quotes, with "para." standing for "paragraph," as counted down from the top of the page.*

Not all possible parenthetical references are shown here. If you have a unique source that doesn't fit these examples, you can usually figure out how to cite it by combining the above reference models.

Servan-Schreiber, D. (2008). *Anti-cancer: A new way of life.* New York, NY: Viking.

Crespi, B., & Badcock, C. (2008). Psychosis and autism as diametrical disorders in the social brain. *Behavior Brain Science, 31*(3), 241–261.

Chew, R. (2008, February 1). Charles Darwin, naturalist, 1809–1882. *Lucidcafe.* Retrieved February 8, 2009, from http://www.lucidcafe.com/library/96feb /darwin.html

Only sources you reference in your document should appear in your References. The reference list is not a bibliography of all the sources you found on your topic.

In a reference list, the entries are listed in alphabetical order, by the authors' last names. When an author's name is not known, the work is alphabetized by the first prominent word in its title. When alphabetizing, ignore words like *The, A,* or *An* if they are the first word in the title.

VAMPIRES IN HOLLYWOOD   12

                              References

Arthen, I. (2005, December 9). Real vampires. *FireHeart, 2*. Retrieved

        from http://www.earthspirit.com/fireheart/fhvampire.html

Barber, P. (1989). *Vampires, burial, and death*. New Haven, CT: Yale

        University Press.

Bluestein, G. (1994). *Poplore: Folk and pop in American culture*.

        Amherst, MA: University of Massachusetts Press.

Keyworth, D. (2006). Was the vampire of the eighteenth century a

        unique type of undead corpse? *Folklore, 117*(3), 1–16.

FIGURE 28.2 Formatting a List of References

The APA Publication Manual *specifies that the heading "References" be centered on the page. The margins should be one inch on all sides. The entries should be double-spaced.*

If you are listing two works by the same author in the same year, they should be alphabetized by the first prominent words in their titles and then distinguished by "a," "b," "c," and so on (e.g., 2007a, 2007b, 2007c).

Formatting a List of References in APA Style

Start the reference list on a new page with the centered heading "References" at the top (Figure 28.2). Entries are then listed double-spaced, in hanging indent format, which means the first line of each entry is not indented, but the rest are indented a half inch.

In professional texts, however, your reference list should match the design of your document. The "References" heading should be consistent with other headings. If you are single-spacing the rest of your document, the reference list should be single-spaced, too, perhaps with spaces between entries.

Citing Sources in the List of References

Watch the Animation on **Citing Sources using APA** at **mycomplab.com**

The following list is not comprehensive. However, we have included models of the most common kinds of entries in a reference list. You can use these examples as models for your own citations. If you do not find a model for a source, you should turn to the APA's *Publication Manual,* 6th edition (2010).

APA List of References

Books and Other Non-Periodical Publications

1. Book, One Author
2. Book, Two Authors
3. Book, Three Authors
4. Book, Corporate or Organization Author
5. Book, Edited Collection
6. Book, Translated
7. Book, Author Unknown
8. Book, Second Edition or Beyond
9. Book, Dissertation or Thesis
10. Book, in Electronic Form
11. Document, Government Publication
12. Document, Pamphlet

Journals, Magazines, and Other Periodical Publications

13. Article, Journal with Continuous Pagination
14. Article, Journal without Continuous Pagination
15. Article, Edited Book
16. Article, Magazine
17. Article, Newspaper
18. Article, Author Unknown
19. Article, CD-ROM
20. Review

Web Publications

21. Web Page, Corporate Author
22. Web Page, Author Unknown
23. Article from an Online Periodical
24. Scholarly Journal Article with a Digital Object Identifier (DOI)
25. Scholarly Journal Article
26. Podcast

Other Kinds of Sources

27. Film or Video Recording
28. Television or Radio Program
29. Song or Audio Recording
30. CD-ROM
31. Personal Correspondence, E-Mail, or Interview

Citing Books and Other Nonperiodical Publications

A book citation will have some of the following features:

1. Name of the author, corporation, or editor with last name first (include "(Ed.)" or "(Eds.)" if the work is listed by editor)

2. Year the work was published, in parentheses (if unknown, use "n.d." for "no date")

3. Title of the work, in italics (capitalize only first word, proper nouns, and any word that follows a colon)

4. City and state or country where the work was published (use standard U.S. Postal Service abbreviations for states; spell out the full names of countries outside of the United States)

5. Publisher

Author Title Publication Online Source

①   ②   ③   ④

Author. (Year of publication). *Title of work.* City and state (or country) of

⑤

publication: Publisher.

1. Book, One Author

Jones, S. (2001). *Darwin's ghost: The origin of species updated.* New York, NY:
Ballantine Books.

2. Book, Two Authors

Pauling, L., & Wilson, E. B. (1935). *Introduction to quantum mechanics.* New York,
NY: Dover Publications.

3. Book, Three or More Authors

Newnan, D. G., Eschenbach, T. G., & Lavelle, J. P. (2008). *Engineering economic
analysis* (10th ed.). Oxford, England: Oxford University Press.

4. Book, Corporate or Organization Author

American Psychiatric Association. (1994). *Diagnostic and statistical manual of mental
disorders* (4th ed.). Washington, DC: Author.

5. Book, Edited Collection

Mueller-Vollmer, K. (Ed.). (1990). *The hermeneutics reader.* New York, NY: Continuum.

6. Book, Translated

Habermas, J. (1979). *Communication and the evolution of society* (T. McCarthy,
Trans.). Boston, MA: Beacon Press.

7. Book, Author Unknown

Handbook for the WorkPad c3 PC Companion. (2000). Thornwood, NY: IBM.

8. Book, Second Edition or Beyond

Williams, R., & Tollet, J. (2008). *The non-designer's web book* (3rd ed.). Berkeley, CA:
Peachpit.

9. Book, Dissertation or Thesis

Simms, L. (2002). *The Hampton effect in fringe desert environments: An ecosystem
under stress.* (Unpublished doctoral dissertation). University of New Mexico.

10. Book, in Electronic Form

Darwin, C. (1862). *On the various contrivances by which British and foreign orchids are fertilised by insects.* London, England: John Murray. Retrieved from http://pages.britishlibrary.net/charles.darwin3/orchids/orchids_fm.htm

11. Document, Government Publication

Greene, L. W. (1985). *Exile in paradise: The isolation of Hawaii's leprosy victims and development of Kalaupapa settlement, 1865 to present.* Washington, DC: U.S. Department of the Interior, National Park Service.

12. Document, Pamphlet

The Colorado Health Network. (2002). *Exploring high altitude areas.* Denver, CO: Author.

Citing Journals, Magazines, and Other Periodical Publications

A citation for a journal, magazine, or other periodical publication includes the following features:

1. Name of the author, corporation, or editor; last name first, followed by initial of first name and any middle initials

2. Date of publication (year for scholarly journal; year, month, day for other periodicals)

3. Title of the work, not enclosed in quotation marks (capitalize only first word, proper nouns, and any word that follows a colon)

4. Title of the periodical in italics (capitalize all significant words)

5. Volume number (italicized) and issue number (not italicized, but enclosed in parentheses). If each issue begins with page 1, include the issue number.

6. Range of page numbers for whole article

    ①   ②   ③   ④   ⑤

Author. (Date of publication). Title of article. *Title of Journal, volume number*

     ⑥   ⑦

(issue number), page numbers.

13. Article, Journal with Continuous Pagination

Boren, M. T., & Ramey, J. (1996). Thinking aloud: Reconciling theory and practice. *IEEE Transactions on Professional Communication, 39,* 49–57.

14. Article, Journal without Continuous Pagination

Kadlecek, M. (1991). Global climate change could threaten U.S. wildlife. *Conservationist, 46*(1), 54–55.

15. Article, Edited Book

Katz, S. B., & Miller, C. R. (1996). The low-level radioactive waste siting controversy in North Carolina: Toward a rhetorical model of risk communication. In C. Herndl & S. C. Brown (Eds.), *Green culture: Environmental rhetoric in contemporary America* (pp. 111–140). Madison, WI: University of Wisconsin Press.

16. Article, Magazine

Appenzeller, T. (2008, February). The case of the missing carbon. *National Geographic,* 88–118.

17. Article, Newspaper

Hall, C. (2002, November 18). Shortage of human capital envisioned, Monster's Taylor sees worker need. *Chicago Tribune,* p. E7.

18. Article, Author Unknown

The big chill leaves bruises. (2004, January 17). *Albuquerque Tribune,* p. A4.

19. Article, CD-ROM

Hanford, P. (2001). Locating the right job for you. *The electronic job finder* [CD]. San Francisco, CA: Career Masters.

20. Review

Leonhardt, D. (2008, November 30). Chance and circumstance. [Review of the book *Outliers*]. *New York Times,* p. BR9.

Citing Web Publications

Citations for Web documents do not need to include your date of access if you can provide a publication date. However, you do need to provide either the URL from which a source was retrieved or a Digital Object Identifier (DOI). When including a URL or DOI, always insert a break *before* a slash, period, or other punctuation mark.

21. Web Site, Corporate Author

U.S. Fish and Wildlife Service. (2008). *Estuary restoration act of 2000.* Retrieved from http://www.fws.gov/coastal/estuaryRestorationAct.html

FIGURE 28.3 CITATION MAP: Citing Part or All of a Web Site

A citation for a Web publication will have some or all of the following features:

① Name of the author, corporation, organization, editor, or webmaster. For authors and editors, last name first followed by initials.

② Date of publication, in parentheses (year, month, date). If no date is given, write (n.d.) to indicate "no date."

③ Title of the individual page, document, or article.

④ Title of the Web site, in italics.

⑤ Retrieval information: the site's URL; the date retrieved (include only if the source could change, e.g., a corporate website or wiki); do not add a period at the end of the URL.

Author of Web site. (Date published.) Title of document or *Title of Page*. *Title of Overall Web Site.*
Retrieved (month date, year) from URL

Pueblo Grande Museum Archaeological Park. (n.d.). Doorways to the Past: Hohokam Houses.
City of Phoenix. Retrieved April 9, 2009, from http://phoenix.gov/PUEBLO/exhouses.html

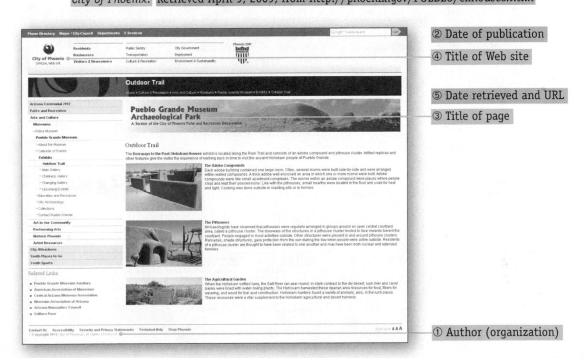

② Date of publication
④ Title of Web site
⑤ Date retrieved and URL
③ Title of page
① Author (organization)

Author Title Publication Online Source

FIGURE 28.4 CITATION MAP: Citing a Journal Article with a DOI

① Name of the author (last name, initials)

② Publication date

③ Title of article

④ Title of the journal in italics

⑤ Volume number in italics, and issue number (in parentheses, not italicized)

⑥ Page numbers

⑦ Digital Object Identifier. (It is easiest to cut and paste the DOI directly from the original document into your text.)

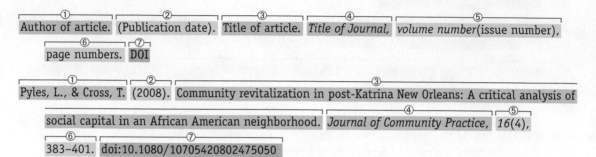

Author of article. (Publication date). Title of article. *Title of Journal, volume number*(issue number), page numbers. DOI

Pyles, L., & Cross, T. (2008). Community revitalization in post-Katrina New Orleans: A critical analysis of social capital in an African American neighborhood. *Journal of Community Practice, 16*(4), 383–401. doi:10.1080/10705420802475050

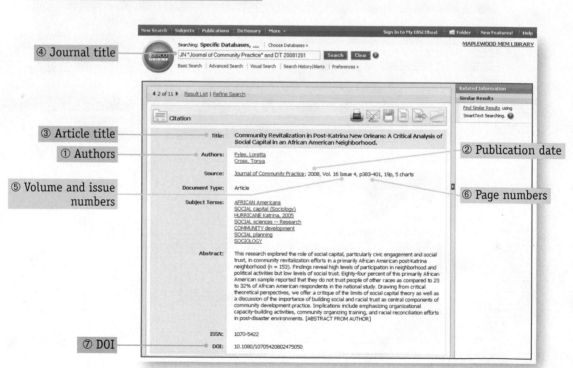

④ Journal title

③ Article title

① Authors

⑤ Volume and issue numbers

⑦ DOI

② Publication date

⑥ Page numbers

22. Web Site, Author Unknown

Clara Barton: Founder of the American Red Cross. (n.d.). *American Red Cross Museum*. Retrieved from http://www.redcross.org/museum/history /claraBarton.asp

23. Article from an Online Periodical

Vaitheeswaran, V. (2009, April 16). Medicine goes digital. *The Economist*. Retrieved from http://www.economist.com/specialreports

24. Scholarly Journal Article with a Digital Object Identifier (DOI)

Blake, H., & Ooten, M. (2008). Bridging the divide: Connecting feminist histories and activism in the classroom. *Radical History Review, 2008* (102), 63–72. doi:10.1215/01636545-2008-013

25. Scholarly Journal Article

The APA no longer requires you to include the name of a database from which you retrieve a journal article. Use the DOI, if available, for such an article.

Ankers, D., & Jones, S. H. (2009). Objective assessment of circadian activity and sleep patterns in individuals at behavioural risk of hypomania. *Journal of Clinical Psychology, 65*, 1071–1086. doi:10.1002/jclp.20608

26. Podcast

Root, B. (2009, January 27). *Just one more book* [Audio podcast]. Retrieved from http://www.justonemorebook.com/2009/01/27/interview-with-neil-gaiman

Citing Other Kinds of Sources

A variety of other sources are available, each with its own citation style. The citations for these sources tend to include most of the following types of information:

1. Name of the producers, writers, or directors with their roles identified in parentheses (Producer, Writer, Director)

2. Year of release or broadcast, in parentheses

3. Title of the work (italics for a complete work; no italics for a work that is a segment, episode, or part of a whole)

4. Name of episode (first letter of first word capitalized)

5. Title of the program (italicized)

Author Title Publication Online Source

6. Type of program (in brackets), e.g., [Film], [Television series], [Song]

7. City and state or country where work was produced

8. Distributor of the work (e.g., HBO, Miramax, New Line Productions)

9. Retrieval information, for works accessed online

27. Film or Video Recording

Osborne, B., Walsh, F., and Sanders, T. (Producers), & Jackson, P (Director). (2002). *The lord of the rings: The fellowship of the ring* [Motion picture]. Hollywood, CA: New Line Productions.

28. Television or Radio Program

Paley, V. (Writer). (2009). Human nature, the view from kindergarten [Radio series episode]. In I. Glass (Producer), *This American Life*. Chicago, IL: WBEZ/Chicago Public Radio.

29. Song or Recording

Myer, L. (1993). Sometimes alone. On *Flatlands* [CD]. Ames, IA: People's Productions.

30. CD-ROM

Geritch, T. (2000). *Masters of renaissance art* [CD]. Chicago, IL: Revival Productions.

31. Personal Correspondence, E-Mail, or Interview

Personal correspondence is not listed in the reference list. Instead, the information from the correspondence should be given in the parenthetical citation:

This result was confirmed by J. Baca (personal communication, March 4, 2004).

A Student's APA-Style Research Paper

Watch the Animation on **APA Formatting** at **mycomplab.com**

The document shown here uses APA style for parenthetical citations and the References list. The student writer followed his professor's requirements for formatting his paper; formatting guidelines in the APA *Publication Manual* are intended for submissions to professional journals.

Running head: ASSORTATIVE MATING   1

Assortative Mating and Income Inequality

Austin Duus

University of New Mexico

Professor Krause

Economics 445: Topics in Public Finance

Assortative Mating and Income Inequality

Paul Ryscavage begins *Income Inequality in America* (1999) on the premise that the growth in income inequality in the United States in the last thirty years is driven by changes in technology, globalization, and family structure. The first two factors seem intuitive. Returns-to-education in an economy where exchange is facilitated by personal computers and BlackBerries is both well-documented and offers explanatory logic on how an educated segment of the population's income gains could outpace those of the less-educated. However, family structure, the final element in Ryscavage's inequality trifecta, seems suspiciously far removed from the typical industrial activities of the economy. At first, this demographic nuance seems more polemical than empirical. The single-mom menace, the erosion of "family values," and the disappearance of the Ozzie-and-Harriet nuclear family seem more like ideological talking points than matters of economic fact.

What is stunning, however, is how small changes in the aggregate makeup of American households can drastically affect the distribution of income in that population. The proportion of single, female-headed households has increased due to the "independence effect" on the dissolution or preemption of marriages among other things. Moreover, this type of household is the most likely to be poor (Cancian & Reed, 1999). Judith Treas (1987) refers to these changes in the context of the "feminization of poverty" (p. 283). This sociology catchphrase makes more sense when considered in the context of trends in female labor force participation and the marriage market.

Even more elemental to the question of family structure and its effects on income inequality are the underlying forces by which individuals choose to partner, and partners choose to sort, in all

> When the author's name appears in the sentence, only the year is parenthetically cited, and the page number is cited at the end of the sentence.

ASSORTATIVE MATING   3

segments of the population. Beyond income inequality (or equality as the case may be), marriage [or nonmarital partnering] has "implications for . . . the number of births and population growth, labor-force participation of women, inequality in income, ability, and other characteristics among families, genetical [sic] natural selection of different characteristics over time, and the allocation of leisure and other household resources" (Becker, 1973, p. 814). In short, household formation is a largely economic decision, which, like other such decisions, is a choice determined by weighing the costs (including opportunity costs) against expected utility.

Theoretical Framework

Individuals do not pair with other individuals to form households randomly. Instead, one can observe traits by which individuals tend to sort themselves and their mates. Garfinkel and McLananhan (2002) define this process of assortative mating as "the tendency of people to choose partners of similar age, race, educational attainment, and other social, psychological, and biological characteristics" (p. 417). More specifically, they are referring to *positive* assortative mating in which individuals choose similar partners. In the literature, this is sometimes referred to as homogamy. Individuals, for various reasons, sometimes find it advantageous to choose partners who are different from them. This is *negative* assortative mating.

The Becker Theory

Gary Becker (1973) was the first to outline a theory of a marriage market. His claims were straightforward. Marriage, like all economic decisions, is an optimized utility function: "Persons marrying . . . can be assumed to expect to raise their utility level above what it would be were they to remain single" (p. 814). Moreover, like all utility functions, a marriage is optimized against a constraint. Potential mates are limited;

Three ellipsis points (...) indicate that some words have been omitted from within a quoted sentence.

Main headings are centered and boldfaced, using both uppercase and lowercase letters.

Secondary headings are flush left and boldfaced, using both uppercase and lowercase letters.

ASSORTATIVE MATING   4

therefore, scarcity drives a market in which "many men and women
compete as they seek mates. . . . Each person tries to find the best
mate, subject to the restrictions imposed by market conditions"
(p. 814).

Use four ellipsis points to indicate material omitted between sentences in a quote.

      Becker (1973) found that people might choose to marry simply
because it is easier to have "sexual gratification, cleaning, and feeding"
(p. 818) in-house than to purchase those services. Also, conveniently,
"love" can "reduce the cost of frequent contact and of resource
transfers" (p. 819). Observations about who marries whom suggest
individuals sort by "IQ, education, height, attractiveness, skin color,
ethnic origin, and other characteristics" (p. 815). Sorting by some
heritable traits may be related to creating "desired" offspring.
Additionally, the choice to separate or divorce is determined by
opportunity cost. If there is more to lose, people will think twice about
going to divorce court.

The findings of credible sources help the author make his point with greater authority.

Negative Assortative Mating

      Becker (1973) speculates there may be negative sorting in regard
to specific "psychological traits, such as a propensity to dominate,
nurture, or be hostile" (p. 824). However, central to Becker's theory of
the marriage market is an assumption of negative sorting in regard to
wages. Jepsen and Jepsen (2002) explain:

> Theories of the sexual division of labor predict that high-
> wage men will pair with low-wage women and that, once the
> couple forms a household, men will specialize in market
> production while women will specialize in home production.
> (p. 442)

For a quotation of 40 or more words, use a block quote without quotation marks.

However, all empirical studies suggest the opposite is true. While
correlations between spousal wages tend to be very small, usually the
smallest of traits studied, they are positive. It is assumed, generally

ASSORTATIVE MATING   5

without warrant, that male wages and female household production are substitutes, and gains in marriage result from this specialization. Becker (1991) finds the sexual division of labor so compelling as to claim in regard to same-sex couples, "households with only men or only women are less efficient because they are unable to profit from the sexual difference in comparative advantage" (p. 38). Becker, however, fails to specify how having a uterus gives one a "comparative advantage" in dishwashing and food preparation or the relationship between a Y chromosome and market work. It is also unclear why partners of the same sex cannot specialize.

When appropriate, author challenges limitations of sources.

Regardless of the problems with assuming gender essentialism in theory, empirically, Lam (1988) found even high-wage women exhibit a tendency to specialize in household production as they prefer even higher wage men. (Thus their opportunity cost to not participating in the labor market is lower in comparison to their spouses.) This means women do not necessarily specialize in household production because they are female. This finding is further validated when female labor force participation data are disaggregated into cohorts. Black women, for example, tend to participate in the labor force regardless of the income of their spouses (Jepsen, 2002; Treas, 1987).

Evidence for Assortative Mating

Traits Studied

Age. While men seek younger women and women seek slightly older men (Jepsen, 2002), on balance, people seek partners of an age similar to their own. Age, in most studies, generally has the "strongest positive assortative mating" (Lam, 1988, p. 478).

Use of multiple heading levels provides access points and makes the text easier to read.

IQ. Jepsen & Jepsen (2002) estimate the correlation as similar to the IQ correlation between siblings.

Education. Lam (1988) calculates schooling being second only to age in positive assortative mating. Strikingly, the particular trait has experienced the largest boost in homogamy. Costa & Kahn (2000) note education as a primary driving force in how couples sort and then where they live. In fact, educational homogamy has increased while homogamy with respect to race, ethnicity, and age has decreased. This could be explained by educational sorting happening later. As individuals marry or partner later in life, they are more likely to partner with someone less like them. While people may choose to partner with someone of a different culture, age, or even weight, level of education seems to be increasingly important as a positive sorting mechanism—at least, among married couples.

Wage. Wage has the weakest correlation coefficient ranging from .02 to .24 (Jepsen & Jepsen, 2002; Treas, 1987).

Differences by Type of Couple

Married Couples. Married couples tend to be the most homogamous in all factors but wage.

Cohabiting Couples. In general, market variables are more positive with unmarried couples than married couples, but less positive with nonmarket traits (Jepsen & Jepsen, 2002). With respect to race, age, and education, unmarried couples tended to be less homogamous than married couples, but more homogamous with earnings and hours worked. This is consistent with the idea of marriage self-selection, whereby financial independence is a disincentive to marry.

While median measures of unmarried couples in regard to age are identical to married couples, there is a much wider distribution of age differences. Unmarried parents tended to have a more substantial education gap than their married counterparts. However, this is

ASSORTATIVE MATING   7

primarily due to the education gap of parents who have never lived together (Garfinkel & McLananhan, 2002).

> Taken as a whole, these results suggest that mothers and fathers who do not marry each other may be less homogamous in terms of age and education than parents who marry. . . . Nonetheless, it appears that a high level of assortative mating still occurs. (p. 429)

Same-Sex Couples. Out of all the types of couples studied, female same-sex couples had the strongest positive assortative mating by wage. Unlike most studies, their wage correlation was statistically significant (Jepsen & Jepsen, 2002). Both male and female same-sex couples had a larger wage correlation than both unmarried and married opposite-sex couples. In contrast, the "estimated coefficient for race and age are noticeably larger for opposite-sex couples than for same-sex couples" (Jepsen & Jepsen, 2002, p. 444).

Black Couples. In many ways, African American family formation is a useful natural experiment on the effects of increased female labor force participation on income inequality. Unlike their White and Latino counterparts, Black women are likely to work regardless of the income of their spouses. Also, "relative to whites, African Americans report less willingness to marry a person of a lower socioeconomic status, and they express less desire to marry" (Jepsen & Jepsen, 2002, p. 437). So while two working spouses would be an equalizing force if upper-income women did not work, this is not the case with Black women.

When it would be unclear what source is cited, the authors' names are included in the parenthetical citation.

While female labor force participation may increase inequality within the African American community, it may actually narrow the race-income gap. According to Danziger (1980), in "1974, nonwhite family income was 78 percent of white's; this ratio would have been only 71 percent if nonwhite wives had not worked more than did white wives" (p. 448).

Analysis

Impact on Income Inequality

Historically we find that female labor force participation was an equalizing force in the United States income distribution. Women's wages were compressed in the phenomenon of the occupational set of nurse/teacher/secretary. However, since World War II (when women first entered the workforce in large numbers), the diversity of market opportunities available to women has substantially increased and as marriage and other assortative mating is delayed well beyond high school, it is increasingly likely pairs will sort by wage as well as by the usual homogamous characteristics.

Conclusion

Currently, empirical data suggest the effects of more high-wage women entering the workforce are mixed (Danziger, 1980). Even for experiments in which all women participated in the labor force, the wage correlation might only increase to around .25 (Treas, 1987), which would have limited effects on the aggregate household income distribution.

Final analyses and conclusions are stated succinctly and prominently.

ASSORTATIVE MATING   9

References

Becker, G. S. (1973). A theory of marriage: Part I. *Journal of Political Economy, 81,* 813–846. doi:10.1086/260084

Becker, G. S. (1991). *A treatise on the family.* Cambridge, MA: Harvard University Press.

Cancian, M., & Reed, D. (1999). The impact of wives' earnings on income inequality: Issues and estimates. *Demography, 36,* 173–184. doi: 10.2307/2648106

Costa, D. L., & Kahn, M. E. (2000). Power couples: Changes in the locational choice of the college educated, 1940–1990. *Quarterly Journal of Economics, 115,* 1287–1315. doi:10.1162/003355300555079

Danziger, S. (1980). Do working wives increase family income inequality? *Journal of Human Resources, 15,* 445–451. doi:10.2307/145294

Garfinkel, I., & McLananhan, S. S. (2002). Assortative mating among unmarried parents: Implications for ability to pay child support. *Journal of Population Economics, 15,* 417–432. doi:10.1007/s001480100100

Jepsen, L. K., & Jepsen, C. A. (2002). An empirical analysis of the matching patterns of same-sex and opposite sex couples. *Demography, 39,* 435–453. doi:10.1353/dem.2002.0027

Lam, D. (1988). Marriage markets and assortative mating with household public goods: Theoretical results and empirical implications. *Journal of Human Resources, 23,* 462–487. doi:10.2307/145809

Ryscavage, P. (1999). *Income inequality in America.* Armonk, NY: Sharpe.

Treas, J. (1987). The effect of women's labor force participation on the distribution of income in the United States. *Annual Review of Sociology, 13,* 259–288. doi:10.1146/annurev.so.13.080187.001355

References begin on new page. All cited works are included and listed in alphabetical order by author.

The DOI is provided whenever available, even for print articles.

6

Getting Your Ideas Out There

PART OUTLINE

Your thoughts and ideas deserve a wider audience.
GET YOUR WRITING OUT THERE *for others to discuss, debate, and respond to. These chapters will show you how to take your writing public.*

29

Using the Internet

In this chapter, you will learn how to—

- create a social networking site.
- start your own blog.
- contribute an article to a wiki and upload a video.

Today people are reading and writing more than ever. They write e-mails, stay up to date on Web sites, update *Facebook* profiles, share opinions on blogs, create podcasts and *YouTube* videos, and text friends with *Twitter*.

In this chapter, you will learn how to use the Internet and new media to put your writing out in the public sphere. There are now more ways than ever to publicize your writing and make an impact on the world through your words.

Is This Writing?

Maybe you are wondering if some of the new media tools we will discuss in this chapter can still be considered writing. Blogging looks like writing, but what about social networking sites or video sharing sites? Can we still call that writing?

We live in a time of great technological change, so we need to expand and change our understanding of what it means to "write" and be "literate." This kind of revolution has happened before. When the printing press was introduced in the fifteenth century, it dramatically changed ideas about what writing looked like. Before the printing press, "writing" meant handwritten texts, such as letters, and illuminated books. The printing press provided access to ideas and texts that were once available only to a privileged few. Then society's understanding of writing changed to fit the new technology.

More than likely, the monks working in the scriptoriums of medieval Europe would have been mystified by the kinds of writing that we take for granted today. Mass-produced books, newspapers, magazines, junk mail, brochures, and posters, would have seemed odd and even threatening. They would have seen computers as a form of magic or witchcraft.

So it's not surprising that we wonder about these media tools. Writing will continue to change, making it look very different than it does now. The new technologies described in this chapter are only the beginning of that change.

Creating a Social Networking Site

Let's start with the easiest way to go public with your writing—creating a profile on a social networking Web site like *Facebook, MySpace, Bebo, LinkedIn,* or *Spoke.* The first three, *Facebook, MySpace,* and *Bebo,* can help you connect and stay in touch with friends and family. Increasingly, these social networking sites are used by nonprofit organizations, political movements, and companies to stay in touch with interested people. For example, your college or university probably has a *Facebook* or *MySpace* site that lets you keep in touch with what is happening on campus.

LinkedIn and *Spoke* are career-related social networking sites that will help you connect with colleagues, business associates, and potential employers.

Choose the Best Site for You

Each social networking site is a little different. As you choose which site is best for you, think about your purpose. Right now, you probably just want to keep in touch with your friends. But as you move through college and into the workplace, your site may become a way to network with other people in your field. Some social networking sites are better at supporting longer genres of writing, such as memoirs, commentaries, reviews, position papers, and other kinds of extended texts.

Be Selective about Your "Friends"

It's tempting to add everyone you know, but that isn't the best approach. You don't want so-called "friends" writing things on your wall that would make you look bad to important people at your university or to future employers.

Add Regularly to Your Profile

Keep your site up to date with your opinions, ideas, passions, and views on current events. However, don't post private information, such as contact information or anything that would allow a stranger to track you down. Any pictures you put on your page should be appropriate for anyone to see (because they will).

Your site will likely evolve into a tool for staying in touch with people in your academic field, other professionals and clients, and people in your community. It will be less about what you did last weekend and more about your long-term interests, your career, and how you're making a difference in the world.

Starting Your Own Blog

A blog is a Web site in which a writer keeps a public journal of his or her experiences, thoughts, and opinions. Blogs are usually made up of words and sentences, but there are also an increasing number of photo blogs, video blogs, and audio blogs.

Choose a Host Site for Your Blog

Don't pay for a blogging site. Some popular free blogging sites include *Blogger, Wordpress, Blogsome,* and *Moveable Type.* Each one has strengths and weaknesses, so you might look at them all to determine which one will fit your needs and reach the people you want to speak to. Another kind of blog is a "microblog," which only allows a small number of words per post. *Twitter* was the groundbreaking microblogging site, but other microblogging services are now available.

Begin Your Blog

Your host site will ask you for some basic information—your name, your blog's name, and an e-mail address. You will then choose the template that fits your personality and the kinds of topics you want to discuss (Figure 29.1).

FIGURE 29.1 Choosing a Blog Template

The template you choose for your blog should fit your personality and the kinds of topics you want to discuss on your blog.

Compose, Edit, and Publish Your Ideas. On your blogging site, you will see tabs or buttons on the screen that allow you to "compose," "edit," and "publish" your comments. Type some of your thoughts into the Compose screen and hit the Post or Publish button. Keep adding more comments when you feel the urge.

Watch the Animation on **Composing Blogs** at mycomplab.com

Personalize Your Blog

You can add photographs, profiles, polls, newsreels, icons, and other gadgets to your blog's layout. Pick features that are appropriate for the kind of blog you want to create, but don't go overboard with extra stuff that distracts readers from your ideas and arguments.

Let Others Join the Conversation. The initial settings for your blogging site will strictly control who can access and post comments to your blog. As you get comfortable with your blog, you might want to allow others to write comments.

When starting out, only allow "registered users" to add comments. If you allow "anyone" to comment, strangers and spammers may contribute posts that annoy or embarrass you, and you will need to spend time cleaning up your blog.

Keep in mind that blogs are public sites that anyone can read. So keep the blog interesting but avoid posts that put you in a bad light. Current or future employers may discover your blog, so you want to only say things that you would say to your current or future boss. Plus, remember that you can be sued for writing slanderous or libelous things about other people. So keep it clean and truthful.

Writing Articles for Wikis

Wikis are collaboratively written Internet sites that users can add to and edit. One of the most popular is *Wikipedia*, an online encyclopedia that allows users to add and edit information about almost any topic. Other popular wikis include *eHow, WikiHow, CookbookWiki, ProductWiki, Uncyclopedia*, and *Wikicars*. Figure 29.2 on page 558 shows a user-written entry from *Wikitravel*. Your professors may ask you to add material to one of these wikis or contribute to a wiki dedicated to your class.

Write the Article

Like any kind of writing, you should begin by thinking about your topic, angle, purpose, readers, and the contexts in which your article will be used. Research your topic thoroughly, draft the article, and edit it carefully. Include any appropriate graphics. You should also have your sources available, so they can be listed in "References," "External Links," and "Further Reading." Draft your wiki article with a word processor. This will allow you to do all the drafting and revising before you add it to the wiki.

Make sure your article is interesting and factually accurate. If your article is about something trivial or mundane, the wiki administrator will simply delete it. If your article is factually inaccurate, other wiki users will rewrite your work.

FIGURE 29.2 Writing for a Wiki

A wiki is a collection of articles written and edited by users. Here is an article about travelling to Quebec from Wikitravel.

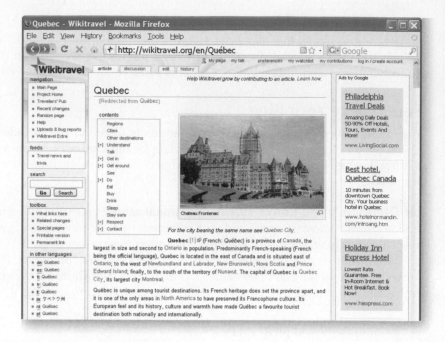

Add Your Article to the Wiki

Look for the button that says, "Create an article" or "Start the X article." Most wikis require you to have an account if you want to add an article. Once you log in, the wiki will provide a box where you can cut and paste your article from your word processor.

Edit and proofread your article. Then click the Save Page button. At this point, your article will be added to the wiki.

You should return to your article periodically to make sure someone hasn't altered it to say something inaccurate. You might be pleasantly surprised to find that someone has expanded your article, providing information you didn't know about.

Putting Videos and Podcasts on the Internet

You can upload videos to Web sites like *YouTube, MySpace Videos, MSN Video, Yahoo! Video, Veoh, Joost, iFilm, Hulu, Metacafe,* and *blip.tv.* Some popular podcasting sites include *Podcast Alley, iTunes, Digg,* and *Podcast Pickle.*

Create Your Video or Record Your Podcast

As with all writing, if you want to make something worth watching or hearing, you should first consider your topic, angle, purpose, readers, and the contexts in which your work will be experienced. Then invent the content and draft a script.

Above all, don't bore your audience. Good planning and tight scripting will allow you to make something worth watching or listening to.

◉ **Watch** the Animation on **Composing Videos** at **mycomplab.com**

Edit Your Work

Edit your work with video– or sound–editing software. Some good video editing software packages include *MS Movie Maker, Adobe Premiere, Final Cut,* and *iMovie.* The most common sound editing software packages for editing podcasts include *Adobe Audition, Audacity, Garage Band,* and *Cubase.*

Upload Your Video or Podcast

When your video or podcast is ready, go to the "upload" link (Figure 29.3). You'll be asked for a title, description, and some keywords called "tags." Try to include as many keywords as you so that people searching the Web site will be more likely to come across your video or podcast.

These sites are public, so don't show, do, or say anything illegal, unethical, or embarrassing. Be careful about your personal information. Even if you limit who can access your work, someone else, including friends, might share them with others.

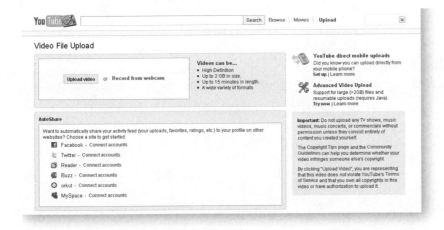

FIGURE 29.3 Uploading a Video

Putting a video on YouTube is easier than ever. This page shows how to load a video by dragging it to the YouTube screen on your computer.

The social media tools you use to manage your personal life can be powerful platforms for sharing your ideas and arguments with a much larger community. Here's what you can do with these tools.

CREATE Your Profile on a Social Networking Site

Choose the social networking site that is most appropriate for your lifestyle and thoughts. Pick one that has the audience you most want to reach.

BLOG about What Matters to You

You're more likely to update your blog often—and write with a passion that engages and involves readers—if you choose a topic of ongoing personal interest.

SHARE Your Online Compositions

Post your work for others to see. But be strategic about who can see or follow you and how (or if) others can comment or participate on your site.

PARTICIPATE in Knowledge-Making on a Wiki Site

Share what you're learning in college by writing entries for wikis—or by correcting erroneous information. Be sure your information is accurate, well-researched, and useful to others.

BROADCAST Your Ideas to the World

Use video and audio recording technologies to capture places, events, and people of interest to you and the community. Upload your work to a site where it can be widely shared and discussed.

1. With your group in class, talk about the different ways you use the new media tools discussed in this chapter. Discuss how these media tools have changed the way people communicate in your lifetime.

2. How are social networking sites, blogging, and audio and video sharing changing the workplace? How do members of your group expect new media to shape their careers?

3. Do you think people learn social skills online that they can use elsewhere? Or, are social media actually harmful to people's abilities to interact in the real world?

Talk About This

1. If you already have a social media site, revise it in ways that would make it appealing (or at least acceptable) to a future employer.

2. With a group of people from your class, shoot a small video or record a podcast. Upload the video or podcast to a video sharing Web site and send a link to your professor.

3. With a group in your class, think of a topic that interests all of you. Then, using three different wikis, read the articles written about that topic. What facts do these wiki articles have in common? What facts are different or missing from one or more of the articles? How do the articles approach the topic from different angles, and what do they choose to highlight?

Try This Out

1. **Learn about a new media tool.** Write a review of one of the new media tools discussed in this chapter. Discuss its future and how you think it will affect your life and your career.

2. **Write your ideas in a blog.** For two weeks, keep a blog in which you write about anything that interests you. Then write an e-mail to your professor in which you explain why you did or didn't enjoy blogging, and whether you think you will continue blogging in the future.

Write This

30

Creating a
Portfolio

In this chapter, you will learn how to—
- collect your materials for your portfolio.
- write a reflection on your work.
- present your materials for academic and career-related purposes.
- create a résumé of your experience and skills.

Portfolios include selections of your best work, packaged for people who need to understand or evaluate your background, abilities, knowledge, and potential. They also give you a chance to reflect on your writing, leading to deeper, more permanent learning. In college, you may need to create a portfolio for a specific course or as a "capstone" to your studies in your major.

Your portfolio will also be an important part of your job application package, because it allows you to show interviewers examples of your work. Throughout your career, your portfolio may be used to track your professional development and determine whether you receive a raise or a promotion.

Two Basic Kinds of Portfolios

There are two basic types of portfolios: *learning portfolios* and *showcase portfolios*.

Learning Portfolios. Learning portfolios focus on your progress toward mastering specific knowledge and abilities. Your learning portfolio is like a movie that leads your readers through a course or your college career to show your progress. Your portfolio demonstrates what and how you have learned. Learning portfolios include finished documents and sometimes drafts and brainstorming notes.

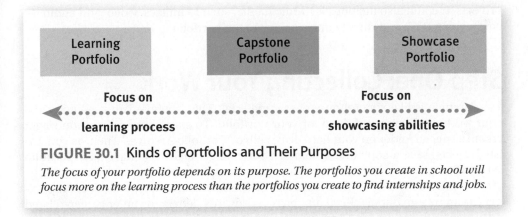

FIGURE 30.1 Kinds of Portfolios and Their Purposes

The focus of your portfolio depends on its purpose. The portfolios you create in school will focus more on the learning process than the portfolios you create to find internships and jobs.

Showcase Portfolios. Showcase portfolios display only finished products that demonstrate your work at its best. They are designed to highlight the knowledge and abilities that you have mastered. They are like a snapshot that provides a rich and detailed depiction of your skills and know-how at the present moment.

A third kind of portfolio, usually called a "capstone portfolio" is a hybrid of these two (Figure 30.1). Like learning portfolios, capstone portfolios show your progress toward mastery. However, capstone portfolios usually do not include drafts or notes because they are designed to show your work at its best.

Getting Started on Your Portfolio

Creating a portfolio is not difficult, but it does take some time and planning. Here are four simple steps to follow:

Analyze the Interactive Document at mycomplab.com

1. **Collect** your work in an ongoing "archive" folder on your computer's hard drive or in a file folder. Each item in your portfolio is called an *artifact*.

2. **Select** those artifacts that best exemplify the knowledge and ability you want your portfolio to exhibit. Your selections depend on who will be viewing your portfolios and why.

3. **Reflect** on what is in the portfolio. Usually professors or supervisors will ask you to write a brief reflection that introduces and reviews the materials in your portfolio.

4. **Present** the portfolio as a complete package. Depending on how it will be used, your portfolio might be print, online, or multimedia.

Your portfolio should include a wide collection of artifacts. It should include documents, of course, but it might also include photographs, presentations, and projects. It could also include electronic media, such as images, video, and audio recorded on a DVD and slipped into a pocket of the portfolio or folder.

Step One: Collecting Your Work

Your archive is like a storehouse of raw material. This is where you keep copies of your work until you need them for your portfolio. To start your archive, you might create a special folder on your hard drive called "Portfolio Archive." Then, as you finish projects, save a copy in that folder. Your college might also have an e-portfolio service that gives students storage space on its computers for their materials.

For print documents, you should also designate a drawer in your desk or file cabinet for archive materials. Keep any projects, awards, letters, or other career-related documents in this drawer. Then at the end of each semester, you can look through these items and decide what to add to your portfolio and what to file for later use.

Right now, early in your college career, is the best time to create an archive. That way, you can get into the habit of saving your best work. As an added benefit, you will always know where your best work is stored. The worst time to start an archive is when you are getting ready to graduate from college. At that point, much of your best work will have been forgotten or lost.

Archiving for a Specific Course

In some courses, your professor will require you to complete a portfolio that shows your work from the class. Make sure you understand what kinds of materials you will need to save for your portfolio. Some professors will ask that you save everything—notes, drafts, and polished copies. Other professors may want just final versions of your work in the portfolio. Here are some things you might be asked to save:

- All notes, including class notes, brainstorming, freewrites, journaling, and so on
- Rough drafts, informal writing, responses, and perhaps your professors' written comments on your drafts
- Peer review, both that you've done for others and that others have done for you
- Final drafts
- Electronic material, such as images, multimedia, blogs, Web-based discussions

Archiving for Your College Career

Your department or college may ask you to create a portfolio at various stages of your college career. For instance, at the end of your sophomore or junior year, your college may require you to submit a portfolio that illustrates your ability to write well and think critically. And at the end of your college career, you may be asked to create a capstone portfolio that illustrates what you have accomplished in your major field of study.

Items that you should save for this portfolio include the following:

- Awards or recognition of any kind

- Letters of reference from professors

- Scholarship letters and letters of acceptance

- Materials and evaluations from internships, co-ops, or jobs

- Copies of exams (preferably ones you did well on)

- Evidence of participation in clubs or special events and volunteer work

You never know what you might need, so keep anything that might be useful. If you regularly save these materials, you will be amazed at how much you did while you were at college.

Archiving for Your Professional Career

Employers often ask job applicants to bring a professional portfolio to interviews. It is also common for professionals to maintain a portfolio for promotions, performance reviews, and job searches. A professional portfolio could include these materials:

- Reflective cover letter that introduces the portfolio by describing your career goals, education, work experiences, skills, and special abilities

- Résumé

- Examples of written work, presentations, and other materials such as images, links to Web sites, and so on

- Diplomas, certificates, and awards

- Letters of reference

For job interviews, you should create two versions of your professional portfolio. The first version, which you should never give away, should hold all your original materials. The second version, called a "giveaway portfolio," should have copies of your materials that you can leave with interviewers.

Step Two: Selecting the Best Artifacts

Once you have created an archive, it's time to begin the process of creating a portfolio. Keep in mind that a single archive can supply the material for several portfolios, each with a different purpose and audience.

Start by considering which artifacts in your archive will allow you to achieve your portfolio's purpose and meet the needs of your readers. Select items carefully because the best examples of your work need to stand out. Choose the key documents that help you achieve your purpose and catch your reader's interest.

Step Three: Reflecting on Your Work

You may be asked to write two kinds of reflections for your portfolio, depending on how it will be used:

Learning-Focused Reflections. These reflections tell the story of your progress in a class or an academic program. They show that you have mastered certain knowledge and abilities. They also give you a chance to understand the course objectives more thoroughly and to master the course content even more completely.

Mastery-Focused Reflections. These reflections focus more on demonstrating how well you have mastered certain bodies of knowledge and abilities. In this kind of reflection, your readers want you to explain what you can do and how well you can do it.

Your Reflection as an Argument

Whether you are creating a learning portfolio or a showcase portfolio, your reflection needs to state an overall claim (i.e., a main point or thesis). Then the reflection should use the items in the portfolio as evidence to support your claim.

Demonstrating these features, Figure 30.2 shows a learning-focused reflection written for a first-year writing course, and Figure 30.3 (on page 569) offers a mastery-focused reflection written by a job candidate. Notice how each reflection makes a claim about the writer's experience and abilities and then points to specific places in the portfolio where they can find evidence supporting those claims. The first reflection, for a writing course, focuses on process and progress. The second, for an interview portfolio, focuses almost exclusively on the job candidate's mastery.

Step Four: Presenting Your Materials

How you present your work is very important. So don't just throw your materials into a manila envelope or fasten them together. That looks sloppy and unprofessional. You need to present your materials in an organized and attractive way, so your readers can find the documents they want to see. Use three-ring binder or a nice folder, or create an e-portfolio that you can put on the Internet or on a disc.

For a Specific Course. Most portfolios for a single course are organized chronologically from the earliest documents to the most recent documents. Your reflection should appear first as an introduction to the portfolio. And if you are asked to include drafts of papers, you should put them *behind* the final versions, not in front of them.

MEMORANDUM

Date: December 2, 2007
To: Greg Evans
From: Josh Kotobi
Subject: Portfolio Memo

English 101 helped me improve my writing in every way, including my rhetoric, grammar, style, and understanding of genres and how to use them. The class objectives included learning about many different genres, and how to present ideas, information, and arguments in each genre. In this cover letter, I will explain my progress and learning in terms of each of the five learning goals for the course.

Reading and Analysis

We read a variety of literary and other writing, and we worked on summarizing, interpreting, evaluating, and synthesizing the ideas in these writings. These activities expanded our writing skills as we learned how to write in different genres and styles. The close analysis of each of these texts allowed us to better understand what constitutes effective writing and ineffective writing.

I believe that the documents that show my progress and ability best in this area are the first and final drafts of my position paper. In the first draft, I just dismissed David Brooks's whole argument. I barely mentioned it, and then didn't even deal with his points. But in the final draft, you'll see that on the first two pages, I summarize, paraphrase, and quote David Brooks's article about marriage. I worked

States purpose and main point.

Highlights learning goals and uses documents to support claims.

continued

FIGURE 30.2 A Student's Learning-Focused Reflection

This reflection, created for a course in first-year writing at the University of New Mexico, exemplifies one approach to the cover letter. The student's professor asked for cover letters that described students' learning progress in terms of the five main course goals.

FIGURE 30.2
A Student's
Learning-
Focused
Reflection
(continued)

very hard to explain his arguments fairly, and I even conceded two points that were very strong. Even so, I went on to use my analysis of his argument to position my own. I didn't just bounce off Brooks's argument—I incorporated it into mine to make my position stronger.

[Kotobi goes on to discuss the other learning goals of the course, omitted here.]

All in all, bit by bit, week by week, I made progress with my writing. The first draft of my first paper, as you can see, was really bad. I was just writing automatically without even thinking. But I think you'll find that as the semester progressed, I wrote more thoughtfully as I learned to frame problems and use the ideas of the authors I read. I'm very pleased about the progress I've made and feel much better about doing well in the rest of my college courses.

> Finishes with main point and looks to the future.

For a Capstone Course. A portfolio for a capstone course can be organized by courses, giving each course its own part and arranged in numerical order. Or you could organize the portfolio by genres (e.g., reviews, analyses, reports, proposals). Drafts are not typically included in capstone portfolios.

For a Job Application Packet. Portfolios used for job searches typically follow the organization of a résumé. After your reflection, you should include parts like Education, Related Coursework, Work Experience, Skills, Awards, and Activities. Each part should have its own divider with a tab.

If you will be presenting your portfolio in person (e.g., in an interview or to a group), you should organize your material in a way that helps you verbally explain your background and experiences. It should also look professional and purposeful.

Creating an E-Portfolio

Increasingly, people are going electronic with their portfolios. Making an e-portfolio is not difficult, especially if you know how to create a basic Web site or if you have access to an e-portfolio service at your university.

Electronic portfolios have several advantages:

- They can be accessed from anywhere there is a networked computer.

- They can include multimedia texts such as movies, presentations, and links to Web sites you have created.

Welcome to My Portfolio

Let me begin by thanking you for reviewing the materials in my portfolio. Here, I have collected examples of my best work to demonstrate my knowledge, experience, and abilities as a civil engineer. These materials will show you that I am well trained and innovative, and I have a solid background in the design, construction, and maintenance of interstate highways and bridges.

> States purpose and main point while acknowledging the readers.

The first section includes examples from my internships and cooperative experiences. I have included two reports that I wrote during my internship with the Michigan Department of Transportation. They show my ability to write detailed, accurate observations of road and bridge conditions, while making clear recommendations. The third document is a proposal for a research project on quick-setting concrete that I helped write as a co-op for New Horizons Construction.

> Explains the content and organization of the portfolio.

The second section shows materials created for my courses at Michigan State. Our professors used projects to teach us how to problem solve and come up with innovative solutions to challenging problems. The reports, proposals, specifications, and technical descriptions included here were selected to demonstrate the range of my abilities and my communication skills.

> Highlights key features of each section.

The third section includes letters of reference, awards, scholarships, and other recognition of my work at Michigan State and my internship and co-op experiences.

My goal in this portfolio is to show you that I am ready to begin contributing to your firm right away. If you would like to see other examples of my work, please call me at 517-555-1855 or e-mail me at rgfranklin@msu.edu.

> Concludes with a main point and contact information.

FIGURE 30.3 A Job Candidate's Mastery-Focused Reflection

In this reflection, a job candidate tries to highlight a few of her strengths and experiences. The reflection serves mostly as an introduction to the portfolio.

- They can include scanned-in documents that show comments that others have handwritten on your work.

- They provide interactivity for the reader. For example, the reflective letter can link directly to the documents in the portfolio or to items on the Internet.

- They include materials and links to information. For example, you might put links to your university and academic department to help interviewers learn about your educational background.

- They can be updated easily, while older versions can be archived.

- They provide customized access features for different readers.

- They eliminate copying costs.

Some e-portfolio services even allow you to maintain an electronic archive from which you can create a virtually limitless number of e-portfolios, each targeted for a specific purpose and audience.

Keeping Your Portfolio Up to Date

This semester, your professor may be asking you to create a portfolio only for your writing class. Right now, though, would be a good opportunity to also create an archive for your portfolio that you can use throughout your college career and beyond.

Each semester, spend a little time updating your portfolio. Look for chances to create documents that fill out any gaps in your portfolio. You can also find opportunities to add to your portfolio by joining clubs, doing volunteer work, and completing internships or co-ops.

It takes an hour or so each semester to update your portfolio. You will be thankful you did when you are nearing graduation and starting to look for a job.

Creating a Starter Résumé

You professor may ask you to include a résumé in your portfolio. At this point in your college career, it probably doesn't seem like you need a résumé—at least not for a few more years. Increasingly, though, résumés are being used for college-related purposes, like scholarships, applications, and internships. Plus, if you create a "starter résumé" now, you can work on filling it out with experiences.

A résumé is a profile of yourself that usually fits on one page (Figure 30.4). Like a profile, your résumé offers basic facts about your life. It should tell a story about your education, work experience, awards, and activities. Your résumé needs to make a good impression, because it is the first item your readers, including employers, will see.

Anne Simmons Franklin

834 County Line Rd.
Hollings Point, Illinois 62905

Home: 618-555-2993
Mobile: 618-555-9167
E-mail: afranklin@unsb5.net

CAREER OBJECTIVE

A position as a naturalist, specializing in agronomy, working for a distribution company that specializes in organic foods.

EDUCATIONAL BACKGROUND

Bachelor of Science, Southern Illinois University, expected May 2012.
Major: Plant and Soil Science
Minor: Entomology
GPA: 3.2/4.0

WORK EXPERIENCE

Intern Agronomist, December 2010–August 2011
Brighter Days Organic Cooperative, Simmerton, Illinois

- Consulted with growers on organic pest control methods. Primary duty was sale of organic crop protection products, crop nutrients, seed, and consulting services.
- Prepared organic agronomic farm plans for growers.
- Provided crop-scouting services to identify weed and insect problems.

Field Technician, August 2010–December 2010
Entomology Department, Southern Illinois University

- Collected and identified insects.
- Developed insect management plans.
- Tested organic and nonorganic pesticides for effectiveness and residuals.

SKILLS

Computer Experience: Access, Excel, Outlook, PowerPoint, and Word. Global Positioning Systems (GPS). Database Management.
Machinery: Field Tractors, Combines, Straight Trucks, and Bobcats.
Communication Skills: Proposal Writing and Review, Public Presentations, Negotiating, Training, Writing Agronomic and Financial Farm Plans.

AWARDS AND ACTIVITIES

Awarded "Best Young Innovator" by the Organic Food Society of America
Member of Entomological Society of America
Vice-President, Entomology Club, Southern Illinois University, 2009–present

REFERENCES AVAILABLE UPON REQUEST

Name and contact information placed up front.

Career objective describes position sought.

Work experience is supported with details.

Skills are listed separately for emphasis.

Awards and activities are listed later in the résumé.

FIGURE 30.4 A Résumé

This resume was created by a graduating senior.

For a college student or recent college graduate, the *archival résumé* is usually the most familiar and appropriate. It includes the following features:

Career objective. A career objective is a sentence or phrase that describes the career you are seeking.

Educational background. Your educational background should list your current college degree and any other degrees in reverse chronological order—most recent to least recent. List your major and minors. Sometimes career-related coursework is listed here.

Work experience. Any jobs, internships, or co-ops that you have held should be listed, starting with the most recent and working to the least recent.

Skills. Résumés often include a section listing career-related skills, such as leadership training, computers, languages, bookkeeping, and so on.

Awards and activities. List any awards you have earned and any organized activities in which you have participated. Scholarships can appear here.

References. Your references are the people who will vouch for you—professors, supervisors, and other professionals. In most résumés, the line "References available upon request" appears at the bottom of the page.

Use this guide to help you begin and complete your portfolio.

COLLECT Your Work in an Archive

Get into the habit of saving your documents and projects in an archive. For a specific course, you may want to save *everything*, from notes to rough drafts to final drafts, from print documents to audio files to images to movies. For a capstone portfolio in the middle or at the end of your academic career, you will want to save a variety of examples of your best work. Some schools allow you to store your work in an electronic archive.

SELECT the Works for a Specific Type of Portfolio

When you have a specific type of portfolio in mind, start selecting the works from your archive that will help you to achieve your purpose and that will be most useful for your readers.

REFLECT on What the Portfolio Shows: Your Learning Process, Your Abilities, and Your Experience

Every portfolio needs some kind of reflection or cover letter that introduces readers to the portfolio. In your reflection, make your argument about what the portfolio shows by pointing out to readers what they should notice.

PRESENT Your Portfolio

If you're using a binder or folder for your portfolio, include a table of contents and tabbed section dividers. If you're creating an e-portfolio, use an attractive Web page design, links, and an easy-to-use navigation system.

KEEP Your Portfolio Up to Date

Revisit your portfolio at the end of each semester. It will be useful when you begin your job search. Many professionals maintain an ongoing portfolio for career development, promotions, and new opportunities.

CREATE Your Starter Résumé

Even if your professor doesn't require a résumé for your portfolio, right now would be a good time to start one. That way, you can fill it in and update it throughout your college career.

1. Brainstorm the development of a portfolio for this course or another course. Describe to your group how you would collect, select, reflect on, and present your work.

2. Analyze the rhetorical situation for a job interview portfolio. Briefly, write down notes that define the topic, angle, purpose, readers, and contexts for this kind of portfolio. Also, discuss how the rhetorical situation might change to suit different kinds of job interviews.

3. Imagine that your major requires that you create a capstone portfolio, including what you learned and how you learned it. Make a list of the kinds of artifacts that you will want to have saved for this portfolio, with a brief explanation of what each artifact would show about you.

1. Go online and find an e-portfolio created by a college student. What kinds of artifacts are included? Is there anything surprising about the documents or projects the student has included? How is the portfolio organized and designed? Does the organization make things easy to find?

2. Go online and find at least two professional e-portfolios from people who are pursuing a career like the one you want to pursue. What is included in their portfolios? How well does the cover letter introduce and explain the contents of the portfolio?

3. Write the résumé you would like to have when you graduate from college. Put down your degree, major, and the year you will graduate. List jobs, internships, and co-ops you would like to do before graduating. Identify the skills you want to develop while you are at college. List the activities you want to participate in while at college. Your résumé should fit on one page.

1. **Create a mini-portfolio.** With your most recent assignment in this course, create a mini-portfolio that charts your progress from prewriting through drafts and feedback to final drafts. Write a cover letter in which you reflect on your writing process for this assignment. In your reflection, make a claim about your learning and support it.

2. **Critique an e-portfolio on the Internet.** Find an interesting e-portfolio on the Internet. Write a three-page rhetorical analysis in which you analyze its effectiveness. How does the author use reasoning (*logos*) to demonstrate his or her knowledge and abilities? How does he or she build up a sense of authority (*ethos*)? Where, if anyplace, does the author use emotion (*pathos*) to add personality to the portfolio?

PEARSON
mycomplab

For support in meeting this chapter's objectives, follow this path in MyCompLab: Portfolio ⟹ Portfolio Building Tips. Review the Instruction and Multimedia resources about building a portfolio, then select Build a New Portfolio to build your own portfolio.

31

Succeeding on
Essay Exams

In this chapter, you will learn how to—

- prepare yourself to succeed on an essay examination.
- begin the exam with confidence, while budgeting your time.
- organize your ideas so you can answer questions quickly and effectively.

Taking essay exams can be a little stressful, but once you learn a few helpful strategies, they will be much easier. You can succeed on essay exams by using some of the time-tested rhetorical strategies you have already learned in this book.

Keep in mind that professors use essay exams to evaluate how well you understand the course materials and whether you can apply what you learned. Exams give you opportunities to demonstrate higher-order thinking skills, such as interpreting ideas, applying concepts to new situations, analyzing solutions, synthesizing knowledge, and evaluating beliefs.

This chapter will help you succeed by showing you what to expect in college essay exams and providing strategies that will help you prepare for and write them. You will learn a four-stage process for doing well on essay exams: preparing, starting the exam, answering the questions, and finishing the exam (Figure 31.1).

Preparing for an Essay Exam

Studying course materials closely and taking good notes during lectures are important first steps for succeeding on exams. In addition, though, you should prepare for an essay exam by *being active* with the material. Here are some strategies for doing so.

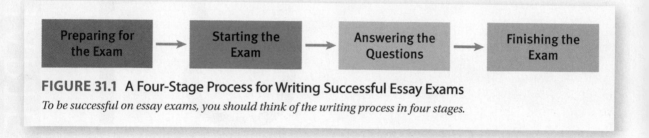

FIGURE 31.1 A Four-Stage Process for Writing Successful Essay Exams

To be successful on essay exams, you should think of the writing process in four stages.

Work in Study Groups

In your class or where you live, find two to five other dedicated students who are willing to meet regularly to study together and collaborate on projects. It helps to find group members who understand the material both better than you and not as well as you. People who have already mastered the material can help you strengthen your own understanding. Likewise, when you help others learn course content, you strengthen your own understanding of the material.

Set up a regular time and place to meet with your study group, perhaps one to three times a week. Your university's student union, a library, or a local café can be good places for regular meetings.

Ask Your Professor about the Exam

You can often improve your chances of succeeding on an exam by asking your professor about it during class or office hours. Your professor may be willing to provide you with sample questions or examples from previous semesters' tests. However, professors don't like it when students "grade grub" by constantly asking, "Will this be on the test?" Instead, ask more open-ended questions like these:

- What kinds of questions are likely to appear on the exam?

- What kinds of things do you expect us to be able to do on the exam?

- How many questions will be on the exam, and how long should each take to answer?

- How do you think we should prepare for this exam?

- Can you give us a list of five to ten concepts or key ideas that we should master for this exam?

- Can you describe what a typical answer to the exam question would look like?

One or two questions like these will almost always be welcome.

Pay Attention to Themes

As you look over your lecture notes and textbook, look for thematic patterns to help you organize and remember the course material.

Ask yourself, what are the fundamental ideas and topics that your professor and textbook have focused on? What are some key points that your professor keeps repeating? What are some larger trends that seem to underlie all the ideas and concepts you have learned in this class?

Create Your Own Questions and Rehearse Possible Answers

Come up with your own questions that you think might appear on the exam and generate responses to them. You can rehearse your responses a few different ways:

- **Talk to yourself:** Mentally run through your responses and, if possible, say your answers out loud.

- **Talk to others:** Talk through answers with members of your study group.

- **Outline or plan out responses:** By yourself or with others, use outlines to map out possible responses. Then express your answers orally or in writing.

- **Simulate the actual exam:** Write a response or two within a set amount of time. If you have test anxiety and tend to go blank before an exam, try to practice in the actual classroom where you will be taking the test.

Starting Your Essay Exam

So the professor has just handed you the exam. Now what? Take a deep breath and relax. Avoid the impulse to just dive right in.

Review the Exam Quickly to Gain an Overall Picture

Take a moment to review the whole exam. Pay attention to the kinds of questions and how much time is recommended for each. Pay special attention to questions that are worth the most so you can leave extra time for them.

As you read each question, jot down a few quick notes or a brief outline of an answer. Then, move on to the next question. These notes and outlines have two benefits: First, they help you warm up by putting your ideas down on the page before you start writing, and, second, they will show your professor where you were going with each answer even if you run out of time. Your professor won't give you full credit for an outline, but he or she might give you partial credit if you were answering the question correctly.

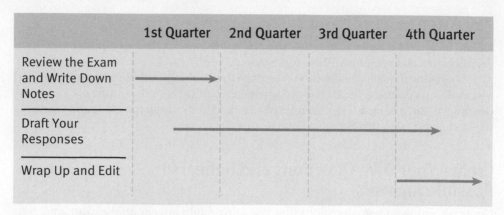

FIGURE 31.2 Budgeting Your Time

Don't just dive in and start writing. Take some of your total time to plan your answers, and be sure to leave time at the end to write conclusions and do some final insertions, editing, and proofreading.

Budget Your Time

Allocate your time properly, so you can answer all the questions. As shown in Figure 31.2, it might help to think in quarters about the time available for your essay exam. Spend a portion of the first quarter considering each question, jotting down some notes, and outlining a possible answer for each question. Devote the second and third quarters to actually drafting your answers one by one. Save some of the fourth quarter for revising, editing, and proofreading.

Answering an Essay Exam Question

When answering an essay exam question, your goal is to demonstrate how much you *know* about the course material and what you can *do* with it. So for most essay exam questions, you will want to keep the organization and style of your response fairly simple and straightforward.

Organize Your Answer

Remember that an essay exam answer should always have an introduction, body, and conclusion. That advice might sound obvious, but under pressure, people often forget these three parts. Instead, they just start writing everything they know about the topic. This often leads to a jumble of facts, names, and concepts that are hard to understand.

As you think about the organization of your answer, keep the basic structure of an essay in mind:

Introduction. Your introduction should state your main claim, which the rest of your answer will support. Your professor should see your best answer to the question up front, preferably in one sentence. In your introduction, you might also restate the question, forecast the organization of your response, and provide some background information (e.g., historical facts, important people, or key terms). Your introduction should only be a few sentences.

Body. The body should be divided into two to five key points, with each point receiving a paragraph or two. Put key points in the topic sentences at the beginning of your paragraphs. Then support each key point with facts, data, reasoning, and examples. Usually, you will find that the professor is asking you to do one of the following things:

- *Explain* a historical event, story plot, or process (narrative or summary).
- *Describe* something or explain how it works (description).
- *Define* something (definition).
- *Divide* something into groups or types (classification).
- *Compare* two or more things (comparison and contrast).
- *Argue* for or against (summary of both sides, argument for one).
- *Solve* a problem (description of problem and argument for a solution).

Once you know what your professor is asking you to do, the structure of your answer will become much more obvious.

Conclusion. Briefly indicate that you are wrapping up (e.g., "In conclusion,") and restate your main point. If time allows, you may also want to raise a new question or problem, describe the implications of your response, state the significance of the problem, or make a prediction about the future.

Above all, keep your answers simple and straightforward. Your professor isn't expecting you to come up with a new theory or an amazing breakthrough. He or she is looking for evidence that you have mastered the materials and can do something with what you have learned.

Finishing Your Essay Exam

Save a little time at the end of the exam for revising and editing. You won't have much time, so focus on completeness and clarity.

Checklist for Revising and Editing Essay Exams

❑ Reread each prompt to make sure you answered the question.

❑ Look for any missing key points and determine if you have time to add them.

❑ Check whether your ideas are clear and easy to follow.

❑ Emphasize key terms and concepts by inserting them or highlighting them.

❑ Proofread for grammatical errors, spelling mistakes, and garbled handwriting.

Remember, you will gain nothing by racing through the exam and being the first person out the door. You won't look any smarter, and your professor really won't be that impressed. So you may as well use all the time available to do the best job you can.

One Student's Essay Exam

To demonstrate some of the ideas from this chapter, here is a typical essay exam response written by a student. His answer is clear and straightforward. The organization is basic, and the style is plain. It's not perfect, but it achieves the student's goals of showing that he understands the course materials and can do something with that information.

Essay Prompt: In your opinion, which world region or subregion has the greatest potential to improve its development status over the course of your lifetime? Why? What environmental, human, and/or economic resources could it depend on in this process?

Prominently identifies which question he is answering.

Shane Oreck

Question 3B

Introduction restates the question, makes a clear main claim, forecasts the answer, and uses keywords from lectures and readings.

The region that has the greatest potential to improve is Latin America. The reasons for this are: its natural resources, technological potential, tourism potential, and human resources.

First, countries within Latin America have a bounty of natural and biological resources. If these countries eventually become able to excavate these minerals in a more efficient manner, then their economy will boom. In the Amazon, many countries are looking toward this uncharted area in hopes of finding biological sources that will help in the areas of science and health. So with time and ingenuity, hopefully this will help Latin America's economy as well.

Second, because Latin America is so close to more technologically advanced countries, they have a great potential for technological advancement. This would be better accomplished through a new trade pact with countries in North America and even Russia. If Latin America can make trade a more viable source of income, then the economy will probably boom, bringing with it technological advance and outside sources that could be of importance for these countries.

> Each body paragraph begins with a strong topic sentence that announces a key point.

Third, tourism has great potential because of Latin America's beautiful oceans, views, landscapes, historical attractions, and architecture. They do face difficulties in terms of modern facilities and safety for Western guests, but if they can create the infrastructure, then, like Mexico, they could enjoy substantial economic relief from the money generated. Some Latin American countries, like Brazil, are already enticing travelers into their areas.

> The writing style is simple and straightforward.

Lastly, Latin America has a vast array of human resources. Although current educational resources are lacking, these countries are heavily populated. With improved educational opportunity and greater availability of birth control (so that women can plan families and enjoy educational opportunities as well), the people of Latin America would be an enormous untapped resource in which to revitalize the region, economically and culturally.

It's true also that many other regions of the world, including China and India, would be candidates for greatest potential for improving their development status. But because of its location, abundance of mineral and biological resources, trade and technological potential, tourism, and human resources, Latin America certainly has the potential for creating a bright future. Besides, Latin America has been so poorly developed for so long, it seems due for a resurgence. Where else can it go but up?

> The conclusion wraps up with its main point and a look to the future.

Pay attention to the straightforward nature of this exam answer. The student used a simple organizational pattern, with a clear introduction, body, and conclusion. The main points are easy to locate in the paragraph's topic sentences. Specific and meaningful facts, details, and reasoning are used to support claims. As demonstrated in this essay exam, your goal is to keep your answers simple, demonstrating that you know the material and can use it to make an argument. Figure 31.3 shows some other typical essay exam questions and a few strategies for answering them.

> ⊙ **Watch** the Animation on **Essay Exam Questions** at **mycomplab.com**

FIGURE 31.3 Sample Essay Exam Questions

Knowing: Understanding the Course Material

Question Cues	Strategy	Examples
Knowing • explain • define • describe • classify • compare	Know the major ideas, dates, events, places, and so on.	**Deaf Studies** Describe the events surrounding the 1880 Milan conference. What were the historical, educational, and philosophical themes that emerged at this conference? Who were the key players and what were their positions? What was the significance for Deaf culture? (12 points) **History** Bradbury describes ten major causes of the Industrial Revolution. List five of them and explain how each contributed to the industrialization of Europe. (5 points) **Sociology** Explain the difference between participant and nonparticipant research, how each is used in sociological research, and for what purposes each is used.
Understanding • summarize • explain • compare	Grasp the meaning of important ideas, facts, and theories. Compare two ideas, positions, or theories.	**Developmental Psychology** Compare the stages of personality development according to Piaget and Erikson. **Management** Identify whether each of the following scenarios is best described as a differential cost, opportunity cost, or sunk cost. (5 points each)

Doing: Applying, Analyzing, Synthesizing, and Evaluating Course Material

Question Cues	Strategy	Examples
Applying • explain • describe • compare • solve	Use information, methods, concepts, and theories in new contexts to solve problems, discover relationships, or illustrate concepts.	**Cost Management** The Pointilla T-Shirt Company produces high-quality casual apparel for a name-brand company in the United States. Management needs an analysis of their product and period costs so they can develop plans for controlling them. Given the following costs, calculate the total product and period costs. . . . **Art History** Use an iconographical analysis to describe the qualities, nature, and history of the statue pictured below.
Analyzing • explain • define • classify	Recognize patterns; interpret causes and effects; identify components.	**American Literature** Compare the essays on Faulker's "A Rose for Emily" by literary critics George L. Dillon and Judith Fetterley. How does each critic explain the uses of literature—i.e., what we *gain* by reading literature? **Nursing** Explain the difference between *glycemic index* and *glycemic load* to two audiences: (1) a class of first-year medical students (who have a good understanding of biochemistry), and (2) the parents of a child with diabetes (who have an eighth grade education and do not know, for instance, the difference between carbohydrates, proteins, and fat). (30 minutes)

continued

FIGURE 31.3 Sample Essay Exam Questions *(continued)*

Question Cues	Strategy	Examples
Synthesizing • combine • create • develop a plan • argue for or against	Generalize from facts; combine knowledge from different areas; make predictions; draw conclusions.	**Literature** Consider William Faulkner's short story "A Rose for Emily" and Maya Quinlan's feminist analysis of Chopin's "Story of an Hour." Using what you've learned about feminist approaches to literature from Quinlan's article, predict how a feminist critic like Quinlan would interpret "A Rose for Emily." Be sure to state her overall interpretation and describe at least three aspects of the short story that she would probably attend to and *why* you think a feminist critic would find those aspects important. **Pharmacy** The chemical formulas and structures for Pharmaceutical A and Pharmaceutical B are shown in the figure below. Explain from a biochemical perspective what would happen if the two drugs were taken simultaneously. In your response, be sure to identify the relevant function groups present in each compound, classify each pharmaceutical, relate some of the structural features of the compound to physical and chemical properties, and discuss the consequences of confusing the two drugs.
Evaluating • assess • argue for or against • solve	Compare and evaluate ideas, models, theories, or plans.	**Introductory Earth Sciences** Describe how the geology, climate, and biology (focusing on plants and animals) of London, England, have changed from the Late Triassic Period to the present. Use the figures below depicting the drift of the continents and apply your knowledge of plate tectonics, climatology, and paleobiology to support your answer. **Geography** In your opinion, which world region or subregion has the greatest potential to improve its development status over the course of your lifetime? Why? What environmental, human, and/or economic resources could it depend on in this process?

Essay exams can be challenging, but you will be more successful if you prepare properly. To do your best, follow these steps.

PREPARE for the Exam

Take good notes on lectures and readings, but also consider the key themes and issues that your professor keeps returning to. Form and regularly meet with a study group. Go to your professor and ask what the exam will look like, and what he or she wants to see in an exam response.

START the Exam

First read through the entire test to get the big picture, making note of how much time you have and the point value for each question. Budget your time so you can outline some answers, write out the exam, and revise and edit.

ANSWER the Questions

Make sure you understand what each question is asking you to do (explain, describe, define, classify, compare, argue for or against, or solve a problem). As you write, stay focused and try to maintain a simple, straightforward organization and style.

FINISH Up with Revising and Editing

Reread the questions and make sure your responses answer them. Make any adjustments needed and highlight places where you address the question directly. Save some time for proofreading.

1. Individually, freewrite an answer to this question: What is hard about writing essay exams? After you've written your response, discuss your answer with your group and come up with three strategies for making essay exams more manageable.

2. In a group or in an informal written response, examine the student example in this chapter. Explain why its structure is appropriate for an essay exam.

3. In a group, talk about the essay exam response as a genre. What other genres does it resemble and in what ways?

1. As an informal writing assignment, create at least two essay exam prompts for another course you are taking. Share them with your group.

2. Find a textbook that has questions at the ends of the chapters and choose one question that you think could be on an essay exam. Make an outline of how you would respond to that question on an essay exam. Discuss your outline with your group.

3. Type "sample essay exam" into an Internet search engine and locate three examples of essay exam questions. Analyze these questions and explain what kinds of content, organization, and style would be appropriate in an answer.

1. **Write a practice essay exam.** As practice, write an essay exam response to a prompt created by your professor. When you are finished, compare your responses with those of your classmates.

2. **Argue for or against essay exams in college.** Write a letter to the editor of your campus newspaper. In your letter, argue for or against the use of essay exams as a way of testing students. If you are arguing against using essay exams, what would be a suitable replacement for them?

32

Presenting
Your Work

In this chapter, you will learn how to—
* get started on developing your presentation.
* organize your presentation with a good introduction, body, and conclusion.
* deliver your presentation with confidence and style.

You will need to make public presentations in your college courses and in the workplace. More and more, professors are asking students to present their projects to an audience. Almost any professional career will require you to present information, ideas, and opinions. Your ability to speak effectively in front of an audience will be an important cornerstone of your success.

In fact, public speaking is becoming more important as new technologies, like video streaming and video conferencing, become common features of the modern workplace. These new media make it possible to present the material in real time and answer your audience's questions.

Most genres go hand in hand with public presentations. For instance, in the workplace it is common for people to present proposals and reports to their clients. In your advanced college courses, you will be asked to present evaluations, commentaries, and arguments as well as research reports.

In this chapter, we are going to show you some easy strategies for turning your documents into public presentations. If you learn and practice a few simple techniques, your presentations will be more effective.

Getting Started

Because this book is about writing, not public speaking, we are going to assume that you have already written a document that you need to turn into a presentation. Now it is time to take that written text and repurpose it into a presentation for an audience.

Ask a Few Key Questions to Get Started

Solid preparation is the key to successful public speaking. A good way to start preparing is to ask the Five-W and How questions:

- *Who* will be in my audience and what do they need?

- *What* do I want to accomplish with my presentation?

- *When* will I be asked to speak?

- *Where* will I be giving my presentation?

- *Why* am I presenting this information to this audience?

- *How* should I give the presentation?

Answer each of these questions separately. Your answers will give you an overview of what you need to do to prepare for your presentation.

Something to keep in mind is that your audience wants more from you than just the information in your document. After all, if they wanted to, they could just read it. So why do they want you to present it to them instead? A presentation gives members of your audience a chance to interact with you and ask questions. Your audience wants to see you in action. They want you to *perform* the material for them.

Ask yourself how you can make your presentation more interactive, more visual, and more entertaining than your original written text.

Choose the Appropriate Presentation Technology

Think about what technology will be available and which would fit your presentation. The technology you choose depends on the audience's expectations and the place where you will be giving your talk.

Each kind of presentation technology offers advantages and disadvantages. Figure 32.1 describes some of the advantages and disadvantages of each.

Allot Your Time

If you are new to speaking in public, a five- to ten-minute presentation might sound like a lifetime. The time, though, will go fast. A ten-minute presentation, for example,

FIGURE 32.1
Pros and Cons
of Presentation
Technologies

	Advantages	Disadvantages	Genres
**Digital Projector**	• Can be dynamic and colorful • Allows for animation and sound • Creates a more formal atmosphere	• Requires a darkened room, which might inconvenience your audience • Diverts attention from the speaker to the screen • Computers are not completely reliable	Memoirs, Profiles, Reviews, Evaluations, Literary Analyses, Rhetorical Analyses, Position Papers, Proposals, and Reports
**Overhead Projector**	• Projectors are available in most workplaces and classrooms • Easy to print transparencies from most home printers	• May seem static and lifeless • Need to manually change transparencies during your presentation	Evaluations, Literary Analyses, Rhetorical Analyses, Position Papers, Proposals, and Reports
**Whiteboard, Chalkboard, Notepad**	• Allows speaker to create visuals on the spot • Audience pays more attention because speaker is moving	• Cannot be used with a large audience • Writing on board requires extra time • Ideas need to be transferred clearly to the board	Evaluations, Commentaries, Position Papers, Proposals, and Reports
**Poster Presentation**	• Allows audience to see whole presentation • Presents highly technical information clearly • Allows audience to ask specific questions	• Cannot be presented to more than a few people • Can be hard to transport	Memoirs, Profiles, Reviews, Evaluations, Literary Analyses, Rhetorical Analyses, Position Papers, Proposals, and Reports
**Handouts**	• Helps reinforce major points • Can offer more detail, data, and statistics • Audience has something to take home	• Handing them out can be distracting in large presentations • Audience members may read the handouts instead of listen to the talk	Profiles, Reviews, Evaluations, Literary Analyses, Rhetorical Analyses, Position Papers, Proposals, and Reports

	5-Minute Presentation	10-Minute Presentation	20-Minute Presentation
Introduction	Half a minute	1 minute	1–2 minutes
Topic 1	1 minute	2 minutes	5 minutes
Topic 2	1 minute	2 minutes	5 minutes
Topic 3	1 minute	2 minutes	5 minutes
Conclusion	Half a minute	1 minute	1 minute
Questions and Answers	1 minute	2 minutes	3 minutes

FIGURE 32.2
Allotting Your Presentation Time

When planning your presentation, allot your time carefully to scale your talk to the time allowed.

is only the equivalent of a four- or five-page paper. So you will need to budget your time carefully to avoid going over the time allowed.

Figure 32.2 shows how to budget the time for a presentation with three major topics. Of course, if your paper has fewer or more than three topics, you should make adjustments in the times allowed for each one. These time limits are flexible guidelines, not rigid rules.

Organizing Your Presentation's Content

The organization of your presentation will typically follow the genre you are using to organize your document. Your talk should have a clear beginning, middle, and end. That advice might seem rather obvious, but public speakers regularly forget to properly introduce their talk to the audience, or they abruptly end without summing up their main points.

Analyze the Interactive Presentation at mycomplab.com

There is an old speechmaking saying you should commit to memory: *Tell them what you're going to tell them. Tell them. Tell them what you told them.*

Introduction: Tell Them What You're Going to Tell Them

The introduction of your talk is almost always the most critical part of your whole presentation. At the beginning of your speech, you have a small window—perhaps a minute or two—to capture the audience's attention while stating your topic, purpose, and main point. If you don't grab the audience at this point, they may tune out for the rest of your talk.

A shorter presentation with a brief introduction will make two or three of the following moves, while a long introduction might include all six:

Identify your topic. Tell your audience what your presentation is about.

State the purpose of your presentation. Explain what you are going to do in your talk.

State your main point. Tell them what you want to prove or support.

Stress the importance of your topic to the audience. Explain why this issue is important to them and why they should pay attention.

Offer background information on the subject. Provide enough information to familiarize the audience with your topic.

Forecast the structure of your talk. Tell them how your talk will be organized.

Even if you are naturally funny, starting your presentation with a joke is risky. The problem with jokes is that they often flop, and they can be offensive in ways you might not anticipate.

Instead of telling a joke, think of a good *grabber* to start out your speech. A grabber states something interesting or challenging that captures the audience's attention. Some effective grabbers include:

A rhetorical question: "Do you ever wonder why child actors tend to have personal problems when they become adults?"

A startling statistic: "A recent survey shows that 74 percent of women students report that they have been sexually harassed at this university. Meanwhile, 43 percent of male students report they have been harassed."

A compelling statement: "If nothing is done about global climate change, it is likely that polar bears will become extinct in the wild during our lifetime."

An anecdote: "Last year, I finally climbed my first mountain over 14,000 feet. In many ways, climbing that mountain affirmed to me that I had triumphed over the injuries I sustained in Iraq two years before."

A show of hands: "Let's see a show of hands. How many of you think the pizza here in town leaves something to be desired?"

A good grabber identifies your topic while giving your audience a little something to think about.

The Body of Your Talk: Tell Them

The body of your presentation is where you are going to state your major points and support them with facts, reasoning, examples, data, quotations, and any other forms of proof you can offer.

In most situations, the body of your presentation should follow the same pattern as the body of your document. Divide your text into two to five major issues that you want to discuss with the audience. If you try to cover more than five topics, you risk overwhelming the audience with more new information than they can handle. So organize the body of your talk to feature the most important things you want them to remember.

Here's a good strategy that might help you strip down your talk to something you can handle in a small amount of time. Look through your document and ask yourself,

"What does my audience *need* to know about this topic to make a decision?" Then cross out any material that goes beyond need-to-know information.

Conclusion: Tell Them What You Told Them

People make this mistake all the time. They finish the body of their talk. Then they shrug their shoulders and say something like, "That's all I have to say. Any questions?" This kind of abrupt ending feels awkward, and it misses an opportunity to drive home the presentation's main point.

Here's a better way to handle your conclusion. Once you clearly signal that you are about to conclude, you will have the audience's heightened attention for the next two minutes. Take advantage of this by repeating your main point in a clear and memorable way. A typical conclusion will include some or all of the following moves:

Signal clearly that you are concluding. Make an obvious transition that signals the end of your talk, such as "Let me wrap up now" or "Finally."

Restate your main point. Tell your audience exactly what you have been trying to explain or prove in your talk.

Reemphasize the importance of your topic to the audience. Be clear about why the audience should care about your topic. Answer their "Why should I care?" questions.

Call the audience to action. If you want the people in your audience to do something, tell them what you think they should do. Be specific about the actions you want them to take.

Thank the audience. When you are finished, don't forget to say, "thank you." This phrase signals the audience that your presentation is done, and it usually prompts them to give you some applause.

Remember to keep your conclusion brief. Once you say something like, "In conclusion," you have one or two minutes to finish up. If you ramble beyond a couple of minutes, your audience will become restless and annoyed.

Question and Answer

At the end of your talk, you should be prepared to answer a few questions from the audience. The question and answer period offers you a good opportunity to interact with the audience and clarify your ideas. During the question and answer period, you should be ready to answer three types of questions:

A Request for Clarification or Elaboration. These types of questions are opportunities to reinforce some of your key points. When you field this kind of question, start out by rephrasing it for the audience. Rephrasing will allow you to put the issue in your own words and state it loudly enough for the whole audience to hear. Then answer the question, expanding on the information you provided in your talk.

A Hostile Question. Occasionally, an audience member will ask a question that challenges the information you provided in your talk. Here is a good three-step strategy for answering these kinds of questions:

1. **Rephrase the question.** State the question in terms that will allow you to answer it in ways that reflect your own beliefs.

2. **Validate the question.** Tell the audience that you understand the questioner's concerns and even share them.

3. **Elaborate and move forward.** Explain that the course of action you are supporting is preferable because it addresses the issue more appropriately or seems more reasonable.

The Heckling Question. In rare cases, an audience member will want to heckle you with hostile questions. In these cases, you need to recognize that the questioner is *trying* to sabotage your presentation. He or she wants you to become flustered. Don't let the heckler do that to you. After trying your best to answer one or two questions from a heckler, simply say, "I'm sorry you feel that way. We have other people with questions. Perhaps we can meet after my talk to discuss your concerns." Then look away from that person. Usually, someone else in the audience will ask a question and you can move on.

When the question and answer period is over, you should briefly thank the audience again. This will usually prompt another round of applause.

Designing Your Visual Aids

Visual aids will help you clarify your ideas and illustrate your main points for the audience. Perhaps the best way to create visual aids is to make slides with the presentation software (*PowerPoint*, *Keynote*, or *Presentations*) that came with your word-processing software.

Format Your Slides

Whether you are presenting in a large lecture hall with a projector or to a few people with a poster presentation, slides are some of the best visual aids available (Figure 32.3). Here are some strategies for formatting your slides:

- Title each slide with an action-oriented heading.

- Put five or fewer major points on each slide. If you have more than five major points, divide that topic into two slides.

- Use left-justified text for most items on your slides. Centered text should only be used for the titles of your slides.

- Use dark text on a white or light background whenever possible. Light text on a dark background can be difficult to read.

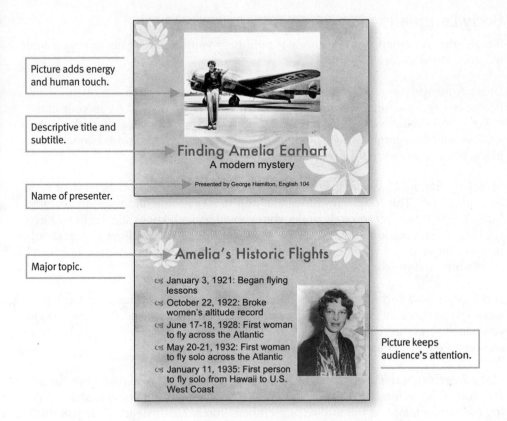

Picture adds energy and human touch.

Descriptive title and subtitle.

Name of presenter.

Finding Amelia Earhart
A modern mystery

Presented by George Hamilton, English 104

Major topic.

Amelia's Historic Flights

- January 3, 1921: Began flying lessons
- October 22, 1922: Broke women's altitude record
- June 17-18, 1928: First woman to fly across the Atlantic
- May 20-21, 1932: First woman to fly solo across the Atlantic
- January 11, 1935: First person to fly solo from Hawaii to U.S. West Coast

Picture keeps audience's attention.

FIGURE 32.3
Creating Slides

Shown here are a title slide and a body slide from a profile paper repurposed as a presentation. The photographs add a strong visual identity to the slides.

- Use bulleted lists of phrases instead of paragraphs or sentences.

- Use photos, icons, and graphics to keep your slides fresh and active for the audience. Make sure your graphics look good on the screen. Increasing the size of a Web-based graphic, for example, can make the image look blurry or grainy.

You will be tempted to pack too much material onto each slide. Effective slides, like the ones shown in Figure 32.3, need to be simple and easy to interpret. You don't want your audience trying to puzzle out the meaning of your complicated slides instead of listening to your talk.

Delivering Your Presentation

How you deliver your talk will make a significant impact on your audience. The usual advice is to "be yourself" when you are speaking in public. Of course, that's good advice for people who are comfortable speaking in front of an audience. Better advice is to "be the person the audience expects." In other words, like an actor, play the role that fits your topic and your audience.

Body Language

Ideally, the movements of your body should help you reinforce your message and maintain the audience's attention.

Dress Appropriately. Your choice of clothing needs to reflect your audience's expectations and the topic of your talk. Even when you are presenting to your classmates, you should view it as an opportunity to practice your workplace and professional demeanor. Dress as though you are presenting in a professional workplace, not as if you were simply going to class.

Stand Up Straight. When speakers are nervous, they tend to slouch, lean, or rock back and forth. This looks unprofessional and makes it difficult to breathe calmly. Instead, keep your feet squarely under your shoulders with knees slightly bent. Keep your shoulders back and down and your head up to allow good airflow. If your shoulders are forward and up, you won't get enough air and the pitch of your voice will seem unnaturally high.

Use Open Hand and Arm Gestures. For most audiences, open hand and arm gestures will convey trust and confidence. Avoid folding your arms, keeping your arms at your sides, or putting both hands in your pockets, as these poses will convey a defensive posture that audiences do not trust.

Make Eye Contact. Everyone in the audience should believe you made eye contact with him or her at least once during your presentation. If you are nervous about making eye contact, look at the audience members' foreheads instead. They will think you are looking them directly in the eye.

Move to Reinforce Major Points or Transitions. If possible, when you make important points, step forward toward the audience. When you make transitions in your presentation from one topic to the next, move to the left or right. Your movement across the floor will highlight the transitions in your speech.

Voice and Tone

As you improve your presentation skills, you should start paying more attention to your voice and tone.

Speak Lower and Slower. When speaking to an audience, you will need to speak louder than you normally would. As your volume goes up, so will the pitch of your voice, making it sound unnaturally high to the audience. By consciously lowering your voice, you should sound just about right. Also, nerves may cause you to speak too quickly. Silently remind yourself to speak slowly.

Use Pauses to Reinforce Your Major Points. Each time you make a major point, pause for a moment to let the audience commit it to memory.

Use Pauses to Eliminate Verbal Tics. Verbal tics like "um," "ah," "like," "you know," "OK?" and "See what I mean?" are nervous habits that fill gaps between thoughts. If you have a verbal tic, train yourself to pause when you feel like using one of these sounds or phrases. Before long, you will find them disappearing from your speech.

Minimize How Often You Look Down at Your Notes. You should try to look at your notes as little as possible. When you look down at your notes, your neck bends, restricting your airflow and lowering your volume. Plus, notes can become a distracting "safe place" that keeps you from engaging visually with your audience.

Practicing and Rehearsing

You should leave plenty of time to practice your presentation out loud. Even better advice, though, is to "rehearse" what you are going to say and how you are going to say it. Rehearsal allows you to practice your presentation in a more realistic setting.

Practice, Practice, Practice

Practice involves speaking your presentation out loud to yourself. As you are working through your presentation verbally, you should memorize its major points and gain a sense of its organization and flow. While practicing, you should:

- Listen for any problems with content, organization, and style.

- Edit and proofread your visuals and handouts.

- Decide how you are going to move around as you deliver the speech.

- Pay attention to your body language and voice.

If you notice any problems as you are practicing your presentation, you can stop and fix them right away.

Rehearse, Rehearse, Rehearse

The secret to polishing your presentation is to rehearse it several times. Unlike practice, rehearsal means giving the presentation from beginning to end *without stopping*.

As much as possible, you want to replicate the experience of giving your real talk. After each rehearsal session, you should make any revisions or corrections.

Recruit friends to listen as you rehearse your presentation. They will provide you with a live audience, so you can gauge their reactions to your ideas. Ideally, they will also give you constructive feedback that you can use to improve the presentation. Another possibility is recording your presentation, with either audiovisual or just audio.

Practicing will help you find any major problems with your talk, but rehearsal will help you turn the whole package into an effective presentation.

Here are some helpful guidelines for developing and giving presentations.

ANSWER the Five-W and How Questions about Your Presentation

Think about the who, what, where, when, why, and how issues that will shape the content, organization, style, and design of your presentation.

CHOOSE the Appropriate Presentation Technology

Depending on the size of your audience and the room in which you will be speaking, consider what kind of presentation technology would best allow you to present your ideas.

ORGANIZE Your Ideas

More than likely, the genre of your document offers a good organization for your talk. Remember to "Tell them what you're going to tell them. Tell them. Tell them what you told them."

DESIGN Your Visual Aids

Slides work well for most presentations. Use presentation software, such as *PowerPoint, Keynote,* or *Presentations,* to convert your paper into a colorful and interesting set of slides. If slides aren't appropriate, you should look into the possibility of using a whiteboard or handouts.

THINK about Your Body Language

Consider issues like how you will dress and how you will stand and move when you are presenting. Practice making eye contact with people.

IMPROVE Your Voice and Tone

Work on speaking lower and slower, while using pauses to reinforce your major points. Also, use pauses to eliminate any verbal tics, such as "um," "ah," "like," and "you know."

PRACTICE and Rehearse

Ultimately, practice and rehearsal are the best ways to improve and polish your presentation. Use practice to help you revise your talk and correct errors. Use rehearsal to polish your presentation and make it as persuasive as possible.

1. In a small group, share your opinions about what works well in a presentation. Discuss effective and ineffective presenters (coaches, teachers, public speakers). What traits made these people effective or ineffective as public speakers?

2. Find a video clip online of a particularly problematic speech. Imagine that you and your group are this person's speaking coach. Being as helpful as possible, what advice would you give this person to improve his or her future presentations?

3. With your group, choose three things from this chapter that you would like to use to improve your presentation skills. Then take turns presenting these three things to your "audience."

1. Find a speech on a video Web site. In a brief rhetorical analysis, discuss the strengths and weaknesses of the presentation. Specifically, pay attention to the content, organization, style, and use of visuals in the presentation.

2. Outline a two-minute speech on a subject that you know well. Then, without much further thought, give a presentation to a small group of people from your class. Practice making the six introductory moves mentioned in this chapter and the five concluding moves.

3. Using presentation software, turn one of the papers you wrote for this class into slides. Break your paper down into major and minor points and add pictures and illustrations that will help your audience visualize your ideas. Print out your slides and look for any inconsistencies in wording or places where you could reorganize.

1. **Evaluate a public presentation.** Attend a public presentation on your campus. Instead of listening to the content of the presentation, pay attention to how it was organized and presented. Then write a review, a rave, or a slam of the presentation. Use the presentation strategies described in this chapter to discuss the strengths and weaknesses of the speaker and his or her talk.

2. **Repurpose a written text into a presentation.** Choose a major project for this course or another one and turn it into a presentation. Choose the appropriate presentation technology. Make sure you develop an introduction that captures your audience's attention. Divide the body of your paper into two to five major topics. Then develop a conclusion that stresses your main points and looks to the future. When you have finished creating your talk, spend some time practicing and rehearsing it. Your professor may ask you to present your talk in class.

PEARSON
mycomplab

For support in meeting this chapter's objectives, follow this path in MyCompLab: Resources ⟹ Writing ⟹ Writing Samples. Review the Instruction and Multimedia resources about presentations, then complete the Exercises and click on Gradebook to measure your progress.

PART 7

Anthology of Readings

This **ANTHOLOGY** provides noteworthy examples of the genres discussed in this book. Read on to discover how genres can be stretched or blended to achieve unique and creative purposes.

PART OUTLINE

33

Memoirs

The Way to Rainy Mountain

N. SCOTT MOMADAY

With his debut novel, House Made of Dawn *(1968), N. Scott Momaday opened doors for other Native American writers to publish their stories. Well known for retelling the history of the Kiowa people, who lived on the American Plains, Momaday was awarded the National Medal of Arts in 2007. The memoir included here, from* The Way to Rainy Mountain *(1969), tells the history of the Kiowa through his and his grandmother's lives. Watch how he uses his grandmother as a lens for telling a richer, more personal story. Like many memoir writers, Momaday uses others to reveal important insights about his own life.*

A single knoll rises out of the plain in Oklahoma, north and west of the Wichita Range. For my people, the Kiowas, it is an old landmark, and they gave it the name Rainy Mountain. The hardest weather in the world is there. Winter brings blizzards, hot tornadic winds arise in the spring, and in summer the prairie is an anvil's edge. The grass turns brittle and brown, and it cracks beneath your feet. There are green belts along the rivers and creeks, linear groves of hickory and pecan, willow and witch hazel. At a distance in July or August the steaming foliage seems almost to writhe in fire. Great green and yellow grasshoppers are everywhere in the tall grass, popping up like corn to sting the flesh, and tortoises crawl about on the red earth, going nowhere in the plenty of time. Loneliness is an aspect of the land. All things in the plain are isolate; there is no confusion of objects in the eye, but *one* hill or *one* tree or *one* man. To look upon that landscape in the early morning, with the sun at your back, is to lose the sense of proportion. Your imagination comes to life, and this, you think, is where Creation was begun.

I returned to Rainy Mountain in July. My grandmother had died in the spring, and I wanted to be at her grave. She had lived to be very old and at last infirm. Her only living daughter was with her when she died, and I was told that in death her face was that of a child.

I like to think of her as a child. When she was born, the Kiowas were living the last great moment of their history. For more than a hundred years they had controlled the open range from the Smoky Hill River to the Red, from the headwaters of the Canadian to the fork of the Arkansas and Cimarron. In alliance with the Comanches, they had ruled the whole of the southern Plains. War was their sacred business, and they were among the finest horsemen the world has ever known. But warfare for the Kiowas was preeminently a matter of disposition rather than of survival, and they never understood the grim, unrelenting advance of the U.S. Cavalry. When at last, divided and ill-provisioned, they were driven onto the Staked Plains in the cold rains of autumn, they fell into panic. In Palo Duro Canyon they abandoned their crucial stores to pillage and had nothing then but their lives. In order to save themselves, they surrendered to the soldiers at Fort Sill and were imprisoned in the old stone corral that now stands as a military museum. My grandmother was spared the humiliation of those high gray walls by eight or ten years, but she must have known from birth the affliction of defeat, the dark brooding of old warriors.

Her name was Aho, and she belonged to the last culture to evolve in North America. Her forebears came down from the high country in western Montana nearly three centuries ago. They were a mountain people, a mysterious tribe of hunters whose language has never been positively classified in any major group. In the late seventeenth century they began a long migration to the south and east. It was a journey toward the dawn, and it led to a golden age. Along the way the Kiowas were befriended by the Crows, who gave them the culture and religion of the Plains. They acquired horses, and their ancient nomadic spirit was suddenly free of the ground. They acquired Tai-me, the sacred Sun Dance doll, from that moment the object and symbol of their worship, and so shared in the divinity of the sun. Not least, they acquired the sense of destiny, therefore courage and pride. When they entered upon the southern Plains they had been transformed. No longer were they slaves to the simple necessity of survival; they were a lordly and dangerous society of fighters and thieves, hunters and priests of the sun. According to their origin myth, they entered the world through a hollow log. From one point of view, their migration was the fruit of an old prophecy, for indeed they emerged from a sunless world.

Although my grandmother lived out her 5 long life in the shadow of Rainy Mountain, the immense landscape of the continental interior lay like memory in her blood. She could tell of the Crows, whom she had never seen, and of the Black Hills, where she had never been. I wanted to see in reality what she had seen more perfectly in the mind's eye, and traveled fifteen hundred miles to begin my pilgrimage.

Yellowstone, it seemed to me, was the top of the world, a region of deep lakes and dark timber, canyons and waterfalls. But, beautiful as it is, one might have the sense of confinement there. The skyline in all directions is close at hand, the high wall of the woods and deep cleavages of shade. There is a perfect freedom in the mountains, but it belongs to the eagle and the elk, the badger and the bear. The Kiowas reckoned their stature by the distance they could see, and they were bent and blind in the wilderness.

Descending eastward, the highland meadows are a stairway to the plain. In July the inland slope of the Rockies is luxuriant with flax and buckwheat, stonecrop and larkspur. The earth unfolds and the limit of the land recedes. Clusters of trees, and animals grazing far in the distance, cause the vision to reach away and wonder to build upon the mind. The sun follows a longer course in the day, and the sky is immense beyond all comparison. The great billowing clouds that sail upon it are shadows that move upon the grain like water, dividing light. Farther down, in the land of the Crows and Blackfeet, the plain is yellow. Sweet clover takes

hold of the hills and bends upon itself to cover and seal the soil. There the Kiowas paused on their way; they had come to the place where they must change their lives. The sun is at home on the plains. Precisely there does it have the certain character of a god. When the Kiowas came to the land of the Crows, they could see the dark lees of the hills at dawn across the Bighorn River, the profusion of light on the grain shelves, the oldest deity ranging after the solstices. Not yet would they veer southward to the caldron of the land that lay below; they must wean their blood from the northern winter and hold the mountains a while longer in their view. They bore Tai-me in procession to the east.

A dark mist lay over the Black Hills, and the land was like iron. At the top of a ridge I caught sight of Devil's Tower upthrust against the gray sky as if in the birth of time the core of the earth had broken through its crust and the motion of the world was begun. There are things in nature that engender an awful quiet in the heart of man; Devil's Tower is one of them. Two centuries ago, because they could not do otherwise, the Kiowas made a legend at the base of the rock. My grandmother said:

> Eight children were there at play, seven sisters and their brother. Suddenly the boy was struck dumb; he trembled and began to run upon his hands and feet. His fingers became claws, and his body was covered with fur. Directly there was a bear where the boy had been. The sisters were terrified; they ran, and the bear after them. They came to the stump of a great tree, and the tree spoke to them. It bade them climb upon it, and as they did so it began to rise into the air. The bear came to kill them, but they were just beyond its reach. It reared against the tree and scored the bark all around with its claws. The seven sisters were borne into the sky, and they became the stars of the Big Dipper.

From that moment, and so long as the legend lives, the Kiowas have kinsmen in the night sky. Whatever they were in the mountains, they could be no more. However tenuous their well-being, however much they had suffered and would suffer again, they had found a way out of the wilderness.

My grandmother had a reverence for the sun, a holy regard that now is all but gone out of mankind. There was a wariness in her, and an ancient awe. She was a Christian in her later years, but she had come a long way about, and she never forgot her birthright. As a child she had been to the Sun Dances; she had taken part in those annual rites, and by them she had learned the restoration of her people in the presence of Tai-me. She was about seven when the last Kiowa Sun Dance was held in 1887 on the Washita River above Rainy Mountain Creek. The buffalo were gone. In order to consummate the ancient sacrifice—to impale the head of a buffalo bull upon the medicine tree—a delegation of old men journeyed into Texas, there to beg and barter for an animal from the Goodnight herd. She was ten when the Kiowas came together for the last time as a living Sun Dance culture. They could find no buffalo; they had to hang an old hide from the sacred tree. Before the dance could begin, a company of soldiers rode out from Fort Sill under orders to disperse the tribe. Forbidden without cause the essential act of their faith, having seen the wild herds slaughtered and left to rot upon the ground, the Kiowas backed away forever from the medicine tree. That was July 20, 1890, at the great bend of the Washita. My grandmother was there. Without bitterness, and for as long as she lived, she bore a vision of deicide.

Now that I can have her only in memory, I 10 see my grandmother in the several postures that were peculiar to her: standing at the wood stove on a winter morning and turning meat in a great iron skillet; sitting at the south window, bent above her beadwork, and afterwards, when her vision failed, looking down for a long time into the fold of her hands; going out upon a cane, very slowly as she did when the weight of age came upon her; praying. I remember her most often at prayer. She made long, rambling prayers out of suffering and hope, having seen many things. I was never sure that I had the right to hear, so exclusive were they of all mere custom and company. The last time I saw her she prayed standing by the side of her bed at night, naked to the waist, the light of a kerosene lamp moving upon her dark skin. Her long, black hair, always drawn and braided in the day, lay upon her shoulders and against her breasts like a shawl. I do not speak Kiowa, and I never understood her prayers, but there was something inherently sad in the sound, some merest hesitation upon the syllables of sorrow. She began in a high and descending pitch, exhausting her breath to silence; then again and again—and always the same intensity of effort, of something that is, and is not, like urgency in the human voice. Transported so in the dancing light among the shadows of her room, she seemed beyond the reach of time. But that was illusion; I think I knew then that I should not see her again.

Houses are like sentinels in the plain, old keepers of the weather watch. There, in a very little while, wood takes on the appearance of great age. All colors wear soon away in the wind and rain, and then the wood is burned gray and the grain appears and the nails turn red with rust. The windowpanes are black and opaque; you imagine there is nothing within, and indeed there are many ghosts, bones given up to the land. They stand here and there against the sky, and you approach them for a longer time than you expect. They belong in the distance; it is their domain.

Once there was a lot of sound in my grandmother's house, a lot of coming and going, feasting and talk. The summers there were full of excitement and reunion. The Kiowas are a summer people; they abide the cold and keep to themselves, but when the season turns and the land becomes warm and vital they cannot hold still; an old love of going returns upon them. The aged visitors who came to my grandmother's house when I was a child were made of lean and leather, and they bore themselves upright. They wore great black hats and bright ample shirts that shook in the wind. They rubbed fat upon their hair and wound their braids with strips of colored cloth. Some of them painted their faces and carried the scars of old and cherished enmities. They were an old council of warlords, come to remind and be reminded of who they were. Their wives and daughters served them well. The women might indulge themselves; gossip was at once the mark and compensation of their servitude. They made loud and elaborate talk among themselves, full of jest and gesture, fright and false alarm. They went abroad in fringed and flowered shawls, bright beadwork and German silver. They were at home in the kitchen, and they prepared meals that were banquets.

There were frequent prayer meetings, and great nocturnal feasts. When I was a child I played with my cousins outside, where the lamplight fell upon the ground and the singing of the old people rose up around us and carried away into the darkness. There were a lot of good things to eat, a lot of laughter and surprise. And afterwards, when the quiet returned, I lay down with my grandmother and could hear the frogs away by the river and feel the motion of the air.

Now there is a funeral silence in the rooms, the endless wake of some final word. The walls have closed in upon my grandmother's house. When I returned to it in mourning, I saw for the first time in my life how small it was. It was late at night, and there was a white moon, nearly full. I sat for a long time on the stone steps by the kitchen door. From there I could see out across the land; I could see the long row of trees by the creek, the low light upon the rolling plains, and the stars of the Big Dipper. Once I looked at the moon and caught sight of a strange thing. A cricket had perched upon the handrail, only a few inches away from me. My line of vision was such that the creature filled the moon like a fossil. It had gone there, I thought, to live and die, for there, of all places, was its small definition made whole and eternal. A warm wind rose up and purled like the longing within me.

The next morning I awoke at dawn and went 15 out on the dirt road to Rainy Mountain. It was already hot, and the grasshoppers began to fill the air. Still, it was early in the morning, and the birds sang out of the shadows. The long yellow grass on the mountain shone in the bright light, and a scissortail hied above the land. There, where it ought to be, at the end of a long and legendary way, was my grandmother's grave. Here and there on the dark stones were ancestral names. Looking back once, I saw the mountain and came away.

A CLOSER LOOK AT
The Way to Rainy Mountain

1. In many ways, Momaday is writing a memoir of a people, the Kiowas, not just himself or his grandmother. How does he use events from his own life and his grandmother's life as a lens through which he can talk about the Kiowas?

2. This memoir is filled with visual imagery. Find five places where Momaday uses detail, especially visual detail, to heighten the reader's experience with the text. Then find one place each in which he uses sound, touch, smell, and taste to describe the world he is remembering.

3. Nature itself is a character in this memoir. Where in this memoir does nature seem to be taking on a living role? In what ways does Momaday use nature to move the story in this memoir forward?

IDEAS FOR
Writing

1. Write a profile of one of your own grandparents (or another older member of your family). As you draft your profile, pay special attention to how *place* shapes your understanding and memories of this person. In other words, how does this person's environment shape and define him or her for you?

2. Write a research report in which you explore where your ancestors came from. Who were your people? Where did they come from and when and why did they decide to move? How did they make the transition from their ancestral way of living to the way you are living now?

The College Hazing That Changed My Life

THOMAS ROGERS

Thomas Rogers contributed this memoir to a series titled "Freshman Orientation" for the online magazine Salon.com, where he is an arts editor. As you read, notice how Rogers uses many of the key features of a memoir to tell a powerful story about his inner conflict that begins with his family, carries on through to his college days, and ends with a surprising resolution and new understanding.

I had no idea college was going to be so much like a gay porn movie. That's what I kept thinking as I stood in the middle of a sun-dappled backyard, dressed in nothing but a spandex unitard and running shoes, preparing to have oil poured over my body. For the last two hours, 10 other young rowers and I had been undergoing "initiation" to my university's varsity crew team. After two weeks of tryouts, we had finally made the grade, and this was our reward: An afternoon of embarrassing hazing activities, followed by a homoerotic climax that seemed to have come straight out of my 17-year-old gay subconscious.

Our team captain, a 200-pound hulk of a man, was walking from freshman to freshman with a large vat of vegetable oil, and letting it cascade all over them one by one. "Be prepared to have the worst acne of your lives over the next week," he warned us. A tarp nearby had also been covered in oil, and other members of the team were streaming into the backyard with bottles of beer to watch what was about to happen. When my turn came, I closed my eyes. As I felt the liquid drip into my shoes, he leaned over and said, "Get ready to wrestle."

College is a strange time. As soon as our parents drive away from our dorms, and leave us alone with our boxes of books and Ikea corkboard, we're free to make an extraordinary number of mistakes and end up in situations that may not teach us much about organic chemistry or Emily Dickinson, but let us figure out who we are and who we want to be. In my case, that situation involved man-on-man oil wrestling.

I had always been my family's black sheep when it came to sports. For as long as I could remember, my mom had been an obsessive long-distance runner. She logged about 50 miles per week, and when her friends ran half-marathons on weekends, she would run along, just to give them "emotional support." My dad, a tall, thin doctor, had competed in triathlons around Western Canada for a large portion of his adult life. And my older sister was a star. Ever since I was a young kid, she had always been an exceptionally talented athlete—a runner, swimmer, biker and rower. By the time I was graduating high school, she had worked her way to the top echelons of Canada's rowing community and was even considering trying out for the Olympic team.

I, on the other hand, was what some of my 5 disappointed sports coaches had consistently described as "physically awkward." Whereas my sister had inherited all of my parents' athletic genes, I had inherited all of their gangliest. I was tall and shaped like a stretched piece of Play-Doh with twigs stuck into it. My limbs had a tendency to do things that I didn't want them to do, like make me fall over boxes and down stairs. And, to make things worse, I was pathetically, pathologically shy. For most of my childhood, I was the wallflower who stood in the corner while the other kids threw balls at each other's faces (apparently I hung out with some pretty violent kids).

On top of that, I'd known I was gay since I was 8. While that discovery didn't send me into paroxysms of panic, it also made me want to keep to myself pretty much all of the time. I spent most of my early teens reading books and listening to a lot of Nine Inch Nails and ABBA. It wasn't that I didn't want to be a jock like the rest of my family—in fact, I was envious of my sister's talents—it's just that I was usually pretty mediocre at the sports I was enrolled in, and practice cut into time spent alone with my Walkman. And then, I discovered rowing.

As far as sports go, rowing is a remarkably bizarre and all-consuming one. You have to get up at 4:30 in the morning to sit in a very skinny boat facing backward and row around in a loop until you get very tired. You have to wear some very revealing spandex outfits. Given that our rowing club was located on a river near farmland, you also have to dodge rocks and tree stumps and the occasional bloated dead cow. And yet there was something magical about it. Every morning, I would get to see the sunrise before I went to school, and I loved the feeling of exhaustion I felt after every practice. In high school, I took the sport more and more seriously until something weird happened: I became sort of good.

Not only did becoming a jock boost my self-confidence, it was an antidote to my anxieties about my burgeoning homosexuality, about the girlish lilt that could emerge in my voice or my occasional extravagant hand motions. I had always been pretty comfortable with the idea that I was gay, but I was still struggling with the implication that it meant being less manly than the other boys. But jocks were manly. They were self-confident, and cool, and, somehow, better than people who weren't jocks. And if I became one, especially at college, I would be like that too.

When I arrived at tryouts, I discovered these people were much larger, more serious and gregarious than me. Everybody seemed to have gone to a private school with a fancy rowing team. One of the older guys, always surrounded by groups of women, kept referring to something called "The Raft," which turned out to be a large bed he used for group sex. Another, an enormous man who went by the nickname "Ice" (apparently he had just discovered "Top Gun"), claimed to be a former Abercrombie and Fitch model and the son of a Dutch ambassador. He would put rubbing alcohol on his blisters to show people how manly he was, and about one

week into the tryouts, he told me to get him a sandwich because "there was a hierarchy on the team," and he was at the top and I was at the bottom. (This comment raised my eyebrows for multiple reasons.)

As different from me as they were, these were precisely the cool jocks I had always dreamed of being. These guys were self-confident, manly and attractive—and nobody seemed to question their abrasiveness. As Ice was fond of saying, while eating large amounts of tuna in the dorm cafeteria, the men on the rowing team could "bring it—athletically, academically and socially." Maybe their chutzpah would rub off on me. One week later, when I finally made the team—as a "bow seat" in the lightweight eight—I felt so much better about myself. Even if it did mean being surrounded by guys I was starting to feel iffy about.

A few days after they announced the lineup, we had to show up at one of our teammates' houses dressed in our unisuits and running shoes. I figured we were in for hazing, but I had hoped it would be more demure, like those trust games where people wear blindfolds and stand on crates and catch each other. Instead, we had to run around campus holding a boat on our shoulders singing "Row, row, row your boat" (unfortunately, this coincided with my university's annual medieval fair). We had to flex in front of the cafeteria during lunch time, and jump in the lake, and perform embarrassing skits in front of the dorms.

Then came the oil wrestling.

When I stepped onto that oil-covered tarp to face off against my opponent, I wasn't preoccupied by the insane homoeroticism of the moment. Instead, I was thinking about how this entire display was predicated on the fact that gay sexuality was laughable and gross. They had clearly chosen it as a hazing activity because the idea of man-on-man contact would make us as uncomfortable as possible. And the more I thought about it, the more I did feel dirty—and resentful.

It was with a tremendous amount of apprehension that I began to grapple with the opponent, a similarly skinny freshman named Kieran. As the crowd began to yell, "wrestle, wrestle, wrestle," we pushed each other over onto our backs, and tried to edge each other to the end of the tarp. Oil wrestling (who knew!) really is quite

10

slippery. So we rolled around and spent a lot of time accidentally elbowing each other in the stomach. By this point, a bunch of twigs had already fallen into the oil, and kept jabbing me in the ribs, and the liquid got into my eyes. Clearly I wasn't putting up much of a show. I heard somebody nearby yell out, "Well, this is lame!"

But by the time Kieran pushed me off the tarp and onto the grass, I had the first great revelation of my freshman year: Being a jock was bullshit. If this was the kind of macho, homophobic stuff I had to tolerate to be on a sports team, there was no point in even trying. If that meant admitting I was a mediocre athlete, that 15 was fine with me. I had to come to terms with the fact that my gayness made me less butch than Ice, and that was better than being a douchebag. When the rowing season ended, I left the sport and turned instead toward outcasts like me—bookish kids, drama nerds and other queer kids. I never turned back.

Now, with some perspective, I can see I discovered something else in that moment, much bigger than my failure to be an all-star jock. I saw that I was never going to be normal. And it was time to stop being embarrassed by that—and start being excited about it.

A decade later, I still am.

A CLOSER LOOK AT
The College Hazing That Changed My Life

1. An effective memoir usually starts fast with a "lead" that draws the reader in and hints at the memoir's overall meaning or "theme." Sometimes, as in this case, it takes the reader right into heart of the main action before backing up and providing background. How effectively does this strategy work in this memoir?

2. Rogers sets the scene with rich and vivid details. He moves from various scenes, painting brief but compelling portraits of key people, from family members to his athletic team members. He also fills scenes with sensory details (sight, touch, sound, and smell). Find specific places where this variety and richness in detail make the memoir more powerful.

3. At the heart of any memoir (or story) is a complication that the author grapples with and needs to resolve. In this memoir, what is the conflict that draws readers in and makes this more than just a personal story? How does he resolve that conflict, and how would you describe his new understanding?

4. Memoirs usually conclude with a point or "implied thesis." How would you describe the author's new understanding? What general point (or points) does the author make?

IDEAS FOR
Writing

1. As we move from the world of family to new situations and friends, all of us face life's complications that we need to resolve for ourselves. Write a memoir that tells the story of your journey from family and youthful friends to new surroundings, how you faced that change and how you arrived at new understandings. Be sure to provide rich details about the scenes and the people in your memoir.

2. In the third paragraph, the author writes shifts the scene from the climactic wrestling scene (his scene-setting lead) to a brief comment about college life: "College is a strange time." In college, he suggests, we learn about more than just the subjects studied in the classroom; we also learn about life and who we are. Drawing on your own personal college experience, write a commentary on this idea about broader learning. How has college experience changed you? Do you think college *should* teach students about more than just subject matter? Should college do more than prepare you for a career?

Growing Up Hard

JOE WILKINS

In this memoir, Joe Wilkins describes his life growing up in Montana. Much of this memoir is a meditation on its first line "Out on the Big Dry, we had to kill to live." Killing was a normal part of life—something that wasn't even thought to be violent. In this memoir, pay attention to how Wilkins uses details and action to tell his stories.

Out on the Big Dry, we had to kill to live:

Come October, we'd herd a yearling lamb into the west pen, throw it some good flakes of alfalfa hay. It'd be grass-fat by then, nearly tame, just chewing, and looking around, and chewing. My father, his black hair bright and wild in the early winter light, would put the rifle barrel in its soft ear and pull the trigger. We were nearly two hours away from the nearest supermarket. And even if we were closer, we couldn't afford it. We ate lamb all winter—lamb chops and leg of lamb and lamb stew with garden peas my mother canned. All kinds of lamb.

But on Sunday, we almost always pulled a fryer out of the freezer for dinner. Butchering chickens was an all-day affair, a late-summer festival of sorts, a kind of prairie celebration. We put on our old jeans and stained snap shirts and ate a big breakfast of hamburger steak, eggs, and potatoes. My mother and grandmother set up aluminum basins of hot water for the plucking. My father and grandfather sharpened knives and hatchets. And when everything was finally ready, they sent us children into the coop.

A moment later we scrambled out slicked with shit and feathers, holding squawking hens to our heaving chests. We gave those orange and brown and piebald hens over to my father or my grandfather, whoever happened to be kneeling behind the pine stump that day, and one-by-one they stretched the hens out on the stump and stroked their necks until they calmed and brought the hatchet down hard. They gave them back to us—still flapping and jerking, blood suddenly everywhere—by their bony feet. There'd be a line of us then, happy children holding headless chickens upside down, blood running out and all over the dust.

But to kill is not necessarily to do violence: 5

I remember my grandfather standing above me, his breath steaming out of him. He was telling me to take my knife and cut the throat of the first antelope I had ever shot. I was twelve years old and confused. This thing laid out on the snow before me was so fine and beautiful; I had no idea it would be like this. I was looking to my grandfather for help, for release from this duty—but he shook his head. I turned back to the buck, took up my eight-inch, bone-handled knife, and eased the bright blade through the skin of the buck's neck and the hollow beneath. There is so much blood in a thing.

After I gutted him and packed him on my back up the ridge and loaded him into the bed of the pickup, I stood in the clear, cold light of the morning, marveling at my blood-crusted jeans, my still blood-wet hands. All winter, I knew, we'd eat breakfasts of antelope steak and fried eggs, earthy-tasting antelope sausage mixed into cream gravy and poured over toast come dinner. My father was years dead by then, and my mother came home from work each day tired in the dark. This blood, I thought, will get us through.

My grandfather broke my reverie. He took me by the shoulders, told me I had done a good, hard thing and done it well. He told me to be careful that it always remained a hard thing to do. "Easy isn't any good," he said. "If it ever gets easy—quit."

Now you're thirteen, old enough to hunt by yourself, so you load an old, bolt-action .22 with shells. You walk north. There is little wind, the sun a white hole in the sky. Beneath your boots the bones of dry grass bend and crack. You feel good about this. Prairie dogs are bad for the fields. They spread disease. A sheep will snap a front leg in a doghole. Your father is dead, your grandfather is old, and you tell yourself you are just doing what a man does. You are taking care of the fields, keeping the stock safe. You tell yourself all kinds of things.

You lay your skinny body down over a pile 10 of rotten fence posts. The prairie dogs run and dash and scamper to their little mounds, now stand and chirp at one another. You close your left eye and snug the butt up against your shoulder, the polished wood cool and smooth on the warm skin of your cheek. There's a fat one not fifty yards away. You steady yourself. There is the smell of creosote, the taste of dust and rank weeds. You sight along the blue barrel and pull the trigger. There is a small pop. The prairie dog flops over and rolls down its mound and is dead.

You are pleased with yourself. You stand for a better look. A cottontail rabbit zigzags out from beneath the pile of old posts some twenty yards and stops. You step back with your right foot and swing the rifle butt up to your shoulder again. There's no need to shoot rabbits. You close your left eye. Rabbits are no good to eat, they don't do any damage to the fields. You drop the open sights over the rabbit's spine. Its long ears twitch one, two, three times. You squeeze the trigger.

The rabbit bucks and jumps, screams. You didn't know rabbits could scream. You shoot again. And again. It's still screaming, back legs kicking at the empty air. You shoot again. The body bucks and jumps and is still.

Your breath comes back to you. That wasn't so bad, you think. But you won't tell your grandfather. He wouldn't like you killing rabbits. He's old, though, and what does he know and who really cares about rabbits anyway? All the older boys you run around with at school shoot them.

It's Saturday night. You are fourteen now, nearly grown, you think—your grandfather older and older yet, his once board-straight shoulders beginning to buckle and slump, and your mother still tired, voiceless and sad-eyed as you slam the screen door and screech the truck's tires on your way out.

You drive on into Melstone and park down 15 by the Sportsman Bar. You get in with that bunch of older boys. They've got cigarettes, beer in the backseat, a bottle of whiskey they're passing around. Boy, they drive fast. They take the corners at a gravelly skid, they raise dust right through the middle of town. Now they race on out to the river. You all pile out and run and yell and knock down the sign that says PRIMITIVE ROAD, now the one that says NARROW BRIDGE. Someone starts throwing beer bottles at the old homesteader's shack off in the willows. They crash and shatter, the glass lovely in the light of the moon. One boy runs up on the bridge and strips off his clothes and jumps. Everyone cheers and swears. From somewhere down in the watery dark, he swears back.

You don't like this. You know this isn't any good. You're all drunk. It's dark. The water's fast and cold this spring. And who knows how deep it is here, anyway? Doesn't anyone remember the Dejagher boy? You've seen him, slouched in his wheelchair, sucking can after can of 7Up through a straw. But all of a sudden—you don't quite know how it happens—you're there with the other boys, in line, laughing right there behind them.

Each jumps in turn, and now it's your turn. You don't know what to do about all this. The other boys cheer and holler. Someone passes you the whiskey bottle. You take a big swig, wing off your t-shirt, edge your toes over the rusted iron—into the dark, you leap.

And for a good while, that's how it goes: you drive fast and wild out into the dark, you coax girls down to your riverbottom bonfire parties, you stand on the beer cooler in the back of Adam's truck and flood the dark trees with a spotlight—your friend, Vinny, shoots and hits the coon between the eyes, hollers, sprays beer foam everywhere.

But then, late one night on your way back from Addie Mae's trailer, where you smoked Winstons and drank Bud Ice and laughed like you knew what you were doing, you come over Hougen's Hill out of Melstone headed west at about ninety miles an hour right down the middle of the road. As your headlights shift from sky to highway, there, straddling the double yellow line, is a big Angus. You're in the old Tercel; that cow's as big as you. You spin the wheel this way and that way and the night spins too around you.

You aren't scared. A little angry, maybe. But mostly it is like a thing coming down that you knew would always come down, the way you know your grandfather will soon die and that skinny sophomore you like will take up with some twenty-seven-year-old ranch hand and Adam will end up knocking over the liquor store in Roundup. There goes basketball, you think. There goes just about everything. 20

And then everything is still: and I am in the middle of the road, facing east instead of west, headlights veering off into the dark. I turn the car around and drive slowly toward home. I make it nearly to our turnoff before the shaking starts. I fall into bed with my jeans on, my arms and shoulders and face and heart jerking, banging like a screen door slapped about in the wind. My breath runs from me in the dark. I don't sleep until I see the sun. Then I dream. Then, miraculously, I wake.

Ten-odd years later the night is dark and shot with stars, the red tracers of lit cigarettes, a scattered rainbow of light from the dance hall.

It's a cover band, mostly George Strait numbers, some old Eric Clapton. And this is the All-School Reunion. Melstone is so small there are no individual class reunions; instead, every ten years or so, anyone who ever graduated from the local high school shows up for two days of handshakes and hellos, Main Street bonfires, beer gardens, and big stories. So that's where I am, at the All-School Reunion, drunk and leaning up against someone's pickup. It's very late. My wife, Liz, has been asking to go. And we should. But maybe just one more beer. A friend of mine from college, who didn't graduate from Melstone but happened to be passing through Montana when we were passing through Montana, is even drunker than I am. He's telling me something, something sad, I think, but I'm not really listening. I'm staring at the stars.

Now two older men are in front of my friend and me. I try to concentrate on them. One is Kevin Kincheloe. I know him. He's a good guy. I used to play with his oldest daughter, Janna, during the noon recess up at school. She was small and dark-haired, and I thought she was beautiful. But when I was in the third grade, just after my father died, they had to move away. The bank foreclosed, and they lost their ranch and everything else. I think Kevin works some kind of wage job up around Billings now.

Anyway, Kevin's a good guy. He says hello, shakes my hand, offers us a pull off his fifth of Southern Comfort. But now the other man shoulders his way up to us. He's big and fat, his face wide and whiskered. His untucked shirt waves over the bulk of his belly. Kevin starts to introduce him, but the fat man cuts him off and says something stupid. My friend says something stupid back. The fat man thumps my friend in the chest with his meaty finger—and the air around us goes glass. 25

Kevin slides back half a step and quits talking, his mouth dropping into a hard line. This man is a father of two daughters, I think, drunkenly surprised to find Kevin readying himself, to find that I too am straightening up, my arms loose, my hands curling into fists at my sides. My friend, stepping toward the fat man, sneering at the fat man, slowly raises the bottle of Southern Comfort and takes a long drink. Then he takes another. He wipes his mouth with the back of his hand, shoves the bottle hard into the fat man's chest, says, "I want to see you drink."

The fat man stands there for a moment. Then drinks—one, two, three, four swallows. My friend, still rigid and pissed and sneering at the fat man, nods with each swallow. The fat man lowers the bottle and hands it to Kevin, who drinks and then hands the bottle to me. So I drink, the syrupy bourbon coating my throat, and somehow, for no decent reason at all, this solves the whole mess: the fat man belches and turns away; my friend laughs and stumbles a bit, sits on his ass in the gravel; I breathe and let my shoulders go soft; Kevin smiles drunkenly and steps back toward me and starts in again on whatever story he was telling in the first place.

I lean back up against the hard, cool steel of the truck to watch the stars open and close their bright and tiny mouths. I am surprised at myself. Here I am: a college professor going soft in the middle thinking I'm going to get into a fistfight. I've never been in a fistfight. Even when I was an idiot-hearted boy, drinking too much and driving too fast and doing stupid things out there in the night, I always stopped before I stepped into that kind of violence. I always turned away. What would I have done tonight? What would have Kevin done? What might have happened?

I'm still idiot-hearted, I think, and then try very hard to quit thinking. Kevin's saying something about how much he misses the people out here, the Sportsman Bar, the good land along the river they used to own.

The land out on the Big Dry was bad, but we 30 tried hard to make it good:

We drained the river for irrigation, we sprayed the fields for knapweed and foxtail, we set out tubs of used motor oil for grasshopper traps. We ran electric fence up the hillsides to make the sheep eat right, we stayed all night in the shed to pull breech lambs, we vaccinated and de-horned and fed tons and tons of corn. And when none of it worked, when the wheat still burned and the grasshoppers came like a plague and the sheep went bone skinny in the sun, when that bad land still beat us, we prayed. And when that didn't work, we cursed. And then we slung the bodies to the boneyard and tried again—harder this time, the wheels greased with another layer of our bile.

Even done well, you couldn't call it a living; it was all a kind of ritualized dying. And that's not to demean a way of life. It's simply to call it like it is. Living off the land, any land, is hard. Living off that bad land, part of that stretch of high plains along the eastern front of the Rockies they used to call the Great American Desert, was nearly impossible. Especially when the rules of agriculture changed under Reagan, which was about the same time the summers got longer and the winters shorter and the creeks that once ran in all the coulees just dried up. And even then we didn't do anything different. We didn't advocate for ourselves or educate ourselves. We just doubled down and got tougher, worked harder—more loans from the bank, more acres grazed to the ground, more chemicals washed across the alfalfa.

We hurt the land, and it hurt us. Sometimes it hurt us physically: I didn't know a man in the valley who wasn't missing a couple of fingers, or maybe recovering from a broken leg after being thrown, again, by that ornery mare. There were boys in wheelchairs, girls with barbed-wire scars down their faces. Women who were forty looked sixty-five, and women who were sixty-five looked downright biblical. Clyde Brewer's heart blew up. Multiple sclerosis took hold of Butch Treible's straight spine and shook it crooked. And when I was nine, my father turned to the wall and died of cancer, probably exacerbated, they told us, by prolonged exposure to potent herbicides.

And sometimes it struck us in other, deeper ways: after my father died, my grandfather, who was one of the last of the old-time cowboys to ride the Comanche Flats before barbed wire, sold the family ranch. We were surprised and broken up about it—I remember my mother and my uncle Tom were especially questioning—but the important thing is my grandfather didn't go bankrupt. He had a choice. He was old but could have waited for me or for my brother, yet of his own will he sold, and then he told us boys a new story: he told us we would leave this place and go off to college. He only had an eighth-grade education, but that's the story he started telling, all about the things we could do if we only buckled down and kept at those books. It was a good story. So many of the other stories weren't working anymore, those ones other men told to their sons and grandsons, the ones about that good land along the river, about how some great-grandfather settled it way back when, about how it was hard going but they made it, about how even in the worst of times the land would see them through, about how the land was theirs and had been theirs and would always be theirs—but then when their boys got ready to start working that land, turned to that land, it was gone. Where'd it go? Ask the Crow, the Northern Cheyenne, the Sioux. See, out West all the old mistakes are new, and many men, good men like Kevin Kincheloe, had to sit at their kitchen tables and watch through the front window as the bank's auctioneer walked their acres, selling everything—from combines to skinny cattle, selling it all right down to the dry grass: imagine it for a moment. Imagine everything you love of the world taken from you. Now imagine it being taken from your child.

It was all about the land. We didn't do right 35 by it. And we lost it: the phone rings, and my mother shakes her head, adds another name to the list of farm foreclosures. The neighbors, the few left, sit silently at the kitchen table, the clink of coffee cups saying all there is to say.

It was a slow, psychic violence. And many turned that violence inward: Over another shot of Rich & Rare at a roadside bar, men hatched a thousand plots for revenge. Boys drove hell-bent down gravel roads. Women left screen doors screeching on their hinges. Girls climbed in with whoever had a fast car headed somewhere else. That's mostly what folks did: they left. And they left like leaving is some kind of answer, like you're not carrying anyway your bad heart out into the hot night, loading into the one pickup the boss won't miss that much a saddle and some tack and that vodka box the kids packed lip-full of toys, and driving through the star-cut dark, trying to decide whether to try Harlowton or Big Timber or maybe up and do it, make for Spokane. On the television politicians talked about this program or that program to help rural America, but someone knew what it was really all about—they set up a suicide hotline strictly for farmers and ranchers who'd gone bankrupt and had to sell and found themselves stuck in a world they didn't recognize.

But too there were those who picked up their rifles and, instead of slipping the barrel under their own chins, shouldered them, drew a bead on that world. Like that bunch in Jordan, Montana, calling themselves The Freemen, barricading themselves in a place they dubbed Justus Township, and holding off the feds for weeks with a big arsenal and bigger threats. The press called them a militia group, a one-time thing, a bunch of crazies, but they were just ranchers who had lost their land, folks like so many who had fallen into reactionary politics. Others got fundamental, went back to the church in a big way, started thinking the books in the library or the new schoolteacher's ideas were to blame. And some just struck out at whoever or whatever happened to be in the way. When the bills piled up too high, my friend Justin's uncle used to take up a logging chain and beat whichever kid happened to be around.

It was historical: smallpox blankets and slaughtered buffalo gave our ancestors the land in the first place. Maybe more blood could get it back.

I was just sixteen the first time I saw a person try to kill another person.

I had parked at the café and was riding 40 around with some older boys in a pickup. One of them had just been dumped by his girlfriend. And he was angry, really angry—swearing and sucking warm beer right from the can and telling us again and again what he ought to do, what he would do. When he spotted her car pulling onto Main Street, he yelled at the boy driving to follow her. *Follow her!*

So we did. We tailed her through town. We yelled when we got close, swore and said all kinds of things. And when she took off down the highway, we came after her. We cranked it up to a hundred and pulled even with her and threw beer cans at her windshield. We followed her when she turned off onto a gravel road, when she turned off into a field of sagebrush, when she skidded to a dusty stop in the middle of nowhere. I was drunk and scared, but I piled out of the pickup like the other boys, ready to yell, ready to stomp around and act mad, ready to do something. And when that girl threw open her car door and shouldered a rifle and started shooting, like the other boys I took off across the prairie.

She was yelling and crying, shaking something terrible. Her father, I knew, was a bad drunk. He'd sold off, leased or lost of most their land and a few months back left the family for a cocktail waitress and an abandoned trailer over near Jordan. I'd still see him sometimes, at ball games or in the café. He'd stumble over to me and shake my hand and try to tell me funny stories about my father, though he couldn't ever remember how they ended and always got them twisted up. Anyway, she must have shot five or six times, maybe more. After a moment, the last report still clanging along the hills, she dropped the rifle and collapsed there beside it in the dust.

We all ran back to the pickup and got in and drove away.

And I thought, as I left for college a few years later, I was getting clean away:

But when I start graduate school, instead of 45 renting an apartment in town, we settle in a little white house down the highway near the cross roads of Bovill, Idaho. Out our backdoor the Bitterroot Mountains rise up with their blue faces of cedar and pine. In the mornings I run along the creek down to the log works, the smell of stone and water and sweet sap strong in the air. Liz brings home buckets of blackberries from the canyon. We make pancakes for dinner, cover them with berries and cream. We've been traveling for a few years, living here and there, and are happy to be back in the West, this place we feel we know, this wide open we both love.

Saturday night we head over to the Elk Bar. It's a one-room joint in the ground floor of the old Bovill Hotel, a pile of bricks that looks like it might collapse if you kicked it hard enough. I order two bottles of High Life and two shots of Jim Beam. We smile at one another, say, "Here's to the West!" Then clink our shot glasses and drink, seal our toast with a whiskey kiss. We take our beers and wander over to the jukebox and lean down to read the yellowing song titles. I pick a Hank Williams tune. Liz goes for Patsy Cline. I start to say something to her, but suddenly she turns and yells.

There are two men—shirtless, stains on their faces, one leaning on a pool cue, the other working a wad of snoose around his mouth. They seem built out of wires and boards, their stringy legs and thick chests and hands. Liz is yelling at them, stepping forward, pointing, her voice high and loud, her face hot. These men are half grinning, half pleading, saying they didn't know who she was, thought she was a girlfriend,

a cousin. And suddenly, as the one with the snoose streak on his chin glances at me and wipes at his mouth, I get it. One of them has felt her up, grabbed her ass or something as we were bent over the jukebox. I feel my whole body go tight and ready. I step forward, in front of Liz, and say, "Leave my wife the fuck alone."

They grin at one another. They step forward too, their shoulders rolling back. The one wraps both hands around his pool stick. "Hey, man, I thought she was my girlfriend. She looks like my girlfriend. Honest mistake, right? No trouble, right? You don't want any trouble, do you?" It's an honest question. Because they do. They've forgotten Liz entirely. They're both staring right at me, the sweat shining on their bare chests. The stains, I see now, are blood bright on their faces. This is what they came for, this is what they wanted all along. And the rest of the bar knows this, too. They have quieted, hunkered down, turned ever so slightly our way. They're waiting, wondering. What will this man do, this skinny man who goes to the university, this man we don't know, this outsider? Will he do the right thing? Will he swing? He ought to swing. That's his wife there. He ought to bust that beer bottle right across that boy's face. He'll get the shit kicked out of him then. Those boys are twice as mean as he is. You can see that plain as day. But that doesn't matter. He ought to swing.

I don't swing. I say, again, "Leave my wife the fuck alone," and I take her arm, and we leave. We walk down the street to the other bar in town, Bailey's, where I drink shot after shot of bourbon, where someone follows us from the Elk and tells us that it's a good thing we left because those boys just got laid off by the local logging company and have been strung out on meth for days and getting meaner each hour. But neither booze nor commiseration helps. I'm in a bad way. I'm in a darkness I haven't ever known. This is as close as I've ever been, and I'm furious that I didn't, furious that in that moment they could have done whatever they wanted, taken what I love most.

Later, as Liz sleeps, I go to the shed behind 50 the house and stand in front of the rough cut boards of the back wall. I swing and swing and my fists crack against the wood and soon the skin of my knuckles is shredded, my fingers swollen and bleeding. I beat the boards with my open hands, my elbows, my chest, my face. At some point, I fall to my knees. I breathe. I stand and walk back with my broken hands into the house.

Go over it again: how it begins with the whims of wind and want, or maybe just some quick moment of stupidity; how failure and shame, even in an instant, become so impossibly heavy, a sack of stones you must shoulder; how this then is fear; and how fear someday detonates you—the slow implosion, the breakneck explosion.

But it doesn't have to be this way. We will fail, we will still act without good reason, we will always be burdened with failure and shame— but that, I think, is where things can change: There is a kind of awful and ready reverence that is some kin to fear but is not fear. It is when we understand the blood drying on our hands, the package of hand-wrapped meat we pull from the freezer. It is when we recognize how stories fail us and how stories save us. It is when we have heard them both and tell, in the moment of our greatest need, the story that will save us.

Like my grandfather. He knew and loved the way it had been, he saw the way it had to be. And always, even in the darkest of my days, my blood remembers his voice. I am here and mostly whole because of the stories he told me. We need to remember how it really was and is out West. And we need to tell those true, new stories.

A CLOSER LOOK AT
Growing Up Hard

1. In this memoir, Wilkins describes several scenes of violence. How does the violence in these scenes differ from the killing he describes at the beginning of the memoir? How does the difference between killing and violence reflect his statement, "But to kill is not necessarily to do violence," which is the thesis of his memoir?

2. Much of this memoir is about the change that has happened to agricultural life in the West. In what ways does Wilkins use his own stories to explain the broader social changes that have happened in the West?

3. Early in the memoir, Wilkins uses the second person view (*you*) and then he shifts to first person view (*I*). Find the place where he makes that shift. How does this shift change the tone of the memoir? How does it change your relationship, as the reader, to the narrator?

IDEAS FOR
Writing

1. Write a review of this memoir in which you explain how well it followed the memoir genre. Look back at the description of the memoir genre in Chapter 4. Did Wilkins's memoir follow the pattern? How well did he use style to hold your attention? In your review discuss whether you thought this memoir was a good example of the genre.

2. Write a memoir in which you use stories to describe how your own hometown has changed during your lifetime. Wilkins ends his story by saying, "We need to remember how it really was and is out West. And we need to tell those true, new stories." Use a memoir to tell the story of your hometown through your own experiences.

The Good Immigrant Student

BICH MINH NGUYEN

In her book Stealing Buddha's Dinner, *Bich Minh Nguyen humorously describes her bittersweet upbringing in Grand Rapids, Michigan. As a child refugee who escaped Vietnam when the war came to an end, she felt like an outsider in Grand Rapids. In this memoir, which was published before her book, she talks about adjusting to school in her new home.*

My stepmother, Rosa, who began dating my father when I was three years old, says that my sister and I used to watch Police Woman and rapturously repeat everything Angie Dickinson said. But when the show was over Anh and I would resume our Vietnamese, whispering together, giggling in accents. Rosa worried about this. She had the idea that she could teach us English and we could teach her Vietnamese. She would make us lunch or give us baths, speaking slowly and asking us how to say water, or rice, or house.

After she and my father married, Rosa swept us out of our falling-down house and into middle-class suburban Grand Rapids, Michigan. Our neighborhood surrounded Ken-O-Sha Elementary School and Plaster Creek, and was only a short drive away from the original Meijer's Thrifty Acres. In the early 1980s, this neighborhood of mismatching street names—Poinsettia, Van Auken, Senora, Ravanna—was home to families of Dutch heritage, and everyone was Christian Reformed, and conservative Republican. Except us. Even if my father hadn't left his rusted-through silver Mustang, the first car he ever owned, to languish in the driveway for months we would have stuck out simply because we weren't white. There was my Latina stepmother and her daughter, Cristina; my father, sister, grandmother, and I, refugees from Saigon; and my half-brother born a year after we moved to the house on Ravanna Street.

Although my family lived two blocks from Ken-O-Sha, my stepmother enrolled me and Anh at Sherwood Elementary, a bus ride away, because Sherwood had a bilingual education program. Rosa, who had a master's in education

and taught ESL and community ed in the public school system, was a big supporter of bilingual education. School mornings, Anh and I would be at the bus stop at the corner of our street quite early, hustled out of the house by our grandmother who constantly feared we would miss our chance. I went off to first grade, Anh to second. At ten o'clock, we crept out of our classes, drawing glances and whispers from the other students, and convened with a group of Vietnamese kids from other grades to learn English. The teachers were Mr. Ho, who wore a lot of short-sleeved button-down shirts in neutral hues, and Miss Huong, who favored a maroon blouse with puffy shoulders and slight ruffles at the high neck and wrists, paired with a tweed skirt that hung heavily to her ankles. They passed out photocopied booklets of Vietnamese phrases and their English translations, with themes such as "In the Grocery Store." They asked us to repeat slowly after them and took turns coming around to each of us, bending close to hear our pronunciations.

Anh and I exchanged a lot of worried glances, for we had a secret that we were quite embarrassed about: we already knew English. It was the Vietnamese part that gave us trouble. When Mr. Ho and Miss Huong gave instructions, or passed out homework assignments, they did so in Vietnamese. Anh and I received praise for our English, but were reprimanded for failing to complete our assignments and failing to pay attention. After a couple of weeks of this Anh announced to Rosa that we didn't need bilingual education. Nonsense, she said. Our father just shrugged his shoulders. After that, Anh began skipping bilingual classes, urging me to do the same, and then we never went back. What was amazing was that no one, not Mrs. Eunice, my first grade teacher, or Mrs. Hankins, Anh's teacher, or even Mr. Ho or Miss Huong said anything directly to us about it. Or if they did, I have forgotten it entirely. Then one day my parents got a call from Miss Huong. When Rosa came to talk to me and Anh about it we were watching television the way kids do, sitting alarmingly close to the screen. Rosa confronted us with "Do you girls know English?" Then she suddenly said, "Do you know Vietnamese?" I can't remember what we replied to either question.

For many years, a towering old billboard 5 over the expressway downtown proudly declared Grand Rapids "An All-American City." For me, that all-American designation meant all-white. I couldn't believe (and still don't) that they meant to include the growing Mexican-American population, or the sudden influx of Vietnamese refugees in 1975. I often thought it a rather mean-spirited prank of some administrator at the INS, deciding with a flourish of a signature to send a thousand refugees to Grand Rapids, a city that boasted having more churches per square mile than other city in the United States. Did that administrator know what Grand Rapids was like? That in school, everywhere I turned, and often when I closed my eyes, I saw blond blond blond? The point of bilingual education was assimilation. To my stepmother, the point was preservation: she didn't want English to take over wholly, pushing the Vietnamese out of our heads. She was too ambitious. Anh and I were Americanized as soon as we turned on the television. Today, bilingual education is supposed to have become both a method of assimilation and a method of preservation, an effort to prove that kids can have it both ways. They can supposedly keep English for school and their friends and keep another language for home and family.

In Grand Rapids, Michigan, in the 1980s, I found that an impossible task.

I transferred to Ken-O-Sha Elementary in time for third grade, after Rosa finally admitted that taking the bus all the way to Sherwood was pointless. I was glad to transfer, eager to be part of a class that wasn't, in my mind, tainted with the knowledge of my bilingual stigma. Third grade was led by Mrs. Alexander, an imperious, middle-aged woman of many plaid skirts held safe by giant gold safety pins. She had a habit of turning her wedding ring around and around her finger while she stood at the chalkboard. Mrs. Alexander had an intricate system of rewards for good grades and good behavior, denoted by colored star stickers on a piece of poster board that loomed over us all. One glance and you could see who was behind, who was striding ahead.

I was an insufferably good student, with perfect Palmer cursive and the highest possible scores in every subject. I had learned this trick at Sherwood. That the quieter you are, the shyer and sweeter and better-at-school you are, the more the teacher will let you alone. Mrs. Alexander should have let me alone. For, in addition to my excellent marks, I was nearly silent, deadly shy, and wholly obedient. My greatest fear was being called on, or in any way standing out more than I already did in the class that was, except for me and one black student, dough-white. I got good grades because I feared the authority of the teacher; I felt that getting in good with Mrs. Alexander would protect me, that she would protect me from the frightful rest of the world. But Mrs. Alexander was not agreeable to this notion. If it was my turn to read aloud during reading circle, she'd interrupt me to snap, "You're reading too fast" or demand, "What does that word mean?" Things she did not do to the other students. Anh, when I told her about this, suggested that perhaps Mrs. Alexander liked me and wanted to help me get smarter. But neither of us believed it. You know when a teacher likes you and when she doesn't.

Secretly, I admired and envied the rebellious kids, like Robbie Andrews who came to school looking bleary-eyed and pinched, like a hungover adult; Robbie and his ilk snapped back at teachers, were routinely sent to the principal's office, were even spanked a few times with the principal's infamous red paddle (apparently no one in Grand Rapids objected to corporal punishment). Those kids made noise, possessed something I thought was confidence, self-knowledge, allowing them to marvelously question everything ordered of them. They had the ability to challenge the given world.

Toward the middle of third grade Mrs. 10 Alexander introduced a stuffed lion to the pool of rewards: the best student of the week would earn the privilege of having the lion sit on his or her desk for the entire week. My quantity of gold stars was neck and neck with that of my two competitors, Brenda and Jennifer, both sweet-eyed blond girls with pastel-colored mono-grammed sweaters and neatly tied Dock-Sides. My family did not have a lot of money and my stepmother had terrible taste. Thus I attended school in such ensembles as dark red parachute pants and a nubby pink sweater stitched with a picture of a unicorn rearing up. This only propelled me to try harder to be good, to make up for everything I felt was against me: my odd family, my race, my very face. And I craved that stuffed lion. Week after week, the lion perched on Brenda's desk or Jennifer's desk. Meanwhile, the class spelling bee approached. I didn't know I was such a good speller until I won it, earning a scalloped-edged certificate and a candy bar. That afternoon I started toward home, then remembered I'd forgotten my rain boots in my locker. I doubled back to school and overheard Mrs. Alexander in the classroom talking to another teacher. "Can you believe it?" Mrs. Alexander was saying. "A foreigner winning our spelling bee!" I waited for the stuffed lion the rest of that year, with a kind of patience I have no patience for today. To no avail. In June, on the last day of school, Mrs. Alexander gave the stuffed lion to Brenda to keep forever.

The first time I had to read aloud something I had written—perhaps it was in fourth grade—I felt such terror, such a need not to have any attention upon me, that I convinced myself that I had become invisible, that the teacher could never call on me because she couldn't see me.

More than once, I was given the assignment of writing a report about my family history. I loathed this task, for I was dreadfully aware that my history could not be faked; it already showed on my face. When my turn came to read out loud the teacher had to ask me several times to speak louder. Some kids, a few of them older, in different classes, took to pressing back the corners of their eyes with the heels of their palms while they chanted, "Ching-chong, ching-chong!" during recess. (This continued until Anh, who was far tougher than me, threatened to beat them up.)

I have no way of telling what tortured me more: the actual snickers and remarks and watchfulness of my classmates, or my own imagination, conjuring disdain. My own sense of shame. At times I felt sickened by my obedience, my accumulation of gold stickers, my every effort to be invisible.

Yet Robbie Andrews must have felt the same kind of claustrophobia, trapped in his own reputation, in his ability to be otherwise. I learned in school that changing oneself is not easy, that the world makes up its mind quickly.

I've heard that Robbie dropped out of high 15 school, got a girl pregnant, found himself in and out of first juvenile detention, then jail.

What comes out of difference? What constitutes difference? Such questions, academic and unanswered, popped up in every other course description in college. But the idea of difference is easy to come by, especially in school; it is shame, the permutations and inversions of difference and self-loathing, that we should be worrying about.

Imagined torment, imagined scorn. When what is imagined and what is desired turn on each other.

Some kids want to rebel; other kids want to disappear. I wanted to disappear. I was not brave enough to shrug my shoulders and flaunt my difference; because I could not disappear into the crowd, I wished to disappear entirely. Anyone might have mistaken this for passivity.

Once, at the end of my career at Sherwood Elementary, I disappeared on the bus home. Mine was usually the third stop, but that day the bus driver thought I wasn't there, and she sailed right by the corner of Ravanna and Senora. I said nothing. The bus wove its way downtown, and for the first time I got to see where other children lived, some of them in clean orderly neighborhoods, some near houses with sagging porches and boarded-up windows. All the while, the kid sitting across the aisle from me played the same cheerful song over and over on his portable boom box. *Pass the doochee from the left hand side, pass the doochee from the left hand side.* He and his brother turned out to be the last kids off the bus. Then the bus driver saw me through the rearview mirror. She walked back to where I was sitting and said, "How come you didn't get off at your stop?" I shook my head, don't know. She sighed and drove me home.

I was often doing that, shaking my head si- 20 lently or staring up wordlessly. I realize that while I remember so much of what other people said when I was a child, I remember little of what I said. Probably because I didn't say much at all.

I recently came across in the stacks of the University of Michigan library *A Manual for Indochinese Refugee Education 1976–1977.* Some of it is silly, but much of it is a painstaking, fairly thoughtful effort to let school administrators and teachers know how to go about sensitively handling the influx of Vietnamese children in the public schools. Here is one of the most wonderful items of advice: "The Vietnamese child, even the older child, is also reported to be afraid of the dark, and more often than not, believes in ghosts. A teacher may have to be a little more solicitous of the child on gloomy, wintery days." Perhaps if Mrs. Alexander had read this, she would not have upbraided me so often for tracking mud into the classroom on rainy days. In third grade I was horrified and ashamed of my muddy shoes. I hung back, trying to duck behind this or that dark-haired boy. In spite of this, in spite of bilingual education, and shyness, and all that wordless shaking of my head, I was sent off every Monday to the Spectrum School for the Gifted and Talented. I still have no idea who selected me, who singled me out. Spectrum was (and still is) a public school program that invited students from every public elementary school to meet once a week and take specialized classes on topics such as the Middle Ages, Ellis Island, and fairy tales. Each student chose two classes, a major and minor, and for the rest of the semester worked toward final projects in both. I loved going to Spectrum. Not only did the range of

students from other schools prove to be diverse, I found myself feeling more comfortable, mainly because Spectrum encouraged individual work. And the teachers seemed happy to be there. The best teacher at Spectrum was Mrs. King, whom every student adored. I still remember the soft gray sweaters she wore, her big wavy hair, her art-class handwriting, the way she'd often tell us to close our eyes when she read us a particular story or passage.

I believe that I figured out how to stop disappearing, how to talk and answer, even speak up, after several years in Spectrum. I was still deeply self-conscious, but I became able, sometimes, to maneuver around it.

Spectrum may have spoiled me a little, because it made me think about college and freedom, and thus made all the years in between disappointing and annoying.

In seventh grade I joined Anh and Cristina at the City School, a seventh through twelfth grade public school in the Grand Rapids system that served as an early charter school; admission was by interview, and each grade had about fifty students. The City School had the advantage of being downtown, perched over old cobblestone roads, and close to the main public library. Art and music history were required. There were no sports teams. And volunteering was mandatory. But kids didn't tend to stay at City School; as they got older they transferred to one of the big high schools nearby, perhaps wishing to play sports, perhaps wishing to get away from City's rather brutal academic system. Each half semester, after grades were doled out, giant dot-matrix printouts of everyone's GPAs were posted in the hallways.

I didn't stay at City, either. When my family 25 moved to a different suburb, my stepmother promptly transferred me to Forest Hills Northern High School. Most of the students there came from upper-middle-class or very well-to-do families; the ones who didn't stood out sharply. The rich kids were the same as they were anywhere in America: they wore a lot of Esprit and Guess, drove nice cars, and ran student council, prom, and sports. These kids strutted down the hallways; the boys sat in a row on the long windowsill near a group of lockers, whistling or calling out to girls who walked by. Girls gathered in bathrooms with their Clinique lipsticks.

High school was the least interesting part of my education, but I did accomplish something: I learned to forget myself a little. I learned the sweetness of apathy. And through apathy, how to forget my skin and body for a minute or two, almost not caring what would happen if I walked into a room late and all heads swiveled toward me. I learned the pleasure that reveals itself in the loss, no matter how slight, of self-consciousness. These things occurred because I remained the good immigrant student, without raising my hand often or showing off what I knew. Doing work was rote, and I went along to get along. I've never gotten over the terror of being called on in class, or the dread in knowing that I'm expected to contribute to class discussion. But there is a slippage between being good and being unnoticed, and in that sliver of freedom I learned what it could feel like to walk in the world in plain, unself-conscious view.

I would like to make a broad, accurate statement about immigrant children in schools. I would like to speak for them (us). I hesitate; I cannot. My own sister, for instance, was never as shy as I was. Anh disliked school from the start, choosing rebellion rather than silence. It was a good arrangement: I wrote papers for her and she paid me in money or candy; she gave me rides to school if I promised not to tell anyone about her cigarettes. Still, I think of an Indian friend of mine who told of an elementary school experience in which a blond schoolchild told the teacher, "I can't sit by her. My mom said I can't sit by anyone who's brown." And another friend, whose family immigrated around the same time mine did, whose second grade teacher used her as a vocabulary example: "Children, this is what a *foreigner* is." And sometimes I fall into thinking that kids today have the advantage of so much more wisdom, that they are so much more socially and politically aware than anyone was when I was in school. But I am wrong, of course. I know not every kid is fortunate enough to have a teacher like Mrs. King, or a program like Spectrum, or even the benefit of a manual written by a group of concerned educators; I know that some kids want to disappear and disappear until they actually do. Sometimes I think I see them, in the blurry background of a magazine photo, or in a gaggle of kids following a teacher's aide across the street. The kids with heads bent down, holding themselves in such a way that they seem to be self-conscious even of how they breathe. Small, shy, quiet kids, such good, good kids, *immigrant, foreigner,* their eyes watchful and waiting for whatever judgment will occur. I reassure myself that they will grow up fine, they will be okay. Maybe I cross the same street, then another, glancing back once in a while to see where they are going.

A CLOSER LOOK AT
The Good Immigrant Student

1. Language is an important theme in this memoir. What are some of the language challenges Nguyen faced as a first-generation immigrant in the United States? How are these challenges different than you might expect?

2. Nguyen felt like an outsider in Grand Rapids. What are five reasons she might have felt like she was not fully a member of this community? What are some of the effects of her feeling like an outsider?

3. Fitting in seemed to be a complicated conflict for Nguyen during her childhood. What are some ways she tried to fit in? Which ways were successful? Which ones were not successful? Does she resolve the conflict?

IDEAS FOR
Writing

1. Nguyen's writing style is intriguing and subtle in this memoir. Write a brief literary analysis in which you discuss how she achieves this style. How does she use diction, simile, and metaphor to illustrate her recollections for readers? How does she create a unique voice or tone that comes through in the words and sentences? What is unique about her style that makes it appropriate to her subject?

2. American society has become increasingly diverse. Write a commentary or position paper in which you discuss how children of immigrants should be brought into the educational system. What are some ways American schools can help new immigrants assimilate without also forcing them to leave their own culture behind?

A FEW IDEAS FOR
Composing a Memoir

1. **Write a transition-to-college memoir.** The decision to attend college usually comes with some tension and even conflict. For you, what social, economic, familial, and personal issues led up to this change in your life? How did you feel about this transition into being a college student? How did it affect the people who are important to you? Describe the emotions you felt (optimism, pride, anxiety, etc.) and what caused those emotions. As you write, think of the larger theme or themes that give meaning to your story.

2. **Write a memoir about a positive turning point.** Describe this turning point by focusing on the "conflict" that you needed to overcome. Then write about how you and others evaluated the conflict and resolved it. How did this event or moment change you? Why was it so important? How did it help define who you are now? What is the broader lesson you learned about life from this experience?

3. **Create a multimodal memoir.** Repurpose a memoir you or someone else has written into a new multi-modal memoir. You could change the medium to a presentation (Chapter 32, "Presenting Your Work"), to a poster, to electronic words and images (on a blog, Web site, etc.), or to audio. Consider supplementing your memoir with images, sounds, and interactivity. Don't simply add images or sounds, and don't simply dump the contents into your new medium. Rather, explore how these changes allow you to transform your original memoir into something new and different. How do these changes allow you to explore new ideas or go more deeply into others?

Profiles

Dave Grohl and the Foo Fighters

CARL WILKINSON

In this profile, Carl Wilkinson provides a rich verbal portrait of rock musician Dave Grohl, who was the drummer in the "seminal grunge band Nirvana" and continues to lead the successful band the Foo Fighters. He also shows how contemporary popular music is changing in response to Internet file sharing. Notice how Wilkinson combines research with rich details about Grohl, his studio, and Grohl's own words to help readers understand what makes Grohl "the perfect rock star."

A group of record company executives, sitting down to sketch the perfect rock star, may well come up with someone a little like Dave Grohl. He has the look—long, thick black hair; he has the talent—he plays the drums, guitar and piano, he sings and he writes his own songs; and, above all, he has both pedigree and credibility.

In the early 1990s, as drummer with seminal grunge band Nirvana, Grohl helped change the face of popular music. Today, as lead singer with stadium-filling rock giants Foo Fighters, he is a multi-millionaire who has sold more than 15 million albums worldwide, won six Grammy awards and is president of his own record label. Alongside Foo Fighters he has a number of side projects (including supergroup Them Crooked Vultures, with Led Zeppelin's John Paul Jones); a documentary about his band shot by Oscar-winning director James Moll was released last month and his seventh album, *Wasting Light*, is out on Monday. Now 42, Grohl—and his brand of rock 'n' roll—has grown up, had kids and settled down.

How did a man who was just a drummer and who never intended to make money from music end up as one of the biggest and wealthiest rock stars of the decade, succeeding in the face of a record industry in crisis?

We meet at Studio 606, the 8,000 sq ft recording space he built in 2005 in the Northridge area of Los Angeles. Outside, the Californian spring sunshine throws stark shadows across a neighbourhood that estate agents would describe euphemistically as "mixed"; from inside this large utilitarian building, with its tinted windows, the blue sky looks almost overcast.

Grohl, who is tall, lean and has grown into 5 his slightly goofy looks, sets down the keys to his decidedly un-rock 'n' roll grey BMW estate, tucks his shoulder-length hair behind his ear and flips the lid on his laptop. "Sorry," he beams. "I've just got to check my e-mail. I want to see if my daughter got into private school." Grohl married Jordyn Blum in 2003, and they have two daughters, Violet Maye, aged four, and Harper Willow, one.

The upstairs lounge looks like a bachelor pad: there's a fridge, jukebox and widescreen TV with an eclectic selection of boxsets: The Office, ACDC and Bon Jovi gigs, and a tape of the Make-up and Effects trade show 1997. Scattered across the purple sofa are cushions covered with old band T-shirts (Slayer, The Police, Black Sabbath, Motorhead, Led Zeppelin) made by Grohl's mother. "She called up and said 'David, what do you want me to do with those T-shirts in the attic?'," says Grohl in a falsetto.

Downstairs, a vast recording studio complete with Persian rugs and a grand piano in the corner leads on to a warehouse filled with carefully labelled guitar cases, drums and assorted equipment. Among the platinum records, framed posters and photographs hanging in the corridor outside the soundproofed control room where we adjourn to talk is the iconic cover of Nirvana's 1991 album *Nevermind*, which celebrates its 20th anniversary in September.

Nevermind (and Nirvana) is both a gift and a curse to Grohl now. "For 16 years I've had to balance these two things: my love and respect of Nirvana and my love and respect of the Foo Fighters." He lifts first his right hand then his left and balances the two, the large feathers tattooed on both forearms gently rising and falling. "I wouldn't be here if it wasn't for Nirvana, there's no question. But I don't know if I'd be alive if it wasn't for the Foo Fighters. I try to keep them at a balance that is very respectful of each other."

Despite Grohl's desire to move on, the legacy of Nirvana's groundbreaking album still haunts him, and for good reason. *Nevermind* changed popular culture. Until the release of that album in 1991, music was dominated by pop giants such as Madonna, Michael Jackson and Whitney Houston. The alternative music scene was just that: lo-fi, raw-sounding and based on a punk DIY ethos that came to be known as grunge.

"Grunge emerged from the Pacific north- 10 west," explains the writer Mark Yarm, whose book *Everybody Loves Our Town: A History of Grunge* will be published in September to coincide with *Nevermind*'s anniversary. "It's unclear who coined the term, but it came to mean guitar bands who had a certain unkempt style and usually came from Seattle. It was a movement that was always supposed to transcend the cash. Success was viewed very warily. People like Nirvana's lead singer Kurt Cobain were resistant to success, yet very much sought it at the same time."

Grohl, who never imagined himself becoming a doctor, lawyer or writer, recorded his first album at 15 in a studio near his parents' house in Springfield, Virginia—a suburb of Washington, DC. "The intention wasn't to become U2, it was to satisfy that need to accomplish something outside of the mainstream system," he says.

That early anti-commercial intent symbolised the ethos of the alternative music scene. In 1990, Grohl became the drummer for Seattle-based band Nirvana, which had been formed by singer Kurt Cobain and bass player Krist Novoselic in 1987. Nirvana had already released a debut album, *Bleach* (1989), and the three-piece—Cobain, Novoselic and Grohl—toured small venues in a tiny van. It was a love of music that fuelled them, not the desire to become rich, famous rock stars.

All that changed when they teamed up with producer Butch Vig on their second album *Nevermind*. Where *Bleach* was a bona fide indie album released on the tiny Seattle-based Sub Pop label to which the band signed for an initial $600

advance, *Nevermind* was released by Geffen, a label owned by the Universal Music Group that was also home to the band's idols Sonic Youth.

"Sonic Youth's major label debut came out in 1990 and sold about 200,000 copies, which was considered a huge number in indie-rock circles back then," explains Yarm. "It was just inconceivable that another 'weird', underground band like Nirvana, who really looked up to Sonic Youth, could sell millions and millions of albums." Yet *Nevermind*, which was expected to sell around 200,000 copies, exploded.

"Many people point to the week in January 15 1992 when Nirvana knocked Michael Jackson— the King of Pop—off the top of the American charts as the moment alternative music truly went mainstream," says Yarm. To date, *Nevermind* has sold more than 26 million copies worldwide.

The album marked a sea-change in popular culture: it was the birth of a sound, a fashion and a lifestyle that was as big as punk or the swinging 60s before it. In the same year as *Nevermind* was released, Douglas Coupland published his famous novel *Generation X* and the theme tune for this new generation was Nirvana's breakthrough single "Smells Like Teen Spirit"—a raw, angry rallying cry that touched a nerve around the world.

Yet, for Grohl—at least initially—little changed. "It was just as much a shock to us as it was to everybody else. I think we were the last ones to believe it. Our world wasn't changing within all of that. We had a gold record and we were still touring in a van. And then it went platinum—we sold a million records— and we were still touring in a van; I was still sharing a room with Kurt when we had a platinum record. Even after we sold 10 million albums I was still living in a back room at my friend's house with a futon and a lamp." He does remember being sent his first credit card though. Never a big spender, he immediately rushed to his local Benihana, the chain of Japanese restaurants.

Thanks to Nirvana's success, record companies descended on Seattle, snapping up any band they could find. "It was a feeding frenzy," says Yarm. "One executive told me that all the flights from LA to Seattle were constantly booked. If one of those planes had gone down, it would have destroyed the music industry."

After the stratospheric success of *Nevermind*, Nirvana released just one further studio album, 1993's *In Utero*, and toured to breaking point. In 1994, lead singer Kurt Cobain, struggling with the pressure, was flown home to the US from Rome after taking an overdose during the European leg of the band's tour. On April 8 1994, Cobain was found dead at the house in Seattle he shared with his wife Courtney Love and their daughter Frances Bean. He had taken a heroin overdose and shot himself. His suicide shook the music world to its core, made global headlines and, in the eyes of many devastated fans, established Cobain as a tragic-romantic figure in the mould of Janis Joplin, Jim Morrison or Jimi Hendrix. He was 27 years old.

In the months after Cobain's death, Grohl 20 couldn't bring himself to play music. "After Nirvana ended in April 1994, I didn't really do much that year," explains Grohl. It wasn't until October 1994 that he felt ready to go back into the studio. "I didn't have a plan or any major career aspiration," he says. "I just felt like I needed to do something."

Over the course of five days, he recorded 13–14 of his songs in a small studio near his house, playing all the instruments and singing every song. Grohl distributed 100 copies of the recording to friends and music industry insiders and, reticent to step into the limelight so soon after Nirvana, he called the project Foo Fighters, the second world war term for an unidentified flying object, as it "sounded more like a band". Those recordings, which cost Grohl around $5,000, became Foo Fighters' self-titled debut album. Released in 1995, it established Grohl as one of the biggest rock musicians in the world.

It's practically unheard of for a drummer to make it as a lead singer—perhaps the only other famous example is Phil Collins, who forged a solo career after his time in Genesis. Yet Collins is not playing stadium gigs 20 years on. When almost every other band of his generation has fallen by the wayside, what is it about Grohl and Foo Fighters that still resonates?

"Their music is no nonsense, blue-collar everyman music," explains Butch Vig, who has produced the band's new album *Wasting Light*. "I think that people feel like they know the band.

They can relate to their songs, but they can also relate to them as individuals." Today, after some personnel changes over the years, Foo Fighters consist of drummer Taylor Hawkins, guitarists Chris Shiflett and Pat Smear, bass player Nate Mendel and Grohl. They are a friendly, close-knit five-piece, who share jokes nonstop and banter about moments on tour. Over the course of 16 years and seven studio albums, the band has honed a particular brand of emotionally charged rock that has transcended their early grunge influences. Grohl writes melodies with the energy of punk rock that form an enviable greatest hits package guaranteed to fill any stadium in the world (in June 2008 the band played two consecutive shows at the 90,000-capacity Wembley Stadium).

The band's new album is in some ways a return to the sound and approach of their early records. "There's no question that history is a big part of this record," admits Grohl. Despite his shiny, well-equipped studio, he decided to record *Wasting Light* in his garage at home, and in a nod to his lo-fi, DIY roots, recorded to tape rather than digitally on a computer. Like *Nevermind*, *Wasting Light* is something of an antidote to the overproduced mainstream pop that currently fills the charts. It's not the only thing that sets the band apart.

The music industry has changed since Foo 25 Fighters released their first album in 1995. "Historically record sales accounted for the majority of band revenues," explains Chris Carey, senior economist at PRS for Music, a not-for-profit organisation which collects and distributes public performance royalties for composers, songwriters and music publishers. "As record sales have suffered in recent years the industry has looked to other areas for revenue. Synchronisations [music used in computer games and TV programmes] and merchandise sales have become increasingly important, and the boom in live music is well reported. It used to be that bands would tour at a loss to sell CDs. Nowadays music is often given away in order to generate buzz and promote live events."

How does this seismic shift in the record industry affect a band such as the Foo Fighters? "They've got an established fan base and a good track record, they're an act coming to the top of the market," says Carey. "Their revenues won't be representative of what a band coming into the market now would experience. That existing fan base, I'd imagine, will still buy physical albums and, I would expect, have a good amount of money to spend on concert tickets so what you can charge for a Foo Fighters gig is more than you could for a newer band. As a result their earning profile will be quite healthy: a good mix of live and recorded."

Today, thanks to industry pressures, many popstars often have to take the money wherever they can get it, whether it's corporate gigs, sponsorship deals or product placement in music videos. In the week I met Foo Fighters, the Libyan revolution was erupting and Beyoncé, Nelly Furtado and Usher had donated to charity their million-dollar fees earned playing for the Gaddafi family. "We've done corporate gigs to pay for touring," says Foo Fighters drummer Taylor Hawkins, "but we've never played for the Gaddafis! There's nothing wrong with getting paid to play music as long as it's in the realms of whatever moral standards you have . . . "

Despite the shift in the music industry, Foo Fighters, with a secure fan base and stable income have been able to pick and choose what they do. "I think at this point we've exceeded any of the expectations we had for this band— musically or financially," explains Grohl. "The most important thing is that we do what we do with the same integrity we had when we started 16 years ago. We're not a financially ambitious band—we're doing just fine. It comes down to how much do you really need?"

Nate Mendel, the band's bassist and longest- serving member after Grohl himself, agrees: "All these ways you can exploit your band commercially, we've done a lot of it, but compared to a band similar to us, we've held back. We wanted to be in a band that didn't have to do that. It's only our generation that's ever had a problem with it. Prior to and after 80s punk rock and the alternative music of the 90s nobody cared. It's only our generation that was cautious about exploiting their music."

"Punk-rock guilt," laughs Hawkins. "I'm flying 30 in this private jet and eating lobster thermidor— but I'm not giving a song to Honda!"

As internet piracy has taken its toll on the record industry, revenue from live gigs and merchandise has become ever more important. "If you're not making money from records you have to make it somewhere else," says Carey. "Merchandise was up more than 20 per cent in 2009 growing at a good rate and in 2008 live music was up about 13-14 per cent which is boom growth."

Piracy and the decline in record sales won't have hit the Foo Fighters as hard as many other newer bands—which may explain why Grohl, who is president of his own label, Roswell Records, is unconcerned about file sharing. When he was growing up Grohl and his friends would swap tapes of their favourite bands despite campaigns warning that "home taping is killing the record industry". Today, the internet has really put a dent in the music business, Grohl acknowledges, but for him file sharing is simply an extension of those home-made mix-tapes. "To me, the most important thing is that people come and sing along when we pull into town on tour," he says. "Sharing music is not a crime. It shouldn't be. There should be a deeper meaning to making music than just selling downloads."

Grohl's experience with Nirvana has coloured the way he now runs Foo Fighters. "I learnt a lot of lessons from being in Nirvana. A lot of beautiful things and a lot of . . ." he pauses, "lessons of what not to do. I'm not a businessman, but when it comes to making music I've kind of figured out a way of doing it without anyone getting hurt." He drums his fingers, performing a short paradiddle against the arm of the leather sofa.

After his death, Cobain's estate passed to his wife, the singer Courtney Love, who in 1997, with Cobain's bandmates, formed Nirvana LLC, a limited liability company to oversee their interests. The three have at times fought over Nirvana's legacy, almost going to court in 2002 (a settlement was reached the day before proceedings were due to begin) and in 2009 scrapping over the use of Cobain's likeness in computer game *Guitar Hero 5*. In April 2006, Love sold 25 per cent of her share in Nirvana's catalogue to Primary Wave Music for a reported $50m.

When he formed Foo Fighters, Grohl set up 35 Roswell Records as a holding company for the band's entire music catalogue, which is then licensed to a record company for a six- to seven-year period at a time. "Unfortunately, a lot of musicians sign away their freedoms when they enter into these big business contracts. It's an age-old story. It's still happening. I don't think there's a place for that kind of outside control when it comes to being creative."

Are you a control freak? I ask. "Absolutely. No question. I am a controlling freak. I'm not a control freak, I'm a controlling freak. This is our baby. When it comes to making music, we have our own process, we have our own crooked democracy . . ."

Democracy? Or is it a benign dictatorship? "Well, yeah. Show me a band of five people where there's no leader . . . I just don't think it could happen. At the end of the day, it's my name at the bottom of the cheque."

Foo Fighters are now embarking on another stadium-filling world tour. As Grohl, the perfect rock star, headed off, I couldn't help thinking of the two fortune cookies I'd spotted earlier pinned to his fridge. "An interesting musical opportunity is in your near future," read one. The other said simply: "Study and prepare yourself and one day, your day will come."

A CLOSER LOOK AT
Dave Grohl and the Foo Fighters

1. Like most profiles, this one has a central theme. It examines not only the actual person (Grohl) but also what the person stands for or typifies. Sometimes the theme involves some sort of tension or an important question. What is the tension for Grohl, and what are the larger questions the profile raises and asks readers to ponder?

2. For the most part, Wilkinson mostly keeps himself out of the picture and lets the facts and his observations of Grohl and his surroundings speak for themselves. However, the author does enter the picture in a few places. Rather than coming out and stating a thesis, he poses three key questions (in paragraphs 3, 21, and 25), and in the final paragraph muses about fortune-cookie messages on Grohl's refrigerator. How do these questions and his final paragraph help direct readers toward certain takeaway conclusions? How would you summarize the thesis of this profile?

3. By citing research from two sources, Wilkinson provides background information that describes the larger social context in which Grohl lives and works. The first source is a history of grunge music by Mark Yarm (paragraphs 10–15), the other an interview with music-industry economist Chris Carey (paragraph 24 and 25). How does this research add to the profile's authority and move the main questions forward?

IDEAS FOR
Writing

1. Write a profile that, like Wilkinson's, not only paints a rich portrait of someone who is a leader in his or her field but also examines a central question about the broader social, cultural, or professional context in which the subject lives and works. Your subject could be an artist or an ordinary person that would interest your readers. Include a memo that states your purpose, your main point, and the readers you are targeting.

2. Choose an artist of performer that you admire and write a rave about that person and his or her work (see Chapter 6). Provide some context about the contemporary scene that helps explain what makes this person and work so extraordinarily exemplary and wonderful.

Prudencia

JODY L. IPSEN

Jody Ipsen is a humanitarian worker for immigrant rights and a freelance writer. A version of this piece appeared in a newspaper, the Tucson Citizen, *titled "Immigration: Why Prudencia Died." Ipsen is collecting her profiles and other work into a book,* When the Women Wept: Cries from the Migrant Trail. *She has adapted one of her book's chapters into this brief profile.*

The tropical jungle, dense with massive tree canopies, palm fronds, mango trees, red coffee berries, tangled vines and creeping ferns against the morning sun explodes like a massive jade from the land. The early morning fog casts the gem in a gauzy film, like an ephemeral phantom that flees when the Maya sun rises. Through the winding roads of the tropics to the highlands of Guatemala, shepherds, dressed in their red and blue trajes (clothing specific to their region) tend their sheep. Small fires coil in vertical rings and roosters rouse the sleep. It is hard to imagine that in 1982, plus or minus a few years, Todos Santos, a village in the clouds, was torched to the ground by U.S.-trained paramilitary, who also massacred thousands of indigenous men, women and children. The civil war that spilt the blood and cut the heads off of thousands continues to haunt the living.

At night the hills of Guatemala heave with grief. Slain victims of the dirty little war weep for their dead children; they cry of starvation and disease; they howl for the pregnant mothers whose babies were cut out of their bellies; they wail when the bullets were shot out of U.S. helicopters; they bawl as they bleed to death from their severed limbs by the cold blooded killers. In the morning the trees drip with tears where their families were hanged.

Unfortunately many men and women flee Guatemala despite the peace accord that was signed in 1996. Under the Freedom of Information Act, the CIA released documents of its covert operations during the Cold War. According to the CIA report titled *Sterilizing a "Red Infection,"* David M. Barret readily admits the United States' clandestine complicity in the civil war resulting in hundreds of thousands of deaths. During the Cold War, the CIA and the U.S. government gained tremendous currency by selling fear that Guatemala was a rising communist country.

Both John Dulles, former Secretary of State, and Allen Dulles, former Director of the CIA, played pivotal roles in the overthrow of the Guatemalan government. Allen Dulles was a shareholder in The United Fruit Company. His investments were threatened by the possible expropriation of land that President Jacobo Árbenz Guzmán wanted returned to peasant farmers.

In December of 1958, John Foster Dulles 5 said, "The United States of America does not have friends; it has interests." The interests of the United Fruit Company were of foremost importance despite an unforeseen turn of heinous events.

CIA documents reported that "Washington used the CIA and U.S. Ambassador John Peurifoy to support and direct certain Guatemalan military leaders in overthrowing Árbenz's government. It was also psychological warfare—cleverly deceptive efforts to persuade Guatemala's citizens and political/military leaders that a major invasion force was steadily moving toward the nation's capital. . . ."

Some eleven years later and thousands of miles away in the Sonoran desert, thirty-three concerned humanitarians caravanned along a dusty road to a remote region approximately twenty miles west of Tucson, Arizona. Discarded backpacks, filthy jeans, brittle water bottles and worn shoes spread across miles of greasewood, mesquite trees, and devil's claws. In the bed of a truck, Father Bob Carney covered his mouth and nose with a bandana to avoid choking on the fine dust that creates the stunning sunsets in Arizona. It was over 100 degrees at 5:30 PM and the heat burned our skin.

Prudencia Martin Gomez was from Todos Santos, Guatemala, a small Maya village in the Cuchumatanes Mountains. At nineteen, Prudencia was migrating to California to join her boyfriend, Ismael. She was abandoned by her group when she fell ill from dehydration and heat exposure. She died on June 15, 2007, in the Tucson Sector of the Sonoran desert. The recorded temperature that day was 115 degrees.

Her boyfriend, Ismael, a young man, had already migrated to the United States when he couldn't find work as a teacher in Todos Santos. Although he was raised by his grandparents near the western coast of Guatemala and was formally educated, he was shunned by his community when he returned, due in large part to his father's grizzly involvement in the civil war.

Prudencia wasn't a casualty of the war, but instead a victim of the devastating consequences that sprouted from the bloody aftermath. Families remain divided, communities are in chaos, and lack of trust for one another creates divisive animosity among the Mayas, especially those families who had ties to the war.

During the 1980's, Todos Santos was scorched to the ground. Crops were burned, homes were seared, Mayas were chopped to pieces. Other families fled to remote regions of the mountains, hiding from the military while subsisting on tree roots and vegetation. Many died from starvation, disease and blight.

Under the auspice of the United States' secret directives during the 1980's, Ismael's father was forced to join the ranks of the military or be murdered, and fought against his own ilk, which had deleterious effects on Ismael's professional opportunities.

Prudencia had heard the gruesome stories juxtaposed to the stories of wealth and of what dreams may come while weighing them against the few jobs available to Maya women, due to the lack of civil rights for women and because of racial tensions that exist between indigenous and non-indigenous peoples of Guatemala. Prudencia was convinced that her future existed inside the United States of America.

Prudencia and Ismael were going to marry once he saved enough money to build them a home in Guatemala. Prudencia, with a petite frame and long black hair that flowed past her hips, had simple pleasures, like gazing at the stars and thinking of the promise of joining Ismael someday. In May of 2007, at the age of 19, she left Todos Santos to surprise her boyfriend, who was living somewhere in California. Like most migrants, she traveled with a coyote (guide), through the veins of Mexico's underground, avoiding immigration police and bandits who rob Central Americans. She then walked approximately fifty miles from the border of Sasabe, Mexico to the outskirts of Tucson, Arizona. With only a gallon of water and the clothes in her backpack, Prudencia trudged through the desert under the scorching summer sun for approximately four to five days. Coyotes often abandon the sick or injured migrants in order to get the remainder of their group across. She was later found dead by humanitarians who were notified by her boyfriend that she was left behind by the group.

By the end of the civil war in 1996, it is estimated that over 200,000 people were murdered. In 2007, three thousand women were murdered in Guatemala. Many believe the murderers are the formerly U.S.-trained Guatemalan military and police. In an attempt to bring back the conservative mano dura party (iron fist), the military instills fear through mutilations in order to persuade the country only the fist can stop the violence. So many of the disappeared women are later found mutilated and remain forever unidentified.

Ostensibly, many of the migrants leaving Guatemala find themselves without work or in Ismael's situation, without a community. The fallout of the civil war continues despite the ongoing efforts of Amnesty International. The legacy of death and destruction due in large part to U.S. covert operations thwarts any mechanisms to restore Guatemalan life to prewar conditions.

According to Intelligence scholar, Christopher Andrew, "The Guatemala affair [was] a disreputable moment—Eisenhower was 'directly responsible' for 'death and destruction, yet showed no signs of embarrassment then or later over his 'bullying of a banana republic.'"

In July of 2008, a shrine was erected at the site where Prudencia died.

A CLOSER LOOK AT
Prudencia

1. Ipsen chooses not to begin with a description of her subject, Prudencia, and does not even mention her until the second paragraph of the second section. How does this delay affect your understanding of Prudencia?

2. Examine the overall structure. Ipsen moves back and forth from the Guatemalan civil war and the United States' role in that war to the story of Prudencia Martin Gomez. In what ways does this complex organization enhance your understanding of her subject?

3. Ipsen chooses not to come out and tell the reader what she believes is the message or theme of this profile. That is, she uses an "implied thesis" that leaves such conclusions to the reader. How would the impact of this piece have changed had she chosen to directly state her thesis?

4. Ipsen has chosen to give this profile a one-word title, not "Prudencia Martin Gomez" or "The Tragedy of Prudencia Martin Gomez," but just "Prudencia." While "Prudencia" refers literally to the person profiled, *prudencia* is Spanish for "prudence," which can mean "discretion, carefulness, and the foresight to avoid danger and mishap"; it can also mean "the habit of mind of discerning what is good and moral." How does this ironic double sense of *Prudencia* enhance the meaning of the profile? What larger questions does it raise? Who has acted prudently and who has not?

IDEAS FOR
Writing

1. Write a brief commentary responding to this profile. Do some research on the Guatemalan civil war and the United States' role in it. Do you believe the United States was justified in taking part in this civil war? When should the United States be involved in these kinds of situations, and when should it stand aside?

2. Ipsen has spent years as a humanitarian helping immigrants who risk their lives migrating to the United States. Obviously, she feels passionately about this social and political cause, and the individuals who are caught up in these issues. Write a letter to the editor in which you express your own views about immigration and the plight of people like Prudencia. When should the United States allow people like Prudencia to enter the country legally? What lines would you draw to keep illegal immigrants out?

Bodies in Motion and at Rest

THOMAS LYNCH

In this profile from Bodies in Motion and at Rest *(2000), Thomas Lynch—a poet, essayist, and undertaker—writes about picking up a corpse and preparing it for burial. Notice how he uses the narrative features of profile to tell a story while making a broader commentary about life and death.*

So I'm over at the Hortons' with my stretcher and minivan and my able apprentice, young Matt Sheffler, because they found old George, the cemetery sexton, dead in bed this Thursday morning in ordinary time. And the police have been in to rule out foul play and the EMS team to run a tape so some ER doctor wired to the world can declare him dead at a safe distance. And now it's ours to do—Matt's and mine—to ease George from the bed to the stretcher, negotiate the sharp turn at the top of the stairs, and go out the front door to the dead wagon idling in the driveway and back to the funeral home from whence he'll take his leave—waked and well remembered—a Saturday service in the middle of April, his death observed, his taxes due.

We are bodies in motion and at rest—there in George's master bedroom, in the gray light of the midmorning, an hour or so after his daughter found him because he didn't answer when she called this morning, and he always answers, and she always calls, so she got in the car and drove over and found him exactly as we find him here: breathless, unfettered, perfectly still, manifestly indifferent to all this hubbub. And he is here, assembled on his bed as if nothing had happened, still propped on his left shoulder, his left ear buried in his pillow, his right leg hitched up over the left one, his right hand tucked up under the far pillow his ex-wife used to sleep on, before she left him twenty years ago, and under the former Mrs. Horton's pillow, I lift to show Matt, is a little pearl-handled .22 caliber that George always slept with since he has slept alone. "Security," he called it. He said it helped him sleep.

And really there is nothing out of order, no sign of panic or struggle or pain, and except for the cardiac-blue tinting around his ears, the faint odor of body heat and a little early rigor in his limbs, which makes the moving of him easier, one'd never guess George wasn't just sleeping in this morning—catching the twenty extra winks—because maybe he'd been up late playing poker with the boys, or maybe he'd had a late dinner with his woman friend, or maybe he was just a little tired from digging graves and filling them, and anyway, he hadn't a grave to open this morning for one of the locals who was really dead.

But this morning George Horton is really dead and he's really being removed from his premises by Matt and me after we swaddle him in his own bed linens, sidle him on to the stretcher, tip the stretcher up to make the tight turn at the top of the stairs and carefully ease it down, trying to keep the wheels from thumping each time the heavier head end of the enterprise takes a step. And it's really a shame, all things considered, because here's George, more or less in his prime, just south of sixty, his kids raised, his house paid off, a girlfriend still in her thirties with whom he maintained twice-weekly relations—"catch as catch can," he liked to say. And he's a scratch golfer and a small business owner with reliable employees and frequent flier miles that he spends on trips to Vegas twice a year, where he lets himself get a little crazy with the crap tables and showgirls. And he has his money tucked into rental homes and mutual funds, and a host of friends who'd only say good things about him, and a daughter about to make him a grandfather for the first time, and really old George seemed to have it made, and except for our moving him feet first down the stairs this morning, he has everything to live for, everything.

And it is there, on the landing of the first 5 floor, only a few feet from the front door out, that his very pregnant daughter waits in her warmup suit to tender her good-byes to the grandfather of her baby, not yet born. And Matt's face is flushed with the lifting, the huffing and puffing, or the weight of it all, or the sad beauty of the woman as she runs her hand along her father's cheek, and she is catching her breath and her eyes are red and wet and she lifts her face to ask me, "Why?"

"His heart, Nancy . . ." is what I tell her. "It looks like he just slept away. He never felt a thing." These are all the well-tested comforts one learns after twenty-five years of doing these things.

"But *why*?" she asks me, and now it is clear that *how* it happened is not good enough. And here I'm thinking all the usual suspects: the cheeseburgers, the whiskey, the Lucky Strikes, the thirty extra pounds we, some of us, carry, the walks we didn't take, the preventive medicines we all ignore, the work and the worry and the tax man, the luck of the draw, the nature of the beast, the way of the world, the shit that happens because it happens.

But Nancy is not asking for particulars. She wants to know why in the much larger, Overwhelming Question sense: why we don't just live forever. Why are we all eventually orphaned and heartbroken? Why we human beings cease to be. Why our nature won't leave well enough alone. Why we are not all immortal. Why this morning? Why George Horton? Why oh why oh why?

No few times in my life as a funeral director have I been asked this. Schoolchildren, the newly widowed, musing clergy, fellow pilgrims— maybe they think it was my idea. Maybe they just like to see me squirm contemplating a world in which folks wouldn't need caskets and hearses and the likes of me always ready and willing and at their service. Or maybe, like me, sometimes they really wonder.

"Do the math" is what George Horton would 10 say. Or "Bottom line." Or "It's par for the course." Or "It's Biblical." If none of these wisdoms seemed to suit, then "Not my day to watch it" is what he'd say. Pressed on the vast adverbials that come to mind whilst opening or closing graves, George could be counted for tidy answers. Self-schooled in the Ways of the World, he confined his reading to the King James Bible, *The Wall Street Journal*,

Golf Digest, the *Victoria's Secret* catalog and the Big Book of Alcoholics Anonymous. He watched C-SPAN, The Home Shopping Network and The Weather Channel. Most afternoons he'd doze off watching Oprah, with whom he was, quite helplessly, in love. On quiet days he'd surf the Web or check his portfolio on-line. On Sundays he watched talking heads and went to dinner and the movies with his woman friend. Weekday mornings he had coffee with the guys at the Summit Café before making the rounds of the half dozen cemeteries he was in charge of. Wednesdays and Saturdays he'd mostly golf.

"Do the math" I heard him give out with once from the cab of his backhoe for no apparent reason. He was backfilling a grave in Milford Memorial. "You gonna make babies, you've gotta make some room; it's Biblical."

Or once, leaning on a shovel, waiting for the priest to finish: "Copulation, population, inspiration, expiration. It's all arithmetic—addition, multiplication, subtraction and long division. That's all we're doing here, just the math. Bottom line, we're buried a thousand per acre, or burned into two quarts of ashes, give or take."

There was no telling when such wisdoms would come to him.

But it came to me, embalming George later that morning, that the comfort in numbers is that they all add up. There is a balm in the known quantities, however finite. Any given year at this end of the millennium, 2.3 million Americans will die. Ten percent of pregnancies will be unintended. There'll be 60 million common colds. These are numbers you can take to the bank. Give or take, 3.9 million babies will be born. It's Biblical. They'll get a little more or a little less of their 76 years of life expectancy. The boys will grow to just over 69 inches, the girls to just under 64. Of them, 25 percent will be cremated, 35 percent will be overweight, 52 percent will drink. Every year 2 million will get divorced, 4 million will get married and there'll be 30,000 suicides. A few will win the lotto, a few will run for public office, a few will be struck by lightning. And any given day, par for the course, 6,300 of our fellow citizens, just like George, will get breathless and outstretched and spoken of in the past tense; and most will be dressed up the way I dress up

George, in his good blue suit, and put him in a casket with Matt Sheffler's help, and assemble the 2 or 3 dozen floral tributes and the 100 or 200 family and friends and the 60 or 70 cars that will follow in the 15 mile per hour procession down through town to grave 4 of lot 17 of section C in Milford Memorial, which will become, in the parlance of our trade, his final resting place, over which a 24-by-12-by-4-inch Barre granite stone will be placed, into which we will have sandblasted his name and dates, one of which, subtracted from the other, will amount, more or less, to his life and times. The corruptible, according to the officiating clergy, will have put on incorruption, the mortal will have put on immortality. "Not my day to watch it" will be among the things we'll never hear George Horton say again.

Nor can we see clearly now, looking into his 15 daughter Nancy's eyes, the blue morning at the end of this coming May when she'll stand, upright as any walking wound, holding her newborn at the graveside of the man, her one and only father, for whom her baby will be named. Nor can we hear the promises she makes to keep him alive, to always remember, forever and ever, in her heart of hearts. Nor is there any math or bottom line or Bible verse that adds or subtracts or in any way accounts for the moment or the mystery she holds there.

A CLOSER LOOK AT
Bodies in Motion and at Rest

1. This profile begins with a description of a dead person, George Horton. Lynch, as the narrator, seems distant and detached from the emotions surrounding this person's death. How does he express this detached feeling in his writing? How does he achieve this tone and the sense that the body is nothing more than a name and a job to do?

2. As the profile continues, it is obvious that Lynch knows more about George than he seems to suggest at the beginning, when George is simply a body to be moved and prepared for burial. Lynch shares facts and quotes with the readers that only someone who knew George or his family would know. What relationship do you think the writer had with the deceased? What does his reaction to George's death tell you about Lynch, as someone who is still living?

3. Late in the profile, Lynch begins reciting a list of demographic numbers that detail how people live and die in the United States. The funeral itself seems like a notable moment in a continuing story of meaningless lives and death in this world. What do you think is Lynch's point here? Does he really feel that life goes on, barely noting people who might have meant so much to others? What is the unstated theme at the heart of this profile?

IDEAS FOR
Writing

1. Find an obituary in today's paper or an obituary of a notable person from the past. Write a commentary in which you discuss how obituaries, as a special kind of profile, are different from typical profiles that describe the living. How do we treat the dead differently, and do you think it is right to do this? What do obituaries focus on, and what do they leave out? What does Lynch's profile of George do differently than a typical obituary?

2. Lynch's description of George's life and death seems rather bleak. Do you find Lynch's profile effective? What do you think is Lynch's point in this profile, and what do you think he wants you to learn or take away from it? Write a rhetorical analysis in which you study the content, organization, and style of this profile. How does Lynch use details and tone to support a broader commentary about life and death in the modern world?

Two Profiles of Griffith Park

These two profiles of Griffith Park, the largest municipal park in the United States, located in the city of Los Angeles, take very different approaches. The first profile appears on the website of Los Angeles Department of Recreation and Parks. The second is written by novelist and nonfiction writer Benjamin Percy for Outside, *a monthly magazine that focuses on outdoor recreation. As you read, notice how they differ in terms of style and content.*

City of Los Angeles Department of Recreation and Parks, General Information for Griffith Park

Times And Regulations:

Griffith Park is open to the public from 5:00 a.m. to 10:30 p.m. Bridle trails, hiking paths, and mountain roads are closed at sunset. The speed limit on all park roads is 25 mph and is strictly enforced. Brush fires present a definite safety hazard, especially from Spring to early Fall, when the natural chaparral and underbrush is very dry. Open fires are prohibited; barbecue pits are provided free of charge at picnic areas. In case of emergency in the park, notify the Ranger Station at (323) 913-4688 or dial 911. The Griffith Park Fire Recovery Blog offers updated park information.

Location:

Griffith Park lies just west of the Golden State Freeway (I-5), roughly between Los Feliz Boulevard on the south and the Ventura Freeway (SR 134) on the north. Freeway off-ramps leading to the park from I-5 are Los Feliz Boulevard, Griffith Park (direct entry) and Zoo Drive. Approaching the park on SR 134 eastbound, take either the Forest Lawn Drive or Victory Boulevard offramps. From SR 134 westbound, take Zoo Drive or Forest Lawn Drive. After leaving freeways, follow the signs into the park.

Narrative

With over 4,210 acres of both natural chaparral-covered terrain and landscaped parkland and picnic areas, Griffith Park is the largest municipal park with urban wilderness area in the United States. Situated in the eastern Santa Monica Mountain range, the Park's elevations range from 384 to 1,625 feet above sea level. With an arid climate, the Park's plant communities vary from coastal sage scrub, oak and walnut woodlands to riparian vegetation with trees in the Park's deep canyons. The California native plants represented in Griffith Park include the California species of oak, walnut, lilac, mountain mahogany, sages, toyon, and sumac. Present, in small quantities, are the threatened species of manzanita and berberis.

Over the years recreational attractions have been developed throughout the Park, however an amazingly large portion of the Park remains virtually unchanged from the days Native American villages occupied the area's lower slopes. Today's Griffith Park offers numerous family attractions, an assortment of educational and cultural institutions, and miles of hiking and horseback riding trails, and provides visitors an ideal environment for enjoyable recreation activities.

Originally a part of the Spanish land grant, 5 Rancho Los Feliz, the park was named for its former owner, Colonel Griffith J. Griffith. Born in Glamorganshire, South Wales, Griffith emigrated to the United States in 1865, eventually, making a personal fortune in California gold mine speculation. In 1882, Griffith settled in Los Angeles, and purchased a 4,071 acre portion of the Rancho Los Feliz, which stretched northward from the northern boundaries of the Pueblo de Los Angeles. On December 16, 1896, the civic-minded Griffith bequeathed 3,015 acres of his Rancho Los Feliz estate as a Christmas gift to the people of Los Angeles to be used as parkland. The enormous gift, equal to five square miles, was to be given to the city unconditionally—or almost so.

"It must be made a place of recreation and rest for the masses, a resort for the rank and file, for the plain people," Griffith said on that occasion.

"I consider it my obligation to make Los Angeles a happier, cleaner, and finer city. I wish to pay my debt of duty in this way to the community in which I have prospered."

Since Griffith's original gift, further donations of land, along with City purchases and the reversion of private land to public domain have expanded the Park to its present size. Col. Griffith died July 7, 1919, however, he had left a sizeable trust fund to complete the dreams he had for the park; specifically designating funds for the construction of a Greek amphitheater (the Greek Theatre, built 1930) and an observatory and hall of science (Griffith Observatory, built 1935.)

Griffith Park stands today a monument to the dedicated vision of one man—Griffith Jenkins Griffith, Park Commission, civic philanthropist, advocate of parklands, and fervent speaker of recreation for the health of Los Angeles.

Welcome to the Jungle

BENJAMIN PERCY

I'm not here for the silicone or Bentleys. I don't want to get my picture taken with a Marilyn Monroe impersonator. I've come to grind my teeth on a little of L.A.'s sweet grit.

My buddy James—a fast-talker with wild eyes and a grizzly bear of a beard—picks me up at LAX. He's lived here for three years but still keeps a GPS on the dash. "This city," he says, "makes no sense." He's talking about more than the tangle of roadways. He's talking about a city that is not so much a city as it is a mess of neighborhoods, each with its own personality, making L.A. a kind of smog-belching, schizophrenic beast.

We park along the L.A. River at Atwater Village and step into the concrete channel. I have alternating views of the freeway and the mist-haloed San Gabriel Mountains. This is not the barren watercourse from *Terminator 2*. Bass populate the river. Horseback riders splash along its banks. There are islands thick with trees that are decorated with garbage. I quickly spot a dozen species of waterfowl.

Ducks honk. Semis blast their horns. A group of spandex-clad bicyclists races by on the riverside path. James and I find a tunnel, full of graffiti and shadows and broken glass, that takes us under the freeway. When we emerge, we are at the doorstep of 4,000-acre Griffith Park, one of the largest urban wildernesses in the country.

We enter the 53-mile network of trails, and soon trees crowd around us, hushing the grumble of the city. At the end of our seven-mile hike, the sun begins to set, and the neon glow of the city makes the sky a bruised purple. We drive to Koreatown and Masan, a restaurant known for its monkfish stew, which we order, along with live octopus. The legs twist on our plates like dying snakes, and I chew them to a paste—if you don't, the suckers can latch on to your tongue.

"You want dessert?" James asks, and I say, "I want to shoot some guns."

Just past Skid Row we find the Los Angeles Gun Club, the kind of nondescript building that could pass for a paper-clip warehouse. Then you approach the door and hear the *snap-snap-snap* of muffled gunfire. Inside, the air is heavy with gun oil, and the walls are busy with racks of every firearm you can imagine. James and I opt for an AR-15, an assault rifle that jerks in my arms like something alive as I fire rounds down lane four. I am surrounded by men with forearm tats who fire pistols while their girlfriends clap and squeal. After blasting my way through three bricks of ammo, my hands are trembling and I can't shake the grin from my face.

"What do you think?" James asks.

"Unreal," I say.

A CLOSER LOOK AT
General Information for Griffith Park and Welcome to the Jungle

1. Profiles belong to a very "stretchy" and versatile genre. These profiles of Griffith Park differ greatly, but they both describe the same place.

   a. How do they differ in terms of the details they describe?

   b. How do they differ in purpose, angle, audience, and style?

   c. How do their titles forecast the content, angle, and style of each?

   d. How do their organizations differ? How do they begin and end?

   e. Finally, compare the two in a single sentence that follows a pattern like this one: "The Recreation and Parks piece makes me feel _____, while Percy's piece makes me feel _____." Then point out or quote specific places in each text that elicit that feeling.

2. The first profile is written for readers who visit the Los Angeles Recreation and Parks website, the second for people who enjoy reading *Outside* magazine. Use Google to find each website and speculate about the values and expectations of each set of readers. How would *Outside* readers react if they found "General Information" in the magazine? How would visitors to the Parks and Recreation website react if they encountered Percy's profile?

3. Which kind of profile would you most enjoy writing? Or would you rather write something that falls between the two? Explain your choice.

4. "Welcome to the Jungle" has more energy and snap partly because it tells a story. What narrative elements does Percy use to make this very short story interesting?

IDEAS FOR
Writing

1. Choose a place you find interesting and write two short profiles of the place. For the first, imagine you work for a business or government agency that needs a serious and restrained profile for their website. The profile should present information clearly and in a way that would be appropriate for a wide range of readers. It should be neutral and objective in tone and style. For the second, imagine you have been asked to contribute a profile to a website or magazine you enjoy reading. Target those readers, using a tone that is energetic and entertaining. Amplify with metaphors and similes. Paint a rich picture with details about what the place smelled, sounded, and looked like. When you've finished, write a memo that explains the strategies you used to match the values and expectations of each reader type.

2. "Welcome to the Jungle" profiles both a place and experience. Write a place profile that also tells an interesting story about one of your personal experiences that happened in a special place. Set the scene in rich detail and use dialogue to provide texture. Your profile should help readers understand what is special about this place.

A FEW IDEAS FOR
Composing a Profile

1. **Write a profile of a place or an object.** While writing your profile, think of this place or object as a *person* rather than as an inanimate thing. Discuss its history, its unique characteristics, its relationships with people, and so on. Relate any stories you know about it. Make sure you keep your readers in mind as you write this profile. Write for readers who are interested in visiting this place or object. How can you make your profile interesting and engaging for them?

2. **Repurpose a profile for children.** Find a profile of a famous person (e.g., Martin Luther King, Clara Barton, Abraham Lincoln, Maya Angelou, Cesar Chavez, Princess Diana) and rewrite it in a way that would be accessible and interesting to children who are five to ten years old. Include the original profile when you hand in your rewritten profile to your professor.

3. **Create a profile of someone in your family for the** *Memory Archive* **(memoryarchive.org).** This site archives personal stories and reflections of everyday people. Use a style that would make your profile especially engaging to readers who don't know you, your family, or your community. Pay special attention to your use of detail, and show your subject in motion or doing things, if possible.

35

Reviews

Harry Potter's Girl Trouble

CHRISTINE SCHOEFER

Most reviews of J. K. Rowling's Harry Potter *books are positive, if not glowing. Some reviewers, however, have raised concerns about the values portrayed in the books. Some Christians complain about Rowling's perceived romanticizing of witchcraft. Meanwhile, critics such as Christine Schoefer, who wrote this review for* Salon, *see problems from a feminist point of view.*

Four factors made me go out and buy the Harry Potter books: Their impressive lead on the bestseller lists, parents' raves about Harry Potter's magical ability to turn kids into passionate readers, my daughters' clamoring and the mile-long waiting lists at the public library. Once I opened *The Sorcerer's Stone*, I was hooked and read to the last page of Volume 3. Glittering mystery and nail-biting suspense, compelling language and colorful imagery, magical feats juxtaposed with real-life concerns all contributed to making these books page turners. Of course, Diagon Alley haunted me, the Sorting Hat dazzled me, Quidditch intrigued me. Believe me, I tried as hard as I could to ignore the sexism. I really wanted to love Harry Potter. But how could I?

Harry's fictional realm of magic and wizardry perfectly mirrors the conventional assumption that men do and should run the world. From the beginning of the first Potter book, it is boys and men, wizards and sorcerers, who catch our attention by dominating the scenes and determining the action. Harry, of course, plays the lead. In his epic struggle with the forces of darkness—the evil wizard Voldemort and his male supporters—Harry is supported by the dignified wizard Dumbledore and a colorful cast of male characters. Girls, when they are not downright silly or unlikable, are helpers, enablers and instruments. No girl is brilliantly heroic the way Harry is, no woman is experienced and wise like Professor Dumbledore. In fact, the range of female personalities is so limited that neither women nor girls play on the side of evil.

But, you interject, what about Harry's good friend Hermione? Indeed, she is the female lead and the smartest student at Hogwarts School of Witchcraft and Wizardry. She works hard to be accepted by Harry and his sidekick Ron, who treat her like a tag-along until Volume 3. The trio reminds me of Dennis the Menace, Joey and Margaret or Calvin, Hobbes and Suzy. Like her cartoon counterparts, Hermione is a smart goody-goody who annoys the boys by constantly reminding them of school rules. Early on, she is described as "a bossy know-it-all," hissing at the boys "like an angry goose." Halfway through the first book, when Harry rescues her with Ron's assistance, the hierarchy of power is established. We learn that Hermione's bookish knowledge only goes so far. At the sight of a horrible troll, she "sinks to the floor in fright . . . her mouth open with terror." Like every Hollywood damsel in distress, Hermione depends on the resourcefulness of boys and repays them with her complicity. By lying to cover up for them, she earns the boys' reluctant appreciation.

Though I was impressed by Hermione's brain power, I felt sorry for her. She struggles so hard to get Harry and Ron's approval and respect, in spite of the boys' constant teasing and rejection. And she has no girlfriends. Indeed, there don't seem to be any other girls at the school worth her—or our—attention. Again and again, her emotions interfere with her intelligence, so that she loses her head when it comes to applying her knowledge. Although she casts successful spells for the boys, Hermione messes up her own and as a result, while they go adventuring, she hides in the bathroom with cat fur on her face. I find myself wanting Hermione to shine, but her bookish knowledge and her sincere efforts can't hold a candle to Harry's flamboyant, rule-defying bravery.

Even though Hermione eventually wins the boys' begrudging respect and friendship, her thirst for knowledge remains a constant source of irritation for them. And who can blame them? With her nose stuck in books, she's no fun. Thankfully, she is not hung up on her looks or the shape of her body. But her relentless studying has all the characteristics of a disorder: It makes her ill-humored, renders her oblivious to her surroundings, and threatens her health, especially in the third volume.

Ron's younger sister Ginny, another girl student at Hogwarts, can't help blushing and stammering around Harry, and she fares even worse than Hermione. "Stupid little Ginny" unwittingly becomes the tool of evil when she takes to writing in a magical diary. For months and months, "the foolish little brat" confides "all her pitiful worries and woes" ("how she didn't think famous good great Harry Potter would 'ever' like her") to these pages. We are told how boring it is to listen to "the silly little troubles of an eleven-year-old girl."

Again and again, we see girls so caught up in their emotions that they lose sight of the bigger picture. We watch them "shriek," "scream," "gasp" and "giggle" in situations where boys retain their composure. Again and again, girls stay at the sidelines of adventure while the boys jump in. While Harry's friends clamor to ride his brand-new Firebolt broomstick, for example, classmate Penelope is content just to hold it.

The only female authority figure is beady-eyed, thin-lipped Minerva McGonagall, professor of transfiguration and deputy headmistress of Hogwarts. Stern instead of charismatic, she is described as eyeing her students like "a wrathful eagle." McGonagall is Dumbledore's right hand and she defers to him in every respect. Whereas he has the wisdom to see beyond rules and the power to disregard them, McGonagall is bound by them and enforces them strictly. Although she makes a great effort to keep her feelings under control, in a situation of crisis she loses herself in emotions because she lacks Dumbledore's vision of the bigger picture. When Harry returns from the chamber of secrets, she clutches her chest, gasps, and speaks weakly while the all-knowing Dumbledore beams.

Sybill Trelawney is the other female professor we encounter. She teaches divination, a subject that includes tea-leaf reading, palmistry, crystal gazing—all the intuitive arts commonly associated with female practitioners. Trelawney is a misty, dreamy, dewy charlatan, whose "clairvoyant vibrations" are the subject of constant scorn and ridicule. The only time she makes an accurate prediction, she doesn't even know it because she goes into a stupor. Because most of her students and all of her colleagues dismiss her, the entire intuitive tradition of fortune-telling, a female domain, is discredited.

A brief description of the guests in the Leaky Cauldron pub succinctly summarizes author J. K. Rowling's estimation of male and female: There are "funny little witches," "venerable looking wizards" who argue philosophy, "wild looking warlocks," "raucous dwarfs" and a "hag" ordering a plate of raw liver. Which would you prefer to be? I rest my case.

But I remain perplexed that a woman (the mother of a daughter, no less) would, at the turn of the 20th century, write a book so full of stereotypes. Is it more difficult to imagine a headmistress sparkling with wit, intelligence and passion than to conjure up a unicorn shedding silver blood? More farfetched to create a brilliant, bold and lovable heroine than a marauder's map?

It is easy to see why boys love Harry's adventures. And I know that girls' uncanny ability to imagine themselves in male roles (an empathic skill that boys seem to lack, honed on virtually all children's literature as well as Hollywood's younger audience films) enables them to dissociate from the limitations of female characters. But I wonder about the parents, many of whom join their kids in reading the Harry Potter stories. Is our longing for a magical world so deep, our hunger to be surprised and amazed so intense, our gratitude for a well-told story so great that we are willing to abdicate our critical judgment? Or are the stereotypes in the story integral to our fascination—do we feel comforted by a world in which conventional roles are firmly in place?

I have learned that Harry Potter is a sacred cow. Bringing up my objections has earned me other parents' resentment—they regard me as a heavy-handed feminist with no sense of fun who is trying to spoil a bit of magic they have discovered. But I enjoyed the fantastical world of wizards, witches, beasts and muggles as much as anyone. Is that a good reason to ignore what's been left out?

A CLOSER LOOK AT
Harry Potter's Girl Trouble

1. The review starts out positive as Schoefer describes her early experiences with the Harry Potter books, especially *The Sorcerer's Stone*. At what point does the review switch from positive to negative? Why do you think she started out the review in a positive way if she was going to say negative things about the books?

2. What are a few of the reviewer's criticisms of the books and why does she think the books are flawed in an important way?

3. One of the reviewer's major complaints is that the books do not include a female villain. Why does she think the lack of a female villain is a problem in the Harry Potter series?

IDEAS FOR
Writing

1. Write a brief memoir about your favorite childhood book, something you read by yourself. Describe the experience of reading this special book and the effects it had on you. What attracted you to the book in the first place? What about the book made it different from other books you read? Which characters did you enjoy and why did they appeal to you? What did you learn from the book, and how did it shape your life?

2. Write a letter to the editor in which you respond to this review. Explain why you think the reviewer did or did not properly review the Harry Potter books, especially *The Sorcerer's Stone*. If you generally agree with the review, what might you add about the book that the reviewer should have mentioned? If you disagree with the review, what are some ways the reviewer got the Harry Potter books wrong?

Why We Crave Horror Movies

STEPHEN KING

This curious article was first published in Playboy *in January 1981 when Stephen King was emerging as one of the great horror writers. It's not a standard evaluation, but it has many of this genre's elements. Watch how King stretches the genre to achieve an interesting purpose.*

I think that we're all mentally ill: those of us outside the asylums only hide it a little better— and maybe not all that much better, after all. We've all known people who talk to themselves, people who sometimes squinch their faces into horrible grimaces when they believe no one is watching, people who have some hysterical fear—of snakes, the dark, the tight place, the long drop . . . and, of course, those final worms and grubs that are waiting so patiently underground.

When we pay our four or five bucks and seat ourselves at tenth-row center in a theater showing a horror movie, we are daring the nightmare.

Why? Some of the reasons are simple and obvious. To show that we can, that we are not afraid, that we can ride this roller coaster. Which is not to say that a really good horror movie may not surprise a scream out of us at some point, the way we may scream when the roller coaster twists through a complete 360 or plows through a lake at the bottom of the drop. And horror movies, like roller coasters, have always been the special province of the young; by the time one turns 40 or 50, one's appetite for double twists or 360-degree loops may be considerably depleted.

We also go to re-establish our feelings of essential normality; the horror movie is innately conservative, even reactionary. Freda Jackson as the horrible melting woman in *Die, Monster, Die!* confirms for us that no matter how far we may be removed from the beauty of a Robert Redford or a Diana Ross, we are still light-years from true ugliness.

And we go to have fun.   5

Ah, but this is where the ground starts to slope away, isn't it? Because this is a very peculiar sort of fun indeed. The fun comes from seeing others menaced—sometimes killed. One critic has suggested that if pro football has become the voyeur's version of combat, then the horror film has become the modern version of the public lynching.

It is true that the mythic, "fairytale" horror film intends to take away the shades of gray. . . . It urges us to put away our more civilized and adult penchant for analysis and to become children again, seeing things in pure blacks and whites. It may be that horror movies provide psychic relief on this level because this invitation to lapse into simplicity, irrationality and even outright madness is extended so rarely. We are told we may allow our emotions a free rein . . . or no rein at all.

If we are all insane, then sanity becomes a matter of degree. If your insanity leads you to carve up women like Jack the Ripper or the Cleveland Torso Murderer, we clap you away in the funny farm (but neither of those two amateur-night surgeons was ever caught, heh-heh-heh); if, on the other hand your insanity leads you only to talk to yourself when you're under stress or to pick your nose on the morning bus, then you are left alone to go about your business . . . though it is doubtful that you will ever be invited to the best parties.

The potential lyncher is in almost all of us (excluding saints, past and present; but then, most saints have been crazy in their own ways), and every now and then, he has to be let loose to scream and roll around in the grass. Our emotions and our fears form their own body, and we recognize that it demands its own exercise to maintain proper muscle tone. Certain of these emotional muscles are accepted—even exalted— in civilized society; they are, of course, the emotions that tend to maintain the status quo of

civilization itself. Love, friendship, loyalty, kindness—these are all the emotions that we applaud, emotions that have been immortalized in
the couplets of Hallmark cards. . . .

When we exhibit these emotions, society 10
showers us with positive reinforcement; we learn
this even before we get out of diapers. When, as
children, we hug our rotten little puke of a sister
and give her a kiss, all the aunts and uncles smile
and twit and cry, "Isn't he the sweetest little
thing?" Such coveted treats as chocolate-covered graham crackers often follow. But if we deliberately slam the rotten little puke of a sister's
fingers in the door, sanctions follow—angry re-
monstrance from parents, aunts and uncles;
instead of a chocolate-covered graham cracker,
a spanking.

But anticivilization emotions don't go
away, and they demand periodic exercise. We
have such "sick" jokes as, "What's the difference between a truckload of bowling balls and a
truckload of dead babies?" (You can't unload a
truckload of bowling balls with a pitchfork . . .
a joke, by the way, that I heard originally from a
ten-year-old.) Such a joke may surprise a laugh
or a grin out of us even as we recoil, a possibility

that confirms the thesis: If we share a brother-
hood of man, then we also share an insanity of
man. None of which is intended as a defense of
either the sick joke or insanity but merely as an
explanation of why the best horror films, like
the best fairy tales, manage to be reactionary,
anarchistic, and revolutionary all at the same
time.

The mythic horror movie, like the sick joke,
has a dirty job to do. It deliberately appeals to all
that is worst in us. It is morbidity unchained, our
most base instincts let free, our nastiest fantasies
realized . . . and it all happens, fittingly enough,
in the dark. For those reasons, good liberals often shy away from horror films. For myself, I like
to see the most aggressive of them—*Dawn of the
Dead*, for instance—as lifting a trap door in the
civilized forebrain and throwing a basket of raw
meat to the hungry alligators swimming around
in that subterranean river beneath.

Why bother? Because it keeps them from
getting out, man. It keeps them down there and
me up here. It was Lennon and McCartney who
said that all you need is love, and I would agree
with that.

As long as you keep the gators fed.

A CLOSER LOOK AT
Why We Crave Horror Movies

1. List the three qualities (criteria) that Stephen King
argues are the characteristics of an excellent horror film. Do you agree with these criteria? Would
you add or subtract some of them? How does King
use these criteria to sort the good horror movies
from the bad?

2. King's style is especially interesting in this article.
He seems to be making a straightforward argument about the difference between good horror
movies and bad horror movies. But occasionally,
he throws a strange sentence at the readers,

creating a pained laugh or a dark thought. Find a
handful of these moments in the article. How does
he use style to bring about this dark humor?

3. The evaluation is about horror movies, but King's
real motive is to explore the psychology behind
people's fascination with such movies. He identifies several reasons why people crave horror films.
Highlight these reasons and discuss them with a
group in your class. Do you agree with King, or do
you think people have other reasons for enjoying
horror movies?

IDEAS FOR
Writing

1. Write a rebuttal to King's article in which you dispute his reasoning or offer different reasons why people like to see horror movies. In your rebuttal, you could challenge King's criteria, or you could question whether he is right about why people enjoy blood and gore. You might even challenge the worth of these kinds of movies altogether. You don't need to completely disagree with King, but you should distinguish your argument from his in a significant way.

2. Rent or go see a horror film, perhaps one based on a Stephen King novel. Write a review of the movie using King's evaluation criteria in this article as the basis of your review. Unlike King's evaluation, your review does not need to define the criteria. Instead, assume King's criteria reflect "common expectations" that most moviegoers will accept. Unlike King, you do not need to make a broader argument about the psychology of these movies. Instead, review the movie as though you were writing for a newspaper or a movie review blog.

"Hawaii Five-O": This Is What Hit TV Looks Like

HEATHER HAVRILESKY

This review is close to a rave. The author, Heather Havrilesky, is very positive about this television show. One of the difficulties of any remake or updated version of a classic show, however, is that it needs to retain the good qualities of the original while offering something new. As you read this review, note the places where Havrilesky compares and contrasts the original Hawaii Five-O *with the new version.*

My youngest daughter, who is 19 months old, has no self-restraint. She can't walk by the dog's water bowl without plunging both of her hands into the water. If she sees a Barbie shoe somewhere, it must go into her mouth immediately, even if there are two other shoes in there already. The second she gets tired of her milk, it's time to pour it all over her chair. If she's naked, then she's looking for a good spot to pee, preferably in some carpeted corner where the smell won't come out.

Network TV writers remind me a lot of my daughter. I imagine them, sometimes, sitting around in the writers room together, shoving Barbie shoes into their mouths, pouring their Fiji bottles into their laps and peeing in the corners of the room, all the while shouting at each other, "The murder victim should either be a stripper with a coke habit or the cheating wife of a very rich, very powerful man!" "No, no, she should be a depressed midget who travels with the county fair as a carnival freak!" "And one of the hostages should definitely have asthma, or a heart condition . . . or leprosy!" "And then the murder victim's son should be so traumatized by what he saw that he can't speak . . . or maybe there are *twin* sons, who *speak a secret language all their own!*"

OK, maybe the writers are shoving pizza in their mouths instead of Barbie shoes, but the level of impulse control is about the same. When your main objective is to capture a national audience's attention and never, ever let it wander, the slightest interest in nuanced storytelling or subtlety or believability falls by the wayside immediately. You don't need a compelling premise or some layers of meaning or a distinct perspective or anything resembling a larger message. What you need is sex, drugs, rock 'n' roll, murder, infidelity, Russian spies, lovable mommies, arrogant businessmen, chicks in bikinis and chain-smoking pimps, all before the first commercial break.

Considering the fact that the needs of the modern audience roughly resemble the needs of your average crack-addicted 14-year-old, it's not hard to understand why CBS's "**Hawaii Five-O**" (10 p.m. Mondays) is one of the big new hits of the fall season. You start with a familiar rock tune (the Rolling Stones "Gimme Shelter," Red Hot Chili Peppers' "Higher Ground,"), cut to an aerial shot of crystal blue water and white sand, skitter over to a close-up of a few juicy butts hanging out of bikini bottoms, pan across a sunny Waikiki skyline, zoom in on a cool surfing stunt, and then start with the story du jour, already in progress. Bad prisoner guy holds guard at gunpoint, escapes from jail, leaving cops confused! Surfing legend catches a wave at an exhibition, then collapses suddenly. He's been shot! Woman is attacked and killed, her husband runs from the cops, holding a bloody knife . . . but did he really do it?

Once you get the basic idea, we cut to that 5 old familiar "Hawaii Five-O" theme song—which is, not incidentally, one of the best theme songs in TV history—and then you've got more crystal blue waves, more juicy butts, plus some macho men running and jumping and shooting. Before you know it, you're hooked. It's like "CSI: Miami" but without the sepia-toned swamps and the alligators reflected in David Caruso's ugly mirrored sunglasses. It's like "Law & Order,"

but with sunshine and delicious tropical fruity drinks where a grumpy Jerry Orbach should go.

But if we're hooked, we're hooked like a toddler with a mouth full of Barbie shoes—eventually, we're either going to choke or projectile vomit all over the room. That's about what it feels like to watch a whole episode of "Hawaii Five-O," too. Because after the guy who just killed his wife (but obviously didn't really do it, since he's holding a bloody knife) goes to the battleship and holds a bunch of tourists hostage, we know that our hunky star McGarrett (Alex O'Loughlin) is going to use his Navy SEAL background to swim under the battleship and climb up the side like a really hot modern pirate, squinting all the while (because that's how macho guys hold their faces, to show that they're tough). Then he's going to put himself in harm's way and save the hypoglycemic hostage and truly *empathize* with the murder suspect and all along, he's going to urge his men to solve the murder, because despite the evidence, he just has a hunch that *this man didn't kill his wife*!

But that alone wouldn't be enough to keep our interest, of course. Along the way, McGarrett also has to meet up with a wise old veteran who overhears his name when he's on the phone and realizes that he once served on the Arizona with McGarrett's grandfather, who died at Pearl Harbor. Suddenly, the action stops completely and the old guy is getting all worked up and patriotic and McGarrett looks deeply moved (because he's not squinting for once). The music swells as the old guy tells McGarrett, "The man that you are named after was a real hero. You should be very proud!" "I *am* proud," McGarrett replies, and the faintest trace of tears come to his eyes. Aww, hot guy *sad*. Patriotism and old guys and honor and stuff. Sniff. *Awesome.*

Even though this tidbit has nothing whatsoever to do with the story, we need it like we need blue skies and Hawaiian shirts and white sand and shave ice. Of course, we *also* need the little girl whose mommy was just killed right in front of her pretty saucer eyes. We need Boomer—err, I mean Kono (Grace Park)—to slowly gain the little girl's trust by taking her out for . . . shave ice!

By the beach! Because then a big Hawaiian guy whom Kono calls "Uncle" can serve the shave ice to them, and the little girl can lament the fact that Daddy loves *lemon* shave ice, and then the little girl can explain that a bad man came and killed Mommy. Right after that, the Bad Man can show up and Bad Men in a van can grab the little girl and drive away, fast! Oh noes!

That's when the writers go from pouring their Fiji bottles into their laps (Wise old patriot remembers your grandfather!) to peeing in the corners (Little girl reveals murderer, then gets snatched off the street by meaty-looking thugs!). Of course, we *knew* they were going to start peeing in the corners soon enough, because from the second Kono met the little girl, she kept telling her, "Don't worry, you're safe with me." and "Nothing's ever going to happen to you, not while I'm around" and "Thugs in vans aren't going to just grab you right off the street in broad daylight, because that wouldn't be remotely believable."

And once the entire writers' room smells 10 like pee, well, then, what can you do? That's when Danno (Scott Caan) chases a private jet down the runway in his sports car and the wise old veteran takes a bullet for McGarrett ("Leave no man behind, remember?" Oh yes, we remember.) and Daddy and daughter are reunited to the gentle strains of State Radio's "Keepsake," probably because they've used Israel Kamakawiwo'ole's rendition of "Somewhere Over The Rainbow" three or four times by now.

And even though it's a little strange that the Hawaii of 2010 so closely resembles the Hawaii of those very special episodes of "The Brady Bunch" where the Bradys fly to Honolulu and become convinced that they're cursed until they return the mysterious idol that they found to the ancient burial ground (which itself closely resembles the last 20 seasons of "Survivor"), there is something vaguely appealing about "Hawaii Five-0." Is it the clear blue waves? Is it the hot ladies in bikinis? Is it the two macho leading men, Danno and McGarrett, who bicker through each scene in the same teasing, testy way that every pair of mismatched cop partners have bickered for the past three decades?

Danno: (on the phone with McGarrett) You miss me, don't you?

McGarrett: Oh yeah, I wish you were here. But you don't swim, do you?

Danno: I don't swim? I swim very well, actually, I just choose not to.

Old veteran: Are you talking to your wife?

McGarrett: I'm talking to my partner.

In case you're unfamiliar with this show or its predecessor, Danno is the goofier, more talkative one, and McGarrett is the tough guy. McGarrett says stuff like, "I will literally pay you cash to stop talking!" and "I want this entire beach on lockdown!" and he's always squinting, because he's tough and he's haunted. Danno is also tough but he *isn't* haunted—except by a hair stylist who insists on combing his hair straight back like Gordon Gekko. And these two might make a good team, really . . . if they were secretly gay, or if one of them was really depressed and slept with the other one's wife on the sly, or if they were up for the same promotion at work and their good-natured ribbing masked a deeper layer of resentment and contempt.

But this isn't "Mad Men," see? This is network television. This is "Fantasy Island," a quarter of a century later, with fewer opportunities to overuse dry ice and demean midgets. The people who create this stuff have no impulse control, and they're handsomely rewarded for it.

But you know what? When you pick up one of those really rubbery Barbie shoes? It sort of begs to be put in your mouth. And it's so soft and springy in there, you just *have* to chew it a little. At that point, are you really going to take the Barbie shoe out of your mouth and dry it off? Are you going to search long and hard for a provocative but subtle way to encapsulate your lead character's frustration with the complicated sociocultural pressures of his position? Or are you going to shoot the surfing legend in the head while he's riding the Pipeline?

Sometimes it's easier to shrug and say, "Let 15 somebody *else* make good TV. I just want to dunk my head in the dog's bowl."

A CLOSER LOOK AT
"Hawaii Five-O": This Is What Hit TV Looks Like

1. The reviewer, Heather Havrilesky, points out that *Hawaii Five-O* is different from other kinds of television shows. What are the main differences she highlights and why does she think they are important?

2. The use of dialogue in this review is important. How does the use of dialogue change the tone of the review? What does dialogue add to it?

3. The reviewer keeps mentioning old television shows, like *The Brady Bunch* and *Fantasy Island*. Do you think readers of this review are familiar enough with these shows to understand the comparisons?

IDEAS FOR
Writing

1. Watch an episode of *Hawaii Five-O*. Write a rebuttal in which you disagree with this reviewer or expand on her comments. Your rebuttal does not need to disagree with her review. If you generally agree with her take on this show, you should find ways to explore further the qualities of the show that she discusses.

2. Write a movie review in which you compare and contrast an original movie and its remake. Usually, old movies are remade because they were good movies in the first place. Does the remake live up to the original? How is it better? Where does the remake fall short? At the end of your review explain which version you like better.

3. The old version of *Hawaii Five-O* has been frequently parodied because of the characters were stereotypical, its theme song was iconic, and some of the tag lines (e.g., "Book 'em, Danno") became features of the popular culture. Choose a movie or television show that has woven its way into our culture. In a commentary, explain how and why the characters and the lines from the show have gone beyond the show itself.

Left Behind, a Virtual Battle for the Souls of Unbelievers

JANE LAMPMAN

In this article, Jane Lampman of the Christian Science Monitor *reviews the video game version of* Left Behind: Eternal Forces. *The video game was controversial, because it was based on the idea that people "left behind," after others (namely, fundamentalist Christians) were raptured to heaven, would need to compete with each other for survival and redemption. As you read this review, keep in mind the cultural politics that underlie this issue.*

"In one cataclysmic moment, millions around the world disappear." Not a bad intro for a dramatic video game. It turns out those millions have been "raptured" into heaven by Jesus. The player's job is to battle to save the ones left behind on earth from the global forces of evil, which are controlled by the Antichrist.

The hitch, though, in this new game aimed at teens, is who constitutes those "forces of evil": activists, secularists, non-Christian rock musicians, and others who resist "recruitment" into the "forces of good"—the believers in a particular kind of Christianity.

Based on the popular Left Behind series of apocalyptic novels, "Left Behind: Eternal Forces" is being marketed for Christmas giving through churches and big-box retailers such as Wal-Mart.

But it has created a stir among Christian, Jewish, and activist groups who disagree with the fundamentalist theology the game presents. They say it will teach children religious intolerance and an "us vs. them" view of the world that is both dangerous for the country and contrary to basic Christian teachings. The game's producers disagree.

The real-time strategy (RTS) game takes 5 place in New York City. "You are sent on a spiritual and military mission to convert people, and nobody is allowed to remain neutral," says Eric Elnes, copresident of Crosswalk America, a progressive Christian group, who says he's explored the game extensively. "You lose spirit points if you kill somebody, but you can hit the prayer button to restore the points."

Mr. Elnes's organization has joined with other Christian groups to petition the game's producers to withdraw it from the market. At the same time, two groups that seek to counter the religious right—the Campaign to Defend the Constitution and Christian Alliance for Progress—have written to Wal-Mart requesting that the PC-based game be taken off the shelves.

"The premillennial theology says there will be religious warfare in our lifetime, and people will be targeting fellow Americans," says Frederick Clarkson, of Talk2Action.org. He worries gamers could come to accept that script for the future.

The game's producers see it very differently. At a time when young people seem less inclined toward Christianity, they say they're trying to reach Christian teens with an alternative to darker video games like "Grand Theft Auto," and hopefully draw other gamers to the faith.

"About 92 percent of kids today are playing games," says Jeffrey Frichner, president of Left Behind Games. "We had the vision to create a game with a positive moral message based on biblical values that parents could embrace and discuss with their kids." He says the game promotes prayer and worship, and deals with "questions of eternal importance."

Producers have spoken with their Crosswalk 10 critics, and Frichner says they'll provide a patch to address one concern.

A review on a website of the conservative group, Focus on the Family, endorses "Eternal Forces" as "the kind of game Mom and Dad can actually play with Junior." Other reviews speak of fairly good production values, but say the game is unwieldy to play and tend to pan it.

The controversy arises largely because the game follows the Left Behind novels, Mr. Frichner says. The 14-book series by Tim LaHaye and Jerry Jenkins has sold more than 63 million copies, including 13 million of The Kids series, a spinoff for children 10 and older. "So we felt we had a bulls-eye market there for the game," he adds.

Dr. LaHaye, one of the most influential leaders in fundamentalist Christianity, conceived the novels as a way to spread to theology called premillennial dispensationalism. First promoted by 19th-century Englishman John Nelson Darby, the theology interprets portions of the Bible as predicting at two-stage return of Jesus.

First, Jesus comes to transport "true Christians" to heaven in what's called "the rapture"; "the tribulation" follows on earth, involving seven years of catastrophe and plagues (as drawn from Revelation).

"It is going to be an unprecedented time of [15] horror of God's judgment on earth," says Terry James, of raptureready.com, the most popular prophecy website.

The period will end with Armageddon and the Second Corning. Those who preach the theology say Jesus' return is imminent. And according to Mr. James, the creation of Israel in 1948 is the most important signal that the End Times have begun. The job of Christians is to convert and save as many people as possible.

The novels focus on the time of the tribulations. The Antichrist is a former head of the United Nations, based in Iraq. His evil minions are called the Global Community Peacekeepers, and are the only people who seek peace treaties. Battles occur around the earth between good and evil forces, leading up to Armageddon in Israel. There, some Jews convert to Christianity and the rest are destroyed along with others who have not accepted Jesus as their savior. Jesus' rule then begins on earth.

The video game engages young gamers as the Tribulation Forces to fight the evil peacekeepers. In multiplayer mode, gamers play on both sides.

"It's ironic the game has been put out for Christmas, which honors the Prince of Peace who said, 'Blessed are the peacemakers, for they shall be called the children of God,'" says Mr. Elnes. "What this game says in 'Cursed are the peacekeepers, for they are children of the Antichrist.'"

The game is the latest facet of a struggle [20] within Christianity over growing promotion of the theology in books, on websites and TV, and in Christian Zionist organizations backing a strong alliance with Israel. Premillennialism is not consistent with Catholic, Eastern Orthodox, or mainline Protestant teachings.

Barbara Rossing, an expert on the book of Revelation at the Lutheran School of Theology in Chicago, says the notion of the rapture is not a biblical idea but a fiction, and the word isn't found in the Bible.

"That's not what the book of Revelation is about, forecasting a sequence of terrifying events that are going to happen," she says. "Also, while Christians say there is evil in the world, we should never say that evil is incarnate in people. . . . The traditional Christian teaching is to be engaged with loving God's world, seeing God's image in people, and taking care of one another."

Some Jews are also troubled by the game. "Jews are often instrumental in rapture theology—war in Israel, Jews converting to Christianity, all other Jews disappearing in the third act of a four-act play," says Rabbi Haim Dov Beliak, of Jews On First, a First Amendment watchdog group. "What happens if no rapture or Second Coming occurs? The classical response in history has been to blame the Jews for somehow foiling everybody's hopes and plans." Jews On First has created a petition opposing the game on its website for people of all faiths to sign; some 500 have done so in the first few days, the rabbi says.

Many critics admit that in America, banning a product is not the best solution. They say they are trying to educate parents about the contents of the game so they can exercise judgment.

There's even a stir among the faithful over [25] the amount of violence they hear is in the game, says James, though neither he nor most of those e-mailing him have yet seen it for themselves.

Frichner says the issue is simply one of different views of Christianity, and the game, which has been approved for teens by the software ratings board, will sell mostly among evangelical Christians.

Yet they are already having success in evangelizing others, he adds. The game has elements that educate players on various issues (such as evolution and intelligent design), and gives them the opportunity to become believers.

"We've already received e-mails from people who have done that," Frichner says.

A CLOSER LOOK AT
Left Behind, a Virtual Battle for the Souls of Unbelievers

1. In this review, the writer is trying to show both sides of a debate about a video game. How does she give both sides an ability to state their positions? Does she seem to take sides on this issue, or does she try to stay in the middle? How does she accomplish this?

2. As in most reviews, Lampman needs to give readers enough information about the game so they can understand it. How does Lampman use description to reveal elements of the game? Do you think she offers enough information? Would you have liked more? Lampman also gives quite a bit of background information on fundamentalists' notions of a world-ending apocalypse. Did you find that information helpful? If so, what did you find helpful and why?

3. What are some of the larger political and cultural issues raised by this video game and referred to in this review? How does the game itself, as described here, go against some of the "common expectations" of some groups while reinforcing the common expectations of fundamentalist Christians? Do you think this kind of video game is an effective recruiting tool for fundamentalist Christians, or do you think it does more harm than good?

IDEAS FOR
Writing

1. Religious groups often try to reach out to young people with new media, like video games, movies, and music. In a position paper, argue for or against some of these attempts to reach out to people. As a college student, how do you feel about these kinds of recruiting efforts, many of them aimed at people just like you? Do you think religious groups should be engaged in using new media to reach out to young people? Or do you think these efforts are already preaching to the choir—that is, entertaining the already convinced and converted?

2. The style of this review makes it more straightforward and perhaps less entertaining than others. Write a rhetorical analysis in which you explore the rhetorical qualities of this review. First pay attention to what the author is trying to accomplish. Then pay attention to the review's content, organization, and style. Look at its use of reasoning (*logos*), authority (*ethos*), and emotion (*pathos*). In what ways is this review effective, and in what ways could it perhaps be more effective (or at least, more entertaining)?

A FEW IDEAS FOR
Composing a Review

1. **Write a review of something you absolutely did not enjoy.** Your topic could be a movie, play, restaurant, book—just about anything. Be creative. Keep in mind, though, that your review will be for public viewing, so you want to be fair while explaining what you did not like about the subject. Then add a brief cover letter written to your professor and your classmates in which you discuss some of the challenges of writing a negative review.

2. **Write a review of three of your favorite movies in a specific genre.** Your review should discuss them together and argue that they are some of the best examples of this genre. What are some of your and your readers' common expectations about this genre? How do these particular movies succeed within the genre, and where do they stray from it? Compare and contrast these three movies to show how they are similar and how they are different.

3. **Find a review on the Internet that you disagree with.** Then write a rebuttal review in which you argue against the other reviewer and show why your subject is actually better or worse than the reviewer said. Your review should be written for the same Web site in which you found the original review.

Literary
Analyses

The Story of an Hour

KATE CHOPIN

Kate Chopin (1851–1904), a writer of short stories and novels, wrote "Story of an Hour" in 1894. During her lifetime, Chopin was sometimes criticized for writing "immoral" stories. More recent critics view her as an early feminist who explored themes of love, marriage, race, and the psychology of women. As you read, pay attention to the way Chopin paints a rich portrait of a character and works out a complete plot in a very short space.

Knowing that Mrs. Mallard was afflicted with a heart trouble, great care was taken to break to her as gently as possible the news of her husband's death.

It was her sister Josephine who told her, in broken sentences; veiled hints that revealed in half concealing. Her husband's friend Richards was there, too, near her. It was he who had been in the newspaper office when intelligence of the railroad disaster was received, with Brently Mallard's name leading the list of "killed." He had only taken the time to assure himself of its truth by a second telegram, and had hastened to forestall any less careful, less tender friend in bearing the sad message.

She did not hear the story as many women have heard the same, with a paralyzed inability to accept its significance. She wept at once, with sudden, wild abandonment, in her sister's arms. When the storm of grief had spent itself she went away to her room alone. She would have no one follow her.

There stood, facing the open window, a comfortable, roomy armchair. Into this she sank, pressed down by a physical exhaustion that haunted her body and seemed to reach into her soul.

She could see in the open square before her house the tops of trees that were all aquiver with the new spring life. The delicious breath of rain was in the air. In the street below a peddler was crying his wares. The notes of a distant song which some one was singing reached her faintly, and countless sparrows were twittering in the eaves.

There were patches of blue sky showing here and there through the clouds that had met and piled one above the other in the west facing her window.

She sat with her head thrown back upon the cushion of the chair, quite motionless, except when a sob came up into her throat and shook her, as a child who has cried itself to sleep continues to sob in its dreams.

She was young, with a fair, calm face, whose lines bespoke repression and even a certain strength. But now there was a dull stare in her eyes, whose gaze was fixed away off yonder on one of those patches of blue sky. It was not a glance of reflection, but rather indicated a suspension of intelligent thought.

There was something coming to her and she was waiting for it, fearfully. What was it? She did not know; it was too subtle and elusive to name. But she felt it, creeping out of the sky, reaching toward her through the sounds, the scents, the color that filled the air.

Now her bosom rose and fell tumultuously. She was beginning to recognize this thing that was approaching to possess her, and she was striving to beat it back with her will—as powerless as her two white slender hands would have been.

When she abandoned herself a little whispered word escaped her slightly parted lips. She said it over and over under her breath: "free, free, free!" The vacant stare and the look of terror that had followed it went from her eyes. They stayed keen and bright. Her pulses beat fast, and the coursing blood warmed and relaxed every inch of her body. She did not stop to ask if it were or were not a monstrous joy that held her. A clear and exalted perception enabled her to dismiss the suggestion as trivial.

She knew that she would weep again when she saw the kind, tender hands folded in death; the face that had never looked save with love upon her, fixed and gray and dead. But she saw beyond that bitter moment a long procession of years to come that would belong to her absolutely. And she opened and spread her arms out to them in welcome.

There would be no one to live for during those coming years; she would live for herself. There would be no powerful will bending hers in that blind persistence with which men and women believe they have a right to impose a private will upon a fellow-creature. A kind intention or a cruel intention made the act seem no less a crime as she looked upon it in that brief moment of illumination.

And yet she had loved him—sometimes. Often she had not. What did it matter! What could love, the unsolved mystery, count for in face of this possession of self-assertion which she suddenly recognized as the strongest impulse of her being!

"Free! Body and soul free!" she kept 15 whispering.

Josephine was kneeling before the closed door with her lips to the keyhole, imploring for admission. "Louise, open the door! I beg, open the door—you will make yourself ill. What are you doing Louise? For heaven's sake open the door."

"Go away. I am not making myself ill." No; she was drinking in a very elixir of life through that open window.

Her fancy was running riot along those days ahead of her. Spring days, and summer days, and all sorts of days that would be her own. She breathed a quick prayer that life might be long. It was only yesterday she had thought with a shudder that life might be long.

She arose at length and opened the door to her sister's importunities. There was a feverish triumph in her eyes, and she carried herself unwittingly like a goddess of Victory. She clasped her sister's waist, and together they descended the stairs. Richards stood waiting for them at the bottom.

Some one was opening the front door with 20 a latchkey. It was Brently Mallard who entered, a little travel-stained, composedly carrying his grip-sack and umbrella. He had been far from the scene of the accident, and did not even know there had been one. He stood amazed at Josephine's piercing cry; at Richards' quick motion to screen him from the view of his wife.

But Richards was too late.

When the doctors came they said she had died of heart disease—of joy that kills.

A CLOSER LOOK AT
The Story of an Hour

1. What makes this a story and not just a sequence of events? In other words, explain how the plot moves from complication to conflict, tension, and resolution to hold the reader's interest. How would the reading experience and the story's significance have been different if the narrator had let it be known at the beginning that Louise Mallard dies in the story?

2. Read the story again, this time paying close attention to and highlighting those parts where the narrator provides details about Louise Mallard's character bit by bit. Notice where the disclosure of certain details are placed. For example, we do not learn the main character's first name until close to the story's end. How does the author's sequencing of disclosures draw the reader into Louise's character?

3. Short stories often describe how characters change or come to a new understanding of themselves or their world. What does Louise Mallard learn in this story? How does her new understanding play a role in her death?

IDEAS FOR
Writing

IDEAS FOR
Writing

1. Write a reading response in which you describe what you believe is the social or political message of "The Story of an Hour." Who were the readers that you think Chopin may have been writing for? What themes or questions did she want her readers to explore? What point, if any, do you think she was hoping to make?

2. In a brief memoir, narrate and describe a significant experience in your life that you reacted to in an entirely unexpected way or in a way that others just couldn't understand. Within the memoir, explain what your reaction to this experience reveals about you, or what it reveals about others' expectations of you.

An Enigma in Chopin's "The Story of an Hour"

DANIEL P. DENEAU

Daniel P. Deneau was a professor of English for many years. As you read his analysis of Chopin's short story, pay attention to the way he poses an interpretive question about the story and then carefully examines a single passage to help answer that question.

The much-anthologized "The Story of an Hour" (1894) is surely Kate Chopin's best-known piece of short fiction. Innumerable students, ranging from the very naive to the very sophisticated, must have grappled with the story in innumerable discussions and essays. As all readers should agree, Louise Mallard receives a great shock, goes through a rapid sequence of reactions, is in a sense awakened and then seems to drink in "a very elixir of life" (354), and finally receives another shock, a reversal, which proves lethal. Probably equally clear to all or to most readers are Chopin's economy, the significance of the open window and the spring setting, the power which she assigns to "self-assertion," and the bold dramatic irony with which the story

concludes. About one issue, at least among readers of anthologies, there may be continuing debate: is Louise a normal, understandable, sympathetic woman, or is she an egocentric, selfish monster or anomaly? And, as more sophisticated readers may ask, is the degree of "self-assertion" or freedom that she thinks she has attained a real possibility in a world of normal human relationships? Obviously readers' preconceptions about love and marriage and independence will dictate different answers to these questions. At one crucial point, however, this relatively clear and realistic story becomes problematic, perhaps even enigmatic—that is, the passage in which Chopin attempts to account for the direct cause of Louise's awakening:

There was something coming to her and she was waiting for it, fearfully. What was it? She did not know; it was too subtle and elusive to name. But she felt it, creeping[1] out of the sky, reaching toward her through the sounds, the scents, the color that filled the air.

Now her bosom rose and fell tumultuously. She was beginning to recognize this thing that was approaching to possess her, and she was striving to beat it back with her will—as powerless as her two white hands would have been.

When she abandoned herself [,] a little whispered word escaped her slightly parted lips. She said it over and over under her breath: "Free, free, free!" The vacant stare and the look of terror that had followed it went from her eyes. They stayed keen and bright. Her pulses beat fast, and the coursing blood warmed and relaxed every inch of her body. (353)

This "something," this "it,"[2] which oddly arrives from the sky, exerts a powerful physical influence on Louise and leaves her with a totally new perspective on her self and her place in the scheme of things. In a limited space, and without the assistance of a psychological vocabulary, Chopin may have been forced to rely on the indefinite, the unidentified, which, as best we can judge, is some powerful force, something supernatural, something beyond the realm of mundane experience or the rule of logic.[3] If immediately after learning of the death of her husband Louise had gone through a rapid logical process leading to a celebration of her total freedom, she might have seemed to be a hard, calculating, and therefore unsympathetic woman. Or to put the point in another way: since she has neither the physical nor moral strength to "beat [. . .] back" her attacker, which she begins to recognize but sadly never names, her responsibility is abrogated. In addition, one of the problems presented by the passage is the fact that Louise meets the "something" with both fear and anticipation. Clearly what occurs is some type of sexual experience, one that at first seems, except for the anticipation, like a terrifying rape, but one that evolves into something sensually stimulating and relaxing, and, of course, spiritually illuminating. In short, a rape seems to have an ironic outcome.

There can be no doubt that the crucial passage becomes a fairly explicit description of a sexual union. One of the meanings of the verb "possess" is "to have sexual intercourse with (a woman)" (OED),[4] and this meaning was certainly known to Chopin, as illustrated by the climactic—that word, unfortunately, is inevitable—passage of "The Storm," the sexual union of Alcée and Calixta: "And when he possessed her, they seemed to swoon together at the very borderland of life's mystery" (595).[5] Moreover, the third paragraph quoted above does suggest coitus and postcoital reactions: the abandonment, the "slightly parted lips," the "keen and bright eyes," and especially the final sentence—"Her pulses beat fast, and the coursing blood warmed and relaxed every inch of her body."

With no male aggressor-partner named in the text, only a "something," readers naturally will speculate. For me, two possibilities exist—both supernatural—of which, time after time, I am reminded as I contemplate the passage: one is classical, pagan; the other, Christian. The former is Leda and the swan-Zeus, a potent, sinister force which creeps from the "sky," attacks, and engenders a world-shaking course of events.[6] But the passage is about more than fear, force, and sex; it is also about anticipation, pleasure, and ultimately enlightenment. Thus, I am also reminded of the descent of the Christian Holy Spirit,[7] who is associated with conception, renewal, empowerment, inspiration, enlightenment, and freedom.[8] Louise does indeed receive an infusion of knowledge from a source that seems beyond human understanding or even naming. Add to these subjective responses Chopin's "belief" that genuine sexual passion itself may help the blind see: after Edna Pontellier first sexual union with Arobin, she has various reactions; however, "above all, there was understanding. She felt as if a mist had been lifted from her eyes, enabling her to look upon and comprehend the significance of life, that monster made up of beauty and brutality" (967).

"The Story of an Hour" lacks the kind of diagrammatic clarity that some readers may expect, mainly or even exclusively, as I have tried to suggest, because of one curious passage. Chopin's desire to transform her protagonist from a woman with a "dull stare in her eyes" (353) to one with "a feverish triumph in her eyes," a woman who carries "herself unwittingly like a goddess of Victory" (354), required a force of exceptional intensity, a force as intense as a combination of a rape, a visitation by the Holy Spirit, and a sexual union—or, in short, a *deus ex machina*. It is no wonder that in a mere seven sentences this force remains perplexing, probably enigmatic. One final point, however, is perfectly clear: having experimented with one very condensed account of an awakening—the account of a mere hour—Chopin later proceeded to create one of the masterpieces of American Literature—the slowly paced, psychologically credible, many-staged awakening of Edna Pontellier.[9]

Notes

1. In one other notable place in her short fiction Chopin used the verb "creeping." See the sexually charged "The Night Comes Slowly" (366).

2. Madonne M. Miner recognizes the importance of the "something" passage (31), but she does not scrutinize it sufficiently. Mary E. Papke seems unclear to me: "The unnameable is, of course, her self-consciousness that is embraced once she names her experience as emancipation and not destitution" (63). Angelyn Mitchell observes that "freedom ravishes" Louise and, quite correctly, that the passage is "loaded with sexual imagery" (62).

3. Cf. "Athénaïse": "If she ever came to such knowledge [of her own mind], it would be by no intellectual research, by no subtle analyses or tracing of actions to their source. It would come to her as the song to the bird, the perfume and color to the flower" (433).

4. The editor of the *OED* adds a surprising note: "this sense [was] suggested in private correspondence in 1969 by Professor W. Empson." The meaning should have been commonly known much earlier.

5. Bert Bender finds the diction "wooden" and "ironically conventional" (266). I doubt that a similar charge could be made about the crucial passage in "The Story of an Hour."

6. Recall Yeats "Leda and the Swan," esp. 11.5 and 6: "How can those terrified vague fingers push/The feathered glory from her loosing thighs?"

7. Chopin would have been well aware of the Christian view of the Holy Spirit (Ghost). See in particular "At Chênière Caminada" (317) and *The Awakening* (893).

8. Various Epistles associate the Holy Spirit with freedom. See, for example, 2 Cor. 3.17, as well as Isa. 61.1.

9. After completing this paper, I was pleased to find Jacqueline Padgett's paragraph in which she refers to an "annunciation" (101) in "The Story of an Hour."

Works Cited

Bender, Bert. "Kate Chopin's Lyrical Short Stories." *Studies in Short Fiction* 11 (1974): 257–66. Print.

Chopin, Kate. *The Complete Works of Kate Chopin*. Ed. Per Seyersted. Baton Rouge: Louisiana State UP, 1969. Print.

Miner, Madonne M. "Veiled Hints: An Affective Stylist's Reading of Kate Chopin's 'Story of an Hour.'" *The Markham Review* 11 (1982): 29–32. Print.

Mitchell, Angelyn. "Feminine Double Consciousness in Kate Chopin's 'The Story of an Hour.'" *CEA Magazine* 5.1 (1992): 59–64. Print.

Padgett, Jacqueline Olson, "Kate Chopin and the Literature of the Annunciation, with a Reading of 'Lilacs.'" *Louisiana Literature* 11.1 (1994): 97–107. Print.

Papke, Mary E. *Verging on the Abyss: The Social Fiction of Kate Chopin and Edith Wharton*. New York: Greenwood, 1990.

"Possess." Def. 3b. *The Oxford English Dictionary*. 2nd ed. 1989. Print.

A CLOSER LOOK AT
An Enigma in Chopin's "The Story of an Hour"

1. What is the interpretive question that Deneau poses in this analysis? How does he set up this question?

2. What exactly does Deneau suggest happens to Louise? Do you find his interpretation persuasive? His interpretation certainly goes beyond the literal meaning of the text. Do you agree with him?

3. The author uses endnotes to note connections with other works by Chopin and with the comments of other literary analyses. How do these endnotes help you understand Chopin's story or Deneau's analysis more fully? How do they enhance the author's authority or *ethos* as an interpreter of Chopin's short story?

IDEAS FOR
Writing

1. Write a rebuttal of Deneau's analysis. While it is true that there are no single correct interpretations of a literary work, any analysis needs to be supported and justified by the words in the literary text itself. Explain why Deneau's analysis might be stretching too far to make its point.

2. Condense this literary analysis into a well-developed one-paragraph summary that provides an objective description of the question Deneau explores, how he explores it, and what he concludes. First, identify Deneau's interpretive question and restate it as clearly and directly as you can. Then describe Deneau's approach to exploring that question and his final conclusions.

Stopping by Woods on a Snowy Evening

ROBERT FROST

Robert Frost (1874–1963) was a popular poet during his lifetime. Many of his poems, like "Stopping by Woods on a Snowy Evening," appear to be simple observations of nature or country life but on other levels address larger philosophical and social themes. Frost considered this among his greatest poems, calling it "my best bid for remembrance." Read this poem several times, paying attention to the scene, the language, what happens, and the feeling that is evoked by the "music" of the poem.

Whose woods these are I think I know.
His house is in the village though;
He will not see me stopping here
To watch his woods fill up with snow.

My little horse must think it queer   5
To stop without a farmhouse near
Between the woods and frozen lake
The darkest evening of the year.

He gives his harness bells a shake
To ask if there is some mistake.   10
The only other sound's the sweep
Of easy wind and downy flake.

The woods are lovely, dark and deep,
But I have promises to keep,
And miles to go before I sleep,   15
And miles to go before I sleep.

A CLOSER LOOK AT
Stopping by Woods on a Snowy Evening

1. Poetry combines the sense of written words with the sound of the spoken words. Read this poem aloud and listen carefully to determine what feeling or mood is created by the sound of the poem. How does the sound match or reinforce the sense of the words?

2. Describe the poem's plot—not just the events that happen but also how character and events create some kind of conflict between characters or within a character. What *conflict* do you think the speaker is experiencing? Point specifically to the poem itself to explain what leads you to that understanding.

3. How do poems like this one, which has no clear resolution, cause you to think more deeply? Does the lack of resolution make the poem frustrating for you or more interesting?

IDEAS FOR
Writing

1. Write a parody of "Stopping by Woods on a Snowy Evening." Imitate the structure, style, and if possible the sound of the poem, focusing on some activity and place in which the speaker finds herself or himself. For instance, you might begin a poem titled "Looking into the Refrigerator on a Sunday Morning" with these lines: "Whose milk this is I think I know./I need it for my cornflakes though. . . ." The point is to play with the poetic form and have fun by using it to describe an incongruous situation.

2. Write a brief review of "Stopping by Woods on a Snowy Evening," another poem, or some other cultural work, such as a song. (See Chapter 6 for more on evaluations.) Early in your review, present a specific set of criteria that you believe any good poem should have.

An Overview of "Stopping by Woods on a Snowy Evening"

STEVEN MONTE

Steven Monte is an associate professor of English at College of Staten Island–City University of New York who has published widely on American poets and poetry. In this interpretation of Frost's great poem, Monte urges readers to look beyond the poem's simplicity to the strangeness and power of the poem to evoke multiple and ambiguous meanings. As you read, pay attention to the way that Monte never strays far from the poem's words (quoting them throughout) to arrive at an interesting and insightful understanding of the poem.

With the exception of "The Road Not Taken," "Stopping by Woods on a Snowy Evening" is probably Frost's best-known poem. As with many well-known poems, we may feel that familiarity equals understanding or that a poem we have read or heard enough times can't surprise us anymore. This is especially the case with "Stopping by Woods," which is not only one of the most popular American poems, but is also one written in a clear and seemingly direct style. We might even say that we like the poem precisely because of its simplicity and effortless feel. But as with a person we've been acquainted with for a long time but don't really know, a familiar poem may change when we encounter it in unfamiliar circumstances. Where once we saw only surface and clearly defined qualities, suddenly we see depths and ambiguity. For this to happen with a poem, we often only need to stop and reflect on our experience, like the speaker in Frost's poem. One of the messages of "Stopping by Woods" seems to be just that pausing and reflecting on experience help us re-enter life with a new understanding and sense of direction.

The plot of "Stopping by Woods" is straightforward: a man (we assume) narrates his experience of driving some sort of horse-drawn vehicle by privately owned woods on a snowy evening. He stops, and then contemplates how strange his halt must seem to the horse, given that it is cold and dark and there is no farmhouse in sight. The horse shakes his harness bell, an action that the man interprets as the animal asking "if there is some mistake." The man then listens to the wind and the snow and ends his account with some remarks on his experience, his responsibilities to the world, and the distance he needs to travel before he sleeps. The story could easily be true—it certainly aims to be "true to life"—but it is hard not to interpret it symbolically. Many readers over the years have felt that the man's journey toward sleep represents life's "journey" toward death, though Frost himself insisted that the last two lines were not an invocation of death. Another popular way of reading the poem is to understand the man's rejection of the woods as an acceptance of social duty and personal responsibility.

But "Stopping by Woods" is a much stranger poem than may appear at first. From the opening lines, we know that the story is being told from the speaker's point of view ("Whose woods these are I think I know"), but we may never bother to consider whom the man is addressing. The addressee of the poem can only be the man himself, who seems to be narrating the events as they occur to him, or thinking "aloud" to himself. This odd, subjective perspective is worth puzzling over, if only because it allows us to see just how self-conscious the man is. Why is he so concerned about being seen stopping by the woods? Is it simply because he fears he will be accused of trespassing on someone else's property? Perhaps he feels guilty that he has temporarily suspended his business and does not wish to be seen or see himself as someone who shirks responsibility. Or it could be that he feels guilty for indulging in a fantasy, for he is attracted to something he feels he should resist. It is hard to say what the woods represent for the man—rest, death, nature, beauty, solitude, oblivion—but it is clear that he feels he should not allow himself to give in to his desire to stay there. There is moreover a sexual dimension to his fantasy: the feminine woods ("lovely, dark and deep") are set against a world of men where promises must be kept—the world of property and business.

Whatever depths "Stopping by Woods" possesses, it gives us the impression of simplicity. How does the poem manage this? Most obviously, its language remains conversational throughout and it generally avoids twisting around the word order of spoken speech. "Stopping by Woods" also contains only one word with more than two syllables. When the poem does alter the expected word order, as in "Whose woods these are I think I know," the sound and the sense of the line help us forget that there is anything odd going on. We don't feel the line should read "I think I know whose woods these are" because we get the sense that the speaker is expressing the thought as it occurs to him: he is especially concerned with remembering who owns the woods, and he expresses his uncertainty by following his first thought with the phrase "I think I know." The insistent rhythms of the poem—every line except one is exceptionally regular in beating out "ta-dum, ta-dum, ta-dum, ta-dum"—and the frequent rhymes add to the illusion of simplicity. Caught in the flow of the poem, we tend not to notice that the lines "Between the woods and frozen lake/The darkest evening of the year" neither follow logically from the lines that come before them nor form a complete sentence on their own. Once again, we might feel that we are listening to the thoughts of the speaker. He is situating himself in place ("Between the woods and frozen lake") and time ("The darkest evening of the year"), where "darkest" may imply the "longest" evening of the year, December 22, the winter solstice. By calling the evening "darkest," the man suggests that he has reached a low point or a moment of crisis.

Another reason why "Stopping by Woods" seems simple is that it is structured around many familiar oppositions. A complete list of these oppositions would be unusually long for such a short poem: man and nature, masculine and feminine, emptiness and fullness, business and pleasure, movement and stopping, society and solitude, life and death, activity and sleep, and so on. Such familiar distinctions may make us feel at home in the poem, but they may also be disturbing. The categories either seem too fixed (should we only associate men with activity and business?) or too fluid (which is empty, life or death?). Oppositions also help determine the poem's organization: "Stopping by Woods" constantly alternates between inner thoughts and descriptions of the world outside. Even within its descriptive mode, the poem shifts from the visual details of the first stanza ("He will not see . . . To watch his woods") to the sounds of the third stanza ("harness bells . . . The only other sound's the sweep"). Meanwhile the second and the fourth stanzas are more reflective. In the second stanza, the man imagines what the horse is thinking. The details of "the woods and frozen lake" may be in the man's line of vision, but they may also be his way of placing the scene on a mental map, just as "darkest evening" may place the day on a mental calendar. The fourth stanza is even more subjective in its description of the woods as "lovely, dark and deep." All of this inward and outward movement and the poem's oppositions make us feel that the man is being pulled in different directions and needs to make a decision.

But before looking at the decision the man makes in the last stanza, it is worthwhile to stop and examine some of the odd features of his descriptions. Why is his horse "little"? Why is the wind "easy" and the flake "downy"? It is not enough to say "because they *are* little, easy, and downy," or even "because they appear that way to the man," for we would still be left wondering why he chose to describe these things and not others. A somewhat more inventive if unkind explanation is that Frost needed to fill up his lines with these adjectives in order to keep the poem's rhythm insistent. But perhaps we can do better. By calling the horse "little," Frost gives us a sense of the smallness of the figures in the landscape. We furthermore sense that the man is not rich and is probably fond of his animal. "Easy" and "downy" may in their own way hint at what the man is feeling. Part of the attraction of the scene seems to lie in its promise of ease and softness, its contrast to the hard world of men.

The description of the woods in the final stanza leads into the strangest and most memorable section of the poem. Why does this last stanza haunt us? It begins innocently enough and even sounds like a cliche: "The woods are lovely." But the vagueness of the description, the pulse of the line, and the repetition of sounds ("dark and deep") suggest that we are entering a kind of dreamworld. The drowsy repetition of "And miles to go before I sleep" completes this effect, and we sense that the poem is enacting what the man is feeling. The poem's close feels satisfying because it deviates from, and then reinforces, patterns that the poem has established earlier. The first three stanzas have rhymes in the first, second, and fourth lines. The third line then rhymes with the first line of the following stanza, helping us feel that all four stanzas connect like links in a chain. But the established rhythms and rhymes are disrupted in the final stanza. The line "But I have promises to keep" is not as rhythmically insistent as the other lines of the poem. It also contains the poem's only three-syllable word, "promises." Just as the man attempts to shake off his dreamy attraction to the woods, we are brought up short with this jarring line. The last two lines then feel like a fade out, not simply because of the repetition, but due to the return of the rhythm and the absence of a new linking word: all four lines of this stanza rhyme.

The speaker in "Stopping by Woods" "wakes up" to a knowledge of what he must do. He apparently decides to return to the real world and cease his dreaming. He is leaving nature and returning to society, and in so doing makes us feel that there is some irony in the poem's title: he was only "stopping by" nature, as if on a social call. At the beginning of the poem he was unsure ("I think I know"); at the end he has gained some kind of knowledge. We can think of the experience he has by the woods as either a temporary diversion or a recurring moment in his life that helps him go on. In this straight reading of the poem, the man's experience, though forcing him to confront the fact of death and the difficulties of life, consoles him (and the reader) in the end. But if this moment is, or has the potential to be, a recurrent moment in life, the poem may not be as consoling as we first thought. In this dark reading of the poem, we can't be sure whether the man has come to a decision or merely postponed it. He never actually says he has moved on and, if anything, he seems on his way to sleep. Even supposing he does continue on his journey, it is not clear that the road ahead represents a more appealing alternative to the woods. Real life may seem emptier now, and all those familiar oppositions that help us make sense of our lives are open to question. If we equate stopping by woods with reading a poem, we will confront a similar dilemma. As the man's experience should suggest, however, it is not a question of choosing between alternatives so much as it is becoming aware of new possibilities. In looking closely at a poem, we don't cancel our first experience of reading so much as we enrich it and make it more strange.

A CLOSER LOOK AT
An Overview of "Stopping by Woods"

1. Read through this literary analysis again, this time noting the places where Monte asks a specific interpretative question about Frost's poem. For instance, in paragraph 3 he asks, "Why is he so concerned about being seen stopping by the woods? Is it simply because he fears he will be accused of trespassing on someone else's property?" He asks similar questions in paragraphs 4, 5, 6, and 7. How does he use these interpretive questions to move his literary analysis forward?

2. Consult Chapter 16, "Choosing a Style." Choose one of these features of style and one two- to five-sentence passage from Monte's literary analysis and explain how Monte's passage illustrates effective style.

For instance, you might wish to explain how Monte weaves the poem's words with his own, or how he tells readers what they should notice about those quotations.

3. Carefully reread Monte's first paragraph, and note especially the final sentence, which states a possible interpretation for—or claim about—Frost's poem. Now reread the final paragraph, which begins by reiterating a similar interpretation but also suggests just as strongly a different interpretation, a "dark reading of the poem." What is Monte's claim? Does he believe one reading is superior to the other? If not, then what exactly does he want us to understand about the poem?

IDEAS FOR
Writing

1. Choose any work from popular culture (a TV show, a song, a movie, a graphic work, etc.) and write a review that interprets that work in parallel fashion to Monte's interpretation of Frost's poem. Specifically, Monte argues that Frost's poem *appears* simple and straightforward, but a more careful reading shows that it is actually complex, meaningful, and interesting. Make a similar argument in your review of your chosen work from popular culture.

2. Monte assumes that a poem that does not lead to a specific reading but allows for multiple ambiguous readings is superior to a poem that has a straightforward meaning or point. Write a position paper that argues for or against Monte's assumption that complex poems are superior.

Touched by a Vampire

LAURA MILLER

Laura Miller is the senior books writer for and cofounder of the Web site Salon. *She also contributes to the* New York Times *and the* New Yorker. *"Touched by a Vampire" was written for* Salon *and reviews the popular* Twilight *series of vampire novels written by Stephenie Meyer. As you read this piece, pay attention to the questions that Miller raises and addresses.*

A minute past midnight on August 2, bookstores across the country will for the first time repeat a ritual once reserved for a single author: J. K. Rowling. They'll stay open late and begin selling copies of *Breaking Dawn* by Stephenie Meyer, the fourth novel of the Twilight series, at the first moment they're officially permitted to do so. Tens of thousands of fans plan to congregate for these release parties, message boards have shut down to guard against leaked spoilers, and as many as a million readers will be blocking out an entire weekend to bury themselves in the book.

The preceding three installments in the series—Twilight, New Moon and Eclipse—occupy the top slots in Publishers Weekly's bestseller list for children's fiction (they are categorized as Young Adult, or YA, titles), and are among the top five overall bestsellers on USA Today's list. In May, Publishers Weekly reported that 5.3 million copies of the Twilight books had sold in the U.S. alone. When a movie based on the first novel comes out in December, expect to see book sales jump to numbers that approach Rowling's eight-figure numbers.

No wonder the media has heralded Twilight as the next Harry Potter and Meyer as the second coming of J. K. The similarities, however, are largely commercial. It's hard to see how Twilight could ever approach Harry Potter as a cultural phenomenon for one simple reason: the series' fan base is almost exclusively female. The gender imbalance is so pronounced that Kaleb Nation, an enterprising 19-year-old radio show host-cum-author, has launched a blog called Twilight Guy, chronicling his experiences reading the books. The project is marked by a spirit that's equal parts self-promotion and scientific inquiry—"I am trying to find why nearly every girl in the world is obsessed with the Twilight books by Stephenie Meyer"—and its premise relies on the fact that, in even attempting this experiment, Nation has made himself an exceptional guy indeed. Bookstores have been known to shelve the Twilight books in both the children's and the science fiction/fantasy sections, but they are—in essence and most particulars—romance novels, and despite their gothic trappings represent a resurrection of the most old-fashioned incarnation of the genre. They summon a world in which love is passionate, yet (relatively) chaste, girls need be nothing more than fetchingly vulnerable, and masterful men can be depended upon to protect and worship them for it.

The series' heroine, Bella Swan, a 16-year-old with divorced parents, goes to live with her father in the small town of Forks, Wash. (a real place, and now a destination for fans). At school, she observes four members of a fabulously good-looking and wealthy but standoffish family, the Cullens; later she finds herself seated next to Edward Cullen in biology lab and is rendered nearly speechless by his spectacular beauty. At first, he appears to loathe her, but after a protracted period of bewilderment and dithering she discovers the truth. Edward and his clan are vampires who have committed themselves to sparing human life; they call themselves "vegetarians." The scent of Bella's blood is excruciatingly appetizing to Edward, testing his ethical limits and eventually his emotional ones, too. The pair fall in love, and the three books detail the ups and downs of this interspecies romance, which is complicated by Bella's friendship with Jacob Black, a member of a pack of Native American werewolves who are the sworn enemies of all vampires.

Comparisons to another famous human girl 5 with a vampire boyfriend are inevitable, but Bella Swan is no Buffy Summers. *Buffy the Vampire Slayer* was at heart one of those mythic hero's journeys so beloved by Joseph Campbell-quoting screenwriters, albeit transfigured into something sharp and funny by making the hero a contemporary teenage girl. Buffy wrestled with a series of romantic dilemmas—in particular a penchant for hunky vampires—but her story always belonged to *her*. Fulfilling her responsibilities as a slayer, loyalty to her friends and family, doing the right thing and cobbling together some semblance of a healthy life were all ultimately as important, if not more important, to her than getting the guy. If Harry Potter has a vampire-loving, adolescent female counterpart, it's Buffy Summers.

By contrast, Bella, once smitten by Edward, lives only for him. When he leaves her (for her own good) at the beginning of *New Moon*, she becomes so disconsolate that she resorts to risking her own life, seeking extreme situations that cause her to hallucinate his voice. This practice culminates in a quasi-suicidal high dive into the ocean, after which, on the brink of drowning, she savors visions of her undead boyfriend: "I thought briefly of the clichés, about how you're supposed to see your life flash before your eyes. I was so much luckier. Who wanted to see a rerun, anyway? I saw *him,* and I had no will to fight. . . . Why would I fight when I was so happy where I was?" After Edward returns, the only obstacle she can see to her eternal happiness as a member of the glamorous Cullen family is his stubborn refusal to turn her into a vampire: He's worried that she'll lose her soul.

Otherwise directionless and unsure of herself, Bella's only distinguishing trait is her clumsiness, about which she makes frequent self-deprecating jokes. But Bella is not really the point of the *Twilight* series; she's more of a place holder than a character. She is purposely made as featureless and ordinary as possible in order to render her a vacant, flexible skin into which the reader can insert herself and thereby vicariously enjoy Edward's chilly charms. (His body is as hard and cold as stone, an ick-inducing detail that this reader, for one, found impossible to get past.) Edward, not Bella, is the key to the *Twilight*

franchise, the thing that fans talk about when explaining their fascination with the books. "Perfect" is the word most often used to describe him; besides looking like a male model, Edward plays and composes classical music, has two degrees from Harvard and drives several hot cars very, very fast. And he can read minds (except, mysteriously, for Bella's). "You're good at everything," Bella sighs dreamily.

Even the most timorous teenage girl couldn't conceive of Bella as intimidating; it's hard to imagine a person more insecure, or a situation better set up to magnify her insecurities. Bella's vampire and werewolf friends are all fantastically strong and fierce as well as nearly indestructible, and she spends the better part of every novel alternately cowering in their protective arms or groveling before their magnificence. "How well I knew that I wasn't good enough for him" is a typical musing on her part. Despite Edward's many protestations and demonstrations of his utter devotion, she persists in believing that he doesn't mean it, and will soon tire of her. In a way, the two are ideally suited to each other: Her insipidity is the counterpart to his flawlessness. Neither of them has much personality to speak of.

But to say this is to criticize fantasy according to the standards of literature, and Meyer—a Mormon housewife and mother of three—has always been frank about the origins of her novels in her own dreams. Even to a reader not especially susceptible to its particular scenario, *Twilight* succeeds at communicating the obsessive, narcotic interiority of all intense fantasy lives. Some imaginary worlds multiply, spinning themselves out into ever more elaborate constructs. *Twilight* retracts; it finds its voluptuousness in the hypnotic reduction of its attention to a single point: the experience of being loved by Edward Cullen.

Bella and her world are barely sketched— 10 even Edward himself lacks dimension. His inner life and thoughts are known to us only through what Bella sees him say or do. The characters, such as they are, are stripped down to a minimum, lacking the texture and idiosyncrasies of actual people. What this sloughing off permits is the return, again and again, to the delight of marveling at Edward's beauty, being cherished in his impermeable arms, thrilling to his caresses and, above all, hearing him profess, over and over, his absolute, unfailing, exclusive, eternal and worshipful adoration. A tiny sample:

"Bella, I couldn't live with myself if I ever hurt you. You don't know how it's tortured me . . . you are the most important thing to me now. The most important thing to me ever."

"I could see it in your eyes, that you honestly believed that I didn't want you anymore. The most absurd, ridiculous concept—as if there were any way that I could exist without needing you!"

"For this one night, could we try to forget everything besides just you and me?" He pleaded, unleashing the full force of his eyes on me. "It seems like I can never get enough time like that. I need to be with you. Just you."

Need I add that such statements rarely issue from the lips of mortal men, except perhaps when they're looking for sex? Edward, however, doesn't even insist on *that*—in fact, he refuses to consummate his love for Bella because he's afraid he might accidentally harm her. "If I was too hasty," he says, "if for one second I wasn't paying enough attention, I could reach out, meaning to touch your face, and crush your skull by mistake. You don't realize how incredibly *breakable* you are. I can never, never afford to lose any kind of control when I'm with you." As a result, their time together is spent in protracted courtship: make-out sessions and sweet nothings galore, every shy girl's dream.

Yet it's not only shy girls who crush mightily 15 on Edward Cullen. One of the series' most avid fan sites is *Twilight Moms*, created by and for grown women, many with families of their own. There, as in other forums, readers describe the effects of Meyer's books using words like "obsession" and "addiction." Chores, husbands and children go neglected, and the hours that aren't spent reading and rereading the three novels are squandered on forums and fan fiction. "I have no desires to be part of the real world right now," posted one woman. "Nothing I was doing before holds any interest to me. I do what I have to do, what I need to do to get by and that's it. Someone please tell me it will ease up, even if just a little? My entire world is consumed and in a tailspin."

The likeness to drug addiction is striking, especially when you consider that literary vampirism has often served as a metaphor for that form of enthrallment. The vampire has been a remarkably fluid symbol for over a hundred years, standing for homosexuality, bohemianism and other hip manifestations of outsider status. Although the connection between the bloodsucking undead and romance fiction might seem obscure to the casual observer, they do share an ancestor. Blame it all on George Gordon, aka Lord Byron, the original dangerous, seductive bad boy with an artist's wounded soul and in his own time the object of as much feminine yearning as Edward Cullen has been in the early 21st. Not only did Byron inspire such prototypical romantic heroes as Heathcliff and Mr. Rochester (a character Meyer has listed as among her favorites), he was the original pattern for the vampire as handsome, predatory nobleman. His physician, John William Polidori, wrote "The Vampyre," a seminal short story that featured just such a figure, Lord Ruthven, patently based on the poet. Before that, the vampires of folklore had been depicted as hideous, bestial monsters.

Bram Stoker's Count Dracula was the English bourgeoisie's nightmare vision of Old World aristocracy: decadent, parasitic, yet possessed of a primitive charisma. Though we members of the respectable middle class know they intend to eat us alive, we can't help being dazzled by dukes and princes. Aristocrats imperiously exercise the desires we repress and are the objects of our own secret infatuation with hereditary hierarchies. Anne Rice, in the hugely popular *Vampire Chronicles*, made her vampire Lestat a bisexual rock star—Byron has also been called the first of those—cementing the connection between vampire noblemen and modern celebrities. In recent years, in the flourishing subgenre known as paranormal romance, vampires play the role of leading man more often than any other creature of the night, whether the mode is noir, as in Laurell K. Hamilton's Anita Blake series of detective novels or chick-lit-ish, as in MaryJanice Davidson's Queen Betsy series.

The YA angle on vampires, evident in the *Twilight* books and in many other popular series as well, is that they're high school's aristocracy, the coolest kids on campus, the clique that everyone wants to get into. Many women apparently never get over the allure of such groups; as one reader posted on *Twilight Moms*, "*Twilight* makes me feel like there may be a world where a perfect man does exist, where love can overcome anything, where men will fight for the women they love no matter what, where the underdog strange girl in high school with an amazing heart can snag the best guy in the school, and where we can live forever with the person we love," a mix of adolescent social aspirations with what are ostensibly adult longings.

The "underdog strange girl" who gets plucked from obscurity by "the best guy in school" is the 21st century's version of the humble governess who captures the heart of the lord of the manor. The chief point of this story is that the couple *aren't* equals, that his love rescues her from herself by elevating her to a class she could not otherwise join. Unlike Buffy, Bella is no hero. "There are so many girls out there who do not know kung fu, and if a guy jumps in the alley they're not going to turn around with a roundhouse kick," Meyer once told a journalist. "There's a lot of people who are just quieter and aren't having the Prada lifestyle and going to a special school in New York where everyone's rich and fabulous. There's normal people out there and I think that's one of the reasons Bella has become so popular."

Yet the Cullens, although they don't live in New York, *are* rich and fabulous. *Twilight* would be a lot more persuasive as an argument that an "amazing heart" counts for more than appearances if it didn't harp so incessantly on Edward's superficial splendors. If the series is supposed to be championing the worth of "normal" people, then why make Edward so exceptional? If his wealth, status, strength, beauty and accomplishments make him the "best" among all the boys at school, why shouldn't the same 20 standard be applied to the girls, leaving Bella by the wayside? Sometimes Edward seems to subscribe to that standard, complaining about having to read the thoughts of one of Bella's classmates because "her mind isn't very original." But then, neither is Bella's. In a sense, Bella is absolutely right: She's not "good enough" for Edward—at least, not according to the same measurements that make Edward "perfect." Yet by some miracle she—unremarkable in every way—is exempt from his customary contempt for the ordinary. Then again, by choosing her he proves that she's *better* than all the average people at school.

Such are the tortured internal contradictions of romance, as nonsensical as its masculine counterpart, pornography, and every bit as habit forming. Search a little deeper on the Internet and you can find women readers both objecting to the antifeminist aspects of *Twilight* and admitting that they found the books irresistible. "Sappy romance, amateurish writing, etc.," complained one. Still, "when I read it, I just couldn't put it down. It was like an unhealthy addiction for me. . . . I'm not sure how I could read through it, seeing how I dislike romances immensely. But I did, and when I couldn't get *New Moon* I almost had a heart attack. That book was hypnotizing."

Some things, it seems, are even harder to kill than vampires. The traditional feminine fantasy of being delivered from obscurity by a dazzling, powerful man, of needing to do no more to prove or find yourself than win his devotion, of being guarded from all life's vicissitudes by his boundless strength and wealth—all this turns out to be a difficult dream to leave behind. Vampires have long served to remind us of the parts of our own psyches that seduce us, sapping our will and autonomy, dragging us back into the past. And they walk among us to this day.

A CLOSER LOOK AT
Touched by a Vampire

1. What are the features and moves that would identify this piece as a literary analysis? What are the features and moves that would identify it as a review? What other genres and genre features are mixed into this literary analysis?

2. In several places, Miller compares the *Twilight* series to the TV show *Buffy the Vampire Slayer* and *Twilight*'s characters (Bella and Edward) to the characters in *Buffy*. Which series does Miller find superior? What criteria does she use to evaluate one as superior to the other? In other words, what is it that makes one better or more interesting?

3. "Touched by a Vampire" can be seen as a "genre-based analysis" of the *Twilight* books, since Miller evaluates the books in relation to how they adhere to the romance genre. Miller writes that the *Twilight* books "are—in essence and most particulars—novels, and . . . represent a resurrection of the most old-fashioned incarnation of the genre." Does Miller, overall, approve or disapprove of the romance genre and of these books? Find specific places in "Touched by a Vampire" that support your conclusions.

IDEAS FOR
Writing

1. Miller takes features from many of the genres described in this book and fuses them into "Touched by a Vampire," which can be seen as a fusion of review, rant, evaluation, literary analysis, and commentary, just to name a few. Using Miller's "genre fusion" strategy, write a similar piece about a book, movie, song, band, television show, or other cultural work that you have found effective or ineffective, or that had a profound influence on you or left you cold.

2. Write a position paper that either challenges or supports Miller's position about the value of and healthfulness of reading romance novels.

A FEW IDEAS FOR
Composing a Literary Analysis

1. Write a literary analysis of a favorite work. Choose a book, poem, movie, play, or other work that you find absolutely wonderful. Invite your readers to consider the work through a new and interesting angle and show them how that angle can lead to new and interesting insights that go beyond the obvious.

2. Write a literary analysis about a persuasive work. Choose a literary work that you feel tries to persuade readers about a certain belief or attitude. Write a literary analysis that focuses on how the literary work persuades its readers (see Chapter 22, "Using Argumentative Strategies"). Very few literary works make explicit claims, but they can often be more influential than straightforward arguments. For instance, it is possible to see Edwidge Danticat's "A Wall of Fire Rising" (page 126) as making an argument against the terrible burden of poverty, or Lawrence Dunbar's "We Wear the Mask" (page 123) as making an argument against racial discrimination. Your analysis should explain what claim the literary work makes and how effectively it makes its case.

3. Write a literary analysis of a nonprint work. Today, you can read printed words on a page, read a text supplemented with images and sound, listen to an audiobook, read a text with an e-book reader or on a Web page, watch a movie version, or experience other multimodal transformations. Experience a literary work both on the traditional printed page and in a digital mode and analyze how these different modes of presentation affect your experience as a reader. In your analysis, focus on how the changes in modes and media change your experience. What is emphasized and what new understandings are made possible? What is de-emphasized or left out?

37

Rhetorical
Analyses

Homer Simpson's Figures of Speech

RICHARD NORDQUIST

Sometimes truths are put in the mouths of simpletons and clowns. The creators of the Simpsons have often used the character of Homer Simpson as a way to tell truths in ironic ways. In this rhetorical analysis, Richard Nordquist uses rhetorical concepts to demonstrate how the writers of the Simpsons use language to make the show clever and insightful.

In this article, we consider some of the ways in which Homeric rhetoric has traveled from *The Odyssey* to *The Idiocy* by way of America's favorite cartoon character. Let's journey to Springfield to review 20 classic figures of speech.

"English? Who needs that? I'm never going to England!"

Woo-hoo! The immortal words of Mr. Homer Simpson—beer-guzzling, donut-popping patriarch, nuclear-power-plant safety inspector, and Springfield's resident rhetorician. Indeed, Homer has contributed far more to the English language than just the popular interjection "D'oh." Let's take a look at some of those rich contributions—and along the way review several rhetorical terms.

Homer's Rhetorical Questions

Consider this exchange from a Simpson family symposium:

Mother Simpson: [singing] How many roads must a man walk down before you can call him a man?

Homer: Seven.

Lisa: No, dad, it's a rhetorical question.

Homer: OK, eight.

Lisa: Dad, do you even know what "rhetorical" means?

Homer: Do *I* know what "rhetorical" means?

In fact, Homeric logic often depends on a 5 rhetorical question for its expression:

Books are useless! I only ever read one book, *To Kill a Mockingbird*, and it gave me absolutely no insight on how to kill mockingbirds! Sure it taught me not to judge a man by the color of his skin . . . but what good does that do me?

One particular type of rhetorical question favored by Homer is erotesis, a question implying strong affirmation or denial: "Donuts. Is there anything they can't do?"

Homer's Figures of Speech

Though sometimes misjudged as a *complete* moron, Homer is actually a deft manipulator of the *oxy*moron: "Oh Bart, don't worry, people die all the time. In fact, you could wake up dead tomorrow." And our favorite figure of ridicule is actually quite handy with figures of speech. To explain human behavior, for instance, he relies on personification:

The only monster here is the gambling monster that has enslaved your mother! I call him Gamblor, and it's time to snatch your mother from his neon claws!

Chiasmus guides Homer to new levels of self-understanding:

All right, brain, I don't like you and you don't like me—so let's just do this, and I'll get back to killing you with beer.

And here, in just five words, he manages to combine apostrophe and tricolon in a heartfelt

669

encomium: "Television! Teacher, mother, secret lover."

Of course, Homer isn't always familiar with 10 the *names* of such classical figures:

Lisa: That's Latin, Dad—the language of Plutarch.

Homer: Mickey Mouse's dog?

But stop snickering, Lisa: the language of Plutarch was Greek.

Simpson Repeats

Like the great orators of ancient Greece and Rome, Homer employs repetition to evoke pathos and underscore key points. Here, for example, he inhabits the spirit of Susan Hayward in a breathless anaphora:

> I want to shake off the dust of this one-horse town. I want to explore the world. I want to watch TV in a different time zone. I want to visit strange, exotic malls. I'm sick of eating hoagies! I want a grinder, a sub, a foot-long hero! I want to LIVE, Marge! Won't you let me live? Won't you, please?

Epizeuxis serves to convey a timeless Homeric truth:

> When it comes to compliments, women are ravenous blood-sucking monsters always wanting more . . . more . . . MORE! And if you give it to them, you'll get plenty back in return.

And polyptoton leads to a profound discovery:

> Marge, what's wrong? Are you hungry? Sleepy? Gassy? Gassy? Is it gas? It's gas, isn't it?

Homeric Arguments

Homer's rhetorical turns, especially his efforts to 15 argue by analogy, sometimes take odd detours:

- Son, a woman is a lot like a . . . a refrigerator! They're about six feet tall, 300 pounds. They make ice, and . . . um . . . Oh, wait a

minute. Actually, a woman is more like a beer.

- Son, a woman is like a beer. They smell good, they look good, you'd step over your own mother just to get one! But you can't stop at one. You wanna drink another woman!

- You know, boys, a nuclear reactor is a lot like a woman. You just have to read the manual and press the right buttons.

- Fame was like a drug. But what was even more like a drug were the drugs.

Yes, Mr. Simpson is occasionally word challenged, as in the malapropism that punctuates this distinctively Homeric prayer:

> Dear Lord, thank you for this microwave bounty, even though we don't deserve it. I mean . . . our kids are uncontrollable hellions! Pardon my French, but they act like savages! Did you see them at the picnic? Oh, of course you did. You're everywhere, you're *omnivorous*. Oh Lord! Why did you spite me with this family?

Consider as well Homer's eccentric (or perhaps dyslexic?) use of hypophora (raising questions and answering them): "What's a wedding? Webster's dictionary describes it as the act of removing weeds from one's garden." And now and then his thoughts collapse before he can make it to the end of a sentence, as in this case of aposiopesis:

> I won't sleep in the same bed with a woman who thinks I'm lazy! I'm going right downstairs, unfold the couch, unroll the sleeping ba—uh, goodnight.

The Master Rhetorician

But for the most part, Homer Simpson is an artful and deliberate rhetorician. For one thing, he's a self-proclaimed master of verbal irony:

> Owww, look at me, Marge, I'm making people happy! I'm the magical man, from Happy Land, who lives in a gumdrop house on Lolly Pop Lane! . . . By the way I was being sarcastic.

And he dispenses wisdom with dehortatio:

The code of the schoolyard, Marge! The rules that teach a boy to be a man. Let's see. Don't tattle. Always make fun of those different from you. Never say anything, unless you're sure everyone feels exactly the same way you do.

Next time you catch *The Simpsons* on TV, 20 see if you can identify additional examples of these rhetorical concepts.

For the complete critical vocabulary required to appreciate the wealth of Homer Simpson's rhetoric, please see our Tool Kit for Rhetorical Analysis (http://grammar.about.com/od/rhetorictoolkit/Tool_Kit_for_Rhetorical_Analysis.htm).

A CLOSER LOOK AT
Homer Simpson's Figures of Speech

1. This rhetorical analysis does not explore the usual *logos, ethos, pathos* triad, although it does mention *pathos*. List out five ways in which humorous shows, including *The Simpsons*, play with reasoning, authority, and emotion to make people laugh.

2. The author uses examples to illustrate the rhetorical terms and concepts mentioned in the article. Do you find these examples helpful? Would more examples be helpful? What are some ways the author could have made these examples easier to understand?

3. Choose one of the rhetorical concepts listed at the website mentioned at the end of the article. Find an example of this concept in a book, magazine, movie, or television show. Bring it to class to share with your group.

IDEAS FOR
Writing

1. Choose a character from a television show or a movie that you like. Write a profile of that character in which you specifically concentrate on how he or she uses language. You can use some of the rhetorical concepts mentioned in this article, or you can discuss how the character uses *logos*, *ethos*, and *pathos* to communicate with others.

2. Pick one of the rhetorical concepts mentioned in this rhetorical analysis and write a brief report about it. Explain the concept and its history. Offer real-world and realistic examples of this rhetorical concept in use.

3. Write a response to this article. Discuss whether you think this kind of analysis is important to learning how language works. Ancient rhetoricians spent a great amount of time learning and exploring these figures of speech. Today, students are rarely taught about them. What has changed, making figures of speech less important? Should they be taught in schools?

Sleuthing Patriotic Slogans

GARY SLOAN

In the United States, slogans are hard to escape. They are ever-present on radio and television, and, when walking or driving, we see them just about anywhere. In this rhetorical analysis, Gary Sloan, a retired English professor, digs a little deeper into the meaning of these slogans. Notice how he questions whether the slogans have any deeper meaning by paying close attention to the words themselves.

In this best of times and worst of times, the American landscape is dotted with signs, billboards, posters, and stickers emblazoned with patriotic slogans. In my hometown, merchants have scrawled on their display windows a smorgasbord of venerable shibboleths: "United We Stand," "Support the Troops," "Pray for the Troops," "Let Freedom Ring," "Home of the Brave," "God Bless America." Taped on many windows is a flyer that reads: "Pro-America Rally in Railroad Park. Bring lawn chairs, flags, and snacks. Dress patriotic."

When I read the flyer, I thought: Shouldn't that be "Dress *patriotically*?"

Because I have spent much of my life studying and teaching language, I respond inappropriately to patriotic slogans: I parse them grammatically and try to explicate them the way I would an obscure fragment in an essay. Like Hamlet, I sometimes become sicklied over with the pale cast of thought when I shouldn't be thinking at all. The slogans are designed to evoke warm feelings of camaraderie and unity, not grimaces and cocked brows.

Yet I persist in my folly. To wit: Many patriotic slogans are in the imperative mood. They issue a command ("Support the Troops," "Pray for the Troops"). Commands are risky. They create resistance in natural-born rebels and in patriophobes (those with an excessive fear of patriotism).

Are "Let Freedom Ring" and "United We 5 Stand" logically compatible? If everyone exercises freedom of speech and conscience, will we all stand united? Instead of assenting to the war against Iraq, some may opt to ring their dissent.

How does one "Support the Troops"? Letters? Pep rallies? Boxes of homemade cookies? Can one support the troops by urging them to obey their consciences even if their consciences conflict with their orders?

"Home of the Brave." Hmm. Brave in what sense? Obviously, many Americans aren't physically brave. Millions are afraid to walk the streets at night or open their doors to strangers. If "brave" refers to moral courage, might the bravest Americans be those who resist the will of the majority? Might it require more bravery to protest Operation Iraqi Freedom than to support it?

"God Bless America" is almost as inscrutable as the utterances of a Delphi oracle. Grammatically, the words are in the subjunctive mood. They express a wish or a prayer: "Please, God, bless America," or "May God bless America."

The real conundrum: What do the words mean? In what sense is God to bless America? With good health, bouncing babies, supportive spouses? Good schools? High IQs? Philosophical wisdom? Fat paychecks, sirloin steaks, sport-utility vehicles, faster computers, more cable channels, bigger boom boxes? Competitive Superbowls? Better face-lifts and liposuction? Speedier cruise missiles, smarter smart bombs, stealthier stealth bombers? Continued monopoly of the planet's natural resources?

And does "America" mean Americans? If so, does it comprise all Americans, including murderers, rapists, thieves, swindlers, embezzlers, muggers, liars, cheats, bullies, pederasts, pornographers, conceited airheads, slobs, slum lords, domestic tyrants, bigots, and racists?

Or does "America" refer to land, spacious 10 skies and amber waves of grain? Or to some platonic ideal of government embodied in the Declaration of Independence and the Constitution, worthy of being blessed even if some Americans aren't?

Now, if I can just figure out how to dress patriotic.

A CLOSER LOOK AT
Sleuthing Patriotic Slogans

1. Sloan suggests that some political slogans have an effect that runs opposite to their intended effect. Sometimes, they command us to do things or think in a particular way. Why do these commands actually undermine their message, according to Sloan?

2. Grammatical issues seem to be at the heart of much of Sloan's irritation with patriotic slogans. What kinds of grammar problems does he suggest cause these slogans to be questionable and less than solid?

3. Toward the end of the article, Sloan questions whether patriotic slogans are really meant for all Americans. When we think of Americans more broadly, including all citizens, what are the problems with these simple slogans?

IDEAS FOR
Writing

1. Look through a magazine or watch television to collect some slogans of your own. How do the slogans that you collected work? When held up to close scrutiny, as in Sloan's article, do they have weaknesses or make questionable assumptions? Write a position paper in which you defend or challenge the use of slogans to persuade people.

2. Find an advertisement on television or *YouTube* that uses a slogan prominently and write a review in which you explain why you think the advertisement is or is not effective. What makes it persuasive? Where are its shortcomings? How might the advertisement be made more effective?

Shooting from the Hip, with a Smile to Boot

LIBBY COPELAND

In the 2008 election, the emergence of Alaska Governor Sarah Palin as a national politician was meteoric. Her acceptance speech for vice-presidential candidate at the Republican National Convention electrified the conservative base, and she became an instant celebrity. In this rhetorical analysis, Libby Copeland, a writer for the Washington Post, *explains Palin's use of style to win people over. Copeland does not use the word ethos, but pay attention to how issues involving reputation and image underlie this analysis.*

The heart of Sarah Palin's appeal is—Wait, did you see that? There! She did it again: wrinkled up her nose in a way that either looks like a sneer or is adorably reminiscent of Samantha from "Bewitched." Depending on whom you talk to.

Next time you see a clip of the Republican vice presidential nominee, try this exercise. Mute your TV and just watch that face. How often do you see someone in political life so extravagantly expressive? The eyebrows go up, the shoulder leans in, the thumb jauntily gestures backward, the tongue actually fixes in the cheek. To mock Barack Obama, she licks her finger and holds it to the imaginary wind! And that smile, that nearly ever-present smile, which either indicates—oh, dear, here we go again—that she's sarcastic and dismissive or that she's letting you in on a very clever joke.

People love her so. People hate her so. At the heart of it is the delivery, a style of speaking we'll see again in tomorrow night's debate, a style that reaches past folksy and veers into the territory of—to hell with it, cue the charges of sexism—cute.

"She's perky, she's spunky," says Republican speechwriter Landon Parvin, who has written for both Presidents Bush. "She has this quality—in a 1950s comedy, her father would call her 'Button.'"

And?   5

"This allows her to get away with murder," he says.

All you wannabe hockey moms who imagine yourselves having coffee with Sarah Palin and swapping five-minute dinner recipes? Who find it endearing when Palin refers to her husband as "my guy"? Who like the smiling certainty in her tone, the determination in her squint? This is for you.

And all you Pal-lergics who dislike not only her hard-edged politics but that spoonful of sugar she serves it with? Who say her manner reminds you of—we'll quote here from a Pal-lergic named Judi Dickerson who coaches actors on dialogue—"the snotty head cheerleader in high school who was untouchable because she was always gonna win"? This is for you, too.

Sarah Palin is many things—somber is not one of them. There's something about her delivery that suggests she's almost always having fun. You know how they call Joe Biden the happy warrior? Palin has a similar quality—the ability to attack without seeming angry. Some of that is the smile on her face and the evident humor in her voice, as Sheila Tate, Nancy Reagan's former press secretary, points out.

But there's a lot more at work. It starts with   10 the way Palin's delivery allows her to leap through the camera into your living room. Perhaps in part because of her background as a television reporter and beauty pageant competitor, she seems to understand how the camera works.

"What she knows is that the camera is a thief," says Republican strategist Ron Bonjean, who has worked for former House speaker Dennis Hastert and former Senate majority leader Trent Lott, among others. "The camera will steal your emotions and make you flat, and what she's doing is over-emphasizing her emotions, over-emphasizing her delivery, in order to get that realness across to the camera."

The realness is what her fans talk about—that she's like them, that she doesn't seem contrived. "We feel like she talks like we do," says Susan Geary, a Richmond retiree who attended a McCain-Palin rally in Fairfax last month. "Like she's sitting in your kitchen."

There's a consistency to Palin's appeal—if you go back and look at old clips of her, you see many of the same stylistic elements—the warmth and the eager delivery, the voice that drops and rises emphatically, the dropped g's.

"That's been her bread and butter for 20 years, from the day she sat down in front of the TV cameras to do her sportscasting," says Anchorage-based pollster Ivan Moore. "Her success in her political career has been based on being able to project this enormously friendly, enormously appealing physical presence—and, some people would argue, use it to conceal this very much more ruthless and nakedly political character."

Palin's fans are drawn to her story, that folk- 15 hero combination of caribou-hunting toughness and traditional femininity that John McCain's campaign has played up. For many Palin supporters, her attractiveness does not weaken her appeal—rather, it balances those tales of valor on the tundra. Supporters have charged her critics with sexism but at the same time, at the GOP convention, delegates wore buttons that said "Hottest VP From the Coolest State." For a while, Cindy McCain was introducing Palin as a "true Western woman," evoking images of pretty prairie wives with rifles who could out-hunt their husbands and still get dinner on the table. (Hot chicks with guns being a beloved American archetype.)

They are also drawn to the notion of Palin's PTA-mom-just-like-you-ness, which is enhanced by the hair, which has not been cut short in the style of many political women, and the voice, which has not been brought down to a deeper register, or stripped of its Alaska-by-way-of-middle-America nasality. Palin does more than mention her five children as biographical fact in appearances—she also speaks in mom language. What other major political figure would attempt what she said at her welcome-home rally in Fairbanks last month?

"I see some of our staff members here and cabinet members," she told the audience at a rally. "I can't wait to give you guys a hug."

Palin's huggability is evidence of her accessibility—or of her lack of gravitas, depending on where you sit. When she met Pakistani President Asif Ali Zardari in New York recently, he called her "gorgeous" and joked he might hug her. In response, she laughed.

Much of Palin's appeal—as well as what some find grating—is about the language she chooses, which is folksy in the extreme. She says "heck" and "darn" and "gosh" and "shoot" and "oh, gee." She says, "Guys and gals, our regulatory system is outdated." And: The nation's financial system "needs some shakin' up and some fixin.'" She pronounces things "awesome" and "cool," as in: "He's an awesome bundle of joy" (baby Trig) and "It was so cool growin' up in this church and gettin' saved here" (the Wasilla Assembly of God). The critics—she calls 'em "haters."

Could central casting produce a more ideal 20 messenger for the new Republican populism?

"I'm sure she's not from Alaska—she's been sitting on a Hollywood sound stage for years waiting for this," says Paul Costello, the former press aide to Rosalynn Carter and Kitty Dukakis. "She's so unbelievably perfect. . . . Even the red ruby shoes that she's been wearing."

In speeches, Palin's comedic timing is spot-on and her intonation is exaggerated, sweeping her audience along on the current of her message. "Very story-timely," says John Neffinger, a communications consultant who coaches corporate speakers and Democratic congressional candidates. "She varies her intonation all over the place so you know exactly what feelings she's trying to convey. Lots of warmth, very sing-songy."

In the few interviews she has given, or when taking question from voters, Palin speaks with speed and a rat-a-tat delivery, as if a pause were a sign of weakness. Sometimes she drops her voice to a rock-and-roll growl. Her hands move in concert, pointing to her lips, jabbing over her shoulder. Her delivery is "decisive, task-focused," says Ken Brousseau, who consults with executive search firm Korn/Ferry International on corporate leadership styles. "Very black and white." Contrast that with Barack Obama's more deliberative style, his long "uuuhs," his concessions to the opposition. ("John, you're absolutely right," in the presidential debate, over and over.)

When she's forced outside her comfort zone, as has happened a few times of late, Palin tends to "slip back to her talking points," as CBS's Katie Couric recently put it. John McCain is a maverick. Lots of things need some shakin' up. Palin may try to turn a question around ("In what respect, Charlie?") or stall when asked for examples to bolster her argument ("I'll try to find you some and I'll bring 'em to ya!").

"Forgive me, Mrs. Palin," faux Katie Couric 25 said to faux Sarah Palin on last week's "Saturday Night Live," "but it seems to me that when cornered you become increasingly adorable."

There's a youthfulness and an enthusiasm there—Palin is all emoticons; Rachel Ray as candidate for higher office. (When she ran for mayor of Wasilla in 1996, her campaign ad boasted upbeat, jazzy music and a slogan reminiscent of daytime TV: "Positively Sarah.") She speaks with supreme confidence (Ya can't blink, Charlie). On Monday, she said she looked forward to meeting Senate veteran Joe Biden at their debate.

"I've been hearing about his Senate speeches since I was in, like, the second grade," she told an audience in Columbus, Ohio—emphasizing her youth, as well as suggesting an unusual attentiveness to the earliest speeches of Biden, who was sworn in when she was 8.

Perhaps, suggests former Miss America Kate Shindle, an undecided Republican, there's a touch of the pageant world to Palin's voice, to her careful adherence to sound bytes, and that "cheerful aggressiveness" that Shindle calls "part cheerleader, part news anchor, and part drill sergeant."

The confidence is underscored by something Palin does frequently at the ends of her sentences. She sets her lips in forceful line (perfectly captured by Tina Fey in her first "Saturday Night Live" impersonation) as if to communicate that the matter is settled.

Now mute the television again. Watch 30 Palin's body. She expresses excitement through encouraging nods as well as what Karen Bradley—a University of Maryland dance professor who studies body movement—calls this "little shoulder wiggle." And watch that nose wiggle—which Parvin, the Republican speechwriter, says sometimes conveys "a cute determination" and sometimes "a cute distastefulness." And sometimes, it operates as a sort of "exclamation point," conveying agreement, he says. He calls her "Gidget goes to Washington."

"She is playing into a cultural stereotype," says Drew Westen, a psychiatry professor at Emory University who also works as a Democratic consultant and wrote *The Political Brain: The Role of Emotion in Deciding the Fate of the Nation*. And the stereotype? Westen cites Marlo Thomas in *That Girl*, Mary Tyler Moore in *The Dick Van Dyke Show*, Sally Field in *The Flying Nun*—a model of perky femininity that "was really salient in the early '60s before the sexual revolution and the cultural revolution took hold."

These physical and rhetorical habits set Palin in relief to Hillary Clinton, who projected great strength but much less of what one Democratic political consultant calls "traditional feminine warmth." Which was why it caused such a splash when Clinton once told a crowd, "I'm your girl"—there is little that's girly about Hillary Clinton's public persona. Palin calls herself a "gal" and it's utterly believable.

"She's not a woman trying to deliver a speech like a man, and there is an integrity to that," says Parvin.

And all of which means Sarah Palin is either great or awful, depending on whom you talk to, because her style and her conservative beliefs are either post-feminist or the antithesis of feminism. If Palin's cuteness is disarming to her supporters, it is troubling to those who worry that she lacks intellectual heft, and infuriating to those who feel she's being coddled. Not too long ago, CNN anchor Campbell Brown suggested the McCain campaign was being sexist by shielding Palin from interviews. Acting coach Dickerson suggests that Palin gets to be as nakedly political as any other candidate while being shielded from retaliation because of the perception that she is, after all, just a gal.

"You have a very glamorous, pretty woman 35 with, actually, a very girly delivery—but what comes out of her are the words of a very savvy, very tough politician," says Dickerson. "It creates a mixed message of allowing her to really say anything that she wants."

Then again, who decides what's fair? Sarah Palin is hugging us all into confusion.

A CLOSER LOOK AT
Shooting from the Hip, with a Smile to Boot

1. In the article, find five rhetorical qualities that Copeland suggests Palin uses to persuade her audiences. Do you agree that Palin uses these qualities in a strategic way? What impact does Palin's style have on you as a viewer?

2. Copeland also suggests that Palin's style has a reverse effect on some people. In other words, some people "hate her so." Why does Palin's style have this effect, according to Copeland?

3. This article relies on some interesting stylistic devices itself. Find five different times when Copeland's own writing style seems to stand out. How does she use detail, metaphors, similes, and other stylistic devices to enhance her message?

IDEAS FOR
Writing

1. Looking back on the 2008 election, what were your reactions to the rhetorical styles of Palin and Obama? Clearly, both of them are formidable public speakers. How are their styles similar? How are they different? Write a response to this article in which you compare and contrast the speaking styles of Palin and Obama.

2. Find a video of Sarah Palin speaking on *YouTube* or another video Web site. Using the qualities highlighted in this article, write a review of her speech in which you critique her style and her use of *ethos* to make her speech more persuasive. Do you find her style effective or not?

Discovering the Truth: The Operation of *Ethos* in Anti-Smoking Advertising

REBECCA FELDMANN

This rhetorical analysis appeared in a journal called Young Scholars in Writing, *which publishes articles on rhetoric and composition written by college undergraduates. Feldmann shows how the popular and effective* Truth *campaign appeals to teens by building* ethos *and challenging the* ethos *of tobacco companies. As you read, look at how she carefully defines concepts up front, which she can then use later in the rhetorical analysis.*

In 1998, the Florida Tobacco Pilot Program (FTPP) launched a $25 million Truth advertising campaign to alert teenagers to the dangers of smoking and to reduce teen tobacco use. The Truth campaign began when studies conducted by the FTPP and other tobacco control efforts determined that smoking is equated with rebellion and teen self-realization and that the theme of "industry manipulation" held broad appeal among young people (Zucker, Hopkins, Sly, Urich, Mendza-Kershaw, and Solan 1). This campaign portrayed the tobacco industry as manipulative and smoking itself as an uncool habit, and it tapped into teens' need to rebel by depicting tobacco use as an addictive habit marketed by an adult establishment (Zucker, Hopkins, Sly, Urich, Mendza-Kershaw, and Solan 2).

The campaign has since spread nationwide, sponsoring advertisements in magazines, television, and radio. It has its own website with a link to a photo blog, a "Find Facts" page where visitors can learn facts that the campaign has gathered about tobacco companies and the effects of smoking[1] and a "Whatta You Think" section where teens can voice their opinions on issues relating to the tobacco industry and smoking.

The reach of these ads has extended across the nation and impacted a number of teens. Between the inception of Florida's Truth campaign and 2000, results within the state included "a 92 percent brand awareness rate among teens, a 15 percent rise in teens who agree with key attitudinal statements about smoking, a 19.4 percent decline in smoking among middle school students, and a 8.0 percent decline among high school students" (Zucker, Hopkins, Sly, Urich, Mendza-Kershaw, and Solan 1). More recently, among 12 to 17-year olds in the U.S., 75% can accurately describe one or more of the Truth ads, 90% reported that the ad they saw was convincing, and 85% responded that the ad gave them good reasons not to smoke (Citizen's Commission). Furthermore, the Commission's website states, "Monitoring the Future, one of the nation's most comprehensive substance abuse surveys, reported dramatic declines in smoking rates among 8th, 10th, and 12th graders, citing Truth as a factor in this public health success story" (Citizen's Commission).

From such statistics, it is easy to conclude that these ads have been effective in drawing teenage audiences, but it is not as easy to conclude *how*. In this article, by turning to Aristotle, I examine these advertisements as contemporary examples of rhetoric to understand how they function. In doing so, I illustrate that the Truth campaign alerts us to the efficacy of rhetoric at its best—rhetoric that alerts us to the truth of a matter rather than manipulates us into being falsely persuaded by appealing images and illustrious wordplay. In a culture where the word "rhetoric" is often associated with scheming political speech or gimmicky advertising, the rhetoric of the Truth campaign aims at something different. Rather than reverting to "that powerful instrument of error and deceit" (827) that John Locke refers to in his *An Essay Concerning Human Understanding,* the rhetoric of Truth's advertising more closely approaches Plato's definition of rhetoric as "an art which leads the soul by means of words" (*Phaedrus* 157).

The use of *ethos*

Aristotle first discusses *ethos* in Book 1 of his 5 work, *On Rhetoric. Ethos,* or persuasion by character, is built "whenever the speech is spoken in such a way as to make the speaker worthy of credence" (38). The rhetor who purports to have the audience's best interest at heart and who successfully conveys this in her speech will persuade by building character (*ethos*) in the speech rather than by relying on a preconceived notion the audience may have of the rhetor. This is the most effective means of swaying an audience; the ethical appeal is "the controlling factor in persuasion" (38), as Aristotle puts it.

An example of the attempt to persuade by invoking *ethos* in the Truth ads is apparent in a series of magazine advertisements, which tell teens, "Their brand is lies. Our brand is truth." This tagline is the most blatant appearance of such character building as it communicates that Truth ads are serving the purpose of truth rather than manipulation. As Aristotle points out, "The true and the just are by nature stronger than their opposites" (34), and the Truth ads build character by upholding this precept.

The visual statements in these ads further build *ethos*. The dual presence of smoking and body-bags in several of Truth's ads illustrate this point, for the message is simple: smoking kills. This message is present in many of Truth's advertisements, including the Marlboro-like ad discussed in more detail below. These visual statements communicate the campaign's *ethos* by pointing out the stark contrast between their advertising and that of tobacco companies. Truth's ads cleverly call attention to the deceitful tactics of tobacco ads that promote a habit that can kill and that target an audience (those

between 12 and 17) which cannot legally engage in that habit.

Practical wisdom [*phronïsis*]

The *ethos* of any speech must contain three components: "practical wisdom [*phronïsis*]," or good sense/knowledge of the subject the speaker is addressing; "virtue [*aretï*]," or good moral character, which also has ties to the desire to communicate "the true and the just" (Aristotle 34); and "good will [*eunoia*]," or having the good of the audience as the speaker's (at least perceived) main interest (121). Aristotle further states that a rhetor may become less persuasive if he fails to demonstrate any one of these parts, but "a person seeming to have all these qualities is necessarily persuasive to the hearers" (121).

In the Truth ads, practical wisdom involves knowledge of the strategies and manipulation used in cigarette advertising and knowledge of the audience (teens between 12–18). Truth communicates practical wisdom relative to Big Tobacco by containing on its website a "find facts" page that enables teens to broaden their knowledge by scrolling through various statements related to tobacco advertising and health risks associated with smoking. It also communicates practical wisdom more subtly by acknowledging and appealing to teens' need for rebellion in encouraging teens to stand up to the adult establishment of Big Tobacco.

Many Truth ads communicate knowledge 10 by alluding to tobacco ads. The newer "Seek truth" advertisements, shown on television and available to view on the website, feature teens set up outside "a major tobacco company in New York" asking hard-hitting questions of the executives from a podium set up on the sidewalk. Their podium has a "Q:" sign attached to the front, and after a question is asked, the camera turns to a podium with an "A:" sign that is situated in front of the tobacco company's building with nobody standing by it. These ads encourage teens to ask questions and rebel against what the smoking advertisements are saying. One particular ad shows a Virginia Slims poster which tells women to "Find Your Own Voice." The young adult in front of the podium introduces her older friend to ask a question to the tobacco company executives. This woman, using her artificial voice box, asks, "Is this the voice you expected me to find?" The camera then flashes over to the empty "A:" podium, followed by silence. The ad ends with script stating, "Ask questions. Seek Truth."

This advertisement resonates with the audience because it shows the campaign's knowledge of its subject and appeals to teens' independent nature. The Virginia Slims advertisement communicates to women that smoking Virginia Slims will lead to independence and finding one's voice. But the Truth ad is a stark reminder that smoking causes cancer, which may attack one's throat and lead to the need for an artificial voice box. Women will lose their physical voices rather than find figurative ones.

To fully succeed in satisfying the "practical wisdom" requirement of *ethos*, the Truth campaign must relate to its audience, teens. Cornelia Pechmann, Guangzhi Zhao, Marvin E. Goldberg, and Ellen Thomas Reibling identify seven recurring themes in antismoking advertisements aimed at teens: Disease and Death, Endangers Others, Cosmetics, Smokers' Negative Life Circumstances, Refusal Skills, Role Model Marketing Tactics, and Selling Disease and Death. They explain that the choice of theme in the advertisement may affect the result the rhetor obtains in persuading the teen to refrain from smoking.

Pechmann, Zhao, Goldberg, and Reibling claim that the most effective message themes are Endangers Others, Refusal Skills Role Model, and Smokers' Negative Life Circumstances. The Endangers Others theme stresses "how secondhand smoke, and smoking in general, can seriously harm smokers' family members, coworkers, and peers" and "convey[s] that smokers may encounter strong social disapproval from nonsmokers" (3). The Refusal Skills Role Model theme operates by explaining why "many attractive role models view smoking as unappealing and demonstrate refusals of cigarette offers" (4). The Smokers' Negative Life Circumstances theme stresses that smoking is a barrier to appearing "mature, independent, savvy, attractive, and cool" (4). Many of the advertisements of the Truth campaign employ the Smokers' Negative

Life Circumstances theme. These commercials revolve around a dictum encouraging teens and young people to "Ask questions" and "Seek truth." By prompting such discourse, the Truth advertisements communicate that, unlike the tobacco firms who encourage youth to passively accept their message, this antismoking campaign challenges them to become "mature, independent, [and] savvy" by prodding these industries for answers and by intelligently drawing out the consequences of smoking. The Truth campaign thus addresses one of the most successful messages in antismoking advertising aimed at youth: rather than telling teens tobacco companies are manipulating them, these ads encourage teens to ask their own questions of this industry, empowering them to be more mature and savvy in a way that tobacco industries discourage.

Good virtue [*aretî*]

In *On Rhetoric*, Aristotle says that virtue "is an ability [*dynamis*], as it seems, that is productive and preservative of goods, and an ability for doing good in many and great ways, actually in all ways in all things [1366b]" (79). The subdivisions of virtue are "justice, manly courage, self-control, magnificence, magnanimity, liberality, gentleness, prudence, and wisdom" (79–80). "The greatest virtues," he continues, "are necessarily those most useful to others. For that reason people most honor the just and the courageous" (80). Indeed, the "just and the courageous" are present throughout all of the Truth ads. Along with wisdom, they comprise the main subdivisions of virtue at work in this form of rhetoric.

One Truth billboard depicts an older man in   15 a bikini holding a cigarette; the caption is "No wonder tobacco executives hide behind sexy models." This advertisement demonstrates both the "just and the courageous" by implying that tobacco companies' ads do not have these qualities. This billboard communicates that tobacco executives are not courageous because they need to hide. The Truth campaign points to the virtue of their counter-advertising campaign, telling their audience, "Their brand is lies. Our brand is truth." This statement appears as a warning, much like the Surgeon General's warning in a cigarette advertisement, suggesting that the Truth campaign does not danger the public. Their product (so to speak) is the quest for knowledge, the desire to point out the lies that are perpetuated by advertising paid for by the tobacco industry.

As James L. Kinneavy and Susan C. Warshauer point out, virtue "is established when speakers give evidence that they are sincere and trustworthy. The audience must be convinced that the speaker will not deceive them" (174). Truth establishes its sincerity: while never directly telling the audience to refuse cigarettes, it does encourage teens to find the facts out for themselves. Thus, Truth is like an ethical orator because it presents its audience with facts they may use to make informed decisions.

Kinneavy and Warshauer also discuss the relationship between *arïte* and the Greek word *Ariston*, which means "nobility" or "aristocracy." This etymological relationship points to the consideration of culture in the ethical argument: "The effectiveness of an ethical appeal thus depends on one's ability to gauge society's values and to display them to affirm them—in one's speech" (175). This explanation reinforces the point that consideration of the group to whom one is speaking is crucial to making a successful ethical argument, specifically in the case of these advertisements for Truth. Kinneavy and Warshauer imply that in persuading the audience that she is virtuous, the rhetor must be able to convince the audience that she would not deceive them. This is also accomplished in the Truth ads, which point to the lies that are perpetuated in the advertisement of cigarettes. Truth recognizes that it must appeal to its teenage audience's values of independence and desire to be neither misled nor controlled by adult or establishment figures.

Good will [*eunoia*]

This intent to clarify rather than deceive leads into the third component of virtue, which is good will [*eunoia*]. As Kinneavy and Warshauer state, good will consists of "the speaker's display of good intentions toward his or her audience" (176). The speaker displays this good virtue by

identifying with his audience by "holding some of their basic aspirations, speaking their language, and if necessary, sharing and affirming their prejudices" (176). In the Truth campaign's parody of a Marlboro advertisement, a cowboy rides through a rugged landscape, followed by three horses carrying body bags instead of three more cowboys. The tagline asks, "What if cigarette ads told The Truth?" At the bottom where the Surgeon General's warning would be in an actual Marlboro ad, a caption states, "YEE HAW! You Too Can Be An Independent, Rugged, Macho-looking Dead Guy." This ad communicates to teens that the cigarette ads are trying to deceive them by stating smoking will make them "independent, rugged, and macho-looking," but that those ads also leave out the crucial point that their product will also kill you, and it's not possible to be any of those things once you are dead. The ad speaks the language of teens and lets them know that the big advertising firms are manipulative.

Kinneavy and Warshauer also point out that another important consideration in a discussion of good will must be its ties to *pathos*, or persuasion by appeal to the emotions. They argue, "By arousing a particular emotion—and sharing it with members of the audience—a speaker may appear more closely identified with them" (176). In addition, and of great import in examining the effectiveness of the Truth advertisements, "having common enemies as the object of shared anger allows the speaker to strengthen this identification" (176). Kinneavy and Warshauer argue that how well a speaker is received by his audience depends upon his ability to communicate his good intent by emphasizing the presence of "common enemies and common friends as well as common values" (177). Many, if not all, of the Truth ads construct Big Tobacco's lies as the enemy.[2]

According to Aristotle, anger may be defined as "desire, accompanied by [mental and physical] distress, for conspicuous retaliation because of a conspicuous slight that was directed, without justification, against oneself or those near to one" (124). This "desire . . . for conspicuous retaliation" is present in the Virginia

Slims and other Truth ads, including one that is a parody of a movie poster. In this poster, one man is in the foreground above the movie title, "Secrets of a Tobacco Executive," with two other executives in the darkness behind him. The tagline states, "Business is war. And he has the body bags to prove it." Underneath the title of the movie is a school hallway with two teens walking through it. This parody suggests that the tobacco executives are targeting teens due to their own selfish business motivations and are selling teens a product that they know to be illegal for those under 18 and lethal for everyone.

This invocation of anger, this appeal to *pathos*, indirectly supports the *ethos* of the Truth campaign. By invoking anger, these advertisements construct a common enemy: an adult establishment that is trying to manipulate youth. As Zucker, Hopkins, Sly, Urich, Mendza-Kershaw, and Solan put it, the program's key message consists of "exposing of the lies and misinformation perpetuated by tobacco industry marketing" (2). The anger that arises out of these ads comes from a sense that tobacco companies are belittling teens by using lies and manipulation. Further, as Aristotle explains, people become angry "against those rejoicing at misfortunes and generally taking pleasure in others' misfortunes; for it is a sign of being either an enemy or a belittler. And [they become angry] against those who do not care if they are suffering" (129). This form of anger is invoked by most of the Truth ads, for in exposing the lies of tobacco firms, the ads imply that these firms do not care that they are harming those who buy their product.

Objections?

One important objection that may be raised against this counter-advertising campaign is whether it creates the same ethical mistake of which it accuses the tobacco industry. That is, as an advertising campaign in a capitalist system, does it accomplish its ends by manipulating the audience? Is the Truth campaign's version of "the truth" merely a means to make more money to keep the campaign alive?

In discussing *ethos* and ethics, Kinneavy and Warshauer state, "The gap between seeming ethical and being ethical may be great" (183). Indeed, this matter of appearance versus reality of *ethos* appears in Aristotle's *On Rhetoric* as well. This is a pressing question, for, according to Aristotle, "it belongs to the same capacity both to see the true and [to see] what resembles the true" (33). Aristotle argues that humans "have a natural disposition for the true" and so a speakerability "to aim at commonly held opinions [*endoxa*] is a characteristic of one who also has a similar ability to regard to the truth" (33). One interpretation of this statement is that a speaker who aims at commonly held opinions of what appears to be true is more likely to be perceived by his audience as persuasive. The skeptic may argue that it makes no difference whether the rhetor speaks or "seems to" speak the truth because the appearance of truth is just as convincing as its reality.

James E. Porter furthers this argument in his work, *Audience and Rhetoric*. He asks, "Is it ethical to change an audience's beliefs without providing them sound reasons and a basis in fact for changing their beliefs?" (18). Porter believes that Aristotle creates a situation in which "a knowledgeable orator facing an ignorant audience is placed in the position of (possibly) manipulating the audience" (18). The orator may try to force her belief upon an ignorant audience without providing much basis for why the audience should believe her. In trying to understand the true, the audience may be misled by the knowledgeable orator.

Do the Truth advertisements end up resorting to this deception? By turning again to Porter and to Truth's website (a soapbox of sorts for our "orator"), we may answer this question with an emphatic "No." Porter explains that the rhetorical situation Aristotle envisions

> involves a knowledgeable rhetor more or less in possession of "the truth" and an ignorant audience. And of course in such a situation, the rhetorician has nothing to learn *from* the audience;

25

she only learns *about* the audience, through audience analysis, in order to better manage their responses. In this view, the rhetor is the privileged entity whose search for knowledge and truth is accomplished prior to the rhetorical act (in dialectic or scientific method), not through it or in conjunction with an audience. (18, emphasis in original)

The Truth ads do not fall subject to this general criticism, as they contradict such a rhetorical situation in two important ways. First, they do *not* assume an ignorant audience. Their success stems from the fact that they effectively communicate that their search for knowledge is incomplete without the participation of their audience. The "About us" page of the website states, "truth is not here to tell you, or anyone else, what to do. We hate when people do that" (*Truth About Us*). These ads suggest that they are aiming for the truth, but it is up to informed teens to complete the quest for truth and knowledge.

The skeptic may raise a question here of whether this is just a marketing tactic. Truth creators know they must appeal to youth who do not like being told what to do; thus the campaign must make it seem like it is not telling teens what to believe, when it fact it is. Immediately after saying that its audience is "never gonna hear any 'just say "no" to cigarettes' stuff from us," it jumps into a tirade about

an industry out there that makes billions of dollars selling a product that's responsible for over 1,200 deaths a day in the U.S. alone. This industry spends more than $34 million each day advertising and promoting those products, and it's entrenched itself in our culture by deceiving and manipulating the public. Truth just thinks everyone ought to know more about that industry and the things they do. (*Truth About Us*)

Isn't Truth an orator that is trying to convince its audience of the credibility of its position? And if it is, is it really that far of a step to say

that the campaign, despite its claims otherwise, is in fact telling its audience what to believe? Further, if one accepts this view, then how is the advertising strategy of the Truth campaign that different from the deceiving strategies employed by tobacco advertising?

Most important, Truth does not attempt to deceive its audience; it is a campaign based on presenting facts to an audience that has already been manipulated. It even broadens its scope to the entire idea of "truth" itself; it is not reaching for an *appearance* of truth, but truth's reality. Again, Truth's website clarifies this claim: the campaign aims to ensure that all the facts are available so that when teens make their own decisions, "they can be based on all the information, not just those things tobacco companies want you to think" (*Truth About Us*). Furthermore, the website states its understanding and support of the individual's right to smoke, but because nicotine is physically and psychologically addictive, it also states its creators' belief that "responsibility should apply not only to the smoker, but to the individuals who choose to make and sell tobacco products as well" (*Truth About Us*). Truth does not merely use appeals to *pathos* in the anger aimed at big tobacco present in many of its advertisements, nor does it resort to a simple version of *ethos* to present itself as a moral entity. Both play important roles but are reinforced by a simple appeal to the *reality* rather than mere *appearance* of truth. As stated on the website, the campaign "gets its information from respected news sources and organizations like the Centers for Disease Control and Prevention, the Food and Drug Administration, and the American Cancer Society" and assures readers that "all of our information undergoes a stringent, multilayered review, stripping it of any and all extraneous assumptions, dangerous leaps in logic, and subjectivity."[3] Truth is not merely trying to persuade its audience, but rather is attempting to shatter manipulation in a quest for the truth about tobacco and its advertising. The campaign centers teens in this quest, stating, "We can't do this without you" (*Truth About Us*).

Conclusion

Truth's advertisements operate using a powerful combination of appeals to *ethos* and *pathos* to resonate with the teenage audience. As a result of the campaign, teenage smoking rates have dropped significantly. Truth's creators recognize that individuals are responsible for their actions and provide teens straightforward facts. The Truth campaign is necessarily tied to Aristotle's ideas of rhetoric but must not be interpreted as mere tactics, as the skeptic may aver. To do so is to miss the goal of the campaign and of rhetoric more generally. While "rhetoric" has come to connote negative images in much of our modern society, it often communicates the true and the just. The Truth campaign is among our society's most convincing examples of this ideal.

Notes

1. Some of the facts mentioned on this page include the following. "About 1 out of every 5 deaths in the US can be attributed to tobacco products"; "Every day about 2000 youths become daily smokers"; and "In 1989 millions of cases of imported fruit were banned after a small amount of cyanide was found in just two grapes. There's thirty-three times more cyanide in a single cigarette than was found in those two grapes."

2. Though it should be noted that Truth takes care not to have smokers or tobacco firms specifically as their target, Truth's website states, "truth is not anti-smoker. We love smokers. . . . truth isn't about passing judgment on people or the choices they make" and further, "truth supports the individual's right to smoke. Tobacco is a legal product in our country, available legally to those above a certain age. It's produced by a legal industry. Truth understands this. You'll never hear us call for a legal ban on smoking" ("About Us").

3. See also the website's "Whatta you think" page, where visitors can write in answers to such questions as "Do you think tobacco companies should list cigarette's ingredients on their packaging?" and "Tobacco

companies won the right, in the Supreme Court, to advertise near schools and playgrounds. Why do you think they would do that?").

Works Cited

"About Us. *Truth.* 23 Nov. 2004. http://www.thetruth.com/index.cfm?seek=aboutUs.

Aristotle. *On Rhetoric: A Theory of Civic Discourse.* Trans. George A. Kennedy. Oxford: Oxford UP, 1991.

The Citizens' Commission to Protect the Truth. *Protect the Truth.org.* 14 May 2005. http://www.protectthetruth.org/truthcampaign.htm.

The Citizens' Commission to Protect the Truth. *Find Facts.* 14 May 2005. http://www.thetruth.com/index.cfm?seek=facts.

Kinneavy, James L. and Susan C. Warshauer. "From Aristotle to Madison Avenue: Ethos and the Ethics of Argument." *Ethos: New Essays in Rhetorical and Critical Theory.* Ed. James S. Baumlin and Tita French Baumlin. Dallas: Southern Methodist UP, 1994. 171–90.

Locke, John. "From *An Essay Concerning Human Understanding.*" *The Rhetorical Tradition: Readings from Classical Times to the Present.* 2nd ed. Ed. Patricia Bizzell and Bruce Herzberg. Boston: Bedford/St. Martin's, 2001. 817–27.

Pechmann, Cornelia, Guangzhi Zhao, Marvin E. Goldberg, and Ellen Thomas Reibling. "What to Convey in Antismoking Advertisements for Adolescents: The Use of Protection Motivation Theory to Identify Effective Message Themes." *Journal of Marketing* 67 (2003): 1–18.

Plato. *Phaedrus.* Trans. H. N. Fowler. *The Rhetorical Tradition: Readings from Classical Times to the Present.* 2nd ed. Ed. Patricia Bizzell and Bruce Herzberg. Boston: Bedford/St. Martin's, 2001. 138–68.

Porter, James E. *Audience and Rhetoric: An Archaeological Composition of the Discourse Community.* Englewood Cliffs: Prentice Hall, 1992.

"The Surgeon General's Report on Reducing Tobacco Use: Tobacco Advertising and

Promotion Fact Sheet." U.S. Department of Health and Human Services. *Reducing Tobacco Use: A Report of the Surgeon General.* Atlanta: U.S. Department of Health and Human Services, Centers for Disease Control and Prevention, 2000. http://www.cdc.gov/tobacco/sgr/sgr_2000/Tobacco Advertising.pdf.

"Seek Truth." *Truth.* 23 Nov. 2004. http://www.thetruth.com/index.cfm?seek=truth.

"Whatta Ya Think? *Truth.* 23 Nov. 2004. http://www.thetruth.com/index.cfm?seek=whattya.

Zucker, David, R. S. Hopkins, David F. Sly, J. Urich, J. Mendza-Kershaw, and S. Solan. "Florida's Truth Campaign: A Counter-Marketing, Anti-Tobacco Media Campaign." *Journal of Public Health Management Practice* 6 (2000): 1–6.

A CLOSER LOOK AT
Discovering the Truth

1. Locate the places early in this rhetorical analysis where the author defines *ethos* in technical and historical terms. How are these definitions helpful for understanding the analysis of the Truth campaign later in the rhetorical analysis?

2. Feldmann suggests that teens, at whom these Truth advertisements are aimed, are different from other kinds of audiences. According to the article, what makes them unique and how does the Truth campaign try to appeal to them by using *ethos* to construct an argument?

3. The word "ethics" is related to *ethos*. Later in the rhetorical analysis, Feldmann argues that advertising campaigns like the Truth campaign can be built ethically on facts. Why does the author think behaving ethically in an anti-smoking campaign is especially important when reaching out to a teen audience?

IDEAS FOR
Writing

1. On *YouTube* or another video-sharing Web site, find some of the anti-smoking advertisements produced by the Truth campaign. Write an evaluation of one of these advertisements, using at least two criteria from Feldmann's rhetorical analysis.

2. In a commentary, discuss how advertisers succeed or fail to use *ethos* to reach out to teens. What are the qualities of an effective advertising campaign, and what makes these kinds of advertisements attractive to teens? Why do some advertisements fail, and how does the concept of *ethos* help us explain those failures?

A FEW IDEAS FOR
Composing a Rhetorical Analysis

1. **Write a rhetorical analysis focused on metaphors.** Chapter 8, "Rhetorical Analyses," talks briefly about how metaphors are used in writing. Find a common metaphor that is used in our society (e.g., "Time is money," "Thought is light," "War on cancer," "Argument is war") and then find examples of that metaphor in public use. In your rhetorical analysis, discuss how the metaphor shapes how people see particular issues. Discuss some of the perhaps unintended meanings or consequences of the metaphor you chose.

2. **Write a rhetorical analysis of three texts.** Compare and contrast the persuasive strategies used in these three texts. Show how different rhetorical strategies are intended to have different persuasive effects.

3. **Critique an ad found on a Web site.** Your ad critique should study the advertisement's uses of rhetorical strategies to persuade people to buy a particular product or use a specific service. How does the advertisement use *logos, ethos, pathos,* and visual appeals to try to be persuasive? Do you find the advertisement effective or not? Turn your ad critique into an electronic document (blog, Web site, *PowerPoint*) and link to the site with the ad.

38

Commentaries

A Gay Man's Case Against Gay Marriage

MICHAEL BRONSKI

In this commentary, Michael Bronski argues that homosexuals, especially gay men, should not become too focused on legalizing gay marriage. He points out that marriage among heterosexuals has been problematic and that homosexuals may have actually learned how to form better relationships outside of marriage. Pay attention to how he uses reasoning to argue against the conventional notion that marriage would be a good thing for homosexuals.

The best argument against same-sex marriage is the argument against marriage.

I've been a gay activist since the gay-liberation Stonewall Riots in 1969, and today I'm a visiting professor of gay and lesbian studies at Dartmouth College. I'm often asked why gay men and lesbians are fighting for same-sex marriage, and my answer is always the same: I don't really know. To me, the fight for same-sex marriage seems not so much shortsighted as beside the point.

Don't get me wrong. I completely support giving gay men and lesbians the right to partake of civil marriage, and the basic economic benefits that come with it, simply as a matter of equality under the law. Within a generation most states will likely follow Massachusetts' bold lead and insure marriage equality for all couples. It's a no-brainer: states that don't allow gay men and lesbians access to the legal status given to heterosexuals blatantly discriminate.

What I don't understand is why gay men and lesbians want to get married. The unswerving fight that gay men and lesbians have waged for marriage equality has been predicated largely on the idea that traditional marriage is the best possible form a relationship can take. For gay-marriage advocates, marriage carries the gold seal of approval: however loving, fruitful, or productive other relationships are, they are, by definition, not as good as marriage.

This is curious, given how deeply ambivalent 5 heterosexuals are about marriage. It's there in the 50 percent divorce rate, the high rates of spouse and child abuse, the incidence of adultery—check the record of the congressmen who voted for the Defense of Marriage Act, never mind average couples. Despite their distinct 1950s ring, jokes about balls-and-chains still abound, and the famous Mae West quip, "Marriage is an institution, I'm just not ready for an institution yet," still gets laughs.

What makes gay people think marriage will work better for them? It probably won't.

I'm not the sort of gay activist who thinks everything heterosexuals do is wrong. I see *Queer Eye for the Straight Guy* as a show about five busybodies who interfere in other people's lives with intrusive product placements. I also recognize that some marriages work marvelously: my parents' 50 wonderfully happy years together ended only with my mother's death a few years ago. But as it is practiced in the United States, we can all agree that marriage is not perfect, and for so many of us marriage no longer suits our current emotional or social needs. We—homosexuals and heterosexuals alike—might do better by spending some time rethinking how we want to live our emotional and sexual, private and public lives. Humans, straight and gay, have an amazing capacity for invention. In the past decades, we have seen myriad variations of expanded and extended families. These have had their flaws, too, but many have worked as well as, if not better, than traditional marriages. By the very fact that we have been forced into the position of outsiders, gay men and lesbians have invented new ways of forming community, of shaping and living our lives. Deprived of the right to traditional marriage, we have proven we can get along without it very well.

Gay-marriage proponents argue we should end these experiments, some saying marriage will "civilize" gay people by making us act more responsibly toward one another. William N. Eskridge titled his 1996 book *The Case for Same-Sex Marriage: From Sexual Liberty to Civilized Commitment.* Well, that just seems silly to me. Heterosexual marriage has not guaranteed better behavior once men and women tied the knot. Not incidentally, it is deeply homophobic to imply that gay people cannot and do not act decently or "civilized" now.

Other gay activists point to the benefits civil marriage brings in the form of tax breaks, inheritance arrangements, access to health care, and guaranteeing loans and credit. But we need to find a way to ensure that these are available to all people, not just those who decide to marry.

Much of the discussion about same-sex 10 marriage concerns deeper economic and social-justice issues: health care, raising children, and protecting family units from outside forces, especially poverty. But these too aren't really the concern of marriage. If you want to ensure that all families are secure and safe, if you want children to be healthy, and well fed and safe, there is plenty to do. You can fight for universal health

care or a higher minimum wage, for a negative income tax that will benefit anyone living close to or under the poverty line, for federally funded childcare, for federal funding to pay parents (both mothers and fathers) who choose to work at home caring for their children. When it comes to fighting for social justice, the right to traditional civil marriage seems pretty low on the agenda.

The gay-marriage movement isn't about these things. Nor is it about commitment or the sanctity of marriage. It is about sentiment and the power of advertising. People—gay and straight, but especially women—have a profound emotional attachment to the idea of marriage. (It is no surprise that close to 75 percent of couples who have applied for same-sex marriage licenses in San Francisco and now in Massachusetts are lesbians.) It is what we have always known, and we have a difficult time thinking of any other way to organize our lives. We also live in a culture that has a multibillion-dollar wedding industry, which inundates us everyday with the message that we will only be happy when we are married.

Equality under the law is nothing to scoff at. But will it make gay men and lesbians happier? In the long run, I doubt it. At least no happier than they are now, and certainly no happier, or unhappier, than heterosexuals. Now that we have it, I wonder if people will think it was worth the fight.

A CLOSER LOOK AT
A Gay Man's Case Against Gay Marriage

1. Early in the commentary, Bronski uses several methods to establish his credibility (*ethos*) to speak on this issue. What are a few methods he uses to build his authority with his likely readers, so they view him as a knowledgeable source of information?

2. Bronski's basic point is that "the best argument against same-sex marriage is the argument against

marriage." What are some of Bronski's arguments against marriage itself? Why does he find the concept of marriage problematic, whether it is between a man and a woman or two people of the same sex?

3. Instead of marriage, what kinds of legal protections and other rights does Bronski believe gays and lesbians should fight for?

1. Write a rhetorical analysis of Bronski's article. Pay special attention to how he uses rhetorical proofs to argue logically (*logos*), establish his authority (*ethos*), and introduce emotion (*pathos*) into his commentary.

2. In a brief proposal, describe a solution to the same-sex marriage issue that you believe all sides would agree is fair. What is the real problem that gays and lesbians are trying to solve by striving for marriage? What approach to this issue would be satisfactory to the majority of Americans? Discuss the costs and benefits of your plan, showing why it would be the best way to resolve this issue.

Female Chauvinist Pigs

ARIEL LEVY

In this commentary, which is from the introduction of Female Chauvinist Pigs, *Ariel Levy argues that women are actually taking steps back by embracing an over-sexualized popular culture. Pay attention to how Levy uses her own experiences and examples from popular culture to press home her main points.*

I first noticed it several years ago. I would turn on the television and find strippers in pasties explaining how best to lap dance a man to orgasm. I would flip the channel and see babes in tight, tiny uniforms bouncing up and down on trampolines. Britney Spears was becoming increasingly popular and increasingly unclothed, and her undulating body ultimately became so familiar to me I felt like we used to go out.

Charlie's Angels, the film remake of the quintessential jiggle show, opened at number one in 2000 and made $125 million in theaters nationally, reinvigorating the interest of men and women alike in leggy crime fighting. Its stars, who kept talking about "strong women" and "empowerment," were dressed in alternating soft-porn styles—as massage parlor geishas, dominatrixes, yodeling Heidis in alpine bustiers.

(The summer sequel in 2003—in which the Angels' perilous mission required them to perform stripteases—pulled in another $100 million domestically.) In my own industry, magazines, a porny new genre called the *Lad Mag*, which included titles like *Maxim, FHM,* and *Stuff,* was hitting the stands and becoming a huge success by delivering what *Playboy* had only occasionally managed to capture: greased celebrities in little scraps of fabric humping the floor.

This didn't end when I switched off the radio or the television or closed the magazines. I'd walk down the street and see teens and young women—and the occasional wild fifty-year-old—wearing jeans cut so low they exposed what came to be known as butt cleavage paired with miniature tops that showed off breast implants and pierced navels alike. Sometimes, in case the overall message of the outfit was too subtle, the shirts would be emblazoned with the *Playboy* bunny or say Porn Star across the chest.

Some odd things were happening in my social life, too. People I knew (female people) liked going to strip clubs (female strippers). It was sexy and fun, they explained; it was liberating and rebellious. My best friend from college, who used to go to Take Back the Night marches on campus, had become captivated by porn stars. She would point them out to me in music videos and watch their (topless) interviews on *Howard Stern*. As for me, I wasn't going to strip clubs or buying Hustler T-shirts, but I was starting to show signs of impact all the same. It had only been a few years since I'd graduated from Wesleyan University, a place where you could pretty much get expelled for saying "girl" instead of "woman," but somewhere along the line I'd started saying "chick." And, like most chicks I knew, I'd taken to wearing thongs.

What was going on? My mother, a shiatsu 5 masseuse who attended weekly women's consciousness-raising groups for twenty-four years, didn't own makeup. My father, whom she met as a student radical at the University of Wisconsin, Madison, in the sixties was a consultant for Planned Parenthood, NARAL, and NOW. Only thirty years (my lifetime) ago, our mothers were "burning their bras" and picketing *Playboy*, and suddenly we were getting implants and wearing the bunny logo as supposed symbols of our liberation. How had the culture shifted so drastically in such a short period of time?

What was almost more surprising than the change itself were the responses I got when I started interviewing the men and—often—women who edit magazines like *Maxim* and make programs like *The Man Show* and *Girls Gone Wild*. This new raunch culture didn't mark the death of feminism, they told me; it was evidence that the feminist project had already been achieved. We'd earned the right to look at *Playboy*; we were empowered enough to get Brazilian bikini waxes. Women had come so far, I learned, we no longer needed to worry about objectification or misogyny. Instead, it was time for us to join the frat party of pop culture, where men had been enjoying themselves all along. If Male Chauvinist Pigs were men who regarded women as pieces of meat, we would outdo them and be Female Chauvinist Pigs: women who make sex objects of other women and of ourselves.

When I asked female viewers and readers what they got out of raunch culture, I heard similar things about empowering miniskirts and feminist strippers, and so on, but I also heard something else. They wanted to be "one of the guys"; they hoped to be experienced "like a man." Going to strip clubs or talking about porn stars was a way of showing themselves and the men around them that they weren't "prissy little women" or "girlygirls." Besides, they told me, it was all in fun, all tongue-in-cheek, and for me to regard this bacchanal as problematic would be old-school and uncool. I tried to get with the program, but I could never make the argument add up in my head. How is resurrecting every stereotype of female sexuality that feminism endeavored to banish good for women? Why is laboring to look like Pamela Anderson empowering? And how is imitating a stripper or a porn star—a woman whose job is to imitate arousal in the first place—going to render us sexually liberated?

Despite the rising power of Evangelical Christianity and the political right in the United States, this trend has only grown more extreme and more pervasive in the years that have passed since I first became aware of it. A tawdry, tarty, cartoonlike version of female sexuality has become so ubiquitous, it no longer seems particular. What we once regarded as a kind of sexual expression we now view as sexuality. As former adult film star Traci Lords put it to a reporter a few days before her memoir hit the best-seller list in 2003, "When I was in porn, it was like a back-alley thing. Now it's everywhere." Spectacles of naked ladies have moved from seedy side streets to center stage, where everyone—men and women—can watch them in broad daylight. *Playboy* and its ilk are being "embraced by young women in a curious way in a postfeminist world," to borrow the words of Hugh Hefner.

But just because we are post doesn't automatically mean we are feminists. There is a widespread assumption that simply because my generation of women has the good fortune to live in a world touched by the feminist movement, that means everything we do is magically imbued with its agenda. It doesn't work that way. "Raunchy" and "liberated" are not synonyms. It is worth asking ourselves if this bawdy world of boobs and gams we have resurrected reflects how far we've come, or how far we have left to go.

A CLOSER LOOK AT
Female Chauvinist Pigs

1. In this article, Levy discusses how being a "feminist" has changed. What are some of the reasons she believes many women who consider themselves liberated have reverted back to objectifying other women and themselves?

2. Levy points out that many women believe the feminist battles have already been won. And now, because women have achieved equality, they believe expressions of their sexuality are part of their earned freedom. Do you agree that women are now equals with men in all ways? If not, what are some ways in which men and women aren't equal?

3. This article relies heavily on examples to support its arguments. Find three examples in the article. What effect do these examples have on the readers? Why are examples sometimes more persuasive than facts or reasoning?

IDEAS FOR
Writing

1. Many people would say that Americans are more conservative now than ever. Often, pundits talk about the United States as being a "center-right" nation. Write an argument in which you explore how and why an overall conservative culture also supports a thriving raunch industry. Or, discuss why you think the United States is not really conservative after all.

2. Write a profile of a public figure who was once known for using his or her looks or sexuality to gain attention. Choose someone who has been out of the spotlight for several years. How did this person rise to fame? When was the turning point in his or her career? What is he or she doing now?

Why Suing College Students for Illegal Music Downloading Is Right

MARCI A. HAMILTON

Marci A. Hamilton, a professor of law, argues that illegal music downloading may seem free to college students but that it has many hidden costs to our society. While reading her commentary, look for the ways she uses costs and benefits to argue that the advantages of suing college students for illegal music downloading outweigh the disadvantages.

Recently, and controversially, the recording industry has switched tactics in its fight against illegal downloading. Despite fear of a public relations debacle, it is planning to sue student downloaders.

First, however, it must identify them, and gather evidence of their illegal activity. Toward this end, subpoenas have already been sent to a number of universities and Internet Service Providers. Hundreds more are expected in September, after school starts.

Meanwhile, the Recording Industry Institute of America (RIAA) has not only led the fight for these lawsuits, but also joined together with campus administrators to educate students on the law and the consequences of violating it.

Some have criticized the RIAA and others in the music industry for going after students. But I will argue that it is entirely right—both legally and morally—for them to do so.

The enduring value of an enforceable copyright law

In a society that enjoys the benefit of a strong, 5 enforceable copyright law, it is too easy to forget what life would be like without it.

While my son went to space camp in Huntsville, Alabama, recently the rest of us went to Nashville, the home of country music and the Country Music Hall of Fame. The museum is excellent at many different levels, but my favorite element was the film of television clips showing country music over the past 50 years. Now, my mother is from Wyoming and my father from Kentucky, so I was destined to be a country-western music fan. The film brought back a million childhood memories; it also reminded me why copyright is such an absolute necessity.

Was it not for copyright's ability to build fences around intangible goods such as lyrics and melodies, a performer like Loretta Lynn would not have been able to leave Butcher Holler, Kentucky, and share her gifts with the world. The list of country music stars that have come from humble beginnings is long, and the best country music never forgets its origins.

The world would have been a lesser place but for copyright's ability to pave the road for these stars to travel from rags to riches, from hillbilly country to the big lights. The Country Music Hall of Fame gives you a real taste of that story as it displays the humble beginnings of some, as well as the gold-plated piano Priscilla Presley gave to Elvis on their first wedding anniversary.

In a culture without copyright, only the rich, or the government-sponsored, could be this culture's full-time creators. Poor artists such as Loretta Lynn would have to flip burgers long into their music careers—and might even give up on music entirely.

For these reasons, imagining a world with- 10 out copyright wouldn't just impoverish the musicians. It would also impoverish the museum, the culture, and music itself.

If the class of creators were winnowed down to the rich and the government-sponsored, and the free market were thus to be replaced by a patronage system, the ability of art to speak to the American people would dwindle precipitously. Artistic works would cater to elites; classical music might survive, but rock and country would encounter grave difficulties.

In the end, then, there is no such thing as cost-free downloading. It may be fiscally free today, but it will cost society dearly in the future.

The advent of the anti-copyright culture

The simple, yet crucial reasons why we have copyright in the first place are easy to forget in the new Information Era. Its utopian early years led adults and students alike to believe that whatever came across their computer screen could be—and ought to be—downloaded cost-free. There was a moment of stunned disbelief: copyright seemed obsolete.

Some saw this simply as a technological reality; others viewed it as a positive social development as well. In fact, it turned out that it was neither. Still, an anti-copyright culture developed—to the shock of the recording industry.

At first, the industry—wary of alienating the 15 young people who were often its best buyers—made a strategic decision to go after the big boys in court. That meant targeting Napster—and soon the industry won its fight.

Nevertheless, the industry continued to hemorrhage, dropping approximately 8 percent in sales last year. The culprits may well be the new Web sites, such as KaZaa, which, unlike Napster, do not depend on centralized servers. These sites accordingly make it nearly impossible to identify the Web host or master.

The industry then had no choice but to go after users—which meant going after students—and it did. As soon as it made the decision, copyright didn't seem so obsolete, after all.

While technology did tend to facilitate illegal downloading, it did not pose infinite obstacles to figuring out who was committing these copyright crimes; universities and ISPs alike tracked their users in certain ways. Although the industry will continue to work on improving the technological protection for works on the Web, for now, the courts will serve them quite well.

That goes to show that, with respect to copyright, new rules are not needed; just enforcement of the old. We were never living in a true legal vacuum, as the "Information Wants to Be Free" contingent suggested; we were living in an enforcement vacuum instead, and that is now changing, as violators are being hunted down.

Even the hunt itself has had a chilling effect. 20 Knowing that one is committing a crime, and may be caught, is scary indeed. Students will back off of illegal copying once they learn that the free ride was an illusion; and if they don't, many parents will step in to ensure that their children don't earn a criminal record along with their college diploma.

Like shoplifting, illegal downloading can be reduced by monitoring and warning.

In a lot of ways, downloading is more like shoplifting than it is like "piracy," the term often used for it. Pirates embrace a life of crime; shoplifters often see their activity (wrongly) as an exciting and slightly risky diversion—a relatively petty vice in an otherwise law-abiding life.

The more seriously society takes shoplifting, the more shoplifters will be deterred. The same is true, I believe, for illegal downloaders. Every law-breaking student has a diploma at stake, and only a scintilla of students is hardened criminals. Like the thrill of shoplifting, the thrill of illegal downloading may fade quickly in the face of serious penalties, and a real risk of getting caught.

Of course, technological "locks" won't be perfect, and some level of crime will remain. But here, again, the shoplifting analogy is instructive. Stores do not lock up every item they offer to prevent shoplifting. Instead, they post signs saying shoplifting is a crime, monitor their customers, and press charges against individual shoplifters. Despite all this, retail stores have had to build into their profit picture losses that will result from undetected shoplifting.

The recording industry will have to use sim- 25 ilar tactics, and like retail stores, they will have to live with a small loss from undetected stealing. But that loss can be minimized, through warnings, monitoring, and enforcement. And word of enforcement spreads. Few will be shoplifting from the store that famously pressed charges against Winona Ryder. Few students will keep downloading once their classmates have famously gotten in deep trouble for doing just that. That is good for them, but even better for us.

A CLOSER LOOK AT

Why Suing College Students for Illegal Music Downloading Is Right

1. According to Hamilton, what are the benefits of copyright laws and why should they be preserved?

2. List three reasons why Hamilton believes that the music industry has the right and the obligation to sue college students who download music illegally.

3. Hamilton calls illegal downloading a crime. What kind of crime does she believe it is similar to?

IDEAS FOR

Writing

1. Do you agree or disagree with Hamilton's argument? Write a letter to the editor in which you argue against or support her position. What are some of the weaknesses and strengths of her argument? As a college student, what kinds of new insights can you offer into this problem of illegal music downloading?

2. Write a brief report for your university's administration in which you discuss the amount of illegal music downloading among college students at your school. Besides online and print sources, also use some empirical sources like surveys and interviews to strengthen your research. Explain whether there is a problem with illegal music downloading and offer some options for handling this issue.

Challenging Veteran Stereotypes

KEN HARBAUGH

Veteran Ken Harbaugh served for nine years as a Navy pilot and was deployed several times to the Middle East. He also graduated from Yale Law School in 2008 after he returned from duty. In this commentary, which first aired on National Public Radio, he argues against the stereotypes of "damaged" veterans that are often used in movies. Pay special attention to the ways he uses reasoning and his own credibility to comment on an issue that troubles him.

America's wars in Iraq and Afghanistan are the most filmed conflicts in history. Already a flood of documentaries and movies have come out, purporting to show what is really happening. On balance, this is a good thing. For a democracy like ours to make the best decisions about war, we must be informed.

I worry though, that the veterans' experience is being portrayed in a way that could hurt for years to come. Most Americans have not seen combat, much less in Iraq or Afghanistan. The prevailing image of today's veteran is gotten through the media, through movies and pictures that often dwell on the trauma of war, the injury it does to the body and the psyche.

This focus on the "damaged" veteran is, for the most part, well intentioned. As a nation, we have no higher moral duty, none, than caring for those we send to do our fighting.

Yet this picture of the veteran scarred by war is incomplete, and often unfair. Some do return physically and emotionally shattered. But not most. Indeed, the vast majority of my former military friends are not only proud of having served, but feel that it made them stronger. This is not a defense of war or the wisdom of our current policies. Still, the act of serving your country, alongside other Americans you would give your life for, I believe changes a person for the better.

After Vietnam, the media created an image ₅ of returning vets as crazed sociopaths, unable to readjust to civilian life. Movies like *Deerhunter* and *Rambo* were standard fare, depicting vets as damaged goods. We're starting to see the same

myth emerge today, with movies like *Ground Truth* and *In the Valley of Elah*.

I applaud anyone who shines light on the plight of those veterans traumatized by war. Their story is important. Americans need to hear it. But pretending that this is every veteran's experience is wrong.

The truth is that many vets adapt extremely well to life after the military. Data from the Bureau of Labor Statistics show vets today are more likely to be employed than their nonveteran counterparts. According to the Justice Department, they're less likely to be imprisoned. And in a survey commissioned by the VA, ninety-one percent of Vietnam veterans who had seen combat said they were "glad they had served their country."

Our veterans are an asset, not a liability. This applies even to those wounded. Many I've talked to would rejoin their units in a heartbeat if they could. That isn't about the justness of our foreign policy. It's about bravery. It's about love. The overwhelming majority of veterans today are proud to have worn the uniform.

I suppose we'll just have to wait for a movie about that.

A CLOSER LOOK AT
Challenging Veteran Stereotypes

1. In what ways does Harbaugh make parallels between the movies made after Vietnam and the movies being made today about the Iraq war? What concerns him about the parallels he sees in these movies from two different eras?

2. Harbaugh is troubled that movies and the media often offer a negative portrayal of "damaged" veterans who return from war. According to Harbaugh, what

exactly is problematic about the kinds of characters these movies and the media are featuring?

3. In a few places, Harbaugh uses concessions to qualify his argument. (See Chapter 22 for more on concession as an argumentative strategy.) Find a few of these concessions and discuss how they strengthen his commentary.

IDEAS FOR
Writing

1. Watch one of the movies Harbaugh lists in this commentary or another movie about soldiers returning from war. Write a review in which you talk specifically about how the movie portrays veterans.

In your review, discuss whether you think the movie relies too much on stereotypes and whether those stereotypes are harmful to veterans and society's understanding of war and its aftermath.

2. Write a brief profile in which you describe the life of a veteran. Your profile could be written about a family member, friend, or acquaintance. Or you can write about a historical figure. In your profile, discuss this person's service. Then discuss his or her life after returning from war.

A FEW IDEAS FOR
Composing a Commentary

1. **Write a commentary for a news Web site.** Choose a controversial issue that interests you and find a relevant story on a news Web site like *CNN, MSNBC,* or *FoxNews.* Do some research on the subject and write a commentary in which you respond to and offer your opinion on this issue.

2. **Write a commentary comparing two views.** Find two commentaries on the same topic in magazines or on a news Web site. Where do these commentaries differ? Where are their views similar? Which commentator do you tend to agree with and why?

3. **Write a letter to the editor for a news Web site.** Choose one of the four commentaries printed in this chapter and challenge or support its argument. What are this person's weakest arguments? Where do you agree with the commentary? What might you add, based on your own experience?

39

Arguments

A More Perfect Union

BARACK OBAMA

Barack Obama delivered this speech on March 18, 2008, before he was nominated as the 2008 Democratic Party presidential candidate. The speech is, in part, a reaction to television and Internet news stories that displayed the speeches of Obama's pastor, Jeremiah Wright. In those speeches, Wright denounced the American government for committing crimes against African Americans and other people of color. Critics of Obama charged that his position must reflect that of his pastor and that his political views, therefore, must be far more extreme than he had indicated. Obama delivered this speech to clarify his views about race in America's past, present, and future. Pay attention to the way he carefully criticizes Wright's statements (calling them both "wrong" and "divisive") but also explains why it is understandable that some people would come to hold such positions.

"We the people, in order to form a more perfect union."

Two hundred and twenty-one years ago, in a hall that still stands across the street, a group of men gathered and, with these simple words, launched America's improbable experiment in democracy. Farmers and scholars, statesmen and patriots who had traveled across an ocean to escape tyranny and persecution finally made real their declaration of independence at a Philadelphia convention that lasted through the spring of 1787.

The document they produced was eventually signed but ultimately unfinished. It was stained by this nation's original sin of slavery, a question that divided the colonies and brought the convention to a stalemate until the founders chose to allow the slave trade to continue for at least twenty more years, and to leave any final resolution to future generations.

Of course, the answer to the slavery question was already embedded within our Constitution—a Constitution that had at its very core the ideal of equal citizenship under the law; a Constitution that promised its people liberty, and justice, and a union that could be and should be perfected over time.

And yet words on a parchment would not be 5 enough to deliver slaves from bondage, or provide men and women of every color and creed their full rights and obligations as citizens of the United States. What would be needed were Americans in successive generations who were willing to do their part—through protests and struggle, on the streets and in the courts, through a civil war and civil disobedience and always at great risk—to narrow that gap between the promise of our ideals and the reality of their time.

This was one of the tasks we set forth at the beginning of this campaign—to continue the long march of those who came before us, a march for a more just, more equal, more free, more caring and more prosperous America. I chose to run for the presidency at this moment in history because I believe deeply that we cannot solve the challenges of our time unless we solve them together—unless we perfect our union by understanding that we may have different stories, but we hold common hopes; that we may not look the same and we may not have come from the same place, but we all want to move in the same direction—towards a better future for our children and our grandchildren.

This belief comes from my unyielding faith in the decency and generosity of the American people. But it also comes from my own American story.

I am the son of a black man from Kenya and a white woman from Kansas. I was raised with the help of a white grandfather who survived a Depression to serve in Patton's army during

World War II and a white grandmother who worked on a bomber assembly line at Fort Leavenworth while he was overseas. I've gone to some of the best schools in America and lived in one of the world's poorest nations. I am married to a black American who carries within her the blood of slaves and slaveowners—an inheritance we pass on to our two precious daughters. I have brothers, sisters, nieces, nephews, uncles and cousins, of every race and every hue, scattered across three continents, and for as long as I live, I will never forget that in no other country on Earth is my story even possible.

It's a story that hasn't made me the most conventional candidate. But it is a story that has seared into my genetic makeup the idea that this nation is more than the sum of its parts—that out of many, we are truly one.

Throughout the first year of this campaign, 10 against all predictions to the contrary, we saw how hungry the American people were for this message of unity. Despite the temptation to view my candidacy through a purely racial lens, we won commanding victories in states with some of the whitest populations in the country. In South Carolina, where the Confederate Flag still flies, we built a powerful coalition of African Americans and white Americans.

This is not to say that race has not been an issue in the campaign. At various stages in the campaign, some commentators have deemed me either "too black" or "not black enough." We saw racial tensions bubble to the surface during the week before the South Carolina primary. The press has scoured every exit poll for the latest evidence of racial polarization, not just in terms of white and black, but black and brown as well.

And yet, it has only been in the last couple of weeks that the discussion of race in this campaign has taken a particularly divisive turn.

On one end of the spectrum, we've heard the implication that my candidacy is somehow an exercise in affirmative action; that it's based solely on the desire of wide-eyed liberals to purchase racial reconciliation on the cheap. On the other end, we've heard my former pastor, Reverend Jeremiah Wright, use incendiary language to express views that have the potential not only to widen the racial divide, but views that denigrate both the greatness and the goodness of our nation; that rightly offend white and black alike.

I have already condemned, in unequivocal terms, the statements of Reverend Wright that have caused such controversy. For some, nagging questions remain. Did I know him to be an occasionally fierce critic of American domestic and foreign policy? Of course. Did I ever hear him make remarks that could be considered controversial while I sat in church? Yes. Did I strongly disagree with many of his political views? Absolutely—just as I'm sure many of you have heard remarks from your pastors, priests, or rabbis with which you strongly disagreed.

But the remarks that have caused this recent 15 firestorm weren't simply controversial. They weren't simply a religious leader's effort to speak out against perceived injustice. Instead, they expressed a profoundly distorted view of this country—a view that sees white racism as endemic, and that elevates what is wrong with America above all that we know is right with America; a view that sees the conflicts in the Middle East as rooted primarily in the actions of stalwart allies like Israel, instead of emanating from the perverse and hateful ideologies of radical Islam.

As such, Reverend Wright's comments were not only wrong but divisive, divisive at a time when we need unity; racially charged at a time when we need to come together to solve a set of monumental problems—two wars, a terrorist threat, a falling economy, a chronic health care crisis, and potentially devastating climate change; problems that are neither black or white or Latino or Asian, but rather problems that confront us all.

Given my background, my politics, and my professed values and ideals, there will no doubt be those for whom my statements of condemnation are not enough. Why associate myself with Reverend Wright in the first place, they may ask? Why not join another church? And I confess that if all that I knew of Reverend Wright were the snippets of those sermons that have run in an endless loop on the television and *YouTube*, or if

Trinity United Church of Christ conformed to the caricatures being peddled by some commentators, there is no doubt that I would react in much the same way.

But the truth is, that isn't all that I know of the man. The man I met more than twenty years ago is a man who helped introduce me to my Christian faith, a man who spoke to me about our obligations to love one another; to care for the sick and lift up the poor. He is a man who served his country as a U.S. Marine; who has studied and lectured at some of the finest universities and seminaries in the country, and who for over thirty years led a church that serves the community by doing God's work here on Earth—by housing the homeless, ministering to the needy, providing day care services and scholarships and prison ministries, and reaching out to those suffering from HIV/AIDS.

In my first book, *Dreams from My Father*, I described the experience of my first service at Trinity:

> People began to shout, to rise from their seats and clap and cry out, a forceful wind carrying the reverend's voice up into the rafters. . . . And in that single note—hope!—I heard something else; at the foot of that cross, inside the thousands of churches across the city, I imagined the stories of ordinary black people merging with the stories of David and Goliath, Moses and Pharaoh, the Christians in the lion's den, Ezekiel's field of dry bones. Those stories—of survival, and freedom, and hope—became our story, my story; the blood that had spilled was our blood, the tears our tears; until this black church, on this bright day, seemed once more a vessel carrying the story of a people into future generations and into a larger world. Our trials and triumphs became at once unique and universal, black and more than black; in chronicling our journey, the stories and songs gave us a means to reclaim memories that we didn't need to feel

shame about . . . memories that all people might study and cherish—and with which we could start to rebuild.

That has been my experience at Trinity. Like other predominantly black churches across the country, Trinity embodies the black community in its entirety—the doctor and the welfare mom, the model student and the former gang-banger. Like other black churches, Trinity's services are full of raucous laughter and sometimes bawdy humor. They are full of dancing, clapping, screaming, and shouting that may seem jarring to the untrained ear. The church contains in full the kindness and cruelty, the fierce intelligence and the shocking ignorance, the struggles and successes, the love and yes, the bitterness and bias that make up the black experience in America.

And this helps explain, perhaps, my relationship with Reverend Wright. As imperfect as he may be, he has been like family to me. He strengthened my faith, officiated my wedding, and baptized my children. Not once in my conversations with him have I heard him talk about any ethnic group in derogatory terms, or treat whites with whom he interacted with anything but courtesy and respect. He contains within him the contradictions—the good and the bad—of the community that he has served diligently for so many years.

I can no more disown him than I can disown the black community. I can no more disown him than I can my white grandmother—a woman who helped raise me, a woman who sacrificed again and again for me, a woman who loves me as much as she loves anything in this world, but a woman who once confessed her fear of black men who passed by her on the street, and who on more than one occasion has uttered racial or ethnic stereotypes that made me cringe.

These people are a part of me. And they are a part of America, this country that I love.

Some will see this as an attempt to justify or excuse comments that are simply inexcusable. I can assure you it is not. I suppose the politically safe thing would be to move on from this episode and just hope that it fades into the woodwork. We can dismiss Reverend Wright as a crank or a demagogue, just as some have dismissed Geraldine Ferraro, in the aftermath of her recent statements, as harboring some deep-seated racial bias.

But race is an issue that I believe this nation 25 cannot afford to ignore right now. We would be making the same mistake that Reverend Wright made in his offending sermons about America—to simplify and stereotype and amplify the negative to the point that it distorts reality.

The fact is that the comments that have been made and the issues that have surfaced over the last few weeks reflect the complexities of race in this country that we've never really worked through—a part of our union that we have yet to perfect. And if we walk away now, if we simply retreat into our respective corners, we will never be able to come together and solve challenges like health care, or education, or the need to find good jobs for every American.

Understanding this reality requires a reminder of how we arrived at this point. As William Faulkner once wrote, "The past isn't dead and buried. In fact, it isn't even past." We do not need to recite here the history of racial injustice in this country. But we do need to remind ourselves that so many of the disparities that exist in the African-American community today can be directly traced to inequalities passed on from an earlier generation that suffered under the brutal legacy of slavery and Jim Crow. Segregated schools were, and are, inferior schools; we still haven't fixed them, fifty years after *Brown v. Board of Education,* and the inferior education they provided, then and now, helps explain the pervasive achievement gap between today's black and white students.

Legalized discrimination—where blacks were prevented, often through violence, from owning property, or loans were not granted to African-American business owners, or black homeowners could not access FHA mortgages, or blacks were excluded from unions, or the police force, or fire departments—meant that black families could not amass any meaningful wealth to bequeath to future generations. That history helps explain the wealth and income gap between black and white, and the concentrated pockets of poverty that persists in so many of today's urban and rural communities.

A lack of economic opportunity among black men, and the shame and frustration that came from not being able to provide for one's family, contributed to the erosion of black families—a problem that welfare policies for many years may have worsened. And the lack of basic services in so many urban black neighborhoods—parks for kids to play in, police walking the beat, regular garbage pick-up and building code enforcement—all helped create a cycle of violence, blight, and neglect that continue to haunt us.

This is the reality in which Reverend Wright 30 and other African Americans of his generation grew up. They came of age in the late fifties and early sixties, a time when segregation was still the law of the land and opportunity was systematically constricted. What's remarkable is not how many failed in the face of discrimination, but rather how many men and women overcame the odds; how many were able to make a way out of no way for those like me who would come after them.

But for all those who scratched and clawed their way to get a piece of the American Dream, there were many who didn't make it—those who were ultimately defeated, in one way or another, by discrimination. That legacy of defeat was passed on to future generations—those young men and increasingly young women who we see standing on street corners or languishing in our prisons, without hope or prospects for the future. Even for those blacks who did make it, questions of race, and racism, continue to define their worldview in fundamental ways. For the men and women of Reverend Wright's generation, the memories of humiliation and doubt and fear have not gone away; nor has the anger and the bitterness of those years. That anger may not get expressed in public, in front of white co-workers or white friends. But it does find voice in the barbershop or around the kitchen table. At times, that anger is exploited by politicians, to gin up votes along racial lines, or to make up for a politician's own failings.

And occasionally it finds voice in the church on Sunday morning, in the pulpit and in the pews. The fact that so many people are surprised to hear that anger in some of Reverend Wright's sermons simply reminds us of the old truism that the most segregated hour in American life occurs on Sunday morning. That anger is not always productive; indeed, all too often it distracts attention from solving real problems; it keeps us from squarely facing our own complicity in our condition, and prevents the African-American community from forging the alliances it needs to bring about real change. But the anger is real; it is powerful; and to simply wish it away, to condemn it without understanding its roots, only serves to widen the chasm of misunderstanding that exists between the races.

In fact, a similar anger exists within segments of the white community. Most working- and middle-class white Americans don't feel that they have been particularly privileged by their race. Their experience is the immigrant experience—as far as they're concerned, no one's handed them anything, they've built it from scratch. They've worked hard all their lives, many times only to see their jobs shipped overseas or their pension dumped after a lifetime of labor. They are anxious about their futures, and feel their dreams slipping away; in an era of stagnant wages and global competition, opportunity comes to be seen as a zero sum game, in which your dreams come at my expense. So when they are told to bus their children to a school across town; when they hear that an African American is getting an advantage in landing a good job or a spot in a good college because of an injustice that they themselves never committed; when they're told that their fears about crime in urban neighborhoods are somehow prejudiced, resentment builds over time.

Like the anger within the black community, these resentments aren't always expressed in polite company. But they have helped shape the political landscape for at least a generation. Anger over welfare and affirmative action helped forge the Reagan Coalition. Politicians routinely exploited fears of crime for their own electoral ends. Talk show hosts and conservative commentators built entire careers unmasking bogus claims of racism while dismissing legitimate discussions of racial injustice and inequality as mere political correctness or reverse racism.

Just as black anger often proved counterproductive, so have these white resentments distracted attention from the real culprits of the middle class squeeze—a corporate culture rife with inside dealing, questionable accounting practices, and short-term greed; a Washington dominated by lobbyists and special interests; economic policies that favor the few over the many. And yet, to wish away the resentments of white Americans, to label them as misguided or even racist, without recognizing they are grounded in legitimate concerns—this too widens the racial divide, and blocks the path to understanding.

This is where we are right now. It's a racial stalemate we've been stuck in for years. Contrary to the claims of some of my critics, black and white, I have never been so naive as to believe that we can get beyond our racial divisions in a single election cycle, or with a single candidacy—particularly a candidacy as imperfect as my own.

But I have asserted a firm conviction—a conviction rooted in my faith in God and my faith in the American people—that working together we can move beyond some of our old racial wounds, and that in fact we have no choice if we are to continue on the path of a more perfect union.

For the African-American community, that path means embracing the burdens of our past without becoming victims of our past. It means continuing to insist on a full measure of justice in every aspect of American life. But it also means binding our particular grievances—for better health care, and better schools, and better jobs—to the larger aspirations of all Americans—the white woman struggling to break the glass ceiling, the white man who has been laid off, the immigrant trying to feed his family. And it means taking full responsibility for our own lives—by demanding more from our fathers, and spending more time with our children, and reading to them, and teaching them that while they may face challenges and discrimination in their own lives, they must never succumb to despair or cynicism; they must always believe that they can write their own destiny.

Ironically, this quintessentially American—and yes, conservative—notion of self-help found frequent expression in Reverend Wright's sermons. But what my former pastor too often failed to understand is that embarking on a program of self-help also requires a belief that society can change.

The profound mistake of Reverend Wright's 40 sermons is not that he spoke about racism in our society. It's that he spoke as if our society was static; as if no progress has been made; as if this country—a country that has made it possible for one of his own members to run for the highest office in the land and build a coalition of white and black; Latino and Asian, rich and poor, young and old—is still irrevocably bound to a tragic past. But what we know—what we have seen—is that America can change. That is the true genius of this nation. What we have already achieved gives us hope—the audacity to hope—for what we can and must achieve tomorrow.

In the white community, the path to a more perfect union means acknowledging that what ails the African-American community does not just exist in the minds of black people; that the legacy of discrimination—and current incidents of discrimination, while less overt than in the past—are real and must be addressed. Not just with words, but with deeds—by investing in our schools and our communities; by enforcing our civil rights laws and ensuring fairness in our criminal justice system; by providing this generation with ladders of opportunity that were unavailable for previous generations. It requires all Americans to realize that your dreams do not have to come at the expense of my dreams; that investing in the health, welfare, and education of black and brown and white children will ultimately help all of America prosper.

In the end, then, what is called for is nothing more, and nothing less, than what all the world's great religions demand—that we do unto others as we would have them do unto us. Let us be our brother's keeper, Scripture tells us. Let us be our sister's keeper. Let us find that common stake we all have in one another, and let our politics reflect that spirit as well.

For we have a choice in this country. We can accept a politics that breeds division, and conflict, and cynicism. We can tackle race only as spectacle—as we did in the OJ trial—or in the wake of tragedy, as we did in the aftermath of Katrina—or as fodder for the nightly news. We can play Reverend Wright's sermons on every channel, every day and talk about them from now until the election, and make the only question in this campaign whether or not the American people think that I somehow believe or sympathize with his most offensive words. We can pounce on some gaffe by a Hillary supporter as evidence that she's playing the race card, or we can speculate on whether white men will all flock to John McCain in the general election regardless of his policies.

We can do that.

But if we do, I can tell you that in the next 45 election, we'll be talking about some other distraction. And then another one. And then another one. And nothing will change.

That is one option. Or, at this moment, in this election, we can come together and say, "Not this time." This time we want to talk about the crumbling schools that are stealing the future of black children and white children and Asian children and Hispanic children and Native American children. This time we want to reject the cynicism that tells us that these kids can't learn; that those kids who don't look like us are somebody else's problem. The children of America are not those kids, they are our kids, and we will not let them fall behind in a 21st-century economy. Not this time.

This time we want to talk about how the lines in the emergency room are filled with whites and blacks and Hispanics who do not have health care; who don't have the power on their own to overcome the special interests in Washington, but who can take them on if we do it together.

This time we want to talk about the shuttered mills that once provided a decent life for men and women of every race, and the homes for sale that once belonged to Americans from every religion, every region, every walk of life. This time we want to talk about the fact that the real problem is not that someone who doesn't look like you might take your job; it's that the corporation you work for will ship it overseas for nothing more than a profit.

This time we want to talk about the men and women of every color and creed who serve together, and fight together, and bleed together under the same proud flag. We want to talk about how to bring them home from a war that never should've been authorized and never should've been waged, and we want to talk about how we'll show our patriotism by caring for them, and their families, and giving them the benefits they have earned.

I would not be running for president if I 50 didn't believe with all my heart that this is what the vast majority of Americans want for this country. This union may never be perfect, but generation after generation has shown that it can always be perfected. And today, whenever I find myself feeling doubtful or cynical about this possibility, what gives me the most hope is the next generation—the young people whose attitudes and beliefs and openness to change have already made history in this election.

There is one story in particular that I'd like to leave you with today—a story I told when I had the great honor of speaking on Dr. King's birthday at his home church, Ebenezer Baptist, in Atlanta.

There is a young, twenty-three-year-old white woman named Ashley Baia who organized for our campaign in Florence, South Carolina. She had been working to organize a mostly African-American community since the beginning of this campaign, and one day she was at a roundtable discussion where everyone went around telling their story and why they were there.

And Ashley said that when she was nine years old, her mother got cancer. And because she had to miss days of work, she was let go and lost her health care. They had to file for bankruptcy, and that's when Ashley decided that she had to do something to help her mom.

She knew that food was one of their most expensive costs, and so Ashley convinced her mother that what she really liked and really wanted to eat more than anything else was mustard and relish sandwiches. Because that was the cheapest way to eat.

She did this for a year until her mom got bet- 55 ter, and she told everyone at the roundtable that the reason she joined our campaign was so that she could help the millions of other children in the country who want and need to help their parents too.

Now Ashley might have made a different choice. Perhaps somebody told her along the way that the source of her mother's problems were blacks who were on welfare and too lazy to work, or Hispanics who were coming into the country illegally. But she didn't. She sought out allies in her fight against injustice.

Anyway, Ashley finishes her story and then goes around the room and asks everyone else why they're supporting the campaign. They all have different stories and reasons. Many bring up a specific issue. And finally they come to this elderly black man who's been sitting there quietly the entire time. And Ashley asks him why he's there. And he does not bring up a specific issue. He does not say health care or the economy. He does not say education or the war. He does not say that he was there because of Barack Obama. He simply says to everyone in the room, "I am here because of Ashley."

"I'm here because of Ashley." By itself, that single moment of recognition between that young white girl and that old black man is not enough. It is not enough to give health care to the sick, or jobs to the jobless, or education to our children.

But it is where we start. It is where our union grows stronger. And as so many generations have come to realize over the course of the two hundred and twenty-one years since a band of patriots signed that document in Philadelphia, that is where the perfection begins.

A CLOSER LOOK AT
A More Perfect Union

1. Read "A More Perfect Union" a second time or watch it on the Internet, noting those portions of the speech that most stand out for you. In some places, Obama begins several sentences in a row with the same word or phrase (a technique that is called *anaphora*). What effect do those passages have on the audience?

2. Find this speech on *YouTube* and watch it. Describe how seeing and hearing the speech was different than reading it. What ideas and key points came through stronger? What did you notice about the speech that you didn't notice while reading it?

3. If you were going to state the main point of this speech in a sentence or two, what would it be? Read the speech again or listen to it with the transcript in front of you. This time, though, highlight or underline the words, phrases, and sentences that seem to state important, larger points. Then look back on what you have highlighted and try to capture in your own words what Obama is trying to convey.

IDEAS FOR
Writing

1. Obama delivered this speech in part to answer public demands that he explain in precise and direct terms his beliefs and guiding principles about race in America. In this sense, the speech could be said to belong to the "manifesto" genre, which is a blend of the commentary, memoir, and other genres such as profiles and proposals. Write a manifesto that makes a public declaration of the principles that you believe in and the values that guide your life. Your response may be political, religious, philosophical, or personal.

2. Write a rhetorical analysis of "A More Perfect Union" that focuses on any aspect of the speech: its use of *ethos, pathos, logos,* or style and arrangement. Use this focus on one or two aspects to arrive at a new insight about the speech that goes beyond the obvious.

Reconsidering Match.com's Sex Offender Ban

TRACY CLARK-FLORY

Genuine arguments engage with others' beliefs, values, and opinions, especially people who disagree with the author. In this argument, Tracy Clark-Flory responds to a tweet from Katha Pollitt, who challenged an article Clark-Flory had published just two days earlier. Notice how Clark-Flory responds to Pollitt's objection, not by changing her position completely but by clarifying the issue she sees as most important and by softening her position somewhat.

When *The Nation's* Katha Pollitt took me to task on Twitter over my piece on *Match .com's* decision to ban sex offenders (Clark-Flory) from the site, I was horrified—but, OK, also kind of honored. She's a writer I admire and respect, and a challenge from her is one I take seriously. "You let perfect be [the] enemy of good," she tweeted (Pollitt). "Women know this isn't complete protection. But it's something." She's right, it *is* something—and something is better than nothing, right? So, I decided to take another look at the issue.

One thing I want to revisit right off the bat is this statement in my original post on the subject: "Besides, we already make it hard enough for offenders to reenter society, and further ostracizing them only encourages recidivism." Looking back at it now, I realize that it might sound like I'm asking women to date rapists to prevent recidivism—which is how Pollitt took it—and I absolutely didn't mean to suggest that. It isn't women's responsibility to romantically reintegrate sex offenders into society. You will not see me signing up for that act of altruism, or whatever you want to call it. What I was trying to get at was that some of our many protective measures—like residence restrictions that in some cities effectively require sex offenders to be homeless—do a real disservice to attempts to reintegrate criminals who have served their time.

The main issue here, as far as I see it, is that sex offender registries clumsily lump together *all* sex crimes. In recent years, a host of less extreme offenses have been included as grounds for registration: "voyeurism, public exposure, adultery, giving obscene material to a minor, displaying obscene material on a bumper sticker, and bestiality," according to a report by the Vera Institute of Justice (Velázquez 2). Also, some states require registration for those "possessing computer-generated images of virtual children." This isn't the case across the board nationwide, but a Human Rights Watch report breaks it down on a state-by-state level, and the results are staggering: "At least five states require registration for adult prostitution-related offenses," 13 "require registration for public urination," 29 "require registration for consensual sex between teenagers," and 32 "require registration for exposing genitals in public."

This has led to the rise of low-risk offenders on registries. Take Georgia, for example: The state's Registration Review Board found that just 5 percent of listed sex offenders were "clearly dangerous" and two-thirds posed a small risk (Economist). Just over 100 of the 17,000 registered sex offenders in the state were considered "predators." HRW explains, "Most states do not make individualized risk assessments before requiring registration. Nor do they offer former offenders a way to get off the registry upon a showing of rehabilitation or years of lawful behavior." The result is that we have nearly 700,000 registered sex offenders in this country. To put that in some perspective, "more than one in 160 adult males are registered sex offenders," according to the Vera Institute's calculations (Velázquez 1).

As far as recidivism goes: 5 percent of all sex offenders were arrested for another sex crime within three years of their release from prison; 5

and 3.5 were convicted. A report in the journal Criminology and Public Policy found that 6.5 percent of sex offenders re-offended within five years of release. As Vera summarizes, "only people arrested for homicide had a lower five-year offense-specific re arrest rate" (Velázquez 6). When you look specifically at sex offenders convicted of forcible rape, things become much more alarming: 25 percent were arrested for a sex crime within 15 years of their release (Matson and Lieb 10).

Our registries desperately need to be reformed, and we could greatly benefit from better data about recidivism for different sex offense types—but that's a much bigger task than simply screening on Match.com. On that front, maybe I *am* making perfect the enemy of good. Eliminating some high-risk predators from the online dating pool is better than nothing. Still, Match.com's approach of banning all registered sex offenders—even those who are low-risk or who committed minor offenses—strikes me as unjust. In the case of Georgia, the site's ban means restricting access to 95 percent of registered offenders who are not "clearly dangerous" and two-thirds who are low-risk. That seems an inept way to screen out men who pose a serious danger to women—especially when you consider that most assaults go unreported and most sex crimes are committed by those without a sex crime record.

It would make a whole lot more sense for Match.com to only ban high-risk offenders. But that is impractical for the same reason that the company avoided instituting any screening procedure for so long: The network of state sex offender databases is a mess. So, in the interest of

(largely) women's safety, and given the lack of options, is it worth banning all registrants, including those who pose a low risk? It just might be—I won't pretend to know the right answer here. In any case, Match.com is a private company and it can do whatever it thinks is best for business—and it's very likely that this is what its customers want. I just think it's important to make sure to keep things in rational perspective, especially when talking about such an emotional subject.

Works Cited

Bureau of Justice Statistics. "Recidivism" United States Department of Justice. No date. Web. 20 Apr. 2011.

Clark-Flory, Tracy. "*Match.com* Bans Sex Offenders—Feel Safe Now?" *Salon.com*. Salon Media Group, Inc. 18 Apr. 2011.Web. 20 Apr. 2011

Economist. "Unjust and ineffective: America has pioneered the harsh punishment of sex offenders. Does it work? The Economist Newspaper Limited. 6 Aug. 2009. Web. 20 Apr. 2011.

Human Rights Watch. "US: Sex Offender Laws May Do More Harm Than Good." Human Rights Watch. 11 Sept. 2011. Web. 20 Apr. 2011.

Matson, Scott and Roxanne Lieb. "Sex Offender Registration: A Review of State Laws. Washington State Institute for Public Policy. July 1996. Web. 20 Apr. 2011.

Pollitt, Katha. Web log post. *Twitter.com*. 19 Apr. 2011. Web. 20 Apr. 2011.

Velázquez, Tracy. "The Pursuit of Safety: Sex Offender Policy in the United States." Vera Institute of Justice. Sept 2008. Web. 20 Apr. 2011

A CLOSER LOOK AT
Reconsidering Match.com's Sex Offender Ban

1. Clark-Flory states her thesis in the final two paragraphs, not at the beginning. After reading the article a second time, play the doubting and believing game, making an argument for each placement of the thesis statement (beginning or end). Would her argument have been more effective and persuasive if the thesis had been placed near the beginning?

2. If you really want to persuade those who disagree with your positions, you need to deal fairly with their arguments and show that you understand them. Does Clark-Flory treat Pollitt's objections fairly?

3. How does Clark-Flory use evidence (facts and the positions of authorities) to back up her argument? Is that evidence authoritative, sufficient, and relevant?

4. In the original article that Pollitt responded to, Clark-Flory criticized Match.com for merely "making everyone else *feel* safe." The issue was Match.com's clumsy and "unjust" lumping together all sex offenders, even those who are not dangerous. Here she restates the issue in paragraphs 6 and 7. What is the issue? What recommended change does the author propose?

IDEAS FOR
Writing

1. Write a rhetorical analysis of Clark-Flory's two articles. You can find the first article on the Web at Salon.com ("Match.com Bans Sex Offenders—Feel Safe Now?"). Using the ideas in "Rhetorical Analyses" (Chapter 8) and "Using Argumentative Strategies" (Chapter 22), explain how and why her second piece ("Reconsidering") is more persuasive and effective than the first—or not. What strategies (*ethos, pathos, logos*) does she use, and how well do they succeed?

2. Write a respectful rebuttal that either refutes or challenges Clark-Flory's "Reconsidering Match.com's Sex Offender Ban." Even if you agree with Clark-Flory, write a rebuttal that highlights any weaknesses in reasoning and explains how they could be made stronger.

The Dangers of the Drinking Age

JEFFREY A. MIRON AND ELINA TETELBAUM

In this article, Miron and Tetelbaum argue against the belief that a drinking age of 21 years old saves lives or keeps students from drinking. Their argument is that raising the drinking age nationally to 21 has had many unintended consequences, such as a rise in binge drinking and disrespect for the law. In this article, pay attention to how the authors use statistics to support their major points and counteract opposing views.

For the past 20 years, the U.S. has maintained a Minimum Legal Drinking Age of 21 (MLDA21), with little public debate about the wisdom of this policy. Recently, however, more than 100 college and university presidents signed the Amethyst Initiative, a public statement calling for "an informed and dispassionate public debate over the effects of the 21-year-old drinking age."

The response to the Amethyst Initiative was predictable: Advocates of restricted access and zero tolerance decried the statement for not recognizing that the MLDA21 saves lives by preventing traffic deaths among 18- to 20-year-olds. The president of Mothers Against Drunk Driving, for example, accused the university heads of "not doing their homework" on the relationship between the drinking age and traffic fatalities.

In fact, the advocates of the MLDA21 are the ones who need a refresher course. In our recently completed research, we show that the MLDA21 has little or no life-saving effect.

To understand why, a bit of history is useful.

When the U.S. repealed the prohibition of 5 alcohol in 1933, states were free to legalize, regulate or prohibit access to it as they saw fit. Most legalized but regulated it. In particular, 32 states adopted an MLDA of 21, while 16 chose an MLDA between 18 and 20. With few exceptions, these disparities persisted through the late 1960s.

Between 1970 and 1976, 30 states lowered their MLDA from 21 to 18. These changes coincided with other national efforts to enfranchise youth, exemplified by the 26th Amendment, which granted those 18+ the right to vote.

In 1984, however, Congress passed the Federal Underage Drinking Act (FUDAA), which withholds transportation funding from states that do not have an MLDA21. The justification given for the act was that higher MLDAs would result in fewer traffic fatalities.

By the end of 1988, after passage of the FUDAA, all states adopted an MLDA21. Several states had adopted an MLDA21 before the FUDAA, but the other states were less eager to change. Several passed MLDA21 legislation but set it up for repeal if the FUDAA were held unconstitutional. Others enacted "sunset provisions" in case federal sanctions expired. But when the Supreme Court upheld the FUDAA, states faced a strong incentive to maintain an MLDA21.

Our research compares traffic fatality rates in states before and after they changed their MLDA from 18 to 21. In contrast to all earlier work, however, we examined separately the impact in states that adopted an MLDA21 on their own and those that were coerced by the FUDAA.

The results are striking. Virtually all the life- 10 saving impact of the MLDA21 comes from the few early-adopting states, not from the larger number that resulted from federal pressure. Further, any life-saving effect in those states that first raised the drinking age was only temporary, occurring largely in the first year or two after switching to the MLDA21.

Our results thus challenge both the value of the MLDA21 and the value of coercive federalism. While we find limited evidence that the MLDA21 saves lives when states adopted it of their own volition, we find no evidence it saves lives when the federal government compels this policy.

This makes sense if a higher MLDA works only when state governments can set a drinking age that responds to local attitudes and concerns—and when states are energized to enforce such laws. A policy imposed from on high, especially one that is readily evaded and opposed by a large fraction of the citizenry, is virtually guaranteed to fail.

The major implication of these results is that the drinking age does not produce its main claimed benefit. Moreover, it plausibly generates side effects, like binge drinking and disrespect for the law—the very behavior that events planned for this month's alcohol awareness theme are designed to deter.

If we are to truly tackle the dangers of youth drinking, we must admit that the National-21 experiment has failed. We welcome the surgeon general's recent call to action to reduce underage drinking, to the extent that it provides tips for families and educators to curb the dangers of alcohol abuse.

The federal government has taken alcohol 15 policy out of these parties' hands, however, by imposing an ineffective policy on everyone. An awareness campaign can only do so much when the most significant impediment to change is not on college campuses but in Washington.

A CLOSER LOOK AT
The Dangers of the Drinking Age

1. In the article, the authors explain how the current drinking age of 21 came about. Review these historical details. How does this historical information help build a context so readers can better understand this issue?

2. According to the authors, why exactly is the minimum drinking age of 21 years not working in most states? Find the places where they make these points.

3. Study this article with a group of others from your class. If you were trying to poke holes in the authors' argument, where are some weak points that you would consider challenging?

IDEAS FOR
Writing

1. Write a proposal in which you argue that states should again have the power to set their own drinking ages. Explain the problem with the national standard of 21 years old and explore its effects. Then, argue that your state should have the power to set its own drinking age. Explain what age you believe is appropriate. Then, argue out the costs and benefits of adopting the age you recommend.

2. Write an argument in which you summarize Miron and Tetelbaum's article and then argue against or for it. Explain both sides of the drinking issue by reviewing research on this subject. Then, argue against their point of view or use their argument as the basis to a broader argument that supports their major points.

The Making of a Divorce Culture

BARBARA DAFOE WHITEHEAD

Barbara Dafoe Whitehead is codirector of the Rutgers University National Marriage Project, whose mission is "to provide research and analysis on the state of marriage in America and to educate the public on the social, economic, and political conditions affecting marital success and child well-being." She is a journalist who speaks to and writes for scholarly, professional, and popular audiences. As you read "The Making of a Divorce Culture," the introduction to her book The Divorce Culture *(1997), pay attention to the way Whitehead defines the causes of America's widespread acceptance of divorce.*

Divorce is now part of everyday American life. It is embedded in our laws and institutions, our manners and mores, our movies and television shows, our novels and children's storybooks, and our closest and most important relationships. Indeed, divorce has become so pervasive that many people naturally assume it has seeped into the social and cultural mainstream over a long period of time. Yet this is not the case. Divorce has become an American way of life only as the result of recent and revolutionary change.

The entire history of American divorce can be divided into two periods, one evolutionary and the other revolutionary. For most of the nation's history, divorce was a rare occurrence and an insignificant feature of family and social relationships. In the first sixty years of the twentieth century, divorce became more common, but it was hardly commonplace. In 1960, the divorce rate stood at a still relatively modest level of nine per one thousand married couples. After 1960, however, the rate accelerated at a dazzling pace. It doubled in roughly a decade and continued its upward climb until the early 1980s, when it stabilized at the highest level among advanced Western societies. As a consequence of this sharp and sustained rise, divorce moved from the margins to the mainstream of American life in the space of three decades.

Ideas are important in revolutions, yet surprisingly little attention has been devoted to the ideas that gave impetus to the divorce revolution. Of the scores of books on divorce published in recent decades, most focus on its legal, demographic, economic, or (especially) psychological dimensions. Few, if any, deal fully with its intellectual origins. Yet trying to comprehend the divorce revolution and its consequences without some sense of its ideological origins, is like trying to understand the American Revolution without taking into account the thinking of John Locke, Thomas Jefferson, or Thomas Paine. This more recent revolution, like the revolution of our nation's founding, has its roots in a distinctive set of ideas and claims.

This book is about the ideas behind the divorce revolution and how these ideas have shaped a culture of divorce. The making of a divorce culture has involved three overlapping changes: first, the emergence and widespread diffusion of a historically new and distinctive set of ideas about divorce in the last third of the twentieth century; second, the migration of divorce from a minor place within a system governed by marriage to a freestanding place as a major institution governing family relationships; and third, a widespread shift in thinking about the obligations of marriage and parenthood.

Beginning in the late 1950s, Americans began to change their ideas about the individual's obligations to family and society. Broadly described, this change was away from an ethic of obligation to others and toward an obligation to self. I do not mean that people suddenly abandoned all responsibilities to others, but rather that they became more acutely conscious of their responsibility to attend to their own individual needs and interests. At least as important as the moral obligation to look after others, the new thinking suggested, was the moral obligation to look after oneself.

This ethical shift had a profound impact on ideas about the nature and purpose of the family. In the American tradition, the marketplace and the public square have represented the realms of life devoted to the pursuit of individual interest, choice, and freedom, while the family has been the realm defined by voluntary commitment, duty, and self-sacrifice. With the greater emphasis on individual satisfaction in family relationships, however, family well-being became subject to a new metric. More than in the past, satisfaction in this sphere came to be based on subjective judgments about the content and quality of individual happiness rather than on such objective measures as level of income, material nurture and support, or boosting children onto a higher rung on the socioeconomic ladder. People began to judge the strength and "health" of family bonds according to their capacity to promote individual fulfillment and personal growth. As a result, the conception of the family's role and place in the society began to change. The family began to lose its separate place and distinctive identity as the realm of duty, service, and sacrifice. Once the domain of the obligated self, the family was increasingly viewed as yet another domain for the expression of the unfettered self.

These broad changes figured centrally in creating a new conception of divorce which gained influential adherents and spread broadly and swiftly throughout the society—a conception that represented a radical departure from earlier notions. Once regarded mainly as a social, legal, and family event in which there were other stakeholders, divorce now became an event closely linked to the pursuit of individual satisfactions, opportunities, and growth.

The new conception of divorce drew upon some of the oldest, and most resonant, themes in the American political tradition. The nation, after all, was founded as the result of a political divorce, and revolutionary thinkers explicitly adduced a parallel between the dissolution of marital bonds and the dissolution of political bonds. In political as well as marital relationships, they argued, bonds of obligation were established voluntarily on the basis of mutual affection and regard. Once such bonds turned cold and oppressive, peoples, like individuals, had the right to dissolve them and to form more perfect unions.

In the new conception of divorce, this strain of eighteenth-century political thought mingled with a strain of twentieth-century psychotherapeutic thought. Divorce was not only an individual right but also a psychological resource. The dissolution of marriage offered the chance to make oneself over from the inside out, to refurbish and express the inner self, and to acquire certain valuable psychological assets and competencies, such as initiative, assertiveness, and a stronger and better self-image.

The conception of divorce as both an individual right and an inner experience merged with and reinforced the new ethic of obligation to the self. In family relationships, one had an obligation to be attentive to one's own feelings and to work toward improving the quality of one's inner life. This ethical imperative completed the rationale for a sense of individual entitlement to divorce. Increasingly, mainstream America saw the legal dissolution of marriage as a matter of individual choice, in which there were no other stakeholders or larger social interests. This conception of divorce strongly argued for removing the social, legal, and moral impediments to the free exercise of the individual right to divorce.

Traditionally, one major impediment to divorce was the presence of children in the family. According to well-established popular belief, dependent children had a stake in their parents' marriage and suffered hardship as a result of the dissolution of the marriage. Because children were vulnerable and dependent, parents had a moral obligation to place their children's interests in the marital partnership above their own individual satisfactions. This notion was swiftly abandoned after the 1960s. Influential voices in the society, including child-welfare professionals, claimed that the happiness of individual parents, rather than an intact marriage, was the key determinant of children's family well-being. If divorce could make one or both parents happier, then it was likely to improve the well-being of children as well.

In the following decades, the new conception of divorce spread through the law, therapy, etiquette, the social sciences, popular advice literature, and religion. Concerns that had dominated earlier thinking on divorce were now dismissed as old-fashioned and excessively moralistic. Divorce would not harm children but would lead to greater happiness for children and their single parents. It would not damage the institution of marriage but would make possible better marriages and happier individuals. Divorce would not damage the social fabric by diminishing children's life chances but would strengthen the social fabric by improving the quality of affective bonds between parents and children, whatever form the structural arrangements of their families might happen to take.

As the sense of divorce as an individual freedom and entitlement grew, the sense of concern about divorce as a social problem diminished. Earlier in the century, each time the divorce rate increased sharply, it had inspired widespread public concern and debate about the harmful impact of divorce on families and the society. But in the last third of the century, as the divorce rate rose to once unthinkable levels, public anxiety about it all but vanished. At the very moment when divorce had its most profound impact on the society, weakening the institution of marriage, revolutionizing the structure of families, and reorganizing parent-child relationships, it ceased to be a source of concern or debate.

The lack of attention to divorce became particularly striking after the 1980s, as a politically polarized debate over the state of the American family took shape. On one side, conservatives pointed to abortion, illegitimacy, and homosexuality as forces destroying the family. On the other, liberals cited domestic violence, economic insecurity, and inadequate public supports as the key problems afflicting the family. But politicians on both sides had almost nothing to say about divorce. Republicans did not want

to alienate their upscale constituents or their libertarian wing, both of whom tended to favor easy divorce, nor did they want to call attention to the divorces among their own leadership. Democrats did not want to anger their large constituency among women who saw easy divorce as a hard-won freedom and prerogative, nor did they wish to seem unsympathetic to single mothers. Thus, except for bipartisan calls to get tougher with deadbeat dads, both Republicans and Democrats avoided the issue of divorce and its consequences as far too politically risky.

But the failure to address divorce carried a 15 price. It allowed the middle class to view family breakdown as a "them" problem rather than an "us" problem. Divorce was not like illegitimacy or welfare dependency, many claimed. It was a matter of individual choice, imposing few, if any, costs or consequences on others. Thus, mainstream America could cling to the comfortable illusion that the nation's family problems had to do with the behavior of unwed teenage mothers or poor women on welfare rather than with the instability of marriage and family life within its own ranks.

Nonetheless, after thirty years of persistently high levels of divorce, this illusion, though still politically attractive, is increasingly difficult to sustain in the face of a growing body of experience and evidence. To begin with, divorce has indeed hurt children. It has created economic insecurity and disadvantage for many children who would not otherwise be economically vulnerable. It has led to more fragile and unstable family households. It has caused a mass exodus of fathers from children's households and, all too often, from their lives. It has reduced the levels of parental time and money invested in children. In sum, it has changed the very nature of American childhood. Just as no patient would have designed today's system of health care, so no child would have chosen today's culture of divorce.

Divorce figures prominently in the altered economic fortunes of middle-class families. Although the economic crisis of the middle class is usually described as a problem caused by global economic changes, changing patterns in education and earnings, and ruthless corporate downsizing, it owes more to divorce than is commonly acknowledged. Indeed, recent data suggest that marriage may be a more important economic resource than a college degree. According to an analysis of 1994 income patterns, the median income of married-parent households whose heads have only a high school diploma is ten percent higher than the median income of college-educated single-parent households. Parents who are college graduates *and* married form the new economic elite among families with children. Consequently, those who are concerned about what the downsizing of corporations is doing to workers should also be concerned about what the downsizing of families through divorce is doing to parents and children.

Widespread divorce depletes social capital as well. Scholars tell us that strong and durable family and social bonds generate certain "goods" and services, including money, mutual assistance, information, caregiving, protection, and sponsorship. Because such bonds endure over time, they accumulate and form a pool of social capital which can be drawn down upon, when needed, over the entire course of a life. An elderly couple, married for fifty years, is likely to enjoy a substantial body of social and emotional capital, generated through their long-lasting marriage, which they can draw upon in caring for each other and for themselves as they age. Similarly, children who grow up in stable, two-parent married households are the beneficiaries of the social and emotional capital accumulated over time as a result of an enduring marriage bond. As many parents know, children continue to depend on these resources well into young adulthood. But as family bonds become increasingly fragile and vulnerable to disruption, they become less permanent and thus less capable of generating such forms of help, financial resources, and mutual support. In short, divorce consumes social capital and weakens the social fabric. At the very time that sweeping socioeconomic changes are mandating greater investment of social capital in children, widespread divorce is reducing the pool of social capital. As the new economic and social conditions raise

the hurdles of child-rearing higher, divorce digs potholes in the tracks.

It should be stressed that this book is not intended as a brief against divorce as such. We must assume that divorce is necessary as a remedy for irretrievably broken marriages, especially those that are marred by severe abuse such as chronic infidelity, drug addiction, or physical violence. Nor is its argument directed against those who are divorced. It assumes that divorce is difficult, painful, and often unwanted by at least one spouse, and that divorcing couples require compassion and support from family, friends, and their religious communities. Nor should this book be taken as an appeal for a return to an earlier era of American family life. The media routinely portray the debate over the family as one between nostalgists and realists, between those who want to turn back the clock to the fifties and those who want to march bravely and resolutely forward into the new century. But this is a lazy and misguided approach, driven more by the easy availability of archival photos and footage from 1950s television sitcoms than by careful consideration of the substance of competing arguments.

More fundamentally, this approach overlooks the key issue. And that issue is not how today's families might stack up against those of an earlier era; indeed, no reliable empirical data for such a comparison exist. In an age of diverse family structures, the heart of the matter is what kinds of contemporary family arrangements have the greatest capacity to promote children's well-being, and how we can ensure that more children have the advantages of growing up in such families. [20]

In the past year or so, there has been growing recognition of the personal and social costs of three decades of widespread divorce. A public debate has finally emerged. Within this debate, there are two separate and overlapping discussions.

The first centers on a set of specific proposals that are intended to lessen the harmful impact of divorce on children: a federal system of child-support collection, tougher child-support enforcement, mandatory counseling for divorcing parents, and reform of no-fault divorce laws in the states. What is striking about this discussion is its narrow focus on public policy, particularly on changes in the system of no-fault divorce. In this, as in so many other crucial discussions involving social and moral questions, the most vocal and visible participants come from the world of government policy, electoral politics, and issue advocacy. The media, which are tongue-tied unless they can speak in the language of left-right politics, reinforce this situation. And the public is offered needlessly polarized arguments that hang on a flat yes-or-no response to this or that individual policy measure. All too often, this discussion of divorce poses what *Washington Post* columnist E. J. Dionne aptly describes as false choices.

Notably missing is a serious consideration of the broader moral assumptions and empirical claims that define our divorce culture. Divorce touches on classic questions in American public philosophy—on the nature of our most important human and social bonds, the duties and obligations imposed by bonds we voluntarily elect, the "just causes" for the dissolution of those bonds, and the differences between obligations volunteered and those that must be coerced. Without consideration of such questions, the effort to change behavior by changing a few public policies is likely to founder.

The second and complementary discussion does try to place divorce within a larger philosophical framework. Its proponents have looked at the decline in the well-being of the nation's children as the occasion to call for a collective sense of commitment by all Americans to all of America's children. They pose the challenging question: "What are Americans willing to do 'for the sake of *all* children'?" But while this is surely an important question, it addresses only half of the problem of declining commitment. The other half has to do with how we answer the question: "What are individual parents obliged to do 'for the sake of their own children'?"

Renewing a *social* ethic of commitment to 25 children is an urgent goal, but it cannot be detached from the goal of strengthening the *individual* ethic of commitment to children. The state of one affects the standing of the other. A society that protects the rights of parents to easy, unilateral divorce, and flatly rejects the idea that parents should strive to preserve a marriage "for the sake of the children," faces a problem when it comes to the question of public sacrifice "for the sake of the children." To put it plainly, many of the ideas we have come to believe and vigorously defend about adult prerogatives and freedoms in family life are undermining the foundations of altruism and support for children.

With each passing year, the culture of divorce becomes more deeply entrenched. American children are routinely schooled in divorce. Mr. Rogers teaches toddlers about divorce. An entire children's literature is devoted to divorce. Family movies and videos for children feature divorced families. *Mrs. Doubtfire*, originally a children's book about divorce and then a hit movie, is aggressively marketed as a holiday video for kids. Of course, these books and movies are designed to help children deal with the social reality and psychological trauma of divorce. But they also carry an unmistakable message about the impermanence and unreliability of family bonds. Like romantic love, the children's storybooks say, family love comes and goes. Daddies disappear. Mommies find new boyfriends. Mommies' boyfriends leave. Grandparents go away. Even pets must be left behind.

More significantly, in a society where nearly half of all children are likely to experience parental divorce, family breakup becomes a defining event of American childhood itself. Many children today know nothing but divorce in their family lives. And although children from divorced families often say they want to avoid divorce if they marry, young adults whose parents divorced are more likely to get divorced themselves and to bear children outside of marriage than young adults from stable married-parent families.

Precisely because the culture of divorce has generational momentum, this book offers no easy optimism about the prospects for change. But neither does it counsel passive resignation or acceptance of the culture's relentless advance. What it does offer is a critique of the ideas behind current divorce trends. Its argument is directed against the ideas about divorce that have gained ascendancy, won our support, and lodged in our consciousness as "proven" and incontrovertible.

It challenges the popular idea of divorce as an individual right and freedom to be exercised in the pursuit of individual goods and satisfactions, without due regard for other stakeholders in the marital partnership, especially children. This may be a fragile and inadequate response to a profoundly consequential set of changes, but it seeks the abandonment of ideas that have misled us and failed our children.

In a larger sense, this book is both an appreciation and a criticism of what is peculiarly American about divorce. Divorce has spread throughout advanced Western societies at roughly the same pace and over roughly the same period of time. Yet nowhere else has divorce been so deeply imbued with the larger themes of a nation's political traditions. Nowhere has divorce so fully reflected the spirit and susceptibilities of a people who share an extravagant faith in the power of the individual and in the power of positive thinking. Divorce in America is not unique, but what we have made of divorce is uniquely American. In exploring the cultural roots of divorce, therefore, we look at ourselves, at what is best and worst in our traditions, what is visionary and what is blind, and how the two are sometimes tragically commingled and confused.

A CLOSER LOOK AT
The Making of a Divorce Culture

1. What are the major points of difference between the way people usually think of divorce in America and the way Whitehead argues we should think about it? You might think about completing a sentence like this: "While most people today believe that divorce _____, in fact, according to Whitehead, we should understand that American divorce _____." Go back to the text and find at least three phrases that accurately reflect Whitehead's position.

2. Using the terminology provided in Chapter 22, "Using Argumentative Strategies," show how Whitehead employs common argumentative strategies to make her case.

3. Drawing on your own knowledge about divorce in the United States, play the doubting and believing game with Whitehead's argument that divorce is primarily due to "an ethical shift" away from social and familial obligation to a focus on "individual fulfillment and personal growth." First, play the believing game: Come up with as many reasons and as much evidence that supports her claim as you can. Then play the doubting game: What evidence and reasons would make a person doubt the accuracy, relevance, or sufficiency of her claims?

IDEAS FOR
Writing

1. Write a concise summary of "The Making of a Divorce Culture." Use the strategies in Chapter 26, "Quoting, Paraphrasing, and Citing Sources," to guide your summary. Describe not only *what* the author says but *how* she argues her point.

2. Write a memoir or profile that draws on your direct personal experience with divorce. Even if it hasn't affected your immediate family, you probably have friends or extended family who have been affected.

As Chapters 4 ("Memoirs") and 5 ("Profiles") point out, people write memoirs or profiles because they want to make a point that can best be conveyed through narrative and description. While Whitehead's argument takes a bird's-eye-view of divorce, you should use this opportunity to take a close personal look at the issues to reinforce, question, or add other dimensions to Whitehead's argument. You may choose to quote or cite Whitehead.

A FEW IDEAS FOR
Composing an Argument

1. **Write an argument on an important issue.** Try to give the topic a local slant by choosing an issue that concerns your campus or your community. It might be the community you physically work or live in, or it might be a virtual community of people who share the same interests. Even if you want to talk about a national or global issue, try to find the local angle. For instance, rather than just writing about global warming generally, approach that issue by discussing what is happening on your campus or within your community.

2. **Write an argument responding to an article.** Find an article that states a position you strongly disagree with. Try to summarize the opposing article's argument so objectively that even

a person who holds that position would agree that you have treated it fairly. Then express your own opinion in a way that shows your views are more reasonable than your opponent's views.

3. **Create a multimedia argument.** Your argument should argue for a specific belief or course of action. Choose an incident from your own life that sets the stage or leads to a lesson about the issue you are arguing. Try to highlight details that allow you to explore both sides of the issue. Consider blending in features of other genres, such as memoirs, profiles, and proposals. Try experimenting with a variety of organizations that creatively use the flexibility of the medium you chose for this project.

Proposals

Diet for a Warm Planet

JULIA WHITTY

Julia Whitty is an award-winning author, journalist, and documentary filmmaker. In this proposal, Whitty identifies some surprising and highly controversial causes of global warming—Americans' wasteful diets and other matters that might be considered personal choice. As you read this, pay attention not only to what Whitty proposes but also to how she makes her argument for her proposal. For instance, what purpose is achieved by including the extended description of the migratory bird?

In 1985 I interviewed James Hansen at his NASA office in New York City about a problem called the greenhouse effect that few outside of science had heard of and fewer would take seriously for another 20 years. He was thoughtful and smart, only 44 years old, though he looked haggard from the battle behind him, as well as the battle he knew lay ahead—one man versus endless rounds of pundits, zealots, oilmen, politicians, journalists, scientists, naysayers, and fools.

The fight that would keep him on the ropes had begun in 1981, when Hansen proposed that the effects of global warming might show up in the real world, instead of just climate models, by 1990—not much later, as many in science were expecting. This early prophecy included uncanny predictions of droughts in North America, melting Antarctic ice sheets, and the opening of the Northwest Passage. More than two decades of bruising battles later, this past spring, Hansen delivered an urgent warning that we must trim atmospheric CO_2 concentrations from 385 parts per million to 350 ppm—right now.

Hansen's number presents a staggering challenge. It insists we dramatically reduce emissions at a time when we're still increasing them by 2 ppm per year, and when little or nothing is happening on the political front. It demands the biggest collaborative effort in the history of our species.

So what can you and I do to set an example for the men who lead the world? How to jump from the Age of Exploitation to the Age of Sustainability and drag the corporate-military-agroindustrial machinery along with us? The path seems paradoxically disconnected—like the business plan of the *South Park* underpants gnomes: Step One, steal underpants . . . Step Three, get rich.

Step Two: Embark upon a fossil fuel diet. We need to tighten up, get fit, get agile, smart, and quick. We need to develop a boxer's stamina if we want to outlast the well-funded heavyweights who will fight us to the death before the referee Nature calls the fight.

In the world of birds, there's a long-distance traveler without equal, the 15-inch-long bar-tailed godwit. It's classified as a shorebird, one of those sandpiper species typically found along coastlines. Yet the bar-tailed godwit has a far more impressive curriculum vitae. It manages its hectic calendar and limited resources with a lithe professionalism that enables it to do what no other animal on earth can do—that is, to leave Alaskan shores and strike out over open water to fly nonstop for eight days and 7,200 miles without feeding or drinking before touching down in another hemisphere (New Zealand) during a different season (spring). Six months later, it repeats the feat in reverse, with a five-week feeding stop in China, for an annual round-trip of 16,500 miles. Each bird makes its first migration only three months after hatching, often in flocks composed solely of first-timers.

We don't know exactly how these pocket Herculeses manage such phenomenal labors. Their skill set includes some form of built-in GPS and a meteorological aptitude that enables them to forecast low-pressure fronts a thousand miles away, and then launch in time to intercept their 60 mph tailwinds days later.

We do know that in every stage of their lives these birds are masters of energy management. They breed on the Alaskan tundra, harvesting berries (including, initially, last year's withered remnants) and seasonal blooms of insects. When their chicks fledge, they move to the shore and overhaul their diet entirely, probing tidal mudflats along Alaskan river deltas, where they transmute marine worms and clams into godwit. Eating is their primary work during these endless summer days, and by the time they launch south they are clinically obese, literally wobbling when they walk, with as much as 55 percent of their 1.5-pound bodies weighing in as fat—the heaviest fat loads recorded in any birds to date.

Yet once airborne they're sleek and efficient fliers. Somehow, just prior to flight, they shrink their digestive organs, while increasing their heart and breast muscles. They follow intelligent pathways through the air, hopping into the slipstream of useful weather systems, slingshotting around counterproductive ones, often clocking along at speeds of 60 mph. They regulate their energy by optimizing altitude, frequenting the cold, dry air at 15,000 feet in order to minimize energy loss through heat and water loss through evaporative cooling. They probably sleep half of their brains at a time, like migrating mallards.

By the time they arrive on New Zealand's 10 tidal estuaries, they're down to half their starting weight, exhausted, bedraggled, and hungry—but just in time for the Southern Hemisphere's spring bounty. They've completed their epic flight without ingesting or combusting a drop of fuel.

They are what we need to be: small of footprint, capable of the long haul.

Our migration from the Profligate to the Sustainable Hemisphere requires us to trim atmospheric CO_2 concentrations from 385 to 350 ppm, which we can do by cutting emissions by the same 10 percent. Right? Not quite. Atmospheric CO_2 concentrations are rife with

long-term feedbacks, both positive and negative, and our current saturation level reflects 250 years of anthropogenic emissions, not just last year's.

So how do we come up with a goal? I'm not a PhD in atmospheric sciences, and neither are you, probably, so this is more in the realm of the hypothetical diet, designed to make a qualitative difference while convincing the world's leaders that we're serious about forcing them to join us in the fight. The United States emits 13.1 trillion pounds of CO_2 a year, 22 percent of the total annual global emissions—about 43,000 pounds per American. But before we start deconstructing the merits of fluorescent lightbulbs, let's consider the bigger picture. Yes, China is catching up and by some estimates has already surpassed us. Yet the vast majority of the 385 ppm clogging the atmosphere was emitted by us.

Since America is responsible for 22 percent of annual emissions, I suggest we set a target of shrinking our personal carbon footprint by 22 percent, or 9,606 pounds. If Americans all did this, it would mean we'd take a disproportionate chunk out of that 385 ppm—which China and India would fairly argue that we should. Twenty-two is a hefty number with an alliterative ring to it and is indicative of serious intentions. If enough of us pull it off, 22 percent has the power to fuel a movement our leaders will follow.

So what would a 22 percent diet look like? 15 Step Two is all about losing weight. Seriously. Body fat. My personal flab is not just a private matter between me and my coronary arteries. Nineteen percent of US energy usage—about as much as is used to fuel our cars—is spent growing and delivering food to the average American who consumes 2,200 pounds of food a year. That's a whopping 3,747 calories a day—or 1,200 to 1,700 more than needed for personal or planetary health. The skinny truth is that as much as 7.6 percent of total energy in the United States today is used to grow human fat, fat that translates to 3,300 pounds of carbon per person.

Sure, liposuction is an untapped fuel source—and New Zealander Pete Bethune extracted 3.38 ounces of his own fat to add to the biofuel powering his carbon-neutral boat, *Earthrace*. But a more sustainable strategy would be to avoid growing the fat in the first place. A comprehensive Cornell University study found that we could cut our food energy usage in half by simply eating less, cutting back on meat and junk food, and considering the source of our food.

For starters, half of our food energy use comes from producing and delivering meat and dairy. If we gave up just meat, we could maintain that hefty 3,747-calorie intake but consume 33 percent less in fossil fuels doing it. If Americans cut just one serving of meat a week, it would equal taking 5 million cars off the road.

One-third of those 3,747 daily calories comes from junk food—potato chips, soda, etc. We can save on fossil fuel costs in this area by installing more efficient lighting, heating, and cooling in the plants that make the stuff and by using less packaging materials. But we'd save a lot more if you and I simply bought less of it. A can of diet soda, for instance, delivers only 1 calorie of food energy at a cost of 2,100 calories to make the drink and the can. Transporting the components and the finished product costs even more, and shipping processed food and its packaging accounts for much of the problem of America's food averaging 1,500 travel miles before it's eaten.

Ideally, we'd eat our recommended 2,000 to 2,500 daily calories from food grown on smaller, traditional, and organic farms—particularly for dairy and meat, which are extremely energy intensive in their nonorganic forms. To make this work, though, we also need to buy locally, since organic can be grown halfway around the world, and that's hardly sustainable. True, local produce could find its way to your table via too many polluting pickup trucks, but buying locally from sustainable farms generally produces a smaller carbon footprint than factory farms with their fuel-heavy pesticides, chemical fertilizers, and travel miles.

But wait, you say, it's too expensive to buy all that local, organic, boutique food. Well, demand drives the market toward affordability. Today nearly 5,000 farmers markets across the 20

US provide fresh neighborhood food to cities, suburbs, and rural areas. The number is growing (up 18 percent between 2004 and 2006) and the farmers are profiting ($1 billion in sales in 2005). The Agriculture Department now provides farmers market vouchers to low-income mothers and seniors—though not yet enough. The next big step in trimming fossil fuel costs is community-sponsored agriculture (CSA), where paid subscriptions support a local small farmer, who supplies his subscribers with weekly deliveries of fresh, neighborhood food. There are now 2,000 CSAs nationwide. What begins as an elite market eventually becomes something common. But it only happens if you and I make it happen.

Our best friend in making it happen is higher fuel costs, which will eventually make some local food cheaper than distant food. Higher gas prices have already prompted Americans to cut back on driving over the last year by just under 5 percent. That's a bigger decline than during the gas crisis of the 1970s, and it was accomplished without too much pain.

To get to our goal we need more like a 25 percent decline in driving. That and one less 1,100-mile plane trip per person would save us each an estimated 2,365 pounds of carbon. Assuming we've saved 3,300 pounds of carbon by going on an actual diet, we've already gotten halfway to that 22 percent reduction in our carbon footprint without sweating. Closing the gap is easy. Even a middling hot water heater produces 3,000 lbs of carbon a year. So when the time comes to replace it, get an on-demand model that doesn't labor to keep 40 gallons of water hot round the clock. Until then, turn down the temperature to 120° F (carbon saved: 500 lbs). While you're at it, turn your thermostat down in winter and up in summer (2,000 lbs) and compensate with sweaters and solar shades or glazes. Hang your clothes to dry; you'll cut 1,440 pounds of carbon, plus gain a few meditative moments with your laundry. My personal favorite: Shop thrift stores. You get to be more of a recycler, less of a consumer, especially if you donate your stuff back when you're done with it. With almost every decision we make, there's a carbon way to look at it. So do an audit. And share your goals with others. Diets work when we support each other. Just as no bar-tailed godwit can make it to New Zealand and back again on its own, neither can we. The secret to Step Two is to learn to flock. Any one of us changing out our lightbulbs is helpful. Many of us acting together becomes a force.

Before their migration, bar-tailed godwits gather on their staging areas to feed, but also to coordinate the group's intentions, demonstrating what we call migratory restlessness—the massed, circling, erratic flights, the constant *kirRUC-kirRUC-kirRUC* calls. Our advantage over the birds is that our voices carry beyond our bodies, allowing us to talk effortlessly across miles and languages.

Except that we don't. On life-and-death matters of sustainability, too many of us remain isolated and silent. A George Mason University study found that while a majority of American health department directors believe their region will suffer serious public health problems from climate change within 20 years, few have made any plans to detect, prevent, or adapt to these health threats partly because they fear they don't *know enough* to speak. The authors conclude that Americans continue to erroneously view climate change as a threat only to species other than our own in part because health professionals remain silent.

When I blogged about this story, angry commenters, some identifying themselves as doctors, complained that health professionals could hardly be expected to solve global warming. That's not the point. Every one of us has a voice, and every one of us is an expert with our own authority to speak. Since when did we give our power away? A doctor can speak of the troubles in sight from increased heat stress, dehydration, migrating diseases. A mental health professional can speak of the post-traumatic stresses that shadow natural disasters. A computer programmer can speak authoritatively of the need to focus our technological skills on life-saving solutions. Parents can speak of the rights of their children to a functioning planet. Children can speak of their fear and anger at our silence. It's not about the right to speak, but the obligation.

25

But free speech is a free-for-all. How do we transition from clamor to consensus? Thomas Malone and Mark Klein of MIT suggest we already have the power to harness computer technology and create a "collective intelligence" to address systemic problems, like climate change, that overwhelm our individual intelligence. They propose a Web-mediated discussion and decision-making forum called the Climate Collaboratium—"a kind of Wikipedia for controversial topics, a Sims game for the future of the planet, and an electronic democracy on steroids."

They suggest four intriguing—and increasingly sophisticated—means to move beyond argument to action: (1) Let online users vote on the issues and run daily simulations of the vote rankings; (2) let users vote within their areas of expertise (scientists within science), except in "values" choices where everyone has a vote, as in "How much economic sacrifice should we make now to reduce sea level rise for our great-grandchildren?"; (3) let users buy and sell predictions about uncertain future events, to be paid only if their predictions are correct; (4) create a "proxy democracy" whereby users could give their voting proxies to others—on scientific issues to the Union of Concerned Scientists, say, or on "values" issues to the Nature Conservancy. Within this cyberflock we might transform our most strident discussions into sound decisions and solid action.

The bar-tailed godwits massing on their staging grounds in Alaska swirl and bunch with elasticized precision. The collective brain of their bodies debates yes and no. On the day of departure, the deliberation rises to 1,500 feet to test the vote up there before descending to the mudflats again. When the decision is finalized, the flocks climb beyond sight, groups of 50 to 100 birds flying in echelons or V shapes, those masterpieces of aerodynamics and communications, each bird gaining lift from the upwash of wings ahead, each bird seeing unimpaired by what lies ahead, all listening to each other's calls.

"We have used up all slack in the schedule for actions needed to defuse the global warming time bomb," writes James Hansen, 20 years after telling Congress that climate change was already, certainly, under way. We're on the mudflats, the tide is rising, the sun is falling, the season is changing, we need to assess those weather systems a thousand miles away. Not one of us can escape the long trip. We still have time—just enough—Hansen says, to tighten up, get fit, get agile, smart, and quick, before the flock is scattered in catastrophic winds that not even the heavyweights will survive.

A CLOSER LOOK AT
Diet for a Warm Planet

1. What is the precise problem Whitty identifies? The larger problem is climate change, but she is addressing a subproblem that is one of many causes of climate change. What is it?

2. What is your initial reaction to her plan to solve the problem she has identified? What do you personally think of it? How do you think Americans generally would react to it? Is her plan realistic?

3. Why has Whitty included a profile of the amazing migratory bird, the bar-tailed godwit? What relevant concept does the bird represent for her? What point is she trying to make with this profile? Try to get into the author's mind and explain why she included this element in her proposal.

IDEAS FOR
Writing

1. Write a brief profile of a nonhuman living thing that illustrates some point you want to make. It might be a remarkable species you know about (like Whitty's godwit). It could also be a specific animal or place that represents something that is relevant for human beings and how they live their lives.

2. Write a rhetorical analysis of Whitty's proposal. Explain how she uses *logos*—appeals to common sense, reason, and values—to win over her readers. Explain also how she uses *pathos*—appeals to emotions such as fear, guilt, hope, etc.—to persuade. In the end, be sure to make an overall assessment about whether her proposal is persuasive or not.

Who Pays for My Time Off? The Costs and Consequences of Government-Mandated Leave

CARRIE L. LUKAS

Carrie L. Lukas is a widely published conservative political writer who has appeared on many television and radio shows, writes for a variety of publications, and has written a book, The Politically Incorrect Guide to Women, Sex, and Feminism. *She also serves as vice president for policy and economics of the Independent Women's Forum. As you read this proposal, pay attention to the way that Lukas carefully frames the issues and identifies problems in the proposals of various (liberal) politicians. Notice also the point at which Lukas first introduces her own plan for solving the problems she identifies.*

Introduction

Balancing the demands of work and family life can be a challenge for any worker. Events such as severe illness or the birth of a child can make working outside the home impossible. People overwhelmingly sympathize with those facing these challenging situations and want society to support such individuals during difficult times.

In recent decades, however, the question has turned not to how civil society can support individuals in times of need, but to how the federal government can dictate how employers must accommodate employees facing these situations. Existing laws require that large employers allow qualified employees to take unpaid leave when facing such circumstances. Some policymakers want to expand these regulations so that they apply to smaller employers and to mandate the availability of additional benefits, such as paid leave.

This paper examines the Family and Medical Leave Act, which mandates that businesses provide unpaid leave to their workers, and considers some of the problems associated with its application. It will also consider the potential consequences of expanding these regulations.

This paper highlights how private entities are voluntarily providing leave benefits and considers ways that policymakers can further encourage businesses and individuals to take actions that will make it easier for individuals in need of leave, without costly government mandates.

The background of the Family and Medical Leave Act

President Clinton signed the Family and Medical 5 Leave Act (FMLA) into law on February 5, 1993, hailing its passage as a victory for families in need: "Today, I am pleased to sign into law H.R. 1, the 'Family and Medical Leave Act of 1993.' I believe that this legislation is a response to a compelling need—the need of the American family for flexibility in the workplace. American workers will no longer have to choose between the job they need and the family they love."[1]

Under this law, employees who meet eligibility requirements are allowed to take up to twelve weeks of unpaid leave during a twelve-month period for reasons related to personal illness, family illness, or the birth or adoption of a child. Employers are required to maintain provided health benefits while employees exercise their right to leave and to allow employees to return to their original job or a comparable position free of any retaliation or loss of job stature.

For employees to be eligible to take this leave, they have to have worked for an eligible employer for a minimum of twelve months and for at least 1,250 hours in the twelve months prior to taking FMLA leave. FMLA applies to private sector employers of fifty or more employees, as well as public agencies and entities.[2]

The law specifies the circumstances in which employees become eligible to take leave under FMLA: for the birth of a child of the employee and to care for the newborn; the adoption (or fostering) of a child and to care for the newly placed child; to care for a spouse, parent, son or daughter under age eighteen with a serious health condition; or, for the employee's own serious health condition. Employees are allowed to choose to use accrued paid leave (vacation, personal, or family leave) for FMLA leave. Employers may also require that employees use these voluntary leave programs for FMLA leave.

If employees feel that their employer has failed to live up to the FMLA requirement, employees can file a complaint with the Department of Labor (DOL) or file a private lawsuit. The DOL was the agency responsible for promulgating the regulations to implement the law.

According to the DOI, 76.1 million workers (or 54 percent of the total 141.7 million workers) were eligible for FMLA leave and 6.1 million workers took FMLA protected leave in 2005.[3]

Problems with the existing FMLA regulations

Those who believe in a limited federal government criticize FMLA as an improper use of federal power. In its essence, FMLA restricts the employment terms that can be offered and accepted by adults. This constitutes a loss of liberty for individuals.

However, putting aside the issue of whether regulations like FMLA are a proper use of government power, there are other problems associated with FMLA's specific terms and enforcement that create challenges for employers and should concern policymakers.

DOL has collected feedback from those affected by FMLA, including employers, administrators, and employees. Employers' complaints have generally focused on a few specific aspects of the law and, more specifically, of the

regulations. DOL notes that employers generally "recognize the value of the FMLA and attempt to comply with its requirements." DOL has not received complaints related to "leave for the birth or adoption of a child" or "the use of scheduled intermittent leave as contemplated by the statute, such as when an employee requests leave for medical appointments or medical treatments like chemotherapy." However, employers report "job disruptions" and "adverse effects on the workforce" resulting "when employees take frequent, unscheduled, intermittent leave from work with little or no advance notice to the employer."[4]

In surveys conducted by the Society for Human Resource Management (SHRM), half of the human-resource professionals responded that they had had to approve leave that they believe was unjustified. One-third also responded that they had received complaints from their employees about co-workers' abuse of FMLA.[5] Two-thirds of respondents said that because of FMLA they had to keep employees who would have been fired because of poor attendance.[6]

While the majority of employers said that FMLA did not have a noticeable effect on their establishment's overall performance, in terms of productivity, profitability, and growth, of those employers that thought it did have an effect, two to three times as many thought the effect on their business's performance had been negative.[7]

Most complaints from employers center on the following issues:

Definition of "Serious Health Condition" Many employers indicate that there is confusion about what constitutes a "serious health condition" under FMLA. And, indeed, DOL's own definition of "serious health condition" has changed while the law has been in effect.[8]

The first regulations promulgated by DOL specified that unless there are complications, many common conditions (such as the common cold, influenza, earaches, upset stomach, minor ulcers, headaches, and so forth) are not considered "serious health conditions" that trigger FMLA protection. However, DOL later revised its position expressing that if such conditions lasted for three days then they meet the threshold of "serious health condition" under FMLA.[9]

Employers can request employees provide documentation from a doctor or a medical professional supporting their claim of having a serious medical condition. According to DOL, employers, healthcare representative, and employees complain that this can be a burdensome process.[10]

Timing of Leave Employees exercising FMLA leave are allowed to take leave intermittently. According to regulations promulgated during the Clinton administration, employers are required to account for leave in the shortest increment used in their payroll system for leave and must account for time taken by the hour or less. When possible, employees are supposed to work with employers to schedule their leave in order to minimize disruptions in the workplace.[11]

An estimated twenty percent of FMLA leave was taken intermittently in 1999–2000, according to DOL.[12] Employers complain about the burden and difficulty of keeping track of these short periods of leave.[13]

In addition to creating an administrative burden for employers, co-workers also often take on additional responsibilities when FMLA leave is exercised. Surveys suggest that overwhelmingly the FMLA leave-takers' workplace responsibilities are shifted to co-workers.

Leave Notification While employees are supposed to provide employers with advanced warning of the need for FMLA leave whenever possible, under the law, employees can report unanticipated leave "as soon as practicable," DOL has interpreted "as soon as practicable" to mean within one to two business days of the incidence of the leave. In other words, employees may take a day off for an FMLA purpose, but not explain this absence to their employer for up to two days after not appearing at work.[14]

According to human-resource professionals responding to the SHRM's survey, less than half of those who used FMLA leave scheduled leave in advance.[15] For employers, the potential problems associated with this provision are clear: it makes it very difficult to plan for unscheduled absence, enforce attendance, and properly account for leave.

Clarifying Existing Regulations—A First Step to Improving FMLA

DOL could ease the burden on employers who administer FMLA by further clarifying employers' responsibilities related to these provisions. For example, DOL could provide additional guidance to clarify the situations in which ailments reach the threshold of constituting a "serious health condition," and ideally this clarification would be returning the law's application more toward Congress's original intent.

DOL could also consider tightening notification requirements or specifying in what instances it is acceptable to inform an employer of FMLA leave *after* the leave has occurred (such as during a health emergency requiring hospital treatment) and when an employee must make an employer aware of leave during the incidence of leave (such as when an employee can easily contact the employer by phone).

Calls for expanded government-mandated leave

Increasingly, policymakers are calling for expanding government mandates for employer-provided leave. For example, in this Congress, Senator Teddy Kennedy (D-MA) and Representative Rosa DeLauro (D-CT) introduced "The Healthy Families Act," which would require that all employers with fifteen or more employees provide full-time workers with seven days of paid leave for their own illness or a family member's illness and part-time workers (who work at least 20 hours per week or 1000 hours annually) pro-rated paid leave. Senator Christopher Dodd (D-CT) has called for creating at least six weeks of paid leave and expanding FMLA to apply to employers with fewer workers.[16] These proposals would entail significant costs for businesses.

The Costs and Potential Consequences of Mandated Paid Leave

Providing employees with paid leave creates costs for business. During the employees' [20] absence, businesses must replace those workers or shift their responsibilities to other employees, resulting in lost productivity. While proponents of expansion would likely highlight that most businesses report that FMLA has had a negligible effect to their bottom line, including productivity, there is reason to assume that a paid leave program would have a greater effect on business.

Workers are more likely to utilize a paid leave benefit than an unpaid leave benefit since the loss of income in the unpaid leave program provides a deterrent to taking leave. So in addition to employers who had not previously provided paid leave facing the additional cost of having to pay absent employees because of this mandate, they would also likely find an increase in the number of absences and greater disruption in the workplace.

The increase in mandated benefits raises the costs associated with hiring an employee. In recent years, benefits have constituted a growing portion of employees' total compensation. As of 2006, more than 30 percent of the average worker's total compensation was paid as benefits.[17] That means employees see less of their compensation in their paychecks. A new mandate increasing benefits will likely mean that workers' take-home pay will be lower than it would have been otherwise, as a greater share of total compensation becomes dedicated to providing these benefits.

If the cost of hiring a worker increases, businesses will have an incentive to hire fewer workers or to outsource jobs to countries where businesses do not have to provide costly benefits. This could mean a loss of job opportunities in the United States, particularly for employees whose job responsibilities can be fulfilled from alternative locations.

The Impact on Small Businesses

The problems experienced by larger employers implementing FMLA would be magnified for smaller companies if they become subject to the law. While an employer of fifty or more employees may be able to shift work from the FMLA-leave taker to co-workers without meaningfully affecting productivity, an organization with just 15 employees would have a more difficult time picking up the slack left by an absent worker, particularly when such a significant portion of leave taken under FMLA is unscheduled.

Small businesses often are more financially vulnerable and will be less able to assume the additional costs of administering and paying for these benefits. Small businesses have been an engine of job growth in recent years, but that could be slowed by imposing costly new mandates.

Solving the problem of the need for paid leave without government mandates

Government mandates are not the only way to address the need for individuals to be able to take and sustain themselves during periods when they cannot work.

Most Employers Voluntarily Provide Leave Packages

Many employers already provide leave packages that are in excess of government requirements. According to DOL, in 2006, 82 percent of the 105 million American workers in the private sector had access to some sort of paid leave, whether it is sick leave, vacation, or personal leave.[18] Not surprisingly, full-time workers were much more likely to have access specifically to paid sick leave than part-time workers (nearly 70 percent of full-time workers had paid sick leave, compared with 20 percent of part-time workers.[19] A DOL survey found that roughly two-thirds of those who took FMLA leave received some compensation, primarily through the employers' paid sick leave plan. Seventy percent of those leave-takers who received compensation received their entire paychecks while they were on leave.

Unfortunately, regulations like FMLA can deter companies from providing or expanding paid leave programs. As the SHRM executive director testified before the Oregon state legislature:

> Companies which have voluntarily provided paid leave prior to the enactment of the FMLA have had dramatic increases in absenteeism rates and have had

more problems with workers providing little or no notice for unscheduled and unplanned intermittent leave pursuant to ongoing or chronic conditions, some of which are questionable under conflicting legal interpretations. . . . Unfortunately, FMLA misapplications have penalized employers with the most generous leave policies and had a chilling effect on the expansion of paid leave.[20]

Addressing the problems with FMLA's application and enforcement may encourage more companies to voluntarily provide paid leave.

Greater Workplace Flexibility

A growing number of employees also enjoy more 30 flexible work schedules and work arrangements. For example, telecommuting was rare a decade ago, but today more than four million Americans telecommute most days and an estimated twenty million telecommute at least once a month.[21] Women are more likely than men to telecommute—2.2 million women worked from home in 2000.[22] Telecommuting provides employees with many advantages, including greater flexibility to care for personal and family needs during the day.

Many workers also have flexible worker schedules, according to the Bureau of Labor Statistics. As of May 2004, 27 million full-time wage and salary workers—or 27.5 percent of all full-time wage and salary workers—worked in arrangements that allowed them to vary their work start and end times.[23] These flexible arrangements make it easier for workers to schedule and make time for important personal duties, such as taking care of personal and family healthcare needs, and other parenting duties, such as participating in educational meetings.

The voluntary move toward greater flexibility signals an important shift in businesses' expectations for their workers: a growing number of businesses are evaluating employees based on output and productivity instead of work hours. It demonstrates that many businesses recognize that flexibility can be a win-win for employers and employees.

Encouraging Private Saving to Provide for Family Leave

While many businesses are providing leave voluntarily, a significant portion of the workforce continues to work in jobs that do not provide provisions for leave. Proponents of expanded government mandates point to these individuals as justification for government action.

Ideally, however, the government shouldn't be involved in encouraging companies or individuals to prepare for periods when individuals are unable to work. All individuals know that they face the potential for problems: severe illnesses can strike employees or their family members, and the birth of a child or the introduction of a new member into the family requires time away from work. Responsible individuals should plan for such circumstances, accruing savings while working so that they can sustain themselves if and when they cannot work for pay. The federal government is not supposed to be our national caretaker.

The federal government should, however, 35 not act as an impediment to responsible actions such as private saving. Unfortunately, the government today does just that by continuing to place onerous taxes on income generated by private savings. When an individual uses after-tax dollars to purchase a new television, they[sic] do not have to then pay a tax every time they watch a program. But when an individual puts money in a savings account or buys a stock, the federal government does tax the income it generates. The double taxation of savings and investment encourages consumption and discourages saving, leaving individuals less prepared to make ends meet during a time of crisis. Policymakers should eliminate the double taxation of savings as a first step to encouraging greater individual responsibility and to help individuals provide for themselves in times of need.

While the federal government creates impediments to many forms of savings, it has embraced measures to encourage individuals to save for specific foreseeable needs and expenses. For example, the federal government has created tax-advantaged savings accounts for retirement, educational expenses, and healthcare costs. Similar efforts could be made to encourage individuals to save to provide for periods of leave. For example, individuals could be allowed to put $5000 per year into a "Paid Leave" savings account tax-free that could then be accessed when an individual takes unpaid, or partially paid, leave. Regulations could require that those funds can only be accessed without tax penalty in specific situations, such as to address a serious illness or for the birth or adoption of a child. Unused funds could then be accessed without a tax penalty once the individual reaches retirement age.

In addition to providing tax incentives to encourage individuals to contribute to "Paid Leave" savings accounts, the federal government could provide additional incentives for businesses to match employees' contributions. The downside of such a policy is that businesses would have an incentive to divert other forms of non-tax advantaged compensation into contributions to "Paid Leave" savings accounts. Employees would likely have less take-home pay as a result. However, such a policy would be preferable to a government mandate on business to provide paid leave directly.

Conclusion

There are situations when individuals need time off from their jobs. While it is tempting to address this legitimate need through government action, there are significant costs to doing so. In the years that FMLA has been in force, many businesses have struggled to make sense of the regulations and have had to bear increased financial and administrative burdens to comply with this law. DOL could help ease the burden of existing regulations by providing some much needed clarity to some of the laws' provisions.

Today there are calls for an expansion of government mandates, including paid leave and expanding FMLA to apply to smaller businesses. These measures would have significant costs for businesses and could have the unintended consequence of making job opportunities scarcer.

There are other ways for policymakers to help individuals sustain themselves during times of leave. First, the federal government ought to stop penalizing savings. Currently, the government discourages individuals from taking the responsible action of setting aside income that can be drawn upon during a period when they cannot work. In addition to ending destructive anti-savings tax policies, policymakers could explore programs that encourage savings specifically to provide for leave. Policymakers have already created tax-advantaged savings vehicles for retirement, health expenses, and education costs, so they could create a similar initiative to deal with situations that require leave.

The primary goals of any government action should be to encourage individuals to provide for themselves and to avoid creating costly mandates that will be a drag on the economy and reduce job opportunities for Americans.

Endnotes

1. President William J. Clinton, "Statement on Signing the Family and Medical Leave Act of 1993," February 5, 1993, available at http://www.presidency.ucsb.edu/ws/index.php?pid=46777.

2. Linda Levine, "The Family and Medical Leave Act: Recent Legislative and Regulatory Activity," Congressional Research Service Report for Congress, Order Code RL31760, January 19, 2007, 2.

3. U.S. Department of Labor Fact Sheet on "Leave Coverage and Usage for U.S. Workers," February 27, 2007, 3.

4. Federal Register, vol. 71, no. 231, December 1, 2006, 69506.

5. Paul Kersey, "Medical Leave Regulations Should Reflect Intent Behind FMLA," Heritage Foundation Web Memo no. 626, December 21, 2004, 1.

6. Linda Levine, "The Family and Medical Leave Act: Recent Legislative and Regulatory Activity," 8.

7. Linda Levine, "Explanation of and Experience Under the Family and Medical Leave Act," Congressional Research Service Report for Congress, Order Code RL30893, February 7, 2003, 14.

8. Federal Register, vol. 71, no. 231, December 1, 2006, 69505.

9. *Ibid.*

10. Federal Register, vol. 71, no. 231, December 1, 2006, 69507.

11. Linda Levine, "The Family and Medical Leave Act: Recent Legislative and Regulatory Activity," 3.

12. Linda Levine, "The Family and Medical Leave Act: Recent Legislative and Regulatory Activity," 9.

13. Linda Levine, "Explanation of and Experience Under the Family and Medical Leave Act," 13.

14. Linda Levine, "The Family and Medical Leave Act: Recent Legislative and Regulatory Activity," 3.

15. Linda Levine, "The Family and Medical Leave Act: Recent Legislative and Regulatory Activity," 9.

16. Senator Christopher Dodd, "Families Need More Paid Leave," *New Hampshire Union Leader*, February 4, 2007, available at http://dodd.senate.gov/index.php?q= node/3727. Senator Christopher Dodd (D-CT) Press Release, "Dodd Introduces Bill to Expand Historic Family and Medical Leave Act," February 5, 2003, available at http://www.senate.gov/~dodd/press/Releases/03/0205.htm.

17. James Sherk, "Shared Prosperity: Debunking Pessimistic Claims About Wages, Profits, and Wealth," Heritage Foundation Backgrounder no. 1978, October 16, 2006, Chart 5.

18. U.S. Department of Labor Fact Sheet on "Leave Coverage and Usage for U.S. Workers," February 27, 2007, 2.

19. *Ibid.*

20. "Specific Recommendations for State Policymakers on Paid Leave Proposals," Excerpts from testimony presented to the Oregon Legislature (Paid Family Leave Task Force, Oregon State Capitol, October 3, 2002), compiled by Deanna R. Gelak, Senior Professional in Human Resources, Executive Director, National FMLA Technical Corrections Coalition, 2.

21. U.S. Census Bureau, available at http://www.census.gov/population/cen2000/phc-t35/tab01-1.xls.

22. U.S. Census Bureau, "Census 2000 PHC-T-35. Working at Home: 2000," Table 1-4, available at http://www.census.gov/population/cen2000/phc-t35/tab01-4.xls.

23. Bureau of Labor Statistics Press Release, "Workers on Flexible and Shift Schedules in 2004 Summary," July 1, 2005, available at http://www.bls.gov/news.release/flex.nr0.htm.

A CLOSER LOOK AT
Who Pays for My Time Off?

1. Reread Lukas's proposal, noting the places where she identifies problems and the places where she proposes solutions. (Mark a small "P" for problems and "S" for solutions.) Are these problems and solutions stated clearly and prominently to help the reader understand what is at stake and make a fair judgment?

2. A good proposal identifies a problem and describes it in a way that helps the reader understand why that problem is important and worth caring about. In addition, a good proposal often analyzes that problem by identifying its causes. According to Lukas, what has caused the problems she addresses? How does her solution address those causes?

3. When a writer establishes an *ethos* of fairness in any communication that aims to persuade, readers will be more open to the writer's ideas and may find them more persuasive. How does Lukas succeed or fail in projecting such an *ethos*? Point to a few specific places in her proposal where you feel she presents the issues fairly or unfairly. Readers also perceive writers to be fair when they have done their research and have documented it. How does Lukas use her sources (the 23 endnotes) to project an *ethos* of fairness?

1. Lukas explores the costs and benefits (mostly costs) of what happens when the federal government strives to become, as she puts it, "our national caretaker." Write either a brief memoir or profile that addresses this issue. Describe a real incident involving the government that happened to you or to another person or to a group of co-workers or acquaintances. You should provide some insight into the concept of government as "caretaker." You can either include or not include an explicit claim about the meaning of your story for this question.

2. Imagine that "Who Pays for My Time Off?" has just appeared in your local newspaper or on your favorite political commentary Web site. Write a letter to the editor that supports or refutes Lukas's argument. State your claim clearly and support it with concrete evidence.

A Modest Proposal

JONATHAN SWIFT

Jonathan Swift (1667–1745) was an Irish clergyman who was among the most skilled satirists ever to write in any language. Like most satires, A Modest Proposal *appears on the surface to approve of something ludicrous in order to attack a real social problem. As you read this selection, keep in mind that it was published anonymously in 1729 and that readers would have been expecting to read a serious and straightforward proposal for addressing the intolerable conditions and treatment of the Irish poor, not a satire.*

For preventing the children of poor people in Ireland, from being a burden on their parents or country, and for making them beneficial to the publick.

It is a melancholy object to those, who walk through this great town, or travel in the country, when they see the streets, the roads and cabbin-doors crowded with beggars of the female sex, followed by three, four, or six children, all in rags, and importuning every passenger for an alms. These mothers instead of being able to work for their honest livelihood, are forced to employ all their time in stroling to beg sustenance for their helpless infants who, as they grow up, either turn thieves for want of work, or leave their dear native country, to fight for the Pretender in Spain, or sell themselves to the Barbadoes.

I think it is agreed by all parties, that this prodigious number of children in the arms, or on the backs, or at the heels of their mothers, and frequently of their fathers, is in the present deplorable state of the kingdom, a very great additional grievance; and therefore whoever could find out a fair, cheap and easy method of making these children sound and useful members of the common-wealth, would deserve so well of the publick, as to have his statue set up for a preserver of the nation.

But my intention is very far from being confined to provide only for the children of professed beggars: it is of a much greater extent, and shall take in the whole number of infants at a certain age, who are born of parents in effect as little able to support them, as those who demand our charity in the streets.

As to my own part, having turned my [5] thoughts for many years, upon this important subject, and maturely weighed the several schemes of our projectors, I have always found them grossly mistaken in their computation. It is true, a child just dropt from its dam, may be supported by her milk, for a solar year, with little other nourishment: at most not above the value of two shillings, which the mother may certainly get, or the value in scraps, by her lawful occupation of begging; and it is exactly at one year old that I propose to provide for them in such a manner, as, instead of being a charge upon their parents, or the parish, or wanting food and raiment for the rest of their lives, they shall, on the contrary, contribute to the feeding, and partly to the cloathing of many thousands.

There is likewise another great advantage in my scheme, that it will prevent those voluntary abortions, and that horrid practice of women murdering their bastard children, alas! too frequent among us, sacrificing the poor innocent babes, I doubt, more to avoid the expence than the shame, which would move tears and pity in the most savage and inhuman breast.

The number of souls in this kingdom being usually reckoned one million and a half, of these I calculate there may be about two hundred thousand couple whose wives are breeders; from which number I subtract thirty thousand couple, who are able to maintain their own children, (although I apprehend there cannot be so many, under the present distresses of the kingdom) but this being granted, there will remain an hundred and seventy thousand breeders. I again subtract fifty thousand, for those women who miscarry, or whose children die by accident or disease within the year. There only remain an hundred and twenty thousand children of poor parents annually born. The question therefore is, How this number shall be reared, and provided for? which, as I have already said, under the present situation of affairs, is utterly impossible by all the methods hitherto proposed. For we can neither employ them in handicraft or agriculture; we neither build houses, (I mean in the country) nor cultivate land: they can very seldom pick up a livelihood by stealing till they arrive at six years old; except where they are of towardly parts, although I confess they learn the rudiments much earlier; during which time they can however be properly looked upon only as probationers: As I have been informed by a principal gentleman in the county of Cavan, who protested to me, that he never knew above one or two instances under the age of six, even in a part of the kingdom so renowned for the quickest proficiency in that art.

I am assured by our merchants, that a boy or a girl before twelve years old, is no saleable commodity, and even when they come to this age, they will not yield above three pounds, or three pounds and half a crown at most, on the exchange; which cannot turn to account either to the parents or kingdom, the charge of nutriments and rags having been at least four times that value.

I shall now therefore humbly propose my own thoughts, which I hope will not be liable to the least objection.

I have been assured by a very knowing [10] American of my acquaintance in London, that a young healthy child well nursed, is, at a year old, a most delicious nourishing and wholesome food, whether stewed, roasted, baked, or boiled; and I make no doubt that it will equally serve in a fricasie, or a ragoust.

I do therefore humbly offer it to publick consideration, that of the hundred and twenty thousand children, already computed, twenty thousand may be reserved for breed, whereof only one fourth part to be males; which is more than we allow to sheep, black cattle, or swine, and my reason is, that these children are seldom the fruits of marriage, a circumstance not much regarded by our savages, therefore, one male will be sufficient to serve four females. That the remaining hundred thousand may, at a year old, be offered in sale to the persons of quality and fortune, through the kingdom, always advising the mother to let them suck plentifully in the last month, so as to render them plump, and fat for a good table. A child will make two dishes at an entertainment for friends, and when the family dines alone, the fore or hind quarter will make a reasonable dish, and seasoned with a little pepper or salt, will be very good boiled on the fourth day, especially in winter.

I have reckoned upon a medium, that a child just born will weigh 12 pounds, and in a solar year, if tolerably nursed, encreaseth to 28 pounds.

I grant this food will be somewhat dear, and therefore very proper for landlords, who, as they have already devoured most of the parents, seem to have the best title to the children.

Infant's flesh will be in season throughout the year, but more plentiful in March, and a little before and after; for we are told by a grave author, an eminent French physician, that fish being a prolifick dyet, there are more children born in Roman Catholick countries about nine months after Lent, the markets will be more glutted than usual, because the number of Popish infants, is at least three to one in this kingdom, and therefore it will have one other collateral advantage, by lessening the number of Papists among us.

I have already computed the charge of nursing a beggar's child (in which list I reckon all cottagers, labourers, and four-fifths of the farmers) to be about two shillings per annum, rags included; and I believe no gentleman would repine to give ten shillings for the carcass of a good fat child, which, as I have said, will make four dishes of excellent nutritive meat, when he hath only some particular friend, or his own family to dine with him. Thus the squire will learn to be a good landlord, and grow popular among his tenants, the mother will have eight shillings neat profit, and be fit for work till she produces another child.

Those who are more thrifty (as I must confess the times require) may flea the carcass; the skin of which, artificially dressed, will make admirable gloves for ladies, and summer boots for fine gentlemen.

As to our City of Dublin, shambles may be appointed for this purpose, in the most convenient parts of it, and butchers we may be assured will not be wanting; although I rather recommend buying the children alive, and dressing them hot from the knife, as we do roasting pigs.

A very worthy person, a true lover of his country, and whose virtues I highly esteem, was lately pleased, in discoursing on this matter, to offer a refinement upon my scheme. He said that many gentlemen of this kingdom, having of late destroyed their deer, he conceived that the want of venison might be well supply'd by the bodies of young lads and maidens, not exceeding fourteen years of age, nor under twelve; so great a number of both sexes in every country being now ready to starve for want of work and service: And these to be disposed of by their parents if alive, or otherwise by their nearest relations. But with due deference to so excellent a friend, and so deserving a patriot, I cannot be altogether in his sentiments; for as to the males, my American acquaintance assured me from frequent experience, that their flesh was generally tough and lean, like that of our school-boys, by continual exercise, and their taste disagreeable, and to fatten them would not answer the charge. Then as to the females, it would, I think, with humble submission, be a loss to the publick, because they soon would become breeders themselves: And besides, it is not improbable that some scrupulous people might be apt to censure such a practice, (although indeed very unjustly) as a little bordering upon cruelty, which, I confess, hath always been with me the strongest objection against any project, how well soever intended.

But in order to justify my friend, he confessed that this expedient was put into his head by the famous Salmanaazor, a native of the island Formosa, who came from thence to London, above twenty years ago, and in conversation told my friend, that in his country, when any young person happened to be put to death, the executioner sold the carcass to persons of quality, as a prime dainty; and that, in his time, the body of a plump girl of fifteen, who was crucified for an attempt to poison the Emperor, was sold to his imperial majesty's prime minister of state, and other great mandarins of the court in joints from the gibbet, at four hundred crowns. Neither indeed can I deny, that if the same use were made of several plump young girls in this town, who without one single groat to their fortunes, cannot stir abroad without a chair, and appear at a play-house and assemblies in foreign fineries which they never will pay for; the kingdom would not be the worse.

Some persons of a desponding spirit are in great concern about that vast number of poor people, who are aged, diseased, or maimed; and I have been desired to employ my thoughts what course may be taken, to ease the nation of so grievous an incumbrance. But I am not in the least pain upon that matter, because it is very well known, that they are every day dying, and rotting, by cold and famine, and filth, and vermin, as fast as can be reasonably expected. And as to the young labourers, they are now in almost as hopeful a condition. They cannot get work, and consequently pine away from want of nourishment, to a degree, that if at any time they are accidentally hired to common labour, they have not strength to perform it, and thus the country and themselves are happily delivered from the evils to come.

I have too long digressed, and therefore shall return to my subject. I think the advantages by the proposal which I have made are obvious and many, as well as of the highest importance.

For first, as I have already observed, it would greatly lessen the number of Papists, with whom we are yearly over-run, being the principal breeders of the nation, as well as our most dangerous enemies, and who stay at home on purpose with a design to deliver the kingdom to the Pretender, hoping to take their advantage by the absence of so many good Protestants, who have chosen rather to leave their country, than stay at home and pay tithes against their conscience to an episcopal curate.

Secondly, The poorer tenants will have something valuable of their own, which by law may be made liable to a distress, and help to pay their landlord's rent, their corn and cattle being already seized, and money a thing unknown.

Thirdly, Whereas the maintainance of an hundred thousand children, from two years old, and upwards, cannot be computed at less than ten shillings a piece per annum, the nation's stock will be thereby encreased fifty thousand pounds per annum, besides the profit of a new dish, introduced to the tables of all gentlemen of fortune in the kingdom, who have any refinement in taste. And the money will circulate among ourselves, the goods being entirely of our own growth and manufacture.

Fourthly, The constant breeders, besides the gain of eight shillings sterling per annum by the sale of their children, will be rid of the charge of maintaining them after the first year.

Fifthly, This food would likewise bring great custom to taverns, where the vintners will certainly be so prudent as to procure the best receipts for dressing it to perfection; and consequently have their houses frequented by all the fine gentlemen, who justly value themselves upon their knowledge in good eating; and a skilful cook, who understands how to oblige his guests, will contrive to make it as expensive as they please.

Sixthly, This would be a great inducement to marriage, which all wise nations have either encouraged by rewards, or enforced by laws and penalties. It would encrease the care and tenderness of mothers towards their children, when they were sure of a settlement for life to the poor babes, provided in some sort by the publick, to their annual profit instead of expence. We should soon see an honest emulation among the married women, which of them could bring the fattest child to the market. Men would become as fond of their wives, during the time of their pregnancy, as they are now of their mares in foal, their cows in calf, or sow when they are ready to farrow; nor offer to beat or kick them (as is too frequent a practice) for fear of a miscarriage.

Many other advantages might be enumerated. For instance, the addition of some thousand carcasses in our exportation of barrel'd beef: the propagation of swine's flesh, and improvement in the art of making good bacon, so much wanted among us by the great destruction of pigs, too frequent at our tables; which are no way comparable in taste or magnificence to a well grown, fat yearly child, which roasted whole will make a considerable figure at a Lord Mayor's feast, or any other publick entertainment. But this, and many others, I omit, being studious of brevity.

Supposing that one thousand families in this city, would be constant customers for infants' flesh, besides others who might have it at merry meetings, particularly at weddings and christenings, I compute that Dublin would take off annually about twenty thousand carcasses; and the rest of the kingdom (where probably they will be sold somewhat cheaper) the remaining eighty thousand.

I can think of no one objection that will possibly be raised against this proposal, unless it should be urged that the number of people will be thereby much lessened in the kingdom. This I freely own, and 'twas indeed one principal design in offering it to the world. I desire the reader will observe, that I calculate my remedy for this one individual Kingdom of Ireland, and for no other that ever was, is, or, I think, ever can be upon Earth. Therefore let no man talk to me of other expedients: Of taxing our absentees at five shillings a pound; Of using neither cloaths, nor houshold furniture, except what is of our own growth and manufacture; Of utterly rejecting the materials and instruments that promote foreign luxury; Of curing the expensiveness of pride, vanity, idleness, and gaming in our women; Of introducing a vein of parsimony, prudence, and temperance; Of learning to love our country, wherein we differ even from Laplanders, and the inhabitants of Topinamboo; Of quitting our animosities and factions, nor acting any longer like the Jews, who were murdering one another at the very moment their city was taken; Of being a little cautious not to sell our country and consciences for nothing; Of teaching landlords to have at least one degree of mercy towards their tenants. Lastly, of putting a spirit of honesty, industry, and skill into our shop-keepers, who, if a resolution could now be taken to buy only our native goods, would immediately unite to cheat and exact upon us in the price, the measure, and the goodness, nor could ever yet be brought to

make one fair proposal of just dealing, though often and earnestly invited to it.

Therefore I repeat, let no man talk to me of these and the like expedients, 'till he hath at least some glympse of hope, that there will ever be some hearty and sincere attempt to put them into practice.

But, as to my self, having been wearied out for many years with offering vain, idle, visionary thoughts, and at length utterly despairing of success, I fortunately fell upon this proposal, which, as it is wholly new, so it hath something solid and real, of no expence and little trouble, full in our own power, and whereby we can incur no danger in disobliging England. For this kind of commodity will not bear exportation, and flesh being of too tender a consistence, to admit a long continuance in salt, although perhaps I could name a country, which would be glad to eat up our whole nation without it.

After all, I am not so violently bent upon my own opinion, as to reject any offer, proposed by wise men, which shall be found equally innocent, cheap, easy, and effectual. But before something of that kind shall be advanced in contradiction to my scheme, and offering a better, I desire the author or authors will be pleased maturely to consider two points. First, As things now stand, how they will be able to find food and raiment for a hundred thousand useless mouths and backs. And secondly, There being a round million of creatures in humane figure throughout this kingdom, whose whole subsistence put into a common stock would leave them in debt two million of pounds sterling; adding those who are beggars by profession to the bulk of farmers, cottagers and labourers, with their wives and children, who are beggars in effect; I desire those politicians who dislike my overture, and may perhaps be so bold to attempt an answer, that they will first ask the parents of these mortals, whether they would not at this day think it a great happiness to have been sold for food at a year old, in the manner I prescribe, and thereby have avoided such a perpetual scene of misfortunes, as they have since gone through, by the oppression of landlords, the impossibility of paying rent without money or trade, the want of common sustenance, with neither house nor cloaths to cover them from the inclemencies of the weather, and the most inevitable prospect of intailing the like, or greater miseries, upon their breed for ever.

I profess, in the sincerity of my heart, that I have not the least personal interest in endeavouring to promote this necessary work, having no other motive than the publick good of my country, by advancing our trade, providing for infants, relieving the poor, and giving some pleasure to the rich. I have no children, by which I can propose to get a single penny; the youngest being nine years old, and my wife past child-bearing.

A CLOSER LOOK AT
A Modest Proposal

1. How closely does Swift adhere to the main features and structure of a proposal? Point to specific passages where the author describes and analyzes the problem, explains the specific plan for solving the problem, and lists the benefits and costs of the plan. What other features of a modern proposal does this satire use?

2. "A Modest Proposal" uses irony to make its argument. In other words, Swift says one thing but means something entirely different. First, summarize what the narrator literally proposes. Then state what you believe Swift really meant for his readers to understand. Finally, describe some of the subtle strategies (such as style, evidence, structure, *ethos, pathos, logos*) Swift uses to make this supposed proposal feel real.

3. As discussed in Chapter 11, writers use proposals to convince readers that a specific plan will solve an important problem. If this is the case, then is "A Modest Proposal" really a proposal? Or is it a piece of writing that uses readers' expectations about proposals to achieve some other purpose? In terms of its purpose, what genre (or microgenre) does it most align with: a commentary, position paper, rant, or some other genre? How does Swift's playing with the genre of the proposal help him (or hurt him) in terms of achieving his intended purpose?

IDEAS FOR
Writing

1. Imitating Swift's "A Modest Proposal," write a mock proposal that on the surface makes a ludicrous proposition but actually criticizes or attacks some injustice or some policy you feel strongly about. Like Swift, you should fashion your mock proposal so that it closely resembles the proposal genre. Include a reflective memo to your professor that describes your true intentions and purpose. This memo should also describe the proposal strategies that you used to play with this genre.

2. Write a rhetorical analysis of Jonathan Swift's "A Modest Proposal." Be sure to define Swift's rhetorical purpose. Is he trying to persuade, and if so, to what beliefs or position? Or is he merely trying to entertain? Or is it some combination? Also, describe the rhetorical strategies that are used. Focus on just one or two rhetorical strategies, such as *ethos, pathos, logos,* or style. Finally, evaluate the work: How effectively does it engage its readers and achieve its rhetorical purpose?

With 7 Billion on Earth, a Huge Task Before Us

JEFFREY D. SACHS

Jeffery D. Sachs, professor of health policy and management and director of the Earth Institute at Columbia University, is a world leader on international economics, sustainability, and poverty alleviation. As you read this brief proposal, written for CNN.com, pay attention to the way he analyzes the global problem we are facing, the methods he uses to convince his readers of its importance, and his proposed solutions.

Just 12 years after the arrival of the 6 billionth individual on the planet in 1999, humanity will greet the 7 billionth arrival this month. The world population continues its rapid ascent, with roughly 75 million more births than deaths each year. The consequences of a world crowded with 7 billion people are enormous. And unless the world population stabilizes during the 21st century, the consequences for humanity could be grim.

A rising population puts enormous pressures on a planet already plunging into environmental catastrophe. Providing food, clothing, shelter, and energy for 7 billion people is a task of startling complexity.

The world's agricultural systems are already dangerously overstretched. Rainforests are being cut down to make way for new farms; groundwater used for irrigation is being depleted; greenhouse gases emitted from agricultural activities are a major factor in global climate change; fertilizers are poisoning estuaries; and countless species are threatened with extinction as we grab their land and water and destroy their habitats.

The economic challenges are equally huge. Population is growing most rapidly in the world's poorest countries—often the places with the most fragile ecological conditions. Poor people tend to have many more children, for several reasons. Many live on farms, where children can be engaged in farm chores.

Poor societies generally suffer from high 5 rates of child mortality, leading parents to have more children as "insurance" against the possible deaths of children. Girls rarely make it to high school, and are often married at a very young age, leading to early childbearing. And modern methods of contraception may be unavailable or unaffordable.

When poor families have six or eight children, many or most of them are virtually condemned to a lifetime of poverty. Too often, parents lack the wherewithal to provide decent nutrition, health care and education to most of them. Illiteracy and ill health end up being passed from generation to generation. Governments in poor countries are unable to keep up, their budgets overmatched by the need for new schools, roads and other infrastructure.

So the arrival of the 7 billionth person is cause for profound global concern. It carries a challenge: What will it take to maintain a planet in which each person has a chance for a full, productive and prosperous life, and in which the planet's resources are sustained for future generations? How, in short, can we enjoy "sustainable development" on a very crowded planet?

The answer has two parts, and each portends a difficult journey over several decades. The first part requires a change of technologies—in farming, energy, industry, transport and building—so that each of us on average is putting less environmental stress on the planet. We will have to make a worldwide transition, for example, from today's fossil-fuel era, dependent on coal, oil and gas, to an era powered by low-carbon energies such as the sun and wind. That will require an unprecedented degree of global cooperation.

The second key to sustainable development is the stabilization of the global population. This is already occurring in high-income and even some middle-income countries, as families choose to have one or two children on average. The reduction of fertility rates should be encouraged in the poorer countries as well. Rapid and wholly voluntary reductions of fertility have been and can be achieved in poor countries. Success at reducing high fertility rates depends on keeping girls in school, ensuring that children survive, and providing access to modern family planning and contraceptives.

Two centuries ago, the British thinker 10 Thomas Robert Malthus famously warned that excessive population growth would cut short economic progress. That is a threat still with us today, but it is a warning, not an inevitable outcome.

We face an urgent task: to adopt more sustainable technologies and lifestyles, and work harder to achieve a stable population of some 8 billion or so by mid-century, rather than the current path, which could easily carry the world to more than 10 billion people by 2100.

A CLOSER LOOK AT
With 7 Billion on Earth, a Huge Task Before Us

1. This proposal, though very brief, follows the classic proposal structure closely. Turn to the At-A-Glance section at the beginning of Chapter 11 and mark the places where Sachs introduces the topic and problem, describes and analyzes the problem, proposes a plan, and concludes by looking to the future. Which features get the most attention? Which features need more explanation?

2. Proposals need to show readers that the problems they address are serious and deserve attention. How does Sachs argue for such importance? Describe his argumentative strategies in terms of ethos, pathos, and logos (consult Chapter 22, "Using Argumentative Strategies"). How effective are his strategies? What other strategies could he have used to convince his readers of his topic's importance?

3. Sachs does not go into much detail about the costs and benefits of his proposed two-part plan. Do you think his plan is feasible? What are the costs and benefits associated with his plan?

IDEAS FOR
Writing

1. Write a rhetorical analysis that explains whether Sachs's proposal successfully meets the writing situation at hand. Be sure to consider the audience and their reading situation (reading this on a website) and how well the brevity meets that situation. How well does Sachs accomplish his overall purpose?

2. In his work as director of the Earth Institute, Jeffrey Sachs attempts to find solutions to enormous global problems. Write a profile of a person who is tackling a major social, political, or economic problem, such as poverty, justice, education, sustainability, and so forth. (You could also profile a group of people or an organization.) Describe the values that motivate your subject and what makes your subject interesting and inspiring.

A FEW IDEAS FOR
Composing a Proposal

1. **Write a proposal to solve a hometown problem.** List five things that irritated you about the place where you grew up. Choose one. Then define the problem or irritation and figure out its causes and effects. Develop a plan for solving that problem and offer a step-by-step solution. Conclude your proposal by explaining why the costs of your plan are worth the benefits of solving the problem. Your proposal should be written for publication in a local newspaper where you grew up.

2. **Write a "modest proposal" of your own.** If you run an Internet search, you will find many proposals titled "A Modest Proposal." Most of them are modeled in some way on Jonathan Swift's "A Modest Proposal," a satire in which he suggests an absurd solution to a real problem. Write your own modest proposal in which you suggest an absurd solution to a serious problem in your community.

3. **Create a podcast proposal for improving your life.** What are the causes and effects of the problem? What would you need to do to fix this aspect of your life? What would be some of the benefits if you followed your plan, and what would be the costs? Although you are the primary reader of this proposal, write it so that others will understand what you are trying to accomplish. Then turn your proposal into a podcast, so you can listen to it in the future.

Reports

CHAPTER 41

Underage Alcohol Use Among Full-Time College Students

OFFICE OF APPLIED STUDIES, SUBSTANCE ABUSE AND MENTAL HEALTH SERVICES ADMINISTRATION

The National Survey on Drug Use and Health (NSDUH) issues new editions of this report every few years. Published by the Substance Abuse and Mental Health Services Administration (SAMHSA) at the Office of Applied Studies (OAS), this study discusses the problem of alcohol use and abuse among underage college students. Pay special attention to how a research question leads to methodology, which leads to results. Also, look at how the design of the report, including its use of color and graphics, makes it more accessible and attractive. The page layout draws the readers' attention to key information in the report while making the text more readable.

National Survey on Drug Use and Health

The NSDUH Report

Issue 31   2006

Underage Alcohol Use among Full-Time College Students

In Brief

- The rates of past month, binge, and heavy alcohol use among full-time college students aged 18 to 20 remained steady from 2002 to 2005

- Based on 2002 to 2005 combined data, 57.8 percent of full-time college students aged 18 to 20 used alcohol in the past month, 40.1 percent engaged in binge alcohol use, and 16.6 percent engaged in heavy alcohol use

- Based on 2002 to 2005 combined data, male full-time students in this age group were more likely to have used alcohol in the past month, engaged in binge alcohol use, and engaged in heavy alcohol use than their female counterparts

During the past decade, increased attention has been directed toward underage alcohol use and binge drinking among college students and the negative consequences related to these behaviors.[1-5] Binge drinking refers to the "consumption of a sufficiently large amount of alcohol to place the drinker at increased risk of experiencing alcohol-related problems and to place others at increased risk of experiencing secondhand effects" (p. 287).[2]

The National Survey on Drug Use and Health (NSDUH) asks respondents aged 12 or older to report their frequency and quantity of alcohol use during the month before the survey. NSDUH defines binge alcohol use as drinking five or more drinks on the same occasion (i.e., at the same time or within a couple of hours of each other) on at least 1 day in the past 30 days. NSDUH defines heavy alcohol use as drinking five or more drinks on the same occasion on each of 5 or more days in the past 30 days. All heavy alcohol users are also binge alcohol users.

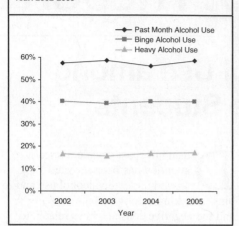

Figure 1. Past Month, Binge, and Heavy Alcohol Use among Full-Time College Students Aged 18 to 20, by Year: 2002-2005

Source: SAMHSA, 2002-2005 NSDUHs.

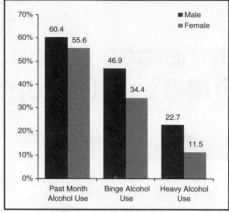

Figure 2. Past Month, Binge, and Heavy Alcohol Use among Full-Time College Students Aged 18 to 20, by Gender: 2002-2005

Source: SAMHSA, 2002-2005 NSDUHs.

NSDUH also asks young adults aged 18 to 22 about college attendance. For this analysis, respondents were classified as college students if they reported that they were in their first through fourth year (or higher) at a college or university and that they were a full-time student. Respondents who were on break from college were considered enrolled if they intended to return to college or university when the break ended.[6]

Data from the 2005 survey indicate that young adults aged 18 to 22 enrolled full time in college were more likely than their peers not enrolled full time (i.e., part-time college students and persons not currently enrolled in college) to use alcohol in the past month, binge drink, and drink heavily.[7]

This report examines trends and patterns in the rates of alcohol use among full-time college students who have not yet reached the legal drinking age (i.e., college students aged 18 to 20) based on data from the 2002, 2003, 2004, and 2005 NSDUHs.

Demographic Characteristics of Full-Time College Students Aged 18 to 20

From 2002 to 2005, an average of 5.2 million young adults aged 18 to 20 were enrolled full time in college each year. This represents 41.3 percent of young adults in this age range. Full-time college students included an average of 2.8 million women aged 18 to 20 (46.0 percent of women in this age group) and 2.4 million men aged 18 to 20 years (36.9 percent of men in this age group) each year. Over half of full-time college students aged 18 to 20 (58.2 percent) lived in the same household with a parent, grandparent, or parent-in-law, while 41.8 percent lived independently of a parental relative.[8]

Past Month Alcohol Use

From 2002 to 2005, the rates of past month alcohol use among full-time college students aged 18 to 20 remained steady (Figure 1), with an annual average of 57.8 percent (3.0 million

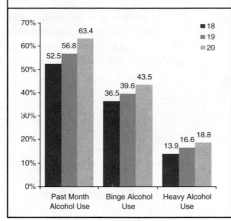

Figure 3. Past Month, Binge, and Heavy Alcohol Use among Full-Time College Students Aged 18 to 20, by Age: 2002-2005

Source: SAMHSA, 2002-2005 NSDUHs.

students) using alcohol in the past month. Male full-time students in this age group were more likely to have used alcohol in the past month than their female counterparts (60.4 vs. 55.6 percent) (Figure 2). Rates of past month alcohol use among this group increased with increasing age (Figure 3). Among full-time college students aged 18 to 20, those living with a parent, grandparent, or parent-in-law were less likely to have used alcohol in the past month than those who were not living with a parental relative (51.2 vs. 67.0 percent).

Binge Alcohol Use

Rates of past month binge alcohol use among full-time college students aged 18 to 20 also remained steady from 2002 to 2005 (Figure 1), with an annual average of 40.1 percent (2.1 million students) engaging in binge alcohol use. In this group of young adult students, males were more likely to have engaged in binge alcohol use than females (46.9 vs. 34.4 percent) (Figure 2).

Rates of binge alcohol use among this group also increased with increasing age (Figure 3). Full-time college students aged 18 to 20 living with a parent, grandparent, or parent-in-law were less likely to have engaged in binge alcohol use than full-time college students aged 18 to 20 who were not living with a parental relative (34.0 vs. 48.5 percent).

Heavy Alcohol Use

From 2002 to 2005, rates of heavy alcohol use among full-time college students aged 18 to 20 also remained steady (Figure 1), with an annual average of 16.6 percent (866,000 students) engaging in heavy drinking. As is true for past month and binge alcohol use, rates of heavy alcohol use were higher among males than females and increased with increasing age (Figures 2 and 3). Among full-time college students aged 18 to 20, those living with a parent, grandparent, or parent-in-law were less likely to have engaged in heavy alcohol use than those who were not living with a parental relative (12.3 vs. 22.5 percent).

End Notes

[1] Reifman, A., & Watson, W. K. (2003). Binge drinking during the first semester of college: Continuation and desistance from high school patterns. *Journal of American College Health, 52*, 73-81.

[2] Wechsler, H., & Nelson, T. F. (2001). Binge drinking and the American college student: What's five drinks? *Psychology of Addictive Behaviors, 15*, 287-291.

[3] Turrisi, R., Wiersma, K. A., & Hughes, K. K. (2000). Binge-drinking-related consequences in college students: Role of drinking beliefs and mother-teen communications. *Psychology of Addictive Behaviors, 14*, 342-355.

[4] Weingardt, K. R., Baer, J. S., Kivlahan, D. R., Roberts, L. J., Miller, E. T., & Marlatt, G. A. (1998). Episodic heavy drinking among college students: Methodological issues and longitudinal perspectives. *Psychology of Addictive Behaviors, 12*, 155-167.

[5] Wechsler, H., Davenport, A., Dowdall, G., Moeykens, B., & Castillo, S. (1994). Health and behavioral consequences of binge drinking in college: A national survey of students at 140 campuses. *Journal of the American Medical Association, 272*, 1672-1677.

[6] Respondents whose current college enrollment status was unknown were excluded from the analysis.

[7] Office of Applied Studies. (2006). *Results from the 2005 National Survey on Drug Use and Health: National findings* (DHHS Publication No. SMA 06-4194, NSDUH Series H-30). Rockville, MD: Substance Abuse and Mental Health Services Administration.

[8] Living with a parental relative is defined as currently living in the same household with a parent, grandparent, or parent-in-law. Respondents who did not live with a parental relative and had unknown information on one or more household relationships were excluded from this analysis.

A CLOSER LOOK AT
Underage Alcohol Use Among Full-Time College Students

1. Find the place where the authors of the report define "heavy alcohol use" and "binge alcohol users." How do these definitions shape their results?

2. Where do the authors describe their methodology? There is no section called "Methods," but the authors have described generally how they went about doing their study. What did they do?

3. Do the authors offer any recommendations about what to do about alcohol usage among college students? If so, locate those recommendations. If not, why didn't they offer any recommendations?

IDEAS FOR
Writing

1. Imagine that you are an administrator at your university who is concerned about alcohol abuse among students. In a proposal addressed to the university president, describe how the school should respond to alcohol abuse. Define the problem, its causes, and its effects. Then develop a plan that will take steps toward solving or containing the problem.

2. Do you think the government and university administrators worry too much or perhaps too little about alcohol use among college students? Write a commentary in which you argue that people are too concerned about alcohol abuse or not concerned enough. You can use the NSDUH report as support for some of your arguments. You will need to do more research to support your claims.

7 Days on Craigslist's Casual Encounters

SAMUEL AXON

Samuel Axon, the Digital Entertainment Reporter at the online magazine Mashable, *takes an empirical approach to finding out who uses and what really happens at the "hookup" section of Craigslist, the best-known national online network of classified advertising. Although this report does not follow the classic organization and style of the report, notice how Axon stretches the genre to fit his readers' needs and values.* **Caution: As a student, you should not conduct an online experiment like this one, because posing as someone else online might be dangerous or violate your university's research ethics policies.**

Many people use Craigslist to find roommates, cheap furniture, used cars or part-time jobs. But there's another function: Sex.

I decided to dive into Craigslist's "Casual Encounters"—a section made for no-strings hookups—to see if any of what I assumed about that virtual place was true. Is it populated entirely by perverted sexual deviants, serial killers, prostitutes and scammers as rumors insist? Or can two regular people really make the connection that the section's name suggests?

I should admit that I had no intention to actually hook up with someone, should the opportunity arise, if for no other reason than it would be inappropriate and manipulative to an unwitting partner to do so and write about it. But it's not a stretch to say that even if you abstain from the goal, spending a week on Casual Encounters can teach you a lot about human beings and how the web has changed how we pursue one of our most essential and important desires.

It goes without saying that the content of this article is not intended for children or those made uncomfortable by such topics. But if you're interested, read on for the story of my seven days on Craigslist's Casual Encounters— my failures, near misses, discoveries, insights and successes. Following that, I interviewed two women to learn how they used the site successfully for their own fulfillment.

The Experiment

I began with a listing announcing myself to the 5 women of my city.

Each day I tried a different approach to see what would be most effective, though I never lied or posted fake photographs. One day my message was intended to be sweet and normal; I suggested starting with drinks and fun conversation to see if we had chemistry, then going back to my place to cuddle on the couch with a movie and see where that led. Another day, I described it as a rebound. In yet another, I explicitly detailed sexual activities and used very aggressive language.

Ultimately, only the "sweet and normal" was successful, even though very few posts by women had that same tone (more on that later). I received about a half-dozen responses each day. Most were scams, some were men, some were prostitutes, and just one was legit.

Barking Up the Wrong Tree

All the responses I got from real people on my first day weren't from women—they were from men. I made it very clear in my post that I was only interested in women, but a large number of men chose to ignore that.

They all offered oral sex. I responded to them politely, saying, "Just interested in women, but thanks for the offer! Have a good one." Most didn't write back after that. One responded: "Really man, can be cool and relaxing."

I began to suspect that no women actually 10 used the site. The stereotype is that women are interested in relationships, and that only men would be interested in totally casual sex, right? We know that's not true, though. In fact, I was inspired to write this article when a friend told me many of her female friends had owned up to using it.

But where were they? I was only getting messages from gay or bisexual men!

An Army of Scammers

Over the next couple of days, I actually received a lot of posts from women. Or at least, they said they were women. To be honest, I doubted the veracity of the claims.

It didn't take long to realize that almost all the replies I received were scams. The situation is so severe on Craigslist Casual Encounters that posts by real women who are actually seeking hook-ups are often flagged for removal at the slightest cause for suspicion.

The most common scams are "safe dating" websites. An alleged woman will write a man saying she's interested, but that because of the Craigslist-based serial killers and rapists in the news, she needs some extra assurance that it's safe. If you follow the link she provides, the website asks you for your credit card number—y'know, so it can do a background check to make sure you're not a criminal. Right.

My favorite scam: One individual tried to 15 get me to buy him or her virtual currency in online games like MapleStory before agreeing to hand over contact information. Yeah, right—moving on!

Taking Initiative

What little luck I'd had so far. The week was half over and I hadn't had a single bite. I decided I would have to take the initiative, so in addition to posting my own ads, I started responding to every ad from any woman who seemed at all interesting.

I cast a wide net in my searches, looking up posts by straight or bisexual women between the ages of 18 and 35 who lived anywhere in Chicagoland—a large metropolitan area that's home to close to five million females. Most of the women wanted something very specific they couldn't find in their normal lives: Someone to help play out a particular fantasy, someone vastly older than them or someone of another race.

Very few of the women who were advertising seemed to be looking for anything I would consider a "normal encounter." Nevertheless, I tailored each response to whatever they were looking for. I typically wrote two or three paragraph replies and matched the tone of their own messages, then attached a couple of tasteful photos of myself.

I didn't get a single reply from an actual prospect this way. It turned out that most of the ads were fakes from scammers, and quite a few fell into another category all together.

Love ~~Don't~~ Does Cost a Thing

Prostitution is what made Craigslist controver- 20 sial. There's technically another section for that—"Adult Services," formerly "Erotic Services"—but that's not the only place you'll find practitioners of the world's oldest profession.

The prostitutes of Craigslist speak in code, but it's not a difficult one to learn. They advertise "French lessons"—an odd thing to advertise under "Casual Encounters," don't you think? Well, it's obviously a euphemism for something else. Many of the ads that weren't from scammers were from prostitutes.

The ads are so obvious that it's surprising the euphemisms are effective in fending off law enforcement. Then again, maybe they *are* law enforcement. What a mess!

Success?

Amidst all those failures, I had one near-success. A woman wrote in response to my sweet "cuddling first" ad saying she was in town for only a couple of months, and that she was frustrated she couldn't find a relationship. When she sent her pictures, she looked plain but attractive.

We exchanged a couple of e-mails over the course of two hours, tossing back and forth lists of interests and the like. She made it clear that she wanted to meet up, and while she talked about starting slow, it was clear that it would indeed be a casual encounter. But when I suggested a time to meet—the last message from me before I would reveal myself and back out—there was no reply.

At least, not yet. The next day, she e-mailed 25 me saying she was deeply apologetic and that she'd fallen asleep. She said she'd like to meet up sometime. So yes, there are women on Craigslist. Well, at least one!

The Other Perspective, Part 1:
My Fake Female Ad

You've probably guessed by now that the experiences for heterosexual men and women on Craigslist's casual encounters are quite different. I observed that for every ad a woman posts, there are at least 20 from men. If nothing else, that imbalance ought to alter the experience.

To get the female perspective, I did two things: I posted a fake ad as a woman to see what kinds of responses I would get, and I interviewed two women who have had success hooking up on casual encounters in the past. First, the ad.

"I just broke up with my boyfriend and while it was the right thing to do, it's been rough because I still have all this physical passion and sexual energy and I don't know where to direct it," I wrote. "I feel this is the best way because I don't want to hurt him by hooking up with someone we both know."

As for potential suitors, I asked only that they supply a photo and "be attractive and not creepy." I clicked "post" and waited. There was a five minute delay before my ad appeared, then I started receiving about one response per minute.

Most of them were careful to say "I don't do 30 this often." Some were attractive, some weren't. Some sent pictures of themselves naked along with the word "Hi." Others wrote a single paragraph making it very clear just how normal and nice they thought they were, and included the sort of photo you would find on a Facebook profile. There were a lot of expressions of sympathy over my fake breakup. I was hearing from men of

all types, and it seemed I had my pick of the litter.

After about thirty minutes, though, my post was flagged for removal. I thought I'd made it look legit, but as we learned earlier, folks have good reason to be hawkish about scammers.

The Other Perspective, Part 2:
Interviews with Craigslist Women

After the end of my test run with Craigslist casual encounters, I decided to get more insight into the female experience with the site by interviewing two women who said they had successes meeting up with men on Casual Encounters.

Their problem was the opposite of mine. They had too many options to pick from, but they both dealt with the numerous choices in the same way.

Both women ultimately responded to men who they felt put effort into writing long, personal messages as opposed to quick notes. Multiple paragraphs of insightful and relatable prose won out—but only after the initial test of physical appearance. One said that only 5 to 10% of the men who responded to her ad made it past the initial, picture-based judgment. Both said they immediately eliminated men who opened with pictures of genitalia—a very common practice. However, looks were important.

My favorite anecdote: One of the women I 35 interviewed said she once had a crush on a client at her job, but couldn't make a move without compromising her professionalism. However, she was looking through Casual Encounters and saw an ad from a man, and she recognized his writing style—it was her old client! She sent him a message to see if it was him, asking a question only he would be able to answer. He proved his identity and they ended up hooking up.

One of the women said she would go to Casual Encounters when she was looking for a very specific sexual experience—something you can't always count on from a one night stand that starts at a club or bar. The other said her reasons could be summed up as "curiosity, boredom, and convenience." She also said "it's a safe way to reach out in ways you might be too shy to in person."

"There are a lot of shady people, or at least people doing shady things on Craigslist," one said. "But once you get over the embarrassment of actually posting or responding to something on Craigslist, it has the potential to be very rewarding. The trick is to keep an open mind and not have any real expectations. At the very least, it's mildly entertaining."

So What Is Casual Encounters Really Like?

After all this exploration, I'll say that Craigslist casual encounters is a place where people go to find very specific things from each other that they might not be able to conveniently locate in the real world. Some of those things are very alternative.

It's a last, best hope for some people who are looking to make a personal connection, but it's full of spam, unwanted attention, crime, and, well . . . crazy people. You might not find what you're looking for, but you're sure to find something interesting regardless.

Put another way, Craigslist casual encounters is a sexual microcosm of the rest of the Internet. 40

A CLOSER LOOK AT
7 Days on Craigslist's Casual Encounters

1. Although this text may not look like some of the other reports in this section, it does conform to the genre's conventions in many ways. Make a list of the ways it does and does not conform.

2. Find the research question and the hypothesis. How clearly are these stated?

3. Axon takes an empirical approach to his research question by conducting a kind of "experiment." How does this approach make the report more or less interesting and persuasive?

IDEAS FOR
Writing

1. You should not do an experiment similar to the one Axon describes, because pretending you are someone else online could be dangerous. Also, you could violate other people's rights or your university's ethics codes for research. Write a commentary in which you discuss some of the ways in which posing as someone else online, especially on Web sites like Craigslist, could put a researcher in jeopardy or violate the rights of others. In your commentary, perhaps you could discuss other ways to gather information about human behavior.

2. Write a rhetorical analysis of "7 Days on Craigslist's Casual Encounters" that explains how well Axon achieves his purpose. First, go to *Mashable* .com and do a full audience analysis (as described in Chapter 3). Now write your rhetorical analysis, focusing on how Axon adapts and stretches the report genre to suit the attitudes, beliefs, and expectations of Mashable readers.

3. Write a "digital-literacy narrative" of your own experience with the World Wide Web. Just as literacy narratives (Chapter 4) focus on formative learning experiences about reading and writing generally, a digital-literacy narrative focuses on the author's experience accessing and sharing information and ideas on the World Wide Web. Be sure to pay attention to any conflicts and resolutions, as well as how your experiences changed you. What new understanding did you come away with?

Freshman Fifteen: Fact or Fiction?

JENNIFER A. CARITHERS-THOMAS, SHELLEY H. BRADFORD, CHRISTOPHER M. KESHOCK, STEVEN F. PUGH

Published in the College Student Journal, *this research report examines the so-called "freshman fifteen," which refers to the average amount of weight that first-year students supposedly gain during their first year of college. The authors of this study used a survey to assess the accuracy of this widespread belief. As you read, pay attention to the way they frame their research question and the methods they use to answer it.*

Abstract

The present study examined the validity of the concept known as Freshman Fifteen. The sample included 52 freshman college students enrolled in a physical education class. Three issues were addressed: a) amount (if any) of weight gain during the first year in college, b) perceptions on the reasons for any weight gain, and c) strategies for losing unwanted weight gain. Results indicated that nearly two-thirds (62%) of the sample reported weight gain (M=10.8 lbs.). These findings did not find strong support for the notion of Freshman Fifteen. Implications for college administrators were noted.

Introduction

The expression "Freshman Fifteen" is a term used to describe the weight gain by students during their first year of study in college (Thomas, 2006). This specific topic has been recently discussed by researchers, clinicians, and nutritionists. Brown (2008) reviewed the extant literature and found more than 140 newspaper articles about freshman weight gain, 20 peer reviewed articles, 141 university newspaper articles and 19 popular magazine articles on this issue, including eight books. A Google search of the term "Freshman Fifteen" yielded 7,630,000 links and articles specifically designed to provide advice, hints, and strategies to help college students avoid gaining the dreaded "Freshman Fifteen" (Google, 2009). With 1.5 million students entering United States colleges or universities each fall, the Freshman Fifteen could be considered an epidemic (Malinauskas, Auinger, & Klein 2006).

The purpose of this study was to validate or negate the premise that freshman college students are likely to gain 15 pounds during their first year of college. Moreover, this study asked respondents to identify the causes of weight gain peculiar to the freshman year and inquired about specific methods that can be implemented to control weight gain. This type of research is necessary to determine if weight gain occurs and, more importantly, what behaviors can be modified to diminish the probability of further weight gain. Furthermore, if the assertion is true that students gain weight, regardless of the specific amount of pounds, universities have an obligation to provide programs, resources, and services to educate their students about the concept of the Freshman Fifteen.

Review of the Literature

The seminal reference to the concept of the "Freshman Fifteen" was found in 1989 that chronicled a college freshman's fight against weight gain (see Brown, 2008). This 15 pounds of perceived weight gain that has been investigated, analyzed, evaluated, and debated for almost two decades and refers to the popular belief that students gain an average of 15 pounds during their first year of college (Hodge, Jackson, & Sullivan 1993). An extensive review of the literature validates that weight gain typically and predictably occurs; yet a weight gain of 15 pounds has not been substantiated by most research endeavors. Some research shows that the average weight gain to be only 8.8 pounds (Howell, Mewborn, Randle & Fowler-Johnson, 1985). A study by Hoffman,

Policastro, Quick, and Lee (2006) found that a mean of 7 pounds is gained during the first year. In another study, 59% of the volunteers gained weight in their freshman year (Graham & Jones, 2000); however, the amount of weight gained was calculated at 4.6 pounds (2000). A study conducted by researchers at Michigan State University revealed that of the 110 respondents, the average weight gain was 7 pounds, again substantially less than the predetermined 15 (Hodge et al., 1993). In fact, the authors concluded that the majority of the female students in the sample remained the same weight during their first six months of college. The Journal of American College Health reported that about 70% of students will gain a significant amount of weight between the start of college and the end of sophomore year (Jung, Bray, & Ginnis 2008). The researchers also found that the average weight gain is closer to 9 pounds as opposed to 15 pounds. Researchers studying men and women found that although both sexes gain weight, men appeared to gain more and experience a larger increase in body mass index (Mihalopoulous , Raedeke, Aeby, Smith, & Dallas 2008).

A recent study found that 90% of first year 5 college students are aware of the freshman 15, yet many students chose to ignore the warning signs related to weight gain (Jung et al., 2008; Wyshak, 2007). The possible reasons of this superfluous weight gain are limitless in the college atmosphere. Many researchers suggest that this weight gain is attributed to the new-found freedom and accompanying stress associated with the shift to college life. Other researchers claim that the excess weight gain is due to an increase in caloric consumption through the intake of alcohol and unhealthy snacking (Jung et al., 2008).

Moreover, few personal characteristics have been found to distinguish women who gain, lose, or maintain their weight. In fact, contrary to predictions, self-esteem, body image, and locus of control were unconnected to weight change among women who gained weight (Hodge et al., 1993). Yet, those women who lost weight and evaluated their appearance, fitness, and health more positively lose less weight. This suggests that a favorable body image may mitigate against a pursuit of slimness (Hodge et al., 1993).

Method

Participants

The participants of this study were students who had completed their freshman year of college at the University of South Alabama. The sample comprised 52 female and male students who were enrolled in tennis and weight training physical education courses.

Instrumentation

Previous researchers who had studied the "Freshman Fifteen" concept had collected measurements such as height and weight, body mass, percentage of body fat, total fat mass, and waist and hip circumferences (Jung et al., 2006; Morrow et al., 2006). The current survey measure sought specific information about the amount of weight gain, loss, or maintenance during a student's freshman year. Another section asked students about factors that contributed to weight gain such as late night snacking, drinking, stress, and social eating. A final section asked students to identify the specific approaches they utilized to lose weight (if they acknowledged that weight had been gained); for example, dieting, increasing one's activity, making better food choices, and decreasing one's amount of stress. These data were collected during the Spring semester of 2009.

Results and Discussion

Nearly two-thirds of our sample admitted to weight gain during their freshman year. Of the 32 students (62%) who reported weight gain, the average weight gain of the respondents was 10.78 pounds (range 2 lbs.-28 lbs.). Only six students reported a weight gain exceeding 15 pounds. Of the 18 females sampled who reported weight gain, the average weight gain was 10.5 pounds. Of the 14 males sampled that gained weight, the average increase in weight was measured at 11.14 pounds. Nine students (17.3%) reported that they actually lost weight during their freshman year. The average amount of weight loss was 9.44 pounds (range 2-30 lbs.). Interestingly, eleven students (21.15%) reported maintaining their weight (7 males; 4 females). Participants identified the most plausible reason or reasons for their weight gain. Table 1 presents the rank order of critical factors.

TABLE 1 Major Factors Identified to Account for Weight Gain

Reasons	Percentage
Late-night snacking	20.8
Cafeteria food selection	12.9
Social eating	11.9
Irregular schedule	11.9
General stress	10.9
Decreased activity	10.9
Lack of "healthy foods"	8.9
Social drinking	6.9

Participants noted several ways that they [10] could lose their weight gain. Students identified increasing activity to be the best way to achieve weight loss (25.24%). Making better food choices (24.27%) and decreasing the amount of fast food consumed (19.42%) also ranked high on the list. In addition, students acknowledged the importance of decreasing snack ingestion (11.65%), dieting (10.68%), decreasing stress (3.88%), and decreasing the amount of drinking (2.91%); interestingly, less than one percent of our sample stated that they would use an over-the-counter diet pill.

The current findings indicated that a sizeable majority of college students gain weight as freshman; however, the amount of weight gain appears to be moderate (about 10 lbs.). Moreover, it seems that young college students are aware of the factors that contribute to their weight gain and various methods that can be implemented which should lead to weight loss.

Also, the current findings support prior research endeavors that reported that many freshman students do not gain weight. In fact, 24% of our sample was able to maintain their weight and 17% were able to lose weight. Further, our findings corroborate the conclusions of earlier research efforts on the "Freshman Fifteen" issue (e.g., Hoffman et al., 2005; Howell et al., 1985; Mihalopoulous et al., 2008).

Implications for College Administrators

College preventative programs that accentuated the importance of good nutrition, consistent exercise, and healthy behaviors could possibly reverse the propensity to gain weight. Dieticians or nutritionists could be more involved in planning meals in the cafeteria setting to provide healthier food selections, such as salads, wraps, and vegetables. Physical education courses could be required for all freshman students to promote the importance of exercise. Colleges could engage nurses or other health care providers to offer seminars on the health benefits of exercise and consistent physical activity in the prevention of chronic diseases associated with obesity. Additionally, colleges should provide exercise equipment and gym facilities that students could use daily in designated areas of student housing. Educational endeavors for all students should consider annual physicals and health fairs that stress proper nutrition, exercise, and the maintenance of healthy behaviors.

The current study has several limitations; for example, the sample size is small and was obtained from one educational setting. Future research should focus on longitudinal data regarding weight loss/gain and concomitant health behaviors that promote stable weight maintenance.

References

Brown, C. (2008). The information trail of "Freshman 15": A systematic review of health myth within the research and popular literature. *Health Information Library*, 25, 1–12.

Google. (2009). Freshman 15. Retrieved February 8. 2009 from www.google.com.

Graham, M., & Jones, A. (2000). Freshman 15; Valid theory or harmful myth? *Journal of American College Health*, 50, 171–173.

Hodge, C, Jackson, L., & Sullivan, L. (1993). The "Freshman 15" facts and fantasies about weight gain in college women. *Physiology of Women Quarterly*, 17, 119–126.

Hoffman, D. Policastro, P., Quick, V., & Lee, S. (2002). Changes in body weight and fat mass of men and women in the first year of college: A study of the "Freshman 15". *Journal of American College of Health*, 55, 52–55.

Howell, M. F., Mewbom, C. R., Randle, Y., & Fowler-Johnson, S. (1985). Risk of excess weight gain in university women: A 3 year community controlled analysis. *Addictive Behaviors*, 10, 15–28.

Jung, M., Bray, S., & Ginis, M. (2008). Behavior change and the Freshman 15: Tracking physical activity and dietary patterns in first-year university women. *Journal of American College Health*, 56, 523–530.

Malinauskas, B., Raedeke, T., Aeby, V., Smith, J., & Dallas, M. (2006). Dieting practices, weight perceptions and body composition: A comparision of normal weight, overweight, and obese college females. *Nutrition Journal*, 5, 11–15.

Mihalopoulos, N., Auinger, P., & Klein, J. (2008). The Freshman 15: Is it real? *Journal of American College Health*, 56, 531–533.

Morrow, M., Heesch, K., Dinger, M., Hull, H., Kneehans, A., & Fields, D. (2006). Freshman 15: Fact or fiction? *Obesity*, 74, 1438–43.

Thomas, J. (2006). Weight gain awareness. The Freshman 15: A nutrition student public speaking project. *Journal of Nutrition, Education and Behavior*, 38, 383–386.

Wyshak, G. (2007). Weight change, obesity, mental health, and health perception: Self-reports of college-educated women. *Primary Care Companion Journal of Clinical Psychiatry*. 9, 48–54.

A CLOSER LOOK AT
Freshman Fifteen: Fact or Fiction?

1. This study examines the accuracy of a belief that is commonly held among college students. List some other beliefs about college life that may or may not be true? How could you design a research study to assess the accuracy of those beliefs?

2. A report's research question should be addressed in its introduction. Reread the introduction, including "Review of the Literature." In a single complete sentence, state this report's research question as a question. Then, explain in your own words what is already known about the topic and why this research would be of interest to college students.

3. Consulting the methods section, describe the participants who were studied and how weight gain was assessed. Do you think this study's results accurately reflect how much weight change occurred and the causes for those changes? Why or why not?

IDEAS FOR
Writing

1. Write a rebuttal that argues that the findings of this research report cannot be entirely trusted. Pay special attention to limitations (weaknesses) of its methods. For instance, you might describe why the participants in this study may not be typical of all college students (hint: use the Internet to learn about "sampling bias"). You might also explain why using surveys may not reveal the truth about weight change or the causes of weight change. Finally, offer some ideas for improving the methods.

2. Write a brief memoir that describes how your dietary or exercise habits changed (or did not) when you first started college or some other new and stressful situation. Like all memoirs, yours should offer insight into the challenges that you faced as well as a main point (or lesson) that provides a new understanding for your readers.

More Than Just a Pretty Face: Men's Priority Shifts Toward Bodily Attractiveness in Short-term versus Long-term Mating Contexts

JAIME C. CONFER, CARIN PERILLOUX, DAVID M. BUSS

Biologists have long studied how various animal species choose their mates. For instance, why are peacocks with the longest tail (a disadvantage for escaping predators) chosen by mates more often than shorter-tailed peacocks? This scientific inquiry asks a similar question about humans: What physical characteristics influence men's and women's choices of partners, and does choice strategy vary across situations?

More than just a pretty face: men's priority shifts toward bodily attractiveness in short-term versus long-term mating contexts

Jaime C. Confer, Carin Perilloux, David M. Buss

Abstract

Studies of physical attractiveness have long emphasized the constituent features that make faces and bodies attractive, such as symmetry, skin texture, and waist-to-hip ratio. Few studies, however, have examined the reproductively relevant cues conveyed by faces and bodies as whole units. Based on the premise that fertility cues are more readily assessed from a woman's body than her face, the present study tested the hypothesis that men evaluating a potential short-term mate would give higher priority to information gleaned from her body, relative to her face, than men evaluating a potential long-term mate. Male and female participants (N=375) were instructed to consider dating an opposite sex individual, whose face was occluded by a "face box" and whose body was occluded by a "body box," as a short-term or long-term mate. With the instruction that only one box could be removed to make their decision about their willingness to engage in the designated relationship with the occluded individual, significantly more men assigned to the short-term, compared to the long-term, mating condition removed the body box. Women's face versus body information choice, in contrast, was unaffected by the temporal dimension of the mating condition. These results suggest that men, but not women, have a condition-dependent adaptive proclivity to prioritize facial cues in long-term mating contexts, but shift their priorities toward bodily cues in short-term mating contexts.

1. Introduction

The importance of physical attractiveness and the biological correlates of various attributes has received much empirical attention since Darwin (1871) noted the precedence given to physical attractiveness, especially in women: "In civilized life man is largely, but by no means exclusively, influenced in the choice of his wife by external appearance" (p. 738). Despite much research having been devoted to attractiveness, most studies have focused on the specific features that contribute to overall attractiveness (for a review, see Sugiyama, 2005). Symmetry (Perrett et al., 1999), averageness (Langlois & Roggman, 1990; but see Grammer & Thornhill, 1994 for sex-specific effects), and sexual dimorphism (Johnston, Hagel, Franklin, Fink, & Grammer, 2001) have been shown to affect facial attractive-

ness. Contributors to bodily attractiveness include waist-to-hip ratio (Singh, 1993) and body mass index (Tovée, Maisey, Emery, & Cornelissen, 1999). Other specific bodily traits, such as muscularity (Frederick & Haselton, 2007), breast size (Furnham & Swami, 2007), and leg length (Sorokowski & Pawlowski, 2008) have been the focus of recent empirical research. Lacking, however, is research on the relative importance of faces and bodies as whole units, and whether the prioritization of facial or bodily attractiveness is dependent upon the intended duration of the mating context (short-term versus long-term mating)—a context of well-documented importance in mate preferences (Buss & Schmitt, 1993).

Aspects of physical attractiveness have been hypothesized to be "attractive" because they have been recurrently and closely associated with individuals' health, age, and hormonal status throughout human evolutionary history (Symons, 1979; Williams, 1975). Certain fitness-dependent cues relating to a woman's *current fertility* and her *reproductive value* (a measure of *future* reproductive potential that is strongly correlated with a woman's age) are conveyed

349

through the face and body with substantial overlap. For example, a woman's current fertility can be assessed through increases in facial (Roberts et al., 2004) and bodily attractiveness (Kirchengast & Gartner, 2002) that occur at ovulation. Similarly, health-correlated cues of reproductive value can be conveyed through both the face and the body. Pocked-marked facial skin, for example, reveals a history of disease (Buss, 1994), while increased leg length is correlated with a multitude of health benefits: lower risks of cardiovascular disease (Gunnell, Whitley, et al., 2003), diabetes (Davey Smith et al., 2001) and cancer (Gunnell, May, Ben-Sholomo, Yarnell, & Smith, 2003). Finally, age-dependent cues also related to reproductive value, such as taut facial skin and firm breasts (Symons, 1979), can be diagnosed through a woman's face and body. Clearly, information regarding a woman's fertility and reproductive value can be gleaned from both her face and body.

Nevertheless, one component, the face or the body, may convey relatively richer information about a particular health or hormonal status variable than the other. Thus, our central hypothesis is that *although many cues regarding a woman's health and fertility can be gleaned from both her face and her body, each component conveys a subset of cues that are not conveyed by the other component.* The results of several studies have indicated that the face and body make independent contributions toward overall attractiveness (e.g., Currie & Little, 2009; Peters, Rhodes, & Simmons, 2007), supporting the tenability of this basic premise. We hypothesized that a woman's face provides relatively richer information regarding her reproductive value; and conversely, that a woman's body conveys stronger cues to her current fertility. These two dimensions peak at different ages, necessitating a tradeoff such that one could not secure a woman who is simultaneously at the pinnacle of reproductive value and fertility. In human populations, reproductive value peaks around age 17, whereas fertility peaks around age 24 (Buss, 1994; Symons, 1979; Williams, 1975). Accordingly, Jones (1996) notes that "...male preferences may have led to the evolution both of cues in the female figure that advertise sexual maturity and of cues in the face that advertise youth" (p. 103; see also Symons, 1979).

Empirical evidence supports the premise that female faces and bodies provide information that is not entirely redundant. Facial features appear to be particularly effective cues of youth and health. Aside from obvious facial indicators of youth, such as homogeneous skin and the absence of wrinkles and sagginess (Fink, Grammer, & Thornhill, 2001), preferences have also been demonstrated for neotenous facial traits (e.g., large eyes; Cunningham, 1986). Features such as these are considered "feminine" because they are sensitive to the rise in estrogen levels that accompanies puberty and persists throughout a woman's reproductive lifespan (Thornhill & Gangestad, 2008). As women age and approach menopause, however, androgens increase relative to estrogen levels, causing their facial features to take a more masculine form (e.g., thinner lips;

Gangestad & Scheyd, 2005), rendering specific facial features effective proxies for assessing a woman's age and consequently, her reproductive value.

Women's bodies provide a window to several variables related to their *current fertility* (as contrasted with reproductive value) that cannot be ascertained through their facial characteristics alone. A woman's body shape is subjected to what Singh (1993) refers to as a "wide first pass filter," a quick heuristic that unconsciously evaluates whether a woman is currently capable of conceiving. For example, information obtained from a woman's waist-to-hip ratio (WHR) informs three concerns paramount to a woman's reproductive condition: (1) pregnancy status, (2) fertility, and possibly, (3) ovulatory status. First, as a woman progresses through pregnancy, her WHR exceeds 1.0, a clear indication that she is currently incapable of conceiving. For example, a young pregnant woman has high reproductive value, but a fertility of zero. This highlights the fact that fertility and reproductive value are partially dissociable, and that bodily cues are a powerful source of information regarding current fertility. Second, women with unusually high WHRs have greater difficulty conceiving than women with sex-typical WHRs (Singh, 1993, Zaadstra et al., 1993); therefore, the hormonal profile necessary for conception can be assessed through a woman's WHR. Finally, based on evidence that women's WHRs may slightly decrease at ovulation (Kirchengast & Gartner, 2002), a woman's figure could also reveal whether or not she is at peak cycle fertility. In addition to waist-to-hip ratio, a woman's body mass index signals her ability to sustain pregnancy and lactation (Lake, Power, & Cole, 1997) as well as her supply of the fatty acids that support fetus neurodevelopment (Lassek & Gaulin, 2008). Bodily traits such as these can be appraised at a glance to assess a woman's current fertility.

Historically, a man's reproductive success depended in part on selecting a mate high in fertility with appreciable reproductive value. However, because there are substantial costs involved in exclusively attempting to secure such a woman (e.g., missed sexual opportunities), men typically make tradeoffs that depend on whether a short-term or long-term mate is sought. Theoretically, for men pursuing a short-term mate, a woman's current fertility is more paramount than her reproductive value (Buss & Schmitt, 1993). Thus, unlike men pursuing a long-term mating strategy, men pursuing short-term mating opportunities should possess evolved psychological mechanisms that are activated less by cues to a woman's reproductive value than by cues to her current fertility. This logic formed the basis of our prediction: *Men assigned to evaluate a woman a short-term mate would give higher priority to information gleaned from her body than from her face, compared to men assigned to evaluate a woman as a long-term mate.*

Although there is compelling evidence that both sexes have evolved short-term and long-term mating strategies (Buss & Schmitt, 1993), individuals naturally differ in the

350

extent to which they pursue one mating strategy over another, a construct labeled sociosexual orientation (SOI-R) (Gangestad & Simpson, 1990). We hypothesized that SOI-R would affect the relative priority given to facial and bodily cues, in addition to the effect of the mating condition to which participants were assigned. Based on the same rationale for the assigned short-term and long-term mating contexts, we anticipated that those who naturally pursue short-term relationships (as measured by the SOI-R, with higher scores indicating less restricted SOI-R; Penke & Asendorpf, 2008) would assign a higher priority to bodily attractiveness than those pursuing mainly long-term committed relationships. Our central hypothesis would receive additional support if both the individual differences in SOI-R and the contextual effects that result from assigning participants to mating conditions produce similar patterns of information prioritization.

We saw no *a priori* grounds for predicting that women would experience an analogous conditional shift in body versus face priority across the two mating contexts for two reasons. First, women were predicted not to differentially prioritize cues of current fertility because men's fertility does not show the same precipitous age-dependent drop-off as women's fertility. As a result, there has been relatively weaker selection pressure on women to attend to such cues. Second, to the degree that women seek physical indicators of good genes in a mate (Gangestad & Thornhill, 1997; Penton-Voak et al., 1999), hormonally dependent characteristics indicative of good genes appear to be equally reflected in men's faces and bodies (Folstad & Karter, 1992; Gangestad, Thornhill, & Yeo, 1994; Thornhill & Gangestad, 1993). Previous research has shown that testosterone-based cues of masculinity (e.g., wide jaw) are correlated with actual and perceived health (Rhodes, Chan, Zebrowitz, & Simmons, 2003). Because such cues have also been correlated with fluctuating asymmetry as assessed through the face and the body (Gangestad, & Thornhill, 2003), information about a man's health can be gleaned from both sources. Thus, in contrast to men, we expected no difference in the priority that women would give to a man's facial and bodily attractiveness as a function of mating context.

2. Methods

2.1. Participants

The sample consisted of 381 university students (194 male, 187 female) who agreed to participate in exchange for course credit. The data from six participants who did not identify themselves as heterosexual were excluded, resulting in a data set of 192 men (age M=18.85, SD=1.29) and 183 women (age M=18.69, SD=1.45). Approximately one quarter of the sample (51 men and 57 women) reported being in a committed romantic relationship.

2.2. Materials and procedure

Two clothed, full body photographs, one of a man and one of a woman, were purchased from a stock photography database for use in the present study. Individual difference measures, including sex, relationship status, and participants' SOI-R (Penke & Asendorpf, 2008), were obtained from participants prior to experimentation.

After accessing the experiment online, participants viewed an image of an opposite sex individual whose face was occluded by a "face box" and whose body was occluded by a "body box." A stick figure was superimposed over the face and body boxes to indicate which part of the photographed individual lied underneath (see Fig. 1). Having been randomly assigned to one of two mating conditions, participants were instructed to first imagine themselves as single and then to consider the possibility of dating the opposite sex individual behind the boxes as either a short-term mate (i.e., one night stand) or a long-term mate (i.e., a committed relationship partner), depending on their assigned condition. To experimentally test the relative importance of facial and bodily attractiveness, participants were instructed that they could only remove one box (the "face box" or "body box") to inform their decision about whether or not they would engage in the designated relationship with the occluded person.

After participants selected a box to remove, they were asked, "When you made your decision about which box to remove, how did you prioritize information gathered from the face versus the body?" Participants responded on a seven-point Likert scale wherein a score of 1 indicated that information from the face was much more important, a score of 4 indicated that information from the face and body was equally important, and a score of 7 indicated that information from the body was much more important. Thus, the two dependent variables were (1) choice of which occluding box to remove, and (2) quantitative judgments about the relative priority of information gleaned from the face versus the body. Although unnecessary, the face or body of the opposite sex individual underneath was subsequently revealed, in accordance with each participant's selection. Participants were fully debriefed as to the purpose of the study.

3. Results

3.1. Face versus body box choice

To evaluate whether participants chose to remove the face or body box more often, we first conducted an exploratory analysis which revealed a general trend to choose the face box over the body box in male participants (face: 61%; χ^2_1=9.19, N=192, p_{rep}=.99, φ=.22) and in female participants (face: 69%; χ^2_1=27.55, N=183, p_{rep}>.99, φ=.39). We then conducted χ^2 cross-tabulation analyses within each sex to examine the effect of mating context on box choice, taking

351

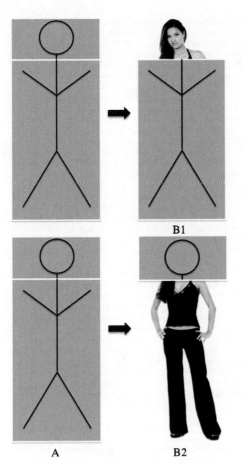

Fig. 1. Demonstration of the box removal procedure (for male participants). Column (A) represents the opposite sex image that is first presented to participants occluded by a "face box" and a "body box." Column (B) represents the image that is presented to participants upon removal of the "face box" (B1) or "body box" (B2).

into account the inherently unequal expected frequencies of box choice. Table 1 presents the observed and expected frequencies for each mating condition by sex. Men removed the face box when told to consider the target as a long-term mate with greater frequency than expected by chance (observed 68; expected 55.5). In contrast, men removed the body box when told to consider the target as a short-term mate with greater frequency than expected by chance (observed 52; expected 39.5), $\chi^2_1=13.81$, $N=192$, $p_{rep}>.99$,

Table 1
Cross-tabulation of box choice by long-term or short-term mating context and sex

Males		Face box	Body box	Females		Face box	Body box
LT	Observed	68	23	LT	Observed	60	22
	Expected	55.5	35.5		Expected	56.9	25.1
	% within LT	75%	25%		% within LT	73%	27%
ST	Observed	49	52	ST	Observed	67	34
	Expected	61.5	39.5		Expected	70.1	30.9
	% within ST	49%	51%		% within ST	66%	34%
Total		61%	39%	Total		69%	31%

LT, long term; ST, short term.

$\varphi=.27$. Women did not differ from chance levels in their choice for box removal, $\chi^2_1=0.99$, $N=183$, $p_{rep}=.75$, $\varphi=.07$. Fig. 2 illustrates box choice within each mating condition by sex, compared to the frequencies expected by chance.

3.2. Rated priority assigned to facial and bodily information

Collecting Likert scale data on the priority that participants assigned to the information from the face and body boxes allowed us to also conduct t-tests within each sex. For this variable, higher scores indicated a greater priority placed on information from the body box. Two females who did not respond to this question were not included in the analyses for the priority variable. In line with the prediction, men who were told to evaluate the target as a short-term mate assigned the body box significantly higher priority (mean±S.E.=3.75±0.15) than did men told to evaluate the target as a long-term mate (mean±S.E.=3.00±0.13), $t_{190}=-3.72$, $p_{rep}>.99$, $d=.52$. Women assigned similar priority to the body box in both the short-term (mean±S.E.=3.21±0.15) and long-term mating conditions (mean±S.E.=2.93±0.15), $t(179)=-1.32$, $p_{rep}=.82$, $d=.19$.

3.3. Individual differences in SOI-R

To explore the hypothesis that the priority given to facial or bodily information is affected by an individual's SOI-R, we correlated participants' priority scores with their SOI-R

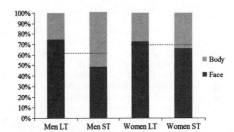

Fig. 2. Frequency distribution of box choice by mating context and sex. Expected frequencies of box choice, based on average frequencies by sex, are indicated with dashed lines.

352

scores, with higher SOI-R scores indicating less restricted sociosexual orientation. For women, only the SOI Desire subscale score was significantly correlated with their box priority ratings, r=.18, N=175, p_{rep}=.963. For men, however, their overall SOI-R score, as well as all subscales, were significantly correlated with their box priority ratings (SOI Total: r=.25, N=183, p_{rep}=.994; SOI Behavior: r=.14, N=188, p_{rep}=.923; SOI Attitude: r=.25, N=189, p_{rep}=.994; SOI Desire: r=.19, N=188, p_{rep}=.971).

4. Discussion

Simply assigning men to a short-term mating condition, as opposed to a long-term mating condition, caused them to increase the priority given to information obtained from a woman's body. Women assigned to the short-term and long-term mating conditions all gave greater priority to information obtained from an opposite sex individual's face. These results, as shown through both box choice and priority ratings, empirically support the hypothesis that men attend to bodily cues more in short-term than long-term mating contexts. In contrast, women's relative preferences were unaffected by mating condition, suggesting that women consistently prioritize facial cues over bodily cues. The adaptive shift in men's mating psychology was also reflected as a stable individual difference in men's SOI scores, with unrestricted men giving greater priority than restricted men to information obtained from a woman's body. Thus, men who most benefit from assessing current fertility, as opposed to reproductive value, showed greater interest in a woman's bodily cues.

Despite the conditional shift that focused men's interest toward a woman's body, both men and women chose to reveal the face of the opposite sex image at greater than chance levels when collapsed across conditions (despite the smaller absolute size of the face box, which one could argue contains less information than the larger body box). If the purpose of removing the face or body box was to assess overall attractiveness, these results are consistent with previous research indicating that the face is a better predictor of overall attractiveness than the body (Furnham & Reeves, 2006; Peters et al., 2007; Riggio, Widaman, Tucker, & Salinas, 1991). Because health is valued in both short-term and long-term mates, and because indicators of a robust immune system, such as symmetry, averageness, and sexual dimorphism, are abundantly accessible from an individual's face, facial attractiveness should be given greater weight, all else equal, than bodily attractiveness. Moreover, the face can convey social signals, such as reciprocal romantic interest, which are valued across sex and mating contexts.

The obtained pattern of results mirrors the findings of Currie and Little (2009) who showed that ratings of facial attractiveness better predicted overall attractiveness than did ratings of bodily attractiveness. Likewise, Currie and Little discovered a context-dependent shift in male raters, wherein ratings of bodily attractiveness better predicted ratings of overall attractiveness in a short-term relationship context than in a long-term relationship context. These findings provide convergent evidence that a woman's face and body convey at least somewhat non-redundant cues of female mate quality (but see Thornhill & Grammer, 1999).

Given that our results were obtained from a relatively young sample, future studies should replicate these results using a more diverse sample of participants. The forced choice procedure used in the present study allowed us to isolate the variables of interest in order to illuminate a context-dependent shift; however, this approach sacrificed ecological validity in regard to the mate assessment circumstances of everyday life. Methods that are more ecologically valid allow multiple cues to be assessed at once, for example, by allowing cues indicative of genetic quality and parental investment capacity to be evaluated simultaneously (Perilloux, Webster, & Gaulin, 2010). Within most cultures, men and women typically utilize cues from both a potential mate's face and body to assess his or her desirability as a mate. Thus, future studies should utilize a methodology that can elucidate how participants simultaneously assign relative priorities to both faces and bodies.

The current study provides evidence that for men, but not for women, priority shifting takes place based on the pursuit of short-term and long-term mating strategies. This methodology is conducive to many avenues of future research which aim to differentiate the relative importance placed on facial and bodily traits in a context-dependent manner, such as whether women's priorities of short-term and long-term mates' faces and bodies vary across the menstrual cycle along with documented fluctuations in sexual desire (Penton-Voak et al., 1999). Traits associated with SOI-R (Thornhill & Gangestad, 2008) and traits associated with parenting effort (Roney, Hanson, Durante, & Maestripieri, 2006) may be expressed in unequal concentrations across a man's face and body.

The present study utilized an evolutionarily informed perspective to hypothesize and document an increase in the relative importance of bodily information to men in a short-term mating context. Our hypothesis received further support when men who were dispositionally inclined to short-term mate showed a similar shift toward bodily cues as men in the assigned short-term mating condition. This study provides the empirical support for the hypothesized sex differences in the prioritization of facial and bodily attractiveness, while adding to a cumulative body of evidence highlighting the importance of temporal context in predicting mating decisions.

Acknowledgments

The authors thank Greg Hixon for his verification of our statistical procedures and members of the Buss Lab for their helpful feedback.

353

References

Buss, D. M. (1994). *The evolution of desire: Strategies of human mating.* New York: Basic Books.

Buss, D. M., & Schmitt, D. P. (1993). Sexual strategies theory: A contextual evolutionary analysis of human mating. *Psychological Review, 100,* 204–232.

Cunningham, M. (1986). Measuring the physical in physical attractiveness: Quasi-experiments on the sociobiology of female facial beauty. *Journal of Personality and Social Psychology, 50,* 925–935.

Currie, T. E., & Little, A. C. (2009). The relative importance of the face and body in judgments of human physical attractiveness. *Evolution and Human Behavior, 30,* 409–416.

Darwin, C. (1871). *The descent of man, and selection in relation to sex.* London: J. Murray.

Davey Smith, G., Greenwood, R., Gunnell, D., Sweetnam, P., Yarnell, J., & Elwood, P. (2001). Leg length, insulin resistance, and coronary heart disease risk: The Caerphilly Study. *Journal of Epidemiology and Community Health, 55,* 867–872.

Fink, B., Grammer, K., & Thornhill, R. (2001). Human (*Homo sapiens*) facial attractiveness in relation to skin texture and color. *Journal of Comparative Psychology, 115,* 92–99.

Folstad, I., & Karter, A. J. (1992). Parasites, bright males, and the immunocompetence handicap. *The American Naturalist, 139,* 603–622.

Frederick, D. A., & Haselton, M. G. (2007). Why is muscularity sexy? Tests of the fitness indicator hypothesis.. *Personality and Social Psychology Bulletin, 33,* 1167–1183.

Furnham, A., & Reeves, E. (2006). The relative influence of facial neoteny and waist-to-hip ratio on judgments of female attractiveness and fecundity. *Psychology, Health, & Medicine, 11,* 129–141.

Furnham, A., & Swami, V. (2007). Perception of female buttocks and breast size in profile. *Social Behavior and Personality, 35,* 1–8.

Gangestad, S. W., & Scheyd, G. J. (2005). The evolution of human physical attractiveness. *Annual Review of Anthropology, 34,* 523–548.

Gangestad, S. W., & Simpson, J. A. (1990). Toward an evolutionary history of female sociosexual variation. *Journal of Personality, 58,* 69–96.

Gangestad, S. W., & Thornhill, R. (1997). The evolutionary psychology of extra-pair sex: The role of fluctuating asymmetry. *Evolution and Human Behavior, 18,* 69–88.

Gangestad, S. W., & Thornhill, R. (2003). Facial masculinity and fluctuating asymmetry. *Evolution and Human Behavior, 24,* 231–241.

Gangestad, S. W., Thornhill, R., & Yeo, R. A. (1994). Facial attractiveness, developmental stability, and fluctuating asymmetry. *Ethology and Sociobiology, 15,* 73–85.

Grammer, K., & Thornhill, R. (1994). Human (*Homo sapiens*) facial attractiveness and sexual selection: The role of symmetry and averageness. *Journal of Comparative Psychology, 108,* 233–242.

Gunnell, D., May, M., Ben-Sholomo, Y., Yarnell, J., & Smith, G. D. (2003). Height, leg length and cancer: The Caerphilly Study. *Nutrition and Cancer, 47,* 34–39.

Gunnell, D., Whitley, E., Upton, M. N., McConnachie, A., Davey Smith, G., & Watt, G. C. M. (2003). Associations of height, leg length and lung function with cardiovascular risk factors in the Midspan Family Study. *Journal of Epidemiology and Community Health, 57,* 141–146.

Johnston, V. S., Hagel, R., Franklin, M., Fink, B., & Grammer, K. (2001). Male facial attractiveness: Evidence for hormone-mediated adaptive design. *Evolution and Human Behavior, 22,* 251–267.

Jones, D. (1996). *Physical attractiveness and the theory of sexual selection.* Ann Arbor, MI: Museum of Anthropology, University of Michigan.

Kirchengast, S., & Gartner, M. (2002). Changes in fat distribution (WHR) and body weight across the menstrual cycle. *Collegium Antropologicum, 26,* 47–57.

Lake, J. K., Power, C., & Cole, T. J. (1997). Women's reproductive health: The role of body mass index in early and adult life. *International Journal of Obesity, 21,* 432–438.

Langlois, J. H., & Roggman, L. A. (1990). Attractive faces are only average. *Psychological Science, 1,* 115–121.

Lassek, W. D., & Gaulin, S. J. C. (2008). Waist-to-hip ratio and cognitive ability: Is gluteofemoral fat a privileged store of neurodeveopmental resources? *Evolution and Human Behavior, 29,* 26–34.

Penke, L., & Asendorpf, J. B. (2008). Beyond global sociosexual orientations: A more differentiated look at sociosexuality and its effects on courtship and romantic relationships. *Journal of Personality and Social Psychology, 95,* 1113–1135.

Penton-Voak, I. S., Perrett, D. I., Castles, D. L., Kobayashi, T., Burt, D. M., Murray, L. K., et al. (1999). Menstrual cycle alters face preference. *Nature, 399,* 741–742.

Perilloux, H. K., Webster, G. D., & Gaulin, S. J. C. (2010). Signals of genetic quality and maternal investment capacity: The dynamic effects of fluctuating asymmetry and waist-to-hip ratio on men's ratings of women's attractiveness. *Social Psychological and Personality Science, 1,* 32–42.

Perrett, D. I., Burt, D. M., Penton-Voak, I. S., Lee, K. J., Rowland, D. A., & Edwards, R. (1999). Symmetry and human facial attractiveness. *Evolution and Human Behavior, 20,* 295–307.

Peters, M., Rhodes, G., & Simmons, L. W. (2007). Contributions of the face and body to overall attractiveness. *Animal Behavior, 73,* 937–942.

Rhodes, G., Chan, J., Zebrowitz, L. A., & Simmons, L. W. (2003). Does sexual dimorphism in human faces signal health? *Proceedings of the Royal Society of London, 270,* S93–S95.

Riggio, R. E., Widaman, K. F., Tucker, J. S., & Salinas, C. (1991). Beauty is more than skin deep: Components of attractiveness. *Basic and Applied Social Psychology, 12,* 423–439.

Roberts, S. C., Havlicek, J., Flegr, J., Hruskova, M., Little, A. C., Jones, B. C., et al. (2004). Female facial attractiveness increases during the fertile phase of the menstrual cycle. *Proceedings of the Royal Society of London, 271,* S270–S272.

Roney, J. R., Hanson, K. N., Durante, K. M., & Maestripieri, D. (2006). Reading men's faces: Women's mate attractiveness judgments track men's testosterone and interest in infants. *Proceedings of the Royal Society of London B, 273,* 2169–2175.

Singh, D. (1993). Adaptive significance of female physical attractiveness: Role of waist-to-hip ratio. *Journal of Personality and Social Psychology, 65,* 293–307.

Sorokowski, P., & Pawlowski, B. (2008). Adaptive preferences for leg length in a potential partner. *Evolution and Human Behavior, 29,* 86–91.

Sugiyama, L. S. (2005). Physical attractiveness in adaptationist perspective. In D. M. Buss (Ed.), *The handbook of evolutionary psychology* (pp. 292–343). Hoboken, NJ: Wiley.

Symons, D. (1979). *The evolution of human sexuality.* New York: Oxford University Press.

Thornhill, R., & Gangestad, S. W. (1993). Human facial beauty: Averageness, symmetry, and parasite resistance. *Human Nature, 4,* 237–269.

Thornhill, R., & Gangestad, S. W. (2008). *The evolutionary biology of human female sexuality.* New York: Oxford University Press.

Thornhill, R., & Grammer, K. (1999). The body and face of woman: One ornament that signals quality? *Evolution and Human Behavior, 20,* 105–120.

Tovée, M. J., Maisey, D. S., Emery, J. L., & Cornelissen, P. L. (1999). Visual cues to female physical attractiveness. *Proceedings of the Royal Society of London, 266,* 211–218.

Williams, G. C. (1975). *Sex and evolution.* Princeton, NJ: Princeton University Press.

Zaadstra, B. M., Seidell, J. C., VanNoord, P. A. H., Te Velde, E. R., Habbema, J. D. F., Vrieswijk, B., et al. (1993). Fat and female fecundity: Prospective study of body fat distribution in conception rates. *British Medical Journal, 306,* 484–487.

A CLOSER LOOK AT
More Than Just a Pretty Face

1. The title of this article has two distinctive parts. The first part before the colon is a familiar and memorable saying. The part after the colon does something different. What does this second part do?

2. How closely do the organization and features of this scientific report follow the reports genre as described in Chapter 12? Highlight places that follow the genre and any places that don't.

3. This report appeared in *Evolution and Human Behavior*, a scientific journal in the field of "evolutionary psychology," which examines how human behavior may in part be influenced by the way evolution has driven human biology. Go to the Web and find one or two articles about this field that are easy to understand but authoritative. When you have a better grasp of the field, discuss whether Confer, Perilloux, and Buss succeed in convincing you that they have reached the correct conclusions? Do you think they have really figured out why people are attracted to others in various situations?

4. This article is addressed primarily to experts in the science of evolutionary psychology. There are parts that a non-specialist, like you and your classmates, might not understand (for instance, the complex statistics in the results section). Even so, if you read closely, you will probably be able to understand the basics. Which parts were most helpful to you as a nonspecialist? Which parts are probably not useful to nonspecialists?

5. The writers begin with the assumption that much of our mate-choosing preferences are based in the biology of reproduction: We choose our mates in part according to the likelihood that they will help us produce offspring that will survive. In other words, we are at least partly similar to birds, reptiles, and other animals. How would you respond to that assumption? For you, is that very idea plausible, ridiculous, or somewhere in between?

IDEAS FOR
Writing

1. Like experts in any field, scientists often need to explain the complexities of their field to wider audiences or ordinary people. A nurse might need talk about nutrition guidelines to a patient, a restaurant chef about food preparation to a food critic, or a lawyer about complex legal issues to a jury. Now it's your turn to play expert. Imagine that you are one of the authors of this study and a journalist wants to do a feature story about how men choose mates, but the journalist is unclear about what the study did and found. Write an e-mail to this journalist explaining, in layperson's terms, what you did and what you discovered in this study.

2. Write a commentary based on this article that encourages your readers either to accept and use the findings or fundamentally question them. If you choose to accept and embrace the findings, explain why the findings are important to your readers. If you choose to question these findings, explain why readers should not make too much of them; for instance, you might be concerned young men will use them to rationalize considering women as sexual objects as "natural." Whichever you choose, be sure to back up your argument with reasoning and evidence.

A FEW IDEAS FOR
Composing a Report

1. **Develop a methods section for a report.** List five questions about life on your campus that you would like to answer. Pick one and develop a methodology for answering that question. Use your methodology to generate facts, data, and other support. Then write a report to the dean of students at your university in which you present and discuss your results and offer recommendations.

2. **Write a summary of a report.** Find a report on the Internet or elsewhere that studies a topic related to your major or a personal interest. Describe what it says in your own words, but do not offer your own opinion. The purpose of your summary is to give an overview of the report's major points, not to offer your own views about the topic.

3. **Create a multimedia report about your major.** Research the topic through the Internet, print sources, and interviews with counselors and professors. Your readers should be college students who might be interested in majoring in this field. Explain the requirements for graduation. Tell them what kinds of careers are available and the demand for people who earn degrees in your major. Then turn your report into a presentation with images, animation, and perhaps video.

42

Research
Papers

The Public Overwhelmingly Wants It: Why Is Taxing the Rich So Hard?

ALYSSA BATTISTONI

Alyssa Battistoni takes on a question that has occurred to many people: Why not ask more from people who already have more than enough money? After all, the gap between the wealthy and the middle class has grown dramatically in the past two decades. By doing research on this question, the author explores the power of the wealthy over politicians and how the rich, as a minority, have more influence on government than others. Look at the ways Battistoni supports her arguments with a balance of facts and emotional appeals.

When even the *New York Times,* the supposed bleeding heart of the liberal media, is asking whether it's more "perilous politically" to accept tax increases for 3 percent of households or benefit cuts for everyone, you'd assume that even Americans who aren't rich are opposed to raising taxes on those who are ("Will Voters," par. 4). But you'd be wrong: nearly three-quarters of Americans support raising taxes on the wealthy ("Washington Post-ABC News Poll," item 14). So why is raising taxes on the wealthy so hard—or why do we think it is?

The obvious answer is that rich people have political clout—but can it really be so simple? A growing mound of evidence suggests that while wealthy people's preferences may not be the only factor in political decision-making, it's a worrisomely important one. In a recent study, Princeton political scientist Larry Bartels found that senators outright ignored the views of their least advantaged constituents while catering to the preferences of the wealthy (4). Princeton's Martin Gilens has also found that policy changes reflect the preferences of the most affluent, while the preferences of poor and middle-income Americans have almost no bearing (794).

Political scientists Lawrence Jacobs and Benjamin Page have found that the preferences of foreign policymakers correspond more to the preferences of executives of multinational companies than to the general public (115). Page and Jeffrey Winters estimate that the top 10 percent of income earners hold about 90 percent of materially based political power, and that "each member of the top 1 percent averaged more than 100 times the power of a member of the bottom 90 percent; about 200 times if the index is calculated in terms of the more politically relevant non-home wealth" (736). These numbers are staggering, and should be seriously troubling to anyone who thinks political equality worth defending. Indeed, by Page and Winter's definition of oligarchy as "the extreme political inequalities that necessarily accompany extreme material inequalities," it's pretty hard to argue that the United States isn't an oligarchic society (732).

The simple fact of the matter is that the people who can afford to fund and engage in Beltway politics, from idea-generating to legislation-drafting, are disproportionately wealthy, so it's difficult to suss out just how much of politicians' deference to the preferences of the wealthy is responsiveness to the wealthy themselves as opposed to the general alignment of rich people's interests with those of influential elites, organized special interest groups, business lobbies, and those of policymakers themselves.

Because of course, plenty of politicians are 5 themselves wealthy—the median net worth of members of Congress is just under a million dollars (Gilson and Perot, sec. 4). Being wealthy doesn't necessarily mean you're a shill for lower taxes—indeed, John Kerry and Jay Rockefeller, two of the richest senators, have advocated more progressive tax rates—but it certainly means that most representatives have a different perspective on economic matters than the average American. Indeed, the 10 richest members of Congress—supporters of progressive taxation or no—all voted to extend the Bush tax cuts. (Gilson and Perot, sec. 4)

Of course, it's no secret that as political campaigns have grown increasingly more expensive, campaign contributions have grown increasingly more important: the 2010 midterms cost $4 billion (Klein, par. 1), and President Obama is already planning to spend a billion dollars on his bid for reelection (Overby, par. 1). Meanwhile, citizens in the top income quarter provide nearly three-quarters of campaign contributions, while those in the lowest quintile account for just 2 percent. But as Bartels notes, campaign contributions don't explain the whole story.

If anything, we probably understate the political influence of the rich. In part, that's because we can't quite comprehend the magnitude of economic inequality and the extent to which political power is correlated with it. The real numbers—like that the wealthiest 300,000 Americans received as much income as the bottom 150 million—sound too crazy to be true (Johnston, par. 5). As a result, proposals to raise taxes on the wealthy are so often dismissed as wild-eyed populist rhetoric—"soaking the rich"—rather than legitimate, reasonable policy prescriptions.

Furthermore, while we take for granted that the wealthy have more political power than the average citizen, we figure that the sheer numbers of middle class and low-income voters can outweigh the preferences of the rich in swaying public officials. Robert Reich, for example, has argued that the rich have the political power to block higher tax rates "only if we let them," saying "here's the issue around which Progressives, populists on the right and left, unionized

workers, and all other working people who are just plain fed up ought to be able to unite" (par. 14). And indeed, that kind of coalition-building is the basis for much progressive politics. But as the wealth and power of the most privileged Americans increases, it's becoming harder and harder for the rest of us to keep up even in the aggregate.

So instead we're getting caught in a negative feedback cycle: as the rich get richer and more powerful, policies are increasingly aligned with their interests, which increases inequality still further. Meanwhile, the middle and working classes are left with shrinking incomes and correspondingly less and less power to demand investment in a more equitable economy—and a broader tax base. Unions used to be able to counter the power of the wealthy, but their decline has left the average worker with little recourse. Instead of presenting an organized alternative to the views endorsed by the rich, average Americans are left to voice their political preferences through the vague format of an opinion poll. It's no wonder that, as political scientists Jacob Hacker and Paul Pierson write, "America's public officials have rewritten the rules of American politics and the American economy in ways that have benefitted the few at the expense of the many" (6).

So while it's absolutely true that the rich pay far more in income taxes than the rest of us (Robyn and Prante, par. 3)—the wealthiest 1 percent of Americans pay 38 percent of income tax—that tiny fraction of the population also receives about 24 percent of income, accounts for about 34 percent of net worth, and holds 42.7 percent of financial wealth (net worth minus the value of one's home) (Domhoff, par. 16). And those are statistics from before the crash—though there are only tentative estimates of current wealth distribution, many economists actually think it's gotten more unequal.

Since average people's wealth is largely tied up in their homes, the wealth of the median household has dropped an estimated 36 percent since the housing bubble popped, while the wealth of the top 1 percent has fallen a comparatively small 11 percent (Wolff, 33). As Bartels concludes, "the economic order of the contemporary United States poses a clear and profound obstacle to realizing the democratic value of political equality" (32). In other words, as long as economic inequality is as extreme as it is now, political equality will remain an ideal rather than a reality. We need to make this case over and over again—right now we're in danger of drawing exactly the wrong lessons from the economic nightmare of the past few years.

In a *Wall Street Journal piece* a couple of weeks ago, former California economic forecaster Brad Williams states "We created a revenue cliff. . . . We built a large part of our government on the state's most unstable income group" (Frank, par. 5). The people protesting with signs reading "We Love Jobs," he suggested, were "missing the real point." But it's Williams who's missing the point: what we really did was build a large part of our economy around an unstable income group and industry, and what we need to do is build an economy with a broader base and more evenly distributed resources.

Indeed, many arguments given against raising taxes are in fact reasons for decreasing the financial and political power of the wealthy. Worried that rich people will leave the state, or even the country, to avoid property or income tax? Don't build an economy that depends on a small number of people who have the resources to leave sticking around. Worried that rich people won't invest in their businesses or create new jobs if we tax them? Don't build an economy that depends on a few wealthy people hiring the rest of us. Worried that rich people's incomes are too volatile? Don't build an economy so heavily dependent on financial markets. And make no mistake: although the Journal would have you believe the distribution of wealth is a naturally occurring phenomenon, state investment and regulation plays an essential role in the structure of the economy. If we want a more equal playing field, we can have it—but we need to start now.

Works Cited

Bartels, Larry. "Economic Inequality and Political Representation." Aug 2005. Web. 25 Apr 2011.

Domhoff, G. William. "Who Rules America: Wealth, Income, and Power." *Who Rules America?* Jan 2011. Web. 25 Apr 2011.

Frank, Robert. "The Price of Taxing the Rich." *Wall Street Journal* 26 Mar 2011. Web. 25 Apr 2011.

Gilens, Martin. "Inequality and Democratic Responsiveness." *Public Opinion Quarterly* 69.5 (2005): 778–796. Print.

Gilson, Dave, and Carolyn Perot. "It's the Inequality, Stupid. *Mother Jones.* Web. 25 Apr 2011.

Haker, Jacob, and Paul Pierson. *Winner-Take-All-Politics.* New York, NY: Simon & Schuster, 2010. Print.

Jacobs, Lawrence, and Benjamin Page. "Who Influences U.S. Foreign Policy." *American Political Science Review* 99.1 (2005): 107–123. Print.

Johnston, David Cay. "Income Gap Is Widening, Data Shows." *New York Times* 29 Mar 2007. Web. 25 Apr 2011.

Klein, Ezra. "More Money, More Problems." *Newsweek* 31 Oct 2010. Web. 25 Apr 2011.

Overby, Peter. "2012: The Year Of The Billion-Dollar Campaigns?" *National Public Radio* 18 Feb 2011. Web. 25 Apr 2011.

Reich, Robert. "Why We Must Raise Taxes on the Rich, ASAP!" *RobertReich.org* 4 Apr 2011. Web. 25 Apr 2011.

Robyn, Mark, and Gerald Prante. "Summary of Latest Federal Individual Income Tax Data." *Tax Foundation.* Web. 25 Apr 2011.

"Washington Post-ABC News Poll." Web. 25 Apr 2011.

"Will Voters Accept Tax Increases?—Room for Debate." 13 Apr 2011. Web. 25 Apr 2011.

Winters, Jeffrey, and Benjamin Page. "Oligarchy in the United States." *Perspectives on Politics* 7.4 (2009): 731–751. Print.

Wolff, Edward. "Recent Trends in Household Wealth in the United States: Rising Debt and the Middle-Class Squeeze—an Update to 2007." Mar 2010. Print.

A CLOSER LOOK AT
The Public Overwhelmingly Wants It: Why Is Taxing the Rich So Hard?

1. One of Battistoni's main arguments is that politicians often overlook the needs of the public, because they share the same views as wealthy and powerful business executives. Why, according to Battistoni, do politicians think and behave this way? According to Battistoni's argument, what are some of the effects of this kind of thinking by politicians?

2. The author sounds angry and frustrated. Identify five places in this research paper where she creates this style or tone. In what ways does Battistoni express her anger and frustration at the power of the rich over politicians?

3. The author also argues that the United States is actually too dependent on the rich to pay taxes. She writes, "What we really did was build a large part of our economy around an unstable income group and industry, and what we need to do is build an economy with a broader base and more evenly distributed resources." Do you think she is contradicting herself at this point? In the end, is she really arguing for more taxes on the rich?

IDEAS FOR
Writing

1. Write a commentary in which you express your own views on taxes. Do you think some people are overburdened with taxes? Do you think some people don't pay enough taxes? Use research to support and explain your views.

2. Write an elevator pitch in which you briefly explain how you would make politicians more responsive to the general public. (The pitch is a microgenre of the proposal, described in Chapter 11.) Right now, most people agree that politicians are overly influenced by special interest groups, wealthy donors, labor unions, and corporate lobbyists, while they are not listening to regular people. In your elevator pitch, explain how you would change the political system so politicians hear about the needs and concerns of all.

Rapture Ready: The Science of Self Delusion

CHRIS MOONEY

In this research paper, Chris Mooney explores why people often believe things that can be proven wrong. Reviewing psychology and political-science research on reasoning and denial, he discusses studies that show how the reasoning processes of conservatives and progressives often depend more on their prior beliefs and expectations than on factual evidence and solid reasoning. Pay attention to the way that Mooney does more than just report his sources' findings; he uses them to inform his own argument and back up his claims.

"A man with a conviction is a hard man to change. Tell him you disagree and he turns away. Show him facts or figures and he questions your sources. Appeal to logic and he fails to see your point" (Festinger, Riecken, & Schacter, 1956, p. 3). So wrote the celebrated Stanford University psychologist Leon Festinger and his coauthors, in a passage that might have been referring to climate change denial—the persistent rejection, on the part of so many Americans today, of what we know about global warming and its human causes. But it was too early for that—this was the 1950s—and Festinger and his coauthors were actually describing a famous case study in psychology.

Festinger and several of his colleagues had infiltrated the Seekers, a small Chicago-area cult whose members thought they were communicating with aliens—including one, "Sananda," who they believed was the astral incarnation of Jesus Christ. The group was led by Dorothy Martin, a Dianetics devotee who transcribed the interstellar messages through automatic writing.

Through her, the aliens had given the precise date of an Earth-rending cataclysm: December 21, 1954. Some of Martin's followers quit their jobs and sold their property, expecting to be rescued by a flying saucer when the continent split asunder and a new sea swallowed much of the United States. The disciples even went so far as to remove brassieres and rip zippers out of their trousers—the metal, they believed, would pose a danger on the spacecraft.

Festinger and his team were with the cult when the prophecy failed. First, the "boys upstairs" (as the aliens were sometimes called) did not show up and rescue the Seekers. Then December 21 arrived without incident. It was the moment they had been waiting for: How would people so emotionally invested in a belief system react, now that it had been soundly refuted?

At first, the group struggled for an explanation. But then rationalization set in. A new message arrived, announcing that they'd all been spared at the last minute. Festinger summarized the extraterrestrials' new pronouncement: "The little group, sitting all night long, had spread so much light that God had saved the world from destruction" (p. 171). Their willingness to believe in the prophecy had saved Earth from the prophecy!

From that day forward, the Seekers, previously shy of the press and indifferent toward evangelizing, began to proselytize. "Their sense of urgency was enormous" (p. 171), wrote the researchers. The devastation of all they had believed had made them even more certain of their beliefs.

In the annals of denial, it doesn't get much more extreme than the Seekers. They lost their jobs, the press mocked them, and there were efforts to keep them away from impressionable young minds. But while Martin's space cult might lie at on the far end of the spectrum of human self-delusion, there's plenty to go around. And since Festinger's day, an array of new discoveries in psychology and neuroscience has further demonstrated how our preexisting beliefs, far more than any new facts, can skew our thoughts and even color what we consider our most dispassionate and logical conclusions. This tendency toward so-called "motivated reasoning" helps explain why we find groups so polarized over matters where the evidence is so unequivocal: climate change, vaccines, "death panels," the birthplace and religion of the president, and much else. (For an overview of the phenomenon of motivated reasoning, see Kunda, 1990.) It would seem that expecting people to be convinced by the facts flies in the face of, you know, the facts.

The theory of motivated reasoning builds on a key insight of modern neuroscience: As Damasio explains, reasoning is actually suffused with emotion (or what researchers often call "affect"). Not only are the two inseparable, but our positive or negative feelings about people, things, and ideas arise much more rapidly than our conscious thoughts, in a matter of milliseconds—fast enough to detect with an EEG device, but long before we're aware of it. That shouldn't be surprising: Evolution required us to react very quickly to stimuli in our environment (p. 144). It's a "basic human survival skill," explains political scientist Arthur Lupia of the University of Michigan (personal communication). We push threatening information away; we pull friendly information close. We apply fight-or-flight reflexes not only to predators, but to data itself.

We're not driven only by emotions, of course—we also reason, deliberate. But reasoning comes later, works slower—and even then, it doesn't take place in an emotional vacuum. Rather, our quick-fire emotions can set us on a course of thinking that's highly biased, especially on topics we care a great deal about.

Consider a person who has heard about a scientific discovery that deeply challenges her belief in divine creation—a new hominid, say, that confirms our evolutionary origins. What happens next, explains political scientist Charles Taber of Stony Brook University, is a subconscious negative response to the new information—and that response, in turn, guides the type of memories and associations formed in the conscious mind (personal communication). "They retrieve thoughts that are consistent with their previous beliefs," says Taber, "and that will lead them to build an argument and challenge what they're hearing."

In other words, when we think we're reasoning, we may instead be rationalizing. Or to use an analogy offered by University of Virginia psychologist Jonathan Haidt: We may think we're being scientists, but we're actually being lawyers (2000, p. 10). Our "reasoning" is a means to a predetermined end—winning our "case"—and is shot through with biases. They include "confirmation bias," in which we give greater heed to evidence and arguments that bolster our beliefs, and "disconfirmation bias," in which we expend disproportionate energy trying to debunk or refute views and arguments that we find uncongenial.

That's a lot of jargon, but we all understand these mechanisms when it comes to interpersonal relationships. If I don't want to believe that my spouse is being unfaithful, or that my child is a bully, I can go to great lengths to explain away behavior that seems obvious to everybody else—everybody who isn't too emotionally invested to accept it, anyway. That's not to suggest that we aren't also motivated to perceive the world accurately—we are. Or that we never change our minds—we do. It's just that we have other important goals besides accuracy—including identity affirmation and protecting one's sense of self—and often those make us highly resistant to changing our beliefs when the facts say we should.

Modern science originated from an attempt to weed out such subjective lapses—what that great 17th century theorist of the scientific method, Francis Bacon, dubbed the "idols of the mind." Even if individual researchers are prone to falling in love with their own theories, the broader processes of peer review and institutionalized skepticism are designed to ensure that, eventually, the best ideas prevail.

Our individual responses to the conclu- 15 sions that science reaches, however, are quite another matter. Ironically, in part because researchers employ so much nuance and strive to disclose all remaining sources of uncertainty, scientific evidence is highly susceptible to selective reading and misinterpretation. Giving ideologues or partisans scientific data that's relevant to their beliefs is like unleashing them in the motivated-reasoning equivalent of a candy store.

Sure enough, a large number of psychological studies have shown that people respond to scientific or technical evidence in ways that justify their preexisting beliefs. In a classic 1979 experiment (Lord, Ross, & Lepper), pro- and anti-death penalty advocates were exposed to descriptions of two fake scientific studies: one supporting and one undermining the notion that capital punishment deters violent crime and, in particular, murder. They were also shown detailed methodological critiques of the fake studies—and in a scientific sense, neither study was stronger than the other. Yet in each case, advocates more heavily criticized the study whose conclusions disagreed with their own, while describing the study that was more ideologically congenial as more "convincing."

Since then, similar results have been found for how people respond to "evidence" about affirmative action, gun control, the accuracy of gay stereotypes (Munro & Ditto, 2010), and much else. Even when study subjects are explicitly instructed to be unbiased and even-handed about the evidence, they often fail. And it's not just that people twist or selectively read scientific evidence to support their preexisting views. According to research by Yale Law School professor Dan Kahan and his colleagues, people's deep-seated views about morality, and about the way society should be ordered, strongly predict whom they consider to be a legitimate scientific expert in the first place—and thus where they consider "scientific consensus" to lie on contested issues.

In Kahan's research, individuals are classified, based on their cultural values, as either "individualists" or "communitarians," and as either "hierarchical" or "egalitarian" in outlook (Kahan, Jenkins-Smith, & Braman, 2011, p. 148). (Somewhat oversimplifying, you can think of hierarchical individualists as akin to conservative Republicans, and egalitarian communitarians as liberal Democrats.) In this study, subjects in the different groups were asked to help a close friend determine the risks associated with climate change, sequestering nuclear waste, or concealed carry laws: "The friend tells you that he or she is planning to read a book about the issue but would like to get your opinion on whether the author seems like a knowledgeable and trustworthy expert" (p. 153). A subject was then presented with the résumé of a fake expert "depicted as a member of the National Academy of Sciences who had earned a Ph.D. in a pertinent field from one elite university and who was now on the faculty of another" (p. 153). The subject was then shown a book excerpt by that "expert," in which the risk of the issue at hand was portrayed as high or low, well-founded or speculative. The results were stark: When the scientist's position stated that global warming is real and human-caused, for instance, only 23 percent of hierarchical individualists agreed the person was a "trustworthy and knowledgeable expert" (p. 163). Yet 88 percent of egalitarian communitarians accepted the same scientist's expertise. Similar divides were observed on whether nuclear waste can be safely stored underground and whether letting people carry guns deters crime. The alliances did not always hold. In another study (Kahan, Braman, Monaha, Callahan, & Peters, 2010), hierarchs and communitarians were in favor of laws that would compel the mentally ill to accept treatment, whereas individualists and egalitarians were opposed.

In other words, people rejected the validity of a scientific source because its conclusion contradicted their deeply held views—and thus the relative risks inherent in each scenario. A hierarchal individualist finds it difficult to believe that the things he prizes (commerce, industry, a man's freedom to possess a gun to defend his family) could lead to outcomes deleterious to society (Kahan et al., 2010). Whereas egalitarian communitarians tend to think that the free market causes harm, that patriarchal families mess up kids, and that people can't handle their guns. The study subjects weren't "antiscience"—not in their own minds, anyway. It's just that "science" was whatever they wanted it to be. "We've come to a misadventure, a bad situation where diverse citizens, who rely on diverse systems of cultural certification, are in conflict," says Kahan (Cone & Kahan, 2010).

And that undercuts the standard notion that 20 the way to persuade people is via evidence and argument. In fact, head-on attempts to persuade can sometimes trigger a backfire effect, where people not only fail to change their minds when confronted with the facts—they may hold their wrong views more tenaciously than ever.

Take, for instance, the question of whether Saddam Hussein possessed hidden weapons of mass destruction just before the US invasion of Iraq in 2003. When political scientists Brendan Nyhan and Jason Reifler (2010) showed subjects fake newspaper articles in which this was first suggested (in a 2004 quote from President Bush) and then refuted (with the findings of the Bush-commissioned Iraq Survey Group report, which found no evidence of active WMD programs in pre-invasion Iraq), they found that conservatives were more likely than before to believe the claim. (The researchers also tested how liberals responded when shown that Bush did not actually "ban" embryonic stem-cell research. Liberals weren't particularly amenable to persuasion, either, but no backfire effect was observed.)

Another study gives some inkling of what may be going through people's minds when they resist persuasion. Northwestern University sociologist Monica Prasad and her colleagues wanted to test whether they could dislodge the notion that Saddam Hussein and Al Qaeda were secretly collaborating among those most likely to believe it—Republican partisans from highly GOP-friendly counties. So the researchers set up a study in which they discussed the topic with some of these Republicans in person (Prasad, Perrin, Bezila, Hoffman, Kindleberger, Manturuk, & Powers, 2009). They would cite the findings of the 9/11 Commission, as well as a statement in which George W. Bush himself denied his administration had "said the 9/11 attacks were orchestrated between Saddam and Al Qaeda."

As it turned out, not even Bush's own words could change the minds of these Bush voters—just 1 of the 49 partisans who originally believed the Iraq-Al Qaeda claim changed his or her mind. Far more common was resisting the correction in a variety of ways, either by coming up with counterarguments or by simply being unmovable:

Interviewer: [T]he September 11 Commission found no link between Saddam and 9/11, and this is what President Bush said. Do you have any comments on either of those?

Respondent: Well, I bet they say that the Commission didn't have any proof of it but I guess we still can have our opinions and feel that way even though they say that. (Prasad et al., 2009, p. 154)

The same types of responses are already being documented on divisive topics facing the current administration. Take the "Ground Zero mosque." Using information from the political myth-busting site FactCheck.org, a team at Ohio State (Nisbet & Garrett, 2010) presented subjects with a detailed rebuttal to the claim that "Feisal Abdul Rauf, the Imam backing the proposed Islamic cultural center and mosque, is a terrorist-sympathizer." Yet among those who were aware of the rumor and believed it, fewer than a third changed their minds.

A key question—and one that's difficult to 25 answer—is how "irrational" all this is. On the one hand, it doesn't make sense to discard an entire belief system, built up over a lifetime, because of some new snippet of information. "It is quite possible to say, 'I reached this pro-capital-punishment decision based on real information that I arrived at over my life,'" explains Stanford social psychologist Jon Krosnick (personal communication). Indeed, there's a sense in which science denial could be considered keenly "rational." In certain conservative communities, explains Yale's Kahan, "People who say, 'I think there's something to climate change,' that's going to mark them out as a certain kind of person, and their life is going to go less well" (Cone & Kahan, 2010).

This may help explain a curious pattern Nyhan and Reifler found when they tried to test the fallacy that President Obama is a Muslim (2010). When a nonwhite researcher was administering their study, research subjects were amenable to changing their minds about the president's religion and updating incorrect views. But when only white researchers were present, GOP survey subjects in particular were more likely to believe the Obama Muslim myth than before. The subjects were using "social desirabililty" to tailor their beliefs (or stated beliefs, anyway) to whoever was listening.

Which leads us to the media. When people grow polarized over a body of evidence, or a resolvable matter of fact, the cause may be some form of biased reasoning, but they could also be receiving skewed information to begin with—or a complicated combination of both. In the Ground Zero mosque case, for instance, a separate study (Nisbet & Garrett, 2010) showed that survey respondents who watched Fox News were more likely to believe the Rauf rumor and three related ones—and they believed them more strongly than non-Fox watchers.

Okay, so people gravitate toward information that confirms what they believe, and they select sources that deliver it. Same as it ever was, right? Maybe, but the problem is arguably growing more acute, given the way we now consume information—through the Facebook links of friends, or tweets that lack nuance or context, or "narrowcast" and often highly ideological media that have relatively small, like-minded audiences. Those basic human survival skills of ours, says Michigan's Arthur Lupia, are "not well-adapted to our information age" (personal communication).

If you wanted to show how and why fact is ditched in favor of motivated reasoning, you could find no better test case than climate change. After all, it's an issue where you have highly technical information on one hand and very strong beliefs on the other. And sure enough, one key predictor of whether you accept the science of global warming is whether you're a Republican or a Democrat. The two groups have been growing more divided in their views about the topic, even as the science becomes more unequivocal.

So perhaps it should come as no surprise 30 that more education doesn't budge Republican views. On the contrary: In a 2008 Pew survey, for instance, only 19 percent of college-educated Republicans agreed that the planet is warming due to human actions, versus 31 percent of non-college educated Republicans. In other words, a higher education correlated with an increased likelihood of denying the science on the issue. Meanwhile, among Democrats and independents, more education correlated with greater acceptance of the science.

Other studies have shown a similar effect: Republicans who think they understand the global warming issue best are least concerned about it; and among Republicans and those with higher levels of distrust of science in general, learning more about the issue doesn't increase one's concern about it. What's going on here? Well, according to Charles Taber and Milton Lodge of Stony Brook, one insidious aspect of motivated reasoning is that political sophisticates are prone to be more biased than those who know less about the issues. "People who have a dislike of some policy—for example, abortion—if they're unsophisticated they can just reject it out of hand," says Lodge. "But if they're sophisticated, they can go one step further and start coming up with counterarguments" (personal communication, April 12, 2011). These individuals are just as emotionally driven and biased as the rest of us, but they're able to generate more and better reasons to explain why they're right—and so their minds become harder to change.

That may be why the selectively quoted emails of Climategate were so quickly and easily seized upon by partisans as evidence of scandal.

Cherry-picking is precisely the sort of behavior you would expect motivated reasoners to engage in to bolster their views—and whatever you may think about Climategate, the emails were a rich trove of new information upon which to impose one's ideology.

Climategate had a substantial impact on public opinion, according to Anthony Leiserowitz, director of the Yale Project on Climate Change Communication. It contributed to an overall drop in public concern about climate change and a significant loss of trust in scientists (personal communication, April 5, 2011). But—as we should expect by now—these declines were concentrated among particular groups of Americans: Republicans, conservatives, and those with "individualistic" values. Liberals and those with "egalitarian" values didn't lose much trust in climate science or scientists at all. "In some ways, Climategate was like a Rorschach test," Leiserowitz says, "with different groups interpreting ambiguous facts in very different ways."

So is there a case study of science denial that largely occupies the political left? Yes: the claim that childhood vaccines are causing an epidemic of autism. Its most famous proponents are an environmentalist (Robert F. Kennedy Jr., 2009) and numerous Hollywood celebrities (most notably Jenny McCarthy [2011] and Jim Carrey). The *Huffington Post* gives a very large megaphone to denialists. And Seth Mnookin, author of the new book *The Panic Virus* (2011), notes that if you want to find vaccine deniers, all you need to do is go hang out at Whole Foods.

Vaccine denial has all the hallmarks of a [35] belief system that's not amenable to refutation. Over the past decade, the assertion that childhood vaccines are driving autism rates has been undermined by multiple epidemiological studies (see Mooney, 2009). It has been undermined as well by the simple fact that autism rates continue to rise, even though the alleged offending agent in vaccines (a mercury-based preservative called thimerosal) has long since been removed.

Yet the true believers persist—critiquing each new study that challenges their views, and even rallying to the defense of vaccine-autism researcher Andrew Wakefield, after his 1998 *Lancet* paper—which originated the current vaccine scare—was retracted and he subsequently lost his license (General Medical Council, 2010, p. 9) to practice medicine. But then, why should we be surprised? Vaccine deniers created their own partisan media, such as the website Age of Autism, that instantly blast out critiques and counterarguments whenever any new development casts further doubt on anti-vaccine views.

It all raises the question: Do left and right differ in any meaningful way when it comes to biases in processing information, or are we all equally susceptible?

There are some clear differences. Science denial today is considerably more prominent on the political right—once you survey climate and related environmental issues, anti-evolutionism, attacks on reproductive health science by the Christian right, and stem-cell and biomedical matters. More tellingly, anti-vaccine positions are virtually nonexistent among Democratic officeholders today—whereas anti-climate-science views are becoming monolithic among Republican elected officials.

Some researchers have suggested that there are psychological differences between the left and the right that might impact responses to new information—that conservatives are more rigid and authoritarian, and liberals more tolerant of ambiguity. Psychologist John Jost of New York University has further argued that conservatives are "system justifiers": They engage in motivated reasoning to defend the status quo.

This is a contested area, however, because [40] as soon as one tries to psychoanalyze inherent political differences, a battery of counterarguments emerges: What about dogmatic and militant communists? What about how the parties have differed through history? After all, the most canonical case of ideologically driven science denial is probably the rejection of genetics in the Soviet Union, where researchers disagreeing with the anti-Mendelian scientist (and Stalin stooge) Trofim Lysenko were executed, and genetics itself was denounced as a "bourgeois" science and officially banned.

The upshot: All we can currently bank on is the fact that we all have blinders in some situations. The question then becomes: What can be done to counteract human nature itself?

Given the power of our prior beliefs to skew how we respond to new information, one thing is becoming clear: If you want someone to accept new evidence, make sure to present it to them in a context that doesn't trigger a defensive, emotional reaction.

This theory is gaining traction in part because of Kahan's work at Yale. In one study (Kahan, Braman, Slovic, Gastil, & Cohen, 2007), he and his colleagues packaged the basic science of climate change into fake newspaper articles bearing two very different headlines—"Scientific Panel Recommends Anti-Pollution Solution to Global Warming" and "Scientific Panel Recommends Nuclear Solution to Global Warming" (p. 5)—and then tested how citizens with different values responded. Sure enough, the latter framing made hierarchical individualists much more open to accepting the fact that humans are causing global warming. Kahan and his colleagues infer that the effect occurred because the science had been written into an alternative narrative that appealed to their pro-industry worldview.

You can follow the logic to its conclusion: Conservatives are more likely to embrace climate science if it comes to them via a business or religious leader, who can set the issue in the context of different values than those from which environmentalists or scientists often argue. Doing so is, effectively, to signal a détente in what Kahan has called a "culture war of fact" (Kahan et al., 2007). In other words, paradoxically, you don't lead with the facts in order to convince. You lead with the values—so as to give the facts a fighting chance.

References

Cone, J. (Interviewer), & Kahan, D. (Interviewee). (2010, June 10). Cultural Cognition Project,

Part 2. [Interview transcript]. Retrieved from http://seagrant.oregonstate.edu/blogs/communicatingclimate/transcripts/Episode_10b_Dan_Kahan.html

Damasio, A. R. (1994, October). Descartes' error and the future of human life. *Scientific American, 271*(4), 144.

Festinger, L., Riecken, H. W., & Schacter, S, (1956) *When prophecy fails: A social and psychological study of a modern group that predicted the destruction of the world.* Minneapolis: University of Minnesota Press.

General Medical Council. (2010, May 24). Determination on serious professional misconduct (SPM) and sanction [Letter to Jeremy Wakefield]. Retrieved from http://www.gmc-uk.org/Wakefield_SPM_and_SANCTION.pdf_32595267.pdf

Haidt, J. (2001). The emotional dog and its rational tail: A social intuitionist approach to moral judgment. *Psychological Review. 108*, 814-834. doi: 10.1037/0033-295X.108.4.814

Kahan, D. M., Braman, D., Monahan, J, Callahan, L., & Peters, E. (2010). Cultural cognition and public policy: The case of outpatient commitment laws. *Law and Human Behavior 34*, 118-140. doi: 10.1007/s10979-008-9174-4

Kahan, D. M., Braman, D., Slovic, P., Gastil, J., & Cohen, G. (2007, October 3). The second national risk and culture study: Making sense of—and making progress in—the American culture war of fact. *The Cultural Cognition Project at Yale Law School.* Retrieved from http://www.scribd.com/doc/3446682/The-Second-National-Risk-and-Culture-Study-Making-Sense-of-and-Making-Progress-In-The-American-Culture-War-of-Fact

Kahan, D. M., Jenkins-Smith, H., & Braman, D. (2011). Cultural cognition of scientific consensus. *Journal of Risk Research 14*, 147–174. doi: 10.1080/13669877.2010.511246

Kennedy, Robert F. Jr. (2009, February 24). Vaccine Court: Autism debate continues. *The Huffington Post.* Retrieved from http://www.huffingtonpost.com/robert-f-kennedy-jr-and-david-kirby/vaccine-court-autism-deba_b_169673.html

Kunda, Z. (1990). The case for motivated reasoning. *The Psychological Bulletin, 108*, 480–498. doi: 10.1037/0033-2909.108.3.480

Lord, C. G., Ross, L., & Lepper, M. R. (1979). Biased assimilation and attitude polarization: The effects of prior theories on subsequently considered evidence. *Journal of Personality and Social Psychology 37*, 2098–2109. doi: 10.1037/0022-3514.37.11.2098

McCarthy, Jenny. (2011, January 10). In the vaccine-autism debate, what can parents believe? *The Huffington Post*. Retrieved from http://www.huffingtonpost.com/jenny-mccarthy/vaccine-autism-debate_b_806857.html

Mnookin, Seth. (2011). *The panic virus: A true story of medicine, science, and fear*. New York: Simon & Schuster.

Mooney, Chris. (2009, May 6). Why does the vaccine/autism controversy live on? *Discover*. Retrieved from http://discovermagazine.com/2009/jun/06-why-does-vaccine-autism-controversy-live-on

Munro, G. D., & Ditto, P. H. (1997). Biased assimilation, attitude polarization, and affect in reactions to stereotype-relevant scientific information. *Personality and Social Psychology Bulletin 23*, 636–653. doi: 10.1177/0146167297236007.

Nisbet, E. & Garrett, K. (2010, October 14). FoxNews contributes to spread of rumors about proposed NYC mosque: CNN and NPR promote more accurate beliefs. Retrieved from http://http://www.comm.ohio-state.edu/kgarrett/MediaMosqueRumors.pdf

Nisbet, E. & Garrett, K. (2010, October 27). Belief in rumors hard to dispel: Fact checking easily undermined by images, unrelated facts. PDF. Retrieved from http://www.comm.ohio-state.edu/kgarrett/FactcheckMosqueRumors.pdf

Nyhan, B., & Reifler, J. (2010). When corrections fail: The persistence of political misperceptions. *Political Behavior, 32*, 303–330. doi: 10.1007/s11109-010-9112-2

Pew Research Center for the People & the Press. (2008, May 8). A deeper partisan divide over global warming. Retrieved from http://people-press.org/files/legacy-pdf/417.pdf

Prasad, M., Perrin, A. J., Bezila, K., Hoffman, S. G., Kindleberger, K., Manturuk, K., & Powers, A. S. (2009). "There must be a reason": Osama, Saddam, and inferred justification. *Sociological Inquiry 79*, 142–162. doi: 10.1111/j.1475-682X.2009.00280.x

Wakefield, A. J., Murch, S. H. Anthony, A., Linnell, J., Casson, D. M., Malik, M., . . . Walker-Smith, J. A. (1998). Lleal-lymphoid-nodular hyperplasia, non-specific colitis, and pervasive developmental disorder in children. *The Lancet 351*,637–641. doi: 10.1016/S0140-6736(97)11096-0

A CLOSER LOOK AT
Rapture Ready: The Science of Self Delusion

1. Mooney is basically arguing that reasoning is not the way people usually figure out what they believe. According to Mooney, how do people form and defend their beliefs—even when their beliefs are provably wrong?

2. According to Mooney's research, what are the basic differences between conservatives and progressives about how they see the world and what they choose to believe? How do these differences sometimes lead them to engage in self-delusion?

3. Late in the article, Mooney offers a few strategies for persuading people to consider ideas that they may disagree with. What are two ways that Mooney mentions to persuade people?

1. Choose one of the examples of self-delusion that Mooney mentions in this research paper. Write a commentary in which you explain and explore this case of self-delusion. Discuss its history and the evidence offered by its believers. At the end of your commentary, explain whether you think this self-delusion is harmful and what you think should be done about it.

2. Write a memoir in which you describe a time when you couldn't persuade someone to do something or believe something. What happened as you made your arguments? Use your memoir to explain why you think this person didn't believe what you were saying.

3. Write an argument in which you try to argue for or against a controversial point. Instead of just expressing your opinion, though, try to "frame" the debate in terms that someone who is politically opposite to you will understand. For example, if you are arguing for "clean energy" with someone who doesn't believe in climate change, how can you reframe the debate in a way that he or she will find more persuasive?

Insufficient Design

HENRY M. MORRIS

As the Founder and President Emeritus of the Institute for Creation Research, Henry Morris has been a prominent creationist for decades. His books against Darwinian evolution are widely read and cited as evidence for creationism. In this research paper, he argues against the Intelligent Design (ID) movement by suggesting it has many of the same problems, in his opinion, as Darwinian evolution. Pay attention to the sources Morris uses to argue against ID and for his view of creationism.

The modern Intelligent Design movement (ID) has been making substantial progress in recent years, at least in terms of public interest. As one evolutionist recently warned his colleagues: The success of the ID movement to date is terrifying. In at least 40 states, ID is being considered as an addition to the required science curriculum in public schools (Shipman, 2005, p. 502).

The "terrified" author of this observation is Professor of Anthropology at Pennsylvania State University. He says he is being stalked by ID advocates! "Now I know that I and my colleagues are being stalked with careful and deadly deliberation. I fear my days are numbered unless I act soon and effectively. If you are reading this, the chances are that you are in the same position" (Shipman, p. 500).

The editor of the prestigious magazine *Science*, in his lead editorial in a recent issue, expressed his alarm thus: Alternatives to the teaching of biological evolution are now being debated in no fewer than 40 states. Worse, evolution is not the only science under such challenge. In several school districts, geology materials are being rewritten because their dates for Earth's age are inconsistent with scripture (too old) (Kennedy, 2005, p. 165). The editor even entitled his diatribe "Twilight for the Enlightenment?"

Similar alarmist articles have been published in numerous other science journals and also in many popular magazines (such as *Newsweek*) and local papers. Our own *San Diego Union Tribune* in a lengthy lead editorial for November 21, 2005, called Intelligent Design "Voodoo Science" in the editorial title. The language seems inflammatory just about everywhere.

One writer becomes unreasonably virulent 5 in his latest editorial. The "Intelligent Design" movement is the most pernicious pseudoscience of our time. It seeks to undermine the teaching of evolution, at a minimum, but at its root is a broad attack on the nature of science itself. . . . (Frazier, 2005, p. 4) He then calls ID "an ancient and long-discredited faith-based idea with zero scientific evidence" (p. 4).

Is ID Really Intelligent?

The reason for calling attention to this almost universally negative reaction to the ID movement among leaders in science, education, law, journalism, and other fields is to note the unrealistic hope that ID leaders have about their movement. Christians have been pointing out for a very long time that the ubiquitous evidences for design in nature constitute strong evidences for God and creation. But atheists and other unbelievers have long hailed Darwinism as their deliverance from this constraint.

Now the ID people think that by distancing their movement from creationism and the Biblical God as the obvious Designer, they can make ID acceptable. They are learning, however, that opposition to ID is even stronger among scientists, if anything, than the opposition to straightforward creationism.

Many evolutionists now regard ID as a hypocritical form of creationism and thus really a religion rather than science. Another skeptic has pointed out what he thinks is a very different reason for rejecting the main ID contention. According to Behe and Dembski, the more complex a system, the more likely it was designed—this is the essence of Point A in Behe's concept. Point B (irreducibility) in Behe's concept asserts that an IC system loses its function if even a single part is missing (Perakh, 2005, p. 34).

That is, a system is irreducibly complex (IC) if it could no longer function if even one part is missing. That, according to these two leaders of the ID movement (Michael Behe and William Dembski) means it must have been intelligently designed.

But this particular writer opines that this 10 would be proof that it was not designed by any kind of intelligence! Thus, it must have been assembled somehow by impersonal time and chance. The simple fact is, though, that if an IC system has been designed, it is a case of bad design. If the loss of a single part destroys the system's function, such a system is unreliable, and therefore, if it is designed, the designer is inept (Perakh, p. 35)

This is a clear example of specious reasoning, but Perakh belabors it at some length. It does lead, however, to an important conclusion. That is, mere complexity is not proof of design. For example, a perfectly cubical object found in a pile of rocks, say, would certainly have been designed for some kind of purpose—say, as a toy block for a child to play with or as one of a pair of dice for a gambler to throw. An irregular rock in that same pile, on the other hand, would be much more complex and therefore more difficult to specify than the cube but it clearly would have been formed randomly by a hodgepodge of forces over a long period of time.

In other words, complexity in itself is not evidence of design. But if it is organized and purposive complexity, then it would surely seem to have been designed. Therefore, instead of wasting time and talent on evolutionary speculation as to how natural selection might have generated a particular animal, say, creationists believe that the scientist would more profitably have tried to determine why the Designer created such an animal.

In any case, evolutionists almost universally conclude that: "As currently promoted, ID theory is neither new nor good science" (Antolin & Herbers, 2001, p. 2383).

Creation and/or Design

The most serious deficiency in the ID movement, however, is its neglect of the most important of the alleged evidences for evolution—that is, the problem of the fossils. These are the remains of billions and billions of once-living plants and animals now preserved in the sedimentary crust of the earth. These all give abundant evidence of suffering and death during all the supposed geological ages which they are supposed to depict. Did the Designer do that? If so, just how and why?

The only adequate answer is in the Bible, in [15] its record of man's sin, the resulting global Curse and eventual Deluge. But the very purpose of the ID movement is to argue for intelligent design without reference to the Bible and the God of the Bible. Without those factors, however, it would seem that the only alternative would be to assume the Designer to be a sadistic producer of global evil as well as the intelligent producer of irreducible complexity.

We so-called "Young-Earth Creationists" also have always believed and taught what seem to us to be irrefutable evidences of intelligent design in nature, but that is not enough. We simply have to take the Biblical record as God's Word, in which He has taught the real and total truth about origins, as well as about sin and death, then providing also the wonderful solution to all such problems in the glorious Gospel of our Lord and Savior Jesus Christ.

Whether these facts are considered scientific or not, they are historical facts which should be considered if Truth is the ultimate goal.

We appreciate the tremendous contribution the ID leaders have made to the origins question, but we feel we must urge them to believe the whole counsel of God and return to the true Biblical record of recent Special Creation, the Fall and Curse, the worldwide Flood, and the promised return of God in Christ to consummate His purposes in Creation.

Although it is unlikely that full-fledged creation will ever be accepted in public schools, it can be argued that Intelligent Design will not be accepted there either. Even if an occasional school board decides to insist on it, it would be a travesty to make teachers who don't believe it try to teach it.

But remember that government schools are [20] unscriptural in the first place. The home is, Biblically speaking, ultimately responsible for the teaching of its youth. The original schools and colleges of our country were always either homeschools or sponsored by Christians, with government schools "evolving" later.

If the options of homeschooling or religious schooling are not available (as was true for my own six children), then the parents should monitor what their offspring are being taught in the public schools and colleges and help them get it all back in Biblical perspective.

Two key Bible texts are appropriate in this connection. "Study to shew thyself approved unto God, . . . rightly dividing the word of truth" (II Timothy 2:15 King James Version). Then, "But sanctify the Lord God in your hearts: and be ready always to give an answer to every man that asketh you a reason of the hope that is in you with meekness and fear" (I Peter 3:15).

References

Antolin, M. F., & Herbers, J. M. (2001). Evolution's struggle for existence in America's public schools. *Evolution, 55*, 2379–2388.

Frazier, K. (2005). Evolution and the ID wars. *Skeptical Inquirer, 29*(2005/11), 4.

Kennedy, D. (2005). Twilight for the Enlightenment. *Science, 308*, 165. doi:10.1126/science.1112920

Perakh, M. (2005). Does irreducible complexity imply intelligent design? *Skeptical Inquirer, 29*, 32–36.

Shipman, P. (2005). Being stalked by intelligent design. *American Scientist, 93*, 500–502.

Voodoo science. (2005, November 21). *San Diego Union-Tribune*. Retrieved April 25, 2011, from http://www.signonsandiego.com/uniontrib/20051121/news_mz1ed-21top.html

A CLOSER LOOK AT
Insufficient Design

1. In this research paper, Morris argues both against Intelligent Design *and* Darwinian evolution. He is arguing for a specific kind of creationism that rejects Intelligent Design as a middle path between creationism and evolution. What is Intelligent Design according to Morris, and how does it differ from other theories of creationism? How does Intelligent Design differ from Darwinian theories of evolution? Where in this research paper does Morris make these distinctions?

2. Look closely at Morris's own arguments *for* creationism. Where and how does he support arguments for creationism? In this research paper, he is mostly arguing against Intelligent Design and Darwinian evolution. Find his evidence for his own beliefs. What kinds of sources is he drawing from?

3. How does Morris use quotations from sources to support his argument and critique the beliefs of others? What kinds of sources does he choose to quote? How does he use these quotations to cast doubt on the other sides of this argument? How do these quotations add an emotional element to his argument?

IDEAS FOR
Writing

1. Write a rebuttal in which you argue for or against Morris's position in this research paper. You could argue for Intelligent Design *or* Darwinian evolution and against Morris's version of creationism. Or, you could back up Morris's argument by adding support for his arguments. Use sources to add support for your rebuttal.

2. Write an explainer (see Chapter 12) in which you explore the arguments for and against "young earth" creationism. How does this version of creationism differ from Intelligent Design? Discuss why the Intelligent Design movement is threatening to creationists like Morris. Also, explain why Intelligent Design is viewed as dangerous by evolutionary biologists. What do you think is the future of this issue in schools?

Charles Darwin's Paradigm Shift

TIM M. BERRA

In this research paper, Tim Berra explains the history of Darwin's theory of evolution. Then, he goes on to discuss some of this theory's implications and impacts on science. The discussion is mostly factual with minimal opinion included. Look closely at the author's strategies for staying objective about a controversial issue.

Charles Darwin (1809–1882) was an extraordinary man by any standard. The theory of evolution by natural selection as elaborated in his book *On the Origin of Species* (1859) is considered by historians and philosophers of science to be one of the most important ideas ever had by the human mind (Dennett 1995). Before exploring this grandiose statement, a brief review of Darwin's life and scientific accomplishments is in order. Then I will address the implications of his very useful insight that extended beyond science and profoundly impacted on the human mind.

An Outline of Darwin's Life

Charles Darwin was born into a wealthy English family on 12 February 1809. His father, Robert Waring Darwin (1766–1848), was a prominent physician as was his grandfather Erasmus Darwin (1731–1802). His mother was Susannah Wedgwood (1764–1817), the daughter of Josiah Wedgwood (1730–1795), the pottery manufacturer and entrepreneur, who was a close friend of Erasmus Darwin.

Darwin's father sent Charles to medical school at Edinburgh University in 1825 and removed him in 1827 when it became obvious that Charles was not interested in a medical career. Robert Darwin then decided that Charles should study to be a clergyman in the Church of England, and sent him to Cambridge University in 1828. Charles graduated 10th in his class in 1831 and then received an invitation orchestrated by his professor, John Stevens Henslow (1796–1861), to be an unpaid naturalist-companion to Captain Robert FitzRoy (1805–1865) on a surveying voyage around the world on H.M.S. *Beagle* (1831–1836). Darwin later described this opportunity as "the first real training or education of my mind".

Upon return from the nearly five-year *Beagle* voyage, Darwin found that he was accepted as a serious scientist, and he had no desire to become a clergyman. He began working on the specimens collected on the voyage. He married his first cousin, Emma Wedgwood (1808–1896), and they eventually moved from London to Down House in Kent (Fig. 1). They had 10 children, seven of whom survived to adulthood. After the voyage, he was often ill, but nevertheless, highly productive. He entered his ideas about how species form in a series of notebooks. This included a branching, tree-like diagram that reflected the common origin and relatedness of organisms. This first evolutionary tree showed that classification should be genealogical. However, he kept his revolutionary ideas private for 20 years except for his closest scientific colleagues: geologist Charles Lyell (1797–1875), botanist Joseph Dalton Hooker (1817–1911), zoologist Thomas Henry Huxley (1825–1895), and his American botanist correspondent at Harvard University, Asa Gray (1810–1888). In 1858 Darwin received of a letter from naturalist Alfred Russel Wallace (1823–1913), who, like Darwin, was inspired by the

FIGURE 1

At rear of montage, wedding portrait of Charles Darwin (watercolour) in 1840 at age 30 by George Richmond. At centre, HMS Beagle drawing by American artist Samuel L. Margolies (1897–1974) from Dibner (1960) in the Burndy Collection at the Huntington Library, San Marino, CA. Used with permission of the Huntington Library. In foreground, one of the last photographs of Charles Darwin, by Elliot and Fry.

writings of Thomas Malthus (1766–1834). Wallace outlined ideas nearly identical to Darwin's. This letter and urging from Lyell and Hooker prompted him to complete and publish *On the Origin of Species* in 1859. Darwin continued to do experiments and publish on a variety of topics right up to the time of his death. He died of heart disease on 19 April 1882 and was laid to rest with pomp and ceremony in Westminster Abby a few feet from Isaac Newton. Further details can be pursued in three of the most comprehensive biographies of Darwin (Desmond and Moore 1991; Browne 1995, 2002), a concise biography (Berra 2009), and, of course, Darwin's autobiography (Barlow 1958).

Synopsis of Darwin's Scientific Achievements

The educated citizen is generally aware of *The Origin* and Darwin's account of his voyage around the world in H.M.S. *Beagle* through his book now universally known as *The Voyage of the Beagle*. These two books have never been out of print.

Most people are surprised to learn that Darwin also made many other major contributions to geology, zoology, and botany through his observations, experiments and writings. His books have been chronicled (Berra 2009), so I will just briefly outline the breadth of his influence. Darwin explained how coral reefs form (1842) and contributed to geological observations on earth movements (1844) and deformation theory of metamorphic rock (1846). In a pioneering four-volume work that took eight years to complete, he described all known barnacle species, fossil and living (1851–1854). Darwin explained how orchids are fertilized by insects (1862), how plants climb (1865), and catalogued the bewildering amount of variation in domestic plants and animals (1868). He explained human origins and sexual selection in ways never before articulated (1870–71), and discussed human and animal emotions in similar terms (1872). The latter work was one of the first books to use photographs to illustrate a point.

Darwin showed how insectivorous plants on impoverished soils utilise nitrogen-rich insects (1875), and demonstrated that the offspring of cross-fertilised plants were more numerous and vigorous than self-fertilised ones (1876, 1877). His observations of climbing plants laid the foundation for the field of plant growth hormones (1880), and his work on earthworms (1881) is a classic study in ecology. Any one of these achievements could constitute a life's work for most scientists.

Darwin's Legacy

Darwin was born and educated at a time when special creation was the prevailing scientific view. That is, God created the universe and all species a few thousand years ago, and they were unchangeable. "Revelation", not research, provided this view. Darwin began the

Beagle voyage with this belief. During his lifetime the age of the earth was increasingly recognised as ancient as suggested by Georges Cuvier (1769–1832) and Charles Lyell (Bowler 1984; Larson 2004). Observations made during the voyage made him question the Genesis creation myth and immutability of species. He found marine fossils thousands of feet above sea level and reasoned that the land had been elevated by earth movements, not inundated in a great biblical flood. The fossil mammals he uncovered in South America resembled living mammals from the same area. He wondered why this should be if each species were specially created. Extinction was hardly recognised in those days. Why did the animals on islands off continental areas resemble those of the nearest land mass if each species were created in place? Why were there so many species in an island group that looked very similar but with slight differences from island to island? It is as if "one species had been taken and modified for different ends", he wrote in *Voyage of the Beagle*. None of these things made sense from a creationist perspective. In 1844 he wrote to Hooker that "I am almost convinced (quite contrary to the opinion I started with) that species are not (it is like confessing a murder) immutable."

The elegant simplicity of Darwin's reasoning can be distilled as follows. There is variation in nature, many more offspring are generated than can survive, therefore there is a struggle for life in which favorable variations are preserved and unfavorable variations are removed. This leads to evolution which he defined as "descent with modification" and to the formation of new species. Nature is doing the selecting for the forms best adapted to a particular environment so he called the process natural selection as opposed to artificial selection that breeders impose. We now know that mutation, chromosomal rearrangements, sexual reproduction, etc. are the sources of genetic variation, but Darwin had no knowledge of such topics. Today we can speak of "descent with modification" as

"a change in gene frequency", and natural selection is simply "differential reproduction",
that is, one genetic variant leaves more offspring than another (Berra 1990). Darwin borrowed the expression "survival of the fittest"
from economist Herbert Spencer (1820–1903).
Evolutionary fitness means reproductive fitness. In modern terms, the fittest is the one who
gets the most genes into the next generation,
not necessarily the biggest or strongest
individual.

By the time of Darwin's death in 1882, most   10
scientists of the world had accepted the concept of common descent, but some were still
skeptical of natural selection as a creative
mechanism (Bowler 1984). The public was less
accepting (Fig. 2).

The publication of *On the Origin of Species*
on 24 November 1859 precipitated one of those
rare events in the history of science, a paradigm
shift. Philosopher Thomas Kuhn used this term
to refer to the replacement of one world view by
another (Kuhn 1962). Examples of a paradigm
shift in science include the replacement of the
earth-centered Ptolemaic system by the sun-
centered Copernican system and the replacement of Newtonian physics by relativity and
quantum physics.

Darwin's work neatly dove-tailed into the
wider pattern of scientific advances that were
occurring during his life. Lyell and others had
provided the necessary geological time for evolution to operate. The writings of Malthus,
Spencer, Wallace, and many others help set the
evolutionary stage.

By 1859 evolution by natural selection was
an idea whose time had come. Darwin and the
publication of *The Origin* closed the deal.
Darwin changed the way humans view their
place in nature. He showed that humans were
not above nature, but part of it. He supplied the
explanation for the great diversity of life and
showed that all life, including human, is related by descent from a common ancestor. His
explanation of evolution via natural selection is
the basis of all of biology and its applied

FIGURE 2

Cartoon of Charles Darwin as a monkey, from Fun, *16 November 1872, just after* The Expression of the Emotions in Man and Animals *was published. Many other similar personal attacks were published during his lifetime.*

subdisciplines of medicine, agriculture, and
biotechnology. No other biologist in the history
of our species has had an impact of this magnitude. In the words of the eminent geneticist
Theodosius Dobzhansky, "Nothing in biology
makes sense except in the light of evolution"
(Dobzhansky 1973).

The paradigm shift from creation to evolu-   15
tion has moved intellectual endeavors from
untestable belief to rational understanding
that flows from the scientific method. This, in
turn, has allowed a vast array of advances in
knowledge.

Darwinian Implications

One of the attributes of a powerful scientific theory is that it enables future research and understanding. Darwinian or evolutionary medicine as formulated by Nesse and Williams (1996) explains how some disease symptoms, such as fever, may be a response favored by natural selection as a defense against pathogens. Some genetic diseases such as sickle cell anaemia may allow differential survival of its victims in malarial zones, a phenomenon called a balanced polymorphism (Berra 1990). Evolutionary thinking explains the arms race waged by pathogens and hosts that prevents either from being completely eliminated. The development of antibiotic resistant bacteria through the flagrant overuse of antibiotics is easily explained by Darwinian reasoning. A drug kills the susceptible bacteria leaving bacteria with a pre-existing resistant mutation to build up the next generation. Then when you actually need the antibiotic for a bacterial infection, you find that the drug is ineffective. This is evolution, pure and simple.

A similar process occurs in agriculture with the over application of pesticides and the formation of pesticide resistant pathogens, insects, and noxious plants. Australians are very familiar with the myxomatosis versus rabbit "arms race" whereby the virus initially killed 99 percent of the rabbits, but given enough time the surviving rabbits returned in force as the virus evolved in the direction of less virulence and the rabbits were selected for more resistance to the virus (Berra 1998).

Evolutionary psychology and evolutionary ethics, as explored by Barkow *et al.* (1992) and popularised by Wright (1994) help explain the origin of morality. Peacemaking among non-human primates by the calming effect of mutual grooming to diffuse aggression may be seen as the precursor of what became morality in humans (de Waal 1989). Modern religions are recent human inventions—a mere few thousand years old. The antecedents of morality, on the other hand, clearly evolved before

humanity as reflected in the empathy exhibited by bonobos (*Pan paniscus*) and the reciprocity of chimpanzees (*P. troglodytes*) (de Waal 2005). Kin selection, whereby an individual sacrifices for a close genetic relative, makes sense in an evolutionary context because some of the same genes of the individual making the sacrifice will be passed on by the kin who survives. This is referred to as inclusive fitness by Hamilton (1972). Realisation that humans share kinship with all animal life has helped to raise consciousness of how we treat other animals (Singer 1977).

The ancestry of the AIDS virus, HIV-1 (human immunodeficiency virus-1) has been traced to SIVcpz (simian immunodeficiency virus) carried by our closest living relative, the chimpanzees, *Pan troglodytes* (Bailes *et al.* 2003). This is not surprising from an evolutionary perspective. Somewhere in high school today there is a student who may contribute to the control of the AIDS epidemic. What chance of that would there be if creationism were taught as science in high school?

Even religion is now being explained as [20] having an evolutionary origin as a natural phenomenon once the brain evolved a critical mass and complexity (Dennett 2006). Bloch (2008) suggested that the evolution of imagination was a requisite for the emergence of religion which he considered a logical extension of human sociality. This occurred about the time of the Upper Palaeolithic "revolution" as manifested by an explosion of image-making and cultural transformations (White 2003). Acceptance of authority necessary for group cohesion and survival enforced by tool use and language combined with confusion of cause and effect and coincidences can result in the establishment of a belief that becomes dominate in a culture (Wolpert 2007).

Those whose religion requires a literal interpretation of the Bible fear that the paradigm shift from supernaturalism to methodological naturalism threatens their beliefs. The 1925 Scopes trial, nicknamed "monkey trial" and "trial of the century" in Dayton, Tennessee, has come to symbolize the struggle of religion against science in popular culture that later inspired the play and film *Inherit the Wind* (Larson 1977). Such creationists are particularly vocal in America which has a long standing tradition of anti-intellectualism (Numbers 1992; Pigliucci 2002). This has resulted in a series of reactionist legal challenges to evolution which have been decided in favor of evolution (Berra 1990). The most recent of these was the Intelligent Design creationist challenge of the Dover, Pennsylvania, School Board. The Intelligent Design creationist philosophy that life is too complex to have arisen by natural means and therefore had a supernatural origin has been critiqued in Pennock (2001) and exposed as a threat to science education by Forrest and Gross (2004). In the conclusion of his decision Judge John E. Jones III determined that the school board's policy of teaching Intelligent Design violated the Establishment Clause of the First Amendment [separation of church and state] of the U.S. Constitution, and he wrote, ". . . in making this determination, we have addressed the seminal question whether Intelligent Design is science (Jones 2005). We have concluded that it is not, and moreover that Intelligent Design cannot uncouple itself from its creationist, and thus religious, antecedents." He further wrote, "The breathtaking inanity of the board's decision is evident when considered against the factual backdrop which has now been fully revealed through this trial." Padian (2007) reviewed three books based on the Dover trial. Biotechnology, whether in the form of genetically modified crops, designer drugs, gene therapy, or the human genome project all derive from Darwin's profound insight. Darwin had no knowledge of genes, chromosomes, or how inheritance worked. This required additional input from the understanding of Gregor Mendel's (1822–1884) genetic work.

The modern evolutionary synthesis grew from Darwin's explanation of natural selection and Mendel's demonstration of inheritance augmented by the research of mathematically oriented population geneticists such as J.B.S. Haldane, Ronald Fisher, Sewall Wright, Thomas Hunt Morgan, Theodosius Dobzhansky, palaeontologist George Gaylord Simpson, botanist G. Ledyard Stebbins, Jr., biologist Julian Huxley (T.H. Huxley's grandson), and the most important evolutionary biologist since Darwin, Ernst Mayr. This fusion of knowledge moved evolutionary science forward to the middle of the 20th century (Larson 2004). James D. Watson's and Francis Crick's 1953 demonstration that the molecular structure of DNA allowed for genetic coding was a huge breakthrough that ultimately made it possible to sequence the three billion chemical base pairs that compose the human genome and identify the approximately 20,000–25,000 genes in human DNA (Lander *et al.* 2001; Venter *et al.* 2001).

Recent discoveries in evolutionary developmental biology, known as evo-devo, have shown that very similar genes are present in very dissimilar animals. These body-shaping genes are controlled by DNA switches called enhancers that turn them on or off at various times in development. Such enhancers are a major factor in the evolution of anatomy (Carroll 2005). The above examples are just a sample of the benefits to society that flow directly from the creative power of Charles Darwin's theory of evolution by means of natural selection.

The paradigm shift instigated by Darwin has made obvious the superiority of the scientific method as a means of understanding the world around us. It is ironic that the legacy of a man once destined for the church has been to replace supernaturalism with methodological naturalism.

References

Bailes, E., Gao, F., Bibollet-Ruche, F., Courgnaud, V., Peeters, M., Marx, P., Han, B. H., & Sharp, P.M. (2003). Hybrid origin of SIV in chimpanzees. *Science,* 300, 1713.

Barkow, J. H., Cosmides, L., & Tooby, J. (Eds). (1992). *The adapted mind.* Oxford: Oxford University Press.

Barlow, N. (Ed.). (1958). *The autobiography of Charles Darwin 1809-1882: with original omissions restored.* New York: W.W. Norton and Company.

Berra, T. M. (1990). *Evolution and the myth of creationism.* Stanford, CA: Stanford University Press.

Berra, T. M. (1998). *A natural history of Australia.* Sydney/San Diego: University of New South Wales Press/Academic Press.

Berra, T. (2009). *Charles Darwin: The concise story of an extraordinary man.* Baltimore, MD: Johns Hopkins University Press.

Bloch, M. (2008). Why religion is nothing special but is central. *Philosophical Transactions of the Royal Society B,* 363, 2055-2061.

Bowler, P. J. (1984). *Evolution: The history of an idea.* Berkelet: University of California Press.

Browne, J. (1995). *Charles Darwin voyaging. Volume I of a biography.* Princeton, NJ: Princeton University Press.

Browne, J. (2002). *Charles Darwin: The power of place. Volume II of a biography.* New York: Knopf.

Carroll, S. B. (2005). *Endless forms most beautiful: The new science of evo devo and the making of the animal kingdom.* New York: W.W. Norton.

Darwin, C. (1859). *On the origin of species by means of natural selection, or the preservation of favoured races in the struggle for life.* London: John Murray.

de Waal, F. (1989). *Peacemaking among primates.* Cambridge, MA: Harvard University Press.

de Waal, F. (2005). *Our inner ape.* New York: Riverhead Books.

Dennett, D.C. (1995). *Darwin's dangerous idea.* New York: Touchstone.

Dennett, D.C. (2006). *Breaking the spell: Religion as a natural phenomenon.* New York: Viking.

Desmond, A., & Moore, J. (1991). *Darwin: The life of a tormented evolutionist.* New York: Warner Books.

Dibner, B. (1960). *Darwin of the Beagle.* Norwalk, CT: Burndy Library.

Dobzhansky, T. (1973). Nothing in biology makes sense except in the light of evolution. *American Biology Teacher,* 35, 125-129.

Forrest, B., & Gross, P.R. (2004). *Creationism's trojan horse: The wedge of intelligent design.* Oxford: Oxford University Press.

Hamilton, W.D. (1972). Altruism and related phenomena, mainly in the social insects. *Annual Review of Ecology and Systematics,* 3, 193-232.

Jones, J.E. III. (2005). Memorandum Opinion. In the United States District Court for the Middle District of Pennsylvania. Tammy Kitzmiller, *et al.* Plaintiffs vs Dover Area School Board Defendants. Case No. 04cv2688.

Kuhn, T. S. (1962). *The structure of scientific revolutions.* Chicago: University of Chicago Press.

Lander, E.S., & 19 coauthors. (2001). Initial sequencing and analysis of the Human genome. *Nature,* 409, 860-921.

Larson, E. J. (1997). *Summer for the gods: The Scopes trial and America's continuing debate over science and religion.* New York: Basic Books.

Larson, E. J. (2004). *Evolution: The remarkable history of a scientific theory.* New York: The Modern Library.

Nesse, R. M., & Williams, G. C. (1996). *Why we get sick.* New York: Vantage Books.

Numbers, R. L. (1992). *The creationists: The evolution of scientific creationism.* New York: Alfred A. Knopf.

Padian, K. (2007). The case of creation. *Nature,* 448, 253-254.

Pennock, R. T. (2001). *Intelligent design creationism and its critics: Philosophical, theological, and scientific perspectives.* Cambridge, MA: Massachusetts Institute of Technology Press.

Pigliucci, M. (2002). *Denying evolution: Creationism, scientism, and the nature of science.* Sunderland, MA: Sinauer Associates.

Singer, P. (1977). *Animal liberation: Towards an end to man's inhumanity to animals.* London: Granada Publishing.

Venter, J. C., & 273 coauthors. (2001). The sequence of the human genome. *Science, 291,* 1304–1351.

White, R. (2003). *Prehistoric art: The symbolic journey of humankind.* New York: H.N. Abrams, Inc.

Wolpert, L. (2007). *Six impossible things before breakfast: The evolutionary origin of belief.* New York: W.W. Norton and Co.

Wright, R. (1994). *The moral animal.* New York: Pantheon Books.

A CLOSER LOOK AT
Charles Darwin's Paradigm Shift

1. In this research paper, Berra writes, "By the time of Darwin's death in 1882, most scientists of the world had accepted the concept of common descent, but some were still skeptical of natural selection as a creative mechanism." According to the author, why were scientists and the public skeptical of Darwin's theories, and why are many people skeptical today?

2. The author includes a great amount of historical information. How is he using this historical information to lay the groundwork for discussing the importance and implications of Darwin's theories?

3. This research paper could be classified as an "expository" research paper, because it mostly explains and offers factual information, while not making an overt argument. Nevertheless, it is argumentative in places. Locate three of those "argumentative" moments in this research paper. How is the author using argument in this otherwise expository research paper?

IDEAS FOR
Writing

1. The cornerstone of Darwin's theory of evolution is the concept of "natural selection." According to the author, what is natural selection and why is it critical to Darwin's theory of evolution? Write a brief in which you explain the concept of natural selection and explain why it is necessary in Darwinian evolution.

2. Create a five-source annotated bibliography about the history of Darwin's theory of evolution. Include only sources that discuss the history of this theory. Do not include articles or books that argue for or against the theory. Combine your annotated bibliography with the bibliographies from your group in class. How many sources did all of you have in common? How many sources were unique to your list? Talk about why you came up with the same or different sources on this topic.

A FEW IDEAS FOR
Composing a Research Paper

1. **Write a Research Paper about a contemporary issue.** Choose an issue that is prominent in the national or local media right now. Your research paper's topic does not need to be new, but you should find a new angle that makes this issue fresh and interesting. Your research paper should be about an issue that you care about but also something you can write about in an informed way. You should ask your professor whether you need to write an "expository" or "argumentative" research paper for this assignment.

2. **Write a research paper that responds to someone else's argument.** Look for an article that makes an argument you consider wrong-headed or at least misinformed. Then, do research on this topic and explain why the facts support a different conclusion and undercut the article you are responding to. Your research paper should use the original article as a starting place, but you should go beyond simply writing a rebuttal. Instead, write a full research paper on the subject that explores the issue in depth.

3. **Develop a research Web site.** In many situations a research Web site is actually more useful than a research paper. These kinds of Web sites collect or make links to sources that readers can use to inform themselves and do their own research on the topic. The Web site you create should gather these sources of information into a usable form. It should also offer some discussion about which sources you found most useful (or not). Try to provide materials and links that address all sides of the issue, not just sources that agree with your opinion.

PART OUTLINE

Do you have questions about grammar, usage, or spelling? Look no further. Your questions will be answered in this **HANDBOOK**.

This handbook is a reference tool for questions about English grammar and usage. It focuses on the sentence as the basic material of written and spoken discourse. It avoids grammatical jargon as much as possible, but it does define terms where they are necessary for understanding important concepts and problems. Refer to this guide while writing and when your professor suggests sections for you to study. It will help you write correctly, clearly, and with an appropriate style.

1 Sentences

Every sentence has at least one subject and at least one verb, begins with a capital letter, and ends with end punctuation (a period, question mark, or exclamation point). In college writing and beyond, you will be asked to communicate complex ideas. You may need to try out new sentence patterns to connect those ideas, and that may lead you to make some sentence errors. Use this handbook to help you understand the wide variety of sentence types while avoiding grammatical errors.

1A Fragments

Sentence fragments are errors in which partial sentences are treated as complete sentences—begun with a capital letter and ended with a period. The fragment may

Watch the
Animation on
Fragments at
mycomplab
.com

be a subordinate clause, a phrase, or a combination of subordinate elements. What makes each a fragment is that it lacks a subject or a verb, or that it begins with a subordinating word. Only independent clauses can make independent statements.

Subordinate Clause Fragment

Recognition. A subordinate clause has a subject and a verb but is not an independent clause because it includes a subordinate connector.

Some common subordinating connectors, grouped by function, include:

Time: *after, before, once, since, until, whenever*

Place: *where, wherever*

Cause: *as, because, since*

Contrast: *although, even though, though, while*

Condition: *even if, if*

Result: *in order that, so, so that*

Alternative: *than, whether*

Relative pronouns, such as *who, whom, whose, whatever, why,* and *unless,* can also be subordinate connectors.

Any clause beginning with one of these words is *subordinate* and should not be written as a sentence. Here are examples of clause fragments (italicized):

The Vikings revolutionized shipbuilding with the keel. *Which allowed their ships to go faster and farther without stopping for supplies.*

Norway's Lapps are believed to be a nomadic people of Asian heritage. *Who follow reindeer herds through Norway's cold, rugged land.*

Because the northern part of Norway is so far north. It has long periods during the summer when the sun shines 24 hours a day.

Correction. There are mainly two ways of correcting clause fragments: (1) attaching them to the preceding or following sentence, and (2) removing or changing the subordinating connector. These sentences illustrate both types of corrections:

The Vikings revolutionized shipbuilding with the keel. *This innovation* allowed their ships to go faster and farther without stopping for supplies. The subordinating word of the fragment is changed.

Norway's Lapps are believed to be of Asian heritage—nomadic people who follow reindeer herds through Norway's cold, rugged land. The fragment is connected to the preceding sentence with a dash.

Because the northern part of Norway is so far north, it has long periods during the summer when the sun shines 24 hours a day. The fragment is connected to the following sentence with a comma.

Phrase Fragment

Phrase fragments lack a subject, a verb, or both. The most common phrases written as fragments are *verbal phrases* and *prepositional phrases.*

Recognition.   A *verbal phrase* is a word group made up of a verb form and related modifiers and other words. As opposed to *verb phrases,* which are made up of verb parts (such as *has been gone*), a verbal phrase is constituted with a *verbal,* a word formed from a verb but not functioning as a verb. *Going,* for example, is a verbal, as is *gone.*

There are three kinds of verbals: gerunds, participles, and infinitives. Gerunds end in *-ing;* participles end in either *-ing* (present) or *-ed* (regular past); infinitives are usually introduced by *to.* Here are a few examples of how verbals are formed from verbs:

Verb	Present Participle and Gerund	Past Participle	Infinitive
snap	snapping	snapped	to snap
look	looking	looked	to look
want	wanting	wanted	to want
go	going	gone	to go
has	having	had	to have

Verbals function primarily as adjectives and nouns, most often in verbal phrases.

In the following examples, the italicized verbal phrases are fragments because they are written as sentences:

Eero Saarinen designed the 630-foot Gateway Arch for the St. Louis riverfront. *Imagining a giant stainless steel arch.* Participial phrase modifying *Eero Saarinen*

Critics said that cranes could not reach high enough. *To lift the steel sections into place.* Infinitive phrase modifying *high*

Saarinen knew that precision was of utmost importance. In *building the arch.* Gerund phrase as object of preposition *In*

Correction.   Verbal phrase fragments can be corrected in one of two ways: (1) by connecting them to a related sentence, or (2) by expanding them into a sentence. Both ways are illustrated below:

Eero Saarinen designed the 630-foot Gateway Arch for the St. Louis riverfront. *He imagined a giant stainless steel arch.* The verbal fragment is expanded to a sentence.

Critics said that cranes could not reach high enough *to lift the steel sections into place.* The verbal fragment is connected to a related sentence.

Saarinen knew that precision was of utmost importance in *building the arch.* The gerund phrase, object of the preposition *In,* is connected to a related sentence.

Recognition.   A *prepositional phrase* is a word group made up of a preposition and its object. Together they contribute meaning to a sentence, usually modifying a noun or a verb. Like subordinating conjunctions, prepositions show relationships, such as time, place, condition, and cause. Common prepositions include *about, above, among, below, but, by, in addition to, into, like, from, out of, past, regarding, toward,* and *until.*

In the following examples, prepositional phrases have been written as sentences and are therefore fragments:

> The Vikings were descendents of Teutonic settlers. *Like most of today's Norwegians.*

> Norway is a land of natural beauty. *From its fjord-lined coast to frigid Lapland.*

Correction.   Prepositional phrase fragments can also be corrected (1) by connecting them to a related sentence, or (2) by expanding them into a sentence.

> The Vikings were descendents of Teutonic settlers, *like most of today's Norwegians.* **or** *Like most of today's Norwegians,* the Vikings were descendents of Teutonic settlers. The prepositional phrase is connected to a related sentence.

> Norway is a land of natural beauty. *Its charm extends from its fjord-lined coast to frigid Lapland.* The prepositional phrase is expanded into a sentence.

Incomplete Thoughts

Sometimes fragments are simply errors in punctuation—the writer uses a period when a comma or no punctuation would be correct. A more difficult type of fragment to correct is the incomplete thought, such as this one:

> A large concrete dock 50 feet short of a wooden platform anchored in the middle of the bay.

With fragments of this sort, the writer needs to insert the missing information. The reader doesn't know what happens—what the dock does or what is done to it. The fragment might be revised like this:

> A large concrete dock *juts out, stopping* 50 feet short of a wooden platform anchored in the middle of the bay.

Acceptable Fragments

You probably encounter fragments every day. Titles are often fragments, as are answers to questions and expressions of strong emotion.

> **Titles:** *Gates of Fire: An Epic Novel of the Battle of Thermopylae*
>
> **Answer to question:** "How many more chairs do we need?" "Fifteen."
>
> **Expression of strong emotion:** "What a great concert!"

And much advertising uses fragments:

> Intricate, delicate, exquisite. Extravagant in every way.

> Another successful client meeting. Par for the course.

Finally, writers quoting spoken words might use fragments:

> Claire asked Erin, "Why would you do that?"

> Erin shrugged. "Because."

Common as they are in everyday life, fragments are usually unacceptable in academic or workplace writing. When you do choose to use a fragment, you should do it intentionally, and only after carefully considering your readers and the effect that you want to achieve.

1B Comma Splices

Comma splices consist of two independent clauses (clauses that can stand alone as sentences) improperly joined together by a comma as one sentence. Here are two examples:

> The economy of Algeria is in trouble, many citizens blame the government.

> The death of any soldier is tragic, however, death by friendly fire is particularly disturbing.

Recognition.   The first step in avoiding comma splices is to identify them. Because they happen only in sentences with at least two independent clauses, you can test your sentences by substituting periods for commas. If you end up with two complete sentences, you probably have a comma splice. In testing the first of the two preceding examples we come up with the following result:

> The economy of Algeria is in trouble.

> Many citizens blame the government.

Both of these clauses obviously qualify as complete sentences, so they must be independent clauses. They therefore cannot be connected with a comma. Remember this simple rule of punctuation: *Periods and commas are not interchangeable*. If a period is correct, a comma is not.

Correction.   You can revise comma splices using five different strategies.

1. Separate the independent clauses using a comma and a *coordinating conjunction*. There are seven—and *only* seven—coordinating conjunctions. As a memory aid, their first letters spell F-A-N-B-O-Y-S:

for	**b**ut
and	**o**r
nor	**y**et
	so

   To correct a comma splice, begin the second independent clause with one of these conjunctions preceded by a comma. For example:

The economy of Algeria is in trouble, *and* many citizens blame the government.

2. Separate the independent clauses using a semicolon (with or without a transitional adverb). Semicolons are often interchangeable with periods and therefore can be used to separate independent clauses. For example:

The economy of Algeria is in trouble; many citizens blame the government.

The death of any soldier is tragic; *however,* death by friendly fire is particularly disturbing.

In the second example, *however* is a transitional adverb. Unlike coordinating conjunctions, *transitional adverbs* are not conjunctions and so do not join sentence elements. They do, however, connect ideas by showing how they relate to one another. Like conjunctions, they can show addition, contrast, result, and other relationships. Some of the most common transitional adverbs are *also, in addition, next, finally, for example, however, meanwhile, therefore,* and *then.*

A semicolon should always precede the transitional adverb that begins the second independent clause. A comma usually follows the transitional adverb, although in some instances, as in the following example, the comma is omitted:

Air bags deflate within one second after inflation; *therefore* they do not interfere with control of the car.

Some comma splices result when writers use transitional adverbs as if they were coordinating conjunctions. If you have trouble distinguishing transitional adverbs from coordinating conjunctions, remember that none of the coordinating conjunctions is longer than three letters, and all of the transitional adverbs are four letters or longer. Also, keep in mind that transitional adverbs are movable within the sentence while coordinating conjunctions are not; for example, the preceding example could be rewritten as:

Air bags deflate within one second after inflation; they do not *therefore* interfere with control of the car.

3. Make one of the independent clauses subordinate to the other by inserting a subordinating conjunction. When one of the clauses explains or elaborates on the other, use an appropriate subordinating conjunction to make the relationship between the two clauses more explicit (see 1A Fragments). Consider the following comma splice and its revision:

Henry forgot to fill in his time card on Friday, he is going to have a hard time getting paid for the overtime he put in last week.

Because Henry forgot to fill in his time card on Friday, he is going to have a hard time getting paid for the overtime he put in last week.

4. Rewrite one of the independent clauses as a modifying phrase. A *modifying phrase* serves as an adjective or adverb within a sentence. By rewriting one of the

independent clauses as a phrase, you can eliminate unneeded words. For example, consider the following comma splice and its revision:

> The celebrity couple smiled for the cameras, they were glowing of wealth and fame.

> The celebrity couple smiled for the cameras, glowing of wealth and fame.
> Here, *glowing of wealth and fame* acts as an adjective modifying the noun *couple*

5. Punctuate each independent clause as a separate sentence. No law of grammar, punctuation, or style says you must present the two independent clauses together within one sentence. The example from before is perfectly acceptable written as follows:

> The economy of Algeria is in trouble. Many citizens blame the government.

It may be to your advantage to divide long and/or complex independent clauses into separate sentences. Doing so may help convey your meaning to readers more clearly.

1C Fused Sentences

Watch the Animation on **Fused Sentences** at mycomplab.com

Fused sentences, sometimes called *run-on sentences,* are similar to comma splices. However, instead of a comma between the two independent clauses, there is no punctuation; the two independent clauses simply run together. For example:

> The United States has 281 lawyers per 100,000 people Japan has only 11 attorneys per 100,000.

> The World Cup is the most popular sporting event in the world you would never know it based on the indifferent response of the average American.

Recognition.   Unlike the comma splice, there is no punctuation in the fused sentence to guide you to the end of the first independent clause and the beginning of the second. As a result, it can be more challenging to identify independent clauses within fused sentences, particularly if the sentence also contains modifying phrases or dependent clauses set off by commas. The best way to do this is to read from the beginning of the sentence (reading aloud may help) until you have found the end of the first independent clause. Consider the following example:

> Even though I was still sick with the flu, I attended the awards banquet as my family watched, the coach presented me with the trophy for most valuable player.

This fused sentence contains two subordinate clauses (*Even though I was still sick with the flu* and *as my family watched*), each one attached to one of the two independent clauses (*I attended the awards banquet* and *the coach presented me with the trophy*).

Correction.   Revise fused sentences using any one of the same five strategies for correcting comma splices (see 1B Comma Splices, for more information on each strategy).

1. Separate the independent clauses using a comma and a coordinating conjunction. For example:

   The United States has 281 lawyers per 100,000 people, *but* Japan has only 11 attorneys per 100,000.

2. Separate the independent clauses using a semicolon (with or without a transitional adverb). For example:

   The United States has 281 lawyers per 100,000 people; Japan has only 11 attorneys per 100,000.

   The World Cup is the most popular sporting event in the world; *however,* you would never know it based on the indifferent response of the average American.

3. Make one of the independent clauses subordinate to the other by inserting a subordinating conjunction. The newly formed dependent clause should explain the remaining independent clause. For example, consider the following fused sentence and its revision:

   I run a marathon my feet get sore.

   Whenever I run a marathon, my feet get sore.

4. Rewrite one of the independent clauses as a modifying phrase. Remember, modifying phrases act as adjectives or adverbs. Consider the following fused sentence and its revision:

   Last night the tomcats fought outside my window they were crying and hissing for what seemed like hours.

   Last night the tomcats fought outside my window, crying and hissing for what seemed like hours. Here, the phrase *crying and hissing* acts as an adjective modifying the noun *tomcats*.

5. Punctuate each independent clause as a separate sentence. As with comma splices, you can write the independent clauses (and their related phrases and dependent clauses) as separate sentences. Indeed, this is often the easiest way to handle fused sentences. For example:

   I attended the awards banquet even though I was still sick with the flu. As my family watched, the coach presented me with the trophy for most valuable player. Here, the subordinate clause attached to the first independent clause *even though I was still sick with the flu* was also moved to the back of the first sentence for better readability.

1D Parallelism

Correctly used parallelism results when two or more grammatically equivalent sentence elements are joined. The sentence elements can be nouns, verbs, phrases, or clauses. (See 1E Coordination and Subordination.)

Watch the Animation on **Parallelism** at **mycomplab.com**

Parallelism becomes a problem when dissimilar elements are joined in pairs, in series, in comparisons using *than* or *as,* or in comparisons linked by correlative conjunctions. Consider the following examples of faulty parallelism:

She did not like rude customers or taking orders from her boss. The two elements in the pair are not parallel.

We were having a hard time deciding what to do in the afternoon: go snorkeling, go fishing, or swim out to the sand bar. The last of the three elements in the series is not parallel.

Michael decided to complete his degree next semester rather than studying abroad for another year. The two elements compared using *than* are not parallel.

My sister not only lost the race but also her leg got hurt. The two elements compared by the correlative conjunction *not only . . . but also* are not parallel. Other correlative conjunctions include *both . . . and, either . . . or, neither . . . nor, whether . . . or,* and *just as . . . so.*

Faulty parallelism can be corrected in various ways:

She did not like *dealing with* rude customers or taking orders from her boss. Words were added to the first element to make it parallel to the second.

We were having a hard time deciding what to do in the afternoon: go snorkeling, go fishing, or *go swimming.* The last element was rewritten to make it parallel with the others in the series.

Michael decided to complete his degree next semester rather than *to study* abroad for another year. The verb form of the second element is changed from a participle to an infinitive to make it parallel with the verb form in the first element.

My sister not only lost the race but also *hurt her leg.* The second element was rewritten to make it parallel with the first element.

1E Coordination and Subordination

When dealing with complex ideas, you will often need to explain relationships among things, ideas, places, people, events, and so forth. Sometimes you will choose to explain those relationships within a single sentence. Most sentence relationships involve either coordination or subordination. That is, sentence elements are either grammatically equal to other elements (coordination) or grammatically dependent on other parts (subordination). For example, two independent clauses in a sentence are coordinate; but in a sentence containing an independent clause and a dependent clause, the dependent clause is subordinate (indeed, dependent clauses are also called subordinate clauses).

Coordination

When two or more equivalent sentence elements appear in one sentence, they are coordinate. These elements can be words, phrases, or clauses. Only parallel elements can be coordinated: verbs linked with verbs, nouns with nouns, phrases with phrases, and clauses with clauses (see 1D Parallelism). For example:

Broccoli and *related vegetables* contain beta-carotene, a substance that may reduce the risk of heart attack. Two nouns are joined by a coordinating conjunction.

We *ran, swam,* and *cycled* every day while we were at the fitness camp. Three parallel verbs are joined in a series with commas and a coordinating conjunction.

American medical devices are equally remarkable, *giving life to those with terminally diseased organs, giving mobility to those crippled with arthritic joints and deadened nerves,* and even, miraculously, *restoring the sense of hearing to those deprived of it.—Atlantic.* The participial (verbal) phrases are joined by commas and a final coordinating conjunction. Also, embedded in the second participial phrase, two coordinate noun phrases are joined by a coordinating conjunction: *arthritic joints and deadened nerves.*

The term "Big Bang" is common usage now with scientists, but it originated as a sarcastic rejection of the theory. Two independent clauses are joined by a comma and a coordinating conjunction.

Subordination

If all sentence elements were grammatically equivalent, the sameness would be tedious. Subordinate elements show where the emphasis lies in sentences and modify elements with independent clauses. A subordinate element—either a phrase or clause—is dependent on the element it modifies for its meaning. At the same time, it often provides a fuller meaning than could be achieved exclusively through the use of independent elements.

For example:

For walking and jogging, the calorie expenditure is greater for people of greater body weight. The subordinate element is a prepositional phrase, modifying *is greater.*

Increasing both speed and effort in aerobic activities, the exerciser burns more calories. The subordinate element is a verbal phrase, modifying *exerciser.*

Because sedentary people are more likely to burn sugar than fat, they tend to become hungry sooner and to overeat. The subordinate clause modifies the verb *tend.*

People *who exercise on a regular basis* change certain enzyme systems *so that they are more likely to burn fat than sugar.* There are two subordinate clauses, one beginning with *who* and modifying *People,* and one beginning with *so that* and modifying the verb *change.*

Effective writing has both coordination and subordination—coordination that sets equivalent elements side by side, and subordination that makes some elements dependent on others. These useful writing tools can be used often or rarely, depending on the rhetorical situation, the genre, and the style you choose to use.

1F Mixed Sentences

A mixed sentence is a problem that occurs when two or more parts of a sentence do not make sense together. It is called faulty predication when a subject and predicate are mismatched. This kind of problem usually occurs when writers are striving to express complex relationships.

The following mixed sentences are common in everyday speech and may not seem inconsistent to you. Indeed, in casual speech they are usually accepted. In standard written English, however, they qualify as grammatical errors.

By driving to the movie was how we saw the accident happen. The prepositional phrase *By driving to the movie* is treated as the subject of the verb *was*. Prepositional phrases cannot serve as subjects.

Just because the candidate once had a drinking problem doesn't mean he won't be a good mayor now. The adverb clause *because the candidate once had a drinking problem* is treated as the subject of the verb *doesn't mean*. Adverbs modify verbs and adjectives and cannot function as subjects.

A CAT scan is when medical technicians take a cross-sectional X-ray of the body. The adverb clause *when medical technicians take a cross-sectional X-ray of the body* is treated as a complement of the subject *CAT scan*—another function adverbs cannot serve.

The reason I was late today is because my alarm clock broke. The subject, *reason,* is illogically linked with the predicate, *is because. Reason* suggests an explanation, so the predicate, *is because*, is redundant.

Revise mixed sentences by ensuring that grammatical patterns are used consistently throughout each sentence. For cases of faulty predication, either revise the subject so it can perform the action expressed in the predicate or revise the predicate so it accurately depicts an action performed by the subject. When you are writing, avoid these patterns: *is when, is where*, and *The reason . . . is because.*

There are often many ways to revise mixed sentences. In each of the following revisions, the grammatical patterns are consistent and the subjects and predicates fit together logically:

While driving to the movie, we saw the accident happen.

Just because the candidate once had a drinking problem, we can't conclude that he won't be a good mayor.

A CAT scan is a cross-sectional X-ray of the body.

The reason I was late today is that my alarm clock broke.

1G Shifts

Shifts occur when writers lose track of their sentence elements. Shifts occur in a variety of ways:

In person

In music, where left-handed people seem to be talented, the right-handed world puts *you* at a disadvantage. Shift from *people,* third person, to *you,* second person

In tense

Even though many musicians *are* left handed, instruments *had been designed for right handers.* Shift from present tense to past perfect

In number

A left-handed *violinist* has to pay extra to buy *their* left-handed violin. Shift from singular to plural

In mood

Every time the *violinist played, she could always know* when her instrument was out of tune. Shift from the indicative mood, *violinist played,* to the subjunctive mood, *she could always know*

In voice

The sonata *was being practiced* by the violinists in one room while the cellists *played* the concerto in the other room. Shift from the passive voice, *was being practiced,* to the active voice, *played*

In discourse type

She said, "*Your violin is out of tune,*" and that *I was playing the wrong note.* Shift from the direct quotation, *"Your violin is out of tune,"* to the indirect quotation, *that I was playing the wrong note*

Once you recognize shifts, revise them by ensuring that the same grammatical structures are used consistently throughout the sentence:

In music, where left-handed *people* seem to be talented, the right-handed world puts *them* at a disadvantage.

Even though many musicians *are* left handed, instruments *have been designed* for right handers.

Left-handed *violinists* have to pay extra to buy *their* left-handed violins.

Every time the violinist *played,* she *knew* when her instrument was out of tune.

The violinists *practiced* the sonata in one room while the cellists *played* the concerto in the other room.

She said, "*Your violin is out of tune and you are playing the wrong note.*"

Watch the
Animation on
**Dangling and
Misplaced
Modifiers** at
mycomplab.com

1H Dangling and Misplaced Modifiers

Dangling and misplaced modifiers are words and word groups that are phrased or positioned in ways that make the meaning of a sentence unclear and sometimes even ludicrous. They are most commonly verbal phrases, prepositional phrases, and adverbs. Here are examples:

Reaching to pick up the saddle, the obnoxious horse may shake off the blanket. The dangling verbal phrase appears to relate to *horse.*

To extend lead out of the eversharp pencil, the eraser cap is depressed. The dangling verbal phrase implies that *the eraser cap* does something.

The eversharp pencil is designed to be used permanently, *only periodically replacing the lead.* The dangling verbal phrase implies that the pencil replaces the lead.

Dick *only* had to pay ten dollars for his parking ticket. The misplaced adverb should immediately precede *ten.*

Theodore caught a giant fish in the very same spot where he had lost the ring *two years later.* The misplaced adverb phrase confusingly appears to modify the last part of the sentence instead of, correctly, the first part.

Errors of this type are difficult for writers to recognize because to the writers they are not ambiguous.

Recognition.   Verbal phrases always have implied but unstated subjects. In other words, somebody or something is performing the action of the verbal phrase, but the phrase itself does not say who or what. For clarity, that implied subject should be the same as the subject of the sentence or clause. In the first example above, the implied subject of *Reaching* is not *the horse.* In the second example, the implied subject of *To extend* is not *the eraser cap.* And in the third example, the implied subject of *replacing* is not *the pencil.* Also check passive voice, because in a passive sentence the subject is not the doer of the action. In the second example, the dangler can be corrected when the verb, changed from passive to active voice, tells who should depress the eraser (see correction that follows).

Correction.   The way to correct dangling and misplaced modifiers depends on the type of error. Misplaced modifiers can often be moved to a more appropriate position:

Dick had to pay *only* ten dollars for his parking ticket.

Two years later, Theodore caught a giant fish in the very same spot where he had lost the ring.

Dangling modifiers usually require some rewording:

As you reach to pick up the saddle, the obnoxious horse may shake off the blanket. The dangling verbal phrase is converted to a clause.

To extend lead out of the eversharp pencil, *depress the eraser cap.* The main clause is revised so that *you* is the implied subject of *depress* (as it is for *To extend*).

The eversharp pencil is designed to be used permanently, *only periodically needing the lead replaced.* The dangling verbal phrase is revised so that the implied subject of *needing* is *pencil.*

1l Restrictive and Nonrestrictive Modifiers

Some modifiers are essential to a sentence because they *restrict,* or limit, the meaning of the words they modify; others, while adding important information, are not essential to the meaning of a sentence. The first type is called restrictive and the second nonrestrictive. The terms usually refer to subordinate clauses and phrases. Here are examples of restrictive and nonrestrictive modifiers:

Watch the Animation on **Restrictive and Nonrestrictive Modifiers** at mycomplab.com

Restrictive

People *who plan to visit Europe* should take time to see Belgium. Relative clause modifying and identifying *People.*

The industrialized country *between the Netherlands and France on the North Sea* is constitutionally a kingdom. Prepositional phrases modifying and identifying *country.*

The Kempenland was thinly populated *before coal was discovered there.* Subordinate clause modifying *was populated* and giving meaning to the sentence.

Language and cultural differences have created friction *that has existed for centuries.* Relative clause modifying and identifying *friction.*

Nonrestrictive

Belgium has two major populations: the Flemings, *who live in the north and speak Flemish,* and the Walloons, *who live in the south and speak French.* Two relative clauses, the first modifying *Flemings* and the second modifying *Walloons.*

With Brussels in the middle of the country, both groups inhabit the city. Prepositional phrases, together modifying *inhabit.*

NATO's headquarters is in Brussels, *where it has been since its beginning in 1950.* Subordinate clause modifying *Brussels.*

Covering southeastern Belgium, the sandstone Ardennes mountains follow the Sambre and Meuse rivers. Participial (verbal) phrase modifying *mountains.*

These examples illustrate several aspects of restrictive and nonrestrictive modifiers:

1. They *modify* a word in the clause or sentence; they therefore function as adjectives or adverbs.

2. They can appear at the beginning, somewhere in the middle, or at the end of a sentence or clause.

3. Most types of subordinate elements can be either restrictive or nonrestrictive.

4. Whether a clause or phrase is restrictive or nonrestrictive depends on its function in the sentence.

5. Restrictive elements are not set off with punctuation; nonrestrictive elements are set off with commas (and sometimes dashes).

If you think the distinction between restriction and nonrestriction is not worth making, consider the following sentences, the first restrictive and the second nonrestrictive:

People who wear braces on their teeth should not eat caramel apples.

People, who wear braces on their teeth, should not eat caramel apples.

Set off with commas, the nonrestrictive *who* clause implies that all people wear braces on their teeth and should not eat caramel apples, which is clearly not the case. It does not *restrict,* or limit, the meaning of *people.* In the first sentence, however, the *who* clause does restrict, or limit, the meaning of *people* to only those who wear braces on their teeth. Often only the writer knows the intended meaning and therefore needs to make the distinction by setting off, or not setting off, the modifier.

Here are a few guidelines that might help you in making this fine distinction:

1. A modifier that modifies a proper noun (one that names a person or thing) is usually nonrestrictive, because the name is sufficient identification. Notice *Flemings* and *Walloons* in the previous example.

2. A *that* clause is almost always restrictive.

3. Adverbial subordinate clauses (those beginning with subordinating conjunctions such as *because* and *when*) are almost always restrictive and are usually not set off with commas when they appear at the end of their sentences. If they appear at the beginning of sentences, they are almost always set off with commas.

4. A nonrestrictive modifier at the beginning of a sentence is followed by a comma, one at the end is preceded by a comma, and one in the middle is enclosed with two commas.

1J Adjectives and Adverbs

Watch the Animation on **Adjectives and Adverbs** at **mycomplab.com**

Adjectives and adverbs, often called *modifiers,* modify nouns and verbs. Adjectives modify nouns; that is, they describe, limit, explain, or alter them in some way. Adverbs modify verbs, adjectives, and other adverbs, telling more than the words by themselves would tell: drive *carefully* (adverb modifying a verb), *unexpectedly* early (adverb modifying an adjective), drive *very* carefully (adverb modifying an adverb). Adverbs usually tell how, where, when, and how much.

Adjectives and adverbs occasionally present some problems for writers. Be careful not to use adjectives when adverbs are needed, as in this incorrect sentence:

The governor suspected that the legislators were not taking him *serious.* The sentence element receiving modification is the verb *were not taking* yet the modifier *serious* is an adjective, which can only modify nouns. The correct modifier for this sentence is the adverb *seriously*. (If you are not sure whether a word is an adjective or an adverb, check your dictionary, which should identify parts of speech.)

Another problem in form concerns the *comparative* and *superlative* degrees. The comparative form of adjectives and adverbs shows a greater degree between two things, as in these correct sentences:

Your luggage is *stronger* than mine. Adjective comparing *your luggage* and *mine.*

Your luggage survives airport baggage handling *better* than mine does. Adverb comparing how the two *survive* handling.

The comparative degree is formed by adding *-er* to shorter adjectives and adverbs (*strong, stronger; hard, harder*). Longer words are preceded by *more* (*beautiful, more beautiful; seriously, more seriously*). Do not use *-er* with *more* (not *more harder*).

The superlative form shows a greater degree among three or more things, as in these correct sentences:

This is the *strongest* luggage I have ever seen. Adjective comparing the present luggage to all other luggage the writer has seen.

Your luggage survives airport baggage handling *best* of all luggage I've seen. Adverb comparing how all luggage the writer has seen survives handling.

The superlative degree is formed by adding *-est* to shorter adjectives and adverbs (*strong, strongest; hard, hardest*). Longer words are preceded by *most* (*beautiful, most beautiful; seriously, most seriously*). Do not use *-est* with *most* (not *most strongest*).

Do not use adjectives and adverbs gratuitously, just to fill space or because you think you ought to. They are effective only when they add meaning to a sentence.

2 Verbs

Verbs are the core of a sentence; together with subjects, they make statements. Verbs often tell what the subject is doing:

The company *agreed* to plead guilty to criminal charges.

Nearly every miner *can name* a casualty of black lung disease.

Another common function of verbs is to link subjects to complements:

Logan *is* an isolated county in the corner of the state.

Sometimes the verb tells something about the subject, as the following passive verb does:

Casualties of mining *cannot be measured* only by injuries.

Through changes in form, verbs can tell the time of the action (past, present, future), the number of the subject (singular or plural), and the person of the subject (first person, *I, we*; second person, *you*; third person, *he, she, it, they*).

2A Tense

Writers can encounter problems with verbs because verbs, unlike most other words in English, have many forms, and a slight shift in form can alter meaning. Notice how the meanings of the following pairs of sentences change when the verbs change:

> The fish *has jumped* into the boat.
>
> The fish *have jumped* into the boat.
>
> The concert *starts* at 8:15 p.m.
>
> The concert *started* at 8:15 p.m.

In the first pair, the meaning changes from one fish to more than one fish jumping into the boat. In the second pair, the first verb implies that the concert has not yet begun; the second, that it had already begun. Observe how the verb *vanish* changes in the following sentences to indicate differences in time, or *tense:*

Present:	Many agricultural jobs *vanish.*
Past:	Many agricultural jobs *vanished.*
Future:	Many agricultural jobs *will vanish.*
Perfect:	Many agricultural jobs *have vanished.*
Past Perfect:	Many agricultural jobs *had vanished.*
Future Perfect:	Many agricultural jobs *will have vanished.*

Omitting an *-ed* ending or using the wrong helping verb can give readers a false message.

Helping (Auxiliary) Verbs.   It is also important to use a form that is a *finite,* or an actual, verb. In the following example, the word that appears to be a verb (italicized) is not a finite verb:

> The fish *jumping* into the boat.

The word *jumping* does not have one of the primary functions of verbs—telling the time of the action, called *tense.* The time of the occurrence could have been the past (*the fish were jumping*), the present (*the fish are jumping*), or the future (*the fish will be jumping*). We also don't know whether the writer meant one fish or many. The *-ing* form is a *verbal* and requires a helping, or auxiliary, verb to make it finite, or able to tell time: words such as *am, is, are, was, were* (forms of *be*). Other helping verbs are *do* (*Do* you *want* the paper? She *doesn't want* the paper) and *have* (I *haven't seen* the paper; *has* she *seen* it?).

Irregular Verbs.   Most verbs change forms in a regular way: *want* in the present becomes *wanted* in the past, *wanting* with the auxiliary *be* (i.e., *is wanting*), and *wanted* with the auxiliary *have* (i.e., *have wanted*). Many verbs change irregularly, however—internally rather than at the ending. Here are a few of the most common irregular verbs:

Base Form	Past Tense	Present Participle	Past Participle
be (is, am, are)	was, were	being	been
come	came	coming	come
do	did	doing	done
drink	drank	drinking	drunk
give	gave	giving	given
go	went	going	gone
grow	grew	growing	grown
lie	laid	lying	lain
see	saw	seeing	seen
take	took	taking	taken
teach	taught	teaching	taught
throw	threw	throwing	thrown
wear	wore	wearing	worn
write	wrote	writing	written

Check your dictionary for the forms of other verbs you suspect may be irregular.

The verb form that is perhaps the most troublesome is the *-s* form in the present tense. This form is used for all singular nouns and the pronouns *he, she,* and *it.* (See 2D Subject-Verb Agreement.)

2B Voice

English sentences are usually written in the active voice, in which the subject of the sentence is the doer of the action of the verb:

> Scott misplaced the file folder. *Scott,* the subject of the sentence, performed the action, *misplaced.*

With the passive voice, the doer of the action is the object of a preposition or is omitted entirely:

> The file folder was misplaced by Scott. *File folder* is now the subject of the sentence.

> The file folder was misplaced. The person doing the action is not named.

As a writer, you need to decide whether to use the active or passive voice. The passive voice requires more words than the active voice, it can hide the doer, and its overuse reduces clarity and increases confusion. This is why you may have been told that you should *never use the passive voice.*

Choose the passive voice when it is appropriate to the genre and to your readers' needs. For genres such as memoirs, profiles, and literary analyses, you will probably choose active voice because readers of these genres usually want to know who is doing what to whom. In other situations, you may choose to use the passive voice, either because you do not know the doer's identity or because the doer's identity is unimportant or obvious to the reader. When writing a lab report in a chemistry course, for instance, your reader does not need to be told who specifically combined the chemicals. Finally, the passive voice can be useful if you want to keep the subjects consistent within a paragraph.

But unless you have good reason to use the passive voice, avoid it. First, look for passive voice by noting *by* phrases near the ends of your sentences. If you find any, determine whether the subject of your sentence performs the action of your verb. If not, revise the sentence so that it does. Another way to find occurrences of the passive voice is to look for forms of *be: am, is, are, was, were, been, being.* Not all these verbs will be passive, but if they function as part of an action verb, determine whether the subject performs the action. If it does not, and if your sentence would be clearer with the subject performing the action, revise to the active voice.

2C Mood

English verbs are stated in one of three moods: indicative, imperative, and subjunctive. In most writing and speaking, the most commonly used mood by far is the *indicative mood*, which is used to make statements, to ask questions, and to declare opinions. For example:

Not many people today *think* the world *is* flat. Makes a statement.

Does anybody today *think* the world is flat? Asks a question.

Members of the Flat Earth Society *should reevaluate* their thinking. Declares an opinion.

Verbs in the *imperative mood* issue commands, requests, or directions. Imperative verbs never change form. When the subject of an imperative verb is not explicitly identified, it is understood to be *you*.

Julia, *stop* teasing your baby brother. Issues command.

Please *complete* this report by tomorrow morning. Issues request.

Turn right at the light and *drive* for another two blocks. Issues directions.

Verbs in the *subjunctive mood* communicate wishes, make statements contrary to fact, list requirements and demands, and imply skepticism or doubt. They usually appear in clauses introduced by *if, that, as if,* and *as though.* Use the base form of the verb for the present tense subjunctive. For the past tense subjunctive of the verb *be,* use *were* for all subjects.

She wishes that her son's best friend *were* more responsible. Communicates wish.

If the world *were* to end tomorrow, we would not have to pay taxes anymore. Makes statement contrary to fact.

The jury summons requires that your cousin *arrive* punctually at 8:00 a.m. and *sign* in with the court clerk. Lists requirements.

His girlfriend talks as if she *were* a pop music diva. Implies skepticism.

Be sure to select the correct verb forms to express indicative, imperative, and subjunctive moods.

2D Subject-Verb Agreement

Clauses are made of subjects and verbs plus their modifiers and other related words. A fundamental principle of usage is that verbs agree with their subjects. In most cases, this principle presents no problem: You say "Birds *have* feathers," not "Birds *has* feathers." But not all sentences are this simple. Before getting into the problem areas, consider first that errors in subject-verb agreement occur only with present tense verbs and the verb tenses that use present tense forms of helping verbs (such as *have* and *be*). And, except for the irregular verb *be* (with its forms *am, is, are, was, were*), the problem centers on third-person singular verbs with their *-s* ending. Here is the problem illustrated. Notice that only the verbs in the third-person singular are different. Unfortunately, all nouns are third person and, when singular, require this form in the present tense.

Watch the Animation on **Subject-Verb Agreement** at **mycomplab.com**

	Present		**Present Perfect**	
	Singular	**Plural**	**Singular**	**Plural**
First person	I work	we work	I have worked	we have worked
Second person	you work	you work	you have worked	you have worked
Third person	he (she, it) works	they work	he (she, it) has worked	they have worked

It is the *-s* form, then, that you need to watch for to avoid errors in subject-verb agreement. Here are some issues that may cause problems.

Intervening Subordinate Element

When a subject and a verb are side by side, they usually do not present a problem. Often, however, writers separate them with subordinate elements, such as clauses, prepositional or verbal phrases, and other elements. The result may be a subject-verb agreement error. The following sentence illustrates this problem:

> The realization that life is a series of compromises never occur to some people. The subject is *realization,* a singular noun, and should be followed by the singular verb *occurs.* The corrected sentence would read "The realization that life is a series of compromises never occurs to some people."

Subject Complement

Subject complements follow some verbs and rename the subject, although they are not always in the same number as the subject. Because a singular subject may have a plural complement, and vice versa, confused writers might make the verb agree with the complement instead of the subject. Here's an example:

> The result of this mistake are guilt, low self-esteem, and depression. The subject is *result,* not *guilt, low self-esteem,* and *depression;* the singular subject should be followed by the singular verb *is.* The corrected sentence would read "The result of this mistake is guilt, low self-esteem, and depression."

Compound Subject

Two or more words may be compounded to make a subject. Whether they are singular or plural depends on their connector. Subjects connected by *and* and *but* are plural, but those connected by *or* and *nor* are singular or plural depending on whether the item closer to the verb is singular or plural. Here are examples:

The young mother and the superior student *are* both candidates for compulsive perfectionism. Two subjects, *mother* and *student,* are joined by *and* and take a plural verb.

Promotions or an employee award *tells* the perfectionist he or she is achieving personal goals. When two subjects, *promotions* and *award,* are joined by *or,* the verb agrees with the nearer one; in this sentence, a singular verb is required.

An employee award or promotions *tell* the perfectionist he or she is achieving personal goals. Here the plural verb, *tell,* agrees with *promotions*, the closer of the two subjects.

Indefinite Pronoun as Subject

Indefinite pronouns are defined and listed under 3C Pronoun Agreement. Although these words often seem plural in meaning, most of them are singular grammatically. When indefinite pronouns are the subjects of sentences or clauses, their verbs are usually singular. Here are examples:

Everyone *has* at some time worried about achieving goals. The singular indefinite pronoun *everyone* takes a singular verb, *has.*

Each car and truck on the highway *was* creeping along on the icy pavement. The singular indefinite pronoun, *each,* requires a singular verb, *was.*

Neither of us *is* going to worry about being late. The singular indefinite pronoun, *neither,* takes a singular verb, *is.*

Nevertheless, some of us *are* going to be very late. The indefinite pronoun *some* (like *all, any,* and *none*) is singular or plural depending on context; compare "Some of the book *is* boring."

Inverted Sentence Order

Inverted sentence order can confuse your natural inclination toward subject-verb agreement. Examples of inverted order are questions, plus sentences beginning with *there*. Sentences like these demand closer attention to agreement.

Have the results of the test come back yet? The plural subject, *results,* takes a plural verb, *have.*

There *are* many special services provided just for kids at hotels, ski lodges, and restaurants. The plural subject, *services,* takes a plural verb, *are. There* is never a subject; it only holds the place for the subject in an inverted sentence.

Intervening Relative Clause

Subordinate clauses that begin with the relative pronouns *who, which,* or *that* present special problems in subject-verb agreement. Their verbs must agree with their own subjects, not with a word in another clause. These subordinate clauses demand special attention because whether the pronouns are singular or plural depends on their antecedents. These sentences illustrate agreement within relative clauses:

> Every person who *attends* the baseball game will receive a free cap. *Who,* the subject of *attends,* means "person," a singular noun.

> John is one of the few people I know who *care* about frogs. *Who,* the subject of *care,* means "people," a plural noun.

> John is the only one of all the people I know who *cares* about frogs. *Who* in this sentence means "one."

3 Pronouns

Pronouns can have all the same sentence functions as nouns; the difference is that pronouns do not have the meaning that nouns have. Nouns name things; a noun stands for the thing itself. Pronouns, however, refer only to nouns. Whenever that reference is ambiguous or inconsistent, there is a problem in clarity.

3A Pronoun Case

Case is a grammatical term for the way nouns and pronouns show their relationships to other parts of a sentence. In English, nouns have only two case forms: the regular form (the one listed in a dictionary, such as *year*) and the possessive form (used to show ownership or connection, such as *year's*; possessive nouns are discussed in 5J Apostrophe).

⊙ **Watch** the Animation on **Pronoun Case** at mycomplab.com

Pronouns, however, have retained their case forms. Here are the forms for personal and relative pronouns:

	Subjective	Objective	Possessive
Personal	I	me	my, mine
	you	you	your, yours
	he	him	his
	she	her	her, hers
	it	it	its
	we	us	our, ours
	they	them	their, theirs
Relative	who	whom	whose
	whoever	whomever	whosever

Notice, first, that possessive pronouns, unlike possessive nouns, do not take apostrophes—none of them. Sometimes writers confuse possessive pronouns with contractions, which do have apostrophes (such as *it's,* meaning *it is* or *it has;* and *who's,* meaning *who is;* for a further discussion, see 5J Apostrophe).

Another problem writers sometimes have with pronoun case is using a subjective form when they need the objective or using an objective form when they need the subjective.

Subjective Case.   Use the subjective forms for subjects and for words referring to subjects, as in these examples:

> Among the patients a nutritionist sees are the grossly overweight people *who* have tried all kinds of diets. *Who is the subject of the verb have tried in its own clause.*

> *They* have a life history of obesity and diets. *They is the subject of have.*

> *He and the patient* work out a plan for permanent weight control. *He and patient are the compound subjects of work.*

> The patient understands that the ones who work out the diet plan are *he* and the nutritionist. *He and nutritionist refer to ones, the subject of the clause.*

Notice that pronoun case is determined by the function of the pronoun in its own clause and that compounding (*he and the patient*) has no effect on case.

Objective Case.   Use the objective forms for objects of all kinds:

> "Between *you* and *me*," said the patient to his nutritionist, "I'm ready for something that works." *You and me are objects of the preposition between.*

> An exercise program is usually assigned to the patient for *whom* dieting is prescribed. *Whom is the object of the preposition for.*

> The nutritionist gives *her* a suitable alternative to couch sitting. *Her is the indirect object of gives.*

> Modest exercise combined with modest dieting can affect *him or her* dramatically. *Him or her is the direct object of can affect.*

> Having advised *them* about diet and exercise, the nutritionist instructs dieters about behavioral change. *Them is the object of the participle having advised.*

Notice again that the case of a pronoun is determined by its function in its own clause and is not affected by compounding (*you and me*).

Possessive Case.   Use the possessive forms to indicate ownership. Possessive pronouns have two forms: adjective forms (*my, your, his, her, its, our, their*) and possessive forms (*mine, yours, his, hers, its, ours, theirs*). The adjective forms appear before nouns or gerunds; the possessive forms replace possessive nouns.

> The patient purchased *his* supplements from the drugstore *his* nutritionist recommended. *Adjective form before nouns.*

> *His* swimming every day produced results faster than he anticipated. *Adjective form before gerund.*

> *His* was a difficult task to accomplish, but the rewards of weight loss were great. *Possessive form replacing possessive noun.*

3B Pronoun Reference

Personal and relative pronouns (see list under 3A Pronoun Case) must refer unambiguously to their antecedents. Pronouns and antecedents must agree.

Ambiguous pronoun reference may occur in various ways:

- More than one possible antecedent.
- Adjective used as intended antecedent.
- Implied antecedent.
- Too much separation between antecedent and pronoun.

Here are sentences in which the pronouns do not clearly refer to their antecedents:

The immunologist refused to admit fraudulence of the data reported by a former colleague in a paper *he* had cosigned. More than one possible antecedent. *He* could refer to *immunologist* or to *colleague.*

In Carolyn Chute's book *The Beans of Egypt, Maine, she* treats poverty with concern and understanding. Adjective used as intended antecedent (possessive nouns function as adjectives). In this case, *Carolyn Chute's* modifies *book* and cannot serve as an antecedent of the pronoun *she.*

It says in the newspaper that the economy will not improve soon. Implied antecedent. There is no antecedent for *it.*

At Ajax *they* have tires on sale till the end of the month. Implied antecedent. There is no antecedent for *they.*

Faulty pronoun reference is corrected by clarifying the relationship between the pronoun and its intended antecedent. Observe how the example sentences have been revised:

The immunologist refused to admit fraudulence of the data reported by a former colleague in a paper *the immunologist* had cosigned. *The immunologist* replaces the unclear pronoun *he.*

In *her* book *The Beans of Egypt, Maine, Carolyn Chute* treats poverty with concern and understanding. The possessive pronoun *her* replaces the possessive noun and refers to the noun subject, *Carolyn Chute.*

The newspaper reports that the economy will not improve soon. The unclear pronoun *it* is replaced by its implied antecedent, *newspaper.*

Ajax has tires on sale till the end of the month. The unclear pronoun *they* is replaced by *Ajax.*

3C Pronoun Agreement

Some pronoun errors occur because the pronoun and its antecedent do not agree. Pronouns must agree with their antecedents in number, person, and gender. (See the list of pronouns in 3A Pronoun Case.)

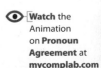

Watch the Animation on **Pronoun Agreement** at **mycomplab.com**

Compound Antecedents

Problems sometimes occur with compound antecedents. If the antecedents are joined by *and,* the pronoun is plural; if they are joined by *or,* the pronoun agrees with the nearer antecedent. Here are examples of correct usage:

In the pediatric trauma center, the head doctor and head nurse direct *their* medical team. The pronoun *their* refers to both *doctor* and *nurse.*

The head doctor or the head nurse directs *his or her* team. The pronouns *his or her* refer to the closer antecedent, *nurse* (because the gender of the nurse is not known, the neutral alternatives are used).

The head doctor or the other doctors give *their* help when it is needed. The pronoun *their* agrees with the closer antecedent, *doctors.*

Indefinite Pronouns as Antecedents

A particularly troublesome kind of agreement is that between personal or relative pronouns and *indefinite pronouns.* As their name implies, indefinite pronouns do not refer to particular people or things; grammatically they are usually singular but are often intended as plural. Some common indefinite pronouns are *all, any, anybody, each, either, everybody, neither, no one, nothing, one, some, somebody,* and *something.*

Like nouns, these pronouns can serve as antecedents of personal and relative pronouns. But because most of them are grammatically singular, they can be troublesome in sentences. Here are examples of correct usage:

Everyone in the trauma center has *his or her* specific job to do. **or** All the personnel in the trauma center have *their* specific jobs to do. The neutral, though wordy, alternative *his or her* agrees with the singular indefinite pronoun *everyone.* The second sentence illustrates the use of the plural when gender is unknown.

Each of them does *his or her* job efficiently and competently. **or** *All* of them do *their* jobs efficiently and competently. *Each* is singular, but *all* can be either singular or plural, depending on context (compare "*All* literature has *its* place").

Shifts in Person

Agreement errors in *person* are shifts between *I* or *we* (first person), *you* (second person), and *he, she, it,* and *they* (third person). These errors are probably more often a result of carelessness than of imperfect knowledge. Being more familiar with casual speech than formal writing, writers sometimes shift from *I* to *you,* for example, when only one of them is meant, as in these sentences:

Last summer *I* went on a canoeing trip to northern Manitoba. It was *my* first trip that far north, and it was so peaceful *you* could forget all the problems back home. The person represented by *you* was not present. The writer means *I.*

See also 1G Shifts.

3D Relative Pronouns

Use relative pronouns to introduce clauses that modify nouns or pronouns. Personal relative pronouns refer to people. They include *who, whom, whoever, whomever,* and *whose.* Nonpersonal relative pronouns refer to things. They include *which, whichever, whatever,* and *whose.*

Use *which* to introduce nonrestrictive clauses and *that* to introduce restrictive clauses (see 1I Restrictive and Nonrestrictive Modifiers). Use *who* to refer to the subject of the sentence and *whom* to refer to an object of the verb or preposition. Following are examples of common errors:

> The lawyer *that* lost the case today went to law school with my sister. Uses impersonal relative pronoun *that.*

> Conflict between the two parties led to the lawsuit *that* was finally settled today. The relative pronoun *that* introduces a nonrestrictive clause that modifies *lawsuit.* Nonrestrictive clauses supply extra information to the sentence, not defining information.

> The case resulted in a ruling, *which* favored the plaintiff. The relative pronoun *which* introduces a restrictive clause that modifies *ruling.* Restrictive clauses supply defining information.

> Later, the lawyer *whom* lost the case spoke with the jurors *who* we had interviewed. The first relative pronoun *whom* refers to the subject *lawyer* while the second relative pronoun *who* refers to the object of the verb *had interviewed.*

Once you recognize relative pronoun errors, it is usually easy to fix them:

> The lawyer *who* lost the case today went to law school with my sister.

> Conflict between the two parties led to the lawsuit, *which* was finally settled today.

> The case resulted in a ruling *that* favored the plaintiff.

> Later, the lawyer *who* lost the case spoke with the jurors *whom* we had interviewed.

4 Style

There is no such thing as "correct style." Style is a choice you make as a writer in response to the rhetorical situation. In Chapter 16, "Choosing a Style," you learned several strategies for using style in ways that are appropriate for your purpose, readers, and genre. Here, you will learn strategies for writing with clarity and conciseness. You will also learn strategies for recognizing when certain kinds of language are and are not appropriate.

4A Conciseness

Nobody wants to read more words than necessary. Concise writing shows that you are considerate of your readers. You do not need to eliminate details and other content to achieve conciseness; rather, you cut empty words, repetition, and unnecessary details.

In the following passage, all the italicized words could be omitted without altering the meaning:

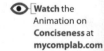
Watch the Animation on **Conciseness** at mycomplab.com

In the final analysis, I feel that the United States should have converted to the *use of the* metric system *of measurement* a long time ago. *In the present day and age,* the United States, except for Borneo and Liberia, is the *one and* only country in the *entire* world that has not yet adopted this measurement system.

You may choose to repeat key words when you are striving for a certain effect (such as setting a tone or establishing character), but take care to avoid pointless repetition, which only bores and slows down your readers.

Follow these guidelines to achieve conciseness in your writing:

1. **Avoid redundancy.** Redundant words and expressions needlessly repeat what has already been said. Delete them when they appear in your writing.

2. **Avoid wordy expressions.** Phrases such as *In the final analysis* and *In the present day and age* add no important information to sentences and should be removed and/or replaced.

3. **Avoid unnecessary intensifiers.** Intensifiers such as *really, very, clearly, quite,* and *of course* usually fail to add meaning to the words they modify and therefore are often unnecessary. Delete them when doing so does not change the meaning of the sentence, or when you could replace the words with a single word (for instance, replacing *very good* with *excellent*).

4. **Avoid excess use of prepositional phrases.** The use of too many prepositional phrases within a sentence makes for wordy writing. Always use constructions that require the fewest words.

5. **Avoid negating constructions.** Negating constructions using words such as *no* and *not* often add unneeded words to sentences. Use shorter alternatives when they are available.

6. **Use the passive voice only when necessary.** Passive constructions require more words than active constructions (see 2B Voice). They can also obscure meaning by concealing the sentence's subject. When there is no good reason to use the passive voice, choose the active voice.

Here are more examples of wordy sentences that violate these guidelines:

If the two groups *cooperate together,* there will be *positive benefits* for both. Uses redundancy.

There are some people *who* think the metric system is un-American. Uses wordy expression.

The climb up the mountain was *very* hard on my legs and *really* taxed my lungs and heart. Uses unnecessary modifiers.

On the day of his birth, we walked *to the park down the block from the house of his mother.* Uses too many prepositional phrases.

She *did not like* hospitals. Uses negating construction when a shorter alternative is available.

The door *was closed* by that man over there. Uses passive voice when active voice is preferable.

Corrections to the wordy sentences above result in concise sentences:

> If the two groups cooperate, both will benefit. This correction also replaces the wordy construction *there will be . . . for both* with a shorter, more forceful alternative.

> Some people think the metric system is un-American.

> The climb up the mountain was hard on my legs and taxed my lungs and heart.

> On his birthday, we walked to the park near his mother's house.

> She hated hospitals.

> That man over there closed the door.

4B Appropriate Language

Effective writers communicate using appropriate language, that is, language that:

1. Suits the genre and rhetorical situation (topic, angle, purpose, readers, context).
2. Avoids sexist usage.
3. Avoids bias and stereotype.

Suitability

The style and tone of your writing should be suitable to your rhetorical situation and the genre you have chosen. Some situations require *formal language.* Formal language communicates clearly and directly with a minimum of stylistic flourish. Its tone is serious, objective, and often detached. Formal language avoids slang, pretentious words, and unnecessary technical jargon. *Informal language,* on the other hand, is particular to the writer's personality or social group and assumes a closer and more familiar relationship between the writer and the reader. Its tone is casual, subjective, and intimate. Informal language can also employ slang and other words that would be inappropriate in formal writing.

Keep in mind that what counts as suitable language always depends on the rhetorical situation you are facing and the genre you are using. Pretentious words might be appropriate if you were writing a parody of someone you feel is pretentious. Certain technical jargon would be not only suitable but also preferable in a technical report written for readers who are experts in the field. Slang could get across just the message you want in a memoir, profile, rave, or argument, especially when you want to identify with a particular group that uses particular terms. Use your genre know-how and rhetorical awareness to help you decide when a certain kind of language is or is not suitable.

As informal language is rarely used within most academic, technical, or business settings, the following examples show errors in the use of formal language:

> The director told the board members to *push off.* Uses informal language.

> Professor Oyo *dissed* Marta when she arrived late to his class for the third time in a row. Uses slang.

The *aromatic essence* of the gardenia was intoxicating. Uses pretentious words.

The doctor told him to take *salicylate* to ease the symptoms of *viral rhinorrhea*. Uses unnecessary jargon.

Employing formal language correctly, these examples could be revised as follows:

The director told the board members to leave.

Professor Oyo spoke disrespectfully to Marta when she arrived late to his class for the third time in a row.

The scent of the gardenia was intoxicating.

The doctor told him to take aspirin to ease his cold symptoms.

Sexist Usage

Gender-exclusive terms such as *policeman* and *chairman* are offensive to many readers today. Writers who are sensitive to their audience, therefore, avoid such terms, replacing them with expressions such as *police officer* and *chairperson* or *chair*. Most sexist usage in language involves masculine nouns, masculine pronouns, and patronizing terms.

Masculine Nouns. Do not use *man* and its compounds generically. For many people, these words are specific to men and do not account for women as separate and equal people. Here are some examples of masculine nouns and appropriate gender-neutral substitutions:

Masculine Noun	Gender-Neutral Substitution
mailman	mail carrier
businessman	businessperson, executive, manager
fireman	firefighter
man-hours	work hours
mankind	humanity, people
manmade	manufactured, synthetic
salesman	salesperson, sales representative, sales agent
congressman	member of Congress, representative

Using gender-neutral substitutions often entails using a more specific word for a generalized term, which adds more precision to writing.

Masculine Pronouns. Avoid using the masculine pronouns *he, him,* and *his* in a generic sense, meaning both male and female. This can pose some challenges, however, because English does not have a generic singular pronoun that can be used instead. Consider the following options:

1. Eliminate the pronoun.

Every writer has an individual style. Instead of Every writer has his own style.

2. Use plural forms.

Writers have their own styles. Instead of A writer has his own style.

3. Use *he or she, one,* or *you* as alternates only sparingly.

Each writer has his or her own style. Instead of Each writer has his own style.

One has an individual writing style. Instead of He has his own individual writing style.

You have your own writing style. Instead of A writer has his own style.

Patronizing Terms.   Avoid terms that cast men or women in gender-exclusive roles or imply that women are subordinate to men. Here are some examples of biased or stereotypical terms and their gender-neutral substitutions:

Biased/Stereotypical Term	Gender-Neutral Substitution
lady lawyer	lawyer
male nurse	nurse
career girl	professional, attorney, manager
coed	student
housewife	homemaker
stewardess	flight attendant
cleaning lady	housecleaner

Biases and Stereotypes

Biased and stereotypical language can be hurtful and can perpetuate discrimination. Most writers are sensitive to racial and ethnic biases or stereotypes, but writers should also avoid language that shows insensitivity to age, class, religion, and sexual orientation. The accepted terms for identifying groups and group members have changed over the years and continue to change today. Avoid using terms that have fallen into disuse such as *Indian* or *Oriental;* instead, use accepted terms such as *Native American* or *Asian American.*

5 Punctuation, Mechanics, and Spelling

Punctuation is a system of signals telling readers how the parts of written discourse relate to one another. Punctuation provides readers with cues for interpreting the writer's words as the writer intended them to be understood.

This section discusses punctuation used within and at the ends of sentences. Other marks, those used within words (apostrophes, hyphens, italics, and slashes) are also explained later in this section.

5A End Punctuation

A period is the normal mark for ending sentences. A question mark ends a sentence that asks a direct question, and an exclamation point ends forceful assertions.

Period .

Sentences normally end with a period.

> Studies suggest that eating fish two or three times a week may reduce the risk of heart attack. Statement.

> Eat two or three servings of fish a week. Mild command.

> The patient asked whether eating fish would reduce the risk of heart attack. Indirect question.

Avoid inserting a period before the end of a sentence; the result will be a fragment (see 1A Fragments). Sentences can be long or short; their length does not determine their completion. Both of the following examples are complete sentences:

> Eat fish. Mild command; the subject, *you,* is understood.

> In a two-year study of 1,000 survivors of heart attack, researchers found a 29 percent reduction in mortality among those who regularly ate fish or took a fish oil supplement. Statement; one sentence.

Question Mark ?

A sentence that asks a direct question ends in a question mark.

> How does decaffeinated coffee differ from regular coffee?

Do not use a question mark to end an indirect question:

> The customer asked how decaffeinated coffee differs from regular coffee.

With quoted questions, place the question mark inside the final quotation marks:

> The customer asked, "How does decaffeinated coffee differ from regular coffee?"

Exclamation Point !

The exclamation point tells readers that the sentence should be interpreted as forceful or dramatic.

> Fire!

> Shut that door immediately!

Because they give the impression of shouting, exclamation points are rarely needed in formal business and academic writing.

5B Semicolon ;

Semicolons are mainly used for connecting two (or sometimes three) independent clauses.

> Dengue hemorrhagic fever is a viral infection common to Southeast Asia; it kills about 5,000 children a year.

Sometimes the second clause contains a transitional adverb (see 1B Comma Splices):

> Dengue has existed in Asia for centuries; *however,* it grew more virulent in the 1950s.

Do not use a comma where a semicolon or period is required; the result is a comma splice (see 1B Comma Splices). In contrast, a semicolon used in place of a comma may result in a type of fragment (see 1A Fragments):

> In populations where people have been stricken by an infectious virus, survivors have antibodies in their bloodstreams; *which prevent or reduce the severity of subsequent infections.* The semicolon makes a fragment of the *which* clause.

Do not confuse the semicolon with the colon (see 5D Colon). While the semicolon connects independent clauses, a colon ordinarily does not.

The semicolon is also used to separate items in a series when the items contain internal commas:

> Scientists are researching the effects of staphylococcus bacteria, which cause infections in deep wounds; influenza A virus, which causes respiratory flu; and conjunctivitis bacteria, which have at times caused fatal purpuric fever.

5C Comma ,

The comma is probably the most troublesome mark of punctuation because it has so many uses. Its main uses are explained here.

Compound Sentences. A comma joins two independent clauses connected with a coordinating conjunction (see 1B Comma Splices):

> Martinique is a tropical island in the West Indies, *and* it attracts flocks of tourists annually.

Do not use the comma between independent clauses without the conjunction, even if the second clause begins with a transitional adverb:

> **Faulty:** Martinique is a tropical island in the West Indies, it attracts flocks of tourists annually. Two independent clauses with no conjunction creates a comma splice.

> **Faulty:** Martinique is a tropical island in the West Indies, consequently it attracts flocks of tourists annually. Two independent clauses with a transitional adverb creates a comma splice.

Introductory Sentence Elements. Commas set off a variety of introductory sentence elements, as illustrated here:

> *When the French colonized Martinique in 1635,* they eliminated the native Caribs. Introductory subordinate clause.

> *Choosing death over subservience,* the Caribs leaped into the sea. Introductory participial (verbal) phrase.

Before their death, they warned of a "mountain of fire" on the island. Introductory prepositional phrase.

Subsequently, the island's volcano erupted. Introductory transitional adverb.

Short prepositional phrases sometimes are not set off with commas:

In 1658 the Caribs leaped to their death.

Sometimes, however, a comma must be used after a short prepositional phrase to prevent misreading:

Before, they had predicted retribution. Comma is required to prevent misreading.

Nonrestrictive and Parenthetical Elements.   Words that interrupt the flow of a sentence are set off with commas before and after. If they come at the end of a sentence, they are set off with one comma.

In this class are nonrestrictive modifiers (see 1I Restrictive and Nonrestrictive Modifiers), transitional adverbs (see 1B Comma Splices), and a few other types of interrupters. Here are examples:

This rugged island, *which Columbus discovered in 1502,* exports sugar and rum. Nonrestrictive *which* clause; commas before and after.

A major part of the economy, *however,* is tourism. Interrupting transitional adverb; commas before and after.

Tourists, *attracted to the island by its climate,* enjoy discovering its culture. Interrupting participial (verbal) phrase (see 1A Fragments); commas before and after.

A popular tradition in Martinique is the Carnival, *which occurs just before Lent each year.* Nonrestrictive *which* clause; one comma.

Martinique is an overseas department of France, *a status conferred in 1946.* An absolute, ending the sentence (participial phrase plus the noun it modifies).

Series

Commas separate items in a series:

Martiniquans dance to *steel drums, clarinets, empty bottles, and banjos.* Four nouns.

Dressing in colorful costumes, dancing through the streets, and thoroughly enjoying the celebration, Martiniquans celebrate Carnival with enthusiasm. Three participial (verbal) phrases.

Martinique has a population of over 300,000, its main religion is Roman Catholicism, and its languages are French and Creole dialect. Three independent clauses.

Various sentence elements can make up a series, but the joined elements should be grammatically equivalent (see 1D Parallelism, which discusses faulty parallelism).

Common practice calls for a comma before the conjunction joining the last item in the series.

Quotations

Commas set off quoted sentences from the words that introduce them:

> "A wise man," says David Hume, "proportions his belief to the evidence."

> According to Plato, "Writing will produce forgetfulness" in writers because "they will not need to exercise their memories." The second clause is not set off with a comma.

> "*X* on beer casks indicates beer which paid ten shillings duty, and hence it came to mean beer of a given quality," reports *The Dictionary of Phrase and Fable*.

Quotations introduced with *that* and other connectors (such as *because* in the second sentence here) are not set off with commas. Commas at the end of quotations go inside the quotation marks.

Coordinate Adjectives

Commas separate adjectives that equally modify a noun:

> The "food pyramid" was designed as a *meaningful, memorable* way to represent the ideal daily diet. Two adjectives modify the noun *way* equally.

When you're not sure about using a comma, try inserting the coordinating conjunction *and* between the two adjectives to see if they are truly coordinate (*meaningful and memorable*). Do not use a comma between adjectives that are not coordinate or between the last adjective and the noun being modified. (See also 1J Adjectives and Adverbs.)

Addresses and Dates

Use a comma to separate city and state in an address, but not to set off the zip code:

> Glen Ridge, New Jersey 07028 *or* Glen Ridge, NJ 07028

In a sentence, a state name is enclosed in commas:

> The letter from Glen Ridge, New Jersey, arrived by express mail.

Dates are treated similarly:

> January 5, 1886 *but* 5 January 1886

> The events of January 5, 1886, are no longer remembered. When other punctuation is not required, the year is followed by a comma.

Commas to Avoid

Some people mistakenly believe that commas should be used wherever they might pause in speech. A comma does mean pause, but not all pauses are marked by commas. Use a comma only when you know you need one. Avoid the following comma uses:

1. To set off restrictive sentence elements:

> People, *who want a balanced diet,* can use the food pyramid as a guide. The restrictive *who* clause is necessary to identify *people* and should not be set off with commas.

2. To separate a subject from its verb and a preposition from its object:

> People who want a balanced diet, can use the food pyramid as a guide. The comma following the *who* clause separates the subject, *people,* from its verb, *can use.* Treat the noun phrase (*People who want a balanced diet*) as if it were a single word.

> The bottom level of the food pyramid contains food from grains, *such as,* bread, cereals, rice, and pasta. The preposition *such as* should not be followed by a comma.

3. To follow a coordinating conjunction (see 1B Comma Splices):

> The food pyramid describes a new approach to a balanced diet. But, the meat and dairy industries opposed it. The coordinating conjunction *but* should not be set off with a comma.

4. To separate two independent clauses (see 1B Comma Splices) not joined with a coordinating conjunction:

> The pyramid shows fewer servings of dairy and meat products, therefore consumers would buy less of these higher-priced foods. The comma should be replaced with a semicolon.

5. To set off coordinate elements joined with a coordinating conjunction:

> Vegetables and fruits are near the bottom of the pyramid, *and should be eaten several times a day.* The coordinating conjunction *and* joins a second verb, *should be eaten,* not a second independent clause; therefore no comma is needed.

5D Colon :

Colons connect two sentence parts, as a hinge connects a door to its frame. Colons tell readers that a second part of the sentence is coming and that the second part will complement the first part by providing either: (1) a list that has been anticipated in the first part, or (2) an explanation, restatement, or elaboration of the first part:

> The space shuttle *Challenger* lifted off on January 28, 1986, with a seven-member crew: Francis R. Scobee, Michael J. Smith, Ronald E. McNair, Ellison S. Onizuka, Judith A. Resnik, Gregory B. Jarvis, and Christa McAuliffe. The list explains *crew.*

A twelve-member investigating team discovered the cause of the disaster: a leak in one of the shuttle's two solid-fuel booster rockets. The phrase explains *the cause of the disaster.*

Do not use colons interchangeably with semicolons (see 5B Semicolon). Semicolons separate two independent clauses that are closely related (see 1B Comma Splices). Colons ordinarily are followed by a phrase or phrases, but they are often followed by an independent clause:

A twelve-member investigating team discovered the cause of the disaster: a leak was found in one of the shuttle's two solid-fuel booster rockets. Both sides of the colon contain an independent clause.

Avoid using colons after verbs and prepositions (see 1A Fragments):

The two causes of the O-ring failure were cold temperatures and design deficiencies. No colon after *were.*

The commission investigating the disaster noted a number of failures in communication, such as one within the National Aeronautics and Space Administration. No colon after *such as.*

Colons have a few other set uses:

Time:	10:15 a.m.
Salutation in a business letter:	Dear Patricia Morton:
Biblical reference:	Genesis 2:3

5E Dash —

The dash separates sentence elements like a comma, but suggests greater emphasis:

In *The War of the Worlds* (1898), science fiction writer H. G. Wells described an intense beam of light that destroyed objects on contact—the laser.

It is also used to set off a nonrestrictive sentence element (see 1I Restrictive and Nonrestrictive Modifiers) that might be confusing if set off with commas:

A number of medical uses—performing eye surgery, removing tumors, and unclogging coronary arteries—make the laser more than a destructive weapon. The three explanatory items separated by commas are set off from the rest of the sentence with dashes.

Like commas that set off nonrestrictive elements within a sentence, dashes are often used in pairs—at the beginning of the interruption and at the end.

A dash is sometimes used in place of a colon when a colon might seem too formal or when you want your reader to pay special attention to what follows the dash:

Besides its medical uses, the laser serves many other functions—reading price codes, playing compact audio discs, and sending telephone messages.

Use the dash with caution; overuse defeats the purpose of giving special emphasis to special parts of your writing. Overuse might also give readers the impression that you aren't familiar with alternative means of punctuation.

Note that a dash (sometimes more specifically called an "em dash") has the width of the capital letter "M"; it is much wider than a single hyphen. Most word processors will automatically replace two hyphens typed between words with a dash.

5F Quotation Marks " "

The main use for quotation marks is to set off direct quotations:

> Professor Charlotte Johnson announced, "Interdisciplinary science is combining fields of scientific knowledge to make up new disciplines."

> "Biochemistry," she went on to say, "combines biology and chemistry."

Quotations within quotations are marked with single quotation marks:

> "The term 'interdisciplinary science' thus describes a change in how processes are investigated," she concluded.

Use quotation marks correctly with other punctuation marks. Periods and commas (see 5C Comma) always go inside the end quotation marks; colons and semicolons almost always go outside the quotation. Dashes, question marks, and exclamation points go inside or outside depending on meaning—inside if the mark applies to the quotation and outside if it applies to the surrounding sentence:

> "Do you know the various branches of the physical sciences?" asked Professor Johnson. Question mark goes inside quotation marks because it applies to the quotation.

> Did the professor say, "Histology deals with tissues and cytology with the fine structures of individual cells"? Question mark goes outside quotation marks because it applies to the surrounding sentence, not the quotation.

Do not use quotation marks to set off indirect quotations:

> The professor said that histology and cytology are different branches of study.

Also, do not use quotation marks when you are using a long quotation. Instead, place the quoted material in its own block of text that is all indented and omit the quotation marks. If you are using APA style, indent quoted material that is more than 40 words in length. If you are using MLA style, indent quoted material that requires four or more lines of your paper. (See Chapter 26, "Quoting, Paraphrasing, and Citing Sources," for more information on properly formatting long quotes.)

Another use for quotation marks is to enclose titles of works that are not published separately, including short stories, poems, songs, chapters, and essays:

> "You Are a Man," by Richard Rodriguez

> "The Incident," by Countee Cullen

Do not enclose titles of your own essays in quotation marks when they are in title position. (See 5K Italics for treatment of titles of works that are published separately.)

Quotation marks are sometimes used to indicate to readers that you are using a word or phrase in a special sense, but be careful not to overuse this function:

> The "right" way to do a thing is not always the best way.

5G Other Marks

Parentheses ( )

Parentheses enclose interrupting elements, setting them off from the rest of the sentence or discourse with a greater separation than other enclosing marks such as commas and dashes. They usually add explanatory information that might seem digressive to the topic.

> The Particle Beam Fusion Accelerator *(PBFA II)* is a device designed to produce energy by fusion. Parentheses set off an abbreviation that will henceforth be used in place of the full term.

> The PBFA II stores up to 3.5 million joules of energy. *(One joule is the amount of energy expended by a one-watt device in one second.)* Parentheses set off an explanation framed as a complete sentence.

Parentheses are always used in pairs. They might have internal punctuation (as in the second example), but marks related to the sentence as a whole go outside the parentheses. Parentheses are almost never preceded by a comma. Note the following example:

> During fusion *(joining of two atomic nuclei to form a larger nucleus),* mass is converted to energy. Parenthetical element is followed by a comma, showing that it relates to *fusion.* If it had been preceded by a comma, it would appear, illogically, to relate to *mass.*

Brackets   [ ]

Square brackets have limited uses and are not interchangeable with parentheses. Their most common use is to indicate to the reader that the writer has inserted words into quoted material:

> Describing the Great Depression, Frederick Lewis Allen says, "The total amount of money paid out in wages *[in 1932]* was 60 percent less than in 1929." The words *in 1932* were not part of the original text.

Some writers use brackets to enclose brief parenthetical material within parentheses:

> Jules Verne (*Journey to the Center of the Earth* [1864]) described giant apes and a vast subterranean sea at the core of the earth. The date of publication is parenthetical to the title of the book.

Ellipsis Dots . . .

Ellipsis dots (spaced periods) are used in quotations to indicate where words have been omitted. Three spaced dots mark omissions within a sentence. If the omission comes at the end of your sentence but not at the end of the original sentence, use four spaced periods.

> One of the legacies of the Great Depression, says Frederick Lewis Allen, is that "if individual Americans are in deep trouble, . . . their government [should] come to their aid." Words following a comma in the original sentence are omitted within the sentence. The brackets enclose an inserted word.

> This idea, adds Allen, "was fiercely contested for years. . . ." Allen's sentence did not end at *years,* where the quoted sentence ends.

Make sure that the omitted words do not distort the meaning of the original selection.

5H Capitalization

Watch the Animation on **Capitalization** at mycomplab.com

The rules for capitalization are relatively fixed. Following are examples of situations calling for capitalization.

1. Beginning of a sentence:

> *In* 1929, the whole credit structure of the American economy was shaken.

2. Proper names or nouns:

> With the onset of the *Great Depression, President Hoover* at first tried to organize national optimism. Historical period or event; person.

> Bankers on *Wall Street,* manufacturers in *Detroit,* and legislators in *Washington* all had an effect on the economy. Place.

> *The Great Depression* was part of a worldwide collapse, ending only with *World War II.* Historical period or event.

> *President Hoover* set up the *Reconstruction Finance Corporation* to aid banks and businesses. Person; institution.

> *Jell-O, Pepsi, Rice Krispies* Trade names.

> *Aunt Beatrice, Grandmother Dietz, Dad* Relationships when they are part of the name; but not *my dad* and *my aunt and uncle.*

3. Titles:

> *Death at an Early Age,* by Jonathan Kozol; *The Dancing Wu Li Masters: An Overview of the New Physics,* by Gary Zukav. Capitalize first and last words, words following colons, and all other words except articles (*a, an,* and *the*) and conjunctions and prepositions of fewer than five letters (*and, but, in, by,* etc.).

Avoid capitalizing common nouns; for example:

> For many people, the *winter* of 1902 was bleak. Seasons.

> Many people moved *south* to a warmer climate. Compass directions.

My *great-grandparents* were among those who moved. Relationships.

Simon Waterson was a *professor of history* at the time. Titles that are not part of proper names.

5I Abbreviation

While abbreviations are part of the language, not all are acceptable in all circumstances. A general guideline is that they are less common in formal prose than in less formal circumstances. The following examples are arranged from most acceptable to least acceptable in written prose.

Watch the Animation on **Abbreviation** at mycomplab.com

Titles with proper names

Dr. Paul Gordon   Paul Gordon, Ph.D.
George Grossman, Jr.

Times and dates

11:15 A.M. *or* 11:15 a.m.   53 B.C.E   C.E. 371

Names of organizations and countries

NATO   CIA   NBC

Use *U.S.* as an adjective (*in a U.S. city*) and *United States* as a noun (*a city in the United States*).

Latin abbreviations (write out except in source citations and parenthetical comments)

etc.   and so forth (*et cetera*—applies to things)
i.e.   that is (*id est*)
e.g.   for example (*exempli gratia*)
cf.   compare (*confer*)
et al.   and others (*et alii*—applies to people)
N.B.   note well (*nota bene*)

Abbreviations to be avoided in most prose

The school board not bd. met on Tuesday not Tues. February not Feb. 3.

William not Wm. Townsend was a guest lecturer in the economics not econ. class.

Townsend arrived from Pittsburgh, Pennsylvania not *PA* or *Penn.,* late last night.

Consult your dictionary when you have questions about specific abbreviations.

5J Apostrophe '

Watch the Animation on **Apostrophes** at mycomplab.com

The apostrophe has two main uses in English—to mark possessive nouns and to show contractions—plus a few specialized uses. Avoid all other uses.

Possessive Nouns

Ownership or connection is marked on nouns with apostrophes:

Norton's résumé is short and concise. The résumé belongs to Norton.

This week's newsletter will be a little late. The newsletter of this week

The article's title is confusing. The title of the article

To make nouns possessive, follow one of these steps:

1. For singular nouns, add *'s* (*nature* + *'s* = *nature's*; *Tess* + *'s* = *Tess's*).
2. For plural nouns ending in *s*, add *'* (*strangers* + *'* = *strangers'*).
3. For plural nouns not ending in *s*, add *'s* (*men* + *'s* = *men's*).

Do not use apostrophes to make nouns plural. (See 5N Spelling.) And do not use apostrophes with possessive and relative pronouns. (See 3A Pronoun Case.)
For example:

The *Harris's* are in Florida. Incorrectly uses apostrophe to make the noun *Harris* plural.

The family lost *it's* home in the fire. Incorrectly uses apostrophe with the pronoun *it* to make it possessive.

Contractions

Apostrophes stand in place of omitted letters in contractions:

doesn't	does not
isn't	is not
I'd	I would
you've	you have
it's	it is *or* it has
who's	who is *or* who has
let's	let us
we'll	we will

Because contractions reflect a casual style, they are usually not acceptable in formal writing. Do not confuse the contracted *it is* (*it's*) and *who is* (*who's*) with the possessive pronouns *its* and *whose*. (See 3A Pronoun Case.)

Special Uses

Plurals of letters, numbers, and words used as terms

I am hoping to get all *A*'s this year.

The memo had four misspelled *there*'s. See 5K Italics, which discusses italicizing words used as terms.

All the *7*'s are upside down in the 1990s catalog. The plural for years is usually formed without apostrophes.

Omitted letters or numbers

We'll never forget the summer of *'78*. Restrict to informal writing.

"Be *seein'* ya," Charlie said. Dialect in quoted speech.

5K Italics

Italic type, which slants to the right, has specialized uses.

Titles of works published independently

The Atlantic Monthly (magazine)

A Farewell to Arms (book)

Leaves of Grass (book-length poems)

The Wall Street Journal (newspaper)

American Idol (television program)

The Glass Menagerie (play)

Ships, aircraft, spacecraft, and trains

Challenger (spacecraft)

Leasat 3 (communications satellite)

San Francisco *Zephyr* (train)

Italics are also used for words, letters, and numbers used as themselves in a sentence:

The process of heat transfer is called *conduction*.

The letter *e* is the most commonly used vowel.

Many people consider *13* to be an unlucky number.

Italics can also be used for emphasis:

"I said, '*Did* you buy the tickets?' not '*Would* you buy the tickets?'"

Although underlining was used as a substitute for italics in the past, writers generally avoid it nowadays because underlining is used for other purposes (for example, to indicate a hyperlink in Web and other electronic writing).

5L Hyphens   -

Hyphens have three main uses: to divide words at the ends of lines, to form compound words, and to connect spelled-out numbers.

Dividing Words

There are three general rules to remember when using hyphens to divide words at the ends of lines: (1) always divide between syllables, (2) don't divide one-syllable words, and (3) don't divide words so that only two letters carry over to the second line. Consider the following examples:

> After the results came back, the doctor sat me down and explained my *condition.*

> While they could not cure the condition, at least they could alleviate its *symptoms.*

> In the end, after months of waiting and mountains of legal fees, the court *ruled* against him. Incorrectly divides the one-syllable word *ruled.*

> Needless to say, when the court ruled against him, he was not *particularly* pleased. Incorrectly divides the word *particularly* so that only the last two letters carry over to the second line.

Forming Compound Words

Knowing when to hyphenate compound words can be tricky because some compound words can be written as single words (for example, *graveyard* or *postmaster*) while others can be written as two separate words (for example, *place kick* or *executive secretary*). Complicating matters further, compound adjectives take hyphens when they precede nouns but not when they follow nouns. Here are some examples of the correct and incorrect use of hyphens:

> My *ex-husband* is a *pro-Communist* crackpot. Use hyphens after the prefix *ex-* and any prefix placed before a proper name, in this case *pro-* before *Communist.* In general, though, most words formed with prefixes are written as one word; for example, *antisocial* or *multicultural.*

> The *post-mortem* revealed that her *brother in law* died of natural causes. This sentence contains two hyphenation errors. First, the compound word *post-mortem* should be written as a single word, *postmortem* (see comment on prefixes in the preceding example). Second, the compound noun *brother in law* should be hyphenated as *brother-in-law.*

> The *secretary treasurer* discouraged the group from making *highly-risky* investments. This sentence contains two hyphenation errors. First, the compound noun *secretary treasurer* requires a hyphen. Second, *-ly* adverbs such as *highly* are written as separate words when they precede adjectives such as *risky.*

Connecting Spelled-Out Numbers

Use hyphens to link compounds of spelled-out numbers and to link numbers to nouns. For example:

twenty-fifth time	six-year-old
nine-page letter	35-year-old
132-page report	

Whenever you have a question about dividing words and hyphenating compound words, use your dictionary. Dots usually mark syllables, and hyphens mark hyphenated compounds.

5M Numbers

Numbers can be spelled out or written as numerals. When to employ one style or the other depends on the writing context. In most academic writing in the humanities, and indeed in most writing geared for a general audience, numbers are usually spelled out. In the sciences, however, numbers are usually written as numerals.

Unless you are asked to follow different conventions, use the following guidelines to handle numbers in writing:

1. Spell out numbers requiring two words or less and write numerals for numbers requiring three or more words. In practice, this means you will write out numbers *one* to *ninety-nine* and write numerals for *100* and above.

2. Spell out numbers that begin sentences. For long numbers this can lead to awkward sentences. In such instances, you should consider revising the sentence to move the number away from the beginning of the sentence so it can be written in numerals.

3. Make exceptions for numbers used in special figures. In these instances, numbers are usually written as numerals. Special figures of this type include days and years; pages, chapters, and volumes; acts, scenes, and lines; decimals, fractions, ratios, and percentages; temperatures; addresses; statistics; and amounts of money.

Consider the following examples:

The company mailed *twenty-one* parcels yesterday.

She bought *2,200* acres of ranch land with her lottery winnings.

One hundred and fifty-two cows drowned in the flood.

The Japanese attacked Pearl Harbor on December *7, 1941*.

You will find the answer on page *87* in chapter *5*.

The famous "To be, or not to be" soliloquy appears in act *3*, scene *1*, of *Hamlet*.

The temperature reached *105* °F yesterday.

The suspect resided at *221* Dolores Street, Apartment *3B*.

The winning margin was *2* to *1*.

With tax, the umbrella cost $*15.73*.

5N Spelling

Your word processor's spelling checker will flag most misspelled words and suggest alternatives, but it will often miss unintended homonyms (for instance, accepting *Brutish Literature* when you meant to type *British Literature*). Because you should not rely solely on a spell checker, here is a review of the most useful and dependable rules of spelling.

Doubling a Final Consonant

When adding a suffix such as *-ing* or *-ed* to a word that ends in a consonant, double the final consonant to keep the internal vowel short (for example, *permit, permitted; stop, stopped*). Double the final consonant when all three of the following are true:

1. The word ends in a consonant preceded by a vowel.
2. The word is one syllable or the accent is on the final syllable.
3. The suffix begins with a vowel.

Here are some other examples:

hop	hopped	begin	beginning
sit	sitting	prefer	preferred
put	putting	occur	occurrence
win	winner	recap	recapped

Words Containing *ie* or *ei*

The familiar rhyme about using *ie* or *ei* is true most of the time—enough times that it is worth remembering: *i* before *e* except after *c* when the sound is long *e*; *e* before *i* when sound is long *a*. Thus, words such as these follow the rule:

receive	believe	weight
ceiling	chief	beige
conceited	siege	eight

There are a few common exceptions: *caffeine, either, neither, seize,* and *weird.*

Final *e*

To add an ending to a word that ends in a silent *e*, drop the *e* when the ending begins with a vowel:

believe + able = believable	believe + ed = believed
move + able = movable	move + ment = movement
hope + ing = hoping	hope + ful = hopeful

When the consonant preceding the final *e* is a soft *c* or *g*, the *e* is dropped only when the ending begins with *e* or *i*:

change + ing = changing	change + able = changeable
notice + ing = noticing	notice + able = noticeable
manage + er = manager	manage + ment = management
nice + er = nicer	nice + ly = nicely

Final *y*

To add an ending to a word with a final *y* preceded by a consonant, change the *y* to *i* except when your ending is -*ing:*

happy + ly = happily	study + ing = studying
apply + es = applies	apply + ing = applying
vary + ous = various	vary + ing = varying
try + ed = tried	try + ing = trying

When the final *y* is preceded by a vowel, keep the *y:*

play + ed = played	play + ful = playful
employ + ed = employed	employ + ment = employment

but

say + s = says	say + d = said
pay + ment = payment	pay + d = paid

Never change the *y* when adding an ending to a proper noun: *the Barrys.*

Plurals

Plural nouns ordinarily have an *s* ending:

boy + s = boys	car + s = cars

Words that end in *ch, s, sh, x,* or *z* require -*es:*

box + es = boxes	church + es = churches

Words ending in *o* are a little more troublesome. If the *o* is preceded by a vowel, add *s:*

radio + s = radios	video + s = videos

If the *o* is preceded by a consonant, ordinarily add -*es:*

hero + es = heroes	potato + es = potatoes

A few common words take either *s* or -*es:*

tornados, tornadoes	zeros, zeroes	volcanos, volcanoes

Some words form their plurals internally or do not have a plural form. Do not add an *s* to these words:

child, children	deer, deer
man, men	fish, fish
mouse, mice	moose, moose

Compound words ordinarily have an *s* at the end of the compound:

textbook, textbooks	snowshoe, snowshoes
text edition, text editions	

But when the first word of the compound is the main word, add the *s* to it:

sisters-in-law   attorneys-general

Whenever you are in doubt about the correct plural ending, check your dictionary.

Homonyms

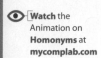 **Watch** the Animation on **Homonyms** at mycomplab.com

Some of the most troublesome words to spell are homonyms, words that sound alike but are spelled differently. Here is a partial list of the most common ones:

accept, except	maybe, may be
affect, effect	of, 've (have)
already, all ready	passed, past
cite, sight, site	than, then
forth, fourth	their, there, they're
it's, its	to, too, two
know, no	whose, who's
lead, led	your, you're

A few other words, not exactly homonyms, are sometimes confused:

breath, breathe	lightning, lightening
choose, chose	loose, lose
clothes, cloths	precede, proceed
dominant, dominate	quiet, quite

Check the meanings of any sound alike words you are unsure of in your dictionary.

Appendix
Readings Arranged by Theme

Credits

Index

Note: Figures are indicated by an *f* following a page number.

Rhetorical Knowledge

By the end of first-year composition, students should

- Focus on a purpose
- Respond to the needs of different audiences
- Respond appropriately to different kinds of rhetorical situations
- Use conventions of format and structure appropriate to the rhetorical situation
- Adopt appropriate voice, tone, and level of formality
- Understand how genres shape reading and writing
- Write in several genres

PART 1 Getting Started provides strategies for analyzing your writing situation in terms of genre, topic, angle, purpose, readers, contexts, and media.

PART 2 Using Genres to Express Ideas covers ten genres commonly taught in college and/or used in the workplace and ten related "microgenres."

PART 3 Developing a Writing Process helps you adapt voice and style to your audience and purpose.

PART 4 Strategies for Shaping Ideas shows how attention to structure and pattern leads to clear writing and persuasive argument.

Critical Thinking, Reading, and Writing

By the end of first-year composition, students should

- Use writing and reading for inquiry, learning, thinking, and communicating
- Understand a writing assignment as a series of tasks, including finding, evaluating, analyzing, and synthesizing appropriate primary and secondary sources
- Integrate their own ideas with those of others
- Understand the relationships among language, knowledge, and power

PART 1 Getting Started focuses on audience and purpose as a way to guide writing decisions.

PART 2 Using Genres to Express Ideas includes invention strategies for each genre and takes you through the writing process reflectively.

PART 3 Developing a Writing Process integrates critical thinking and writing strategies with the writing process stages.

PART 5 Doing Research takes you through the research process practically but reflectively.

PART 7 Anthology of Readings includes questions and writing assignments that will have you considering rhetorical strategies, inquiry, and critical thinking.

Processes

By the end of first-year composition, students should

- Be aware that it usually takes multiple drafts to create and complete a successful text
- Develop flexible strategies for generating, revising, editing, and proofreading
- Understand writing as an open process that permits writers to use later invention and rethinking to revise their work
- Understand the collaborative and social aspects of writing processes
- Learn to critique their own and others' works
- Learn to balance the advantages of relying on others with the responsibility of doing their part
- Use a variety of technologies to address a range of audiences

PART 2 Using Genres to Express Ideas is structured so that each chapter mirrors the writing process, beginning with an overview and moving from invention to organizing and drafting, choosing the appropriate style and design, and revision.

PART 3 Developing a Writing Process provides a detailed description of the stages of the writing process, from invention and prewriting to revising and editing.

PART 5 Doing Research helps you understand how to responsibly use sources and the ideas of others to inform your own work.

PART 6 Getting Your Ideas Out There helps you use electronic and other media to make your writing public.

Throughout the book, you have opportunities to communicate in a variety of media and genres.